Business Marketing Strategy
Cases, Concepts, and Applications

The Irwin Series in Marketing

Gilbert A. Churchill, Jr., Consulting Editor
University of Wisconsin, Madison

Alreck & Settle
The Survey Research Handbook, 2/E

Arens & Bovee
Contemporary Advertising, 5/E

Bearden, Ingram, & LaForge
Marketing: Principles & Perspectives, 1/E

Belch & Belch
Introduction to Advertising and Promotion: An Integrated Marketing Communications Perspective, 3/E

Berkowitz, Kerin, Hartley, & Rudelius
Marketing, 4/E

Bernhardt & Kinnear
Cases in Marketing Management, 6/E

Bonoma & Kosnik
Marketing Management: Text & Cases, 1/E

Boyd, Walker, & Larréché
Marketing Management: A Strategic Approach, 2/E

Burstiner
Basic Retailing, 2/E

Cadotte
The Market Place: A Strategic Marketing Simulation, 1/E

Cateora
International Marketing, 8/E

Churchill, Ford, & Walker
Sales Force Management, 4/E

Cole & Mishler
Consumer and Business Credit Management, 10/E

Cravens
Strategic Marketing, 4/E

Cravens & Lamb
Strategic Marketing Management Cases, 4/E

Crawford
New Products Management, 4/E

Dillon, Madden, & Firtle
Essentials of Marketing Research, 1/E

Dillon, Madden, & Firtle
Marketing Research in a Marketing Environment, 3/E

Engel, Warshaw, & Kinnear
Promotional Strategy, 8/E

Faria, Nulsen, & Roussos
Compete!, 4/E

Futrell
ABC's of Selling, 4/E

Futrell
Fundamentals of Selling, 4/E

Hawkins, Best, & Coney
Consumer Behavior, 6/E

Lambert & Stock
Strategic Logistics Management, 3/E

Lehmann & Winer
Analysis for Marketing Planning, 3/E

Lehmann & Winer
Product Management, 1/E

Levy & Weitz
Retailing Management, 2/E

Mason, Mayer, & Ezell
Retailing, 5/E

Mason, Mayer, & Wilkinson
Modern Retailing, 6/E

Mason & Perreault
The Marketing Game!, 2/E

McCarthy & Perreault
Basic Marketing: A Global-Managerial Approach, 11/E

McCarthy & Perreault
Essentials of Marketing: A Global-Managerial Approach, 6/E

Meloan & Graham
International and Global Marketing Concepts and Cases, 1/E

Patton
Sales Force: A Sales Management Simulation Game, 1/E

Peter & Donnelly
A Preface to Marketing Management, 6/E

Peter & Donnelly
Marketing Management: Knowledge and Skills, 4/E

Peter & Olson
Consumer Behavior and Marketing Strategy, 3/E

Peter & Olson
Understanding Consumer Behavior, 1/E

Quelch
Cases in Product Management, 1/E

Quelch, Dolan, & Kosnik
Marketing Management: Text & Cases, 1/E

Quelch & Farris
Cases in Advertising and Promotion Management, 4/E

Quelch, Kashani, & Vandermerwe
Cases in European Marketing Management, 1/E

Smith & Quelch
Ethics in Marketing, 1/E

Stanton, Buskirk, & Spiro
Management of a Sales Force, 9/E

Thompson & Stappenbeck
The Marketing Strategy Game, 1/E

Walker, Boyd, & Larréché
Marketing Strategy: Planning and Implementation, 1/E

Weitz, Castleberry, & Tanner
Selling: Building Partnerships, 2/E

Business Marketing Strategy
Cases, Concepts, and Applications

V. Kasturi Rangan
Harvard University

Benson P. Shapiro
Harvard University

Rowland T. Moriarty, Jr.
Chairman, Cubex Corporation

Chicago • Bogotá • Boston • Buenos Aires • Caracas
London • Madrid • Mexico City • Sydney • Toronto

© Richard D. Irwin, Inc., 1995

All rights reserved. No part of this book may be reproduced, stored in a retrieval system, or transmitted, in any form or by any means, electronic, mechanical, photocopying, recording, or otherwise, without the prior written permission of the copyright holder. The copyright on each case in this book unless otherwise noted is held by the President and Fellows of Harvard College and they are published herein by express permission. Permissions requests to use individual Harvard copyrighted cases should be directed to the Permissions Manager, Harvard Business School Publishing, Boston, MA 02163.

Case material of the Harvard Graduate School of Business Administration is made possible by the cooperation of business firms and other organizations which may wish to remain anonymous by having names, quantities, and other identifying details disguised while maintaining basic relationships. Cases are prepared as the basis for class discussion rather than to illustrate either effective or ineffective handling of an administrative situation.

Senior sponsoring editor:	Stephen M. Patterson
Editorial coordinator:	Christine Scheid
Marketing manager:	Jim Lewis
Project editor:	Paula M. Buschman
Production manager:	Ann Cassady
Designer:	Michael Warrell
Cover designer:	Ellen Pettengell
Interior photographs:	Weimer Graphics
Art studio:	Mary Jo Szymanski
Graphics supervisor:	Heather D. Burbridge
Compositor:	Graphic Sciences Corporation
Typeface:	10/12 Times Roman
Printer:	Buxton Skinner Printing Company

Library of Congress Cataloging-in-Publication Data

Rangan, V. Kasturi.
    Business marketing strategy : cases, concepts, and applications / V. Kasturi Rangan, Benson P. Shapiro, Rowland T. Moriarity, Jr.
       p.   cm. — (The Irwin series in marketing)
    Includes index.
    ISBN 0-256-16911-X
    1. Marketing—Management. 2. Product management. 3. Industrial marketing—Management. 4. Marketing—Management—Cases studies.
I. Shapiro, Benson P.   II. Moriarty, Rowland T.   III. Title.
IV. Series.
HF5415.13.R268   1995
658.8′02—dc20   94–22561

Printed in the United States of America
1 2 3 4 5 6 7 8 9 0 BX 1 0 9 8 7 6 5 4

Preface

This book is based on the extremely successful business marketing course at the Harvard Business School. We three co-authors have taught the course for over a decade and a half, from the mid-70s to the early 90s, and almost every year it has been among the best rated of the second-year MBA electives.

In organizing the book, we mulled over the several frameworks used in the past years. The most obvious way to organize the material appeared to be by marketing mix topics, such as market segmentation, customer selection, product policy, pricing, channels of distribution, and so on. What we found, however, was that second-year MBA students, having studied the principles of marketing by the marketing mix framework in the core course, realize that it is highly interactive and are anxious and eager to jump ahead and take a holistic view of the marketing function. Moreover, we have seen from our various consulting experiences that marketing decisions are integrative, and rarely separable as an exclusive market selection or pricing or distribution issue. So from both a pedagogical point of view and a practitioner point of view, the classic marketing mix organization did not appeal to us very much.

At the other extreme, we were also aware of business-to-business marketing curriculums that have tended to specialize by distinctive topic areas. The notion of industrial buying behavior, for example, was quite important and widely researched and taught in the late 70s and early 80s. The topic of distribution channels rose in prominence in the mid-80s. Then in the late 80s, high-tech marketing became the rage. We did not want to specialize this book by any such interest focus either, because its primary purpose is to serve students, professionals, and practitioners who practice business marketing across a wide range of industry settings. What we sought was a pedagogically wholesome and managerially motivating framework that would appeal to a broad cross section of business marketers. Our organization of the book, therefore, has a very simple logic: the product life cycle.

Business-to-business marketing concepts and challenges vary in importance over the life cycle of the product. While the process of new product development is critical early on, the task of managing the order fulfillment cycle is more important at the tail end of the life cycle. Similarly, while the task of selecting and building a sales-and-distribution channel is of paramount importance in the early stage, issues of channel management and distribution cost efficiency become more important in the later stage. The book, therefore, has three core modules—"Managing New Products," "Managing Mature Products," and "Managing Product Market Diversity"—to reflect the market maturation process. Within each of these core sections there are a variety of conceptual issues that cut across the entire spectrum of the marketing mix. The organizing framework is simple, it is holistic, and it treats the marketing mix as interactive and integrative, yet at the same time special topics and issues facing business marketers are picked up at appropriate points in the product life cycle. For example, in the "Managing Mature Products" module, there is an extensive discussion on how to manage the commoditization trend. The challenges and scope of business-to-business marketing are set out and the basic concepts in customer segmentation and organization buying behavior are reviewed in the opening section, "Introduction."

This book has an equal representation of readings and cases. They work together to complement each other. The readings are almost evenly split between practical applications and thoughtful conceptual frameworks. Similarly, the cases reflect a range of strategic/conceptual issues as well as those that address tactics and implementation. While each of the four sections has been written to represent a cogent collection of challenging conceptual and practical material, the articles may be read as stand-alone pieces and are intended to be of value to graduate students as well as practicing managers who think and deal daily with issues and problems such as those portrayed in the book.

The cases have been chosen for their strong managerial underpinnings and therefore to some extent are protected from the passage of time. They vary from small entrepreneurial start-ups such as Ring Medical to global conglomerates such as Northern Telecom and GE Plastics. The range of products also vary widely, from traditional heavy industrial products to high-technology components. We provide a brief overview of each of the cases and readings in the book in Chapter 1 (see Tables 1 and 2 on pages 13–14).

As is obvious from the table of contents, in a venture of this magnitude several people contribute to the product. We would like to thank Tom Bonoma for "Major Sales: Who *Really* Does the Buying?" and also his coauthored piece, "How to Segment Industrial Markets." We are grateful to our colleagues Steven Wheelwright and Kim Clark for allowing us to use their article "Creating Project Plans to Focus Product Development"; to Dorothy Leonard-Barton, Edith Wilson, and John Doyle for releasing "Commercializing Technology: Understanding User Needs"; to Bob Dolan for letting us have his Northern Telecom case series, as well as his article "Industrial Market Research: Beta Test Site Management"; to Melvyn Menezes for his "Xerox Corporation: The Customer Satisfaction Program," as well as the Techsonic Industries, Inc. case; to Jeffrey Rayport for the Rank Xerox case; to Anirudh Dhebar for "Intel Corporation: Going into OverDrive™"; to Frank Cespedes for our use of "Once More: How Do You Improve Customer Service?" as well as his co-authored case "Becton Dickinson & Company: VACUTAINER® Systems Division"; to Ray Corey for his coauthored Ingersoll-Rand case; and to Jay Misra and Cliff Fitzgerald for letting us revise their original Rolm case. We would like to thank our other colleagues who coauthored several of the articles that are contained in this book, namely, Gordon Swartz, John Sviokla, Elliott Ross, Ursula Moran, Tom Kosnik, Nitin Nohria, Barbara Jackson, Kevin Bartus, Eric Beinhocker, George Bowman, Raphael Carty, Craig Cline, Kim Crawford, Christopher Fay, Joseph Finegold, Bruce Isaacson, Susan Lasley, Robert Lightfoot, David May, Krista McQuade, Steven Michael, Dominic Palmer, Jon Serbin, Paresh Shah, Jon Skofic, and Joep VanThiel. While many people contributed to it, the manuscript itself was put together by Susan Brumfield and Morgan McCurdy, our cheerful assistants. A special thanks to them, especially Susan Brumfield, who carefully proofread our manuscripts and efficiently coordinated the production process with our publishers. At Richard D. Irwin, we owe our appreciation to Paula Buschman, who firmly and effectively guided our project, and to Steve Patterson for his encouragement, commitment, and support.

Our gratitude in no small measure is due to Dean John McArthur for encouraging field research and case writing, the backbone of this book and several of the articles we have written. We appreciate the Division of Research at the Harvard Business School for so generously funding our field research and for giving us permission to use the cases and articles. We thank the *Harvard Business Review, Journal of Marketing, Business Horizons, Sloan Management Review,* and *Industrial Marketing Management* for granting permission to use a number of articles that were originally published in their journals. And last but not least we would like to thank our students over the various years who have helped us refine our thinking by their active class participation. This helped us work through the concepts carefully and helped in clarifying and enhancing our communication of them.

The book itself, however, would not have been possible without the help of the case protagonists, practitioners, and managers who kept us challenged by directing us to topical issues and problems. We are forever indebted to them for their time and their willingness to share a slice of their professional lives with us.

This book is gratefully dedicated to the several people who inspired and influenced our personal and professional lives. That list is long and obviously different for each of us. In this volume, we would like to acknowledge: Vijayaraghavan and Sushila Raghavan, Balaji Chakravarthy, Gopal Rathnam, and Prabha Sridhar (V. Kasturi Rangan); Ernest L. and Rose P. Shapiro, and Sidney and Rose Weinstock (Benson P. Shapiro); and Rowland T. Moriarty, Sr., and Nancy and William Fitz (Rowland T. Moriarty, Jr.).

Contents

Preface vii

SECTION I

Introduction

1. **Scope and Challenge of Business-to-Business Marketing** 3
   V. Kasturi Rangan and Bruce Isaacson

2. **Norton Group PLC (A): To Be or Not to Be in the Motorcycle Business** 15
   V. Kasturi Rangan and Jon Skofic

3. **How to Segment Industrial Markets** 35
   Benson P. Shapiro and Thomas V. Bonoma

4. **Major Sales: Who *Really* Does the Buying?** 46
   Thomas V. Bonoma

SECTION II

Managing New Products

5. **New Product Commercialization: Common Mistakes** 63
   V. Kasturi Rangan and Kevin Bartus

6. **Techsonic Industries, Inc.: Humminbird—New Products** 76
   Melvyn A. J. Menezes and Eric D. Beinhocker

7 **Millipore New Product Commercialization: A Tale of Two New Products** 99
   V. Kasturi Rangan and Kevin Bartus

8 **Ring Medical: Organizing New Product Marketing** 124
   V. Kasturi Rangan and Christopher Fay

9 **Rohm and Haas (A): New Product Marketing Strategy** 148
   V. Kasturi Rangan and Susan Lasley

10 **Northern Telecom (A): Greenwich Investment Proposal (Condensed)** 163
   Robert J. Dolan

11 **Northern Telecom (B): The Norstar Launch** 171
   Robert J. Dolan

12 **Rolm: The SIGMA Introduction** 198
   V. Kasturi Rangan, Jay Misra, and Cliff Fitzgerald

13 **Green Marketing at Rank Xerox** 215
   Jeffrey F. Rayport and Joep VanThiel

14 **Intel Corporation: Going into OverDrive™** 244
   Anirudh Dhebar

15 **Creating Project Plans to Focus Product Development** 264
   Steven C. Wheelwright and Kim B. Clark

16 **Commercializing Technology: Understanding User Needs** 281
   Dorothy Leonard-Barton, Edith Wilson, and John Doyle

17 **Industrial Pricing to Meet Customer Needs** 306
   Benson P. Shapiro and Barbara B. Jackson

18 **Industrial Market Research: Beta Test Site Management** 320
   Robert J. Dolan

19 **Designing Channels of Distribution** 330
   V. Kasturi Rangan

Section III

Managing Mature Products

20 **Beating the Commodity Magnet** 345
   V. Kasturi Rangan and George T. Bowman

21 **Cumberland Metal Industries (A): Model Year 1978 Negotiations with Beta Motors** 360
Benson P. Shapiro and Craig E. Cline

22 **Peak Electronics (A): Vendor Relationship with the Ford Motor Company** 377
V. Kasturi Rangan, Kim Crawford, and Paresh Shah

23 **The BOC Group: Ohmeda (A)** 397
Rowland T. Moriarty and Gordon Swartz

24 **Atlas-Copco (A): Gaining and Building Distribution Channels** 422
V. Kasturi Rangan

25 **Ingersoll-Rand (A): Managing Multiple Channels, 1985** 437
V. Kasturi Rangan and E. Raymond Corey

26 **Computervision—Japan (A)** 452
Rowland T. Moriarty

27 **Signode Industries, Inc. (A)** 476
Rowland T. Moriarty, Jr., David May, and Gordon Swartz

28 **Becton Dickinson & Company: VACUTAINER® Systems Division** 495
Frank Cespedes and V. Kasturi Rangan

29 **Manage Customers for Profits (Not Just Sales)** 513
Benson P. Shapiro, V. Kasturi Rangan, Rowland T. Moriarty, and Elliot B. Ross

30 **Close Encounters of the Four Kinds: Managing Customers in a Rapidly Changing Environment** 525
Benson P. Shapiro

31 **Segmenting Customers in Mature Industrial Markets** 548
V. Kasturi Rangan, Rowland T. Moriarty, and Gordon Swartz

32 **Once More: How Do You Improve Customer Service?** 559
Frank V. Cespedes

33 **Automation to Boost Sales and Marketing** 573
Rowland T. Moriarty and Gordon S. Swartz

34 **Reorienting Channels of Distribution** 586
V. Kasturi Rangan

35 **Managing Hybrid Marketing Systems** 599
Rowland T. Moriarty and Ursula Moran

Section IV

Managing Product Market Diversity

36 **Managing Market Complexity: A Three-Ring Circus**   619
V. Kasturi Rangan

37 **Barco Projection Systems (A): Worldwide Niche Marketing**   632
Rowland T. Moriarty and Krista McQuade

38 **Fabtek (A)**   653
Benson P. Shapiro, Rowland T. Moriarty, and Craig E. Cline

39 **Xerox Corporation: The Customer Satisfaction Program**   668
Melvyn A. J. Menezes and Jon Serbin

40 **Millipore Corporate Strategy**   692
Nitin Nohria, V. Kasturi Rangan, and Robert W. Lightfoot

41 **GenRad, 1990 (A): At a Crossroads in Electronic Tests**   715
Raphael R. Carty and Benson P. Shapiro

42 **General Electric Plastics: Organizing the Marketing Function**   745
V. Kasturi Rangan and Steven Michael

43 **Variety versus Value: Two Generic Approaches to Product Policy**   765
Benson P. Shapiro

44 **What the Hell Is "Market Oriented"?**   783
Benson P. Shapiro

45 **Staple Yourself to an Order**   792
Benson P. Shapiro, V. Kasturi Rangan, and John J. Sviokla

46 **High-Tech Marketing: Concepts, Continuity, and Change**   806
Rowland T. Moriarty and Thomas J. Kosnik

47 **The Logic of Global Business: An Interview with ABB's Percy Barnevik**   823
William Taylor

Index   842

Section I Introduction

CHAPTER 1

Scope and Challenge of Business-to-Business Marketing

This chapter identifies six key linkages that distinguish business-to-business marketing: three with respect to the external environment (i.e., derived demand, complex buying process, and concentrated customer base) and three with respect to the internal organization (emphasis on technology, high level of customization, and order fulfillment mechanism). These linkages give rise to unique challenges in the analysis and execution of marketing decisions. After these challenges are discussed, the organization of the book is explained. The three core sections, following this introductory section, reflect the product life cycle theme: managing new products, managing mature products, and managing product market diversity.

Industrial or business-to-business marketing is the marketing of goods and services to commercial enterprises, governments, and other nonprofit institutions for use in the goods and services that they, in turn, produce for resale to other industrial customers.[1] Implicit in this definition is the type of customer in business-to-business markets as well as the use of the goods purchased. In industrial markets, goods are usually bought for enhancement and subsequent resale, whereas in consumer markets, goods are bought for their final consumption or use.

Because most economic activity is directly or indirectly geared to serving consumers' needs, it is hard to estimate the size of the economy for industrial products and services. Certain activities, however, do predominate in the industrial sector, for example, chemicals, primary metals, and machinery manufacturing. One estimate suggests that business-to-business activity represents about one-third of the U.S. 1989 GNP of $5,200 billion.[2] In less-developed economies, the percentage can be

---

V. Kasturi Rangan and Bruce Isaacson prepared this note.
Copyright © 1994 by the President and Fellows of Harvard College.
Harvard Business School note 594–125.

[1] E. Raymond Corey, *Industrial Marketing Cases and Concepts,* 4th ed. (Englewood Cliffs, N.J.: Prentice Hall, 1991), p. xi.

[2] V. Kasturi Rangan and Bruce Isaacson, "What Is Industrial Marketing?" Harvard Business School note No. 592-012.

even higher, because a thriving industrial sector, be it manufacturing or trading, is needed first, so consumers will get products of acceptable quality and value.

Products sold in industrial markets are usually classified as:[3]

- *Heavy equipment* such as radiology instrumentation or diesel engines.
- *Light equipment* such as hand tools or personal computers.
- *Systems* such as database networks, where the equipment is of secondary importance to the solution being delivered.
- *Raw materials* such as crude oil or cotton fiber.
- *Processed materials* such as rolled steel or plastic polymer that have undergone further processing from raw materials.
- *Consumable supplies* such as coolants, abrasives, or medical syringes.
- *Components* such as electrical motors or disk drives.
- *Services* such as management consulting and contract maintenance.

The above categories are neither exhaustive nor mutually exclusive. They are listed merely to suggest the scope and range of industrial products.

Aspects Distinguishing Industrial Marketing

The industrial marketing system can be considered in terms of two key linkages. The first is the external interface between the seller's marketing/sales function and the end user. The second is the internal interface between the seller's marketing/sales function and its manufacturing operations (see Figure 1).

While each of these linkages is highly complex (e.g., the role of research and development [R&D] in the internal interface and the role of distribution channels in the external interface), the two sets of linkages serve as convenient handles to explore the major challenges of business-to-business marketing.

The External Linkages

The three important considerations with respect to external linkages are derived demand, complex buying/selling process, and concentrated customer base.

Derived Demand. The demand for industrial products tends to be driven by the primary demand for consumer goods. For example, an automobile is built from hundreds of components—engines, wheels, the exterior body, the dashboard, and so forth. Each of these in turn is the end result of a supply chain consisting of many other components and raw materials. The dashboard, for

---

[3]This classification scheme is based on one offered by Robert W. Haas, *Industrial Marketing Management* (Boston: Kent Publishing Company, 1982), chap. 1.

FIGURE 1

Key linkages

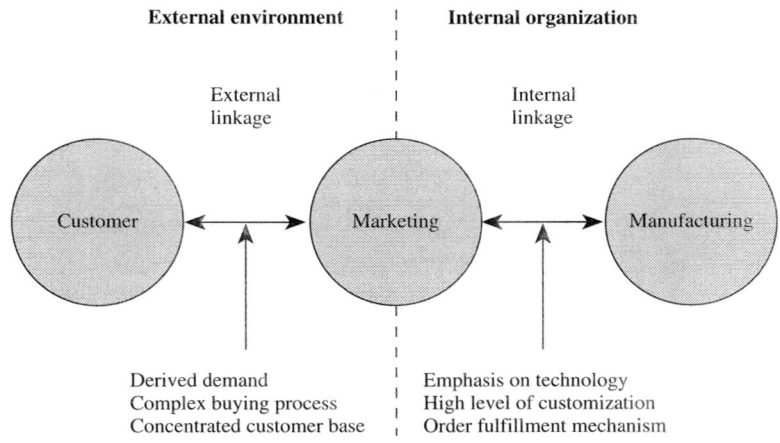

instance, is usually molded from a plastic called ABS. ABS is made from three chemicals, one of which is styrene. The styrene is made from ethylene, and ethylene from petroleum. Thus, the demand for each of these intermediate goods is influenced by the consumer demand for automobiles. When the demand for automobiles slumps (or peaks), so does the demand for ABS. Although consumer preferences, economic cycles, and social trends all affect industrial products demand, given its derived nature, it is possible to estimate demand for industrial products with a greater degree of rationality. Industrial firms must purchase in anticipation of the economic and market conditions; industrial buying, therefore, has a longer-range orientation.[4]

Complex Buying/Selling Process. In consumer markets, the decision-making unit purchasing any particular item is often the individual and is rarely larger than the household. In industrial markets, the decision-making unit is usually much more complex. The purchase of one piece of industrial equipment might involve a host of departments, such as purchasing, engineering, finance, and manufacturing, and might also require top-management approval. Generally, the complexity of the buying process is increased by the following factors:

- The influence of the formal organization.
- The strategic importance of the item being purchased.
- The cost of the item being purchased.
- The complexity of the need being serviced.

---

[4]Fred E. Webster, *Industrial Marketing Management,* 2nd ed. (New York: John Wiley & Sons, 1984), chap. 1, pp. 5–19.

The complexity of the buying decision increases the time, expense, and skills required of companies selling to industrial customers. Also, industrial customers, unlike consumers, often buy for multiple operations from multiple locations. Each individual unit may use the same basic product, but unique requirements may necessitate service at the buying headquarters as well as at the individual plant locations. Needless to say, aggregating of the selling tasks at two or more levels only makes selling more complicated.

While the selling and buying process is more complex, several aspects of the industrial sale make it easier to establish close customer relationships. Industrial purchases tend to be relatively rational and based on specific performance characteristics or benefits sought by the customer:

> Industrial or business customers have economic requirements, not wants. Unlike consumer products, industrial products do not make anyone look or feel better, and they generally do not have any significant aesthetic value. Industrial products are bought only to help the user manufacture, distribute, or sell more effectively.[5]

Concentrated Customer Base. Since consumer marketers often reach millions of consumers, any individual consumer may not dominate the selling process. By contrast, industrial marketers generally have a much smaller base of potential customers, and in many industrial markets a small number of customers represent a large percentage of the industry's buying potential. Industrial marketers selling big-ticket items like power generation equipment can literally count their customers on their fingers. Also, given the special infrastructural support often required, many industrial product manufacturers may be concentrated in geographical areas, such as California's Silicon Valley, for high-technology electronics. The targeted and concentrated nature of the industrial customer base makes direct marketing and face-to-face selling an effective and economically viable proposition. By contrast, many consumer marketers use mass-media communication techniques to reach a broad and dispersed consumer base.

The Internal Linkages

The following considerations are important to internal linkages.

Emphasis on Technology. Technology and performance superiority can give the industrial product competitive advantages in its marketplace, and product improvements in successive generations of industrial products are strongly emphasized. Manufacturers of semiconductors and disk drives, for instance, are constantly improving the performance-to-price ratio of their components over successive generations so that their end users can make better products for subsequent sale. While many consumer product manufacturers may also be constantly offering innovations

---

[5]B. Charles Ames and James D. Hlavacek, *Managerial Marketing for Industrial Firms* (New York: Random House, 1984), p. 22.

in their markets, the emphasis is on solutions and not on technology per se. In industrial markets, performance, functions, and features are of primary importance in the design, manufacturing, and marketing of the product.

High Level of Customization. The customization of consumer products is usually limited to packaging, labeling, or promotion, with the basic product standardized over a broad range of customers and markets. By contrast, because industrial products are used in the further manufacture or assembly of the next level of products, it is quite important to meet the technical requirements of the user. Many industrial product manufacturers will even tailor their operations facilities to meet the unique requirements of key customers. Engineers and design teams may often be assigned to learn the needs of key end users and customize products accordingly. Industrial firms will often sell standard products as well, but the complexity of the machinery or system may cause the accompanying technical support to be customized.

Order Fulfillment Mechanism. A large variety of industrial products are made to order. Even if produced to standard specifications, the actual manufacturing may commence only after the customer order is received. Thus, a high proportion of industrial goods manufacturing is essentially job-shop oriented, whereas production for consumer items such as packaged food tends to be based on large scale, batch, or continuous flow operations. While the raw material and work-in-process inventory levels may vary with the type of industrial products and markets being served, the finished-goods inventory levels are likely to be lower for many industrial goods manufacturers. As a result, when an industrial customer initiates an order, the order fulfillment chain often triggers a manufacturing operation directly linked to the order somewhere on the factory floor. Consumer goods manufacturing, on the other hand, is often linked to finished-goods inventory because the product specifications are usually standardized. Manufacturing of consumer products is usually geared to meeting a sales forecast, rather than an individual customer order, so when a customer initiates an order, the order fulfillment warehouse or customer-service department is the trigger point for fulfillment. Consumer product manufacturers use finished-goods inventory to insulate manufacturing from day-to-day changes in customer demand.

Management Challenges

Given the distinguishing characteristics of both internal and external linkages, the formulation and execution of the marketing mix poses unique challenges in industrial markets.

   1. *New product commercialization.* New product development and commercialization is the lifeline for many industrial businesses. Regis McKenna, a leading high-tech marketing consultant, points out that it took more than 75 years for the fractional horsepower motor to appear in nearly a dozen household gadgets, but the semiconductor chip has already appeared in as many gadgets in less than 20 years.

As the pace of technology development has speeded up, the rate of product obsolescence has accelerated. Such time-to-market pressures have forced many industrial companies to offer a regular stream of innovations just to play in the market. An effective new product development and commercialization process is critical to survival in such environments. Since technology plays such an important role, a key function in industrial markets is customer education and market development. Industrial customers might not, a priori, express appreciation or enthusiasm for an untested new product, and it is the marketer's responsibility to demonstrate a product's use and value to the customer. Because industrial products are often technically complex and may require a change in the buyer's operations, recognition of use and value usually comes only after intense application trials and productivity analysis. Many industrial marketers actually create and build a market for their products, rather than merely serve existing needs.

2. *Market segmentation.* Consumer markets can be segmented by psychological or sociological factors such as lifestyle or attitudes, but industrial markets are more likely to be segmented by industry characteristics, purchase quantities, or technical requirements. More recently, industrial marketers have realized the need for benefits-based or, better still, buying behavior–based market segments. Unfortunately, such a segmentation scheme is often very difficult to implement in industrial markets because industrial customers, unlike consumers, will not self-select themselves into a segment and shop accordingly, but rather have to be approached with the appropriate marketing mix at the outset. Consider, for example, a consumer who needs a dress for a special occasion. She is likely to visit a specialty retailer rather than a discount store to buy the dress. It is the opposite in the industrial situation, where the salesperson rather than the customer has to make the visit and offer the appropriate product.

3. *Product policy/pricing.* Industrial products are often sold on the basis of technology, product features, or other functional properties. This, as noted, is the result of a more rational buying approach on the part of industrial buyers. Thus, prices, while reflecting customers' value perceptions, may vary from near cost to a healthy surplus over costs. It will usually be possible to price high in a new product environment. However, when core product advantages wear out over time (e.g., the patent expires), there's little to differentiate the various suppliers in the marketplace. In mature industrial markets, competitive price pressures are common. The marketing effort to arrest such a commoditization is a key aspect of industrial product policy for many suppliers. Product differentiation in industrial markets comes either through physical product improvements or through the service that accompanies the product. In consumer markets, by contrast, careful product positioning, niche marketing, and brand pull advertising can maintain the value of the franchise even without any major improvements in product or service. Industrial products are often broadly viewed as *specialties* or *commodities.* Price is the dominant buying criterion for commodities because all suppliers' products appear essentially the same to the buyer, whereas buying criteria for specialties often transcend price. Vendor relationship, technical characteristics, or service may provide the necessary differentiation.

The intense competitive environment of the 1990s, coupled with increasing customer sophistication, is likely to make product differentiation very hard to achieve in many mature industrial businesses. From chemicals to banking, customers expect more service, more support, and more convenience. The level of service, support, and convenience provided to the customer via channels of distribution is likely to provide the differentiation point. Competition will be on the augmented product rather than the core product. But the challenge is to offer product augmentation that has value to customers and does not significantly raise costs; mere add-on services at a higher cost are unlikely to be received very positively.

4. *Channels of distribution.* Industrial markets usually have narrower customer bases than consumer markets, making it economically viable to reach at least a segment of the end users, especially the large ones, directly. Moreover, given the technical nature of the product and the complex buying process, it is often a sales team rather than a lone salesperson who closes the sale to an industrial customer. Thus, industrial marketers frequently deploy key account (or customer) sales teams consisting of technical as well as commercial people.

Because many options are available to the industrial marketer looking for a channel to distribute a product, selecting the right method of distribution is difficult. In general, an industrial marketer will prefer a direct sales force to external channels when:

- There is a manageable (small) number of customers.
- The purchase value is significant.
- Customers are concentrated geographically.
- The sales process is long and complex.
- Customers require a lot of information and training in product use.

When using its own sales force to sell directly, manufacturers are likely to receive better feedback about market needs and will have better control over the marketing mix in the channel. The cost of running such a sales force, however, has been estimated to vary between $150 and $250 per sales call, restricting its deployment in situations requiring extensive market coverage. An indirect (or distribution) channel will be preferred when:

- The customer base is dispersed.
- The product is bought as part of a larger assortment of complementary products.
- The product information is relatively straightforward to communicate.
- The customers require local and convenient product/service availability.

This strictly dichotomous direct versus distribution view, however, is rapidly disappearing in the 1990s. Traditionally, channels were viewed as a collection of intermediaries to take the product to market efficiently, that is, at the lowest cost. The emphasis has shifted from low cost to effective fulfillment of customers' needs. Now, instead of viewing channels as a collection of intermediaries, managers consider channels as a collection of tasks, such as providing information, fulfilling a service warranty, or breaking up bulk. This perspective has had two effects. First, companies now manage a wide variety of channel members. For example, instead of using either independent or company-owned distributors, companies now manage hybrid channels composed of many diverse intermediaries, each of which may specialize in fulfilling specific channel tasks. Second, companies no longer look at their distributors as adversaries to be controlled but rather as partners. Management of multiple channels and hybrid channels is a significant challenge for the 1990s, because such a transformation requires the manufacturers to view channel systems in their entirety, rather than viewing them piecemeal.

5. *Cross-functional and interdepartmental coordination.* Given the emphasis on technology, higher product customization, and the nature of the order fulfillment cycle, the selling and operations functions of an industrial marketing firm usually need much closer integration. This may be achieved by a supporting field organization of technical people who assist sales representatives in developing customer applications and solving customer engineering problems. As mentioned, large customers may be served by a joint team of salespeople and technical people. Depending on the nature of the industrial product and complexity of the buying process, such a team approach may be appropriate for some smaller customers as well. Thus, there is a heavy emphasis on teamwork in industrial marketing.

The need for closer marketing and operations integration often means that industrial marketers have to make or assist in decisions that cut across functional lines in a general management fashion. Product development, applications engineering, capacity planning, and quality assurance are only a few among the many nonmarketing functions that an industrial marketing manager has to participate in. By contrast, the consumer marketing function tends to be more specialized. Setting the promotion plan or advertising schedule for a brand of soap or toothpaste could often be a full-time job in itself, but industrial marketers tend to be involved in a wider range of activities.

6. *Managing social responsibility.* Consumers in industrialized economies such as the United States, Canada, Europe, and Japan are showing increasing concern for environmental issues like pollution, waste disposal, and global warming. Both consumer groups and their elected government representatives are likely to demand higher standards of social responsibility from businesses. Thus, manufacturers of products such a chlorofluorocarbons (CFCs), which are known to deteriorate the earth's protective ozone layer, must find alternative and environmentally safe substitutes. Similarly, plastics manufacturers must find an answer to the solid waste problem (many forms of plastics are currently nonbiodegradable). Perhaps the design of recycling systems and reverse channels from consumers to convenient recycling points could be an answer. Product design must include creative ways to use recycled parts and components. Industrial markets in the 1990s must clearly go beyond narrow profit-maximizing objectives and demonstrate how their business mission, in addition to serving their stockholders, addresses society's needs.

Framework for the Book

While the concepts, cases, and frameworks offered in the book are meant to illuminate the six management challenges described above, the organization of the book reflects the dynamics of the product life cycle (PLC). The fundamental task of reading the market and developing a new product is significantly different from that of maintaining or increasing share in a mature market.[6] The former involves creativity in interpreting customers' latent needs, while the latter requires the sensitivity to listen to customers' manifest needs. The former might require customer education and market development, while the latter might require product differentiation and market segmentation. New products might require a value-enhancing pricing approach, while mature products might need a price/service adjustment. Each of the six management challenges described above has a somewhat different flavor for new product-markets as compared to mature product-markets. It is a fact of life that products, markets, and functional departments, rather than elements of the marketing mix, are the more commonly used units of decision making at many firms. Taking a longitudinal PLC view encourages and reinforces this holistic orientation. We have therefore chosen to organize the book on the model of the product life cycle. Within each stage of the PLC, we present concepts, frameworks, and cases that best illustrate the six management challenges described above.

The Three Core Sections of the Book

The introductory Section I is meant to provide readers a basic understanding of how industrial marketing differs from consumer marketing, and to reinforce classic concepts in market segmentation and organizational buying behavior. Sections II, III, and IV comprise the core of the book.

Industrial markets, like all other markets, naturally mature along the product life cycle. At the start of the PLC, manufacturers must face and overcome a considerable amount of uncertainty. Some of the uncertainty may be caused by the new product configuration or technology itself and how to valuate its true benefits. But a large part of the variance may also be market driven, for example, a lack of product knowledge and acceptance in the targeted markets. Only as the product-market context matures is information available to plan and approach marketing activities with greater deliberation. For instance, in the early part of the PLC so little information is

---

[6]While the concept of managing the product over its life cycle is not new, as can be seen from Theodore Levitt, "Exploit the Product Life Cycle," *Harvard Business Review,* November–December 1965, and Philip Kotler, "Marketing Strategies for Different Stages of the Product Life Cycle," chap. 12, pp. 347–76, *Marketing Management: Analysis, Planning, Implementation, and Control,* 6th ed. (Englewood Cliffs, N.J.: Prentice Hall, 1988), our approach of emphasizing the conceptual differences is unique. We not only explore the differences in management prescriptions, but we attempt to understand the rationale for the underlying differences.

available on how customers buy and use the product that firms usually target markets by clearly identifiable demographic variables such as company size or industry type. But, as the PLC advances, better information begins to emerge on customer usage and buying behavior patterns. Firms able to use this information to their advantage are likely to be more successful.

As the product matures, a similar increase in knowledge of several marketing facets, such as product positioning and channel networks, becomes available, enabling firms to be more thoughtful in their marketing options. But that does not mean that decisions are any less complicated because by now competition is keen, customers are more knowledgeable and demanding, and prices and margins are usually declining. This raises a different set of management challenges; maintaining market share and profits becomes an arduous task. Early in the PLC, a firm's success depends on how skillfully its management is able to anticipate the product-market trends and absorb the associated uncertainties and risks. By contrast, when the PLC matures, management success depends on how accurately it is able to read the already available product-market information and deploy resources to retain strengths and overcome weaknesses. This difference leads to different emphases on the various aspects of the marketing mix. Two of the three core modules, Section II, "Managing New Products," and Section III, "Managing Mature Products," are organized to cover this spectrum of issues and challenges facing industrial marketers as the product-market evolves from new to mature.

The evolution of the PLC is usually accompanied by other related changes in the product-market context. Customers, who are by now completely familiar with and knowledgeable about the product, demand special services to fulfill their unique requirements. As manufacturers scramble to differentiate their products in different segments, product variety, customer segments, buying behavior, and channel arrangements begin to proliferate. Managing this complexity requires one to view the industrial marketing system in its entirety and not by specific product lines or channels. Coordination among products, markets, and channels becomes a significant management task. The third core module, Section IV, "Managing Product Market Diversity," takes a macro view of an organization's entire marketing activity whereby marketing decisions are integrated and synchronized with general management's resources, constraints, and objectives. Product decisions have to be viewed in the context of the business units' other products, sales force decisions must be harmonized in the context of a firm's overall distribution channels, and marketing decisions have to be made in the context of a firm's corporate strategy. Tables 1 and 2 provide a chapter-by-chapter plan of the book organized by the PLC theme. We also provide a brief description of the major topics and challenges covered in each case or reading.

TABLE 1 Cases

Company Case Study	Business Unit Size*	Product	Case Theme
Introduction			
1. Norton Group PLC (A)	Small	Rotary engines	Allocating limited product development resources over several projects, some in consumer and some in industrial markets.
Managing New Products			
2. Techsonic Industries, Inc.	Small	Sonar depth sounders	Selecting among three new product development projects.
3. Millipore New Product Commercialization	Large	Analytical instruments and industrial membranes	Launch planning for two new products in two different business divisions.
4. Ring Medical	Small	Information systems	Entrepreneurial start-up facing new product positioning and channeling problems.
5. Rohm and Haas (A)	Small	Chemicals	Resurrecting a failed product launch: marketing mix management.
6. Northern Telecom (A)	Medium	Phone systems	Project planning for a product line extension.
7. Northern Telecom (B)	Medium	Phone systems	Developing and launching the new product.
8. Rolm	Large	PBX equipment	Implementing product launch (when to announce and what to announce).
9. Green Marketing at Rank XEROX	Large	Copiers	Launching a new product built from recycled parts.
10. Intel Corporation	Large	Semiconductors	Coordinating distribution channels for supporting new products.
Managing Mature Products			
11. Cumberland Metal Industries (A)	Small	Automobile components	Managing price and customer relationship over the product life cycle.
12. Peak Electronics (A)	Small	Automobile components	Managing relationship with a large customer (Ford).
13. The BOC Group: Ohmeda (A)	Large	Medical equipment	Reorienting channels away from distributors to direct sales force.
14. Atlas-Copco (A)	Large	Air compressors	Building and managing a distribution network.
15. Ingersoll-Rand (A)	Large	Air compressors	Industry leader's efforts in gaining share and building multiple channels.
16. Computervision—Japan (A)	Medium	CAD/CAM computers	Channel strategy for new market (Japan).
17. Signode Industries, Inc. (A)	Large	Packaging supplies	Managing price and share in a commoditizing market.
18. Becton Dickinson & Company	Medium	Medical supplies	Negotiating a customer's (large hospital buying group) price, product, and distribution requests.
Managing Product Market Diversity			
19. Barco Projection Systems (A)	Medium	Projection equipment	Product and price response to SONY's market entry.
20. Fabteck (A)	Small	Fabrication	Managing order selection and prioritization.
21. Xerox Corporation	Large	Copiers	Managing customer satisfaction.
22. Millipore Corporate Strategy	Large	Analytical instruments and industrial membranes	Developing a product-market strategy and organizational structure for a multidivisional organization.
23. GenRad, 1990 (A)	Large	Semiconductor testing equipment	Developing a product-market strategy for a product line.
24. GE Plastics	Large	Engineering plastics	Developing a global organization strategy to support new product entrepreneurship as well as mature product leadership.

*Business units with greater than $100 million in sales are classified as large, between $10 million and $100 million as medium, and less than $10 million as small.

TABLE 2 **Readings**

Reading	Theme

Introduction

1. Scope and Challenge of Business-to-Business Marketing — Highlights distinctive aspects of business-to-business marketing.
2. How to Segment Industrial Markets — Proposes the concept of nested indicators to understand and implement industrial market segmentation.
3. Major Sales: Who *Really* Does the Buying? — Discusses the nature and scope of the buying decision-making unit.

Managing New Products

4. New Product Commercialization: Common Mistakes — Discusses four common mistakes in new product development and launch.
5. Creating Project Plans to Focus Product Development — Discusses ways to plan and prepare a portfolio of new product development projects.
6. Commercializing Technology: Understanding User Needs — Discusses several methods of incorporating customer needs in new product development.
7. Industrial Pricing to Meet Customer Needs — Discusses pricing strategies ranging from "cost plus" to "customer's valuation of benefits."
8. Industrial Market Research: Beta Test Site Management — Beta test site management.
9. Designing Channels of Distribution — Offers a systematic six-step methodology for designing new product channels.

Managing Mature Products

10. Beating the Commodity Magnet — Discusses four generic strategies to avoid the commodity pull.
11. Manage Customers for Profit (Not Just Sales) — Offers a framework for managing customer profitability.
12. Close Encounters of the Four Kinds: Managing Customers in a Rapidly Changing Environment — Proposes models for obtaining and sustaining customer relationships.
13. Segmenting Customers in Mature Industrial Markets — A practical application of buying behavior segmentation.
14. Once More: How Do You Improve Customer Service? — Offers a framework for constructing and managing service activities after the sale is over.
15. Automation to Boost Sales and Marketing — Discusses productivity enhancements made possible by marketing/sales automation systems.
16. Reorienting Channels of Distribution — Projects trends and challenges in managing distribution channels.
17. Managing Hybrid Marketing Systems — Provides guidance on how to compose hybrid channels.

Managing Product Market Diversity

18. Managing Market Complexity: A Three-Ring Circus — Highlights the organizational difficulties of managing product-market diversity.
19. Variety versus Value: Two Generic Approaches to Product Policy — Discusses two generic, somewhat opposite, approaches to product policy.
20. What the Hell Is "Market Oriented"? — Looks at interfunctional aspects of market orientation.
21. Staple Yourself to an Order — A practical approach to reengineering the order generation and fulfillment process.
22. High-Tech Marketing: Concepts, Continuity, and Change — Looks at how managers can adapt fundamental marketing techniques to address high-tech environments.
23. The Logic of Global Business: An Interview with ABB's Percy Barnevik — An interview with Asea Brown Boveri's CEO, Percy Barnevik, on the logic of its global organization structure.

CHAPTER 2

Norton Group PLC (A): To Be or Not to Be in the Motorcycle Business

Norton, a once famous motorcycle manufacturer, soundly beaten by Japanese competition, turns its attention to developing rotary engines. The company is acquired by Norton Group PLC, which is headed by a dashing entrepreneur. The new management must decide what direction to give the company and what projects to concentrate on, especially because the company's financial resources are limited. The menu of projects involves application of the rotary technology to motorcycles as well as to several aviation products.

On June 15, 1987, the Extraordinary General Meeting held in the British Motorcycle Museum went well for the directors of Norton Group PLC (NG). Called to approve the £1.64 million[1] acquisition of Norton Motors Limited (Norton) from Manganese Bronze Holdings by NG,[2] the meeting resulted in passage of the resolution. Philippe Le Roux, the 36-year-old entrepreneur who headed the publicly quoted NG, and who had masterminded the takeover, returned to his office to map out the company's future. With him were Jack Johnson, director of sales and marketing, and David Gnodde, director of finance.

"Jack, the waiting game is over," said Le Roux, with a sigh of relief. "We've now got the shareholders behind us. It's time to make some crucial decisions on markets and products. I need you to develop a plan of what products and market segments should get the highest priorities. With our monthly burn rate of close to £100,000 for manufacturing and administrative overhead, we can't wait forever to put revenues on the income statement. I want this company to break even in 1987–1988,[3] which means generating £1.2 million of contribution."

Jon Skofic prepared this case under the direction of V. Kasturi Rangan.
Copyright © 1988 by the President and Fellows of Harvard College.
Harvard Business School case 589-013 (revised February 10, 1992).
[1]The exchange rate at the time of the acquisition was U.K.£ = U.S.$1.65.
[2]In spite of similar names, the two companies had no connection.
[3]NG's financial year ran from September 1 to August 31.

He continued: "In 1988–1989, I'm looking for pretax profits of £400,000 and, in 1989–1990, £900,000. We have the products and recognition to get sales—what we now need is a strategy and a plan."

Philippe Le Roux had left a career in merchant banking in mid-1986 to pursue entrepreneurial investment and management opportunities in a family-controlled venture capital company. By the end of that year, having identified an opportunity to transform Norton, he had become its managing director and a significant stockholder[4] in NG, the vehicle used to bid for Norton.

James Lansdowne Norton had formed the Norton company in England in 1898, and until the mid-1970s, Norton was a prominent player in the world motorcycle market. But in 1977, Norton closed its Wolverhampton factory and withdrew from producing a large range of motorcycles, realizing that the deteriorating performance of its motorcycle business could not be readily reversed in the face of stiff Japanese competition. Norton then concentrated on developing rotary-engine technology begun in 1969. By 1983, the company had developed a rotary-engine motorcycle, the Norton Interpol 2, sold mainly to the British police and armed forces. Since entering into a conditional agreement to buy Norton in February 1987, NG management had considered other high-performance motorcycle segments, namely, civilian touring machines and racing bikes.

Though Norton had sold more than 300 Interpol 2 motorcycles by 1987, Le Roux doubted whether the future of the company lay in motorcycle manufacturing. Also, the rotary engine's characteristics, such as its high power-to-weight ratio, gave it considerable advantages in many other applications. Le Roux was particularly interested in applications for military drones (unmanned aircraft) and light and ultralight manned aviation. Moving in this direction would take the company away from its basic dependency on the motorcycle business, where it had long been overtaken by Japanese and German manufacturers. But conventional wisdom in corporate strategy indicated that a fledgling company such as NG was better off focusing on one market as its primary business opportunity. Said Le Roux: "There is a constant struggle between focus and opportunities. It is not that we cannot focus, but that we do not fully understand the opportunities and the degree of difficulty of pursuing them."

Company History

The Norton company's history throughout the 20th century was one of brilliant engineering. The first major motorcycle launch in 1908 was the Big Four Norton, promoted under the slogan "The Unapproachable Norton." Then followed years of successful motor racing, culminating in 1939 when Norton set the lap record at 91 mph on the 35-mile Isle of Man Tourist Trophy circuit, at the time the preeminent international competition.

---

[4]He owned 20 percent of its stock in June 1987.

From 1939 to 1945, Norton's production was dedicated to military requirements. Several thousand Norton motorcycles were made during World War II and used by the Allied Armed Forces.

After the war, the company developed a range of motorcycles, which gained a reputation for their high performance, quality styling, and handling capabilities. In the 1960s, ironically, Norton benefited from the market invasion of the Japanese manufacturers, including Honda, Suzuki, Yamaha, and Kawasaki. Initially, the Japanese introduced a range of small, inexpensive motorcycles of less than 500-cubic-centimeter (cc) engine capacity; these companies, together, grew the recreational market in the United States and Europe successfully. Norton, with other U.S. and European manufacturers of larger and more expensive motorcycles, exploited this growth as new motorcycle riders, initiated by the Japanese vehicle, traded up to larger machines. The company's sales volume went up from 1,500 units (£0.85 million) in 1960 to 15,000 units (£12 million) by 1972. But soon thereafter, as the Japanese manufacturers introduced their own competitively priced motorbikes in the 500-cc-plus category, Norton's market share began to fall off steeply. The combined U.S. market share of the British producers, Norton, Triumph, and BSA, declined from almost 50 percent in 1969 to under 10 percent in 1973. By 1975, Norton, which had merged in 1972 with BSA and Triumph, was finding itself under pressure from Japanese producers offering additional features such as rear disk brakes and electric starters. In 1977, Norton withdrew from the motorcycle business; from producing 350 complete motorcycles per week, Norton cut back to producing only spare parts.

Thus shorn of its manufacturing and marketing operations, Norton largely became once again, from 1977 to 1983, a research and development center under the wing of Manganese Bronze Holdings, a British industrial conglomerate. Norton focused on the development of a rotary engine for motorcycle use in police and military applications. By targeting these two segments, it intended to avoid head-on competition with the Japanese motorcycle industry. In 1983, it sold the first 50 motorcycles incorporating a rotary engine to the British police force. Norton, however, did not return to profitability through this business, and the pattern of pretax losses continued. (Exhibit 1 shows Norton's financial statements from 1983 to 1986. Exhibit 2 shows Norton's sales by geographic area.)

Rotary Engines

A type of internal combustion engine, the rotary engine was, however, very different from the familiar reciprocating engine. It had neither the pistons nor the valve gear of a reciprocating engine; instead, it relied on the circular motion of the rotor to provide shaft power (see Exhibit 3 for further details and a comparison of the rotary's competitive edges). In spite of inherent advantages, rotary engines had raised a number of performance questions over time. Rotaries were commonly held to have a higher fuel consumption than reciprocating engines, and there had been reliability problems associated with the seals (the equivalent of the piston rings in a reciprocating engine) between the rotor housing and the rotor. Norton's development thrust had been successful in solving these problems. Norton's rotary inventions

Exhibit 1 Norton Motors Limited's Financial Statements 1983 to 1986

	1986	1985	1984	1983
Income Statement (for year ending August 31—amounts in £)				
Net sales	1,289,164	899,807	783,897	384,702
Cost of goods sold	(363,754)	(378,471)	(192,660)	(23,166)
Gross margin	925,410	521,336	491,237	361,536
Operating costs	(1,153,269)	(1,174,725)	(1,271,881)	(821,081)
Exceptional items	—	—	(235,388)	—
Operating profit	(227,859)	(653,389)	(916,032)	(459,545)
Taxation	—	—	—	—
Profit after tax	(227,859)	(653,389)	(916,032)	(459,545)
Extraordinary items	—	3,083,262[a]	7,000	525,022
Profit/(loss)	(227,859)	2,429,873	(909,032)	65,477
Balance Sheet (for year ending July 31—amounts in £)				
Cash	26,624	63,228	104,582	297,608
Accounts receivable	248,134	343,446	224,136	134,606
Inventory	404,063	256,742	279,534	269,774
Properties for disposal	—	—	94,970	264,665
Current assets	678,821	663,416	703,222	966,653
Property, plant, and equipment	122,097	93,151	83,543	70,915
Investments in subsidiaries	20,000	20,000	115,003	155,103
Total assets	820,918	776,567	901,768	1,192,671
Accounts payable	712,005	501,526	452,579	336,164
Long-term liabilities	393,277	331,546	3,023,447	2,521,733
Called-up share capital	100,000	100,000	12,120	12,120
Profit and loss account	(384,364)	(156,505)	(2,586,378)	(1,677,346)

[a] Relates to sale of real estate assets.

Exhibit 2 Norton Motors Limited's Net Sales by Geographical Area: 1983 to 1986 (for year ending August 31—amounts in £)

	1986	1985	1984	1983
United Kingdom	733,454	572,595	566,227	286,768
North America	466,133	245,688	120,752	37,931
Australasia	17,375	3,485	16,876	10,022
Western Europe	92,202	78,039	80,042	48,791
Other	—	—	—	1,190
Total	1,289,164	899,807	783,897	384,702

EXHIBIT 3 Background on the Rotary Engine

In a reciprocating engine, a piston moves back and forth in a combustion chamber and that motion is translated into rotary power by the action of a crankshaft (see Figure A). In a rotary engine, rotary power is generated directly—with no need for translation—by the movement of a rotor in a trochoid-shaped chamber (see Figure B).

This makes the rotary engine fundamentally simpler than the reciprocating engine; it also has significantly fewer parts, which contributes to its superior power-to-weight ratio. Another advantage over the reciprocating engine is that the forces in a rotary engine are balanced at all times, which makes it quieter and gives it much greater smoothness.

FIGURE A

In a reciprocating engine the up-and-down motion of a piston in a cylinder is translated to rotatory power by a crankshaft.

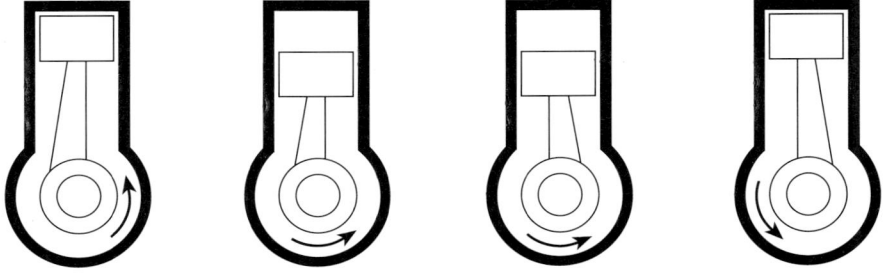

FIGURE B

In a rotary engine, circular motion of a rotor provides energy to the shaft directly.

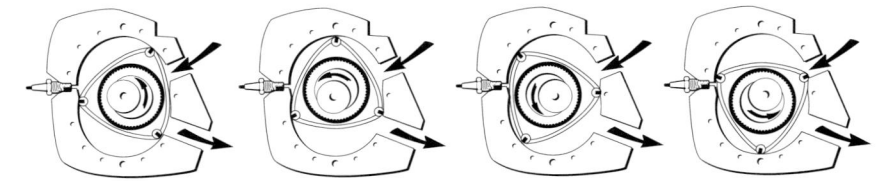

were protected by patents until about 1995. The company considered itself the worldwide leader in the under-100-bhp (brake horsepower) rotary technology.

Mazda, a Japanese company, was the dominant company in the mid-range engine size (100 bhp to 450 bhp), which it used in its automobiles. John Deere, a U.S. manufacturer, held leadership in technology for larger engines, and was designing diesel-fueled rotary engines suitable for agricultural tractors and military vehicles.

A *Forbes* magazine article summed up the situation:

> Unlike most other challengers to the reciprocating piston engine through the years, the rotary actually works. But so great is the world's investment in piston engines that without spectacular cost savings—which the rotary doesn't offer—it doesn't pay to switch. Hence, most of the companies that tried to develop a rotary car engine in the early 1970s, including General Motors, ended up dropping the technology.

Acquisition of Norton

With the ratification by NG's shareholders of the purchase of Norton Motors Limited, Le Roux's next mission was to return Norton, the sole remaining British motorcycle company of consequence, to profitability by applying NG's management and marketing talents.

To pay for the acquisition and to transform the company from an R&D to a manufacturing and sales mode, the company required a significant injection of cash. Whichever strategic option was selected for Norton, funding was needed to upgrade and expand production capacity, increase working capital, and meet the front-end expenses of launching new products. Le Roux backed a hunch about the popular appeal of the Norton name: He elected to raise £3.75 million by going direct to his existing 8,000 NG shareholders and to new investors without the backing of an underwriting institution. By mid-June 1987, Le Roux had indications that his fund-raising drive would be successful.

He planned to use the capital as follows:

TABLE A   NG's June 1987 Stock Offering

	£ million
Proceeds from stock offering	3.75
Less cost of acquisition	1.64
Less cost of Norton's debts	0.36
Cash in hand after acquisition	1.75
Planned investment in plant and equipment	0.50
Funds available for R&D/manufacturing/marketing projects	0.75
Reserved for contingencies	0.50
Total	1.75

The investment in expanding production capability, including the purchase of a Heller CNC machining center, was to take place in July 1987 and the new capacity would be online by October. Norton would then be able to produce annually on a single shift 1,000 of its larger engines of the type used in motorcycles (P41 and P52 engines) or of the type planned for the light aircraft market (P64 engine). Alternatively, Norton could make 2,000 of its smaller engines of the type proposed for the drone market (P73 engine).

Norton's motorcycle plant had the capacity to assemble 500 motorcycles annually, on a one-shift basis. If the company chose to produce 1,000 motorcycle engines per year, bike assembly could be expanded at a cost of £500,000 to keep pace with the engine output. The bulk of the expenditure would go toward financing the increased working capital needs (in parts and work-in-process inventory).

Moving from one to two production shifts would involve a one-time expense of £200,000, largely to cover hiring and training of new workers. Moving from two to three shifts would entail similar expenses. Workers on both the second and third shifts would have to be paid double time.

Scope of Norton's Operations in 1987

In 1987, Norton's two primary areas of activity were the Commando motorcycle spare parts business and the rotary-engine motorcycle business.

Commando spares business: Although the Norton Commando, a 750-cc motorcycle, had been out of production for 10 years, an estimated 25,000 motorcycles were still in working condition worldwide, and sales of spare parts had grown at a rate of 14 percent per annum since 1983. This business accounted for an estimated £500,000 in sales revenue in 1986; gross margins were in excess of 30 percent.

Most parts were made under subcontract in the United Kingdom; finished stock was stored adjacent to the company's only factory at Shenstone, West Midlands. Parts were distributed through a network of 102 authorized Norton dealers, 61 of whom were located in the United Kingdom. The remainder were located overseas and serviced the aging fleet of Commandos exported in the 1960s and 1970s.

Rotary motorcycle business: By 1987, Norton's only motorcycle under production was the rotary-engine Interpol 2; 239 had been sold to local police forces and the armed forces. In June, Norton was completing an order for a further 96 motorcycles from the British Ministry of Defense. No export sales or retail sales of the Interpol 2 had occurred.

In 1986, the Interpol 2 motorcycle accounted for about £450,000 in sales revenue. Combining the attractive power-to-weight ratio and smoothness of the Norton rotary engine with the Norton bike's traditional handling qualities, it proved to be reliable and popular with riders. Norton had many inquiries about the bike from the United Kingdom and abroad. Dealers and motorcyclists in the United Kingdom showed interest in the prospect of a civilian version, and interviews with both confirmed that a high-performance, high-quality Norton superbike might be sold to the top end of the market.

Income from Licensing Arrangements

In 1985, Norton had signed licensing arrangements with a large, $2.5 billion diversified U.S. producer of military and industrial equipment and machinery, granting to this company a transfer of rotary engine technology and rights, until 1995, to manufacture and market rotary engines to military and industrial buyers in North and South America. The agreement was structured to yield an annual fee of about £150,000, and, in addition, a 3 to 7 percent royalty on all sales of rotary engines. Norton also had income from a range of quality consumer products sold by mail under the name "Norton Collectables."

To Be or Not to Be in the Motorcycle Business

Though Philippe Le Roux rated the Norton name as an invaluable asset, he was not convinced that the motorcycle business would sustain the company in the long run. A 1986 study done by a prominent management consulting firm for Norton had recommended shutting down the motorcycle business because of the company's poor competitive position in comparison to global suppliers from Japan and Germany. On the other hand, Le Roux recalled a conversation with Sir John Egan, managing director of Jaguar Cars Ltd., a top-of-the-line British auto manufacturer. Egan had warned: "Stay clear of the airy-fairy aviation stuff. Norton has neither the products nor the reputation. Stick to the knitting. Build a good motorcycle and it will sell."

Upon acquisition of Norton, there were four product/market segments of interest to Le Roux: (1) the motorcycle market; (2) the drone, or remote-pilot vehicles, market; (3) the light aviation market; and (4) the ultralight aviation market.

Motorcycle Market

Paramilitary Motorcycles

Norton had the option in 1987 to continue marketing its on-road paramilitary bike, the Interpol 2, as before or to transform it into a civilian machine. (Exhibit 4 is a

EXHIBIT 4   Interpol 2

photograph of the Interpol 2.) The paramilitary market segment was limited to four-stroke machines in the greater-than-500-cc class; the Interpol 2's P41 engine had a capacity of 588 cc. In Britain, where Norton had an advantage as an indigenous producer, the market was flat. U.K. paramilitary demand was estimated as follows:

TABLE B   Forecast U.K. Paramilitary Motorcycles Sales

	1987	1988	1989	1990	1995
Police forces	320	340	280	330	290
Armed forces	96	—	—	75	88
Total	416	340	280	405	378

Norton had either sold machines or had had machines under test with 36 of the 48 police forces in the United Kingdom using motorcycles, and had averaged an approximate 20 percent market share in 1985 and 1986. Its competitor, BMW of West Germany, held the remainder of the market with two products: the R75, a two-cylinder, 705-cc bike with a strong reputation for being a reliable workhorse; and the K100, a four-cylinder, 1,000-cc bike, which had been introduced in 1986. Both BMW bikes were also sold in civilian form as touring machines. (BMW worldwide had sold 3,200 R75s and 12,800 K100s in 1986.) British police forces had grown accustomed to the R75 as it had been around since the 1970s, and the bike had developed a strong following when the Norton Commando exited the market. The K100 was a smoother, easier-to-handle machine with a premium finish. As the top-of-the-line BMW, it was priced in the United Kingdom at £6,200, including taxes. British police, to the surprise of observers, had begun to buy the K100 (approximately 40 in 1987); it was believed the bike might be overspecified for their use of it.

Pricing in the paramilitary market segment was tight, and on its return to the market in 1983, Norton had been obliged to match BMW's prices. In 1987, it sold the Interpol 2 at the same average price as the R75—£3,900 excluding sales and road taxes. Given Norton's standard costing of £3,600 (see Table C), little margin was allowed for profit or error. With over 2,000 components and 20,000 manufacturing processes required to produce the Interpol 2, the company needed to keep a close watch on costs to make sure that the bike came in on budget.

TABLE C   Standard Cost of Interpol 2

Materials	£1,928
Labor	816
Direct manufacturing cost	686
Marketing expense[a]	164
Total	£3,594

[a] The 1986 fully loaded cost of one sales representative spread over 85 bikes.

The margin of £300 also had to cover the cost of the three-year, complete warranty on parts and labor, which Norton had been obliged to offer to match BMW's terms of sale. When NG's David Gnodde, director of finance, arrived at Shenstone in 1987, he found that no one had calculated the precise cost to Norton of offering the warranty; experience told him it amounted to several hundred pounds per machine.

Civilian Motorcycles

Sales of civilian superbikes (typically over 500 cc and costing above £4,000) were the only buoyant sector of an otherwise depressed U.K. market for two-wheelers. As elsewhere in the developed countries, the trend in the United Kingdom toward off-road machines in the recreational market had abated, and by 1987 consumers sought street machines with high performance and quality. The U.K. market for this kind of motorcycle, split by brand and price and including taxes, is given below.

TABLE D   U.K. Civilian Superbike Sales in 1986

Retail Price	£4,000–4,500	£4,500–5,000	£5,000–5,500	£5,500–6,000	£6,000+
Kawasaki	1,050	340	0	0	0
BMW	355	0	890	0	0
Suzuki	0	620	0	0	0
Honda	0	0	0	100	50
Other	55	40	90	0	50
Total	1,460	1,000	980	100	100

Certain overseas markets had had much larger sales of motorcycles over 500 cc in 1986; for example, 17,000 were sold in the United States and 26,000 in West Germany, compared with 3,640 sold in the United Kingdom.

Norton felt that it could develop, at a cost of £200,000, a rotary-engine superbike positioned as a classic touring machine competitive with BMW and the top Japanese machines in time for launch at the fall 1987 Bike Show, the most important British bike exhibition. The bike would be based on the Interpol 2 and would emphasize comfort, no-nonsense handling, and all-day rideability rather than raw acceleration and top-end speed. A limited edition "Norton Classic," it was felt, would appeal to the customer seeking an alternative to a Japanese or BMW tourer.

The bike could be priced at around £6,000 including taxes (about 5 percent), a level competitive with the more expensive BMW and Japanese models, which had been rising in price as their currencies appreciated against the pound. After taxes, Norton would net an approximate £2,100-per-bike contribution toward its manufacturing and administrative overheads. (This calculation assumed that Norton sold the limited edition direct and provided after-sales support from the factory, allowing it to keep the normal distributor's margin of 25 to 30 percent.)

If, over the longer term, Norton sought to exploit the international superbike market, certain design changes would be required, including the development of the

P52 water-cooled engine for the bike. At a total cost of £200,000 for development, this unit could then be offered in the Interpol frame during the second half of 1988. With the water-cooled engine bike, Norton could consider taking on the might of BMW and the Japanese manufacturers in the international arena. It had to win, say, 10 percent of the U.S. superbike market to sell 1,500 to 2,000 bikes a year. Provided the bike met U.S. emission standards, the potential existed to sell bikes with a variable cost of £3,600 for up to £5,500 to £6,000 retail. Selling 2,000 bikes a year would, however, require an advertising and promotions budget of nearly £1 million and a phenomenal effort in terms of coordinating distribution channels. And with dealers requiring margins of 25 to 30 percent, Norton's gross margin would be cut to an average of £575 per bike.

Production Racer Motorcycles

A production racer was a special class of a highly tuned, 120-plus bhp bike capable of speeds in excess of 140 mph. With a limited budget, the P41 rotary engine had already been tuned to produce 155 bhp in the test workshop; the engine had then been installed in a racing frame and had run over 200 miles at high speeds at a test track. It would take, at estimate, until mid-1988 at a cost of £200,000 to iron out its bugs so that it could be marketed to the biking public, assuming no other major development program was being simultaneously conducted.

Though the U.K. market for production racing bikes was small (less than 50 were sold in 1986), prices in this segment were high. A motorcyclist who raced on the weekends and was not sponsored by one of the major manufacturers would pay upward of £15,000 for a top machine. Norton's manufacturing engineers calculated that they could produce a bike for a variable cost of £8,000 to £10,000 with the potential to compete with the top Honda production racer priced at £15,000. And marketing a small number of specialist machines sold with high gross margins fitted well with Norton's hand-built, job-shop manufacturing process.

Launching a production racer would require Norton to invest at least £300,000 in its own racing team program in the 1988 summer season to prove the bike in championship competition. Although this was a high investment, racing success would have a spillover effect to other Norton products.

Jack Johnson estimated that demand for production racers would be relatively flat at a level of some 50 units per annum in the United Kingdom for the next few years. The U.S. market was estimated to be more than 500 units/year and the European market (excluding the United Kingdom), about 150 units/year.

Drone Aircraft

Drones, used by all branches of the military in most countries, with North America, Western Europe, Israel, and the Middle East as significant markets, would be a new market for Norton. Drones were remotely controlled by ground-based personnel and fell into two main categories: expendable drones and surveillance drones.

Expendable Drones

Expendable drones flew in one of two roles: as aerial targets or as offensive missiles used in combat.

Aerial target drones as a concept had been around for many years and had benefited from the advent of microelectronics, which permitted the miniaturization of the avionics system used to guide the craft. They were used for training ground-based artillery operators or surface-to-air weapon systems operators. A target drone served as a mock-up of enemy aircraft to be shot at by ground-based soldiers.

Combat drones were more recent. Their role was offensive, either to carry a warhead and act as a cruise missile, or to carry jamming equipment that interfered with the enemy's intelligence-gathering and communications systems.

Power for drones had traditionally come either from two-stroke engines or gas turbine engines chosen for their power output. The world market for target drones was estimated to be from 3,000 to 5,000 units per annum, split evenly between two-stroke-powered drones and turbine-powered drones. In 1987, the target market was thought to be growing quite slowly at less than 5 percent per annum.

Engine manufacturers sold to original equipment manufacturers (OEMs), such as Boeing, Northrop and smaller companies, who integrated the engine into the drone airframe. (Engine cost was approximately 20 to 30 percent of the total system cost; the electronics payload usually made up the bulk of the cost.) The OEM, in turn, sold the target system to the procurement arm of the armed forces.

Two major combat drone engine contracts were to be bid in 1988. In 1987, the U.S. Air Force had awarded a contract to Boeing to manufacture up to 10,000 anti-radar combat drones for delivery from 1990 to 1995. Boeing had not yet selected the engine suppliers. Simultaneously, the British and West German armies were collaborating on a joint program pioneering the development of a combat drone designed to neutralize enemy radar installations; it offered the prospect of 6,000 to 9,000 units to be processed over a period of three years in the early 1990s.

By June 1987, Norton had developed, specifically for the drone market, a small, 22-pound, 38-HP rotary engine, known as P73 (see Exhibit 5 for a picture of the P73 installed in an expendable target drone). The development of P73, however, was not complete; it was estimated that by early 1988 and at a further cost of £350,000, Norton would be in a position to supply prototype engines to interested OEMs. Table E shows a comparison of the characteristics of the P73 with its three main competitors (which shared 80 percent of the world market):

TABLE E   Drone Engine Comparison

	Power (bhp)	Weight (lb)	Power-to-Weight Ratio	Fuel Consumption (lb/bhp hr)
Norton P73 (rotary)	38	22	1.7	0.6
Dixon (2-stroke)	25	19	1.3	0.8
Weiss (2-stroke)	26	18	1.4	0.8
K.A.N. (2-stroke)	26	18	1.4	0.8

EXHIBIT 5 P73 Drone Engine

A.

B.

Dixon of the United Kingdom and Weiss of West Germany were both aviation engine subsidiaries of large, diversified industrial holding companies. K.A.N. was a relatively small, family-controlled engineering firm based in the United States that specialized in short-life engines.

The price of a standard two-stroke drone engine to the OEM averaged around £1,250. The Norton P73 in its basic form had the following structure:

TABLE F   **P73 Cost Structure**

	£
Materials	£620
Labor	180
Direct manufacturing cost	256
Total	£1,056

Surveillance Drones

Designed for surveillance missions and to collect intelligence in combat zones, these drones had become popular in military circles following their deployment over Lebanon by Israel in 1982. They were a lower-cost alternative to sending a manned aircraft over enemy territory and had no attendant risk of loss of life. It had been forecast that the global surveillance drone market would be in the region of 500 to 1,000 units per annum by 1990 and would grow at a rate of 25 percent per annum.

Three criteria were important to the OEM and the military customer in considering the purchase of a surveillance drone. First, OEMs such as Lockheed of the United States and the United Kingdom's GEC believed the engine to be the weakest aspect of the drone and were concerned about engine reliability; the two-stroke engines used in expendable drones dominated the nascent surveillance drone market, and these were prone to failure. Engine failure in a surveillance drone was catastrophic: the philosophy of expendability did not apply here as it did with target and combat drones. Since the vehicles carried sensitive electronic equipment worth several hundred thousand dollars, it was critical that they returned to base at the end of each mission. Second, the amount of fuel consumed was important. The average mission length was around an hour for an expendable drone compared with three to eight hours for a surveillance drone. Inefficient engines reduced mission length capability or required more fuel to be carried on take-off, in turn reducing the amount of space and weight otherwise taken by the electronic payload. Third, a low vibration level was required from the engine in order to minimize interference transmitted to the sensitive camera and electronic payload.

Norton felt that in the P73 it had the edge over its two-stroke competition on the question of engine dependability. Moreover, the P73 had already achieved 25 to 35 percent better fuel consumption in engine trials than two-strokes (see Table E). Finally, the rotary was inherently the better balanced engine and vibration had been reduced to a much lower level than in the two-stroke. Gaining market share at the expense of the incumbent two-strokes, however, would be a long process because of lengthy testing and evaluation procedures demanded by the OEMs.

In 1987, Norton had no one assigned to the task of marketing to the military procurement officers and OEMs who purchased drone engines. In each case, the sales process would involve liaisons to be established with those who developed the drone, those who marketed the system, those who used the system, and those who procured the system for the military. In all, this was a new market requiring a decision-making process that Norton did not fully understand.

Light Aviation

Light aviation also represented a new market opportunity for Norton. Light aircraft, defined by the Federal Aviation Agency as weighing less than 12,500 lbs., were typically capable of carrying one to four people. Some 172,000 light aircraft were in use in the United States, and 20,000 in Europe, and new pilots were being trained on both continents in large numbers as interest in aviation grew.

But despite the high level of interest in private aviation, a decline in sales of new light aircraft had occurred since 1978. Cessna, Piper, and Beech, commonly referred to as the "Big Three," had dominated worldwide production of light aircraft since World War II. By 1987, however, all three had ceased to manufacture these aircraft in the face of rising labor costs (a significant portion of overall cost) and product liability insurance. See Table G for annual U.S. general aviation aircraft shipments by type of aircraft.

Industry experts predicted that the decline in light aviation sales would reverse over time: The stock of aircraft in use was getting older and numbers of new pilots were demanding new aircraft designs. Pent-up demand existed for aircraft with lower operating costs.

TABLE G U.S. General Aviation Aircraft Shipments*

	Single-Piston Engine	Twin-Piston Engine	Turboprop	Jet	Total
1965	9,873	1,780	87	112	11,852
1970	5,942	1,159	135	56	7,292
1975	11,579	2,116	305	194	14,056
1980	8,640	2,116	778	326	11,877
1983	1,811	417	321	142	2,691
1985	870	193	321	145	2,029
1986	985	138	250	122	1,495
1987 (forecast)	643	87	263	122	1,085

*The light aircraft class spans all four columns but is predominantly covered in the single-piston engine column.

In addition, opportunities existed for Norton in retrofitting engines in aircraft undergoing overhaul, which was carried out after every 1,500 hours of operation. The 90 bhp Norton P64 rotary engine (see Exhibit 6) with its superior power-to-weight ratio and aerodynamic shape (the barrel-shaped rotary could easily be cowled in the nose of light aircraft), presented an attractive opportunity. By June 1987, only the gearbox of the P64 engine needed additional development. With six months' development time and testing at a cost of £150,000, Norton was confident that it would have a reliable and highly competitive power unit (see Table H for a comparison to three leading competing light aircraft engines).

TABLE H **Light Aircraft Engine Comparison**

Engine	Type	Power (bhp)	Weight (lbs)	Power-to-Weight Ratio
Norton	rotary	90	105	0.9
EngTech (U.K.)	2-stroke	75	135	0.6
Wimer (WG)	4-stroke	65	165	0.4
Benson (U.S.)	4-stroke	105	235	0.4

The Norton P64 rotary engine had commenced an engineering and flight trial with a small U.K. aircraft manufacturer that could lead to U.K. type-certification in mid-1988,[5] necessary for Norton to install it in light aircraft. The aircraft manufacturer had agreed to a letter of intent to purchase 150 engines over a five-year period commencing in 1988, dependent on certification.

Though the certification process was not costly and only involved engine trials, Norton would also be required to install an information system to track to its source every component used in the engine. On an average, an engine of the capacity that Norton made consisted of about 200 component parts. A consulting company had offered to install such a system, including the computer hardware, for £300,000; it claimed that the system's benefits would be felt in all operations. In particular, said the consultants, the system would reduce the inventory of the 2,000 parts necessary for assembling a motorcycle.

Since the Big Three were unlikely to reenter the light aviation market, the manufacturing companies in the light aviation class of the future were likely to be fragmented, and European OEMs stood as good a chance of winning a significant share of the world market as U.S. OEMs. This meant that if Norton were to sell its P64 engine directly to the OEMs, it would require a large sales force and field engineering staff.

---

[5]Type-certification is the process of establishing the plane and engine's airworthiness under a range of operating conditions to the satisfaction of the U.K. Civil Aviation Authority, equivalent to the U.S. Federal Aviation Administration.

Exhibit 6 Norton P64 Aero-Engine

A.

B.

Given the pricing of competitive engines in the 65 to 105 bhp bracket around the £3,600 to £4,250 level, Norton could make a gross margin of £1,000 per engine, assuming it priced head-to-head with the competition (at £4,000) and allowed a distributor's margin of 25 percent.

Ultralight Aviation (Kitplanes)

Ultralight aircraft, a category of aircraft weighing less than 254 lbs., were, strictly speaking, single seaters, though over the years the designation had come to encompass twin-seat vehicles. A pilot's license was not required to fly an ultralight, and neither the airframe nor the engine required type-certification. Therefore, it was an inexpensive way for a newcomer to get airborne.

To meet its weight limits, the plane was constructed of aluminum structural members with a dacron skin (rather than the aluminum ceconite skin of conventional light aircraft) and typically had an open cockpit and a minimum of instrumentation (often only a fuel gauge, engine revolution counter, and altimeter).

Ultralights were usually sold by the manufacturer in kits for the buyer to assemble at home, retailing at about £4,500, excluding engine. If the buyer carried out more than 50 percent of the construction work, the manufacturer could describe his product as a "kit" and not be held responsible for construction defects, thus avoiding the exposure to product liability litigation (which had crippled the light aviation business in the 1980s).

The engine for an ultralight was usually bought from an engine distributor; the buyer then installed it into the airframe. Since the manufacturer specified a particular engine as suitable for a particular airframe, Norton would need to work with the manufacturers to get its engine approved and included in the assembly drawings provided with the kit.

The ultralight movement had begun in the 1970s when hang-gliding enthusiasts had literally strapped small engines to the gliders in order to gain altitude. It had initially started with the American Cuyuna two-stroke engine, replacing that in the 1980s with the Austrian Rotax two-stroke engine. By 1987, 90 percent of ultralights were powered by Rotax engines in the 27-bhp-to-65-bhp range. None of Norton's competitors in the light aircraft segment were present in the ultralight segment since their power-to-weight ratios were not suitable for ultralights.

There were 13,000 single-seat ultralights and 9,000 twin-seaters in the U.S. market; the European market was estimated to be about a fifth of the size. Twin-seat vehicles, requiring more power than single-seaters, tended to use engines of 50 bhp and above and more power was sought by many fliers, both to enhance the capability of their craft and to satisfy their egos. Ultralight flying was a recreational/sports activity for 80 percent of those who used the vehicles, and the status and image of equipment flown mattered to the flyer. Commercial flyers who performed such tasks as crop spraying and traffic and crowd surveillance comprised the remaining 20 percent; this group of users valued reliability and extra power and would pay a premium to have those advantages.

Early market research carried out by Norton verified that the ultralight market might be receptive to more powerful engines, and that as the perceived trend from single- to twin-seat vehicles developed, more engines with greater than 50 bhp would be required. Ultralight shipments in the United States amounted annually to 2,000 to 2,500 units, of which 60 percent to 75 percent were single-seaters. It was estimated that by 1990, twin-seaters would make up 50 percent of new sales.

Pricing in this market was different from pricing in the light aviation market. The top-of-the-line Rotax engine, a 65-bhp two-stroke engine, retailed at £1,350. For Norton to compete with its £4,000, 90-bhp engine, superior presentation of the Norton benefits would be required. The pluses were that the P64 would be a more reliable engine with a longer life than the Rotax two-stroke line, and that improved fuel economy and lower vibration levels would provide for the justification of the price premium.

Jack Johnson had detected some dissatisfaction with the Rotax line among users, and OEMs especially, concerning reliability. Engine failure was a relatively common occurrence with two-strokes. (Since ultralights would plane without power, failure was not usually a catastrophic event unless it occurred on takeoff.) Equally, certain features of the two-stroke, such as the corrosion-prone muffler system, compromised the quality of the engine. Johnson sensed that just as ultralights had evolved from powered hang-gliders to aircraft using two different generations of two-stroke engines, the movement might be ready for the next evolutionary step—to a more powerful, more reliable, and higher quality engine. He was plagued, however, by the changes that would be required in the Norton sales and marketing function. The buyer type would be a new one, a sales force would have to be recruited, the channels of distribution would be new, and, above all, pricing would require careful presentation to the buying public. Johnson knew he needed to look more closely at Norton's economics.

The Dilemma

Developing the motorcycle market appealed to Jack Johnson's sense of history and matched the aspirations of many of the workforce and shareholders. Philippe Le Roux's sense, on the other hand, was that the aero-engine market would yield the greatest return. He believed that the engine would be ready for launch in the summer of 1988 at the large civilian airshows in the United States if Norton used the time until then on gearbox engineering work. He felt that the superior power-to-weight ratio of the Norton engine and disillusionment with the competitors' range would make acceptance easier to accomplish.

Le Roux was also tempted by the drone market. Military sales were less prone to economic cycles, and once the engine was specified in a military vehicle, the OEM, to whom Norton supplied the power plant, would be carrying out all the expensive marketing effort.

Le Roux had often said, "Management's objective is to run a portfolio of opportunities in the first year and then decide whether the various opportunities have any potential." Constrained resources, however, had raised serious questions regarding the shotgun approach. David Gnodde, finance director, had put together a list of projects requiring Le Roux's attention:

	(£s)
1. Development of the Norton Classic.	200,000
2. Development of P52 motorcycle engine.	200,000
3. Marketing expenditure for launching Norton Classic worldwide.	1,000,000
4. Development of engine for prototype racer.	200,000
5. Marketing expenditure for launching racer.	300,000
6. Development of P73 drone engine.	350,000
7. Development of P64 aero-engine.	150,000
8. Installation of information system (to track components).	300,000

Le Roux had access to £750,000 for capital expenditure. He would only very reluctantly touch the £500,000 set aside for contingencies. Given the company's current financial position, raising debt would be quite costly. How to break even in the short run while maintaining strategic direction in the long run was the problem he saw for Norton to solve just as soon as possible.

Chapter 3: How to Segment Industrial Markets

The difficulty of segmenting industrial markets has dissuaded companies from trying, despite the benefits they could gain in terms of market selection and focus. The problem is to identify the most useful variables. One way to do this is to arrange the five general segmentation criteria—demographics, operating variables, customer purchasing approaches, situational factors, and personal buyer characteristics—into a nested hierarchy. The segmentation criteria of the largest, outermost nest are general characteristics about industries and companies. Innermost nests are specific, subtle, and hard-to-assess traits.

As difficult as segmenting consumer markets is, it is much simpler and easier than segmenting industrial markets. Often the same industrial products have multiple applications; likewise, several different products can be used in the same application. Customers differ greatly and it is hard to discern which differences are important and which are trivial for developing a marketing strategy.

Little research has been done on industrial market segmentation. None of the 10 articles in the *Journal of Marketing Research*'s special August 1978 section, "Market Segmentation Research," for instance, deals with industrial market segmentation in more than a passing manner. Our research indicates that most industrial marketers use segmentation as a way to explain results rather than as a way to plan.

In fact, industrial segmentation can assist companies in several areas:

- **Analysis of the market.** Better understanding of the total marketplace, including how and why customers buy.

This reading was prepared by Benson P. Shapiro and Thomas V. Bonoma.

Copyright © 1984 by the President and Fellows of Harvard College. All rights reserved. Reprinted with permission from *Harvard Business Review*, May–June 1984, pp. 103–10.

- **Selection of key markets.** Rational choice of market segments that best fit the company's capabilities.
- **Management of marketing.** The development of strategies, plans, and programs to profitably meet the needs of different market segments and to give the company a distinct competitive advantage.

In this article we integrate and build on previous schemes for segmenting industrial markets and offer a new approach that enables not only the simple grouping of customers and prospects, but also more complex grouping of purchase situations, events, and personalities. It thus serves as an important new analytical tool.

Consider the dilemma of one skilled and able industrial marketer who observed recently:

"I can't see any basis on which to segment my market. We have 15 percent of the market for our type of plastics fabrication equipment. There are 11 competitors who serve a large and diverse set of customers, but there is no unifying theme to our customer set or to anyone else's."

His frustration is understandable, but he should not give up, for at least he knows that 15 percent of the market purchases one product and that knowledge, in itself, is a basis for segmentation. Segments exist, even when the only apparent basis for differentiation is brand choice.

At other times, a marketer may be baffled by a profusion of segmentation criteria. Customer groups and even individual customers within these groups may differ in demographics (including industry and company size), operating differences (production technology is an example), purchasing organization, "culture," and personal characteristics. Usually, a marketer can group customers, prospects, and purchase situations in different ways depending on the variables used to segment the market. The problem is to identify relevant segmentation bases.

We have identified five general segmentation criteria, which we have arranged as a *nested* hierarchy—like a set of boxes that fit one into the other or a set of wooden Russian dolls. Moving from the outer nest toward the inner, these criteria are: demographics, operating variables, customer purchasing approaches, situational factors, and personal characteristics of the buyers.

Exhibit 1 shows how the criteria relate to one another as nests. The segmentation criteria of the largest, outermost nest are demographics—general, easily observable characteristics about industries and companies. Those of the smallest, inmost nest are personal characteristics—specific, subtle, hard-to-assess traits. The marketer moves from the more general, easily observable segmentation characteristics to the more specific, subtle ones. This approach will become clearer as we explain each criterion.

We should note at this point that it may not be necessary or even desirable for every industrial marketer to use every stage of the nested approach for every product. Although it is possible to skip irrelevant criteria, it is important that the marketer completely understand the approach before deciding on omissions and shortcuts.

Exhibit 1 Nested Approach

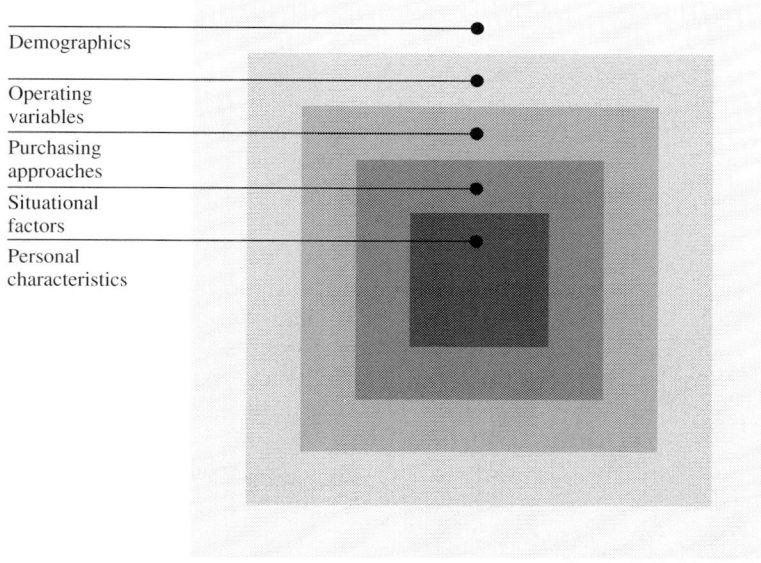

Demographics
Operating variables
Purchasing approaches
Situational factors
Personal characteristics

Demographics

We begin with the outermost nest, which contains the most general segmentation criteria, demographics. These variables give a broad description of the company and relate to general customer needs and usage patterns. They can be determined without visiting the customer and include industry and company size, and customer location.

The Industry. Knowledge of the industry affords a broad understanding of customer needs and perceptions of purchase situations. Some companies, such as those selling paper, office equipment, business-oriented computers, and financial services, market to a wide range of industries. For these, industry is an important basis for market segmentation. Hospitals, for example, share some computer needs with retail stores and yet differ markedly from them as a customer group.

Marketers may wish to subdivide individual industries. For example, although financial services are in a sense a single industry, commercial banks, insurance companies, stockbrokerage houses, and savings and loan associations all differ dramatically. Their differences in terms of product and service needs, such as specialized peripherals and terminals, data handling, and software requirements, make a more detailed segmentation scheme necessary to sell computers to the financial services market.

Company Size. The fact that large companies justify and require specialized programs affects market segmentation. It may be, for example, that a small supplier of industrial chemicals, after segmenting its prospective customers on the basis of company size, will choose not to approach large companies whose volume requirements exceed its own production capacity.

Customer Location. The third demographic factor, location, is an important variable in decisions related to deployment and organization of sales staff. A manufacturer of heavy-duty pumps for the petrochemical industry, for example, would want to provide good coverage in the Gulf Coast, where customers are concentrated, while putting little effort into New England. Customer location is especially important when proximity is a requirement for doing business, as in marketing products of low value per unit weight or volume (corrugated boxes or prestressed concrete), or in situations where personal service is essential, as in job shop printing.

As noted, a marketer can determine all of these demographic variables easily. Industry-oriented and general directories are useful in developing lists of customers in terms of industry, size, and location. Government statistics, reports by market research companies, and industry and trade association publications provide a great deal of demographic data.

Many companies base their industrial marketing segmentation approach on demographic data alone. But while demographics are useful and easily obtained, they do not exhaust the possibilities of segmentation. They are often only a beginning.

Operating Variables

The second segmentation nest contains a variety of segmentation criteria called operating variables. Most of these enable more precise identification of existing and potential customers within demographic categories. Operating variables are generally stable and include technology, user-nonuser status (by product and brand), and customer capabilities (operating, technical, and financial).

Company Technology. A company's technology, involving either its manufacturing process or its product, goes a long way toward determining its buying needs. Soda ash, for example, can be produced by two methods that require different capital equipment and supplies. The production of Japanese color televisions is highly automated and uses a few, large integrated circuits. In the United States, on the other hand, color TV production once involved many discrete components, manual assembly, and fine-tuning. In Europe, production techniques made use of a hybrid of integrated circuits and discrete components. The technology used affects companies' requirements for test gear, tooling, and components and, thus, a marketer's most appropriate marketing approach.

Product and Brand-Use Status. One of the easiest ways, and in some situations the only obvious way, to segment a market is by product and brand use. Users of a particular product or brand generally have some characteristics in common; at the very least, they have a common experience with a product or brand.

Manufacturers who replace metal gears with nylon gears in capital equipment probably share perceptions of risk, manufacturing process or cost structure, or marketing strategy. They probably have experienced similar sales presentations. Having used nylon gears, they share common experiences, including, perhaps, similar changes in manufacturing approaches.

One supplier of nylon gears might argue that companies that have already committed themselves to replace metal gears with nylon gears are better customer prospects than those that have not yet done so, since it is usually easier to generate demand for a new brand than for a new product. But another supplier might reason that manufacturers that have not yet shifted to nylon are better prospects because they have not experienced its benefits and have not developed a working relationship with a supplier. A third marketer might choose to approach both users and nonusers with different strategies.

Current customers are a different segment from prospective customers using a similar product purchased elsewhere. Current customers are familiar with a company's product and service, and company managers know something about customer needs and purchasing approaches. Some companies' marketing approaches focus on increasing sales volume from existing customers, via either customer growth or gaining a larger share of the customer's business, rather than on additional sales volume from new customers. In these cases, industrial sales managers often follow a two-step process: First, they seek to gain an initial order on trial, and then to increase the share of the customer's purchases. Banks are often more committed to raising the share of major customers' business than to generating new accounts.

Sometimes it is useful to segment customers not only on the basis of whether they buy from the company or from its competitors, but also, in the latter case, on the identity of competitors. This information can be useful in several ways. Sellers may find it easier to lure customers from competitors that are weak in certain respects. When Bethlehem Steel opened its state-of-the-art Burns Harbor plant in the Chicago area, for example, it went after the customers of one local competitor known to offer poor quality.

Customer Capabilities. Marketers might find companies with known operating, technical, or financial strengths and weaknesses to be an attractive market. For example, a company operating with tight materials inventories would greatly appreciate a supplier with a reliable delivery record. And customers unable to perform quality-control tests on incoming materials might be willing to pay for supplier quality checks. Some raw materials suppliers might choose to develop a thriving business among less-sophisticated companies, for which lower-than-usual average discounts well compensate added services.

Technically weak customers in the chemical industry have traditionally depended on suppliers for formulation assistance and technical support. Some suppliers have been astute in identifying customers needing such support and in providing it in a highly effective manner.

Technical strength can also differentiate customers. Digital Equipment Corporation for many years specialized in selling its minicomputers to customers able to develop their own software, and Prime Computer sells computer systems to business users who do not need the intensive support and "hand holding" offered by IBM and other manufacturers. Both companies use segmentation for market selection.

Many operating variables are easily researched. In a quick drive around a soda ash plant, for example, a vendor might be able to identify the type of technology being used. Data on financial strength is at least partially available from credit-rating services. Customer personnel may provide other data, such as the name of current suppliers; "reverse engineering" (tearing down or disassembly) of a product may yield information on the type and even the producers of components, as may merely noting the names on delivery trucks entering the prospect's premises.

Purchasing Approaches

One of the most neglected but valuable methods of segmenting an industrial market involves consumers' purchasing approaches and company philosophy. The factors in this middle segmentation nest include the formal organization of the purchasing function, the power structure, the nature of buyer–seller relationships, the general purchasing policies, and the purchasing criteria.

Purchasing Function Organization. The organization of the purchasing function to some extent determines the size and operation of a company's purchasing unit. A centralized approach may merge individual purchasing units into a single group, and vendors with decentralized manufacturing operations may find it difficult to meet centralized buying patterns.[1] To meet these differing needs, some suppliers handle sales to centralized purchasers through so-called national account programs, and those to companies with a decentralized approach through field-oriented sales forces.

Power Structures. These also vary widely among customers. The impact of influential organizational units varies and often affects purchasing approaches. The powerful financial analysis units at General Motors and Ford may, for example, have made those companies unusually price-oriented in their purchasing decisions. A company may have a powerful engineering department, for instance, that strongly influences purchases; a supplier with strong technical skills would suit such a customer. A vendor might find it useful to adapt its marketing program to customer strengths, using one approach for customers with strong engineering operations and another for customers lacking these.

---

[1] See E. Raymond Corey, "Should Companies Centralize Procurement?" *Harvard Business Review*, November–December 1978, p. 102.

Buyer–Seller Relationships. A supplier probably has stronger ties with some customers than others. The link may be clearly stated. A lawyer, commercial banker, or investment banker, for example, might define as an unattractive market segment all companies having as a board member the representative of a competitor.

General Purchasing Policies. A financially strong company that offers a lease program might want to identify prospective customers who prefer to lease capital equipment or who have meticulous asset management. When AT&T could lease but not sell equipment, this was an important segmentation criterion for it. Customers may prefer to do business with long-established companies or with small independent companies, or may have particularly potent affirmative action purchasing programs (minority-owned businesses were attracted by Polaroid's widely publicized social conscience program, for example). Or they may prefer to buy systems rather than individual components.

A prospective customer's approach to the purchasing process is important. Some purchasers require an agreement based on supplier cost, particularly the auto companies, the U.S. government, and the three large general merchandise chains, Sears Roebuck, Montgomery Ward, and J.C. Penney. Other purchasers negotiate from a market-based price and some use bids. Bidding is an important method for obtaining government and quasi-government business; but because it emphasizes price, bidding tends to favor suppliers that, perhaps because of a cost advantage, prefer to compete on price. Some vendors might view purchasers that choose suppliers via bidding as desirable, while others might avoid them.

Purchasing Criteria. The power structure, the nature of buyer–seller relationships, and general purchasing policies all affect purchasing criteria. Benefit segmentation in the consumer goods market is the process of segmenting a market in terms of the reasons why customers buy. It is, in fact, the most insightful form of consumer goods segmentation because it deals directly with customer needs. In the industrial market, consideration of the criteria used to make purchases and the application for these purchases, which we consider later, approximate the benefit segmentation approach.

Situational Factors

Up to this point we have focused on the grouping of customer companies. Now we consider the role of the purchase situation, even single-line entries on the order form.

Situational factors resemble operating variables but are temporary and require a more detailed knowledge of the customer. They include the urgency of order fulfillment, product application, and the size of order.

Urgency of Order Fulfillment. It is worthwhile to differentiate between products to be used in routine replacement or for building a new plant and emergency replacement of existing parts. Some companies have found a degree of urgency useful for market selection and for developing a focused marketing-manufacturing approach leading to a "hot-order shop"—a factory that can supply small, urgent orders quickly.

A supplier of large-size, heavy-duty stainless steel pipe fittings, for example, defined its primary market as fast-order replacements. A chemical plant or paper mill needing to replace a fitting quickly is often willing to pay a premium price for a vendor's application engineering, for flexible manufacturing capacity, and for installation skills that would be unnecessary in the procurement of routine replacement parts.

Product Application. The requirements for a 5-horsepower motor used in intermittent service in a refinery will differ from those of a 5-horsepower motor in continuous use. Requirements for an intermittent-service motor would vary depending on whether its reliability was critical to the operation or safety of the refinery. Product application can have a major impact on the purchase process, purchase criteria, and thus on the choice of vendor.

Size of Order. Market selection can be based at the level of individual line entries on the order form. A company with highly automated equipment might segment the market so that it can concentrate only on items with large unit volumes. A nonautomated company, on the other hand, might want only small quantity, short-run items. Ideally, these vendors would like the order split up into long-run and short-run items. In many industries, such as paper and pipe fittings, distributors break up orders in this way.

Marketers can differentiate individual orders in terms of product uses as well as users. The distinction is important as users may seek different suppliers for the same product under different circumstances. The pipe-fittings manufacturer that focused on urgent orders is a good example of a marketing approach based on these differences.

Situational factors can greatly affect purchasing approaches. General Motors, for example, makes a distinction between product purchases—that is, raw materials or components for a product being produced—and nonproduct purchases. Urgency of order fulfillment is so powerful that it can change both the purchase process and the criteria used. An urgent replacement is generally purchased on the basis of availability, not price.

The interaction between situational factors and purchasing approaches is an example of the permeability of segmentation nests. Factors in one nest affect those in other nests. Industry criteria, for instance, an outer-nest demographic description, influence but do not determine application, a middle-nest situational criterion. The nests are a useful mental construct but not a clean framework of independent units because in the complex reality of industrial markets, criteria are interrelated.

The nesting approach cannot be applied in a cookbook fashion but requires, instead, careful, intelligent judgment.

Buyers' Personal Characteristics

People, not companies, make purchase decisions, although the organizational framework in which they work and company policies and needs may constrain their choices. Marketers for industrial goods, like those for consumer products, can segment markets according to the individuals involved in a purchase in terms of buyer–seller similarity, buyer motivation, individual perceptions, and risk-management strategies.

Some buyers are risk averse, others risk receptive. The level of risk a buyer is willing to assume is related to other personality variables such as personal style, intolerance for ambiguity, and self-confidence. The amount of attention a purchasing agent will pay to cost factors depends not only on the degree of uncertainty about the consequences of the decision but also on whether credit or blame for these will accrue to him or her. Buyers who are risk averse are not good prospects for new products and concepts. Risk-averse buyers also tend to avoid untested vendors.

Some buyers are meticulous in their approach to buying—they shop around, look at a number of vendors, and then split their order to assure delivery. Others rely on old friends and past relationships, and seldom make vendor comparisons.[2] Companies can segment a market in terms of these preferences.

Data on personal characteristics are expensive and difficult to gather. It is often worthwhile to develop good, formal, sales information systems to ensure that salespeople transmit the data they gather to the marketing department for use in developing segmented marketing strategies. One chemical company attributes part of its sales success to its sales information system's routine collection of data on buyers. Such data-gathering efforts are most justified in the case of customers with large sales potential.

Reassembling the Nest

Marketers are interested in purchase decisions that depend on company variables, situational factors, and the personal characteristics of the buyers. The three outer nests, as Exhibit 2 shows, cover company variables, the fourth inner-middle nest, situational factors, and the inmost nest, personal characteristics.

As we move from the outer nests to the inner nests, the segmentation criteria change in terms of visibility, permanence, and intimacy. The data in the outer nests are generally highly visible, even to outsiders, are more or less permanent, and require little intimate knowledge of customers. But situational factors and personal characteristics are less visible, are more transient, and require extensive vendor research.

---

[2]For further discussion of these, see Thomas V. Bonoma, "Major Sales: Who *Really* Does the Buying?" *Harvard Business Review,* May–June 1982, p. 111, and Benson P. Shapiro and Ronald Posner, "Making the Major Sale," *Harvard Business Review,* March–April 1976, p. 68.

EXHIBIT 2 Classification of Nests

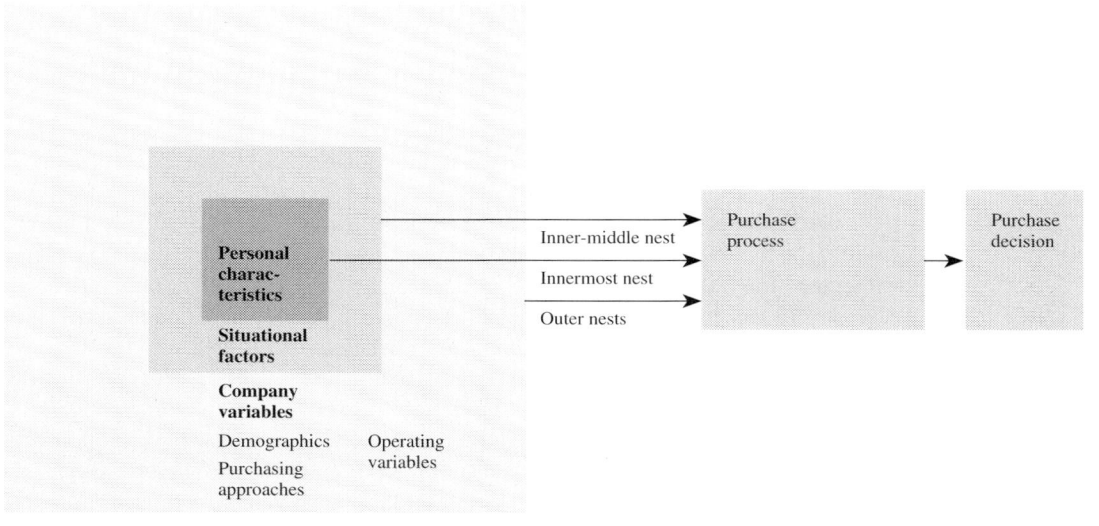

An industrial marketing executive can choose from a wide range of segmentation approaches other than the nested approach and, in fact, the myriad of possibilities often has one of the four following outcomes:

- No segmentation. "The problem is too large to approach."
- After-the-fact segmentation. "Our market research shows that we have captured a high share of the distribution segment and low shares of the others; thus we must be doing something right for customers in high-share segments."
- Superficial segmentation. "While we know all banks are different, it's easier to organize marketing plans around banks because we can identify them and tell the salespeople whom to call on." This dangerous outcome gives a false sense of security.
- Obtuse, convoluted, and disorganized segmentation. "We have a 300-page report on market segmentation and customer buying patterns, but there is just too much data in there. So we have decided to focus on insurance companies and hospitals to avoid another two-day market planning meeting."

Our approach using a hierarchical structure is easy to use. Marketers can, in most cases, work systematically from the outer nests to the inner nests. They can run through the whole set of criteria and identify important factors that otherwise might be neglected. And they can balance between reliance on the easily acquired data of the outer nests and the detailed analyses of the inner nests.

We suggest that a marketer begin at the outside nest and work inward because data are more available and definitions clearer in the outer nests. On the other hand, the situational and personal variables of the inner nests are often the most useful. In our experience, managers most frequently neglect situational criteria. In situations where knowledge and analysis exist, a marketer might decide to begin at a middle nest and work inward or, less probably, outward.

After several attempts at working completely through the process, companies will discover which segmentation criteria are likely to yield greater benefits than others and which cannot be considered carefully without better data. A warning is necessary, however. A company should not decide that an approach is *not* useful because data are lacking. The segmentation process requires that assessments of analytic promise and data availability be made independently. The two steps should not be confused. When the necessary data are gathered, managers can weigh segmentation approaches.

A fine line exists between minimizing the cost and difficulty of segmentation by staying in the outer nests on the one hand and gaining the useful data of the inner nests at appreciable direct and indirect cost on the other. The outer-nest criteria are generally inadequate when used by themselves in all but the most simple or homogeneous markets because they ignore buying differences among customers. Overemphasis on the inner-nest factors, however, can be too expensive and time-consuming for small markets. We suggest achieving a sense of balance between the simplicity and low cost of the outer nests and the richness and expense of the inner ones by making the choices explicit and the process clear and disciplined.

Executive Decision Making

"Unless we admit that rules of thumb, the limited experience of the executives in each individual business, and the general sentiment of the street are the sole possible guides for executive decisions of major importance, it is pertinent to inquire how the representative practices of businessmen generally may be made available as a broader foundation for such decisions, and how a proper theory of business is to be obtained. The theory of business, to meet the need, must develop to such a point that the executive, who will make the necessary effort, may learn effectively from the experiences of others in the past what to avoid and how to act under the conditions of the present. Otherwise, business will continue unsystematic, haphazard, and, for many men, a pathetic gamble, with the failures of each serious business depression made up largely of the best moral risks.

"No amount of theory can be a substitute for energy, enthusiasm, initiative, creative ability, and personality, nor will it take the place of technical knowledge. Now, however, all of these personal qualities may be coupled with an adequate technical equipment, and yet the executive of wide experience may fail through our inability to grasp the broad underlying forces controlling business, a knowledge of which would give a sound basis for judgment. It is a serious criticism of our business structure that it so long lacked an adequate method by which these broad forces may be appraised, their probable course charted, and their applications to individual executive problems made reasonably clear."

From Wallace B. Donham, "Essential Groundwork for a Broad Executive Theory," *Harvard Business Review,* October 1922, p. 1.

Chapter 4

Major Sales: Who *Really* Does the Buying?

Seemingly well-planned, well-executed selling strategies may fail if management does not understand the human side of selling. Marketing managers can get at the human factors of purchasing decisions by answering four questions: Who is in the buying center? Who are the powerful buyers? What does each buying-center member want? How do they perceive us? Sales managers should listen to the sales force, emphasize homework and details, and make productive sales calls the norm.

> You don't understand: Willy was a salesman. . . . He don't put a bolt to a nut. He don't tell you the law or give you medicine. He's a man way out there in the blue, riding on a smile and a shoeshine. And when they start not smiling back—that's an earthquake.
>
> Arthur Miller
> *Death of a Salesman*

Many companies' selling efforts are models of marketing efficiency. Account plans are carefully drawn, key accounts receive special management attention, and substantial resources are devoted to the sales process, from prospect identification to postsale service. Even such well-planned and well-executed selling strategies often fail, though, because management has an incomplete understanding of buying psychology—the human side of selling. Consider the following two examples:

• A fast-growing maker and seller of sophisticated graphics computers had trouble selling to potentially major customers. Contrary to the industry practice of quoting high list prices and giving large discounts to users who bought in quantity, this company priced 10 to 15 percent lower than competitors and gave smaller quantity discounts. Even though its net price was often the lowest, the company met

---

This reading was prepared by Thomas V. Bonoma.
Copyright © 1982 by the President and Fellows of Harvard College.
Reprinted with permission from *Harvard Business Review* 60, no. 3, May-June 1982, pp. 111–19.

resistance from buyers. The reason, management later learned, was that purchasing agents measured themselves and were measured by their superiors less by the net price of the sophisticated computers they bought than by the amount deducted from the price during negotiations. The discount had a significance to buyers that sound pricing logic could not predict.

• Several years ago, at AT&T's Long Lines division, an account manager was competing against a vendor with possibly better technology who threatened to lure away a key account. Among the customer's executives who might make the final decision about whether to switch from Bell were a telecommunications manager who had once been a Bell employee, a vice president of data processing who was known as a "big-name system buster" in his previous job because he had replaced all the IBM computers with other vendors' machines, and an aggressive telecommunications division manager who seemed to be unreachable by the AT&T team.

AT&T's young national account manager was nearly paralyzed by the threat. His team had never seriously considered the power, motivations, or perceptions of the various executives in the customer company, which had been buying from AT&T for many years. Without such analysis, effective and coordinated action on short notice—the usual time available for response to sales threats—was impossible.

Getting at the Human Factors

How can psychology be used to improve sales effectiveness? My contention is that seller awareness of and attention to the human factors in purchasing will produce higher percentages of completed sales and fewer unpleasant surprises in the selling process.

It would be inaccurate to call the human side of selling an emerging sales concern; only the most advanced companies recognize the psychology of buying as a major factor in improving account selection and selling results. Yet in most industries, the bulk of a company's business comes from a small minority of its customers. Retaining these key accounts is getting increasingly difficult as buyers constantly look not only for the best deal but also for the vendor that best understands them and their needs. It is this understanding and the targeted selling that results from it that can most benefit marketing managers.

Buying a Corporate Jet

The personal aspects and their complexities become apparent when one looks closely at an example of the buying process: the purchase of a business jet, which carries a price tag in excess of $3 million. The business-jet market splits obviously into two segments: those companies that already own or operate a corporate aircraft and those that do not.

In the owner market, the purchase process may be initiated by the chief executive officer, a board member (wishing to increase efficiency or security), the company's chief pilot, or through vendor efforts like advertising or a sales visit. The CEO will be central in deciding whether to buy the jet, but he or she will be heavily influenced by the company's pilot, financial officer, and perhaps by the board itself.

Each party in the buying process has subtle roles and needs. The salesperson who tries to impress, for example, both the CEO with depreciation schedules and the chief pilot with minimum runway statistics will almost certainly not sell a plane if he or she overlooks the psychological and emotional components of the buying decision. "For the chief executive," observes one salesperson, "you need all the numbers for support, but if you can't find the kid inside the CEO and excite him or her with the raw beauty of the new plane, you'll never sell the equipment. If you sell the excitement, you sell the jet."

The chief pilot, as an equipment expert, often has veto power over purchase decisions and may be able to stop the purchase of one or another brand of jet by simply expressing a negative opinion about, say, the plane's bad weather capabilities. In this sense, the pilot not only influences the decision but also serves as an information gatekeeper by advising management on the equipment to select. Though the corporate legal staff will formulate the purchase agreement and the purchasing department will acquire the jet, these parties may have little to say about whether or how the plane will be obtained, and which type. The users of the jet—middle and upper management of the buying company, important customers, and others—may have at least an indirect role in choosing the equipment.

The involvement of many people in the purchase decision creates a group dynamic that the selling company must factor into its sales planning. Who makes up the buying group? How will the parties interact? Who will dominate and who submit? What priorities do the individuals have?

It takes about three months for those companies that already own or operate aircraft to reach a decision. Because even the most successful vendor will sell no more than 90 jets a year, every serious prospect is a key account. The nonowners, not surprisingly, represent an even more complex market, since no precedent or aviation specialists exist.

The buying process for other pieces of equipment and for services will be more or less similar, depending on the company, product, and people involved. The purchase of computer equipment, for example, parallels the jet decision, except that sales prospects are likely to include data processing and production executives and that the market is divided into small and large prospects rather than owners and nonowners. In other cases (such as upgrading the corporate communications network, making a fleet purchase, or launching a plant expansion), the buying process may be very different. Which common factors will reliably steer selling-company management toward those human considerations likely to improve selling effectiveness?

Different buying psychologies exist that make effective selling difficult. On the one hand, companies don't buy, people do. This knowledge drives the seller to analyze who the important buyers are and what they want. On the other hand, many individuals, some of whom may be unknown to the seller, are involved in most major purchases. Even if all the parties are identified, the outcome of their interaction may be unpredictable from knowledge of them as individuals. Effective selling requires usefully combining the individual and group dynamics of buying to predict what the buying "decision-making unit" will do. For this combination to be practical, the selling company must answer four key questions.

1. Who's in the "Buying Center"?

The set of roles, or social tasks, buyers can assume is the same regardless of the product or participants in the purchase decision. This set of roles can be thought of as a fixed set of behavioral pigeonholes into which different managers from different functions can be placed to aid understanding. Together, the buying managers who take on these roles can be thought of as a "buying center."[1]

Exhibit 1 shows six buying roles encountered in every selling situation. I have illustrated these roles by using the purchase or upgrading of a telecommunications system as an example. Let's consider each triangle, representing a buying role, in turn.

The *initiator* of the purchase process, whether for a jet, paper towels, or communication services, recognizes that some company problem can be solved or avoided by acquiring a product or service. A company's turboprop aircraft may provide neither the speed nor the range to get top management quickly to and from scattered operations. The prospective buyer of communications equipment may want to take advantage of technological improvements or to reduce costs through owning instead of leasing.

One or more *gatekeepers* are involved in the purchase process. These individuals, who may have the title of buyer or purchasing manager, usually act as problem or product experts. They are paid to keep up on the range of vendor offerings. In the jet example, the chief pilot will ordinarily fill this role. In the telecommunications example given in Exhibit 1, corporate purchasing, the corporate telecommunications staff, or, increasingly, data processing experts may be consulted. By controlling (literally keeping the gate open or shut for) information and, sometimes, vendor access to corporate decision makers, the gatekeepers largely determine which vendors get the chance to sell. For some purchases the gatekeeping process is formalized through the use of an approved-vendors list, which constitutes a written statement of who can (and who, by absence, cannot) sell to the company.

Influencers are those who "have a say" in whether a purchase is made and about what is bought. The range of influencers becomes increasingly broad as major purchases are contemplated, because so many corporate resources are involved and so many people affected. In important decisions, board committees, stockholders of a public company, and even lowly mechanics can become influencers. One mining-machinery company encountered difficulty selling a new type of machine to its

---

[1]The concept of the buying center was proposed in its present form by Frederick E. Webster, Jr. and Yoram Wind in *Organizational Buying Behavior* (Englewood Cliffs, N.J.: Prentice Hall, 1972), pp. 75–87.

Exhibit 1 Members of the Buying Center and Their Roles

Initiator	Division general manager proposes to replace the company's telecommunications system
Decider	Vice president of administration selects, with influence from others, the vendor the company will deal with and the system it will buy
Influencers	Corporate telecommunications department and the vice president of data processing have important say about which system and vendor the company will deal with
Purchaser	Corporate purchasing department completes the purchase to specifications by negotiating or bidding
Gatekeeper	Corporate purchasing and corporate telecommunications departments analyze the company's needs and recommend likely matches with potential vendors
Users	All division employees who use the telecommunications equipment

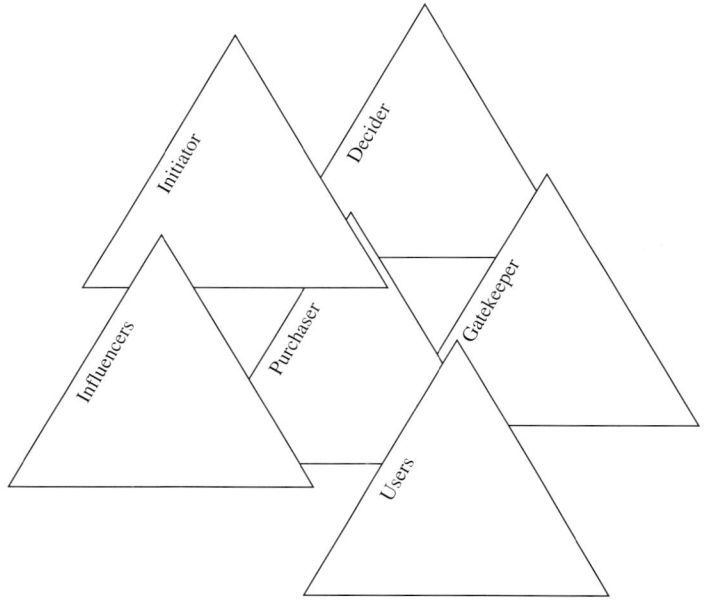

underground-mining customers. It turned out that mine maintenance personnel, who influenced the buying decision, resisted the purchase because they would have to learn to fix the new machine and maintain another stock of spare parts.

The *deciders* are those who say yes or no to the contemplated purchase. Often with major purchases, many of a company's senior managers act together to carry out the decider role. Ordinarily, however, one of these will become champion or advocate of the contemplated purchase and move it to completion. Without such a champion, many purchases would never be made. It is important to point out that deciders often do not sign off on purchases, nor do they make them. That is left to others. Though signers often represent themselves as deciders, such representation can be deceptive. It is possible for a vendor with a poor feel for the buying center to *never* become aware of the real movers in the buying company.

The purchase of executive computer work stations clearly illustrates both the importance of the champion and the behind-the-scenes role of the decider. A high-level executive who has become interested in using computers at his or her job after reading a magazine article or after tinkering with a home computer might decide to try out microcomputers or time-sharing terminals. The executive might then ask the company's data processing group—which is likely to be quite resistant and averse to executive meddling—to evaluate available microcomputer equipment. When trial purchases are made, the high-level executive will quietly help steer the system through the proper channels leading to acceptance and further purchases. The vendor, dealing directly with the data processing people, may never be aware that this decider exists.

The *purchaser* and the *user* are those concerned, respectively, with obtaining and consuming the product or service. The corporate purchasing department usually fills the purchaser role. Who fills the user role depends on the product or service.

Remember that I am discussing social roles, not individuals or groups of individuals. As such, the number of managers filling the buying roles varies from 1 to 35. In very trivial situations, such as a manager's purchase of a pocket calculator on a business trip, one person will fill all six roles. The triangles in Exhibit 1 would overlap: The manager initiates (perceives a need), gatekeeps (what brand did I forget at home?), influences himself or herself (this is more than I need, but it's only $39.95), decides, buys, and uses the equipment.

In more important buying situations, the number of managers assuming roles increases. In a study of 62 capital equipment and service acquisitions in 31 companies, Wesley J. Johnston and I quantified the buying center.[2] In the typical capital equipment purchase, an average of four departments (engineering and purchasing were always included), three levels of management hierarchy (for example, manager, regional manager, vice president), and seven different persons filled the six buying roles. For services, the corresponding numbers were four departments, two levels of management, and five managers. As might be expected, the more complex and involved the buying decision, the larger the decision unit and the more careful its decisions. For example, when packing supplies were ordered, little vendor searching or postsale evaluation was involved. When a new boiler was bought, careful vendor comparisons and postsale audits were undertaken.

2. Who Are the Powerful Buyers?

As useful as the buying-center concept is, it is difficult to apply because managers do not wear tags that say "decision maker" or "unimportant person."[3] The powerful are often invisible, at least to vendor representatives.

---

[2]Wesley J. Johnston and Thomas V. Bonoma, "Purchase Process for Capital Equipment and Services," *Industrial Marketing Management* 10 (1981), p. 253.

[3]In the interest of saving space, I will not substantiate each reference to psychological research. Documentation for my assertions can be found in Thomas V. Bonoma and Gerald Zaltman, *Management Psychology* (Boston: Kent Publishing Company, 1981). See chap. 8 for the power literature and chap. 3 for material on motivation.

Unfortunately, power does not correlate perfectly with organizational rank. As the case of the mine maintenance personnel illustrates, those with little formal power may be able to stop a purchase or hinder its completion. A purchasing manager who will not specify a disfavored vendor or the secretary who screens one vendor's salespeople because of a real or imagined slight also can dramatically change the purchasing outcome. Sales efforts cannot be directed through a simple reading of organizational charts; the selling company must identify the powerful buying-center members.

In Exhibit 2, I outline five major power bases in the corporation. In addition, I have categorized them according to whether their influence is positive (champion power) or negative (veto power).

Reward power refers to a manager's ability to encourage purchases by providing others with monetary, social, political, or psychological benefits. In one small company, for instance, the marketing vice president hoped to improve marketing decisions by equipping the sales force with small data-entry computers. Anticipating objections that the terminals were unnecessary, he felt forced to offer the sales vice president a computer of his own. The purchase was made.

Coercive power refers to a manager's ability to impose punishment on others. Of course, threatening punishment is not the same thing as having the power to impose it. Those managers who wave sticks most vigorously are sometimes the least able to deliver anything beyond a gentle breeze.

Attraction power refers to a person's ability to charm or otherwise persuade people to go along with his or her preferences. Next to the ability to reward and punish, attraction is the most potent power base in managerial life. Even CEOs find it difficult to rebut a key customer with whom they have flown for 10 years who says, "Joe, as your friend, I'm telling you that buying this plane would be a mistake."

EXHIBIT 2   Bases of Power

Type of Power	Champion	or	Veto
Reward: Ability to provide monetary, social, political, or psychological rewards to others for compliance	●		
Coercive: Ability to provide monetary or other punishments for noncompliance	●		
Attraction: Ability to elicit compliance from others because they like you	●		●
Expert: Ability to elicit compliance because of technical expertise, either actual or reputed			●
Status: Compliance-gaining ability derived from a legitimate position of power in a company			●

NOTE: These five power bases were originally proposed over 20 years ago by psychologists J.R.P. French, Jr. and Bertram Raven. See "The Bases of Social Power" in D. Cartwright, ed., *Studies in Social Power* (Ann Arbor: University of Michigan Press, 1959).

When a manager gets others to go along with his judgment because of real or perceived expertise in some area, *expert power* is being invoked. A telecommunications manager will find it difficult to argue with an acknowledged computer expert who contends that buying a particular telephone switching system is essential for the "office of the future"—or that not buying it now eventually will make effective communication impossible. With expert power, the skills need not be real, if by *real* we mean that the individual actually possesses what is attributed to him or her. It is enough that others believe that the expert has special skills or are willing to respect his or her opinion because of accomplishments in a totally unrelated field.

Status power comes from having a high position in the corporation. This notion of power is most akin to what is meant by the word *authority*. It refers to the kind of influence a president has over a first-line supervisor and is more restricted than the other power bases. At first glance, status power might be thought of as similar to reward or coercive power. But it differs in significant ways. First, the major influence activity of those positions of corporate authority is persuasion, not punishment or reward. We jawbone rather than dangle carrots and taunt with sticks because others in the company also have significant power which they could invoke in retaliation.

Second, the high-status manager can exercise his or her status repeatedly only because subordinates allow it. In one heavy-manufacturing division, for example, the continual specification of favored suppliers by a plant manager (often at unfavorable prices) led to a "palace revolt" among other managers whose component cost evaluations were constantly made to look poor. Third, the power base of those in authority is very circumscribed since authority only tends to work in a downward direction on the organization chart and is restricted to specific work-related requests. Status power is one of the weaker power bases.

Buying centers and individual managers usually display one dominant power base in purchasing decisions. In one small company, an important factor is whether the manager arguing a position is a member of the founding family—a kind of status power and attraction power rolled into one. In a large high-technology defense contractor, almost all decisions are made on the basis of real or reputed expertise. This is true even when the issue under consideration has nothing to do with hardware or engineering science.

The key to improved selling effectiveness is in observation and investigation to understand prospects' corporate power culture. The sales team must also learn the type of power key managers in the buying company have or aspire to. Discounts or offers of price reductions may not be especially meaningful to a Young Turk in the buying company who is most concerned with status power; a visit by senior selling-company management may prove much more effective for flattering the ego and making the sale. Similarly, sales management may wish to make more technical selling appeals to engineers or other buying-company staff who base their power on expertise.

The last two columns of Exhibit 2 show that the type of power invoked may allow the manager to support or oppose a proposal, but not always both. I believe status and expert power are more often employed by their holders to veto decisions with which they do not agree. Because others are often sold on the contemplated purchase, vetoing it generally requires either the ability to perceive aspects not seen by the average manager because of special expertise or the broader view that high corporate status is said to provide. Reward and coercive power are more frequently used to push through purchases and the choice of favored vendors. Attraction power seems useful and is used by both champions and vetoers. The central point here is that for many buying-center members, power tends to be unidirectional.

Six Behavioral Clues

Based on the preceding analysis of power centers, I have distilled six clues for identifying the powerful:

1. Though power and formal authority often go together, the correlation between the two is not perfect. The selling company must take into account other clues about where the true buying power lies.

2. One way to identify buying-center powerholders is to observe communications in the buying company. Of course, the powerful are not threatened by others, nor are they often promised rewards. Still, even the most powerful managers are likely to be influenced by others, especially by those whose power is based on attraction or expertise. Those with less power use persuasion and rational argument to try to influence the more powerful. Managers to whom others direct much attention but who receive few offers of rewards or threats of punishment usually possess substantial decision-making power.

3. Buying-center decision makers may be disliked by those with less power. Thus, when others express concern about one buying-center member's opinions along with their feelings of dislike or ambivalence, sellers have strong clues as to who the powerful buyer is.

4. High-power buyers tend to be one-way information centers, serving as focal points for information from others. The vice president who doesn't come to meetings but who receives copies of all correspondence about a buying matter is probably a central influencer or decider.

5. The most powerful buying-center members are probably not the most easily identified or the most talkative members of their groups. Indeed, the really powerful buying group members often send others to critical negotiations becase they are confident that little of substance will be made final without their approval.

6. No correlation exists between the functional area of a manager and his or her power within a company. It is not possible to approach the data processing department blindly to find decision makers for a new computer system, as many sellers of mainframes have learned. Nor can one simply look to the CEO to find a decision maker for a corporate plane. There is no substitute for working hard to understand the dynamics of the buying company.

3. What Do They Want?

Diagnosing motivation accurately is one of the easiest management tasks to do poorly and one of the most difficult to do well. Most managers have lots of experience at diagnosing another's wants, but though the admission comes hard, most are just not very accurate when trying to figure out what another person wants and will do. A basic rule of motivation is as follows: all buyers (indeed, all people) act selfishly or try to be selfish but sometimes miscalculate and don't serve their own interests. Thus, buyers attempt to maximize their gains and minimize their losses from purchase situations. How do buyers choose their own self-interest? The following are insights into that decision-making process from research.

First, buyers act as if a complex product or service were decomposable into various benefits. Examples of benefits might include product features, price, reliability, and so on.

Second, buyers segment the potential benefits into various categories. The most common of these are financial, product-service, social-political, and personal. For some buyers, the financial benefits are paramount, while for others, the social-political ones—how others in the company will view the purchase—rank highest. Of course, the dimensions may be related, as when getting the lowest-cost product (financial) results in good performance evaluations and a promotion (social-political).

Finally, buyers ordinarily are not certain that purchasing the product will actually bring the desired benefit. For example, a control computer sold on its reliability and industrial-strength construction may or may not fulfill its promise. Because benefits have value only if they actually are delivered, the buyer must be confident that the selling company will keep its promises. Well-known vendors, like IBM or Xerox, may have some advantage over lesser-known companies in this respect.

As marketers know, not all promised benefits will be equally desired by all customers. All buyers have top-priority benefit classes, or "hot buttons." For example, a telecommunications manager weighing a choice between Bell and non-Bell equipment will find some benefits, like ownership, available only from non-Bell vendors. Other desired benefits, such as reputation for service and reliability, may be available to a much greater degree from Bell. The buyer who has financial priorities as a hot button may decide to risk possible service-reliability problems for the cost-reduction benefits available through ownership. Another manager—one primarily concerned with reducing the social-political risks as a result of service problems—may reach a different decision. Exhibit 3 schematically shows the four classes into which buyers divide benefits; the telecommunications example illustrates each class.

Outlining the buyer's motivation suggests several possible selling approaches. The vendor can try to focus the buyer's attention on benefits not a part of his or her thinking. A magazine sales representative, for instance, devised a questionnaire to help convince an uncertain client to buy advertising space. The questionnaire sought information about the preferred benefits—in terms of reach, audience composition, and cost per thousand readers. When the prospective buyer "played this silly game" and filled out the questionnaire, he convinced himself of the superior worth of the vendor's magazine on the very grounds he was seeking to devalue it.

Conversely, sellers can de-emphasize the buyer's desire for benefits on which the vendor's offering stacks up poorly. For example, if a competing vendor's jet offers better fuel economy, the selling company might attempt to refocus the buyer's attention toward greater speed or lower maintenance costs.

EXHIBIT 3 Dominant Motives for Buying a Telecommunications System

The benefits in bold type are more highly valued than the others and represent the company's "hot button."

Benefit Class			
Financial	*Product or Service*	*Social or Political*	*Personal*
Absolute cost savings	**Pre- and post-sales service**	Will purchase enhance the buyer's standing with the buying team or top management?	Will purchase increase others' liking or respect for the buyer?
Cheaper than competitive offerings	**Specific features**		How does purchase fit with the buyers' self-concept?
Will provide operating-cost reductions	**Space occupied by unit**		
Economics of leasing versus buying	**Availability**		

The vendor can also try to increase the buyer's confidence that promised benefits will be realized. One software company selling legal administrative systems, for example, provides a consulting service that remote users can phone if they are having problems, backup copies of its main programs in case users destroy the original, a complete set of input forms to encourage full data entry, and regular conferences to keep users current on system revisions. These services are designed to bolster the confidence of extremely conservative administrators and lawyers who are shopping for a system.

Finally, vendors often try to change what the buyer wants, or which class of benefits he or she responds to most strongly. My view of motivation suggests that such an approach is almost always unsuccessful. Selling strategy needs to work with the buyer's motivations, not around them.

4. How Do They Perceive Us?

How buyers perceive the selling company, its products, and its personnel is very important to efficient selling. Powerful buyers invariably have a wide range of perceptions about a vending company. One buyer will have a friend at another company who has used a similar product and claims that "it very nearly ruined us." Another may have talked to someone with a similar product who claimed that the vending company "even sent a guy out on a plane to Hawaii to fix the unit there quickly. These people really care."

One drug company representative relates the story of how the company was excluded from all the major metropolitan hospitals in one city because a single influential physician believed that one of the company's new offerings was implicated in a patient's death. This doctor not only generalized his impressions to include all the company's products but encouraged his friends to boycott the company.

A simple scheme for keeping tabs on how buyers perceive sellers is to ask sales officials to estimate how the important buyers judge the vending company and its actions. This judgment can be recorded on a continuum ranging from negative to positive. If a more detailed judgment is desired, the selling company can place its products and its people on two axes perpendicular to each other, like this:

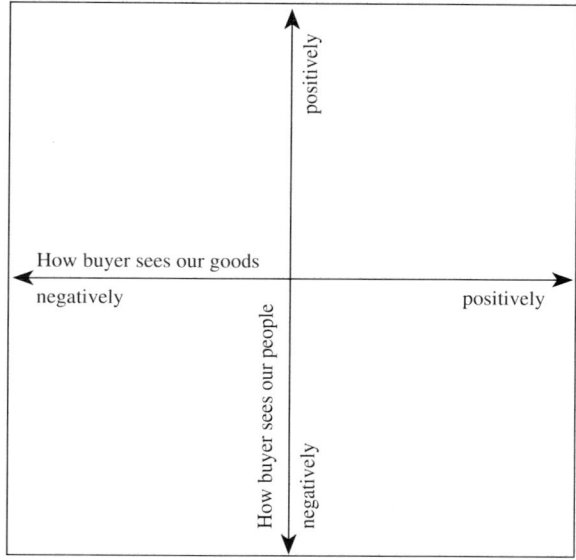

The scarcity of marketing dollars and the effectiveness of champions in the buying process argue strongly for focusing resources where they are likely to do the most good. Marketing efforts should aim at those in the buying company who like the selling company, since they are partially presold. While there is no denying the adage, "It's important to sell everybody," those who diffuse their efforts this way often sell no one.

Gathering Psychological Intelligence

While I would like to claim that some new technique will put sound psychological analyses magically in your sales staff's hands, no such formula exists. But I have used the human-side approach in several companies to increase sales effectiveness, and there are only three guidelines needed to make it work well.

Make Productive Sales Calls a Norm, Not an Oddity

Because of concern about the rapidly rising cost of a sales call, managers are seeking alternative approaches to selling. Sales personnel often do not have a good idea of why they are going on most calls, what they hope to find out, and which questions will give them the needed answers. Sales-call planning is not only a matter of minimizing miles traveled or courtesy calls on unimportant prospects but of determining what intelligence is needed about key buyers and what questions or requests are likely to produce that information.

I recently traveled with a major account representative of a duplication equipment company, accompanying him on the five calls he made during the day. None of the visits yielded even 10 percent of the potential psychological or other information that the representative could use on future calls, despite the fact that prospects made such information available repeatedly.

At one company, for example, we learned from a talkative administrator that the chairman was a semirecluse who insisted on approving equipment requests himself; that one of the divisional managers had (without the agreement of the executive who was our host) brought in a competitor's equipment to test; and that a new duplicator the vendor had sold to the company was more out of service than in. The salesperson pursued none of this freely offered information, nor did he think any of it important enough to write down or pass on to the sales manager. The call was wasted because the salesperson didn't know what he was looking for or how to use what was offered him.

Exhibit 4 shows a matrix that can be used to capture on a single sheet of paper essential psychological data about a customer. I gave some clues for filling in the matrix earlier in the article, but how sales representatives go about gathering the information depends on the industry, the product, and especially the customer. In all cases, however, key selling assessments involve (1) isolating the powerful buying-center members, (2) identifying what they want in terms of both their hot buttons and specific needs, and (3) assessing their perceptions of the situation. Additionally, gathering psychological information is more often a matter of listening carefully than of asking clever questions during the sales interview.

Listen to the Sales Force

Nothing discourages intelligence gathering as much as the sales force's conviction that management doesn't really want to hear what salespeople know about an account. Many companies require the sales force to file voluminous call reports and furnish other data, which vanish, never to be seen or even referred to again unless a sales representative is to be punished for one reason or another.

To counter this potentially fatal impediment, I recommend a sales audit. Evaluate all sales force control forms and call reports and discard any that have not been used by management for planning or control purposes in the last year. This approach has a marvelously uplifting effect all around; it frees the sales force from filling in forms it knows nobody uses, sales management from gathering forms it doesn't

EXHIBIT 4 Matrix for Gathering Psychological Information

Who's in the buying center, and what is the base of their power?	Who are the powerful buyers, and what are their priorities?	What specific benefits does each important buyer want?	How do the important buyers see us?	Selling strategy
_____	_____	_____	_____	_____
_____	_____	_____	_____	_____
_____	_____	_____	_____	_____
_____	_____	_____	_____	_____

know what to do with, and data processing from processing reports no one ever requests. Instead, use a simple, clear, and accurate sales control form of the sort suggested in Exhibit 4—preferably on a single sheet of paper for a particular sales period. These recommendations may sound drastic, but where management credibility in gathering and using sales force intelligence is absent, drastic measures may be appropriate.

Emphasize Homework and Details

Having techniques for acquiring sales intelligence and attending to reports is not enough. Sales management must stress that yours is a company that rewards careful fact gathering, tight analysis, and impeccable execution. This message is most meaningful when it comes from the top.

Cautionary Notes

The group that influences a purchase doesn't call itself a buying center. Nor do decision makers and influencers think of themselves in those terms. Managers must be careful not to mistake the analysis and ordering process for the buyers' actions themselves. In addition, gathering data such as I have recommended is a sensitive issue. For whatever reasons, it is considered less acceptable to make psychological estimates of buyers than economic ones. Computing the numbers without understanding the psychology, however, leads to lost sales. Finally, the notion implicit throughout this article has been that sellers must understand buying, just as buyers must understand selling. When that happens, psychology and marketing begin to come together usefully. Closed sales follow almost as an afterthought.

SECTION II Managing New Products

CHAPTER 5
New Product Commercialization: Common Mistakes

This article addresses the common mistakes made in new product development and launch. Many times customers' and suppliers' perceptions of the degree of product/market innovation do not match. One of them may view the innovation as a breakthrough, but the other may view it only as an incremental improvement of an existing solution. Such a mismatch will inevitably lead to faulty commercialization. But even if the match is perfect, this article argues that breakthroughs and incremental new products require quite different new product development processes to enable commercial success.

It is widely acknowledged that a constant supply of new products and their successful commercialization are key to a firm's survival. But studies by Booz Allen and others have found that after all the time, effort, and money spent in screening and developing new products, 50 to 67 percent of them fail in the commercialization process.[1] Why do so many new products fail? In some cases, the product development process is flawed to start with. In others, the product concept is very poorly backed by market research. In some others, the launch process and its execution are at fault. In any case, the failure statistic highlights the need for close management attention to the new product development and commercialization process. As a noted expert concluded, "If half of a factory's output ended up as defects, you'd shut the place down."[2]

Various remedies have been offered for streamlining and improving the new product development process. The concept of creating a team consisting of members

---

V. Kasturi Rangan and Kevin Bartus prepared this note.
Copyright © 1994 by the President and Fellows of Harvard College.
Harvard Business School note 594-127.
[1]Booz Allen & Hamilton, Inc., *New Product Management for the 1980s* (New York: Booz Allen & Hamilton, 1982).
[2]Robert G. Cooper cited in "Flops: Too Many New Products Fail. Here's Why—And How to Do Better," *Business Week,* August 16, 1993.

FIGURE 1 New product development stages

1. Initial screening	The initial decision to go ahead with the project, the idea having been screened in from several alternatives.
2. Preliminary market assessment	The preliminary market study: a "quick and dirty" situation analysis of the marketplace, possible market acceptance, and competitive assessment.
3. Preliminary technical assessment	An initial technical appraisal, addressing questions such as, "Can the product be developed? Can it be manufactured?" and so on.
4. Detailed market study	Marketing research: detailed market studies such as user needs-and-wants analysis, concept tests, positioning studies, and competitive analyses.
5. Preliminary business analysis	Comprehensive business analysis with projected net present values, pro forma income statements, and the like.
6. Product development	The actual development of the physical product leading up to a prototype.
7. Alpha tests	Testing the product in-house under controlled or laboratory conditions.
8. Beta tests	Testing the product with customers in field trials.
9. Test market	An attempt to sell the product to a limited market area or customers, to gauge product acceptance in a real market context.
10. Trial production	A limited trial, or batch production run, designed to prove production facilities.
11. Final business plan	A final business and financial analysis prior to launch.
12. Production ramp up	Full-scale production.
13. Market launch	The implementation of a comprehensive marketing plan.

SOURCE: Adapted from Robert G. Cooper, *Winning at New Products* (Reading, Mass.: Addison-Wesley, 1993), p. 29.

from different functions is probably the single most widely accepted concept in accelerating new product development. Such a team is able to solve potential problems early in the development cycle and engender commitment more easily from all of the involved functions.[3] The need for a product champion or a project manager to coordinate the team has also been highly recommended.[4] The whole idea, of course, is to move the project along its various phases (see Figure 1) as smoothly and efficiently as possible.

While the dedication of a cross-functional team under the leadership of a project manager/product champion is necessary, it is insufficient to ensure new product success.[5] A careful matching of the product development process to the type of product is required. See Figure 2. Edward Krubasik suggests different processes for

---

[3]Many articles and books have been written on the subject. The following are representative: Hirotake Takeuchi and Ikujiro Nanaka, "The New Product Development Game," *Harvard Business Review*, January–February 1986; Steven C. Wheelright and Kim B. Clark, *Revolutionizing Product Development* (New York: Free Press, 1992), pp. 165–217; Preston G. Smith and Donald G. Reinertsen, *Developing Products in Half the Time* (New York: Von Nostrand Reinhold, 1991), pp. 111–51.

[4]The new product literature is flooded with stories of product champions, from Tom West of the Eclipse project, portrayed in Tracy Kidder, *The Soul of a New Machine* (New York: The Atlantic Monthly Press, 1982), to the dozens of fascinating protagonists in *Breakthroughs* (San Diego: Mercury, 1993), by P. Ranaganath Nayak and John M. Ketteringham.

[5]For more on this see E. W. Larson and David H. Gobeli, "Organizing for Product Development Projects," *Journal of Product Innovation Management* 5 (1988), pp. 180–90.

[6]Edward G. Krubasik, "Customize Your Product Development," *Harvard Business Review*, November–December 1988.

FIGURE 2

Matching development process to product type

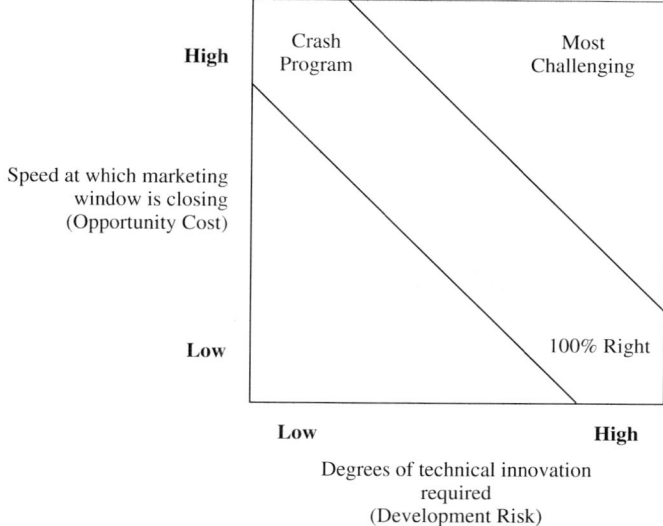

SOURCE: Edward G. Krubasik, "Customize Your Product Development," *Harvard Business Review,* November–December 1988.

different product contexts.[6] While they all have to systematically navigate the 13 stages of a new product's development and launch, different levels of formal management sign-offs and checkpoints are appropriate for the different new product contexts. When the development risks are high and the opportunity costs are low, it is not particularly advantageous to accelerate product development. Such a process could boost project expense and jeopardize product performance and cost. A carefully controlled transition across each stage may make sense. Popularly called the stage-gate system, such a process involves staging the development over several "gates."[7] The project may proceed to the next gate only and only if it clears certain well-specified hurdles. At the other extreme, when the development risk is low and opportunity costs are high, it is absolutely important to speed up the process. Several steps may have to run concurrently. Fortunately, the risks of development failure are also low. The hardest process to manage is when the risks as well as the opportunity costs are high. While technology and cost considerations will necessitate a carefully staged process, market considerations demand speed. The process has to carefully blend caution and aggression.

In summary, the new product literature offers us a wealth of guidelines on how to better manage the development and commercialization process, when to accelerate the steps, and how to effectively manage the teamwork. In this article, we focus on some common product-development and launch mistakes committed by firms that are fully cognizant of, and firmly committed to, the various

---

[7]Robert G. Cooper, *Winning at New Products* (Reading, Mass.: Addison-Wesley, 1993), pp. 95–120.

prescriptions referred to above. Even though the problems we describe here are executional, several of them are driven by a poor understanding of the development concept to start with.

Marketing Mistakes

A Framework

As shown in Exhibit 1, over the years many new product taxonomies have been offered. Products have been classified along various dimensions, such as newness of product/technology, newness to market, newness to company, extent of product change, extent of process change, and so forth. But curiously enough every one of these definitions assumes that the originator of the innovation and the customer are in complete agreement on the newness of the product or its breakthrough nature. But anecdotal evidence suggests that a significant number of new products fail precisely because suppliers and customers do not see eye-to-eye on what the product is supposed to do. There is a disjunction between the seller and the buyer. Consider the case of NeXT, a desktop computer developed by Steve Jobs, the legendary founder of Apple Computer.[8] Customers did not want the optical drive instead of the usual floppy drive. The new feature made it tough for them to switch work from a PC to NeXT. Even though the machine had other nifty features, such as hi-fi sound, customers never overcame their initial resistance. Students found it too expensive, while engineers thought that workstations delivered better performance and value. Thus, after spending $200 million to develop the product, Steve Jobs was forced to drop the product. Yet if he had listened to customers and gone with more standard technology earlier on, some analysts say he might have succeeded. The moral of the story is simple: The new product development process has to start with the voice of the customer, and in this case the customers were seeking an incremental rather than a radical innovation.[9] They were not prepared for the "next generation" product. They did not see the need for it, nor were they willing to pay for it.

In order to understand such supplier–customer misperceptions, we offer a framework to diagnose the problem. See Figure 3. On one axis we map the supplier's perception of the new product, and the customer's on the other. For simplicity, we divide the world into "breakthrough" inventions and "incremental" innovations, knowing full well that many intermediate positions are feasible. Breakthrough is an idea that is so different that it cannot be compared to any existing practices or perceptions. It employs a new technology and creates a new market. Breakthroughs are conceptual shifts that make history.[10] Incremental innovations, on the other hand, are

---

[8] Adapted from "Flops: Too Many New Products Fail."

[9] Vincent P. Barabba and Gerald Zaltman, *Hearing the Voice of the Market,* (Harvard Business School Press, 1991), pp. 19–35.

[10] Nayak and Ketteringham, *Breakthroughs,* p. 1.

Exhibit 1   New Product Taxonomies

	Existing Products	New Products
New Markets	Market Development	Diversification
Existing Markets	Market Penetration	Product Development

SOURCE: Ansoff H. Igor, "Market Strategy Given Newness of Markets and Products," *Harvard Business Review*, September–October 1957.

Newness to Market

Newness to Company	Low	High	
High		New Product Lines (20%)	New-to-World Products (10%)
	Improvements/Revisions to Existing Products (26%)	Additions to Existing Product Lines (26%)	
Low	Cost Reductions (11%)	Repositionings (7%)	

SOURCE: Booz Allen & Hamilton, *New Products Management for the 1980s* (New York: Booz Allen & Hamilton, 1982).

continuations of existing methods or practices. Both suppliers and customers have a clear conceptualization of the product and what it can do. Existing products are sufficiently close substitutes.

When both the supplier and the customer view the new product context as a breakthrough, or as incremental, we then have the perfect match running from east to west in Figure 3. The mismatch is represented by the north–south axis.

Breakthroughs and Incrementals

Breakthrough products require intensive technology and/or applications development. Customers are awed by the new product's potential. It is often doubtful at this stage if a large number of customers really understand how the product usage

Exhibit 1 (concluded)

	Process Changes			
Product Changes	New Core Process	Next Generation	Upgrade	Tuning/Incremental
New Core Product	Breakthrough			
Next Generation Product		Platform		
Addition to Product Family				
Add-ons and Enhancements				Derivative

SOURCE: Steven C. Wheelwright and Kim B. Clark, "Creating Project Plans to Focus Product Development," *Harvard Business Review,* March–April 1992.

characteristics will evolve and what usage patterns it will involve. It is important to have a technology vision at this stage in anticipation of market development. While a few "opinion-leader" customers may share that vision, most customers may not have a clue. It would be futile, for example, to seek extensive customer opinion on product attributes and features because the product concept may appear too distant to be of immediate use. A bulk of the product development work, therefore, has to

FIGURE 3

New product types

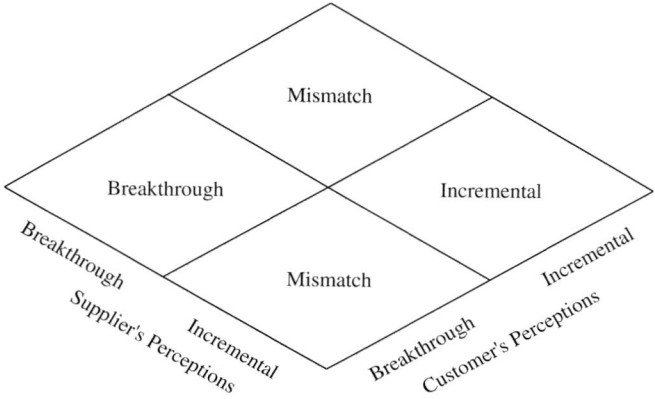

be undertaken with input from only a handful of customers. The effort is typically an "inside out" process, with the technology people playing an important role. A projective vision and a keen sense of market anticipation, which are known as empathic design, are required in the product development process.[11]

In contrast, customers will be able to play a major role in providing input for incremental products. These are, typically, evolutionary development from their viewpoint. Based on their own product-usage history, customers usually will have a precise definition of what improvements they need in the product. Because of their experiences in making the previous-generation product, manufacturers will be able to fairly accurately estimate the technological and manufacturing changes required to serve the customers' needs. In short, the customer's voice becomes the dominant impetus for new product design. Tools and techniques such as quality function deployment (QFD) and conjoint analysis are useful for such new product development activity.[12] Because customers know what they want, and because alternative solutions are usually available in the market, incremental innovations are often designed to meet narrow cost targets. Performance at a price, rather than performance alone, becomes an important design criterion. Even if it did not apply to the whole product, certainly component parts could benefit from reverse engineering key competitors' products. The voice of the distribution channel has to be factored into the product launch. The product design and pricing have to be sensitive to channels' profit considerations. The key differences are captured in Figure 4.

Wrongly interpreted, Figure 4 could misdirect managers into believing that minimal marketing input is required of breakthrough new products. Nothing could be further from the truth. Even though only a few customers may be able to connect with the company's technology visions, it is important to remember that the success of the new product depends on the crucial element of the manufacturer's being able to envision and build a market for its products. This often requires careful marketing thought up-front. One has to identify potential markets and customers; a program to educate them on the benefits of the new technology must be mounted to coincide with the new product's launch. At times a radically new sales and distribution system may be necessary. All this means that even though only a few customers may lend their voice to technology development, the new product introduction process must recognize and incorporate the market building and development activity.

In contrast, sales and manufacturing functions have a crucial role to play in developing and marketing incremental new products. That is because the sales/distribution channel is often the one that is closest to the customer and in the best position to read customer feedback. Many of the customer requirements may not necessitate fundamental technological innovation as much as feature and function improvements. Engineering/manufacturing could often be in a position to build these

---

[11]Dorothy Leonard-Barton, Edith Wilson, and John Doyle, "Commercializing Technology: Imaginative Understanding of User Needs," Harvard Business School Working Paper 93-053.

[12]Robert J. Dolan, *Managing the New Product Development Process* (Reading, Mass.: Addison-Wesley, 1993).

FIGURE 4

Nature of the marketing tasks

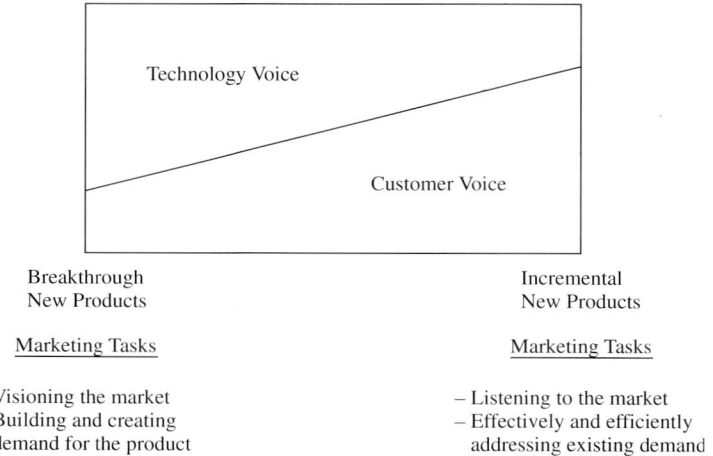

upgrades without resorting to an intense research/technology effort. Thus while R&D and marketing may play the lead role in breakthrough new product development, usually sales and manufacturing/engineering have a larger role to play in incremental new product development.

Mistake No. 1. The most common mistake is the utter lack of sensitivity to the differences in the management tasks required of incremental versus breakthrough projects. There is an overwhelming tendency to treat them all alike. It is important to realize that cross-functional involvement is not a panacea to all new product development problems; what matters is the nature of the cross-functional involvement (such as those shown in Figure 4). Time and again we found short-term-results-oriented line people assigned to breakthrough development teams. Not only were they unable to envision how the market would develop, their pessimistic forecasts dampened the teams' enthusiasm. They in turn were extremely frustrated because the teams were unable to meet their request for hard customer-data or precise product-cost estimates. The solution is not to leave the line functions (like production and sales) out, but instead to incorporate the right kind of marketing and manufacturing thinking into the team. But it certainly would be dangerous to leave it all to the inventors. Technical people who are thrilled with the breakthrough idea may be short-sighted with respect to its commercial feasibility. Their market forecasts may have a higher correlation to their aspirations for the product than to market realities. At the other extreme, incremental product teams may find themselves saddled with thinkers and visionaries who question the value of the new product concept, who often ask for a thorough systemwide evaluation of every product or process change. "What's so new about this new product?" they often ask. Yet the field-level salespeople or the operations people on the team will vouch for its viability and urge a quick clearance to the next stage. They know the product will work and their customers will buy if only the new product is brought speedily into the market. They are shocked by the project's snail's pace. The moral of the story is simple: Cross-functional teams require people of appropriate cross-functional abilities.

Mistake No. 2. Though not as common as No. 1, Mistake No. 2 is a tendency to assume that breakthrough projects equate with high-profile activities needing resources and top-management support, and that incremental projects are less important and need only back-pocket support.

This is untrue. The resource allocation decision has to be based on the long-term financial attractiveness of the project. Some breakthrough innovations may not have a large market potential to start with. The market will have to develop and grow with the adoption of the innovation. This being the case, it may be prudent to stage the allocation of resources on such projects. On the other hand, many incremental innovations may absolutely require a major investment up front. This is usually the case when the firm's existing product is hopelessly out-of-date in a very large market. Reengineering the product may require heavy manufacturing investments. The point is simple: Do not confuse the nature of the project with potential payoffs. While it is almost inevitable that top management would have to get involved in high-investment projects, it is not entirely desirable to delegate all low-investment projects. Some of them may involve technologies or anticipated market niches that could be of great strategic importance to the company, and without top management's support in the early stages, such projects may flounder. Thus, top management's involvement has to be selective and on a case-by-case basis, but certainly independent of the nature of the product.

In Figure 3, we referred to the north–south direction as the axis of mismatch. In this instance, the manufacturer's and customer's perception of the product's newness are divergent. In one case, the supplier of the technology may see the product as an incremental innovation, whereas the customer may perceive it as a breakthrough—we call this the shadowed new product (because the supplier may not see its true potential). In the other case, the supplier may see the product as an incredible breakthrough, whereas the customers may be lukewarm toward it—we call this the delusionary new product. See Figure 5.

Shadowed New Products[13]

By *shadowed,* we do not mean that the product's technical merit or the customer's potential benefit is negligible, but that the product's contribution in economic terms to the company's portfolio is relatively minor in the short run. These are products that the company's engineers and R&D scientists discovered while pursuing other, more central projects. Alternatively, these are products that the company's sales force thought would serve some of the unmet needs of its existing customers. Either way, these products are not the central thrust of a company's

---

[13]A large part of this discussion is drawn from V. Kasturi Rangan, Rajiv Lal, and Ernie P. Maier, "Managing Marginal New Products," *Business Horizons* 35, no. 5, pp. 35–42.

FIGURE 5

Seller–customer mismatch

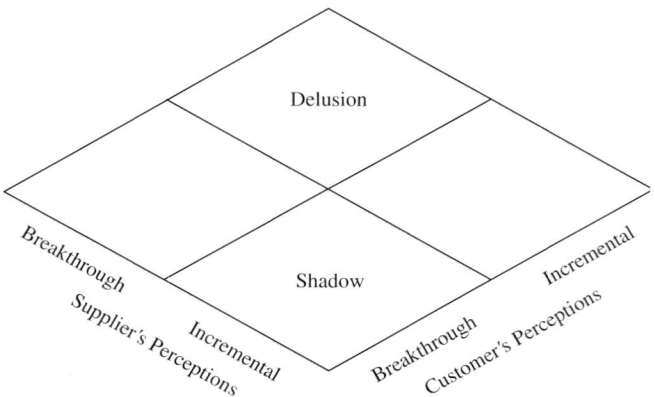

R&D or sales strategy. These are products discovered in the shadow of more important activity. Consequently, such products are not intended to account for a significant chunk of the company's revenues or profits. An example is the Post-It note at 3M Company.

The story goes that the original Post-It application came out of division manager Arthur Fry's desire to keep the bookmark from falling out of his hymn book. There is a similar story regarding 3M's Scotch brand transparent tape. It was apparently invented for an industrial customer who used it to seal insulation in an airtight package. When first developed, both of these products had limited application, and in fact the company was not even sure where the market was for such products. The products were invented for a specific use, rather than to serve a whole market. But today Post-It and Scotch brand tape are in the top five office supply items in the United States, and represent a multimillion-dollar business for 3M company. When initially launched, many such innovations appear marginal. All are small contributors individually, but down the road they can well turn out to have significant impact on a company's bottom line. However, very few companies pay attention to proactively marketing such products.

What reasons underlie the failed launches of so many shadowed new products? The fundamental reason is that these products do not generate the same sense of urgency or focus that accompanies "central" new products. Even though the product idea may have clear champions, because the product was invented relatively cheaply, the new product development team usually will not subject it to the same taxing commercial feasibility and test-marketing standards as the other central products in its pipeline. Many times such products bypass established processes to fall right into the hands of day-to-day line management. Commercialization usually follows organizational routines. And therein lies the crux of the problem.

Mistake No. 3. Because managers already handle a portfolio of other products through existing manufacturing/sales systems, it makes sense to adopt the same for the new product. But the true appreciation for the new product comes in many cases from new customers in new segments, and even if they come from current customers, a different buying unit with different buying criteria may be responsible for its adoption. Using existing organizational systems often means completely missing the boat on the real customer's real needs. This is the customer who values the product as a breakthrough.

A frequent practice is to "make a little, sell a little" until the opportunity is crystal clear. Since the product is not central to the company's short-term financial well-being, there is a tendency to look for some signs of success toward which further attention and resources may be directed. Taking advantage of the existing organizational routines is certainly the cost-minimizing approach; sharing product management, sales management, and distribution is one outcome. Using common marketing and sales resources makes the most economic sense at the outset, with the intention of ultimately tailoring a program for the new product. But the product must show some initial signs of success, so managers wait and see. Meanwhile, a huge opportunity is being missed. It is sold as an incremental innovation to existing customers, when with a little imagination and creativity, an entirely new problem for an entirely new customer may be addressed. Market segmentation and channel selection are usually wrong, and because the product is anchored to existing solutions, it is usually underpriced. A higher price can be obtained, but that requires active customer education for the right customers.

Marketing is as much about creating and shaping customer needs as it is about serving well-identified customer requirements. Good marketers learn about and shape customer needs, even as they implement their marketing programs. The business-as-usual approach completely violates the interactive nature of this market development process.

While the wait-and-see and business-as-usual attitudes may be interpreted as a failing of management execution, top management must take its share of the blame, too. It is responsible for providing a corporate environment/culture that encourages entrepreneurship with rewards for success that outweigh the risks of failure. With a strategic new product, top management involvement is easily obtained. Decisions involving development, introduction, marketing, and sales occur at the top level. This allows senior management to make far-reaching choices and motivate the organization to reflect its priorities. In the case of shadowed new products, the decision to launch has neither strategic urgency nor the routine expediency of a product enhancement. Under these circumstances, lower level management has no incentive to take initiative either, because success may not get the attention of the top brass, whereas a failure will only unnecessarily diminish an existing reputation. The end result is a vicious cycle of wait-and-see and business-as-usual which accelerates the death of the product, followed by a quiet burial. This is a pity because these products cost very little to invent and make, but with imaginative marketing they could add significant new customer segments and new products for the company. Each new product by itself may not immediately be a significant contribution to the bottom line, but put together, they certainly can bring about significant new sales.

Delusionary New Products

We take up these products last because they represent the largest proportion of new product failures. These are innovations where the suppliers of the technology have grandiose visions for the product, but their customers often do not share the same euphoria. We already outlined the predicament of NeXT, but there are literally hundreds more examples like that.[14] Vincent Barabba and Gerald Zaltman describe the VideoDisc fiasco:[15]

> Another example of how technology cannot stand on its own, no matter how advanced, is provided by RCA's $580 million VideoDisc venture. R&D made a major technological breakthrough that had many technological merits, such as a higher-quality (relative to VCR technology) means for watching movies at home; yet, because of improper analysis of the desires of the market, the venture failed. . . .
>
> . . . RCA's VideoDisc strategy had been heavily dependent on a few key assumptions: that the traditional mass-market customer would prefer a low price to more features, that dealers could clear up any consumer confusion about multiple formats, that VCR producers could not substantially reduce the price gap between their players and disc players, that dealers would welcome disc systems as they had VCRs, and that consumers would want to own video programming just as they owned LP records and audio tapes. . . .
>
> . . . In fact, the outcome quickly revealed that most of the key assumptions on which RCA had based its VideoDisc strategy were no longer valid. . . . Had the plan been for a stable product in a familiar business, it would have been well-conceived and well-executed, but for an innovative product in a marketplace destabilized by changing technologies, it was an approach that allowed little room for adjustment.

Why are there so many products with more "show" than "tell"? Don't these firms understand the discipline of knowing the customer? Don't they collect market research? Many do, but the disconnect, unfortunately, comes because of an inside-out process rather than a lack of customer information. As a result, the data interpretation is faulty, not necessarily the data collection. Because of the newness of the product, the technology, or the manufacturing process, to the company there's a justifiable air of expectation and excitement within. But the real question is whether the potential customer is equally excited. To customers, this product may be just one more additional line for consideration among the various available alternatives. They would perhaps like to know why the said offering is superior to competitive products—as far as they know they are viewing an incremental innovation rather than a breakthrough invention.

Mistake No. 4. Such supplier misperceptions lead to faulty product positioning. There is an attempt to break new ground with the product, when in fact a "new and improved" positioning would be more palatable to the customer. The Sony Walkman product launch process is a nice illustration of how to do it right.[16] The product

---

[14]Donald W. Hendon, *Classic Failures in Product Marketing* (New York: Quorum Books, 1989).
[15]Barabba and Zaltman, *Hearing the Voice of the Market,* pp. 31–32.
[16]Nayak and Ketteringham, *Breakthroughs,* pp. 94–111.

development effort required tricky coordination between its tape recorder and headphone divisions. The whole idea of making a cassette player without a speaker or a recorder, but instead with a headphone, seemed quite at odds with Sony's product traditions. The concept itself would not have been commercially viable without the amazing speed of its product development team. The scale-up required innovative manufacturing techniques. Yet when the product was launched, it was priced at a modest $165, with a clear goal to bring it down to less than $100 within three years. The product was sold through broad-line electronic distribution channels. In short, the product was positioned, priced, and sold as through it was an additional offering in the mass distributed, modestly priced consumer electronic category of tape recorders, radios, and cameras.

Of course, we are not suggesting that all potential delusionary products should be priced and marketed through mass-market channels. Our argument is that they should be positioned and priced appropriately with respect to existing solutions in the marketplace. If such an effort in fact requires the company to go upmarket for a specific customer niche where the product outperforms existing solutions, by all means it should be marketed and channeled to reflect its premium status. Our point is that the positioning strategy be driven by the market, rather than by the ambitions of the product champions. The outcome of such an exercise could lead to the conclusion that there are no equivalent customer solutions in the market, and that in fact the product is a radical new idea. The inventors then have a clear breakthrough on their hands, and marketing resources would be needed to develop and create a market.

Conclusions

The mismatches, that is, the shadows and delusions, could be corrected by aligning them with breakthroughs or incrementals. But it is important to drive the analysis at all times from the customers' viewpoint. A proper alignment will not automatically lead to new product success. It requires a careful piloting through the 13 steps indicated in Figure 1. The nature of the new product development process and the composition of the teams and the nature of their tasks will have to carefully reflect the nature of the new product. All this is hard work and creative work. But at least if the ideas are right, and when accompanied by good execution, the chances of success are maximized. On the other hand, if the alignment is mismatched, no amount of creativity and executional excellence can remedy a guaranteed failure.

Chapter 6
Techsonic Industries, Inc.: Humminbird—New Products

After several new product failures, the company began using customer input to help develop new products. In 1989, the fishing electronics industry is experiencing a downturn, and the company's sales and profits are slipping. The company, which has one product line (depth sounders) and a strong brand (Humminbird) has conducted substantial market research on three new products. Of these, one is an extension of the existing line, while the other two would be new product lines for the company. Top management is deciding which one or more of the three new products it should proceed with.

In July of 1989, the top management of Techsonic Industries, Inc., of Eufaula, Alabama, met to make plans for an important industry trade show coming up in October. Techsonic, a privately held company, was the leading manufacturer of depth sounders, devices that used sonar to help sports fishers measure the depth of the water beneath their boats and locate fish. Techsonic sold its products under its well-known Humminbird brand name. The upcoming annual trade show was often used to introduce new products to the market, and it was a company tradition to have something at the show each year to excite its customers and the industry.

The company had three new products in various stages of development: a new depth sounder—the 901, a VHF (very high frequency) marine radio, and a navigation device based on newly available satellite technology. Whereas the 901 would be an extension of Techsonic's existing line of depth sounders, the radio and the navigation device would be the start of two new product lines. The company had completed substantial market research on all three of these products and had to decide which ones it would proceed with and the priorities it would attach to each. In addition, Techsonic's chairman, Jim Balkcom, and president, Tom Dyer, wanted to see marketing plans for the new products before the trade show.

This case was prepared by Eric D. Beinhocker under the direction of Melvyn A.J. Menezes. Copyright © 1990 by the President and Fellows of Harvard College.
Harvard Business School case 591-007.

Company Background[1]

In 1989, Eufaula, Alabama, was a small southern town with stately old homes, beautiful dogwood trees, and numerous bass boats on trailers headed toward the town's lake. Techsonic Industries, located on the shores of Lake Eufaula, was founded in 1971 by Yank Dean IV, an inventor, Eufaula native, and bass fisher. During the early 1970s, bass anglers began using sonar depth sounders to measure the depth of the lake bottom beneath their boats. The depth sounder would also display the depth of objects such as logs, sea grass, and, anglers hoped, fish. The type of depth sounder most commonly used was called a flasher because it indicated the depth of objects with flashing lights on a circular display. Dean's and his fishing friends' dissatisfaction with existing flashers spurred Dean to develop one that they themselves would like to use. The Humminbird Super 60 was introduced with a waterproof case, an easy to read display, sturdy components, and a three-day repair guarantee (see Exhibit 1 for product photos). Although incremental, these improvements struck a chord with anglers, and the Super 60 became a legendary product in the bass fishing community.

Though pleased with the Super 60's success, the company's very profitable $2 million a year in revenues, and the regional customer base, Dean knew that the company had greater potential. In 1976, he recruited Jim Balkcom, an Atlanta banker, West Point graduate, and Harvard Business School MBA, to join Techsonic as a vice president. Although Balkcom was an Atlanta native and a nonfisher, Dean convinced him of the opportunity to build a business in Eufaula. Eleven months after

---

[1]In addition to field interviews, the first two sections draw on material from Joshua Hyatt, "Ask and You Shall Receive," *Inc.,* September 1989, pp. 90–97.

Exhibit 1

 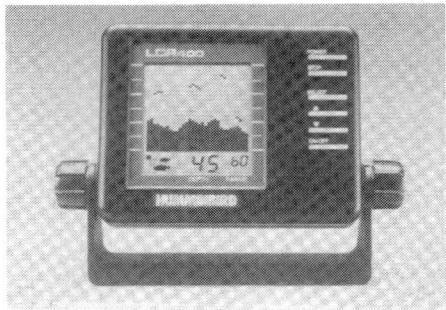 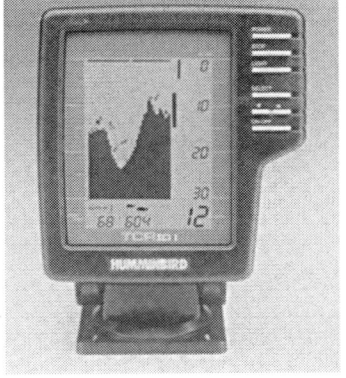

Balkcom joined, Dean died of a heart attack while jogging. In 1977, Balkcom found himself president of a company that needed new products but had just lost its only inventor, engineer, and source of market knowledge.

Despite these difficulties, Balkcom had ambitious plans for Techsonic. His long-range vision focused on growth through new products and customer loyalty through outstanding service. He poured money into efforts to enhance the existing product line and enter the market for a different type of depth sounder known as a chart recorder.[2] During the six-year period from 1977 to 1982, Techsonic introduced nine new products, all of which turned out to be, as one executive put it, "half-dead dogs." The new flashers did not offer any new features that were truly useful, and the chart recorders were too expensive, complicated, and unreliable for Hummin-bird's customer base.

Fortunately for Techsonic, the Super 60's reputation for quality and the company's high standards of service kept customers loyal. When Yank Dean was alive, customer service often consisted of his crawling under customers' boats on a Saturday morning to get their Super 60s working. Techsonic developed a reputation for standing behind its products. After Dean's death Balkcom worked to develop an organization and culture that could build on that image in the market as the company grew.

In 1978, while Techsonic was still struggling to develop new products, Balkcom hired his West Point classmate Tom Dyer to head sales and marketing. Over the next several years, Balkcom and Dyer greatly expanded distribution from local sporting goods and fishing shops to mass market retailers such as Wal-Mart and Kmart, catalogers such as Bass Pro, and marine and sporting goods stores nationwide. Although revenues increased to $19.6 million in the fiscal year ended June 30, 1983, the Super 60 still accounted for 97 percent of the company's sales (a summary of Techsonic's financial history from 1985 appears in Exhibit 2).

New Product Development

In early 1984, Techsonic's management took a step that was unprecedented in their $55-million-a-year industry. They began a deliberate effort to research their customer base—both existing and potential. Although concerned about spending $20,000 for "a folder with some stuff in it," they commissioned a market research firm (MRF) to perform market research using focus groups and telephone interviews.[3] The MRF ran focus groups in nine cities across the country and oversaw 2,500 phone interviews. They found that Techsonic's customers wanted a product that was easier to read in sunlight and that had a graphic representation like that of a chart recorder, but was as reliable and inexpensive as a flasher. Techsonic's

---

[2]Instead of flashing lights on a depth scale, chart recorders trace an image showing the location of fish with a pen on paper moving between two rollers.

[3]In a focus group, an interviewer spends time with a group of customers to gauge reactions to new product or advertising concepts.

Exhibit 2   Summary Financial Statements

	(Year Ending June 30)				
	1985	1986	1987	1988	1989
Income ($000)					
Net sales	52,063	94,792	106,155	122,534	107,089
Gross profit	23,975	45,546	47,602	46,968	32,001
Sales and marketing	8,146	12,949	14,125	17,272	19,239
Engineering	1,345	1,949	2,289	3,590	3,851
General and administration	4,452	5,953	5,678	5,742	5,076
Other expenses	3,652	6,217	6,742	0	0
Interest expense	0	0	0	9,591	16,240
Refinance expense	0	0	0	12,415	0
Pretax profit	6,380	18,478	18,768	(1,642)	(12,405)
Income tax	2,210	8,016	8,371	850	(5,253)
ESOP contribution	340	510	510	0	0
Discontinued operations	1,387	184	(26)	0	0
Net income	2,443	9,768	9,913	(2,492)	(7,152)

The company's balance sheet as of June 30, 1990, showed $798,000 in cash, current assets of $33.3 million, current liabilities of $16.8 million, long-term debt of $29.7 million, subordinated debt of $33.1 million, and stockholders' equity of $3.7 million.

Source: Company records.

management was surprised to learn that most of their customers really did not know how to use their flashers and wanted a simpler product. They had always assumed that their customers liked lots of buttons and features.

Techsonic's management soon realized that the solution to these customer needs lay in a new technology, liquid crystal displays (LCDs). LCDs, which in 1983 were found mostly in digital watch and calculator displays, would allow a graphic representation of the bottom, fish, and other objects. But, unlike a chart recorder, there would be no moving parts to break down or paper that could get wet. The unit could be waterproof, sturdy, and, with its large display, easy to read in sunlight. In addition, the product could be easy to use with an "automatic mode," allowing anglers simply to turn the unit on and use it, but still have the option of changing settings if they wanted to.

By the fall of 1984, Techsonic began to build prototypes and, consistent with its new philosophy of listening to its customers, returned to focus groups to test reactions to the product. The reactions were positive, though not exactly what management expected. The majority of the participants said they would not remove their old flashers and replace them with this new product. Instead, they would mount the two side by side on their boats.

In June 1984, a month before the new product's introduction, the company began to build interest and demand in the distribution channel through heavy advertising in the top fishing magazines. Rather than positioning the product as competing with flashers, the advertising copy, with the slogan "Bridging the gap—between flashers and charts," was based on data from the focus groups. Each point that had emerged as important in the focus groups—for example, ability to view in sunlight—was addressed in the ads. Techsonic introduced the product in July 1984 as the Humminbird LCR (liquid crystal recorder) (photo in Exhibit 1) at the American Fishing and Tackle Manufacturers Association trade show, with the largest booth it had ever had.

By the end of fiscal year 1985, 11 months after the introduction, the company had sold 238,000 LCR units. The most Super 60s it had ever sold in a year was 163,780. Revenues increased more than two and a half times, to $52.7 million, with the Super 60 accounting for only 25 percent of unit sales. Management was surprised to learn that almost half of the LCR's sales were to first-time buyers. The LCR product had not only increased Humminbird's market share, but had also brought new buyers into the market, increasing the total market size.

The LCR's success helped make listening to the customer the foundation of the company's culture. Balkcom and a group of employees developed a "corporate values" card for every employee to carry, which featured the company motto, "The quality of any product or service is what the customer says it is." "The Customer" was placed at the top of the organizational chart in Techsonic's lobby, and management began to believe that its lack of fishing experience was actually an advantage in an industry in which most executives were avid anglers. As Al Nunley, vice president of marketing, described it, "We don't have any preconceived ideas, and our emotions about our own likes and dislikes in fishing don't get in the way. Others in this industry think they know what the customer wants. We're about the only ones who actually ask and listen."

According to Dyer, "Now we had a secret weapon. We were stupid enough to think that if it worked for us once, it could work for us again." In the spring of 1985, the MRF returned to focus groups to start the product development cycle again, this time using warranty cards from LCR purchasers to select the groups. With these groups, a single theme repeatedly appeared. Claiming that it was too difficult to distinguish fish from rocks and other objects, participants suggested displaying the "fish in red." The LCD supplier developed a new black and red LCD, and Techsonic quickly built a series of prototypes.

Focus groups were held for the new products, trying different symbols and mixes of red and black to depict different sizes of fish and varying bottom hardness. Their message was to "Keep it simple. Show fish in red and the bottom in black."

Techsonic introduced its new 4-ID product in July 1986 with this slogan, "If it's red, it's fish. It's that simple."

Data from focus groups and telephone interviews showed a very positive response to the new product. However, the company could not believe that it would repeat the LCR's success. For one, at $350 the new 4-ID was significantly more expensive than the LCR, which in 1986 sold for $200. Techsonic shipped 163,000 4-ID units from January to June. By December end it had shipped 230,000 4-ID units, with total company sales growing to $95 million. Once again, the company had both increased its market share and brought new buyers into the market by introducing an easier-to-use, more functional product.

As new Humminbird products expanded the market, competitors began to enter, mimicking Humminbird features. Prices began to erode and product life cycles shortened.

During 1987, the product development cycle at Techsonic was repeated. But this time the focus groups and interviews with Humminbird users revealed fewer and less substantial problems to be solved. Customers were pretty satisfied with their LCRs, 4-IDs, or their imitators.

Thus, the next product in the Humminbird line, the TCR, was much the same as the 4-ID, but with some incremental improvements to the resolution of the sonar, the mounting system, and the product's ease of use. Although the improvements were useful, none had the impact of the first LCR or "fish in red." The positioning statement for the TCR was The Next Generation, and the product line was introduced in August 1988.

In addition to its middle- and low-end TCR products, Techsonic introduced a high-end product, the TCR Color-1, which used a new eight-color LCD technology. However, anglers were not sufficiently interested in color to justify the product's higher price and it failed to become a mainstream hit.

The TCR line sold at a rate just under its target until April of 1989, when the entire marine market went into a nosedive. As Balkcom described it, "Everything stopped." A large portion of Techsonic's sales were to new-boat buyers, so that when new-boat sales diminished, its sales were strongly affected, causing a buildup of inventory in the company's sales channels. Because most of Techsonic's competitors were similarly affected, significant price reductions occurred as manufacturers and dealers attempted to clear the excess inventory from the channel.

Depth Sounder Market

The total depth sounder market in 1989 was approximately $286 million, up from $20 million in 1976 and $55 million in 1983. The product breakdown was: LCDs: $264 million, 1,050,000 units; flashers: $17 million, 110,000 units; chart recorders: $5 million, 10,000 units. In 1989, the depth sounder market and the entire U.S. fishing electronics industry experienced a sharp downturn, with sales and profits dropping an average of 15 percent. A slowdown in the new-boat market and increased competition led to a significant erosion in depth sounder prices.

Competition

Competition in the depth sounder market increased from a handful of companies to more than 30 in 1989, with Humminbird and MorPal the dominant ones. There were seven others that competed directly with Humminbird (see Exhibit 3).

In the low end of the market (below $135 retail price), a number of smaller companies had come out with products copying Humminbird features. As Balkcom described it, depth sounders in the low end were about as differentiated as

Exhibit 3   U.S. Market Share and Industry Advertising Expenditures, 1989

Company	Total (% $)	LCDs (% Units)		Flashers (% Units)		Chart (% Units)		Advertising Expenditure ($)
		F	S	F	S	F	S	
Techsonic Industries	38	31	16	22	12	6	4	$1,700
MorPal	26	12	10	29	18	35	25	674
Hammertech Electronics	9	na	na	na	na	na	na	721
PAR Digital	6	4	5	5	5	—	14	383
Marmen	6	na	na	na	na	na	na	374
Lisotech	4	10	22	1	2	—	—	199
Navsonic	4	na	na	na	na	na	na	753
FindFish Electronics	na	8	1	7	9	—	8	346
Jules Marine Technology	na	1	0	3	0	1	0	1,020
All Others	7	34	46	33	54	58	49	3,256
Total	100	100	100	100	100	100	100	$9,426

F = freshwater market.   S = saltwater market
na = not available.   — = Company does not manufacture a product in this category.
SOURCE: Techsonic Industries, Inc.

"jellybeans." Meanwhile, the high end of the market was involved in a "feature war," with new technologies and features being added to products at a rapid pace and vendors unable to increase their prices to reflect the additional functionality. Some of the features Techsonic's competitors were adding in 1989 included split screens that showed both an LCR-like graph and a flasher-like display, touch screens replacing buttons for function selection, and digital water temperature, speed, and depth indicators.

End-Users

In early 1987, Techsonic commissioned a market research firm (MRF) to gather information on the end-users of depth sounders. It conducted telephone interviews of 605 noncommercial power boat owners. A summary of that survey's findings is presented in Exhibit 4.

Marketing

Distribution

Techsonic sold its products through multiple sales channels. To reach these channels, it used a sales force of 29 people in the United States, including three regional managers. Most Techsonic sales were through mass merchants and catalogers. Other channels used by Techsonic included marine distributors, marine dealers, sporting goods distributors and dealers, and OEM.

Exhibit 4   End-User Telephone Survey, 1987: Summary Results

- Noncommercial power boat owners were predominantly male (94%), average age 45, and average annual income $40,000. Their occupations were professional or managerial (50%), blue collar (24%), or retired (18%).
- Noncommercial power boat owners used their boats primarily for sports fishing (89%). They fished primarily in freshwater (95%), and to a much lesser extent in saltwater (14%) or in the Great Lakes (14%). On average, they spent $900 a year on boating and fishing equipment, not including major purchases such as boats and trailers.
- Most of the respondents watched boating- and fishing-related TV programs (72%) and attended boat shows (59%).
- Unaided brand awareness and brand preference for depth sounders were as follows:

	Unaided Awareness	Most Preferred	Also Considered
Humminbird	70%	28%	37%
MorPal	73%	40%	28%
Jules Marine Tech.	32%	5%	34%
PAR Digital	20%	2%	15%
FindFish Electronics	17%	1%	12%

- Seventy-seven percent of the respondents owned depth sounders, and the average number of depth sounders owned was two. Of those who owned a depth sounder, 75% owned a flasher, 28% an LCD, and 26% a chart.
- Among depth sounder owners, Humminbird was owned by 47%, MorPal by 41%, and Jules Marine Tech. by 12%. Humminbird was popular in LCDs (57% share) and flashers (41%), but was weak in charts (15%). On the other hand, MorPal was strong in charts (54%) and flashers (42%), but not so strong in LCDs (25%).
- Respondents purchased their depth sounders from a variety of outlets: marine stores (28%), sporting goods stores (16%), mass merchants (15%), catalogs (15%), OEM as part of the boat (13%), and another fisher (5%).

Source: Company records.

Mass merchants and catalogers operated with lower gross margins (1 to 15 percent) than did the other channels (20 to 40 percent). Consequently, the volume of Humminbird product sold through mass merchants and catalogers resulted in heavy discounting of the products in the marketplace. As a result, many marine dealers and distributors were unable to make an adequate return on Humminbird. Although a few marine dealers made 20 percent margins on Humminbird, most of them broke even or lost money. They wanted to make a 30 to 40 percent margin on the products they stocked, but believed that a margin of at least 20 percent was necessary for survival. In 1989, many marine dealers were dropping the Humminbird line and stocking competing brands that were not sold by mass merchants, even though they often had to put in greater efforts to sell them.

Most distribution channel members viewed Humminbird as a mid-level product, both in technology and price. Although Techsonic had pioneered many of the innovations in the industry, many of its dealers perceived MorPal as the technological leader, and some considered Humminbird's "fish in red" a sales gimmick that seemed to work well with customers. They considered the Humminbird brand to be a good value with high customer acceptance, believing it most appropriate for first-time buyers and weekend fishers.

Communications

Techsonic spent approximately $1.7 million on print advertising in 1989, the highest in the industry. Humminbird products were advertised regularly in fishing and outdoor magazines such as *Bass Masters, Field & Stream, Fins and Feathers,* and *Bassin'* and occasionally in publications such as *USA Today* and *Sports Illustrated.* Favorable product reviews in trade magazines were important, and Techsonic had a public relations firm assist it in communicating with the press.

Boat shows and industry trade shows also played an important role in promoting Humminbird products. Techsonic used them to demonstrate its products to dealers and customers, as well as to introduce new products, assess the competition, and get feedback from the market.

Techsonic also sponsored the Humminbird Sports Team, a group of well-known professional bass fishers and other athletes. In addition, it sponsored a number of sporting events carried on cable television, including: "Humminbird Bass & Golf" (fishing and golf competition), "Humminbird Bass & Race" (fishing and car racing), and an annual celebrity bass-fishing tournament.

New Product Options: Project 901

In 1989, to reassert its position as the market and technological leader, Techsonic's R&D team developed a revolutionary new fish-finding system. The product, referred to internally as Project 901, had taken years to develop and was aimed at satisfying two important benefits that Techsonic believed anglers sought in a depth sounder: to find fish faster and to see fish better. The product provided the first truly three-dimensional view of the water ever available in a depth sounder, allowing anglers to distinguish more easily between fish and other objects, as well as to locate the fish more precisely.

Market Study

Techsonic commissioned a market research firm at a cost of $50,000 to conduct a market study on the 901. The objectives were to determine the customer's intention to buy and the perceived uniqueness of the product, the market and sales potential for the first three years, and a profile of the potential customer, and to provide guidelines for product positioning, features to be included in the standard and deluxe models, and the best price for each model.

Methodology

MRF conducted 375 interviews in three key markets: freshwater, saltwater, and the Great Lakes. The respondents were boat owners who planned to buy a depth sounder during the next three years. The interviews, lasting 15 minutes, were conducted at the boat owners' homes by experienced interviewers. Respondents were paid $15 for their participation and were not informed that the research was being conducted for Humminbird.

After a few questions obtaining demographic information and the brand of depth sounder they would consider buying, participants were shown a short video of the 901. They were then asked about (*a*) their likelihood of buying the 901 if it were available at a reasonable price (no price was stated), (*b*) the perceived uniqueness of the 901, (*c*) pricing, and (*d*) their likelihood of buying the 901 within the next year if it were available at $449.

Next, participants were shown another short video explaining some additional or optional features of the 901. For each feature, participants were asked whether they believed that (*a*) it was essential to the product and had to be included for them to purchase the product; (*b*) it increased the value of the product, for which they would pay more if it were included; or (*c*) it had no effect on whether or not they would buy the product. They were then asked questions about pricing the deluxe model (which had all the features they wanted), and how likely they were to buy it within the next year if it were available at $629.

Analysis and Recommendations

Customer Interest. The market research firm concluded that the 901 was a clear winner because it scored high on the dimensions of uniqueness and purchase likelihood (see Exhibit 5). In addition, the 901 results compared very favorably with those of past new products from Techsonic. It earned the highest uniqueness score of any Techsonic product and the highest intention-to-buy score since the original LCR in 1984.

Freshwater fishers and mid-sized boat owners were the most likely to buy the product. Those who did not own a depth sounder and those who currently owned an LCD or chart recorder indicated they were most likely to buy the 901.

Market and Sales Potential. MRF estimated the total market potential for the first three years to be 320,000 units and Humminbird's sales potential at 139,871 units (including 93,030 standard units and 46,841 deluxe units) during that period (see Exhibit 6). Based on Techsonic's retail pricing plans of $449 for the standard unit and $629 for the deluxe unit, the 901 would represent retail sales of $71.2 million over three years.

Important assumptions in the calculation of the market and sales potential given in Exhibit 6 were:

1. All respondents who said that they were "very likely to buy" the 901 at a reasonable price were considered potential customers for year one. Respondents who indicated they were "somewhat likely" to buy the 901 at a reasonable price were considered potential customers for years two to three.
2. For participants for whom Humminbird was not the first-choice vendor for the next depth sounder purchased, for each manufacturer the proportion of

EXHIBIT 5 Project 901 Product Test: Customer Interest

The average respondent was 45 years old, most likely a professional, executive, or manager and had an average annual income of $50,000, a profile which was similar to the general population of boat owners.

Participants were asked the following two questions:

"You said you were considering buying a depth sounder. If this new product were available to you at a reasonable price, how likely would you be to *buy it* during the *next year?* Would you be: *very likely to buy; somewhat likely to buy; not very likely to buy;* or *not at all likely to buy* it during the next year?"

"How different or *unique* would you say this product is compared to what is now available to you to buy? Would you say it is: *Very unique; somewhat unique; not very unique;* or *not at all unique* or different from what is available now?"

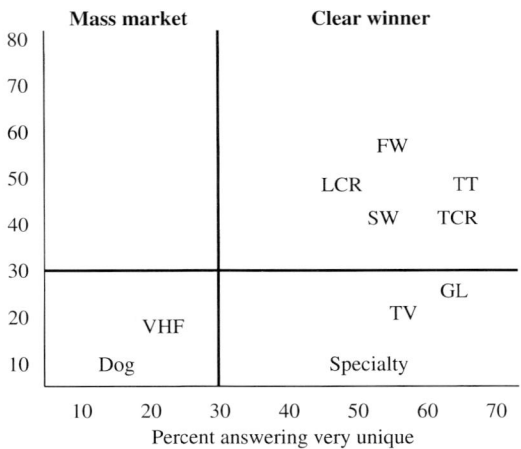

901 Test results:
TT = Total market
FW = Freshwater
GL = Great Lakes
SW = Saltwater

Past results:
LCR = Where LCR scored when tested
TCR = Where TCR scored when tested

Test controls (other products used to gauge reaction):
TV = A random LCD television
VHF = A random saltwater VHF marine radio

SOURCE: Company records.

respondents who said they would consider Humminbird was applied to that manufacturer's potential market share to estimate Humminbird's potential sales.

Product Positioning.   Based on the responses to the product description, MRF concluded that despite the 901's technological wizardry, its most important perceived benefit was that it helped customers find fish faster and see them better.

Exhibit 6 Project 901 Test: U.S. Market Potential

Total Market Potential for Humminbird 901

	Number of Boats	Percent (%)	Basis
A. Boats whose use makes them eligible to own depth sounders.	4,000,000		Past experience
B. Boats likely to purchase depth sounders in next 1–3 years.	320,000	8% of A	Past experience
Total market potential	320,000 units		

First-Year Sales Potential for Humminbird 901

Stated First Choice	"Very Likely" First Year	"Would Buy" Humminbird	Total Units
(31%) Humminbird = 99,200	× 49%	× 100%	48,608 (Humminbird share)
(20%) MorPal = 64,000	× 27%	× 38%	6,566 (MorPal, but would buy Humminbird)
(14%) Jules Marine = 44,800	× 48%	× 71%	15,268 (Jules Marine, but would buy Humminbird)
Humminbird Sales Potential in First Year:			70,442

Based on responses, sales of standard units at $449 each were estimated to be 47,530 units and sales of deluxe units at $629 each were estimated to be 22,912 units.

Second- and Third-Year Sales Potential for Humminbird 901

	"Somewhat Likely"	"Would Buy" Humminbird	Total Units
(31%) Humminbird = 99,200	× 45%	× 100%	44,640 (Humminbird share)
(20%) MorPal = 64,000	× 47%	× 38%	11,430 (MorPal, but would buy Humminbird)
(14%) Jules Marine = 44,800	× 42%	× 71%	13,359 (Jules Marine, but would buy Humminbird)
Humminbird Sales Potential in Second and Third Years:			69,429

According to responses, sales of standard units at $449 each were estimated to be 45,500 and sales of deluxe units at $629 were estimated to be 23,929.

Source: Company records.

Respondents' comments indicated that although technology played an important role in the 901's perceived uniqueness, they had come to expect technology and were no longer amazed by it. The MRF felt that although people responded to the 901's novelty and many considered it their next great toy, these considerations were secondary to the ease factor (see Exhibit 7). They recommended emphasizing that the 901 made fishing easier, and thus more fun.

Product Features.   Customer evaluations of the various 901 features are shown in Exhibit 8. Based on these responses, MRF recommended that the standard 901 model should include: 3-D view to 240 feet, a video operator's manual, a temperature gauge, and ability to match display speed and boat speed. They recommended that the following additional features be included in the deluxe model: bottom hardness indicator, ability to program the display to show different fish sizes, three simultaneous views of the bottom from different angles, marine plotter connection, and a speedometer.

Exhibit 7 Project 901 Study: Product Positioning

The interviewer read the following: "I now will read you four different ways this new product could be described. Please listen carefully and choose the *one* description which *best* matches *your perception* of this new product." Questions were read in order. Cards with questions written on them were placed on the table for the respondents to study.

Question	Response
a. It's the next hot item for fishermen. Anyone who values having the very latest equipment would just have to have it.	15%
b. It's much easier to understand what's on the screen. It looks as though it would be easy to use, and it would make catching fish easier.	48%
c. It's fascinating to watch the bottom and fish move across the screen. It would be fun to have this product on a boat.	12%
d. It's the next generation of fish-finding technology. It's obviously light years ahead of anything else on the market.	25%

SOURCE: Company records.

Exhibit 8 Project 901 Study: Product Features

Feature	Available with Competitive Products	Essential for Purchase (%)	Would Pay More for (%)	No Effect on Purchase (%)
1. View three different angles	No	39	22	39
2. Instructions on videotape	No	38	23	39
3. Temperature gauge	On some	36	46	18
4. Display speed matches boat speed	No	28	39	39
5. Show fish size	On some	29	50	21
6. Bottom hardness indicator	No	29	39	32
7. Distance display from back to front	On some	28	31	41
8. 3-D view to 240 feet	No	28	47	25
9. Speedometer	On some	22	26	52
10. 6" × 4" screen	On some	18	37	45
11. Regular view 240–600 ft.	On some	18	19	63
12. Bottom alarm	Yes	13	28	59
13. Marine plotter connection	On some	11	40	49

SOURCE: Company records.

Pricing. Before seeing or hearing about the 901, the amount of money people said they planned to spend on their next depth sounder ranged from $219 to $560. The suggested "best prices" for the 901 indicated that Techsonic was on target with the $629 price for the deluxe model, but that they could charge substantially more than the previously considered $449 for the standard model. Considering all this, MRF suggested retail prices of $529 and $629 for the standard and deluxe models, respectively.

Margins. Techsonic management expected dealer margins to be anywhere from 15 to 40 percent, depending on the channel. In planning for the product, they decided to use a net price to dealers of $390 for the standard model and $440 for the

EXHIBIT 9   Project 901: Profit and Loss Forecast

	(Year Ending June 30)			
	1991	1992	1993	Total
Standard Model				
Unit sales	28,000	32,000	60,000	120,000
Net price per unit	$390.00	$330.00	$280.00	$319.00 avg.
Net sales	10,920,000	10,560,000	16,800,000	38,280,000
Gross profit	4,914,000	4,224,000	5,880,000	15,018,000
Percent (%)	45.00%	40.00%	35.00%	39.23%
SG&A (25%)	2,730,000	2,640,000	4,200,000	9,570,000
Other	933,000	426,000	271,000	1,630,000
EBI&T	$1,251,000	$1,158,000	$1,409,000	$3,818,000
Deluxe Model				
Unit sales	4,000	12,000	20,000	36,000
Net price per unit	$440.00	$375.00	$320.00	$351.67 avg.
Net sales	1,760,000	4,500,000	6,400,000	12,660,000
Gross profit	792,000	1,800,000	2,240,000	4,832,000
Percent (%)	45.00%	40.00%	35.00%	38.17%
SG&A (25%)	440,000	1,125,000	1,600,000	3,165,000
Other	217,000	146,000	101,000	464,000
EBI&T	$135,000	$529,000	$539,000	$1,203,000

Capital expenditures for both products combined:

Packaging	$36,000
Tooling	136,000
Equipment	38,000
R&D	400,000
Total	$610,000

SOURCE: Company records.

deluxe model, and unit sales levels of 120,000 and 36,000, respectively, over the next three years (see Exhibit 9).

At a similar stage, the company's last two products to be introduced, the TCR ID-1 and TCR ID-10, had been projected to sell approximately 21,600 units each over three years. The average price over the same period for both products was forecast at about $260, with gross margins of 42 percent and 46 percent, respectively. The total capital expenditures for both products was $151,643, and the total projected earnings before interest and taxes was $2.08 million.

The VHF Marine Radio

In 1988, Techsonic's board of directors decided that it would be in the company's interest to move beyond its dependence on depth sounders and to make additional use of its powerful brand name and distribution network. The board believed that marine communications, in particular VHF radios, presented an opportunity because of the relatively small degree of penetration in Humminbird's customer base. The VHF radio market was fragmented, with no dominant competitor, and weakly represented in Humminbird's distribution channels. Finally, Techsonic felt it could build a differentiated product using its brand name and reputation for waterproofing, durability, and service.

Market Study and Methodology

Techsonic commissioned the MRF at a cost of $26,000 to do a market study to determine the market potential for a Humminbird radio and to define an appropriate product. The MRF interviewed three groups of potential buyers: recreational boaters, sports fishers, and Humminbird customers.

VHF Market

VHF radios were used primarily for safety: to communicate for help in an emergency and to find out the weather. However, in addition to providing a "lifeline for survival," VHFs provided a "social pipeline." A popular method of communication among boaters, they were used to talk to friends on the shore, to contact other boaters, and to find out where fish were, what bait was working, and who was catching what. Although fishing was often characterized as a solitary sport, most fishers appreciated the opportunity to interact with others (see Exhibit 10).

The study confirmed the fragmented nature of the market. FindFish Electronics was owned by 17 percent of the respondents, STEBOB Radio by 7 percent, IGM Communications by 5 percent, and various other brands (none of which had more than 3 percent market share) by 45 percent. The remaining 26 percent did not know the brand of their VHF radio.

End-Users

More than two-thirds of the respondents had a VHF and about one-third had a CB (citizens band) radio. The MRF concluded that most boaters would therefore be purchasing a VHF radio as a replacement for an older unit. Although the demographic profile of VHF owners was very similar to that of depth sounders, only 7 percent of Humminbird's customers owned a VHF, and 42 percent owned a CB radio.

A majority (56 percent) of the respondents purchased their VHF radios from marine dealers. The other major channels of distribution included mail order catalogs (14 percent), department stores (6 percent), sporting goods stores (6 percent), and catalog showrooms (5 percent). About two-thirds of the respondents installed the radios themselves.

Nearly two-thirds of the respondents attended a boat show within the previous year. About 25 percent participated or watched fishing tournaments, and about as many belonged to a fishing or boating club that held regular meetings.

EXHIBIT 10 VHF/Marine Radio Market Study: What Would You Like to Do?/What Would You Use a Radio For?

	Recreational Boaters		Fishermen		Humminbird Customers	
	A %	B %	A %	B %	A %	B %
Get the weather	62	56	67	66	42	33
Radio for help in emergency	56	56	56	57	33	39
Find out where the fish are biting	27	23	38	34	26	23
Know what bait is working	25	21	36	33	27	23
Talk to friends on shore	19	21	36	29	20	13
Know who's catching what	18	14	34	26	23	14
Talk with other boaters	24	11	24	15	18	8
Touch base with home	19	24	26	27	11	15
Schedule meeting with other boaters	21	17	13	13	11	8
Order supplies from offshore	8	8	13	8	4	4

A = Would like to be able to do often.
B = Would use a marine/VHF radio to do.
SOURCE: Company records.

Product Features

A vast majority (88 percent) of the respondents purchased fixed-mount radios, as opposed to hand-held radios, and bought an antenna at the same time (90 percent), though in most cases (57 percent) not as a package.

The major problems VHF owners faced concerned the radio's durability, the battery's dying, and the absence of waterproofing. However, it was not clear exactly what impact solving these problems would have on brand choice.

Concerns

Techsonic management was concerned about a few problems regarding the distribution channels. First, radios were typically purchased through marine dealers, a channel in which Techsonic was quite weak, accounting for only 11 percent of Humminbird depth sounder sales. The trend for depth sounders was moving away from marine dealers as price competition from the mass merchants and catalogers was driving dealers away from the Humminbird line. Techsonic's management had in the past encouraged this trend because research had indicated that product availability was a major sales bottleneck, a problem that the mass merchants could solve.

Techsonic management believed that there was an opportunity to increase the number of radios sold in the mass merchant channels and that it had the right product to do so. At the same time, the MRF research indicated that a strong presence in marine dealers would be critical for success. However, there was some expectation

EXHIBIT 11   VHF/Marine Radio: Profit and Loss Forecast

	(Year Ending June 30)			
	1991	*1992*	*1993*	*Total*
Unit sales	5,600	20,000	24,000	49,600
Net price per unit	$195.00	$175.00	$157.00	$168.55 avg.
Net sales	1,092,000	3,500,000	3,768,000	8,360,000
Gross profit	218,400	1,225,000	1,507,200	2,950,600
Percent (%)	20.00%	35.00%	40.00%	35.29%
SG&A (25%)	273,000	875,000	942,000	2,090,000
Other	240,000	48,000	0	288,000
EBI&T	($294,600)	$302,000	$565,200	$572,600
Capital expenditures				
Packaging	$18,000			
Tooling	318,000			
Equipment	60,000			
R&D	180,000			
Total	$576,000			

SOURCE: Company records.

that marine dealers would be quite wary about being burned by Humminbird again, especially if they saw Techsonic pushing the radios through the mass merchants.

The second problem centered around the mass merchants. A small number of mass merchants that moved significant amounts of Humminbird products traditionally allocated three SKUs (stock keeping units) to Humminbird. They had communicated strong resistance to increasing this number of SKUs, leading the MRF to believe that a Humminbird radio would potentially force the removal of another Humminbird product from these retailers' shelves.

The third problem centered around pricing through the mass merchant channel. Pricing was not addressed in the MRF survey, but Techsonic had decided to set $269 as the expected retail price, based on a competitive analysis of similarly featured radios (though some Humminbird features such as waterproofing were unique) and Techsonic's internal profit targets. Management expected dealers to make 15 to 35 percent on the product and used a net dealer price of $195 in their internal profit forecast (see Exhibit 11).

Early discussions with Humminbird dealers revealed a potential problem with these prices. Mass merchants traditionally viewed Humminbird as the mid-point in their lines, and wanted to sell the radio at $199. At $269, a Humminbird radio would be at the high-end of the radios they were selling. Although they felt that the Humminbird VHF was an attractive product with some differentiating features, they were skeptical as to the value of its brand name at the high end of the radio market.

Finally, there was some concern among Techsonic managers that the radio would be the first Humminbird product manufactured outside the company. At least initially, the radio's electronics would be manufactured in the Philippines by an experienced, low-cost producer. Final assembly, testing, and packaging would be done in Eufaula.

Navigation Products

In addition to radios, Balkcom and Dyer were considering expanding into marine navigation electronics, in which they believed there was significant opportunity because of a new technology that would be introduced to the market in late 1990.

Navigation Market

In 1989, the most commonly used navigation system for recreational boating and sports fishing was LOCATOR. Boats equipped for LOCATOR had a device that received LOCATOR signals and displayed an estimate of the boat's position. By timing the differences in the reception of signals transmitted from three or more of the LOCATOR network's ground-based stations, the receiving unit on the boat could estimate the boat's position.

The LOCATOR market was small (estimated 1989 sales of 80,000 units) and very fragmented. Only two brands (PAR Digital and Onkar Marine) held more than a 10 percent market share. LOCATOR products had a retail price beginning at about $300 and required a considerable amount of skill to operate. Most LOCATOR receivers were not user-friendly, and owners complained of having to refer to the manual constantly. Some of the problems LOCATOR users faced were performance-related: accuracy tended to degrade in bad weather, signals were subject to interference, it was often unusable because a transmitter was not operating, and the transmitters were concentrated along the coasts, leaving most inland lakes and waterways with poor or no coverage.

GPS (Global Positioning System) was a new satellite-based navigation system sold in the commercial market and priced between $3,000 and $5,000. A GPS receiver in a boat used time differences in its reception of signals from a group of satellites to determine the boat's location. The major advantages of GPS over LOCATOR were that its readings were more accurate, its signals were much less susceptible to interference or weather problems, and it would cover the entire world. Although limited in 1989 to approximately 10 hours per day, GPS was expected to become 24-hour effective by late 1990, with worldwide coverage expected to be completed in late 1991.

Balkcom and Dyer believed that the shift in navigation technology from LOCATOR to GPS presented Techsonic with two opportunities. The first was to enter the navigation market by introducing a product based on GPS technology. Techsonic hoped to introduce GPS to the recreational boating and sports fishing market by developing a user-friendly version priced to consumers at about $1,000.

The second opportunity was to attempt to expand the LOCATOR market significantly by introducing a more user-friendly version of LOCATOR and selling it at $50 less than competitively priced products. They believed that the LOCATOR market had been limited by operational complexity and price. They felt they could take advantage of Humminbird's reputation among freshwater fishers and smaller-boat owners, where LOCATOR had a low level of penetration.

Market Study

Balkcom and Dyer commissioned a market research firm (MRF) at a cost of $33,000 to study the market for navigation devices and help identify appropriate market opportunities. Specifically, the study sought (*a*) to examine whether the LOCATOR and/or GPS markets were worth pursuing, and (*b*) to determine for the LOCATOR and GPS systems appropriate product positioning, desired features and configurations, comparative ratings and purchase intentions, and price expectations and sensitivities.

Methodology

The study was conducted using 308 mailed questionnaires to noncommercial powerboat owners, of whom 205 owned LOCATORs and 103 owned no navigation system. Both groups contained saltwater and freshwater boat owners.

Analysis and Recommendations

Navigational Problems. LOCATORs were purchased primarily for navigational purposes, especially for navigating in bad weather, for determining the boat's exact position, and for returning to favorite fishing or diving spots. The problems frequently mentioned by LOCATOR owners were "having to refer to the manual all the time" (62 percent), "not being able to use the LOCATOR because a transmitter was not operating" (43 percent), "forgetting which waypoint number identifies a particular position" (39 percent), "taking a long time to warm up and lock on to a signal" (38 percent), "not being able to use it because of interference or bad weather" (37 percent), and "getting incorrect readings" (37 percent).

The predominant reasons for not purchasing a LOCATOR were price (50 percent) and the lack of a need (32 percent). The problems faced by LOCATOR nonowners are summarized in Exhibit 12.

Brand Preferences and Product Design. There was considerable lack of involvement with the product category. Half the respondents were unable to give a specific answer when asked which brand of LOCATOR they would purchase. Among LOCATOR owners, PAR Digital (14 percent) and Onkar Marine (12 percent) had the highest market shares. Other popular brands were Global Navigation (9 percent), Navsonic (8 percent) and Marmen (7 percent). LOCATOR units were purchased either as stand-alone units (79 percent), or as combinations: LOCATOR/depth sounder (13 percent) or LOCATOR/plotter (8 percent). However, regarding what they would like to buy, respondents' preferences were: stand-alone units (40 percent), LOCATOR/depth sounder (26 percent), LOCATOR/marine plotter (23 percent), and LOCATOR/GPS (8 percent). Nonowners were significantly more interested in a depth sounder combination, whereas LOCATOR owners significantly preferred a marine plotter combination.

Respondents were asked to evaluate various attribute and benefit statements in terms of both desirability and impact on the selection of a system. The MRF then combined impact and desirability ratings to come up with a "motivating power" score for each product feature or benefit. Comparing the motivating power score with desirability (see Exhibit 13), MRF concluded that although performance characteristics emerged as the most critical, respondents sometimes tended to understate

EXHIBIT 12   Global Positioning System: Problems Faced by LOCATOR Nonowners

	Frequent Problem (%)	If Occurs, Major Problem (%)
Not being able to determine your exact position	67	30
Not being able to navigate in the fog	67	72
Not being able to tell how much time it will take to get to a particular destination	62	16
Not being able to tell someone your position, or find someone according to their position	60	39
Not being able to return to favorite fishing/diving spot	58	33
Not being able to find your way in strange/new waters	49	48
Not being able to navigate through difficult channels	40	54
Not being able to determine your course heading	40	39
Not being able to find your way back to harbor in bad weather	34	54
Not being able to find your way back to harbor at night	32	67

SOURCE: Company records.

EXHIBIT 13   Global Positioning System: Purchase Motivators and Feature Desirability

	Rankings					
	Total Sample		LOCATOR Owners		Nonowners	
Features	MP	D	MP	D	MP	D
Works in all weather	1	1	1	1	1	1
Provides the highest level of accuracy	2	4	2	3	3	9
Not affected by interference	3	7	3	6	5	6
Won't become obsolete	4	6	6	7	2	3
Provides total coverage	5	3	4	2	6	11
Locks on to weak signals	6	12	5	9	11	15
Best value	7	2	11	4	4	2
Most technologically advanced	8	13	8	13	10	14
Clearly displaying all information at the same time	9	11	9	11	9	12
Being the easiest to learn how to operate	10	8	7	8	14	5
Being serviced and returned within three days	11	9	12	10	8	7
Quickly installed by you, yourself	12	10	14	12	7	4
Being priced appropriately for needs	13	5	10	5	15	8
Saltwater proof, submersible	14	14	13	14	16	13
Showing the shoreline, position, and course	15	16	15	16	12	10
Allowing for software update	16	15	16	15	13	16

MP = Motivating power of feature in purchase decision.
D = Desirability of feature.
SOURCE: Company records.

the importance of not being affected by interference, being able to lock on to weak signals, and being the most technologically advanced system. They also concluded that respondents overestimated the importance of price dimensions such as best value and being priced appropriately for navigation needs.

LOCATOR versus GPS. The awareness of LOCATOR (90 percent unaided, 98 percent aided) was substantially higher than that of other navigation systems: SATNAV (27 percent and 65 percent), Compass (20 percent and 88 percent), and GPS (12 percent and 76 percent). Nearly half the respondents who were aware of GPS did not know how it worked. Respondents rated LOCATOR and GPS systems on various attributes and benefits. The two systems were then compared along the continuum of motivating power. On many of the most motivating performance characteristics, GPS was judged superior to LOCATOR. LOCATOR had a big advantage over GPS on price, which, according to the MRF's analysis, played only a relatively modest role in selecting a navigation system.

The purchase intentions of respondents in terms of the percentage who said that they would definitely or probably purchase during the next three years is given in Table A.

TABLE A Purchase Intention for LOCATOR and GPS

Time Period	LOCATOR Owners	LOCATOR Nonowners	Total
Next Year:			
LOCATOR	11%	34%	19%
GPS	7%	14%	9%
Years 2–3:			
LOCATOR	19%	37%	25%
GPS	24%	30%	26%

Respondents who indicated a greater purchase interest in GPS tended to have higher incomes.

Pricing. To provide guidelines on the optimal price for a LOCATOR or GPS system, respondents were asked a series of questions such as: At what price does a LOCATOR/GPS begin to be expensive? To be cheap? To be so expensive that you would never consider using it? To be so cheap that you would question its quality? Responses to these questions indicated that for LOCATOR owners, the optimal price for a LOCATOR ranged from $780 to $915, and for a GPS system, it ranged from $910 to $1,399. For nonowners the corresponding optimal price ranges were $480 to $580 and $580 to $960.

Recommendations

Given the results of this study, the MRF recommended that Techsonic immediately pursue the development of a GPS system rather than a LOCATOR system. According to them, the GPS system represented the best solution to many of the problems experienced by boat owners regarding navigation and positioning. The MRF also noted that both LOCATOR owners and nonowners were concerned with LOCATOR obsolescence.

The MRF concluded that it expected interest to build in GPS as it became fully operational and as costs declined. The Humminbird GPS system should be positioned as the most state-of-the-art and user-friendly system available, and, the MRF believed, it could be priced at $1,000 or more.

Margins. Management expected dealers to realize margins of anywhere from 15 to 40 percent on GPS products and estimated its net sales price to dealers at $800 during the first year of sales. The expected retail price for a LOCATOR product was $630 with a net dealer price of $450. An analysis of Techsonic's expected margins on the GPS and LOCATOR products appear in Exhibit 14 on page 98.

Joint Venture. To facilitate entry into the GPS market, Balkcom and Dyer had discussed the possibility of a joint venture with Standard Telecommunications, Inc. (STel), of Palo Alto, California. STel, which had worked on GPS-based navigation systems as a U.S. Department of Defense contractor, was interested in diversifying into civilian applications of GPS and agreed to develop low-cost GPS products for Techsonic for a $1 million "development fee." If the joint venture went through, STel would be responsible for the GPS electronics, and Techsonic would specify features and develop the user interfaces, displays, and casings for the products. Techsonic would have exclusive rights to manufacture and market all STel GPS products for the consumer market. Such exclusivity would not extend to commercial or military markets.

Balkcom and Dyer believed that this joint venture would put Techsonic in a unique position for entering the GPS market. None of STel's competitors that were experienced in working with GPS, such as Trimble, Magellan, or Sony, had any presence in the consumer market for marine electronics. Similarly, none of Humminbird's competitors that were considering GPS, such as MorPal, Onkar Marine, ESTAP-Sonic, or PAR Digital, had any expertise with the technology.

The Decision

On July 30, Techsonic's senior management met to decide the fates of the three new products. Al Nunley, vice president of marketing, was scheduled to make a presentation of his recommendations and marketing plans. He had asked his marketing manager, Mike Centers, to assist him in the preparation as well as in the presentation at the meeting.

EXHIBIT 14 Navigation Systems: Profit and Loss Forecast

	(Year Ending June 30)			
	1991	1992	1993	Total
Global Positioning System				
Unit sales	400	6,000	16,800	23,200
Net price per unit	$800.00	$704.00	$620.00	$644.83 avg.
Net sales	320,000	4,224,000	10,416,000	14,960,000
Gross profit	114,688	2,407,680	4,999,680	7,522,048
Percent (%)	35.84%	57.00%	48.00%	50.28%
SG&A (25%)	80,000	1,056,000	1,249,920	2,385,920
EBI&T	$34,688	$1,351,680	$3,749,760	$5,136,128
Capital expenditures:				
Packaging	$28,000			
Tooling	80,000			
Equipment	36,000			
R&D	220,000			
Joint Venture Investment	400,000			
Total	$764,000			

	(Year Ending June 30)			
	1991	1992	1993	Total
Locator				
Unit sales	4,000	12,000	5,600	21,600
Net price per unit	$450.00	$375.00	$300.00	$369.44 avg.
Net sales	1,800,000	4,500,000	1,680,000	7,980,000
Gross profit	630,000	1,440,000	470,400	2,540,400
Percent (%)	35.00%	32.00%	28.00%	31.83%
SG&A (25%)	450,000	1,125,000	420,000	1,995,000
EBI&T	180,000	315,000	50,400	545,400
Capital expenditures:				
Packaging	$21,600			
Tooling	88,000			
Equipment	72,000			
R&D	120,000			
Total	$301,600			

SOURCE: Company records.

CHAPTER 7
Millipore New Product Commercialization: A Tale of Two New Products

The case details two new product development efforts at Millipore, a high-technology market leader in the value-added "separations" industry. The two products in two separate divisions have each adopted a different process. The two products, LC/MS and Viresolve, are now ready for commercialization, and their respective product managers have to make several marketing decisions to ensure success.

In 1993, Millipore was poised to launch several innovative product lines. Company executives had particularly high hopes for the liquid chromatography/mass spectrometry (LC/MS) product line in the Waters Chromatography Division and Viresolve in the Process Membranes Division. Much of the potential success of these products rested on commercialization decisions made in the past three years by their respective protagonists: Dave Strand, VP for new business development at Waters, and Paul Sekhri, product manager for Viresolve at the Process Division.

In early 1990, Dave Strand was given the task of commercializing Millipore's innovative LC/MS product line. Strand had come to Waters Chromatography Division a few years earlier, when the software firm he helped found was purchased by Waters. A rising star in the division, he hoped that successful introduction of these products would reestablish Waters' claim to technological leadership in the liquid chromatography (LC) marketplace. That title had been challenged for the first time in 1983, when Hewlett-Packard, until then a small player in the LC market, had beaten Waters to market with the photodiode array (PDA) detector for liquid chromatography systems. Waters still dominated the LC market that they gave birth to in 1958 with 40 to 50 percent of the global LC market to HP's 22 to 23 percent. With the introduction of new technologies like LC/MS they sought to place a lock on the LC market that would make it unprofitable for any firm to challenge their position. As Dave Strand put it, "We want to make the view not worth the climb."

Kevin Bartus prepared this case under the direction of V. Kasturi Rangan.
Copyright © 1993 by the President and Fellows of Harvard College.
Harvard Business School case 594-010.

In October 1990, Paul Sekhri, a young marketing manager with several years of experience working for start-ups in the biotech industry, was hired to commercialize a newly developed membrane system capable of removing viruses from protein drugs developed using biotechnology. Over the last few years Millipore had been struggling to better serve the rapidly growing biotechnology industry, and the virus removal product was one of the most promising biotechnology products that Millipore had yet developed. While "market characterization" and beta tests had been a central part of the development process, when Sekhri arrived he was met with many remaining commercialization issues. "When I started, my boss, Tim Leahy, said, 'Your job is to commercialize this product.' So I asked, 'What's the name of it?' He said, 'That's up to you.' I asked, 'What are you charging for it?' He said, 'That's up to you.' I asked, 'How are you distributing it?' He said 'That's up to you.' There was just a big, clean slate." Millipore's leading competitor in virus removal was Asahi, a small Japanese company. Asahi's membrane products, except for the virus removal membrane, were distributed in the United States by Pall. Worldwide, Pall was Millipore's leading competitor with a 13 percent share. Millipore (with $174 million in sales) had 22 percent.

Millipore Corporate Background

With worldwide sales of $750 million in 1991, Millipore was the market leader in the $3.4 billion separations industry. Millipore's products were primarily based on two separations technologies: membrane technology and chromatography.

Membrane technology separated the components of a substance primarily according to the size of those components. A substance, such as water, air, or chemicals, was filtered through thin screens called membranes, which were made of various materials and had small holes of different sizes. The pores allowed components (molecules, ions, or particles) of certain sizes to pass through, while others were trapped on the surface of the membrane. Millipore offered a wide range of membrane types, sizes, and configurations.

In a typical chromatographic separation, the substance or sample to be separated was injected into a fluid such as water. This solution was then pumped through a tube called a column which was packed with chemical materials. As the sample traveled through the column, the chemical packing separated the sample into its individual chemical molecules or components. As each component left the column, it was sensed by a detector, which transmitted a signal to a recording device. Information about each component was then depicted on a chart called a chromatogram. The total system was composed of an injector, a pump, a column, a detector, and a recorder. Millipore participated in a wide range of liquid chromatography applications.

The membrane separation and chromatography technologies were used in two types of customer applications: analysis and purification. Products for analytical applications were used to gain knowledge about a sample by detecting, identifying, and/or quantifying its chemical, physical, or biological components. Products for purification applications were used to help manufacture or process a customer's product by removing contaminants or by isolating and purifying specific components from complex mixtures.

Exhibit 1 provides an overview of the corporation's sales by customer application, customer segment, and geography. As can be seen from Exhibit 1, while chromatography technology was used predominantly in analytical applications, membrane technology was used for both analytical and purification applications. Millipore grouped its customers into eight major markets: pharmaceutical (e.g., Pfizer), biotechnology (e.g., Genentech), life sciences (e.g., Massachusetts Institute of Technology), food and beverage (e.g., Coca-Cola), microelectronics (e.g., IBM), chemical (e.g., Dow), environmental (e.g., U.S. Environmental Protection Agency), and patient care (e.g., Massachusetts General Hospital). Its customers included corporations of all types and sizes, government agencies, hospitals, universities, and research institutions.

EXHIBIT 1 Five-Year Revenue Review by Technology/Market/Geography ($ in thousands)

	1991	1990	1989	1988	1987	Five-Year Growth Rate
Sales by Product Line and Technology						
Analytical:						
Membranes	$145,909	$139,358	$124,612	$123,241	$110,773	9%
Chromatography	265,412	259,693	242,574	230,741	207,944	8%
Other	42,429	38,638	29,698	18,824	6,392	96%
Subtotal	453,750	437,689	396,884	372,806	325,109	11%
Purification:						
Membranes	257,476	226,156	186,981	170,307	130,084	19%
Chromatography	26,454	26,669	24,739	29,059	20,884	10%
Other	10,299	12,648	7,726	6,751	12,405	—
Subtotal	294,229	265,473	219,446	206,117	163,373	17%
Total	$747,979	$703,162	$616,330	$578,923	$488,482	13%
Sales by Market						
Industrial[a]	$512,219	$476,104	$427,617	$399,406	$329,015	14%
University/government	178,016	172,504	139,568	133,195	110,810	15%
Patient care/medical research	57,744	54,554	49,145	46,322	48,657	3%
Total	$747,979	$703,162	$616,330	$578,923	$488,482	13%
Sales by Geographic Area						
United States	$274,718	$267,627	$250,218	$230,010	$203,827	9%
Western Europe	234,201	230,391	183,824	176,077	152,085	14%
Japan	171,279	136,205	120,123	112,838	86,206	18%
Other[b]	67,781	68,939	62,165	59,998	46,364	11%
Total	$747,979	703,162	$616,330	$578,923	$488,482	13%

[a] Under "Industrial" was included industries such as pharmaceutical, biotechnology, chemical, and microelectronics.
[b] This included sales to Latin America, Africa, Eastern Europe, and other countries in Asia except Japan.

Profit-and-loss responsibility at Millipore Corporation was organized by three major product divisions:

1. Chromatography Division (also called Waters Chromatography Division, after Jim Waters, its founder). The LC/MS project was being developed under this division.
2. Process Systems Group (purification applications of membrane technology). The virus removal project was being developed under this division.
3. Analytical Systems Division (analytical applications of membrane technology).

A separate division, called Intertech, handled operations in Latin America, Eastern Europe, Africa, and Asia (except Japan, which was handled by Nihon Millipore).

See Table A below for an approximation of sales by each product division as constructed from Exhibit 1.

Each of the first three divisions had profit-and-loss responsibility with independent marketing, sales, R&D, and manufacturing operations. Because of common membrane technology, Analytical Systems and Process Systems shared manufacturing facilities. The company as a whole operated in 70 countries worldwide, with its world headquarters for Process Systems and Analytical Systems at Bedford, Massachusetts, and its Waters Chromatography division at Milford, Massachusetts. See Exhibit 2 for a corporate organization chart.

As can be seen from Exhibit 2, core R&D, under Jack Johansen, was a key corporate function. Core R&D supplied divisions with short-term and long-term research support for product development as well as conducting some research of its own on core technologies with potential long-term payoffs. Approximately 80 percent of the corporation's $66 million R&D budget was spent on divisional product development projects and the rest on core R&D. The divisional R&D budgets were allocated more or less in proportion to their sales revenues. According to Millipore's technology VP, roughly 50 percent of the R&D budget was spent on incremental new products and the other half on "change the name of the game" kinds of innovations.

Sales and marketing functions at Millipore were organized under each division (see Exhibit 3). In each country, one of the divisional sales managers also acted as country manager, a position which included responsibility for administrative functions such as order-entry, shipment, and invoicing. For example, Art Caputo acted both as the North American sales manager for Waters and as the country manager

TABLE A   Sales History by Product Division, 1987–1991 ($ millions)

	1991	*1990*	*1989*	*1988*	*1987*
Waters	291	287	267	260	228
Process	267	238	194	177	142
Analytical	188	178	154	142	118
Intertech	67	68	62	59	46

Exhibit 2 Millipore Organization Chart, March 1992

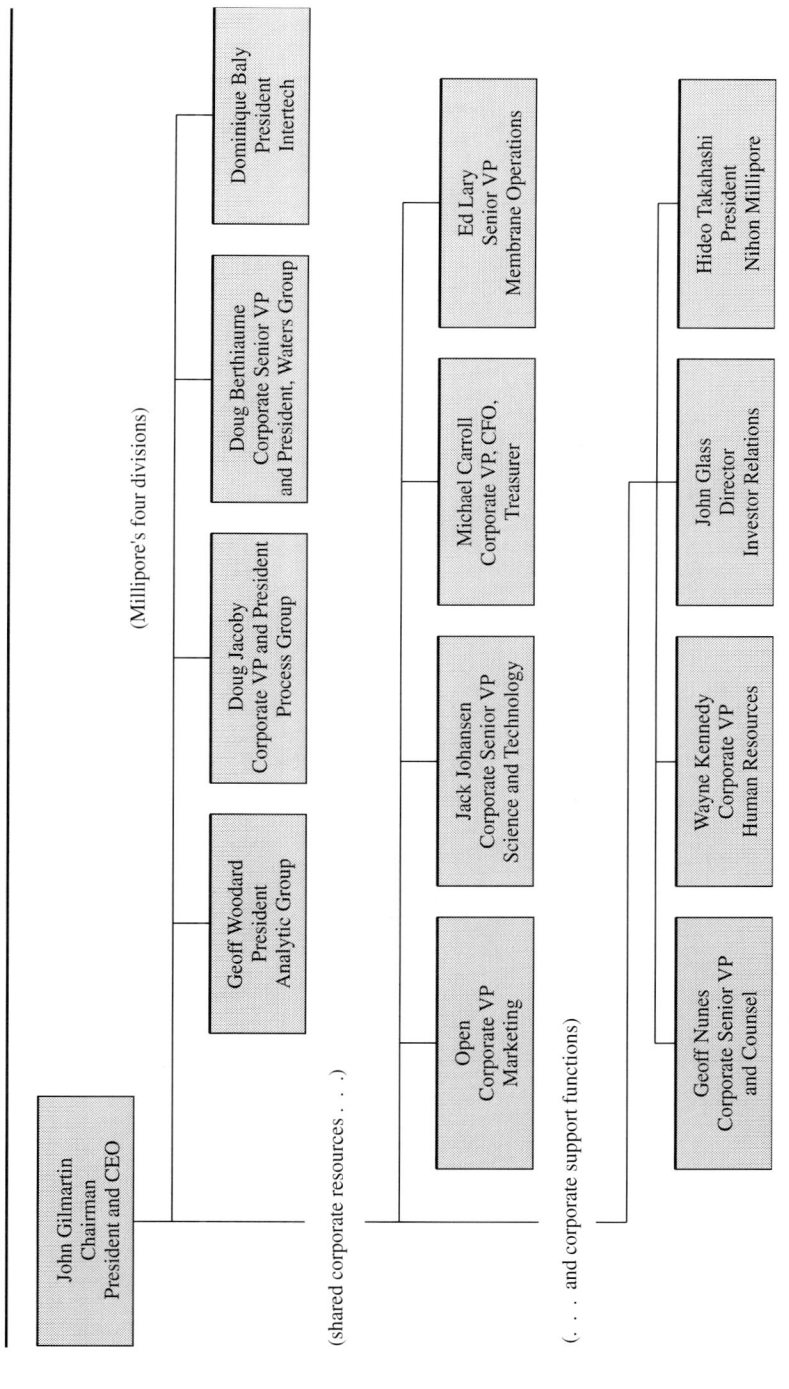

SOURCE: Casewriter depiction of organization from company data.

EXHIBIT 3 Organization of Sales and Marketing Functions at Millipore

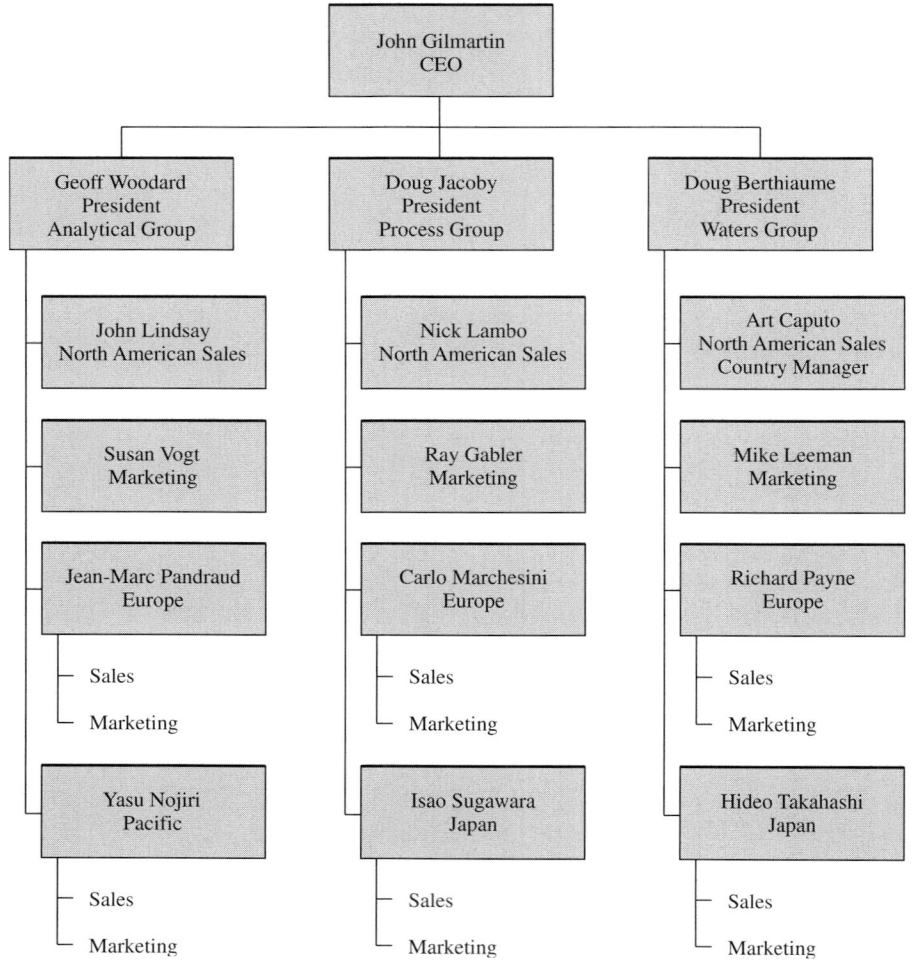

for North America. The three major Millipore divisions shared common distribution warehouses and logistics facilities worldwide. The North American sales operation was headquartered at Marlborough, Massachusetts.

New Product Development

The initiative for division product development came up from the division. Each of the three divisions had its own unique new product development system. The Analytical and Process Groups were decentralized into market-focused business units. Project ideas

EXHIBIT 4 New Product Evaluation Criteria at Analytical Group

		Weights	0 points	1 point	2 points
	Return Analysis				
S	Market size (potential market-current year)	7	<$5M	$5M–$20M	>$20M
S	Market growth (five years out)	9	<15%	15%–30%	>30%
S	Market share (third year after K.O.)	5	Base <$5M	Base = $5M–$20M	Base >$20M
S	Strategic importance to base business	15	All business pertains to base	Some potential for new customer base	Totally new customer base
S	Potential for new market segment	10	<$1M	$1M–$4M	>$4M
F	Third year sales (net of cannibalization)	9	<$4M	$4M–$15M	>$15M
F	Total five years sales (net of cannibalization)	12	<$0M	$0M–$1.5M	>$1.5M
F	Net present value	14	One geography	Two geographies	Worldwide
M	Potential geographies for sales	4	Competitor has similar and superior	Similar, but ours superior	We are the only one in market
M	Potential for product differentiation	9	No patent position	Weak patent position	Strong patent position
M	Potential patent protection	6			
		100			
	Risk Analysis				
C	Total R&D cost (five years—only MAG)	6	<$.75M	$.75M–$3M	>$3M
C	Total capital cost (five years—only MAG)	3	<$.5M	$.5M–$2.5M	>$2.5M
C	Market development cost (five years marketing and promotion)	4	<$.25M	$.25M–$1.5M	>$1.5M
R	Technology risk	9	We already own technology	Technology exists	Technology requires invention
R	Strength of technology skills	7	Have skills and necessary quantity	Have skills, not necessary quantity	Do not have necessary skills or quantity
R	Product/engineering development risk	4	We do it everyday	Others do it, we have to acquire	No one has done it
R	Strength of development skills	4	Have skills and necessary quantity	Have skills, not necessary quantity	Do not have necessary skills or quantity
R	Manufacturing technology risk	4	We do it everyday	Others do it, we have to acquire	Requires manufacturing invention
R	Strength of manufacturing skills	4	Have skills and necessary quantity	Have skills, not necessary quantity	Do not have necessary skills or quantity
R	Sales and service skills	4	Sales force well trained	Significant training and redirection	Add specialists
R	Regulatory impact	3	Not regulated	Regulated, we're in	Regulated, we're not in
Cmp	Presence of dominant competitor	3	Competitor has <15% share	Competitor has 15%–40% share	Competitor has >40% share
Cmp	Number of competitors	2	<3	three–five	>5
Cmp	Risk of existing competitive technology	4	No existing competitive technology	Exists, but not fully developed	Competitive technology already commercialized
Cmp	Risk of alternative new technology	4	No existing alternative new technology	Exists, but not fully developed	Alternative new technology commercialized
		65			

Weighing Breakdown

Return

Strategic (S)	46%	Risk - Cost (C)	20%
Financial (F)	35%	Risk (R)	60%
Miscellaneous (M) - 19%		Competition (Cmp) - 20%	

were submitted by marketing, sales, and R&D people, and allocation of resources was made by the general managers of the business units and divisional presidents. Resources for new membrane development to support divisional projects were allocated by the Core Membrane VP for R&D, who was also responsible for allocating resources to core research projects. The process was iterative, often involving ranking of projects based on their market potential and strategic importance, with the final cut being made by budgetary constraints. See Exhibit 4 for the evaluation framework used at the Analytical Group involving quantification of returns versus risks. At the Process Group, the procedure was more informal, but addressed similar issues. At Waters, the procedure was somewhat different. Top managers from each functional area constituted a New Product Committee. Marketing, sales, R&D, manufacturing, and overseas country heads were all part of this committee. They each brought in ideas supplied to them by their constituencies, and the committee as a whole then decided on how to allocate its resources.

John Gilmartin, the CEO of Millipore Corporation, had set a goal of 15 percent growth in sales accompanied by a 10 percent return on sales and assets. This had to be achieved in an environment where the industry was only growing at about 8 percent. The corporation, therefore, was focused on exploiting niche marketing opportunities with new products. John Gilmartin had set a target of achieving 40 percent of annual sales from products introduced in the recent three years. Figures compiled by the corporate planning department indicated that such a target had not been achieved in the last five years.

Table B below provides a brief description of the 11 key new product introductions in 1991.

TABLE B

Waters Chromatography Division
1. *717 Auto Sampler:* Upgrade of existing Waters autosampler line, redesigned and repositioned to address recurring reliability problems.
2. *996 Photo Diode Array (PDA) Detector:* An in-house redesign of a product originally sourced from a Japanese vendor.
3. *Millennium Software:* First chromatography software to integrate essentially all data collection and analysis functions required by liquid chromatographers. First Waters product to run on Windows. Required for use on 996 PDA. Only useful with other Waters products.

Analytical Division
4. *Analyzer Feed System (AFS):* Water purifier for laboratory systems. Redesign of a previously failed product launch; 1992 revenues of $700,000.
5. *Base Station—Automated DNA Sequencer:* Developed by a now-defunct division as part of a broad effort to exploit the growing biotech market. Effort undermined by early field problems and a dominant competitor.
6. *ConSep/1:* A liquid chromatography system developed at Analytical to allow customers to take advantage of Memsep technology. Memsep, a technology recently purchased by Millipore, incorporates a membrane (versus the more typical gel or treated beads) in a chromatographic column. Memsep's recent sales had been flagging, presumably because existing chromatography systems were not capable of utilizing the new technology to its full potential. Consep/1 was developed to address this need.
7. *Expedite:* An automated DNA synthesizing station. Developed in part to promote sales of specialty chemicals used to manufacture DNA, which are manufactured by a wholly owned subsidiary.

TABLE B   (concluded)

Process Division
8. *Viresolve:* Novel virus removal system developed for the biopharmaceutical market.
9. *Opti-Seal:* Replacement for existing product.
10. *Opti-Cap:* Replacement for existing product.
11. *IntegriTest:* Novel method for testing the integrity of membranes. Launch challenged by design problems and demanding training requirements.

The LC/MS Project at the Waters Division

The LC/MS project at Waters had a checkered history. In 1990, Dave Strand inherited a program in tatters. No working mass spectrometer prototypes had been developed. Little systematic marketing research had been done, and there were no agreements with component vendors. See Exhibit 5 for a brief history of the previous product development effort.

As can be seen from Exhibit 5, the LC/MS effort first originated with a desire to build an interface to feed into the mass spectrometer. A liquid chromatography system could separate different chemicals from a compound solution, and the typical chromatography detector could tell the analyst how much of each chemical was present. But identification of each chemical could only be done on the basis of comparison to a standard; if it was known that caffeine took 30 minutes to travel through a chromatography column made of silica gel, then the analyst had reason to believe that an unknown chemical taking 30 minutes to pass through silica gel was in fact caffeine. Mass spectrometry took identification a significant step further. A chemical

EXHIBIT 5   **History of the LC/MS Project**

1985:	A marketing manager and a scientist at Waters collaborated to develop liquid chromatography systems tailored specifically for use with the mass spectrometers and interfaces offered by mass spectrometry firms.
1986:	Sales of tailored LC's begin.
1987:	Sales of tailored LC's hit $500,000. Funding officially assigned to development program. Waters begins a series of meetings with component vendors with the aim of eventually building mass spectrometers in-house using purchased components. A favorite idea involves developing a smaller version of the full-scale mass spectrometer offered by other firms. Scientists at Waters also begin to develop proprietary LC/MS interfaces.
1988:	Newly hired project manager from outside builds a team of scientists capable of developing a full-scale mass spectrometer in-house. Interface development scaled back. New strategy is to aim for the high end of the analytic market with a full-scale machine, eventually offering a smaller mass spectrometer in addition. Vendor agreements are pursued, some as a temporary measure until component manufacture can be brought in-house.
1989:	Project manager is dismissed amid financial and strategic concerns. Much of the scientific team he assembled disperses.
1990:	Dave Strand inherits the LC/MS program.
1992:	Extrel acquired.

like caffeine was broken into ionic components and flung against a screen (an electromagnetic field was used, thus differentiating between components on the basis of mass and charge). The pattern on the screen formed a unique fingerprint for each chemical, identifying the chemical with certainty. While conventional LC detectors were adequate for identifying a spectrum of 25 compounds or less, mass-specific detectors were enormously cost-efficient over a larger range, exceeding 75 compounds.

In order for the output of an LC system to be fed directly into a mass spec, an interface had to drastically reduce the amount of liquid flow and turn the remaining liquid molecules into gaseous ions. Interfaces such as thermospray and particle beam had been developed for use with small molecules such as caffeine, but these interfaces often destroyed the big molecules, such as proteins, typically analyzed by the biotechnology industry. At the close of the 1980s, the electrospray interface became commercially available for the biotechnology market. By 1993, the most common LC/MS interfaces for small molecules were particle beam and thermospray, and electrospray for large molecules.[1]

There were approximately 10,000 mass spectrometrists in the United States, most of whom had PhDs. There were 100,000 chromatographers in the United States, most of whom did not have PhDs.

The two types of scientists usually worked for the same companies, and often worked on the same development project. A large pharmaceutical company trying to discover a new drug, for example, might have a chromatography lab work on the more routine analysis and have the mass spectrometrists work on the more difficult problems. The mass spectrometrists might use their own chromatography equipment, but they usually treated it as another input to their MS. Should the chromatographers require mass spectrometry, they would take a tray of samples up a floor or across the hall to the mass spectrometrists, who might charge a few hundred dollars per sample.

An integrated LC/MS system offered advantages to both mass spectrometrists and chromatographers. Mass spectrometrists, generally considered the more elite of the two groups due to more rigorous education and training requirements, already used liquid chromatography to separate compounds into pure samples prior to analysis by mass spectrometry. To them, an integrated system offered greater efficiency. Chromatographers often asked mass spectrometrists to positively identify chemicals for them on a mass spectrometer. To them, an integrated system, especially one that was easy enough for a chromatographer to run, offered the advantages of mass spectrometry without having to bother mass spectrometrists.

Customer Perceptions

One of the first tasks Dave Strand concentrated on when he took over the job in 1990 was better understanding customer interest in LC/MS systems. Two focus group sessions were conducted.

---

[1] Molecules were characterized by their molecular weight as small or big. Amino acids, drug conjugates, neurotransmitters, carbohydrates, surfactants, peptides, proteins, and DNA represent a range of molecules from small to big.

The first session, held in February 1991, involved a group of chromatographers from the pharmaceutical, industrial chemical, and consumer products industries. These potential LC/MS customers were asked what they wanted in an LC/MS, and how purchasing decisions might be made. Attributes of an ideal system included something "easy, straightforward, and rugged," and several chromatographers expressed a desire for a "table top model." There was general agreement that the lower the price was, the more input the chromatographer would have on the purchasing decision, and the more widely used the unit would be. "On a benchtop for $50,000," said one chromatographer, "we'd have one for each of our development chemists." Others cited $100,000 as the price point that would allow chromatographers, not mass spectrometrists, to make the ultimate decision.

The second session, held in December 1991, was conducted individually with scientists (predominantly PhD's) in the pharmaceutical and biotechnology industries. Participants were questioned on their desire for alternative LC and MS technologies, on their perception of Waters, and on their perceptions of potential LC/MS vendors. Several scientists voiced a desire for a smaller-scale LC system. "It fills a niche for biomolecules, small samples for research," said one participant (later market research indicated that in fact about 9 percent of the LC market was interested in smaller-scale LC). When asked to give their perceptions of Waters, reactions were mixed. "They're people who know HPLC," said one scientist. "Waters has a good reputation with us," said another.

Situation at the Start of 1993

With these concerns of focus session participants in mind, and given the difficulty Waters continued to have in making arrangements for sourcing mass spec components, in 1992 Waters purchased Extrel, a $12 million manufacturer of laboratory analysis equipment. Extrel had built a credible reputation in mass spectrometry, with sales of about 30 research grade, full-function mass spectrometers per year. As 1993 began, Waters and Extrel engineers were working hard to develop the lower-tier, mass-specific detector that Waters managers had sought for so many years. Meanwhile, sales of tailored LCs continued.

Commercialization of LC/MS

Market Definition: Chromatographers versus Mass Spectrometrists

By offering a "mass spec adapted for LC utilization," Waters planned to take advantage of its dominance in the LC marketplace. Although the centerpiece of Strand's launch, a scaled-down mass spectrometer, was aimed at chromatographers and not the mass spectrometrists, there was an important relationship of influence between the two customers. Mass spectrometrists were in a sense the prima donnas of the analytical laboratory, generally more highly educated and more highly paid than the chromatographers. Because of this status and because of their knowledge of the science of mass spectrometry, the purchase of a scaled-down mass spectrometer was likely to require their blessing, if not their official approval.

Although Strand's detector-level mass spectrometer (so called because of its intended similarity to the other detectors used by chromatographers) was clearly aimed at lowering the dependence of chromatographers on mass spectrometrists, the latter were expected to feel no threat. Strand recalled the reaction of mass spectrometrists to the introduction of detector-level mass spectrometers for gas chromatography in the mid-80s. Mass spectrometrists "looked at them as helpful, because they filtered out the mundane problems and allowed them to work on the more interesting problems." Far from feeling threatened, Strand expected mass spectrometrists to help chromatographers choose a good detector-level mass spectrometer. "There's a feeling," suggested Strand, "that you have to have their tacit blessing, that this is a good product. It may not be as powerful as their million dollar machine, but for $100,000, this is a good beginner's tool and an acceptable adjunct to an LC system."

Strand felt that he had a good sense of what customers expected and desired. "I've attended probably every scientific conference there is and talked to a lot of people. We've done three rounds of focus sessions which have been very helpful in understanding what the product issues were. We think we know based on focus session work what it would take to get customers to buy from us, and what price range and technology trade-offs they would be willing to accept."

Although the detector-level mass spectrometer (called MSD, or mass-specific detector) had not yet been tested at any customer site, in late 1992 Waters conducted a focus session with mock-ups of the product to get feedback on size, serviceability, accessibility, and integration. The feedback was quite positive.

Segmentation

In 1991, the market for MSD integrated with LC systems was estimated to be $50 million. Although no one firm currently sold detector-level mass spectrometers for liquid chromatography, the market for these products was expected to be $110 million by 1996. The research grade, full-function mass spectrometer integrated with gas or liquid chromatography sold for about $250,000 to $500,000. Competitors like Finnigan, VG, Sciex, and Hewlett-Packard occupied this $300 million market. HP and Varian also made an MSD integrated with gas chromatography; this, however, was a smaller market, worth $150 million.

Dave Strand divided the potential market for LC/MS in two ways, both largely derived from Waters' experience with liquid chromatography. One approach segmented users into four groups, each consisting of about a quarter of the existing LC/MS market: pharmaceutical, industrial chemical, biopharmaceutical, and environmental. This segmentation was not based so much on SIC classifications as it was on the application that the LC was used for; for example, many traditional pharmaceutical companies had begun to use biotechnology to develop biopharmaceutical drugs.

Waters was already strong in both the pharmaceutical and the industrial chemical segments of the chromatography market. In 1989, the size of the pharmaceutical segment of the chromatography market was $319 million, of which Waters held 27 percent. The industrial chemical segment was $438 million, of which Waters held 19 percent. Strand felt that LC/MS products would do particularly well in industrial chemicals, because "industrial is sort of mundane; often those sales for us are unopposed. But if you go into the pharmaceutical or any of the biopharmaceutical companies, there's brisk competition to get in there."

Strand also divided the market according to how research oriented the chromatographer was. Sixty percent of all chromatographers were involved in quality control or quality assurance (QC/QA), involving tasks such as ensuring that each production batch had a desired level of a certain chemical. More research oriented were the methods developers (30 percent), who designed procedures for QC/QA. Most research oriented were the researchers (10 percent), who were involved in developing new chemicals or drugs. Many Waters managers saw a rough progression of influence from the researchers down to the methods developers and then to QA/QC, but no vendor had actively exploited that progression. Eighty-eight percent of current LC/MS sales were to researchers and methods developers, but Strand hoped that eventually his detector-level mass spectrometer would appeal to the much larger but much more conservative QC/QA market.

Comparable Introductions in the Past

Waters' managers expected sales for the detector-level mass spectrometer market to grow from $0 to $110 million in four years. This estimate was based on two similar introductions in the past: GC-MSD and PDA detectors. HP had introduced GC-MSD, a detector-level mass spectrometer (MSD, or mass-specific detector) for gas chromatography in 1983, and later introduced PDA detectors. As illustrated in Exhibit 6, the GC-MSD market grew from zero to over 1,200 units in five years, an annualized growth of over 400 percent. Recalling these historic market growth rates played a large role in helping Strand estimate sales of the detector-level mass spectrometer. The estimate was also based on the expectation that 10 to 12 percent of all LC systems would include a mass detector within four years, just as in 1992 10 to 12 percent of all LC systems had PDAs.

Launch

Strand had received several suggestions for the LC/MS introduction, though specific launch dates and details were yet to be finalized. One suggestion was to stage the launch. That is, the company would first tailor the Extrel mass spectrometer (named Benchmark) to capillary-scale liquid chromatography. This would be particularly appealing to biopharmaceutical researchers who worked with small sample sizes. Building on this experience, Waters could then launch the conventional scale LC tailored to the mass-specific detector (code-named Mercury). This would appeal to the industrial chemicals segment. This detector was expected to measure only 20″ × 20″ × 15″ and weigh 150 lbs. compared to Benchmark at 3′ × 2′ × 2′ and 350 lbs. It was considered ambitious, but not impossible, to introduce Benchmark at the

EXHIBIT 6 Growth Rates of Two Similar Products: GC-MSD and LC-PDA

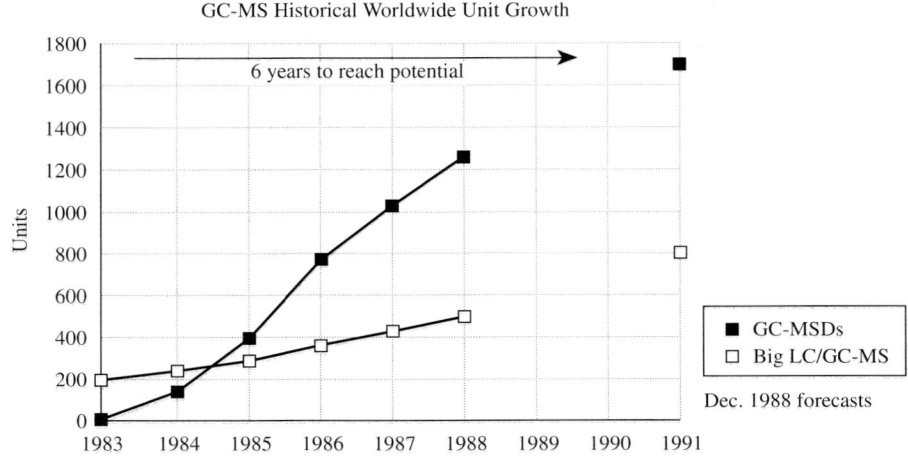

Source: Company records.

1993 Pittcon trade show for chromatographers, followed by the Mercury launch about six to nine months later at the American Society of Mass Spectrometrists.

Art Caputo, the Waters sales manager, was involved in virtually all of the major decisions on LC/MS development. His plan was to initially rely on Extrel salespeople and a handful of specialists, but slowly train his entire sales team of nearly 200 salespeople. "That is the only way we can ramp up Mercury sales from 50 units in 1991 to nearly 300 units by 1996," concluded Caputo.

Remaining Commercialization Issues

Waters managers believed that where chromatographers had the authority to purchase their own equipment, it was generally only for instruments costing $100,000 or less. While Benchmark was priced at $180,000 to $200,000, Mercury had to be priced below the $100,000 point. HP typically sold their GC/MSD for under $75,000, and although a detector-level mass spectrometer for LC systems was likely to sell for more, Waters took the GC/MSD as a starting point for calculating target cost. "We took the pieces apart on an HP GC/MSD and estimated that it could be built for about $20,000. We have set for ourselves a manufacturing target somewhat more than that, and achieving that would be very important for our success in this marketplace," reasoned Dave Strand. "It is an interesting industry," he added. "Competition is based on value added and technology, and participants usually respect each other's market position. There's been little disruption throughout the last decade. That's why we are keen to have that technological lead in Mercury," he concluded.

Virus Removal Commercialization at the Process Group

When Paul Sekhri inherited the virus removal project in 1990, several working beta sites were already installed, and the original developers of the product idea were still involved in assisting him in the launch phase.

See Exhibit 7 for a brief history of the virus removal product development.

In 1985, Tony DiLeo, an R&D manager, knew that Millipore had only begun to exploit the tangential flow membrane technology that his team had developed. In tangential flow filtration, fluid circulated across the membrane surface and was slowly pulled through the membrane by suction. Because of their more sophisticated designs, tangential flow systems were not as simple for users to operate as conventional dead-end filters, such as coffee filters. Tangential flow did, however, offer less clogging and thus better performance when used to discriminate between particles of similar size.

At DiLeo's request, Ray Gabler, a top marketing manager, spoke with many of Millipore's key biotech and pharmaceutical customers to identify a list of 11 promising applications for this technology. Running preliminary experiments and investigating each application's complexity and probable length of development time, DiLeo and his group narrowed the list to three promising applications. One of these applications was virus removal.

Virus removal had always been a problem in the development of biotechnology drugs. Some drugs were derived directly from mammalian blood plasma or cells. When these substances were extracted from the body, viruses often came along for the ride. In 1985, for example, human growth hormone extracted from the pituitary glands of cadavers contained undetected Creutzfeldt-Jakob viruses, which infected and killed several treated patients. Another class of biotech drugs, such as Genentech's tPA for heart attacks, was developed using recombinant DNA, in which gene fragments from a mammalian cell were spliced into rapidly reproducing organisms.

EXHIBIT 7 History of the Viresolve Project

1985:	Tangential flow expert at Millipore searches for additional applications of tangential flow technology. A top marketing manager generates a short list of potential applications. Technical team tests feasibility of potential applications.
1986:	Promising virus removal trials are presented to top management. Proponents of virus removal gather further customer information, and a major Millipore customer makes a presentation to top management requesting development of a virus removal product.
1987:	Project is officially funded, and development work begins. Membrane manufacturing process is altered to enable production of membranes with fewer defects in pore size.
1988:	Development work continues. Decision made to focus on membrane development before firming designs for a device to deploy the membrane.
1989:	Formal project plan constructed by project leader, allowing different sections of project team to more effectively work in parallel.
1990:	Working membrane developed. In all, six tests at customer sites are conducted between 1987 and 1990. Paul Sekhri hired to commercialize product.

Monoclonal antibodies like Centacor's Centoxin for septic shock were also developed using mammalian cells, but instead of using only a gene fragment, the entire cell was used. In the development of both recombinant DNA drugs and monoclonal antibodies, viruses were often unintentionally removed from the mammal along with the original source cells. In addition, viruses sometimes inhabited the media used to grow cell cultures. Finally, viral contamination was a potential result of careless laboratory procedures.

When DiLeo and Gabler spoke with customers about this problem, it became apparent that these biopharmaceutical customers were highly dissatisfied with current methods of virus removal, and were very interested in more effective solutions to this problem. Indeed, two key customers were instrumental in convincing top management at Millipore to put resources into developing a membrane system capable of removing viruses in a consistent and validatable fashion. Validation, or proof of virus removal, was expected to become an increasingly important part of the FDA approval process.

The virus removal project was established with division funds in 1987. Day-to-day project management was handled by DiLeo, with Gabler handling customer contacts and negotiation of a total of six test sites. A detailed Program Plan that DiLeo developed in 1989 played a critical part in ensuring that development went smoothly. The plan included PERT charts developed by the scientist in charge of each facet of development, as well as estimates of performance parameters that enabled each of the subproject teams to work in parallel. Although the original completion target was missed by about six months, the relative smoothness of the development project could be attributed to an accurate early product definition, continual contact with the market, and access to development resources.

Industry

At least half of all of Millipore's business was directly or indirectly tied to the pharmaceutical market. Viresolve was one of several new products specifically designed to tap into a fast-growing segment of that market, biopharmaceuticals, which were therapeutics produced through genetic engineering. Both traditional pharmaceutical companies and recently founded biotech companies were taking part in the research. In 1992, the biopharmaceutical market was about $3 billion, expected to grow to $30 billion by the year 2000.

Competition

Inactivation of Viruses

The most prevalent ways of dealing with harmful viruses involved inactivating them instead of actually removing them. Viruses exhibited many of the characteristics of living organisms, and so inactivating a virus was tantamount to rendering it lifeless, and hence harmless. Methods of inactivation included physical techniques such as heat and ultraviolet radiation, but these methods could also harm or destroy the proteins that drug manufacturers wanted to process.

Chemical inactivation techniques were much more prevalent. The solvent detergent method, developed by the New York Blood Center, broke down the lipid (fat) coat that enveloped many viruses (in a manner very similar to the way soap breaks down oils). "I'd say every blood product company, and most pharmaceutical companies, use the solvent detergent method," said Paul Sekhri. "They have a very nice track record. In the three million units of product that have used solvent detergent, they have never had one incident of infection. But there's a drawback to that. You have to know the virus you're removing. Many viruses have no lipid coats, for example, and were thus unaffected by solvent detergent."

Millipore emphasized that any virus unaffected by inactivation methods such as solvent detergent represented an accident waiting to happen. "My approach to marketing Viresolve is that we can remove even unknown viruses," said Paul Sekhri. "That sounds really strange. But it's been interesting to see how the market is slowly embracing that thought. Every single major virological accident in the past 10 years has been because of a virus that the manufacturer didn't know was there. We can address that with this system. With an inactivation method you can't."

Physical Removal of Viruses

Membranes were generally considered the most effective manner of physically removing viruses. Size exclusion membranes, like Viresolve, worked by allowing smaller molecules, like proteins, to pass. Larger particles, like viruses, were retained. Exhibit 8 shows the virus removal properties of Viresolve/70. The size of a virus is characterized by its diameter in nanometers (one billionth of a meter). Viresolve's effectiveness is measured in terms of log reduction value (i.e., "7 log removal" meant that the membrane would miss one virus particle out of every 10 to the seventh power, or 10 million virus particles). Providing validation of virus removal was the competitive advantage that Millipore had chosen to emphasize in Viresolve over other membranes. There were two important types of validation. One

EXHIBIT 8 Viresolve/70 Qualification: Predicted Minimum System Performance

	Virus Diameter (nm)	One-Stage (log removal)	Two-Stage (log removal)
Virus Removal			
Parvovirus	22	1.5–1.8	2.7–3.0
Hepatitis C	40	3.3–3.4	6.5–6.7
BVD	40	3.3–3.4	6.5–6.7
HBV	42	3.5–3.8	6.8–7.1
Adenovirus	70	6.0–6.3	
HIV	100	7.4–7.7	
Herpes virus	100	7.4–7.7	

involved providing published proof that a specific virus had been removed to a specific degree using the membrane product in the manufacturer's test facilities. This type of validation was instrumental in helping Millipore compete against conventional multiuse membranes. A second type of validation involved providing a method for the customer to test each purchased membrane to assure that it would remove viruses as advertised. Millipore had developed a "correlating integrity test" to meet this latter need, which appeared to be a substantial asset.

Some manufacturers of conventional filtration membranes had recently repositioned their existing membrane lines to take advantage of the growing interest in virus removal. While their advertising emphasized the familiarity of their approach to virus removal, their technical documentation conceded less-effective performance than the newer Viresolve technology. For example, their 1990 literature claimed to remove the Murine (Mouse) Leukemia Virus to about 4 logs, while the Viresolve/70's 1992 literature claimed removal of the same virus to about 7 logs. This was far more virus particles than most drug raw materials contained. Moreover, the Pall membrane admittedly was not effective against the smallest known virus, polio, which Viresolve/70 could remove to 3.5 logs. Exhibit 9 illustrates the perfor-

EXHIBIT 9   New Membrane Provides Validatable Performance

Millipore, the world leader in membrane technology, has developed the Viresolve virus removal module, the first technology to deliver validatable viral clearance.

Viresolve modules consist of unique nanoselective membranes that can remove 4–6 logs of 40 nm-sized viruses and 8+ logs of retroviruses, while recovering greater than 90% of proteins the size of human albumin and smaller. In fact, log reduction values can be almost doubled by running Viresolve modules in series.

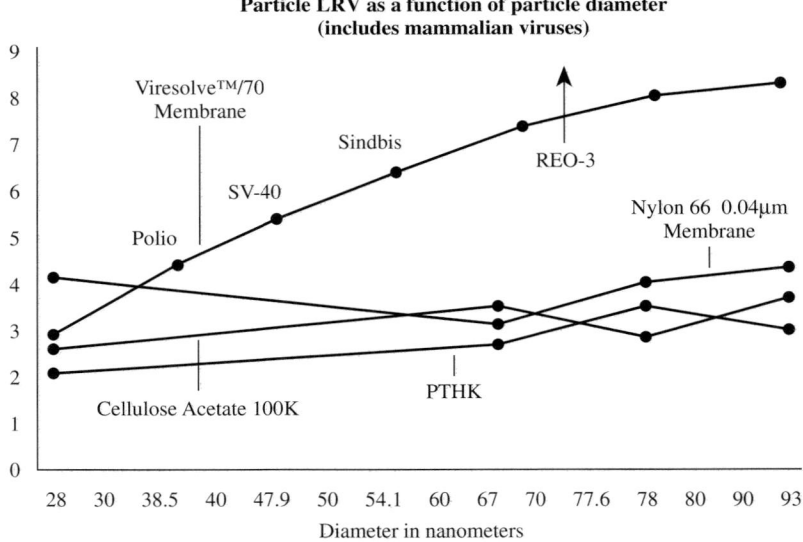

NOTE: LRV = log reduction value.
Minimum virus removal using Viresolve/70 system.

mance of Viresolve against competitors, including Pall's Nylon 66 membrane. The exhibit plots virus size against removal rate by Viresolve. For example, Viresolve removed the Sindbis virus, a particle about 54.1 nanometers (billionths of a meter) in size, to 6 logs, whereas Pall's membrane was only effective to 3 logs.

Millipore managers were much more concerned about the new product developed by Asahi. Laboratory tests appeared to indicate that Asahi's Planova was effective in virus removal. Moreover, their membrane used the more familiar dead-end filtration technology (e.g., coffee filter). In Viresolve's tangential flow technology, liquid flowed perpendicularly to the surface and was drawn through the filter using suction. Because tangential flow systems were still relatively unfamiliar and because there were more process variables involved, they were generally more challenging for the customer to properly install. However, a key advantage that tangential flow provided was that it allowed Millipore to use membranes which held viruses back on the surface of the membrane. Asahi used a hollow-fiber approach, which captured viruses within the membrane's depth. Taking advantage of their simpler membrane design, Millipore scientists developed a correlating integrity test to verify (or validate) that a given Viresolve membrane would actually work as promised. The test was nondestructive, and so the tested membrane could later be put to use with absolute confidence in its performance.

Asahi also had an integrity test that customers could use, but the test was destructive and so the membrane could only be tested after it had been used. Hence, the customer could never be certain of the membrane's performance until after it had been used. "We won a battle for a contract with a major British pharmaceutical company about three months ago," recalled Sekhri. "We went head to head with Asahi. They liked a lot of things about Asahi, but it came down to the integrity test. They didn't feel comfortable without absolutely knowing what their log values were. They thought of our test as being something really new, really special in the marketplace, and they went with Viresolve."

Commercialization Issues

Market Segmentation and the Viresolve Product Line

The pores in the Viresolve membrane were small enough to prevent viruses from passing but large enough to allow most proteins through. The smaller the protein, the more likely that a size exclusion approach would work for removing viruses. One type of market segmentation, therefore, was based on the size of the protein. There were three broad segments of the protein purification market.

First were the makers of proteins using recombinant DNA technology, in which genes were spliced into a host cell to enable that cell to manufacture the desired protein. These proteins tended to be small, generally under 70,000 daltons (unit of molecular weight). The Viresolve/70 was targeted at these customers—makers of interferons, growth factors, clotting stimulating factors, interleukins, and hormones.

A second segment was the makers of proteins using monoclonal antibodies, in which a cell which produced a desirable protein was fused with a cancerous ("immortal") cell to produce a hybrid cell capable of producing the desired protein and multiplying spontaneously to produce many more identical hybrid cells. These proteins were of moderate size, typically under 180,000 daltons. The Viresolve/180 was targeted at these customers—makers of monoclonal antibodies and Ig fragments.

The third segment was blood processors, and Millipore had not yet developed a Viresolve type of product to meet this need. "It's probably the bigger part of the market," Sekhri conceded. "I get at least one call every week from a major blood company." The problem was that the principle of size exclusion, the method by which the Viresolve membrane operated, could not be readily applied to blood processing. Blood contains proteins that are as large, or larger, than the largest commonly found viruses. Techniques other than size exclusion had certainly been used in virus removal, but not as reliably. "We are working on that. It's kind of the next phase, maybe 'Viresolve 3.'"

Naming the Product

Soon after arriving at Millipore, Sekhri distributed a companywide memo requesting a name for a "new technology capable of removing viruses from proteins." Names like Virex, Viratain, and Virecut were submitted. Some, like Virex, were already used; Virex was a software program to remove computer viruses. At the conclusion of a meeting with about 20 Millipore people, Sekhri made the final choice to go with Viresolve.

Understanding Customer Needs—Installing "Specials"

Sekhri personally handled the first few sales. During 1991 and 1992, Sekhri and three applications engineers, trained to ensure that Viresolve performed optimally, helped the first 50 or 60 customers worldwide install prelaunch versions of Viresolve. These early versions of the product were known internally as "specials." Sekhri sought to ensure that the first industry impressions of Viresolve would be positive ones. "It's a brand new technology in a very conservative market. We could not afford to have any failures in the marketplace. If a customer just got one of these things and ran it and then said, 'It doesn't work,' it could very well be because the customer didn't know what he or she was doing. If that customer started telling the very small, close-knit biotech market that Viresolve doesn't work, that would be the death blow to us."

The novel tangential-flow technology that Viresolve employed was a bit trickier to run than the traditional dead-end flow technology used by competitors. "You don't just press a button," explained Sekhri. "There's optimization involved. So we thought that we would actually go out to every customer in the field ourselves, and do the trials, and write them up a full report, and then say, 'Great, now you know how to do it and you're on your own.'" This approach seemed to be succeeding in building appreciation for Viresolve, and for tangential flow technology. "If there is an existing perception on the part of customers, it may be that dead-end filtration is easiest, but our educated customers know that tangential flow filtration makes a lot of sense for this application."

The list of customers targeted for specials was developed by Sekhri with help from Nick Lambo, the Process Division sales manager. "We identified customers that had the highest potential for Viresolve products," Lambo recalled. But the actual sales calls were done by Paul Sekhri; the three applications engineers (one each in the United States, Europe, and Japan) handled installation. "We didn't really want to get our salespeople turned on to a product that was in alpha stages."

Costs and Pricing

Sekhri calculated a price for Viresolve by looking at what Millipore charged for its ultrafiltration membranes and calculating a premium based on what advantages Viresolve offered over ultrafiltration and the other membranes that competitors used to remove viruses. These filters often had relatively inconsistent pore sizes and had, typically, been designed nearly a decade earlier for other applications. "I knew that we had a three-part package. We had a membrane that was dedicated to the removal of viruses from proteins, and could do that reproducibly and predictably. We had validation data, which I have found to be almost as valuable as the membrane itself. Our competitors are running into problems with that right now. Their customers are saying, 'It's great, we're using your membrane, so give us all of the validation data.' But they don't have the data. And the third part was that we could verify the membrane's use through what's called a correlating integrity test. So in thinking of what we charge for standard ultrafiltration membranes, I figured we could charge a premium."

Another pricing consideration was whether or not to sell the membrane modules as disposable. "I asked a number of customers this: 'Would you rather spend more money for a single-use disposable, or spend less money for a reusable?'" although reusing a membrane meant having to prove that all of the previously retrieved viruses had been cleaned off. Acceptable tests for this were not reliable enough for some customers. "So they said, 'We'd rather have a single-use disposable, even if we have to pay a little bit more money for it.'" Viresolve modules were sold as single-use plastic devices and membranes, although the metal housing was permanent. One exception to this indifference to prices was the 10-foot-square module, which was considered by some customers to be too expensive for such frequent disposal. "So we compromised by validating five-time reuse."

The prices for Viresolve were as follows: ⅓-square-foot module: $500; 1-square-foot module: $1,200; 10-square-foot module: $2,000. For the 1-square-foot module, the comparable price for an ultrafiltration membrane (the technology that Viresolve replaced for this application) was $500–$600. For the 10-square-foot module, it was $1,000–$1,200. Ultrafiltration membranes could be reused 10 to 20 times. The 1-square-foot module processed 20 to 30 liters, and the 10-square-foot module about 100 liters, with times varying by process. Prices on both of the smaller units had been raised once since initial introduction.

For many customers, the price of a Viresolve unit was a trivial part of their production costs. Interferon, for example, was worth $1.5 million a liter by the time it reached the Viresolve membrane in the process. Millipore recommended that Viresolve be installed in the downstream processing of biopharmaceuticals, after completion of steps like filtration, chromatography, centrifugation, extraction, flocculation, and electrokinetic separation.

Launch

"We define a launch as: Product is on the shelf, with a full complement of training and literature in place," said Nick Lambo. To Paul Sekhri, this translated into two chief tasks: "preparing the customer to buy, and preparing applications specialists [the salesforce] to sell."

Preparing Customers to Buy

Preparing customers to buy was done largely through word-of-mouth advertising and promotion. Sekhri had seeded the word-of-mouth process by ensuring that the first customers had favorable experiences. Promotion was done through the scientific press, conferences, and the trade press. Several of the product's developers wrote technical papers for prestigious scientific journals. Sekhri traveled extensively to attend trade conferences and make presentations, and also hired a public relations firm. "We hired a PR firm because this is what I would consider really exciting news, a really good story. They helped us conduct a number of press conferences, and because of the press conferences we had a number of articles written into some pretty reputable journals. From reading these articles, people have called me up directly."

Viresolve Module Size

Millipore planned to introduce three different sizes of Viresolve: the $\frac{1}{3}$-square-foot, 1-square-foot, and 10-square-foot modules. The smallest size was primarily for research work, the largest primarily for production work. Although tests at customer sites had taken place exclusively in R&D labs with small Viresolve modules, sales to production facilities were traditionally the Process Division's strength. The forthcoming 10-square-foot module would also allow Millipore salespeople to address the full life cycle of customer needs—from development of a new therapeutic to its production.

Preparing the Sales Force to Sell

Training the sales force (applications specialists) to sell Viresolve consisted chiefly of preparing training materials, conducting a two-day training seminar, and responding to follow-up questions from the field. During 1992, Sekhri prepared a *Launch*

Manual and *Reference Materials* for each salesperson involved. The material included a description of the product line, prices, detailed answers to commonly asked questions, copies of Viresolve and competitive advertisements, published validation studies for Viresolve versus its competitors, and a step-by-step guide through the sales cycle. "I've launched the product in Europe and Japan, and they're kind of running by themselves," said Paul Sekhri. "I get maybe three to five faxes a day from salespeople around the world with questions."

The U.S. launch was originally scheduled for the fourth quarter of 1992, but was delayed until spring 1993. In October 1992, a scaled back version was conducted. One representative from each of four to six regions was brought in and given specialized training in Viresolve. These representatives had "the best and most concentrated opportunities for the product initially," according to Nick Lambo, who had approximately 20 sales representatives dedicated to pharmaceuticals.

"The next step is to train the full U.S. sales force, and that's going to happen in April 1993. We're going to do this whole dog-and-pony show that we did in Europe for two days again." The training included presentations and teaching sessions, as well as "wet work" with actual Viresolve modules.

A crucial part of the sales cycle was the conducting of a feasibility study using actual customer samples. The launch package described how the salesperson was to go about arranging these studies. Once the initial contact was made, the customer filled out a form explaining their virus removal needs. The salesperson faxed the form to Millipore application engineers, who let the salesperson know within 48 hours whether or not the application appeared to make sense. Once a mutually convenient date was set, the application engineer, customer, and salesperson all met to conduct the feasibility study at the customer site, using a sample of the material to be purified. Within two weeks, application engineers completed a report and forwarded it by overnight mail to the customer, who then made the decision whether or not to purchase Viresolve. From this point on, the salesperson kept in touch with the application engineers for any further technical assistance.

Launch Strategy

Two elements of the launch strategy were considered particularly crucial. First, Lambo and Sekhri wanted biopharmaceutical firms to use Viresolve in the R&D process, so that there was a natural progression to using it in production. This would happen both because of familiarity with the product and because of the product's inclusion in the FDA approval process. "What you want to do, ideally, is work with the customer as they develop the processes for drugs, to educate and inform them of our technology, to prove it on a small scale so that it carries through into the process step," said Nick Lambo. "If you miss that opportunity to get it inserted early, there's a lot more work to be done."

The historic strength of Lambo's sales force made this particularly challenging. "My organization tends to focus on the production scale end," which was where the 10-square-foot version might be used. "But products like Viresolve have to be inserted in the R&D stages, early on. By the time production has begun, getting them retroactively inserted is difficult." To improve his organization's ability to handle this challenge, Lambo had hired an R&D engineer in California to concentrate strictly on R&D insertion of Millipore products, including Viresolve. "If that's successful, and we think it will be, then I'll rapidly apply for another headcount in other parts of the world."

The other crucial element of the launch strategy was to push the Viresolve/70 hardest in the initial stages of the launch. Because the disparity between protein and virus sizes was greatest for the applications that Viresolve/70 was targeted at, Sekhri felt that the chances for dramatic success were best with this product. Such dramatic success, it was felt, could help set the stage for the commercial success of later products in the Viresolve line.

Forecasting Sales

Sekhri had forecast sales of $200,000 in 1992. Viresolve had achieved $300,000 in sales by the middle of the fourth quarter.

Many managers at Millipore couldn't help but contrast Viresolve with launches of product line extensions, many of which began with sales in the millions of dollars. Nick Lambo expressed these sentiments: "Viresolve is an exciting product because it is a major leap of faith. It's something no one else has on the market. The frustrating part is, you're not going to see a rapid sales ramp."

Remaining Commercialization Issues

Repeating Viresolve's European Successes in the United States

To date, interest in Europe had been particularly strong. "In Europe, the government has already published guidelines for virus removal," explained Sekhri. "The United States has not yet published guidelines. That's why some U.S. customers say, 'We'll use it when we're told we need to use it.' Well, in Europe they're being told to use it. All of the early adopters came out of Europe." The absence of U.S. regulations made the U.S. launch of Viresolve all the more challenging.

Millipore was working on the development of the 10-square-foot module which could be sold to manufacturing facilities. The smaller Viresolve modules were more suited to R&D facilities. "We've got to have the 10-square-foot module," insisted Nick Lambo. "This is not an R&D tool, and unless you can show a clear path to production scale, the product will have short-term interest." The 10-square-foot Viresolve module was one of the top development priorities of the R&D manager in the Pharmaceutical Group of the Process Division.

Millipore was already looking into several promising extensions of the Viresolve product line. A similar system might be designed to remove nucleic acids or pyrogens—"Any time you have a product stream that could be contaminated by a biological agent there's need for a Viresolve type of a membrane," explained

Sekhri. Millipore was also very interested in designing a system to provide virus removal to blood processing companies, using a technology different from size exclusion.

While Viresolve would undoubtedly meet with a measure of success, some managers at Millipore were concerned that the product might have a limited window of opportunity. "There are some people in my organization who think that this product may have a short life cycle," noted Nick Lambo. "You're talking about mammalian cell technology and the viruses present in that. As technology moves away from that, as more products are being built through other kinds of technology, it may not be an issue." As genetic engineers gained the ability to chemically synthesize more proteins instead of modifying mammalian cells to produce them, these managers felt that there would be correspondingly less risk of viral infection. Other managers, however, argued that research on new biotechnology drugs would probably always involve the use of mammalian cells, and thus the need for virus removal products would continue.

CHAPTER 8
Ring Medical: Organizing New Product Marketing

This case describes the progress of a new product launch, HCS-100, a hospital communication system. Ring Medical has sold only 5 systems in six months against an annual target of 30. There is a lack of agreement internally on how the new product effort should be organized. In the context of a severely constrained resource situation, the Norwegian parent had to decide whether the entrepreneurial Ring Medical should operate independently or under the auspices of its U.S. subsidiary. In addition, there are differences of opinion on how the product should be positioned and what distribution channels should be used. These issues have to be resolved before the board meeting scheduled on the following day.

On Wednesday, May 4, 1988, Paul Ruggieri, president and CEO of Ring Group, a wholly owned subsidiary of Scanvest Ring, Norway, faced two highly challenging issues as he prepared for the May 5 board meeting. Ruggieri strongly believed that the HCS-100 product, for which he had nominal responsibility, could well represent the single major opportunity for Ring Group to turn a profit for the first time since 1984. (See Exhibit 1 for Ring Group financial statements.) Moreover, the HCS-100 would enable Ring Group, headquartered in Great Neck, New York, to break its dependence on mature products and markets and position the company for future growth. Before this might happen, however, board members would have to (1) resolve how the organizational responsibilities for the HCS-100 product should be divided, and (2) approve a marketing plan of action.

Currently, the HCS-100 product was housed at Ring Medical, a division of Ring Group (see Exhibit 2 for an organization chart). From its inception in July 1986 until recently, Ring Medical had operated autonomously, headquartered in

---

Christopher Fay prepared this case under the direction of V. Kasturi Rangan.
Copyright © 1988 by the President and Fellows of Harvard College.
Harvard Business School case 589-046 (revised June 1993).

EXHIBIT 1 Ring Group Statements of Income and Retained Earnings

	1987	1986	1985	1984
Net sales	$3,265,194	$2,103,552	$2,363,468	$2,953,590
Cost of sales	2,049,763	1,341,233	1,313,959	1,717,108
Gross profit	1,215,431	762,319	1,049,509	1,236,482
Selling, general and administrative expenses	2,804,306	2,289,033	1,571,457	1,335,162
Operating profit (loss)	(1,588,875)	(1,526,714)	(521,948)	(98,680)
Income (loss) from foreign currency transactions	(85,698)	(101,639)	(59,203)	96,145
Interest expense	(45,496)	(206,421)	2,048	7,005
Other income	20,032	11,296	(32,839)	(3,935)
	(111,162)	(296,764)	(89,994)	99,215
Extraordinary gain[a]	—	1,352,870		
Net income (loss)	(1,700,037)	(470,608)	(611,942)	535
Retained earnings (deficit), beginning of year	(1,260,169)	(789,561)	(163,531)	(164,066)
Retained earnings (deficit), end of year	$(2,960,206)	$(1,260,169)	$ (775,473)	$ (163,531)

[a] Trade payables forgiven by Scanvest Ring.

Billerica, Massachusetts. In January 1988, Ed Owens, formerly in charge of product development, was promoted to head Ring Medical, reporting directly to Paul Ruggieri. The entire management team at Ring Medical—and especially Ed Owens and Dave Forster (technical director), the two men credited with designing, engineering, and launching the HCS-100 product—strongly wanted their autonomy to continue. Reporting up through Ring Group would destroy the entrepreneurial spirit of their group, they argued.

Much was expected of Ring Medical's development and launch period initiated in October–November of 1987. On average, two to three units a month were expected to be sold, yielding total revenues of approximately $150,000 per month at average gross margins of nearly 50 percent. As of April 1988, however, only 5 systems had been sold versus a budgeted annual sales volume of over 30. Revenues totaled about 15 percent of the targeted annual amount of over $1.7 million. Management's attention focused on the HCS-100's sales and distribution system. The company had recruited eight manufacturers' reps who were offered a 20% commission rate on sales for each installed system. In the six to seven months that the manufacturers' rep network had been operational, only one system had been sold by any rep; the other four systems had been sold by Ed Owens. Both Owens and Forster were critical of the efforts of national sales manager Charlie Witteck, who was located in Great Neck, New York. "Either the rep concept is lousy, or Charlie Witteck is not doing his job," argued Forster. Matters came to a head in April 1988 when Witteck, touring the Massachusetts area for a trade show, refused to visit the

EXHIBIT 2 Ring Group, Inc., Organization Chart, Effective 2/23/88

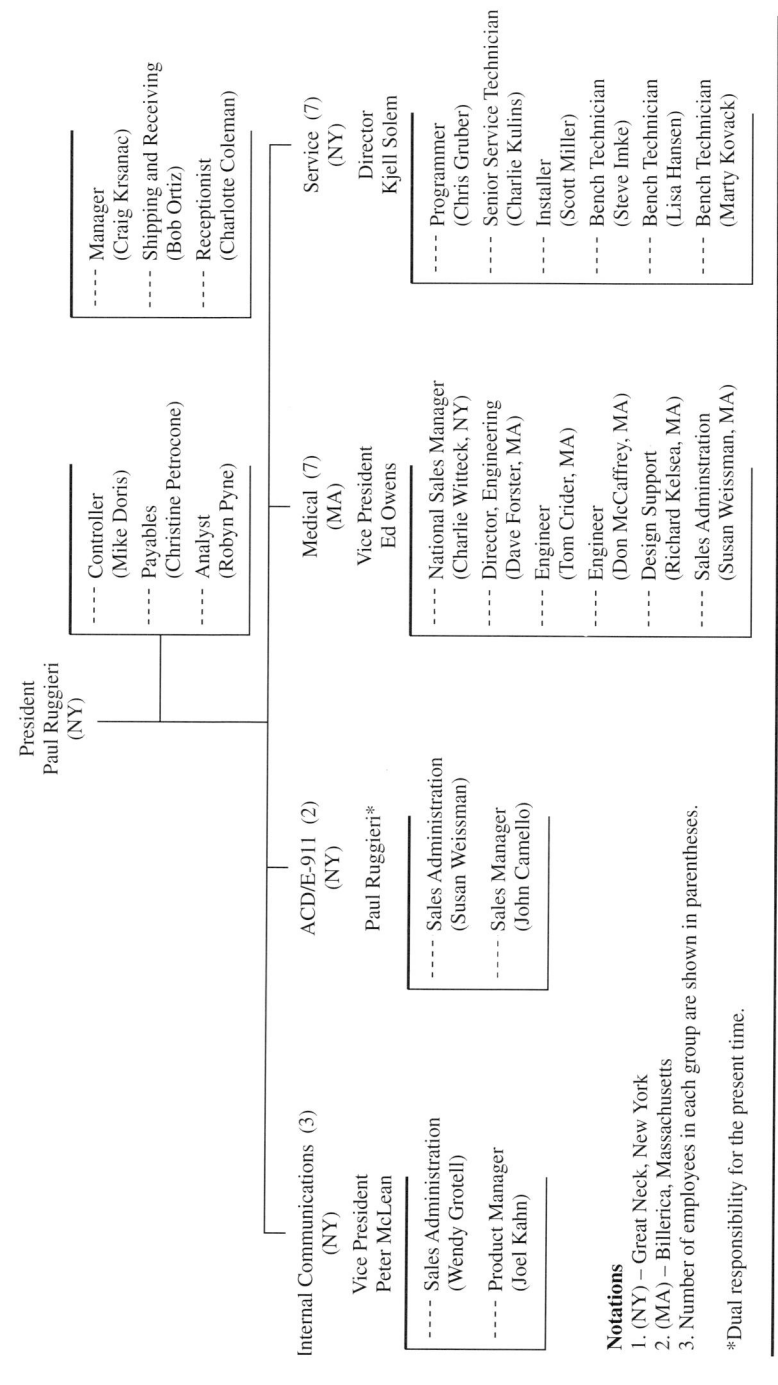

Notations
1. (NY) – Great Neck, New York
2. (MA) – Billerica, Massachusetts
3. Number of employees in each group are shown in parentheses.

*Dual responsibility for the present time.

division headquarters at Billerica. He instead reported back to Paul Ruggieri at Great Neck that "a problem with our HCS-100 sales effort is the utter lack of consistency in product policy, pricing, and customer support from Billerica. Without sorting out these problems, it would be futile to expect our reps to work miracles in the field."

To date, Scanvest Ring had spent in excess of $700,000 on the HCS-100 effort, and its CEO, Helge Midttun, and other board members were hesitant to invest further in a project that had so far shown lackluster results. Ring Group was the only subsidiary of Scanvest Ring not located in Scandinavia. Its board had recently been quite forthright in announcing a strategy of focus on Scandinavian markets, both to shareholders and management. The historical tendency of tolerating its U.S.-based "problem child" was not likely to continue.

Helge Midttun had a general philosophy of separating new and mature products in Scanvest Ring's efforts in Norway. Indeed, there had been a marked tone of approval in Midttun's voice as he described the vibrant, upbeat culture—complete with a background of Beatles music—he witnessed on his last visit to Ring Medical. Ruggieri felt that the key to any course of action regarding the organization of the HCS-100 product effort was consistency—not only across all aspects of marketing management but also with Ring Group's current strategy and operation.

Ring Group of North America, Inc.

Ring Group of North America, Inc., was established in 1971 as a wholly owned subsidiary of Scanvest Ring, one of Scandinavia's largest information technology companies, with 1987 profits of $12.7 million on sales of $138 million. (See Exhibit 3 for Scanvest Ring financial statements.) Ring Group's charter was to develop U.S. markets for selected Scanvest Ring products. Its preeminent business base quickly came to be selling and servicing a "hands free" duplex intercom system. Intercom sales topped $2 million in 1987, giving Ring Group in excess of 20 percent of the estimated market. While this market, composed mainly of hospitals, was considered mature, new markets for the latest generation intercom products had been identified. An intercom system had recently been sold to the brokerage division of a leading New York investment bank. An average configuration of the latest generation intercom system, the Tridex, sold for about $10,000 and contained 20 extensions (see Exhibit 4). Some larger systems had over 300 extensions. All system functions were controlled by a microprocessor which is not shown in the exhibit.

Approximately 60 percent of intercom sales in 1987 were made to end-users through five or six manufacturers' reps, under the direction of Peter McLean, vice president of the Internal Communications Division of Ring Group. Direct sales earned a gross margin of 50 to 60 percent. Nearly 60 national distributors constituted an additional branch of the intercom distribution effort, accounting for about 35 percent of sales, with a contribution margin of roughly 35 percent. Most of these distributors were audio contractors, who merely bid on products such as intercom

EXHIBIT 3 Scanvest Ring Income Statement (in thousands of kronas)

	1978	1979	1980	1981	1982	1983	1984	1985	1986	1987
Sales	27,548	55,065	92,582	131,675	183,156	647,123	957,991	1,133,405	705,097	860,361
Cost of goods sold	9,574	23,294	40,040	50,272	68,228	260,445	413,076	439,398	272,346	342,021
Wages and other personnel expenses	8,197	15,735	22,897	35,074	52,716	220,343	307,596	373,398	221,061	271,256
Other operating expenses	6,322	9,089	13,575	21,677	31,892	110,315	162,285	282,438	112,808	148,583
Ordinary depreciation	659	1,790	2,065	2,482	3,029	11,080	17,060	30,676	22,785	22,701
Bad debts	—	—	201	2	201	1,260	4,732	19,104	7,658	2,271
Changes in stocks	—	—	—	—	—	(5,081)	(12,553)	4,533	466	(1,366)
Total operating expenses	24,752	49,908	78,778	109,507	156,066	598,362	892,196	1,149,547	637,124	785,466
Operating profit (loss)	2,796	5,157	13,804	22,168	27,090	48,761	(65,795)	(16,142)	67,883	74,895
Net financial items	105	1,393	2,794	5,236	12,990	14,428	9,069	41,756	16,694	(4,121)
Profit (loss) ordinary activities	2,691	3,764	11,010	16,932	14,100	34,333	56,726	(57,898)	51,189	79,016
Net extraordinary items	—	528	—	1,500	1,542	967	2,430	102,001	9,811	24,952
Profit (loss) before year-end allocations	2,691	3,236	11,010	15,432	12,558	33,366	54,296	(159,899)	41,378	54,064
Year-end allocations	2,442	2,596	9,007	12,893	10,752	28,886	60,176	(36,786)	3,991	21,734
Net profit (loss)	249	640	2,003	2,539	1,806	4,480	(5,880)	(123,113)	37,387	32,330
Ordinary result	2,368	2,995	8,880	14,148	12,102	29,789	51,889	(55,061)	50,177	77,407
Earnings per share (unadjusted)	4,736	922	1,076	1,715	112.06	22.22	4.96	(4.71)	4.28	6.45
Earnings per share (adjusted)	0.51	0.55	1.70	2.75	1.91	2.64	4.46	—	4.28	6.45
Average number of shares	500	3,250	8,250	8,250	108,000	1,340,564	10,453,940	11,687,410	11,716,643	12,008,310

NOTE: The 1987 exchange rate was $ = K6.2.

EXHIBIT 4   Intercom System

A TRIDEX STATION FOR ANY LOCATION

The TRIDEX system is designed to function efficiently in all ambient conditions – quiet offices, noisy industrial areas, or for example, hospitals where discreet, low-level sound is often a necessity.

Lifting the TRIDEX unit automatically gives the user a confidential handset – an essential feature in the medical profession, in banks and in other fields where discretion is needed.

Other models: Singlebutton keyboards, flushmounted stations, industrial stations, sub-stations restricted to receive calls, remote microphone units – in fact a full range of stations to answer the needs of any organisation. Reserve your telephone for essential external services and use TRIDEX for efficient internal communication.

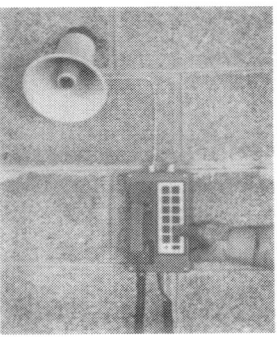
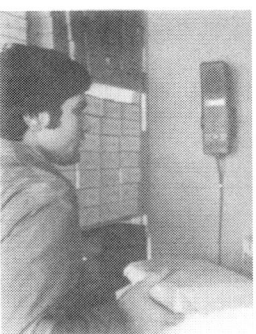

RING GROUP, INC.
230 Community Drive, Great Neck, New York 11021
(516) 487-0250 / (800) 645-9690

systems and therefore did not carry inventory. Bids were submitted from 60 to 90 days in advance of approval and delivery. Ring Group maintained the appropriate inventory to serve this demand. OEM (original equipment manufacturers) arrangements represented the final channel for the intercom product. Sales to OEMs, such as the Contel Executone Group, had a margin of less than 20 percent. OEMs generally sold the intercom product under a private label.

The second major family of products handled by Ring Group consisted of a variety of telephone switches known as automatic call distributors (ACD).[1] An ACD switch could distribute a large volume of incoming phone calls evenly across internal operators. This feature made the ACD attractive to such users as airlines, car rental agencies, and catalog houses, who relied on high-volume telephone response. The ACD market, with an estimated size of $600 million in 1988 and $1 billion in 1990, had attracted a range of competitors, from companies such as Northern Telecom, AT&T, and Rockwell to much smaller firms, such as Redcom and Suma-Four. Ring Group sold a customized version of the ACD, known as E-911, to several cities, towns, and municipal counties. E-911 service enabled citizens to dial 911 on any telephone to report an emergency requiring medical, fire, or police assistance. The system was so configured that the call receiver was able to locate the call source automatically.

The E-911 and other ACD products were sold directly by Ruggieri and a field sales representative. Seven manufacturer representatives, coordinated by a sales administrator, also sold ACD products. Currently, there was no sales coverage in the western region of the United States. The E-911 and ACD products had a long sales cycle: from 6 to 18 months from initial contact to installation. While the decision maker for the E-911 product—the city, town, or county officials—generally endeavored to become well acquainted with Ring Group people and products, a crucial influence for basic ACD products was often a local telephone company that configured, installed, and maintained the system of which Ring Group equipment was a part. ACD products ranged in price from under $100,000 to over $5 million, depending on size and complexity. A typical Ring ACD is pictured in Exhibit 5.

In addition to the intercom and switch product lines, Ring Group marketed peripheral and other ancillary telephony equipment with a less-concerted effort. Product design and assembly were the concern of Norwegian management. All products were manufactured by Kitron, a Scanvest Ring manufacturing subsidiary based in Norway; after the manufacturing stage, switches, intercoms, and other products were sent to Brekke, the Norway-based Scanvest Ring distribution division. Brekke paid a transfer price to the manufacturing division at a level above cost, but below Norway market price. Brekke then added a margin of 20 to 30 percent and distributed product to the Norway market, Ring Group, and other international markets.

Ring Group management cited two sources of frustration in its operating relationship with Scanvest Ring. First, Ruggieri estimated that a Ring ACD was priced from 50 to 80 percent above U.S. competition. "While the relatively high Norwegian labor costs account for some of Ring's cost disadvantage, Kitron's practice of channeling product through Brekke substantially adds to our procurement costs," he

---

[1] An ACD was a variety of a general class of telephone switch called private branch exchange (PBX). A PBX functioned to connect incoming telephone lines, or trunks, to internal telephone extensions at the site of a telephone user. PBXs ranged widely in capacity and expense, according to the total number of trunks and extensions serviceable (trunks and extensions were collectively referred to as ports). For a user who received many more incoming calls than made outgoing calls, a PBX, or an ACD, was often needed. An ACD that relied on digital technology was referred to as a digital call distributor, or DCD.

EXHIBIT 5   ACD Switch

DCD 600: DIGITAL CALL DISTRIBUTOR

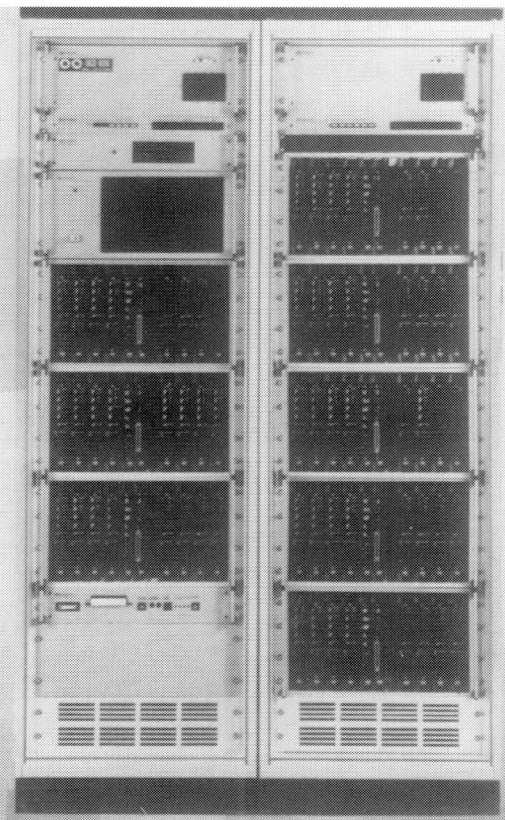

The Ring Digital Call Distributor (DCD) 600 is a technologically advanced digital automatic call distributor that operates in today's predominantly analog environment. Yet it can be configured to operate equally well in tomorrow's digital environment.

By automatically routing incoming calls, queueing calls, recording traffic loads, providing printed hard-copy statistics and real-time, on-screen management information, the DCD 600 solves the problems of handling large numbers of incoming calls. And it does it efficiently, effectively and reliably.

In addition to a wide array of standard features, the DCD 600 offers a number of optional features to meet specialized operating needs and requirements.

added. In effect, Ruggieri felt his hands were somewhat tied as he tried to show Scanvest Ring a reasonable profit.

A second source of frustration for Ring Group management was Scanvest Ring's general unwillingness to allow Ring Group to make revisions to, or otherwise customize, Scanvest Ring products. According to Ruggieri, Scanvest Ring maintained that the benefits from modification of completed product designs were outweighed by the R&D and manufacturing cost advantages that Scanvest Ring would enjoy through product standardization. Ruggieri suspected that Scanvest Ring's near-monopoly position in Norway accounted substantially for its unwavering adherence to this policy. "Because the Norwegian market is essentially uncontested, competitive product features are either not demanded by Norwegian customers, or at the very least, such features are not required for success in Norway," Ruggieri thought.

Helge Midttun disagreed. Scanvest Ring had grown in leaps and bounds from 1982 to 1985 through a series of acquisitions and opening of several foreign subsidiaries in Europe. The company's profit performance, however, plummeted. On taking over as CEO in 1986, Helge Midttun consciously chose a strategy of focusing on the two core businesses of telecommunications and information systems. While telecommunications products and markets were mature, information systems technology and markets were new and rapidly growing. Through strategies of cost reduction, product line rationalization, and focus on Scandinavian markets, Scanvest Ring management had achieved a turnaround (see Exhibit 3). Scanvest Ring had divested all its foreign holdings; Ring Group was the lone foreign subsidiary.

It was in the context of this unique relationship to its corporate parent that Ruggieri would have to address the pressing issues relating to the budding HCS-100 effort.

Ring Medical

In the spring of 1986, Charlie Witteck, a sales representative then working for Telphi, Inc., approached Paul Ruggieri with what both men saw as a terrific opportunity for Ring Group. Witteck's firm had developed a computerized internal communications system for the hospital market. The product would both enhance the quality and reduce the cost of communication between physicians, patients, hospital administrators, and others connected to the hospital's community.[2] Because of the proprietary nature of the product's operating system, as well as a shortage of cash, the product seemed doomed to failure if left in the hands of Telphi. Encouraged that Ring's engineering expertise and experience in selling, when combined with the Telphi product, could add up to success, Ruggieri convinced Scanvest Ring to acquire the intellectual property rights to the Telphi product. In July of 1986, Scanvest Ring paid $25,000 to complete that acquisition. The new division, Ring Medical, was to be operated independently from Ring Group for legal and financial reasons. Scanvest Ring was to make an initial cash contribution of $200,000, and if certain goals were met, an additional $500,000 for working capital in the form of a loan.

Former Telphi vice president of sales and marketing, Ed Owens, 50, was hired with overall responsibility for product and market development, operating out of Billerica, Massachusetts. Owens had had offers from four companies for Telphi's intellectual property rights. It was apparent to bidders that the real "intellectual" value was that of Ed Owens, and an acquisition of Telphi would be incomplete with-

---

[2]Operating system is the building block (or language) which enables a computer to configure and run application programs. Telphi's software was based on its proprietary operating system. By 1988, AT&T's UNIX operating system was fast emerging as the industry standard for the size range of computers discussed in this case.

out him. Of all the offers he received, the one from Ring Group was most attractive. Charlie Witteck, 60, also a former Telphi employee, was initially hired by Ring Group at Great Neck, New York, to assist in ACD sales, but in March 1987 was appointed national sales manager for Ring Medical.

Dave Forster, 25, left an engineering position at Northern Telecom to become director of engineering at Ring Medical in Billerica. A promising young engineer with strong interest in management, Forster too was not without ample career options. His confidence in the Telphi product was strong testimony to its potential value.

The HCS-100

In the broadest sense, the HCS-100 served to improve the cost effectiveness and quality of communication between various participants in a hospital's operations, including physicians, patients, administrators, and maintenance workers. The HCS-100 was an assembly of telephone and computer hardware and software, all of which were available off the shelf, with the exception of the digital call distributor (DCD). The DCD employed in the HCS-100 was the DCD-601, manufactured by the Norwegian Scanvest Ring subsidiary, Kitron.

In addition to the DCD-601, the HCS-100 was made up of a 32-bit minicomputer manufactured by Convergent Technologies. The computer used a relational database management system (RDBMS), based on the widely standardized UNIX operating system. The fourth major component of the HCS-100 was a terminal and customized keyboard, manufactured by Wyse Technologies. An emergency manual backup system, touchscreen, and other interconnecting software for the HCS-100 were developed by Ring Medical.

DCD-601

Of the four main building blocks of the HCS-100, the DCD-601 was considered to be of greatest strategic importance. It was one of only a handful of DCDs made that was architecturally suitable for U.S. telephony equipment and sufficiently economical for an HCS-100-type product. Only two United States–based firms manufactured such a switch, Redcom, in Rochester, New York, and Suma-Four, in Manchester, New Hampshire. The remaining firms were based in Europe, and none of their switches were of suitable construction for U.S. telephony hardware. Ed Owens was convinced that to modify a foreign-made DCD for application in the United States would be grossly uneconomical. He and Dave Forster also felt that it would be uneconomical for a North American manufacturer of large DCDs, such as AT&T, Rockwell, or Northern Telecom, to custom-engineer a DCD either for a would-be Ring Medical competitor or for the DCD maker's own entry into the HCS-100's target market. "The current hospital market is simply too specialized and small for large players to exploit economically," argued Ed Owens.

HCS-100 Modules

The arrangement of the HCS-100's four key building blocks, in addition to the specific software, determined the function that the system would perform. There were six general, distinct functions for which the HCS-100 could be configured as modules. Ring Medical intended to offer modules independently or in any combination. (See Exhibit 6 for a schematic diagram of a full HCS-100 system, and a listing of the offerings of each module.) A fully configured system with all modules was priced at about $70,000.

Telephone Answering Service (TAS)

The TAS, priced at about $55,000, allowed for efficient handling of physicians' phone calls dialed to their private offices during hours when the office was unattended. The office attendant programmed the office phone to forward calls to a special number that dialed the HCS-100 system at the physician's hospital. By virtue of a special kind of trunk, known as a direct inward dialing (DID) trunk, the HCS-100 system recognized from which doctor's office the call had been forwarded. The HCS-100 terminal screen then immediately displayed a file of information on the physician. This information included how the physician would like the phone answered, how the physician could be reached, and special instructions for handling emergency calls. The operator was then able to carry on a normal conversation with the caller, providing information according to instructions the physician had filed in the TAS, and simultaneously type a message into the physician's TAS file. The physician could then easily access message information without directly contacting the operator by checking a registry terminal, printer, or fax machine located at the physician's home or office at the hospital. Messages could also be transmitted to physicians' digital pagers.

Ring Medical management was confident that the HCS-100 TAS was both superior to competing products and preferable to alternative solutions, largely because of its flexibility in screen design. The hospital was not constrained to a standard series of screens but could request custom-designed screens. The HCS-100 software was so adapted that Ring Medical could provide this at nominal cost. No current Ring Medical competitor had this degree of flexibility. A hospital-run TAS such as the HCS-100 was also expected to offer a more professional service to physicians than would a "mom and pop" answering service. The hospital TAS operator would answer calls exclusively for physicians affiliated with one hospital. The TAS operator was therefore expected to be more informed and of greater assistance to a caller than would a third-party answering-service operator who handled calls for a number of physicians affiliated with a variety of hospitals.

Target Market

Ring Medical managers claimed that the primary reason for choosing hospitals as a target market for the HCS-100 was based on fundamental facts and characteristics about the hospital business. Changes in hospital reimbursement procedures

Exhibit 6   HCS-100

*Our integrated HCS-100 system means **substantial** savings, over time, for the health care organization that is planning ahead.*

After implementing one module, you can add others at minimal cost—certainly much less than the cost of purchasing them from separate vendors.

And the modules you add will interact with each other to increase staff efficiency—giving you further reductions in operating costs and an increasingly effective communications system.

- **a portable printer** available for the physician's convenience. It will reduce the number of check-in calls and enable operators to provide a higher standard of service to the physician's private patients.
- **a physician registry** that allows physicians to view their messages on any touch terminal screen.
- **printouts** that can be made at the hospital and picked up by the physician or distributed through the internal mail system.

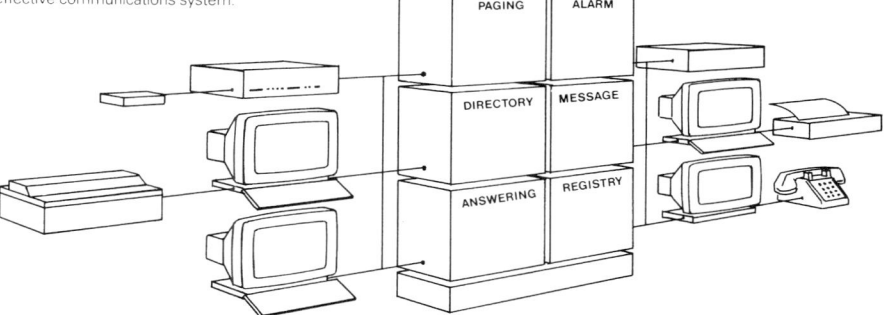

You also get more value for each dollar you invest because our systems are designed *specifically* for the health care environment. We know that no two health care institutions are alike, so we've built a variety of options into our systems so they can be customized to meet your specific needs—at *no* additional cost.

Physicians' Telephone Answering Message Service:

With a RING HCS-100 system, you can offer physicians in your area a personalized and professional answering/message service tailored to their specific needs.

When a call is forwarded from a physician's office, RING HCS-100 automatically displays the physician's account data, a personalized answering phrase, and message pad.

To reduce call-handling time, several standard message phrases can be accessed at the touch of a single key. And, on completion of the call, the system automatically "stamps" the message with the operator's initials, date, and time.

To further increase efficiency—while still providing a high quality service—the system incorporates several message delivery options, including:

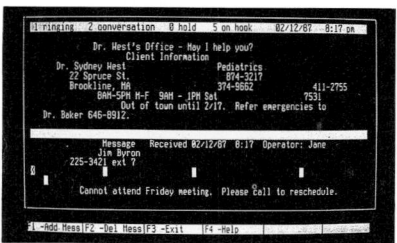

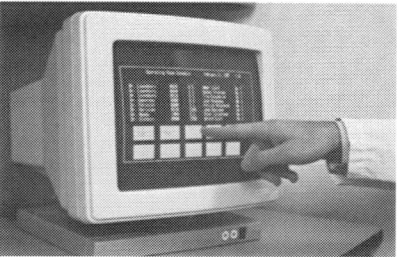

This touch-activated color terminal makes it easier for physicians to register their status. When it is used in conjunction with our Physicians' Telephone Answering Service/Message Center, physicians will be encouraged to sign in because the screen will display their messages and provide access to other important information. (They also have the option of registering from a telephone inside or outside the hospital.) Physicians using the registry to retrieve messages will not have to bother the answering service operator with a check-in call.

Exhibit 6 (concluded)

If a message is urgent, RING's HCS-100 complete call-out and patching capability allows the operator to reach the physician directly—or to patch the call through to the emergency room or the on-call physician.

And to ensure continuity of service, operators can key in reminders that will alert the next shift to wake-up calls or to unanswered pages that need to be repeated.

SUMMARY OF KEY FEATURES

- PBX interfaces
- supports both DID and secretarial lines
- speed dialing
- remote printing
- call out and patching
- statistical reports
- message printout at client offices
- automatic "no message" indication at check-in
- automatic display of account data
- automatic time stamping
- timed reminders
- customized message prompts
- billing package for your personal computer
- single key message input
- automatic call distribution
- color display terminal

Registry

RING's HCS-100 physician Registry system does a better job of keeping track of physicians and other key staff members—while giving them instant access to important messages and to each others' whereabouts.

Physicians are encouraged to "sign in" because the system is engineered for touch access and rapid delivery of messages and hospital bulletins geared to the physicians' needs. For added convenience, the system has a telephone interface with stored voice instructions so a change in status can be registered from any Touch Tone® phone.

Key information available through the Registry:

- department bulletins
- patient roster
- in-house staff
- operating room schedules
- meeting announcements
- messages from answering service or message center

The Registry system helps switchboard personnel handle calls more efficiently. The RING HCS-100 terminal will display the status and location of any physician—so that operators can easily determine whether to page, take a message, or refer the caller to someone else.

The Registry display can be customized to fit the different categories you use (e.g., "in and available," "in and not available," "in delivery room," etc.). And information is labeled with the time of the last update or sign-in so users can see if the physician's status is current. The system can also be set up to automatically delete information that hasn't been updated in the last twenty-four hours.

Paging

RING's HCS-100 Paging system, consisting of one or more encoders, will interface with your existing transmitter control equipment. Paging can be initiated from any designated terminal on the system, or with the proper access code, from any Touch Tone® telephone. This dial access feature allows a high percentage of pages to be initiated without involving the operator. The system supports multiple/mixed coding formats so your tone, tone and voice, numeric and

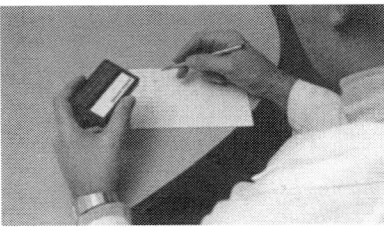

RING helps you strengthen ties with physicians by offering a medically-oriented, cost efficient answering service/message center.

alphanumeric display pagers need not be replaced. An optional voice storage module will provide added efficiency if you do a lot of voice paging.

In addition, for flexibility in group paging, individuals can belong to multiple groups—with mixed pager types included in a single group.

For convenience, and in compliance with F.C.C. regulations, station identification is automatically broadcast. To provide the documentation you need, all pages are logged and the log may be printed at any time.

Directory

A computerized Directory system dramatically reduces operators' call handling time by enabling them to find information in less than two seconds—and to respond to callers' requests more professionally and accurately.

The Directory may contain more than 100,000 records in ten customized files, which may include, for example:

- staff directory
- patient directory
- corporate directory
- on-call schedules
- physician directory
- volunteer directory
- benefactors directory

In addition, printed directories can be produced on the premises at no additional expense. Updates are easy, and those staff who need the critical information have it at their fingertips.

Alarm Monitor

Engineered to *supplement* existing alarm systems, the RING HCS-100 alarm system reduces emergency response time.

When a security, fire, electrical, mechanical, or environmental problem occurs, operators are alerted instantly via a message on the screen and an audible tone.

With the touch of a button, they receive both the problem location and precise instructions—pre-written by your own staff. They are told whom to notify, under what circumstances (including pertinent telephone and pager numbers), and any follow-up action they should take—from beginning full-scale hospital evacuation to transmitting lifesaving information to fire, police, or repair personnel.

Touch Tone is a registered trademark for AT&T.

EXHIBIT 7 Ring Medical's Target Market

Product

Hospital communication system (HCS). System unit price $70,000 with six integrated modules:

Directory	Telephone answering	Message
Alarm/Security	Registry	Paging

U.S. Hospital and Health Care Market

Present number: 6,988 hospital sites in United States
Small size, 6–99 beds: 3,239 small sites
Medium size, 100–399 beds: 2,847 medium sites
Large size, over 400 beds: 902 large sites

Market Potential

Percent with automated telephone answering systems: Less than 5% penetrated.
Percent to be upgraded: 50% estimated medium and large sites.
Hospital totals: 2,847 + 902 = 3,749 sites with over 100 beds.
Financial potential: 3,749 sites × $70,000 per site = $262 million.
Percent to be upgraded: 50% estimated = $131 million.

SOURCE: American Hospital Association.

---

introduced in April 1983 and new forms of competition from groups like HMOs (health maintenance organizations) were forcing hospitals to operate more efficiently and cut costs. An HCS-100-type system was believed to be a useful tool in that regard. Nearly 7,000 U.S. hospitals spent over $1.4 billion on telecommunications equipment in 1987. Other potential markets existed for an HCS-100-type product, however, and a number of Ring Medical competitors had made inroads into the commercial telephone answering market.

Ring Medical's preliminary strategy was to target large- and medium-sized hospitals (see Exhibit 7). Of all U.S. hospitals, only 5 percent had an automated telephone answering system. Under Ring Medical's current pricing scheme, the remaining 95 percent, unpenetrated medium- and large-sized hospitals, represented a market of some $260 million (see Exhibit 7). Internal company estimates projected that at least half of these hospitals would be upgraded to offer an automated TAS service within the next five years.

Customer buying behavior in the hospital industry was complex. Many hospitals were part of multihospital buying groups, and purchase negotiations were often centralized. Equipment buying, however, tended to be more decentralized, and the hospital administrator invariably was involved. While large hospitals often included many managers and clinical people in their decision-making units (DMUs), small hospitals tended to have smaller DMUs. Typically, purchasing an HCS-100 product would involve the administrator and the telecommunications manager in hospitals, although others might participate, depending on the module configuration.

Exhibit 8 Ring Medical's Hospital Communication Competitors and Their Product Offerings

HCS-100 System Features	A.I.S.	AMTELCO	CANDELA	STARTEL	MULTITONE
1. Telephone answering	RA	X	X	X	X
2. Message storage/retrieval	RA	X	X	X	X
3. Directory	RA	RA	RA	RA	RA
4. Touch screen registry	O	O	O	O	O
5. Dial access registry	X	O	O	O	O
6. Remote alarm monitoring	X	X	X	X	X
7. Premise alarm monitoring	O	O	O	O	O
8. Paging encoder	X	O	O	O	O
System Price ($000)	$80–$100	$50–$150	$30–$75	$50–$150	$70–$100
Annual Revenue	$3M–$5M	$12M	$11M	$10M	$5M–$8M

Feature Descriptions:
1. System interconnects to Bell Network and PBXs to provide automatic display of account information and all standard call-handling functions.
2. Computer storage, retrieval, and counting of text messages.
3. Allows databases to be created, modified, displayed, and printed in different formats.
4. Provides facility for physicians and staff to register location and availability status via touch-sensitive terminal screens. Terminals also provide access to a wide variety of information, including messages.
5. Provide facility for physicians and staff to register location and availability status via Touch Tone® telephone.
6. System will display alarm-response instructions when alarm condition occurs in physician's office. The alarm sensor triggers an auto-dialer to call a specific number that will be answered by the system.
7. Provides hard-wire interface to on-premises hospital alarm systems. Senses alarm conditions through dry contact closure and automatically displays notification and response instructions.
8. Allows pages to be initiated from any designated system terminal. Accommodates all common paper types and coding formats.

NOTE: RA = ring competitive advantage; O = feature not offered; X = no ring competitive advantage.

Competition

Ring Medical had five principal competitors, of which only one, A.I.S., focused exclusively on the hospital market. Ring's product offerings and those of its five competitors are shown in Exhibit 8.

A.I.S. Waltham

A.I.S., privately held, was established in 1981, employed 40 people, and had estimated 1986 sales of $3M. A.I.S. was a designer and marketer of an integrated hospital communication system; all software, paging, and voice board designs were proprietary. All hardware was based on Data General Computers. Five of the six HCS-100 modules were offered; no premise alarm module was offered. Distribution was direct to hospitals and also via telecommunications distributors. Direct sales effort covered New England, New York, and Chicago. Ring management estimated 80 A.I.S. installations.

A.I.S. relied on the PBX switch already installed for other telecommunications devices at the hospital as the basic building block for its systems. Ring management considered this to be a severe disadvantage. While an HCS-100 switch was independent of the hospital telephone switch and therefore operational even when the main switch failed, an A.I.S. system was totally dependent on the PBX. A second benefit of an independent TAS switch was that data on incoming and outgoing TAS-related calls were tracked separately from other call traffic. This meant a hospital using an A.I.S. system would be forced to charge a flat fee for subscription, while the user of the HCS-100 could opt for a fee based on usage.

Progress of the HCS-100 Effort

Ring Medical's efforts to date could be summarized in three phases. The first phase, commencing in July 1986, pertained mainly to legal and administrative issues in connection with the formation of the company. Phase two, initiated in January 1987, was considered remarkable: In just six months, the company was able to develop and sell its first system to Yale University Medical Center, under the assurance of comprehensive service (referred to as a Beta test site). While the Yale system was being installed, the company geared itself to commercializing the product concept. Research and product development was still considered a priority issue. By late September 1987 the company was ready to enter the product-launch and commercialization phase. After long arguments, members of Ring Medical's management team agreed that a manufacturers' representative network was the best way to reach the customer. Ring Medical needed to preserve its internal capital for product development, and manufacturers' reps cost the company nothing in terms of fixed cost. A 20 percent commission would be paid on orders generated. There were at least 100 manufacturers' reps in the industry selling a wide array of telecommunications products. However, since the company was headquartered at Massachusetts, the New England area (consisting of Vermont, Maine, New Hampshire, Massachusetts, Connecticut, and Rhode Island) was reserved as headquarters sales territory, to be sold and developed directly by Ed Owens. In addition to the Yale system, four more systems were sold in the launch phase. A brief description of the sales process for each of the five systems is provided below:

1. Yale University Medical Center, 829 beds, sold June 1987.

Ed Owens contacted Cathy Johnson, director of telecommunications at Yale, in February 1987. Owens already knew Johnson, for he had sold her a product much like Ring Medical's Directory module while he was at Telphi. The Telphi Directory product was essentially useless to Yale, primarily because the operating system was proprietary and could not be supported. Aware of Johnson's dismay with her purchase, Owens suggested that he replace the Telphi Directory with a Ring Medical Directory. Additionally, he would sell Johnson a Message module. The price of the entire package was $58,000. Johnson was free to return the system for a complete refund if not satisfied.

Between the time of initial contact in February 1987 and closure of the sale in June, Owens and Forster devoted an estimated 60 hours each to the Yale account, making three presentations. In addition to Johnson, Doris Cousins, chief PBX operator, and a couple of consultants attended the presentations. The buyers' primary concerns were the system's reliability and Ring Medical's reputation and history. While the consultants' and PBX operator's input seemed important to Johnson, she alone was responsible for the decision to buy.

2. St. Anthony's Hospital, Ohio, 404 beds, sold November 1987.

This account was sold by Judy Petty, a manufacturer's representative. Petty first became acquainted with the St. Anthony's director of telecommunications while she was employed by Tascom, a Ring Medical competitor, as a salesperson. Petty left Tascom expressly to be a manufacturer's representative and largely to be able to carry the Ring Medical line. Her strong confidence in the superiority of the HCS-100 was encouraging to Ed Owens.

After brief training, conducted by Ed Owens, Petty was assigned the Midwest sales territory and issued a modem and terminal—standard equipment for all of Ring Medical's reps. These sales aids allowed Petty to access a "canned" demonstration package at the Billerica headquarters, which provided the decision makers with a very realistic display of the various HCS-100 modules.

The key decision makers at St. Anthony's were the director of telecommunications and the administrative VP. Petty noted that the sales process was very difficult, for the DMU was quite familiar with competitive offerings. After five months, a TAS and Registry were sold. St. Anthony's paid $73,000 for the package.

3. Winchester Hospital, 223 beds, sold February 1988.

After a nine-month sales effort, Ed Owens sold a TAS and Registry to this Massachusetts hospital. Like the Yale sale, this was a replacement of a formerly installed Telphi unit as well as an additional Ring Medical sale. The price was $54,000.

Like that of St. Anthony's, Winchester's was a highly competitive sales process. Five players were known to have bid for the business. Although the hospital DMU comprised the director of telecommunications, vice president of finance, and the PBX operator, the decision to buy the HCS-100 was largely influenced by Nancy Aldrich, a prominent industry consultant, with the consulting firm TMC. Aldrich, with over 150 client hospitals, deemed HCS-100 the most technologically advanced product available.

4. Danbury Hospital, 366 beds, sold April 1988.

This Connecticut-based account was closed by Ed Owens after one presentation. The time from contact to close was two months, primarily due to the hospital's budgeting and capital appropriations process. A TAS module was purchased for $40,000.

The director of telecommunications contacted Owens by reference of Cathy Johnson at Yale, and also on the advice of a representative of Homisco, a value-added reseller which had recently sold the hospital a computerized accounting system to track and bill outgoing long-distance calls. Owens knew the president of Homisco from past business dealings and had apprised him of the HCS-100 package. Because both the HCS-100 and Homisco's key products were based on the same UNIX operating system, Homisco considered the products complementary and mutually beneficial to each company's sales efforts. Danbury had been in the market for a TAS-type product, and Owens's assessment was that the DMU was generally well informed as to the available products and technologies.

    5. Dow Jones, 32 users.

Ed Owens contacted Norm Smith, director of telecommunications for Dow Jones Corporation, to interest him in replacing Dow's existing directory product. One remote demonstration in Dow's corporate offices in Princeton, New Jersey, and one visit to Ring Medical's office by Stephanie Matthews, a communications manager under Smith, convinced Dow to replace its Telphi computer with Ring's UNIX-based Convergent computer and HCS-100 Directory System.

  Since Dow was an OEM user of Wyse terminals, it was able to retain the 20 existing operator position terminals for use with the Ring system. The Directory module was purchased for $30,000 (utilizing existing Dow Jones terminal hardware, as explained above).

Marketing Challenges

Organizational issues apart, there were two distinct marketing challenges that the HCS-100 product launch faced. The first was the question of product policy; the second issue concerned channels of distribution.

Product Policy

For most hospitals, a TAS represented an incremental investment, a new addition, as opposed to an expenditure to replace an existing activity with new technology. Thus, the question was whether the HCS-100 should be positioned as a source-efficiency (i.e., cost reduction), or a source-effectiveness (i.e., quality enhancement) system.

In addition to eliminating a physician's need for a separate answering service, TAS was considered a potential source of hospital revenue, as physicians could be charged for system use. Management estimated that an average physician spent $100 monthly on an answering service. A physician TAS subscriber should therefore be expected to pay at least this amount. For a TAS capable of servicing 65 physicians, the incremental operating expenses incurred by a hospital would be salary and benefits for one full-time equivalent HCS-100 attendant (estimated to be $30,000 to $35,000 annually), plus one-time costs of added telephone company–supplied hardware and Ring Medical–supplied servicing fees of about $10,000. With a basic TAS price of $55,000, the decision maker could readily calculate a satisfactory payback period as well as impressive contribution levels.

Beyond the "hard dollar" revenue from physician fees, Ed Owens and Dave Forster were particularly convinced that potentially larger "soft dollar" revenues would accrue to the hospital offering a TAS. Physicians were ultimately responsible for "filling beds" in the fixed-cost–intensive hospital. Any measures a hospital's administration took to make its hospital more desirable for physicians should be rewarded by greater utilization. The TAS was seen as a significant hospital enhancement.

Ruggieri, Owens, and Forster were in agreement that the HCS-100 should be positioned as the unequivocal high-end hospital internal communications system for large- and medium-size hospitals. Relative to the competition, the HCS-100 was considered to have both the cutting-edge and most dependable hardware, and the greatest number of module offerings. The current thinking was to couple a clear quality edge (i.e., high-end) with a low relative price point. As Exhibit 8 shows, the HCS-100 was priced well below chief rival A.I.S., and at parity with, or moderately below, all other competitors.

Another issue concerned line extension into add-on products. Owens anticipated extremely attractive margins from add-on sales, consisting of service, spare parts, additional modules, and new generation software. On an installed base of 24 hospitals, add-on sales alone could account for an additional $1 million in gross margins (see Exhibit 9). The critical question, however, was how should Ring Medical organize its sales and distribution efforts now to position itself to take advantage of an add-on market to be developed later.

Channels of Distribution

While there was strong consensus that gaining access to the complex decision-making unit at large- and medium-size hospitals posed a significant challenge, there was disagreement about the most appropriate channels of distribution. Three fairly distinct schools of thought prevailed.

The first approach centered on the aggressive deployment of manufacturers' representatives and was most embraced by Charlie Witteck, national sales manager. At 60, Witteck had logged more time in the field than any other Ring Medical manager. He was confident in his ability to understand the type of people in the hospital buying environment and therefore to know what sort of people should be deployed to sell in that environment. "In short, they must be seasoned. Young salespeople simply do not have the aplomb or personal bearing for the job," Witteck had argued. In keeping with this philosophy, he had recruited eight manufacturers' reps in November 1987. Their backgrounds and assigned territories are presented in Exhibit 10.

On the organization of the marketing effort, Witteck felt that time had come for the bright, young, enthusiastic product development team in Massachusetts to turn the sales responsibility for HCS-100 over to the more stable, seasoned New York management team. He had often expressed his opinion:

> Even though you'd think this thing would sell itself—it's so damn good—it requires a great deal of patience and maturity. You can't just go to the PBX operator; she has no authority. The telecommunications director, on the other hand, has authority, but she has no motivation to invest in something for the sake of cutting costs, let alone creating a new function and source of profit for the hospital. For concerns like these, you need to find the appropriate hospital administrator, maybe a vice president of finance. But chances are that person knows nothing about telecommunications. . . . Sometimes, you even have to get the MIS people involved, or perhaps outside consultants.

EXHIBIT 9 Projected Add-On Sales

Installed Customer Hospital Base Worksheet 3/10/88	Initial Sale	Second Year Add-On Sale Spare Parts	Second Year Add-On Sale Modules	Second Year Add-On Sale Service	Second Year Total Add-On Potential	Third Year One Module and Service	Fourth Year One Module and Service	Fifth Year One Module and Service	Fourth Year Total Add-On Potential
Assumptions		(A)	(B)	(C)	(A,B,C)	(B,C,D)	(B,C,D)	(B,C,D)	(A,B,C,D)
Yale University Medical Center	$ 58,000	$9,000	$6,000	$6,000	$21,000	$12,600	$13,860	$15,246	$62,706
St. Anthony's Medical Center	73,000	9,000	6,000	6,000	21,000	12,600	13,860	15,246	62,706
Winchester Hospital	54,000	9,000	6,000	4,000	19,000	12,600	13,860	15,246	60,706
Danbury Medical Center	40,000	9,000	10,000	6,000	25,000	12,600	13,860	15,246	66,706
Total sales—four hospitals	$225,000	36,000	28,000	22,000	86,000	50,400	55,440	60,984	252,824
Estimated gross margin (%)		50%	80%	70%		75%	75%	75%	
Estimated gross margin ($)		18,000	22,400	15,400	55,800	37,800	41,580	45,738	180,918
Installed base of 24 hospitals	Add-on sales	216,000	168,000	132,000	516,000	302,400	332,640	365,904	1,516,944
Estimated gross margin ($)		108,000	134,400	92,400	334,800	226,800	249,480	274,428	1,085,508
Installed base of 48 hospitals	Add-on sale	432,000	336,000	264,000	1,032,000	604,800	665,280	731,808	3,033,888
Estimated gross margin ($)		216,000	268,800	184,800	669,600	453,600	498,960	548,856	2,171,016
Installed base of 96 hospitals	Add-on sale	864,000	672,000	528,000	2,064,000	1,209,600	1,330,560	1,463,616	6,067,776
Estimated gross margin ($)		432,000	537,600	369,600	1,339,200	907,200	997,920	1,097,712	4,342,032

Projected five-year market share of system sales and installed base:

1988 = 24 projects sold.
1989 = 40 projects sold.
1990 = 60 projects sold.
1991 = 80 projects sold.
1992 = 100 projects sold.
Total five-year sales = 304.

Hospital Profile of Installed Base	Location State	Number of Beds	Number of Admits	Annual Expenses (in $000)	Number of Personnel
Yale Med Center	Connecticut	829	31,004	$187,744	3,715
St. Anthony's Med Center	Ohio	404	11,867	$ 57,548	1,220
Winchester Hospital	Massachusetts	223	7,848	$ 29,133	666
Danbury Hospital	Connecticut	366	16,460	$ 87,551	1,742

Assumptions:

(A) = Hardware sales of spare parts package @ $9,000 @ 50% margin.
(B) = Add-on sale of one new software feature module and moderate system expansion @ $6,000 @ 80% margin.
(C) = Annual service revenue and software upgrade @ $500/month @ 70% margin.
(D) = Estimated 10% price increase per year in third, fourth, fifth years.

Exhibit 10 Manufacturers' Reps

Rep	Prior Selling Experience	Region	Age
Ms. Petty	Telephony (TAS com)	Ohio, Kentucky, Pennsylvania	40
Mr. Dunne	Contel Executone	Maryland, Washington, D.C., Delaware, Eastern Pennsylvania	64
Mr. Kline	Data and Telephony Systems	Florida	65
Mr. Hirsch	Data and Telephony Systems	New York, New Jersey, Connecticut	50
Mr. Mawn	Hospital Intercoms	Georgia, Alabama, South Carolina, Tennessee	50
Mr. McCadden	Northern Telecom Sales	New York, Long Island	55
Mr. Schmidt	Contel Executone	Colorado, Nevada	55
Mr. Smith	Computer and Oil Industry Sales	Texas	55

According to Witteck, one had to endure the mire of bureaucracy presented by the target hospital's organization and successfully bring all relevant parties together so that they could see the tremendous worth of the HCS-100. To Witteck, this challenge would be most effectively met by representatives "who've been around a while." The obvious choice of distribution strategy entailed a complement of able manufacturer's reps, reporting to an administrator at the New York Ring Group headquarters. Witteck further supported the manufacturer rep scheme by arguing that "we simply do not have the resources to deploy a direct sales force. No matter what you do, each salesperson will end up costing the company at least $60,000 to $75,000."

Ed Owens and Dave Forster, on the other hand, saw a direct sales force as a necessity that had to be afforded. Their view was that

> with a decision-making unit of this complexity, and a product with such a high price tag, you've got to have dedicated field salespeople. Sure, the manufacturer's rep might make a pretty penny, but if he or she gets frustrated with the process, attention can easily be shifted to other products, for other companies. We also need to have assurance that these people in the field are well trained. Training can make all the difference, and with the manufacturer's rep, you've got no control.

Owens further argued that the direct sales force should report to a sales director at the Ring Medical headquarters at Billerica. Well aware of the intensive effort by design and service personnel in the Billerica office over the last two years, Owens was concerned at the loss of momentum, lack of coordination, and general shock to the entrepreneurial culture in Billerica that would surely result if the sales effort were not administered from his office. Moreover, "nearly everything else is handled from here in Massachusetts, why not sales as well?" Owens asked.

Paul Ruggieri disagreed. Ruggieri was compelled by a number of reasons to believe that the HCS-100 product launch would run much more smoothly if many important functional tasks were administered from the Ring Group's Great Neck, New York, headquarters. Service was a prime example. From his experience with users of other Ring Group products, Ruggieri felt strongly that a well-staffed service center, complete with a warehouse of spare parts, was immediately needed in New York. Ruggieri also envisioned a network of similar dedicated service centers in due course, strategically located all over the country. In addition, other support functions would clearly be less costly and executed more efficiently, Ruggieri thought, if handled out of Ring Group headquarters. At least in the near term, services such as warehousing, shipping, and secretarial support could be absorbed by excess capacity in New York.

Reacting to Paul Ruggieri's concerns about service, Ed Owens commented:

> We entirely agree that without satisfactory postinstallation service, the technological edge of the HCS-100 will be for naught. Presently, we have two full-time software engineers devoted fully to service. Most of it has taken the form of answering questions and removing program bugs via a modem. But we really don't need a full-fledged field service operation. That's where Paul is wrong. He's used to selling mature hardware-oriented systems; a large part of HCS-100 is the software. All we need to do is make a phone call, and then via modem fix the problem from here. In addition, Dave Forster spends a substantial portion of his time in the field performing services that cannot be accomplished otherwise.

"On-site service will not be required," added Owens, "because most hospitals anyway have a sophisticated maintenance crew to handle their various complex hardware. On-site inventory of critical parts and telephone instructions should more than suffice to handle emergencies."

Dave Forster noted that the servicing process tends to spur creativity and enhance the product development process. "Let's not forget," he said, "we are dealing with a high-tech product in a new market. It would be foolish for the product development people to be separated from customers' problems."

Perhaps more compelling than the economies from shared overhead functions, however, was the ability to coordinate Ring Medical activities with other Ring Group activities to achieve strategic goals. This could happen only if the operations were housed in New York. Ruggieri argued

> Why restrict the HCS-100 to hospitals? There are a number of good opportunities out there that make sense. I am making inroads into several of these with other products we've got here. Take the business market, for instance. It's huge by comparison to hospitals, and what's more, we just sold an intercom system to a major corporate client. The way I see it, we've got some mature markets which we have been chasing with hardware-intensive product. The HCS-100 is different; the money there is in the software, especially the add-on sales. It's a product that would make a great fit for us here as we try to transition from hardware to the software side.

While Ruggieri acknowledged that the engineers and other staff in Billerica had done a great job of bringing the HCS-100 to its current market-ready state, he was of the opinion that it was time to make a change. He was not enamored of the manufacturer's rep distribution option, which seemed most consistent with a New York–based sales administration. Ruggieri advocated a third distribution strategy altogether—a network of telecommunications distributors, such as Introlink, a West Coast–based reseller with experience in telecommunication products, and a reasonable clientele of health care customers.

Ruggieri had spoken with Introlink in the past about selling Ring intercoms to West Coast hospitals, where Ring Group was not represented. The distributor would take responsibility for marketing the HCS-100. A few issues would still have to be resolved with this option. Would Ring allow Introlink to carry the HCS-100 under its own brand name if demanded? What would their margins be? How could Ring ensure uniform pricing levels across the nation if Introlink had free rein in the West Coast, while Ring's own sales force of manufacturers' reps sold on the East Coast?

Decisions

As Ruggieri recalled the views of Witteck, Owens, and Forster, he thumbed through the latest revision of the 1988 Ring Group budget he had sent to Scanvest Ring (see Exhibit 11). He knew that in contrast to the sanguine projections for HCS-100 sales, he would tomorrow confirm that a scant five systems had been sold. A quick look at the budget would also indicate to board members that cash generated from Ring Group operations would not sustain operating and other expenses projected for Ring Medical. His audience would be cautious, if not skeptical, from the start. His answers to the interdependent organizational and marketing plan issues would have to be airtight.

EXHIBIT 11 1988 Ring Group Budget ($000)

	Total
Gross Sales:	
Commercial ACD	$ 600
911	1,100
Intercom dealer	1,300
Intercom direct	400
Contel	500
Schools	200
Medical (HCS-100)	1,720
Total gross	$5,820
Returns and Allowances	6
Total net	$5,814
Cost of Sales:	
ACD	$ 811
Intercom	1,572
Medical	640
Total cost of sales	$3,023
Operating Expense:	
ACD	$ 206
Intercom	374
Medical	885
Technical services	335
Shipping and receiving	37
General and administration	677
Total operating expense	$2,514
Net Income	$ 277

CHAPTER 9

Rohm and Haas (A): New Product Marketing Strategy

Rohm and Haas's sales of a new biocide, Kathon MWX, was utterly disappointing. This was all the more puzzling since sales of a similar product—Kathon 886 MW, a liquid biocide used only in large-capacity tanks—was well on target and held a steady 30 percent market share. In May 1984, about five months after the new product was launched, management was reviewing the product's marketing strategy with a view to bringing Kathon MWX sales closer to target. Of particular concern were the distribution and communication strategies used for the new product.

On May 15, 1984, Joan Macey, Rohm and Haas market manager for Metalworking Fluid Biocides, was reviewing distributor purchases of Kathon MWX, a new biocide that killed microorganisms in metalworking fluids. She found that total sales to distributors for the first five months were 74 boxes against a first-year target of 1,350 boxes. "I have a super product but I can't sell it," she said. "I am in the process of reviewing our approach of taking this product to market, but at this point I am not convinced we have a better alternative."

Macey was also responsible for the marketing of Kathon 886 MW, a liquid biocide used in large metalworking fluid tanks (above 1,000-gallon capacity). Kathon 886 MW was a powerful biocide, and very small quantities were sufficient to treat large tanks. Because of its low-use level, Kathon 886 MW was unsuitable for smaller-capacity tanks, and Kathon MWX was developed specifically for use in tanks with less than 1,000-gallon capacity.

Kathon 886 MW had a sales volume of $5.4 million in 1983; sales for the first five months of 1984 were at the budgeted level of $2.1 million. Kathon MWX had been launched in December 1983, with a targeted sales volume of $0.2 million in

---

This case was prepared by V. Kasturi Rangan and Susan Lasley.
Copyright © 1986 by the President and Fellows of Harvard College.
Harvard Business School case 587-055 (revised May 25, 1993).

1984; sales in the first five months were about $12,000. Macey estimated the market potential for Kathon 886 MW to be $18 million and Kathon MWX to be $20 million. Explaining the poor sales of Kathon MWX, she said:

> The total usage of Kathon MWX and its substitutes is nowhere near the $20 million potential for this market. Many small users are either unaware or don't see the need for biocides in their metalworking fluid treatment. We do poorly because we do not have enough competition to build primary demand.

Company Background

In 1906, Otto Rohm and Otto Haas founded the company in Germany to sell chemicals to that country's leather tanning industry. The U.S. branch opened in Philadelphia in 1909. At the end of World War I, Otto Haas incorporated the American branch as an independent company. Over the years it became a leader in chemical technology, especially in acrylic emulsion polymers.[1] In 1983, the American company reported worldwide sales of $2 billion derived from four business segments:

1. Polymers, resins, and monomers—for applications in paints, industrial finishes, decorative coatings, and construction products
2. Plastics—for applications in signs, skylights, containers, and automotive products
3. Agricultural chemicals—herbicides and fungicides for crop diseases
4. Industrial chemicals—for lubricants and fuels, water treatment, and the formulation of a wide variety of industrial and consumer products

The company's product lines consisted of over 500 different products. Exhibit 1 gives the trend of sales and profits by business segments.

The Industrial Chemicals business segment consisted of three product groups: Fluid Process Chemicals, Petroleum Chemicals, and Specialty Chemicals. The Kathon microbiocide products with 1983 sales of $25 million were part of the Specialty Chemicals Group. Surface active chemicals (called surfactants) and water-soluble polymers were the other products marketed by the Specialty Chemicals Group (see Exhibit 2 for an organization chart). Joan Macey was market manager for microbiocide applications in the metalworking fluid and latex/adhesives markets. Latex/adhesives biocides (1983 sales of $2 million) were sold directly by the Specialty Chemicals sales force to about 50 compounders for use in emulsions, paints, sealants, and adhesives. The metalworking fluid biocides—Kathon 886 MW and Kathon MWX—were sold through a network of formulator/distributors. All of them

---

[1] The technology involves dispersing, or emulsifying, certain monomers in a fluid such as water. Then the monomers are polymerized—linked together through a chemical reaction. The resulting emulsion polymer retains the viscosity of water. When exposed to air, the water evaporates and a continuous, tough film remains.

EXHIBIT 1   Sales and Profits by Business Segments, 1979–1983 (millions of dollars)

	1983	1982	1981	1980	1979
Net sales:					
Polymers, resins, and monomers	$ 745	$ 707	$ 753	$ 665	$ 626
Plastics	390	353	376	345	345
Industrial chemicals	336	331	324	303	265
Agricultural chemicals	337	336	308	295	243
Other industries	68	101	124	117	111
Total	$1,876	$1,828	$1,885	$1,725	$1,590
Net earnings:					
Polymers, resins, and monomers	$ 79	$47	$45	$53	$50
Plastics	33	9	14	16	27
Industrial chemicals	22	12	23	23	20
Agricultural chemicals	18	24	21	20	16
Other industries	(11)	2	(6)	(9)	(1)
Corporate	(3)	(8)	(4)	(9)	(16)
Total	$138	$86	$93	$94	$96
RONA[a]:					
Polymers, resins, and monomers	19.7%	12.9%	11.5%	12.8%	12.1%
Plastics	13.9	3.7	5.2	7.3	13.2
Industrial chemicals	12.6	7.4	13.1	13.8	12.0
Agricultural chemicals	7.2	9.1	7.2	9.8	9.7
Other industries	(6.3)	1.2	(4.2)	(6.1)	(1.0)
Total	10.5%	7.6%	7.9%	8.9%	9.6%

NOTE: Net earnings are from continuing operations (before extraordinary credit in 1979) and are after the allocation of corporate expenses and income taxes. Income taxes are allocated based on the tax effect of transactions included in pretax income. Corporate consists mainly of after-tax interest income and expense.

[a]Return on net assets (RONA) equals net earnings from continuing operations plus after-tax interest expense, divided by year-end total assets.

SOURCE: Company records.

manufactured and sold metalworking fluids as well as any auxiliary products such as biocides and corrosion inhibitors. As market manager, Macey was responsible for formulating the marketing strategies for the three products under her charge, all of which were sold by the Specialty Chemicals sales force.

Fourteen of the 40 salespeople employed by the Industrial Chemicals business unit worked for the Specialty Chemicals Group and were responsible for selling all the products of the group (surfactants, biocides, and polymers) to various markets. Salespeople were assigned to exclusive territories and were supervised by three district managers who reported to a national field sales manager based at the Philadelphia headquarters.

All members of the sales force had college degrees in chemistry, chemical engineering, or related fields. The salesperson's role was to offer help and advice to the user in formulation or process design; for example, they recommended appropriate chemical levels for cooling tower treatment or detergent formulations. Starting salaries for trainees ranged from $20,000 to $27,000 annually, and the experienced

EXHIBIT 2 Organization Chart: Specialty Chemicals Group

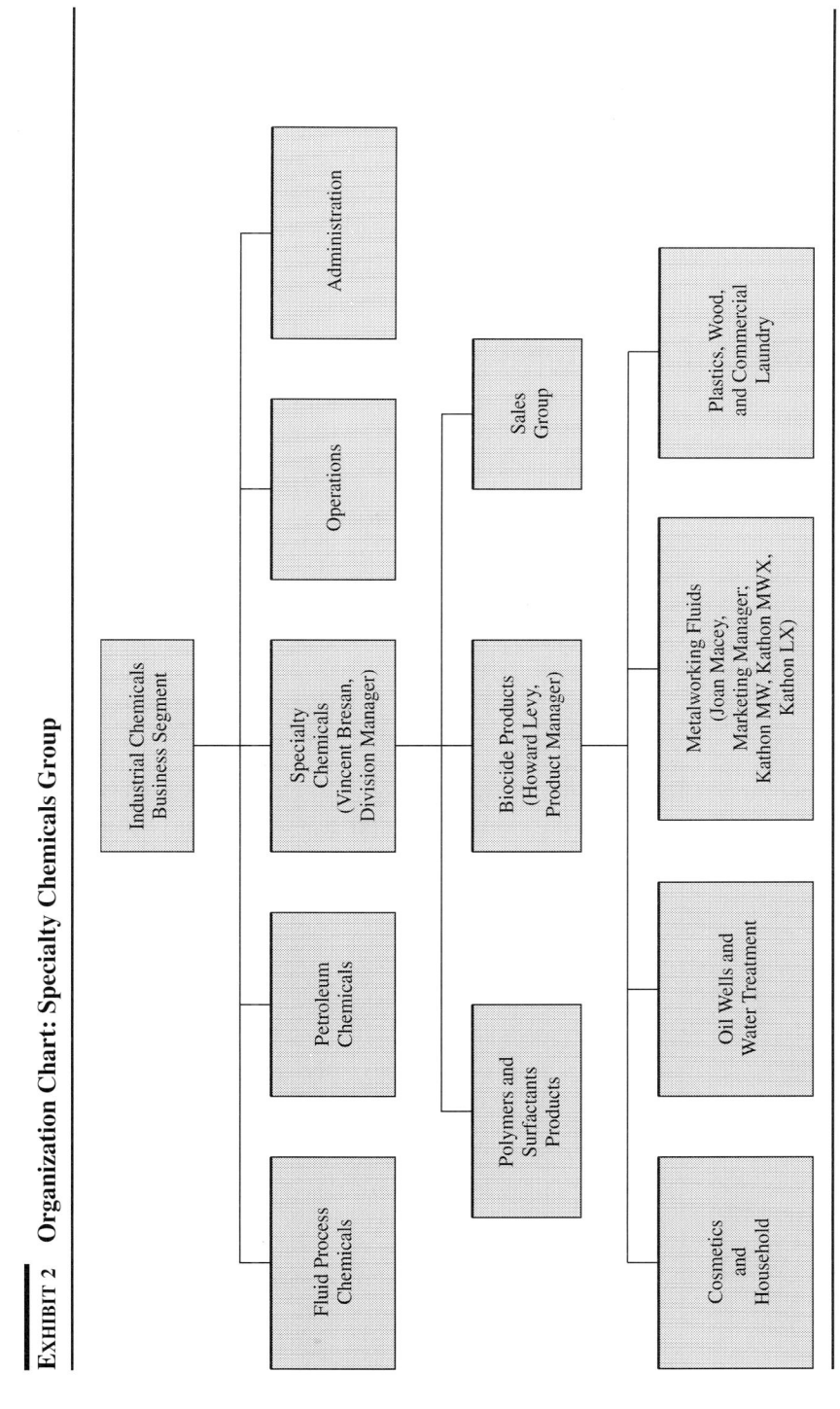

salesperson could earn $50,000 to $70,000. Salespeople were evaluated on several objectives, including new account activity, market penetration, and quantity sold in pounds. Six of the 14 salespeople had most of the biocide customers in their respective territories. On average, they spent about 20 to 30 percent of their time on all biocide customers; approximately one-third of this time was spent on metalworking fluid formulators (the primary customers for Kathon 886 MW and Kathon MWX). The rest of the time was spent visiting users. Many of these calls were made jointly with the formulators' salespeople.

Metalworking Fluid Biocides

Metalworking fluid, as the name implies, is used in operations such as turning, milling, grinding, honing, and drilling. The fluid is directed onto the surface of the metal being machined to lubricate and cool the workpiece and the machine tool and to remove chips and debris from the work area.

In 1983 about 60 million gallons of metalworking fluid concentrate were produced in the United States. Nearly all of it had to be diluted with water by the user. Water was typically 90 to 95 percent of the mixture after dilution. The diluted fluid was then placed in a reservoir and pumped to a nozzle that directed the fluid to the machined piece (see Exhibit 3). A tray built into the workstation caught chips, and the used fluid was filtered and returned to the reservoir for reuse.

Microorganisms such as bacteria, fungi, and yeast flourish in the warm aqueous environment of metal machining, and their growth increases with poor shop maintenance. They break down the metalworking fluids, and as the microorganisms develop, they multiply in long chains to clog filters, flow lines, and drains. Their foul-smelling, metabolic by-products stain and corrode workpieces and pollute the work environment.

Biocides are chemicals that kill the microorganisms in water-based metalworking fluids without affecting fluid performance. They have many applications in manufacturing products such as cosmetics, paper detergents, and latex paints. They are used, as well, in water treatment and oil field drilling.

Chemical companies formulate metalworking-fluid concentrates by mixing emulsified oils and special additives. Formulators often add biocides to the metalworking fluid concentrate to provide some initial protection against contamination. The concentrate is then sent to users, who dilute it for their machining operations. Metalworking fluids are depleted by water evaporation and fluid loss and must be replenished each day. As the fluid ages, the concentrate biocide no longer adequately protects it, and a maintenance biocide must be added to extend fluid life. A metalworking system kept free of bacteria, yeast, or fungi uses fluid for a much longer period of time—one or two weeks longer than the three to four weeks for a less well-maintained system. Regular treatment with maintenance biocides and makeup metalworking fluid (every one or two weeks) extends fluid life almost indefinitely and does not require a complete flushing of the fluid tank.

Exhibit 3 Metalworking Fluid

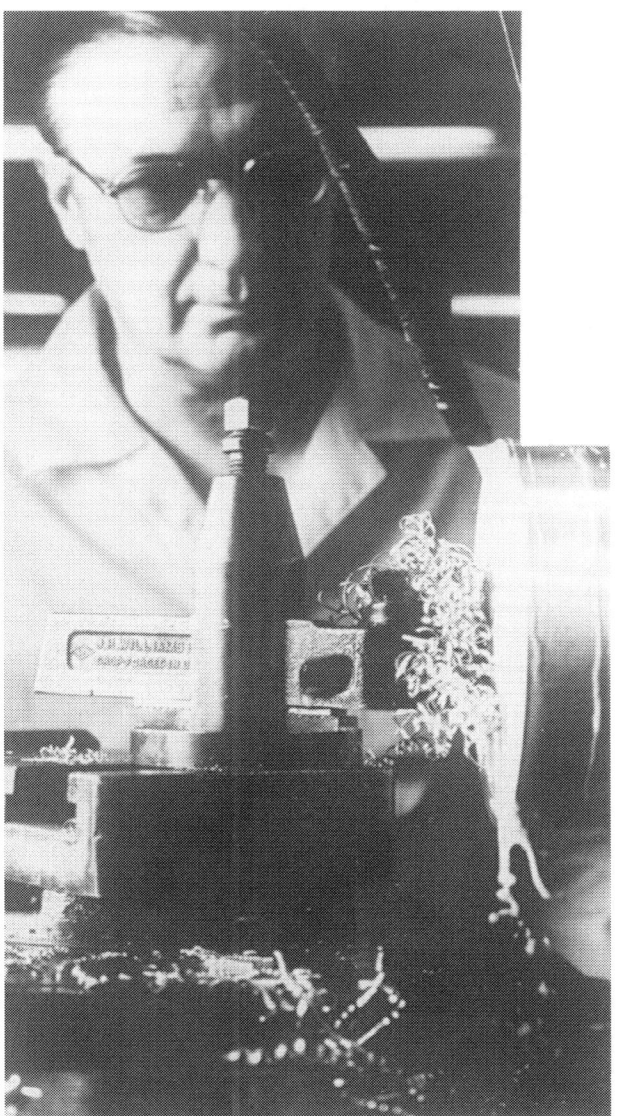

Source: Company material.

The *concentrate biocide* market was estimated to be $30 million in 1983. Industry sources predicted a downward sales trend, however, because of the growing use of maintenance biocides. The *maintenance biocide* market was estimated to be about $38 million in 1983, but if industry predictions were right, it would replace nearly all of the concentrate biocide market in 10 years.

Kathon Metalworking Fluid Biocides

Kathon 886 MW, a liquid, was the primary maintenance biocide on the market. Too reactive to be used in the metalworking fluid concentrate, it extended the life of diluted fluids in central system reservoirs. Kathon 886 MW was a broad-spectrum biocide generally 10 times more effective than competitive biocides. One gallon of Kathon 886 MW protected 8,000 to 10,000 gallons of metalworking fluid in a central reservoir initially for three weeks. About 10–15 gallons of a competitive product would be required to do the same job. In 1983, Kathon 886 MW had a 30 percent share of the $18 million maintenance biocide market for large systems. It was distributed by 12 major metalworking fluid formulators, who sold it as part of a fluid maintenance package to their customers. From a practical standpoint, because of its low use level and toxic properties, it could not be used in metalworking fluid reservoirs smaller than 1,000 gallons without creating misuse problems and safety risks.

Customers who were satisfied with the performance of Kathon 886 MW had asked for a convenient, safe-to-use version for their smaller (50- to 100-gallon) reservoirs. A market survey revealed that this was the most common reservoir size for small machines. Rohm and Haas technicians responded with an intense product development effort that led to the development of Kathon MWX.

After attempts to formulate a water-soluble solid product had failed, a unique packaging design to deliver liquid biocide was developed (Exhibit 4). It was a 5.5-×-7.5-inch water-permeable plastic packet containing two ounces of diatomaceous earth[2] soaked with Kathon 886 MW. The packet was designed to hang into the metalworking fluid reservoir by a strap suspended on a plastic hook and could treat 25 to 75 gallons of metalworking fluid for 2 to 4 weeks. The customer simply placed the packet in the metalworking fluid; water then flowed through the packet and gradually transferred the biocide from the diatomaceous earth to the fluid. The used packet could be removed from the reservoir for disposal at the first sign of failure (odor) or in one month. No maintenance was required, and the packet was safe to handle and dispense. In expanding the fluid maintenance market to include small machine applications, it was estimated that the potential existed for $20 million in added sales volume.

Although Kathon 886 MW and MWX were maintenance biocides, they could be used in only 70 percent of the metalworking fluids. Incompatibility with the concentrate biocide in the original formulation rendered them ineffective with the other 30 percent. By comparison, however, competitive maintenance biocides were compatible in only about 45 percent of commercial metalworking fluids.

---

[2] An inert solid that when mixed with Kathon had the consistency of moist sand.

EXHIBIT 4   Kathon MWX User Information

Kathon® MWX
Biocide Packets
for small machine maintenance

Extends fluid life
Extends fluid life
Extends fluid life
Extends fluid life
Extends fluid life
Extends fluid life
Extends fluid life

- **Extends fluid life**
- **Controls bacteria and fungi**
- **Eliminates odor**
- **Minimizes machine downtime**
- **Effective over a wide pH range**
- **Easy to use, safer to handle**
- **Does not release formaldehyde**
- **Readily disposable**
- **EPA registered for metalworking fluids**

Customers

In 1983, there were about 325 potential customers for Kathon 886 MW or equivalent products, and an estimated 150,000 potential customers for Kathon MWX. Table A on page 157 breaks down the metalworking industry by machine size.

Exhibit 4 (concluded)

What is Kathon MWX?

It is a safer-to-handle plastic packet containing a highly water soluble biocide which controls bacteria and fungi, including the odors they produce.

How should you use Kathon MWX?

Simply attach the packet to the hook provided and suspend it from the edge of the sump into a 50 gallon reservoir of dilute soluble, semi-synthetic or synthetic metalworking fluid.

How many Kathon MWX packets should be used?

For noticeably rancid fluids, use 1-2 unopened 2 ounce packets for every 50 gallons of fluid every 1-2 weeks. Follow this with a maintenance dose of one packet for every 50 gallons every 2-4 weeks.

How does Kathon MWX work?

When the packet is submerged in the fluid, the aqueous fluid enters the packet through the small pores and carries the active ingredient back out into the fluid where it destroys bacteria and fungi, including the odors they produce. This flow action will continue to release active ingredient from the packet to the reservoir until it reaches equilibrium (about 3 days). After this, the active ingredient will gradually be depleted as it continues to prevent the development of rancidity.

How will you know that Kathon MWX is doing the job?

Since the active ingredient in Kathon MWX begins to act immediately, any odor produced by the rancid fluid will be significantly reduced within several hours. Slime and other biological debris will pull away from the sides and bottom of the reservoir and disperse in approximately 3 days.

When should the Kathon MWX packet be removed from the reservoir?

The packet should be left in for a minimum of 3 days to reach equilibrium. At this time, the level of active ingredient in the packet is the same as the level in the fluid. This level – 20 ppm – is non-hazardous and similar to the level used in many consumer products. The packet may be left in place for an additional 2 to 4 weeks since it will continue to provide rancidity control until the active ingredient is essentially gone.

How should you dispose of Kathon MWX?

If the packet is removed in fewer than three days, it should be treated with a deactivating solution (see product literature) before disposal. If the packet is removed after three days, it will consist of the plastic packet, diatomaceous earth and a non-hazardous level of active ingredient. It may be disposed of as trash, unless prohibited by state or local authorities.

SOURCE: Company records.

Biocide users worked with either *nonferrous metals* such as aluminum, copper, tungsten, and titanium or *ferrous metals* such as iron and steel.

Nonferrous Metals. In the domestic market, nonferrous metals were used primarily to make aluminum sheet, foil, and cans in large-scale, fully automated, high-speed manufacturing facilities. Central systems used metalworking fluid in reservoirs as large as 150,000 gallons. Nonferrous operations required the metalworking fluid to be kept completely free of bacteria because of the sensitivity of the

TABLE A Metalworking Industry Fluid Systems

Metalworking Fluid System	Reservoir Capacity (gallons)	Number of Metalworking Machines	Number of Plants
Central system	50,000 to 250,000	170	25
Central system	8,000 to 30,000	1,530	300
Individual system	50 to 1,000	1,701,000	150,000

metal to staining, and microbiologists and chemists were often employed to develop biocide treatments and monitor systems closely. Kathon 886 MW was the favored biocide of many of these companies and held about 70 to 80 percent of a $3 million to $5 million market.

Ferrous Metals. The ferrous metal industries ranged broadly from the large-scale automated manufacture of products such as automotive and farm equipment to the smaller-scale production of pumps, instruments, aircraft parts, and nuts and bolts. Customers with large-scale manufacturing facilities had central systems similar to those in the nonferrous industries, but bacteria levels in the metalworking fluid were not as critical to ferrous metals as they were to nonferrous metals.[3] Though Kathon 886 MW was adopted by many for its cost-effectiveness, its overall share of the $12 million to $16 million ferrous market (only central systems) was only 15 to 20 percent.

Competition

Table B lists the major competitors in the biocide market. In 1983, Rohm and Haas, Lehn and Fink, Dow Chemical, and Angus Chemical each had approximately 15 to 20 percent of the maintenance biocide market.

It was assumed that Lehn and Fink and Angus Chemical each employed three salespersons for metalworking biocides. Lehn and Fink sold directly to distributors and end-users, and distributors were supplied at 10 percent off list price. Angus Chemical sold to distributors and end-users at the same price.

Olin Corporation's Triadine-10, introduced in 1983, was well received by the market. Two other major chemical companies were planning entries into the maintenance biocide market: Union Carbide, with Gluteraldehyde, and ICI, with Proxel, both for central systems. Rohm and Haas chemists conducted comparative tests (see Exhibit 5) to demonstrate that Kathon 886 MW was still the most cost-effective biocide for central systems.

---

[3]The ferrous industry generally accepted up to 50,000 cfu/ml of bacteria (50,000 colony-forming units of bacteria per milliliter of metalworking fluid).

Section II Managing New Products

Table B Competitors' Products

Company	Concentrate Biocide	Maintenance Biocide	
		Central Systems	Stand-Alone Systems
1. Lehn and Fink	Grotan	Grotan	—
2. Dow Chemical	—	Dowicil 75 DBNPA	Dowicil 75 —
3. Angus Chemical	Bioban P-1487	Tris Nitro	Tris Nitro
4. Olin Corporation	Triadine-10	Triadine-10	—
5. Millmaster Onyx	—	Onyxide 200	—
6. RT Vanderbilt	—	Vancide TH	—
7. Merck	—	Tektamer 38 A.D.	—

The most widely known product for individual systems was Tris Nitro "Sump Saver" tablets, an Angus product. One two-ounce tablet treated 25 gallons of metalworking fluid. Macey estimated that distributors paid $4.00/pound (eight tablets) and sold them to customers for $7.75/pound. Unlike Kathon MWX, these tablets dissolved in the metalworking fluid. They were generally considered less effective against bacteria and ineffective against fungi, and they worked for only about three days.

Another product, Dowicil 75, came in water-soluble packages that were dropped into the reservoir. Each 2.5-pound package treated 500 gallons of fluid. Macey estimated the cost to distributors at $2.34/pound and a resale price of $10/pound. While Dowicil 75 performed well against both bacteria and fungi, it had a heavy ammonia odor, released formaldehyde, and could not be safely used in reservoirs with capacities less than 500 gallons.

Some metalworking operators in small shops, in a makeshift effort to control the odor released by bacteria, poured household bleaches, disinfectants, deodorants, and similar materials into their smaller reservoirs. The odors of these materials usu-

Exhibit 5 Kathon 886 MW Cost-Effectiveness

Comparative Cost of Treating a 10,000 Gallon System with Biocide (for one cycle)

I. With Dowicil 75
10,000 gallons[a] × 8.4 pounds[b]/gallon × 0.15%[c] × $2.14[d]/pound = $269.64

II. With Grotan
10,000 gallons × 8.4 pounds/gallon × 0.15% × $1.20/pound = $151.20

III. With Kathon 886 MW
10,000 gallons × 8.4 pounds/gallon × 0.01% × $8.50/pound = $71.40

[a]This corresponds to approximately 400 gallons of metalworking fluid concentrate.
[b]Weight of metalworking fluid per gallon.
[c]Biocide concentration required for treatment.
[d]Biocide price to end-user.
Source: Company records.

ally combined with the bacterial odor to make the working environment even worse for the workers. These substitute materials also interfered with the cooling and lubricating performance of the metalworking fluid.

Distribution Channels

The metalworking fluid formulators were the first level of distributors in this industry. They purchased biocides, both concentrate and maintenance, directly from the manufacturers. The concentrate biocide was incorporated into the metalworking fluid at the time of its formulation. The formulators then sold the metalworking fluid directly to large companies and to other dealers who resold it to smaller accounts. Metalworking fluid generally accounted for more than 90 percent of a formulator's business. As a service to customers with large central reservoir systems, distributors provided a maintenance package that usually included delivery, fluid preparation, weekly monitoring for microorganisms, and maintenance biocide treatments. Other special-purpose chemicals such as pH adjusters and corrosion inhibitors were provided as needed. Many of these products were sold under the formulators' private brand names. Most formulators engaged in R&D, acceptance testing of manufacturers' additives, and systems monitoring.

In 1983 the total sales of 10 large national formulators were roughly $200 million. Another 20 to 30 formulators had a combined sales volume of some $100 million. Several hundred small formulators had sales of $0.5 million to $1 million each. Because of the number and fragmentation of the ferrous metalworking industries, large formulators distributed their products through a secondary distribution network, consisting primarily of industrial supply houses and machine tool shops.

Industrial supply houses ranged from small, family managed companies in rural areas to large, professionally managed companies in urban areas. Some specialized in serving particular industry sectors. They were "supermarkets" for their customers. A supply house servicing a ferrous metalworking industry, for example, might carry several brands of biocides, safety accessories, uniforms, small general-purpose tools, shop cleaning and maintenance supplies, worktables, hand trucks, concrete blocks, spill absorbents, and hand soaps.

The 1982 Census of Wholesale Trade listed 14,327 industrial supply houses in the United States. A major metropolitan area might have over 100 supply houses serving a variety of industries. Industrial supply house sales in 1982 amounted to approximately $40 billion. Inside salespeople took telephone orders from regular customers and over-the-counter orders from walk-in customers. Outside salespeople generated new accounts and called on regular customers.

Machine tool shops specialized in distributing and servicing machine tools and items used with them like spare parts, tool bits, metalworking fluids, and biocides. Some also served as sources of metals. There were 3,654 such companies in the United States, and in 1982 their sales were $8.7 billion.

Typically, large industrial companies (e.g., General Motors, Caterpillar Tractor) purchased biocides directly from manufacturers or from their distributors (formulators). They used the secondary network of industrial supply houses and machine tool shops for miscellaneous items (such as safety equipment or paper towels) that were not critical to their line of business. Small companies, however, often relied exclusively on industrial supply houses and machine tool shops for all their needs.

Marketing Strategy for Kathon MWX

Ten of Rohm and Haas's 12 distributors (formulators of metalworking fluid) agreed to distribute Kathon MWX in addition to Kathon 886 MW. The company offered private branding on Kathon 886 MW, but not on Kathon MWX. Though many formulators asked for private branding, only one distributor declined to carry Kathon MWX when turned down on a request for its own-brand product. Explaining the rationale for this policy, a company manager said:

> Kathon MWX is the industrial equivalent of a consumer packaged good; it is a "baggie" product packaged at the factory. We need some uniformity in package design. Moreover, we want the end-user to know it's a Rohm and Haas product. Our end-users hardly see the Kathon 886 MW drum because our formulators include the product as a part of their maintenance service. But Kathon MWX is different; we expect the end-users to do the maintenance themselves.

Kathon MWX was packed in boxes containing 144 packets, each packet weighing two ounces. Quantity prices to distributors per box of 144 packets were as follows:

1–2 boxes	$180.00
3–4 boxes	$165.00
5+ boxes	$145.00

Joan Macey estimated the manufacturing cost per packet to be about 50 cents. The company did not specify a price to end-users, but most formulators charged end-users and other dealers $2/packet. Some formulators had a strong secondary distribution network consisting of 200 to 300 industrial supply houses, and in such instances, the secondary level of distribution was known to add a 10 percent margin. One of the company's distributors with a sales force of 700 commissioned reps claimed that he could sell each packet for $6 to the end-users.

The product launch (December 1983) was accompanied by a press release in 40 metalworking industry journals announcing the availability of Kathon MWX. The announcement included information about characteristics of Kathon MWX and its benefits. Full-page advertisements costing $3,800 each were placed in five issues of *American Machinist* between February and June 1984. Interested readers could get further information and a two-packet sample by filling out a reader service coupon. Over 200 such inquiries were received from the February, March, and April advertisements. All inquiries were forwarded to distributors. Rohm and Haas responded directly with a copy of the very colorful ad, a material safety data sheet, a set of technical notes, and a how-to-use booklet (see Exhibit 4). Distributors were expected to follow up on the leads and generate orders.

In spite of all these efforts, the sales in the first five months of the launch period barely touched $12,000.

Joan Macey's Dilemma

Disappointed with Kathon MWX's sales performance, Macey began a review of her marketing plan to take any necessary corrective steps. She also sought opinions from two of her colleagues in the Specialty Chemicals division who had successfully launched and established new products. Her first colleague advised:

> You are too hard on yourself, Joan. New products don't succeed overnight. It takes years for the product to get market acceptance and longer still to get dealer support. If you feel comfortable about your original marketing plan, it's worthwhile giving it a chance. We are in the business of specialty chemicals, we offer solutions to customers' problems. We are not in the fashion business!

Her second colleague felt differently; he agreed that Kathon MWX's initial marketing approach was probably not best suited for the product. He encouraged Macey to review the marketing plan, saying, "The only good news on Kathon MWX is that you know there is a problem; therefore you can fix it."

Regardless of what she might ultimately do about her strategy for marketing the product, Macey thought it would be a good idea to contact the 200 prospects who had responded to the reader service coupons. Macey employed a summer trainee who was working toward an MBA to conduct a telephone survey. Explaining her rationale for the survey, she said:

> I wish I could thoroughly research the market, but that's not possible. Frankly, what else can I do with the limited budget I have for support activities? Kathon MWX has to show some initial movement before further resources are justified. It is imperative that I make a quick decision. After all, I have other products to manage and my boss has the entire biocide business to manage. One has to place Kathon MWX in its proper perspective. A quick survey should do that.

The survey revealed several major facts:

1. On average, customers discarded used metalworking fluid after three weeks. Rancidity and dermatitis[4] were the primary reasons for this, and most customers believed that bacteria, not metal particles or harsh chemicals, caused the dermatitis.

2. Although most survey participants had their used fluids hauled away, few knew how much this service cost. Those who did know gave figures of $0.29, $0.55, $1.80, and $2.00 per gallon of used fluid.

---

[4]Dermatitis symptoms are skin eruptions and rashes that last anywhere from a few hours to a few weeks.

3. Only about 20 percent of the participants remembered receiving the Kathon MWX information packet. When asked about the image of the product conveyed by the promotional literature, many said that the product was worth trying. Despite their inclination to use Kathon MWX, they expressed some apprehension about its safety. An explanation of the proper handling technique usually overcame these fears.
4. Users obtained metalworking fluids from tool shops, oil companies, formulators, and industrial supply shops. The majority sourced from two or more small, local tool or supply shops within 30 miles of their businesses, as well as one of the large national formulators. Users occasionally found it necessary to write to a large national distributor for supplies that were not locally available.
5. About 50 percent of the users used products ranging from household disinfectants to metalworking fluid biocides to kill odor-causing bacteria in their machine sumps. The majority of these products did not seem to work, yet the end-user, typically, continued to use the product. Only half of the participants who had tried a biocide could remember its name. None had tried Kathon MWX.

From the summer trainee's survey report, Macey extracted the cost information that she thought would be useful in a review of Kathon MWX's marketing strategy (see Exhibit 6). She wondered if raising the price would increase end-user perception of the product's value. She wondered what short-term and long-term sales and market share targets were appropriate for Kathon MWX. Concerned about the appropriateness of the current channels of distribution for Kathon MWX, she considered other options. Finally, of course, she wondered if Kathon 886 MW was a help or hindrance in developing a market for Kathon MWX, especially since marketing plans for Kathon 886 MW projected a healthy growth in distribution and market share.

EXHIBIT 6 Cost Information Gathered from Survey Data

	Average Cost
Metalworking fluid concentrate	$5.68/gallon[a]
Waste disposal	$1.36/gallon[b]
Kathon MWX	$2/packet

- 1 packet of Kathon MWX treats 25–50 gallons of diluted metalworking fluid.
- A typical small machine shop had 22 machines, each with a reservoir capacity of 50 gallons. It discarded fluid every four weeks. By using Kathon MWX they could keep the fluid 2–5 weeks longer.
- Machine downtime, labor, and water costs were negligible for small machines. Costs of other additives (buffers, corrosion inhibitors) were not considered in a differential analysis.

[a] Per gallon of undiluted fluid. A dilution ratio of 1:24 is assumed.
[b] Per gallon of diluted fluid.

CHAPTER 10
Northern Telecom (A): Greenwich Investment Proposal

The general manager for the Business Products Division proposes to replace an existing loss-making product with a new product, code-named Greenwich. At an investment of $54 million he hopes to succeed in this very-price-competitive market served by nearly 100 suppliers.

Proposing significant new investment in the Business Products Division (BPD) had not been part of Mike Ennis's mandate. Installed as the general manager of this Northern Telecom division in February 1985, his assignment was clear: to "stop the bleeding." The Calgary, Canada-based division had generated negative cash flow of $61 million over the past three years manufacturing and marketing the Vantage[1] key system, a telephone system targeted to small businesses. Vantage had achieved the Number 1 share position in Canada but it was eroding, and the product had failed to achieve any significant sales in the United States, holding less than a 1 percent share.

Now, in November 1985, Ennis had prepared a proposal entailing an additional $54 million investment by Northern to develop a completely new key system product line to replace Vantage. Ennis's business plan for this new product line, code-named Greenwich, included arresting the decline and modestly improving Canadian market share, achieving a 15 percent share in the United States by 1991, lowering production costs, and greatly improving product reliability. The North American key systems market had over 100 suppliers. Ennis's proposal was for Greenwich to become the product of choice for resellers and end-users by virtue of its simplicity.

This case was prepared by Robert J. Dolan.
Copyright © 1993 by the President and Fellows of Harvard College.
Harvard Business School case 594-051.
[1]Vantage is a registered trademark of Northern Telecom.

Background

A variety of equipment was involved in connecting all the world's telephone sets to one another. Each terminal had to be "switched" to connect to any other terminal (see Figure 1).

FIGURE 1

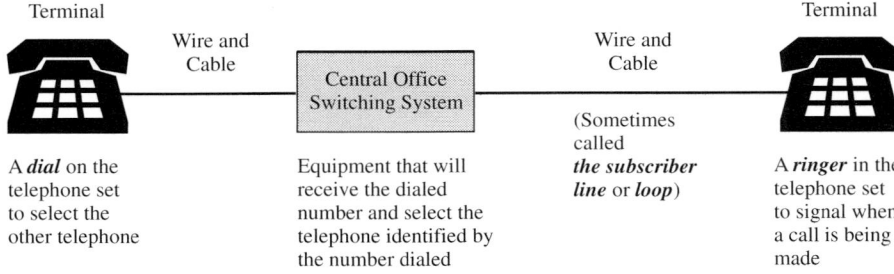

A major city may have had several central office switches, and each significant population center usually had one switch. For each terminal to reach any other terminal, the central office switches must be connected to each other. This was accomplished with wire and cable or electronic equipment (see Figure 2).

Many telephone or terminal users were associated with each other in an office environment (in a business, hospital, etc.), with most of the communication needs being between fellow employees rather than with the outside world. Under these circumstances, it was often uneconomical to connect each telephone or terminal to a central office which might be several miles away. Instead, switching equipment was placed on the business subscriber's premises. This type of switching equipment was often called a private branch exchange (PBX).

The equipment needed to provide this overall networking capability is grouped under the heading of Business Communications and Networks (see Figure 3).

FIGURE 2

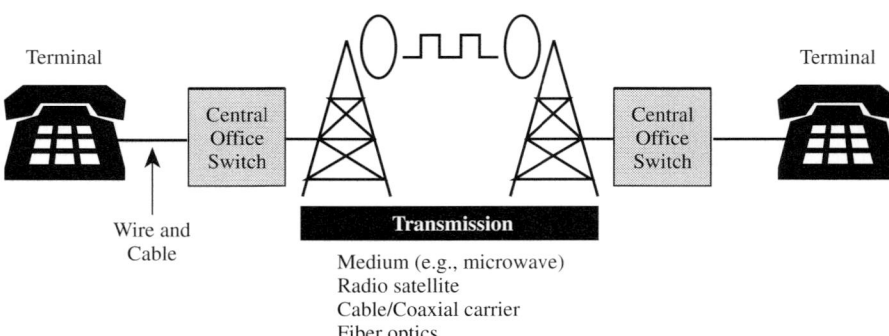

FIGURE 3

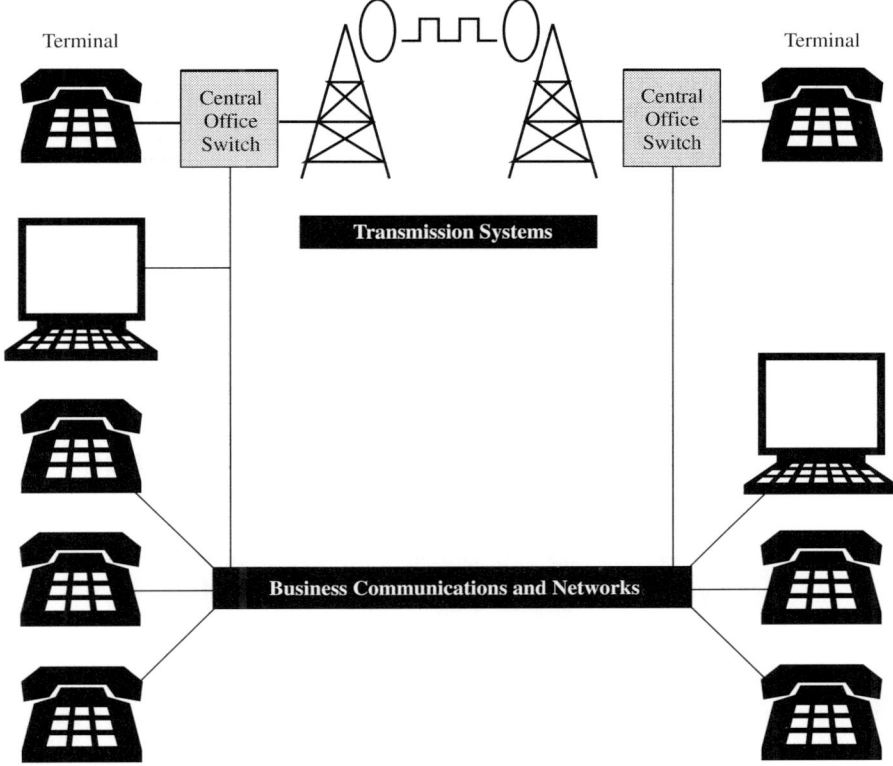

Northern's 1984 sales revenue of $3.4 billion was largely divided among these three product lines:

1. Central office switches (50 percent of sales revenue).
2. Business communication systems (30 percent of sales revenue): This product line was made up of private branch exchanges, commonly known as PBXs, and key systems.
   a. Key systems were designed for small businesses with between 2 and 100 employees and, unlike the PBX business, were a highly fragmented business with over 100 different suppliers. (Only Northern and AT&T had manufacturing operations in North America. All other suppliers were offering product produced in the Pacific Rim.) A key system consisted of a set of telephone stations and a central control unit, called a key system unit (KSU). A key system needed access either to a Central Office Switch or PBX for "outside calls." It offered small firms the advantage over Centrex of handling calls within the organization without access fees; in addition, multiple stations (i.e., telephone sets) could be linked to the system. The key system business was not as

technologically demanding for suppliers as the Centrex or PBX business, and entry barriers were low.

    b. PBXs were targeted to organizations with 100 or more employees. Northern was one of the leaders in the PBX market in North America, along with AT&T, Rolm, and MITEL. PBX systems were, typically, sold through and installed by local telephone companies. A PBX system investment could range up to $15 million for a large organization.

3. Transmission equipment (12 percent of sales revenue).

Through its participation in the Central Office and PBX markets, Northern had good relationships with local telephone companies (telcos) throughout North America. These firms were Northern's major customers for Central Office systems and major resellers or distribution networks for PBXs. In the 1980s, the U.S. market had undergone a drastic change when AT&T was forced to divest its 23 local companies. These 23 companies were reorganized into 7 Regional Bell Operating Companies (RBOCs): Ameritech, Bell Atlantic, Bell South, NYNEX, Pacific Telesis, Southwestern Bell, and U.S. West. As part of the legal process creating the RBOCs, they were forbidden from manufacturing telephone equipment. AT&T kept its long-distance network and maintained the right to manufacture equipment, thus being a competitor of Northern.

Business Products Division

The Vantage System was designed to be state-of-the-art in electronic key systems. Vantage, AT&T's Merlin system, and the systems of many Pac-Rim suppliers represented significant advances over the "plain old telephone set." They offered the small-business user features such as speed dialing, call forwarding, conferencing, intercom, and volume controls. Vantage was targeted at the business user needing between 2 and 50 stations within the organization. However, the Vantage product line had difficulty from the beginning. A Northern document written to capture the "Learning from Vantage" chronicled the product's history as follows:

> Ultimately a good system, the Vantage key system came too slowly and too late. . . . Launched in 1977 in London, Ontario, and moved out to Calgary when the Business Products Division (BPD) was created, Vantage took a glacial seven years to cover the small-business market. During that time, its technological superiority vanished; what remained was a potentially attractive system with severe cost and quality problems. Deregulation aggravated the cost problem. Once a multitude of offshore products became available from telcos and interconnect dealers (the sales channels),[2] consumers began to

---

[2]The regional telephone companies (telcos) were important resellers in the North American market, particularly so in Canada. In Canada, they handled 70 percent of key systems sales. Independent dealers sold the other 30 percent. The distribution channels in the United States were more complex since AT&T sold its own brand, Merlin, directly to end-users. This accounted for 42 percent of sales. Telcos accounted for 25 percent—18 percent by RBOCs and 7 percent by independents. Dealers sold the other 33 percent.

make their own choices. All else being roughly equal, they chose overwhelmingly on the basis of price.

Vantage was expensive all across the size range, and particularly in the sensitive lower end. The first Vantage had been a mid-sized system, and the small system bore many of its expensive characteristics. To price-sensitive buyers, these superior features meant nothing. The absence of a full-range product (and particularly the lack of a viable entry-level system that could grow with a new company), then the crushing blow of deregulation hobbled the business; a division staffed and equipped to handle the North American market was actually handling only a shrinking portion of the Canadian market. Economies forced by the division's perilous financial position slowed the redesign work that was essential to improve the quality and lower the cost. Suppliers' efforts to improve their quality were hampered by traditional supplier/customer attitudes compounded by distance and the division's siege mentality. An unhelpful attitude to the sales channels' problems further tarnished a lackluster reputation. All key systems were plagued by a variety of technical problems, plus the unanticipated complexity of training technicians and users. Effective resolution of these problems was important to the telcos, because just two service calls a year to a customer site will eliminate their margins. The division, however, disavowed responsibility for nontechnical issues; telcos and dealers were effectively forced to demonstrate a genuine technical issue before a problem would be addressed.

While the strong reputation of Northern Telecom in Canada propelled Vantage to be the best-selling key system in the Canadian market at one time, it failed to achieve even 1 percent share in the United States. The Calgary operation had been set up in anticipation of this appreciable U.S. market penetration. This, plus all the "fix up" problems in Canada, led to continuing losses:

	Vantage Sales	Net Income
1982	$29MM	($23MM)
1983	$50MM	($20MM)
1984	$72MM	($18MM)

Thus, when Ennis took over in February 1985, he was asked to analyze four options:

1. Abandon key systems.
2. Maintain status quo with better controls.
3. Shut down Calgary and consolidate key systems into another division.
4. Keep Calgary operating—but as a cost center, subordinated to another division's P&L.

Ennis explained his philosophy:

I am an old banker. I knew that if you are into a bank for $70 million as we were, they would like to find a way to work with you to turn it around—rather than just walk away from it. None of these options I was supposed to look at had a chance of turning it

TABLE B Comparison of Key Market Statistics for 1985 and 1991 Projection

	1985	1991 Projection
U.S. market (units sold per year)	5.5 million	5.5 million
Canadian market (units sold per year)	455 thousand	539 thousand
Total dollar market value	1.6 billion	1.1 billion
Manufacturer's average net revenue received per station	$268.00	$182.00

SOURCE: Company records.

around. So, that's why I decided to look at the "Expand" option even though nobody asked me to. What would it cost to do key systems right, and what kind of impact could we expect if we did it right? It was obvious we needed a new product. I figured it would cost $35 million to get a first release to market and $50 million to deliver a full product line. Six million dollars of this was to revamp internal processes. With this kind of investment, you would have to get 20 to 25 percent market share in the United States in the longer term. Then, to have a really important business, you'd have to build off the North American market and compete globally. Could we do it?

Key statistics on the market in 1985 and projected changes by 1991 are given in Table B.

A variety of market research procedures delivered the same conclusion: the Key Systems industry had failed to deliver *useable* functionality to the desktop. A Northern study concluded: "Simplicity has not been adequately addressed by any competitor. Lack of simplicity is the greatest source of end-user dissatisfaction and a significant source of cost to the channel. Simplicity is focused on self-evident feature usage and system administration via terminal displays."[3]

The net of the consumer research was that Ennis and his team perceived an opportunity with consumers if Northern provided a product with an "appropriate price, absolute simplicity, and useable functionality."

Reseller Analysis

End-users were not particularly knowledgeable about the key systems. While price sensitive, the typical buyer's search-and-acquisition process for a key system was: "I called the telephone company and they came out and put one in." This made achieving distribution and reseller support key for manufacturers. The reseller situation was dramatically different in the Canadian and U.S. markets. In Canada, the re-

---

[3] Self-evident feature usage: making a feature work as a user would intuitively think it would without reference to a manual. System administration via terminal displays: having liquid crystal display on the phone set which could walk a user through how to access a particular feature. (This would obviate the need for reference to a manual.)

EXHIBIT 1   Key System Distribution Channels in the United States, 1984

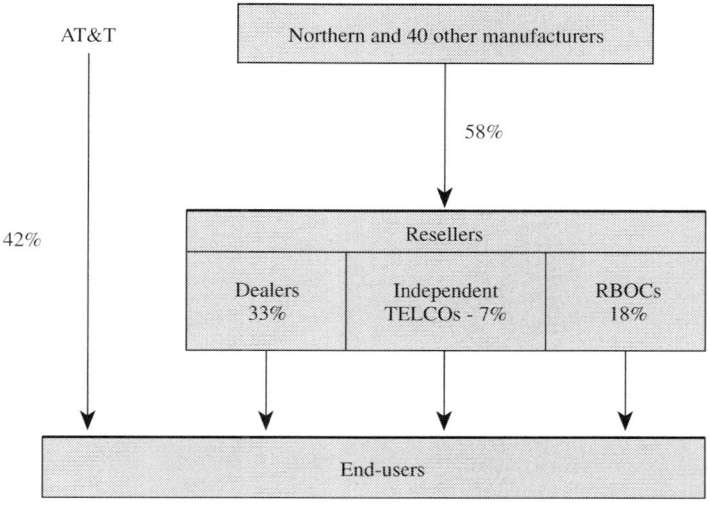

gional telephone companies sold 70 percent of units, while independent dealers sold the remaining 30 percent. As shown in Exhibit 1, the dominant channel in the United States was AT&T selling its own product direct to end users. AT&T was a fully integrated supplier offering its own branded product (Merlin) supported by an AT&T sales and service organization. With divestiture in 1984, AT&T chose not to sell its PBX or key system equipment to the Regional Bell Operating Companies. Regulations precluded the RBOCs from manufacturing their own equipment. The other 58 percent of the market was sold through dealers (33 percent), independent telecommunications companies such as GTE (7 percent), and the RBOCs (18 percent). While there were about 100 manufacturers of key systems worldwide, 40 suppliers actively vied for the business of these resellers. With the exception of Northern Telecom, all of these manufactured in the Pacific Rim. The two dominant ones in 1984 were TIE with 19 percent share of the total U.S. key system market and MITEL with 16 percent.

While the key systems market had grown rapidly in the early 1980s, resellers had not been able to make satisfactory profits. The lack of simplicity in useability with respect to the end-user resulted in many calls to resellers for additional training. Many repair requests turned out to have been made for properly functioning equipment not being used properly. Since the products were typically under warranty, "repairs" were a cost, not a source of revenue, for resellers. Although the number of potential vendors and lack of significant product differentiation led to continual price wars, this did not translate into satisfactory levels of reseller profit, due to these "repair" and other costs. Also, resupply from the Pac-Rim was unreliable. The Pac-Rim manufacturers operated on a four-month replenishment cycle.

EXHIBIT 2 Key Financial Projections for Expand Option (US$ millions)

	Plan Year				
	1986	*1987*	*1988*	*1989*	*1990*
Total sales ($):	68.3	74.7	108.1	186.1	240.2
Canada	39.1	35.8	39.4	50.5	59.8
United States	27.6	37.5	67.3	124.3	159.2
International	1.6	1.4	1.4	11.3	21.2
Cost of sales (% sales)	75	70	65	61	61
Sales and marketing (% sales)	12	15	13	13	12
R&D ($)	8.7	12.4	11.0	11.2	10.9
EBT	(4.9)	(2.9)	6.2	22.6	32.7
Cash flow	(3.7)	(2.3)	(.7)	(2.4)	12.7

Market growth patterns were irregular, making the resellers' forecasting task difficult. In most cases, inventory was badly managed. In 1985, many resellers were in heavily overbought positions. The mentality was that large levels of inventory were one's only protection against demand uncertainty and the long replenishment cycle from the Pac-Rim. New vendors and new products also obsoleted resellers' inventory. In general, Northern's research showed widespread reseller dissatisfaction, centering around the complexity of running a key systems business. The question was whether Northern could convert this reseller dissatisfaction into a viable key systems business throughout North America.

Ennis developed the financial projections for the investment option shown in Exhibit 2. This plan represented an early 1988 launch of Greenwich and 1990 market shares of 53 percent and 15 percent in the Canadian and U.S. markets, respectively. Ennis believed that a $54 million R&D investment could deliver a full Greenwich product line—starting with an entry-level system with the right cost level and then modular additions to this basic architecture to reach more performance-oriented, larger customers. In 1986 and 1987 some of the R&D allocation would be to the Vantage line to reduce its cost and improve its quality. Ennis believed it was crucial for the launch of Greenwich to be preceded by satisfactory performance of the Vantage line, which would continue to be sold in 1986 and 1987 as the Greenwich system was being developed.

CHAPTER 11

Northern Telecom (B): The Norstar Launch

Describes the new product development and commercialization process for Norstar, the outcome of a $54 million project to replace an existing unsuccessful product in the very competitive key systems market. The development program, the business model, and the marketing program are all detailed. One has to assess the chances of the new product's success, and recommend changes to the marketing program where necessary.

In March 1988, Mike Ennis, general manager of Northern Telecom's Business Products Division (BPD), prepared the final details for the launch of the first product in the Norstar key systems family.[1] Two and a half years earlier, Ennis's plan to develop the Norstar line, then code-named Greenwich, had been accepted by Northern Telecom's Executive Committee, though some members regarded it as a high-risk proposition. It was strategically important for Northern to be in the key systems business. However, the $70 million in losses incurred by Vantage, Norstar's predecessor, created some concerns within the corporation about the wisdom of investing $50 million in the development of another key system product family.[2]

As the outlines of Northern's plans came to be known, some securities analysts expressed their surprise at the investment and Northern's goal of challenging AT&T for leadership in the U.S. market. In an article headlined "Setting Skyhigh Goals for Meridian Norstar," the *Financial Times of Canada* noted one analyst's concern

---

This case was prepared by Robert J. Dolan.
Copyright © 1993 by the President and Fellows of Harvard College.
Harvard Business School case 593-104 (revised June 30, 1993).

[1]Meridian, Norstar, and Vantage are registered trademarks of Northern Telecom.
[2]Key systems were telephone sets designed for the small-business market, that is, organizations needing between 2 and 100 telephone sets or stations. Those with requirements for more sets would, typically, be better served by purchasing a private branch exchange (PBX). Details on the key systems market and Northern's considerations to develop the Norstar line are given in "Northern Telecom (A)," Harvard Business School case 9-594-051.

about Northern's lack of a distribution channel in the United States, referring to Northern as a "tiny, inconsequential player in key systems for years. And then last year we heard rumors that they were spending millions of dollars on key system development. Frankly, we thought they were crazy."[3] Roy Merrills, president of Northern's U.S. operations, in Richardson, Texas, reiterated Northern's goals for Norstar: "It's the right product at the right time. We are firmly committed to success in the key system market. We're in it for one reason and one reason only—to be Number 1. Our goal is leadership."

Ennis had directed the product development activities aimed at making Norstar the "right product at the right time" and the vehicle for both global leadership and profitability in key systems. The Norstar Compact System for users that needed up to 16 stations was now ready for market. Ennis had to be sure BPD's marketing strategy supporting Norstar would achieve sales in an intensely competitive marketplace. The proposal to invest $50 million in Norstar development had been justified on the basis of attaining 55 percent share in Canada and 15 to 20 percent in the United States. He recognized enormous differences between the Canadian and U.S. markets. While he believed that the Norstar product fit the needs of both, there would have to be some customization of the supporting elements of the marketing mix to the individual markets. In Canada, Northern held the leading market share in virtually every telephone-related product category, was well-known to consumers, and had strong relationships with the telephone companies. These telcos held 70 percent of the key system business and would be the prime resellers of the Norstar line. In contrast, Northern was virtually unknown to small-business customers in the United States. The Vantage system held only a 1 percent share, placing it no. 18 in market-share ranking. In addition, the Regional Bell Operating Companies (RBOCs), whom Northern was targeting to be prime resellers, held only 20 percent of the U.S. key system market.

Since 70 percent of the demand for key systems was outside of North America, Canada and the United States would be only the first challenges for Ennis. However, he knew that success here was a necessary platform to approach markets worldwide. Similarly, he had recognized two years earlier that, like it or not, the Vantage product line was the platform from which he had to stage his Norstar effort.

Vantage Product Line

The financial impact documented in black and white on BPD's profit and loss statements since 1982 was only one of the negative effects of the Vantage product line. Northern people associated with the line were dispirited and feared for their jobs, resellers were disgruntled with it, and end users favored less-expensive models. Once the decision was made for Northern to continue in the key systems business, Ennis appointed two key managers to rectify the Vantage problems. Fouad Aziz, director

---

[3]*Financial Times of Canada,* March 21, 1988, p. 3.

of Customer Service, and Alan Stewart, director of Quality, were responsible for turning the Vantage experience into a positive position from which to launch the Norstar line.

Aziz explained:

> There was a major learning cycle for everybody with Vantage—users, resellers, and us. It was one of the first pure electronic key systems in the marketplace. There was a general lack of understanding about how to make, sell, install, and maintain these systems. Vantage had some problems initially, no doubt about it. From 1985 to 1987, when everybody else around here was working on Norstar, my job was to focus on Vantage: Get costs down, fix it in the field, and figure out what Vantage was telling us about how to do it better for the next-generation product. While development of Norstar was a big investment, we knew we also had to invest in fixing Vantage.

Figure 1 documents the results of investment in Vantage research and development to "get the costs down." It shows the manufacturing cost per station for Vantage for 1984–1987.

The success of the cost-reduction program had a parallel with respect to customers. In 1985, Quality director Alan Stewart instituted BPD's first systematic measurement of customer satisfaction. The survey, distributed to a variety of people within resellers' organizations, asked for an overall rating on Northern's performance and specific ratings in the areas of hardware, documentation, services, sales and marketing, and software. Previously, the quality effort had been focused on the inspection of incoming parts from suppliers. The customer satisfaction survey represented the redefinition of quality to a customer-based concept. This formal interaction with resellers and Stewart's personal follow-up on any problem areas served to improve Northern's understanding of the resellers' business situation and their perceptions of Northern. It also changed the customers' attitude toward Northern.

Stewart related the importance of this change:

> Vantage gained market share back in Canada and together with the cost-reduction program, this got us more support for Norstar from corporate; but, more important, all our activities with Vantage during this time got us our customer credibility back. When

FIGURE 1

Vantage cost per station

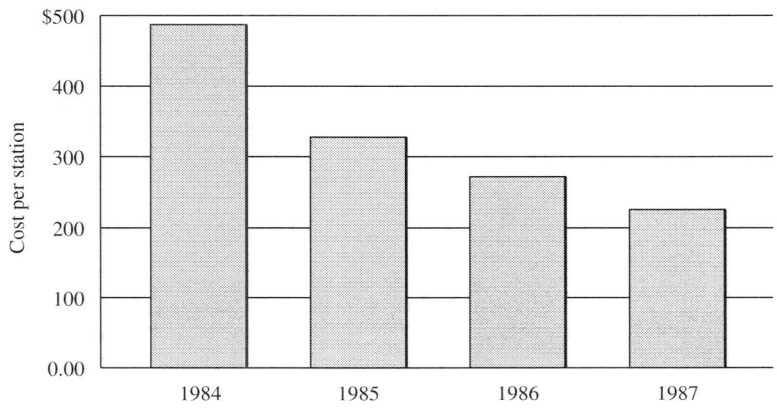

Vantage first started to have problems in the field, we adopted the attitude that the product was fine and the resellers just were not installing it right or training end-users well. This really hurt us and we had to rebuild those relationships if the next product we offered was going to have any chance with these customers.

In addition to the customer credibility, Aziz emphasized the significant learning about the resellers from this development of a closer association:

> We really came to understand how they work, how they are organized, how they communicate or don't communicate within the organization, what was their attitude toward training courses, how the installation and repair group worked. . . . It also helped us to establish the right links in the organization. We learned a lot which will help us with marketing Norstar.

The Norstar Development Program

Ross Matthews, BPD's manager of Manufacturing Engineering during the development of both Vantage and Norstar, explained how the development program for Norstar was a direct result of the Vantage experience.

> Vantage was the outcome of a product-development program based on a serial delivery concept. First, the product group develops a commercial specification. This basically says what the product is supposed to do. Then, the designers come in. At Northern, our design house is Bell Northern Research [BNR], an organization which is 70 percent owned by Northern and 30 percent by Bell Canada. The design group takes the commercial specification and goes off and develops the product specification. In this case, the design group is located two time zones and 2,000 miles away from the product group. They get together again with the product group, iterate through it, and ultimately hash it out. The design group sometimes adds some neat features they think would be good, something that's really differentiating based on the latest technology they have developed. Finally, after lots of discussion usually, the product group accepts the product specification and signs off on it. Now here we are in manufacturing. The first involvement we have in this thing is as the design document flies over the wall. Vantage's problems were evidence of the deficiencies in this system of product development. It had cost problems, it had quality problems, and it was in the middle of the pack on MTBF.[4] There was just no way the product as designed could be manufactured in Canada at competitive cost and quality levels.

Norstar's development process was designed to overcome this situation by a team effort of the product/marketing group, design, and manufacturing to fulfill the basic business proposition of "appropriate price, absolute simplicity, and useable functionality." Ennis and Howie Bender, vice president of BNR, became cochairs of monthly program reviews. As the client of BNR, Ennis insisted that all members of the BNR team assigned to Norstar work in the same location and only on Norstar.[5]

---

[4]MTBF: an acronym for "mean time between failures"—a measure of a product's reliability.

[5]BNR's policy was to have development spread over multiple locations and a designer simultaneously assigned to multiple projects.

The design team was to understand the entire Norstar business plan. Second, the specific client of the design team within Northern's BPD was redefined to include not just the product group but also manufacturing. The design job was conceived of as the codesign of both the product and the manufacturing process. The team was told to zero-base the manufacturing operation, forgetting about how the factory currently operated, the people skills on hand, and the available equipment. The mandate was to find the optimal combination of product and manufacturing process to achieve the business objective.

Matthews commented on the change in philosophy:

> This was a very new role for us in manufacturing. Manufacturing was now being pulled into the product development process well ahead of the product definition stage. Being in on the conceptual stage of things was not anything we had done before. At first, it sounds great—you will be able to voice your concerns earlier and get people to think about your issues. But it's a big change too. For the first time, we had to understand the whole business process because we had to figure out what manufacturing should be. What cycle time targets, overhead levels should we have? Having "ease of manufacture" become a design criterion of the people at BNR wasn't easy either. Many of the BNR designers had never been in a factory. You can't design something for ease of manufacturing if you don't really understand how manufacturing works. So, we brought them all here to see what goes on; first the lead designers, then the rest. It cost about $1,500 in expenses for each of the 30 of them and two days of their time and ours, but it was well worth it to have them just look at an assembly operation. They then quickly understood the implications of the various design actions on us.
>
> This whole process of coordination and the team concept was not smooth by any means. Everybody had new responsibilities. At first, BNR took the insistence on colocation of all members of the design team as a challenge to their ability to manage technology development. But Ennis was eventually successful in making these people feel part of the team, not just a subcontractor.
>
> There were battles, but survival is a great motivator and to survive we knew we had to make the business model work and that became the common focus. Not how do you do manufacturing or how do you do design, but how do we together make the business model work out.

The Business Model

From the beginning, the rationale for Norstar development was the failure of any of the approximately 100 key system suppliers to deliver simplicity to users and resellers. BPD's contact with end-users, begun in the "Monitor, Measure, Assess, and Decide" stage of Ennis's tenure during May–November 1985, continued in the form of a formal market research program and contact with Vantage customers in the field. BPD elaborated upon the end-user needs and inferred the resulting commercial requirements and specifications summarized in Exhibit 1.

1. "Appropriate price" remained paramount. The intensely competitive environment among key system manufacturers, the lack of sophisticated selling

EXHIBIT 1   Summary of End-User-Needs Input to Norstar Development

End-User Needs	Commercial Requirement	Commercial Specification
1. Appropriate price	• Low distribution price • Low end-user price	• Low-cost manufacturing
2. Absolute simplicity	• Learning with no user guide • East-to-use features • Easy to change	• Ergonomic layout • Set feature walk-through • Direct feature access • Single-button access to key functions • Automatic relocation

3. Reliability	• Does not break
	• No maintenance required
		• MTBF:
		  KSU—6 years
		  Sets—12 years
		• Repair-call rate: Less than 1 call per 100 stations/month
		• No periodic maintenance schedule

4. Flexibility	• Growth capability • Obsolescence protection	• Functional terminals • Evoluable architecture • Family of systems • Software cartridges
5. Quality	• Set fulfills purpose • Style	• Different sets for different needs • Absolute simplicity • Styling

techniques, and little product differentiation led to regular price cutting and continued focus on price by end-users. Gaining significant share without meeting the price level of the competition was not feasible—whatever the value provided. Hence, BPD had to target low reseller and end-user prices, leading to the commercial specification of a low-cost manufacturing facility.

2. "Absolute simplicity" was made concrete in three commercial requirements. First, end-users were averse to printed user guides. Any learning or guide to features should be delivered through the telephone set itself. Second, users wanted feature utilization to be self-evident: "It works like you think it should work." Finally, changes, such as moving from one office to another, should be easy to make. Out of these requirements, the team defined the specifications of an ergonomic layout for the set with built-in user guide, "direct feature access," meaning that any feature can be easily programmed onto a button for one-button access, key functions such as speed-dialing delivered through touching one button, and automatic set relocation. Automatic relocation meant that a set could be picked up by the user, moved from one office to another, plugged back in, and function just as in the original location.

3. "Reliability" needs set the standards for the mean-time-between-failures on equipment and established a limit on expected repair calls at one per 100 stations per month. Thus, a user with eight stations should have a maximum of one repair call per year. The system was to require no periodic maintenance.
4. "Flexibility" grew out of users' expectations of their changing needs over time. The most common reason for a small-business customer to change equipment was growth. Users wanted the capability to grow their systems and functionality in an efficient fashion. This led to the commercial specification of feature-laden terminals to be accessed as needs arose. Second, it established the requirement for a family of systems built from an architecture that allowed easy migration to larger systems. The system should allow functionality to be delivered by software cartridges "dropped into" sets.
5. "Quality" meant simply that the set did what the user wanted it to do and had a nice appearance. Given the heterogeneity of the customer base, this led to a specification for different sets for different customers.

Similar study of resellers' needs lead to identification of four key areas and resulting requirements and specifications as summarized in Exhibit 2. The first reseller need was "competitive product cost." Resellers understood the dominance of price in the end-users' purchase decision just as Northern did. This resulted in a price-to-resellers goal of $225 per station, driving the target manufacturing cost to $107 per station. Resellers perceived the profit margins to be razor thin in key systems, with no possibility of relief via gaining higher prices from end-users. Consumers were clearly uninterested in premium-priced systems.

EXHIBIT 2 Summary of Reseller-Needs Input to Norstar Development

Distribution/Reseller Needs	Commercial Requirement	Commercial Specification
1. Competitive product cost	Purchase Price—$225/station	Cost—$107/Station

2. Low installation/ maintenance cost	• Simple installation
	• No user training
	• No maintenance
	• Low failure rate
		• MTBF:
		  KSU—6 years
		  Sets—12 years
		• Automatic relocate
		• Repair-call rate: Less than 1 call per 100 stations/month
		• Set provided training

3. Low selling cost	• Brand awareness • High close rate • No training—salesperson/customer	• NT/Meridian name • Simplicity • Low price • Obsolescence protection • Applications • Common family features
4. Reduced materials management costs	• Minimal parts • Low nonrevenue earning investment	• Common sets • Software cartridges • Low failure rate • Simplistic troubleshooting

BPD's only way to make resellers profitable and hence interested in selling Norstar was through working on the reseller's own cost structure. As shown in Exhibit 2, the three major cost components were installation/maintenance, selling, and materials management. Delivery of the low installation/maintenance cost resulted in many of the same commercial specifications as those dictated by meeting user needs (i.e., low MTBFs), user training provided through the station itself, and the automatic relocate function so a reseller would not be required to move a set from one location to another. When electronic key systems such as Vantage replaced electro-mechanical ones, resellers had expected simpler service operations; instead, they had become unmanageable. Electronic systems were far more complex than expected, and they brought a whole new set of problems. Technicians were ill-prepared for the new issues, and service costs often wiped out any anticipated margins.

The second major component was selling costs. Low selling costs required end-user awareness of the brand name and/or manufacturer. Superior product features had the role of enabling resellers to achieve a high "close" rate—given that the end-user's demand for low price was met. Again, meeting this reseller requirement dictated a commercial specification consistent with that derived from studying end-user needs (i.e., low price, simplicity, and functionality to meet the end-user's specific needs).

The third cost was materials management. These were high for resellers because the low-cost Pacific Rim suppliers operated on four-month replenishment times. Some of the more popular brands were demanding 180-day stocking commitments. Resellers' difficulty in forecasting demand had resulted in maintenance of large buffer stocks. Coupled with a spate of new products hitting the market and continually declining prices, the effective inventory holding cost was extremely high. Simplifying and reducing the cost of materials management required common sets for multiple applications to minimize the number of separate stockkeeping units. Low failure rates would reduce spare part requirements.

The concept of basing the Norstar product and delivery system design on providing the reseller a profit opportunity was formalized in a "value model" of the resellers (see Figure 2). Analysis of the typical reseller's cost structure showed that product cost to the reseller represented about 40 percent of the end-user price; target profit margin was about 10 percent. The other 50 percent was divided among five components of cost: installation and repair, materials management, sales costs, training, and overhead.

The 10 percent target profit margin was problematic in two respects. First, even if achieved, it did not compare favorably to margins on other products being sold by the telephone companies. Second, considering all the unanticipated problems with electronic systems, even that slim margin was frequently wiped out by repair or training cost increases. Some resellers were even considering leaving the key system business. As shown in Figure 2, the end-user price was viewed as a fixed ceiling that could not be pushed up to provide more reseller margin. The only option was to deliver value by reducing the reseller's cost elements.

The Norstar business proposition was summarized in *simplicity:* simple for resellers to understand, stock, sell, install, and maintain, and simple for end-users to

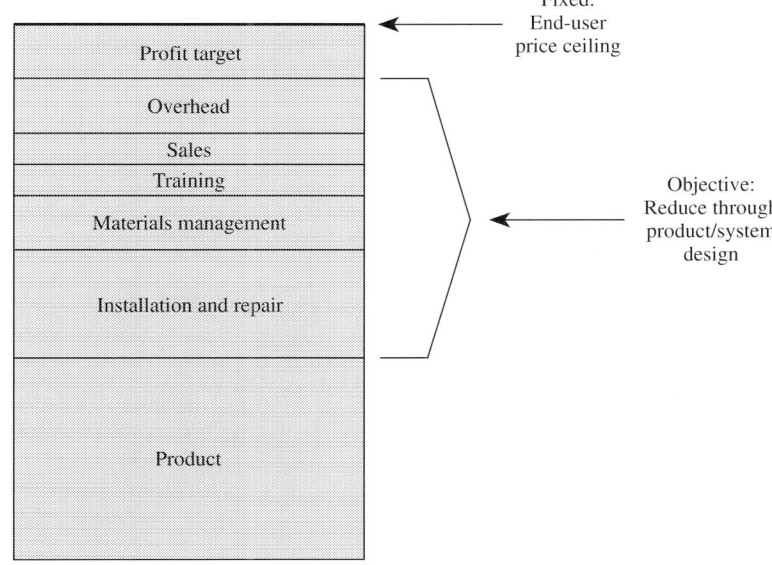

FIGURE 2

Norstar value model

use. While many issues were debated among the team members from product/marketing, design, and manufacturing, this dual-simplicity as the core of the business proposition was "nailed to the wall."

Converting the Business Proposition into a Marketing Program

Product development followed a structured "gating" procedure with three gates:

G1: Product definition.
G2: Field tests with customers.
G3: Product launch.

Ennis's philosophy was to build a multidisciplinary team that stayed with the product from conception stage through the first release at G3 and beyond. After G3, the team would work to fill out the product line, then simplify and cost-reduce the entire manufacturing and delivery system.

With the dual-simplicity business proposition firmly established, the multidisciplinary team continued interaction with resellers and end-users to develop the product definition. Northern's study of end-users had multiple benefits. In addition to providing product design input to the team, it helped to gain credibility with resellers and induce them to cooperate in the design process. As Carl Price, Norstar product manager, related:

We went around to the telcos and started showing them what we had found out about their customers. They were really impressed that we had done our homework, and this also showed them we were serious about key systems. That got them to commit to us in the design. Early on, we had help from Bell Canada, and from the United States, Bell South, and Centel.

In the words of one manager, "Although the goals were shared, the means provoked heated argument. The definition of the system's user side simmered on the far edge of open battle for months." For example, product/marketing was adamant on the price aspect—that features added could not push price above the customer-dictated ceiling. BNR designers, to meet the demand for self-instructing terminals, proposed a liquid crystal display (LCD) be incorporated in the more fully featured terminals in the line. The cost/benefit trade-off was resolved via a simulation developed on a Macintosh to test the control and ease of use made possible by the LCD. By firsthand observation of the user testing, the product/marketing group concluded that the impact on users and reseller cost justified the manufacturing cost of including LCDs. Four months were spent hammering out the details of a set of product definitions that blended the market requirements with most appropriate technologies and most cost-effective manufacturing methods. The G1 product definition gate was officially passed in fall 1986. The level of detail of the definition at G1 was such that manufacturing was required to sign off on a manufacturing cost at "G3 + 3" (i.e., the three months after product launch date at G3).

G1: The Product Definition

The product definition incorporated a number of BNR technical advances. The most significant of these was based on the concept of silicon-intensive design. A custom-silicon large-scale integrated circuit (CLSI) packed several functions onto one chip. For example, one of the nine CLSIs in Norstar was the digital station-set chip which incorporated four functional blocks: the codechip, microprocessor interface, control for hands-free operation, and interface to the communications loop. Eight of the nine CLSIs were newly developed for Norstar. CLSI reduced the number of components to manage and the required testing time and promised cost reductions relative to Vantage sets of up to 50 percent for the larger systems in the 2- to 100-set range.

At G1, several key product definition decisions were made:

1. System software would be embodied in plug-in cartridges in the key system unit (KSU) and in the telephone set CLSI. This distributing of system intelligence out to the sets, rather than building into the key system unit only, provided great flexibility in features provided.[6]

---

[6]As described more fully in the "Northern Telecom (A)" case, a key system is composed of a central control unit—called a key system unit (KSU)—and the telephone sets. Conceptually, the system intelligence could be contained in the KSU and accessed by the telephone sets or placed in the sets and more limited intelligence placed in the KSU. The latter approach, made practical and cost-efficient by BNR technological developments, offered more flexibility.

2. To reduce the number of stockkeeping units, many options of other vendors would be standard in all Norstar sets; for example, each set would have:
   - Liquid crystal display.
   - Hands-free operation.
   - Headset jack.
   - Volume control in the handset.
   - Extra-long cord.
   - Built-in wall mount plate.
3. The system would have a modular design, to cover the 2- to 100-station market. Two base systems would be developed: "Compact" would serve users with a need for only 16 sets or less, and "Modular" would cover the 16- to 100-set part of the market. The base KSU in the modular system would support 24 sets. Up to six modules could be added, each providing support for 16 additional sets as needed by the end-user.
4. To simplify installation, sets would plug in to the KSU with standard jacks and be fully functional at default settings. All wiring would be polarity-insensitive single-pair to minimize installer's time in wiring systems.
5. The system would be developed to interface with personal computers to allow for PC-driven applications.
6. Easy access would be provided to over 70 features. (The Appendix shows a Norstar brochure which lists the principal features and associated benefits.) These features were designed to make it easy for Norstar-system end-users to:
   - Make calls.
   - Take calls.
   - Manage calls.
   - Manage the system.
   - Add the options you want.

The product definition at G1 was coupled with the definition of certain system requirements.

1. Manufacturing cycle time, to meet the reduced-inventory requirement of resellers, had to be less than 48 hours at product launch (compared with 8 weeks for Vantage). This would allow resellers to order based on their booked, rather than forecasted, business.
2. Manufacturing facility had to meet global needs with varying preferences for different models, colors, languages, and "random volume orders"; hence, minimal product-switchover times were essential.

Moving to G2: The Field Test with Customers

The first product developed was the Compact System, for small businesses with need for fewer than 16 stations. It was the most price-sensitive segment of the market. Meeting the cost challenge here would ensure being able to meet it in larger systems.

User testing was extensive through the prototype stage. BNR designers made particular use of a technique called co-discovery learning. In this research, designers videotaped two people who, without aid of a user guide, worked together to discover how to use a product. The conversation between the two provided valuable diagnostic information beyond that attainable from just watching one person alone attempt to use the equipment. The G2 gate required the product to pass extensive beta tests in which representative users tested the system in their own work environments. Northern conducted beta testing through resellers. The first large-scale field tester was GTE. Ross Matthews explained:

> GTE was first to show real interest, and that was fine because we regarded them as a "tough customer"—in the good sense of having demanding requirements. So, they came up and met with the whole Norstar team. They explained what their criteria were—how they would measure performance and what they expected from us. We got it all squared away in two days because all the necessary players from marketing, design, and manufacturing were at the table. Without the multifunctional team, just getting the test set up with GTE would have dragged on for a full quarter [of a year]. So, we got them started and then repeated the whole process with Bell South and Ameritech in the United States as well as working with the Canadian telcos.
>
> In September 1987, we had 60 three-month field tests of Norstar going on. Our old philosophy on beta tests was, No news is good news. We hoped we would not hear anything from anybody and inferred from that that things were working out fine. With Norstar, we took a very disciplined and proactive approach. We studied the sites so we knew we had a good, representative portfolio of users. We did lots of interviews and formal questionnaires. The net result was clear: People loved what they had. We could not get the test units away from them.

Preparing for G3: Product Launch

By March 1988, the 100 work years of development and 20 work years of verification on Norstar had resulted in:

1. A product that obtained rave reviews in field tests.
2. A new manufacturing process built around the principles of Flexible Manufacturing Systems and short-cycle just-in-time manual assembly: 54 computers, 17 robots, and assembly people combined to provide a 10,000 set-per-week capacity. Capacity growth to 20,000 sets per week was planned by the end of 1989. All this was to happen within the current 100,000-square-foot plant.
3. Costs per station at launch were on target. Relative to an index of total costs at the end of 1988 set at 100, costs per station were projected to evolve as follows:

	Material	Labor	Overhead	Total
End 1988	74%	6%	20%	Index = 100
End 1989	61%	5%	16%	82%
End 1990	45%	4%	10%	59%
End 1991	37%	4%	10%	51%

The table indicates that total cost at the end of 1989 was expected to be 82 percent of what it was at the end of 1988. Material cost per station at the end of 1989 was expected to be 61 percent of the *total* cost at the end of 1988. These cost declines were to be achieved by a program of (1) worldwide sourcing, (2) development of vendor partnerships, and (3) "communicating our customers' needs to our vendors." Vendors were to be held to a zero-defect standard and on-demand delivery, in return for which Northern would buy the requirements exclusively from that vendor.

The initial product available was to be the Compact System with a key system unit to accommodate up to six telephone lines and 16 stations. Two sets, as pictured in Exhibit 3, would be available initially. The M7208 Square Set was the basic system and considered "the main runner" in the price-sensitive market. It featured a one-line, 16-character LCD display and eight program keys. The M7310 Feature Set had a two-line, 16-character per line LCD display, 10 program keys, and 12-dual program keys (see the top of the set in Exhibit 3). These 12 keys with a shift key provided easy access to 24 additional commonly dialed numbers or frequently used features. The features accessible were the same regardless of set; the larger set just provided more flexibility in use.

Ennis's Launch Decisions

In March 1988, product development was continuing on the Modular line for larger systems, with completion scheduled for early 1989. It would utilize the M7208 and M7310 sets and, in addition, a larger M7324 set would be available at that time. By spring 1989, the introduction of the personal computer interface card would permit Norstar to work with personal computer applications. Northern itself was developing a Dial by Name program in which a user typed in the first few letters of a person's name, using the telephone dial; this would access a computer-stored directory of names and phone numbers, and the person's number would be automatically dialed. Northern also planned to promote third-party software development.

While these systems held promise for the future, Ennis was concerned about today. Throughout Norstar's two-and-a-half-year development process, the rumored development programs of competitors reminded the Norstar team of the criticality of time. Ennis believed he had a strong product advantage over competitors' current offerings. He had to seize the window of opportunity by quickly ramping up sales in both the United States and Canada. The development team still expected no growth

EXHIBIT 3   Two Stations Sets for Launch System

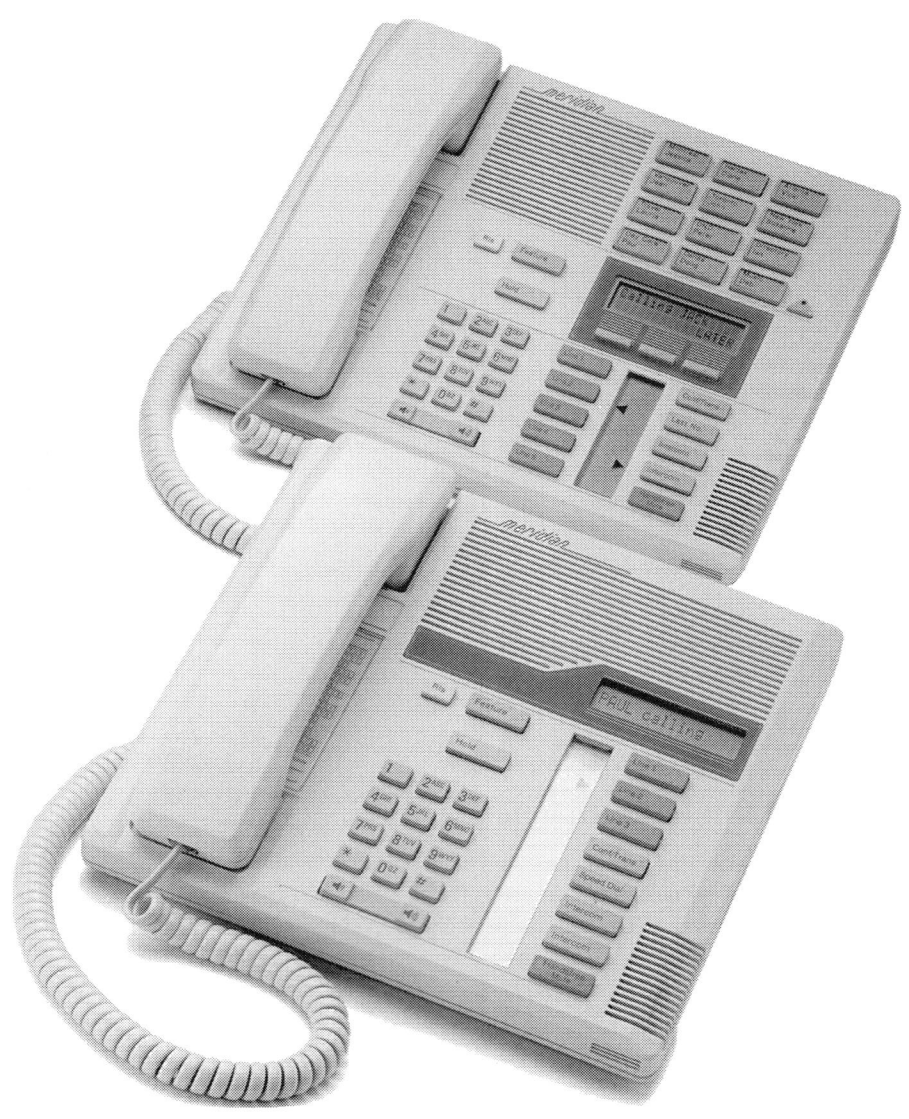

in unit sales rate in the North American market overall. Thus, Northern would have to take share away from others.

In Canada, the regional telephone companies held 70 percent of the key system business. Northern had good relations with these resellers, though many had turned away from the Vantage product, given its problems. For the Canadian market the marketing team had proposed a large-scale consumer advertising campaign budgeted at $3 million and using television ads under the tag line, Norstar: Simply the best. This would be the first time Northern had used television for a business product. Magazine ads were to be double-page full color. Proposed advertising copy was developed based on the field test units' desire to keep their test Norstar units (see Exhibits 4 and 5). Ennis felt this program would help develop brand preference for Norstar but he wondered if it was sufficient to "own" the telco channel and have Norstar become the system of choice. Anticipating likely improved competitive product in the not too distant future, he wanted to quickly establish a strong telco/Norstar relationship.

In the United States, the situation was quite different. The team had been successful in involving major resellers in the Norstar product development effort and several had agreed to take on the Norstar line. However, Northern Telecom was still a virtual unknown in the small-business market. With Vantage's share less than 1 percent, Norstar had no viable distribution structure; nor did it have its own sales and service infrastructure. The recommendation for the U.S. market was not to use television or magazines but to put on a trade show for resellers and some potential buyers. One proposal was for a "Dallas Spectacular" for about 400 resellers and potential major buyers. Developed along a *Star Wars* theme, the high-tech show was to invite these key parties for an all-expenses-paid trip to "Take a look at a brilliant new star." Estimated cost was $1 million. In the United States, the main distribution channel would be the RBOCs, who currently held only 20 percent share of the market. To achieve its share goals, Norstar would have to become the dominant system sold by the RBOCs and also enable the RBOCs to grow their own share (in contrast to AT&T's direct-selling organization and dealers).

The whole Norstar effort had been developed in accord with Northern's philosophy and motto, Quality means business. Ennis had decided to price Norstar at competitive levels so that sales efforts could focus just on selling quality and value, rather than attempting to justify a price premium. In particular, distributor list prices would be $450, less appropriate discounts in both markets. Resellers were expected to sell the system in a price range at approximately distributor list. While key system prices had decreased 10 percent per year for the last five years, Ennis's strategy was to hold Norstar prices at those established at the launch. He knew this would require substantiating the impact Norstar was having on the resellers' cost structure. Otherwise, the continued price decreases of other vendors would lead resellers to press for Norstar price decreases as well. Holding prices up while Norstar's cost-reduction program had its impact on product cost would provide the margins he needed to attain profitability.

The Norstar team believed the $50 million investment and their efforts had produced the "right product at the right time and at the right cost." That investment had been justified on the basis of attaining 53 percent and 15 percent, respectively, of the Canadian and U.S. markets within several years. Now, Ennis and his team just had to translate that quality product into significant share gains in a market with 100 competitors and no projected unit growth. If successful, they would then have the opportunity to turn Norstar into a reasonably profitable business by penetrating global markets.

EXHIBIT 4 Example of Proposed Advertising Copy for Canadian Market

EXHIBIT 5 Example of Proposed Advertising Copy for Canadian Market

APPENDIX

Features and Benefits

- Easy to Make Calls
- Easy to Take Calls
- Easy to Manage Calls
- Easy to Manage the System
- Easy to Add the Options You Want

APPENDIX *(continued)*

Easy To Make Calls

norstar

FEATURE	BENEFIT
DIAL INTERCOM Allows 2-digit intercom calling.	Provides easy access to all persons on the system.
DIRECT STATION SELECTION (DSS) User presses one programmed key to automatically call another person in the office. 	Saves time because user can directly access a person in the office by pressing the button with his/her name on it. No need to remember the intercom number.
END-TO-END SIGNALLING Generates Dual Tone Multi-Frequency (DTMF) tones on external lines so user can signal external device or network.	Improves communications efficiency by allowing user to directly access and activate devices such as voice recording devices.
EXTERNAL LINE ACCESS Outside lines can be directly accessed by keys on individual phones, or indirectly via a line pool.	Saves time and improves business communication. Anyone who has his/her line programmed for external calls does not have to go through a receptionist to make outside calls.
LAST NUMBER REDIAL Always stores in memory the last number dialed on the dial pad. User can dial it automatically (without picking up the handset) by pressing the LAST NUMBER button. 	Saves time.
LINE POOL A group of phones share a group of external lines. An idle line is released to a set for one call only.	Saves money since several people can share a group of lines.
MANUAL LINE SELECTION Any desired idle or ringing line can be selected by pressing the line key. This overrides the *Automatic Line Selection* feature.	User can access the line of his/her choice. User can answer calls which come in on something other than the his/her "usual" line.
MEMORY BUTTON KEYS Touching a *Memory button* automatically speed dials the external and internal calls or system features selected. 	One-button dialing is faster, simpler and more accurate Faster feature access with no codes to remember

189

APPENDIX *(continued)*

Easy to Make Calls

FEATURE	BENEFIT
ON-HOOK DIALING A user can activate the set and dial digits on an external or internal line without lifting the handset or pressing the *Handsfree* key. On hearing the party answer, the user lifts the hand-set or presses *Handsfree* to converse.	No need to pick up the handset. Saves time and increases productivity.
PAGING Norstar sets can make paging announcements three ways: *Internally*, through the set speakers. *Externally*, through a customer-supplied amplifier and speaker. Both *internally* and *externally* at the same time.	Saves time; makes it easier for the user to find the needed party.
PAUSE Allows the user to insert a 1.5 second waiting period between digits being dialed. Used when programming Speed Dial numbers.	Easier programmed dialing.
PRIME LINE SELECTION For outgoing or incoming calls, the user lifts the receiver or presses the *handsfree* key. The set will automatically select an open line.	For incoming calls, the user doesn't have to decide which line is ringing. It's second nature to just pick up the phone. For outgoing calls, the user doesn't have to select a line, it is done for him automatically.
As an inside call is made, the display shows whether the phone being called is busy, using *Do Not Disturb*, or on *Call Forward*. The name of the party being called is also displayed.	Provides information to help the caller assess the telephone status of the called party; personalizes and improves office communications.
RING AGAIN ON BUSY Ring Again on Busy Set alerts a user when a busy internal set becomes available. Ring Again on Busy Line Pool alerts a user when a line in a line pool becomes available.	Saves time. Increases productivity because the user doesn't have to keep checking to determine if a set or line is available.
RING AGAIN ON NO ANSWER Alerts a user when the next activity occurs at an internal set that previously failed to answer a call from the user.	Saves time. Increases productivity since the caller doesn't have to keep trying to reach the person who didn't answer his phone.
SPEED DIAL – SET Allows user to program and dial up to 24 Speed Dial numbers of their own choice. An outside line is selected automatically and the number dialed is displayed.	Saves time; prevents misdialing. Every user can have his/her own private speed dial numbers.
SPEED DIAL – SYSTEM Any set can access 30 Speed Dial numbers shared by the system, and the number dialed is displayed	Provides fast access to numbers frequently used by everyone in the office.

APPENDIX   *(continued)*

Easy To Take Calls

norstar

FEATURE	BENEFIT
CALL IDENTIFICATION On an inside call, the name of the calling party is displayed.	Personalizes office communications. Allows the called party to prepare himself/herself for the call. Increases office efficiency. On call forward, allows professional answering of colleagues' phones.
CALL PICKUP (GROUP) Any user in a pickup group can answer external or internal calls ringing at another telephone without leaving their work station. The user either presses the pre-programmed CALL-PICKUP button on a set so equipped, or presses FEATURE 75. 	Better customer service; less irritation from the sound of unanswered ringing phones.
CALL TIMING The display shows the length of the current or most recent call in minutes and seconds when queried by the user.	Can be used to record time charges.
DISCRIMINATING RINGING Internal and external calls have different ringing cadences.	the user can distinguish internal from external calls
DISTINCTIVE RINGING The set can be programmed to ring with one of four distinct tone combinations, so that the user can distinguish the ringing of the user's set from that of other sets nearby.	Eliminates confusion. Useful in open office environments
DO NOT DISTURB If the user activates this feature while a call is ringing his or her phone, the call will ring at the Prime phone. This is a selective form of *Call Forward*.  Activating DND puts the user in DND mode, which suppresses: voice calls, ringing, paging announcements, and *Ring Again* offers. It stops all tones and ringing, except *Held Line Reminder*. In DND mode, incoming calls still appear on the line indicators, but *Call Identification* for incoming inside calls is not displayed.	User can work uninterrupted without worrying about calls going unanswered. Because all visual signals still appear on the set, user can decide to answer any call. User can still make outside calls.
TIME/DATE DISPLAY The time and date appear on the display when the user is not on a call.	Provides extra convenience; saves space on user's desk.
VOICE CALL DENY User can prevent the set from receiving Voice Calls. All internal calls to that set will then be received as ringing calls.	User can prevent interruptions from voice calls, while still being alerted to the fact that there is an incoming internal call

191

APPENDIX *(continued)*

Easy To Manage Calls

norstar

FEATURE	BENEFIT
AMPLIFYING HANDSET Amplifying handset allows users who have hearing impairments or who are in a noisy environment to boost volume.	Ensures communications effectiveness.
AUTOMATIC HOLD A busy line will automatically be placed on hold if the user, without pressing the HOLD button or hook switch, presses a second line button, an INTERCOM button, or the CONF/TRANS button.	Prevents internal and external calls from being accidentally cut off during a transfer or when the user inadvertently presses another button.
CALL FORWARD - ALL CALLS The user can forward internal and external calls to another set.	Ensures user's calls will be answered if he/she wants to leave the workstation or work uninterrupted. Improves customer service.
CALL FORWARD OVERRIDE When one set is forwarded to another, this feature allows the forward destination to call the forwarding set. Also called *Secretarial Filtering*, this feature lets a secretary take calls for a supervisor and call him or her periodically to give messages.	Allows the secretary to convey important messages even when the phone is forwarded to the secretary.
CALL STATUS DISPLAY The line lamp on a telephone shows the line status in one of these ways: LAMP OUT — The line is idle. STEADILY LIT — The line is in use. SLOW FLASH — An incoming call is ringing on the line FAST FLASH — A call is on hold on the user's station. SLOW FLICKER — A call is on hold on the line at another station.	Allows the user to effectively manage a flow of calls by being able to tell at a glance the status of lines/calls.
CALL PROGRESS TONES Audible indication of telephone numbers dialed.	Allows user to discern whether button depression was recorded by the set
CONFERENCING This feature lets the user establish a three party conference by connecting two calls to the user's set. To create a conference, the user: (1) Makes the first call. (2) Presses the CONF/TRANS button. (3) Makes the second call. (4) Presses the CONF/TRANS button. (5) Presses the line button of the first held call. Alternatively, the user can call up step-by-step instruction on the display panel. 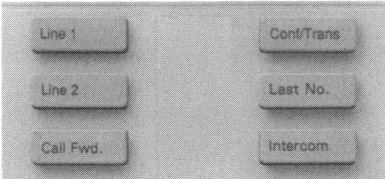 Once a conference call is established, any of the following operations can be carried out:	Saves time and avoids miscommunication by having three parties privy to the same conversation. User does not have to remember codes or sequence of operations. The phone guides the user through each step.

APPENDIX *(continued)*

FEATURE	BENEFIT
Split the conference: The conference originator can talk privately with either of the two parties involved, while the second party is on hold. The originator can also put the other parties on hold independently, preventing them from talking to each other. *Force release a conference party:* Lets the user disconnect one party. *Transfer from the conference:* Lets the user drop out of the conference, leaving the other two parties connected. If the other Parties are both outside the office, the user must put the Conference on hold, and disconnect only after both parties have hung up. *Consultation:* User can put a conference call on hold to make or answer another call. User presses another line button: conference call is automatically put on hold.	Allows user to temporarily interrupt a conference to deal with another matter; then easily reactivate the conference.
EXCLUSIVE HOLD When the user places an external call on exclusive hold, it cannot be picked up on any other set.	Allows total system-wide privacy and confidentiality.
HANDSFREE ANSWERBACK ON INTERCOM This feature allows the user to respond to a voice call without physically answering the call.	User can answer the phone without touching it and continue working, if desired.
HANDSFREE/MUTE CAPABILITY Handsfree operation allows the user to participate in a telephone call with the receiver on the hook by speaking to the telephone set in a normal voice and listening to the other party over the telephone set loudspeaker. The user may confer privately with people near the telephone by depressing the Handsfree/Mute button, which suppresses voice transmission to the other party.	Handsfree operation lets the user answer calls hands-free, so the user can continue working. Handsfree also allows one or several people near the set to converse with the party on the line. Pressing the mute button lets the user conduct in-office conversations privately from the caller.
HEARING AID COMPATIBLE The receivers on all Meridian Norstar sets are compatible with hearing aids.	Allows users with hearing aids to use any Norstar phone in the system comfortably and effectively.
HELD LINE REMINDER When the user places an external call on hold, this feature generates periodic reminder tones until the call is removed from hold.	Reminds the user that he/she has a caller on hold. Improves customer service.
HELD CALL REMINDER TRANSFER TO PRIME After two minutes, a held call will signal the prime set.	Improves customer service.
I-HOLD/U-HOLD INDICATION The set that places a line on hold flashes at a faster rate. Other sets will flash at the regular rate for that line.	Set user can easily differentiate the call he or she has put on hold from calls put on hold by other set users sharing the same group of external lines.
LEAVE MESSAGE/LIST The user can send a personalized display message requesting another person in the office to call back. The user can display up to four sent messages, and cancel any if desired When leaving a message, the user is guided by the display.	Saves time, since the user doesn't have to keep calling back.

APPENDIX *(continued)*

Easy To Manage Calls

FEATURE	BENEFIT
LINK KEY The user can have the system generate a timed hookswitch flash to communicate with a host PBX or Centrex by pressing the link key or dial pad code.	Allows the system to interface behind a larger telephone switch. Individual departments/locations can have all the features of a Meridian Norstar system, yet still easily access the features of the larger system.
LISTEN ON HOLD If the user has been placed on hold by the other party, the user can depress the HANDSFREE button and place the handset on hook while waiting for the other party to return. When the other party announces his or her return, the user hears the announcement through the loudspeaker and can then pick up the handset and resume the conversation.	The user can continue working, with both hands free, if placed on hold, and can easily resume the call when the other party returns.
MESSAGE WAITING/LIST The set display tells the user when a message has been received. The set can automatically place an internal call to the party that sent the message, or can cancel the message without calling back.	Improved internal communications.
NIGHT SERVICE This feature permits incoming calls, normally directed to the attendant/Prime set, to be routed to a preselected Night Service set. Any set can be the night phone.	Better customer service; better staff communications.
PRE-SELECTION/CALL SCREENING The user can select a ringing line on the set by pressing the ringing line key. Then the identifier ‹name› calling" (for internal calls) and "Line ‹x›" (for external calls) is displayed.	Allows the user to determine who is calling or which line is being used.
PRIME LINE Administration can assign a prime line to a set. If a set has a prime line, Automatic Outgoing Line Selection occurs and external dialing features (Autodial, Speed Dial, Last Number Redial) will select an outgoing line automatically. Automatic Incoming Line Selection will automatically select a prime line call before calls ringing on other lines.	The user does not need to select a line when making a call.
PRIVACY When the user is on a line, no other set can access the call. This feature is automatic on all calls.	Security and confidentiality.
RELEASE The release key disconnects an active call.	Allows the user to disconnect a call without lifting/replacing the handset. Saves time.
TRANSFER To transfer a call to an internal local, the user calls the internal local, touches the *Conf/Trans button*, and the first party button after the call is answered. The user touches the disconnect button to disconnect from the call.	Makes it very difficult to lose a party being transferred. Better customer service; more professional image.
USER PROGRAMMABLE FEATURE KEYS Each user of each set can assign many desired features to programmable keys. On Meridian M7310, each of the larger "Memory" buttons (non-indicator programmable keys) can store two phone numbers or features. The triangular button shifts between the two.	Each user can customize a set to his/her needs, and change the programming as those needs change.
VOLUME CONTROL The individual user has complete volume control of handset receiver, handsfree speaker, headset, ringing, incoming background music, and set paging.	User can adjust volume for his/her own personal preference. Improves comfort and efficiency.

APPENDIX *(continued)*

Easy To Manage The System

norstar

FEATURE	BENEFIT
AUTOMATIC SET RELOCATION User can move phones from jack to jack. Phone number and individual programming moves with the phone.	Saves time since no features have to be reprogrammed. Saves money since there is no need to call an installer to move phones.
CENTREX/PBX REACHTHROUGH When behind Centrex or BPX, users can access features which require tone signals in addition to dialing. These features include: Timed Release: A code signals Centrex or the PBX (longer duration than a flash) to disconnect the call and then give a dial tone. The code can be included in an autodial sequence, speed dial bin, or the last number redial buffer. Run/Stop: A code allows the user to store two or more sequences in the same key, with successive depressions of the key sending out successive sections of the stored sequence.	Allows Centrex features to be accessed in a convenient fashion.
CUSTOMER TEMPLATES Button overlays which the System Coordinator places on individual sets when programming system features. The overlays identify buttons which take on the functions named on the overlay when used in conjunction with an administration code. A programming sheet supplied by the installer is used to record phone numbers and features assigned to each phone.	Simplifies programming tasks done by the System Coordinator.
DEFAULT ADMINISTRATION Defaults are features programmed into buttons before delivery. They make the system operational immediately upon installation. The System Coordinator can reprogram any button setting except for inside and outside line buttons and Handsfree/Mute.	Makes the phone system operational immediately upon installation
DELAYED RING TRANSFER After three full ring cycles, an external call will transfer to the prime set.	Improves customer service since unanswered calls transfer automatically to the prime set.
EXECUTIVE FLEXIBLE CALL RESTRICTION OVERRIDE The user can override any call restriction on any phone by entering a 3-digit password.	Improves convenience and efficiency for selected personnel by allowing them to bypass Call Restrictions on any phone.
EMERGENCY TRANSFER/POWER FAIL CUT-THROUGH If there is a commercial power failure, this feature provides basic telephone service via a single-line phone acting independently from the system.	Ensures continued basic telephone service will be available in the event of a power loss.
FLEXIBLE CALL RESTRICTIONS The user can prevent any phone or line from accessing specific numbers (eg. long distance).	Improves cost control.
FLEXIBLE CALL RESTRICTION OVERRIDE The user can establish specific numbers which are exceptions to the restrictions.	Maintains general call restrictions cost control, yet provides system-wide access to selected numbers within the restricted categories.
MULTIPLE LINE KEYS Each call is accessed on a separate line key. Multiple line keys allow the user to manipulate calls easily. By allowing calls to provide visual alerting and be answered easily when the user is active on another call, these line keys also serve a 'call waiting' function.	Allows the user to handle calls easily, as each telephone may have up to 6 lines on it.

APPENDIX *(continued)*

Easy To Manage The System

FEATURE	BENEFIT
MUSIC/TONE/SILENCE ON HOLD This feature allows held external calls to be presented with music or a periodic tone.	By presenting the party on hold with music or a periodic tone, the user can re-assure customers that they have not been forgotten.
PAGE ORIGINATION/RECEPTION – INTERNAL Through the set speakers, the user can make a page or be paged internally.	A paging announcement can be easily sent to all phone sets.
PAGE ORIGINATION – EXTERNAL Through set speakers connected to a user-supplied amplifier and speaker, the user can make external paging announcements.	A paging announcement can easily be sent to all phone sets and to staff in rooms or areas without phone sets.
PRIME SET A prime set is a set which receives unanswered calls. A prime phone supports these call management features: *Delayed Ring Transfer:* transfers external calls to the Prime Phone if they go unanswered after the third ring. *Held Line Reminder:* begins at the Prime Phone two minutes after an outside call is put on hold, if the Prime Phone has the outside line. *Do Not Disturb:* transfers incoming external calls to the Prime set.	More efficient call handling because one set gets all unanswered calls.
PRIVATE LINES An external line can be assigned to one set as a private line. It can appear only on that set and the Prime Set. Calls that are put on hold or left unanswered on this line cannot be picked up by any other phone.	Provides extra privacy, as well as better access (since only one person has the line, that user will always have access to one outside line).
PROGRAMMABLE USER NAMES The System Coordinator can program user names to appear on the LCD Display during inside calls. The display shows the name of the person calling or the name of the person the user is calling.	Professional handling of calls forwarded by colleagues. Enhanced message waiting.
PULSE/TONE DIALING Dialing numbers are automatically sent as pulse or tone signals, whichever is most appropriate for the trunk lines receiving the transmission.	Allows the system to operate regardless of the type of signalling used by the user's telephone exchange.
RINGING LINE PREFERENCE When a person picks up the handset to answer a call, if two or more lines are ringing, he will automatically be connected to the first call.	Allow the user to answer calls without first selecting a line.
SET BASED ADMINISTRATION General administration (programming activities normally done by the user's System Coordinator) include time and date, system speed dial entries, night service set designation, name assignment to sets, call restrictions and overrides, executive password.	Allows fast, accurate administration set-up and changes by remote access.
SHOULDER REST The shoulder rest holds the receiver comfortably and securely on either shoulder.	Improves comfort and efficiency for users who are on the phone a lot and who prefer hand-held operation.
SIMULTANEOUS VOICE/DATA CAPABILITY Facsimile, answering machines, credit card terminals and other services can be accommodated on the same line that handles voice calls.	No separate dedicated line required to accommodate phone-linked equipment.
SQUARE/NON-SQUARE/HYBRID CONFIGURATION The system can be configured as a square, non-square or hybrid system. In a square system, all sets have direct access to all external lines (up to six). In a non-square system, fewer programmable keys are used for line access, so not all external lines can be directly accessed by each set.	Square system configuration can provide tariff advantages, satisfy a user need for direct control of external lines, or conform to traditional user expectations. Other configurations make more programmable keys available for direct feature access.

APPENDIX *(concluded)*

Easy To Add The Options You Want

norstar

FEATURE	BENEFIT
ANALOG TERMINAL ADAPTOR This device allows the user to accommodate analog equipment including answering machines, credit card readers, modems, fax machines, and other standard analog tip-and-ring devices without the need for a separate dedicated line. In addition to providing analog terminal connectivity, the ATA will enable off premise extensions. Whether on or off-site, the ATA will allow the analog terminal to access many of the Meridian Norstar features. These features include: C.O. and intercom lines (prime is programmable), Hold, System speed dial, Conference, Call forward, Paging, Call restrictions. The ATA can be connected to any Meridian Norstar digital station port. The number of ATA's which may be connected to a Meridian Norstar system is limited only by the number of available ports.	Maximizes efficiency while keeping hardware costs as low as possible.
AUXILIARY LOUD BELLS An auxiliary ringer supplied by the user can be connected to ring on internal and/or external calls.	Ensures that a ringing phone will be heard in noisy areas.
BACKGROUND MUSIC Background music can be connected to the KSU to play through Meridian Norstar telephone speakers. Music automatically disconnects when the set is in use. User can program background music on or off.	Can improve the general office working environment.
BUSY LAMP FIELD UNIT This module attaches to the Meridian M7310 set. It allows the user to see the busy/not busy status of other sets on an ongoing basis.	Helps to ensure that calls are handled efficiently and that no calls are missed.
CONFIDENCER For noisy locations, this unit replaces the standard handset and filters out excessive background noise.	Makes it easy to hear calls in noisy locations.
HEADSET An approved headset can be plugged into the special jack built into every Meridian Norstar phone. No additional wiring or power is required. The Handsfree/Mute button controls the headset in the same way that it controls Handsfree calls. Volume is adjusted using the Volume button.	Plug-in headset makes it easy to provide handsfree privacy and convenience at any phone.
LANGUAGE CHOICE ON DISPLAY LCD Display panel contains built-in bilingual message capability. Display language can be changed in seconds on a per set basis.	Saves money when people speaking the alternate language are employed (no need to keep changing sets to accommodate new employees).
NIGHT SERVICE BELLS Any set can be the night phone. This phone can also be programmed to ring the Auxiliary Ringer for all ringing calls at the Night Service phone while active.	Ensures night calls from customers will be heard in noisy locations.
OFF-PREMISE EXTENSION The OPX capability of the system allows the user to have a single line set operational at other than the main system location.	Better customer service.

CHAPTER 12

ROLM: The SIGMA Introduction

ROLM's product development team had to prepare a detailed plan for launching a new product, code-named SIGMA. The new product, though superior in features, had the potential to drastically affect ROLM's relationship with its existing customer base because it was technically incompatible with its current product line. Decisions had to be made on five key launch issues ranging from announcement timing to backlog management.

In January 1987, Bob Lundy was sizing up the progress he and the SIGMA team had made on the new PBX development at ROLM Corporation. Lundy had joined ROLM late in 1984, a few months before International Business Machines Corporation acquired 100 percent of the 15-year-old company's stock. On arriving at ROLM, Lundy had taken charge of a system development project that was intended to improve ROLM's cost competitiveness. After two years of effort, Lundy was pleased that his project, which had been given the code name SIGMA, had become the centerpiece of ROLM's future product line.

In many ways the SIGMA system promised significant improvements over the company's existing product line. It would be less costly to build and less costly for customers to operate. But SIGMA also presented problems because it would be technologically incompatible with ROLM's earlier PBX systems. Essentially, for the first time in the company's history, ROLM was planning to introduce a next-generation product that could not be integrated with any of the 20,000 installed systems of its customer base. ROLM's share of the installed base was about 12 to 15 percent.

V. Kasturi Rangan prepared this revised case. The original case was prepared by Cliff Fitzgerald under the supervision of Jay Misra.

Copyright © 1990 by the Board of Trustees of the Leland Stanford Junior University, and Copyright © 1990 by the President and Fellows of Harvard College.

Harvard Business School case 590-082 (revised Nov. 2, 1992).

By 1987, ROLM was committed to introducing SIGMA, but controversy remained concerning the introduction strategy and implementation. Lundy's task was to propose solutions for several critical implementation issues associated with the SIGMA introduction. And, because senior management had widely differing views about SIGMA, he had to build a consensus for how the SIGMA introduction would be managed.

Company Background

ROLM Corporation was founded in June 1969 by four electrical engineers who had recently graduated from Rice University.[1] Sharing an entrepreneurial interest, the founders started ROLM with the goal of developing a military specification, or mil-spec, computer. By using newly available minicomputer technology, ROLM's founders believed they could design a computer that would cost 80 percent less to build than the mainframe systems that dominated the mil-spec market. After nine months of development, the company shipped the first units of its new mil-spec computer, priced approximately 50 percent below the closest competitor.

In those early years, ROLM was committed to maintaining its technical leadership in the mil-spec business and to building responsive service and support capabilities. By combining technical leadership, superior service, and unrivaled price/performance, ROLM quickly earned a reputation as a leading mil-spec supplier. By 1973, however, Ken Oshman, ROLM's president, became concerned about the prospects for future growth at ROLM. Oshman predicted the mil-spec computer market would be nearly saturated by the time ROLM reached $10 million–$20 million in sales. Driven by higher ambition, Oshman and his fellow founders decided to investigate other markets where the company's computer expertise could be applied.

After considering several alternatives, ROLM became interested in private branch exchanges (PBXs) as a promising market to diversify into. A PBX is a customer-oriented telephone switching system that connects telephone extensions within an organization to the local telephone company's switching office or directly to other extensions within the organization. A simple PBX system would consist of desktop telephones, wires that link the telephone to the PBX cabinet, and the cabinet itself. By owning a PBX rather than paying the local telephone company for individual telephone lines for each extension, a company could reduce the costs of using and maintaining its telephones. A PBX also provided a company with greater flexibility and management control of its telecommunications systems.

Business users that did not own a PBX had to access a central office switching service (Centrex) offered by the local telephone companies. Central office switches were located at the telephone company. The customer did not pay for the equipment or its maintenance, but paid a line fee every time the switch was used. PBX, on the other

---

[1]The name ROLM is an acronym for the founders' last names: Gene Richeson, Ken Oshman, Walter Lowenstern, and Bob Maxfield.

hand, was located at the customer site. Although customers paid for the equipment, they did not pay a fee for intraoffice use because the switching was done internally.

In 1973, an estimated 40,000 PBX systems were installed in the United States, supporting approximately 10 million telephone lines. Most of these systems had been supplied by AT&T and were based on analog technology that had been developed in the 1960s or earlier. ROLM's project assessment team identified several shortcomings of analog PBX systems that they believed could be remedied by a digital, or computer-controlled, PBX. They also believed a computer-controlled PBX would become a necessity for supporting the technology-leading PBX applications of the future. Finally, they believed that developing such a system would be an easier job for ROLM than it would be for AT&T. Weighing the advantage of being first to market, Oshman decided to commit his company to developing a computer-controlled PBX. In April 1975, after little more than a year of development, ROLM introduced its first CBX (computer-controlled private branch exchange) with a capability of serving customer installations requiring up to 800 extensions.

Growth Years: 1975–1982

Between 1975 and 1982 ROLM's revenues grew from $11 million to $380 million, 85 percent of which was contributed by sales of the CBX product line. During this period of rapid growth, ROLM spent aggressively to expand and enhance the CBX product line. The company added software releases every year that provided customers with a succession of innovative, industry-leading features. ROLM also adapted the CBX hardware platform to serve a broader range of customer installation sizes. (See Exhibit 1 for ROLM product lines and launch data.)

Because of rapid changes in technology during this period, telecommunications managers were uneasy about the possibility of their PBX equipment becoming obsolete as soon as a new and better system was announced. An investment in a single PBX system installation could amount to as much as $15 million for a large organization, and a minimum useful life for the asset was generally expected to be five years. In response to this concern about obsolescence, ROLM designed its new products so that any customer could easily upgrade to the company's latest, full-feature system. Therefore, customers were able to incorporate the currently available state-of-the-art technology without losing their present investment in an installed CBX. This capability became a hallmark of the company and was emphasized by ROLM executives and salespeople. Exhibit 2 illustrates how this theme was used in ROLM's advertising.

Several trends were shaping the competitive environment in the PBX market during the 1970s and 1980s. First, deregulation in the telecommunications industry was dissolving the legal monopoly AT&T had enjoyed since the 1930s. This trend had facilitated ROLM's entry to the PBX market, but it also made the business increasingly attractive to new competition. Second, increased reliance by businesses on information systems was creating a need for accessing and moving data within the organization. Many people considered the PBX to be the most promising system

EXHIBIT 1   ROLM: Product Lines

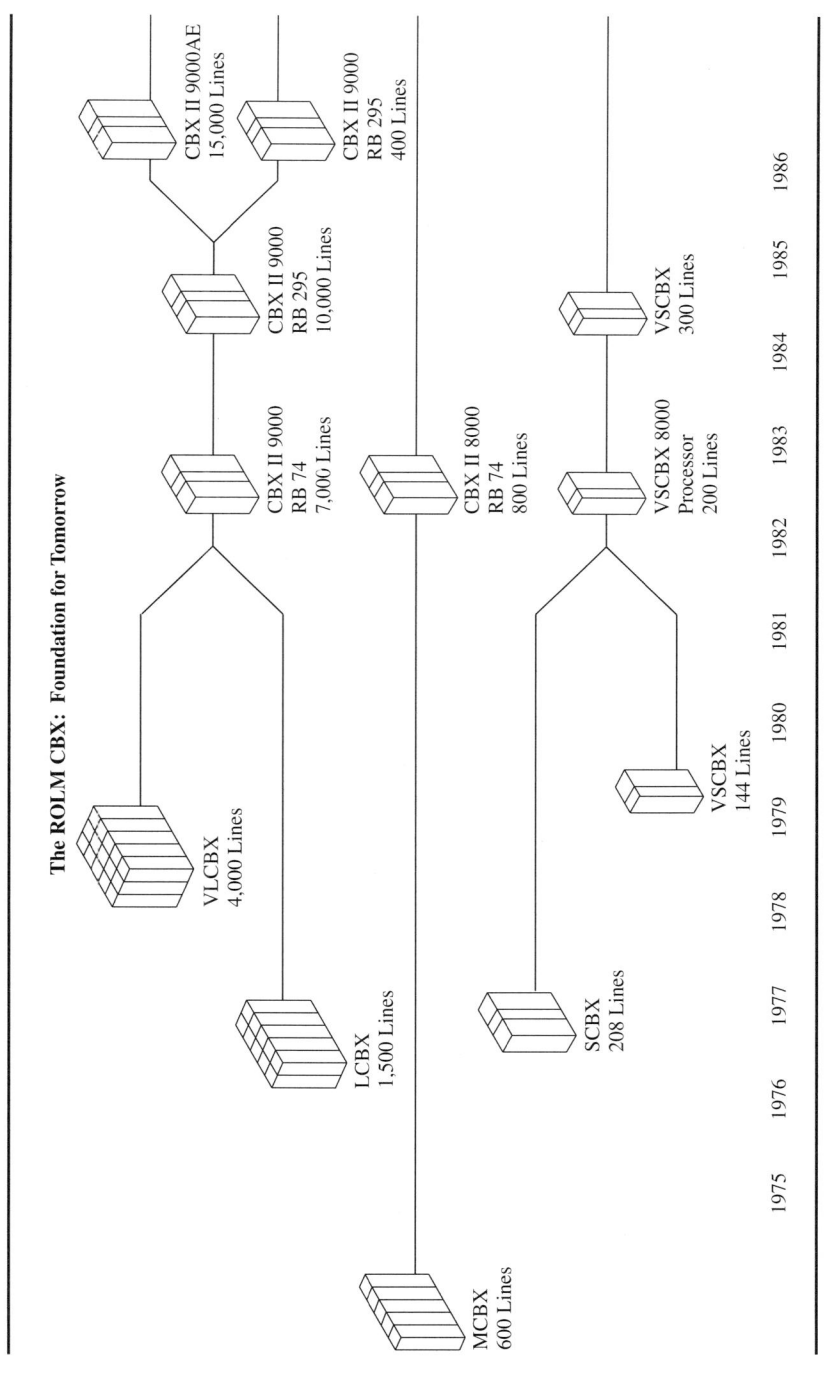

EXHIBIT 2   ROLM: Advertising

DON'T LET THE STEPS KILL YOU.

Take The Ramp. ROLM has perfected a breakthrough communications controller: The CBX II.

It's the centerpiece for a spectacular new ROLM* business telephone system — the fastest, most advanced way to manage voice and data in the world.

Instead of the typical stops, starts, steps and plateaus of expansion, CBX II lets you grow smoothly, easily and very, very cost-effectively.

You can move up The Ramp from sixteen phones to more than ten thousand phones, terminals and personal computers. You can store and forward messages. You can monitor costs. You can have the least expensive long distance routes automatically, instantly. You can even network networks, from Dow Jones to the IBM Infonet. And we're plugged into IBM and HP and DEC and Data General and the other movers and shakers to guarantee that we can take their new products and new systems in stride.

The CBX II is just the latest reason why ROLM is the choice of more than two-thirds of the *Fortune 500* companies, why more than fourteen thousand ROLM systems are up and running today.

When it's all said and done, the best thing about The Ramp is that it ends that recurring nightmare that you may be buying a business communications system that can't grow, can't change or has a big, gee whiz capability missing.

Make your life a lot simpler. Just skip the steps and take The Ramp. **ROLM** for tying information together, particularly because of its already installed wiring and access to public network. This potential opportunity also increased competitive interest in the PBX market.

As a consequence, Northern Telecom, a Canadian start-up, and several other companies had become active in marketing digital PBX systems that were increasingly competitive with ROLM's CBX. AT&T introduced a series of new PBX systems in the 1970s, but these systems were based on outdated analog technology, and AT&T's share of the PBX market slid from 50 percent in 1976 to 27 percent in 1982. Lacking a competitive digital offering, AT&T was beginning to show signs that it would fight its loss of market share through aggressive pricing.

Technological Concerns

By 1982, a significant technology concern had developed at ROLM due to the prevalent use by the company's principal competitors of a sampling rate different from the one used in the CBX product line. *Sampling rate* refers to the number of times per second a digital PBX converts voice (analog) signals into a digital form, or vice versa. The electronic chip that performs this operation is known as a coder-decoder, or codec for short. When ROLM introduced the CBX in 1975, it used a sampling rate of 12,000 samples per second (also called 12 kilohertz, or 12 kHz), which was then the standard for the industry. Later, when ROLM's competitors were developing their own digital PBX technology, 8 kHz emerged as the preferred sampling rate and became the de facto industry standard.

ROLM's use of nonstandard 12 kHz sampling was increasingly perceived as a technical liability of the CBX line. Some customers began to view ROLM as offering old and obsolete technology that was poorly positioned for the future of telecommunications. While ROLM was in fact able to modify its CBX systems to convert between 12 kHz and 8 kHz samplings—and therefore could support any current and future 8 kHz applications—doing so required extra circuitry and development expense.[2] Furthermore, not only were 12 kHz codec chips less plentiful and more expensive then 8 kHz codec, but 8 kHz codec prices were continuing to fall, while 12 kHz codec prices had leveled off.

A second technological problem at ROLM concerned the aging of CBX technology. Much of ROLM's R&D effort through 1982 had been directed at developing software and hardware enhancements that would maintain the company's product leadership while remaining compatible with existing CBX technology. Over the years, the company's competitors were building entirely new systems that incorporated the latest available technologies. As a result, competitive PBX offerings were smaller and required less power and air conditioning than the CBX, making

---

[2]Several new telecommunications technology standards, including ISDN (Integrated Services Digital Network) and T-1 bypass, incorporated 8 kHz sampling. ROLM could accommodate these emerging standards with extra circuits, but customers were increasingly skeptical of ROLM's position for the future.

them less expensive for customers to operate. Also, using newer technologies often meant that competitors experienced lower manufacturing and service costs. ROLM's disadvantage in hardware technology had become a serious drawback in competitive bidding situations, resulting in lost business and wasted effort on the part of account people who had to explain ROLM's position to customers.

Late in 1983, ROLM announced it would introduce a new version of the CBX, dubbed the CBX II, which would consolidate its product line and offer advance performance. However, the CBX II would not address either the concerns about aging technology or ROLM's use of 12 kHz sampling. Nevertheless, the CBX II would remain technologically compatible with earlier CBX systems.

Competitive Considerations

Prior to 1981, AT&T was the monopoly provider of both long-distance telephone service (through its long-lines division) and local area service (through its 22 Bell operating companies). Judge Harold Greene's 1984 Modified Final Judgment decreed that the Bell operating companies be spun off into seven regional holding companies (RHCs) that would be independently operated. As a result, the local telephone companies were no longer obliged to buy AT&T equipment. (AT&T's Western Electric division manufactured central office switching as well as PBX equipment.) By 1985, while several manufacturers offered keen competition in the PBX market, the central office switching market was still dominated by AT&T and Northern Telecom, with market shares of 45 percent and 40 percent, respectively. ROLM did not manufacture central office switching equipment.

After the 1984 divestiture, initially the local telephone companies aggressively pushed PBX technology (by acting as distributors for PBX manufacturers), but by 1985 had realized that more revenues and profits could be made by pushing Centrex services. There was little distribution margin left because of aggressive price competition among PBX manufacturers. The RHCs began to pressure AT&T and Northern Telecom to upgrade their installed central office switching equipment's business features. This involved mainly software, and some hardware, upgrades. Both AT&T and Northern Telecom were able to respond quite quickly to this need, forcing end-users to wonder about the economics of owning PBX equipment instead of renting Centrex (central office switching) services from the local telephone companies. This move further hurt the PBX market development and sharpened the competition in the PBX market.

SIGMA

Late in 1984 IBM acquired ROLM in order to accelerate the development of PBXs that could interact with IBM computers. The end of 1984 also marked Bob Lundy's arrival at ROLM. Lundy, an electrical engineer and a Stanford MBA, joined ROLM from Hewlett-Packard to manage a product development and introduction program that was in early concept phase. (See Exhibit 3 for an organization chart.) The

EXHIBIT 3   ROLM: Organization Chart

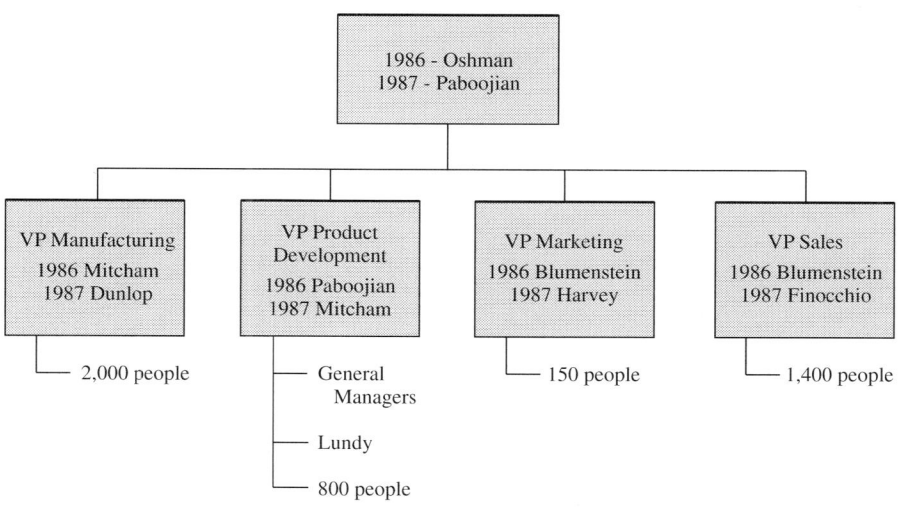

principal goal of Lundy's new program was to reduce the life cycle cost of the CBX. (*Life cycle cost* refers to the total of the customer's cost of owning and ROLM's cost of manufacturing, maintaining, and servicing the CBX.)

As product manager, Lundy led a product development team consisting of managers from hardware and software engineering, reliability and maintainability engineering, planning, and manufacturing. In four months of all-out effort, this tightly focused group completed a new product definition and set a development schedule. As proposed, the new product would be an entirely new system that would preserve the best of the CBX technology. Most important, it would be able to run the same software applications that CBX customers already knew how to use.

However, the new system would utilize the industry standard 8 kHz sampling rate rather than the 12 kHz sample rate used in the current CBX product line. Although 8 kHz sampling would reduce hardware costs and facilitate product development, the resulting system would be incompatible with the 20,000 CBXs currently installed. To upgrade from the CBX to the new system, ROLM's customers would need to replace their CBX controllers with new controllers, an operation that was known as a "forklift upgrade." To preserve security over these plans, Lundy adopted the code name SIGMA for his program.

Not all of the CBX system components would be incompatible with the SIGMA system, however. The telephone lines themselves and the wiring that connected the controller to the individual telephone extensions could be used with the SIGMA system. For small installations, the cost of purchasing and installing these components amounted to 40 percent of the hardware system cost, while the costs for installation of 10,000 or more lines accounted for 60 percent of the bill.

Exhibit 4 ROLM: SIGMA versus Competition

Factors	Sigma	"Best of Breed"
<600 Lines Segment		
Reliability	=	A
Cost of ownership	−	A
System coverage	+	SIGMA
Function/feature	=	A/SIGMA
Connectivity/data support	+	SIGMA
>600 Lines Segment		
Reliability	=	A/SIGMA
Cost of ownership	+	SIGMA
System coverage	+	B/SIGMA
Function/feature	=	C/SIGMA
Connectivity/data support	+	SIGMA

Source: Company records.

The development team believed the SIGMA system would deliver the following improvements compared to the CBX:

- Switching capacity: 70 percent higher.
- Reliability: 100 percent higher.
- Service cost: 55 percent lower.
- Power requirements: 50 percent lower.
- Physical space requirement: 50 percent lower.

Lundy felt strongly that these improvements would answer the criticisms that had been directed at the CBX. Concerns about obsolete technology, air-conditioning requirements, and physical bulk would be resolved. Moreover, Lundy believed that SIGMA's increased performance would enable ROLM to capture a higher win ratio in the market and would provide an excellent foundation for developing future industry-leading applications. (See Exhibit 4 for management's assessment of SIGMA's strengths with respect to competition.)

By late 1985, SIGMA had emerged as ROLM's best bet for the future. The new design would save manufacturing costs and potentially improve current gross margins by as much as 50 to 75 percent. The SIGMA team had completed the specifications for the new system, and Ken Oshman had made the decision to go ahead with further development. Oshman also decided that the target market for SIGMA should be extended across the entire range of the current CBX line, covering installations from 600 to 20,000 lines. The SIGMA team had reason to be pleased with the importance that their program had taken on. Moving ahead, Lundy prepared for the next management checkpoint meeting, scheduled for January 1986 with the vice president of systems development.

Implementation Issues

At the management checkpoint meeting of January 1986, Lundy presented his team's specifications and product development plans for SIGMA. During the presentation, Lundy stressed that the general goal of the SIGMA program was to increase revenue and profitability at ROLM, and he listed the following specific objectives of the program:

1. Increase ROLM's win ratio in competitive bidding situations.
2. Increase margins.
3. Avert any decline in orders and revenue during the introduction period.
4. Minimize value erosion of ROLM's installed base of CBX.
5. Maximize customer confidence.
6. Avoid confusion in the marketplace.

After listening to the presentation, Dennis Paboojian, ROLM's VP of systems development, was very concerned about how the introduction of SIGMA would be managed. He believed the SIGMA introduction was vastly more difficult than any previous new product introduction at ROLM. This stemmed from two principal facts: (1) SIGMA was technologically incompatible with ROLM's installed base, and (2) the SIGMA rollout would span the entire range of the CBX II product line, which provided the majority of ROLM's revenues. Paboojian believed an introduction that was anything less than superbly orchestrated would place ROLM's entire business at risk. (See Exhibit 5 for ROLM-installed systems as of 1987.)

EXHIBIT 5   ROLM: Installed Base (1987)

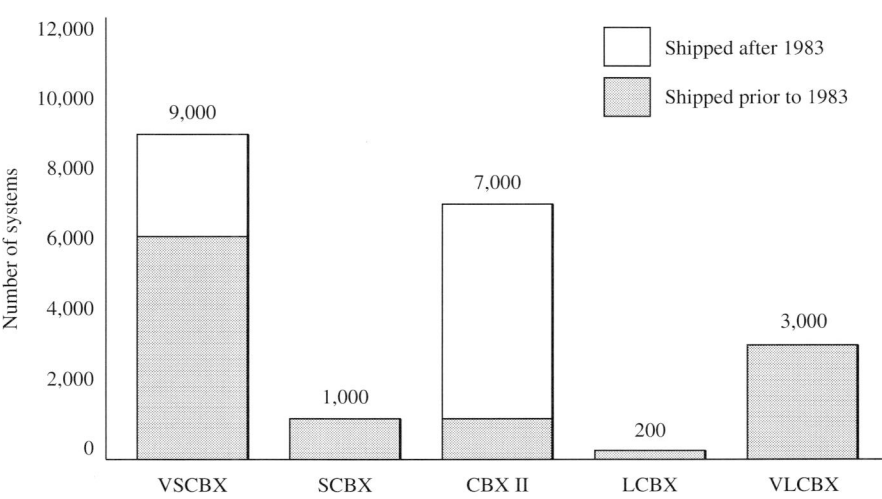

- Systems of greater than 400 lines represented 30 percent of unit systems sales but 70 percent of revenue.
- Shipments of approximately 200 systems per month were planned for 1987.

With development work continuing on the SIGMA system, Lundy and his team spent much of the next 12 months addressing the concerns Paboojian had raised. By January 1987, Lundy believed his team had enough information to fully characterize these issues, and he knew that engineering and manufacturing had committed to rolling out production units of SIGMA in December. Lundy framed the following five critical implementation issues.

1. *Security.* ROLM managers were apprehensive about how customers would react when they learned that SIGMA was incompatible with the CBX line. Most thought that a premature leak of information about SIGMA would result in a significant reduction of revenue. Customers would be afraid that the new system would signal a reduction in ROLM's efforts to support the CBX. Customers bought systems from ROLM not only for their current capabilities but also with the expectation of adding future system expansions and software updates as was done on a yearly basis to enhance mainframe computers.

Until 1986, knowledge about SIGMA had been kept to a small number of inside people. Maintaining security would become increasingly difficult, however. For example, during 1987 SIGMA would be installed for testing at ROLM and at eight different IBM locations; thus, an increasing number of inside staff would have to know about the new system. Also, 20 demonstration sites, requiring six weeks of installation time, would need to be in place throughout the United States prior to announcement day. Third, a number of market-leading, large-system contracts were being vied for at this time—installations that SIGMA would be capable of handling but the CBX II would not. On these contracts, ROLM could either decline to bid or bid and risk broad disclosure about the new system. Fourth, account managers at IBM, whose primary interest was to secure IBM computer sales, were being asked by their clients to reveal the ROLM subsidiary's new product plans. Finally, ROLM managers thought that divulgence of product plans, even to major existing customers, would inevitably constitute a general announcement.

Despite tight security measures, Lundy was aware that rumors about SIGMA had already appeared in trade journals (see Exhibit 6). These rumors were being used by ROLM's competitors to undermine the company's sales efforts. Prompted by the rumors, major customers were requesting ROLM to allow guarantees in purchase contracts providing assurance that their CBX II systems would not become obsolete.

2. *Announcement.* Lundy faced three basic issues concerning the SIGMA announcement: whether to announce quietly or with a splash, and what information to emphasize in the announcement. Lundy surveyed several senior managers on these issues and received differing views, as indicated in the following excerpts:

> Dennis says don't splash. Thinks we would lose control, and believes big splash announcements lead to a very complex situation for the sales force to handle. For example, maybe we wouldn't be able to deal with customers who are in the process of installing a CBX II system but who want to convert their orders to a SIGMA system [from interview with Dennis Paboojian, Vice President of Systems Development].

> Dick thinks we have to prepare to announce but seems to imply that we may end up with something less than a major splash. After discussion, he pointed out that a splash had

EXHIBIT 6   ROLM: News Reports

Is Rolm readying CBX III?
Switch maker denies CBX II successor in beta test.

BY PAM POWERS
Senior Editor

Despite Rolm Corp.'s staunch contention that the rumored successor to its CBX II private branch exchange is a figment of the industry's imagination, observers close to the company insist the IBM subsidiary is on the verge of making a significant announcement, possibly involving a new generation PBX.

According to one anonymous source, Rolm is already beta testing a CBX III architecture that will be introduced soon. Other analysts believe pending announcements will simply involve enhancements to the existing CBX II.

All observers, however, voiced strong opinions regarding Rolm's CBX II failings, noting that an upgrade or new switch would serve to strengthen the company's position in the PBX market.

Rolm's introduction of the low-end Redwood PBX in June represented a departure from the company's proprietary architecture, rekindling speculation that Rolm would eventually shift its larger, mainstream switch products to industry standards. Rumors of a CBX III have dogged Rolm ever since, although the company has never indicated such a product was slated for introduction.

Rolm's current PBX architecture samples analog voice signals 12,000 times per second and represents each sample with a 12-bit digital word. Industry-standard pulse-code modulation samples analog signals 8,000 times per second and represents each sample with an 8-bit byte. Some analysts contend Rolm's break with the industry standard is creating compatibility problems with the data processing products of parent company IBM and bodes ill for Rolm's compatibility with Integrated Services Digital Network environments.

According to Jerry Eisen, president of Office Sciences International, Inc. of Iselin, N.J., Rolm has been aware for some time that the CBX II architecture had to change. Eisen, who has been in discussions with Rolm over the last four months, said, "We told Rolm, and they agreed, that the switch has to support 64K bit/sec ISDN, the footprint has to change and the power requirements have to change."

Rolm's admission of architectural shortcomings, he said, would probably result in a new architecture with the same digital interface, enabling users to retain CBX II station equipment but requiring new racks and cards. Eisen said he would be surprised not to hear an announcement in the immediate future. "Rolm is overdue as far as the market is concerned."

Donald Dittberner, president of Dittberner Associates, Inc., a consultancy located in Bethesda, Md., said he, too, is expecting an announcement. "I see Rolm having serious problems in competition from ISDN Centrex," he said. "I would think that IBM, which has never supported ISDN, now sees the handwriting on the wall. If something isn't announced by spring, I think Rolm will be in very difficult straits." A new switch should support local-area network capabilities and IBM protocols and be ISDN-compatible, he said.

Doane Perry, senior telecommunications analyst with International Data Corp., said he believes Rolm is poised to make an announcement. "On the inside of the switch, it will have to be more IBM Systems Network Architecture-compatible, and on the outside, more ISDN- and T-1-compatible. Rolm has had problems achieving T-1 compatibility," he added.

Lee Goeller, president of Communication Resources, Inc., of Haddonfield, Conn., elaborated on the T-1 point. "Everybody else who had a chance made a T-carrier-compatible PBX," he said. "To not do this is foolish; all Rolm has to do is change the switching matrix."

If Goeller's assertion is correct, Rolm might accomplish the necessary enhancements by introducing a new processor for the CBX II in lieu of a completely new machine.

That, said Joaquin Gonzalez, service director of Enterprise Networking Strategies at Gartner Group, Inc. in Stamford, Conn., is the far more likely scenario. "Rolm has taken great pains to talk about the CBX II as its only high-end PBX now and forever," Gonzalez said. He refuted the possibility of a CBX III introduction, but said, "I think Rolm will come out with more powerful processors under the existing architecture, with enhancements enabling network management of voice." □

SOURCE: Reprinted from *Network World.* Copyright 1986 by Network World, Inc., Framingham, Massachusetts 01701.

ROLM held a press conference in New York in early 1986 to squelch speculation about a "CBX III" development program. The delegation was lead by vice president Jack Blumenstein, who emphasized the following point: ROLM would be foolish to develop any new PBX that was incompatible with or would obsolete the company's installed base of some 20,000 CBX systems. "Our customer base was one reason IBM bought us; the guy who bought the first CBX 10 years ago will still be able to get everything," insisted Blumenstein.
SOURCE: *MIS Week,* January 13, 1986.

better have a lot of content, and we need to assess what the promotable value of SIGMA really is. At first he did not think a splash announcement would help in increasing the win ratio [from interview with Dick Moley, Vice President of Marketing].

Ken thinks it would be a major mistake to announce at all. Very concerned about the installed base. Suggests making the announcement a year late. Proposes that we highlight what we've got in the new product, but recognize that good release materials (sales and support documentation) without a big splash announcement accomplishes the same thing. After all, we win deals across the desk, talking with customers [from interview with Ken Oshman, president and founder].

By comparison, Lundy felt very strongly that SIGMA should be announced as an exciting new hardware platform for the future. A further question Lundy faced was whether to portray SIGMA in an announcement as an entirely new system or simply as an upgrade in the cabinet and hardware. Here, again, he favored the more aggressive story.

3. *Timing*. To study the question of when to announce, Lundy considered a number of scenarios. The first assumed an announcement three months ahead of general availability. This scenario had the advantage of putting ROLM in the running for certain large contracts that were in the bidding process at the end of the year.

The second scenario Lundy considered also assumed announcement three months in advance of product availability, but in this case he assumed a gradual ramping up of production over three months after the SIGMA introduction.

The third assumed an announcement timed to coincide with general product availability. Lundy wondered about the pros and cons of each scenario with respect to the goals and objectives of the program.

Lundy also began to consider how an announcement might work in December. On close examination, he became discouraged about announcing then because of problems with doing business at the end of the year. December was the end of the accounting year for both IBM and ROLM, and usually there was frenzied business activity at that time, though it was difficult to get anything done in the last 10 days because of the holidays. At the same time, pressure was building to push the announcement forward to October. An October announcement would coincide with the announcement of a new European CBX system that would also be based on 8 kHz sampling technology. This schedule would leave less than nine months for planning and would require manufacturing to push forward their commitment date.[3]

In contemplating when to announce, Lundy was aware that SIGMA had already missed its original introduction date of January 1987.

4. *Backlog*. A major issue for Lundy's team was how to manage ROLM's backlog of orders in the months leading up to the announcement. Orders in the pipeline could be categorized according to four stages: ordered but not shipped, shipped but not installed, installed but not paid, and paid. The amount of time the average order spent in each of the first three stages was 90 days, 40 days, and 60

---

[3]Manufacturing planning faced six-month lead times for procuring certain parts.

days, respectively. ROLM typically would begin production on an order as soon as the order was received.

Lundy already had a general idea about what the backlog would look like during the middle of the year. He knew, however, that he would need better information about the types of installations and customers if his team was going to be able to manage the backlog effectively. To collect this information and to manage the various accounts, he formed the Backlog Management Team (BMT). Its goals were as follows:

- Plan to convert 95 percent of the backlogged orders from the CBX II system that was ordered to an equivalent SIGMA installation.
- Ensure complete secrecy about SIGMA before announcement.
- Take all steps necessary to avoid customer confusion.

The BMT believed many customers in the backlog could be convinced to accept a SIGMA system in lieu of a CBX because SIGMA would cost the same at purchase but would be less expensive to operate over the product's life. Also, while SIGMA would require less floor space and air conditioning than customers had installed for the CBX, SIGMA's applications were functionally equivalent to the CBX. Generally, therefore, a customer could accept a SIGMA installation as a direct replacement of a CBX, and the primary impact would be that in some cases less than half of the area that was allocated for the system would be utilized.

However, Lundy's team did not expect all customers to willingly convert to a SIGMA system. Customers would be reluctant to buy a new system that might have glitches in it. In fact, most buyers rated system reliability as the most important criterion for selecting a PBX. As a result, a major question for Lundy was whether or not ROLM should continue marketing and/or shipping its widely accepted CBX II line after the SIGMA announcement. Continuing to market the CBX II would help safeguard ROLM's backlog of orders, but it would also complicate ROLM's manufacturing efforts and would confuse customers. Lundy favored the higher-risk solution of stopping active marketing of the CBX II. Under Lundy's plan, the company would continue to ship CBX II system expansions to its installed base and new CBX II systems on a special request basis only.

Perhaps a larger problem was how to keep sales and installation activity going through the summer. While ROLM was making every attempt to contain information about SIGMA within the company, there was widespread speculation in the industry that a new ROLM product was coming on-line. Customers were becoming wary and demanding assurances that their investments would not be made obsolete by a new ROLM product. In the worst case, Lundy's team worried about the reactions (and careers) of telecommunications managers whose CBX systems would be installed and paid for just before SIGMA was announced.

ROLM's regional sales managers, who took the brunt of customers' concerns, demanded the ability to disclose ROLM's product plans to key clients and to offer some form of financial incentive to keep sales rolling. Lundy and the team members began to work on a program that would guarantee a trade-in allowance on any recently installed CBX system. Such a program would take the sting out of the SIGMA announcement, but it would also negatively impact ROLM's bottom line.

Exhibit 7   ROLM: Investment Protection Plan

Customer Economics

In a system purchase scenario, a customer accepts a CBX II in July 1987 for a total cost of $2 million. The chart below indicates the proportions of component cost.

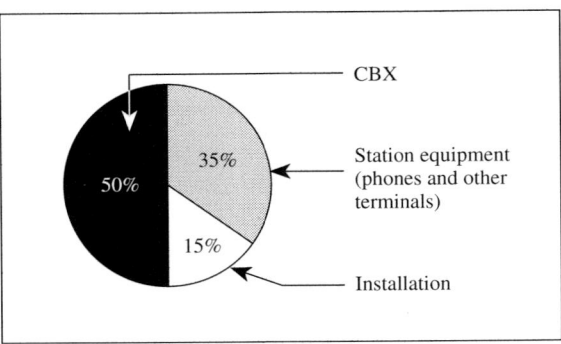

In December 1987 the customer decides to trade in the CBX II controller for a SIGMA controller costing an additional $500,000 (without IPP discount). The component costs are as follows:

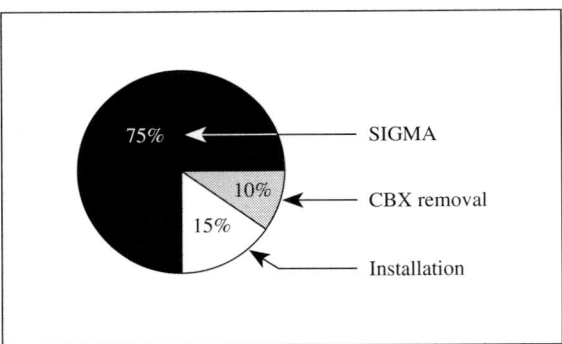

To buy an equivalent new system in December 1987 from one of ROLM's competitors would cost:

Competitor	Cost
X	$2.8 million
Y	$2.0 million
Z	$1.8 million

To better appraise the economic effects of such a program, Lundy devised a preliminary investment protection plan (IPP) that would provide a discount option to current customers of 55 percent off the incremental cost of upgrading to SIGMA (see Exhibit 7). Lundy was not certain how successful he would be in selling a 55 percent discount program to senior management, considering ROLM's sales executives wanted a discount of 80 to 100 percent, while IBM executives—who had never before provided this kind of benefit—wanted a discount of not more than 10 to 15 percent. There were also several questions of timing: namely, how many months prior to announcement should the IPP be grandfathered, and how many months after announcement should the option expire. Another issue was whether to compute the discount on the cost of the controller only or on total system cost, including installation.

Lundy knew his team would face tremendous challenges in persuading backlogged customers to convert to SIGMA, once the new system was announced. To accomplish its goals, the backlog management team would need to actively manage each account, learning as much as possible about each account's circumstances and gauging the likelihood of conversion without divulging ROLM's plans about the new product. If the team was not thoroughly prepared to manage this challenge, Lundy expected the resulting confusion would seriously injure ROLM's standing in the market and result in losses and deferrals in orders and revenues.

5. *Installed base.* ROLM's installed base of 20,000 CBX systems presented another major problem to Lundy's group. Because of ROLM's historic high growth-rate, most of the company's installed systems had not yet been fully depreciated by its customers. These customers expected that ROLM would continue its policy of protecting their investment by providing an easy and relatively inexpensive means of incorporating ROLM's latest-available technologies. The SIGMA announcement, however, would be perceived by these customers as a signal that ROLM was ending its commitment to enhance the CBX II line, and they would expect that future developments would be available only on the SIGMA platform. Lundy's team had to find ways to minimize this perception of value erosion among existing customers.

ROLM would continue to ship and support system expansions to its installed base. This activity was projected to account for 25 percent of revenue in 1987. ROLM was committed to providing the same level of service to these customers as it had done before. But ROLM did in fact plan to reduce development efforts on the CBX II in favor of developing future capabilities for SIGMA. This meant that installed base customers would have no other option than a "forklift upgrade" if they wanted to utilize the capabilities ROLM was developing for the future. This promised to add considerably to the expense of staying up-to-date with PBX technology.

To soften the blow to installed base customers, Lundy's team worked on a migration incentive plan that would provide some value to customers who wanted to trade in their CBX II systems for SIGMA systems. The preliminary plan called for a 20 percent allowance, although Lundy thought older systems should receive less of an allowance than newer systems. While he hadn't yet decided how to structure the allowance schedule, he did conclude that only CBX systems installed after 1984 would qualify for any benefit under this program.

Next Steps

In recent months, AT&T and Northern Telecom each had announced extremely competitive products in the 100–600 line range. In particular, the new AT&T System 75 family had earned the "best of breed" status in the low-end segment by

Exhibit 8 ROLM: PBX Market Statistics, 1982–1986

	1982	1983	1984	1985	1986
Market size (thousands of lines shipped)	3,200	3,700	4,400	4,800	5,000
Market size (billions of dollars)	2.90	3.30	3.50	3.50	3.50
ROLM PBX revenue (millions of dollars)	380	500	560	540	550
ROLM gross margin after sales and marketing expense (millions of dollars)	60	75	78	72	65

NOTE: Gross margin before sales and marketing expenses were 45% to 50% of sales.

Market Share of Top Eight Competitors

	1982	1983	1984	1985	1986
AT&T	27	23	19	23	22
Northern Telecom	13	17	22	23	23
Rolm	13	15	17	15	16
MITEL	12	12	10	9	9
NEC	4	5	6	7	8
GTE	5	4	4	4	4
Siemens	4	4	4	3	4
Intecom	1	2	3	3	2

SOURCE: Adapted from Roger G. Noll and Bruce M. Owen, "United States vs. AT&T: An Interim Assessment," in Stephen Bradley and Jerry Hausman, eds., *Future Competition in Telecommunications* (Cambridge, Mass.: HBS Press, 1989); and *Business Week,* Information Processing section, July 10, 1989.

offering compact digital systems that had low power requirements. Furthermore, these competitors had announced that their new products would support ISDN.[4] As a result, competition in the low-end segment was expected to be severe, if not brutal. (See Exhibit 8 for PBX market statistics from 1982–1986.) Nevertheless, Lundy felt SIGMA would still lead the industry on the following key attributes:

- Seamless architecture: Through SIGMA, ROLM had the unique capability of covering the entire line range with a single product.
- Superior performance: SIGMA's advanced processor offered 70 percent more traffic capacity than the competition.
- Voice and data integration: SIGMA offered superior solutions and support for voice and data standards.
- Desktop devices: SIGMA would be compatible with ROLM's industry-leading product line of digital phone sets and terminals.

Although the SIGMA team had made considerable progress in framing the five critical issues, Lundy still had to set a clear direction for each one. Once his choices were set, he would need to actively campaign to win approval from senior management.

---

[4] Although SIGMA would not ship with ISDN capability, ROLM planned to issue a statement of direction.

CHAPTER 13

Green Marketing at Rank Xerox

Management at Rank Xerox had put together an innovative line of copiers made partially from reassembled parts. This was seen as a step toward manufacturing and marketing environmentally friendlier products. Several issues, however, still remained to be addressed, such as customer acceptance, compliance with national regulations, pricing aspects, and product guarantees.

Introduction

On April 16, 1992, Val Govaerts, reprographics marketing manager at Rank Xerox headquarters in Marlow, United Kingdom, found himself confronted with a difficult decision. The European market seemed ready for the introduction of an environmentally friendly product line, but several problems were influencing the decision. Little market data existed about actual customer preferences, making the positioning of such a line difficult. There was also a need to describe such a product line in a legally consistent manner in all markets, such that customers would be made aware of the inclusion of reprocessed parts. Finally, although the concept of a Green line was revolutionary in the industry—and would allow Rank Xerox to capitalize on being the first in the market with such a line—it also exposed the company to unknown liabilities and possible public dismay if things went wrong. Govaerts sat back in his chair and mulled over the issues once more.

Joep VanThiels prepared this case under the supervision of Jeffrey F. Rayport.
Copyright © 1993 by the President and Fellows of Harvard College.
Harvard Business School case 594-047 (revised May 12, 1994).

Company Background

The Xerox group consisted of Xerox Corporation, marketing products in the North American continent; Fuji Xerox, marketing in Japan, Korea, Southeast Asia, and Australia; Modi Xerox, marketing in India; and Rank Xerox, marketing in Europe, Africa, the Middle East, and the rest of Asia (see Exhibit 1).

Following the introduction of its first copier in 1959, Xerox held a firm grip on the copier market with market shares close to 100 percent. However, when patents on Xerox's xerographic technology expired during the 1970s, several Japanese companies started to exploit the technology and quickly introduced small, inexpensive, low-volume copiers. This was the first real competition Xerox had ever faced after

EXHIBIT 1 Organization Chart

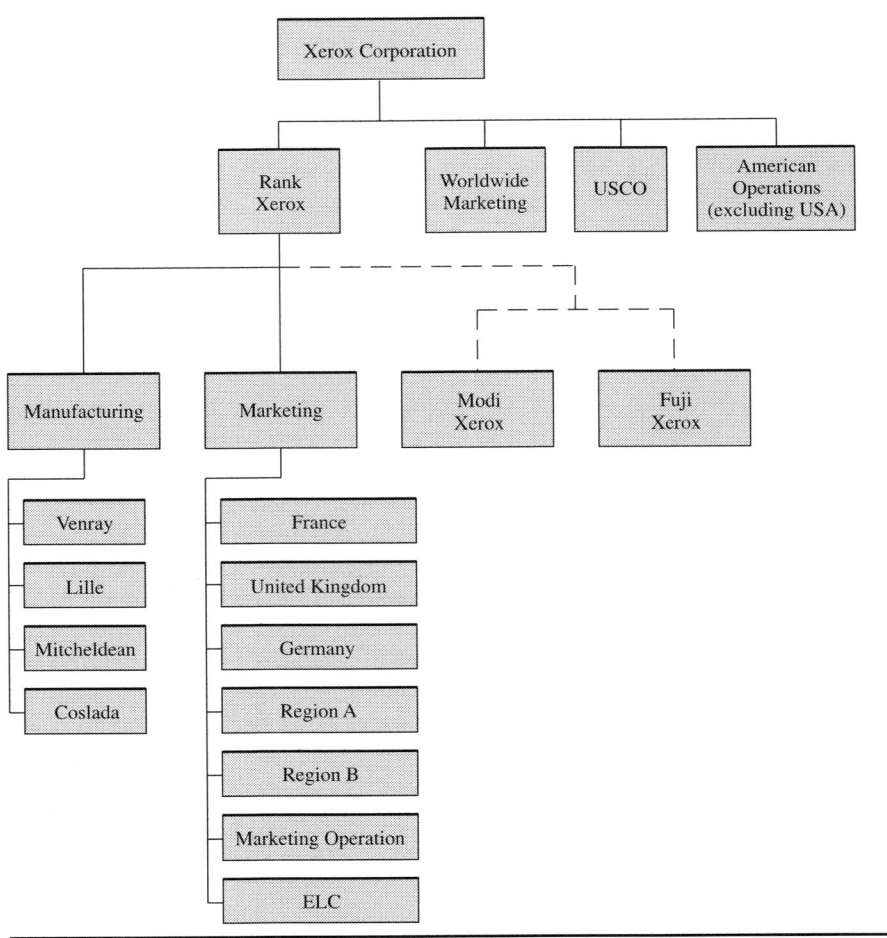

Exhibit 2 Xerox Group Consolidated Financial Results (in millions of dollars)

	1985	1986	1987	1988	1989	1990
Revenues:						
Document processing	8,676	9,355	10,320	11,688	12,431	13,583
Financial services	3,085	3,691	4,274	4,753	5,204	4,390
Total operating revenue	11,761	13,046	14,594	16,441	17,635	17,973
Income from operations	381	488	578	388	704	605
Return on sales	3.2%	3.7%	4.0%	2.4%	4.0%	3.4%
Assets:						
Document processing	7,247	7,517	10,657	12,203	13,276	14,168
Financial services	10,126	12,394	11,793	14,238	16,812	14,216
Total assets	17,373	19,911	22,450	26,441	30,088	28,384
Return on assets	2.2%	2.5%	2.6%	1.5%	2.3%	2.1%

years of virtual monopoly in the low-end copier market. As a result, it did not have the proper infrastructure and people mentality to compete in an increasingly competitive environment. Xerox was also hampered by an uncompetitive low-volume copier line that could not compete directly with the Japanese. In the meantime, the Japanese were gaining ground by slowly expanding their presence through a dealer distribution network, thus eating away more Xerox market share.

The situation was aggravated by the ability of Japanese companies to offer products at low prices in the United States and Europe while obtaining high profits in their own protected Japanese market. During that time, the Japanese exercised great creativity and also found other ways to penetrate the European markets through joint ventures with European copier manufacturers (Olivetti-Canon and Develop-Minolta) and/or through assembly operations on the European continent.

In light of the foregoing, Xerox's total market share plummeted to below 20 percent (see Exhibits 2 and 3 for selected financial results).[1] David Kearns, CEO, recognized Xerox's lack of customer focus and market connectedness, and implemented a quality process called Leadership Through Quality. The process was also aimed at stopping market share erosion. In addition, many organizational changes were made, and Xerox entered the low-volume market in order to compete at the base of the Japanese product lines. However, even though market share erosion was slowed by these actions, it was not enough.

The Japanese proved more responsive than Xerox to changing customer needs through more rapid new-product commercialization. New products were essential to respond to evolving customer requirements, yet product development was only part of the challenge. Marketing programs were necessary to accompany each introduction. On both fronts, Xerox achieved dramatic reductions in time to market for new products.

Xerox repositioned the corporation to appeal to customers with a statement that was both memorable and distinctive—Xerox, The Document Company. The

[1]SOURCE: Dataquest.

Exhibit 3 Rank Xerox Consolidated Financial Results (in millions of dollars)

	1985	1986	1987	1988	1989	1990
Revenues:						
Document processing	2,078	2,661	3,325	4,029	4,225	4,734
Financial services	18	41	85	a		
Transfers	188	168	184	324	333	290
Total operating revenue	2,284	2,870	3,594	4,353	4,558	5,024
Income from operations	58	45	81	97	74	143
Return on sales	2.5%	1.6%	2.3%	2.2%	1.6%	2.8%
Assets:						
Document processing	2,344	2,533	2,980	4,258	4,648	5,586
Financing/banking	131	302	778			
Total assets	2,475	2,835	3,758	4,258	4,648	5,586
Return on assets	2.3%	1.6%	2.2%	2.3%	1.6%	2.6%

^aAs of 1988, Xerox Corporation took full responsibility of the financial services division.

refocusing stressed Xerox's core competence. Xerox also initiated several programs during the 1980s, such as benchmarking, employee involvement, and a new set of corporate priorities. The new priorities were customer satisfaction, improved return on assets, increased market share, and employee satisfaction. In addition, Xerox redefined quality to meet customer requirements, thus increasing efficiency and flexibility. Within just a few years, financial results responded and Xerox was awarded many quality awards, including the prestigious Malcolm Baldrige Award (1989) in the United States and the European Foundation of Quality Management (EFQM) award (1992) in Europe (see Exhibit 4). These awards were direct results of Xerox's aggressive and successful Leadership Through Quality process, which has since become the core of Xerox's business strategy.

Exhibit 4 Quality Awards

1980	Fuji-Xerox won Japanese Deming Award for Quality.
1983	Rank Xerox factory in Venray received the CIMEI quality award from the Dutch government.
1984	Rank Xerox factory in Mitcheldean awarded the British quality award.
1986	Rank Xerox factory at Welwyn Garden City won the British quality award.
1987	Rank Xerox factory in Lille won the French quality award.
1989	Xerox won the USA's Malcolm Baldrige National Quality Award.
1989	Xerox Canada won the Award for Business Excellence.
1990	Australian group awarded the Australian quality award.
1990	Rank Xerox in Venray won Nevbat-Misset Co-purchaser Award for Best Purchasing Policies.
1990	Xerox won the National Quality Award in Mexico.
1992	Rank Xerox won the Total Quality Award from the European Foundation of Quality Management (EFQM).
1992	Asset Recovery Operation in Venray received an ISO-9002 certification (a process control standard awarded to companies in process manufacturing industries), making ARO one of the world's first recycling operations to meet ISO standards.
1992	Rank Xerox service organizations in the United Kingdom, France, Belgium, and the Netherlands received national quality awards.

As a result of all these changes, Xerox became more competitive and financial results improved accordingly. Market share also stabilized and even improved slightly. Xerox was ready for a counterattack.

Organization. The Rank Xerox organization was broadly divided into two major functions: manufacturing operations and marketing operations. The latter included marketing, sales, and service. The logistics for the entire company were monitored by the European Logistics Center (ELC) in Venray, the Netherlands. In addition, both marketing operations and manufacturing had access to such Xerox functions as R&D, finance, and worldwide manufacturing.

Manufacturing Operations. Rank Xerox had four manufacturing sites in Europe. Venray in the Netherlands, which also housed the ELC, was the largest site with 2,200 employees and built the midvolume (based on copies per minute) copiers. Mitcheldean in the United Kingdom (1,700 employees) produced the low-volume and high-volume copiers. Lille in France (650 employees) produced input/output devices. Coslada in Spain (100 employees) was the smallest operation and responsible for toner production and laser printer assembly. Some high-volume copiers sold in Europe were supplied by Xerox plants in the United States.

Marketing Operations. Rank Xerox marketing operations was subdivided into 25 national companies and local regions, called European operating units (EOUs) (see Exhibit 5). Each EOU sold the full line of products, but differences in

---

EXHIBIT 5   Rank Xerox European Operating Units (EOUs)

United Kingdom
Germany
France
Region A
   Austria
   Belgium
   Denmark
   Finland
   Greece
   The Netherlands
   Italy
   Norway
   Portugal
   Spain
   Sweden
   Switzerland
Region B
   Rest of Europe
   Africa
   Parts of Asia
   India

NOTE: When excluding Region B, the United Kingdom, Germany, and France each represented about 20% of Rank Xerox's business and Region A the other 40%.

Exhibit 6 Rank Xerox Revenues per Market Segment (1991), Excluding Region B

Market Segment	Revenue ($ million)	Percentage
Low volume	$ 643	(14%)
Mid volume	2,389	(53%)
Mid/high volume	502	(11%)
High volume	978	(22%)
	$4,512	(100%)

NOTE: Data is disguised and thus not representative of actual situation.

languages, national legislation, and customer expectations required different marketing and service approaches in each national market.

Distribution. The EOUs sold Xerox products through both a direct sales force for the key accounts (60 percent of revenues) and through the same direct sales force as well as dealers to smaller accounts and the general public (40 percent of revenues). There were two types of dealers: concessionaires, who were authorized to sell Xerox products only, and regular dealers, who carried other brand names too.

Communications Programs. The marketing approach to each of these distribution points was different. The company focused on its larger accounts through direct sales. Smaller accounts received communications largely through targeted corporate advertising. Dealers were encouraged to do their own advertising, but they also benefitted from advertising by Rank Xerox in the form of brochures, magazine and newspaper advertisements, and the (Rank) Xerox brand name.

Products in Line with (Rank) Xerox's Corporate Image as "The Document Company." Rank Xerox produced and sold copiers, fax machines, printers, and high-quality Xerox-branded paper. Industry analysts traditionally divided the copier market into four segments: personal desktop copiers, and low-, medium-, and high-volume copiers. Exhibit 6 shows Rank Xerox products in each segment in which it had an interest, together with their respective sales volumes. Most products had a field life of 3 to 7 years, and a product family was usually marketed for 5 to 15 years, depending on its success. In the past, an old product family used to be replaced by a complete new product line (product revolution), but over the years, old lines were superseded more and more by upgraded product families (product evolution). One of the reasons for this shift was the increase in reusable content of returned copiers due to the similarity of its successor lines.

Competitors. Within Europe, Rank Xerox's major competitors were Canon in the low-volume market and Kodak in the high-volume market. Exhibit 7 provides a listing of the most important competitors and their market shares for each of the market segments.

EXHIBIT 7	Market Share per Market—1991	
Segment	Company	Percentage
Low	Canon	49.8%
	Rank Xerox	42.1
	Oce	2.3
	Polaroid	2.0
	Sharp	1.9
	Other	1.8
		100.0%
Mid	Canon	48.3%
	Rank Xerox	41.3
	IBM	5.3
	Minolta	1.6
	Kodax	1.0
	Other	1.4
		100.0%
High	Rank Xerox	87.8%
	Kodak	10.1
	IBM	0.8
	Pitney Bowes	0.4
	Konica	0.3
	Other	0.6
		100.0%

NOTE: Data is disguised and thus not representative of actual situation.

None of the Japanese competitors had any substantial manufacturing base in Europe. Some, like Canon and Minolta, had assembly operations or joint ventures with European copier manufacturers, but the most major sourcing and value-added manufacturing was still performed in Japan.

Green Consumerism

Besides competition based on price, value, service, and quality, another important competitive factor was emerging in Europe. Over the last decade, environmental awareness in Europe had skyrocketed and public outcry (see Exhibits 8, 9, and 10) for protection of the environment had become a major political and business priority. Spurred by numerous environmental disasters, individual European countries as well as the European Community set out to develop new environmental legislation and regulations. Unfortunately, the disparity between the countries' physical and regulatory infrastructures aimed at protecting the environment was enormous. For example, Germany, Denmark, the Netherlands, and Austria were, on average, much more environmentally active than Europe's more southern countries such as Spain, Italy, and Greece. Others, including France and the United Kingdom, were somewhere in between. As a result, landfill sites were being closed, the cost of disposal

EXHIBIT 8   Most Important Environmental Problems Facing the Nation (Volunteered)

Q.5 Thinking about our nation as a whole, what is the most important environmental problem facing our nation? If you feel that there are no serious environmental problems facing our nation, please feel free to say so. (OPEN-ENDED)

Problem Mentioned

	Most Often	Percent (%)	Second Most Often	Percent (%)	Third Most Often	Percent (%)
North America:						
Canada	Air pollution	24%	Water quality	20%	Global warming	17%
United States	Air pollution	23	Water quality	15	Waste disposal	14
Latin America:						
Brazil	Loss of natural resources	53	Water quality	9	Air pollution	6
Chile	Air pollution	33	Water quality	22	Pollution (general)	21
Mexico	Air pollution	41	Pollution (general)	12	Water quality	7
Uruguay	Waste disposal	22	Water quality	21	Air pollution	11
East Asia:						
Japan	Air pollution	15	Pollution (general)	15	Waste disposal	14
Korea (Rep.)	Water quality	34	Air pollution	25	Waste disposal	14
Philippines	Loss of natural resources	41	Air pollution	13	Water quality	11
Other Asia:						
India	Air pollution	49	Water quality	13	Population-related	10
Turkey	Air pollution	29	Pollution (general)	26	Waste disposal	11
Eastern Europe:						
Hungary	Air pollution	53	Water quality	10	Toxic waste	9
Poland	Air pollution	46	Water quality	23	Waste disposal	12
Russia	Air pollution	25	Pollution (general)	15	Toxic waste	12
Scandinavia:						
Denmark	Water quality	36	Air pollution	18	Pollution (general)	8
Finland	Air pollution	32	Pollution (general)	22	Water quality	13
Norway	Pollution (general)	30	Air pollution	19	Water quality	5
Other Europe:						
Germany (West)	Air pollution	31	Waste disposal	21	Loss of natural resources	11
Great Britain	Air pollution	21	Pollution (general)	15	Water quality	13
Ireland	Pollution (general)	15	Air pollution	13	Water quality	12
Netherlands	Air pollution	38	Waste disposal	18	Water quality	6
Switzerland	Air pollution	56	Waste disposal	14	Loss of natural resources	6

SOURCE: Gallup poll (1992).

was skyrocketing (up to $20 per cubic meter in the Netherlands), and more and more legislation was aimed at reducing waste by promoting recycling and reuse.

Meanwhile, in Eastern Europe, the recent fall of Communism was not only opening up that market, but also revealed enormous environmental problems beyond imagination with no apparent solution. It was unclear how this was going to affect their relationship with Western Europe, as their markets would undoubtedly begin to interact more and more or even merge. Either way, it was clear that environmental performance would become an important competitive factor in these markets too.

In Western Europe, some companies—and in one case a whole industry (chemicals)—had already become proactive in their response to environmental

Exhibit 9 Relative Importance of Environmental Issues—Corporate Respondents

Corporate Respondents

Industrial pollution is the top issue for the corporate respondents in terms of *very important* replies. Over 8 out of 10 of these respondents consider the issue to be *very important*. Industrial pollution and *energy conservation* are the leading issues when *very important* and *important* replies are added together.

Environmental Issue	Very Important	Important	Not Very Important	Unimportant
Industrial pollution	69	13		NA
Recycling of materials	25	49	8	1
Use of recycled paper	9	44	27	3
Improved working environment	15	59	9	
Quality of design	26	43	13	NA
VDU screens	3	26	49	5
Noise reduction	12	53	17	1
Cutting out waste	39	39	5	
Waste disposal	42	36	5	
Greenhouse effect	46	28	7	2
Energy conservation	59	23	1	
Ozone depletion	45	33	4	NA
Congestion	24	44	12	3
Environmentally friendly purchasing	7	56	19	1
Consumer lobbies	9	46	24	4
State regulation and control	30	42	9	2
Others (please specify):				
Acid rain	1			
Animal testing		1		
Population	1			
Attitude of people	1			

SOURCE: Adaptation Limited, *Managing the Relationship with the Environment* (1990).

problems that may be caused by their processes and products. Often, these proactive measures came from internal sources as employees pressured their employers. Consumers, too, were demanding more environmentally responsible behavior from the companies they bought their products from. In Germany, for example, consumers responded en masse to a public call to remove secondary packaging from consumer goods while at the store and leave it at the counter. Given Germany's new packaging law, the store owners were ready and the ultimate producers were eventually forced to take back the packaging. Similar developments were evident in the Netherlands, Denmark, and Austria, too. Other driving forces for change include critical but cooperative attitudes from environmental groups and research institutes.

It was obvious that a company's environmental performance had become a major competitive factor in Europe. Yet few companies had become responsive to these pressures beyond mere intent. Rank Xerox was one of these few.

Exhibit 10 Public Opinion on Most Important Political Issues in the EC

Importance of Protecting the Environment

Asked to put 12 main political issues in order of importance, respondents to an opinion poll throughout the European Community made protection of the environment second only to unemployment. Asked to grade how important it was, 94 percent of those questioned thought environmental protection very important.

The five most important national and international issues per country. Percentage of public who think issue is very important.

	B	DK	D	GR	E	F	IRL	I	L	NL	P	UK
Unemployment	94	95	95	93	98	97	98	96	92	94	95	94
Environmental policy	90	97	98	92	94	93	91	94	95	97	91	93
Stable prices	87	84	90	93	93	83	93	89	91	—	94	86
Personal security	80	—	—	—	—	—	—	—	—	—	—	—
Arms limitation	75	79	89	86	87	—	—	82	—	82	—	—
Balance of payments	—	88	—	—	—	—	—	—	—	—	—	—
Pension security	—	—	95	—	—	—	—	—	—	—	—	—
Education	—	—	—	88	—	96	—	—	—	—	—	—
Terrorism	—	—	—	—	95	—	—	—	—	—	—	—
Social protection	—	—	—	—	—	94	—	—	—	—	—	—
Emigration	—	—	—	—	—	—	93	—	—	—	—	—
Northern Ireland	—	—	—	—	—	—	84	—	—	—	—	—
Tax reform	—	—	—	—	—	—	—	81	—	—	—	—
Site advantage	—	—	—	—	—	—	—	—	91	—	—	—
Pensions	—	—	—	—	—	—	—	—	85	—	—	—
Equal rights	—	—	—	—	—	—	—	—	—	85	—	—
Law of labor	—	—	—	—	—	—	—	—	—	—	90	—
Housing/homeless	—	—	—	—	—	—	—	—	—	—	—	94
Health services	—	—	—	—	—	—	—	—	—	—	—	94
Health reform	—	—	—	—	—	—	—	—	—	—	91	—
Combat crime	—	—	—	—	—	—	—	—	—	—	94	—

Source: ZEUS Report, January 1990; based on the Eurobarometer opinion poll, conducted for the European Commission in the 12-member states of the European Community in the summer of 1989.

Asset Recovery Operations at Rank Xerox

Rank Xerox had refurbished copiers or their parts for almost 25 years. It started in 1967 with a single model, the 914. Throughout the 1970s, the refurbishing process was continuously improved, expanded to other products, and "new build" manufacturing lines. The contract term, used to disclose that a product was refurbished, was *reconditioned*.

In 1987, Rank Xerox established the Asset Recovery Operations (ARO) program at its Venray facility. At the time, ARO was a local initiative to rebalance the asset pool of returned copiers. As most machines were rented or leased to customers, Rank Xerox would take back old machines at the end of the contract or when the contract was upgraded to a higher or newer model. These returned copiers were useful and operational, but had little market value. Refurbishing them added little benefit to the company's product lines. This led to the belief that these copiers might still be valuable if parts or materials could be recovered and reused in the "new build" production line. As a result, ARO was created as a small pilot operation staffed with a handful of people (see Exhibit 11).

The concept of recovering parts from old equipment soon proved to be very feasible and within just four years, ARO grew to a full-fledged facility with more than 140 employees in Venray and more personnel throughout the corporation. Volume grew accordingly, which also created structural problems, such as the documentation of thousands of different parts recovered and limited understanding of ARO's cost structure. But these problems were to be expected given ARO's phenomenal growth rate.

ARO's results were impressive. In 1990, ARO delivered almost half a million parts back to the manufacturing lines and the outlook for 1992 was close to three quarters of a million parts. In addition, the waste stream was reduced tremendously. A study in 1991 revealed that for the 1050 model, more than 95 percent (measured by weight) of the parts were being recovered, independent of the internal demand from manufacturing. If manufacturing didn't take the parts, they were sold to external contractors for other applications or material scrap value. These contractors also included Rank Xerox suppliers, who would reuse the materials to produce parts for Rank Xerox (Exhibits 12A and 12B).

The ARO concept proved to be the right answer (economically and environmentally) to the increasing pool of old, outdated copiers. Similar yet smaller facilities were set up in Lille and Mitcheldean to supply parts and materials to their local newly built production lines as well. In the mean time, ARO Venray obtained an industry-first ISO-9002 Quality System Assessment and Certification award. ARO was one of the world's first businesses involved in the recovery of usable items (not just materials) to receive such an internationally respected quality certification. Again, this was the result of Rank Xerox's relentless pursuit of Leadership Through Quality.

Other actions aimed at future asset recovery included the design for reuse and disassembly, increased commonality of parts from different models (increasing useful life within the company), and phased product development with new and independent project assessment and assurance teams (PAAT), which determined whether the new product conformed with Xerox's high environmental standards at various points in the development process.

Xerox's Environmental Leadership Program

In 1991, Bernard Fournier, managing director of Rank Xerox, signed the Principles for Environmental Management on behalf of Rank Xerox. The charter was developed by the ICC (International Chamber of Commerce) to proactively improve the environment in order to save our future (see Exhibits 13 and 14). In addition, Rank Xerox vowed to implement a new program that would enable lifetime responsibility (from cradle to grave) for its products. This, however, would take several years to fully realize. Exhibit 15 shows the policy statement of the Environmental Leadership program initiated at Rank Xerox in 1990. This program was consistent with the Leadership Through Quality approach at Rank Xerox: Employees benefitted from the high degree of employee involvement and the empowerment required by both the program and Leadership Through Quality; and customers, who increasingly demanded environmentally friendly products and services, benefitted, too, as Rank Xerox aimed to comply with and/or exceed national and international laws and regulations.

EXHIBIT 11 A New Manufacturing Mind-Set

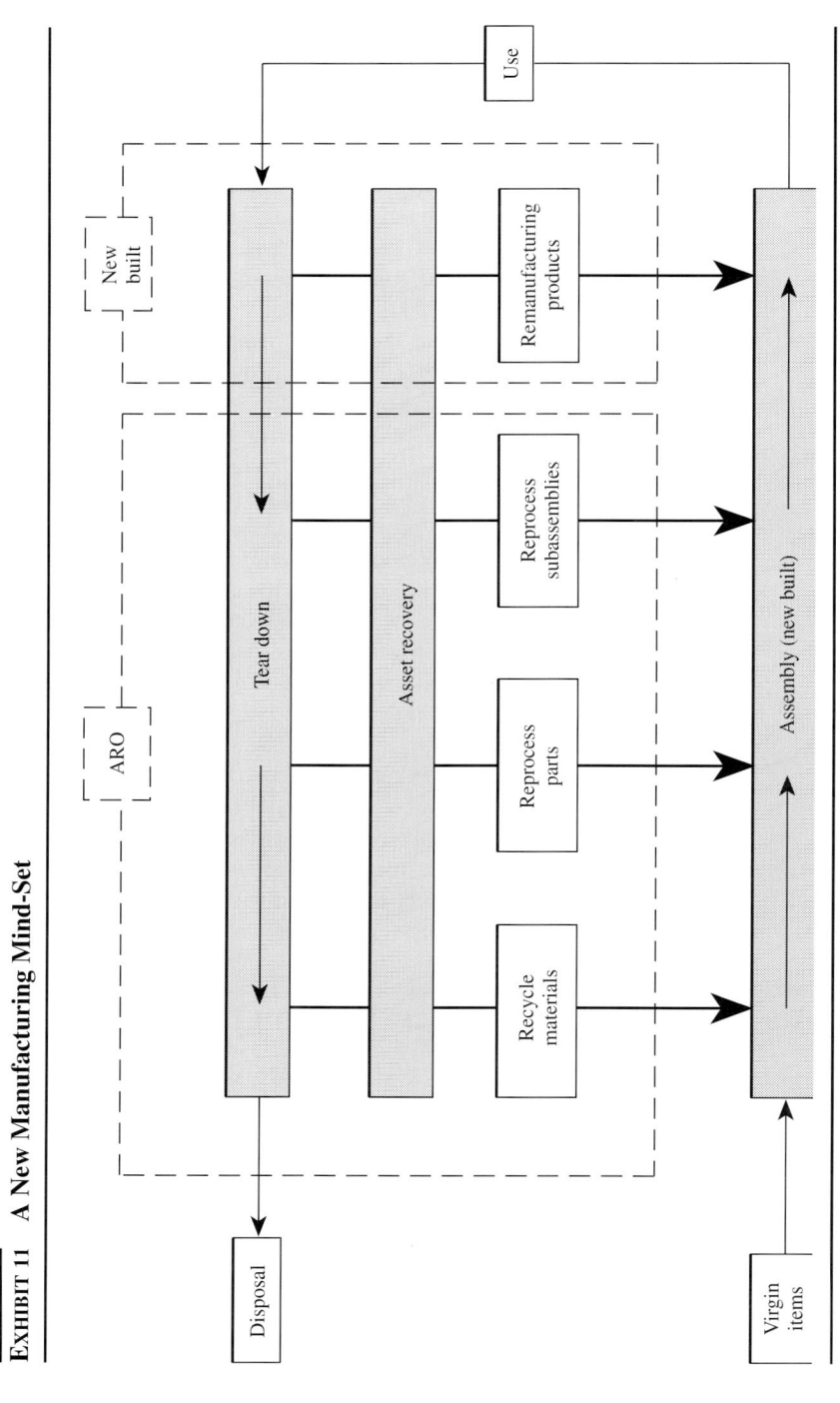

EXHIBIT 12A Asset Recycle Management

	Xerox	Supplier	Other
Repair product	Field life extension	N/A	3rd party
Remanufacturing product	Control	Supplier	3rd party
Reprocess S/As parts	To new build	Sell	Sell
Recycle raw materials	Regrind plastics	Salvage (sell) metals, papers, glass, etc.	
Disposal waste	Landfill incinerate		

The program was also consistent with Rank Xerox's business priorities of customer satisfaction; employee motivation and satisfaction; increasing market share; and improving return on assets. The latter two would be obtained through creating a competitive advantage based on environmental leadership and reduced manufacturing costs due to reuse/recycling.

Environmental Marketing Team. As customers and legislation demanded more environmentally friendly products, it became clear that Rank Xerox had to respond. The success of ARO and the resulting capacity to reuse high quantities of reprocessed parts seemed to provide a solution. But in each country the demands and requirements were different and it seemed impossible to find a uniform solution that would apply to the entire European market.

In January 1992, Olivier Grouès, director of marketing at Rank Xerox, put together a special environmental marketing team (EMT) whose task it was to determine if and how Rank Xerox could capitalize on its recycling efforts. He gave the group until May 1, 1992, to come up with a workable solution. The solution was to include how Rank Xerox should position itself and its products in a uniform way while preserving flexibility to serve individual market needs.

The EMT consisted of Valentin (Val) Govaerts, Repro Marketing manager; Karl Kummer, Environment director; Carole Shephard, legal counsel; and Frank Crowley, manager of Recycling Operation Support. The EMT first decided to determine all of the relevant issues prior to making any decisions.

Exhibit 12B MRT Cartridge Reclaim

Examples of parts and material recovery at ARO

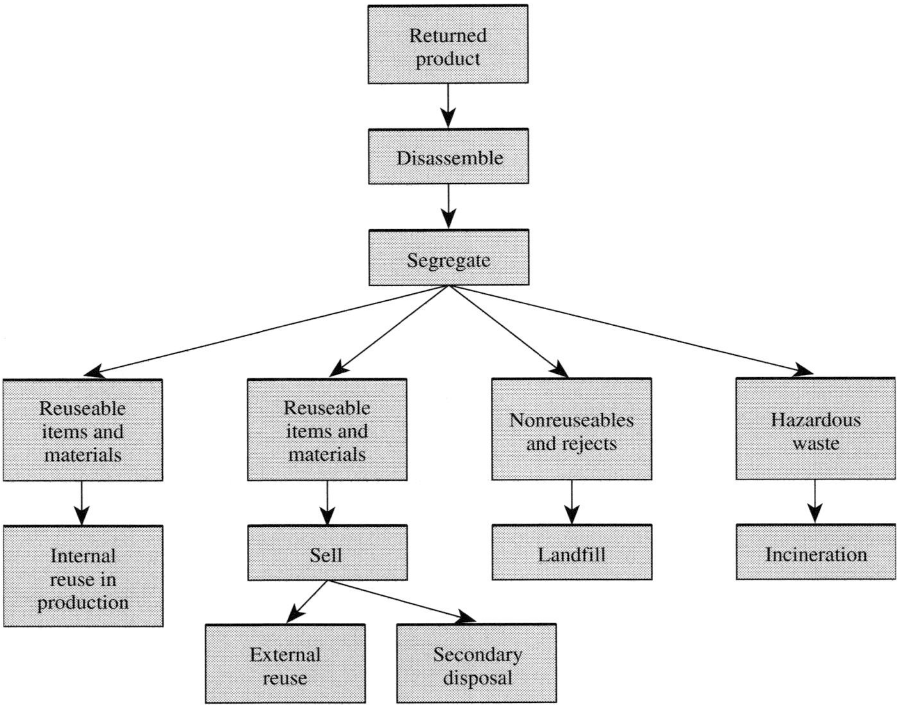

```
Returned product
    ↓
Disassemble
    ↓
Segregate
    ↓
┌──────────────┬──────────────┬──────────────┬──────────────┐
Reuseable      Reuseable      Nonreuseables   Hazardous
items and      items and      and rejects    waste
materials      materials
    ↓              ↓              ↓              ↓
Internal       Sell           Landfill       Incineration
reuse in       ↓
production   External / Secondary
             reuse     disposal
```

Some examples (by weight-percentages)

Product	Internal production	External reuse	Secondary disposal	Landfill	Incineration
1040	14–24%	65–70%	10–5%	10–0%	1%
1050	22–32%	56–61%	10–5%	10–0%	2%
5052	38–48%	40–45%	10–5%	10–0%	2%
CRUs	83–85%	5–10%	5–3%	5–0%	2%

Customers

It was clear that the customer expectations were changing, but the level of acceptance of products with recycled parts still varied greatly in the various countries. Several surveys indicated change (see Exhibit 16), but insufficient data on Rank Xerox customers existed. The only customer information available at this point was the results of several focus groups in Canada (see Exhibit 17). Karl Kummer was in the process of developing a customer environmental survey (see Exhibit 18) but no

EXHIBIT 13 The Business Charter for Sustainable Development
Principles for Environmental Management

Foreword

There is widespread recognition today that environmental protection must be among the highest priorities of every business.

In its milestone 1987 report, "Our Common Future," the World Commission on Environment and Development (Brundtland Commission), emphasized the importance of environmental protection in the pursuit of sustainable development.

To help business around the world improve its environmental performance, the International Chamber of Commerce established a task force of business representatives to create this Business Charter for Sustainable Development. It comprises 16 principles for environmental management which, for business, is a vitally important aspect of sustainable development.

This charter will assist enterprises in fulfilling their commitment to environmental stewardship in a comprehensive fashion. It was formally launched in April 1991 at the Second World Industry Conference on Environmental Management.

Introduction

Sustainable development involves meeting the needs of the present without compromising the ability of future generations to meet their own needs.

Economic growth provides the conditions in which protection of the environment can best be achieved, and environmental protection, in balance with other human goals, is necessary to achieve growth that is sustainable.

In turn, versatile, dynamic, responsive, and profitable businesses are required as the driving force for sustainable economic development and for providing managerial, technical, and financial resources to contribute to the resolution of environmental challenges. Market economies, characterized by entrepreneurial initiatives, are essential to achieving this.

Business thus shares the view that there should be a common goal, not a conflict, between economic development and environmental protection, both now and for future generations.

Making market forces work in this way to protect and improve the quality of the environment—with the help of performance-based standards and judicious use of economic instruments in a harmonious regulatory framework—is one of the greatest challenges that the world faces in the next decade.

The 1987 report of the World Commission on Environment and Development, "Our Common Future," expresses the same challenge and calls on the cooperation of business in tackling it. To this end, business leaders have launched actions in their individual enterprises as well as through sectoral and cross-sectoral associations.

In order that more businesses join this effort and that their environmental performance continues to improve, the International Chamber of Commerce hereby calls upon enterprises and their associations to use the following principles as a basis for pursuing such improvement and to express publicly their support for them.

Individual programs developed to implement these principles will reflect the wide diversity among enterprises in size and function.

The objective is that the widest range of enterprises commit themselves to improving their environmental performance in accordance with these principles, to having in place management practices to effect such improvement, to measuring their progress, and to reporting this progress as appropriate internally and externally.

Principles

1. Corporate priority. To recognize environmental management as among the highest corporate priorities and as a key determinant to sustainable development; to establish policies, programs, and practices for conducting operations in an environmentally sound manner.

2. Integrated management. To integrate these policies, programs, and practices fully into each business as an essential element of management in all its functions.

3. Process of improvement. To continue to improve corporate policies, programs, and environmental performance, taking into account technical developments, scientific understanding, consumer needs, and community expectations, with legal regulations as a starting point; and to apply the same environmental criteria internationally.

4. Employee education. To educate, train, and motivate employees to conduct their activities in an environmentally responsible manner.

5. Prior assessment. To assess environmental impacts before starting a new activity or project and before decommissioning a facility or leaving a site.

6. Products and services. To develop and provide products or services that have no undue environmental impact and are safe in their intended use, that are efficient in their consumption of energy and natural resources, and that can be recycled, reused, or disposed of safely.

NOTE: The term *environment* as used in this document also refers to environmentally related aspects of health, safety, and product stewardship.

EXHIBIT 13 *(concluded)*

7. Customer advice. To advise and, where relevant, educate customers, distributors, and the public in the safe use, transportation, storage, and disposal of products provided; and to apply similar considerations to the provision of services.

8. Facilities and operations. To develop, design, and operate facilities and conduct activities taking into consideration the efficient use of energy and materials, the sustainable use of renewable resources, the minimization of adverse environmental impact and waste generation, and the safe and responsible disposal of residual wastes.

9. Research. To conduct or support research on the environmental impact of raw materials, products, processes, emissions, and wastes associated with the enterprise and on the means of minimizing such adverse impact.

10. Precautionary approach. To modify the manufacture, marketing, or use of products or services or the conduct of activities, consistent with scientific and technical understanding, to prevent serious or irreversible environmental degradation.

11. Contractors and suppliers. To promote the adoption of these principles by contractors acting on behalf of the enterprise, encouraging and, where appropriate, requiring improvements in their practices to make them consistent with those of the enterprise; and to encourage the wider adoption of these principles by suppliers.

12. Emergency preparedness. To develop and maintain, where significant hazards exist, emergency preparedness plans in conjunction with the emergency services, relevant authorities, and the local community, recognizing potential transboundary impacts.

13. Transfer of technology. To contribute to the transfer of environmentally sound technology and management methods throughout the industrial and public sectors.

14. Contributing to the common effort. To contribute to the development of public policy and to business, governmental, and intergovernmental programs and educational initiatives that will enhance environmental awareness and protection.

15. Openness to concerns. To foster openness and dialogue with employees and the public, anticipating and responding to their concerns about the potential hazards and impacts of operations, products, wastes, or services, including those of transboundary or global significance.

16. Compliance and reporting. To measure environmental performance; to conduct regular environmental audits and assessments of compliance with company requirements, legal requirements, and these principles; and periodically to provide appropriate information to the Board of Directors, shareholders, employees, the authorities, and the public.

Support for the Charter

The ICC is undertaking an extensive campaign to encourage member companies and others to express their support for the charter. It has also invited certain international organizations to provide supportive messages.

A list of these companies, and the messages received from international organizations are given in separate leaflets which are normally circulated together with the charter. They may also be obtained from ICC Headquarters or ICC National Committees in nearly 60 countries. The Business Charter for Sustainable Development was prepared by the ICC in 1990 for launching at the Second World Industry Conference on Environmental Management (WICEM II) in April 1991. It provides a basic framework of reference for action by individual corporations and business organizations throughout the world.

The charter is also published by the ICC in Dutch, French, German, Portuguese, and Spanish. Other editions are in preparation, or may be available from ICC National Committees.

SOURCE: The International Chamber of Commerce.

EXHIBIT 14

Rank Xerox Limited
Parkway
Marlow
Buckinghamshire SL7 1YL
Telephone 0628-893832
Telex 846666 RXEROX G

Managing Director

Mr. Jean-Charles Rouhrer
Secretary General,
INTERNATIONAL CHAMBER OF COMMERCE,
38 Cours Albert 1er.
75008 Paris,
FRANCE.

1st May 1991

Dear Mr. Rouhrer,

Rank Xerox International Headquarters is pleased to support the International Chamber of Commerce Business Charter for Sustainable Development—Principles for Environment Management.

We believe that our environmental policies are consistent with the principles of the International Chamber of Commerce Charter. For example, our Corporate Environmental Health and Safety Policy includes a commitment to the continual improvement of performance in environmental protection and resource conservation, in both company operations and product design.

Yours sincerely,

B. D. Fournier

Registered Office:
Parkway, Marlow,
Buckinghamshire SL7 1YL
Registered in England No. 575914

---

results would be available for at least a few months. Govaerts wondered how transferable Canadian information would be to the European market. The past had shown that the customer requirements varied tremendously between the European countries. Recent feedback from the EOUs indicated that these differences were still prevalent. But Govaerts also considered another point of view:

> Does it really matter what the current differences are? Isn't it obvious that the integration of the EC market will continue to converge customer expectations over the next few years? In that case, Rank Xerox could go ahead with a uniform approach throughout

> **EXHIBIT 15 Rank Xerox Environmental Health and Safety Policy**
>
> Rank Xerox is committed to the protection of the environment and health and safety, primarily of its employees, customers, and neighbors. This commitment is applied worldwide in developing new products and processes.
>
> - Environmental health and safety concerns take priority over economic considerations.
> - All Rank Xerox operations must be conducted in a manner that safeguards people's health, protects the environment, and conserves valuable materials and resources.
> - Rank Xerox is dedicated to the continual improvement of its performance in environmental protection and resource conservation.
> - Rank Xerox is dedicated to designing products for maximum conservation of resources, and to taking every opportunity to recycle or reuse waste materials generated by its operations.
>
> **Rank Xerox's Environmental Principles**
> We are committed to leadership in environmental protection: a commitment which is applied worldwide in developing new products and processes.
>
> The standards we set ourselves go beyond the controls of even the most stringent EC regulations and our policies have set benchmarks for our industry.
>
> There is a fundamental realization in the company that we can change the way things are made and the way business works, in order to protect our world.

Europe and not worry about national differences. This would also be in line with the goals of the Environmental Leadership strategy, which aims at presenting the company as a proactive environmental leader and that requires the company to apply the strictest environmental regulations in any of its markets worldwide. If this applies to design, development, and manufacturing, then why not to marketing?

Communications Strategy

Besides the question of whether to unify the positioning of Rank Xerox and its products, the EMT also had to decide on how to communicate this both internally throughout the company and externally throughout their markets.

Employee motivation and satisfaction was one of the company's business priorities and communicating the Environmental Leadership program throughout the company was key to its success. In the last few years, employee awareness of environmental issues was increasing and adherence to good environmental practices by the company became a major part of employee satisfaction. Kummer asserted:

> It is imperative that the internal message be clear, concise, and nonambiguous. If we decide to communicate a different message to each of our operating units based on their individual needs, how can we then tell our own employees yet another story? Whatever message we convey internally cannot be in contradiction to our message to our customers.

The issue of how to communicate externally seemed less contradictory: Extreme care needed to be taken in the wording of the message and the ability to back up any claims with proof. Several companies had already been making claims about their environmental practices. For example, BMW was criticized for suggesting that

Chapter 13   Green Marketing at Rank Xerox

EXHIBIT 16   Environment Facts—Various Surveys

- 53% of Europeans (i.e., France, Germany, and the United Kingdom) would buy a product less harmful to the environment even if it costs more than other kinds (1990 McCann Erickson Harris Research Center).
- 51% of Europeans would sacrifice some quality to buy a product that would cause less damage to the environment (1990 McCann Erickson Harris Research Center).
- 59% of companies feel that Green consumerism will play a significant role in their companies' marketing plans over the next five years (1991 FIND/SVP).
- 62% of Americans name environmental pollution as a "very serious threat" to American society, up from 44% in 1984 (1989 Roper Study).
- 82% said they would pay 5% or more extra for environmentally friendly products, compared to 49% in 1989 (1990 J. Walter Thompson Study).
- 64% were less likely to buy from a company with a poor environmental record, and 27% have already boycotted a product because of a poor record (1990 J. Walter Thompson Study).
- 49% bought products made from recycled materials and 31% bought a product because it is supposed to be good for the environment (1990 J. Walter Thompson Study).

---

its cars were more capable of being recycled than rival models. In reality this was not true, nor did BMW provide the infrastructure to recycle the cars beyond a small pilot plant in Landshut, Germany.

Another example was the McDonald's fast food chain, which was taken to task in the United Kingdom for claiming that its foam packaging was more environmentally friendly than paper coated with plastic, wax, or silicone, which could not be recycled. Yet its advertisement showed a paper french fries box with the recycling

---
EXHIBIT 17   Major Results from Focus Groups in Canada

- The marketplace is ready for a major supplier to play a leadership role in the environmental area. Being first also has important positive image implications.
- The concept of production and marketing of remanufactured products was rated favorably (8.2 on scale of 10).
- Buyers want and expect the vendor to be *open* in the marketing of such product or line. They believe that it is to the benefit of both the vendor and themselves that they understand the environmental implications.
- People like to believe that they are doing something positive environmentally, and that their decisions to dispose are not adding to global waste.
- The primary issue in their minds is that remanufactured products perform as new. If that is the case, they will have no sensitivity about acquiring them.
- Decision makers estimate that on average almost 60% of parts and components of a photocopier can be recycled.
- Almost two-thirds believe that the process will result in less having to be manufactured from raw materials and that the end price (cost) will be lower than for a copier built from new parts and components.
- The attitudinal area is not showing signs of growing stale. People are concerned, and are exhibiting more concern about it in the workplace. Whatever programs Xerox can efficiently implement and communicate will be well received in the marketplace and signal leadership in *this area.*

Exhibit 18 Environmental Survey for Rank Xerox Customers

Excerpt of Proposed Questions (draft)
1. Does your organization have, besides a health and safety policy, an environmental policy?
2. Do you prefer to buy from a supplier which has a written environmental policy which is available to you on request?
3. Which company, in your judgment, cares most for the environment?
4. What is your view in respect to office machines like computers, copiers, and printers:
   ___ I insist on a high amount of reused or recycled parts.
   ___ I expect a certain amount of reused or recycled parts.
   ___ I would only buy a product with recycled parts after an open and convincing explanation by the supplier.
   ___ I would not buy a product with reused or recycled parts.
   ___ I am not concerned about these issues.
5. If a product has reused or recycled parts to help the environment with the same warranty and performance as a product made from 100% new parts, what do you expect to pay for it? Less, equal, more, or don't know?
6. Some countries and the European Commission have, or will have, environmental labels. Do you take these into account in your purchasing decision?
7. What are your requirements for paper used by your copier(s) and/or printer(s): white premium only, white but environmentally friendly, gray, or brownish tone helping to protect the environment? Is price a factor to you in purchasing paper?
8. What is your most important environmental requirement?

---

logo on the side, indicating recyclability. In both of these examples, the issues may have seemed trivial, but they clearly indicated how critical consumers had become regarding environmental claims made by manufacturers. However, Frank Crowley did not see this as a problem:

> With our design for reuse, advanced return flow infrastructure, and already high levels of reuse of raw materials and individual parts, we have the ability to go public with our efforts and back them up with tangible proof. And anybody who doesn't believe us can come to Venray and take a look at ARO and our fully integrated remanufacturing activities in the "new build" lines!

Kummer agreed, but Shephard was less enthusiastic:

> The existing culture in R&D and manufacturing matches our corporate environmental intentions, but I am not sure whether that is also the case within marketing, especially when you look at the terminology used in our contracts. There is a real disparity between our manufacturing capabilities ("gray") versus our marketing efforts ("black and white"). For example, a high proportion of 1050 machine parts coming back from customers after their lifetime can be used for the newly introduced 5051, but we are referring to them in our contracts as "reconditioned." This understates the quality of the remanufacturing process, representing a lost opportunity to capitalize on our recycling and reuse efforts.

All agreed that rectifying the "gray versus black and white" culture and capabilities should be high on the agenda, and the EMT had already put in a lot of effort to balance the terminologies and definitions. But, according to Kummer, this current imbalance should not inhibit Rank Xerox from going public with its efforts:

There is a clear lack of environmental leadership in any market as no company is recognized by the general public as an environmentally conscious organization. Even the Body Shop, whose whole image is based on the environment, only has a 9 percent recognition as an environmentally conscious company (Exhibit 19). That means that there is a great window of opportunity for us here and we should not wait too long by trying to work out all the details.

Canon is said to be already recycling cartridges in China and is planning a remanufacturing plant in Scotland. And the word is that the other Japanese manufacturers are planning to combine their efforts through a new cooperation that will provide the infrastructure for retrieving and disassembling their returned copiers. Also, at the last Hannover Fair, Kodak presented its refurbishing and recycling activities. They may not be as advanced as we are, but they are definitely working on it.

Crowley was less worried:

Hold on a minute. Nobody comes close to what we are doing. Yes, Canon may be taking back cartridges from their customers, but there's no way that they are actually recycling them. It's just not cost-effective to ship 'em all the way to China for recycling. I'm sure that they're just dumping them.

Shephard joined the conversation: "Does it matter what they are doing exactly? Karl [Kummer] is right. The point is that they are working on it and we should not sit back and wait for them to catch up. We are ahead and should make sure that we stay ahead."

Crowley agreed, adding:

I see your point. We have a definite advantage with our European manufacturing base, which allows us to fully exploit the benefits from the reuse of parts and subassemblies. The best the Japanese can do is to disassemble their machines and sell the materials for recycling of raw materials, which has the lowest financial benefits. And shipping parts back to Japan or China cannot be cost-effective.

Kummer nodded in agreement: "Mere recycling of raw materials is also the least environmentally friendly option."

It was quiet for a few seconds, after which Govaerts concluded: "Superb! I am now more convinced than ever that we should try to capitalize on our recycling efforts. Let's move forward on how we should go about it." An intense meeting followed.

Potential Product Lines

The disparity in readiness between manufacturing and marketing needed to be either corrected or contained within limits to fully exploit the range of manufacturing capabilities. The marketing terminology and product positioning had to be flexible enough to capitalize on the range of recycled contents in the products, yet had to be simple enough to avoid confusion and be usable in each of the national markets with different environmental regulations and customer requirements.

Exhibit 19 Company Environmental Policy on the Office

Question 4. *What companies can you think of which are particularly environmentally conscious?*

	Total	Directors	Buyers	Users
Body shop	9%	10%	5%	11%
ICI	7	13	4	3
BP	4	9	2	2
Shell	3	6	4	0
Marks and Spencer	3	7	1	1
Petro/oil companies	3	4	4	1
Tesco	2	4	2	1
Sainsbury	2	4	2	1
Volkswagen	2	1	3	2
Rank Xerox	2	0	5	0
Water Boards	2	3	1	1
IBM	2	3	2	0
Waste disposal companies	2	1	3	1
Power/electric companies	2	2	3	0
Car companies	1	1	1	2
None	53	41	52	66

See Attachment for other companies mentioned.

Base: All Respondents   Apart from the fact that nearly 100 organizations were named in response to this question, over half of those questioned could not think of an environmentally conscious organization. This indicated that no one organization or group of organizations is implementing environmental practices in such an effective manner as to be recognized as a role model.

Attachment: Other Companies Mentioned
Those Who Were Mentioned by 1% of the Sample

Esso	ICL
Boots	National Power
BT	Saab
Charity shops	3M
Chemical companies	Household products companies
Greenpeace	Remokil
Safeway	McDonalds
Audi	Paper companies
Unilever	Lever
BMW	B & Q
Arc	Leigh Environmental
Glaxo	

Those Who Were Mentioned by Less Than 1% of the Sample

Gibbs	Printing companies
Securicor	Superdrug
McCains	British Coal
Beechmams	Lexmark
John Laing	CMB
British Gas	Crown Agents
Tarmac	Asda
Econwaste	John West
Southern Electric	Rank Havis Corp

After a productive brainstorming session, the EMT gradually narrowed down their options and finally concluded that they would recommend to develop three product categories based on recycled content:

1. **Premium class:** Newly built products with less than 5 percent reprocessed parts (based on value) and the latest technology incorporated.
2. **Green class:** Products that result from partial disassembly and reassembly of existing models. The value of reprocessed parts could exceed 5 percent. These remanufactured units were to be fully tested against new-built quality and inspection criteria and would be positioned to the customer as a product with the same quality, reliability, performance, and guarantee as a Premium class product. However, these products do not necessarily incorporate the latest technological advances.
3. **Silver class:** Products that have been used at trade shows or as demos in showrooms. Upon return to the EOU, they would be locally refurbished, repaired, or cleaned by the EOUs and sold as the same model again. The number of reprocessed parts would be limited to those items replaced during repair. The Silver class was estimated to be about 2 to 3 percent of newly built machines.

In general, the EMT felt that this categorization addressed the problem of black and white marketing terminology sufficiently and in a workable and easy-to-understand manner. Several issues still had to be resolved, such as customer acceptance, compliance with national regulations, pricing aspects, and product guarantees (especially for the Green class). In addition, prior to launch, the names of each product class would have to be reassessed as well, but for now they would be used as working titles.

Customer Acceptance

At this point, it was unknown how the customer would respond to the new product categorization. It was very well possible that different marketing approaches would be required in each country. But the EMT felt confident that the proposed system allowed enough flexibility for Rank Xerox to service all markets and meet their customer requirements and expectations. Crowley commented:

> Germany will love it, Italy will hate it. But that's the beauty of it: We will sell more Green class machines in Germany and wait for Italy to develop acceptance of the product. This also gives us time to expand our capacity for more Green class products in order to be ready when other markets develop demand for them. As you know, we continuously feed back disassembly and reassembly problems incurred at our remanufacturing lines and ARO to the design engineers, who use the knowledge in each next design. This guarantees a continuous improvement in the remanufacturability of our future products and thus in our capabilities to further expand the Green line.

Kummer acknowledged the match between gradual market acceptance and remanufacturing ramp-up and added:

The concept is revolutionary. It allows us to capitalize on our recycling efforts *and* develop a positive environmental company image. The only problem I see is: how Green is Green? I mean, no business is ever 100 percent environmentally friendly. Copiers produce visible paper (waste), malodorous ozone, noise, heat, and dust. Does a Green line create the perception that we are trying to conceal our real environmental impact—as little as it is?

The others agreed, and Govaerts continued:

That will depend a lot on how we word our campaign and position the Green product line. But you're right, we have to be very careful. That does not mean that we should cancel the concept. We have £1.2 million[2] in our advertising budget and we should use it wisely. I suggest we allocate about one-third for the introduction and the rest for follow-up advertising during the remainder of the year. I would rather underpromote the line than go all out and get burned. In other words, I do not want to create the impression that we can offer such a Green line for all our product families as of today. It takes time to implement this concept and we do not have the resources nor the infrastructure to do this overnight, especially for our current products. Future products are different; this concept can be worked out as part of the design and start-up phases. So let's be very careful about what we proclaim!

National Regulations

Within Europe, all countries were very clear on the legal requirement to disclose recycled content to the customer, but how this was to be disclosed and with which metric was not always clear. In addition, language differences created terminology problems. Shephard explained:

The word *recycling* has a different legal definition in almost every country and could thus misstate our intended meaning. The best example is Italy, which defines recycling to include waste incineration with the purpose of energy generation. Other countries do not view this as recycling and neither do we. We might be able to stick with the definitions used by the European Community, which are in line with our definitions. But will they be accepted in non-EC countries?

A similar problem exists with our positioning to the customer. Some languages have a limited vocabulary to describe various forms of environmental efforts. From what I understand, in Finland there is really only one word: recycling. In contrast, the English language probably tops the list with more than 20 different words: recycling, reuse, reprocess, remanufacture, refurbish, regrind, reclaim, salvage, and so on (Exhibit 20). This makes a homogeneous approach toward the whole European market rather complicated.

The EMT agreed that customer contract definitions as well as the wording of any marketing campaign should receive careful consideration.

---

[2] At the time of the case, £1 equaled approximately $1.80.

EXHIBIT 20

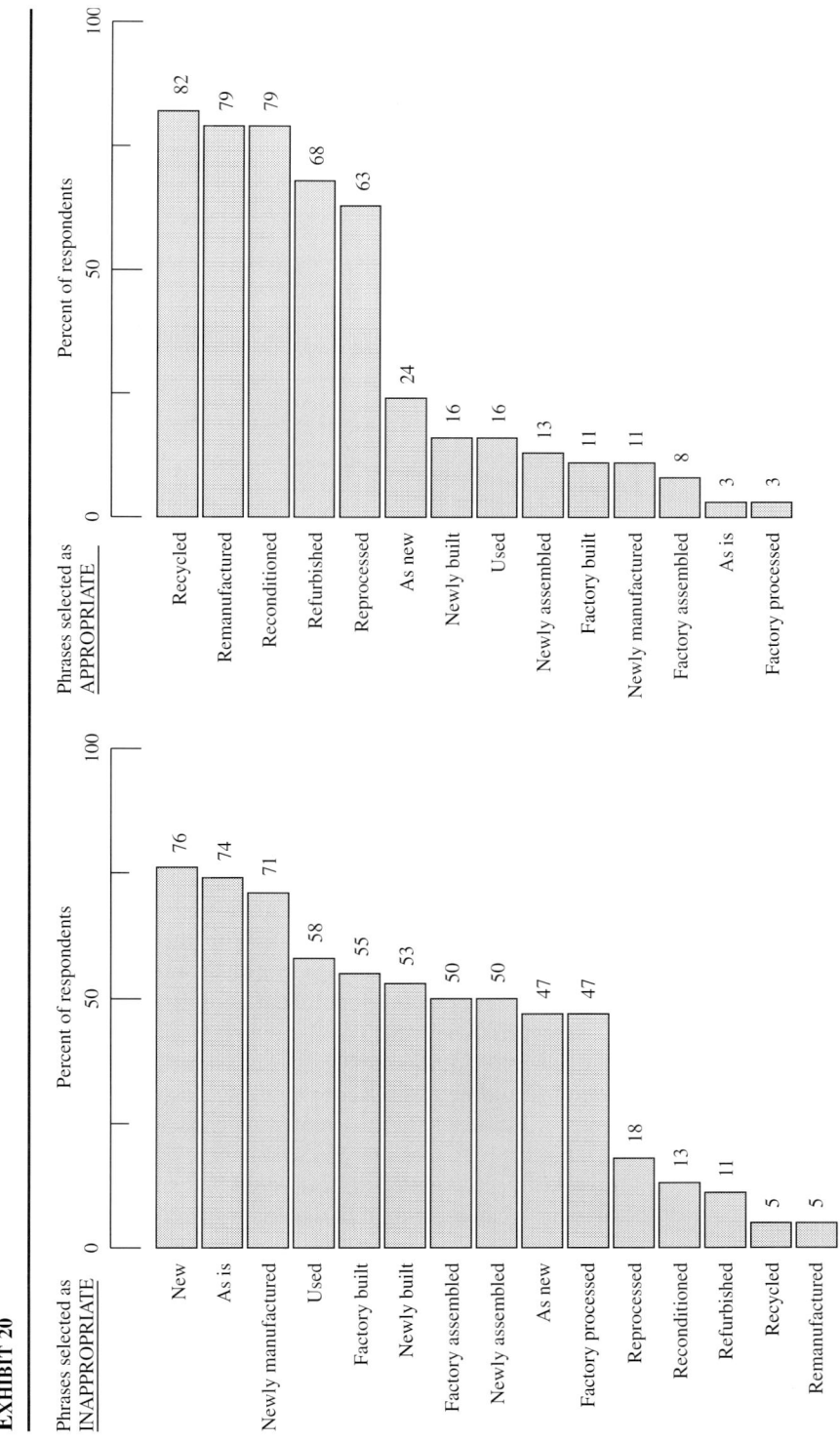

Exhibit 21   Production Schedule for Green Class Copiers

Copier Type	1992 Q2	Q3	Q4	1993 Q1	Q2	Q3	Q4	1994 Q1
Low	440	490	620	760	910	1,020	1,040	1,030
Medium	1,110	1,470	1,830	2,340	3,100	3,540	3,960	4,410
Medium/high	120	120	120	140	230	250	250	250
High	0	0	50	50	100	140	170	190
Total	1,670	2,080	2,620	3,290	4,340	4,950	5,420	5,880

NOTE: Data is disguised.

Pricing Policy

Pricing of the Green line had yet to be resolved. Customer perception played a great role in this. In some countries, such as Germany, the Netherlands, Austria, Switzerland, and Denmark, customer acceptance of and demand for the Green line was expected to be high and customers might even be willing to pay a premium. But in most other countries, especially in the United Kingdom and Southern Europe, customer enthusiasm would be much lower and they would demand a discount for what they perceived as a non-new product.

In addition, Rank Xerox was not yet able to determine the exact manufacturing cost of individual Green class machines. Parts were transferred from ARO to manufacturing based on a standard manufacturing transfer price (MTP), but the actual cost associated with each part had not been quantified precisely. To correct this problem, ARO was in the process of implementing a computerized cost accounting system, but this had proven more difficult than expected due to the enormous complexity of thousands of different items processed by ARO. As a result, Rank Xerox had thus far only been able to determine that the bottom line impact of its ARO activities had been positive. A better understanding existed of the financial impact of remanufacturing, but the combination of the two was rather complicated.

Govaerts knew that the Green line might jeopardize existing sales, but it would also generate additional sales to environmentally conscious customers whose only option would be Rank Xerox's Green class copiers. Crowley had been able to put together estimates for the production capacity of Green class products (see Exhibit 21), but the real question was whether the combined sales revenue and total income from the three product classes would increase. If not, should Rank Xerox go ahead anyway because the market would eventually require such products?

Product Guarantees

This new set of product categorizations brought forward new questions on the guarantees, especially concerning the Green class. The concept of a separate line with high reprocessed content was so revolutionary that no market-based examples

Exhibit 22 Feedback from Focus Groups in the United States on Types of Guarantees

Four service guarantees were presented to focus groups in New York City, Columbus, Ohio, and Raleigh, North Carolina:
1. **Service Guarantee.** If your machine is not operating 98% of the time, you will receive 10% off your next invoice.
2. **Product Performance Guarantee.** We guarantee that your machine will perform at its original specifications or better for at least five years. If not, we will replace your unit at no charge.
3. **Product Fit Guarantee.** The vendor guarantees that the product will meet your needs. If it doesn't, you can trade it in for full credit toward any other product.
4. **Money Back Guarantee.** If you are not satisfied with the product or vendor, you can return your machine, no questions asked.

The focus group preferences were as follows:
1. If Xerox would offer any of the above guarantees, is it believable?
   91% believable   9% not believable
2. If Xerox would offer your choice of guarantees, how likely would you be to consider them?
   55% very likely   35% somewhat likely   10% not likely
3. Guarantees are a meaningful way to protect the customer.
   90% agree   10% disagree
4. A company that offers a better guarantee makes a better product.
   35% agree   65% disagree
5. All guarantees are pretty much the same.
   30% agree   70% disagree
6. Dealer guarantees are easier to enforce than manufacturer guarantees.
   53% agree   47% disagree
7. Guarantees cannot be enforced by small customers.
   22% agree   78% disagree
8. Is a guarantee more or less important in your decision process than the following?

	More	Equal	Less
Price	27%	19%	54%
Features	31%	11%	58%
Experience	37%	9%	54%
Reputation	40%	10%	51%

9. Have you done any of the following as a result of hearing about a guarantee?
   Called for more information   37%
   Demo or trial   45%
   Considered new vendor   32%
   Switched vendor   29%
   Done nothing/no response   37%

existed on how to deal with customer guarantees. Little data was available; only the results of a phone questionnaire completed in the United States (Exhibit 22), which revealed different customer guarantee requirements in different markets. But the questionnaire did not address what the customer expects from a product with a high content of reprocessed parts.

This concerned Shephard:

How can we continue our Total Satisfaction Guarantee[3] program if we don't know yet whether our Green class products can live up to it or whether the customer requires the same guarantee for such products? The Total Satisfaction Guarantee has been a critical subset of our marketing approach over the last few years.

The fact that the guarantee is critical was well known to Govaerts:

The copier market is becoming like a commodity market: All of the products out there are starting to look alike and they all have pretty much the same features. Therefore, the only way to differentiate your product from the competition is by focusing on everything around it: service, warranty, performance, price, and so on. To this extent, Rank Xerox implemented its Total Satisfaction Guarantee program. Having an advantage in these peripherals to the product is the only way to gain market share in an industry that is growing at 1 to 2 percent annually.

I agree with Carole [Shephard] that we will most likely have to apply our Total Satisfaction Guarantee to the Green class products too. In that case, are we setting ourselves up for future problems and costly liabilities or is the inspection and release system for reprocessed parts tight enough to guarantee performance equivalent to the Premium class? If not, how are we to compensate for that? Through reduced pricing, shorter guarantee contracts, or other instruments?

Crowley interrupted:

I am confident that our quality inspection and release systems for remanufacturing, reprocessing, and recycling are adequate enough to guarantee performance equivalent to new parts for at least one more life cycle. At this time we have the luxury that the supply of parts from returned equipment exceeds our production demand for reprocessed parts. This allows us to apply very tight requirements for the parts and for those which demand has taken off. We have not yet had any problems from the field beyond statistically similar problems with new parts.

In addition, we will continue to monitor reliability in the field and if new problems pop up, we'll trace them back to their cause and correct the problem. Even if that means that we will have to go back to the drawing board.

But Shephard rebutted:

I understand that we have the proper infrastructures, given our current situation, but my problem is: What confidence level do we have such that we can honestly guarantee—and I don't mean in writing—that our Green line will perform as well as newly built Premium class models? What if we find out two years from now that there is a problem with a certain reprocessed part that requires a manufacturer recall? Or, even worse, what if we find out some day that a material or process deemed environmentally friendly today turns out to have damaging environmental effects after all? Such negative public exposure could really undermine the whole concept of the Green line, not to mention the financial implications.

---

[3]The Total Satisfaction Guarantee, introduced in 1990, allowed the customer to decide whether equipment installed and serviced by Xerox performed to his or her standards and expectations during the three years following the purchase. If not, Xerox would deliver an identical or comparable replacement at no cost to the customer, no questions asked.

EXHIBIT 23 Excerpts from Electronic Mail to Val Govaerts

Date: April 16, 1992
To: Val Govaerts
Copies: Karl Kummer
Sender: Peter Smith
Note: Canon CRU Recycling

Today, I received a copy of a video tape of the Canon cartridge recycling plant in Tai-lien City, China. Canon allowed us to video the cartridge processes during a plant tour. There were other activities going on as well, but we were not allowed to see them.

According to Canon, the plant employs about 1,300 people with only about 10 Japanese residents. The factory is large and modern and Canon claimed they plan to expand by up to 50 percent over the next few years.

The cartridge recycling process consists of disassembly, cleaning, repair, and manual inspection, and about 90 percent of the parts are claimed to be reused in new cartridges. The plastic parts are ground and then added to virgin material (50/50 ratio) and remolded into new cartridges.

Peter

Crowley was about to argue that such uncertainties will always remain and that this could happen to newly built products as well, but the silence after Shephard's comment made it clear that she had struck a sensitive and volatile issue.

With this, the meeting quietly ended and Govaerts returned to his office. He sat down and noticed that the in-basket icon on his computer screen was flashing, indicating urgent incoming electronic mail. His thoughts still at the meeting, Govaerts called up the document and scanned through it. But it didn't take long before the document (excerpts shown in Exhibit 23) grabbed his full attention. "Well, there you have it!" he sighed, leaning back into his chair. He knew that a decision had to be made very soon and that it would have a major impact on Rank Xerox's marketing strategy for the next 5 to 10 years.

CHAPTER 14
Intel Corporation: Going into OverDrive™

In May 1992, Intel Corporation, the leading supplier of microprocessors for IBM-compatible personal computers, announced the retail availability of OverDrive™ Processors, a new line of performance upgrades for Intel486 microprocessors. With the availability of this product, broader questions regarding product line management arose. How does a firm manage a product line in the context of rapid technological change? How should Intel develop the OverDrive business? How will the OverDrive offering affect the company's microprocessor business? And what will be the organizational implications of the new business?

Intel Announces First OverDrive™ Processors for Retail Market: Increases PC Speed up to 70 Percent

Folsom, California, May 26, 1992—Intel Corporation today announced the retail availability of OverDrive™ Processors—a line of single-chip performance upgrades that boost all software applications.

OverDrive Processors can easily be installed by the PC [personal computer] user and fill the vacant OverDrive Processor socket found in most Intel486 SX microprocessor-based systems. . . .

Based on Intel486 DX2 "speed doubling" technology, these first OverDrive Processors allow users . . . to double the internal speed of their computer's CPU [central processing unit] by adding a single chip, without upgrading or modifying any other system components. . . .

"OverDrive Processors are both cost-effective and the simplest way to upgrade. Depending on system design, PC users can install . . . [them] in five minutes," said Mike Fister, general manager of Intel's End User Components Division. Fister explained that traditional upgrades, like proprietary CPU upgrade cards, are expensive, ranging from $800 to $2,000, compared to the $500 range of OverDrive Processors. Other CPU upgrades can also be difficult to install. . . .

This case was prepared by Anirudh Dhebar.
Copyright © 1993 by the President and Fellows of Harvard College.
Harvard Business School case 593-096 (revised May 11, 1993).

In addition to the OverDrive Processors for Intel486 SX CPU-based systems announced today, Intel is developing single-chip OverDrive Processors for both Intel486 DX and DX2 microprocessor-based systems.

On May 26, 1992, Intel Corporation's Folsom, California-based End User Components Division (EUCD) announced the immediate availability of two versions of OverDrive Processors—one for 16- and 20-MHz Intel486™ SX CPU-based systems and the other for 25-MHz Intel486 SX CPU-based systems. The extract above is from the press release accompanying the product announcement.

The May 26 press release also included information on Intel's benchmark tests on a 20-MHz Intel486 SX CPU-based system: The new processor was found to be 62 percent faster when running WordPerfect Corporation's WordPerfect 5.1 word processing software, 77 percent faster with Borland International's Paradox database-management software, and 481 percent faster in the case of Lotus Development Corporation's Lotus 1-2-3 spreadsheet software. When running Lotus 1-2-3, the OverDrive processor was also 67 percent faster than the Intel487™ SX math coprocessor, a performance-enhancing processor that the user could (and might) have installed in the vacant socket intended for the OverDrive Processor. These speed improvements at the processor level promised up to a 70 percent improvement in the speed of the complete personal computer system.

EUCD expected to announce the availability of OverDrive Processors for Intel486 DX CPU-based systems in late 1992 and Intel486 DX2 CPU-based systems in 1993. Industry observers saw the new OverDrive processors as part of a new trend at Intel: microprocessor upgradability, with each new microprocessor being followed some time later by an OverDrive Processor. An important motivation for the new processor was the chorus of end user demand for a cost-effective way to enhance the computer-system performance without having to invest every so often in entirely new systems. The *cause célèbre* of the end user demand was the relentless pace of product improvement in the personal computer industry: The different industry players were introducing new-and-improved products every two to three years, and this was at least twice as fast as the normal asset depreciation and replacement cycles for most corporate end users. Prior to the OverDrive Processor, a number of systems manufacturers who used Intel microprocessors in their systems had introduced upgradable systems, but the performance enhancement solution differed from manufacturer to manufacturer, and there was no standard way that was cheap, easy, and nondisruptive. Intel, with the new OverDrive Processor, was offering an industrywide solution that was less expensive ("$500 range" versus "$800 to $2,000"), easy ("depending on system design, . . . in five minutes"), and nondisruptive ("adding a single chip [in a vacant OverDrive Processor socket], without upgrading or modifying any other system components").

If the OverDrive Processor strategy proved to be a winner, it would have a significant impact on Intel and its relationship with its customers: the microprocessors that would be "overdriven" were the company's main line of business (and the responsibility of the Microprocessor Products Group, or MPG—a separate products group that was older, larger, and more powerful than EUCD); the original-equipment manufacturers (OEMs) who employed these microprocessors in their personal-computer products were MPG's most important customers; MPG and its OEM customers had well-defined product design, pricing, positioning, and evolution strategies; and the new OverDrive Processors called into question some, if not many, of these strategies. Furthermore, the new processors launched Intel into an entirely new line of business—OverDrive Processor sales to end users owning systems made by MPG's OEM customers. EUCD—and not MPG—was responsible for OverDrive Processor sales and, as the newly appointed general manager of EUCD, it was Mike Fister's responsibility to develop the OverDrive Processor business such that it was congruent with—and not in opposition to—the strategic interests of MPG and its relationships with the OEM customers.

Intel Corporation—An Overview

Santa Clara, California-based Intel Corporation was founded in 1968

with the vision of designing and manufacturing very complex integrated circuits, or silicon "chips." . . . In 1971 Intel introduced the world's first microprocessor, a development that changed . . . much of the industrial world. . . . Today, . . . [m]ost of the company's activities are focused on extending and enhancing the worldwide business computing hardware standard that started with the introduction of the Intel microprocessor-based IBM PC 10 years ago. . . . Intel's mission is to supply the building blocks that allow this "new computer industry" to grow.[1]

One of the most important building blocks was the microprocessor, the "brain" that served as the computer's central processing unit (CPU), and where all computer-program instructions were executed. Intel was the world's leading supplier of microprocessors, and microprocessors were a significant part of the company's business (contributing an estimated 55 percent of Intel's sales and the bulk of its profits).[2]

As important as *microprocessors* were as a product category, they were not the only building blocks that Intel offered to the PC industry. The company's other building blocks for the industry were:

- *Microprocessor peripherals,* which worked with microprocessors and handled specific functions such as the control of disk drives and memory devices.

---

[1]*Annual Report 1991* (Santa Clara, Calif.: Intel Corporation, 1992), p. 6. Much of the information in this section is based on the "Intel in Brief" discussion on p. 6 of the annual report.

[2]Microprocessors were used, not only in personal computers, but also in a wide range of consumer-electronic, household, industrial, telecommunications, and transportation equipment. In this case study, the term *microprocessors* refers to microprocessors used as central processing units in personal computers. The revenue share estimates for Intel's different product groups are drawn from the article "Inside Intel," *Business Week,* June 1, 1992, pp. 86–94. The article quotes a Robertson Stephens & Co. estimate of $3.1 billion in microprocessor sales in a total 1992 revenue estimate of $5.5 billion. The revenue estimates for the other product groups mentioned in the case were other chips (principally microcontrollers), $1.4 billion; flash memory, $200 million; personal computers, $380 million; PC enhancement products, $310 million; and supercomputers, $150 million.

- *Multimedia products,* which brought multimedia capability to PCs.
- *PC enhancement products,* including add-in boards, PC-networking products, components for boosting PC computing power ("math coprocessors"), and selective software. OverDrive Processors were PC enhancement products.

Just as microprocessors were not Intel's only PC products, PC products were not the company's only major product offerings. Intel's other products were:

- *Flash memory devices* and *"EPROMs,"* which stored programs for microprocessors and microcontrollers and retained data even when power was turned off.
- *Microcontrollers,* which were microcomputers programmed to perform specific functions in automobile engines, laser printers, disk drives, home appliances, consumer-electronic equipment, household appliances, and so on.
- *OEM modules and systems,* which were based on Intel components and sold to OEMs for integration into their products.
- *Supercomputer systems,* which were high-performance computers based on "massively parallel" processing on many microprocessor modules.

Intel sold the above products through a number of distribution channels:

- *Original equipment manufacturers,* who incorporated Intel's microprocessors, microcontrollers, components, modules, and systems into their products.
- *Electronics distributors,* who sold replacement microprocessors, microcontrollers, components, modules, and systems for the OEM customers' products.
- *Retail computer stores,* which sold Intel's enhancement products (the company distributed these products through a network of over 8,400 retailers).
- *End users,* who directly purchased Intel's supercomputers and certain networking products.

For the year ending December 31, 1991, 49 percent of the company's sales were in the Americas, 22 percent in Europe, 19 percent in Asia Pacific, and 10 percent in Japan.

Exhibit 1 presents Intel's financial highlights for the five years 1987–91.

EXHIBIT 1 Intel Corporation: Financial Highlights

	1987	1988	1989	1990	1991
Five Years Ended December 28, 1991					
Net revenues ($ in millions)	1,907	2,875	3,127	3,921	4,779
Cost of sales ($ in millions)	1,044	1,506	1,721	1,930	2,316
Net income ($ in millions)	248	453	391	650	819
Return on average stockholder's equity	19.7%	27.0%	16.9%	21.2%	20.4%
Research and development ($ in millions)	260	318	365	517	618
Employees at year-end (in thousands)	19.2	20.8	21.7	23.9	24.6

Exhibit 2 Intel Corporation: Different Groups in Corporate Organization

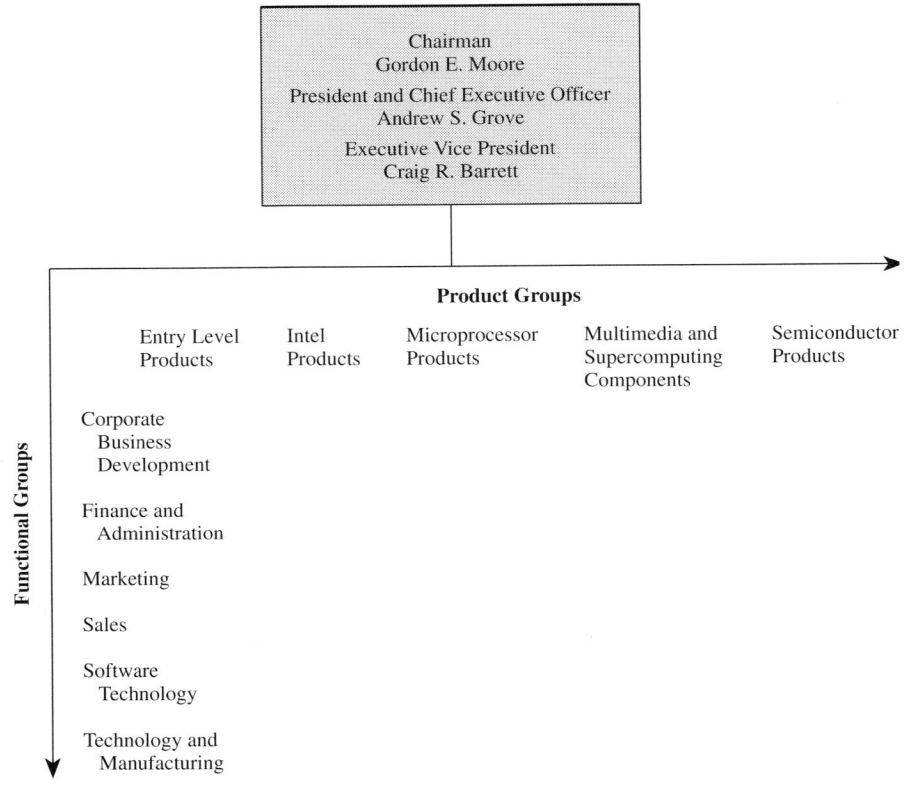

Intel was organized in a "matrix" form, with products and functional groups. Exhibit 2 identifies the different groups in the corporate organization. The two products groups directly relevant to this case study—the Microprocessor Products Group and the Intel Products Group—are identified in boldface. EUCD was one of five divisions in the Intel Products Group (the other four divisions were Networking Products, PC Enhancement Products, OEM Modules and Systems, and Supercomputer Systems). Mike Fister, general manager, EUCD, reported to Frank K. Gill, senior vice president and general manager, Intel Products Group. Fister was new to EUCD. When the OverDrive Processor was first conceived and the decision was made to go ahead, Dennis L. Carter was the general manager of EUCD; by May 1992, however, Carter had moved to a different position in the Intel organization.[3]

---

[3] Vice president and director of marketing in the Architecture Marketing and Applications Group.

Intel Microprocessors and Math Coprocessors

The Microprocessor[4]

The microprocessor was where the action was in a personal computer: it was the computer's central processing unit (CPU), the module in which all the instructions of a computer program were executed, including numerical processing, logical operations, and timing functions. The microprocessor consisted of three functional units: registers, which provided temporary storage for memory addresses, status codes, and information used during program execution; an arithmetic/logic unit, which performed all the numerical processing and logical operations; and control circuitry, which used a clock input to coordinate activity and maintain the proper sequence of operations in program execution.

For the personal computer to work effectively, the microprocessor had to be correctly and efficiently linked with the computer's memory (where programs and data were stored), and input/output devices (keyboard, display monitor, printer, floppy disk, etc.). The link was achieved through "buses," and one of the most important buses was the data bus, which was used for transporting data. There were two types of data buses: (1) the internal data bus, which carried data inside the microprocessor, and (2) the external data bus, which shuttled data between the microprocessor and the other parts of the computer.

The "width" of the data bus was an important determinant of performance: the wider the bus, the more "powerful" the computer. Data-bus width was measured in bits (an abbreviation for *bi*nary dig*it*s, the smallest unit of information in computers), and the smallest width in personal computers was 8 bits (1 computer "word"). While internal and external buses were typically of the same width, they did not have to be so: microprocessor manufacturers often followed up a new-generation chip with an entry-level, low-cost version that had the same internal bus width but a narrower external bus width. The Intel386™ SX microprocessor is a good example: it was introduced over two-and-a-half-years after the nearly three times as expensive Intel386 DX microprocessor, it had the same internal bus width as the DX version (32 bits), but it had a narrower external bus width (16 bits versus 32 bits). In general, the less-expensive version was less powerful than its more-expensive counterpart, but more powerful than a previous-generation microprocessor.

As the microprocessor executed a program, data were transferred from one subsystem of the computer to another. Each instance of data transfer was called a bus cycle, or machine cycle. Cycle timing was kept by a microprocessor clock signal, and the frequency of the signal (the number of cycles per unit of time) was another determinant of computer performance. Clock frequencies for Intel microprocessors ranged from 5 MHz to 50 MHz (1 MHz = 1,000,000 cycles per second).

---

[4]This section draws on the discussion in the chapter "Introduction to Microcomputers," *8086/8088 User's Manual* (Santa Clara, Calif.: Intel Corporation, 1989).

The Evolution of Intel Microprocessors: 8086/88 to Intel486 SX

Intel introduced its first 16-bit microprocessor for the personal computer—the 8086 chip—in 1978, but it was a later 8-bit chip—the 8088—that made its way into the first IBM PC, the computer that set the IBM PC-compatible standard and led the personal computer revolution of the 1980s. The 8088 chip had an 8-bit external bus width, a 16-bit internal bus width, and—in its initial version—a 5-MHz clock frequency. It was a fairly advanced microprocessor for its time.

In subsequent years, Intel improved the 8086/8088 microprocessor line in two ways: (1) It introduced new versions with higher clock frequency (8 MHz and 10 MHz in the case of the 8086, and 8 MHz in the case of the 8088); and (2) it introduced a next-generation 80286 in February 1982. As the product line evolution information in Exhibit 3 indicates, the company followed the same two-pronged product improvement strategy for the 80286 chip. Thus, there were faster versions of the 80286 (up from 8 MHz to 10 MHz and 12 MHz) and, in October 1985, the Intel386™ DX.

The evolution of the Intel386 series was different from that of the previous two generations (8086/8088 and 80286) in one very important respect: In June 1988, Intel introduced the Intel386 SX, a lower-performance, lower-priced chip that would bring

EXHIBIT 3   Evolution of Intel's Microprocessors Product Line

Chip Series	Date of Introduction	Clock Frequency	Internal Bus	External Bus	Number of Transistors	Typically Used In
8086	June 1978	5 MHz 8 MHz 10 MHz	16-bit	16-bit	29,000	Portable computing
8088	March 1979	5 MHz 8 MHz	16-bit	8-bit	29,000	Desktop computing
80286	February 1982	8 MHz 10 MHz 12 MHz	16-bit	16-bit	130,000	Portable computing
Intel386 DX	October 1985 February 1987 April 1988 April 1989	16 MHz 20 MHz 25 MHz 33 MHz	32-bit	32-bit	275,000	Desktop computing
Intel386 SX	June 1988 April 1989	16 MHz 20 MHz	32-bit	16-bit	275,000	Entry-level desktop and portable computing
Intel386 SL	October 1990 September 1991	20 MHz 25 MHz	32-bit	16-bit	855,000	Portable computing
Intel486 DX	April 1989 May 1990 June 1991	25 MHz 33 MHz 50 MHz	32-bit	32-bit	1,200,000	Desktop computing and servers
Intel486 SX	April 1991 September 1991 September 1991	20 MHz 16 MHz 25 MHz	32-bit	32-bit	1,185,000	Desktop computing

SOURCE: Intel Corporation.

the new Intel386 technology to entry-level systems (for which the DX version was too expensive). Now, Intel had a three-pronged product improvement strategy: continuing improvements in the speed of the up-market DX microprocessor, continuing improvements in the speed of the entry-level SX microprocessor, and, in April 1989, the introduction of the next-generation microprocessor. In October 1990, the company added a fourth prong to the Intel386 strategy: the Intel386 SL for low-power consumption (and, therefore, ideal for the new breed of portable personal computers).

The Intel486 series added another variation to the product evolution theme. Like the Intel386 series, the company increased the speed of the DX version and introduced an entry-level SX version. Five months after the 20-MHz SX was introduced, Intel added to the SX line in two opposite directions—a slower 16-MHz version and a faster 25-MHz version.

While the Intel486 SX and Intel386 SX were similar in that they were entry-level versions of the corresponding DX chips, the two were realized in dissimilar ways. In the case of the Intel386 SX, the chip had the same 32-bit internal bus as the DX chip, but a narrower 16-bit external bus (instead of 32 bits for the DX). The Intel486 SX was based on a totally different approach: it eliminated the Intel486 DX's "floating-point unit," a module that gave the DX an extra zip when performing numerical analysis.[5]

Until March 1991, Intel microprocessors—either manufactured directly by Intel or manufactured under license by large OEM customers and other chip manufacturers—were the only microprocessors used in IBM PC-compatible personal computers. One chip manufacturer producing Intel microprocessors under license was Santa Clara, California-based Advanced Micro Devices (AMD). In March 1991, AMD introduced its own version of the 386 microprocessor—a version that AMD claimed was up to 32 percent faster than Intel's.[6] The new processor proved especially popular among the low-price IBM PC clone manufacturers and grabbed an estimated 30 percent of the 386 market in the fourth quarter of 1991. AMD was also working on a clone of the 486 chip, though shipment was not expected until the fourth quarter of 1992, by which time Intel was expected to be selling its next-generation "P5" microprocessor.

AMD's entry foreshadowed a number of other competitive entries:

> Led by . . . [AMD], cloners of Intel chips are denting its bottom line. In May [1992], the No. 3 U.S. chip-maker, Texas Instruments Inc., announced two souped-up microprocessors. MIPS Computer Systems Inc. and [Mountain View, California-based] Sun

---

[5] In fact, when the Intel486 SX was first introduced, the die for manufacturing the new chip was not ready, and Intel made the chip by disabling the floating-point unit in the DX. When word of the disablement reached the press, the company was criticized for offering a less-expensive version of the DX chip that was a DX chip with the floating-point unit disabled. Once the SX manufacturing die was ready, subsequent Intel486 SXs were manufactured without the floating-point unit. Perhaps because of this controversy, the Intel486 SX chip acquired the reputation of being a "hobbled" chip and was not popular—until, that is, plans were announced for a forthcoming upgrade; demand was also spurred by a substantial reduction in the processor's price.

[6] The information in this and the next two sentences is drawn from Stephen K. Yoder, "Intel—AMD Clash Is Close to a Climax," *The Wall Street Journal,* January 31, 1992.

Microsystems Inc. have new designs that outrace Intel's—and will even run the same huge library of programs. Even IBM, Intel's No. 1 customer, has joined with Apple Computer Inc. and Motorola Inc., maker of Apple's microprocessors, to build a new desktop brain. . . .

. . . [Milpitas, California-based] Cyrix Corp. and [Richardson, Texas-based] Chips & Technologies Inc. have re-created—and improved—Intel386 without, they say, violating copyrights or patents.[7]

Intel Math Coprocessors

One reason why Intel did not choose to realize the Intel386 SX chip in the same way as the Intel486 SX was that the Intel386 DX chip did not have a floating-point unit (and, therefore, there was no question of coming up with a version without the floating-point unit). The 8086/8088 and 80286 series did not have a floating-point unit either, and this was a problem when it came to numerical computations. To overcome this deficiency, from the very beginning, Intel had offered a separate math coprocessor, a single-chip floating-point microprocessor that interfaced with the main microprocessor. Thus, there was the 8087, the 80287, the 80387 DX, and the 80387 SX (for the 8086/8088, the 80286, the Intel386 DX, and the Intel386 SX, respectively). The Intel486 DX did not need a math coprocessor. Finally, the Intel486 SX was an entirely different story. When it announced the chip, Intel also introduced the 80487 SX. But, for all practical purposes, the 80487 SX was the Intel486 DX—since all that differentiated the Intel486 SX from the Intel486 DX was the absence of the floating-point unit in the former.[8]

While Intel's math coprocessors complemented the company's corresponding microprocessors, the two product lines were managed by two different products groups. The Microprocessor Products Group (MPG) managed the microprocessors line; the End User Components Division (EUCD), the math coprocessor line. Harry Laswell, marketing manager, EUCD, talked about the math coprocessor business:

> You might think that the math coprocessor business was some brilliant strategy on Intel's part. It wasn't; the business just happened. The motivation for a separate chip with a floating-point unit came from our microcontrollers for factory automation equipment. Even then, the chip was never intended for the PC. But IBM introduced a vacant socket in the PC, and there you have it: A math coprocessor market developed.
>
> Now that we had the market, we had to manage it. The math coprocessor was not a branded product; price competition was intense; a number of competitors were promising a superior socket-compatible product; and, with the Intel486 DX architecture, we foresaw the eventual death of the product category.

---

[7]"Inside Intel," pp. 86–87. Cyrix was also taking another page out of Intel's book: In August 1992, Jim Chapman, Cyrix's vice president of marketing, was quoted as saying that the company was working on a clock-doubling line of 386 chips; clock-doubling was the technology that Intel had employed in the OverDrive Processor to soup up its performance.

[8]This was even more reason for dissatisfaction among the initial Intel486 SX buyers: at least initially, they were already buying the DX chip, albeit with its floating-point unit disabled; in the 487 SX, they would have to buy what was effectively another DX chip so that the original SX chip would perform like the DX chip—which, in a sense, it already was.

As early as 1989, we were thinking about what to do with the math coprocessor line. Then the question was, how to increase the coprocessor's performance to compete effectively with the imitators. We had two options: "add more transistors" and/or "make the transistors run faster." We couldn't choose the second option in 1985, when the 80387 came out. But, by 1991, we could. That realization had a major impact on our plans for the Intel486 SX: yes, we could worry about the math coprocessor for the chip; but now, we were onto something more important: the OverDrive Processor.

The OverDrive Processor

Genesis

Until mid-1991, Dennis Carter was general manager, EUCD. In that capacity, he too was concerned about the future of the division's math coprocessor business. Carter remembered talking about this with Laswell and Bill Rash, then a marketing manager in the Microprocessor Products Group:

Until the 80387, Intel's math coprocessor business was good, but not great. The 80387 did well. But what next? With the advent of the floating-point unit in the Intel486 DX, there was no need for a math coprocessor. Even in the resulting shrinking market, there was an increasingly strong competition from look-alikes. What would happen to this business? What could we do?

And then, Harry [Laswell] and Bill [Rash] came up with this idea of *speed doubling*. Harry can explain it better than I can; basically, their idea was to improve—enhance—microprocessor performance by doubling the speed inside the processor. Harry actually thought of speed doubling in the context of the math compressor. Later, Bill argued, if we can pull off this trick in the math coprocessor, why not in the microprocessor itself? This thought led to two new chip series: the OverDrive Processor, and the Intel486 DX2 microprocessor. But, MPG was not ready for the DX2, and we had to hold off.

It was the OverDrive Processor that caught EUCD's imagination. We had surveyed many customers and corporate MIS [management information systems] managers about our math coprocessors, and we had some very interesting data. When asked why someone purchased a math coprocessor, the answer was not "for the ability to do floating-point arithmetic." Most customers didn't even know what floating-point arithmetic was. Most were buying a math coprocessor for "better" performance. Indeed, most customers were comparing the math coprocessor with other enhancement products, and it soon became clear to us that the math coprocessor was mispositioned.

The same MIS managers also told us they were concerned about the rapid pace of product improvement. Microprocessors improve significantly every couple of years, while most corporations depreciate their PCs over five years—a mismatch that caused many users to look for some way to upgrade their systems without having to scrap the system before its depreciation life has expired.

There were plenty of upgrade options around: One could upgrade the graphics, one could add in modules to accomplish specific tasks, one could add memory, and one could even upgrade the central processing unit. A number of system vendors offered the last option in their "upgradable" systems. These vendors designed CPU-level upgradability in

EXHIBIT 4 Speed-Doubling Technology

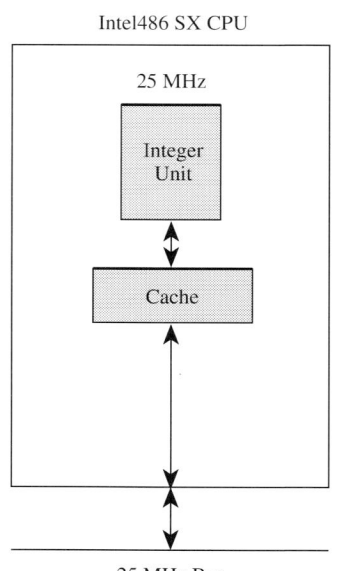
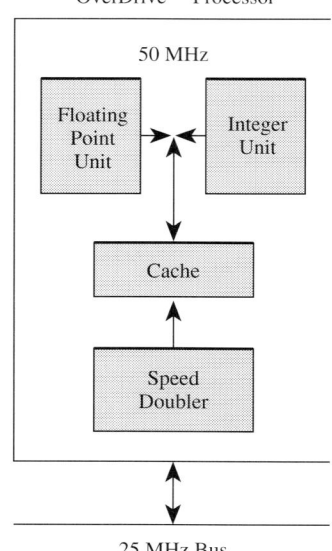

	Speed-Doubling Technology: Implementation	
	Intel486 DX2	**OverDrive Processors for Intel486 SX and DX Systems**
Positioning	• Available only to OEMs for manufacturing new systems • Not available for end-user purchase	• Retail upgrade product sold through resellers • End-user purchase as upgrade for existing systems
Pinout	• 168-pin 486 DX pinout	• 169-pin Intel487 SX and 168-pin Intel486 DX pinout
Versions	• Intel486 DX2-50 MHz	• For 16/20-MHz Intel486 SX and 25-MHz Intel486 SX systems (May 1992); for Intel486 DX systems (2nd half, 1992)
After-sales support	• As offered by OEM	• Intel lifetime warranty • 1-800 phone support • End-user collaterals, including user's manual, installation instructions, etc.

SOURCE: Intel Corporation.

one of three ways: swap system boards, add "turbo" cards, or install new, proprietary CPU modules. All three methods were risky. Each system vendor offered its own proprietary upgrade scheme; imagine the plight of the MIS manager supporting systems supplied by 10 to 15 different vendors. Furthermore, upgrading required the end user (or a special service facility) to tinker with the CPU. Some call the CPU the computer's heart; some call it the brain; in either case, a transplant is very risky. Finally, at $800 to $2,000, upgrades were expensive.

So, we asked, why not an upgrade processor that would fit into a separate "upgrade-ready" socket? This would assuage the MIS managers' concern about doing a heart or brain transplant with the original microprocessor and yet offer the end user a standard way to upgrade to an increased performance level across all applications. The OverDrive Processor was the solution. Of course, we had not coined the term *OverDrive Processor* yet. The brand name would come later.

"The basic idea of speed doubling is quite simple," said Laswell as he explained the speed-doubling concept alluded to by Carter. Laswell elaborated:

> Take the 80387 math coprocessor. It has two clocks: one for coordinating communications with the Intel386 microprocessor, and the other for the floating-point unit. We couldn't do anything to the first clock, but supposing we ran the second clock faster. That would soup up the coprocessor. As math coprocessors go, that would differentiate our product. There was only one problem: In the time frame of the 80387 coprocessor, we were already pushing the two clocks as fast as we could, and the only way to enhance the math coprocessor's performance was by increasing the number of transistors.
>
> The same logic did not apply when the Intel486 SX came along. By then, semiconductor process technology had advanced so we could speed up—double—the second clock. The result: a souped up 80487 SX coprocessor [see "Example" in Exhibit 4].
>
> Of course, the Intel486 SX was a bad example to begin with: The chip was made possible by [first disabling and then] eliminating the floating-point unit in the Intel486 DX, and the unsouped-up 80487 SX was essentially the Intel486 DX. If we souped up the 80487 SX, then the Intel486 SX-80487 SX combination would outperform the Intel486 DX. In any case, if we could soup up the original 80487 SX, and if this was essentially the Intel486 DX, then we should be able to soup up the latter chip as well. By now, Bill [Rash] was really into the *bigger* picture. "Why," he argued, "can't we speed up the Intel486 DX and make way for an Intel486 DX2?"
>
> Rash's idea of a DX2 chip made sense for another reason: There was a performance gap in Intel's product line between the then fastest DX chip and the forthcoming "P5" chip series, and the DX2 chip could fill the gap.

Interregnum: The Intel486 DX2 Microprocessor

Laswell's and Rash's analysis suggested two implementation paths for the speed-doubling technology: a new Intel486 DX2 microprocessor, and upgrades for the Intel486 DX and SX. As sensible as the analysis appeared, it posed all kinds of implementation problems. One of them was that the Microprocessor Products Group (MPG) was not ready for the Intel486 DX2: the new chip would throw a monkey wrench into their and their customers' product-evolution plans (and the customers' upgradable systems product offerings); the new chip would divert design, development, and manufacturing resources; and, in any case, it takes time to launch a new product that must fit into someone else's systems product. Intel's management committee gave its go-ahead for the Intel486 SX and DX OverDrive Processors in March 1991, but until MPG was ready to go public with its plans for the DX2, EUCD could not officially announce the OverDrive Processors for the Intel486 SX and DX.

The introduction of the Intel486 DX2 in the context of the SX and DX OverDrive Processors also posed some knotty marketing problems. For the same clock speeds, there was not much to differentiate a DX2 chip from the corresponding SX- or DX-plus-OverDrive Processor combination; in which case, how should the DX2 be positioned, and why would MPG's OEM customers even bother building systems around the DX2 chip? Would a gray market develop for the new chips? What about the differences in aftersales support for OEM and retail products? The lower half of Exhibit 4 offers some answers.

OverDrive Processor Implementation: Architecture and Road Map

While the pieces were being positioned for the Intel486 DX2 chip, EUCD was planning the eventual implementation of the OverDrive Processor concept. Carter, Laswell, and others realized that they could not test the concept with the Intel486 DX: While this would be the logical place to start (rather than the SX chip), the chip was first issued before the OverDrive Processor concept was articulated and, therefore, the OEMs had not designed their PCs with an empty socket. The only way to install the OverDrive Processor in these PCs would be by pulling out the old chip and replacing it with a new chip—precisely the kind of transplant that end users had cautioned against.

That left only one alternative: to introduce the concept with the Intel486 SX chip. While this introduced a new set of product-positioning problems (the SX-plus-OverDrive versus the DX), it was an especially viable alternative because many SX systems already had an empty socket for a math coprocessor.

The decision to use the math coprocessor socket for the OverDrive Processor raised a new set of questions. The socket had 169 holes for the math coprocessor's 169 pins. This was one hole (and one pin) more than the main microprocessor socket. The extra pin was originally added on the math coprocessor to make sure that the coprocessor was oriented correctly (the locator pin was on one of the four corners of the coprocessor). Since EUCD decided to make the Intel486 SX OverDrive Processor pin-compatible with the 80487 SX, it could not serve as an OverDrive Processor for Intel486 DX systems (which were not intended to have a vacant socket) or for those Intel486 SX systems where the OEM vendors had decided not to include a vacant socket; these required a 168-pin connector.

Finally, once the idea of OverDrive Processors as enablers of upgradability had gained currency, it quickly transcended the speed-doubling concept: Speed doubling was a solution that applied to the Intel486 DX and SX; other chips might warrant other solutions. For example, the Intel486 DX2 chip already had speed doubling and, therefore, could not be further upgraded by speed doubling. As

EUCD envisioned it, there would be an OverDrive Processor for the DX2 chip, but performance enhancement would be realized in that case by the use of next-generation technology. Exhibit 5 illustrates EUCD's OverDrive Processor strategy for the Intel486 series.

OverDrive Processor Implementation: Getting the Systems Manufacturers' Buy-In

Bob Bennett, OverDrive Product manager, was responsible for working with the systems manufacturers so that their systems would be designed with an OverDrive Processor in mind. Bennett talked about the challenges in getting the systems manufacturers to buy into the concept:

> For starters, we couldn't even talk to them about the OverDrive Processor. We told them "something" was in the works, but we could not be specific until MPG went public about the DX2 chip. And even then, it was not clear they would be exactly happy about the OverDrive Processor idea: the microprocessor upgrade would threaten *their* upgradable products. Of course, we could talk about the 80487 SX math coprocessor, but there was already a lot of confusion about the positioning of the Intel486 SX.
>
> The OEMs were also not enthused about giving away premium real estate space on a rapidly shrinking CPU board to a vacant socket for which Intel was promising—wink, wink, nudge, nudge—"something." And it was not only a matter of space. With speed doubling, the OverDrive Processor would generate a lot of heat. Would there be enough space for cooling? What about product warranties and other issues? Who would be responsible if an end user makes a mistake when installing the OverDrive Processor and damages the system? In any case, was the OverDrive Processor a consumer product or an OEM product?
>
> To see why the last point was relevant, consider pricing. The OEMs typically dealt with MPG, which had an established pricing formula: a price schedule that offered discounts depending on the quantity purchased (for the OverDrive Processor, we would only have two prices: distributor cost and manufacturer's suggested list price); MPG practices dynamic pricing, where a chip starts off with a high price and then drops in price as it gets older and new-and-improved chips come along (in the retail market, you can't drop prices every quarter); and, given the vast increase in the offering of equivalent products (for example, a 50-MHz Intel486 DX2 was equivalent to a 25-MHz Intel486 SX with an OverDrive Processor), how are we going to maintain price equivalence to minimize arbitrage opportunities?
>
> Then take product positioning. How were we going to position the OverDrive Processor? If we positioned it as a CPU upgrade, then we would be pitting it directly against the systems manufacturer's upgrade scheme. If we positioned it as akin to a math coprocessor, then Intel would not get the maximum impact from the new product. Or should we position it as a performance booster?

Cesar Pun was compatibility manager, EUCD. It was his job to make sure that once a systems manufacturer signed on, its vacant socket was mechanically and logically compatible with the OverDrive Processor. Pun talked about his challenge:

> Things became easier once we could discuss our plans openly with the systems manufacturers. But, for the older systems—especially the Intel486 DX CPU-based systems,

Exhibit 5 OverDrive Processor Strategy: A Roadmap

A. *OverDrive™ Processor Product Roadmap*

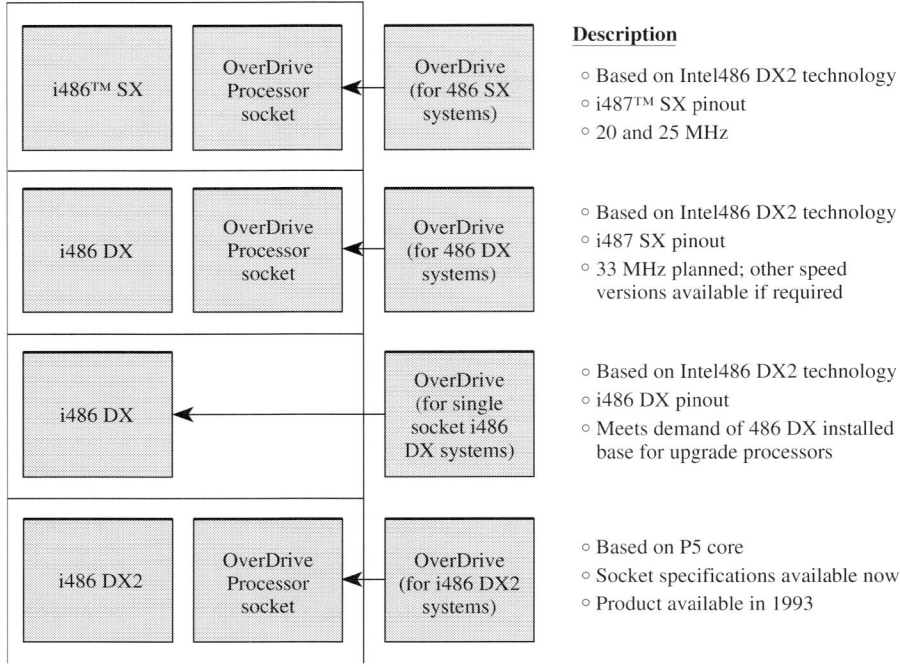

Description

- Based on Intel486 DX2 technology
- i487™ SX pinout
- 20 and 25 MHz

- Based on Intel486 DX2 technology
- i487 SX pinout
- 33 MHz planned; other speed versions available if required

- Based on Intel486 DX2 technology
- i486 DX pinout
- Meets demand of 486 DX installed base for upgrade processors

- Based on P5 core
- Socket specifications available now
- Product available in 1993

which were designed before even we knew about the OverDrive Processor—compatibility was a major concern.

On the mechanical side, we had to test for heat emission, air flow, heat sinks, insertion forces, and what have you. Even if we could get mechanical compatibility, there was logical compatibility to worry about. Individual systems and microprocessors have their own windows of tolerance when it comes to electronically interacting with each other, and the windows must have a large enough overlap for the PC to function effectively. Some systems, especially inexpensive ones supplied by down-market OEMs, have narrow tolerance windows, and while the system might be jury-rigged to work with DX or SX microprocessors, it might experience difficulty with the OverDrive Processor. For example, of the 18 25-MHz DX systems we tested, 3 or 4 failed.

We have established a compatibility council and have been testing systems on the basis of their market shares, but there are issues we haven't settled yet. For example, who should pay for the testing: Intel, or the systems manufacturers? How does the answer change if the OverDrive Processor concept catches on, and it is in the systems manufacturers' interest to have their system qualified for compatibility? For our part, we plan to regularly publish a list of qualified vendors [see Exhibit 6 for a list as of May 26, 1992].

EXHIBIT 5   (concluded)

B. Intel OverDrive™ Processors—Part of Future Architectures

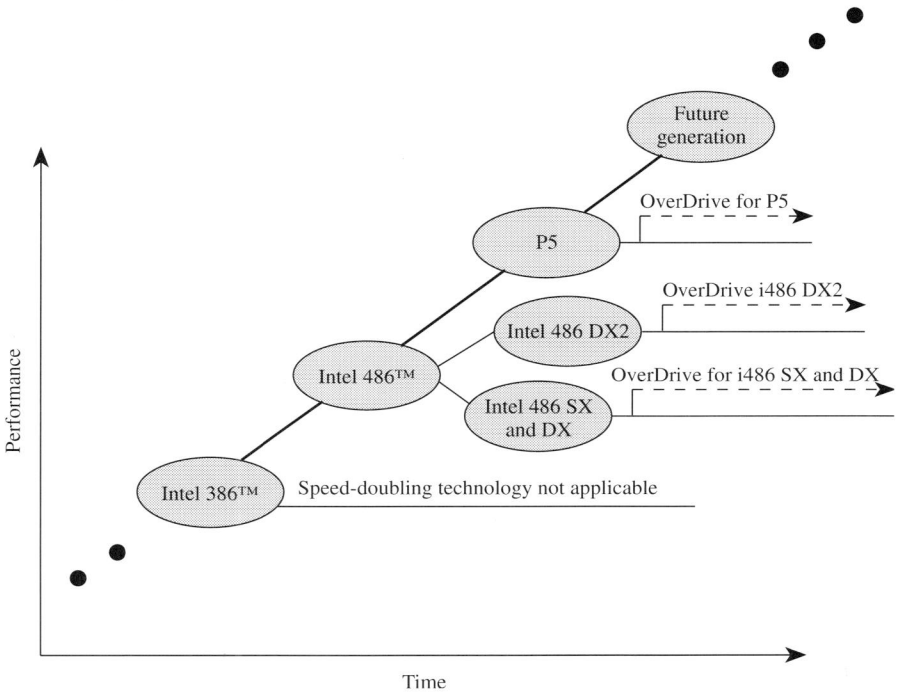

SOURCE: Intel Corporation.

Cheryl Beninga was product manager for a future DX2 OverDrive Processor. Being responsible for a future rather than an existing or past product, she had a relationship with the systems manufacturers that was different than that of Bennett and Pun. Like Bennett, Beninga was new to EUCD (and to Intel; Bennett joined the company in early 1991, Beninga in November 1991). Beninga talked about her job, the relationship between EUCD and the systems manufacturers, and the challenge of managing the OverDrive Processor line in the long run:

> I work with Intel's engineering team on product design and the OEMs on the design of the OverDrive Processor socket. The Intel486 DX2 microprocessor was released in March 1992, and the volume build-up has been quite good. I believe that a full 75 percent of the new DX2 systems will be designed with an OverDrive Processor socket. Ideally, we would like a branded, "OverDrive ready" socket in all systems.
>
> You have probably heard a lot about OEMs and the OverDrive Processor. But, if you think of it, we need the OEMs. They are our channel to the market: If they don't include

EXHIBIT 6   Intel486 SX CPU-Based Systems Supporting OverDrive Processor*

U.S. System Manufacturers

3D Microcomputers	ECS	PC and C Computer Corporation
ALR	Eltech	PC Designs
Altos	Epson	Philips
AMI	Everex	Reply
ARES	Fountain Technologies, Inc.	Rogentech
AST	Fujikama	Sceptre Technologies
Austin	Hewlett-Packard Corporation	Sefco East
BCC	IBM	Swan
Blackship	Kama	Tandon
Cemtech	Leading Technology	Tandy
Club American	Micronics	Tangent
Commodore Business Machines	Mylex	Touche
Compaq	Mynix	Tri-Star
Compuadd Computer Corporation	NCR	Tricord
Cumulus	NEC Technologies, Inc.	Vtech
Dell Computer Corporation	Northgate	Win Labs, Ltd.
Digital Scientific	Novas	Zenith Data Systems
Easy Data	Packard Bell	Zeos International

European System Manufacturers

Actebis	ITOS	Schneider
Akhter GMBH	NCR	Siemens Nixdorf
Apricot Computers	NEC Technologies, Inc.	Tandon
Aquarius System Int'l GMBH	Normerel	TCI Trident Computer GMBH
ASEM	Olivetti	TMC Technology Electronics GMBH
ECS Germany	Opus Technology PLC	
Elonex PLC	Osicom	Triumph-Adler
Escom Computer Vertriebs GMBH	Peacock Computer GMBH	Tulip Computers
	Philips PCS	Viglen LTD.
Hewlett-Packard Corporation	Research Machines	Worx
ICL Personal Systems	Schmidt Computer GMBH	Zenith Data Systems

Asia Pacific System Manufacturers

ACER	ECS	Juko
ACT	FIC	Micro Computer Systems
Altos	GES	Mitac
Arche	GVC	SVT
Asus	Handjade	Tatung
CAF	HCL	Trigem
Copam	Infocom	Twinhead
DTK	Informtech	Videotech
		Wipro

Rest of the World System Manufacturers

Itautec Informatica S.A.	Microtec S.A.	Monydata Teleinformaticia LTDA

*Partial as of May 1992.
SOURCE: Intel Corporation.

a socket, we can't sell the OverDrive Processors. Perhaps the best way to encourage the OEMs to include an OverDrive socket is to generate end user enthusiasm for the concept.

OverDrive Processor Implementation: Reaching Out to the End User

Two people in the EUCD organization were charged with the responsibility for generating end user enthusiasm for the OverDrive Processor concept: Kristin Bailey, marketing communications manager, and Bill Bidal, acting worldwide channel marketing manager. Bailey talked about the marketing communications support for the OverDrive Processor concept:

> The OverDrive Processor concept was supposed to apply to all three lines in the Intel486 series—the DX, the SX, and the DX2—and we had a different problem in each case: DX was an older chip, and most DX CPU-based systems did not have an OverDrive socket; the SX was introduced in April 1991 with a math/OverDrive socket in mind, but the chip had acquired a reputation as a hobbled chip; and no one was ready to talk about the DX2 until early 1992. Indeed, we couldn't even talk in specific terms about the OverDrive Processor until MPG was ready to announce the DX2 chip. What do you tell people?
>
> Furthermore, whom do you tell? How do you tell them? And when do you tell them? The OEM customers read publications like *Electronic Design* and *EDN;* the end user reads *PC Magazine, Byte,* and *PC World.* People typically purchased math coprocessors—the product with which EUCD has lots of experience—at the time of system purchase, but we expect them to purchase the OverDrive Processor one to two years after purchasing their PC.
>
> There was an additional element of confusion as marketing communications go. We had to decide whether to launch the DX2 and the OverDrive Processor at different times or at the same time. If the answer is at different times, which should come first? Whichever way you cut it, there was bound to be some confusion. It was decided that MPG would introduce the DX2 in March [1992] and we would follow with the OverDrive announcement in May. In a sense, the DX2 served the role of placating the system manufacturers; announcing the OverDrive before the DX2 would have defeated that goal.
>
> We began advertising a "vacancy" slot beginning September–October 1991. Since we couldn't talk about the OverDrive Processor at this time, the advertisement was subtle: we promised the audience that Intel will have "something" next year for the slot, and that "something" will be of value and help protect the system-owner's investment in the system. The "vacancy" ads were specifically targeted to the nontechnical audience. We placed them in *The Wall Street Journal, Business Week,* and so on. In January [1992], we even had TV commercials during the Super Bowl.

If it was Bailey's job to make the systems manufacturers, the end users, and the distribution channels aware of the OverDrive Processor product, it was Bidal's job to make sure that the product was correctly priced, the distribution channels got the product, and it was packaged so that it was indeed easy for the end user to install. Bidal commented on these aspects of his functions:

> Let's start with price. Actually, price is not something I decide: Mike [Fister] and Harry [Laswell] worry about that. But it affects channel marketing, and I worry about it. From

Section II Managing New Products

EXHIBIT 7 OverDrive Processor: An Installation Guide

The instructions on this card pertain only to computers with an empty OverDrive Processor socket. If your computer does not have an empty OverDrive Processor socket, see the *User's Guide*.

- The diskette included with your OverDrive Processor contains an animated installation demonstration. You may wish to see this before proceeding. Read the diskette label for instructions.
- This *Quick Installation Card* is for customers who are familiar with installing computer upgrade products; other customers should use the more detailed instructions in the *User's Guide*.

1. Remove the cover from your computer. Be sure to ground yourself.

Warning! Danger to you! Turn off the computer's power switch and unplug the power cord from the wall outlet. If you don't you could electrocute yourself.

2. Check the pins. Examine the connector pins on the OverDrive Processor. If any pins are bent, carefully straighten them as shown. Note that the 25MHz OverDrive Processor has a heat sink attached to ensure proper heat dissipation; the 16/20 MHz version does not need a heat sink.

OverDrive Processor 16/20 MHz version   OverDrive Processor 25 MHz version

3. Find the empty OverDrive Processor socket. Some typical socket types are shown here. If your system does not have an empty OverDrive Processor socket, see *Installation Procedure* in the User's Guide.

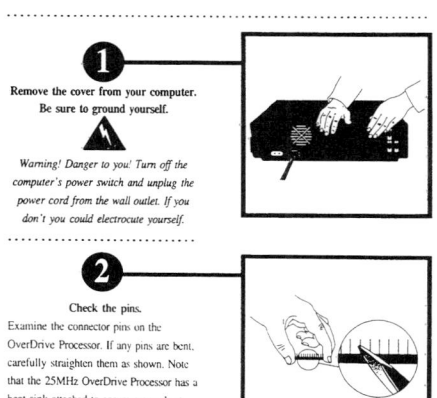

LIF or standard socket   ZIF sockets

4. Orient your OverDrive Processor correctly. A keyed socket will have three rows of pin holes and a key pin hole. Match the key pin on the chip with the key pin hole on the socket.
If your socket has less than or more than three rows of pin holes, or does not have a key pin hole, your computer may still be upgradable with the OverDrive Processor. Contact your computer dealer or manufacturer for more information.

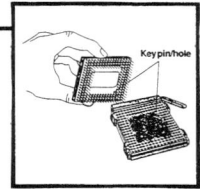 Key pin/hole

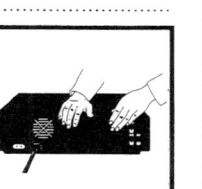
Pull lever to unlock; push to lock.

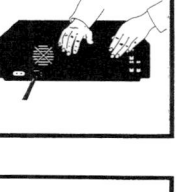
Turn socket screw to release, then insert the OverDrive Processor. Then turn screw to lock to secure the chip.

LIF or standard socket; push firmly and evenly as shown here.

5. Insert the OverDrive Processor in the empty socket. If your computer has a Zero Insertion Force socket like the ones shown here, be sure to unlock or release the socket before inserting the chip. After inserting the chip, close the lock/unlock lever or turn the lock/unlock screw (or hex-head screw) to the closed position. If your system does not have a Zero Insertion Force socket, you may have to press firmly to "seat" the pins in the socket. Your computer's system board should not bend under the pressure of inserting the OverDrive Processor.

6. Set jumpers or switches on the system board. You may need to set switches, jumpers, or both on your computer's system board to let the computer know you've added an OverDrive Processor. Refer to your computer's manual for information.

7. Put the cover back on the computer. Reconnect all the cables and cords, and plug the power cord into the wall outlet. Turn on the computer. If your computer requires it, run the computer's setup or configuration program.
If you have problems with your computer after installing the OverDrive Processor, see *Troubleshooting* in the User's Guide.

8. Test your OverDrive Processor. Use the diagnostics included on the utilities diskette. If you already installed the Installation Demo, you *do not* need to reinstall the diagnostics. To install the tests, insert the disk in drive A (drive B on some computers) and type:

A: and press **Enter**
Then type **install** and press **Enter**

Follow the directions on the screen. After installation is complete, type **overdrive** and press **Enter** to start the programs.

intel

OverDrive is a trademark of Intel Corporation. This literature is subject to change without notice. Intel assumes no rights or responsibilities for errors or omissions herein. © 1992 Intel Corporation. All rights reserved.

Source: Intel Corporation.

SOURCE: Intel Corporation.

the outset, we had decided that something in the $500 to $600 range made sense: It was cheaper than the end user's other options, and it was within the purchase-requisition authority of many end users. We didn't want people to have to go to their bosses or an executive committee just to buy an OverDrive Processor.

As for distribution channels, in the United States our customers are (1) OEMs like Dell and Gateways [discount PC vendors], who have indicated their desire to sell the OverDrives through their channels; (2) 40 direct accounts; and (3) national distributors (the major 3), regional distributors, direct resellers, superstores, and so on. We are reaching these channels directly and also through the usual catalogs that the different distributors use. In Japan, the strategy is somewhat different. There, most of our customers are the systems manufacturers, though we also distribute through a few resellers. In Europe, we rely more on distributors, who are seen as partners in making the OverDrive business happen.

Finally, product packaging. Here's what we have come up with [he said, holding a 6-×-8½-inch envelope]: a small box ["Chip Removal Kit"] containing the OverDrive Processor and a chip removal tool [in case the socket in which the processor would go was not empty], a *Quick Installation Card* [see Exhibit 7], a *User's Guide,* a *Utilities* diskette, a *Warranty Registration Card,* and some aftersales support and promotional materials.

Given Intel's matrix organization, EUCD did not directly handle the sales function for the OverDrive Processor—or, for that matter, the math coprocessor or any other product. Sales for all five Intel Products Group divisions (EUCD, Networking Products, PC Enhancement Products, OEM Modules and Systems, and Supercomputer Systems) were centralized at the group's headquarters in Portland, Oregon.

Concluding Comments

Mike Fister, general manager, EUCD, commented on the OverDrive Processor's broader implications for Intel:

> MPG has microprocessor product line evolution, positioning, pricing, and so forth, down to a science. Over the last couple of years, they have also adopted an aggressive "Intel Inside" branding strategy. How will OverDrive affect the MPG business? Also, how will it change the way people perceive of CPUs, computer obsolescence, and Intel's role in managing the consequences of rapid change in microprocessor technology?

CHAPTER 15
Creating Project Plans to Focus Product Development

The long-term competitiveness of most manufacturers depends on their product development capabilities. Yet few companies approach the development process systematically or strategically. They end up with an unruly collection of projects that do not match long-term business objectives and that consume far more development resources than are available. The aggregate project plan methodology attempts to address this problem. It helps managers to allocate resources, sequence projects, and build critical development capabilities.

The long-term competitiveness of any manufacturing company depends ultimately on the success of its product development capabilities. New-product development holds hope for improving market position and financial performance, creating new industry standards and new niche markets, and even renewing the organization. Yet few development projects fully deliver on their early promises. The fact is, much can and does go wrong during development. In some instances, poor leadership or the absence of essential skills is to blame. But often problems arise from the way companies approach the development process. They lack what we call an aggregate project plan.

Consider the case of a large scientific instruments company we will call PreQuip. In mid-1989, senior management became alarmed about a rash of late product development projects. For some months, the development budget had been rising even as the number of completed projects declined. And many of the projects in the development pipeline no longer seemed to reflect the needs of the market. Management was especially troubled because it had believed its annual business plan provided the guidance that the marketing and engineering departments needed to generate and schedule projects.

Steven C. Wheelwright and Kim B. Clark prepared this article.
Copyright © 1992 by the President and Fellows of Harvard College. All rights reserved. Reprinted from *Harvard Business Review,* March–April 1992, pp. 70–82.

To get to the root of the problem, the chief executive first asked senior managers to compile a list of all the current development projects. They discovered that 30 projects were under way—far more than anticipated and, they suspected, far more than the organization could support. Further analysis revealed that the company had two to three times more development work than it was capable of completing over its three-year development planning horizon. (See the chart "PreQuip's Development Predicament: Overcommitted Resources.")

With such a strain on resources, delays were inevitable. When a project ran into trouble, engineers from other projects were reassigned or, more commonly, asked to add the crisis project to their already long list of active projects. The more projects they added, the more their productivity dropped. The reshuffling caused delays in other projects, and the effects cascaded. Furthermore, as deadlines slipped and development costs rose, project managers faced pressure to cut corners and compromise quality just to keep their projects moving forward.

The senior management team also discovered that the majority of PreQuip's development resources—primarily engineers and support staff—was not focused on the projects most critical to the business. When questioned, project leaders admitted

PreQuip's Development Predicament: Overcommitted Resources

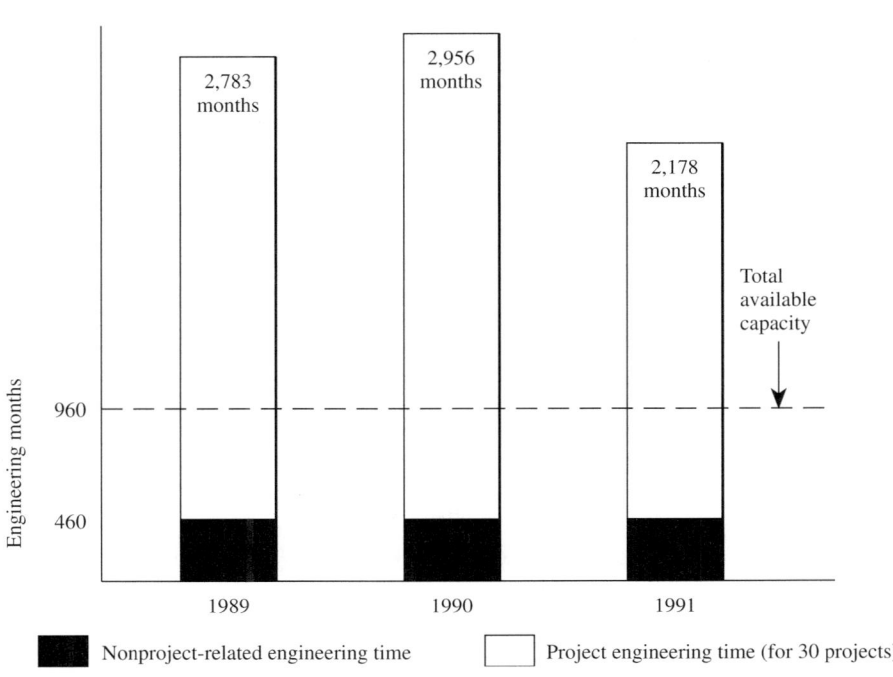

PreQuip had 960 engineering months each year to allocate to development work. But combining the time it would take to keep its current 30 projects on schedule with the time engineers spent doing nonproject development work, the company found it had overcommitted its development resources for the next three years by a factor of three.

that the strategic objectives outlined in the annual business plan had little bearing on project selection. Instead, they chose projects because engineers found the technical problems challenging or because customers or the marketing department requested them. PreQuip had no formal process for choosing among development projects. As long as there was money in the budget or the person making the request had sufficient clout, the head of the development department had no option but to accept additional project requests.

Many engineers were not only working on noncritical projects but also spending as much as 50 percent of their time on nonproject-related work. They responded to requests from manufacturing for help with problems on previous products, from field sales for help with customer problems, from quality assurance for help with reliability problems, and from purchasing for help with qualifying vendors. In addition to spending considerable time fixing problems on previously introduced products, engineers spent many hours in information and update meetings. In short, they spent too little time developing the right new products, experimenting with new technologies, or addressing new markets.

PreQuip's story is hardly unique. Most organizations we are familiar with spend their time putting out fires and pursuing projects aimed at catching up to their competitors. They have far too many projects going at once and all too often seriously overcommit their development resources. They spend too much time dealing with short-term pressures and not enough time on the strategic mission of product development.

Indeed, in most organizations, management directs all its attention to individual projects—it micromanages project development. But no single project defines a company's future or its market growth over time; the set of projects does. Companies need to devote more attention to managing the set and mix of projects. In particular, they should focus on how resources are allocated between projects. Management must plan how the project set evolves over time, which new projects get added when, and what role each project should play in the overall development effort.

The aggregate project plan addresses all of these issues. To create a plan, management categorizes projects based on the amount of resources they consume and on how they will contribute to the company's product line. Then, by mapping the project types, management can see where gaps exist in the development strategy and make more informed decisions about what types of projects to add and when to add them. Sequencing projects carefully, in turn, gives management greater control of resource allocation and utilization. The project map also reveals where development capabilities need to be strong. Over time, companies can focus on adding critical resources and on developing the skills of individual contributors, project leaders, and teams.

Finally, an aggregate plan will enable management to improve the way it manages the development function. Simply adding projects to the active list—a common practice at many companies—endangers the long-term health of the development process. Management needs to create a set of projects that is consistent with the company's development strategies rather than selecting individual projects from a long list of ad hoc proposals. And management must become involved in the development process *before* projects get started, even before they are fully defined. It is not appropriate to give one department—say, engineering or marketing—sole responsibility for initiating all projects because it is usually not in a position to determine every project's strategic worth.

Indeed, most companies, including PreQuip, should start the reformation process by eliminating or postponing the lion's share of their existing projects, eventually supplanting them with a new set of projects that fits the business strategy and the capacity constraints. The aggregate project plan provides a framework for addressing this difficult task.

How to Map Projects

The first step in creating an aggregate project plan is to define and map the different types of development projects; defining projects by type provides useful information about how resources should be allocated. The two dimensions we have found most useful for classifying are the degree of change in the product and the degree of change in the manufacturing process. The greater the change along either dimension, the more resources are needed.

Using this construct, we have divided projects into five types. The first three—derivative, breakthrough, and platform—are commercial development projects. The remaining two categories are research and development (R&D), which is the precursor to commercial development, and alliances and partnerships, which can be either commercial or basic research. (See the chart "Mapping the Five Types of Development Projects.")

Each of the five project types requires a unique combination of development resources and management styles. Understanding how the categories differ helps managers predict the distribution of resources accurately and allows for better planning and sequencing of projects over time. Here is a brief description of each category:

Derivative projects range from cost-reduced versions of existing products to add-ons or enhancements for an existing production process. For example, Kodak's wide-angle, single-use 35mm camera, the Stretch, was derived from the no-frills Fun Saver introduced in 1990. Designing the Stretch was primarily a matter of changing the lens.

Development work on derivative projects typically falls into three categories: incremental product changes, say, new packaging or a new feature, with little or no manufacturing process change; incremental process changes, like a lower-cost manufacturing process, improved reliability, or a minor change in materials used, with little or no product change; and incremental changes on both dimensions. Because design changes are usually minor, incremental projects typically are more clearly bounded and require substantially fewer development resources than the other categories. And because derivative projects are completed in a few months, ongoing management involvement is minimal.

Mapping the Five Types of Development Projects

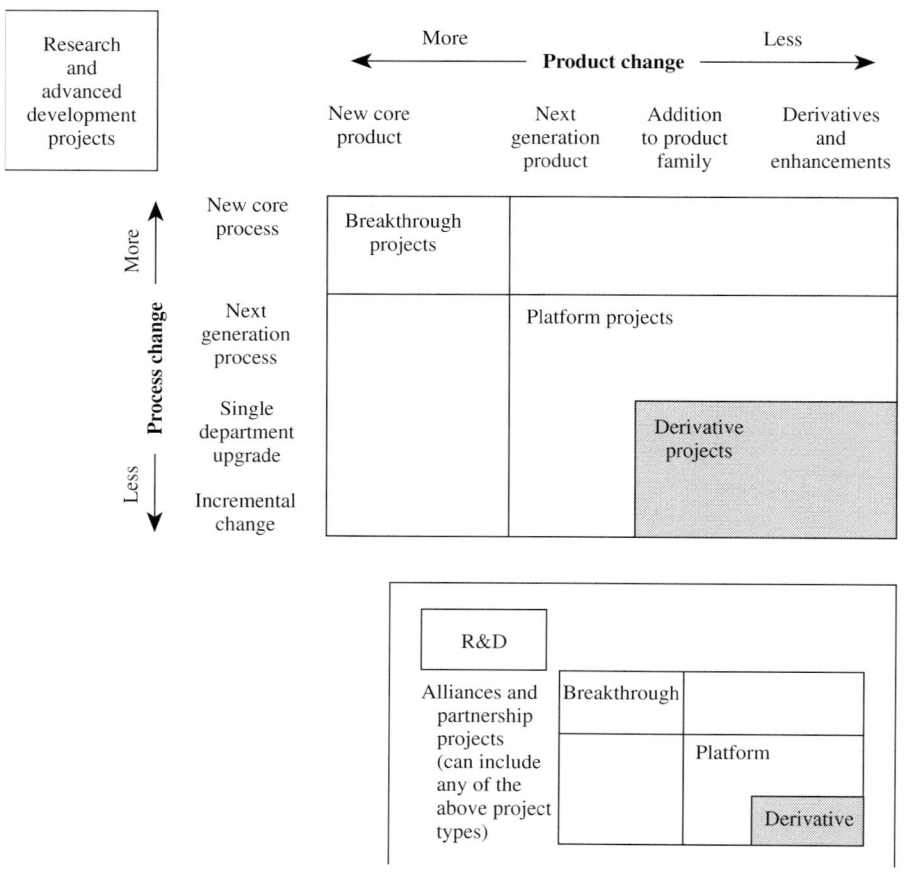

Breakthrough projects are at the other end of the development spectrum because they involve significant changes to existing products and processes. Successful breakthrough projects establish core products and processes that differ fundamentally from previous generations. Like compact disks and fiber-optics cable, they create a whole new product category that can define a new market.

Because breakthrough products often incorporate revolutionary new technologies or materials, they usually require revolutionary manufacturing processes. Management should give development teams considerable latitude in designing new processes, rather than force them to work with existing plants and equipment, operating techniques, or supplier networks.

Platform projects are in the middle of the development spectrum and are thus harder to define. They entail more product and/or process changes than derivatives do, but they don't introduce the untried new technologies or materials that breakthrough products do. Honda's 1990 Accord line is an example of a new platform in the auto industry: Honda introduced a number of manufacturing process and product changes but no fundamentally new technologies. In the computer market, IBM's PS/2 is a personal computer platform; in consumer products, Procter & Gamble's Liquid Tide is the platform for a whole line of Tide brand products.

Well-planned and well-executed platform products typically offer fundamental improvements in cost, quality, and performance over preceding generations. They introduce improvements across a range of performance dimensions—speed, functionality, size, weight. (Derivatives, on the other hand, usually introduce changes along only one or two dimensions.) Platforms also represent a significantly better system solution for the customer. Because of the extent of changes involved, successful platforms require considerable up-front planning and the involvement of not only engineering but also marketing, manufacturing, and senior management.

Companies target new platforms to meet the needs of a core group of customers but design them for easy modification into derivatives through the addition, substitution, or removal of features. Well-designed platforms also provide a smooth migration path between generations so neither the customer nor the distribution channel is disrupted.

Consider Intel's 80486 microprocessor, the fourth in a series. The 486 introduced a number of performance improvements; it targeted a core customer group—the high-end PC/workstation user—but variations addressed the needs of other users; and with software compatibility between the 386 and the 486, the 486 provided an easy migration path for existing customers. Over the life of the 486 platform, Intel will introduce a host of derivative products, each offering some variation in speed, cost, and performance and each able to leverage the process-and-product innovations of the original platform.

Platforms offer considerable competitive leverage and the potential to increase market penetration, yet many companies systematically underinvest in them. The reasons vary, but the most common is that management lacks an awareness of the strategic value of platforms and fails to create well-thought-out platform projects. To address the problem, companies should recognize explicitly the need for platforms and develop guidelines for making them a central part of the aggregate project plan.

Research and development is the creation of the know-how and know-why of new materials and technologies that eventually translate into commercial development. Even though R&D lies outside the boundaries of commercial development, we include it here for two reasons: It is the precursor to product and process development and, in terms of future resource allocation, employees move between basic research and commercial development. Thus, R&D projects compete with commercial development projects for resources. Because R&D is a creative, high-risk process, companies have different expectations about results and different strategies for funding and managing it than they do for commercial development. These differences can indeed be great, but a close relationship between R&D and commercial development is essential to ensure an appropriate balance and a smooth conversion of ideas into products.

Alliances and partnerships, which also lie outside the boundaries of the development map, can be formed to pursue any type of project—R&D, breakthrough, platform, or derivative. As such, the amount and type of development resources and management attention needed for projects in this category can vary widely.

Even though partnerships are an integral part of the project development process, many companies fail to include them in their project planning. They often separate the management of partnerships from the rest of the development organization and fail to provide them with enough development resources. Even when the partner company takes full responsibility for a project, the acquiring company must devote in-house resources to monitor the project, capture the new knowledge being created, and prepare for the manufacturing and sales of the new product.

All five development categories are vital for creating a development organization that is responsive to the market. Each type of project plays a different role; each requires different levels and mixes of resources; and each generates very different results. Relying on only one or two categories for the bulk of the development work invariably leads to suboptimal use of resources, an unbalanced product offering, and eventually, a less-than-competitive market position.

PreQuip's Project Map

Using these five project types, PreQuip set about changing its project mix as the first step toward reforming the product development process. It started by matching its existing project list to the five categories. PreQuip's product line consisted of four kinds of analytic instruments—mass spectrometers, gas and liquid chromatographs, and data handling and processing equipment—that identified and isolated chemical compounds, gases, and liquids. Its customers included scientific laboratories, chemical companies, and oil refineries—users that needed to measure and test accurately the purity of raw materials, intermediate by-products, and finished products.

PreQuip's management asked some very basic questions in its attempt to delineate the categories. What exactly was a breakthrough product? Would a three-dimensional graphics display constitute a breakthrough? How was a platform defined? Was a full-featured mass spectrometer considered a platform? How about a derivative? Was a mass spectrometer with additional software a derivative?

None of these questions was easy to answer. But after much analysis and debate, the management team agreed on the major characteristics for each project type and assigned most of PreQuip's 30 projects to one of the five categories. The map revealed just how uneven the distribution of projects had become—for instance, less than 20 percent of the company's projects were classified as platforms. (See the chart "Before: PreQuip's Development Process Was Chaotic. . . .")

Management then turned its attention to those development projects that did not fit into any category. Some projects required substantial resources but did not represent breakthroughs. Others were more complicated than derivative projects but did not fall into PreQuip's definition of platforms. While frustrating, these

Before: PreQuip's Development Process Was Chaotic . . .

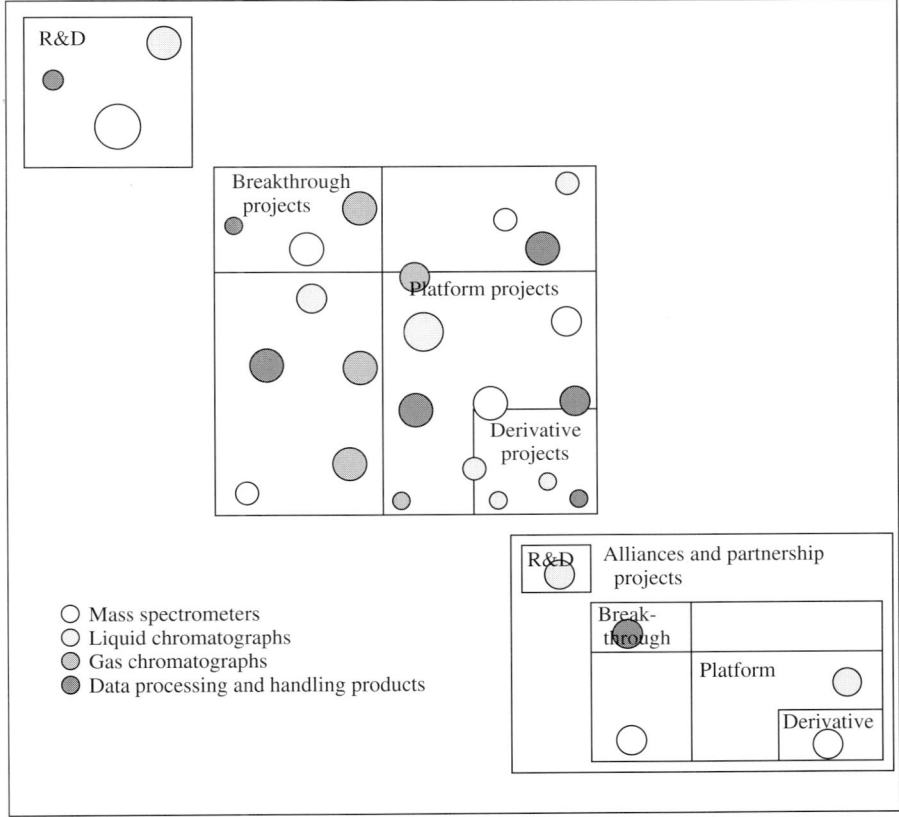

dilemmas opened managers' eyes to the fact that some projects made little strategic sense. Why spend huge amounts of money developing products that at best would produce only incremental sales? The realization triggered a reexamination of PreQuip's customer needs in *all* product categories.

Consider mass spectrometers, instruments that identify the chemical composition of a compound. PreQuip was a top-of-the-line producer of mass spectrometers, offering a whole series of high-performance equipment with all the latest features but at a significant price premium. While this strategy had worked in the past, it no longer made sense in a maturing market; the evolution of mass spectrometer technology was predictable and well defined, and many competitors were able to offer the same capabilities, often at lower prices.

Increasingly, customers were putting greater emphasis on price in the purchasing decision. Some customers also wanted mass spectrometers that were easier to use and modular so they could be integrated into their own systems. Others demanded units with casings that could withstand harsh industrial environments. Still others required faster operating speeds, additional data storage, or self-diagnostic capabilities.

Taking all these customer requirements into account, PreQuip used the project map to rethink its mass spectrometer line. It envisaged a single platform complemented with a series of derivative products, each with a different set of options and each serving a different customer niche. By combining some new product design ideas—modularity and simplicity—with some features that were currently under development, PreQuip created the concept of the C-101 platform, a low-priced, general-purpose mass spectrometer. In part because of its modularity, the product was designed to be simpler and cheaper to manufacture, which also helped to improve its overall quality and reliability. By adding software and a few new features, PreQuip

. . . After: PreQuip's Development Process Was Manageable

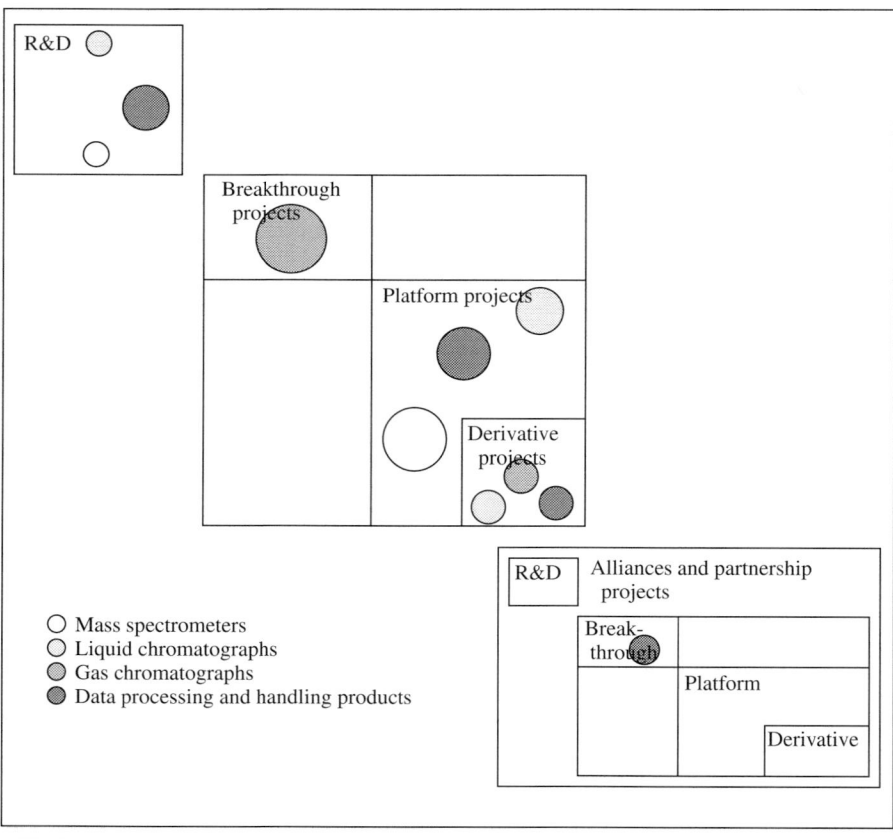

could easily create derivatives, all of which could be assembled and tested on a single production line. In one case, a variant of the C-101 was planned for the high-end laboratory market. By strengthening the casing and eliminating some features, PreQuip also created a product for the industrial market.

Mapping out the new mass spectrometer line and the three other product lines was not painless. It took a number of months and involved a reconceptualization of the product lines, close management, and considerable customer involvement. To provide additional focus, PreQuip separated the engineering resources into three categories: basic R&D projects; existing products and customers, now a part of the manufacturing organization; and commercial product development.

To determine the number of breakthrough, platform, derivative, and partnered projects that could be sustained at any time, the company first estimated the average number of engineering months for each type of project based on past experience. It then allocated available engineering resources according to its desired mix of projects; about 50 percent to platform projects, 20 percent to derivative projects, and 10 percent each to breakthrough projects and partnerships. PreQuip then selected specific projects, confident that it would not overallocate its resources.

In the end, PreQuip canceled more than two-thirds of its development projects, including some high-profile pet projects of senior managers. When the dust had settled in mid-1990, PreQuip had just 11 projects: 3 platforms, 1 breakthrough, 3 derivatives, 1 partnership, and 3 projects in basic R&D. (See the chart ". . . After: PreQuip's Development Process Was Manageable.")

The changes led to some impressive gains: Between 1989 and 1991, PreQuip's commercial development productivity improved by a factor of three. Fewer projects meant more actual work got done, and more work meant more products. To avoid overcommitting resources and to improve productivity further, the company built a "capacity cushion" into its plan. It assigned only 75 full-time-equivalent engineers out of a possible 80 to the eight commercial development projects. By leaving a small percent of development capacity uncommitted, PreQuip was better prepared to take advantage of unexpected opportunities and to deal with crises when they arose.

Focus on the Platform

PreQuip's development map served as a basis for reallocating resources and for rethinking the mix of projects. Just as important, however, PreQuip no longer thought about projects in isolation; breakthrough projects shaped the new platforms, which defined the derivatives. In all four product lines, platforms played a particularly important role in the development strategy. This was not surprising considering the maturity of PreQuip's industry. For many companies, the more mature the industry, the more important it is to focus on platform projects.

Consider the typical industry life cycle. In the early stages of growth, innovative, dynamic companies gain market position with products that have dramatically superior performance along one or two dimensions. Whether they know it or not, these companies employ a breakthrough-platform strategy. But as the industry develops and the opportunity for breakthrough products decreases—often because the technology is shared more broadly—competitors try to satisfy increasingly sophisticated customers by rapidly making incremental improvements to existing products. Consciously or not, they adopt a strategy based on derivative projects. As happened with PreQuip, this approach ultimately leads to a proliferation of product lines and overcommitment of development resources. The solution lies in developing a few well-designed platform products, on each of which a generation of products can be built.

In the hospital bed industry, for example, companies that design, manufacture, sell, and service electric beds have faced a mature market for years. They are constantly under pressure to help their customers constrain capital expenditures and operating costs. Technologies are stable and many design changes are minor. Each generation of product typically lasts 8 to 12 years, and companies spend most of their time and energy developing derivative products. As a result, companies find themselves with large and unwieldy product lines.

In the 1980s, Hill-Rom, a leading electric-bed manufacturer, sought a new product strategy to help contain costs and maintain market share. Like other bed makers, its product development process was reactive and mired in too many low-payoff derivative projects. The company would design whatever the customer—a single hospital or nursing home—wanted, even if it meant significant commitments of development resources.

The new strategy involved a dramatic shift toward leveraging development and manufacturing resources. Hill-Rom decided to focus on hospitals and largely withdraw from the nursing home segment, as well as limit the product line by developing two new platform products—the Centra and the Century. The Centra was a high-priced product with built-in electronic controls, including communications capabilities. The Century was a simpler, less-complex design with fewer features. The products built off each platform shared common parts and manufacturing processes and provided the customer with a number of add-on options. By focusing development efforts on two platforms, Hill-Rom was able to introduce new technologies and new product features into the market faster and more systematically, directly affecting patient recovery and hospital staff productivity. This strategy led to a less chaotic development cycle as well as lower unit cost, higher product quality, and more satisfied customers.

For companies that must react to constant changes in fashion and consumer tastes, a different relationship between platform and derivative projects makes sense. For example, Sony has pioneered its "hyper-variety" strategy in developing the Walkman: it directs the bulk of its Walkman development efforts at creating derivatives, enhancements, hybrids, and line extensions that offer something tailored to every niche, distribution channel, and competitor's product. As a result, in 1990, Sony dominated the personal audio system market with over 200 models based on just three platforms.

Platforms are critical to any product development effort, but there is no one ideal mix of projects that fits all companies. Every company must pursue the projects that match its opportunities, business strategy, and available resources. Of course, the mix evolves over time as projects move out of development into production, as business strategies change, as new markets emerge, and as resources are enhanced. Management needs to revisit the project mix on a regular basis—in some cases every six months, in others, every year or so.

Steady Stream Sequencing: PreQuip Plans Future Development

Periodically evaluating the product mix keeps development activities on the right track. Companies must decide how to sequence projects over time, how the set of projects should evolve with the business strategy, and how to build development capabilities through such projects. The decisions about changing the mix are neither easy nor straightforward. Without an aggregate project plan, most companies cannot even begin to formulate a strategy for making those decisions.

PreQuip was no different. Before adopting an aggregate project plan, the company had no concept of project mix and no understanding of sequencing. Whenever someone with authority had an idea worth pursuing, the development department added the project to its active list. With the evolution of a project plan, PreQuip developed an initial mix and elevated the sequencing decision to a strategic responsibility of senior management. Management scheduled projects at evenly spaced intervals to ensure a "steady stream" of development projects. (See the chart "PreQuip's Project Sequence.")

PreQuip's Project Sequence

Project Type	Development Resources Committed at Mid-1990 (% of Total Engineering Time)	Project Description	Project Number	Sequencing (1990–1991)
R&D	(Separate)	Advanced pump	RD-1	
		Electronic sensors	RD-2	
		Software	RD-3	
Breakthrough	12.5%	Fully automated self-diagnostic system for gas chromatograph	BX-3	
Platform	52.5	Liquid chromatograph	A series	A-502
		Gas chromatograph	B series	B-502
		Mass spectrometer	C series	C-101, C-201
		Data processing and handling equipment	D series	DX-52, DX-82
Derivative	18.75	Liquid chromatograph	A series	A-311, A-321, A-502X
		Gas chromatograph	B series	B-22, B-32
		Mass spectrometer	C series	C-1/X, C-1/Z, C-101X
		Data processing and handling equipment	D series	D-333, D-433
Partnership	10.0	Medical/chemical diagnostic system	VMH	

A representative example of PreQuip's new strategy for sequencing projects is its new mass spectrometer, or C series. Introduced into the development cycle in late-1989, the C-101 was the first platform conceived as a system built around the new modular design. Aimed at the middle to upper end of the market, it was a versatile, modular unit for the laboratory that incorporated many of the existing electromechanical features into the new software. The C-101 was scheduled to enter manufacturing prototyping in the third quarter of 1990.

PreQuip positioned the C-1/X, the first derivative of the C-101, for the industrial market. It had a rugged casing designed for extreme environments and fewer software features than the C-101. It entered the development process about the time the C-101 moved into manufacturing prototyping and was staffed initially with two designers whose activities on the C-101 were drawing to a close.

Very similar to the C-1/X was the C-1/Z, a unit designed for the European market; the C-1/X team was expanded to work on both the C-1/X and the C-1/Z. The C-1/Z had some unique software and a different display and packaging but the same modular design. PreQuip's marketing department scheduled the C-101 to be introduced about six months before the C-1/X and the C-1/Z, thus permitting the company to reach a number of markets quickly with new products.

To leverage accumulated knowledge and experience, senior management assigned the team that worked on the C-1/X and the C-1/Z to the C-201 project, the next-generation spectrometer scheduled to replace the C-101. It too was of a modular design but with more computer power and greater software functionality. The C-201 also incorporated a number of manufacturing process improvements gleaned from manufacturing the C-101.

To provide a smooth market transition from the C-101 to the C-201, management assigned the remainder of the C-101 team to develop the C-101X, a follow-on derivative project. The C-101X was positioned as an improvement over the C-101 to attract customers who were in the market for a low-end mass spectrometer but were unwilling to settle for the aging technology of the C-101. Just as important, the project was an ideal way to gather market data that could be used to develop the C-201.

PreQuip applied this same strategy across the other three product categories. Every other year it planned a new platform, followed by two or three derivatives spaced at appropriate intervals. Typically, when a team finished work on a platform, management assigned part of the team to derivative projects and part to other projects. A year or so later, a new team would form to work on the next platform, with some members having worked on the preceding generation and others not. This steady-stream sequencing strategy worked to improve the company's overall market position while encouraging knowledge transfer and more rapid, systematic resource development.

An Alternative: Secondary Wave Planning

While the steady-stream approach served PreQuip well, companies in different industries might consider alternative strategies. For instance, a "secondary wave" strategy may be more appropriate for companies that, like Hill-Rom, have multiple product lines, each with its own base platforms but with more time between succeeding generations of a particular platform.

The strategy works like this. A development team begins work on a next-generation platform. Once the company completes that project, the key people from the team start work on another platform for a different product family. Management leaves the recently introduced platform on the market for a couple of years with few derivatives introduced. As that platform begins to age and competitors' newer platforms challenge it, the company refocuses development resources on a set of derivatives in order to strengthen and extend the viability of the product line's existing platform. The wave of derivative projects extends the platform life and upgrades product offerings, but it also provides experience and feedback to the people working on the product line and prepares them for the next-generation platform development. They receive feedback from the market on the previous platform, information on competitors' platform offerings, and information on emerging market needs. Key people then bring that information together to define the next platform and the cycle begins again, built around a team, many of whose members have just completed the wave of derivative products.

A variation on the secondary wave strategy, one used with considerable success by Kodak, involves compressing the time between market introduction of major platforms. Rather than going off to work on another product family's platform following one platform's introduction, the majority of the development team goes to work immediately on a set of derivative products. This requires a more compressed and careful assessment of the market's response to the just-introduced platform and much shorter feedback loops regarding competitors' products. If done right, however, companies can build momentum and capture significant incremental market share. Once the flurry of derivative products has passed, the team goes to work on the next-generation platform project for the same product family.

Before 1987, Kodak conducted a series of advanced development projects to explore alternative single-use 35mm cameras—a roll of film packaged in an inexpensive camera. Once used, the film is processed and the camera discarded or recycled. During 1987, a group of Kodak development engineers worked on the first platform project which resulted in the market introduction and volume production of the Fling 35mm camera in January 1988. (The product was later renamed the Funsaver.) As the platform neared completion, management reassigned the front-end development staff to two derivative projects: the Stretch, a panoramic, double-wide image version of the Fling, and the Weekend, a waterproof version.

By the end of 1988, Kodak had introduced both derivative cameras and was shipping them in volume. True to the definition of a derivative, both the Stretch and the Weekend took far fewer development resources and far less time than the Fling. They also required less new tooling and process engineering since they leveraged the existing automation and manufacturing process. The development team then went to work on the next-generation platform product—a Funsaver with a built-in flash.

No matter which strategy a company uses to plan its platform-derivative mix—steady stream or secondary wave—it must have well-defined platforms. The most advanced companies further improve their competitive position by speeding up the rate at which they introduce new platforms. Indeed, in a number of industries we've studied, the companies that introduced new platforms at the fastest rate were usually able to capture the greatest market share over time.

In the auto industry, for example, different companies follow quite different sequencing schedules, with markedly different results. According to data collected in the late 1980s, European car companies changed the platform for a given product, on average, every 12 years, U.S. companies every 8 years, and Japanese companies every 4 years. A number of factors explain the differences in platform development cycles—historical and cultural differences, longer development lead times, and differences in development productivity.[1]

In both Europe and the United States, the engineering hours and tooling costs of new products were much higher than in Japan. This translated into lower development costs for Japanese car makers, which allowed faster payback and shorter economic lives for all models. As a consequence, the Japanese could profitably conduct more projects and make more frequent and more extensive changes than both their European and U.S. competitors and thus were better positioned to satisfy customers' needs and capture market share.

The Long-Term Goal: Building Critical Capabilities

Possibly the greatest value of an aggregate project plan over the long term is its ability to shape and build development capabilities, both individual and organizational. (See chart for eight steps of an aggregate project plan.) It provides a vehicle for training development engineers, marketers, and manufacturing people in the different skill sets needed by the company. For instance, some less-experienced engineers initially may be better suited to work on derivative projects, while others might have technical skills more suited for breakthrough projects. The aggregate project plan lets companies play to employees' strengths and broaden their careers and abilities over time.

Thinking about skill development in terms of the aggregate project plan is most important for developing competent team leaders. Take, for instance, an engineer

---

[1]Based on research by Kim B. Clark and Takahiro Fujimoto. See their article, "The Power of Product Integrity," *Harvard Business Review,* November–December 1990, p. 107.

Eight Steps of an Aggregate Project Plan

1. Define project types as either breakthrough, platform, derivative, R&D, or partnered projects.
2. Identify existing projects and classify by project type.
3. Estimate the average time and resources needed for each project type based on past experience.
4. Identify existing resource capacity.
5. Determine the desired mix of projects.
6. Estimate the number of projects that existing resources can support.
7. Decide which specific projects to pursue.
8. Work to improve development capabilities.

with five years of experience moving to become a project leader. Management might assign her to lead a derivative project first. It is an ideal training ground because derivative projects are the best defined, the least complex, and usually the shortest in duration of all project types. After the project is completed successfully, she might get promoted to lead a larger derivative project and then a platform project. And if she distinguishes herself there and has the other required skills, she might be given the opportunity to work on a breakthrough project.

In addition to creating a formal career path within the sphere of development activities, companies should also focus on moving key engineers and other development participants between advanced research and commercial development. This is necessary to keep the transfer of technology fresh and creative and to reward engineers who keep their R&D efforts focused on commercial developments.

Honda is one company that delineates clearly between advanced research and product development—the two kinds of projects are managed and organized differently and are approached with very different expectations. Development engineers tend to have broader skills, while researchers' are usually more specialized. However, Honda encourages its engineers to move from one type of project to another if they demonstrate an idea that management believes may result in a commercially viable innovation. For example, Honda's new lean-burning engine, introduced in the 1992 Civic, began as an advanced research project headed by Hideyo Miyano. As the project moved from research to commercial development, Miyano moved too, playing the role of project champion throughout the entire development process.

Besides improving people's skills, the aggregate project plan can be used to identify weaknesses in capabilities, improve development processes, and incorporate new tools and techniques into the development environment. The project plan helps identify where companies need to make changes and how those changes are connected to product and process development.

As PreQuip developed an aggregate project plan, for example, it identified a number of gaps in its capabilities. In the case of the mass spectrometer, the demand for more software functionality meant PreQuip had to develop an expertise in software development. And with an emphasis on cost, modularity, and reliability, PreQuip also had to focus on improving its industrial design skills.

As part of its strategy to improve design skills, the company introduced a new computer-aided design system into its engineering department, using the aggregate project plan as its guide. Management knew that one of the platform project teams was particularly adept with computer applications, so it chose that project as the pilot for the new CAD system. Over the life of the project, the team's proficiency with the new system grew. When the project ended, management dispersed team members to other projects so they could train other engineers in using the new CAD system.

As PreQuip discovered, developing an aggregate project plan involves a relatively simple and straightforward procedure. But carrying it out—moving from a poorly managed collection of ad hoc projects to a robust set that matches and reinforces the business strategy—requires hard choices and discipline.

At all the companies we have studied, the difficulty of those choices makes imperative strong leadership and early involvement from senior management. Without management's active participation and direction, organizations find it next to impossible to kill or postpone projects and to resist the short-term pressures that drive them to spend most of their time and resources fighting fires.

Getting to an aggregate project plan is not easy, but working through the process is a crucial part of creating a sustainable development strategy. Indeed, while the specific plan is extremely important, the planning process itself is even more so. The plan will change as events unfold and managers make adjustments. But choosing the mix, determining the number of projects the resources can support, defining the sequence, and picking the right projects raise crucial questions about how product and process development ought to be linked to the company's competitive opportunities. Creating an aggregate project plan gives direction and clarity to the overall development effort and helps lay the foundation for outstanding performance.

CHAPTER 16
Commercializing Technology: Understanding User Needs

Research managers in the 1990s are challenged to produce more relevant, potentially profitable knowledge and to produce it faster. This reading argues that imaginative understanding of user needs is a primary key to success. The chapter draws upon evidence from studies of new product development by Hewlett-Packard and others to substantiate that assertion and to explore its implications. A typology of technology commercialization situations is suggested, ranging from those in which technological potential aligns well with current markets to those requiring the creation of whole new businesses. Varying degrees of uncertainty and risk are associated with these commercialization situations and therefore each situation requires different tools for eliciting user needs.

Introduction

Statistics

The statistics on technology commercialization in the United States are fairly grim. On average, as much as 46 percent of all resources devoted to product development and commercialization are spent on products that are canceled or fail to yield adequate financial returns.[1] A Booz Allen report estimates that for every 100 projects that enter development, 63 are canceled, 25 become commercial successes, and 12 are commercial failures.[2] However, some companies boast a success rate of 70 to 80 percent in new product launches; clearly it is possible to beat the averages through a superior product development process.[3]

This reading was prepared by Dorothy Leonard-Barton, Edith Wilson, and John Doyle.
Copyright © 1993 by the President and Fellows of Harvard College
Harvard Business School working paper 93-053.

[1] See Robert G. Cooper, *Winning at New Products* (Reading, Mass.: Addison-Wesley Publishing, 1986), p. 16.
[2] Booz Allen & Hamilton, "New Product Management for the 1980s," Booz Allen & Hamilton report, New York, 1982.
[3] Cooper, *Winning at New Products,* p. 17.

Shorter Market Windows

The development process must be more efficient as well as more effective. One of the major forces driving an increasing focus on improving development practices is the ever shortening product life cycles in many industries.[4] Hewlett-Packard documented this tendency among their own products, as Figures 1 and 2 demonstrate. In Figure 1, each line on the graph represents the sales history over time for all HP products that were launched in the year where the line originates. Thus, for example, the cohort of products launched in 1979 brought in about $250 million worth of orders that first year, and increased to $600 million in 1980, which was their highest year; thereafter, sales very gradually dwindled off throughout the 1980s and into 1990. In contrast, the cohort of products introduced into the market in 1987 and in 1988 produced a very steep rise in sales the following year, but also dropped off dramatically thereafter.

Bringing their expertise in measuring waveforms to the analysis, Hewlett-Packard managers translated the data in Figure 1 into sales windows for Figure 2. In Figure 2, each point in the graph indicates the number of years that fall between two points: (1) the year that the sales of a particular cohort of products first reached one-half their eventual sales peak and (2) the year that sales again fell to that level after peaking. As the graph in Figure 2 indicates, that "sales window" has been narrowing over time as the curve describing the rise and fall of sales orders for a given cohort of products has become both shorter and steeper.

FIGURE 1

*Product sales history**

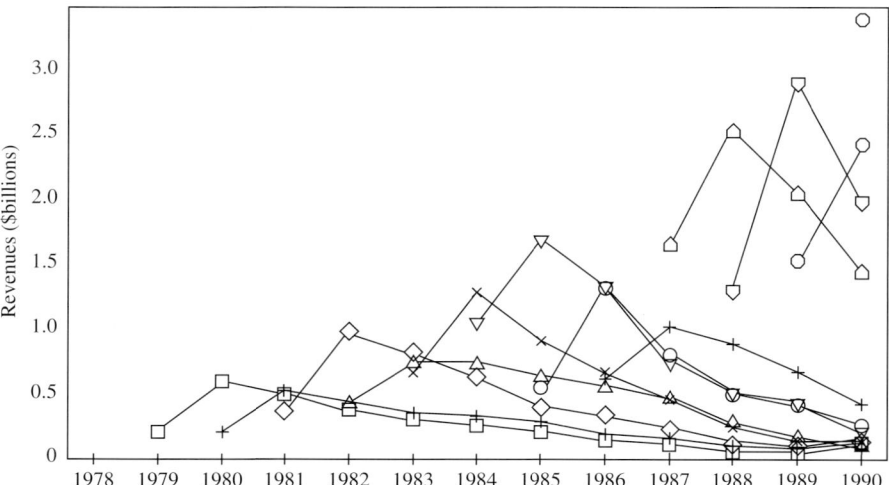

*Each line on the graph represents the sales history over time of all those products launched the year at which the line originates.

SOURCE: Courtesy of Hewlett-Packard.

---

[4]See Christoph-Friedrich von Braun, "The Acceleration Trap," *Sloan Management Review* 32, no. 1 (1990), pp. 49–50.

FIGURE 2

*Sales windows for product cohorts**

*Each point on the graph indicates the number of years between: (1) the year that sales of a particular cohort of products first reached one-half their subsequent sales peak, and (2) the year when sales again fell to that one-half peak level.
SOURCE: Courtesy of Hewlett-Packard.

Time-Based Competition

Such shorter product life cycles have led companies to emphasize time as the basis of competition,[5] vying with each other to publicize bringing product to market in record time. However, in recounting such successes, managers sometimes conveniently overlook the reservoir of knowledge tapped for the final push to commercialization. That is, the publicized project time lines do not include the time spent developing support tools or conducting laboratory experiments. Nor are abortive prior attempts to build similar products acknowledged, although such projects may have yielded critical knowledge. For example, Digital Equipment brought their first engineering workstation, the 3100, to market in an unheard-of eight months. Besides departing from tradition to buy a MIPS company semiconductor chip, DEC also utilized UNIX-based computer-aided design tools available only in their research laboratories and mined graphical interface designs developed for prior, canceled projects. Developers candidly admitted they could not have made their frenetic dash to the market without the information garnered in these prior projects.[6] Similarly, Kodak brought out their Funsaver, single-use camera in only nine months

---

[5]For example, see Joseph Bower and Thomas M. Hout, "Last-Cycle Capability for Competitive Power," *Harvard Business Review* 66 (November–December 1988), pp. 110–18; Brian Dumaine, "How Managers Can Succeed through Speed," *Fortune* 119 (February 13, 1989), pp. 54–74; George Stalk, Jr., "Time—The Next Source of Competitive Advantage," *Harvard Business Review* 66 (July–August 1988), pp. 41–51.

[6]Kent Bowen, Kim Clark, Charles Holloway, and Steven Wheelwright, eds., *Visions and Capability: High Performance Product Development in the 1990s* (New York: Oxford University Press, forthcoming).

when they were challenged by Fuji. However, they were able to do so principally because an engineer had been working on the camera for two years with no official encouragement or even sanction.[7]

Distinctive Competencies of the Corporation

As these examples suggest, speed to market often depends upon the development team's ability to pull from the knowledge warehouses of their corporation unutilized but technically developed concepts, designs, and tools. Such reservoirs of knowledge build up over time, shaped by the norms and values of the corporation, the skills of personnel, and the particular incentive systems in place; they can constitute unique technological competencies.[8] The notion that companies possess distinctive competencies that can be systematically deployed for competitive advantage has existed for decades.[9] However, it has received renewed attention lately because of disenchantment with strategies based on accumulating unrelated businesses, because of the recognition that Japanese competitors have exploited their capabilities very shrewdly,[10] and because successful new products often build on those competencies.[11]

From Basic Research Toward Applied

At least superficially, this renewed interest in the accumulation of unique knowledge seems to conflict with another trend: the move by many corporations away from investments in central laboratories. Multiple arguments for this move are cited; principally, the inability of corporations to turn knowledge into practical applications and profit. Laboratories are therefore under increasing pressure to demonstrate their utility. Moreover, managers are increasingly aware that the distinctive competencies of a firm depend upon knowledge diffused throughout the organization—not just in the research laboratory. Some even denounce the idea of a special research facility. Chaparral Steel, one of the most successful United States–based minimills, is acknowledged as extremely innovative and has patented a number of inventions, yet they do not separate research and development from production.[12] Their CEO, an

---

[7]Ibid.

[8]Dorothy Leonard-Barton, "The Case for Integrative Innovation: An Expert System at Digital," *Sloan Management Review* 29, no. 1 (1987), pp. 7–19.

[9]Richard Rumelt, *Strategy, Structure, and Economic Performance* (Boston: Harvard Business School Press, 1974, 1986); Robert Hayes, "Strategic Planning—Forward in Reverse," *Harvard Business Review,* November–December 1985, pp. 111–19; Michael Hitt and R. Duane Ireland, "Corporate Distinctive Competence, Strategy, Industry, and Performance," *Strategic Management Journal* 6 (1985), pp. 273–93.

[10]C. K. Prahalad and Gary Hamel, "The Core Competence of the Corporation," *Harvard Business Review* 68 (May–June 1990), pp. 79–91.

[11]Modesto A. Maidique and Billie Jo Zirger, "The New Product Learning Cycle," *Research Policy* 14, no. 6 (December 1985), pp. 229–313.

[12]Dorothy Leonard-Barton, "The Factory as a Learning Laboratory," *Sloan Management Review* 34, no. 1 (1992), pp. 23–36.

outspoken former R&D director and a PhD metallurgist from MIT, maintains that research laboratories are idea graveyards—"not because there are no good ideas there, but because the good ideas are dying there all the time."[13]

Organization of the Chapter

The research manager in the 1990s is thus challenged to produce more relevant, potentially profitable knowledge—faster. In this chapter, we focus on an activity critical to successfully meeting that challenge: understanding user needs. We first examine the evidence from Hewlett-Packard's investigation of their development practices and from academic studies that link imaginative understanding of user needs to successful technology commercialization. We next explore what it means to understand user needs, including the management dilemmas inherent in that process. The fourth section of the chapter proposes a typology of technology commercialization situations and associated mechanisms for understanding user needs when the products are developed in advance of the current market. These situations and sources range from aligning new products with a known market through traditional market research to creating whole new businesses through market intuition or applications identification.

Hewlett-Packard's Product Definition Project

In the late 1980s, Hewlett-Packard (HP) faced a major shift in market focus from test and measurement to computers. This change necessitated a concomitant emphasis on increasing productivity and shareholder value. The corporation issued a challenge to each of the businesses: Halve the time to break-even (when cumulative product profits equal development costs) by simultaneously reducing product development time, increasing revenue streams, and controlling expenses. The challenge initiated much thought about the sources of overly long break-even times. Senior managers could identify a number of problems that recurred across multiple projects: "creeping elegance" of product definitions as enthusiasm for technical potential overwhelmed simplicity, "poor positioning because of poor feature sets," "user needs being incompletely understood," "competitive knowledge being inadequate," and "falling short of targeted performance." All such problems pointed, these managers believed, to an underlying weakness in the product definition phase of new product development. Product definitions were unstable during the course of the development projects, wasting resources and time when they shifted. Corporate engineering at HP therefore decided to develop a product definition process that would address these issues (see Figure 3).

---

[13]Cited in Alan Kantrow, "Wide-open Management at Chaparral Steel: An Interview with Gordon E. Forward," *Harvard Business Review* 29, no. 1 (1987), pp. 7–19.

FIGURE 3

Product definition: a domino effect

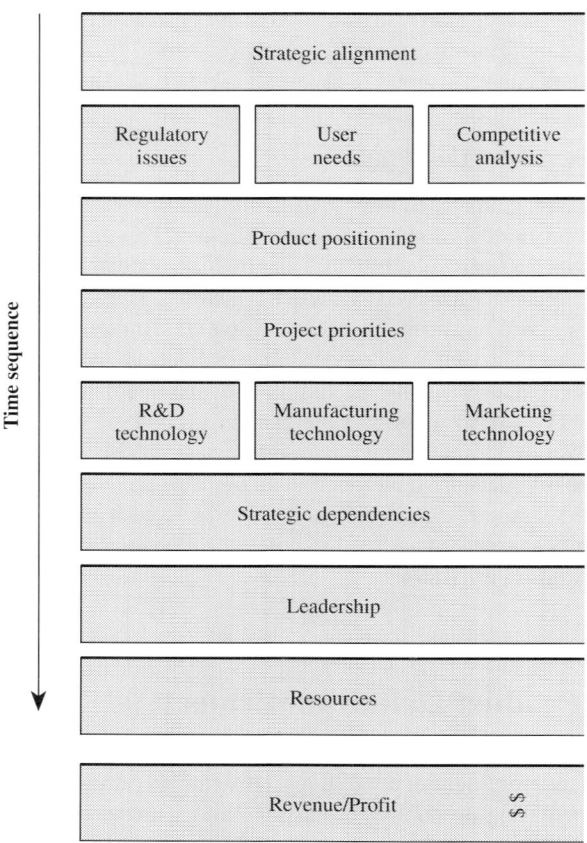

SOURCE: Courtesy of Hewlett-Packard.

Research into studies of new product development quickly revealed that problems with product definition were endemic to development.[14] One study particularly intrigued the Hewlett-Packard staffers. The University of Sussex had conducted a study to determine the factors leading to marketplace success of new products. Project SAPPHO[15] identified 29 product pairs in the first phase of their study, and 43 in a second phase; each pair consisted of one product that succeeded in the marketplace and one that did not. The key findings of the Project SAPPHO team were that:

1. Successful innovators have a much better understanding of user needs.
2. Successful innovators pay more attention to marketing and publicity.

---

[14]Ashok Gupta and David Wilemon, "Accelerating the Development of Technology-based New Products," *California Management Review,* Winter 1990, pp. 24–44; Cooper, *Winning at New Products;* Roy Rothwell et al., "SAPPHO Updated—Project SAPPHO Phase II," *Research Policy* 3 (1974), pp. 258–91.

[15]"Project SAPPHO—A Comparative Study of Success and Failure in Industrial Innovation," report on Project SAPPHO by the Science Policy Research Unit, University of Sussex, Brighton (London: Centre for the Study of Industrial Innovation, 1974).

FIGURE 4

Product definitions in unsuccessful projects

Unsuccessful Products	Project Number						Percent Failing
	180	150	120	110	100	210	
Users' needs understanding	O	X	O	O	O	X	66.7
Strategic alignment and charter consistency	X	O	O	X	O	X	66.7
Competitive analysis	O	O	X	X	O	X	50
Product positioning	O	O	X	O	X	X	50
Technical risk assessment	X	O	X	O	X	O	50
Priority decision criteria list	X	X	X	O	O	O	50
Regulation compliance	O	O	X	X	X	X	33.3
Product channel issues	O	O	X	X	X	X	33.3
Project endorsement by upper management	X	X	O	X	X	X	16.7
Total organizational support	X	X	O	X	X	X	16.7

Legend:
X = Successfully completed.
O = Inadequately completed.
SOURCE: Courtesy of Hewlett-Packard.

3. Successful innovators perform their development work more efficiently than failed ones, but not necessarily more quickly.

4. Successful innovators use outside technology and scientific advice, not necessarily in general, but in the specific area targeted.

5. In successful development projects, the responsible individuals are usually more senior, with greater authority than their counterparts on failed projects.

Since the probability that these five factors distinguished between successful and unsuccessful projects by chance was less than 0.1 percent, the Project SAPPHO authors assert that the five factors significantly differentiate project success from failure. The SAPPHO project offered hope that a systematic investigation of successes and failures could enable Hewlett-Packard to construct a roadmap for better product definition. Therefore, in 1989, one of the authors, Edith Wilson, undertook case studies of 19 successful and unsuccessful projects in 9 of HP's 14 business groups. All the projects had been completed and the products introduced to the marketplace. Information was gathered through a combination of interviews and questionnaires directed toward engineers, middle-level managers, managers from the functions of R&D, marketing and manufacturing, and the division's general manager. Three major questions were asked: (1) What steps were taken to develop the product definition? (2) In hindsight, what went right and what wrong in the development and use of the product definition? (3) How was the product definition used during the development phase?

From the answers to these questions, Wilson documented the process used by successful project teams to define their products (Figure 4) and noted what differentiated the practices of successful teams from unsuccessful ones (Figure 5). Team performance

FIGURE 5

Product definition in successful projects

Successful Products	Project Number					
	190	170	160	140	130	200
Users' needs understanding	X	X	X	X	X	X
Strategic alignment and charter consistency	X	O	X	X	X	X
Competitive analysis	X	X	X	X	X	X
Product positioning	X	X	X	X	X	X
Technical risk assessment	X	X	X	X	X	X
Priority decision criteria list	X	X	X	X	X	X
Regulation compliance	X	X	X	X	X	X
Product channel issues	X	X	X	X	X	X
Project endorsement by upper management	X	X	X	X	X	X
Total organizational support	X	X	X	X	X	X

Legend:
X = Successfully completed.
O = Inadequately completed.
SOURCE: Courtesy of Hewlett-Packard.

on 11 product definition factors appeared to account for the difference.[16] (See Table 1.) The primary cause of difficulties in the marketplace identified in both the original study and the follow-up research conducted by Bacon, Beckman, Mowery, and Wilson in other companies was a failure to understand user needs.[17] This failure was not always, or even usually, attributable to a lack of effort. Some teams spent months and millions of dollars in a vain attempt to answer some fundamental questions about their customers. They faced problems in identifying the target user, the actual buyer who controlled the financial decision, and other stakeholders who affected the buying decision. The less-successful teams were unable to determine exactly what problems had to be solved to satisfy each link in the set of customers, from the factory to the end users. They could not translate user needs into product.

Understanding User Needs

Research on Product Success and Failure

The important elements of the process identified in the Hewlett-Packard study (and the SAPPHO project that inspired it) have also been remarked by a number of other new product development studies. A Conference Board study found inadequate market analysis most commonly cited as a cause of new product failure.[18] In a number of

---

[16]Only 10 factors were originally identified. The 11th was added in a follow-up study funded by the Sloan Foundation at five other companies (IBM, GE, GM-Delco, Motorola, and Xerox).

[17]Glenn Bacon, Sara Beckman, David Mowery, and Edith Wilson, "Managing Product Definition in High-Technology Industries: A Pilot Study," in press.

[18]D. S. Hopkins and E. L. Bailey, "New Product Pressures," *Conference Board Record* 8 (1971), pp. 16–24.

TABLE 1 **Factors in New Product Development**

Factors

1.	Strategic alignment	How does the project contribute to the business unit's strategic objectives?
2.	Users' and customer needs	Is there a specific market segment targeted for the product? Can the team articulate the problems that the product must solve for it to be successful?
3.	Compliance issues	Has the team identified all the relevant compliance issues that the product must adhere to, including the manufacturing and recycling issues?
4.	Competitive analysis	Has the team identified the product's top three competitors (by market share) and thoroughly identified what their business and product strengths and weaknesses will be at the time of market release?
5.	Product positioning	Is the product defined to solve your customers' problems better than the competitors can and at greater value to the customers?
6.	Project priorities	What is the hierarchy of priorities for the project? Prioritize cost, date of market release, and features to identify what you would trade off for what.
7.	Risk management	Is the team taking the appropriate level of risk in R&D, marketing, and manufacturing?
8.	Market channels	Will the market channel required to be successful in this business be established by the time of market release?
9.	Management leadership	Does upper management know about this project, support the efforts, and provide the team guidance in making decisions?
10.	Resource availability	Do you have the staffing and funding needed to meet the goals of the project within the allotted amount of time?
11.	Dependency management	Are all internal and external strategic dependencies established and functioning well enough to assure yourselves that there will be no integration or schedule problems?

studies conducted over the past two decades, Robert Cooper and his colleagues have identified inadequate attention to market as a primary factor leading to failure.[19] In a study of 235 new product development projects, William Souder similarly noted that a primary condition for technical success was the clarity of problem definition, which he equates with clarity of understanding user requirements.[20]

There is, therefore, a very strong consensus that understanding user needs is one of the key factors leading to commercialization success. However, opinions vary widely as to how that understanding may be achieved. In their study of 252 product development projects in 123 firms, Robert Cooper and Elko Kleinschmidt found that preliminary market assessments were conducted in the successful product development projects.[21] However, formal market studies, done in only a quarter of the projects, were usually rated as "poorly handled." Moreover, the studies tended to take the form of reactive competitive comparisons in over a fourth of those projects.

---

[19] Robert G. Cooper, "Why Industrial New Products Fail," *Industrial Marketing Management* 4 (1975), pp. 315–26; R. Canlantone and Robert G. Cooper, "A Discriminant Model for Identifying Scenarios of Industrial New Product Failure," *Journal of the Academy of Marketing Science* 7 (1979), pp. 163–83; Robert G. Cooper and Elko J. Kleinschmidt, "An Investigation into the New Product Process: Steps, Deficiencies, and Impact," *Journal of Product Innovation Management* 3 (1986), pp. 71–85; and Cooper, *Winning at New Products*.

[20] William Souder, *Managing New Product Innovations* (Lexington, Mass.: Lexington Books, 1987, p. 68).

[21] Cooper and Kleinschmidt, "An Investigation into the New Product Process."

There were almost no concept tests, that is, studying customer reactions to a proposed new product in concept form. Less than a fifth of the project teams studied what customers actually wanted or needed in order to generate product specifications. Moreover, there was at least as much detailed market research done for the failed projects as for the successful ones. Therefore, merely increasing emphasis on market research may not lead to better understanding of user needs and a higher probability of product success.

There are at least three major barriers to successfully introducing market-derived information into a new product development project: corporate core rigidities, the tyranny of the current market, and user myopia.

Core Rigidities

As suggested above, the core competencies of a firm often aid the commercialization of technologies. However, the very same core technical capabilities that have made a company great, can also constitute core rigidities and hinder new product development.[22] New product ideas built on familiar technologies, using traditional, comfortable sources of information are more easily commercialized. In fact, synergy with the firm's capabilities (technological resources and skills) has been identified as one of the factors "fundamental" to new product success.[23] However, new product ideas built on unfamiliar technologies are more likely to be seen as "illegitimate"[24] and therefore see a more difficult birthing. In recognition of that fact, such ventures are often isolated from the rest of the organization.[25]

The core capabilities of a firm can constitute a core rigidity to technology commercialization in very subtle ways. Well-entrenched routines and ingrained culture favor certain technologies and information sources. In "technology-driven" companies, information about user needs often goes unheeded unless it comes from a source with status in the organization. The same characteristics and practices that constantly reinforce the ability of engineers to influence product design simultaneously undermine the ability of marketing (or manufacturing) people on the team to be heard.

Companies such as Kodak, Digital Equipment, and Hewlett-Packard owed their original marketplace success to technological innovation, and the primary sources of that innovation were the technologists. In such companies, the product design intuition of founders and other technical gurus early in corporate history is legendary. Some researchers in Hewlett-Packard Laboratories can still recall their skepticism

---

[22]Leonard-Barton, "The Factory as a Learning Experience."

[23]Cooper and Kleinschmidt, "An Investigation into the New Product Process"; also see Robert G. Cooper and Elko J. Kleinschmidt, "New Product Success Factors: A Comparison of 'Kills' versus Successes and Failures," *R&D Management* 20, no. 1 (1990), pp. 47–63; and Souder, *Managing New Product Innovations.*

[24]Deborah Dougherty and Trudy Heller, "The Illegitimacy of Successful Product Innovation in Established Firms," *Organization Science,* in press.

[25]Rosabeth Moss Kanter, "When a Thousand Flowers Bloom: Structural Collective, and Social Conditions for Innovation in Organizations," in *Research in Organizational Behavior,* vol. 10, ed. Barry M. Staw and L. L. Cummings (Greenwich, Conn.: JAI Press, 1988).

that the handheld calculator vigorously championed by Hewlett could ever function better than their slide rules; Gordon Bell at Digital Equipment is credited with the "one architecture" strategy that made their VAX line of minicomputers so popular. The success of such products came from anticipating what the market would buy, and the engineering function dominated.

Over time, these companies grew a strong technological capability that included not only skilled engineers but proprietary physical equipment—simulation systems, process equipment—that embodied years of accumulated, specialized knowledge. Hiring practices, incentive systems, and the values and norms of the company strengthened that capability by enabling the corporation to attract and hold the best technical minds—in certain fields. For instance, skilled chemical engineers migrated to Kodak, where they could aspire to the pinnacle of success represented by the top 5 percent of engineers who became film designers. Electrical and mechanical engineers headed for Digital or Hewlett-Packard. In contrast, for years (some would say still), software engineers entered any of these companies at a disadvantage, knowing their profession was not highly regarded. And in all of these companies, marketing people entered the company at their own peril. Their salaries, their status, their ability to influence key product design decisions were all subordinate to researchers and design engineers. Marketing skills were not part of the original distinctive competencies of these firms.

An initial lack of information from the market often causes unnecessary delays when it is uncovered and assimilated late in the project. For instance, during the design of the Deskjet printer at Hewlett-Packard, marketers tested early prototypes in shopping malls to determine user response. They returned from their studies with a list of 21 changes they believed essential to the success of the product; the engineers accepted 5. Unwilling to give up, the marketers persuaded the engineers to join them in the mall tests. After hearing the same feedback from the lips of the users that they had previously rejected, the product designers returned to their benches and incorporated the other 16 requested changes. Similarly at DEC, early in the development of a local area network switch, marketing personnel suggested a number of features that were rejected by engineers as unnecessary. Just one month before expected release of the product, a respected senior engineer visited several customers and discovered the rejected features were absolutely essential. The schedule was slipped several months to allow the design to be retrofitted. In both these cases, information about user needs was available, but the marketing people lacked the experience and status to influence product design. As a consequence, the product definition was altered late in the development process and the products reached the market later than necessary.[26]

The Tyranny of Current Markets

On the other hand, listening too closely to current markets can also constitute a barrier to commercializing technology. Responding to a flood of marketplace demands for improvement along current product performance curves can leave too

---

[26]Dorothy Leonard-Barton, "Core Capabililties and Core Rigidities: A Paradox in Managing New Product Development," *Strategic Management Journal* 13 (1992), pp. 111–25.

few resources to assess the possibility that those curves are being fundamentally altered by new technologies. Therefore, traditional sources of market information and influence on new product development can constitute as substantial a core rigidity for a company as the traditional dominance of the engineering function or proprietary technological knowledge bases. Clayton Christensen observed this type of core rigidity in an extensive study of the computer disk drive industry.[27] He researched four architectural transitions represented by the reduction in disk diameter from 14 to 8, 5.25, 3.5 and 2.5 inches. Each reduction entailed not only "shrinking" individual components, but rearchitecting the relationships of components within the system.

Noting the tendency for these architectural changes to be introduced by new firms entering the market rather than by established firms, Christensen found a primary reason to be the disinterest of existing firms' customers in the smaller disks.

> The sluggishness or failure of established disk drive manufacturers faced with architectural change seems rooted . . . in the inability of their marketing and administrative organizations to find customers who valued the attributes of the new-architecture drives . . . not . . . because their architecture-related engineering knowledge was rendered obsolete. . . . Rather, the changes in product architecture seem to have rendered obsolete the established firms' knowledge of market.[28]

In the very few cases in which the new technological architectures did appeal to a firm's current customers, existing rather than entrant firms dominated. For example, Conner Corporation was able to make a "very smooth transition into 2.5-inch drives [from 3.5 inch]" because the smaller disks appealed to current customers.[29] The situation studied by Christensen exemplifies a common problem in many companies: "Outbound" marketing efforts (i.e., selling) tend to supersede "inbound" marketing efforts (i.e., market research and development). The impact on the bottom line of the outbound selling is much more visible and immediate than that of inbound. Managers very rationally emphasize those activities for which they are most directly rewarded. Moreover, more training is devoted to outbound promotion and selling activities, both in academia and within corporations, than is devoted to gathering and translating market information into feasible commercialization steps.

Users' Natural Myopia

As the example of the computer disk industry suggests, the greatest challenges to understanding user needs are to select the right users as informants and to recognize when their suggestions may limit product design. Users are often myopic in a number of logical and natural ways. First, they see the potential to apply technology within their own bounded context and will naturally influence the design of the new

---

[27] Clayton Christensen, "The Innovator's Challenge: Understanding the Influence of Market Environment on Processes of Technology Development in the Rigid Disk Drive Industry," unpublished PhD thesis, Harvard Business School, 1992.
[28] Ibid., pp. 114–15.
[29] Ibid., p. 150.

product or process to meet needs within that particular environment. Software designers habitually face this problem. For example, a vendor designing a purchasing module for a manufacturing resource planning (MRPII) system to order and monitor purchased parts for a multiplant corporation solicited the help of users in a certain plant in the Northeast, assuming it was representative of all corporate plants. The vendor spotted the flaw in this assumption only after managers of shipping docks in a dozen other plants angrily reported being so buried every four months with thousands of long-lead-time purchased parts that they had to hire extra help. At the plant that served as the model of usage, only 15 percent of the parts ordered were long-lead-time items; a regularly scheduled delivery point of every four months was adequate. For all the other plants in the system, such parts represented over 40 percent of their purchased parts; they required that the flow be spaced out over time.[30]

Second, users are not all equally proximate to the latest trends in usage patterns. Designers of a system to monitor the progress of work-in-process inventory within a factory worked hard to make sure their software could accommodate the variety and volume of components moving down the line. Within weeks of installation, their system was obsoleted because the factory moved to a just-in-time system for which any buildup of inventory was anathema. When the factory workers pared the stream of components down to a thin, steady flow, they no longer needed a complex system to monitor voluminous work-in-process; a simple visual system sufficed.[31]

Finally, and most difficult, users cannot see their world through the eyes of the technologist and therefore cannot know what solutions, functions, enhanced features, or capabilities a technology may offer. Technology always offers more possibilities than can be recognized and commercialized. Examples range from establishing paternity through DNA tests of blood samples (not the most obvious application of the discovery of DNA) to holographic greeting cards (not the most profound application of holography). Therefore, technologists often cannot simply ask users what they want. However, ignoring user needs is clearly not the answer. Rather, developers need a whole range of identification, listening, and translation skills to translate user needs into commercialization opportunities. We turn now to a discussion of a proposed typology of technology commercialization situations.

Design in Advance of the Market: From Alignment to Creation

Technology commercialization situations range from those in which technological potential aligns well with current markets (far left in Figure 6) to those which require the creation of new markets—sometimes even the creation of whole new businesses, with new infrastructure, standards, procedures (far right in Figure 6). In

---

[30] Dorothy Leonard-Barton, "Implementing New Production Technologies: Exercises in Corporate Learning," in *Managing Complexity in High Technology Industries: Systems and People,* ed. Mary Von Glinow and Susan Mohrman (New York: Oxford University Press, 1989).

[31] Dorothy Leonard-Barton and Deepak Sinha, "Dependency, Involvement, and User Satisfaction: The Case of Internal Software Development," Harvard Business School Working Paper 91-008, 1990.

FIGURE 6

Typology of technology commercialization situations

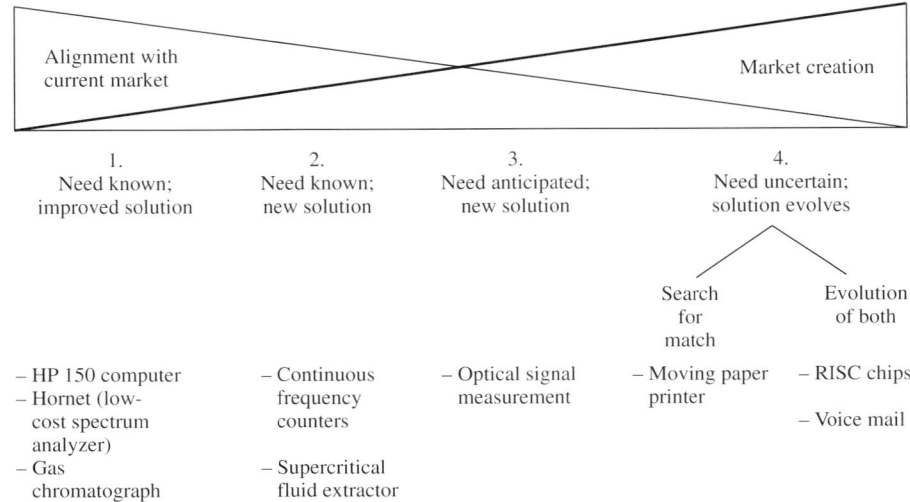

those situations at the left, product definition and development follow quite well known paths; in contrast, in those situations represented by the far right side of Figure 6, commercialization is realized only through a combination of trial, perseverance, and serendipity. In the following pages, we describe each of the four commercialization situations and illustrate them with examples, many from Hewlett-Packard's experience. Thereafter, we will discuss some of the commercialization risks associated with designing in advance of the market and then briefly describe some methods of ascertaining user needs all along the spectrum from alignment with current markets to creation of new markets.

An Improved Solution for a Known Need

Competition or explicit customer demands often drive technological improvements along known performance parameters for current products. In such cases, with or without extensive market research, developers often know that lower costs, more features, or better quality are likely to win in the marketplace. HP's Signal Analysis Division, which produces spectrum analysis devices used for testing and analyzing radio-frequency and microwave signals, had traditionally competed on product quality and performance rather than price. However, in the mid-1980s, the commercial market expanded, particularly at the low end, where Japanese offerings threatened HP products. Although a low cost spectrum analyzer existed in the laboratory (the Hornet), there was little interest in commercializing it until an R&D manager returned from a plant visit with a customer in Italy who pointed out that the Japanese had produced a low cost product with features comparable to HP's high-priced spectrum analyzer. Intent on bringing the Hornet to market within 18 months, the team nonetheless took time to conduct a totally unprecedented price study. Moreover, marketing personnel accompanied engineers on customer visits to assess user needs, although R&D maintained responsibility for product definition. The Hornet met both cost and schedule goals and was a marketplace success.

Less successful was the Hewlett-Packard 150, an early attempt to produce a personal computer. The day after HP introduced the HP120, a terminal for use with the HP3000 minicomputer, IBM introduced its first PC. HP responded by changing the project charter for the HP150, a follow-on to the 120. Rather than simply being a terminal, the 150 was now expected to have enough computing power to stand alone and be capable of supporting MS-DOS, the operation system for the IBM PC. One of the problems faced by the development team was that the marketing plan for the HP150 as a terminal for the HP3000 was not altered to reflect the very different set of users now targeted. Therefore, the product development team continued to optimize on the performance characteristics suitable for the customers originally envisioned. As a terminal, the HP150 was quite successful. However, as a personal computer, it was never profitable.[32]

In both of these cases, the developers established user needs in reactive mode. That is, the competition defined the meaningful parameters, on which the development team then attempted to achieve parity if not superiority. There were clear benchmarks against which to design. The challenge lay in identifying the right set of users to interview. Once correctly identified, those users could readily communicate their needs so as to guide design trade-offs.

A current need in the marketplace can be obvious to developers, even in the absence of direct competition or customer demand, just from knowing current cost or functionality barriers to usage. In such cases, developers proactively decide to "delight" their customers with leaps in performance that no competitors have attempted and no users directly requested. The challenges of pushing beyond current technical barriers can be very significant. In the early 1980s, HP was market leader in gas chromatographs, which was an old, mature market. In about 1983, managers in the analytical business decided on a bold target: a chromatograph with one-third the components of the current model and three times the quality—for one-third the price. Such a product was not just a logical enhancement of the current chromatograph. The design required a tremendous leap in performance. In fact, it "wasn't even on the same price/performance curve," yet the developers believed strongly that the customers would want it.[33] Customer forums and site visits to observe user practices helped developers identify critical features. As expected, the product was highly successful, not only in its traditional market, but also in new application areas because of its lower cost.

New Solution to a Known Need

Users may have a need for which they would be incapable of imagining a solution without knowing about a particular technological advance. They could not ask for the solution because they do not know the technological potential exists.

---

[32]Bowen et al., *Visions and Capability*.

[33]Quotes from interview with Dr. James Serum, group R&D manager, Analytic Group, Hewlett-Packard, November 1992.

For instance, HP researchers took the initiative to develop a supercritical fluid extractor for the environmental testing market, knowing that current techniques for analyzing toxic residues in soils involved dangerous solvents and unpleasant, labor-intensive techniques such as boiling the soil and reconcentrating it to analyze the residue. By passing carbon dioxide in a supercritical, near-liquid state through the soil, they could extract the pesticides from the dirt. Once the carbon dioxide was released from the pressure that rendered it supercritical, it returned to an easily vented gaseous state, leaving behind the extracted organic sample. The extractor will connect to other HP analytical instruments and its use will improve productivity significantly. Only researchers aware of the laboratory experimentation conducted under supercritical conditions could have imagined this application. After conducting market research to establish uses of the technique, the team built a prototype and had lead customers run their samples through it. Currently used in Environmental Protection Agency laboratories, the extractor is not as high volume and profitable as the gas chromatograph. However, it solved an array of real customer problems.

The HP continuous frequency counter first introduced in 1986 originated in a somewhat similar situation. Traditional frequency counters for monitoring various types of waves gradually became outdated as transmitters generating frequencies increased in accuracy. One HP engineer envisioned a counter analogous to an oscilloscope that could read frequencies continuously as a series of digits which could then be plotted on an X/Y display and could track drift in frequency signals. However, even this analogy did not help communicate with prospective users, who responded very unenthusiastically when marketing described the new concept. Convinced that a current (if nonobvious) need did in fact exist, the engineers constructed a functional prototype which they persuaded marketing to take to the field. Somewhat to everyone's amazement, the prototype was seized by users with such enthusiasm that marketing sometimes had a hard time retrieving the models. Users saw immediate applications—including many the engineers had not anticipated. One customer wanted to hook the counter up to his radar system to check its functioning. The product became a great commercial success, representing approximately 15 percent of the division's sales. Most important to HP, this product halted the decline of a product line and reinvigorated it.

A New Solution to an Anticipated Need

If meeting nonobvious but current user needs is a challenge, peering into the future to identify as yet unarticulated future needs of a given market is even harder. By extrapolating societal, technological, environmental, economic, or political trends, developers attempt to foresee what users will need in the future when those trends mature. To someone who understands both industry and societal trends, the needs themselves may be fairly obvious. However, timing is often extremely unclear. When will there be enough users or complementary technology or adequate infrastructure to justify development? Moreover, of course, the trends interact. For instance, society's demand for faster, more proximate means of communication interacts with the technological trends that are driving computers to become commodities and communications to become wireless.

Researchers at HP track a number of trends that may be harbingers of future markets. Long before fiber optics was a reality, or optical signaling technologies were on the market, Hewlett-Packard was designing optical signal measurement equipment to be ready when their customers needed it.

Many companies are tracking environmental trends which have reemerged in the 1990s as a likely potent influence on new product design. For instance, legislation in Europe mandating that companies accept back their products for recycling may foretell similar moves in U.S. markets. Yet currently, the supply of recycled materials outstrips both our capacity to process them and also the demand for their reuse. Industry is thus caught in a catch-22: Companies cannot recycle materials economically until they can process them on a large scale and consumers do not want to buy recycled goods because they are still too expensive. Companies have multiple chores to create a market for recycled materials: Create collection processes, create new process technologies to accommodate recycled materials, and stimulate demand for products designed from recycled materials.

An Evolving Solution to an Uncertain Need

At times, technologists run far ahead of consumers by developing an application for which they initially identify the wrong market. When HP Laboratories first recognized their ability to develop a printer that moved not only the pen across a plotter, but also the paper underneath in the other direction, they were enthusiastic. The opportunity for small-scale, high-resolution printers seemed obvious to them. However, they were dismayed to find no interest from the division producing large printers. Only when they were able to engage the interest of the medical division for use in plotting electrocardiographs was a market identified. That technology has, however, been very successful. It repaid the relatively modest costs of its development many times over when it was incorporated into HP's pen plotters.

Such cases are often called—disparagingly—"technology push," because the technical possibility preceded any known user need. Laboratories and the basements of home inventors are full of failed solutions to unknown problems. However, the negative connotation of the phrase is misleading in two ways. First, many products on the market satisfy needs no user had felt or expressed and that embody no technology. The notorious pet rock, sold in the 1970s, perhaps best exemplifies "sellers push" product development. Second, of course, many extremely well known inventions initially had no user demand, although many people today would insist they need them—such as xerography or Post-it pads. Sometimes need and solution evolve together. For example, two widely used technologies that started life in quite different forms at IBM were shaped by trial and error and through the brutal help of internal corporate selection processes and the marketplace. The voice mail systems that are so ubiquitous today originated at IBM when a remote dictation system was designed so that traveling managers could relay their correspondence back over telephone lines to a pool of specially skilled typists in a manuscript center. The so-called Advanced Dictation System was not used as expected. Both managers and documentation preparation people disliked it. However, people started sending messages back to their secretaries using the system, which was consequently retitled the Audio Distribution System. In the very early 1970s, this system became a Speech Filing System—the prototype of current voice mail.[34]

The Reduced Instruction Set Chip (RISC) so widely used today similarly started life in a form very different from today's. In the early 1970s, when the eventual intersection of telephones and computers was foreseen, researchers at IBM saw a clear need to apply digital computing technology to digital switching for telephones. Since such switches have extremely long lives, the computer software that underlay their design needed to be structured to be able to evolve. Moreover, the hardware needed to be scalable. The computer architecture invented to meet this need was not used for this original purpose because of IBM business decisions, but was generalized and extended for less-specialized uses. It became the basis in the mid-1970s for what is known today as RISC architecture. Thus, a project originally aimed at helping IBM get into the telephony business was the origin for the architecture that evolved into RISC.[35]

At this right side of the spectrum pictured in Figure 6 is a strong element of serendipity. Technological potential and market need have to coincide in both time and place for the necessary synergy to occur.

Challenges in Designing in Advance of the Market

The challenges in commercialization become increasingly more acute from left to right in Figure 6, that is, from alignment with current markets to the definition and creation of totally new markets (see Figure 7).

FIGURE 7

Challenges of designing in advance of the market

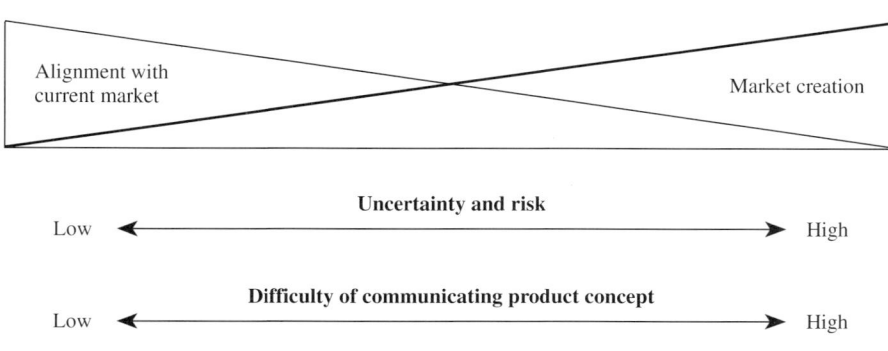

[34]Interview with Dr. Joel Birnbaum, vice president and director, Hewlett-Packard Laboratories, November 1992.
[35]Ibid.

Uncertainty and Risk

Even alignment situations are not without risk. There is always the possibility that the competition will design a better product or get to market faster. Another risk is that the nature of the market segment will change. When HP first sold test and measurement equipment, each piece was a stand-alone "box," with independent functionality. However, today's customers want an integrated, total measurement system. Voltmeters or spectrum analyzers are regarded as components in total testing systems. As this example illustrates, alignment with a current market is far from a static process; the target is continually moving. However, commercialization of technology when no known market exists is obviously riskier and more costly. The fact that many corporations are scaling back on basic research suggests that they do not believe they can afford this type of wandering toward markets. The question then emerges: Who will fund the discovery process and where will it take place? The usual answers—universities, small companies, and national laboratories—all are somewhat facile. However, it is beyond the scope of this chapter to explore that issue.

Communicating Product Concept

Communication of the product concept and elicitation of user reactions become progressively difficult and potentially more expensive as the commercialization situation departs from market alignment and moves toward market creation. Therefore, much more attention and many more resources must be invested in creatively interacting with potential users.

HP researchers could ask their current customers about a vastly cheaper and better gas chromatograph (Situation 1) because customers had a very clear concept of this instrument—what it looks like, what it does, and the like. A simple description of the proposed new chromatograph, combined with a two-dimensional sketch, conveyed enough information to the users, who could extrapolate mentally to a three-dimensional, functioning instrument.

However, customers could not imagine the continuous frequency counter (Situation 2) from mere description. Even analogy with a familiar tool (the voltage oscilloscope) was not enough. A two-dimensional sketch would not help, because it was the new functionality that they failed to grasp—not the physical shape of the invention. Only when they saw a three-dimensional, fully functioning prototype did they grasp the instrument's potential to meet their current needs.

Obviously, when the needs are not yet even felt, as in Situation 3, users may have an even more difficult time thinking ahead to assess whether they will want the technology and, if so, in what form. Like the technologists, they are uncertain about when and if necessary supporting infrastructure may be developed and they are often unsure how much they would pay for certain future products. General Electric Plastics (GEP) faces such a situation in stimulating interest in recycled plastics. GEP built a "house of the future" in Pittsfield, Massachusetts, using recycled plastics in such applications as countertops and faux slate shingles on the roof. Although the investment is considerable, such three-dimensional, functioning demonstrations of technologies in situ, as they would actually be used, are necessary to help customers understand the commercial potential. GEP has also worked on designing products for disassembly so that the component parts can be easily separated at the end of the product life in preparation for recycling. For example, in a joint venture with the design house Fitch RichardsonSmith, GEP designed an electric tea kettle explicitly for disassembly.[36]

In Situation 4, the problem is not only communicating a potential product concept, but also eliciting enough information through demonstration and use of a functioning prototype for developers to identify users and adapt their proposed solution to need. Obviously, this is a very-high-cost effort in terms of both time and money. Increasingly, technological tools such as virtual reality software may help developers present alternative potential futures without actually building products. Currently, prospective clients can walk through simulated buildings of the future; advanced computer-aided design tools allow viewers to revolve a three-dimensional object on the screen and view it from different perspectives; stereolithography enables immediate transformation of design specifications into three-dimensional (but, of course, nonfunctioning) solid models. However, none of these tools yet allow prospective users to actually experience the object being developed. Moreover, it is to everyone's benefit to develop better methods for anticipating market need rather than matching solution to need after the fact.

Tools and Mechanisms for Understanding User Needs

When the product is well aligned with current markets, traditional market research can help track customers' needs quite well, for the needs are clear, current, and communicable. At the opposite end of the spectrum, when the uncertainty of investing in technology for an unknown market is so great, market intuition and serendipity play a large role, and it is not clear the process can be as systematized and structured. Situations 2 and 3, falling in the middle of Figures 6 and 7, are candidates for considerably more managerial attention. Here lie largely unexplored opportunities to considerably improve the process of technology commercialization through empathic design.[37]

Empathic design, as the term implies, means understanding user needs through empathy with the user world rather than from user articulation of needs. The significance of empathic design is lower at the two extremes of the technology commercialization situations—but still important to understand (see Figure 8). Even when the product being designed is aligned with current markets and the users are well known (far left of Figure 8), there are desirable product attributes that the user is often unable to articulate—or even imagine. Users are often totally unaware of their

---

[36]See Karen Freeze and Dorothy Leonard-Barton, *GE Plastics: Selecting a Partner* (Boston, Mass.: Design Management Institute, 1991).

[37]Dorothy Leonard-Barton, "Inanimate Integrators: A Block of Wood Speaks," *Design Management Journal* 2, no. 3 (1992), pp. 61–67.

FIGURE 8

Tools and mechanisms for understanding user needs

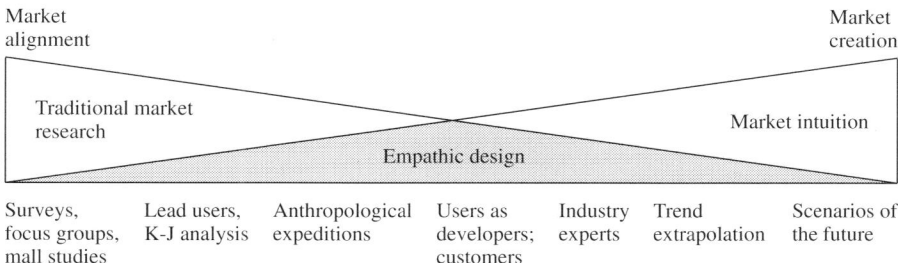

own psychological and cultural responses to symbols and forms and are unable to describe what they want until they see it. Therefore, so-called intangibles such as shape, appearance, and feel are usually determined by expert designers through empathic design. At the market creation end of the spectrum (far right of Figure 8), the ability of developers to imagine a future user environment in which their technology could usefully function requires some degree of empathic design. The ability of industrial designers to embody their imagination in sketches or models is particularly useful in envisioning potential futures. However, since the market is still being created, no real users have been reliably identified.

Empathic design is most powerful when developers are proposing new solutions, either to known or anticipated user needs (middle of Figure 8). In such situations, when product designers develop a deep understanding of the current user environment, they can then extrapolate about the way that environment may evolve in the future and imagine the future need their technology can satisfy. However, as discussed below, the mechanisms for creating an empathic design capability are less well known than those employed in traditional market research.

Tools to help explore user reactions to products at the market alignment end of the spectrum are widely researched and taught. Marketing departments in the western hemisphere are expert at conducting surveys and focus group interviews. So-called mall studies, mentioned earlier in the description of the changes made to the HP deskjet, exemplify more ambitious but still widely used techniques. Less widely employed are interviews with so-called lead users,[38] who are already at the cutting edge of current products. By anticipating their own immediate needs, they foretell the more distant needs of less-advanced users and guide the design of radically improved solutions. Other techniques are most helpful when users can identify a product concept, but important dimensions are unclear. An example is the "K-J" analysis, a highly structured process for gathering and analyzing qualitative data first developed by a noted Japanese anthropologist, Jiro Kawakita. It has been applied to quality improvement programs in Japan and the United States with the help of Professor Shoji Shiba of Tsukuba University[39] and to "concept engineering" at the Center for Quality Management in Cambridge, Massachusetts. Another example of

---

[38] Eric von Hippel, "Novel Product Concepts from Lead Users: Segmenting Users by Experience," M.I.T. Sloan School of Management Working Paper 1476-83, 1983.

[39] Shoji Shiba, Richard Lynch, Ira Moskowitz, and John Sheridan, "Step by Step KJ Method," CQM Document No. 2, Wilmington, Mass.: The Center for Quality Management, Analog Devices, 1991.

systematic need elicitation is the proprietary Value Matrix used by a group of design houses, the Design Consortium, to uncover the often latent desires of a wide spectrum of user/stakeholders in a client firm.[40]

The most powerful aid to empathic design is an anthropological expedition of some kind. Technologists immerse themselves in the user world, much as anthropologists do when they inhabit native villages in unfamiliar parts of the world. Designers or developers with a thorough knowledge of technological potential live in the user environment long enough and absorb enough understanding of that environment to empathize with user needs. They see how users cope with unnecessarily inconvenient, uncomfortable, inefficient, or inaccurate tools and consider how to solve the unspoken problems. Products designed through this process present users with functionality, ease of use, and other benefits they would not have thought to ask for themselves. One of the most famous designers in U.S. history, Henry Dreyfuss, used to require his designers to live with whatever tool they were designing. They rode corn pickers and prowled factories. Similarly, today, Hewlett-Packard product developers in the medical division spend time in intensive care units and hospital clinics. It was on such a visit recently that a product developer noticed the way that nurses, in the course of their duties, inadvertently blocked the surgeon's view of the television screen which the physicians used to guide their intricate work. To solve this problem, the product designer conceived of a tiny screen mounted on a surgeon's helmet, to keep the image directly and constantly in view. In a different type of anthropological expedition, Xerox has employed trained anthropologists and other behaviorists to investigate exactly how people actually interact with sophisticated copier machines, and to report their findings to the corporation as a whole. These explorations resulted in knowledge about users' assumptions and mental models that was very pertinent to machine design, but had never before been systematically gathered.[41]

One very obvious way to commercialize technology is for those who have experienced a problem to apply technology in its solution, that is, for users to become developers. Eric von Hippel has documented hundreds of cases in which users were the primary inventors of a new tool or process.[42] In order to bring user innovation in-house, companies employ in their development organizations customers or individuals who have extensive experience in the user world. At HP, for example, the product line manager for mass spectrometry and infrared spectroscopy systems has a PhD in organic chemistry with a specialty in mass spectrometry. "Most of our senior managers have been born and raised in the [analytical chemistry] business . . . when we speak with customers, the full implications of every word are immediately relevant to us; . . . we can feel the pulse of the customer."[43]

---

[40]See John R. Hauser and Don Clausing, "The House of Quality," *Harvard Business Review* 66, no. 3 (May–June 1988), pp. 63–73. Such techniques are often used as the "front end" for Quality Function Deployment processes that translate user requirements into engineering specifications.

[41]John Seely Brown and Susan E. Newman, "Issues in Cognitive and Social Ergonomics: From Our House to Bauhaus," *Human-Computer Interaction* 1 (1985), pp. 359–91.

[42]Eric von Hippel, *The Sources of Innovation* (New York: Oxford University Press, 1988).

[43]Interview with Dr. James Serum, Hewlett-Packard, November 1992.

Rather than bringing customers in-house to represent the user world, some companies have pursued a policy of commercializing their basic technologies through partnering with customers. ALZA Corporation is noted for its nontraditional drug-delivery systems, that is, ways to deliver drugs into the bloodstream over time at a continuous rate. They partner with specific customers to design customized delivery systems for a particular drug. For example, Janssen Pharmaceutica sells transdermal patches for which ALZA tailored their membranes to deliver a painkiller, Duragesic, for cancer patients. Similarly, ALZA partnered with Pfizer to deliver medicine for the treatment of angina that may be taken just once, instead of three times, a day.

Another lens into the user world can be provided by industry experts. Allegheny Ludlum, a highly profitable specialty steel producer, set up a market development group almost 30 years ago. While the mandate for group members has changed somewhat over the years, their basic task is to entrench themselves in the personal networks of the customer base they serve. Each member of the group is a walking compendium of several vital kinds of information: intense technical knowledge about certain alloys and their application; widespread personal contacts among industry experts and customer companies; deep knowledge about standard-setting and regulation in their industry. This understanding of the user world is mostly tacit (i.e., in their heads).

When the user world lies in the future, developers need to extrapolate current trends and anticipate a world none can confidently predict. While technology commercialization in this situation usually depends upon the market intuition of well-informed gurus, techniques exist for formal scenario-construction.[44] The intent of such scenarios is less to predict exactly a future state than to stimulate consideration of nonobvious futures, to force "out-of-the-box" thinking (i.e., to divorce thought from a straight, unwavering trend line).

All of these tools and mechanisms have limits and costs. The inability of even very sophisticated market research to reliably predict actual user behavior on occasion is well known. There are many explanations, including the basic facts that attitudes do not predict behavior and that, as mentioned before, people are unable to articulate some of their aesthetic and even functional needs. Anthropological expeditions are time-consuming and require special skills. Experts hired in from the user world can become so enmeshed in daily business activities that they can eventually lose touch with the cutting edge.[45] The major limitation to creating industry experts

---

[44]Peter Schwartz, *The Art of the Long View: Planning for the Future in an Uncertain World* (New York: Doubleday Currency, 1991).

[45]This possible danger is exacerbated if high-level senior officials try to micromanage technical project details. In one company studied by Dorothy Leonard-Barton, project teams frequently complained that senior management "swooped down" midway through projects to tinker with technical details which they were no longer in a position to judge. Senior managers can also remain personally invested in an obsolete technology. In another company, a major move from glass to plastic materials was delayed at huge cost to the corporation. The principal reason, according to company informants, was that a critical senior official could not bear to desert his primary skill base and expertise in glassmaking. Only when he left the company was the switch finally made—some years after competition had already proven the profitability of the move.

is that their expertise is held in their heads. Such tacit knowledge is difficult to evaluate financially since commercialization ideas planted in a certain year may not yield sales for 5 or 10; moreover, tacit knowledge is not easily codified or transferred. Industry experts can also become too narrowly focused and adopt the same myopic view of the world that their users have. In short, they may go "native." Customer partners may engender similar risks, in that they can direct technology commercialization into narrow, self-serving niches. And, finally, market scenarios are only intended to provoke possibilities—not predict the future with any assurance.

Corporations are therefore well advised to pursue a wide range of these techniques to understand user needs. The wider the range available to guide technology commercialization, the more opportunity there is to apply the most appropriate technique to a given situation.

Conclusions

Not all new products and processes are alike. They may arise either through a process of invention or innovation.[46] While innovation has the characteristics of "being both demandable and predictable within a finite time," invention does not.[47] If one represents the life of a particular technology through the useful oversimplification of an S-shaped curve (see Figure 9), it is clear that products and processes arising through invention potentially have a much longer life span than those arising through the more derivative process of innovation.[48] Therefore, inventive products are very desirable (albeit not to the exclusion of innovative ones). The dilemma addressed in this paper is that understanding user needs is absolutely critical to successful technology commercialization of both invention and innovation. Since innovative products and processes are derivative, users can directly help shape their design. Extensive tools and methods exist for eliciting user needs—even uncommunicated ones—for such products. Usefully channeling user input into the design of inventive products and processes is much more difficult, and we have far fewer tools and methods to apply to the process.

Our current ability to imaginatively understand user needs (i.e., to commercialize technology through empathic design and market intuition) is constrained by the limited number of people in our organizations who are capable of this art. The observations in this chapter suggest that the next managerial frontier for technology commercialization is to explore methods for better understanding uncommunicated, nonobvious but current user needs and unarticulated, nonobvious future needs. If

---

[46]Either of these may be preceded, of course, by a process of discovery. However, technological discoveries only provide opportunities; they must be shaped into useful products and processes.

[47]John Doyle, "Commentary: Managing New Product Development: How Japanese Companies Learn and Unlearn," in *The Uneasy Alliance: Managing the Product-Technology Dilemma,* ed. Kim Clark, Robert Hayes, and Christopher Lorenz (Boston, Mass.: Harvard Business School Press, 1985).

[48]Brian Dumaine, "How Managers Can Succeed through Speed," *Fortune* 119 (February 13, 1989), pp. 54–74.

FIGURE 9

The S-curve of technology maturation

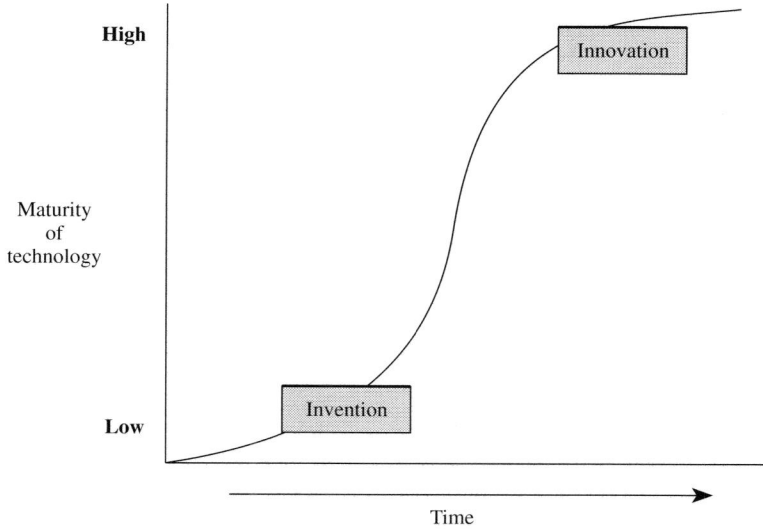

one primary method for creating this understanding is harnessing the creative imagination of individual gurus, then we need to consider how we identify such individuals and develop their skills to the highest degree possible. Another challenge is figuring out how to design various kinds of anthropological expeditions into user territory. Finally, we need better understanding of the limits and possibilities of market scenarios.

In this decade, companies globally confront the need to wring unnecessary buffers of time out of their development processes, but without destroying creativity. The capability to develop new products and processes quickly and effectively will distinguish industry leaders. Truly understanding user needs—not just their demands—enables speed without sacrificing inventiveness.

CHAPTER 17
Industrial Pricing to Meet Customer Needs

When a customer buys a product, he or she goes through a complex process of balancing the price of the product against the perceived benefits, costs, risks, and value in use of the product. If the customer thinks this way when analyzing a purchase, it makes great sense for marketers to set prices with the same items in mind. To do this, marketers need to understand the use to which their customers put the products, the performance benefits, both physical and service, that are most important, and the different cost variables that the customer perceives, such as risk of product failure. To help marketers apply a customer approach in determining a price, the authors have provided a list of important concepts.

Even back in "the good old days" of the very early 1970s, industrial marketers found pricing to be a great challenge. Then both customers and competitors were applying pressure, and since that time government price controls, double-digit inflation, a sudden recession, and finally an economic malaise combining some amount of inflation and recession have simply caused the situation to get worse. A cover article in *Business Week* stressed these changes:

> The chief characteristics of the new price strategy are flexibility and a willingness to cut prices aggressively to hold market shares. On the way out the window are many of the pricing traditions of the U.S. industrial giants.[1]

Our purpose in this chapter is *not* to explore the reasons behind these changes in pricing practice, nor is it to provide a set of pet solutions and perfect techniques managers can use to respond to the situation. Instead, we present a philosophy to help managers approach pricing situations, a coherent, rational framework in which

---

This reading was prepared by Benson P. Shapiro and Barbara B. Jackson.
Reprinted from *Harvard Business Review* 56, no. 6, November–December 1978, pp. 119–27.
Copyright © 1978 by the President and Fellows of Harvard College. All rights reserved.
[1]"Flexible Pricing," *Business Week*, December 12, 1977, p. 78.

managers can make pricing decisions, and finally some tools and constructs that will facilitate the application of the framework.

Although the general approach we suggest can be applied to pricing consumer goods, especially the more complex ones such as appliances and furniture, managers in companies making industrial products—that is, products not resold in their existing form directly to consumers—will find it most useful. These products include items sold to institutional markets such as hospitals and universities, as well as the more typical components, capital goods, supplies, and raw materials sold to manufacturers.

Pricing Strategies

Managers normally set prices one of three ways. The first is for management to maintain a strong internal orientation, basing prices on its own costs, and, usually, adding some standard industry markup to average costs. Cost-plus is a simple system, but it fails to consider competitors, customers, or the volume, price, and profit relationships among costs. A well-known sophisticated version of this approach, target rate-of-return pricing, was developed at General Motors during the 1920s and 1930s. While it included consideration of volume fluctuations through the business cycle and the cost of the capital involved in the business, target rate-of-return prices were still based totally on internal costs, not on the market.

The second approach is to let competitors set prices, and then to meet them head-on. This strategy assumes that a marketer's company, its products, its image and position in the marketplace, and its cost structure are exactly like the competition's. A slightly more sophisticated version of this approach involves maintaining a set dollar or percentage differential between one's prices and the competitor's. A manager might, for instance, maintain a price of 5 percent below the market "leader" to allow for the leader's stronger reputation. However, this approach is mechanistic and does not allow managers either to build on their products' and company's unique strengths or to adjust for their unique weaknesses.

The third approach, which is more difficult than the other two, focuses on the customer. It requires marketers to assess carefully the value customers place on the product. Typically, industrial marketers have shied away from this approach, but now, given the difficult market conditions we have described, the need for such a thorough, customer-based approach seems clear. Fortunately, the opportunity for its application has been advanced by the emergence of new concepts and techniques. In what follows we will go into the customer-based approach and these concepts in more detail.

How Customers Evaluate Products

The basic idea behind our customer-based approach may appear quite simple: Customers balance the benefits of a purchase against its costs. When the benefits outweigh the costs and when the particular product under consideration has the best relationship of benefit to cost, the customer purchases the product. Though the concept is simple, it is difficult to make operational; in particular, it is difficult to define product benefits and costs in terms of the customer's perspective.

In the industrial marketplace, the benefits can be functional (utilitarian aspects that might be attractive to engineers), operational (a product's reliability and durability would be important to manufacturing and operating managers), or financial (aspects attractive to purchasing agents and controllers). Benefits for individuals can also be personal; for example, the ego satisfaction of doing a job well or protection from the risk of termination.

The costs a customer perceives are just as diverse. They include clearly defined acquisition costs: seller's price, incoming freight, installation, and order handling costs. They also include less clearly defined costs such as the risk to the customer of a product failure (which can include the personal risk of making a poor decision, as well as the risk to the company of shutting down a production line or repairing a piece of equipment), fear of late or inaccurate delivery, custom modification after receipt of the item, and so forth.

The important point here is that the benefits are more complex and subtle than marketers often realize and the costs for the prospective customer are a great deal more than just the seller's price. A customer's decision to purchase a product is an exceedingly complex process involving perceptions and not merely hard and fast realities. Price is only a part of this process.

Simply, then, the marketer must determine the highest price that the customer would be willing to pay for the product. One could view that as:

Benefits − Costs other than price = Highest price the customer will pay.

To determine that price, the marketer needs to understand the customer's perception of benefits as well as his or her perception of the costs other than price. The marketer also needs to remember that his or her cost is unimportant in determining the customer's perceptions. The customer cares about the marketer's price, not cost. In fact, to make the statement even more accurate, the customer cares about his or her own costs, much more than about the marketer's price.

Furthermore, marketers need to be aware of the choices their competitors are offering the customer. Those options help determine the environment in which customers perceive benefits and costs, and, of course, they are possible substitute purchases.

This customer-based orientation has been called *utility* or *value* pricing. With this approach, a marketer looks at the utility or value of the product to the customer and compares that with the utility or value offered by competitors. A particular example, which involves a published case study on E. I. duPont de Nemours & Co.,[2] illustrates how important value pricing is.

In July 1954, DuPont introduced Alathon 25, a new polyethylene resin used in pipe manufacture. Until that time, all polyethylene pipe had been made from a by-product off-grade resin. While pipe produced from Alathon 25 looked exactly like

---

[2] E. Raymond Corey, "E. I. duPont de Nemours & Co.," in *Industrial Marketing: Case and Concepts,* 2nd ed. (Englewood Cliffs, N.J.: Prentice Hall, 1976), p. 179.

pipe made from off-grade resin, it had a longer life than competitive pipe and could withstand greater pressure.

After the product's shaky entry into the market, DuPont developed a strong promotional program for Alathon 25 which communicated its notable benefits to a careful selection of the extruders who made the resin into pipe. Alathon 25 sales grew strongly despite the fact that extruders sold the pipe to distributors for between $9.50 and $13.00 per 100 feet versus the $5.00 to $7.00 price for pipe made from off-grade resin. This price ratio, almost 1.9, is greater than the relative lives of the pipes would suggest.

An advertisement reproduced in the case study shows the secret of this strategy's success. It shows a farm application, a typical use of the pipe, where the pipe goes underground. It is clear that if the pipe bursts, it would have to be dug up—a time-consuming, expensive chore. The value or utility of the pipe is great because it is part of a complex system.

We can, then, restate our simple concept in marketer's terms: With a complete understanding of the end use, set a price based on the product's utility or value in use.

Obviously, such an approach requires that a marketer have considerable knowledge of his or her customers to completely understand their applications, including their subtle operational and organizational relationships. A marketer can get that knowledge by analyzing the customers' cost–benefit trade-offs.

Analyzing the Customer's Perceptions

In setting prices, marketers of industrial products need to do the following:

1. Understand the total use of the product.
2. Analyze the benefit variables.
3. Analyze the cost variables.
4. Make cost–benefit trade-offs.

Although the first area is perhaps the most important, it is the least easy to generalize about because each application is so different. The marketer will simply have to study each end use. If the product is a raw material or component, it will be part of both the ultimate product and the process by which the product is made. If it is a piece of capital equipment, it is often only a part of a larger production system. The polyethylene pipe just mentioned is a good example. It was part of two important larger systems; the complex and tedious installation process and the completed system for transporting water.

Focusing on Benefit Variables

A marketer can begin to develop a more complex sense of a product's utility as he or she analyzes the benefits to customers. In doing this analysis, the marketer will find it useful to regard the product as a set of physical attributes and as a set of "soft" service

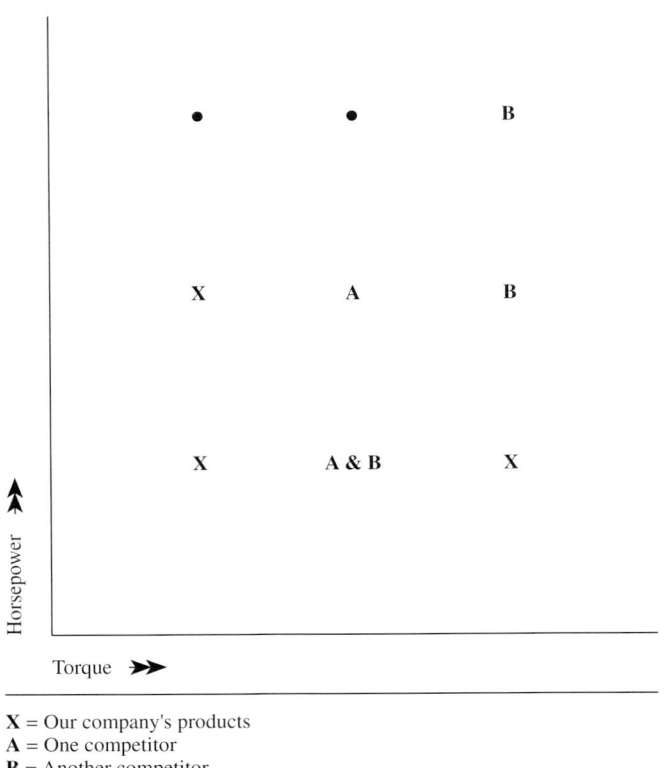

EXHIBIT 1 Product Space for Electric Motors

X = Our company's products
A = One competitor
B = Another competitor

attributes. Theodore Levitt has referred to this latter bundle of characteristics as the "augmented product."[3] Let us first consider the product's physical attributes.

One of the best ways to analyze a set of competitive products is to put them in a performance space (or map or graph) where the axes represent different performance variables.[4] Even though at the first cut one may think of many different dimensions along which to describe product offerings in a marketplace, on further analysis a marketer will usually find that two carefully selected variables tell most of the story.

In the case of electric motors, for example, the variables might be horsepower and torque. Exhibit 1 shows such a space. Each item in the competitive product lines

---

[3]*The Marketing Mode: Pathways to Corporate Growth* (New York: McGraw-Hill, 1969), chap. 1.
[4]The basic concept of placing products in a product or performance space was suggested by Wroe Alderson in 1957 in *Marketing Behavior and Executive Action* (Homewood, Ill.: Richard D. Irwin). Part of his thinking was apparently the result of earlier work by Hans Brems ("The Interdependence of Quality Variations, Selling Effort, and Price," *Quarterly Journal of Economics,* May 1948, pp. 418–40).

could be placed on a point in the space. Construction of such a space has three advantages. First, it forces the marketing manager to define explicitly the product's primary attributes. Second, it provides a visual way to compare competing lines. And third, and perhaps most important, it encourages the manager to develop an explicit product policy based on the main product characteristics.

As Exhibit 1 shows, products usually do not appear at all points in the product space. Instead, they appear at points that have particular technical significance or historical tradition. Thus, motors might be offered at 5 hp and 10 hp but not at 8.273 hp; printing presses would always be sized to match paper dimensions. This fact makes the product space much easier to work with. The space in Exhibit 1, for example, has nine feasible products, seven of which are being produced. Sometimes, of course, managers might choose to break with the established traditions of product positioning, but such situations are rare.

The product space is a particularly powerful tool when it is used as a visual technique for segmenting a market. Returning to our electric motor example, we can map different market segments in the space. Exhibit 2 shows how such a map might look. In some industries, where a small number of specific accounts make up the

EXHIBIT 2 Product Space for Motor Pumps Showing Two Market Segments

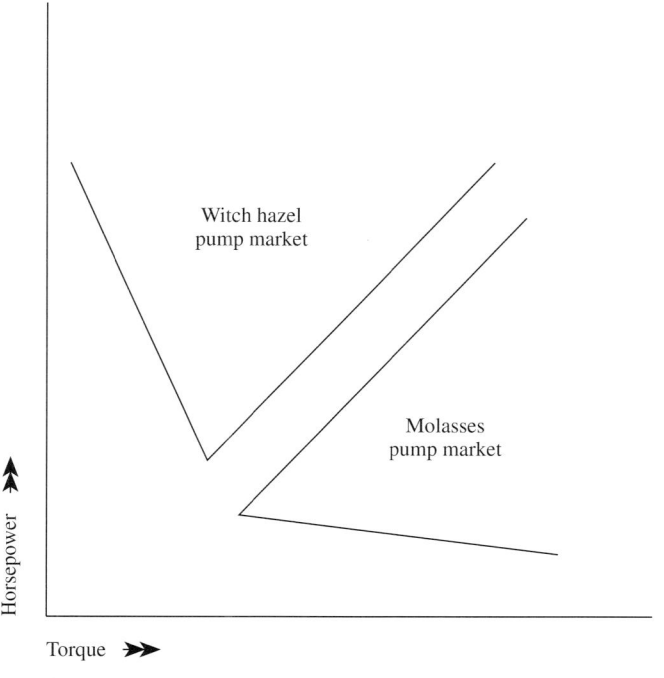

NOTE: In this idealized product space, motors for the witch hazel industry pump market would be of high horsepower and low torque because witch hazel is not viscous. Molasses, on the other hand, is gooier, has more viscosity, and companies making it need pumps of high torque (or turning power) relative to horsepower.

market, or a large share of it, the needs of individual accounts can even be mapped in the space.

But so far we have discussed only the physical attributes of competitive products, which in many industrial markets are identical or almost identical. The products are often purchased to specification. In those situations, the products are not differentiated, but the companies can be by the services they offer. One company might stress reliability of delivery and another quality of technical support. These service attributes can be mapped in much the same way that the physical characteristics are mapped in the product space. For example, in the copier marketplace the variables might be total price per copy and repair service responsiveness.

With most industrial products, the customer is purchasing an exceedingly complex system with many variables. While it is possible to study the trade-off explicitly[5] by conducting surveys, as would certainly be justified in large markets, it is often possible for a marketer to identify the important purchase criteria just by knowing intimately his or her customers' needs.

Focusing merely on product attributes and company services can, however, lead marketers into a very dangerous trap—that of marketing features and not benefits. Even though every good sales manager stresses to his or her salespeople that the customer buys benefits, most salespeople and many marketing managers stress features and forget benefits. To quote a familiar phrase, "The person who buys the ¼-inch drill bit does not want the drill bit but wants the ability to drill ¼-inch holes."

Thus, to the customer, "durability" refers to the ability to drill more holes before the bit must be replaced, not the hardness of the bit. Many marketing managers (and salespeople), however, would mistakenly stress the newer, harder alloy the bit is made of rather than the benefit of more holes between bit changes.

A very clever way to avoid the trap is to develop the performance space dimensions based on customer needs (i.e., number of holes drilled by the bit) instead of physical or service attributes. This procedure carries the customer orientation one important step forward.

Calculating Cost Variables

Just as benefits are a complex group of physical and service attributes, perceived in different ways by different people, costs are much more than just the "price" the customer pays. In trying to calculate costs, it is useful to begin with the purchase price, and then add on the clear, explicit acquisition and use costs such as inbound transportation, installation, repair, labor, power, and so forth. Employing the concept of life cycle costing, the manager can consider all of the costs associated with a piece of equipment or a manufacturing process over the life of a product.

While life cycle costing has typically been used for capital equipment, it can be applied to almost any purchase, including that of a service or supply item. Most

---

[5]Paul E. Green and Yoram Wind, "New Ways to Measure Consumers' Judgments," *Harvard Business Review,* July–August 1975, p. 107; and Brian T. Ratchford and Gary Ford, "A Study of Prices and Market Shares in the Computer Main Frame Industry," *The Journal of Business,* April 1976, p. 194.

major make-or-buy analyses have the elements of life cycle costing in them if they are performed correctly. Applying the concept, a manager can trade off his or her customer's operating costs, power, or labor against capital investment.

But doing an effective cost analysis includes looking at less-obvious costs. For instance, if a product failure or an interruption in a manufacturing process presents a great risk to the customer, he or she is much more likely to pay a high price to ensure reliability than someone who does not perceive the same risk. Some companies, for example, purchase good components for their products because they know that their customers are very sensitive about performance. If the product fails, the customer has lost more than the monetary value of the component, and the company's relationship with the customer is lessened by that amount as well.

Creative ways of looking at the customer's perception of cost can lead to powerful, yet sometimes simple, marketing approaches. One manufacturer of laboratory instruments was plagued by a high number of very small orders for a limited variety of repair parts for one particular product line. On analysis, the product manager found that customers were annoyed at having to order small parts because the ordering cost was greater than the parts prices. Furthermore, the company was losing money on the parts for the same reason.

Even more costly, customers were upset at the downtime caused by not having the correct parts in stock. A few customers with many instruments seemed capable of keeping the right mix of parts in stock but others with limited experience could not develop good inventory rules. To alleviate the problem, the product manager developed repair kits with several different assortments of parts and offered them to customers using a large variety of instruments. The company's costs went down, customer costs decreased, and customer satisfaction increased because instruments were available more of the time.

Making Cost–Benefit Trade-Offs

If the customer makes cost–benefit trade-offs in analyzing a purchase, then it seems sensible for the marketer to do the same in analyzing how to approach the customer. The simplest way to begin to understand the trade-off is first to look at only physical product attributes and at price. Leave for later a consideration of the service variables and the other factors that make up the customer's cost.

In many industrial markets, it is possible to define and examine a general price–performance ratio. A major performance variable in crawler tractors, for example, is horsepower. The price–performance ratio here thus becomes dollars per horsepower. A low ratio (1:0) indicates greater horsepower per dollar than does a higher ratio (2:0).

A marketer can use the performance space described earlier to do this kind of analysis by replacing one variable of the product's performance with price. On the graph in Exhibit 3, each item in a product line can be represented by a point. Any particular product line can be represented by joining together the points for each item in the line to form a curve. Price performance curves have been used in the computer industry with some success to show the development of the industry over

Exhibit 3 Price–Performance Curves

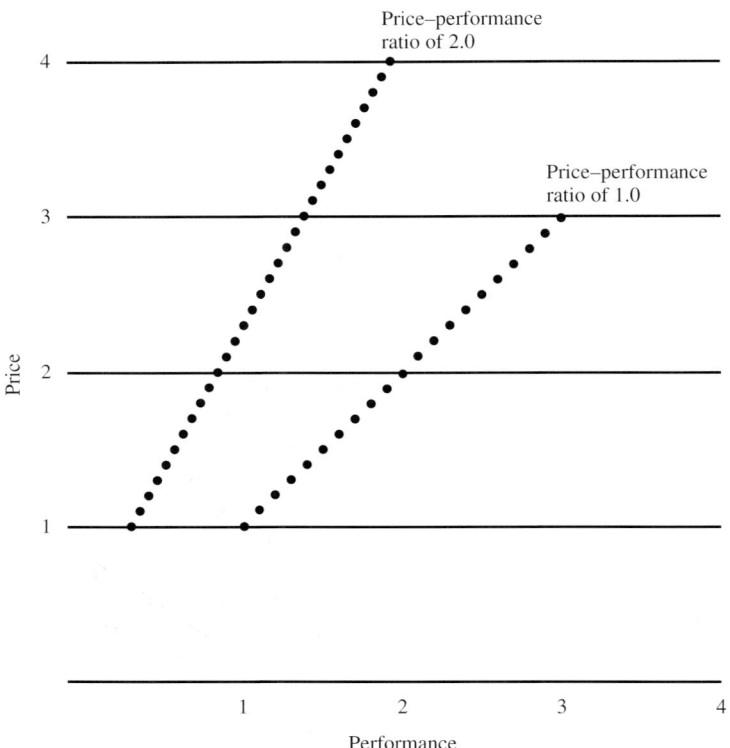

time. There, for example, one can see the greater performance per dollar (or productivity) resulting from each successive generation of computers.

Theoretically, it would be possible to build a three dimensional (or more) price–performance space, with several dimensions of product performance plotted against one price dimension. But as it is impossible for managers to visualize the three dimensional space, let alone more dimensions, it is more practical for them to select one primary performance characteristic.

The most clear-cut price–performance curve, however, leads one into the features versus benefits trap again. The performance attribute graphed in price–performance curves is usually a feature, not a benefit. The crawler tractor buyer, for example, is not really interested in horsepower, but in amounts of earth moved per hour. Here again, the space can be defined in customer-oriented terms such as yards of earth moved per hour.

TABLE 1	A Customer Approach to Pricing

1. A commitment to the philosophy that the customer chooses products by measuring benefits against costs.
2. An understanding that benefits involve a great deal more than physical attributes and that in many industrial situations it is the "soft" services which differentiate products.
3. A realization that cost involves more negative aspects of the purchase than price alone.
4. The perspective of benefits and costs in terms of a complete usage system, not in terms of an isolated part of that system.
5. Cognizance of the fact that different customers view benefits and costs in different ways, thus necessitating careful market segmentation.
6. The application of graphic techniques to understanding the position of products and product lines in terms of customer needs and competitive offerings.

Thus, instead of contrasting price with features or performance, the marketer should remember the end use of the product and look at price together with benefits and costs. To assess meaningfully the benefits and costs of a complex system requires a great deal of creativity and meticulous calculation. Throughout, the marketer should keep his or her eye on customers and their perceptions.

Furthermore, the marketer may have to consider as possible costs customer concerns which one usually does not even consider quantifying. For instance, if one is marketing a piece of capital equipment critical to a total manufacturing system, in considering the benefits of reliability a marketer might very well have to assess the cost to his or her customer of shutting down the whole production system if that risk is important to the customer. Different customers clearly will have different concerns and will use the product in different systems. As a result, they will likely perceive the same product as having different benefits and costs. For a summary of the important concepts of an analysis of cost-benefit trade-offs see Table 1.

How Marketers Should Determine Price

To the industrial marketer, the price-determining process is much more complicated than just selecting a price. As the customer looks at price as an integral aspect of the product, so must the manufacturer. Thus, price should be seen as a design variable in planning the product, as one of several critical performance attributes. The intimate relationship between price and product policy makes a great impact on the whole product planning-pricing process.

For a particular example, let us look again at the crawler tractor business.[6] In the U.S. market, Caterpillar had traditionally dominated the market for large tractors

---

[6]For more on this particular situation, see the case study entitled "Deere & Company: Industrial Equipment Operations," Intercollegiate Case Clearing House, Boston, Mass. 02163, Order no. 9-577-112.

over 100 horsepower. On the other hand, Deere & Company had dominated the market for small utility machines under 100 horsepower. Then, at about the same time, Deere and Caterpillar entered each other's market domains. The new Deere large tractor unit had a hydrostatic transmission which, according to Deere management, provided about 15 percent better productivity per horsepower than the comparable existing units. Deere, however, was unfamiliar with the large tractor market and somewhat of an unknown to the customer in this marketplace.

In designing its new tractors, Deere had four courses of action open to it:[7]

1. It could introduce units slightly larger in horsepower than the competitive Caterpillar unit.
2. It could introduce units with the same horsepower as the Caterpillar units.
3. It could introduce units slightly smaller than the Caterpillar units.
4. It could place its entries between existing Caterpillar units.

The last option would require reeducating the marketplace, an ambitious undertaking in the face of such competent, well-entrenched competition.

Because this product was so complex, involving several years of design time and millions of dollars in engineering and tooling costs, Deere's decision was difficult and important. It was clearly both a product policy and a pricing decision. In the crawler tractor industry, part of price is determined by manufacturing cost. Cost, in turn, is determined by the size of the product as well as by other variables such as unit volume. Another important point is that the price can be changed, especially lowered, much more easily and quickly than the product can be changed.

(The general inflationary tenor of the economy has made it much easier to raise prices than it was previously, however. A price increase is not the shock it once was. In addition, if price is raised too high at one point, it can be readjusted by skipping a future industry price increase.)

The basic product design itself is the most difficult thing to change in any material way.

In considering these options, it is important to note the role of the customer's perception of performance. The appropriate pricing strategy might be different in a situation where the customers view horsepower as the primary variable than in one where they view productivity (yards moved per hour) as the key variable.

According to the case study (in which some data are disguised), Deere apparently introduced its tractor at about equal price and at slightly greater horsepower than Caterpillar's competing unit. To encourage rapid trial and adoption of its product, Deere management apparently passed on to the customer all of the benefit of higher productivity resulting from new technology. In addition, it seemingly did not want to stray far from industry-established tractor sizes.

---

[7]We very much appreciate the help of Ken Kessler of the Deere engineering staff for explaining these options to us.

Pricing and Product Planning

If one accepts the basic importance of the customer's view in setting price, and the concept of the customer balancing benefits and costs, then it becomes clear that product planning and pricing become one process. In fact, in industrial marketing, it is almost impossible to separate them. To a great extent, price defines a product's market, competition, and potential application. It is influenced strongly by cost, which, in turn, is related to unit volume and performance. In the other direction, price affects unit volume.

Once a product is in a price–performance space, it is not fixed there forever; it can be moved either by changing its price, or by changing its physical or service performance attributes. Regardless, product planning and pricing must be managed simultaneously.

Perhaps two examples would be useful here. In one, a manufacturer of an expensive engineered plastic developed a new version of the product that provided some clear performance advantages over the existing version. Furthermore, on a direct cost basis, the new version was cheaper than the older one. However, when amortization of the development expenditure was added to the direct cost, the total was greater than the fully allocated cost of the older version.

The company had several clear choices involving the pricing of both items as well as the timing of the new product's introduction. It was possible, for instance, to introduce the new product at a premium price compared with the older one while holding the older one at its current price. Or management could reduce the older one's price. That option seemed especially interesting because company engineers expected to cut the processing costs of the old product through a new manufacturing process not applicable to the new version. If the price were to be cut, management had to decide whether to do so before the introduction of the new version or concurrent with it.

Finally, the company could simply replace the older version with the newer one. In approaching this situation, the managers involved had to consider benefits, customer costs, the usage systems, and customer perceptions, not just the company's own costs.

In another situation, a manufacturer of a specialized type of electric motor was under pressure from a new competitor who offered a lower-priced, lower-quality unit designed for the needs of a rapidly growing segment of the market. In this case, management could either develop a specialized motor for the same segment or could meet its competitor head-on by reducing the prices of its whole line. Management chose to develop a new motor for this segment rather than cut the price and sacrifice margin on its whole line. Fortuitously, the manufacturer then discovered other market segments, where its penetration had been low, which had applications for the new, cheaper, lower-quality motor.

As a competitive tool, pricing has a particularly strong advantage over product planning—as has been said, it is almost always quicker and easier to change the price than to change the product or the service. Changes in the "soft" service part of the product take a great deal of time to implement. One cannot easily develop a

EXHIBIT 4   **Planning Factors to Consider When Changing Prices on Product Lines**

	Action		
Planning Factors	Price Change	Reengineering of Existing Product or Processes	New Product Development or Major Process Change
Longer-term impact	Low*	Moderate	High
Investment necessary	Low	Moderate	High
Risk	Low?	Moderate?	High?
Ease of competitive response	High	Moderate	Low

NOTE: It is important to note that the term risk as used here may not be true risk. We have focused on short- and moderate-term risk. The true long-term risks may be quite different. In situations of rapid change, especially technological, it may be far riskier to make small product and process changes than to make substantial ones.
*To be read, the longer-term impact of a price change is low.

better applications engineering capability, upgrade a sales force, or implement a rapid order processing and delivery program. Thus, in the electric motor situation just described, if the problem were urgent and development of a new line a lengthy process, the manufacturer would almost have been forced to respond with price cutting.

Pricing changes are, however, easy for competitors to copy. Unless a company has an underlying cost advantage over another company, it is hard to develop a strong position solely on the basis of price. Exhibit 4 shows the impact, cost, risk, and ease of competitive response for various kinds of product line and price changes.

Relating Price to Cost Structure

Up to this point our focus has been almost totally on the customer. But a company's own structure also plays an important part in the pricing-planning process.

A pricing policy should be structured in such a way that it takes maximum advantage of the company's cost structure and, wherever possible, builds on the company's distinctive competitive competence. It should be noted, however, that in most situations price can be used to shape demand, but not to change it radically. There are, after all, other elements of the customer's costs, as well as the benefits, to be considered.

A company that has a highly automated manufacturing plant, for instance, and an expensive sales force might want to generate large orders, giving substantial volume discounts to help do so.[8] Large orders, which make good use of the equipment's

---

[8]The Robinson-Patman Act makes it illegal for a company to favor one customer over another competing customer. But it does allow pricing which reflects costs savings. For more on this exceedingly complex law, see Richard A. Posner, *The Robinson-Patman Act: Federal Regulation of Price Difference* (Washington, D.C.: American Enterprise Institute for Public Policy Research, 1976).

economical long runs, justify the high cost of the sales call. On the other hand, another company with a broad product line, a more labor-intensive manufacturing operation, and a large distribution network with its attendant high fixed cost, might have a much more gentle slope to its volume-discount curve.

Managers cannot assume, however, that the large company–large order, small company–small order relationship always applies. In many situations, a small company can carve out a specialized niche around large orders and long runs. With top-level managers acting as account managers, a small company can service customers capable of placing large orders on a direct basis. The large manufacturer, on the other hand, can cover all segments of the market with a broad product line and intensive distribution. In doing so, it serves the small user as well as the large user.

The manager should base his other product policy, view of market segmentation, and price on the use (as measured by the size of a single-line entry on the order form) the customer is going to make of the product, rather than on the customer's size or total business it gives the manager's company.

There are many other situations where managers build a pricing policy around an existing cost structure. For example, managers can design a cost structure and its underlying manufacturing, marketing, sales, and distribution strategies to complement a particular product policy and pricing strategy. It seems to us that if a product policy and pricing strategy are indeed responsive to customer needs, the best long-term approach is to build the cost structure to fit them. While perhaps appropriate in the short term, market strategies that sacrifice customer benefits to protect the company's interests, such as an existing cost structure, are doomed in the long term.

Concluding Note

We began this chapter discussing a basic philosophy built around customers and their perceptions of benefits and costs. That concept is the truly important one. Pricing must be done on the basis of customers' perceptions of the value of the product, which depend on their total usage systems.

Techniques such as the performance space and price–performance curves help to implement the concept of customer primacy. But they are techniques, not ends in themselves. Industrial marketers win or lose in the customer's mind.

CHAPTER 18
Industrial Market Research: Beta Test Site Management

The purpose of this chapter is to set out guidelines for maximizing the value of a beta test program. The authors identify a variety of uses and purposes of such a testing program. They then set out the major benefits and costs to both vendors and test sites, based on an analysis of over 20 beta test programs. Finally, they provide management guidelines for effective implementation.

Introduction

The new product development process for a 50-cent candy bar and that for a $500,000 piece of computer hardware are the same—or so the textbooks say. In each situation, the manufacturer is advised to proceed through a number of sequential steps: idea generation → initial screening → concept testing → product use testing → market testing → introduction. In practice, however, the processes are quite different. Somewhat ironically, the process for the candy bar entry would likely follow the suggested model more closely and have a more scientific, rigorous appearance.[1] This is because candy bar buyers:

- Are numerous and easy to identify.
- All use the candy bar for the same basic purpose.
- Follow a short decision-making process in purchasing.
- Likely decide whether or not to buy a bar on their own.

Robert J. Dolan prepared this note.
Copyright © 1991 by the President and Fellows of Harvard College.
Harvard Business School note 592-010.
[1]See, for example, a description of the likely processes to be followed in "Note on Concept Testing" (HBS case no. 590-063) and "Note on Pre-Test Markets" (HBS case no. 588-052).

- Can easily articulate whether they like the bar or not after use.
- Need only a short time to use up the bar and become a candidate for a repeat purchase.

In contrast, possible adopters of the $500,000 computer system may be few in number and hard to find, vary in the intended application of the system, have a decision-making process characterized by broad participation by individuals across the company and long gestation time, and take a long time in deciding how well the product fits their needs.

These contrasts in buyer behavior cause significant differences in the effective implementation of the steps of the development process. The product use and market test phases for a candy bar would commonly involve large samples, rigorous statistical analysis, and carefully designed market experiments. The same phases for computers will usually find a handful of "respondents"—not selected with statistical analysis in mind. This handful is the vendor's beta test sites.[2]

R. G. Cooper's survey shows that money invested in the beta test phase of the new product development process is one of the key differentiators between industrial product successes and failures.[3] The frequent use of beta programs suggests their importance. However, there are no well-articulated guidelines for management of such tests. In practice, beta site selection and management seem ad hoc at many firms—driven by convenience rather than recognition of the trade-offs involved. This lack of effective management leads J. B. Elmer to refer to beta site testing as "an informal method that's really not research" and to suggest prototype-testing research as a way to avoid the "significant potential marketing hazards" of beta testing.[4]

The purpose of this chapter is to set out guidelines for maximizing the value of a beta test program. We begin by identifying the variety of relationships between vendors and sites. We then set out the major benefits and costs to both vendors and test sites, based on an analysis of over 20 beta test programs. Having established potential costs and benefits, we then provide management guidelines for effective practice. The small sample sizes inherent in beta test programs and the multiplicity of purposes possibly served to preclude reducing beta site management to a simple formula. However, specific prescriptions of value can be made.

Briefly stated, our guidance on effective beta management is this:

1. Carefully define the purpose of the program. In the next section, we set out and illustrate five major purposes of beta testing. Clarity in purpose aids in determining the number of sites required, the desired characteristics of sites, the length of the test, and data collection methods.

2. Design the testing program to guard against the significant threats to validity of a program. Central here is that beta sites are usually few in number and

---

[2]Alpha testing refers to the prior usage of in-house product testing.
[3]R. G. Cooper, "Identifying Industrial New Product Success: Project Newprod," *Industrial Marketing Management* 8 (1979), pp. 124–35.
[4]J. B. Elmer, "Software Developers Can Benefit from Prototype-Testing Research," *Marketing News*, January 1989, pp. 5–6.

selected purposively by the firm rather than randomly. The section called "Threats to Test Value" provides the major issues to be considered in this.

3. Understand and manage the sites' motivation for participating in the test. This can help in recruiting sites and designing the program to be implemented. This is the subject of the section named "Threats to Test Value."

The final section provides a summary and conclusions.

Beta Test Purposes

By definition, a beta test is "a real world test of a system after it has passed all its laboratory tests."[5] Implicit in this definition is the fact that this test precedes the general availability of the product. An example of a basic function check of a system is Accu-Chek's testing of its electronic shelf pricing system for grocery stores.[6] The 90-day test provided Accu-Chek:

1. Validation of the basic concept of half-inch electronic labels changed by handheld computers replacing manual systems.
2. Diagnostic information on specific aspects of the program. Specifically, Accu-Chek obtained information pertaining to four constituent groups:
   a. Its *own field force* found that the labels were not easily installed.
   b. The size and position of the labels were not appealing to *consumers*.
   c. *Shelf-stockers* found the labels hung over too far, making item placement difficult.
   d. *Store management's* experience with the test system raised accuracy and security concerns which had to be overcome before large-scale adoption would be achieved.

Figure 1 shows this function and diagnostic check at the center of a beta site purpose diagram. While this purpose is at the heart of most test programs, important supplementary purposes are also served as indicated. As shown, the three major purposes served are:

1. Product.
   a. Basic function check.
   b. Refinement of core product design.
   c. Added features desired in core product.
2. Augmented product design.
   a. Support features.
      (1) Training required.

---

[5] J. G. Sweetland, "Beta Tests and End-User Surveys: Are They Valid?" *Database,* February 1988, pp. 27–32.

[6] "Technology Hits Shelf Pricing," *Discount Merchandising* (September 1989), pp. 72–74.

FIGURE 1

Beta test purposes

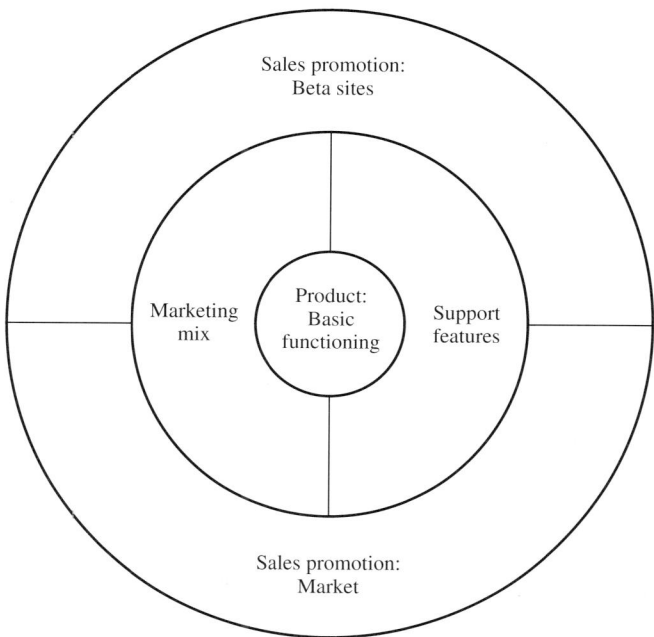

(2) Documentation adequacy.
(3) Other features.
  b. Marketing mix to support product introduction, especially:
    (1) Positioning.
    (2) Pricing.
3. Sales promotion.
  a. To beta sites:
    (1) Develop account relationship.
    (2) Trial path to purchase.
  b. To general market:
    (1) Publicity/credibility from passing test.
    (2) Reference accounts/demo sites.
    (3) Equivalent to preannouncement.

In addition to the data on the core product, a beta program can test and refine augmentation of the core. For example, in the software industry the core product becomes commoditylike after a short time and hence support programs are key. For example, Lotus's "agreements on support, connectivity, communication between vendor and user" were arrived at after "extensive beta testing of various arrangements."[7]

---

[7]E. Bender, "Software Hits, Lower Profits," *Computerworld,* May 12, 1986, pp. 35, 44.

Beta programs can also provide input to determining the appropriate marketing mix to support the product. Especially useful is testing to permit the calculation of the economic value to the customer, a key input to product pricing.[8] For example, the Cumberland Metals Industries case reports the field testing of a new type of pile driver pads.[9] Via collection of data on pile-driving efficiency in the two test sites, the company was able to calculate precisely the value of the pads to the customer. This would be the upper bound on what any individual would pay. Systematic analysis of the variance in the value can be the key to market segmentation, product positioning, and target market selection.

Finally, the outer ring of Figure 1 shows beta's use as a sales promotion device—to beta sites themselves and the market more generally. Xerox recently used 26 sites as betas for its $220,000 Docutech Production Publisher.[10] While Xerox's usual practice was to beta at five or six sites, the quintupling of the number of sites was due to the fact that "the company used the new product as a tool for building closer relationships with key customers." These closer relationships achieved through beta testing can result in sales as effectively as the beta test is a trial run for the test site. For example, the first four U.S.–based purchasers of Elran Technologies' ACE artificial intelligence software—AT&T, Pennwalt, General Dynamics, and Unisys—were all beta sites originally.[11]

Betas can have a market impact for the system more generally as a successful beta program reduces the uncertainty about the product in the eyes of potential adopters. For example, Data Communications (1987) labeled AT&T the "League Leader" as it "moved to nail down a significant piece of business by passing initial beta tests . . . at General Electric Corp."[12] Beta test results are news in the high technology area and can generate invaluable publicity as in a *Computerworld* article headlined "First Beta Test User Lauds Kontact for 'Smarts.' "[13] The first paragraph of the article read: "The first beta test use of Mitel Corp.'s $4,000 executive workstation said it has more 'smarts' than the Northern Telecom Inc. Displayphone and is more 'truly' an executive workstation than the more expensive Xerox Corp. 8010 Star."[14]

Beta test sites can be useful to the general market as reference accounts or demo sites for potential adopters. For example, Feredata sold their data base machine to National Resource Management, an oil and gas company in Dallas, based on a demo at Wells Fargo Bank. NRM Management commented: "We are impressed that Feredata took us to see the system at Wells Fargo. They [the bank] have different appli-

---

[8]For details, see J. L. Forbis and N. T. Mehta, "Value-Based Strategies for Industrial Products," *Business Horizons* 3 (May–June 1981), pp. 32–42.

[9]"Cumberland Metal Industries," Harvard Business School case 9-580-104, Boston, Mass., 1980.

[10]B. J. Feder, "A Copier That Does a Lot More," *The New York Times,* October 3, 1990, pp. 1, D8.

[11]J. Stein, "An Author's ACE in the Hole?" *Computerworld,* June 5, 1989, p. 104.

[12]"Timeplex's Link/100 Draws Mixed Industry Response," *Data Communications,* August 1987, pp. 85–86, 88–90.

[13]B. Hoard, "First Beta Test User Lauds Kontact for 'Smarts,' " *Computerworld,* January 24, 1983, p. 13.

[14]Ibid.

cations but the same type of thing, high-level inquiry."[15] The Apparel Technology Center was set up in Raleigh, North Carolina, to act as a beta test site for advanced apparel technology and to document performance of systems for reference by member companies.[16] Easingwood and Beard suggest that using a prestigious firm as a beta is a good way to "legitimize" a product, which is important for very new/complex products.[17]

Beta testing with Morgan Guaranty and Manufacturers Hanover has led to the establishment of Light Signatures as the standard of the industry in stock certificate fraud detection.[18] Light Signatures' system takes a fiber fingerprint of a stock certificate. Testing with Morgan and Manufacturers (and improving the system based on that test) facilitated obtaining the commitment of 25 major securities processors, getting banknote companies to design their documents in a way compatible with the system, and gaining the endorsement of the Securities Transfer Association.

Finally, Rabino and Moore not only position beta programs as serving the above purposes but also note their signaling properties—they "serve the important function of alerting selected customers to an imminent product launch."[19] Later, this "plays a critical role in enhancing product awareness as information about technical aspects begins to leak out and rumors are generated by the press."[20]

In summary, beta site testing serves a multiplicity of purposes, not just as a "checking-out" of the functioning of the product, as many propose. It is important, however, to give explicit priority to the desired purposes. The purpose to be served determines the type of site desired (e.g., "representative" for purpose 1, "large account" for purpose 3a, and "prestigious" for purpose 3b), number of sites (e.g., "few" for purpose 1's basic function check, "many" for purpose 2b, due to segmentation, and for purpose 3), the data collected from the site, and the agreement about confidentiality of results. Since different purposes lead to vastly different optimal designs, it is crucial to have these set prior to the start of the test.

Threats to Test Value

There are four major issues to consider in designing a valid test:

1. Selecting the proper sites.
2. Timing the test at the right stage of the product development cycle.
3. Managing account relationships.
4. Managing the information flow from the sites.

---

[15]E. Myers, "Database Machines Take Off," *Datamation,* May 15, 1985, pp. 53–54, 58, 63.

[16]F. Fortess, "Squaring Off with the Competition," *Bobbin,* May 1988, pp. 104–6, 108, 110.

[17]C. Easingwood and C. Beard, "High Technology Launch Strategies in the U.K.," *Industrial Marketing Management* 18 (1989), pp. 125–38.

[18]T. C. Crane, "Shedding Light on Certificate Fraud," *ABA Banking Journal,* May 1988, pp. 22, 25.

[19]S. Rabino and T. E. Moore, "Managing New Product Announcements in the Computer Industry," *Industrial Marketing Management* 18 (1989), pp. 35–43.

[20]Ibid.

Due to the cost of managing a beta site, it is typical that few are chosen. The danger in using a small sample is well illustrated by Jaben's discussion of banks as beta sites: "One software development company, for example, chose only one beta site to test a new product. To please that bank, the developer made several changes. The only problem was, that particular bank was not representative of the industry, and the product became so customized that it could not be marketed to other financial institutions."[21]

While most firms do protect against this type of situation by using more than one site, it is crucial in segmented markets to understand (through other research) the variation in customers' requirements and evaluation criteria. Beta sites should be representative of the product's key target markets and be firms which will push the product to its useful limit in the test.

The second major issue is properly trading off the issues involved in timing of the beta test. One argument is to push the test toward the early stages of the new product development process where the results of the test are most easily incorporated into the design of the product. On the other hand, the argument is not to jeopardize an account relationship by sending out a product with lots of bugs in it as a beta. The need to make this decision reinforces the major point of the last section (i.e., be explicit about the goals of the beta test). When Westinghouse was offered a chance to beta IBM's 3090 scientific processing capability, its computer center director assessed the likely impact of a Westinghouse test on product design to be "about zero."[22] IBM was testing late in the process, apparently after much in-house testing, and the design was reasonably fixed. On the other hand, Jenkins reports that "performance issues they discovered in beta test" led Lotus to delay shipping Release 3.0 of 1-2-3.[23] One software industry consultant lays some of the blame for "vaporware" on the lateness of actual customer contact in the development process.

Third, there are account relationship issues not directly related to product performance. In the course of a beta test, a customer relationship may be built or it may be destroyed. The vendor has information needs which the tester can find intrusive. For example, if the vendor is using the beta for the purpose of doing an economic-value-to-the-customer calculation, the vendor must understand the economics of the tester's business to translate product performance into dollar returns. Similarly, assessing product performance may require more than unobtrusive measures (e.g., it may involve survey work with a wide variety of people within the tester's organization).

Account relationship considerations extend to nonsites as well. Frequently (for reasons to be detailed in the next section), potential testers view being a beta site as a great advantage. Hence, not being considered or selected can upset potential customers.

Finally, one must manage the information flow from a beta site. Nondisclosure agreements have grown increasingly difficult to work out and thus general publicity and information to competitors can flow from beta sites. For example, the head-

---

[21] J. Jaben, "Banks as Beta Sites," *United States Banker,* December 1987, pp. 31, 33–34.

[22] D. Stamps, "Beta Site Politics," *Datamation,* April 1, 1986, pp. 62–63, 66, 70.

[23] A. Jenkins, "Long Overdue—The Reasons behind Vaporware," *Computerworld,* October 5, 1988, pp. 11–13.

line on *Computerworld*'s article on CIGNA's beta testing of Lotus's Symphony was "Symphony gets mixed reviews from beta test site" and included CIGNA's judgment that "it is difficult to master, does not easily integrate data, and lacks the versatility of stand-alone packages."[24] Similarly, the *Computerworld* article on Chase Manhattan, "the first U.S. beta test site to go public with its Wangnet experience," had Chase's vice president of telecommunications strategy describing Wang as having been pushed "into a future for which it was not entirely prepared," noting "there have been a series of delays. . . . In the overall, Wang never even could have made the original dates," and "Wang has a lot of work to do with its operating system."[25] Whatever Wang learned from the test, one has to wonder how it could be enough to net out positively over this kind of publicity.

While nondisclosure agreements have historically functioned reasonably well in non-technology-laden environments, now the number of interconnects with a multiplicity of vendors makes this unworkable generally. Consequently, one must be aware that the fact that one is testing, and the general nature of the results of those tests, are not secret for long.

The Test Site Interests

An effective beta test requires close cooperation from the test sites. Gaining this participation and cooperation requires understanding a site's motive for being part of a test. Firms consider and sometimes even compete to be part of a beta test program in order to do the following:

1. Get experience with the newest technology ahead of competitors.
2. Have the opportunity to influence product design to yield a product which better fits the firm's particular needs.
3. Have the added attention of vendor personnel in learning how to use the new technology.
4. Develop a relationship with the vendor in anticipation of preferential treatment such as price breaks.
5. Enhance their reputation as a pioneer on the forefront of technology.

The most common reason to seek experience as a beta site is to be first with new technology. The University of Pennsylvania Library was a beta site for a do-it-yourself online search system from Telebase Systems because previous experience with similar systems indicated a latent constituent need which could be satisfied with an upgraded system.[26] Gillette approached Digital Equipment to become a beta

---

[24]P. Korzeniowski, "Symphony Gets Mixed Reviews from Beta Test Site," *Computerworld,* August 13, 1984, p. 6.
[25]B. Hoard, ". . . But Beta Test Site Encounters Rough Seas," *Computerworld,* May 16, 1983, p. 7.
[26]E. G. Fayen, "The Answer Machine and Direct Connect: Do-It-Yourself Searching in Libraries," *Online,* September 1988, pp. 13–16, 19–21.

site for an office automation and communications software package. Gillette's director of MIS commented: "We begged them [to allow Gillette to be a beta site]. They had a system that no one else had that solved our particular need at the time."[27] Alper also reports that General Electric approached Coefficient Systems to beta their product. In this situation, General Electric did achieve the second benefit noted above. It explained its later adoption of the Coefficient Systems' product by saying: "We had tested their software. . . . As a matter of fact, they took most of the suggestions we gave them and incorporated them into the next version of the product."[28]

It is clear from these first two benefits sought by test sites that vendor and test site interests do not always perfectly align themselves with one another. A site may wish a long test period to keep the product from general availability to competitors. More important, though, the sites want customization. This places a heavy burden on the vendor to make sure that these benefits are widely sought by the market.

Important secondary benefits 3, 4, and 5 provided added impetus. Stamps reports that some firms try to develop a reputation as a beta tester in order to attract the top technical personnel in the computer industry.[29]

Understanding these inducements is necessary if the firm is to overcome the perceived barriers to being a test site. The president of Remington Shavers and Knives is not atypical in his view: "I don't like being a beta site."[30] The most common concerns are these:

1. The benefits to the test site are all uncertain. The product may never come to market or the test may reveal that it is not very well suited to the purpose of the tester.
2. If the function being performed by the beta system is a critical one for the tester's operation, a parallel system may have to be run because the beta system cannot be relied upon to do the job with the required accuracy.
3. The participation does involve a time commitment in learning how to use the system and provide the desired information to the vendor.

Explicit awareness of these potential barriers and attractions to being part of a beta program is very useful in terms of constructing a test so that the desired type of site is willing to be part of the program.

Summary

Beta tests are a staple of industrial new product development. Their effective execution can be crucial to the proper design and ultimate market success of product. This chapter has set out explicitly the vendor and test site perspectives on beta programs.

---

[27] A. Alper, "Beta Sites: Pioneer Users Take Risks to Grab Technical Edge," *Computerworld,* August 25, 1986, pp. 1, 15.
[28] Ibid.
[29] "Beta Site Politics."
[30] "POS Flexibility Keep Remington Sharp," *Chain Store Age Executive* (July 1990), pp. 49–50.

The purpose of the test—which can vary markedly from one situation to the next—drives the optimal program design and thus must be set clearly. The incentives presented by the vendor yield certain participation and cooperation levels from potential sites programs. The relationship of the elements is as follows:

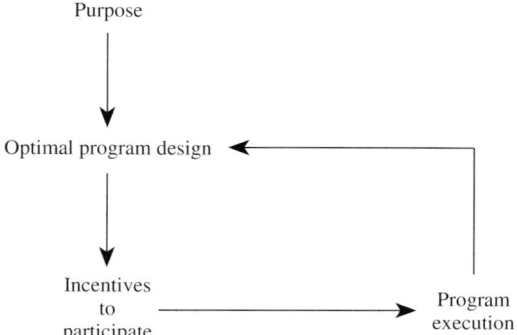

Many beta programs yield substantially less benefit (and in some cases have a negative net impact) to vendors than could be obtained. This chapter argues for more systematically setting priorities on purposes, guarding against threats to validity, and better understanding test site motivations as a path to greater contribution from this stage of the new product development process.

CHAPTER 19
Designing Channels of Distribution

We present a framework and a method for addressing the new product channel choice decision. We offer a six-step method that involves:

- *Disaggregating and prioritizing a distribution channel by customers' channel function requirements.*
- *Obtaining and combining customers' (and key informants') evaluations of the channel functions.*
- *Benchmarking existing channels (one's own as well as competitors').*
- *Identifying and constructing effective channel alternatives.*
- *Quantifying the short-term and long-term benefits and costs of each alternative.*
- *Selecting the appropriate channel by trading off the opportunities versus constraints posed by existing channel networks (if applicable).*

The method requires extensive management participation to facilitate its implementation. We provide an illustrative application to demonstrate its managerial usefulness.

For many businesses, the successful launch of new products is critical to maintaining market leadership. Unfortunately, empirical data indicate that one-third to one-half of all new products fail to meet a firm's financial and marketing goals.[1] A survey of 183 Fortune 1,000 firms indicated that nearly half of them had new product failures exceeding 40 percent.[2] This result is indeed surprising because these

---

V. Kasturi Rangan prepared this note.
Copyright © 1994 by the President and Fellows of Harvard College.
Harvard Business School note 594-116.

[1] Booz Allen & Hamilton, *New Product Management for the 1980s* (New York: Booz Allen & Hamilton, 1982).

[2] G. Dean Kortge (1989), "Simultaneous New Product Development: Reducing the New Product Failure Rate," *Industrial Marketing Management* 18, no. 4 (1989), pp. 301–6.

failed products had been screened for technical soundness and commercial feasibility. Various explanations have been offered for these failures: insufficient attention to the commercialization process, lack of management support, and poor marketing planning and execution. In this chapter, we focus on one aspect of the launch decision: the choice of distribution channels. We offer a method to systematically evaluate, plan, and execute the channel choice decision for new industrial products.

The primary question is about channel structure; that is, which intermediary, or intermediary combination, is best suited to take the new product to market? There is an equally important corollary question: How should the intermediary network be managed once it is up and running? This and related management issues are dealt with in greater detail in Chapter 34, "Reorienting Channels of Distribution."

Fundamentally, the approach that we offer is similar to that suggested by Stern and Sturdivant[3] and Rangan, Menezes, and Maier.[4] The starting point is the customer and the building block is the channel function. In our experience the method has worked best when implemented by a cross-functional task force headed by a senior executive reporting directly to the CEO. The new product development team in many cases could double up as the channels task force. It is important for the task force, however, to commission appropriate teams to participate in the various steps, rather than assume all the expertise themselves. We first present a schematic overview of the design method, highlighting its six important steps, followed by an illustrative application.

The Channel Design Framework

Step 1 consists of identifying homogeneous customer segments. Obviously, customers with similar requirements will need similar channel sources. It is important to keep in mind, however, that a customer is usually an end user and rarely a channel intermediary. For example, producers of agricultural chemicals should target the farmer and not the dealer. But producers of plastic pellets for making milk bottles should probably focus on the "dairy," not the "consumer," because that is where the product has value in the eyes of the end user. A dairy, especially a large one, will certainly need to worry about the cost and quality of the milk bottles. In some cases (e.g., a small dairy), the molder who manufactures the bottle might be the more appropriate end user. In any case, there should be a thoughtful end user, rather than intermediary, focus.

While advocating an emphasis on the end user may appear rather obvious, in our experience this has been a hotly debated issue in several business applications of this approach. Many industrial marketers have long looked upon their distribution channels as "customers" and rarely bothered to look beyond. Yet the primary

---

[3]Louis W. Stern and Frederick D. Sturdivant, "Customer-Driven Distribution Systems," *Harvard Business Review* (July–August 1987).

[4]V. Kasturi Rangan, A.J. Menezes, and Ernie Maier (1992), "Channel Selection for New Industrial Products: A Framework, Method, and Application," *Journal of Marketing* 56 (July 1992), pp. 69–82.

TABLE 1 Eight Generic Channel Functions

1. **Product information.** Customers seek more information on certain kinds of products, particularly products that are new and/or technically complex and those that have a rapidly changing technological component.

2. **Product customization.** Some products inherently need technical modification; they require customization to fit the customer's production requirements (e.g., special steel for a maker of surgical instruments). Many times, however, even a standard product may need to fulfill specific customer requirements or factors such as size or grade.

3. **Product quality assurance.** A customer emphasizes product integrity and reliability because of product consequences for the customer's own operations; for instance, a standard chemical may be of utmost importance to pharmaceutical manufacturers, given the liability associated with a defective final product. This is a measure of the application's importance to the customer.

4. **Lot size.** This function reflects the customer's dollar outlay for the product. If it has a high unit value or is used extensively, it is likely to represent a significant financial decision for the customer and is likely to lead to a concentrated purchasing effort.

5. **Assortment.** A customer may need a broad range of products and may require one-stop shopping. For example, an electrical contractor may need products that satisfy different electrical codes, depending on the nature of the project. At other times, assortment needs may simply be related to the breadth of the product line (e.g., size) and availability of complementary products (e.g., wires with electrical switches).

6. **Availability.** Some customer environments require the channel to support a high degree of product availability. These are usually customers whose product-usage rate is difficult to predict (e.g., spare parts, because they are required only when a machine breaks down), or customers who will switch to competition rather than wait when the product is unavailable. Notions of demand uncertainty and requirements of buffer inventory are related to this function.

7. **After-sales service.** Customers need services such as installation, repair, maintenance, and warranty. Often the quality and availability of such postsales services will influence the initial sale. The nature of this service will obviously differ by industry. For example, in the computer industry the compatibility and availability of hardware and software upgrades may serve as a key purchasing influence.

8. **Logistics.** Transporting, storing, and supplying products to the end user involve levels of complexity. For example, transshipping and transporting hazardous chemicals may require special investments likely to increase handling costs. Moreover, once such investments are in place, governing their effective use will involve additional transaction costs.

purpose of the distribution channel is to satisfy customer/end user needs, and intermediaries are conduits to effect this goal. The recommended method here is not intended to undermine the role of the intermediary, only to view them as a means to an end and not an end in itself.

Step 2 consists of identifying and prioritizing the customer's channel function requirements. A generic list appears in Table 1, but it should be treated only as a starting point. Each product-market context is unique, and channel function requirements that best represent customers' reality are most likely to lead to effective channel solutions. This information should be elicited from customers in as fine-grained detail as possible. For instance, it would be useful to know how keen customers are for the three-year warranty instead of the one-year, and how much they would be willing to pay for it; how sensitive they are for a two-hour versus a six-hour service response time; and so on. Table 2 provides an example.

TABLE 2   Example: Channel Function Priorities and Operational Detail

Most Important

1. **Product information.** Customers would like complete technical knowledge of product construction. They would prefer the availability of an expert to supervise installation as well as initial use. After the initialization, customers would be satisfied to exchange performance characteristics via computer, seeking assistance only when necessary.

2. **Product warranty.** Customers would prefer a 3-year warranty and are not willing to pay more than a 5% price premium to receive the same. In case of a product breakdown, they would like it repaired within 4 hours, and in any case not beyond 24 hours. Customers are willing to pay for the labor charges if repaired within 4 hours.

Somewhat Important but Not Critical

3. **Application engineering.** Customers would like application engineers to visit installations every month to assist in optimizing the system in operation.

4. **Availability of complementary products.** Customers would like to source complementary products simultaneously from the same channel source if possible.

5. **Credit terms.** Customers would like a 90-day credit term, if possible, but they can live with 30-day credit terms.

In our experience, the data for this step are most effectively gathered simultaneously with Step 1 (segmentation data). This way, segmentation and channeling strategies are consistent with each other and reflective of customers' needs.

Data gathering in Step 2 has to be based on customer input. For new products, this equates to potential customers, but depending on the nature of the innovation, these potential users may or may not be able to provide reliable feedback. In these cases, we suggest using a team of experts who have special knowledge of the products and how customers are likely to buy and use them. There are two such groups of experts. First are customer lead users. Eric von Hippel[5] identifies them as "users whose present strong needs will become general in a marketplace months or years in the future. Since lead users are familiar with conditions that lie in the future for most others, they can serve as a need-forecasting laboratory for marketing research." A second group of experts is often found in-house.[6] In the new-product channel context, judgmental projections of experienced salespeople, product managers, sales managers, and product development engineers can compensate for the absence of extensive customer data on purchases and usage behaviors.

Step 3 consists of benchmarking the seller's existing channel capabilities as well as competitors' channels with respect to customers' channel function requirements. Data from Step 2 will serve to prioritize and anchor customers' desired (or ideal) level of channel functions. A supplier executing at that level can therefore be assured of the lion's share of the business. But the supplier's channel capabilities may not match this functional profile. The larger the deviation on the important

---

[5]E. Von Hippel, "Lead Users: A Source of Novel Product Concepts," *Management Science* 32, no. 7 (1986), pp. 791–805.

[6]Jean-Claude Larreche and Reza Moinpour, "Managerial Judgement in Marketing: The Concept of Expertise," *Journal of Marketing Research* 20 (May 1983), pp. 110–21.

TABLE 3 Channel Benchmarking

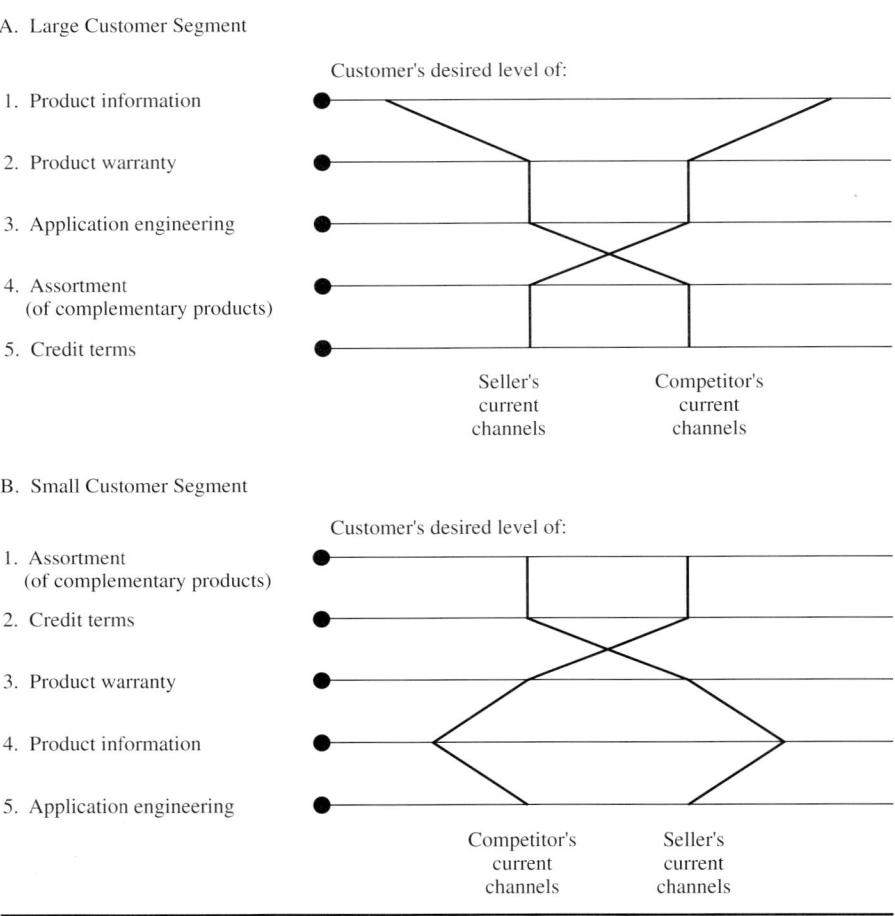

functions, the less the chances of attracting customers. It is a good idea at this stage to also benchmark the channel capabilities of leading competitors. This will provide a comprehensive map of the company's relative channel strengths and weaknesses.

In the example in Table 3, the leading competitor uses a direct salesforce channel and is therefore able to provide a relatively high level of customer intimacy with respect to product information, product warranty, and application engineering functions, whereas the target firm uses a distributor channel and is therefore able to provide a better level of service with respect to availability of complementary products and credit terms. The firm's relative channel profile for two customer segments is shown. But because the large customers and small customers prioritize channel functions differently, the target company is likely to do poorly with the large customers if it were to sell the new product through its existing channels. On the other hand, it has a stronger profile with small customers because its distributors provide superior "assortment" and "credit terms."

When the various product options in the market are comparable in product functions, features, and price, Step 3 serves as a direct calibration of channel effectiveness. If there are product differences, however, the relative deviations from the customers' channel function requirements will not neatly map onto projected sales/market share. This is why some companies prefer to have product development people on the channels task force. Having the benchmarking and calibration step executed by the same team that identified, clarified, and prioritized customers' channel function requirements ensures measurement consistency and reliability.

Step 4 consists of creatively interpreting the output from Steps 2 and 3 to arrive at the feasible channel options that would satisfy customers' requirements. For example, large customers' needs from Table 3 could be potentially served by a direct salesforce, and small customers by a distributor channel. But it is also possible to serve large customers with a combination of direct salesforce and distributors, whereby the direct salesforce would handle the product information, product warranty, and application engineering functions, and the distributors would handle the product assortment and credit terms. Usually, various channel alternatives will be available to take a product to market (e.g., agents, brokers, manufacturers' reps, value-added resellers). The role of the channels task force here is to creatively identify channel alternatives with the potential of getting closer to customers' ideal requirements. For the example, in Table 4, Option 1 (seller → sales force → distributor → customer) is the current capability. Options 2 and 3 are hybrid combinations whereby the salesforce/agents perform a set of channel functions, and the

TABLE 4   **Generating Alternatives**

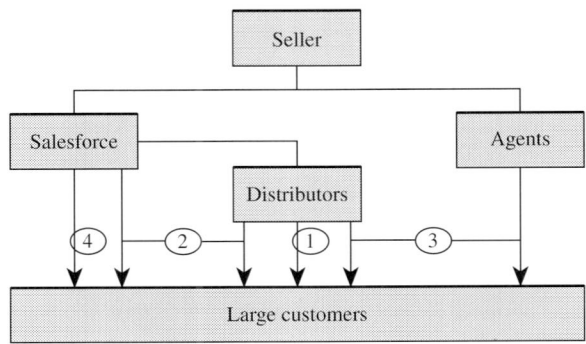

Option 1   Current method of going to market.
Option 2   Salesforce and distributors sharing channel functions among them.
Option 3   Agents and distributors sharing channel functions among them.
Option 4   Salesforce performing all channel functions.

distributors supplement the rest. It would be ideal for the salesforce/agents to deliver the product information, product warranty, and application engineering functions, and for the distributors to deliver the product assortment and credit function. This way both the large and small customers would be happy. Finally, Option 4 is a pure direct salesforce alternative, which would please the large customers.

It is important at this stage not to be restricted by real or imagined constraints. Issues of channel cost or conflict should be strictly deferred to Step 5. For example, one may conclude that under Option 1, the seller's existing distributors would be unable to adequately satisfy customers' product information, product warranty, and application engineering needs. But that should be no reason to rule out the option. If feasible, one should assume that with appropriate investments and training, distributors could rise to the desired level. Such an option should then be considered in the choice set at this stage.

Step 5 consists of systematically evaluating the benefits and costs associated with each option. Revenues, market share, market penetration, transaction costs, start-up costs, and opportunity costs must all be considered. Channel costs are not only influenced by the depth and extent of channel functions to be performed, but also by competitive behavior that influences the availability of channels. Varying investment strategies for each option from Step 4 will lead to differing customer satisfaction levels and consequently varying levels of outputs (revenue, profits, share, etc.). Investment options that push the profile in Table 3 closest to the customer's ideal will lead to the best outcomes, but that may come at a huge cost. Thus the options being considered here will have to be a multiple of those from Step 4—varying investment levels for each option. This analysis should be as quantitative and as specific as possible. An estimate of intensity (and number) of distributors, for example, is useful information. Qualitative factors such as channel motivation and level of conflict/cooperation may be considered as well. The appropriate channel, of course, is a sensible trade-off between output (e.g., revenues) and input (e.g., transaction costs). Companies with multiple product-market segments may draw up a short list of appropriate strategies for each segment rather than prematurely locking in on one. The reason for this becomes clear in Step 6.

Step 6 consists of elaborating the channel overlaps for multiproduct, multimarket businesses by aggregating the output from Step 5. Channel synergies and dysfunctionalities across product-market segments should be discussed, and trade-offs made within the pool of appropriate strategies. This discussion is likely to be productive and objective if Step 5 data are largely quantitative. Channel designers then have an estimate of the systemwide cost for trading each best option from Step 5. Benefit–cost analysis then becomes more meaningful, and if necessary the company might be better off investing in conflict resolution mechanisms rather than skipping customer-oriented optimal channels. Strategic long-run factors become very important at this stage of the evaluation. The key question is, "Do the channels provide a market advantage? Does it reflect strategy?"

Table 5 shows three different optimal channels for the three different target segments of a company. There are likely to be practical difficulties in the coexistence of these three channels. First, Segments 1 and 2 may be somewhat hard to demar-

TABLE 5 Optimal Channels for Three Segments

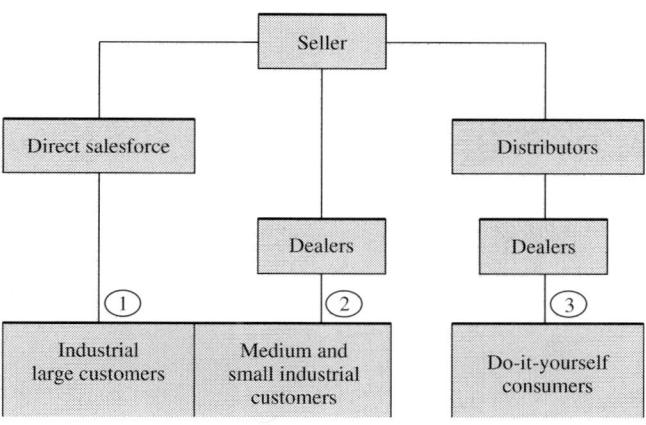

cate, especially with respect to the medium-sized accounts. Second, "dealers" for the industrial and consumer markets may overlap in some cases. But if the company's strategic focus was on the industrial market and, say, this accounted for 80 percent of the market potential, it may make a lot of sense to serve Segment 3 through industrial dealers (Channel 2) as well. Again, knowing the potential conflicts between the direct salesforce and dealers for the medium-sized accounts, it may be wise to negotiate dealer agreements carefully up front. Alternatively, as shown in Table 6, if a hybrid approach was second best for both of the industrial segments, and if the projected decrease in revenues and profits is less than the anticipated conflict costs of the ideal channel, it may simply make sense to go with the second best solution.

TABLE 6 The Second Best Option: Hybrid Channel for Industrial Customers

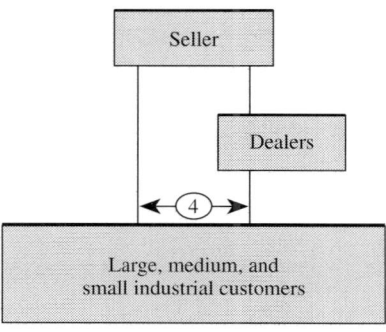

The key to effectively implementing this step is totally dependent on the care used and detail undertaken in the previous steps. In the absence of well-calibrated channel maps and concrete financial data, this crucial final step could deteriorate into a slugfest of personal hunches, which is exactly what this systematic procedure tries to overcome.

Application: A Description of the Process[7]

What follows is a brief description of how the channel design method was implemented in a division of a large industrial company.

Manufacturing process changes had enabled this company to develop a new product, Scotchfiber (disguised name). Customers used Scotchfiber-type products for a variety of applications such as deburring metal parts; deflashing plastic and paper utensils; cleaning golf balls, tiles, and rubber articles; gripping fabric in textile mills; and containing components for assembly. Management was convinced of Scotchfiber's superiority, especially in the $100 million industrial cleaning and finishing market, which consisted of many specialty applications. The new product was to be directed originally only at large industrial users in various industries. Independent market research confirmed that these customers uniformly sought a high level of technical benefits. The product launch team headed by the director for marketing operations served as the channels task force.

Scotchfiber was a new product line for this company. Potential customers currently used alternative solutions to address their needs, and Scotchfiber applications had little overlap with the company's existing product lines. About 95 percent of the company's current products were sold to end users through a network of more than 500 independent distributors with the help of the company's 100 salespeople. Because of the new product's numerous potential applications and the strength of its distribution channels, management was inclined to route Scotchfiber through existing channels, which consisted of general-line finishing distributors.

With the help of the marketing manager, product manager, and two sales representatives, we worked out operational definitions for each of the eight channel functions identified in Table 1 to reflect the Scotchfiber marketing context. The function "product information," for example, was characterized by the degree of information a customer sought on (1) roll fiber length, fiber property, and construction density, and (2) usage properties, such as the ability to finish irregularly shaped pieces and interiors. The operational definitions for each function were typed on separate cards to be used as the basic interview guide.

We chose as key respondents 10 potential "customer experts" who were at the leading edge of adopting and using the new product. These lead users were considered the trendsetters in their industry and either had already started to use Scotch-

---

[7] A large part of this section is extracted from V. Kasturi Rangan, A. J. Menezes, and Ernie Maier, "Channel Selection for New Industrial Products: A Framework, Method, and Application," *Journal of Marketing* 56 (July 1992). Printed with permission of the American Marketing Association.

fiber in production trials or were in the process of placing the trial order. In addition, we selected 11 individuals from the company who had special knowledge about the product and/or its customer applications. Some of these "producer experts" were intensely involved in Scotchfiber product and application development, and the rest were involved in marketing the product to lead users.

Experts were interviewed individually to obtain their evaluations of customers' anticipated channel function requirements and priorities as they saw them. We chose three years as the time horizon for the new product channel study because the company's top management estimated this to be the time frame in which Scotchfiber, if successful, could establish itself in the market.

Combining the experts' evaluations is essential to making a good channel decision because knowledge is generally dispersed in the early stages of the product life cycle. Two broad approaches are used for combining experts' opinions: (*a*) group-oriented, where experts interact, inform, and build consensus, such as the Delphi method,[8] and (*b*) analytical (statistical), when interaction among the experts is impossible because of physical separation or confidentiality. Because some of the lead-use customers were considering proprietary applications of the Scotchfiber technology, we did not use the interactive Delphi method, but instead chose a mathematical "consensus" method developed by Robert Winkler.[9]

The new product channel profiles were presented to the new product launch team, which was made up of six members of the division's marketing and sales staff who were responsible for drafting an initial Scotchfiber marketing plan. None had participated as experts in the earlier evaluations. The launch team also benchmarked the capabilities of its existing channels as well as Scotchfiber's indirect competitors. This was done by a subcommittee of the task force aided by a market research firm. Armed with these data, the launch team met several times to reach the following conclusions:

- The anticipated customer requirements on product information, product customization, and product quality assurance for the new product considerably exceeded the current capabilities of the division's general-line finishing distributors.
- The anticipated channel function profile after the product was established (i.e., 3 years) matched that of the division's other products currently being routed through general-line finishing distributors.
- A new class of distributors, fiber specialists, which the company did not currently use, would also be able to satisfy the functional requirement for the established product. However, they would have difficulties fulfilling the first three functional requirements for the new product, but to a lesser degree than the current distributors.

---

[8]H. A. Linstone and M. A. Turoff, *The Delphi Method: Techniques and Applications* (Boston: Addison-Wesley, 1975).

[9]Robert L. Winkler, "Combining Probability Distributions from Dependent Information Sources," *Management Science* 27 (April 1981), pp. 479–88.

TABLE 7 **Feasible Channel Options**

	Now (when product is new)	Three Years Later (when product is established)
Option 1	Salesforce	• General-line finishing distributors
Option 2	Salesforce	• Fiber specialist
Option 3	Salesforce and general-line finishing distributors	• General-line finishing distributors
Option 4	Salesforce and fiber specialists	• Fiber specialists
Option 5	Salesforce and general-line finishing distributors	• Fiber specialists
Option 6	Salesforce and fiber specialists	• General-line finishing distributors

Six channel paths were initially identified as feasible options for taking the product to market (see Table 7): two of these were pure options, while the other four were hybrid combinations of salesforce and distributors sharing channel tasks for the new product. Options 5 and 6, however, were eliminated as the group thought both of these options would entail very high switching costs and channel conflicts given the required change from one class of distributor to the other. It just didn't make sense to start with fiber specialists and switch to general-line distributors and vice versa. The costs of taking back inventory and any legal fees for rewriting and defending new contracts would far surpass the benefits. Thus, the choices for the optimal channel were reduced to four.

At this company, new products were assigned sales and profit targets: Line managers were expected to achieve or surpass both. The division's area sales managers and their key sales representatives were contacted for revenue and cost estimates of going to market using each of the four channel options. Instead of estimating variations in sales revenues through each option, area sales managers felt more confident in estimating the intensity of channel coverage each option required for achieving the fixed sales target. Knowing this, managers could estimate the cost of each channel option. Distribution costs were disaggregated into seven elements: demand generation (salesforce time, marketing, and advertising), distributor technical training, distributor administrative training, sales support (inventory carrying and customer credit), logistics (order processing, transportation, and warehousing), distribution margin, and opportunity costs (of salesforce time taken away from selling existing products).

Many cost elements, such as logistics, sales support, and distribution margin, can be computed once the channel options and the details of its implementation are known. But others, such as distributor training costs and opportunity costs, are essentially judgments for new products and channels that were obtained from area sales managers and subsequently refined by headquarters' accounting staff. We aggregated the costs for each channel option. Because the sales target was identical for all four options, the optimal channel in this case was the cost-minimizing option. The relative cost numbers are shown in Table 8. Option 3 was the optimal choice.

TABLE 8 **Relative Costs of Feasible Channel Options**

	Demand Generation Costs	Distributor Training and Maintenance Costs		Sales Support Costs	Logistics Costs	Distribution Margin	Opportunity Costs	Total Cost Index
		Technical	*Administrative*					
Option 1	High	Low	Low	High	Medium	Low	Medium	102
Option 2	High	Medium	High	Medium	Medium	Medium	High	110
Option 3	Medium	Medium	Low	Medium	Low	High	Low	100
Option 4	Medium	Medium	High	Medium	Medium	High	High	111

In Option 3, the salesforce and the general-line finishing distributors together called on end users to establish the product and effect sales. In three years, these same distributors would be expected to take on full responsibility for the product line; by then, it was assumed that the distributors would be sufficiently trained to service and maintain the several applications for the product.

Conclusion

To evaluate the usefulness of the proposed method, we went back to the company a year after the new product launch to obtain information on how Scotchfiber was performing. We interviewed several members of the original launch team and a cross section of the field sales management and sales reps directly involved in the Scotchfiber marketing effort. A full year after launch, Scotchfiber sales were running 25 percent ahead of sales targets and profits were running 34 percent above expected levels.

Although these results pertain to evaluations at the end of the first year of a three-year planning horizon model, management believed the suggested method helped them make a good decision. Without the aid of this method, the company would have distributed the product through its 500 distributors, which, managers thought on hindsight, would have been a mistake. The company's decision makers initially underestimated the channel support required for the new product's launch. Formally incorporating customer judgments, an essential part of the method, helped remedy management misperception.

Our interviews also identified factors such as effective communication between headquarters and field sales as key reasons for Scotchfiber's success. But two of the top three reasons were "involvement of the direct sales force" and "the channel selection process." A key contribution of this research was the process itself. Other than bringing a conceptual framework to the new product channel decision, the research process integrated judgments from three important constituencies:

- Lead-use customers (the potential early adapters of the product).
- In-house experts (such as the product manager and distribution development manager).
- Line managers (sales reps and sales managers).

The process combined channel concepts with experts' judgments and managers' inputs to arrive at an appropriate channel for the new product. The managers' active participation generated substantial commitment to the method and facilitated its implementation. The very process of systematically focusing on the new product channel problem led to the discovery and improvement of several related (but not central to the method) tasks, all of which magnified the impact. There is a valuable lesson in this: The process of method development and implementation is perhaps as important as the underlying conceptual framework. While the method outlined here may be immediately more applicable to new product markets, the same principles have been used in several channel audits of mature product markets as well. Steps 1 to 3 are particularly useful. Knowing the capability of existing channels with respect to customers' channel function requirements and benchmarking them with competitors' channels provide useful diagnostics. While a structural change may not be feasible in some cases given long-established channel relationships, distribution managers can at least infer specific guidelines on how to manage existing channel networks to enhance their profile to be more in tune with customer needs.

SECTION III Managing Mature Products

CHAPTER 20 Beating the Commodity Magnet

All markets follow a cycle of growth and maturity, then commoditization and decline. In this chapter we argue that while commoditization of an industry may seem inevitable, the better-managed firms find a way to make money in the commodity cycle. These firms know how and when to differentiate their products through innovation, service, and customer partnerships, and how and when to offer a no-frills product and seek cost leadership. Four such strategic options are detailed and discussed.

Introduction[1]

According to conventional wisdom, all markets follow a cycle of growth and maturity, then commoditization and decline. Profits are to be found in the specialty industries—electronics, scientific equipment, and aerospace—while more mature industries beset by declining demand and overcapacity cannot sustain comparable profitability. Hence, many corporations throughout the 1980s had sought to divest their mature or commodity-type businesses, while redeploying resources into something more promising. Our research refutes this conventional wisdom. Many companies in commodity businesses perform as well as or better than their counterparts in specialty businesses because they have learned how to demonstrate value for their customers. They have mastered the art of beating the commodity magnet.

These firms in an increasing number of commodity businesses—blood collection products, replacement motors, and steel strapping, among others—are

---

V. Kasturi Rangan and George T. Bowman prepared this reading.
Copyright © 1994 by the President and Fellows of Harvard College.
Harvard Business School note 594-122.
[1]Reprinted by permission of the publisher from V. Kasturi Rangan and George T. Bowman, "Beating the Commodity Magnet," *Industrial Marketing Management* 21 (1992), pp. 215–24. Copyright © 1992 by Elsevier Science Inc.

becoming consistently profitable by knowing how and when to differentiate their products through innovation, service, and customer partnerships, and how and when to offer a no-frills product and seek cost leadership. These companies understand that commoditization can be a self-fulfilling prophecy in which lower price, profits, service, and customer loyalty interlock in a cycle of decline. While commoditization of an industry may seem to be inevitable, the better-managed firms find a way to make money in the commodity cycle, as the following examples suggest.

Blood Collection Products.[2]   Becton Dickinson & Company (BD) has maintained a commanding market share with a price premium in the market for needles, collection tubes, and lancets, despite low-price competition from a Japanese competitor, Terumo, Sherwood Medical, and entry attempts by Abbott Labs, Johnson & Johnson, and Corning Glass. Key success factors include stress on quality and the direction of its selling efforts to the lab technicians who actually use their products. One BD sales representative noted several instances when hospital administrators attempted to purchase less-expensive products but were rebuffed by bench technicians, who insisted on BD's well-known VACUTAINER® and MICROTAINER® name.

Replacement Motors.[3]   The replacement motor market for consumer durables has few entry barriers, hundreds of competitors, and distributors who have introduced private-label brands. When industry-leader GE began losing market share in the mid-1980s, it sought to learn more about customer requirements and discovered that 30 percent of all customers left the point-of-sale without the motors they had come to buy. In response, GE increased stock levels and efficiency of order fulfillment; it also fought price erosion by providing training and unique product information for wholesale counter personnel, and by creating a computerized cross-reference system that enabled wholesalers to determine which GE motor could be used as a replacement.

Steel Strapping.[4]   Despite low-cost competition from numerous competitors and fluctuating steel prices, Signode Industries has long maintained profitable industry leadership by taking a partnership approach to customer strapping requirements. Key elements in Signode's strategy are the study of each industry's strapping needs, the design of specialized equipment to meet those needs, and the service and sales of strapping consumables. Because of this systems sales approach, the Signode sales force maintains multiple contacts with customer organizations, ranging from vice presidents of manufacturing to plant managers and purchasing agents. In this way, Signode has become the standard-bearer of steel strapping; its competition has to provide products that fit into Signode equipment.

---

[2]Frank V. Cespedes and V. Kasturi Rangan, "Becton Dickinson and Company: Vacutainer Systems Division," Harvard Business School case no. 592–037.
[3]E. Raymond Corey, "GE Component Motors," Harvard Business School case no. 586-059.
[4]Rowland T. Moriarty, "Signode Industries," Harvard Business School case no. 587-157.

Commodity Magnet

The product life cycle concept is well known. It traces the evolution of new product markets from the product introduction stage through growth to maturity.[5] See Figure 1. The theory is that product adoption is slow at the beginning as early adopters try out the product. There is usually a need for customer education and close supplier assistance to tide over the early technical uncertainties. Over time, as these uncertainties are debugged, more customers adopt the product and the market begins to grow more rapidly. But wider market acceptance will often attract new competitors and the ensuing battle leads to price deterioration. Customers, who are by now quite knowledgeable about the product may not need the same hand-holding they required in the earlier stages. Consequently, they may seek price concessions, adding to the competitive price pressures in the market. In an attempt to seek and hold customers, some suppliers may attempt to differentiate their follow-on services such as quick shipment, product warranty, product availability, and so on. But provision of these services costs money, and not all customers may see the value in paying the higher price. Worse still, some customers, especially the large ones, may demand all these services at the lower price, and some suppliers will acquiesce to these demands to keep their factories running in an intensively competitive environment.

FIGURE 1

Product life cycle: implications

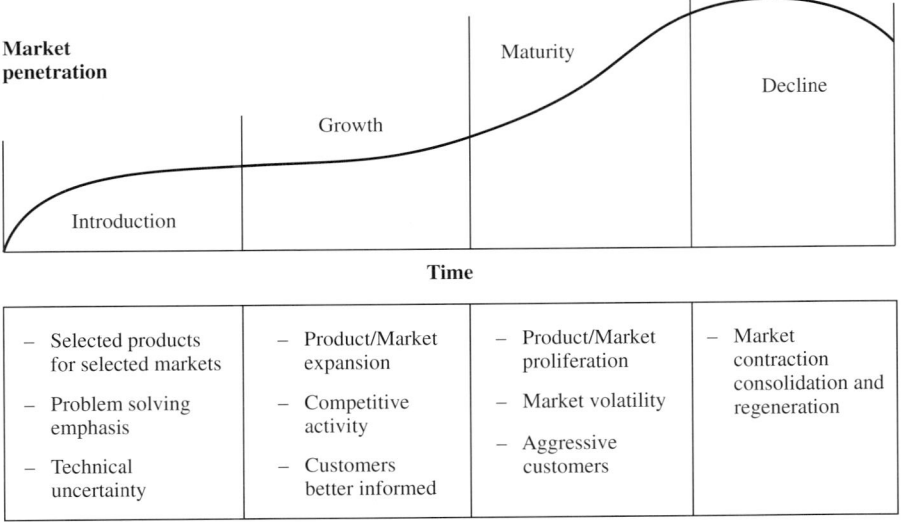

[5] See, for example, Philip Kotler, "Managing Products through Their Product Life Cycle," in *Marketing Management: Analysis, Planning, Implementation, and Control,* 7th ed. (Englewood Cliffs, N.J.: Prentice Hall, 1991), pp. 347–73.

FIGURE 2

Market life cycle: alternative framework

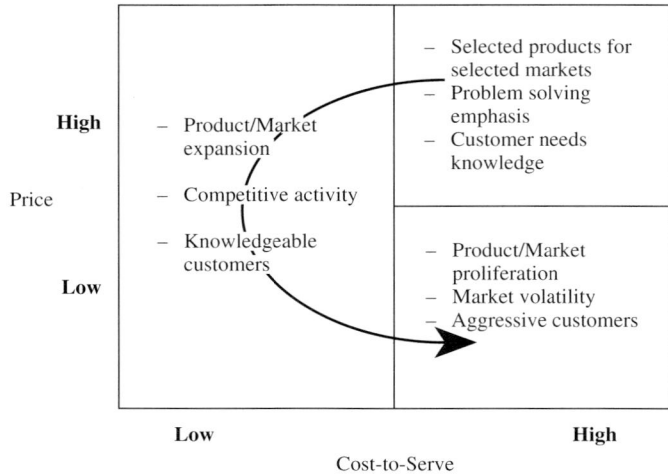

This description of the product life cycle sketched in Figure 1 has significant implications for managers when viewed along the two dimensions of price and cost-to-serve.[6] See Figure 2. The price dimension reflects the relative price of the product offering in comparison to other similar competing solutions. For a new product, the comparison is with existing, often inferior ways of solving the same problem. The cost-to-serve dimension again is a relative measure and reflects the marketing, sales, distribution, and customer service intensity needed to support the product during its life. It is easy to see from Figure 2 how the commodity trend could have grave implications for company profitability. As the market matures, relative prices tend to drop even as the cost-to-serve increases.

Figure 2 to some extent is a simplified explanation of the product life cycle dynamic. In some markets—for example, pharmaceuticals—there may be a significant pent-up demand for a new product, and if the product is protected by patents or technological advantages, the product may be able to command high prices at a relatively low cost-to-serve. Thus, the product could be launched as a "specialty" rather than an "augmented" offering. The offering may be augmented later when the pharmaceutical goes off patent. In other cases, the market evolution may proceed in other different ways, as indicated in Figure 3. In general, the commodity magnet has the tendency to pull the business from the northwest to the southeast quadrant, that is, from a specialty to a commodity.

But regardless of the nature of the product—grain or a computer—it is the market dynamics that distinguish a commodity. Most managers recognize the early warning signs of commoditization—increasing competition, availability of "me-too" products, customers' reluctance to pay for unnecessary features and services

---

[6]The matrix in Figure 2 is adapted from Benson P. Shapiro, V. Kasturi Rangan, Rowland T. Moriarty, and Elliot Ross, "Manage Customers for Profits (Not Just Sales)," *Harvard Business Review,* September–October 1987.

FIGURE 3

Market types and market evolution

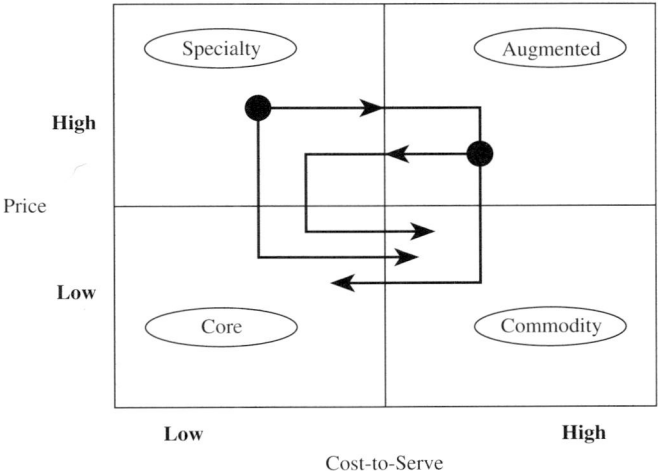

accompanying the product, and pressure on prices and margins in general.[7] Steadily and deliberately as the market transitions to a commodity type, many buyers begin to perceive the product and its suppliers to be homogeneous, and price becomes the predominant buying criterion.

A few key points that are worth highlighting: The commodity trends described above and sketched in Figures 1, 2, and 3 are inevitable in all product markets. The pace of commoditization may vary—six months in semiconductors to nearly 15 years in certain specialty chemicals, but every product market will eventually face the pull of the commodity magnet. It is important to note, however, that not every firm in the said product market will necessarily follow in the market trend. Each firm will take positions that are consistent with its capabilities and strategies. For example, while the personal computer industry may be rapidly commoditizing, individual players such as Apple, IBM, Compaq, and Dell may all take different positions on the product map shown in Figure 3. Thus, in a commodity market, there will coexist high-price–high-service players as well as low-price–low-service players. Different players will be offering augmented product, specialty products, and core products all at the same time.

Key Concepts

In order to formulate marketing strategies that are appropriate to avert the commodity magnet, it is important to understand a couple of key concepts that underlie the dynamic of the commodity trend. This is explained in Figure 4. The

---

[7]Benson P. Shapiro, "Specialties versus Commodities: The Battle for Profit Margins," Harvard Business School working paper no. 587-120.

FIGURE 4

Key concepts

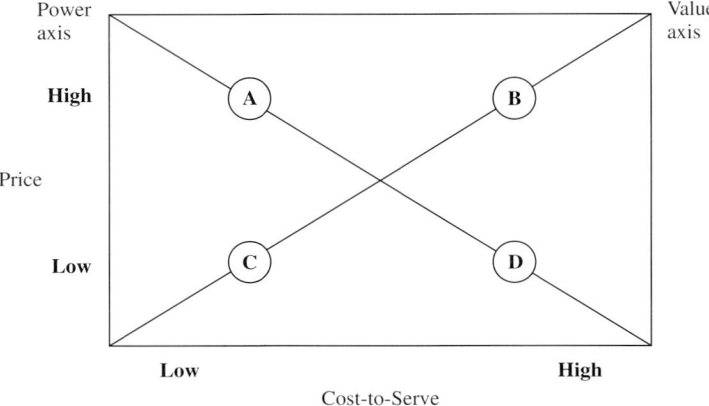

diagonal that runs from southwest to northeast represents an axis of value where a company charges a price that reflects the value of the service it provides. The southwest quadrant (C) represents a core, no-frills product that is not accompanied by highly augmented services. Correspondingly, the price paid by the customer is relatively low. On the other hand, the northeast quadrant (B) represents a product accompanied by intensive value-added services, for which the customer pays a higher price. All locations above the value diagonal signify that the company is able to extract a higher value than the services it renders, because customers perceive the firm's product as being superior to competitive offerings or substitutes. In short, all positions above the value diagonal reflect a product differentiation strategy. Positions below the value diagonal usually indicate that the firm is unable to extract the full value of the services it renders with its product. At the southeast corner (D), the company essentially gives away all its services free, perhaps in an effort to retain market share in a very competitive market environment. Thus, the cross diagonal represents an axis of power: the manufacturer is more powerful (differentiated) in the northwest and the customer in the southeast.

Clearly, strategy A would be the most advantageous for any firm, and will likely lead to the highest profits; the strategy is based on product feature/function superiority. Strategies B and C ensure an adequate and fair return to the firm, with B emphasizing differentiation through augmented services, and C emphasizing a low cost approach. Which strategy a firm should adopt, B or C, depends on its relative strengths and weaknesses with respect to other competitors in the field. Strategy D is rarely consciously adopted by any firm. Because of the customer and competitive environment, a firm reluctantly sinks to that quadrant. While a firm may be able to survive that environment in the short run, it is guaranteed to lead to losses in the long run because no business can afford to give away services without correspondingly increasing prices.

When a product is dragged down to a commodity status, the conventional marketing wisdom is to attempt to push it back up again by differentiating the physical product,[8] or adding value by innovating the product delivery system. There are several problems with that prescription. Some low-tech products may not have any further scope for product improvements. And even for high-tech products, not all firms have the resources to effect the necessary innovations. Moreover, investments in systems to add value are often costly (e.g., computerizing the order entry and inventory systems). Most of all, it is not entirely obvious that customers will place value on the improved product or service features—after all, it is a commodity market! Under such circumstances, what does a manager do to preserve the firm's profit position? How does one manage to beat the commodity cycle?

Differentiation Strategies

Firms with differentiated products operating from quadrant A (in Figure 4) often cannot resist the temptation to charge high prices even as the market rapidly gravitates toward a commodity status. We believe that in a true commodity market, firms would be unable to sustain the A position without seriously undermining their market share. If a firm does not offer a real customer benefit or product differentiation, customers, as they become knowledgeable, are likely to switch to competition rather than stay with a firm that is apparently overpriced for the services it offers. It is much easier to move toward the value diagonal from A, before commoditization occurs. Once the market has already moved in that direction, to rise up from the D quadrant to the value diagonal is far more difficult for reasons we discuss later in this chapter. On the other hand, if the A position is sustainable because of true product advantages, it would be financially unwise to surrender the extra margins prematurely. One needs to keep a close eye on the market trend for signs of commoditization.

The key idea is to move toward a stable position along the value diagonal so that the manufacturer is firmly entrenched in quadrant B providing an augmented product, or in quadrant C providing a core product. In either case, both the firm and its customers are involved in a fair exchange. Although it may seem that there are unlimited directions to move toward the equilibrium axis, Figure 5 shows that a firm has only four really feasible options. Any other strategy would be difficult for either a firm or its customers to adopt. A firm in position A, for instance, attempting to move toward a position along the value diagonal, would find it impossible to pull off any movement in the AB to AC range, because that would require the company either to drop price or increase service, or both. This is likely to cause a strain on profits in what is already a tough market. Management is hardly likely to approve a plan that voluntarily surrenders profits when other potential options are available. Similarly, for a firm in position D, attempting to move its customers to the equilibrium axis along the DB to DC range would involve increasing price or decreasing service, or both. This is likely to lead to a steep loss in customers and market share.

---

[8]Theodore Levitt, "Differentiation of Anything," *Harvard Business Review,* January–February 1980. Also see Philip Kotler, *Marketing Management: Analysis, Planning, and Control,* 6th ed. (Englewood Cliffs, N.J.: Prentice Hall, 1988), p. 448.

FIGURE 5

Strategies to beat the commodity magnet

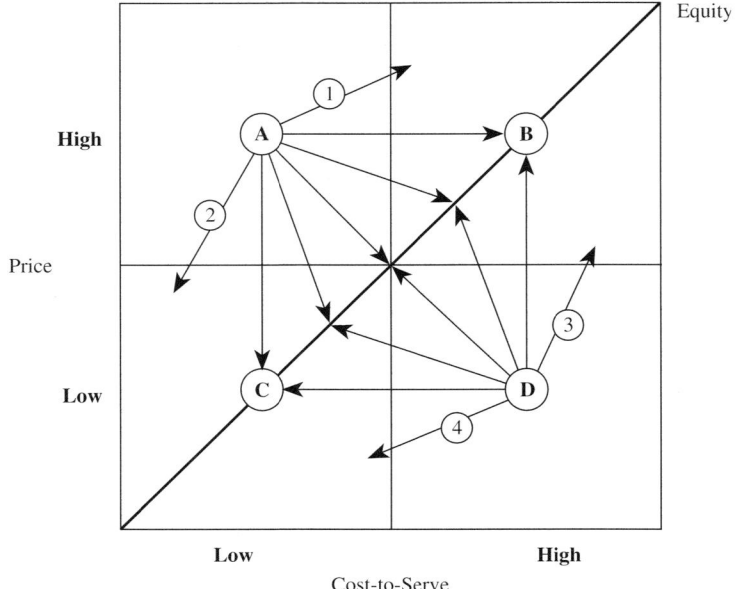

In the final analysis, there are only four feasible strategies, two that can be implemented before the onset of commoditization and two after. These are:

1. *Value-added strategy:* Moving to the value diagonal by increasing price as well as augmenting services.
2. *Process innovation strategy:* Moving to the value diagonal mainly by decreasing price and some cost-to-serve as well.
3. *Market focus strategy:* Moving to the value diagonal by focusing on customers who would pay the additional price for augmented services because they value them.
4. *Service innovation strategy:* Moving to the value diagonal mainly by decreasing cost-to-serve. Again, like the market focus, this strategy will lead to a reorientation of the customer base.

Value-added Strategy. Value-added strategy allows a firm to forestall price erosion by providing value-added services to the product. Such services necessarily should go beyond those that a customer would normally expect (e.g., on-time order fulfillment). Installation, training, and technical support are among the many that are often used. Effective differentiators begin by asking what the buyer values. Learning may require formal research and should generate a comprehensive list of possible product and service offerings for each customer segment. Effective differentiators then critically evaluate the list of possible service offerings, choosing those with the greatest potential to leverage customer value over cost-to-serve. In any case, the strategy's purpose is to pamper the customer with a lot of services, enabling the supplier to earn a price premium over competition. The basic approach is one of bundling: The product and services when combined form a unique package that the customer values and is willing to pay extra money for.

The value-added strategy was central to the success of Becton Dickinson's VACUTAINER trademark systems division. Given the increasing competition and increasing customer sensitivity to price, the company consciously built its brand name and reputation. The wide assortment of needles and tubes, and their unique color-coded product identification schemes for the dozens of blood tests doctors performed, gave it a quality edge and image. The company complemented this strong product quality with an intense relationship effort at the bench level. That is, the company's sales force called on and cultivated hospital laboratory technicians who actually used the product. The combined effect of the value-added strategies has helped the company retain market leadership and profits even in a rapidly commoditizing market.

We should emphasize, however, that value-added strategies that do not provide real value to the customer are not likely to survive as the market deteriorates to a commodity status. Successful marketers like Becton Dickinson, by constantly enhancing the product and the delivery system, had so trained the customer to their standards and services that switching to a competitor's product would involve substantial retraining costs.

Customers' costs of possession and usage, in addition to acquisition, should be made an inherent part of the selling proposition. For instance, the benefit of providing just-in-time inventories may outweigh the price premium. Thus, the point here is not one of additional services alone, but value added, in such a way that the customer benefits are quantifiable. In short, value-added strategies that can clearly demonstrate added savings to the customer are likely to be sustainable in the long run.[9] Customers' costs of switching (to a competing product) are an important part of the cost calculation under this strategy. The seller attempts to minimize the buyers' costs of acquisition, possession, and switching. We call this value-in-use to distinguish it from the simple value-added strategy described earlier.

The value-in-use strategy was successfully employed in GE's replacement motors business. To improve customer service, GE helped its dealers to measure and improve fill rate (percentage of time customer orders are successfully filled in from stock) and average delivery time of in-stock and nonstock items (i.e., items that distributors get from GE after receipt of customer order). In addition, it installed a stocking and ordering information system for improving customer service. Contractors seeking GE motors could now obtain them easily, and the little extra they paid in price was more than offset by the near elimination of delay, costs of waiting, inconvenience, and uncertainty. The system helped customers routinize their procurement functions, enabling them to concentrate on their primary business-providing maintenance and repair services. The gain in alternative revenue far outweighed the extra price of motors.

---

[9]John L. Forbis and Nitin T. Mehta, "Value-Based Strategies for Industrial Products," *Business Horizons* 24, no. 3 (1981).

Process Innovation Strategy. The crux of this strategy is to offer customers product at dramatically lower prices for the few services that are now stripped away. Usually such a steep drop in price is only feasible if the firm is able to innovate its design at considerably lower manufacturing costs, without significantly altering, and if possible enhancing, the features and performance of the current product. Such a strategy is often possible in new high-technology industries, where the component parts have rapidly improving performance-to-price ratios. The table below, for example, shows the significant jump in the performance/price ratios of successive generations of Intel's semiconductor chips for personal computers.

Intel Chip	Launch	MIPS	Price ($)	Performance/ Price Index
286	1982	1	$ 100	1.0
386	1985	5	200	2.5
486	1989	20	400	5.0
(586) Pentium	1993	100	1,000	10.0

Similar performance-to-price gains have been obtained in other key components like disk drives as well. The end result is a dramatic reduction in cost and increase in performance for each successive generation of personal computers. But even in traditional industries, such an improvement is possible because of innovative manufacturing technologies that firms are often able to develop. The dramatic gains made by innovative assembly line technology in the auto industry are a case in point.

The net effect of a process innovation strategy is usually an increase in market share and a rapid buildup of a loyal customer base. An example of the price innovation strategy was Digital Equipment Corporation's (DEC) VAX 11/780 minicomputer introduction. In the late 1970s, just before the proliferation of the minicomputer market and the invention of microcomputers, DEC came out with the VAX minicomputer. Instead of going head-to-head with market leader IBM's service offerings, DEC's managers reasoned that a segment of highly knowledgeable customers would be willing to take additional responsibilities for servicing the product and developing software applications. DEC's early insight enabled it to offer a highly desirable machine that had a much lower price, with fewer services, than IBM, but at a very attractive performance specification for the price. The company was quickly able to capture significant market share and profits as a result.

Sony's introduction of the 1270 superdata projector in 1989 is another example of the process innovation strategy.[10] Until then Barco Projection Systems, a Belgian company, and Electrohome, a Canadian company, shared worldwide leadership for overhead video projection equipment capable of reading and transmitting graphic signals. But unlike its competitors, Sony was not a niche player, but a mass-marketer with dominant share in the lower-end video and data markets. In addition,

---

[10]"Barco Projection Systems," Harvard Business School case no. 9-591-133.

Sony also produced a critical component, the picture tube, in-house. With a projected sales volume of about five times Barco or Electrohome, Sony brought the 1270 projector to the higher-end graphic market at prices 30 to 40 percent below existing levels, a clear attempt to widen the market and capture significant share. Because of its mass production and marketing capabilities, Sony was operating on a cost curve that was different from that of its smaller rivals, who were batch producers for niche markets.

Market Focus Strategy. While the earlier two strategies were proactive responses in anticipation of market commoditization, the market focus strategy is a reactive effort to stem the tide after a firm has already been dragged down to the D quadrant. The thrust of this strategy is to increase price more than the accompanying improvements in service. To be successful, this approach inevitably involves a careful review of a firm's customer base to select only those customers for future relationship who value its augmented service offering.

Signode Corporation, which performed a similar study in 1984, after its market share and profits had steadily slumped over the last 10 years, found that a core group of customers highly valued its bundled offering of strapping equipment, supplies, and engineering service. Signode was the only company in 1984 that provided strapping equipment and engineering advice (on a customer's packaging needs), in addition to supplying commodity strapping. Some customers found this service most valuable, and the savings they derived as a result far exceeded the price premium they paid on Signode's strapping. Signode's managers realized that their uniform across-the-board marketing policies did not allow it to segment its customer base by customer benefit derived. Subsequent segmentation enabled it to offer a bundled product-service combination to its value-seeking customers and an unbundled offering to its price-seeking customers.

The market focus strategy usually leads to a decrease in overall market share because of the clear focus on selected accounts, but an increase in profits because service is now provided only to those customers who value it. While the market focus strategy, like the value added strategy, results in providing the customer with a benefit that is valued, one is a proactive approach in anticipation of the commodity trend, while the other is a reactive approach to stem the tide. With the market focus strategy, a firm's augmented services will have to provide a true customer benefit, rather than a perception of value. The value-in-use approach is the only way to demonstrate true savings for the customer. Product augmentation that cannot be translated into true cost savings will not work, because customers by now are fully familiar with competitive offerings and perceptual benefits will not soothe customers' desire for value. Communicating true value may require intense and prolonged product trials, but most importantly, it requires demonstrated superiority. Not everybody, therefore, can flippantly elect this strategy. Only some have the capability. Firms adopting this market focus strategy usually tend to have a narrow customer base of large accounts with deep partnerships. The firm may decide either to forgo the rest of its customer base or handle them separately as a price-sensitive segment (as the following discussion on service innovation will reveal).

Service Innovation Strategy. With this strategy, services judged to be uneconomical to provide in a price-competitive market are stripped away. Because significant price erosion has already occurred, this is often the only way to improve one's profit. To some extent, this strategy is a complement of the market focus strategy. Just as some customers find a true benefit from the augmented service offering, some others would rather take a price break instead of paying for costly services accompanying the product. If a firm is either not well positioned to offer augmented services, or does not have the desire to do so, it would make much more sense for it to adopt the service compression strategy.

Signode's main competitor in the steel strapping market, "Alpha," pursued this strategy in the face of rapid commoditization in the steel strapping industry. Alpha Company first halved its expensive sales force and switched a large proportion of its sales through less-expensive distributor channels. Next, it cut back ancillary services like custom designing of packaging equipment for its customers. In fact, the company stopped making packaging equipment entirely, preferring to source it from outside. It simply produced and sold steel strapping with no frills at 5 to 10 percent discounts below Signode. This strategy was meant to ensure profit gain for the company. And, like the market focus strategy, it is likely to lead to a market share loss as some service-seeking customers will certainly be turned away. But this need not always be the case.

Dell Computer Corporation, an Austin, Texas-based personal computer manufacturer, has established an extremely successful mail order marketing program that strips away much of the unnecessary presales service functions computer dealers usually provide, such as product demonstration and installation. These services were not necessary in the 1990s, as many computer buyers were already computer literate and did not require the hand-holding characteristic of the market in the early 1980s. Customers, however, regard postsales servicing of hardware as essential, and manufacturers unable to provide that are judged poor on product reliability. In order to address this customer need, Dell established an extensive telephone support program, which is linked to on-site servicing provided by another company's (Xerox Corporation) sales force. By splitting up postsales from presales service requirements and innovating its on-site service delivery, Dell reduced overall service costs, which enabled it to offer steep price discounts. As a result, Dell's profits as well as market share have steadily increased in the last three years.

Tough Choices

From an individual firm's point of view, the critical issue is one of timing, especially for those operating with a differentiated product. If a firm in position A, for instance, moves too quickly toward the value diagonal, it may miss the opportunity to reap profit gains from its superior product. At the same time, if it moves too late, it may find itself abandoned by its customers. Worse still, if these customers had felt cheated by the firm's high prices, they may resist switching back even after the firm makes a more value-oriented offering. Thus, the firm may be left with the costly alternative of stealing away competitors' customers. In a commodity market, such an action is certainly likely to provoke competitive reaction and a downward price spiral, and a rapid pull to quadrant D.

For firms in position D, the critical issue is one of having the resolve and determination to bite the bullet while attempting to beat the commodity cycle. Either of the two strategies, market focus or service compression, requires the firm to carefully segment its customers by price, service, and value requirements so that the firm may focus on a selected group of customers, allowing the rest to leave the system. Such a decision is often painful because of the intricate web of relationships that may exist with some of those customers, and also because of opposition from vested parties within the company who continue to advance their cause. Moreover, the roles and responsibilities of several members of the marketing and sales team may now have to be curtailed, or even terminated.

An interesting question is whether the same firm can operate at the two extremes of the equity diagonal. It can, but rarely will a small firm with limited resources be able to position itself as a value-added supplier as well as a no-frills low-cost supplier. Being all things to all people is a difficult proposition. A large firm, usually the market share leader, will attempt to do both. It may concentrate its efforts in one position, but it can certainly afford to participate in the other segment too.

In any case, it is worth noting that strategies 1 and 3 (value-added and market focus) are demand-side strategies. The thrust is to effectively differentiate the product in the mind of the customer by appropriate augmentation. It is a strategy of bundling product and service, and in some cases product and other complementary products. It requires careful customer and channel selection and niche marketing. On the other hand, strategies 2 and 4 (process innovation and service innovation) are supply-side strategies. The thrust is efficiency in manufacturing and marketing the product to customers who are price-sensitive. It is a strategy of unbundling product from unnecessary services. It requires market coverage and mass-marketing expertise. Fundamentally, they are very different approaches to gaining profits. They can be mixed only with careful demarcation of managerial roles and responsibilities within the organization.

Industry Dynamics

Even though we have presented the availability of four discrete options for industry participants to control their own destiny and beat the commodity cycle, competitive dynamics often can influence the pace of an industry's commoditization. Market leaders can profoundly affect the maturity and commoditization of the entire industry depending on what strategy they select. A comparison of IBM's strategies in the mainframe and PC markets provides a good example. IBM established its market leadership in mainframes in large part through it reputation for world-class service and dependability. Customers understood that they were overpaying for the core hardware product. But they continued to purchase IBM even after the entry of low-cost plug-compatible Amdahl and NEC because they trusted IBM's service orientation. Although IBM occasionally used price reductions to compete with plug-compatible producers, overall it maintained its high-value-added strategy; a bottom-of-the-line 3090 cost approximately $800,000, plus service and maintenance contracts until very recently (1990). Although the mainframe market is projected to grow only at 2.6 percent through 1998, the market avoided the severe price/performance erosion much longer than technical workstations, minicomputers, and personal computers. We believe a large part of this stability was due to IBM's leadership in maintaining a value-added approach. It was not until the early 1990s that this market began to commoditize as well, mainly because of customers' push for open systems.

IBM's PC strategy differed strikingly. In choosing to license its technology to other manufacturers and sell its PC through dealer channels, the company opened the door for intensive distribution and price competition. In a sense, the company indicated its willingness to unbundle product from follow-on services. As many have argued, mass-marketing was probably the only feasible strategy at that time. IBM's focus may have been on volume rather than margin. In any case, we believe IBM's strategy encouraged the rapid commoditization of this industry. As product technology has matured, niche players Dell, Blackship, Northgate, and a host of foreign low-cost producers have found an even lower service position, ignoring the retail channel altogether and going through direct mail.

In short, the commoditization of the industry is dependent on how the leading players conduct themselves. If such leaders cut price to increase share, the pace of commoditization quickens, leaving only a few niche markets for product differentiators. But if the leader creates a service-oriented climate and resists dropping price, the decline is usually slowed.

Conclusions

This article has challenged the conventional belief that industry commoditization is inevitable and is accompanied by deteriorating profits. While an industry might slowly and steadily slide to a commodity status, not all firms operating in that industry should necessarily suffer the same fate. By adding value or by seeking a low-cost position, firms may continue to show good profit margins. In fact, we argue that even after an industry reaches a commodity status, firms can innovatively break the cycle and return to profitable levels.

While the strategy literature[11] recommends a choice of "differentiation," "focus," and "cost leadership" at the business unit level, we offer its marketing variations at the product level. In the differentiation mode, the tactic has to change with

---

[11]Michael E. Porter, *Competitive Strategy* (New York: Free Press, 1980), pp. 34–44.

the state of commoditization. In the early stages, a value-added strategy could serve as a defensive shield around the core product, whereas in the latter stages a firm would necessarily have to demonstrate to the customer savings from the added services that surround its core offerings. Similarly, a cost-leadership strategy in the early stages of market commoditization would have to focus on price/performance advantages and lower manufacturing costs, whereas in the latter stages an efficient deployment of marketing and sales resources is often an attractive option.

While some firms reconcile themselves to lower sales and profits with the onset of commoditization, many well-managed firms have learned to beat the commodity cycle. Our analysis and action strategies provide the framework for achieving such success.

CHAPTER 21

Cumberland Metal Industries (A): Model Year 1978 Negotiations with Beta Motors

This chapter provides the background on Cumberland Metal Industries' entry into the automotive components market as a supplier of emission control equipment parts. Cumberland Metal must decide what bid to quote on Beta Motors' new business. The company, which innovated the product, had a three-year contract for 100 percent of Beta's business, but is now faced with a competitive situation in which a rival supplier is being actively courted by Beta to serve as the second source.

At the end of October 1976, Mr. John Bach, president of Cumberland Metal Industries (CMI), was considering what price to quote to Beta Motors, a large U.S. automaker, for its 1978 model year Slip-Seal business. CMI's three-year arrangement for the supply of 100 percent of Beta's Slip-Seal requirements was due to expire at the end of the 1977 model year.[1] Mr. Bach knew that Beta was anxious to secure a second source, and that a major competitor was engaging in an all-out campaign to obtain a portion of Beta's business for 1978. Furthermore, it was likely that tougher emission standards would be enacted when the new Congress convened in January, thereby doubling the volume of Slip-Seal used by Beta in its 1979 model year cars. Mr. Bach commented on the current situation:

> In one sense, our business has never been better. We have orders for 8.4 million pieces from all of our customers for model year 1977—5.2 million from Beta alone. Still, we are faced with two problems: (1) Should we reduce our price in the 1978 model year further to meet potential competition, and (2) if somebody does get a chunk of the business in the 1978 model year, will our 1979 quote, which would then have to be competitive,

---

This case was prepared by Craig E. Cline under the supervision of Benson P. Shapiro.
Copyright © 1978 by the President and Fellows of Harvard College.
Harvard Business School case 578-170 (revised June 1986).
[1]*Model year* was defined as the automaker's annual production period. For example, the 1978 model year was scheduled to commence July 1, 1977, and terminate June 30, 1978.

make sense to Beta? I don't want to leave them feeling like we *were* reacting to competitive pressure, and hence have been ripping them off all along.

The Company

Cumberland Metal Industries was one of the largest manufacturers of curled metal products, having more than tripled its sales since its entry into the automotive market in 1973. The company was located in western Maryland, and employed 250 people. Over the past five years, sales had grown at an average of 43 percent per year, and earnings at a 77 percent average rate. Total sales for 1976 were expected to reach $22 million, with a return on sales of 20 percent. CMI stock was traded on the Boston Stock Exchange.

Originally a small company that manufactured wire clothes hangers, mine detector screens, chemical process filters, and special metallic substrates for conveyor belts, CMI was bought by Mr. Bach and a group of financial backers in 1963 when sales were about $250,000 per year. Mr. Bach had a doctorate in physical metallurgy and had been a metallurgist with the company; he was 28 when he took over the business. Under his direction, the company aggressively pursued chemical process filter applications in the industrial sector, enabling the company to grow to $5.5 million in sales and a $400,000 after-tax profit by 1973. The company currently manufactured industrial products using curled metal as a base material, catering primarily to manufacturers and users of special industrial springs, gaskets for high- and low-temperature applications, and a special self-lubricating sealing composite trademarked Slip-Seal for automotive EGR (exhaust gas recirculation) valves. A typical order for curled metal products (aside from automotive products) was in the $200–$300 range.

The company was organized into three divisions: Metal Products, Slip-Seal, and Filter Systems. Each had an extensive capability to develop new products and provide applications engineering in depth. Marketing was conducted along product lines, using product managers who combined specialized technical and marketing skills. Sales, except in the automotive business, were made through manufacturers' representatives.

Curled Metal

Curled metal was a continuous metal wire that had been "flattened" and then curled into tight ringlets. The continuous ringlets allowed the curled metal to stretch in both length and width, and gave it three-dimensional resiliency. CMI purchased the wire from outside vendors, and performed the flattening and curling operations in-house. Because it could be made of various materials, such as copper, monel, and stainless steel, curled metal could be made to withstand almost any temperature or chemical. Stacking many layers could produce a shock mount, an air flow corrector, or a highly efficient filter for coalescers. Tightly compressing curled metal could produce an oil filter or, when impregnated with graphite and mica, an exhaust seal.

Entry into the Automotive Market

EGR Development

The exhaust gas recirculation valve was developed by the major automotive companies in the early 1970s to reduce nitrogen oxides (NO_x) emissions in compliance with standards established by the Clean Air Act of 1970. (Exhibit 1 shows the history of emission control standards up to October 1976.) The EGR valve served as a control mechanism in the vehicle's exhaust gas recirculation system. This system returned a portion of the engine's exhaust to the intake manifold, where it was mixed with incoming air and fuel. The quantity of recirculated exhaust was controlled by a metering valve. The resulting air-fuel-exhaust mixture burned at a lower peak combustion temperature, thus reducing the formation of NO_x.

However, the EGR systems on 1973 and 1974 model year cars were rather crude and decreased fuel economy by as much as 25 percent compared with similar cars made in precontrol years. This situation was aggravated by the gasoline shortage caused by the embargo by most Arab oil-producing nations. Thus, although the Environmental Protection Agency (EPA) extended the 1973–1974 NO_x standards to 1975–1976, most of the automotive companies decided to redesign their EGR systems in conjunction with the introduction in 1975 of catalytic converters, which were used to reduce hydrocarbon and carbon monoxide emission levels.

Two of the automakers, Alpha Motors and Beta Motors, designed a vacuum-sensing EGR valve (vsEGR). In it, a vacuum signal from the carburetor activated a diaphragm to open the valve. The vacuum signal and exhaust backpressure determined the quantity of exhaust flowing through the valve. Although the temperature of the exhaust gas was ultimately reduced significantly, the companies' engineers estimated that the temperature of the exhaust flowing through the valve opening would be somewhere in the 900°–1,200°F range. Therefore, the material used to

Exhibit 1 Emission Standards through the Years (as of October 1976)

	Hydrocarbon	Percent Cut*	Carbon Monoxide	Percent Cut	Nitrogen Oxides	Percent Cut
Average precontrol emissions	8.7 grams/mile		87.0 grams/mile		3.5 grams/mile	
1970–71	4.1	52.9%	34.0	61.0%	5.0	43.0% increase
1972	3.0	65.5	28.0	67.8	5.0	43.0 increase
1973–74	3.0	65.5	28.0	67.8	3.1	11.4
1975–76	1.5	82.8	15.0	82.8	3.1	11.4
1977	1.5	82.8	15.0	82.8	2.0	43.0
Ultimate**	0.41	95.3	3.4	96.0	0.4	88.6

*Percent cut from the average precontrol emissions.
**These are the standards mandated by the Clean Air Act of 1970 that originally were to have gone into effect in 1975.

hold the valve shaft in place had to both lubricate the shaft and prevent the escape of exhaust into the vacuum chamber while withstanding high temperatures (for a schematic diagram, see Exhibit 2). (Kappa Cars, the largest automaker, developed an air-pressure-operated EGR valve that avoided the valve seal problem.)

CMI's Opening to the Automotive Market

Slip-Seal had been developed by CMI to provide a lubricated, resilient seal at high temperatures. It was made from compressed curled metal that had been impregnated with a special composition of graphite and mica. At the end of 1972, Beta ordered Slip-Seal samples from CMI for possible use in its vsEGR valve units. Initially, there was a great deal of skepticism at CMI that Beta's Slip-Seal business would amount to anything. CMI was having financial problems, having recently divested itself of several unprofitable ventures, and some people believed that the company was too small to handle production on Detroit's scale. It was also assumed that competition would be intense.

But in February 1973, Mr. Joe Polinsky, CMI's director of sales, went to Detroit to size up the situation at Beta. He reported back to Mr. Bach: "I'm very concerned. Beta's engineering group is really in trouble, and we're not doing enough to help them. This project is for real." Mr. Bach thereupon decided to rent an apartment in Detroit and assign four people—two in Detroit, and two at CMI headquarters—to act as liaison between CMI's and Beta's engineering groups. Mr. Bach commented on this decision:

> After Joe returned from Detroit, I decided to almost let the rest of the business go down the tubes and focus exclusively on getting the Beta business. Since Alpha Motors was using a similar EGR design, we decided to go after their business too. I sensed that this program had such political sensitivity at Alpha and Beta that they could not afford to make a mistake.
>
> So I decided that our best strategy would be to hold the program in engineering until the last possible moment to preempt the competition. By holding it in engineering[2]—by working hand-in-hand with them to refine the specifications, etc.—we were able to keep the program out of purchasing until it was too late for competitors to qualify[3] in time for Job 1.[4]

Mr. Bach knew that Alpha and Beta would have to start shipping 1975 cars with the new EGRs in August 1974, and that CMI would have to start shipping Slip-Seals in February 1974. To secure commitments from suppliers for the large volumes of metal wire, graphite, and mica necessary to meet Job 1, Mr. Bach calculated that he would need a commitment from the automotive companies no later than May 1, 1973.

---

[2]"Engineering" refers to Beta's Engineering Department. "Purchasing" is used similarly.
[3]All emission- or safety-related products affected by government-mandated standards had to be extensively tested before going into production. Qualification of a component usually took nine months to one year and cost approximately $500,000.
[4]"Job 1" was the target date for shipment of seals to be used in 1975 EGR units.

EXHIBIT 2   vsEGR Valve

Exhaust Gas Recirculation (EGR)

A.

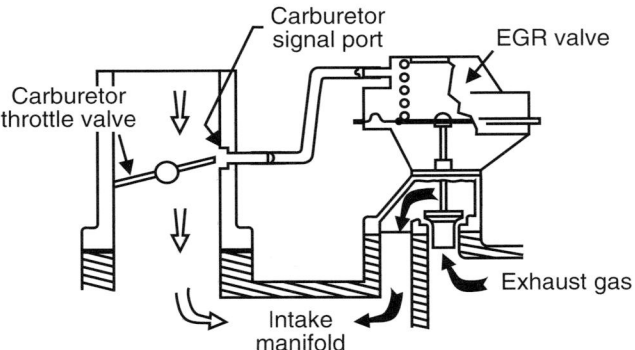

B.

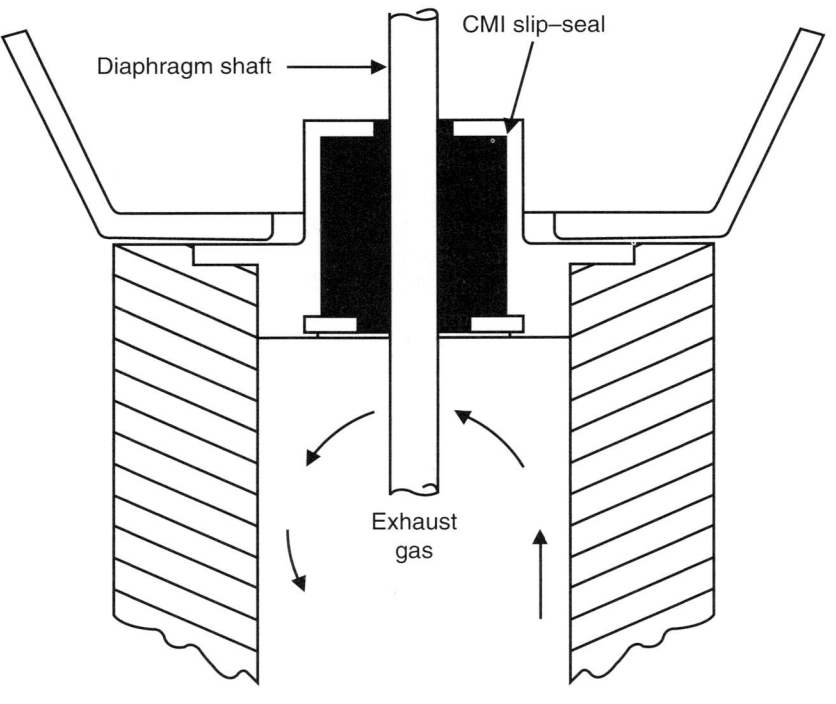

A. vsEGR valve operation.
B. Detailed view of a vsEGR valve, showing location of EGR valve seal.

On April 21, 1973, Mr. Polinsky and Ms. Wendy Pickering, who had been named manager of the automotive program at CMI in March, went to purchasing at Beta Motors, introduced themselves, and explained what CMI was prepared to do for Beta's vsEGR program. Mr. Polinsky concluded his presentation by warning that "if we don't get started by May 1, we cannot guarantee that we'll deliver on Job 1." The Beta purchasing agent was alarmed: "What do you mean you can't deliver?" Ms. Pickering replied, "We need nine months, an irreducible minimum. We've been through this fully with engineering. We've got to get a kickoff—you've got to get us going." After mulling it over, the purchasing agent asked if CMI would accept an indemnification for 30 days while purchasing worked on it. Mr. Polinsky said CMI would. The purchasing agent asked how much. He said, "$120,000." The same scene was repeated at Alpha. CMI received telegrams from the two automakers on April 30 indemnifying it on a month-by-month basis for all nonrecoverable expenses resulting from the program up to $120,000. Mr. Bach said:

> We had learned the magic words in Detroit—job stopper. All we had to do was to say that we couldn't be ready for Job 1 without their immediate action, because this program had high visibility at their corporate level, the EPA, and Congress. If you said these magic words, doors opened up for anything you needed. We did not take advantage of them—but we did find that this was the way to break logjams.

Precontract Negotiations

CMI began negotiations with wire suppliers to secure purchase agreements for the large quantities of wire needed for the program. Concerned about the uncertainty surrounding the temperatures to which the Slip-Seals would be subjected, Beta engineers wanted CMI to use a better quality wire than the standard stainless steel curled metal ordinarily used in Slip-Seals. CMI engineers suggested, and Beta chose, copper-flashed nickel, which had greater tensile strength and elasticity, and could withstand higher temperatures (up to 1,800°F). Alpha, however, elected to use stainless steel. Copper-flashed nickel had never been drawn[5] before, and all of the commercial wire drawers were "afraid of it." Furthermore, they were reluctant to accept an order for such large quantities of wire from CMI without a guarantee of payment in case the program should fail. Mr. Bach noted that

> Up to this time, we had been ordering quantities of 10,000 pounds of metal when feeling flush, and usually less, and suddenly we proposed to order a million pounds, half of that being an exotic metal. Therefore, I encouraged our copper-flashed nickel supplier to include all the technical risks in the price to give him an economic incentive to deliver the wire. He gave me a price of $10.00 per pound.

---

[5]The drawing of wire—that is, the progressive reduction of metal from rod form to fine wire—involved a two-part process at each state of reduction. Wire (e.g., .024-inch diameter) was first broken down by drawing it through a die to reach the next smaller diameter (e.g., .012 inch). Since this made the wire hard and brittle it had to be heated to high temperatures (annealed) to make it soft and malleable enough to be redrawn. Wire was usually stocked in certain standard diameters and redrawn to smaller diameters for individual customer orders.

> We then went to Alpha and Beta and told them that we had no way of swinging this deal unless they helped us. They subsequently agreed to indemnify us so that we could borrow the money from a bank to pay the wire suppliers and obtain the tooling and facility. We obtained a $3.2 million secured bank loan, and our debt/equity ratio jumped from 0.7:1 to 3:1.

Concurrently, having stayed out of the negotiating process until CMI received the initial go-ahead from the two automakers, Mr. Bach joined Mr. Polinsky and Ms. Pickering in the weekly meetings to negotiate the terms of the supply contracts with Alpha's and Beta's purchasing departments in Detroit.

> I went to Beta shortly after we received the indemnification from purchasing and announced there were two things we *must* have to do business with them: (1) Beta had to buy the tooling for us and give us title to it, and (2) Beta had to pay us back the money we put into building the facility in a short period of time. Everything else, we told them, was negotiable. I told Alpha the same thing the next day.

He also told the two automakers that CMI would be willing to establish a second source, but only if CMI retained title to the tooling transferred to the latter. Beta's purchasing agent was shocked: "What, are you kidding? You can't do business in Detroit that way!" Mr. Bach recalled:

> They attacked me. You don't know what it's like. Did you ever see *In the Heat of the Night?* Sidney Poitier played a black detective from Philadelphia down in the South. A local sheriff said to him, "Boy, you down South now, boy, and you got to deal with us Southerners now, boy," just like that. And I got that feeling, "Boy, you in *Detroit* now, boy, who do you think you are talking about us buying tooling for you?" That's the kind of credibility problem we had. I mean, here we were, a $5 million company, and we were going to supply Beta with a critical component of a new emissions control device that had incredible visibility on all levels, and we were asking them to pay back all of our start-up costs and give us title to the tooling to boot.

At that the CMI team got up and left. The following week Beta indicated that it would be willing to make this arrangement if it could retain title until the expiration of the contract, and could amortize the start-up costs over the three years of the contract. Mr. Bach agreed, but said he wanted payback in two years. Beta agreed. Alpha, on the other hand, gave CMI title to the tooling for its production from the start.

Overall, Beta agreed to indemnify CMI for a maximum of $6 million of nonrecoverable expenses. Alpha agreed to indemnify CMI for $1.5 million. CMI leased a plant to house the production of both automakers' Slip-Seals requirements, with a minimum combined capacity of 9 million pieces. Tooling start-up, labor, and facility expenses eventually amounted to $2.3 million. CMI also agreed to supply tooling at cost for a second source for both automakers if it were guaranteed at least two-thirds of each company's seal business.

Pricing. Prices were to be quoted on three different parts, since the Slip-Seal design differed somewhat for different car and light truck models. CMI's first problem was convincing purchasing that the seal was an engineered product that could not be obtained as a commodity item from just any vendor. CMI also had to educate them about its costs. According to Mr. Bach:

> Purchasing conducted an evaluation of the cost of the product to determine what they thought the part should cost. This is done to make sure they are buying the product at a reasonable price. We went through this analysis with both companies and the pricing we came out with was a combination of negotiating with the purchasing people on the one hand, and the product engineering evaluators on the other. This involved trying to get them to accept certain basic costs from us since they had no experience in the curled metal business on which to base their opinions. They were applying standard rates of production, and so on. We had to present them with certain throughput information, and from that they would come up with overhead rates, G&A,[6] and standard scrap rates, and allowing for profit, they would then have "priced" the product. There was a little bit of a cat and mouse game here. Purchasing would calculate what they thought the price should be, based on the elements of cost, and would distort it so that they could negotiate a little better deal.

In July 1973, Mr. Bach was able to obtain the elements of the costing formula Beta's purchasing department used to determine acceptable costs and prices from a product engineering evaluator through the course of normal business negotiation. Consequently, Mr. Bach developed the "L formula,"

> which was after the guy's name. After that, every change in price we made we first passed through the L formula. We skewed our prices to match their estimates, rather than to reflect our factory costs. It meant that on certain parts we got less and on other parts we got more. It just happened fortuitously that the parts we got more on were the high-volume ones. I made millions of dollars for this company just by knowing how Beta's elements of cost were assembled.

Several problem areas remained. The price of each product was based on a certain volume—3.5 million for Beta and 4.7 million for Alpha. CMI negotiated an agreement whereby volume changes of more than ±10 percent would necessitate a change in price. "By knowing the elements of their costs, I could tell them the price changes I wanted based on the volume shortfall that would slide through the formula safely. Therefore, we got our investment back by 1976." Scrap rates were also a problem, since copper-flashed nickel had a terrible yield initially (88 percent) because of the wire suppliers' and CMI's unfamiliarity with drawing it. After much debate, Mr. Bach proposed that prices be based on a scrap rate of 9 percent, with protection up to 12 percent. Over 12 percent, "we eat it; under 9 percent, and we give them back the difference. We were putting through 35,000 pounds of copper-flashed nickel a month, and at $15 a pound, 3 percent meant big money." In addition, Mr. Bach negotiated a formula whereby material price changes were to be passed through to the automakers. This was considered critical in the inflationary spiral of the period.

Wire costs—and availability—were another problem. Shortages of both copper-flashed nickel and stainless steel were forecast for 1973 and 1974, with lead

---

[6]"G&A" were the general and administrative overhead costs.

times increasing to perhaps 8–10 weeks from less than three. Moreover, the prices of both metals were unstable. CMI had quoted copper-flashed nickel to Beta at $10, but it had risen to $15 by August 1973. Consequently, CMI estimated that the cost of stainless steel would rise to $2.60/pound by the time production would begin on Alpha's pieces, and based Alpha's contract on that price. Mr. Bach recalled:

> Our copper-flashed nickel supplier—National Rod and Wire—was very aggressive. He wanted to be Alpha's second source, but Alpha wasn't having any part of it—he was nowhere near to qualifying. But they asked him what stainless was going to cost, and he told them $2.00/pound, which was the current price. They hit the roof. They called me, made me come to Detroit—it was Sidney Poitier all over again—"Who do you think you *are,* boy, talking $2.60 a pound?" So I apologized and said we'd change it to $2.30. The first shipment came in at $2.15, and it wound up at $2.40, which is where it is today.

When the contracts were signed for the 1975 model year (with Beta in August and Alpha in November 1973), the following prices had been established for each part (see Exhibit 3 for cost work sheet).

	Alpha			Beta		
	Price (without amortization factor)	Gross Margin	Amortization Factor*	Price (without amortization factor)	Gross Margin	Amortization Factor*
Part A	$.60	$.238	$.140	$2.30	$.868	$.140
Part B	.80	.377	.140	2.60	.839	.140
Part C	1.00	.477	.140	3.10	.793	.140

*The amortization factor was based upon a two-year payback schedule and was added to the selling price of each part sold in model years 1975 and 1976. The $.140-per-unit factor was obtained by dividing the $2,300,000 start-up cost by the expected 16.4 million units to be used in 1975 and 1976 model years. The actual amortization factor was $.213 because only 10.8 million units were sold in 1975 and 1976. All start-up costs were paid back by the end of model year 1976.

Competition

CMI was concerned about three competitors in 1973: Anvil Products, Inc., a privately held company with $12 million in sales; Wireworks Corporation, a public company with $4 million in sales; and Fabricated Metals Corporation (FMC), a publicly owned company controlled by the founder and his son, with $3 million in sales in curled metal products. Wireworks Corporation was a direct competitor to CMI in the filter products business; FMC competed in the coalescer business; and Anvil Products was not a direct competitor.

Mr. Bach feared Anvil Products and Wireworks the most during this period—especially Anvil Products, because it was very strong financially and had enough curling capacity to handle the vsEGR seal program. Anvil, however, expressed no interest in the automotive business. Wireworks did make a proposal to Alpha and Beta Motors, but after submitting samples it did not follow up with engineering support. Mr. Bach noted

EXHIBIT 3   Price/Cost Projections for the 1975 Model Year

Part	Number of Projected Units (millions)	Material Cost per Unit*	Direct Labor Cost per Unit	Overhead per Unit	Total Variable Cost per Unit
Alpha Motors					
A	3.3	$.230	$.036	$.096	$.362
B	1.0	.287	.040	.096	.423
C	.4	.383	.044	.096	.523
Total	4.7				
Beta Motors					
A	2.4	1.300	.036	.096	1.432
B	.8	1.625	.040	.096	1.761
C	.3	2.167	.044	.096	2.307
Total	3.5				

*Material cost is based on $15.00 per pound for copper-flashed nickel and $2.30 per pound for stainless steel. Adjustments have been made for yield.

They might have gotten the business initially had they pursued engineering rather than just submitting samples and going to Detroit once or twice. They were not aware that the anxiety level was so high at Alpha and Beta, and that it wasn't a matter of price and delivery, but of price, delivery, reliability, hand-holding, engineering support, and constant presence. Therefore they did not pursue engineering, but waited for engineering and purchasing to go back to them. But engineering and purchasing didn't get back to anyone—if you wanted the business, you had to go after it. If they had gone after it—had they made eight trips there—they would have gotten 40 percent of the business.

FMC went to Beta in the beginning and said that it would sell Beta Slip-Seals for 10 percent less than whatever CMI was quoting. But FMC wanted Beta's engineering people to supply specifications and provide support for making the part, and engineering responded, "Nothing doing—you're going to have to make your own piece, your way, and bring it in here. We're not helping you make the piece." FMC fell by the wayside, and by the time CMI signed the supply contracts with Alpha and Beta (formally, for 75 percent and 60 percent of the business, respectively), no other competitor was anywhere near qualifying for 1975 model year production.

The Contract Period

Economic Factors

By the end of its first month of production (May 1974), CMI's automotive program was operating in the black. As a result, Mr. Bach disbanded the launch group and created a cost reduction group. Mr. Bach particularly wanted to replace copper-flashed nickel, since the fluctuations in its availability and price had irritated Beta (because of the price change pass-through formula in its contract with CMI) and threatened delivery. Moreover, Beta had discovered that Alpha had used a stainless-steel-based Slip-Seal in its EGR valves when it had dissected a production model it had bought for analysis. CMI's engineers had known all along that Alpha's engineering design was superior on both cost and performance bases, but CMI had not been able to discuss the relative merits of Alpha's confidential design with Beta, nor could it imply any superiority. To be sure, CMI had frequently questioned the need for so sophisticated a material as copper-flashed nickel, but Beta's engineers had been so caught up in meeting its production Job 1 deadline with a guaranteed, successful material that they totally and repeatedly precluded consideration of alternative materials, irrespective of apparent cost savings.

After it was determined that Beta's EGR operated at temperatures below the upper limit for stainless steel, Beta and CMI agreed to replace copper-flashed nickel with stainless steel. This enabled CMI to terminate its supply contract with National Rod & Wire. CMI subsequently brought in a third source for stainless "to keep the other two honest" and was shipping stainless-steel-based Slip-Seals to Beta by April 1975. Mr. Bach explained that

> We then passed through only the direct savings resulting from going to a $2.30/lb. material from the $15.00/lb. material, keeping the markup and scrap percentages from the copper-flashed nickel. The net effect was that material costs as a percentage of sales for product A, which was better than two-thirds of unit volume, dropped from 57 percent to about 19 percent, and the gross profit remained at $.868 (but as a percentage, it went from 38 percent to 71 percent). The new prices were $1.23 for product A, and $1.26 and $1.32 for products B and C, respectively. Coincidental with the change in material, Beta made the decision to refine the vsEGR's design to improve fuel economy even more, thereby increasing the number of Slip-Seals used in each one.

CMI sold the 60,000 pounds of copper-flashed nickel it had stockpiled (and had bought from Beta for its salvage value of $5.00 per pound) to a European automaker at full market value.

Because of the recession in 1975, the two automakers ordered far fewer Slip-Seals from CMI than had been specified in the initial supply contracts (see Exhibit 4). Thus, although prices had been adjusted upward according to the pass-through formula, CMI nevertheless had to close its automotive plant from December 1974 until April 1975. But with the changeover from copper-flashed nickel to stainless

EXHIBIT 4 EGR Seal Requirements by Customer, 1975–1981 Auto Model Year (million units)

	1975	1976	1977	1978*	1979*	1980*	1981*
Alpha	1.6	2.4	3.2	3.2	5.8	6.5	6.5
Beta	2.6	4.2	5.2	4.6	12.0	12.2	12.5
Kappa	0	0	0.1	0.1	0.7	2.5	5.0–14.0[a]

*Projected.
[a] Mr. Bach felt that Kappa's 1981 requirements would be nearer the higher end of this range.

steel and Beta's decision to use additional Slip-Seals, CMI's overall unit production increased by 57 percent in model year 1976 and 27 percent in model year 1977 (Exhibit 4), and pre-tax dollar gross margin nearly tripled from 1975 to 1977.

Costs were reduced even further in 1976 when CMI integrated backward into wire drawing.[7] Average unit variable cost for Beta's product A subsequently dropped from $.330 in model year 1976 to $.270 in model year 1977, whereas prices were decreased from $1.23 to $1.20 for the same period. Similar cost reductions were effected for Alpha Slip-Seals, but margins were reduced proportionately.[8]

Company Reorganization. CMI had originally established the Slip-Seal group as a separate division to isolate it; in the event the Slip-Seal program died—for whatever reason (such as political reversal of the Clean Air Act requirement and/or timetable, or CMI technical inability to meet future shipments at competitive prices)—nothing else would be affected. Previously, the company had been divided internally into separate product groups. But with the success of the Slip-Seal program, CMI embarked on an ambitious expansion effort whereby the company was split along market lines (July 1976) identified as separate divisions, each operating out of its own plant. Slip-Seal was maintained as a separate, dedicated division. Each division had its own marketing, post-curling assembly, and engineering organizations. At this time, all non-Slip-Seal automotive parts were taken from Slip-Seal (which had begun manufacturing fuel filters for Kappa cars in early 1976) and placed in the Metal Products Division to keep wire drawing, flattening, and curling capacity available for the increases in the seal program forecast for the next four years. The expansion was entirely financed from Slip-Seal's contribution. Company officials generally expected that the non-Slip-Seal Divisions would show a positive cash flow by 1979, and that the company as a whole would grow to $48 million sales by 1981. Ms. Pickering, who had been with CMI for the past 10 years, thought these forecasts were much too optimistic. Current financial data for the company and the Slip-Seal Division are shown in Exhibit 5.

Relations with Beta Motors

Relations with Alpha and Beta Motors during the first two years of the contract were good. This was partly responsible for CMI's having gotten 100 percent of both companies' EGR seal business during the period of the contract. Beta had intended to qualify a second source sometime during the 1975 model year, but the recession diverted Beta's attention away from this issue. When the question arose again in the 1976 model year, CMI had proved its ability to perform well (no seals were rejected or had failed in the field), and the economics appeared adverse to splitting the business. Therefore, when CMI sought to negotiate out of its contractual obligation to establish a second source, Beta was willing to do so in exchange for the return of the $100,000 fee it had originally given CMI for that purpose.

---

[7]For an explanation of wire drawing, see footnote 5.

[8]CMI's margin and scrap percentages on Alpha Slip-Seals had been based on stainless steel from the start.

EXHIBIT 5 Projected Income Statement, 1976 (in millions)

	Automotive Division 1976 Projection	Corporation 1976 Projection	Corporation 1975 Actual
Net sales*	$5.1	$22.0	$15.7
Cost of goods sold	1.7	15.5	13.1
Gross margin	3.4	6.5	2.6
General, sales, and administrative expenses**	.4	2.3	1.8
Income before income tax	3.0	4.2	.8
Nonoperating income†	.2	.2	
Total	$3.2	$ 4.4	$ .8

NOTE: Projections for 1976 were made on October 20, 1976, based upon actual results for 9 months and forecasts for October, November, and December.

*Automotive unit sales totaled 5.4 million.

**Net of amortization factor, which paid for start-up costs, and depreciation on plant leasehold improvements, tooling, and equipment.

†Resulted from sale of copper-flashed nickel wire not needed for operations.

CMI's relationship with Beta's Purchasing Department took a turn for the worse toward the close of the 1976 model year program. (CMI's relationship with Beta's Engineering Department remained strong throughout the entire contract period.) When Beta had begun the vsEGR program, management had assigned top purchasing and engineering people to the program because of its sensitivity. But once the program was solidly established, Beta brought in "maintenance people" to handle subsequent supply negotiations. Mr. Seth Brilliant, the new Beta purchasing agent, was described by Ms. Pickering as a "crew-cut, military drill sergeant."

Mr. Bach had difficulty dealing with the new people in Beta's Purchasing Department. They would often keep him waiting for hours for scheduled appointments, and occasionally did not show up for a meeting at all. Ms. Pickering observed that "John is a free swinger. He's got the authority and the ability to make decisions for CMI on the spot. He brings out the defensiveness in people who can't match his self-confidence."

Model Year 1978 Negotiations with Beta Motors

Because of the difficult relationship that now existed between CMI and Beta's Purchasing Department, Mr. Bach decided to initiate negotiations with Beta for its 1978 model year EGR seal supply contract long before the current contract had terminated. He anticipated pressure from competitors in this round of negotiations, and suspected that they were being encouraged by Beta. However, no competitor had yet begun the qualification process at Beta to Mr. Bach's knowledge. Since Beta's EGR seal business was expected to constitute a significant share of the overall seal business during the next five years, Mr. Bach thought it imperative to formulate a comprehensive and far-sighted strategy for use in the upcoming negotiations with Beta:

> We were facing the third year of the supply contract and already feeling pressure from competitors attracted by the obvious fact that the curled metal business was more than a $4 or $5 million specialty business. We knew who our competitors were and we anticipated that they would price a part we were selling for $1.20 at 60 cents, but that there was little chance a competitor could qualify before model year 1979. We thus knew that under no condition could we lose the entire order in 1978, because Beta would not go to an untried competitor for sole source, or they wouldn't go to two new sources and leave themselves without an experienced supplier. So right at the beginning I decided that the basic problem was not only how should we price our product for 1978, but also how could we use 1978 as a leverage to secure as large a share of model year 1979 business as possible—while avoiding competitive pricing. This last condition was important, because our investments in wire drawing and the other divisions made it imperative that we guarantee our position in the business—both in terms of volume and margins—as long as possible.

Therefore, at the beginning of the 1977 model year program (April 1976), Mr. Bach notified Ms. Pickering and all other concerned personnel that he would personally handle the negotiations with Beta Motors for 1978 model year and beyond. During the next four months, CMI submitted quotes to Beta for various combinations of model year 1978, 1979, and even 1980 business, on an unsolicited basis. Beta, however, returned each quote with a note indicating that it was not ready "to consider 1978 model year proposals from potential EGR seal vendors at this time."

On September 3, 1976, Alpha announced that it was awarding a two-year supply contract to CMI for 70 percent of its seal business. Relations with Alpha had been amicable since the beginning, and Ms. Pickering had little trouble negotiating prices satisfactory to both CMI and Alpha:

	Estimated Variable Cost	Price
Model Year 1978 and 1979		
Part A	$.270	$.50
Part B	.333	.65
Part C	.429	.80

Mr. Bach had expected that Alpha would secure a second source for the 1978 model year, since in late 1975 Alpha's Engineering Department had let it be known that it was actively working to qualify one of its regular automotive suppliers that had recently gotten into the curled metal business, the Andrew Dennison Company, a publicly owned company with $35 million in sales. Mr. Bach knew that Andrew Dennison would be preoccupied with developing sufficient capacity to supply Alpha's seal needs in the 1978 model year, and thus would be unlikely to solicit a part of Beta's 1978 business.

On October 15, 1976, CMI received a request from Beta Motors to quote on 50 percent, 75 percent, and 100 percent of the 1978 model year EGR seal business. The deadline for submitting a quote was November 1. Beta also requested that CMI provide 100 percent supply protection (against a 50 percent supply volume) through April 1, 1977, in the event a second source was unable to qualify. With regard to a potential second source, Mr. Bach had known for some time that the owner of the Fabricated Metals Corporation (FMC) "desperately wanted a piece of Beta's 1978 model year business." But because of the late date, Mr. Bach thought that FMC only had a 10 percent chance of qualifying in time.

Mr. Bach estimated that the unit costs of the Beta Slip-Seals used in 1978 cars would be as follows:

		1977 Model Year (for comparison)	
	Unit Cost[a]	Unit Cost	Price
Part A	$.296	$.270	$1.20
Part B	.343	.333	1.23
Part C	.439	.429	1.29

[a] These costs differed slightly from those for Alpha because of slight variations in product design introduced by Beta in the 1978 model year.

Exhibit 6 shows data developed from material available in early 1976.

EXHIBIT 6 Internal Cost Estimates as of April 1976

	Factory Costs*				Unit Sales Ratio**	
Part	Material	Direct Labor	Factory Burden	Total	1976 (to November)	1975
Alpha Design						
A	$0.164	$0.036	$0.070	$0.270	0.71	0.70
B	0.227	0.036	0.070	0.333	0.24	0.23
C	0.323	0.036	0.070	0.429	0.05	0.07
					1.00	1.00
Beta Design						
A	$0.190	$0.036	$0.070	$0.296	0.68	0.67
B	0.237	0.036	0.070	0.343	0.25	0.24
C	0.333	0.036	0.070	0.439	0.07	0.09
					1.00	1.00
				Fixed Costs		
Selling expenses				$7,300 per month		
General and administrative				$30,000 per month		

*This is actual data for the first three months of 1976.
**The ratio of unit sales for Alpha and Beta tended to be stable as shown (calendar year data).

In deciding what strategy to pursue in responding to Beta's request for a quotation on 1978 model year business, Mr. Bach felt it important to consider the following areas of concern:

Competition. In July 1976, Mr. Bach learned that FMC had approached Beta with an offer to pay for tooling and to cut the product's price to 60 cents for part A (and equivalent prices for parts B and C) in exchange for 50 percent of Beta's 1978 seal business. In August, CMI's purchasing agent learned from a supplier that representatives of FMC had approached him and asked to buy "the wire CMI is buying," and offered him "anything he wanted" in return. CMI had created its own wire specifications, which had been developed in such a manner that it would have been very uneconomical for a competitor to duplicate it, so FMC's approach was to attempt to buy CMI's material directly. As far as Mr. Bach knew, none of CMI's wire suppliers thus far had given in to FMC's pressure.

Mr. Bach had met the president of FMC at trade shows on several occasions, and knew he was willing "to spend as much as much as $1 million to get a piece of the action." Mr. Bach characterized the president of FMC as

> schlock. He's from the "Boys, have I got a bargain for you—can I get you a girl or some money?" school, anything that is necessary to get the job. We immediately became enemies. He didn't like me because I refused to play ball with him—I'm not going to get involved in price-fixing, I'm not going to collude—I'm not going to buy from him or sell to him, he's a competitor, the enemy.

None of the other competitors that Mr. Bach was concerned about in 1973 seemed to be competitive threats in the 1978 model year business.

Federal Standards and New EGR Design. A compromise proposal that would have amended the Clean Air Act to relax the NO_x standard for the 1978 model year was killed by a Senate filibuster at the beginning of October 1977, thus saddling the automakers with the tough standards established in existing law (see Exhibit 1). It was generally accepted that the automakers did not have the technological means of attaining the ultimate 0.4 gram/mile NO_x standard in either the 1978 or 1979 model year. Thus, it was assumed that Congress would extend the 1977 NO_x standard to 1978, though it seemed likely that environmentalist forces would successfully pressure Congress to tighten the 1979 NO_x standard (to 1.0 gram/mile).

To meet the anticipated 1979 NO_x standard, Beta engineers were actively pursuing an alternative EGR design that would use three times as many seals as the present vsEGR valve. The new design was the sonic EGR valve, which performed the same function as the vsEGR, except that the valve was now regulated by the change in pitch or frequency caused by the flow of exhaust gases.

It was expected that the environmentalist forces would encounter stiff opposition from a faction, representing the automakers, supporting an extension of 1977 NO_x standards into the 1980s. But Mr. Bach was confident that the more stringent NO_x standard for 1979 would be enacted when the next Congress convened, especially if a Democratic administration was in power.

Alternative Technology. The introduction of a sonic EGR, however, could conceivably make a noncurled metal EGR seal competitive. The sonic EGR unit was to be mounted between the exhaust manifold and the exhaust pipe. By placing the EGR at this point, the valve would now be exposed to temperatures around 1,200°F, with extremes approaching 1,600°F. If it were decided that stainless steel wire was inadequate for the projected temperature extremes, a return to the use of copper-flashed nickel would have to be made. Recent advances in noncurled metal-based seal technology had made it price and performance competitive with copper-flashed nickel-based seal technology, although it was still more expensive than stainless-steel-based seal technology. It was unlikely that noncurled metal seals could qualify before 1979, but Mr. Bach was disturbed to learn that Beta was considering using them in a portion of its 1978 vsEGR valve production to gain familiarity with their performance, despite their substantially higher price (compared with stainless-steel-based seals).

Unionization. In mid-1975, organizers from the Teamster's Union had attempted to unionize the workers in the various CMI divisions. National Labor Relations Board certification elections were held in each division in December 1975. Although the union won the other divisions by a combined vote of 112 to 51, it lost the Slip-Seal Division by a vote of 27 to 6. Ms. Pickering thought that the union might try again to organize the Slip-Seal Division in early 1977, but was confident that the results would be the same. Nevertheless, Mr. Bach was concerned about their activities, since the establishment of a union in the Slip-Seal Division would almost certainly cause Beta to seek a second source.

Kappa Cars as a Potential Customer. During the past year, CMI engineers had been working in conjunction with Kappa's Engineering Department to develop a variation of the vsEGR valve for use on Kappa cars. A small number of vsEGR-equipped Kappa cars were to be manufactured in model year 1977. Mr. Bach did not expect Kappa to make a decision to convert to full vsEGR or sonic EGR use in the next two years, but anticipated that Kappa would represent the largest seal market by the end of the decade (Exhibit 4).

Chapter 22: Peak Electronics (A): Vendor Relationship with the Ford Motor Company

This chapter chronicles Peak Electronics' relationship of two years with Ford. Peak, a minority-owned business, was developed by Ford to supply printed circuit boards used in assembling antilock brake systems for selected Ford cars. The chapter traces the evolution of the relationship from its birth, and has its ups and downs. But at this time, the relationship has taken a turn for the worse.

On July 2, 1991, Earl J. Yancy was pacing restlessly in his elegantly furnished office in Woodbridge, Connecticut. As he gazed about the flowers, plants, and fine photographs, he fixed on a picture entitled *The Honeymoon*. Yancy, the owner of Peak Electronics, believed that his business marriage to Ford Motor Company, not two years old, was in trouble already. As he noted to his plant manager, Bill Neale, "I can't believe it, but the honeymoon is over. They [Ford Electronics Division management] are not positively disposed to our loan request, and this will automatically shut down our business. We have to give them a response by 5:00 PM today, and get out of this mess."

Peak Electronics, Inc., a printed circuit board operation wholly owned by Earl Yancy, was in deep financial trouble. If Peak's biggest customer, the Ford Motor Company, did not come to its rescue with some form of financial assistance, not only would it go under, but it could also take Yancy's other company, Yancy Minerals, Inc., along with it. In July, Peak Electronics had not yet reached profitability, reporting a loss of $911,500 on sales of $2,735,991 (see Exhibit 1 for a statement of operations for the first six months of 1991). In addition, Peak was unable to make $150,000 in loan payments currently due to Ford and $300,000 in trade payables, interest, and principal loan repayments due to creditors. Though the holiday weekend was around the corner, relaxation, much less celebration, was hardly on Yancy's mind.

V. Kasturi Rangan prepared this case with research assistance from Kim Crawford and Paresh Shah. Copyright © 1993 by the President and Fellows of Harvard College.
Harvard Business School case 594-006 (revised June 3, 1994).

Exhibit 1 Peak Electronics Financial Statements for First Six Months of 1991

	January	February	March	April	May	June	Six-Month Total
Sales:							
Ford	$215,947	$330,747	$391,240	$324,527	$422,029	$393,720	$2,078,210
Premiums	205,333	327,461	53,392	0	0	0	586,186
Other customers	4,598	15,098	11,985	6,855	24,501	8,558	71,595
	$425,878	$673,306	$456,617	$331,382	$446,530	$402,278	$2,735,991
Cost of sales:							
Inventory—beginning of period	333,683	305,303	261,143	306,619	350,745	369,020	333,683
Labor	106,002	122,185	142,391	126,005	169,334	121,857	787,774
Other purchases	120,597	99,373	221,448	151,275	215,306	215,724	1,023,723
Manufacturing—indirect	175,654	212,270	226,261	217,421	237,626	176,763	1,245,995
Subtotal	$735,936	$739,131	$851,243	$801,320	$973,011	$883,364	$3,391,175
Inventory—end of period	305,303	261,143	306,619	350,745	369,020	389,669	389,669
	$430,633	$477,988	$544,624	$450,575	$603,991	$493,695	$3,001,506
Gross profit	(4,755)	195,318	(88,007)	(119,193)	(157,461)	(91,417)	(265,515)
Expenses:							
Selling	6,161	11,192	12,915	6,081	11,716	11,230	59,295
Administrative	81,871	68,413	79,891	88,875	74,651	29,906	423,607
Financial	24,143	31,431	27,840	23,873	28,784	27,012	163,083
Subtotal	$112,175	$111,036	$120,646	$118,829	$115,151	$68,148	$645,985
Earnings (loss) before income taxes	(116,930)	84,282	(208,653)	(238,022)	(272,612)	(159,565)	
Provision for income taxes	0	0	0	0	0	0	
Net earnings (loss)	($116,930)	$84,282	($208,653)	($238,022)	($272,612)	($159,565)	($911,500)
Gross profit (%)	−95.26	−38.21	−35.07	−35.97	−35.26	−22.72	
Production days	17	18	20	18	24	20	
Revenue/panel	$89.15[a]	$74.81[a]	$45.66[a]	$36.82	$40.40	$39.79	
Panels/month	4,777	9,000	10,000	9,000	11,052	10,109	
Panels/day[b]	281	500	500	500	461	505	
Direct labor/panel	$22.19	$13.58	$14.24	$14.00	$15.32	$12.05	
Material cost/panel	$31.19	$15.95	$17.60	$11.91	$17.83	$19.30	

[a]Includes premiums.
[b]According to Peak's auditors, Ernst and Young, Peak had a maximum capacity of 1,200 panels/day.

Earl Yancy[1]

Earl J. Yancy was born into a modest-income, working-class, African-American family in Lafayette, Louisiana. The son of a Creole construction foreman, Yancy was among the first males in his family to attend college. But he dropped out after his sophomore year to take a series of dead-end jobs where, according to Yancy, "I spent most of my time moving from one minimum-wage dead-end job to the next."

---

[1]Portions of this section have been drawn from "The Renaissance Man as Entrepreneur," *New England Business* 77 (October 1989), pp. 34–36; and "The Success of Earl Yancy," *Connecticut,* April 1985.

Viewing the military as the only way out of this situation, Yancy joined the Marines and decided that if he could survive boot camp he could do anything.

After his stint with the U.S. Marines, Yancy completed his college degree and obtained an advanced degree from the School for Building Art & Architecture in Berlin, followed by a master's degree from Yale University. As a Loeb fellow at Harvard, he worked on a dissertation in educational-behavior research and, following his studies, taught architecture at both Harvard and Yale.

At the age of 31, he was disenchanted with his academic career. The practically flat pay scales, despite the level of one's individual contributions and achievement, were particularly annoying to Yancy. He sought both higher compensation and fulfillment by applying his solid education in the business world.

He founded Yancy Minerals, Inc., in 1977 to market commodities. He chose the mineral commodities business because it did not require much money to get started. He steadily built the business to $40 million in revenues and $1.2 million in profits by 1989. Yancy Minerals purchased commodities such as bituminous coal, metals, and chemicals from major producers and then maintained or subcontracted warehousing, distribution, and fabricating facilities for reselling to customers. Due to market cyclicality, both revenues and profits at Yancy Minerals were somewhat lower in 1990.

Yancy's friends described him as tenacious and as someone who rarely took no for an answer. During his first year in business, Yancy set out to win a coal contract with Pittston Company. For a few months he unsuccessfully deluged Pittston's CEO, Nicolas Camicia, with phone calls and letters. He practically camped out in the corporate lobby for a week trying to get an appointment with Camicia. Nothing worked. Finally, he heard that Camicia was an early riser, so Yancy waited in the parking lot at 5:30 AM for Camicia to arrive at work. At 6:30 AM when Camicia arrived, Yancy introduced himself, was invited in, and by 10:30 AM left Pittston with a contract in hand.

During the 1960s, Yancy had grown interested in the martial arts, which he eventually taught while in Cambridge. The discipline and focus imparted by this martial arts training and teaching were incorporated into his business philosophy, as he sought to hire employees who were secure, unintimidated by criticism, and would extend themselves. He exhorted his staff to follow his lead, take calculated risks, and be willing to be "perceived as a tenacious competitor." He aimed for a firm that would "outwork and outsmart" rather than "outmuscle" the competition.

Peak Electronics

Peak Electronics was founded in 1989 when Yancy purchased a plant to supply printed circuit boards to the Ford Motor Company. Peak's products formed the interconnection in electronic circuits that went into making the antilock brakes on rear wheels of selected Ford cars. Peak was 100 percent owned by E. J. Yancy, who had invested a total of $705,000. This included equity as well as closing costs. In addition, $1.3 million in loans were provided by various sources to complete the initial financing of the business. Of this $1.3 million, Ford Motor Company's lending arm, Dearborn Capital, had provided $400,000, and Printed Boards (the seller of the plant to Peak Electronics) had agreed to accept $352,000 in deferred payments. Yancy Minerals had about $350,000 tied up at Peak Electronics—about half in direct loans and the other half indirectly through loans to Yancy.

Yancy had no experience in printed circuit board manufacturing. His main asset, in addition to his business acumen (according to a close friend and adviser), was "his stodgy tenacity and an ability to cultivate and exploit the rich relationships he establishes. That is what Yancy is good at, be it Yancy Minerals or Peak Electronics."

According to Yancy:

> One of the main reasons we got into the business was to offset the cyclicality of the minerals business. We needed something more steady, and I was also keen to get us into the major leagues. This seemed like a challenging higher-technology opportunity. Moreover, I had a keen interest in a business that relied on strict adherence to utilizing the manufacturing discipline.

Ford's Minority Supplier Development Program

Ford Motor Company, one of the largest automobile manufacturers in the world, with 1989 sales revenue of $82.8 billion and profits of $3.8 billion,[2] was widely hailed as the American answer to the Japanese automotive challenge. According to *Incentive* magazine,[3] Ford was winning awards by recognizing that 60 to 75 percent of automobile customers' satisfaction depended on quality. Ford's quality focus was reinforced with a variety of programs, including dealer incentive plans, employee involvement teams, supplier ratings and awards, and customer suggestion programs. These efforts resulted in the following:

- Ford showed the biggest gains in domestic loyalty among buyers—from 35 percent in 1980 to 47 percent in 1988.
- Ford achieved significant market share gains—from 16.9 percent in 1982 to 21.3 percent in 1988.

The company manufactured nearly 55 percent of its components in-house and sourced about 45 percent from outside. Nearly 85 percent of the outside purchase dollars was for parts and components that went into the automobile. Ford preferred to structure strategic partnerships with vendors of such items, called production parts because they went directly into the manufacturing line. Ray Jensen, Ford's minority supplier manager, explained:

> We take anywhere from 30 months to 36 months to bring a car from concept to market. So we have a pretty good idea of the design features of the various components well before the model comes up for production ramp-up. We use this lead time to structure

---

[2]*1991 Moody's Industrial Manual* (New York: Dun and Bradstreet, 1991), p. 2,968.
[3]Todd Englander, "Ford: Quality Driven," *Incentive* 163, no. 1 (January 1989), pp. 23–34.

EXHIBIT 2   Ford Motor Company Purchasing Organization

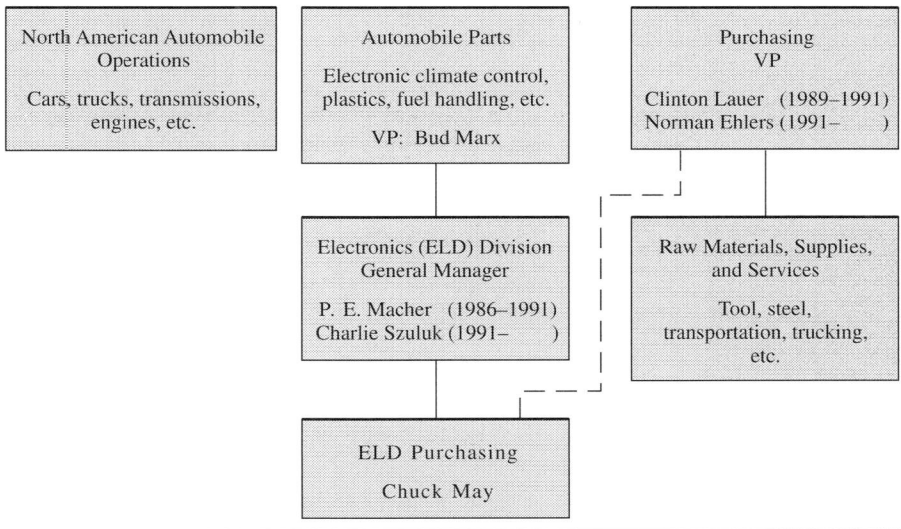

long-term contracts with suppliers to get their technical expertise and production capabilities ready for model launch. We see them all as strategic alliances.

In contrast, supply items constituted only 15 percent of Ford's outside purchases and were not usually used directly in the automobile itself. For example, Yancy Minerals had a supply contract to provide coal to Ford's steel production plant, Rouge Steel, in Dearborn, Michigan.

Broadly speaking, Ford's purchasing operations were organized into three distinct areas. Within each area, division managers were responsible for organizing and executing the purchasing effort (see Exhibit 2). Norman Ehlers, formerly the purchasing executive director of NAAO (North American Automobile Operations) had recently taken over as vice president, purchasing and supplies staff (with responsibility for nonproduction purchasing), from Clinton Lauer, who had retired after 25 years of service with Ford. Though Norman Ehlers and his staff had line responsibility for only the raw materials, supplies, and service portion of Ford's overall purchases, he and his staff had dotted-line responsibility for ensuring consistency and coordination of purchasing policies across the three purchasing organizations. Ray Jensen, an African-American and the minority supplier development program manager, reported dotted line to Norman Ehlers, vice president of purchasing.

Tracing the genesis of the Peak Electronics partnership, Ray Jensen added:

> We had a healthy business relationship with nearly 350 minority suppliers. But most of them were small, and only about 80 to 90 of them supplied production parts. While our top 200 vendors accounted for nearly $14 billion in purchases, all our minority vendors put together supplied us only about $750 million annually. We had to break this trend.

Our goal is to build each and every one of our production parts minority suppliers to at least $20 million to $30 million businesses within three years. At that level, efficiencies start kicking in, and our vendors are able to make profits. We end up benefiting too. We get a steady and reliable supply of high-quality parts.

According to Norman Ehlers, there were three important reasons for Ford's efforts to increase minority vendor participation:

- Business sense.
- Government guidelines.
- Social responsibilities.

Henry Ford II himself had stated in the early 1980s the need for business to aid in the task of building a well-balanced American society. The government had specific incentives and regulations in place to promote minority hiring and reduce discrimination within American businesses. Ray Jensen had added: "About 25 percent of the U.S. consumers are minorities. A one point share increase in Ford's market share is a healthy $20 million in profits for an auto manufacturer. Our minority vendor program is important to us morally as well as financially."

In order to aid the minority business development effort, the Ford Motor Company began a Sponsorship Program with a select group of minority-owned businesses. Rather than continuing to actively manage and monitor relations with many small, often struggling minority suppliers, Ford decided to select and focus on about 50 minority-owned companies. These core companies were targeted for growth within Ford's buying patterns if they consistently delivered high-quality products. This growth was intended to help provide them with stability. Ideally, these suppliers would qualify for a sole-source contract with the Ford Motor Company, depending upon their capabilities. Corporate management paid particular attention to the success of this program.

1987: The Courtship Is Initiated

E. J. Yancy had developed relationships with many influential managers at Ford through Yancy Minerals, a long-time supplier to the Raw Materials, Supplies, and Services Purchasing Group at Ford Motor Company. Yancy maintained friendly professional and social relations with many managers at Ford with whom he negotiated coal contracts. He made it a point to cultivate these relationships as these managers progressed up the Ford ranks. In 1987, E. J. Yancy, as a minority business owner and well-regarded Ford supplier, was asked to join Ford's Minority Supplier Development program. This program was revitalized by Ford in the mid-1980s to further enhance Ford's efforts to purchase more supplies from minority-owned companies.

According to Chuck May, supply office manager for Ford's Electronics Division, in 1988 his division sought to aggressively increase its purchases from minority-owned businesses. The Electronics Division was currently dealing with 15 small minority suppliers, who were all competing in less-technical, smaller value components. May selected printed circuit boards as a potential product area in which to create a minority-owned supplier for his division because this product was relatively easy to manufacture and at the lower end of the high-technology spectrum. (See Exhibit 3 for information on the manufacturing process for printed circuit boards.)

Chuck May felt that a minority operation could be successful in this business given the initially relatively low technology requirements. In addition, he knew of a printed circuit board manufacturing plant geographically close to Yancy Minerals that was for sale, which could, after modifications, produce two-sided printed circuit boards. This plant was owned by Printed Boards, a major supplier of printed circuit boards to his division at Ford.

Sponsored suppliers were typically existing Ford suppliers or a new company (to Ford) with a fairly well developed non-Ford customer base. Judged by these standards, Peak was atypical. It neither supplied electronic components to Ford nor to other customers. However, May assumed that a potential minority-owned printed circuit board manufacturer like Peak Electronics, with a high-quality rating (Q1) within Ford's well-known quality system, would have little trouble expanding its revenue base to other corporate accounts. May felt, however, that a broad range of other corporate accounts would be crucial to the survival of this newly created Ford supplier given the inevitable volatility which usually accompanied Ford's purchases.

The Electronics Division devised a detailed plan which considered the effects upon and possible involvement of their current suppliers in this effort. Because the Electronics Division expected aggressive growth in Ford's new car sales, it estimated that the purchases of printed circuit boards would increase annually at a rate of 8 percent for the next several years. The division expected to bring the new supplier up to speed without any net reductions in its purchases from existing suppliers given this anticipated growth.

E. J. Yancy had built his business through his drive and ability to provide needed products at market prices without defects or delay. He had also quickly established relationships with key business decision makers. Through Yancy's early involvement in the Ford Minority Supplier Development Program at Yancy Materials, he was introduced to Chuck May. May selected Yancy because of his strong reputation at Ford as an effective businessperson. In addition, Yancy indicated a strong interest in expanding to meet Ford's needs by confirming his interest in entering the printed circuit board business. Yancy later stated that prior to this meeting he had never even seen a printed circuit board manufactured, but "it doesn't matter what you are making as long as you have a Quality Improvement Plan." May and other managers at Ford's Electronics Division encouraged Yancy to select and prequalify a site in anticipation of becoming a sponsored minority supplier to the Electronics Division. However, Yancy said he would not move forward with Printed Boards without a demonstrated commitment from Ford.

EXHIBIT 3 An Overview of the Basic Process for Building Printed Circuit Boards at Peak Electronics

A printed circuit board is a single or multilayer card made of nonconducting fiberglass laminate which forms the basic foundation for electronic subassemblies. The bare printed circuit board provides the functional structure which will hold electronic components as well as the required circuitry pattern which will connect the components electrically. Several steps are involved in manufacturing the printed circuit board from raw board stock (laminate):

1. Precutting: Raw copper-clad fiberglass laminate is precut to panel sizes.
2. Drilling: Holes are drilled in specified locations where electronic component leads (ends) will be inserted and soldered in place.
3. Copper deposition: To provide a surface to allow electric current to flow from one side of the board to the other, a layer of copper is applied over the surface of the board and through the holes.
4. Surface preparation: A mechanical brush scrub is performed to provide a surface which will allow for adhesion of a photo-resistant chemical.
5. Laminate, print, and develop: The board is coated with the photoresist and an image of the required final circuitry generated via CAD/CAM is laid over the board. It is then exposed to light through the circuitry image so that areas that are not to be circuitry will retain the photoresist chemical and become polymerized. The areas that are to be actual circuitry (nonpolymerized because no light penetrated through the film over these areas) then are chemically removed.
6. Electrolytic plating: The board now has polymerized photoresist (now acting as a plating resist) in areas where final circuitry will not be required. A layer of copper is plated over the circuitry (the plating-resist areas will not bind copper). Once this step is complete, the circuitry has been laid down where needed (particularly in the holes).
7. Tin lead plating: A layer of tin lead plating is then plated over the circuitry. This works as an etch resist.
8. Resist strip: The board now looks like an all-copper board with circuitry in gray tin lead. Next, the photoresist polymerized film is removed from the noncircuit areas.
9. Copper etch: Next, all remaining copper is removed, etched off, except for where the tin etch resist has been applied over the circuitry. The board now has only circuitry on it and no other copper.
10. Tin strip: Sometimes the tin that covered the copper circuitry is taken off, leaving only copper traces on the circuitry.
11. Soldermask: To prevent any circuits from bridging with solder and to protect the copper circuitry, a layer of rugged, nonconducting epoxy is applied over the surface of the board except where components will be attached.
12. Legend: As a means for technicians to identify component locations, a legend is silk-screened over the board to provide component numbers and other information.
13. Blank/Rout: The parts are then trimmed to their finished size so that they will fit in the designated location. Often at this step, the panel is punched into 8 or 12 smaller circuit boards.
14. Electrical test: To ensure that the circuit board functions electrically the way the design intended, an electrical/continuity test is performed.
15. Final inspection: A final check is performed to verify that all operations in production were performed properly.

Printed Circuit Board Applications

Starting with bare printed circuit boards, electronics manufacturers insert specific electronic components such as resistors, transistors, and computer chips into preestablished locations on the board according to the design requirements. Once the printed circuit board has been populated with all of its components (either manually or via automatic insertion machinery), these components are soldered into place by hand or with automatic wave-soldering machinery. Once the components have been secured into their respective positions with solder, the overall assembly is tested to ensure that all of the proper connections have been made to achieve the designed electronic function of the assembly. Applications of printed circuit boards are as numerous and varied as electronic applications themselves. Some of the more common uses include computer cards in PCs and larger systems, controllers for machinery and vehicles, electronic stereo components, and processing equipment for sensors. Peak Electronics manufactured only the bare printed circuit board.

September 1988—The Marriage is Proposed

On September 15, 1988, Ray Jensen, Ford's Minority Supplier Development Manager, confirmed Ford's intentions for the minority sponsorship of Yancy as a printed circuit board supplier. This was the first agreement entered into by the Electronics Division with a new supplier, 100 percent sourced on specific production parts, who had no previous manufacturing experience with an automotive company. In the letter reproduced below, Jensen essentially "conveyed corporate management's support to the Electronics Division on their decision to select Yancy as the Electronics Division's sponsored supplier for printed circuit boards and the need for the sponsored supplier and sponsoring division to work together in order for the program to be successful."

Ford Motor Company
The American Road
P.O. Box 1899
Dearborn, MI 48121-1899

September 15, 1988

E. J. Yancy, President
Yancy Minerals, Inc.
1768 Litchfield Turnpike
Woodbridge, CT 06525

Dear Yancy:

I am writing to emphasize the commitment we, at Ford Motor Company, have made to the minority business community in the form of our Minority Supplier Development program. As you are aware, the central and most effective feature of this program is our sponsorship activity. Under sponsorship, Ford Motor Company attempts to extend long-term contracts to those selected minority suppliers who have a demonstrated capacity for producing and delivering quality products and services.

To date, this program has been very successful and is one that we at Ford intend to continue.

As this program relates to Yancy Minerals, this office has conveyed to Bill Graning of the Electrical and Electronics Division (EED) its support of EED's decision to select Yancy as EED's sponsored supplier for Electrical and Electronic components—primarily printed circuit boards. As you will recall in our meeting with yourself, Graning, and several members of his staff and supply base, I emphasized the importance of the sponsoring division and the sponsored supplier mutually working toward reaching the long-term goals of competitive pricing and consistent quality that is monitored by a stringent statistical process control format.

At this writing, it is my understanding that Yancy and its technical advisers, Printed Boards, have identified and are in negotiations to purchase one of several manufacturing plant locations. It is further my understanding that based on product samples, specification drawings, prices, and the projected purchase volumes Yancy has received from EED, that Yancy has formalized agreements with key technical personnel and financing sourcing to support its efforts to make this sponsorship agreement with EED a success within the seven-year term of your sponsorship agreement.

Please keep us informed of your progress.

Sincerely,

R. M. Jensen, Manager
Minority Supplier Development
Purchasing and Supply Staff

November 1989: The Union Takes Place

Despite the general framework for Ford's sponsorship program, the details of a specific contract between Peak Electronics and the Electronics Division of the Ford Motor Company needed to be agreed upon. E. J. Yancy represented Peak Electronics as the sole owner. With many years in the coal supply business, Yancy was an experienced deal maker with a very aggressive, can-do attitude. Although they were given direction by Clinton Lauer, then VP of purchasing and supplies staff, the principal negotiators for Ford were Charlie Szuluk and Chuck May. The Ford representatives expected a quick, relatively simple negotiation. They thought that the standard terms of a minority supplier sponsorship were very clear and fairly generous. In addition, the Electronics Division was facilitating Yancy's purchase of the printed circuit board plant from Printed Boards with the anticipation of significant volumes to be ordered from him. Finally, this entire sponsorship effort was a part of Ford's supplier partnership program. In the experience of Ford managers, partnership meant less detail in written agreements through long negotiations but more trusting, handshake-type agreements between business partners.

E. J. Yancy entered the negotiations with a clear focus on the expected competitive position that his new company would face. All of the surviving Ford suppliers of printed circuit boards seemed to be large, entrenched companies with significant experience and well-established relationships with the managers at Ford's Electronics Division. Furthermore, raw materials and direct labor were over 60 percent of the production cost for printed circuit boards. This could potentially give the larger competitors a significant advantage over Peak Electronics through volume discounts on these raw materials. In addition, the Printed Boards facility was a multilayered board operation which had to be converted to a two-sided board facility, and this would involve retraining labor and reorienting shop flow practices.

The negotiations, which began in November 1988, were finally concluded in November 1989. During this interim period, Yancy agreed to cover Printed Boards' operating costs of running the plant. Yancy reasoned that a plant shutdown would have involved tremendous start-up costs. One difficult aspect of the negotiation revolved around financial assistance in the form of outright, nonrepayable, price premiums based on actual volume delivered, which Ford would give Peak "for purposes of assisting and sustaining Peak Electronics during its initial launching period." One Ford manager commented, "The basic contract was agreed on early in 1989. Delay was due to Yancy not agreeing with Ford's premium offer and method of disbursement." Yancy believed that he needed $3.5 million over three years to achieve stand-alone profitability. During the final negotiations with senior corporate executives, Ford said it would not pay more than $3 million in premiums, so Yancy agreed to $2.9 million. Selected excerpts from the November agreement between Ford and Yancy are presented below:

Chapter 22 Peak Electronics (A)

Audio Systems: Electronics Division
Ford Motor Company
17000 Rotunda Drive
Dearborn, MI 48121

November 7, 1989

Earl J. Yancy, President
Peak Electronics, Inc.
51 Carlson Road
Orange, CT 06525

Dear Yancy:

Ford Motor Company, acting through its Electronics Division, is willing to enter into a multiyear contract with Peak Electronics, Inc., Orange, Connecticut, with regard to the supply of printed wiring boards to Ford Motor Company. This contract is for the "printed wiring board" types described in this contract for which Ford has delegated the authority to the Electronics Division to purchase on their behalf. . . .

Purchase/Supply Commitment. Ford's obligation to purchase printed wiring boards is contingent upon successful completion of both process and product approvals as measured by Ford Motor Company's Q101 System Survey Engineering Sample Evaluation Report (form 2913,), and Initial Sample Report (form 292a). Ford will purchase and Peak Electronics will manufacture and supply 100% of Ford's original equipment requirements per the attached Estimate of Annual Usage of printed wiring boards (and replacements) identified in the table below . . . during the term of this five-year contract, commencing during Ford's 1990 model year and extending through model year 1994. These obligations apply to goods of the current design level and to those goods modified by normal engineering changes.

Ford estimates that its purchases for such goods will have an annualized value of $6,400,000 in model year 1991 and $8,500,000 in model year 1992.

Model years for Ford generally ran from mid-August of one year to the next. That is, model year 1991 cars were shipped in August 1990. Parts procurement and manufacturing would therefore typically start in March 1990. To help Peak Electronics get started, according to Yancy, Ford had promised a $3.6 million revenue base for Model Year 1990 cars. But an Electronics Division manager disagreed: "Ford Motor issues purchase orders for specific part numbers at a unit price and a percent of part requirements. Volume is a result of the vehicle sales using the individual part. Ford does not commit or promise dollar amounts."

These estimates are preliminary and will change as Ford acquires more information about the marketplace for its vehicles and these goods.

The part numbers from which Ford will attempt to qualify Peak Electronics and the base prices to be paid by Ford to Peak Electronics therefore are as follows:

			Model Year		
Part Numbers	1990	1991	1992	1993	1994
101	$11.11	$11.11	$11.11	**	**
102	14.16	14.16	14.16	**	**
103	8.04	8.04	8.04	**	**
104	7.11	7.11	7.11	**	**
105	11.19	11.19	11.19	**	**
106	6.77	6.77	6.66	**	**
107	7.23	7.23	7.23	**	**
108	19.60	19.60	19.60	**	**
109	17.20	17.20	17.20	**	**
110	2.79	2.79	2.79	**	**
111	10.18	10.18	10.18	**	**

NOTE: Part numbers represented the actual board placed in a vehicle, but often several boards were made in a batch on a large panel and shipped as a panel. A panel could represent anywhere from 4 to 24 final boards. A price realization of about $45 per panel was usually a reasonable assumption.

**Part numbers and pricing have yet to be identified for model years 1993 and 1994, and will be the same as for prior years unless other part numbers are substituted by Ford. Peak Electronics agrees to develop a program wherein Peak's prices are fully competitive by model year 1993. Provided that Peak remains a qualified Ford supplier, after 1992 Ford will permit Peak Electronics to compete for additional products, in an estimated range of 15% per year to be purchased by Ford.

Should Ford's requirements for such parts decline substantially, Ford will attempt to identify and substitute replacement business to achieve the level of purchases contemplated by this contract.

Premiums and On-Going Productivity. As Peak supplies printed wiring boards, starting during the model year 1990, Ford will pay Peak maximum premiums of $1,800,000 on a schedule of one dollar for each dollar on the first $1,800,000 of the purchase price paid to Peak for goods sold hereunder. Premium payments for model year 1991 of $900,000 will be prorated over the 1991 model year or over the remaining portion of the 1991 model year after completion of payment of the $1,800,000. In no event shall the premium in model year 1991 exceed 25 percent of the purchase price, nor shall the payment period be less than 10 months (which could extend payments into the 1992 model year). A premium of $200,000 will be paid on a prorated basis for model year 1992. It is agreed duplicate premiums will not be paid.

It is agreed by both parties that payment of premiums by Ford is for the purpose of assisting and sustaining Peak Electronics during its initial launching period. When Peak Electronics becomes profitable and does not require said premiums, then it is agreed that negotiations would be initiated to determine an appropriate accelerated premium reduction schedule.

Further, in pursuit of never-ending improvement, Ford and Peak agree to negotiate, beginning in the 1992 model year, an ongoing commitment for annual price reductions based on the projected ability of Peak to achieve annual productivity improvements.

Term and Extension of Term. This contract will provide for a continuing supplier/customer relationship between Peak Electronics and Ford. Accordingly, Ford and Peak Electronics will meet in June of each year to discuss and consider an extension of this contract beyond its initial expiration date at the end of Ford's model year 1994 or any extended expiration date. . . .

Economics for Supplier's Labor and Purchased Goods. Prices are based on Peak Electronics' cost for labor, purchased material, and parts as of July 15, 1989. From time to time, but no more frequently than annually, Ford or Peak Electronics may initiate negotiations to adjust prices to recognize changes in Peak Electronics' cost. To facilitate orderly negotiations, Peak Electronics will provide such data as may be reasonably requested by Ford to substantiate any requested adjustment. Any proposed price adjustments will be submitted at least 45 days prior to the requested effective date. Price adjustments during the first three years of the contract will be based upon an average of competitive adjustments granted to Ford's other suppliers of printed wiring boards for labor, purchase materials, and parts, and will be effective 30 days after peak Electronics' accrual date. For purposes of this section, labor will be deemed to be 20% and purchase materials and parts will be deemed to be 40% of the price of supplies (exclusive of premiums) of this purchase agreement.

Delivery. The delivery of printed wiring boards will be F.O.B. carrier seller's plant (Peak Electronics).

Changes. In pursuit of never-ending improvement, Ford and Peak Electronics both agree that design improvements to reduce the above prices are desirable and should be aggressively pursued. If Ford initiates design or other changes which result in decreased production cost, prices will be decreased to reflect the entire effect of the decreased production costs. If Peak initiates design or other changes which result in decreased production costs, prices will be decreased after recovery of nonrecurring expenses (for tooling, amortization, etc.) for the first year to reflect equal sharing of the decreased production costs and thereafter to reflect the entire effect.

QOS/Q1. Peak Electronics will develop a quality operating system plan (QOS) for printed wiring boards and review it with the appropriate Ford SQA (supplier quality assurance) engineer within 120 days after the date of execution of this agreement. Ford SQA is available to provide direction and consultation to Peak Electronics on the plan. Also, Peak Electronics must establish a plan for achieving the Q1 quality rating within one year of beginning production and must submit the plan to Ford within 120 days after the date of execution of this agreement. Peak Electronics will provide timely progress on the quality plan and will review such progress with the SQA engineer at appropriate intervals. . . .

Ford Technical Assistance. Upon request, Ford will provide Peak Electronics with technical advice regarding SPC (statistical process control) and other matters mutually agreed upon by Ford and Peak Electronics. However, Peak Electronics bears the ultimate responsibility for achieving and maintaining Ford quality requirements. Such assistance could consist of on-site personnel to help implement statistical systems for production control, process assistance, or other areas as appropriate. It is understood by Ford that Peak Electronics will also retain the services of Printed Boards to assist in these areas. One particular area for immediate assistance will be the joint Ford/Peak Electronics development of a plan with milestones for the development and implementation, over an 18-month period, of an SPC program which Ford agrees to monitor over this period. . . .

Termination. . . . If during this agreement, (*a*) Peak Electronics does not meet Ford's quality standard, (*b*) Peak Electronics does not remain competitive in quality and delivery with other responsible suppliers or potential suppliers, or (*c*) Ford can substitute supplies of significantly advanced design or processing, Ford may terminate its purchase obligations in whole or in part without further liability. Ford shall provide written notice to Peak Electronics, which outlines its causes for termination, and specify a termination date of at least six months after the date of the notice. If Peak Electronics demonstrates to Ford, prior to the specified date of termination, that Peak Electronics will correct the causes by the termination date or a subsequent date acceptable to Ford, termination will be suspended and this agreement will continue.

If you are willing to accept the terms and conditions noted above, please indicate your concurrence below.

Respectfully submitted,

Richard J. Vitale
Purchasing Specialist
Electronics Division

Pursuant to this contract, both Ford and Yancy agreed upon an initial business plan for Peak Electronics, which projected $5 million in revenues with a loss of $0.9 million in 1990 and $10.9 million in revenues with profits of $1 million in 1991. These projections included the portion of Ford premiums allocated to each year. According to Yancy, much of Peak's initial business plan was put together by Printed Boards for Peak. Below are the profitability projections submitted in Peak's initial business plan:

Peak Electronics Initial Business Plan

(In thousands)	1990			1991		
	1st Six Months	2nd Six Months	Full Year	1st Six Months	2nd Six Months	Full Year
Revenue (including premiums)	$1,999	$3,005	$5,004	$4,995	$5,862	$10,857
Direct costs	1,053	1,445	2,498	2,462	3,316	5,778
Gross profit	946	1,560	2,506	2,533	2,546	5,079
Total overhead	1,614	1,805	3,419	2,055	2,041	4,096
Net income	$(668)	$(245)	$(913)	$478	$505	$983

January 1990—Peak Electronics Begins Operations

Peak Electronics began operations in January 1990. E. J. Yancy carefully built Peak's management team primarily from existing Printed Boards managers but assigned a new chief financial officer who was recommended by Printed Boards as having strong analytical skills and solid experience in financial management. Finally, Bob Holloway, a retired Ford employee and an expert on Ford's Q1 quality systems, was hired by Ford as a consultant to assist Peak in setting up its quality control systems.

Yancy and his new management team recognized at the outset that a likely key to Peak's success would be its ability to install and adhere to manufacturing disciplines. As a start, the team laid special emphasis on improving communication and relations between management and labor. Yancy had toured the facility with Ford personnel during Printed Boards' ownership and had concluded that the plant was being treated as a "stepchild" in the Printed Boards' family and that a better human resource policy would greatly improve the operation. Daily shift meetings were instituted for all employees to facilitate better communication. Campaigns to encourage all employees to generate and share ideas on improving the operation and/or the product's quality were also instituted. A plantwide incentive program was begun to pay employees based upon actual results. Finally, training was enhanced with each employee receiving 10 hours of training per month.

The new management practices paid off for Peak Electronics. The team at Peak became one of its most valuable assets. Every Ford manager praised Yancy for his ability to build a cohesive and effective team at Peak Electronics. Chuck May stated that Peak Electronics was "amazingly effective at managing teams and people." He acknowledged that Yancy built a surprisingly solid team with very low turnover in a shorter-than-expected time frame.

The facility was converted from multisided to double-sided board production by June 1990. According to Chuck May, this conversion required upgrading the facility from a job shop to an assembly operation. The first significant order was received from the Electronics Division of the Ford Motor Company in late February 1990. Peak Electronics' processes and equipment had to be inspected and approved and the engineering department of Ford's Electronics Division had to qualify the plant's pilot output before large production run orders could be placed. As Peak began production in February 1990, its output underwent the following engineering qualifications:

- A sample lot of a minimum of 325 pieces had to be manufactured and analyzed, and trial run samples forwarded to project engineers at the manufacturing plant that would use the boards.
- Analysis would take place at Peak, at an outside laboratory, at Ford's Product Engineering Division offices, and at the user manufacturing plant. Some of the outside laboratory tests required life and environmental testing of up to 45 days.
- After the above tests were completed and the results accepted, a production validation quantity of 2,000–2,500 boards had to be shipped to the user plant for further validation of quality.

Although before the plant was acquired from Printed Boards it had achieved a minimum acceptable Ford quality rating of 140 points out of 200, Peak Electronics, under the November agreement, had to begin the important effort to achieve Q1 qualification within Ford's supplier system. The Q1 designation was the top quality status for a Ford supplier. (See Exhibit 4 for more details of the Q1 qualification process at Ford.) According to Chuck May, the typical time required for Q1 designation was 12 months. Peak Electronics achieved the required Q1 score of 165 in June of 1990, only six months into the process, which was the minimum qualification time possible. May indicated that this achievement was particularly notable given the condition of Peak Electronics' equipment, which was "adequate but older than most." Peak Electronics' quality was consistently praised by all of the Ford managers, including Chuck May. According to Yancy, as of November 1990, Peak was making major strides in achieving its business plan objectives:

Yancy's Goals	Achievement
Peak will be nominated for Q1 rating by 12/1/90:	Nominated by 10/90
—Peak will achieve at least 85E on monthly rating	Achieved 94E
—Peak will earn a quality survey score greater than 165	Achieved 165
Peak will institute manufacturing disciplines:	
—Peak will achieve 95% true yield by 12/90	Achieved 76% by 9/90
—Peak will achieve 10-day cycle time by 12/90	Achieved 12 days as of 9/90
—Peak will be in control and capable of 75% of significant characteristics by 1/91	Achieved 62% as of 9/90

Exhibit 4 Ford's Q1 Quality Qualification Process

As part of a reformulation of its quality improvement methods, in the early 1980s Ford shifted its approach to quality from defect detection to one of defect prevention and continuous improvement with particular emphasis on the use of statistical process controls. It established the Ford Q1 Preferred Quality Award for outstanding suppliers. Below is a description of the evaluation process Peak Electronics completed in order to achieve a Q1 rating in six months, the minimum time period possible.

Award Criteria
To qualify for a Q1 award, a supplier must meet or exceed all of the following threshold criteria:
- Have had all initial samples approved during first-time presentation.
- Maintain an 85 Excellent overall supplier rating for over six months based on the Supplier Quality Rating System which weighs three areas of performance as follows:

Criteria	Points	Elements of Criteria
I. • Adequacy of Supplier Quality System (Q101)	30	• 20 Questions (Quality System Survey)
II. • Supplier Management Awareness and Commitment	20	• Continuous Improvement —Understanding/Commitment —Training —Management Controls • Response to Quality Concerns
III. • Ongoing Quality Performance Total	50 100	• Quality of Products and Services

Category I
30 Points: The Adequacy of the Supplier Quality System. (As measured by 20 questions on a Quality System Survey.) A supplier must earn a total score of 160 points or above with a score of 7 or greater (on a scale of 0–10) for all questions on the Quality System Survey, and earn 40 out of 50 points for the five questions pertaining to statistical methods. Ford provided its quality assessors detailed guidelines and clear directives on the evaluation criteria to make ratings as objective as possible. An example of a typical question is:
  Is statistical process control (SPC) utilized for significant product characteristics and process parameters?
- How are the significant characteristics chosen?
- Describe the SPC methods used. Are they appropriate to the factors being controlled?
- Evaluate the supplier's reaction to out-of-control conditions.
- Evaluate the supplier's application of SPC.

Category II
20 Points: The Supplier Management Awareness and Commitment to Continuous Improvement and Response to Quality Concerns. Four major question groups were rated on a 0 to 5 scale. An example of a typical question is:
  Does a training plan exist to provide statistical methodology training to employees, including a timing chart for implementation?
- Is a qualified specialist available as a resource?
- Have training manuals in statistical techniques been developed, and are they available to all affected personnel?
- Is training in advanced statistical techniques planned/implemented?
  Similar to the other categories, Ford provided its quality assessors a detailed evaluation guideline.

Category III
50 Points: Ongoing Quality Performance in Products and Services. (Must earn 45 out of 50 points.) Specific points are deducted from 50 based on past six months' product and service performance including factors such as rejection rates, deficient deliveries, and field service requirements.

EXHIBIT 5 Peak Electronics Shipment Performance

	Boards Shipped	Cumulative Shipped	Panels Returned
1990			
February	38,176	38,176	0
March	30,982	69,158	0
April	58,325	127,483	0
May	60,081	187,564	20
June	64,931	252,495	1
July	19,680	272,175	0
August	62,979	335,154	1
September	120,867	456,021	3
October	111,549	567,570	0
November	88,192	655,762	1
December	89,604	745,366	7
1991			
January	52,470	797,836	0
February	92,660	890,496	0
March	106,230	996,726	12
April	87,480	1,084,206	3
May	93,069	1,177,275	17
June	115,109	1,292,384	0

True yield percentage is roughly defined as total first pass conforming output quantity divided by input quantity. *Ship yield* is roughly defined as total conforming quantity shipped to customer (including product which has been reworked) divided by input quantity. Although Peak had difficulties achieving the 95 percent true yield goal, when panels were defective its production management was able to identify the problem areas and rework a large percentage of problem boards to achieve higher ship yields (see Exhibit 5).

First Quarter 1991: Financial Difficulties Challenge the Relationship

Despite Peak Electronics' solid start in improving quality and reducing costs, it experienced serious financial difficulties during its first year of operation. First, Peak had to pay $800,000 to Printed Boards toward operating costs for the November 1988 to November 1989 time frame when it was negotiating a vendor agreement with Ford. This figure was almost twice what Yancy had expected. Second, due to a nationwide recession, Ford experienced a major sales downturn which prevented it from ordering the anticipated number of circuit boards from Peak during 1990. Actual purchases from Peak for model year 1990 were $700,000 versus the projected $1,800,000. May indicated that the car models to which Peak Electronics con-

EXHIBIT 6 Ford Overall Automobile Sales in Units and Dollars for 1989, 1990, and 1991

Ford Motor Company and Subsidiaries

Operating Highlights	1991	1990	1989
Worldwide factory sales of cars, trucks, and tractors (in thousands):			
United States	2,869	3,284	3,721
Outside United States	2,490	2,588	2,687
Total	5,359	5,872	6,408
Sales and revenues (in millions):			
Automotive	$72,050.9	$81,844.0	$82,879.4
Financial services	16,235.4	15,806.0	13,266.5
Total	$88,286.3	$97,650.0	$96,145.9
Net (loss)/income (in millions):			
Automotive	$(3,185.5)	$98.7	$3,174.7[a]
Financial services	927.5	761.4	660.3
Total	$(2,258.0)	$860.1	$3,835.0[a]

[a]Includes an after-tax loss of $42.4 million from the sale of Rouge Steel Company.
SOURCE: Ford Motor Company, 1991 Annual Report.

tributed were particularly hard hit. (See Exhibit 6 for Ford overall sales in 1989, 1990, and 1991.) At a November 1990 review meeting with Dearborn Capital, one of its financiers, Peak raised the issue of liquidity and the possible need for refinancing. Peak also needed to identify and obtain non-Ford customers to enlarge its sales base to ensure profitability, and Ford's help would be enlisted to make introductions to other firms.

In order to meet his initial cash needs, Yancy was able to convince Ford corporate management to accelerate its premium payments to Peak Electronics. The initial agreement involved only $1.8 million in premium payments during model year 1990 out of a total of $2.9 million in premium payments over three years. However, Peak Electronics was actually paid all $2.9 million in premium payments in the 1990 model year. Yancy convinced senior Ford corporate management to accelerate this premium despite the initial objections of the operating managers in the Electronics Division. Subsequently, however, Electronic Division management concurred based on their assumption that Ford volume would return shortly. According to Yancy:

> These negotiations were difficult and strenuous because of the unique nature of the purchasing organization of large corporations like Ford. I sensed a serious conflict between mandates sent from Ford corporate to divisions regarding their purchasing practices and the corporation's expectations of how the divisions would relate with sponsored suppliers. One is a long-term vision and the other is a short-term performance orientation.

In March and April of 1991, Peak's financial forecasts understated expenses by $300,000. An additional $400,000 accounting error was also uncovered in 1990.

The shortfall placed additional cash strains on Peak Electronics. To overcome this setback, Ford provided an additional $300,000 in premiums and $500,000 in price increases in April. Ford paid an advance of $100,000 against these price increases in May. It continued to provide revolving financing for raw material, and on two occasions provided cash advances against inventories.

July 1991: Ford's Electronics Division Seeks to Discontinue Its Relationship with Peak Electronics

In July 1991, Peak Electronics was continuing to experience financial difficulties. Unfortunately, revenues from other corporate accounts had not yet materialized. Ford managers had made personal phone calls to CEOs of major companies and had written letters of introduction to corporate buyers in different industries on behalf of Peak Electronics (see Exhibits 7 and 8). Chuck May was particularly perplexed by

---

EXHIBIT 7 Ford Introductory Letter to Hewlett-Packard

P. E. Macher
General Manager

Electronics Division
Ford Motor Company
16900 Executive Plaza Drive
Dearborn, MI 48126-8200

John Young, CEO
Hewlett-Packard Company
3000 Hanover Street
Palo Alto, CA 94304

Dear John:

    I would like to solicit your personal support in assisting a new minority company. This new company, Peak Electronics, manufacturers printed circuit boards. The company was started in January 1990 and is an Electronic Division-sponsored minority supplier.

    We have been receiving products from Peak Electronics since last April and have just recently nominated Peak for Ford's Q1 Award. I am sure you can appreciate that finding qualified minority suppliers in the electronics component area is very difficult. We believe Peak represents a unique opportunity for purchasing quality products at competitive prices. (Reference attached brochure.)

    In order to pursue a business relationship with Peak Electronics, please have your people contact C. L. May at Ford Electronics (390-8454) or Earl Yancy, President, Peak Electronics (203-795-0241). I am confident that with your personal support, your people will find that Peak is a high-quality, competitive-cost supplier.

                              Sincerely,

                                P. E. Macher
                                General Manager

cc: E. Yancy
    C. L. May—ELD

SOURCE: Peak Electronics.

EXHIBIT 8 Ford Introductory Letter to Digital Equipment Corporation

P. E. Macher
General Manager

Electronics Division
Ford Motor Company
16900 Executive Plaza Drive
Dearborn, MI 48126-8200

Ken Olsen, President
Digital Equipment Corporation
146 Main Street
Maynard, MA 01754-2571

Dear Ken:

I would like to solicit your personal support in assisting a new minority company. This new company, Peak Electronics, manufacturers printed circuit boards. The company was started in January 1990 and is an Electronics Division-sponsored minority supplier.

We have been receiving products from Peak Electronics since last April and have just recently nominated Peak for Ford's Q1 Award. I am sure you can appreciate that finding qualified minority suppliers in the electronics component area is very difficult. We believe Peak represents a unique opportunity for purchasing quality products at competitive prices. (Reference attached brochure.)

In order to pursue a business relationship with Peak Electronics, please have your people contact C. L. May at Ford Electronics (390-8454) or Earl Yancy, President, Peak Electronics (203-795-0241). I am confident that with your personal support, your people will find that Peak is a high-quality, competitive-cost supplier.

Sincerely,

P. E. Macher
General Manager

cc: E. Yancy
    C. L. May—ELD

SOURCE: Peak Electronics.

Peak Electronics' difficulty in securing other business, given Peak's Q1 quality rating from Ford. "It is not that simple to go out and get outside business," countered Yancy. "It is a long lead time sales process. Moreover, there is a minority bias which is not helpful, especially when it comes to technology components."

Peak was experiencing a severe cash shortfall and again sought $150,000 in assistance from the Ford Motor Company. On hearing of Yancy's requests for additional support, the Electronic Division's purchasing management recommended to Corporate Purchasing that it be denied because at that time, the Ford Motor Company itself was struggling with profit and cash flow difficulties. Chuck May of the Electronics Division described the very careful evaluation made of suppliers requesting loans: "Ford must evaluate the request like a bank would, by specifically assessing the likelihood that the loan will be repaid. Any previous investments or loans have to be considered sunk costs for Ford to prevent them from pouring good money after bad money." Chuck May added that the specific assessment of Peak

Electronics involved asking the central question: Given its history of financial problems, overhead costs, and complete reliance on Ford for business, is Peak Electronics a viable business? Although direct financial assistance was ultimately granted by Ford's corporate management, the actual cost was transferred to the division doing business with that supplier.

A Ford Supply Office Manager noted:

> Ford had profiled Peak as a $10 million business with 60 percent Ford and 40 percent outside sales. Yancy had developed a philosophy for Peak of full employment of a well-trained staff. Also, if quality was maintained, business would come to him. When outside sales failed to materialize and Ford business did not ramp up as originally projected, Peak failed to reduce direct labor and overhead compatible with the reduced level of business.

Earl Yancy summarized the situation:

> There has always been a huge gulf in the Ford people's understanding of the issues and problems facing a small business. What is called a variable cost (direct labor) has a fixed component when you get well below capacity. Differences in business scale and stage of development are at the core of the difficulties in our relationship. As well-intentioned as some people at Ford have been in extending their support, the fact remains that we at Peak Electronics are on the verge of going out of business.

CHAPTER 23

BOC Group: Ohmeda (A)

 *The president of Ohmeda, a wholly owned company of the BOC Group, plans to increase the company's medical equipment sales from $95 million in 1985 to $158 million in five years by focusing on the sale of high-tech equipment. At the same time, the president expects to sell Ohmeda's medical supplies business ($22 million in sales) and transfer its medical gases business ($27.2 million in sales) to another business unit of the BOC Group. The changes in Ohmeda's products combined with the planned growth in medical equipment cause the president to reassess Ohmeda's marketing system. The new strategic thrust requires him to review the role of Ohmeda's direct sales and dealer sales coverage. In doing so, he evaluates the economics of three options: (1) continuing with Ohmeda's present system, (2) eliminating dealer sales coverage, and (3) specializing salespeople by product group.*

On March 24, 1986, W. Dekle Rountree, president of Ohmeda, a wholly owned company of the BOC Group, nodded and smiled as he read the finance officer's memo. After 11 months of informal searching, Ohmeda had located a health services company interested in acquiring its medical supplies business. Given the initial offer of $19 million, Rountree believed that the sale could be negotiated and signed before October 1, 1986—the beginning of Ohmeda's fiscal year 1987.

Rountree had waited anxiously for this day. Shortly after joining the company in November 1984, he had decided to focus Ohmeda's marketing on new, high-tech medical equipment. In particular, he intended to increase the company's equipment revenues from $95 million in 1985 to $158.5 million in 1990.

Rountree was doubly pleased because the memo arrived at an opportune moment. Desmond O'Connell, managing director of the BOC Group's health care businesses, had just confirmed that Ohmeda's industrial gases business would be

---

This case was prepared by Gordon Swartz under the supervision of Rowland T. Moriarty.
Copyright © 1986 by the President and Fellows of Harvard College.
Harvard Business School case 587-080.

reorganized under another BOC business unit beginning in fiscal year 1987. Thus, if the supplies-business sale went through, Ohmeda would begin the new year with only its medical equipment product line.

In light of these changes, Rountree wondered whether this might also be an appropriate time to terminate most of Ohmeda's dealers. According to a study by a consulting firm, Health Care Industries, he could improve Ohmeda's margins by direct selling. The study also recommended specializing Ohmeda's salespeople by product groups.

Since 1976 Ohmeda had been losing market share in its major equipment market, anesthesia systems. In addition, Ohmeda's ability to sell new, high-tech products had been brought into question by its troubled 1985 launches of the Infant Care Incubator and the CPU-1 ventilator. Although Rountree thought that specialization might improve the sales force's knowledge of clinical applications and increase overall sales effectiveness, he was worried that it might also confuse customers and overly complicate Ohmeda's transition to its equipment focus. In fact, Ohmeda's vice president of sales had argued that specialization would reduce sales efficiency, and the vice president of finance had questioned the economics of product specialization.

Rountree knew that changes in Ohmeda's product line, its dealer ranks, or the organization of its sales force would require a reassessment of the company's direct sales coverage and a complete review of its management systems for selecting, motivating, evaluating, and compensating its salespeople. Rountree recognized that this analysis would provide a critical foundation for the future of Ohmeda's medical-equipment business.

Company Background

Ohmeda manufactured and marketed medical equipment and supplies. It was headquartered in Murray Hill, New Jersey, and operated manufacturing facilities in Madison, Wisconsin; Boulder, Colorado; Denver, Colorado; Ft. Meyers, Florida; and Columbia, Maryland. In fiscal year 1985[1] Ohmeda revenues topped $160 million and pretax income was about $13 million. In the United States, the company employed over 2,000 people, including 130 sales representatives.

Ohmeda was an autonomous division of a London-based multinational, the BOC Group, whose business areas included industrial gases, health care, welding and carbon-based products, vacuum engineering, and educational and food services. In 1985, it had revenues of $2.8 billion and operating profits of $302 million. After industrial gases, health care was the BOC Group's largest business area and accounted for more than $595 million in 1985 revenues and $96 million in operating profits. (See Exhibit 1 for financial data on Ohmeda and the BOC Group.)

---

[1]Ohmeda's fiscal year ran from October 1 to September 30. Throughout the case, all financial data are presented by fiscal year.

Exhibit 1 Income Statements for the BOC Group and Ohmeda

(In millions of dollars)	1983	1984	1985
The BOC Group[a]			
Revenues:			
Gases	$ 1,164	$ 1,744	$ 1,713
Health care	454	566	595
Carbon products	181	281	211
Other	683	333	279
Total revenues	$ 2,482	$ 2,924	$ 2,798
Operating profit	$ 191	$ 270	$ 302

(In thousands of dollars)	1983	1984	1985
Ohmeda—United States Only			
Revenues:			
Equipment	$ 79,859	$ 87,088	$ 95,160
Supplies	20,321	21,224	22,449
Gases	24,625	26,663	27,235
Service	11,400	13,267	15,975
Total revenues	$136,205	$148,242	$160,819
Cost of goods sold	83,479	82,696	93,729
Gross profit	$ 52,726	$ 65,546	$ 67,090
Distribution expense	15,033	15,196	15,072
	$ 37,693	$ 50,350	$ 52,018
Operating expenses:			
Administrative	$ 12,770	$ 14,193	$ 15,579
R&D	3,336	4,089	5,332
Corporate charges	2,171	2,724	3,396
Sales	14,207	13,856	14,248
Total operating expense	$ 32,484	$ 34,862	$ 38,555
Other income	—	—	5
Operating profit	$ 5,209	$ 15,488	$ 13,468

NOTE: BOC Group and Ohmeda fiscal year began October 1 and ended September 30. For example, FY 1983 began October 1, 1982, and ended September 30, 1983.

[a]BOC Group financials were converted from British pounds to U.S. dollars: £1.00/$1.25.

SOURCE: Company records.

Other BOC health care companies manufactured and sold anesthetic pharmaceuticals, intravenous therapy equipment, and home health care products. These product lines were marketed independently of Ohmeda.

Ohmeda History

Ohmeda's experience as a medical equipment and supplies manufacturer stretched back to the beginning of the Ohio Chemical and Manufacturing Company. In 1910, Ohio Chemical was founded in Cleveland to manufacture and sell nitrous oxide, oxygen, carbon dioxide, and epsom salts.

Because hospitals were major users of pure gases, Ohio Chemical played an important role in the supply of gases and gas equipment for hospital applications, especially anesthesia procedures. Ohio Chemical also introduced several innovations in gas-handling equipment and promoted research on the anesthetic properties of gases. In 1938, Ohio Chemical merged with the Heidbrink Company, a well-known maker of anesthesia machines. During the next 30 years, Ohio Chemical expanded its gases business nationwide and enlarged its medical equipment product line to include architectural products, surgical equipment, infant incubators, and disposable hospital supplies. In 1978, the company was acquired by the BOC Group, and in 1984 it was renamed Ohmeda.

Ohmeda Organization

As the president of Ohmeda, Rountree reported directly to the BOC Group's managing director of health care, Desmond O'Connell. Before joining Ohmeda in November 1984, Rountree had been with Baxter-Travenol for 10 years. He had a BS degree from the Georgia Institute of Technology and an MBA from the Harvard Business School (1973).

Ohmeda was organized into seven functions: manufacturing, finance, human resources, sales, service, research and development, and marketing. In September 1985, the sales and service functions were combined to form Ohmeda's North American field operations (NAFO) group. In addition, financial tasks related to sales expenses, order entry, and customer billing were transferred from the finance group to NAFO. (See Exhibit 2 on pages 402 and 403 for an organizational chart of the BOC Group and Ohmeda.)

Changes in BOC/Ohmeda's Marketing

After its 1978 purchase of Ohmeda, the BOC Group began to rationalize its international manufacturing capacity and to reorganize its product lines. In addition to eliminating redundant manufacturing facilities and reorganizing BOC's health care businesses by patient therapy, the plan called for all gas products to be grouped within BOC's industrial gases business unit. However, this regrouping was only now being implemented.

The transfer of gases to another BOC business unit would reduce Ohmeda's total revenues by $27.2 million (17 percent), but Rountree was enthusiastic about the change. Now, with the sale of the $22.4 million medical supplies business, he would be able to focus Ohmeda's marketing entirely on medical equipment.

In early 1985, Rountree had decided to reduce the company's involvement in medical supplies. Although supplies accounted for 14 percent of Ohmeda's total revenues of $160.8 million, Rountree believed that Ohmeda's future in supplies was extremely limited. Survival in the supplies market was based increasingly on low price, and Ohmeda had little chance of competing with multibillion-dollar supplies companies such as Baxter-Travenol.

With changes affecting both supplies and gases, Ohmeda would lose $49.6 million in sales. However, unless Rountree purposely resized the sales force, Ohmeda would still have 130 direct salespeople to concentrate on equipment sales. While the two changes would not force a reduction in personnel, Rountree expected that most salespeople would be upset over lost commissions on gases and supplies. To the sales force, the lost sales translated to a loss of $843,000 in commissions. Still, Rountree anticipated that these losses would be quickly offset by the growth of the equipment business.

Five-Year Plan

By reorienting the company to the development and marketing of advanced medical equipment, Rountree planned to expand Ohmeda's medical equipment business from $95 million in 1985 to $158.5 million in 1990—a compound annual rate of 11 percent. In particular, Rountree intended to reestablish Ohmeda's dominance in anesthesia equipment and to reinvigorate the company's recent attempts to introduce new infant care and respiratory therapy products. Table 1 presents Rountree's five-year goals by product line.

TABLE 1

	1985 Actual			1990 Goals		
	Sales ($ million)	Market Share	Market Size ($ million)	Sales ($ million)	Market Share	Market Size ($ million)
Anesthesia	$ 29.5	45%	$ 65.1	$ 45.6	65%	$ 70.1
Infant care:						
Thermoregulators	10.4	39	27.0	13.5	46	29.3
All other	5.8	13	46.0	7.6	15	49.3
Respiratory therapy:						
Low-tech	5.6	15	37.0	6.1	15	40.9
Ventilator	0.1	0	57.8	2.7	4	66.9
Patient monitors[a]	6.7	4	166.0	34.2	16	211.9
Suction	14.3	60	24.0	16.8	65	25.9
Architectural products	22.8	34	68.0	32.0	45	71.0
Equipment total[b]	$ 95.2			$158.5		
Service	16.0			26.9		
Gases	27.2			–		
Supplies	22.4			–		
Total	$160.8			$185.4		

[a]Major growth in monitors is a combination of acquisition and new product introductions.
[b]The equipment product lines are described individually on pages 410–15.

EXHIBIT 2 Organizational Structure of The BOC Group and Ohmeda

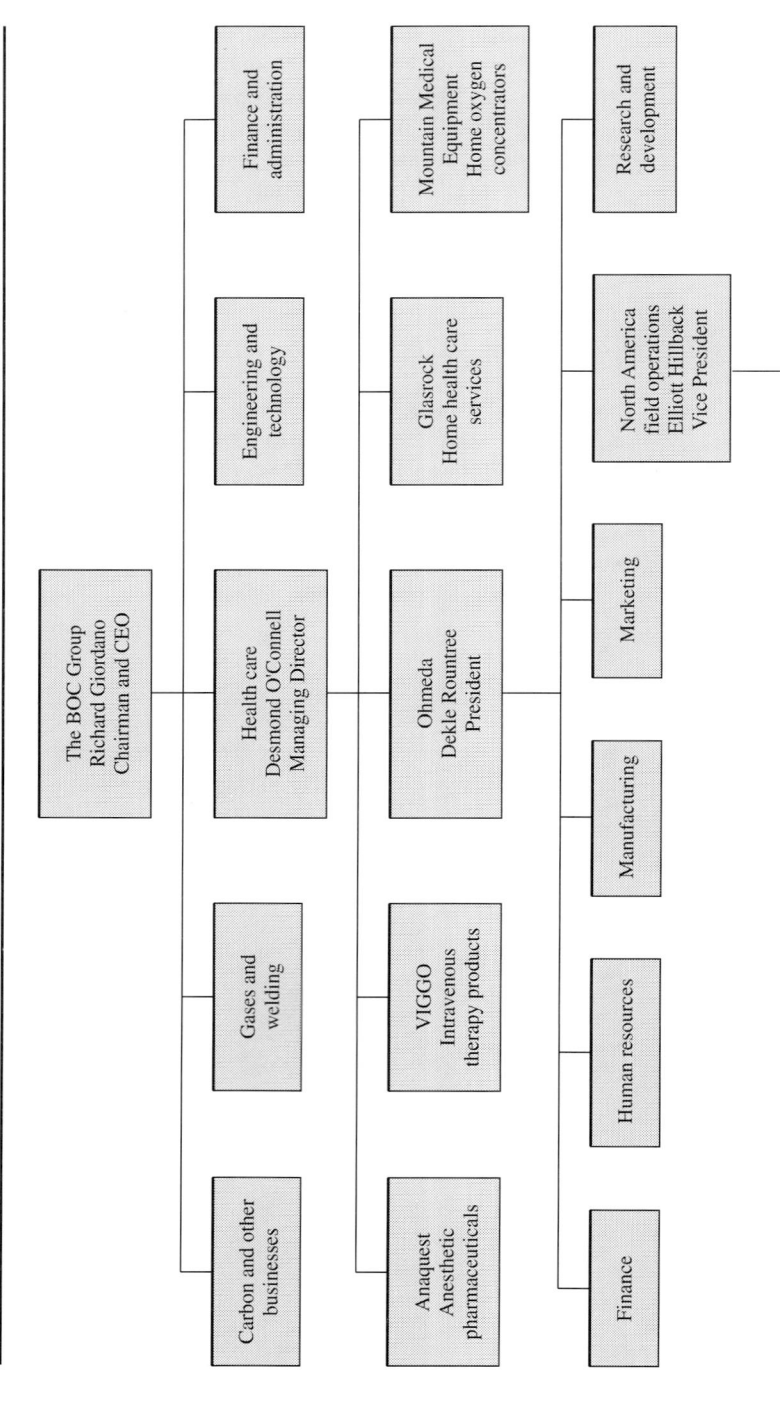

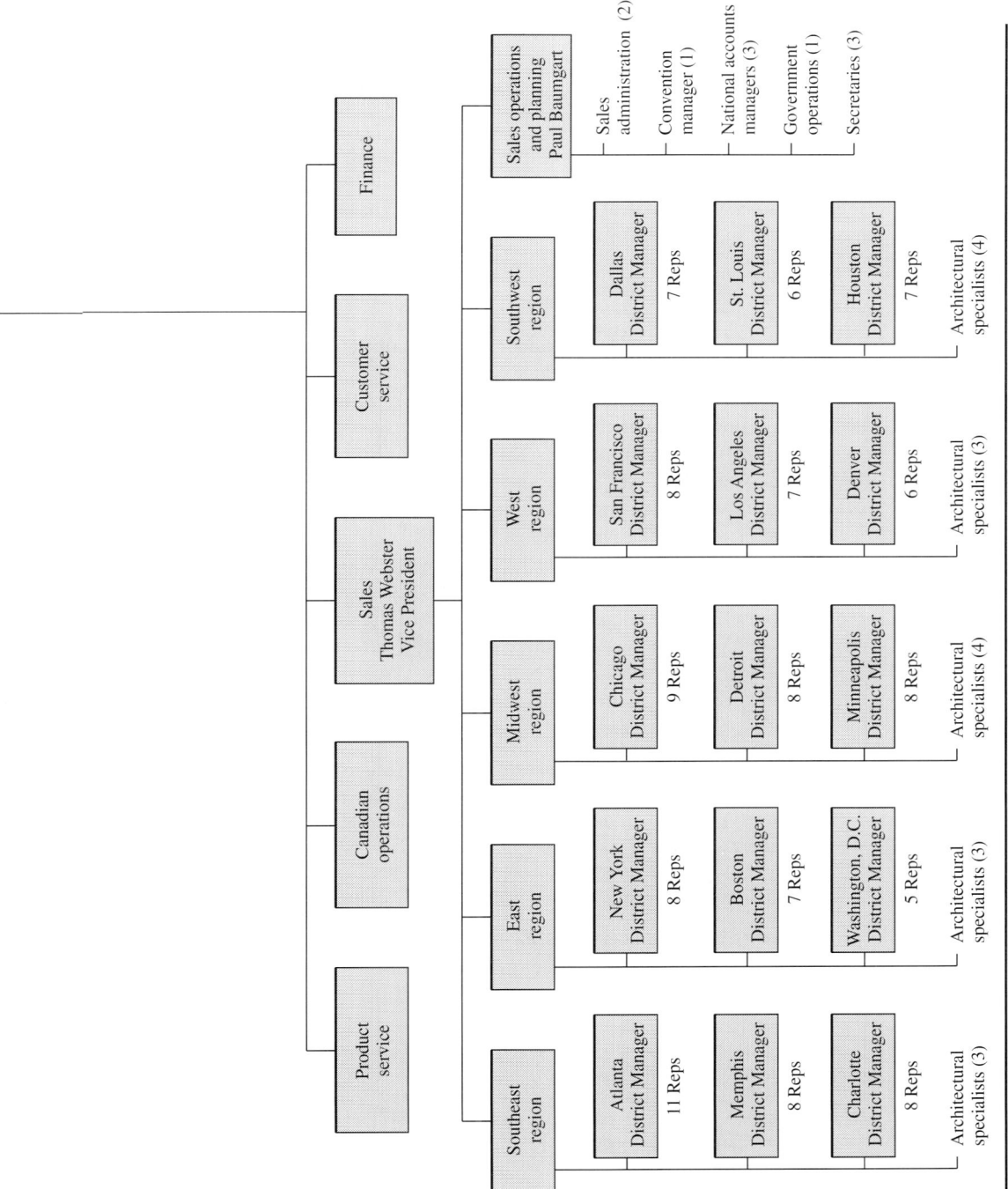

SOURCE: Company records.

Marketing Channels

In anticipation of focusing Ohmeda on medical equipment, Rountree in June 1985 had commissioned a consulting firm, Health Care Industries (HCI), to perform a detailed analysis of Ohmeda's dealers and sales force.[2] Historically, Ohmeda had generated over 50 percent of its equipment and supplies revenues through its 109 dealers. However, Rountree suspected that dealers were becoming less effective at selling Ohmeda's increasingly complex products. He also believed that direct selling might be more effective and profitable, especially in the long term.

Ohmeda's Dealers

HCI's analysis of dealer sales produced a number of troubling statistics. First, an increasing percentage of each product line was being sold through dealers. Consequently, a growing percentage of Ohmeda's sales reflected the 21 percent dealer discount as compared with an average 6 percent discount on direct sales.

Second, 30 percent of dealer sales were made from dealer inventory; the other 70 percent were "built to order" by Ohmeda's manufacturing group and then shipped directly to the customer. In this way, Ohmeda's dealers maintained average demonstration and stock inventories of $30,000.

Third, dealer sales efforts overlapped the efforts of Ohmeda's direct reps and occasionally each other. Moreover, Ohmeda's dealers did not provide specialized product knowledge or focus their selling efforts on Ohmeda's weaker products. (Exhibit 3 compares dealers' and direct sales reps' time allocation by product.)

One particularly unsettling part of this overlap was the collaboration of Ohmeda's direct reps with its dealers. Will Hirama, a 19-year veteran of the Ohmeda sales force, explained:

> I don't carry demonstration equipment. So when I need to perform a sales demo, I ask the dealer to deliver a demonstrator unit to the prospect hospital. At the appointed time, the dealer arrives with the equipment, and I use it to close the sale. To compensate the dealer for hauling around 400-plus pounds of hardware, I let the dealer book the order. Believe me, if I'm selling an anesthesia system that lists for $25,000, the $64 reduction in my commission[3] is a bargain compared with the trouble of lugging around a demo unit.

A fourth item of concern was the relative cost of sales. As shown in Exhibit 4, dealer sales were about twice as expensive as direct sales. In addition, when all

---

[2]Data for the study were collected from Ohmeda's midwest region, but the results of the study were believed to be reasonably representative of all Ohmeda regions. The midwest region was chosen for three reasons: (1) hospitals in the region covered the full range of hospital sizes, from very large urban hospitals to small rural hospitals; (2) Ohmeda's competitors were neither especially strong nor especially weak in the region; and (3) relationships between Ohmeda's midwest sales reps and its dealer organizations were typical for all regions.

[3]A system with a list price of $25,000 would sell at an average discount of 6 percent ($23,500), if sold direct. At an average commission rate of 1.7 percent, the salesperson would receive $399.50. If sold to the dealer, the same system would be discounted 21 percent to $19,750, and the salesperson would receive $335.75. The difference in commissions was $63.75.

EXHIBIT 3 Time Allocation of Direct and Dealer Salespeople

	Direct Sales		Dealer Sales	
	All Products	Equipment Only	All Products	Equipment Only
Anesthesia	32%	37.6%	26%	40.0%
Infant care	7	8.2	8	12.3
Respiratory therapy	7	8.2	6	9.2
Patient monitors	7	8.2	7	10.8
Suction	8	9.4	10	15.4
Architectural products	24	28.2%	8	12.3%
Equipment	85%	100.0%*	65%	100.0%
Supplies	7%		35%	
Gases	8%		0	
	100%		100%	

NOTE: Data indicate allocation of selling time only. For example, direct salespeople had 2,000 available work hours; 860 hours (43%) were spent with customers. Of the 860 hours, 32% were allocated to sales of anesthesia equipment.
*Column does not total 100% due to rounding.
SOURCE: Health Care Industries consulting study.

effects of dealer/direct sales overlap were removed, Ohmeda's direct sales force was estimated to account for about 30 percent of dealer equipment sales. (Exhibit 5 provides estimates of true direct and dealer equipment sales.)

While HCI's analysis presented some economic justification for terminating Ohmeda's dealers, Rountree was also concerned that reduced account coverage might translate into a major loss of sales. This concern was reinforced by Thomas Webster, NAFO's vice president of sales. Webster was adamantly opposed to terminating any dealers because he believed that terminated dealers would respond by taking on competitive products.

> We have a 70-year relationship with some of our dealers. Although some of these companies derive only 5 percent of their revenues from Ohmeda's products, others depend on us for 95 percent of their sales. If we simply terminate them according to our 30-day notice privilege, they're not going to take it sitting down. They'll go over to our competitors and take our customers with them! If we cut our dealers, we'll be cutting our own throat.

Webster had also prepared some preliminary estimates to demonstrate that the dealers provided important coverage. Based on his calculations, which are given in Exhibit 6, Webster estimated that in the next six months Ohmeda would have to hire at least 35 new salespeople to cover the dealers' customers. Given that Ohmeda was currently recruiting only seven new salespeople per year, Webster argued that such an increase in staffing would be practically impossible.

EXHIBIT 4 **Comparison of Direct and Dealer Sales Profitability with the Potential Profitability of All Direct Sales**

(In thousands of dollars)	1985 Direct Sales	1985 Sales to Dealers	1985 Total Sales	Potential Sales, If All Direct
A. Ohmeda revenues:				
Supplies	$2,030	$20,419	$22,449	
Equipment	53,827	41,333	95,160	
Total	55,857	61,752	117,609	$129,334[a]
B. Average discount	6%	21%		6%
C. List price of goods sold to end-users (A/(1–B))	59,422	78,167	137,589	137,589
Selling Costs				
D. Discount amount (C × B)	3,565	16,415	19,980	8,255
E. Sales commission (A × 1.7%)	950	1,050	1,999	2,199
F. Other sales costs (%)	3.2%	2.4%	2.8%	3.8%[b]
G. Other sales costs (A × F)	1,787	1,482	3,269	4,978
H. Sales administration (%)	6.1%	5.8%	5.9%	6.1%
I. Sales administration costs (A × H)	3,407	3,582	6,989	7,889
J. Total	9,709	22,529	32,238	23,321
K. Sales costs as percent of list price revenues (J/C)	16.3%	28.8%	23.4%	16.9%
L. Sales cost as percent of Ohmeda's revenues (J/A)	17.4%	36.5%	27.4%	18.0%

[a]Total direct revenues are "backed into" by multiplying the current list price of goods sold ($137.6 million) by one minus the average direct sales discount (1 − 0.06).

[b]Cost of going all direct does *not* include salaries or overhead for additional salespeople if necessary. Increased rate for other sales costs includes additional inventory expense, estimated at $654,000, and additional distribution expense, estimated at $1,055,000.

Formulas: Added inventory = 109 dealers × $30,000 × 20% = $654,000.
            Added distribution = ($129,334 − $117,609) × 9% = $1,055,000.

SOURCE: Health Care Industries consulting study.

Ohmeda's Direct Sales

As a result of their analysis, HCI had also suggested that Ohmeda's equipment sales could be improved by organizing the sales force into three specialized product groups: anesthesia; critical care (infant care, respiratory therapy, and suction); and architectural products. According to HCI's suggestion, the anesthesia and critical care units would both sell patient monitors.

HCI reasoned that selling sophisticated medical equipment required strong product and clinical knowledge and that Ohmeda's current general line sales organization was insufficiently focused. Indeed, HCI anticipated that the rapid pace of technical innovation would eventually force medical equipment companies to specialize their salespeople by product. In the meantime, specialization would enable Ohmeda's salespeople to develop a better understanding of their equipment and its clinical applications and, as a result, would increase sales.

Exhibit 5 Equipment Sales to End Users Adjusted to Remove Direct/Dealer Overlap

(In thousands of dollars)	Ohmeda's Direct Sales to End Users	Ohmeda's Sales to Dealers	Estimated Dealers' Sales to End Users at Direct Discount
A. List price of equipment sold	$57,263	$52,320	$52,320
B. Average discount	6%	21%	6%
C. Current equipment revenues [A × (1 −B)]	$53,827	$41,333	$49,181
D. Adjustment for direct/dealer overlap [30% of dealers' sales to end users ($49,181) made by Ohmeda's direct reps]	14,754		(14,754)
E. Sales to end users with overlap removed	68,581		34,427

SOURCE: Health Care Industries consulting study.

Exhibit 6 Calculation of Ohmeda's Requirement for Additional Direct Salespeople to Offset Lost Dealer Sales Coverage

Direct Sales Force Equipment Sales per Selling Hour

A. Ohmeda's direct equipment sales after dealer overlap is removed[a] — $68,581,000

B. Ohmeda direct sales time spent on equipment [130 reps × 2,000 hours/year × 43% of time with customers × 85% of time spent on equipment] — 95,030 hours

C. Ohmeda direct equipment sales per equipment selling hour (A/B) — $722/hours

Dealer Equipment Sales Converted to Hours of Direct Equipment Sales and Total Hours of Work

D. Dealer equipment sales to end users[a] — $34,427,000

E. Direct sales hours necessary to cover dealer equipment sales at Ohmeda's current direct sales/hour (D/C) — 47,683 hours

F. Direct equipment sales hours converted to direct work hours (E/43%) — 110,890 hours

Equivalent Direct Reps Necessary to Cover Dealer Sales

G. Direct reps (F/2,000 hours/representative) — Loss = 55 reps

Direct Salespeople Gained by Focusing on Equipment

H. Equivalent direct salespeople currently focused on supplies and gas (130 reps × 15% of time spent on supplies and gas) — Gain = 20 reps

Net Change in Sales Force Size

I. Necessary hires to cover current dealer sales (G–H) — 35

J. Additional district sales managers (I/8.5) — 4

K. Total change in sales personnel (I + J) — 39

[a]Exhibit 5 provides data on direct and dealer equipment sales with overlap removed.

SOURCE: Company records.

Webster, however, was even more critical of HCI's sales force analysis.

Baxter-Travenol is the largest medical supplies and equipment company in the world. They specialized their sales force in 1981, and now they're back to a general sales organization. If specialization is the answer, why then did Baxter-Travenol switch back?

Another thing—right now our salespeople spend 43 percent of their time with customers. That's a pretty good efficiency figure for industrial selling. The main reason our efficiency is so high is that every Ohmeda salesperson sells a broad line of products. If we specialize, then Ohmeda will have to send three different salespeople to every hospital. What's that going to do to our efficiency? We'll be lucky if we can maintain our current selling time and keep our efficiency above 32 percent.

Ohmeda's vice president of finance, Valerie Ruttenberg, had also questioned HCI's analysis. Based on Webster's estimate that time spent with customers would decrease from 43 percent to 32 percent of a salesperson's total time, Ruttenberg estimated that maintaining Ohmeda's current direct equipment sales coverage with a specialized sales force would cost an additional $3.2 million per year and would require the company to recruit more than 40 sales professionals during the next six months. Ruttenberg also noted that the required increases would be substantially larger if dealers were to be eliminated. (Exhibit 7 provides the finance VP's calculations.)

Ohmeda's Markets

Ohmeda's products were sold direct and through distributors to 5,789 hospitals in the United States. These customers ranged from urban hospitals[4] with more than 700 beds to rural hospitals with less than 50 beds. Because hospitals were strictly regulated, they faced constant pressure to cut costs. As a cost-control measure, all purchases of supplies and medical equipment required budgetary approval of the hospital administration. However, the purchasing influence of hospital administrators was generally inversely related to the complexity of the item. Thus, for purchases of disposable supplies and gases, a hospital purchasing agent often awarded the contract based on low price. In contrast, capital equipment was invariably selected by the hospital's medical specialists and clinical area end users. Because any machine malfunction was potentially life-threatening, medical specialists were especially concerned with precision, reliability, and safety. In addition, both the sophistication of clinical procedures and the technical expertise and interest of medical specialists were increasing. Consequently, the product and clinical knowledge required to sell medical equipment was also increasing. This trend was especially evident in high-technology markets such as anesthesia machines, infant incubators, and respiratory ventilators. (Exhibit 8 summarizes hospital purchasing influences by purchase type and functional responsibility.)

---

[4]Urban hospitals were those institutions which were located within a Standard Metropolitan Statistical Area of more than 100,000 people.

EXHIBIT 7 **Calculation of Needed Equipment Sales Hours to Cover Ohmeda's Current Direct Customer Base with a Specialized Sales Force**

Hospital Type	Number of Hospitals	Average Number of Hospital Calls per Year	Percent of Hospitals Called	Average Number of Accounts	Length of Average Account Call (minutes)	Needed Hours of Equipment Sales Time	Percent of Total Sales Time
Current Equipment Sales Coverage							
Urban:							
≥700 beds	239	27.4	100%	4.1	39	17,452	18%
500–699 beds	371	17.6	100	3.4	36	13,320	14
200–499 beds	1,018	14.7	92	3.0	39	26,846	28
<200 beds	1,067	9.8	81	2.9	31	12,691	13
Rural:							
>100 beds	951	8.8	76	3.5	35	12,986	14
≤100 beds	2,143	7.6	55	2.8	28	11,705	12
Total	5,789					95,000ª	

	Current Direct Sales Coverage (equipment only)	Specialized Coverage (equipment only)	Change
A. Total work hours per year per rep	2,000	2,000	0
B. Percentage of time spent selling (efficiency)ᵇ	43%	32%	−11%
C. Available selling hours per salesperson (A × B)	860	640	−220
D. Total hours of direct equipment sales coverage needed (from table above)	95,000	95,000	0
E. Number of salespeople needed (D/C)	110	148	38
F. Cost per salesperson ($000)	$85	$85	0
G. Total cost of salespeople ($000) (E × F)	$9,350	$12,580	$3,230
H. District sales managers needed (E/8.5)	13	17	4

ªEquipment selling time was actually 95,030 hours per year, that is, 2,000 work hours × 43% selling time × 85% equipment × 130 reps.
ᵇEfficiency was defined as the ratio of (1) time spent with customers to (2) total work time. The current average was 860/2,000, or 43%.
SOURCE: Company records.

In 1985 Ohmeda's $160.8 million in U.S. revenues were derived as follows: $27.2 million from gases (17 percent), $22.4 million from supplies (14 percent), $95.2 million from equipment (59 percent), and $16 million from service (10 percent). Ohmeda sold a wide range of medical equipment and accessories, including anesthesia systems and accessories ($29.5 million), patient monitors ($6.7 million), respiratory therapy products ($5.7 million), suction therapy equipment ($14.3 million), infant care equipment ($16.2 million), and architectural products ($22.8 million). Many of these items were unrelated and were considered to be specialty products. (Exhibit 9 illustrates the variety of Ohmeda's medical equipment products.)

The breadth of Ohmeda's equipment line was evident, in part, in the range of its high-tech and low-tech products. For example, anesthesia machines, patient monitors, respiratory ventilators, and infant incubators featured state-of-the-art technology, including modern electronics, data processing capacity and/or computer

EXHIBIT 8 Summary of Purchase Influences

Decision Makers	Infant Care Incubators	Respiratory Therapy Ventilators	Anesthesia Equipment	Suction Equipment	Architectural Products	Patient Monitors
Head nurse/unit supervisor	●	◐	◐	●		●[a]
Nursing staff	●			●		
Anesthesiologist			●			
Neonatologist	◐					
Respiratory therapist	◐	●				
Purchasing			○	◐	◐	◐
Biomed tech	◐	◐	◐	○	○	
Hospital engineer					●	
Architect/contractor					●	

Key:
Primary ●
Secondary ◐
Some Involvement ○

[a] Patient monitors were selected by the supervisor of each therapy unit. Thus, monitors that were used with anesthesia equipment were chosen by the chief resident in anesthesiology.

SOURCE: Health Care Industries consulting study.

interfaces, and modular designs that enabled the medical specialist to group equipment into advanced systems. These major systems attracted most research and development funds and were continuously updated. By contrast, Ohmeda's entire suction therapy product line and most accessories for its capital equipment were standard items and were less-frequently updated.

The diversity of Ohmeda's competitors matched its products. Competitors ranged from small companies focusing on one medical equipment niche, such as North American Drager in anesthesia equipment and Healthdyne/Air Shields in infant care, to large medical equipment multinationals such as Hewlett-Packard and Siemens. While many of these competitors sold through a combination of direct salespeople and specialized dealers, the larger companies relied more heavily on their direct sales. (The strengths and weaknesses of Ohmeda's major competitors are summarized by product line in Exhibit 10.)

Anesthesia Equipment

The Products. Anesthesia machines were used to monitor and control the delivery of anesthetic agents and oxygen to a patient during surgical procedures. With 70 years of experience in anesthesia products, Ohmeda was a leading developer and supplier of sophisticated anesthesia technology. Its anesthesia machines had been adopted by most hospitals, and company officials estimated that Ohmeda equipment was used in most of the 20 million surgical procedures performed each year.

Ohmeda offered three anesthesia machines, ranging in price from $18,000 for a low-end machine to $26,000 for the top-of-the-line Modulus-II Anesthesia System

EXHIBIT 9 **Examples of Ohmeda Equipment**

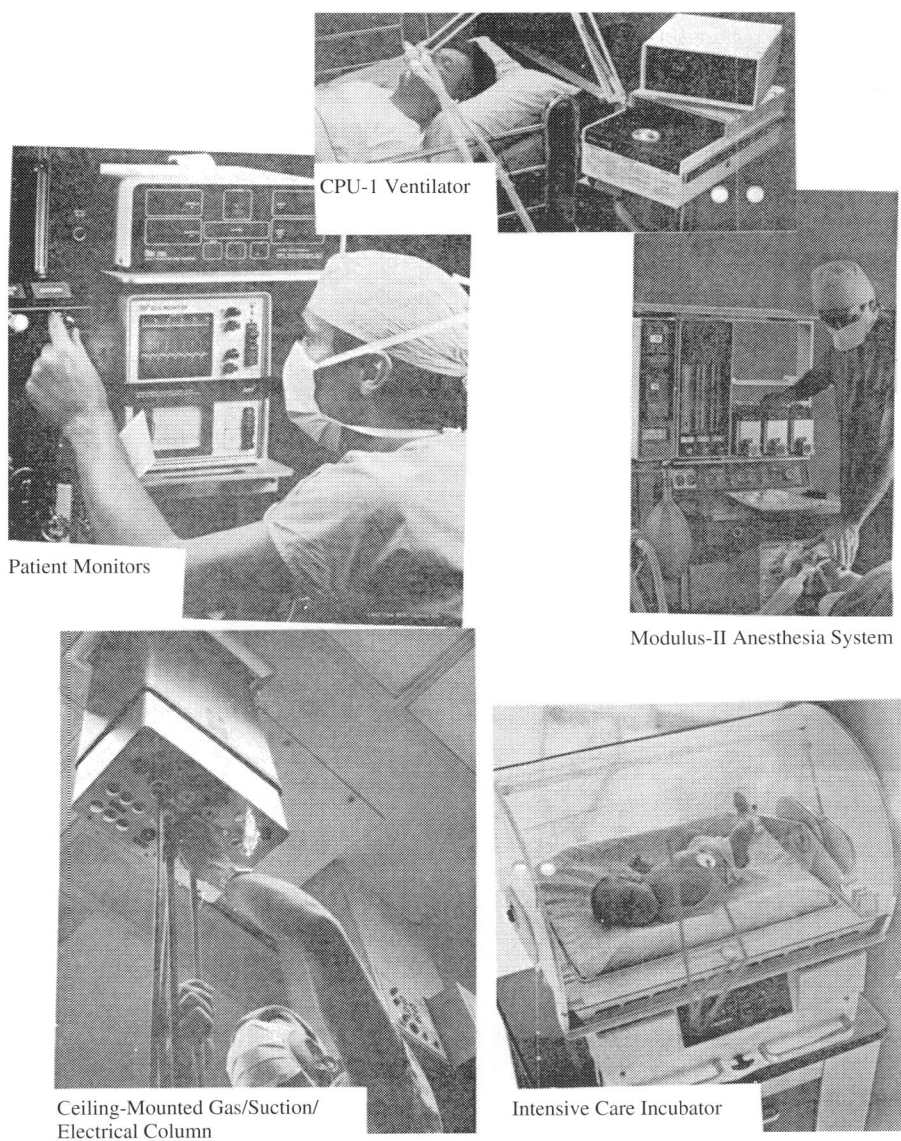

SOURCE: Company product literature.

(Mod-II). The Mod-II was introduced in October 1985 and, unlike other anesthesia machines, it combined electronic patient monitors with the gas delivery unit. The Mod-II also featured an "open" design that would allow the integration of new monitoring and electronic modules as they became available.

EXHIBIT 10 Ohmeda's Major Competitors

Market ($ size; units) [Ohmeda market share]	Ohmeda's Competitors	1985 Market Share (%)	Pricing	Sales and Distributor Channels	Sales Coverage and Development	Comments
Anesthesia ($65.1 million; 3,200 machine/year) [45%]	N.A. Drager	35	$16,000–$20,000	20 exclusive dealer organizations	Focused in Ohmeda's eastern and western regions	All dealers service Drager machines; dealers must meet minimum sales hurdles
Infant Care Thermoregulators ($27 million; 4,550 units/year) [39%]	Healthdyne/Air Shields (H/AS)	61	$5,040–$6,490	24 explicitly nonexclusive dealer organizations, providing 100 dealer reps; also 15 direct salespeople	Deployed around metropolitan areas	Dealers must meet quarterly sales targets; contracts exclusive *in practice*; 90% of dealers service H/AS machines
All Other ($46 million) [13%]	H/AS	34	Competitive*			
Respiratory Therapy Low-tech ($37 million) [15%]	Baxter-Travenol	45+	Low†	Very large direct sales force	National	N/A
Ventilator ($57.8 million; 3,500 units/year) [0%]	Puritan-Bennett	42	$16,000	30 dealer organizations; 20 direct salespeople	National	Sells "standard" design ventilator
	Bear Medical	28	$16,000	30 dealer organizations; 10 direct salespeople	National	Sells "standard" design ventilator
	Siemens	22	$17,000–$18,000	Large direct sales force (>300 reps)	National	Entered U.S. in 1977 with European design ventilator; spent estimated $5 million on communications and training; market share expected to grow by 2%/year for next 2–3 years
Patient Monitors ($166 million) [4%]	Hewlett-Packard	25+	Competitive	Large direct sales force	National	Sales force sells all Hewlett-Packard medical equipment
	Siemens	25+	Competitive	Same as for ventilators	National	Sales force sells all Siemens medical equipment
Suction ($24 million) [60%]	Chemetron	25	Low	About 100 dealer reps; 12 direct salespeople	Focused in Ohmeda's eastern and western regions	Introduced new product line six months ago; gained market share at 1–2% per year in 1983–84
Architectural Products ($68 million) [34%]	Chemetron	23	Competitive	Same as for suction	Same as for suction	
	Hill-Rom	15	Competitive	85-person direct sales force	National	Originally a maker of hospital beds
	Square-D	13	Competitive	Combination of direct and dealer reps; no. unknown	Focused in Ohmeda's eastern, western, and southeastern regions	Designed and manufactured custom electrical switchgear; often bundled switchgear with other products; most direct salespeople held college degrees in engineering

*Denotes that prices were very close to Ohmeda's across a wide range of products.
†Denotes that prices were 10% lower than Ohmeda's across a wide range of products.
SOURCE: Company records.

Market Trends. Until 1976, Ohmeda had clearly dominated the anesthesia equipment market and had maintained a market share of more than 65 percent. Since 1976, however, its market share had slipped to 45 percent. Meanwhile, North American Drager, established in 1974 by a West German medical equipment company, had increased its share from nothing in 1976 to 35 percent in 1985. Drager had capitalized on the increasing sophistication of the anesthesia market by emphasizing "advanced technology and reliable, German engineering." Rountree was particularly concerned with Drager's penetration of large urban hospitals and teaching institutions, where Drager's share of purchases had reached 42 percent.

Patient Monitors

The Products. Patient monitors performed such diverse tasks as monitoring a patient's heart rate and rhythm (electrocardiography) during surgery, tracking a patient's blood pressure during the critical stages of recovery, or watching for subtle changes in the body temperature of a premature infant. Less-obvious functions of patient monitors included tracking and recording respiratory volume, concentration of oxygen in a patient's blood (oxygenation), and concentration of CO_2 in a patient's breath. Some type of monitor was used in almost every hospital setting.

Technical innovations were rapidly expanding the capabilities of patient monitors. Many advanced monitors now included: (1) electronic displays capable of graphically illustrating current values or trends in patient parameters, (2) data processing capacity or computer interfaces for collecting and analyzing patient data, and (3) integrated/modular designs enabling several monitors to share data to provide more accurate readings. Depending on their clinical application and technological sophistication, monitors ranged in price from $700 to $6,000.

Market Trends. Ohmeda was not a market leader in patient monitors, but it competed in segments totaling almost $166 million and maintained respectable shares (12 to 17 percent) in a few specialized markets. Ohmeda currently sold its monitors mainly as accessories to other medical equipment; however, Rountree expected the company to grow substantially through independent sales of advanced monitors.

Respiratory Therapy

The Products. Respiratory therapy products provided support for patients with impaired breathing. These products ranged from simple, handheld resuscitators and low-tech accessories to long-term critical care ventilators. Ohmeda manufactured and sold a variety of low-tech items, such as mechanical flow meters and humidifiers, with prices ranging from $35 to $200.

In October 1985, Ohmeda had also introduced an advanced microprocessor-controlled respiratory ventilator, the CPU-1. Priced at $11,000, Ohmeda's new CPU-1 provided extended respiratory support in critical and intensive care cases. Because the CPU-1 tracked the patient's response to the therapy and was self-monitoring, a trained respiratory therapist could operate it with little continuous intervention. Despite disappointing sales, Ohmeda's sales planning and operations manager, Paul Baumgart, believed that the innovative CPU-1 could have an important impact:

> The CPU-1 was developed by a Paris-based subsidiary of the BOC Group. It was introduced in France in 1978, and it's still the most advanced respiratory therapy system on the market. In addition to the most advanced technology, the CPU-1 embodies an important clinical innovation: mandatory minute volume (MMV).[5]
>
> MMV is accepted throughout Europe as a critical measure of patient respiration but has not yet been adopted in the United States. We are attempting to convince respiratory therapists that important patient care and safety information is contained in the MMV measure. So far, the going has been slow. Our price is lower, but we've sold only 10 units in the past six months; that's 10 percent of plan.

Market Trends. The market for low-tech respiratory therapy equipment was based on low price; Baxter-Travenol dominated the segment. Because Rountree saw little long-term potential in this segment, he was satisfied with Ohmeda's 15 percent share of these low-tech sales. However, with the CPU-1, Rountree planned to expand Ohmeda's ventilator sales from $110,000 in 1985 to $2.7 million by 1990—an annual compound growth of more than 90 percent. Rountree believed that timing was critical: The ventilator installed base was coming due for replacement, and annual sales were expected to increase from 3,500 to 4,200 units during the next three years.

Suction Therapy

The Products. Suction therapy products were used in surgeries and in the care of critically ill patients. For example, during surgery a suction tube would remove a patient's saliva to prevent choking. The amount of suction was controlled by a vacuum regulator assembly.

As a result of its expertise in gas delivery systems, Ohmeda had entered the suction therapy business early. In addition to vacuum regulators, Ohmeda sold a broad line of suction accessories. Prices ranged from a few dollars for simple fittings and connectors up to $200 for vacuum regulators. Ohmeda's suction equipment was widely recognized as reliable and sturdy; more than half of the operating rooms and intensive care units in the United States had installed its suction regulators. Many hospitals continued to buy Ohio Chemical's suction equipment as a matter of course, and suction continued to be one of Ohmeda's most profitable product lines.

Market Trends. Although its suction products had not been revised since 1978, Ohmeda had a 60 percent market share in the $24 million market for suction products. Ohmeda's primary competitor was Chemetron, a privately owned company

---

[5]In MMV, the therapist specifies a minimum respiration volume, and the CPU-1 tracks the patient's exhaled volume minute by minute. If the minimum volume is not maintained, an alarm sounds. However, most U.S. respiratory therapists have been trained on equipment that estimates a patient's respiration volume based on measures of exhale pressure and breath rate.

with a 25 percent market share. During the past six months, Chemetron had introduced a completely new product line; however, Mark Halpert, Ohmeda's general manager for suction products, believed the threat posed by Chemetron was not in its new products:

> Sure, they're trying to upgrade quality, but our products are still better. Instead, they sell by cutting their prices to 10 percent or more below ours. What really concerns me is the rumor that we're going to terminate our dealers. Chemetron has tremendous sales coverage; overall they've gained 1 to 2 percent of the market during each of the past two years.
>
> Unlike other Ohmeda products, suction equipment is not complex. If Rountree eliminates our dealers, I'm not sure that we will be able to maintain "share of mind," and that could be disastrous. Simple reorders, "onesie-twosies," constitute more than half of our suction business.

Infant Care

The Products. Infant care products provided a controlled environment for premature infants or for babies suffering from other medical difficulties. These products ranged in complexity from simple accessories such as mist tents to advanced microprocessor-controlled thermoregulation systems. Thermoregulators, which included infant warmers and incubators, maintained the patient's body temperature within a very precise range. Incubators were the most sophisticated thermoregulation systems, because they covered the infant with a transparent hood that also enabled accurate control of the incubator atmosphere. The hood, however, reduced visibility and access to the patient.

Ohmeda's newest infant care product, the Intensive Care Incubator (ICI), was the result of a major development effort. Using an entirely new, double-walled hood design, the ICI addressed two important clinical problems: infant radiant heat loss and the need for improved patient access and visibility. The ICI also replaced conventional-incubator thermostats and thermometers with electronic monitors and a microprocessor-based temperature controller. The ICI was compatible with a wide variety of other medical equipment and was priced at $6,500.

Ohmeda had expected its new ICI to take sales from less innovative Healthdyne/Air Shields (H/AS) products. However, in the six months since its October 1985 introduction, Ohmeda had sold only a few hundred units. Most salespeople attributed the disappointingly low ICI sales to the difficulty involved in explaining the concept of radiant heat loss. Ohmeda's salespeople also felt that the ICI's all-new design made this a "completely different kind of equipment purchase."

Market Trends. With the very low growth in the U.S. birthrate, the market for infant care equipment was expected to grow at less than 2 percent per year for the foreseeable future. Nevertheless, Rountree planned to grow Ohmeda's share of the thermoregulation segment by at least 5 percent per year. In 1986, H/AS and Ohmeda were the only competitors in the infant thermoregulation market. Both companies also received revenues from other infant care products, but in Ohmeda's case these revenues were essentially add-ons to sales of thermoregulators.

Architectural Products

Ohmeda's architectural products were used for hospital construction and remodeling. For example, when a hospital added new facilities, it would require specialized piping for gas and vacuum delivery, special wiring for secure electrical power supply, and for surgical areas special ceiling-mounted service columns or movable overhead service pendants that reduced operating-room clutter.

Ohmeda offered a line of "completely integrated architectural systems," including vacuum pumps, air compressors, and modular walls. All Ohmeda salespeople sold architectural products, but three or four salespeople in each region focused on assisting hospital engineers, contractors, and architects in planning and designing new hospital systems. Many architectural products were big-ticket items; average orders ranged from $40,000 to $60,000.

North American Field Operations

Ohmeda's North American Field Operations (NAFO) group was responsible for all Ohmeda sales, service, and customer support in North America. Elliott Hillback, Jr., age 38, joined Ohmeda in March 1985 and was now vice president of NAFO. Hillback had earlier been vice president of artificial organs at Baxter-Travenol, where he had worked with Rountree. He held an undergraduate degree in anthropology and a Harvard MBA (1972).

NAFO was divided into five departments: Canadian operations, finance, product service, customer service, and U.S. sales. Canadian operations constituted less than 10 percent of Ohmeda's business, and it was run independently of U.S. sales and service. The finance department dealt with sales expenses, order entry, and customer billing.

Product Service

Product service maintained and serviced Ohmeda's medical equipment in the field. The company employed more than 200 factory-trained service representatives, deployed nationwide through five regions: West, Southwest, Southeast, Midwest, and East. Ohmeda's service reps were trained on all products and worked exclusively on Ohmeda equipment. Their technical skills were continually upgraded through company training in new service procedures and new medical technology. No dealers were allowed to service Ohmeda equipment.

Customer Service

Customer service was responsible for: (1) answering customer inquiries regarding product features, prices, delivery lead time, and status of current orders; (2) processing all orders and coordinating them with production scheduling to determine delivery dates; and (3) handling all misorders, misshipments, and returns of defective or damaged goods.

U.S. Sales

Thomas Webster, head of NAFO's sales, had been with the company for 33 years, including 12 years as vice president of sales. During this time, total sales had increased by 8 to 15 percent per year, and Webster credited much of this success to the sales force. He also questioned the necessity of changing the sales organization:

> Our salespeople are a major source of competitive advantage. They are independent and aggressive, and they mesh well with our dealers. Why fix something if it's not broken? If we cut the dealers, the result will be lower account coverage and lower sales for Ohmeda. If we go a step further and specialize, our customers will be completely confused and our sales force will be in total disarray.

The sales department was organized into a sales planning group and five sales regions. The planning group was responsible for sales administration, convention attendance, and national account management. Ohmeda had 14 national accounts, including major hospital management groups such as Humana, Hospital Corporation of America, and American Medical International. In addition, as a result of industry consolidation, sales to these customers had grown at an average annual rate of 30 percent during the last five years.

Average compensation for Ohmeda's three national account managers was $60,000, including salary of about $45,000 and commission of $15,000. In addition, all sales to national accounts were counted toward the territory sales totals of Ohmeda's sales reps and were included in their commission calculations.

The five sales regions—West, Southwest, Southeast, Midwest, and East—were each headed by a regional vice president. Three of the regional vice presidents had been with the company for more than 20 years; the other two each had 10 years of experience at Ohmeda. Key statistics for each region are given in Table 2.

TABLE 2 Sales Region Statistics

	Southeast	East	Midwest	West	Southwest
Equipment sales (in millions of dollars)	$ 26	$ 16	$ 18	$ 15	$ 20
Sales representatives	30	23	29	24	24
Total hospitals	1,236	958	1,450	1,046	1,099

Sales regions were divided into three districts, each with a district manager and 5 to 11 sales reps. The average district manager had been with the company for 15 years. A typical district contained about 400 hospitals and was covered by eight salespeople. Each sales rep had an exclusive geographic territory and was responsible for the full Ohmeda product line; some also managed dealer operations in their territories. Exclusive territories ranged in size from 30 to 160 hospitals; an average territory contained about 50 hospitals.

Each region also had 3 to 4 specialists helping the sales force sell architectural products. (Exhibit 11 provides a midwest region map and data by sales territory.)

EXHIBIT 11 Ohmeda's Midwest Region Territories

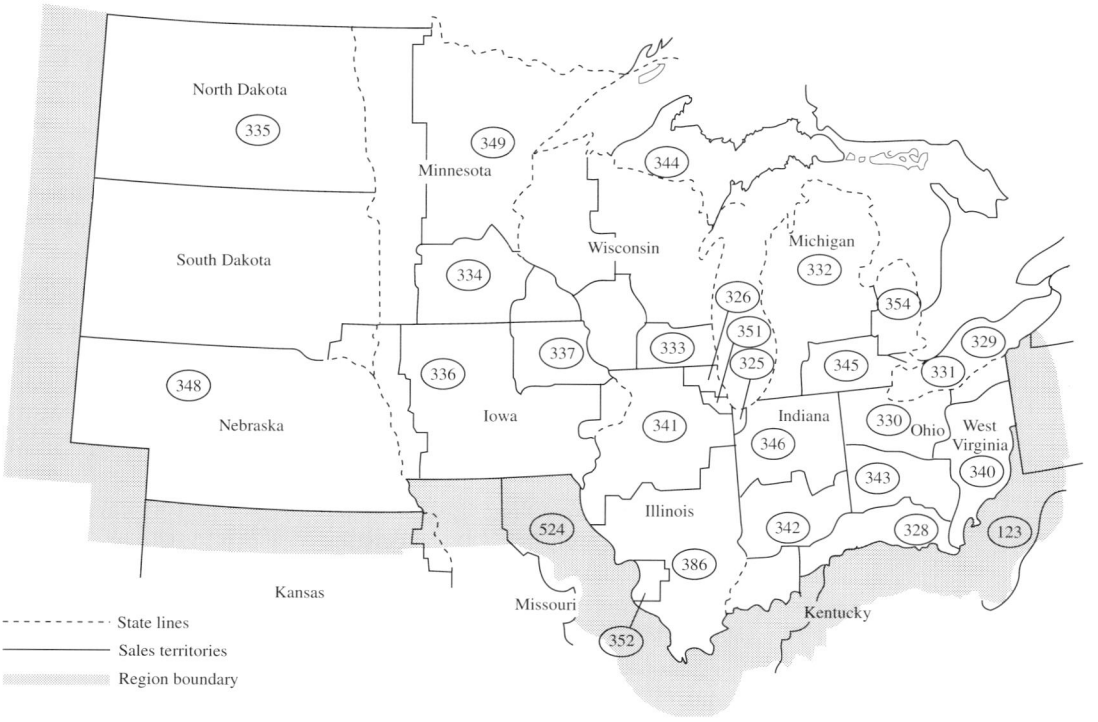

The Sales Force

Ohmeda's sales force was composed of experienced professionals whose length of service with Ohmeda averaged just over 10 years. Most had joined the company with experience in sales, but only a few had previously sold medical equipment or supplies. Sixty percent of Ohmeda's salespeople were high school graduates; 40 percent were college graduates. Their average age was 42; about half were over 50 and 25 percent were under 35.

New sales reps received two weeks of product training, covering all products in Ohmeda's line. All reps were also given refresher training as Ohmeda's product line expanded or as general changes in medical technology occurred. Ohmeda's product training was given high marks, but few salespeople mastered the entire product line. Instead, most focused their efforts on those products with which they were most knowledgeable and successful.

In general, Ohmeda's strong reputation for product quality made it easy to recruit and retain salespeople. Within NAFO, sales turnover was low, averaging less than 5 percent per year.

EXHIBIT 11 (concluded)

Territory Number	Number Hospitals by Size (beds)			Total <200	Total Hospitals	Total Beds	Total Surgeries (000s)
	>700	500–699	200–499				
Data for Midwest Region Territories							
325	4	4	14	8	30	12,525	205
326	1	3	22	15	41	12,138	211
328	1	5	13	23	42	9,907	216
329	4	0	18	14	36	11,273	218
330	1	1	17	40	59	9,817	200
331	2	3	10	11	26	8,282	166
332	0	1	15	50	66	8,517	185
333	1	4	22	14	41	11,515	240
334	2	2	7	42	53	7,503	138
335	0	0	10	150	160	10,073	142
336	1	3	12	74	90	10,445	177
337	2	0	6	40	48	6,126	122
340	1	4	21	22	48	11,799	216
341	1	2	22	44	69	12,675	258
342	2	3	8	22	35	8,862	193
343	4	6	9	17	36	11,514	239
344	0	2	10	62	74	8,493	165
345	1	2	19	17	39	9,909	219
346	0	4	11	44	59	10,110	205
348	0	4	12	101	117	11,230	195
349	2	0	11	78	91	10,117	162
351	4	2	19	10	35	12,875	208
352	2	4	11	14	31	10,150	174
354	1	3	14	19	37	8,700	221
386	2	2	11	72	87	11,315	197
Totals	39	64	344	1,003	1,450	255,870	4,872

Sales Territories

Because hospital densities varied considerably from territory to territory, district managers and sales reps worked together to establish hospital calling frequencies. Of 2,000 hours per year, Ohmeda reps spent 43 percent of their available time with customers, 26 percent traveling, and 31 percent with administrative duties, on the telephone, or away on training or vacation.

Overall, sales reps averaged about five calls per day. Given Ohmeda's broad product line, a sales rep who visited a hospital's anesthesia department, nursery, hospital engineer, purchasing agent, and critical care unit could perform five sales calls within a single institution.

Most Ohmeda sales reps saw its extensive product line as a major advantage in selling. Robert Carroll, an 18-year veteran in the metropolitan Chicago area, commented:

> With our products, it's a rarity if I'm not received at a hospital. I have 41 hospitals, and I visit each one 8 to 10 times a year. At every one I have long-standing relationships with

10 to 12 people—from the hospital engineer in the basement to the head of anesthesia on the top floor. All these people know that Ohmeda offers a range of products. If they need something, or if they know that one of their colleagues needs something, they're likely to tell me. Even though purchasing is trying to limit all sales calls to very specific purposes, my network at these hospitals keeps me in touch.

Statistics collected for HCI's study revealed that account coverage and call frequency declined with hospital size. While these statistics displayed an emphasis on large accounts, HCI's analysis of market share by hospital size suggested that Ohmeda's reps were less effective in large accounts. For example, in sales of anesthesia machines, Ohmeda's market share among very large urban hospitals was only 22.7 percent; however, its market share among medium and small urban hospitals was more than 50 percent. In addition, for each anesthesia machine sold, Ohmeda's very large accounts required 36 hours of contact sales time, while small urban accounts required only 15 hours. (Exhibit 12 summarizes Ohmeda's selling time and market share by hospital size.)

Evaluation and Compensation

Sales reps were responsible for maximizing the sales volume within a specified territory, and their performance evaluation was based on total revenues. Provided that a sales rep was deemed effective by Webster, territories which were consistently under- or overforecast were respectively increased or decreased in size to equalize revenues. Although reps were also responsible for informing management of com-

EXHIBIT 12 Summary of Ohmeda's Selling Time and Market Share by Hospital Size (anesthesia equipment)

Type of Hospital	Actual Selling Hours per Machine Sold	Ohmeda's Share of 1985 Sales	Percent of Total Market	Ohmeda's Share of Total Market	Percent of Ohmeda's Total Sales
Urban:					
>700 beds	35.8	22.7%	21%	4.8%	10.6%
500–699 beds	27.3	39.8	17	6.8	15.1
200–499 beds	27.9	56.1	27	15.1	33.8
<200 beds	15.4	53.9	10	5.4	12.0
Urban total			75	32.1	71.5
Rural:					
>100 beds	23.3	49.7	17	8.4	18.9
≤100 beds	50.8	53.3	8	4.3	9.5
Rural total			25	12.7	28.4
			100%	44.8%	100.0%[a]

[a] Column does not actually total 100% due to rounding.
SOURCE: Health Care Industries consulting study and company records.

petitive changes in their territories, this was not linked to evaluation and information collection was limited. In fact, as one district manager noted, "competitor information and product suggestions from the field are generally ignored by headquarters."

Total compensation averaged $42,000, including salary and commission. In addition, each rep received a company car. Annual salaries ranged from $19,200 to $28,800 and were based on seniority and performance. Commissions ranged from $10,000 to $60,000 and were determined by a three-stage formula: (1) 1.5 percent commission on all sales up to the previous two-year average for the territory; (2) 2 percent commission on all sales from the two-year average to the territory forecast—generally about 15 percent greater than the two-year average; and (3) a 5 percent commission on sales over forecast. Given these stages, the average rate of commissions paid was 1.7 percent. The average cost of a salesperson was $85,000, including salary, commissions, expenses, company car, and overhead.

Options

As Rountree reread the finance officer's memo, he contemplated how the changes in Ohmeda's product line would affect the company's marketing systems. If the sale of the supplies business was successful, Ohmeda would be focused on medical equipment beginning October 1, 1986. Including the transfer of gas revenues and the supplies divestiture, Ohmeda's current revenues would be reduced by 31 percent.

In light of these product-line changes and the company's five-year goals, it would be necessary to reassess Ohmeda's direct-sales and dealer-sales account coverage. If he decided to emphasize direct sales or specialize the salespeople by product groups, Rountree would need to resize Ohmeda's direct sales force. He also recognized that these changes would require a complete review of Ohmeda's management systems for selecting, motivating, evaluating, compensating, and developing sales personnel.

At first glance, Rountree had thought that emphasizing direct sales through a specialized sales force might improve the company's sales effectiveness. Now, however, he was very uneasy. Webster's comments that efficiency would suffer and that terminated dealers would become Ohmeda's competitors were especially haunting, and Ruttenberg's economic analysis had added yet another dimension to his worries. Even more troubling was the notion that changes made in the next six months would spell the success or failure of Ohmeda's $95 million medical equipment business.

CHAPTER 24

Atlas Copco (A): Gaining and Building Distribution Channels

Atlas Copco, a Swedish company, held the highest market share for air compressors worldwide. However, its attempts to enter U.S. markets had been unsuccessful in the past. The chapter describes a series of strategic distribution maneuvers which enabled the company to improve market share from 1 percent to 10 percent in 10 years. Management must now reassess its distribution strategy, and if necessary, formulate a new one to improve the company's current position from No. 4 to No. 1 or No. 2 in the U.S. market. The objective is to gain an understanding of what is involved in building distribution strength.

Introduction

On December 10, 1984, Arthur Droege, vice president for marketing and sales of Atlas-Copco's Industrial Compressors Division, started to draft a letter to his distributors introducing a new franchising policy that created four levels of franchise. The basic franchise would be for distribution of compressors below 200 horsepower. The second level of franchise would include larger compressors, but it would be offered only to distributors who performed according to mutually accepted targets on the basic franchise. Similarly, a third level of franchise for specialized product lines would be offered selectively to distributors at the second level, based on performance. The fourth level of franchise, a general service franchise, would be offered only to distributors willing to invest in equipment and facilities necessary to maintain Atlas-Copco's installed compressors in the field. Depending on their performance and capabilities, distributors would be offered one or several franchises.

V. Kasturi Rangan prepared this case.
Copyright © 1987 by the President and Fellows of Harvard College.
Harvard Business School case 588-004 (revised May 21, 1993).

Chapter 24   Atlas Copco (A)

The draft letter began:

Dear ———,

Now that 1984 is nearly behind us, we can look back at a most successful year for marketing industrial compressors. Most of our markets have expanded considerably during the year, and our invoiced sales increased significantly.

For 1985 we are forecasting continued modest growth and have been busy during the past months developing our marketing plans to capitalize on this increasing market potential with our sights set on increased market share.

Our product charter for 1985 has been expanded and puts us in a position to satisfy almost every air requirement in the industrial marketplace. In order to accomplish this, our primary channel of sale for the coming years will be industrial distribution. In fact, our plans for 1985 are to market 90 percent of our budgeted units and 80 percent of our budgeted sales dollars through our distributor network. Our distributor marketing effort will be supplemented with a direct sales staff that will be responsible for calling on a defined customer list. The direct sales channel will be aimed at markets and customers that are normally best developed with a direct relationship between customers and manufacturers. All distributors whose franchised territory includes customers with whom we wish to establish a direct sales relationship will be notified as to our activity in order to prevent duplication of effort and customer confusion.

As Droege continued to write, the phone rang. Dean Pope, the division's president, was on the line. "Art, have you had a chance to put the finishing touches on our new franchising policy? Can we include it in our agenda for the afternoon's strategy meeting?"

"Sure," replied Droege. "I know you've been interested in evaluating our distribution strategy for a long time, and this new proposal gives us the opportunity to do so."

Stationary Air Compressors

Like electricity and gas, compressed air is a utility with a wide range of applications. Stationary air compressors provide compressed air for three main purposes: powering tools and other machinery (plant air), powering and controlling pneumatic systems in certain types of equipment (special machinery), and supplying air for certain manufacturing processes (process air). Industry convention was to classify compressors by horsepower size (small, below 25 hp; medium, 25 to 300 hp; and large, above 300 hp) and by compression technology (reciprocating, or recip; rotary screw, or rotary; and centrifugal).

Reciprocating compression occurred when a piston moved within a cylinder. Air was drawn into the cylinder on the intake stroke; on the return stroke, the air was compressed and discharged at high pressure for further use. Rotary compression was achieved by means of two intermeshing rotors within a casing. Rotation of the assembly caused air to enter through the inlet port, and as rotation continued the entrapped air moved along the length of the rotor shaft and was discharged under pressure for further use. Centrifugal compression was the result of an impeller rotating at high velocity. The air particles discharged from the tip of the impeller were

TABLE A Air Compressors: User Cost Comparisons

	Recip	Rotary	Centrifugal
Cost of compressor per hp	$300	$200	$225
Estimated life	10–12 yrs.	5–7 yrs.	10–12 yrs.
Installation cost as a percent of initial cost	20%[a]	10%	12%
Spare parts and maintenance cost per year	6%	2.5%	2%
Energy costs at 7 cents/kwh and 300 days operation in a year	$400/hp	$460/hp	$435/hp

[a] The installation costs for recips were relatively high because special foundations were required to reduce machine vibrations.

stacked one against the other to produce high pressure for further use. See Exhibit 1 for cross-sectional drawings of the three types of compressors. Table A compares the average user cost for reciprocating, rotary, and centrifugal air compressors.

Company and Industry Background

In 1984, Atlas-Copco, with worldwide sales of $1.25 billion (40 percent derived from the compressor business), was one of the world's leading companies in the field of compressed air and hydraulics. Atlas-Copco North America, jointly owned by Atlas-Copco Airpower, Belgium, and Atlas-Copco, Sweden, operated five businesses in the United States, accounting for about 14 percent of the company's worldwide revenues. The Industrial Compressor Division, one of the company's five business units, manufactured and marketed medium- and large-hp compressors using recip and rotary technologies. Table B ranks the various competitors by their share of the U.S. market.

TABLE B Stationary Air Compressor Manufacturers: Ranking by Estimated Market Shares, 1984

Machine Size	
Medium (25–300 hp)	*Large* (above 300 hp)
Recip	
Ingersoll-Rand	Ingersoll-Rand
Joy	Joy
Gardner-Denver	Gardner-Denver
Quincy	Atlas-Copco
Atlas-Copco	
Rotary	
Ingersoll-Rand	Ingersoll-Rand
Sullair	Sullair
Atlas-Copco	Atlas-Copco
Joy	Joy
Gardner-Denver	

EXHIBIT 1 Compression Technologies

Reciprocating Compressor

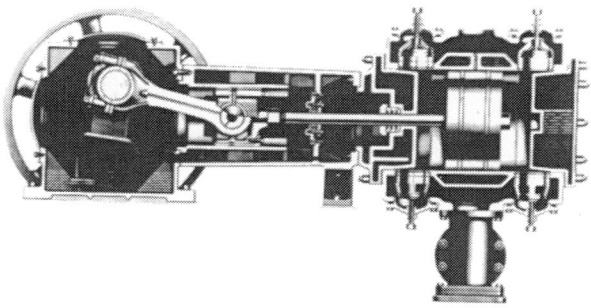

Rotary Screw Compressor

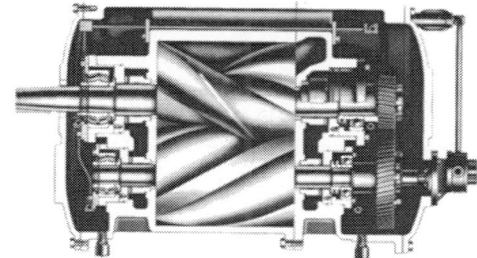

Centrifugal Compressor

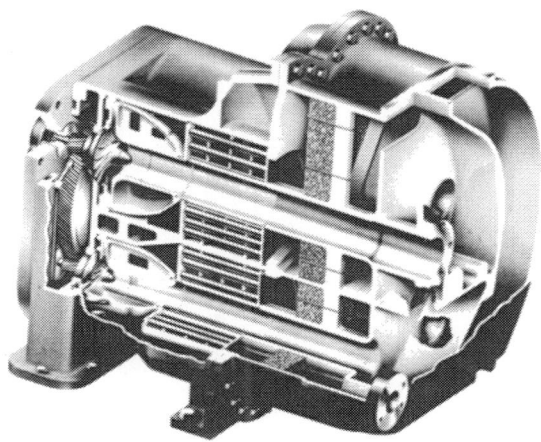

Although Ingersoll-Rand and Atlas-Copco had an equal share of the world market, Ingersoll-Rand was the market leader in the United States with a 30 percent share. Joy Manufacturing sold mainly in the United States, and had held second place behind Ingersoll-Rand for the last 35 to 40 years. Sullair Corporation, founded in the mid-1960s, was an active challenger to Joy. Sullair's founder, Donald Hoodes, a former Joy employee, pioneered the rotary screw technology and actively promoted it as a replacement for the recip technology. Because well-established distributors in the industry were not initially enthusiastic about carrying Sullair's product lines, the company initiated a company-owned distribution system to take its products to market. Joy and Sullair were each estimated to have a market share of 10 to 15 percent. Atlas-Copco ranked fourth with a 10 to 12 percent market share. Another half-dozen suppliers accounted for the remaining 30 percent of the market.

Industry sources estimated the market for the type of compressors listed in Table B to be about $285 million in 1984 (not including spare parts and accessories, which were estimated to be another $125 million). Although the market for recip and rotary compressors was more or less evenly divided, the trend seemed to favor rotary compressors. Another emerging industry trend was the demand for "dry air." Although limited in terms of market size, this highly specialized requirement had forced manufacturers to design machines to be completely free of oil particles used in lubricating the bearings. Dry air or oil-free air was used in applications such as food processing, electronic assembly, and pharmaceutical packaging.

The customer-buying process for compressors in the 300-hp range was distinct from those in the 25-hp range. At the larger end of the spectrum, customers usually put out requests for quotations on fairly well defined compressed air requirements. Prospective bidders needed the technical ability to construct a solution to customer problems and address their specification needs quite closely. The selling cycle averaged 3 to 6 months and multiple decision makers (such as engineers and purchasing managers) were usually involved. The smaller compressors, on the other hand, were bought on the basis of availability, credit terms, and maintenance support. The decision was usually authorized by the owner directly. While small customers rarely ever bought the large compressors, the converse was not always true. A large company like Monsanto or Polaroid, in addition to buying the large compressors, also purchased the small compressors for specific operations in their plants.

Atlas-Copco North America: Industrial Compressors Division

The Industrial Compressors Division was headed by Dean Pope, president. Reporting to him was Arthur Droege, vice president of marketing and sales (see Exhibit 2). A national sales manager in charge of all field sales supervised four regional managers and reported to Droege. The four regional managers were responsible for sales to 85 distributors through 12 salespersons. The regional managers were also responsible for direct sales to end users through seven salespersons.

EXHIBIT 2 Atlas-Copco Organization Chart

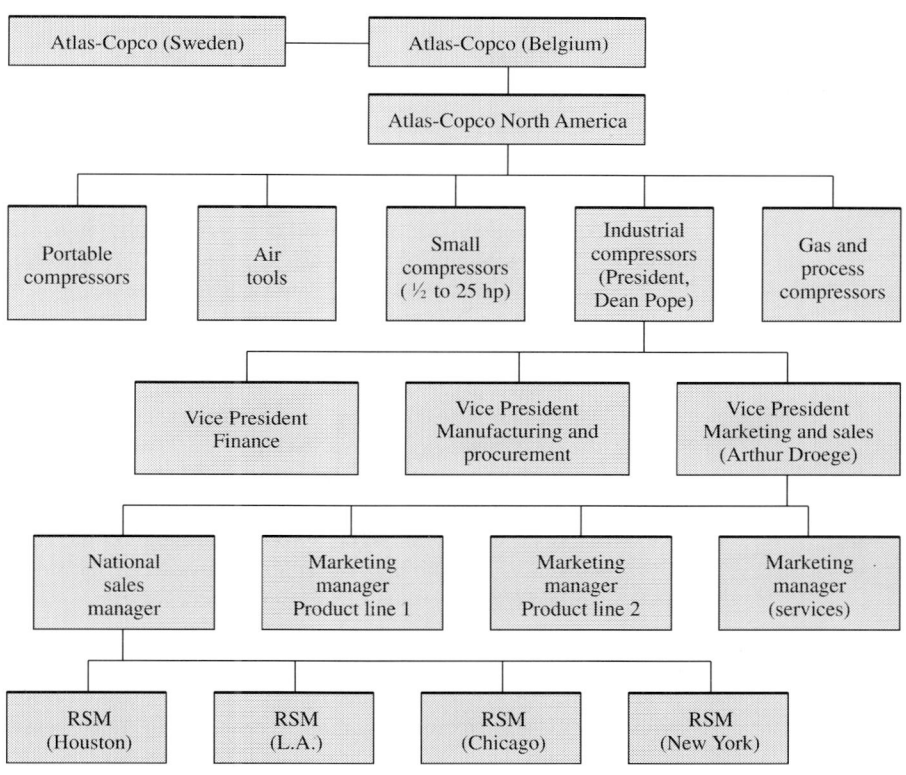

There were three marketing managers reporting to the vice president:

1. Marketing manager in charge of recips up to 125 hp and lubricated (or nonoil-free) rotaries up to 200 hp.
2. Marketing manager in charge of all oil-free rotaries, recips in the 125 to 700 hp range, and centrifugal compressors.
3. Marketing manager in charge of after-sales service, spare parts, and distributor service training.

In 1984, sales of the industrial compressor business unit were $50 million. Of this amount, $13 million came from sales to end users and the other $37 million from sales through the company's 85 distributors. Atlas-Copco had improved its overall share from 1 to 3 percent in 1970 and 10 to 12 percent in 1984. Atlas's share of the rotary compressor segment was about 20 percent, but its share of the oil-free rotary compressor segment was even higher at 60 percent. In 1985, the company's management set itself the goal of becoming the leading challenger to Ingersoll-Rand in the United States.

Distribution Strategy

In contrast to other foreign manufacturers of compressors, Atlas-Copco had been able to enter the U.S. markets and establish an effective sales and service organization. The company achieved this through four distinct phases in the entry strategy.

Phase One

Atlas-Copco began operations in the United States in 1950. The company had concentrated on products for the mining and construction industries—primarily portable air compressors, handheld rock drills, and specialized drill steel. The company's initial share of the stationary air compressor market was under 1 percent. Meanwhile, the company's share of stationary air compressors had steadily improved in Europe, Asia, and South America. By 1972, Atlas-Copco had achieved substantial market shares in Sweden, Norway, France, Germany, Italy, Spain, Brazil, the Philippines, Korea, and Japan. The company's top management decided to focus on North America as the next strategic market. At that time, Atlas-Copco made a range of recip compressors, but the machines were designed to European engineering standards and were not adapted to the American industry. Thus one of management's first tasks in 1972 was to develop a line of compressors suitable for the U.S. market.

By 1975, the company had adapted several of its recip compressors to meet U.S. standards; the company's strength, however, was in rotary screw technology. Management considered this an advantage for Atlas-Copco because the recently established Sullair Corporation was aggressively promoting the rotary screw design as a substitute for 25 hp to 300 hp recips. Improvements in rotor design, rotor cutting, and rotor meshing technology made it possible for rotary screw designs to be used in stationary air compressors that previously required reciprocating technologies. The parent company, Atlas-Copco, had strong interests and investments in machine tools in Europe, and this gave the company an edge in the design and manufacture of rotary screw compressors.

Since Atlas-Copco now had a broad line of compressors for the U.S. market, the company's managers felt that its strength in the rotary screw design would enable it to build market share, if only the company had a strong distribution network. The company's managers approached this task in two ways. First, they attempted to appoint more distributors, and second, they streamlined existing distributor operations. The company identified target markets for development, such as pharmaceuticals, pulp and paper, and electronics. Distributors were encouraged to call on customers in these key market segments. For its part, the company supported the distributor effort with technical assistance and field sales support.

In spite of these efforts, the first attempt to get distribution was considered a complete failure. In the words of one company manager: "Some of us learned about distributors and distribution, but we didn't get the distribution we wanted, either in terms of quality or numbers of distributors."

Management cited the lack of an installed base of machines as the single most important reason for the failure. Most installed machines were of the reciprocating type, which needed constant maintenance, repair, and spare parts. Distributors provided these functions and normally earned high margins on such services (30 to 35 percent). A machine base was crucial to the distributor's economic viability. Distributors usually carried only one manufacturer's product line, and in return manufacturers usually provided distributors with exclusive territories. Given the underlying distribution arrangement and the attractiveness of the spare parts and services market, most distributors were unwilling to entertain a new entrant like Atlas-Copco—accepting a new line would jeopardize existing distribution arrangements with their primary suppliers. Anyway, Atlas-Copco's broad line of compressors would only make up for the loss of revenue from complete machines. A sizable portion of distributors' revenues were earned from sales of spare parts and services required of already installed machines, some of which were 25 years old. Unfortunately, Atlas-Copco's installed base of machines at that time was close to nil.

Phase Two

Beginning in 1976, the company altered its strategy for gaining distribution in the U.S. market. Instead of offering prospective distributors a broad line of products, the company focused on its foremost product, the oil-free rotary screw compressors. The Z series, as these compressors were known, were offered in 30 models ranging from 100 to 2,500 hp (see Exhibit 3). Because of the parent company's interests and investments in machine tool technology in Belgium, Atlas-Copco was able to design and manufacture rotor profiles that were of higher precision and quality compared with the competition's. In addition, because of its worldwide position, the company was able to produce a broader range of oil-free compressors at lower cost than the competition. The company's Z series compressors were reportedly the best-designed oil-free rotaries available in the U.S. market. Its competitors believed that the oil-free market required a high degree of product customization and service; hence, they preferred to approach this market directly rather than through distributors. This gave Atlas-Copco an additional selling point with prospective distributors: the company would sell only its large (above 350 hp) Z series machines directly; the rest would be sold through distributors.

Atlas-Copco also offered distributors a 15 percent margin on list price. In contrast, oil-lubricated recips and rotaries, because of intense price competition, earned distributors only an 8 to 10 percent margin. The higher margin was to offset the downstream loss on spare parts, an important consideration in the sale of reciprocating machines. Distributors were also introduced to the notion of end user maintenance contracts. Because the oil-free rotaries were used in special applications, machine downtime was costly for end users. Customers, therefore, were willing to pay for maintenance contracts that insured reliable performance. Income from these maintenance contracts further offset the distributor's loss of spare parts margins.

Atlas-Copco's field sales force approached prospective distributors and explained the superiority of their product and its unique margin structure. Describing this drive to get distribution, a company executive explained:

EXHIBIT 3 Z Compressor

Oil-free air packaged for delivery.

Inlet filter/Silencer
Easily accessible for inlet filter changeout. Located high inside the compressor package, it receives the coolest, cleanest air possible.

Discharge grating
All the ventilation air is discharged through this one opening, allowing for easy heat recovery adaptation.

Discharge damper
Located at the outlet of the high pressure stage, the discharge damper reduces outlet noise and ensures a smooth air supply.

Intake valve
A combined inlet throttle valve and blow-off valve is used to regulate the compressor using full load/no load control.

Low pressure stage
Compresses the inlet air to an intermediate pressure. Absence of oil in this compression chamber ensures totally oil-free air.

Cooler block
The oil, inter- and aftercoolers are combined in one compact cooler block. The compressed air and oil are cooled directly by ventilating air. This simple, reliable method eliminates the need for an intermediate coolant system.

High pressure stage
Compresses cooled air from low pressure stage to final pressure.

Check valve
A discharge check valve is provided to prevent "blow back" while compressor is unloaded or stopped.

Inlet grating
All the air used for compressing and cooling enters through this single grate. This eliminates dust and dirt being pulled in from the plant floor and allows air to be ducted in from another location.

Instrument and control panel
All controls, gauges and instrumentation are conveniently located at one end of the compressor package.

Canopy
The complete compressor package is enclosed in a sound attenuating canopy. Large gull-wing doors and panels facilitate routine maintenance.

Driver
The motor driver is mounted to the compressor casing with a standard NEMA D flange. By using a flexible coupling to connect it to the bull gear shaft, no radial loads are transmitted to the motor bearings.

Vibrationally isolated
Compressor casing and motor are vibrationally isolated from the main package frame. The floor need only support the static weight of the unit and the unit need not be bolted down.

430

We would have liked to sign up Ingersoll-Rand and Joy distributors. However, our earlier experience had indicated that these distributors had too much to lose by switching over. We saw Worthington, Chicago-Pneumatic, and Quincy distributors as strong possibilities—especially Worthington. First, they all had similar product lines. Second, they had a loyal network; 75 percent of their distributors were former employees. But Worthington was a dying company; their cost structure was totally uncompetitive and their distributors could see the writing on the wall. We saw an opportunity to emphasize our worldwide leadership in air compressors and our intention to stay and compete in the U.S. market long term. Further, although it was customary for distributors to carry only one supplier's medium and large compressors, we did not require our distributors to be exclusive. Also, we did not require our distributors to carry a full line, so they could pick and choose the products they wanted.

The second campaign for distribution was successful, and by 1979 the company signed 50 distributor agreements.

In 1979 Worthington Industries, owner of two air compressor factories and many other engineering businesses, was acquired by McGraw Edison. In 1980, McGraw Edison sold Worthington's air compressor plant at Holyoke, Massachusetts, to Atlas-Copco. As part of the deal, Atlas-Copco was allowed to use the Worthington name and designs for 18 months; during the same period it also agreed to supply Worthington's distribution network with Worthington compressors and spare parts. Atlas-Copco's managers considered this an opportunity to gain access to a fully developed distribution network. Pooling its own distribution network with that of Worthington, the company now had about 100 distributors. In 1980, the company also acquired Turbonetics, Inc., a Voorheesville, New York, manufacturer of centrifugal compressors. With these acquisitions, Atlas-Copco now had the domestic manufacturing capacity and the distribution network to be an important competitor in the North American stationary air compressor market.

Phase Three

Having gained a network of 100 distributors in a short time, Atlas-Copco's managers set about rationalizing their distribution network. After much deliberation, they decided that intensive distribution was not advantageous; given the nature of the product and the market, a single distributor for a market area was considered preferable, primarily because a distributor in a local market needed the assurance of the spare parts business. As noted, a distributor's margin on spare parts was 30 to 35 percent, whereas on complete compressors, it was 15 percent for the Z series and 8 to 10 percent for the rest. Spare parts income was crucial to the distributor's overall economic viability, and intensive distribution would certainly threaten this income flow. Moreover, Atlas-Copco's managers were eager to avoid intrabrand competition at this stage of the company's growth; it was more important for them to gain market share. Atlas-Copco also recognized that exclusive territories were customary in the industry, and distributors were reluctant to change.

Many overlaps were created by the merger of Atlas-Copco's and Worthington's distribution systems. The company's policy of exclusive sales territories meant that these overlaps had to be resolved. Since the company planned to eliminate the

Worthington designs in 18 months and replace them with Atlas-Copco equivalents, it was all the more important to resolve the overlaps quickly. Twenty distributors who were members of both the Atlas-Copco and Worthington systems and whose market areas did not overlap with that of other distributors were immediately selected for inclusion in the rationalized network. Fifty other distributors who were either Atlas-Copco or Worthington distributors and whose territories did not overlap with other distributors were also chosen for the rationalized system. This left 30 distributors and 15 remaining sales territories. The final 15 were chosen on the basis of several considerations. A distributor was given preference:

1. If it was a branch of a multiple-location distributor who already had been selected to be part of the rationalized system.
2. If it had been associated with Atlas-Copco for a long period of time.
3. If it had more than 50 percent of its business revenues from sales of air compressors and spare parts.
4. If it had more than 10 percent market share in its served area.
5. If it was aggressively calling on customers and building business.
6. If it had technical service capability.

In spite of the company's best efforts, distributor overlaps in some territories remained. Atlas-Copco managers contended that, as long as the product lines were segregated, there would be no intrabrand competition. Hence, in market areas with distributor overlaps, the company tried to maintain exclusive product lines for each distributor. For example, if one sold recip compressors, then the other would sell rotary compressors.

There were a few areas where this policy of segregated product lines was not feasible and distributors carried identical product lines. In Ohio, for instance, Dayton Electric covered Cincinnati and Dayton, averaging $250,000 annually, while Ohio Transmission covered Columbus, Mansfield, Louisville, Dayton, and Cincinnati, and averaged $750,000 annually. Dayton Electric was a loyal Atlas-Copco distributor that had provided efficient and aggressive support for the company. Ohio Transmission had come aboard during the Worthington merger. Although the two distributors sold identical Atlas-Copco product lines, the company's managers recommended retaining both distributors. Several exceptions such as these were handled on an individual basis rather than by a general distribution policy.

By 1981, the company finally settled on 85 distributor agreements, and the selected distributors were invited to conferences in their respective regions. One purpose of these meetings was to convey to the distributors a sense of well-being and stability. A company manager remarked, "Distributors like to know that big daddy [Atlas-Copco] is alive and well. They like stability and steady growth, and they don't like too many changes." A second purpose was to exchange ideas on how Atlas-Copco and its distributors could help each other achieve their objectives. These meetings covered the following four broad topics.

Service. Distributors pointed out that many end users thought Atlas-Copco was an offshore manufacturer and believed that shipments of compressors came all the way from Europe. Atlas-Copco urged its distributors to counter this perception by always carrying sufficient stock of small and medium compressors (less than 100 hp) and spare parts. The company did not, however, insist on stock norms or guidelines. End users normally purchased the larger-than-100-hp compressors as capital equipment, and distributors had a six- to eight-week lead time for delivery. Distributors were not required to carry any stock of these machines; Atlas-Copco was responsible for delivering these compressors in time for its distributors to meet customer orders. The company's managers assured the distributors that the company carried a 120-day stock of spare parts and a 45-day stock of compressors at the company's U.S. stocking locations.

Display. Atlas-Copco's managers encouraged distributors to maintain attractive display and demonstration facilities. Although a compressor was evaluated ultimately on its performance, Atlas-Copco paid a great deal of attention to the external appearance of its compressors: They were painted, finished, and packaged with great care. It was hoped that end users would infer strong internal performance from this attractive external appearance. Facilities for machine displays were therefore a crucial distributor requirement, and distributors agreed to maintain adequate displays and demonstrations for the various models.

Direct Accounts. Atlas-Copco's stated policy was to allow a distributor to sell the full range of products, regardless of machine size, as long as the distributor had the technical competence to sell and support the product. The company, however, also sold direct to about 150 of its large national accounts like Fluor, Bechtel, and Anheuser Busch. These accounts bought their compressor requirements centrally at their national headquarters. The accounts' several manufacturing units in their various locations sent in their compressed-air requirements to a central purchasing committee for coordination. In order to minimize conflicts between the distributor's sales force and the direct sales force in the service of such accounts, it was agreed that an account list would be made available to distributors. The company sales force would call only on these accounts; the distributors would receive all other sales leads and orders. Atlas-Copco agreed that every account they wanted to add to this list would be reviewed and discussed with the local distributor before the company's sales force took over.

"We have never had a problem with the direct account list," commented Droege. "Some accounts want a direct relationship, and it is often a three-year investment before the order materializes; distributors are not geared to this type of selling. Whenever distributors have demonstrated the ability, we have transferred accounts back to their list."

Training. At the request of its distributors, Atlas-Copco agreed to launch a communication program to convey information on the company and the objectives of its various programs. Distributor organizations would be provided with training, education, and technical support.

Atlas-Copco's consolidation efforts began to pay dividends, and the company's market share improved from 2 percent in the early 1970s to about 7 percent in 1981. Recalling the gain in market share, Droege said:

It is important in this business to have a threshold market share; we believe 5 to 8 percent is an appropriate threshold. You need a foot in the door before you can grow in this market. Of course, there is a tremendous word-of-mouth effect in this business: Engineers talk to one another. If one firm has an Atlas-Copco machine, the other firm will at least get a quote on an Atlas-Copco compressor before making the purchase decision. As we get more inquiries we convert more business.

Phase Four

Primary demand for air compressors suffered from the 1981–1982 economic recession in the United States. When the recession ended and industry demand picked up between 1983 and 1985, Atlas-Copco found it still had certain advantages over purely domestic competitors. Since the U.S. dollar was strong and had gained 25 percent in value over the Belgian franc, the company found it cheaper to source from its parent in Belgium than to manufacture compressors in the United States. Even after deducting about 5 percent for shipping costs, the company still had a 20 percent exchange rate advantage. Company management decided as a matter of long-term strategy not to drop prices in order to gain market share. The parent company's president was quoted as saying, "You can build market share with prices, but not a company or a market." Instead, the Industrial Compressor Division approached its markets with heavy promotion and end user advertising. In 1983, the company spent a half million dollars on advertising in trade journals and trade shows. Until that time, the company had spent virtually nothing on advertising and promotion.

The company's market share steadily climbed, and by the end of 1983 it had reached about 10 percent. Field salespeople reported that distributors had begun to perceive Atlas-Copco as a long-term supplier in the marketplace, and industry observers agreed that Atlas-Copco's objective of becoming a leading challenger to Ingersoll-Rand was not unrealistic. Meanwhile, company managers wondered whether their distribution channels could sustain the volume growth of the past few years. Though many distributors did an excellent job on the large compressors and the Z series rotaries, some did not devote enough attention and resources to the more difficult products in their line. Atlas-Copco's share of the oil-lubricated recips and rotaries (less than 125 hp) was about 7 percent, while its share in the above-125 hp segment was about 16 percent. The company's managers were convinced that to compete with Ingersoll-Rand, Joy, and Sullair, they needed to be uniformly strong over a broad line of products. As a first step, the company performed a distribution audit to analyze its current network.

Distributors who had more than 80 percent of their sales from air compressors, accessories, and service were categorized as A distributors. Distributors in the 10 to 80 percent range were categorized as B; the rest were categorized as C. Of Atlas-Copco's 85 distributors, 28 were A; 18 were B; and 39 were C. The A distributors generally offered better technical support and service and focused their time and resources on the compressor business. At the other extreme, C distributors sold a wide range of products, including pumps, motors, and other machinery. This categorization scheme helped Atlas-Copco define the nature and quality of the selling effort

EXHIBIT 4 Atlas-Copco's New Franchising Policy

Several different types of distributor franchises will be available to Atlas-Copco distributors in 1985. The franchises vary by product line and provide for an enhancement of the basic franchise by successfully performing to the criteria associated with each level of product.

I. The basic franchise will include the following product lines:
- Rotary compressors 15–200 hp: RS, GA100, GAI, GAII, ZT2, ZE2.
- Reciprocating compressors 7½–200 hp: H, B, BP3, D, C, N, ER5.
- Other products: FD refrigerant air dryers—PD, DD oil and particulate removal filters.

Distributors for the basic franchise will be responsible for maintaining an inventory of prime equipment and spare parts and ensuring an in-house service capability in order to successfully satisfy the demands of the local market. Any distributor who performs according to the normal annual budget agreements for the products in the basic franchise can, if it desires, take advantage of the enhanced distributor franchise.

II. The enhanced distributor franchise will include the following product lines:
- Rotary compressors 100–350 hp: ZR3, ZT3, ZR4, ZT4, ZA3, ZA4.
- Reciprocating compressors 200–700 hp: ER6-9, ET6-7.
- Air dryers: MD3, MD4.

There will be no inventory requirement for prime equipment for the enhanced franchise; however, distributors will be responsible for maintaining a spare parts inventory and a service capability to successfully support the existing and future machine population in their territory. For those distributors who possess the sales, marketing, and service capability to handle these engineered products but do not have the necessary credit history with Atlas-Copco, an agency agreement is also available at a reduced commission rate.

III. Distributors who satisfy the requirements of the basic franchise and the enhanced franchise will become eligible for an agency agreement. The agency agreement will include the following product lines:
- Rotary compressors 450–2500 hp: ZR5-8, ZA5-8.
- Air dryers: MD5-6.
- Plant air centrifugal compressors.

The intent of the agency program is to allow distributors with the sales and marketing expertise required to handle larger compressor sales participate in this segment of the market. Agents will communicate directly with Holyoke Marketing in much the same way as our direct sales force, and are expected to be able to sell the larger compressors with minimal participation from the field sales department. The agency program will not include a requirement for inventory of prime equipment or spare parts, nor will the agent be responsible for warranty or postwarranty service. Quotations for products covered by the agency agreement and subsequent purchase orders will be prepared in the name of Atlas-Copco Industrial Compressors, Inc.

IV. An authorized service center program will be available for agents who are prepared to make the necessary investment in equipment, personnel, and training to become an extension of Atlas-Copco's direct service efforts. Authorized service centers will be able to conduct warranty and postwarranty service and participate in the revenues generated through the sale of the spare parts. An inventory format will be part of the service center program and will be based on the installed population in the territory.

---

and resources that the distributors provided. The company's managers thought that Ingersoll-Rand and Joy had a much higher percentage of A and B type distributors.

As a result of this analysis, the company initiated a distributor development program. Droege described its objective: "We ultimately wanted each of our 85 distributors to be A class and carry a full range of our compressors."

The C distributors were encouraged to allocate more resources for Atlas-Copco products and were provided technical and service support for expanding their compressor business. Since the C distributors' salespeople carried several product lines, they made presentations for many products in one call. Atlas-Copco initiated a training program to assist distributor sales reps in making an effective compressor presentation in the limited call time available. Atlas-Copco also employed 12 marketing reps solely to provide technical assistance and service to the distributors who wanted to move up the product line.

Several of the A and B distributors were doing well in terms of the company's annual quotas, but their performance was uneven over the product line. In the words of a company manager, "They were concentrating on the easier-to-sell big machines. This helped them meet their revenue and profit goals. But it didn't help us; we were growing stronger in the strong product lines but not so with our commodity products." Atlas-Copco encouraged its distributors to carry a full line by providing advertising and promotion support for products at the lower end of the line.

The New Franchising Policy

The four-level franchising policy (see Exhibit 4) emerged as a direct result of the distribution audit and the distributor development program. Droege explained the spirit of the proposal:

> Like any other company, we have our strong product lines and our commodity product lines. Our Z series of rotary screw compressors are unique products, the best available in the market. They are big-ticket items, easier-to-sell products with good margins. Our GA series of lubricated rotary compressors, for instance, are commodity products. The competition is very intense in this market. Here's where our distributors can help us by providing customer contacts and service. We want our distributors to concentrate uniformly on all product lines. We want to reward distributors who sell our small-ticket compressors with the franchise for the big-ticket compressors. Creaming the line is unfair; we don't want free riders in our distribution system.

As Droege readied himself for the afternoon's meeting, he pulled out three sets of documents he had prepared in support of the policy. The files were entitled "What the Policy Does for Customers," "What the Policy Does for Distributors," and "What the Policy Does for Us."

CHAPTER 25

Ingersoll-Rand (A): Managing Multiple Channels, 1985

Ingersoll-Rand (I-R), the leading firm in the U.S. stationary air compressor industry with a 30 percent share, marketed a broad range of compressors through a multiplicity of channels. Its management had been confronted periodically since 1960 with decisions about which air compressor types and sizes should be marketed through which channels. Thus, in late 1985, with the development of a new centrifugal, the Centac-200, a decision had to be made on whether this model would be marketed through the I-R direct sales force or through the distributor network.

Ingersoll-Rand (I-R), the leading firm in the stationary air compressor industry with a market share of 30 percent, marketed three types of compressors, reciprocating (recips), rotary screw (rotaries), and centrifugal, ranging in size from ¾ to 6,000 horsepower (hp). I-R air compressors were sold by the company sales force to OEMs (original equipment manufacturers) and user-customers and also through a network of independent distributors as well as I-R-owned distributors (air centers). In addition, small compressors (up to 5 hp) were sold through manufacturers' reps (MRs) to retail chains and catalog houses. With its broad product line and multiplicity of channels, the management of I-R's Stationary Air Compressor Division (SACD) had been confronted periodically since 1960 with issues regarding what air compressor types and sizes should be marketed through which channels. Before 1960, all products had been sold by I-R sales reps directly to OEMs and users.

Thus, in late 1985, with the development of a new 200 hp centrifugal, the Centac-200, a decision had to be made as to whether this model would be marketed through the I-R sales force or through the distributor network. James Clabough, SACD vice president of marketing and sales, explained:

V. Kasturi Rangan and E. Raymond Corey prepared this case.
Copyright © 1989 by the President and Fellows of Harvard College.
Harvard Business School case 589-121 (revised January 17, 1992).

As of now, we sell *all* centrifugal compressors through the direct sales force. Now we have a new 200 hp centrifugal. While that falls in the hp range that our distributors and air centers carry, some of our managers think that all centrifugals should continue to be sold only through the direct sales force. The distributors haven't had experience with centrifugals, and we're not sure they can provide the technical support needed to service these units in the field.

The Stationary Air Compressor Market

Compressed air, like electricity and gas, is a utility with a wide range of applications. Stationary air compressors provide compressed air for three main purposes: powering tools and other machinery (plant air), powering and controlling pneumatic systems in certain types of equipment (special machinery), and supplying air for certain manufacturing processes (process air). Industry convention was to classify compressors by horsepower size: small (below 25 hp), medium (25 to 300 hp) and large (above 300 hp) and by compression technology: reciprocating (recip), rotary screw (rotary), and centrifugal. See Exhibit 1 for cross-sectional drawings of the three types of compressors. Table A compares the average user cost for reciprocating, rotary, and centrifugal air compressors.

The large compressors were generally sold by manufacturers' direct sales forces because of the need to coordinate sales effort in several locations and the heavy engineering component of the sale. A majority of the medium, and almost all of the small compressors, were sold through independent distributors. Industry distribution channels consisted of 600 large specialist distributors (called air houses) and over 5,000 small general-line dealers. The air houses tended to handle the full scope of medium and small compressors, while the dealers were generally limited to the small compressors.

The small compressors could be further broken down by application: DIY (do-it-yourself) and industrial. The DIY market consisted of many consumer hobbyists who used compressors for odd jobs around the house such as home repair or painting. The DIY market was predominantly sold through large retail chains like Grainger, Lowe's, and Grossman's and was concentrated in sizes ½ to 5 hp. Industrial customers were normally sold through industrial distributors.

TABLE A User Cost Comparisons for Three Types of 200 Horsepower Air Compressors

	Recip	*Rotary*	*Centrifugal*
Cost of compressor per hp	$300	$200	$225
Estimated life	10–12 years	5–7 years	10–12 years
Installation cost as a percent of initial cost	20%[a]	10%	12%
Spare parts and maintenance cost per year	6%	2.5%	2.0%
Energy costs at 7 cents/kwh and 300 days operation in a year	$400/hp	$460/hp	$435/hp

[a] The installation costs for recips were relatively high because special foundations were required to dampen machine vibrations.

EXHIBIT 1 Compression Technologies

(1) Reciprocating Compressor

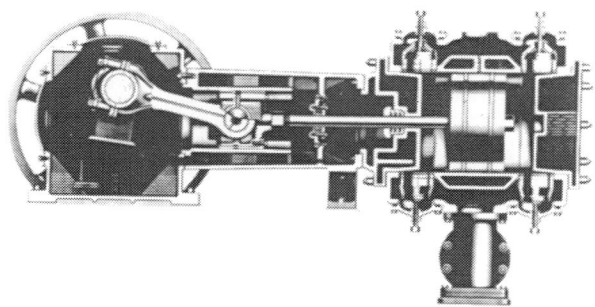

(2) Rotary Screw Compressor

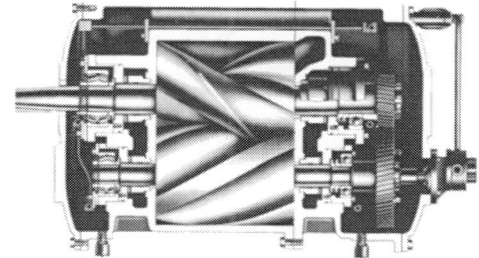

(3) Centrifugal Compressor

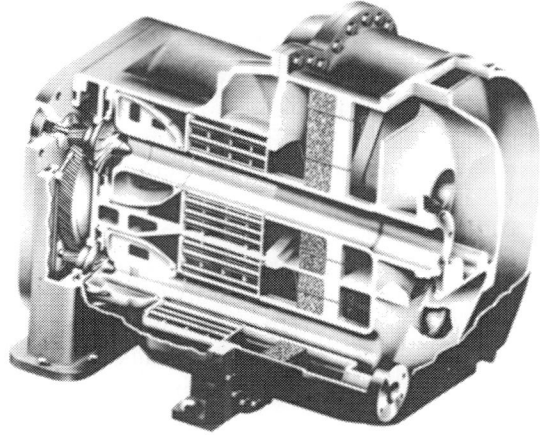

TABLE B **Stationary Air Compressor Manufacturers Listed by Product Segments in Order of Estimated Market Shares in the United States, 1984**

	Small (below 25 hp)	Medium (25–300 hp)	Large (above 300 hp)
Recip	Campbell-Hausfeld Ingersoll-Rand Quincy Kellogg-Compair Sanborn Curtiss Gardner Denver Atlas-Copco	Ingersoll-Rand Joy Atlas-Copco Gardner Denver Quincy	Ingersoll-Rand Joy Atlas-Copco Gardner Denver
Rotary	Sullair Kaesar (technology only partially developed)	Ingersoll-Rand Sullair Atlas-Copco Joy Gardner Denver	Ingersoll-Rand Sullair Atlas-Copco Joy
Centrifugal	N/A	(technology under development)	Ingersoll-Rand Joy Elliot
1984 market size[a]	$175 million	$175 million	$110 million
Number of end users	50,000[b]	25,000	2,500

[a]The market sizes shown are for complete compressors. Accessories and spare parts represented an additional 10% and 35% of the market, respectively.

[b]This number represents institutional customers such as retail stores. This does not include actual end users, many of whom were individual do-it-yourself consumers.

As Table B indicates, I-R was the leading supplier in the United States for each product segment except small recips for the DIY market. I-R's share was estimated at 30 percent of an approximately $660 million market in 1985 (including about $200 million for parts and accessories). Joy, Sullair, and Atlas-Copco competed for the second spot, each with an estimated 10 to 12 percent share.

Joy was a billion dollar (in sales) company producing petroleum and mining equipment. Its air compressor division had been in business since 1946, and was particularly strong in centrifugal compressors where its share matched that of I-R. Sullair was founded in the late 1960s by Donald Hoodes, a former Joy employee, who pioneered the commercial use of rotary technology in stationary air compressors. The company, which made both portable and stationary compressors using rotary technology, had a strong share in that segment, matching that of I-R. Atlas-Copco, a $1.5 billion (sales) Swedish company, was the worldwide leader in stationary compressors (along with I-R), but its marketing and sales efforts in the United States had not been as successful as its European operations.

Because of the industrial recession in 1982–1983, sales of complete compressors in the U.S. market had declined from $500 million in 1980 to $460 million by 1985. The number of units sold, however, had gone up from about 600,000 to 900,000. This was a result of intense price competition in the lower horsepower range (especially less-than-25 hp) which accounted for nearly 850,000 units in 1985.

The Stationary Air Compressor Division (SACD)

Ingersoll-Rand, with sales of $2.64 billion in 1985, had manufacturing operations in 16 countries, sales offices in 40 countries, and distribution arrangements in 80 others. The company operated three business groups. The Stationary Air Compressor Division was a business unit in the Standard Machinery group.

James Clabough, marketing and sales vice president, was responsible for marketing all stationary air compressors in North America. (See Exhibit 2 for an organization chart of the Stationary Air Compressor Division.) Reporting to him were the following seven departmental managers:

1. A direct sales manager (DSM) was responsible for sales to users of all centrifugal compressors, rotary compressors above 450 hp, and reciprocating

EXHIBIT 2 SACD Organization Structure

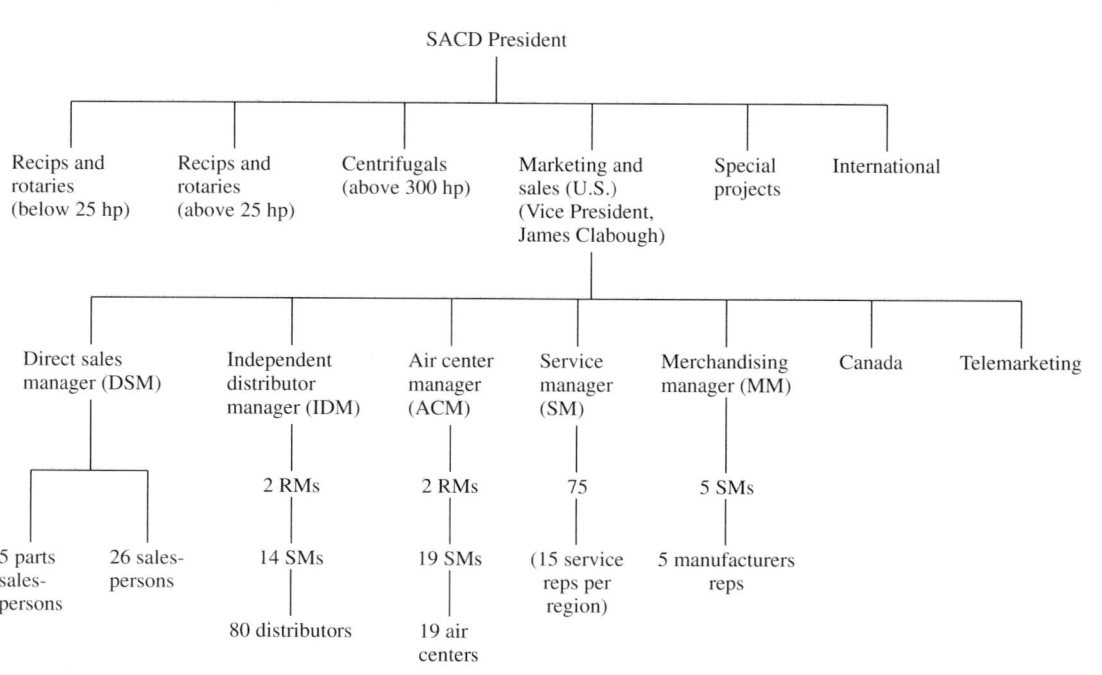

compressors above 250 hp. The DSM's organization included five regional managers and two industry managers. The industry managers marketed compressors to certain customer segments—the ski industry and government accounts.[1]

    a. Each of the five regional managers supervised five to seven salespersons. Of the 26 direct salespersons, four handled about eight large accounts each; the others had about 60 smaller accounts each. Sales reps were paid commissions of 1 to 3 percent on sales of all complete compressors. Approximately 70 percent of a salesperson's compensation was by way of commission income. All members of the direct sales team had technical degrees and were highly competent in technical selling. Due to economic conditions, the direct sales force had been reduced in size from 35 to 26 reps during the 1980–1985 period.

    b. Five parts salespersons were solely responsible for the sale of parts to the company's large direct customers.

2. An independent distribution manager (IDM) directed sales activities through independent distributors who sold reciprocating compressors below 250 hp and rotary compressors below 450 hp. Distributors did not sell centrifugal compressors at all. Reporting to the IDM were two regional managers each of whom supervised seven area managers whose sole responsibility was selling to and servicing the 80 I-R independent distributors.

3. A national air center manager (ACM) supervised sales through company-owned distributors. Like the independent distributor, each branch or air center sold and serviced reciprocating compressors below 250 hp and rotary compressors below 450 hp. Air centers did not sell centrifugal compressors. Reporting to the ACM were two regional managers each of whom had six or seven local air center managers. In all, there were 19 air centers, each having a sales manager, a service manager, four or five sales representatives, four to eight service personnel, and three administrative assistants. Air centers and distributors generally did not overlap each other's territories.

4. A service manager (SM) directed a team of direct field service supervisors. There were 10 to 20 of these highly skilled technicians in each of the five direct sales regions.

5. A merchandising manager (MM), was responsible for sales of do-it-yourself (DIY) products, mainly reciprocating compressors less than 5 hp. Five sales managers reported to the MM. The company sold its products through five manufacturers' representatives (MRs) to retail chain stores and catalog houses. MRs were paid a 3 percent commission on sales. SACD's typical

---

[1] Air compressors were used in the ski industry for snow making. Most ski resort operators preferred to buy snow-making equipment through about a dozen specialized consultants. Ingersoll-Rand's sales force called on these consultants. I-R compressors set the standards in this industry and, as a result, the company sold a very large share of compressors for snow making. The government business was placed under a separate industry manager because of its unique bidding and buying process.

manufacturers' rep organization represented 10 to 15 suppliers and averaged $40 to $50 million in sales a year. Large hardware retail chains with over a hundred stores, such as Lowe's, were among their important customers. Display, special packaging, promotion, and co-op advertising were all used in marketing small air compressors to consumers, small contractors, and repair persons.

6. Two departmental managers reporting to Clabough were responsible for sales to Canada and telemarketing respectively.

Distribution System

The direct sales force was organized into 26 territories. Within their territories, they were responsible for sales of complete compressors above 250 hp recips, 450 hp rotaries, and all centrifugals to all end users. In some cases, large national accounts preferred to buy their requirements of smaller-sized compressors also through the direct sales force, and the company generally obliged. The direct sales force was only indirectly responsible for sales of parts and service, which were handled by a separate national sales force with a dotted-line relationship to the (direct sales) regional managers.

Distributors and air centers sold the below-250-hp recips and below-450-hp rotaries in their assigned geographical territories. By and large, there were no territorial overlaps. Each was expected to stock compressors, accessories, and spare parts, resell them to end users, and provide the required technical and service support. Independent distributors and air centers were sold identical products and accessories at identical prices. Most of the company's independent distributors carried compatible lines of air compressors and accessories in addition to I-R lines. However, over 50 percent of their revenues and profits were derived from Ingersoll-Rand lines. The air centers, on the other hand, carried only I-R lines.

The areas covered by the independent distributor network and air centers were about equal in geography, but the territories for which the independents had primary responsibility represented 70 percent of the potential. Distributor and air center sales to end users and OEMs accounted for 55 percent of SACD's sales revenues in 1985. Many distributors and air centers had networks of 10 to 12 dealers each. These were typically auto jobbers, paint supply houses, mill supply houses, and wagon jobbers. About 30 percent of the below-25-hp units were sold through the dealer networks.

Both distributors and air centers were invoiced at 20 percent off list price, and in special cases I-R sales managers could authorize an additional 5 percent discount off list to meet competitive prices. Both set their own resale prices. Typically, distributors and air centers earned a gross margin of 10 to 15 percent on compressors, and 30 to 35 percent on spare parts and services.

Air center sales reps were paid a commission of 20 percent of gross margin on bookings. On average, 75 percent of their compensation was earned as commissions. Distributors' sales personnel were on similar compensation plans. Exhibit 3 indicates the relative growth in sales revenues realized through the direct sales force,

Section III   Managing Mature Products

EXHIBIT 3   Sales Index by Channel of Distribution, 1980–1985

	1980	1981	1982	1983	1984	1985
1. Direct sales force	100	100	80	70	75	75
2. Independent distributors	100	100	75	95	110	110
3. Air centers	100	110	110	110	150	160
4. Merchandising team	—	—	—	100	140	350

NOTE: The index presents dollar sales for a given year as a percentage of the 1980 sales for the channel (except for the merchandising team, which is indexed on 1983 sales). Of the division's 1985 sales, approximately 35% went through independent distributors, 30% through the direct sales force, 20% through air centers, and 15% through the merchandising team.

independent distributors, air centers, and MRs for 1980–1985. Exhibit 4 provides comparable data by type of channel as well as by class of product.

Evolution of the Distribution System

The company's channel system had evolved over a quarter-century with respect to types of reseller organizations and the Ingersoll-Rand products each carried, as Table C indicates.

During the 1960s the company's distribution system consisted of a direct sales team and a network of independent distributors. All recips above 50 hp were sold by

EXHIBIT 4   Sales Index by Type of Product and Channel, 1980–1985

	1980	1981	1982	1983	1984	1985
Recips (below 25 hp)						
1. Independent distributors	100	110	80	100	115	110
2. Company air centers	100	115	130	150	200	210
3. Merchandising team	—	—	—	100	135	350
Recips (above 25 hp)						
1. Direct sales force	100	120	90	80	80	80
2. Independent distributors	100	80	50	75	85	85
3. Company air centers	100	90	100	90	110	110
Rotaries (all hp)						
1. Direct sales force	100	130	140	80	80	80
2. Independent distributors	100	90	80	90	105	125
3. Company air centers	100	115	115	130	160	175
Centrifugals (all hp)						
1. Direct sales force	100	95	80	80	80	80

NOTE: The index presents dollar sales for a given year as a percentage of the 1980 sales for the channel (except for the merchandising team, which is indexed on 1983 sales). Of the division's 1985 sales, approximately 40% was from recips below 25 hp. Recips (above 25 hp), rotaries, and centrifugals each accounted for approximately 20% of sales.

TABLE C **Allocation of Sales Responsibility for Stationary Air Compressors by Type and Size to Sales Channels for 1960, 1973, and 1984**

	1960	1973	1984
Direct sales force	Recips 50 hp and over	Recips 150 hp and over Rotaries 150 hp and over All centrifugals	Recips 250 hp and over Rotaries 450 hp and over All centrifugals
Distributors	Recips under 50 hp	Recips under 150 hp Rotaries under 150 hp	Recips under 250 hp Rotaries under 450 hp
Air centers		Recips under 150 hp Rotaries under 150 hp	Recips under 250 hp Rotaries under 450 hp
Manufacturers' reps			Recips 5 hp and under

the direct sales team; all recips below 50 hp, called distributor-class products, were sold by the distributors. Certain master distributors were selling up to 125 hp recips in 1967–1968. In 1968 the company introduced centrifugal technology in some of its larger-than-500-hp compressors. These were sold only by the direct sales team.

There was no change in distribution policy until 1971, when SACD managers decided to offer the 150 hp recip to distributors for resale because many distributors' customers wanted to trade up to larger machines. By 1973 all recips up to 150 hp were made exclusively distributor class products, since distributors had demonstrated their ability to service the larger units.

In 1968 Sullair, a new competitor, introduced the first rotary screw stationary air compressor and established a company-owned distribution system to market the product. By 1973, Sullair was aggressively promoting the rotary screw machine as a replacement for recips in the 25- to 300-hp range. I-R managers speculated that Sullair had elected to go through company-owned channels because (1) it had a "better mousetrap" and wanted to develop the market aggressively, and (2) its product line was limited and it had no installed machine base to generate spare parts business. For these reasons, the new line might not be attractive to independent distributors.

In the 1971–1973 recession, Ingersoll-Rand discovered that a number of its distributors were overextending their working capital and some were even on the verge of bankruptcy. I-R managers set up the first company-owned air center in late 1971, following a failure of an independent distributor, when no suitable replacement was found. Four other locations were established by 1973, all of which were independent distributorships which I-R had acquired. An I-R manager commented: "There was no master plan for establishing the air centers. Air center locations evolved from failed private distributors in an ad hoc fashion."

In 1974, Ingersoll-Rand introduced a range of rotary screw compressors, and the division general manager decided that all rotary compressors up to 300 hp would be primarily distributor class products. In 1976, recips up to 200 hp were also put in this category. The company's direct sales force retained responsibility for sales of all recips above 200 hp, all rotaries above 300 hp, and all centrifugal compressors. Meanwhile, the company's managers continued to expand their air center operations to territories where suitable distributors could not be found, and by 1976 there were a dozen air center locations. I-R also altered the structure of its sales force. Prior to 1976, each sales rep was responsible for direct sales, as well as distributor sales. In 1976, separate sales organizations were established for direct, distributor, and air center sales, respectively. The structural change was in large part a result of pressure from independent distributors for equal representation. The emergence of air centers, with a reporting relationship directly to the vice president of sales, had created concern over the long-term future of independent distributors. The AIRD (Association of I-R Distributors) organization lobbied for and received equal representation through the creation of the distributor area sales managers. The residual direct sales organization was therefore consolidated as the separate direct channel.

During the next three years, the market share for the distributor class products jumped from 17 percent to 30 percent and I-R's market share for the direct sales products remained at about 45 percent. Then came the 1981–1983 recession. The air centers reported a slight increase in revenues, while distributor sales dropped by 25 percent, and direct sales by 15 percent. Air centers had been pushed by I-R management to maintain sales volume even at the cost of loss in margins.

In 1983, the cutoff for distributor class products was raised to 250 hp for recips and 450 hp for rotaries. The centrifugal machines, however, continued to be sold only by the direct sales team, although the horsepower range of distributor class products was now nudging the lower boundaries of the centrifugal machine. Meanwhile, in 1982 a merchandising team had been set up to focus on the sales of below-5-hp compressors directly to institutional customers. Large OEM buyers of the small compressors, such as Johnson Controls, were identified and approached directly. This effort proved only partially successful. The company's managers wished to expand their reach of the small hp market and in 1984, five manufacturers' reps were appointed to sell directly to retail chains.

Spare Parts Sales

While company distributors and air centers offered spare parts for the size of machines they sold as "completes," spare parts for the larger machines were generally ordered directly from Ingersoll-Rand. Users of the large compressors, however, were sometimes frustrated by delays in spare parts deliveries and procured parts from "pirate parts" vendors. These were often parts suppliers to air compressor manufacturers. They sold to distributors generally at a 10 to 15 percent discount under existing market prices. As a result, nongenuine Ingersoll-Rand parts were available to any distributor regardless of its supplier affiliation. This forced Ingersoll-Rand distributors to compete with other distributors in their own market areas for the spare parts business. In addition to loss of margin on spare parts, I-R managers and distributors were both seriously concerned about the opportunity that this provided for competitors to gain a foothold in Ingersoll-Rand's customer base.

The company's management, therefore, structured a trial parts program to address this problem. The plan, to be introduced in 1986, was to authorize a selected list of 19 distributors to carry spare parts for the large compressors (even though the direct sales force sold the machine). Since each distributor on an average had 5 field reps, this would add 95 persons to I-R's overly burdened 5 parts sales reps who now did the job. These same distributors were also given larger recips and small centrifugals as part of this trial.

Rationale for the Multiple Channel System

The rationale for the four-channel distribution system (direct sales force, independent distributors, company-owned air centers, and manufacturers' reps) was explained by a company manager: "The fundamental reason for going through distribution at all is purely economic. We realized way back in the 1960s that any machine that sold for less than $5,000 was not economical for a direct sales approach."

Another manager added:

> Frankly, the rotary versus recip distinction is more complex than that. Reciprocating compressors require more spare parts than rotary machines and there are good margins on spare parts for us. Every time we increase the horsepower range of recips for distributors to carry, we are essentially handing over to them a lucrative spare parts business for already-installed machines.
>
> But going beyond that, probably the most important factor has been the differences in buying behavior among our several types of customers and our attempts to service their different needs through different channel systems.

Buying Behavior

The large compressors (above 300 hp) were generally used in custom-designed applications. Contractors like Bechtel and large manufacturers like General Motors routinely put out inquiries for their air compressor requirements. These requests for quotations contained detailed specifications, and a high degree of technical expertise and coordinated sales effort was necessary to submit bids on such inquiries and to negotiate prices. The service requirements on some of these machines were also complex and machine failure could result in costly downtime. All of these considerations favored the use of a direct sales force channel.

I-R marketing managers believed that buyer behavior was less complex, and specifications less demanding, in the case of the medium and small machines. Off-the-shelf availability was important, however, especially for the under-100-hp machines since customers often required delivery within a week. Buying decisions were generally made by the owner or the plant engineer. Many smaller customers did not have maintenance teams in their plants; it was important, therefore, to provide the convenience of locally available spare parts and service.

Compressors at the higher end of the distributor class product range (about 300 hp) were sold to larger customers who were relatively sophisticated in their buying behavior. Since these machines were priced in the range of $100,000 each, the buying decision was most often taken by a group rather than by an individual. Most were purchased as capital equipment, requirements were planned ahead, and a six- to eight-week lead time on delivery was acceptable to the user. Ingersoll-Rand preferred, however, to go through distributors for such customers because they were widely dispersed and numerous. Further, many distributors had demonstrated their ability to sell and service these accounts. The company's air centers were also capable of serving the same kind of buyers.

The small machines (less than 5 hp) went to a completely different set of customers, mainly small contractors, plumbers, or moonlighting repair persons using compressed air for small jobs. Many consumers used small compressors for jobs such as spray painting or home repair, and typically shopped at hardware stores, home service centers, and other retail outlets like Sears and Lowe's. As noted earlier, Ingersoll-Rand reached these outlets through MRs who had extensive market contacts and long experience in selling to retail outlets. For a detailed description of Ingersoll-Rand's distribution policies and guidelines, see Exhibit 5.

Historic Accident

"The buying behavior argument sounds good, but is mostly rationalization, and has little basis in fact," suggested a senior I-R manager.

> We had a rotary product as early as 1971. It was a foster child to the various divisions in successive moves. The product performed poorly, and none of the divisions wanted to do anything with it.
>
> In 1974, the company introduced a much improved version of the product under a general manager in charge of the newly formed Rotary Division. The general manager unilaterally offered rotaries to distributors in larger sizes, in an attempt to sell a product that the direct team had previously lost faith in. At this point, division and personal rivalries produced a series of moves and countermoves, which escalated distributor product responsibility to 300 horsepower. There was no grand strategy.

Managing Multiple Channels

The company faced certain challenges in managing its distribution channel system because of the multiple modes of reaching the market. For one, even though the product lines for the different channels were clearly defined, the company's channels at times competed directly with each other. A direct sales rep, for example, might submit a bid on an order for a 400-hp machine while a distributor competed for the sale by quoting a price for two 200-hp compressors. At the lower end, distributors and air centers competed with the merchandising team on the under-5-hp compressor line. Commenting on the consequences of a direct-distributor conflict, an I-R product manager commented:

EXHIBIT 5 Distribution Channels: Policies and Guidelines

For distributor franchising purposes, I-R managers classified the air compressor line into eight groups, as follows:

Distributor Type		Product Classification
Type 30	Full service	(5–25 hp recip)
Type 40	Completes	(25–125 hp recip)
ESH-V	Completes	(25–125 hp recip)
PHE/LLE	Completes	(75–150 hp recip)
XLE	Completes	(150–250 hp recip)
SSR-1000	Completes	(15–40 hp rotary)
SSR-2000	Completes	(40–450 hp rotary)

Individual distributor agreements covered one or more product classifications.

It was the stated policy of the company not to compete with its independent distributors in the sale and service of equipment that was covered by the distributor agreement. There were a few exceptions to the above policy as stated in the company's sales manual:

1. It is the policy of Ingersoll-Rand Company to sell directly to all users those items of equipment not specifically described in the selling agreement. Inasmuch as Ingersoll-Rand calls on these customers directly to sell engineered products, we also reserve the right to sell all products on a direct basis to accounts which are designated as Special Accounts.
2. It is the marketing policy of Ingersoll-Rand Company to sell our equipment directly to original equipment manufacturers and national accounts, where this best serves the interest of the customer.
3. It is the policy of Ingersoll-Rand Company to encourage and assist established and officially designated distributors to sell equipment of the type described in the selling agreement to state, county, and city governments. However, Ingersoll-Rand reserves the right to sell to state and local governments direct if the distributor is not properly representing us or is unable or unwilling to handle the sale.
4. It is the policy of Ingersoll-Rand Company to sell directly all of its products to the United States government and all of its agencies, including the armed forces.
5. It is the policy of Ingersoll-Rand to sell distributor products through privately owned distributors. However, when the privately owned distributors are not growing or showing sufficient market penetration or where we cannot find private capital or expertise, Ingersoll-Rand reserves the right to operate company-owned distributor stores. Ingersoll-Rand will discuss anticipated changes with the appropriate distributors if changes are to be made. The performance of each privately owned distributor will be reviewed once a year and the private distributor must demonstrate to Ingersoll-Rand its growth and penetration in the marketplace. If the growth and penetration is unsatisfactory a suggested plan and time must be set for improvement.

I-R managers recognized that sound, durable, and mutually productive relationships between the company and its distributors required acceptance by each of certain fundamental responsibilities to the other. Accordingly, the company took responsibility for providing its independent distributors with a product line that would yield a good return on investment. The company's warranty policy, while protecting the user's interest, was designed also to compensate distributors for the costs of in-warranty repairs. In addition, the company offered special plans and terms designed to aid in the financing of I-R inventory. Periodic consultation was also provided to determine distributor stocking levels, and excess stocks could be returned for credit. Further, I-R provided such promotional materials as:

- Complete pricing catalogs.
- Product application bulletins.
- Product promotional literature.
- Display material for point-of-sale use.
- Product exhibits for trade shows.

Company-owned air centers received comparable sales and service support.

Just the other day, I heard from a direct salesperson on a heartbreaking loss of a 1,000 hp compressor. This fellow had been working on the inquiry for over six months, providing the necessary engineering backup. But looks like the customer's sister division had a poor experience with an I-R distributor on a 50 hp off-the-shelf compressor. That image ruined our big sale, and the order was lost.

To reduce interchannel competition, I-R managers initiated the Full Partner Program: If a direct sales rep referred an inquiry to a distributor or an air center, he or she would get a 1 percent commission on the sale if the order materialized. The commission was increased to 2 percent if the salesperson actively assisted in securing the order for the distributor or the air center. Commissions were also available to distributors and air centers for referring inquiries to direct sales reps. A lead that was ultimately converted to an order yielded a 2 percent commission; if the distributor actively assisted in getting the order he or she received a 5 percent commission. Under the Full Partner Program, the company paid out $70,000 in 1984.

"It is too early to judge the effectiveness of the Full Partner Program," an I-R sales manager remarked. "The payout could be monumental. Distributors and salesmen are buddies. They could indiscriminately pass commissions to each other. We'll only end up paying more commissions for the same level of sales."

Even though the company implemented sales policies for its independent distributors and air centers, each perceived the other to be receiving favored treatment. Distributors contended that because air centers were company owned, they got better prices, better information, and better service. The company's air center managers countered that separate sales territories kept air centers out of competition with distributors, and as they saw it, the company's policies heavily favored distributors.

One air center manager said:

> In fact, air centers have been started in areas where distributors were not interested or could not do a good job of distribution. In a sense, we start with poorer territories, and the company's sales policies make it even worse. When machines are in short supply, they go to the distributors; the factory prefers to do it that way because the transaction is scored as a sale. Products shipped to an air center are invoiced only after the final sale is made to a user.

I-R managers estimated that overall, it cost the company about 19 percent of sales to run the air center operation, 21 percent of sales to run the distributor operation, and 11 percent of sales to run the direct sales force operation. Though air center overheads were generally high, management believed that certain economies were achieved because of the centralized order entry system and inventory transfer facility among the 19 air centers. However, Clabough thought the difference in cost between the two channels was not that important as long as they provided market coverage and penetration in difficult-to-reach areas.

Clabough was also of the opinion that the current allocation of sales and market potential between SACD's independent distributors and its air centers was ideal. Increasing the number of air centers, he argued, could demoralize the independent distributors. On the other hand, decreasing their numbers would make the air centers less economical to operate and ineffective as an alternate channel to independent distribution.

The Decision on Centac-200

As vice president of marketing and sales, Clabough had to consider several factors before deciding whether the 200-hp centrifugal machine should go to distributors/air centers or to the direct sales team. One consideration was that the spare parts requirements could be as low as 2 to 3 percent of initial cost on an annual basis. Distributors, generally, thrived on spare parts and repair services, and such a low number was unlikely to be attractive to them. Another problem was that since the Centac-20 operated at high speeds (50,000 revolutions per minute), inadequate repair carried the risk of serious damage. Clabough was confident of the technical support his service department would provide, but less certain of his distributors in this regard. According to Clabough:

> In favor of distributors, we have a well-established network. Centac-200 would be a good reward to our loyal distributors. More than anything else, it would be consistent with our hp assignment. On the downside, the new product would probably take our distributors' attention away from the smaller compressors. Further, the product is such that intensive distributor training would be required. Finally, we run the risk of being dependent on a channel we cannot completely control.
>
> In favor of keeping the Centac-200 in the direct sales category, we have well-established service capabilities and the Centac-200 would be a good addition to a shrinking line of direct sales products. On the downside, we run the risk of our sales reps ignoring the Centac-200. They tend to be elephant hunters; they go for the big kills. The Centac-200 would be on the lower end of their line.

Another consideration related to competition. Centrifugal machines provided oil-free air (i.e., the air supply was free of oil particles generally used in lubricating the compressor bearings). "Dry air" or "oil-free air" was used in applications such as food processing, electronic assembly, and pharmaceutical packaging. The Centac-200 would give Ingersoll-Rand an oil-free machine to go head-to-head with Atlas-Copco's extremely successful Z series rotary compressor which was sold through distributors. Atlas-Copco's Z series machines were considered top quality in the industry. As a result, Atlas had over a 30 percent share of the small but specialized oil-free market. It was expected that sooner or later Ingersoll-Rand would expand the Centac line to include other machines at lower hp ratings. Further, the overall market for Centac-200 went well beyond its estimated $9 million (200 units) in the respect that it could also replace some oil-flooded rotaries and the market for that product was estimated at another $35 million.

Last and most important, Clabough wondered what effect his decision would have on the relationship between direct sales force, distributors, and air centers. "Frankly, with our market position, we will be able to carry off any arrangement, but we want to do what is right and best for the company."

CHAPTER 26
Computervision—Japan (A)

Computervision (CV) must define a sales and distribution strategy that will restore its position as a leading competitor in the Japanese computer-aided design and computer-aided manufacturing (CAD/CAM) market. Management was considering a wide range of possible actions: (1) strengthening or expanding CV's 10-year relationship with its current exclusive distributor, Tokyo Electron Limited (TEL); (2) reorganizing the role of its Japan-based sales support group; and (3) replacing TEL with other distribution arrangements.

In early May 1983, Patrick Alias was returning to the United States from his third trip to Japan in as many months. Ever since his promotion in February to vice president, Americas–Far East (AFE), of Computervision (CV) Corporation, he had been shuttling back and forth between Boston and Tokyo. With each trip to Japan, his concern about CV's competitive position had increased. Although CV's exclusive Japanese distributor believed it was doing a good job of marketing the CV product line, there were clear signs that the competition—especially IBM and Fujitsu—was gaining market share at CV's expense. Costs for CV's marketing support organization in Japan had also risen dramatically, from $200,000 per quarter in 1979 to $1,400,000 for the first quarter in 1983.

When Jim Berrett, president of Computervision, promoted Alias to his new position, he made the following comment:

> Japan is by far the largest market in the AFE organization. It certainly is the fastest growing in the AFE and possibly the world, yet our market penetration there is substantially below what we have in the United States and Europe. If we don't take immediate steps to improve our position, we could wind up as a minor player in the Japanese market.

Rowland T. Moriarty prepared this case.
Copyright © 1985 by the President and Fellows of Harvard College.
Harvard Business School case 585-155 (revised April 30, 1991).

Just before Alias's most recent visit to Japan, Berrett had asked him to prepare a detailed plan for improving CV's penetration of the Japanese market. The Japanese market was becoming so important to CV's overall strategy that Jim Berrett wanted Alias to be ready to present his recommendations to CV's board of directors at their May 26 meeting.

Computervision Corporation

With 1982 revenues of $325 million, CV was the worldwide leader in CAD/CAM turnkey systems. Headquartered in Bedford, Massachusetts, the company was engaged in designing, manufacturing, marketing, and servicing computer-aided design and computer-aided manufacturing (CAD/CAM) products and systems. These systems were used for increasing productivity and product quality. They shortened the cycle for developing and manufacturing new products by automating many complex or repetitive tasks previously performed manually. CAD/CAM was one of the core building blocks in the newly emerging concept of computer integrated manufacturing (CIM). The objective of CIM was to automate and computerize all aspects of product design, engineering, and production. CAD/CAM equipment was the fastest growing segment of the industrial automation business. The worldwide market for CAD/CAM equipment was forecast to be a $4 billion to $6 billion business by 1987 with an estimated growth rate of 30 to 50 percent per year.

Company History

CV was one of the first entrants into the CAD/CAM industry in 1969, when its cofounders developed an automatic integrated circuit network generator. During the 1970s, CV developed and marketed several leading-edge CAD/CAM products and grew at an annual compound rate of more than 50 percent. However, in 1981 CV's sales had begun to slow. By 1982, CV's sales grew only 20 percent over 1981. (See Exhibit 1 for selected financial data on the company.)

CV claimed to have a 35 percent share of the turnkey system's market in the United States, where it had focused most of its efforts on the large (Fortune 500) manufacturing companies. CV also had a strong position in Europe with more than 60 percent of the market in some countries.

Products

CV's products were known for their quality and reliability. Its newest high-performance product line was the Designer V system shown in Exhibit 2. The price of the system in the United States ranged from $200,000 to $600,000, depending on the system's application and its particular hardware/software configuration. The company also marketed a medium-scale system called the Designer M series that sold for approximately $120,000.

EXHIBIT 1   Computervision Corporation Five-Year Summary of Selected Financial Data
(in thousands except per share data)

	1982	1981	1980	1979	1978
Revenues	$325,185	$270,706	$191,086	$103,004	$48,432
Operating income	48,181	55,339	40,761	24,184	9,722
Income from continuing operations	32,381	35,748	23,464	12,874	4,811
Income per share from continuing operations	$ 1.18	1.30	$ .91	$ .52	$ .24
Research and development expenses as percent of revenues	11.2%	10.0%	9.9%	8.6%	7.9%
Operating income as percent of revenues	14.8	20.4	21.3	23.5	20.1
Income from continuing operations as percent of revenues	10.0	13.2	12.3	12.5	9.9
Return on average stockholders' equity	19.9	25.3	33.8	39.3	37.5
Revenues by geographic areas:					
United States	54.5%	54.3%	59.6%	64.6%	63.3%
Europe	34.7	36.5	33.7	29.7	30.4
Other	10.8	9.2	6.7	5.7	6.3
Total assets	$274,140	$228,838	$167,479	$86,876	$49,112
Long-term debt and capitalized leases	30,689	29,645	19,521	15,934	6,382
Stockholders' equity	179,780	144,993	108,480	40,659	26,447
Current ratio	2.5	2.5	2.8	1.9	2.2
Debt to total capital	15%	17%	15%	28%	19%

Income statement data for all periods reflect the results of continuing operations only. Balance sheet data and return on average stockholders' equity reflect the financial position and net income of the total company.

No cash dividends have been declared. Applicable data have been restated to reflect two-for-one stock splits in 1981, 1980, and 1979.

CAD/CAM systems, like most computer-based systems, had three primary components—the computer hardware, the operating system software, and the application software. The quality, performance, and reliability of a CAD/CAM system depended heavily upon how well the system's hardware and software components were integrated. Most of CV's competitors were systems integrators. They created turnkey systems by adding their software to another company's hardware.

Unlike its competitors, CV designed and produced a substantial portion of the minicomputer-based hardware for the Designer product line. Because much of this hardware was custom-designed for CAD/CAM systems, the software was often easier and less expensive to develop. CV believed their resulting systems were better integrated and provided more features than comparable competitive products.

The operating system software in the Designer product line was specifically developed by CV to enable users to create, design, manipulate, edit, and store data for both two- and three-dimensional diagrams. CV had also developed a variety of specialized software packages for the following applications:

1. Mechanical design.
2. Manufacturing and process control.
3. Electronic design of printed circuits, integrated circuits, and wiring diagrams.

Exhibit 2 Designer V System

  4. Architecture, engineering, and construction (including piping).
  5. Mapping.

In addition to being vertically integrated, CV distinguished itself from the competition by offering a complete spectrum of support services to its customers, including:

- Preinstallation consulting.
- Educational services.
- Audiovisual training materials.
- Equipment delivery and installation.
- Acceptance testing.

- On-site consultation and guidance.
- Documentation.
- Productivity services.
- Contract maintenance.
- International parts centers.
- Remote diagnostics.

International Operations

Computervision's international expansion followed the typical pattern for fast-growth, high-technology companies. In 1972, CV hired agents to sell its products in the United Kingdom, France, and Holland. Since they generated little sales volume, CV appointed a European sales manager in 1973. Shortly after his arrival in Europe, the sales manager fired the French agent and hired Patrick Alias as CV's first direct sales representative in Europe. Alias was a 28-year-old Frenchman with master's degrees in electronics and mathematics and three years of experience working for a small American computer company in France. In his first year he booked three times the orders of all the European agents combined.

Alias's success led to CV's decision to phase out the European agents over the next two years and build a European sales, service, and marketing support organization. By 1977, CV-Europe was generating a third of the company's sales revenues and had 150 employees. By 1982, CV-Europe had 450 employees and was generating 35 percent ($113 million) of the company's yearly revenue.

Alias's career growth paralleled the rapid development of the European market. During the 1970s, he held a variety of sales and marketing positions within CV-Europe and was appointed VP marketing for Europe in 1981. CV's senior management felt that Alias's leadership, management, drive, and ambition played an important role in the rapid development of the European sales organization.

In February 1983, when Jim Berrett promoted Alias to the position of VP-AFE, he had high expectations that he would have a significant impact on CV's competitive situation in Japan. Unlike Europe, CV had always marketed products in Japan through an exclusive distributor, Tokyo Electron Limited (TEL).

Tokyo Electron Limited

Founded in 1963, TEL had grown rapidly by aggressively marketing imported high-technology systems in Japan. When CV entered the market in 1973, TEL had become its exclusive distributor.

Headquartered in Tokyo, TEL had 1982 sales of $256 million (U.S. dollars) and net profit of $28.1 million. It had been growing at a sustained rate of 25 percent per year for the last 10 years. Exhibits 3 and 4 contain selected financial data on TEL. TEL's operations were divided between production and marketing. Production was carried out by its subsidiary, Telmec Inc., and four affiliates based on joint venture

Exhibit 3 Tokyo Electron Limited Nonconsolidated Statements of Income (years ended September 30, 1982 and 1983)

	(in thousands of U.S. dollars)	
	1982	1981
Net sales	$256,008	$204,277
Operating expenses:		
Cost of sales	192,780	149,152
Selling, G&A expenses	35,055	30,759
Net profit from operations	$ 28,173	$ 24,366

production agreements with U.S. high-technology companies. The marketing operation had four separate sales divisions whose 1981 and 1982 results are shown in Exhibit 4. CV's products were sold through the Computer Controlled Systems (CCS) division of TEL, whose revenues were up 28 percent in 1982 to $40.3 million. CV's CAD/CAM systems represented about 80 percent of the CCS division sales.

The director of CCS was Jim Nomura, who joined TEL in 1967 after working for Sumitomo Electric for seven years. He had headed TEL's CAD/CAM sales operation since its beginning in 1973. Having worked in the United States for three years, Nomura spoke excellent English and was familiar with the American style of management. Over the years, CV had assigned responsibility for the Japanese market to a number of different managers, many of whom now held senior management positions. Because Nomura had always handled TEL's relationship with CV personally, he knew many of CV's current executives.

The 10-year relationship between CV and TEL had been uneven. Up until 1977, CV sales in Japan grew slowly and the TEL/CV relationship was amiable. Senior management at CV had been focused primarily on the fast-growth markets in the United States and Europe. However, in 1977 a newly appointed CV manager for Japan undertook a complete review of the CV/TEL arrangement. He was dissatisfied with many aspects of TEL's handling of the CV product line, including market

Exhibit 4 TEL's Sales by Sales Division

Sales Division	Sales (millions)		Percent Change	Percent of Total 1982 Company Sales
	1982	1981		
Semiconductor Production Equipment	$105.8	$93.4	13.3%	41.3%
Measurement Analysis Systems	41.3	27.6	49.6	16.1
Computer-Controlled Systems (CCS)[a]	40.3	31.4	28.3	15.7
Electronic Parts and Components	68.6	51.8	32.4	26.8
Total	**$256.0**	**$204.2**	**25.4%**	**100.0%**

[a] 1979 sales = $12.6 million. 1980 sales = $18.5 million.

penetration, market coverage, customer support, customer service, new product introduction, new product adaptation, and pricing policies. After a complete review of the options available to CV in the Japanese market, including the establishment of a direct CV sales organization and an analysis of alternative distributors, CV decided not to sever its relationship with TEL. CV felt the overall size of the market at that time did not warrant the risks, the management time, and the expense of switching distributors or establishing its own sales operation. Since that time, the situation in Japan had been under constant review by CV's senior management. A continuing concern that the Japanese CAD/CAM market was about to explode, and that CV-Japan (CVJ) was not well positioned to be the market leader, led to tension in the CV/TEL relationship.

Along with growth and expansion over the past 10 years, TEL's strategic orientation had migrated away from just being an exclusive distributor for American high-technology companies. It now had a strong preference for manufacturing or assembling as well as selling American high tech products in Japan. In September 1981, TEL established a 50/50 joint venture with GenRad (TEL-GenRad Limited) to begin domestic production of GenRad's electronic testing systems. Similar joint ventures had been established with other U.S. high-tech companies operating under the names TEL-Varian Limited, TEL-Thermco Limited, and TEL-Tre Limited. TEL's complete line of products were sold through its four separate sales divisions.

TEL's joint ventures put additional pressure on the TEL/CV relationship in several ways. First, TEL was assured a long-term relationship with its joint venture partners, whereas its exclusive distribution contract with CV had lapsed two years earlier, and had never been replaced. TEL and CV had only a temporary agreement requiring a written 30-day notice by either company to cancel their arrangement. Second, becoming a manufacturing company had significantly increased TEL's prestige and profile within the Japanese business community. This had helped TEL greatly in competing with Japan's largest employers for the best university graduates each year, but now the limited availability of university recruits was constraining TEL's growth. TEL's uncertain relationship with CV was making it increasingly difficult for Jim Nomura to compete internally with the other TEL sales divisions for new people to expand sales coverage. Third, TEL management believed that joint ventures helped its long-term stability by transferring American technologies into the company. This in-house technical knowledge would also increase its options whenever a joint venture agreement expired. Finally, TEL believed that joint ventures gave it a competitive edge in the marketplace. The company's better understanding of the technology improved its ability to adapt American products for their Japanese customers and also helped it provide better applications and service support.

Ever since the mid-70s, Nomura had been proposing a joint venture with CV. Several factors caused CV senior management to be unreceptive to this idea: (1) CV had no other joint ventures, (2) Japan represented a small proportion of its overall revenues, and (3) the company was extremely concerned about safeguarding its proprietary technology. As a result, Jim Berrett told Alias that a joint venture with TEL would not be possible in the foreseeable future.

CAD/CAM equipment was clearly an important source of revenues and profits for TEL. In spite of the various ups and downs in the TEL/CV relationship, Nomura felt TEL was doing an excellent job for CV in the Japanese CAD/CAM market. Sales results for the CCS division over the past few years were impressive—47 percent increase in 1980, 70 percent increase in 1981, and 28 percent increase in 1982. Nomura also pointed to the large increase and projected increase in staffing for his division as evidence of TEL's ongoing commitment to CV (see Exhibit 5 for staffing projections and Exhibit 6 for CCS organization).

CV sold its systems to TEL at about 35 percent below the U.S. list price. TEL, typically, sold the system in Japan at U.S. list price plus 15 percent for shipping, tariffs, and insurance. A typical system that sold in Japan for $500,000 and in the United States for $425,000 was purchased by TEL for $275,000 F.O.B., Bedford, Massachusetts. CV management believed that the high Japanese prices for this equipment hurt their market penetration in Japan. TEL discounted the CV systems anywhere from 0 to 30 percent, depending on the customer, the size of the order, and the date the order was placed in the quarter. Aware of pressure on CV from security analysts for steady and dramatic increases in quarterly revenue, TEL tended to hold back orders until just before the end of CV's quarter in order to obtain additional discounts and concessions. After all discounting and negotiation, CV averaged 53 percent gross margin on TEL shipments. This did not include any of the expenses for the CVJ operation.

CV-Japan

CV-Japan (CVJ), headquartered in Tokyo, was by far the largest operation within CV's Americas–Far East organization.

CV's total installed base of systems in the AFE was 282, with 198 in Japan (70 percent), 21 in Australia, 18 in Singapore, 15 in Taiwan, and 30 in the other 14 countries covered by the AFE. In 1982, the AFE produced about 10 percent of CV's revenue—$34.8 million—of which $17 million (49 percent) came from Japan (TEL). Jim Berrett's strategic plan projected CV's revenues from Japan to grow 47 percent in 1983 to $25 million, 36 percent in 1984 to $34 million, and 62 percent in 1985 to $55 million. In the first quarter of 1983, CV's sales to Japan (TEL) were $6.7 million with CVJ expenses of $1.4 million and a cost of goods of $3.2 million. See Exhibit 7 for TEL's CAD/CAM 1978–1982 sales performance.

The CVJ organization, shown in Exhibit 8, had grown from 25 people in 1980 to 75 people in 1983. In order to support TEL's efforts in Japan, CVJ had added 20 people to marketing, 14 to software development, 5 to software support, 3 to hardware support, and 8 others to various staff functions. The marketing function was divided into sales and sales support. The salespeople were assigned to specific geographic areas and were responsible for achieving monthly, quarterly, and yearly sales plans by supporting TEL's sales representatives. The sales support account executives were also assigned geographically to support TEL's sales representatives through demonstrations, presale customer consultation, system proposals, and other functions required in promoting sales and closing an order. The software development function

EXHIBIT 5 TEL Staffing Chart for CCS Sales Division

	1973	1974	1975	1976	1977	1978	1979	1980	1981	1982	1983	1984	1985	1986	1987
Sales and sales A.E.[a]	1	2	2	3	5	7	7	14	21	25	37	46	64	88	125
Service C.E.[b] and A.E.	—	3	3	3	6	10	13	16	22	25	31	37	44	53	64
Subcontract	—	1	2	2	4	5	5	8	10	15	26	35	48	66	90
										(4)	(13)	(21)	(32)	(47)	(68)
Programmer subcontract	—	—	1	1	1	1	1	2	3	11	11	14	16	18	20
								(2)	(15)	(21)	(34)	(36)	(40)	(45)	(50)
General management	0	2	3	1	1	1	2	2	2	4	4	5	6	7	8
Administration						1	1	2	2	3	4	5	6	6	6
secretaries	1	1	1	1	3	3	4	5	7	12	18	23	26	33	39
Grand total	2	9	12	11	20	28	33	51	82	120	178	222	282	363	470
Average	(1.17)	(7.17)	(10.9)	(10.83)	(14.00)	(24.83)	(28.58)	(42)	(70)	(107)					
Growth rate	—	350%	33%	(8%)	82%	40%	18%	55%	61%	46%	48%	25%	27%	29%	29%
												Plan			

[a] A.E. indicates account executive.
[b] C.E. indicates customer engineer.

EXHIBIT 6 TEL Computer Controlled Systems Division Functional Organization Chart (May 1, 1983)

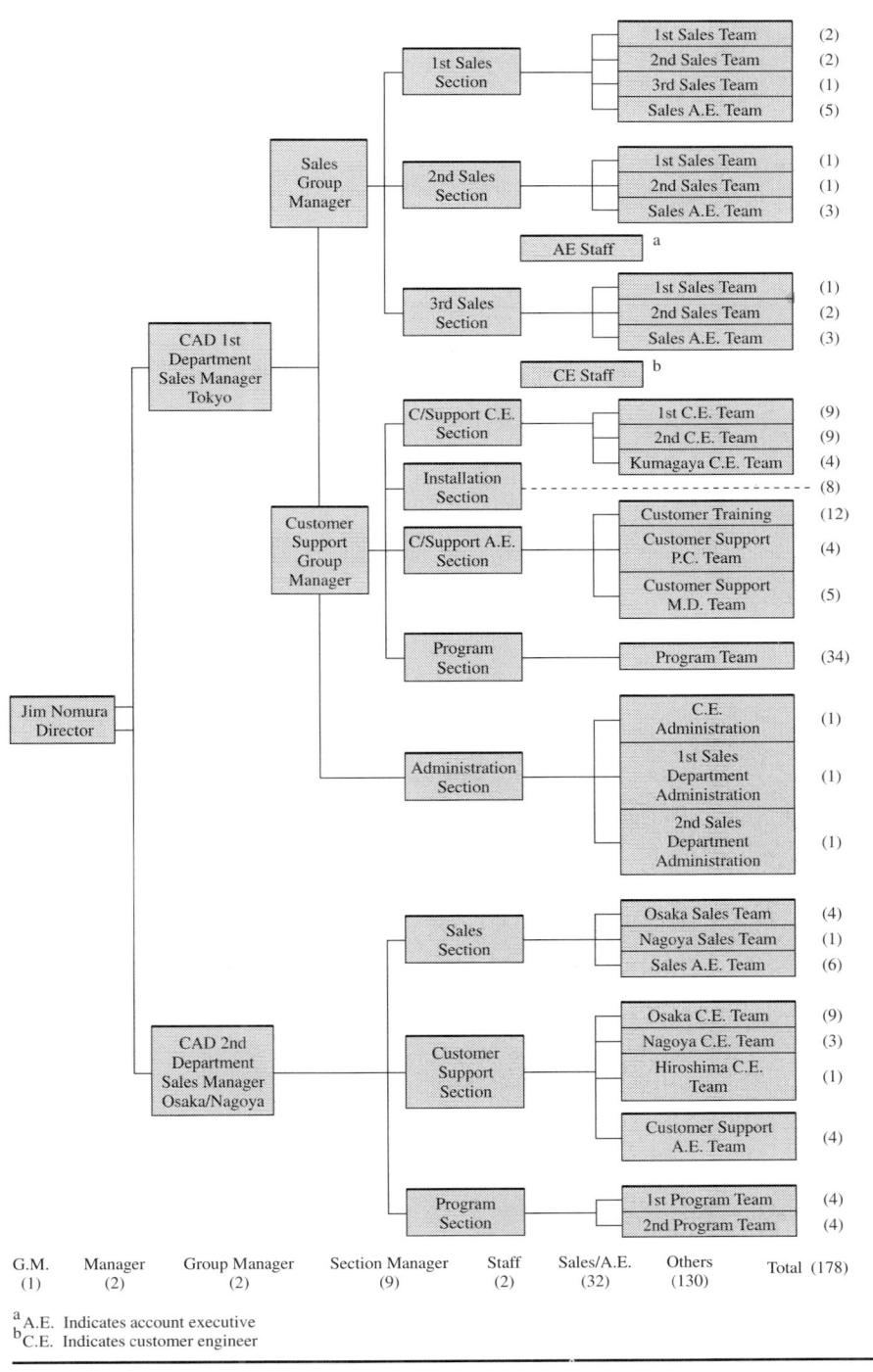

[a] A.E. Indicates account executive
[b] C.E. Indicates customer engineer

Exhibit 7 TEL's CAD/CAM Sales Performance (in millions of dollars)

	1982	1981	1980	1979	1978
TEL system sales	31.54	19.13	11.47	6.96	5.76
TEL service revenues	1.23	.83	.43	.25	.09
Total TEL sales from CV systems	32.77	19.96	11.90	7.21	5.85
Percent increase	+64%	+68%	+65%	+23%	
Number of systems sold	63	39	23	14	11
CV's revenue from TEL	17.1	13.5	8.2	4.9	4.0

Exhibit 8 CV-Japan Organization

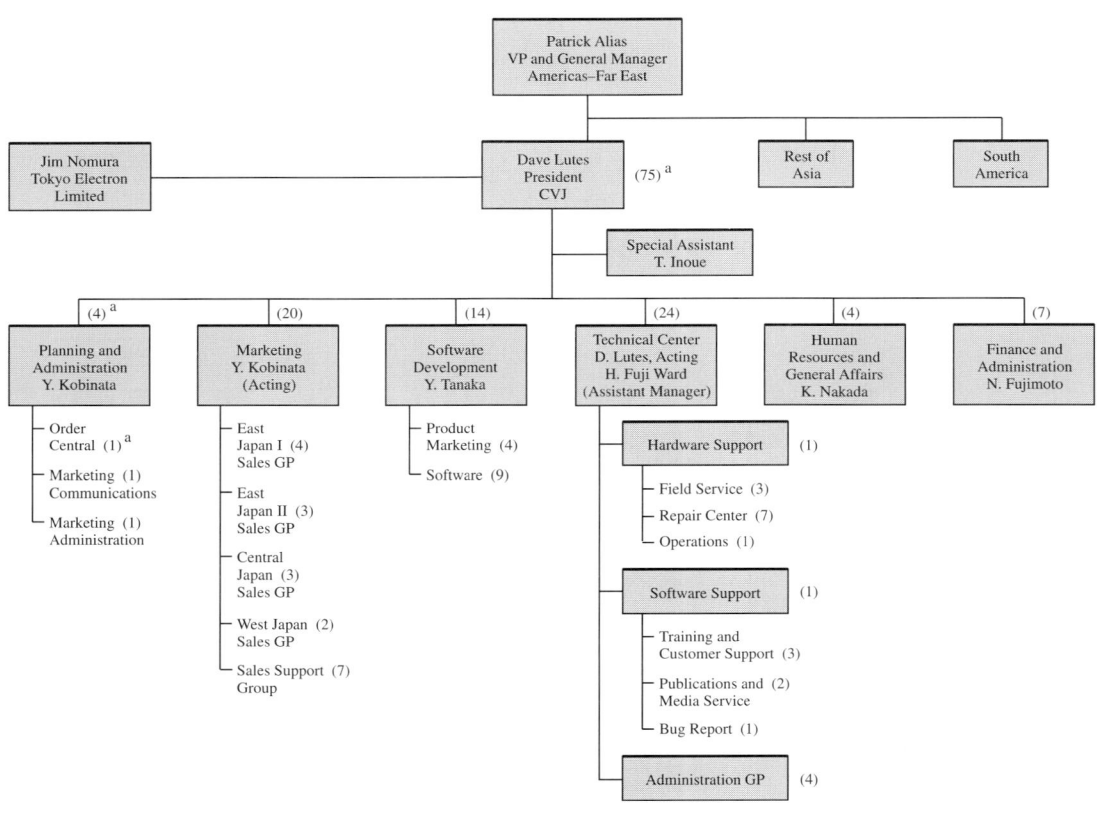

[a] Indicates total number of employees in the department.

was responsible for helping TEL develop special software programs for the Japanese market. Product marketing was a new department within the software development function. Its objectives were stated as follows:

- Survey and analyze customer problems and the competitive situation in all applications areas.
- Help develop the marketing strategy for each application category and promote sales in cooperation with sales management.
- Introduce new CV products to Japanese users and prospects.
- Feed back information to CV's product development group at headquarters.
- Offer consulting services to customers and the sales force.

Competition in Japan

American companies dominated the market in Japan—although many of them had affiliated themselves with various Japanese companies to facilitate their own entry into the market. About 25 companies were competing in the Japanese CAD/CAM market. An independent market research firm estimated the Japanese-installed base of CAD/CAM systems to be distributed as follows:

Research Firm's Estimated 1982 Installed Base

Company	Units	Percent (%)
Computervision, Japan	130	20%
Calma/C. Itoh	120	19
Applicon/Marubeni Hytech	100	15
IBM-Japan	80	12
Fujitsu (Facom)	80	12
Daini Seikosha (Seiko)	70	11
Other	70	11
Total	**650**	**100%**

Calma

Calma was a United States–based turnkey systems company with estimated 1982 worldwide sales of about $100 million. Recently acquired by General Electric, it was now part of GE's Industrial Automation Systems group. Calma's products focused heavily on the electronics industry, although it also had systems for mapping and for architecture, engineering, and construction (AEC) applications. In Japan, Calma was the leading supplier for the integrated circuit (IC) application, which represented 60 percent of its installed base of systems. Shortly after GE acquired Calma, it entered into a joint venture agreement with C. Itoh—the third largest independent trading company in Japan. The agreement included subassembly, service support, sales, and distribution of its systems as well as some new product development. A large number of Calma/C. Itoh's sales and sales management people had recently left to join Digital Equipment Corporation in Japan.

Applicon

Applicon was also a United States–based turnkey systems supplier. In 1982, it was acquired by Schlumberger, a leading supplier of data services to the oil industry. Applicon's worldwide sales revenue was estimated to be $75 million. Applicon produced systems for most of the major CAD/CAM applications, but it had been most successful in the electronics industry. In Japan, 80 percent of its installations were used for integrated circuit (IC) or printed circuit (PC) board design. Marubeni Hytech was Applicon's exclusive distributor responsible for sales, service, and support in Japan. Marubeni was the fourth largest independent trading company in Japan. During 1982–83, most of Applicon's orders had come from its existing customer base.

IBM-Japan

IBM-Japan was a wholly owned subsidiary of IBM. Its CAD/CAM systems were sold through a large direct sales force as part of its broad offering of data processing products. During the past two years, IBM-Japan had increased its CAD/CAM sales effort dramatically. In addition to its large staff of CAD/CAM specialists in Tokyo, it also had CAD/CAM sales teams and support groups in Osaka and Nagoya (Japan's second and third largest cities). Industry sources estimated that Japan's CAD/CAM potential was located 50 percent in the Tokyo area, 20 percent in the Osaka area, and 20 percent in the Nagoya area.

Dataquest, a market research company, estimated that in 1982 IBM-Japan had the largest CAD/CAM revenues in the Japanese market, with Fujitsu being number two. While both companies had a smaller installed base of CAD/CAM systems than the traditional turnkey vendors such as CV, Calma, and Applicon, they had a large installed base of mainframe computers and well-established reputations. Unlike the turnkey vendors, IBM and Fujitsu systems were not based exclusively on minicomputers. Their systems also ran on large IBM and IBM plug-compatible mainframes. Both companies used the CADAM software system that Lockheed had developed for its internal use. The CADAM system provided a two-dimensional drafting ability primarily used for mechanical design applications. IBM and Fujitsu marketed CADAM under a licensing agreement with Lockheed. Fujitsu also sold a three-dimensional software system, called ICAD, that had originally been developed for Fujitsu's internal use. It was estimated that 90 percent of IBM's and Fujitsu's installations were used for the mechanical design/drafting application.

Fujitsu

In 1982, the Facom division of Fujitsu surpassed IBM as the largest seller of computers in Japan. All of Fujitsu's mainframe computers were considered IBM plug-compatible. Like IBM-Japan, its CAD/CAM systems were sold through a large direct sales force. Facom invested heavily in the training and support of its customers. Although Facom had been selling CAD/CAM systems only since late 1981, it already had a large group of support people located in the four major cities of

Japan—Tokyo, Osaka, Nagoya, and Kita-Kyushu. All of Facom's training, training literature, and training exercises were provided in Japanese—unlike most of the American CAD/CAM suppliers that provided Japanese-language training, but English-language text. While Facom was behind IBM in CAD/CAM revenues and units for 1982, it had made major inroads into the Japanese market. Although not known exactly, its 1982 CAD/CAM revenues in the Japanese market were estimated at approximately $50 million.

Seiko

Daini Seikosha (Seiko) was a worldwide leader in the watch industry as well as a major supplier in Japan of graphics plotters, graphics terminals, and other graphics peripherals. In 1981, it entered the CAD/CAM market by using a variety of approaches. First, it became the exclusive distributor for the Create 2000 printed circuit board design systems that had been developed by another Japanese company—Zuken. Second, Seiko decided to market its own internally developed system for designing integrated circuits called the SX8000 system. Finally, it agreed to be a nonexclusive distributor for the McAuto Unigraphics product used for mechanical design. This product had been developed for internal use by McDonnell Douglas and was now being marketed by its McAuto division. In Japan, McAuto was also selling the product through a small direct sales force and other distributors. Seiko had shown a strong commitment to diversifying into the CAD/CAM area from its base in the manufacture of watches and other fine machinery. Many executives believed that Seiko would grow more rapidly than many United States–based companies in Japan because of its large investment, the local content of its hardware, and the company's support philosophy. Like Fujitsu, Seiko was providing heavy support for all three of its products. This was a considerable challenge because the Create 2000 was based on Hewlett-Packard equipment, while the SX8000 and the McAuto systems used DEC or Data General equipment. The declining cost of central processors combined with Seiko's locally manufactured peripherals allowed the company to price its systems much lower than CV, Applicon, or Calma. It was estimated that 60 percent of Seiko's installations were used for mechanical design and 40 percent for printed circuit board design.

Competitive Overview

The recent success of IBM and Fujitsu in the Japanese CAD/CAM market reflected the increased worldwide competition for this fast-growing market. Most of the large computer hardware companies were forward integrating into the CAD/CAM market by licensing third-party software. In addition to the large computer companies, the traditional turnkey systems suppliers (CV, Calma, Applicon, etc.) were encountering new competition from many other directions, including:

- Third-party software houses that packaged their software on hardware stipulated by the customer.

- Component integrators working on a specialized niche. For example, many of the recent start-ups in the field focused on the automated drafting function in order to gain a foothold in the overall CAD/CAM market.
- Some large companies like GM, GE, and Lockheed had developed a leading edge CAD/CAM technology internally in order to gain a competitive advantage in their industry. Similar to Fujitsu, these companies were starting to sell and/or license their proprietary CAD/CAM knowledge.

In the past two years the Japanese market had attracted the attention of most of the new CAD/CAM suppliers.

The Japanese CAD/CAM Market

Japan had a population of 116 million people and a gross national product roughly one-half that of the United States. Robotics was heavily used in the manufacturing process in Japan, and its use in manufacturing surpassed the use of CAD/CAM in the design and engineering process. This reflected the strong Japanese emphasis on manufacturing quality and cost control, as well as the easier cost justification for robotics. Because it was hard to put a cash value on fast design turnaround and multiple design iterations, costs of CAD/CAM systems were more difficult to justify. The market situation was just the reverse in the United States where total revenues generated by CAD/CAM sales were much larger than total revenues generated by robotics sales.

A Dataquest research report estimated the total installed base of CAD/CAM systems in Japan at the end of 1982 to be distributed by application as follows:

Distribution by Application

Application[a]	Installed Systems Base	Percent of Installed Base
Mechanical design	426	64%
IC design	130	20
PC design	65	10
AEC	32	5
Mapping/other	7	1
Total	**650**	**100%**

[a]In Japan, 60% of CV's systems were used for mechanical design, 20% for PC design, and 20% for all other applications.

The total installed base in the United States was estimated to be 5,800 units. Adjusting for the difference in GNPs, the current Japanese installed base was equivalent to that of the United States in 1977. From 1977 to 1982 the U.S. market grew at a compound annual rate of 47 percent for systems sold, 53 percent for workstations sold, and 71 percent for total annual revenue. During this same period, the compound annual growth rate by application was as follows: mechanical design—87 percent; PC board design—67 percent; IC design—62 percent; mapping—60 percent; and AEC—57 percent. As with the United States, mechanical design applications were forecast to be the fastest growing area in Japan, followed by printed circuits (PC), integrated circuits (IC), mapping, and architecture, engineering, construction (AEC).

Pricing

Historically, CAD/CAM systems cost much more in Japan than in the United States. For example, a typical CV system with four terminals in Japan cost approximately $500,000 versus $425,000 in the United States. The Japanese prices of the other American turnkey vendors were slightly less but in the same general range. However, Japanese systems did not have to pay import duties and shipping, which could add 15 percent to the price of a system. In the long run, both TEL and CV expected prices to decline in Japan between 5 and 15 percent per year.

Another factor was the type of central processor used. The first four to eight workstations driven off a large mainframe computer cost about the same as a turnkey system driven off its own minicomputer. However, for an installation involving more than eight workstations, the incremental cost could be as low as $100,000 per workstation if the mainframe computer had unused processing capacity.

Unique Market Characteristics

The structure of Japanese industry gave the Japanese market several unique characteristics:

1. Japanese industry was centered around 16 industrial groups which employed 16 percent of all workers and accounted for approximately 29 percent of goods sold by Japanese companies. Exhibit 9 shows revenue and employment figures for the 16 groups. Many of these powerful industrial groups had developed out of the pre-WWII Zaibatsu companies, such as Mitsui, Mitsubishi, and Sumitomo. During the postwar occupation of Japan, Allied forces had broken up the Zaibatsu in an effort to diffuse political power in Japan. However, in the 1950s and 1960s the old Zaibatsu companies and some of the larger post-WWII companies began to form industrial groups centered around banks (for financing) and trading companies (for import/export). The newly formed groups, in compliance with the antimonopoly laws imposed by the Allied occupation, did not recombine into single companies. Instead, they formed company groups through loans, trade agreements, distribution arrangements, and interlocking directories. Each company acted independently and was targeted at some specific industry or service. The overall group strategy was coordinated by monthly or quarterly meetings of the president's councils, called Sacho-Kai. In some cases, the industrial groups were associated with each other through common trading companies or banks. For example, the Matsushita group was loosely connected with the Sumitomo group through its use of Sumitomo Bank.

EXHIBIT 9 Japan's 16 Largest Industrial Groups

Group	Number of Companies	Number of Turnover (yen–billions)		Employees (1,000 persons)	
Mitsubishi	136	22,336	(4.8)	387	(2.4)
Mitsui	102	16,058	(3.4)	200	(1.2)
Sumitomo	108	16,407	(3.5)	325	(2.0)
Fuyo	103	14,962	(3.2)	256	(1.6)
DKB	64	16,654	(3.6)	317	(1.9)
Sanwa	80	13,552	(2.9)	217	(1.3)
Tokai	25	3,440	(.7)	38	(.2)
IBJ	19	1,699	(.4)	34	(.2)
Nippon Steel	40	5,310	(1.1)	144	(.9)
Hitachi	37	3,514	(.8)	143	(.9)
Nissan	27	4,370	(.9)	119	(.7)
Toyota	36	8,960	(1.9)	162	(1.0)
Matsushita	24	3,692	(.8)	97	(.6)
Toshiba-IHI	38	3,119	(.7)	131	(.8)
Seibu	21	1,542	(.3)	60	(.4)
Tokyu	19	1,167	(.2)	41	(.3)
Subtotal	879	136,782	(29.3)	2,671	(16.4)
Japan total	209,195	467,145	(100%)	16,330	(100%)

SOURCE: Dodwell industrial groupings in Japan 1980/81.

Hitachi, Ltd., was a member of the presidential council of the DKB, Fuyo, and Sanwa groups, and it borrowed equally from each group's bank.

The largest industrial group in Japan was Mitsubishi with 136 companies and 387,000 employees. The smallest of the 16 major groups was Seibu with 22 companies and 58,000 employees. It was difficult to directly compare the Japanese groups with large American companies. Unlike divisions in U.S. companies, each group member in Japan was usually targeted at one industry and its stock was individually traded. Consequently, a great deal of information was available for doing industry analysis and targeting industry-specific marketing activities. The Japanese industrial groups were a considerable economic force because in addition to controlling all of their own companies each group also had considerable influence over an additional 200 to 500 nongroup companies that were sole source suppliers or subcontractors. It was not unusual for the primary industrial group companies to decide what type of equipment the supplier companies would use.

2. Most Japanese industries were fairly concentrated. In some cases, the top 10 companies controlled 90 percent of the industry.

3. The revenue/employee ratio for most industries was much higher than in the United States because (1) the extensive use of subcontractors reduced the number of employees involved in producing the goods sold by each company, and (2) many firms did not market their products to the end user, but relied on closely aligned

trading companies to handle the labor-intensive task of sales and services. The trading companies associated with the 16 industrial groups often played a very significant role in selling their group's products both within their group (to other group companies, suppliers, and subcontractors) and to outside markets (domestic and foreign). In addition, the trading companies often acted as distributors' agents or brokers for nongroup products.

4. Cost of capital, return on investment, and rates of profitability were substantially below those in the United States.

Japanese Market Potential

Lack of reliable information on the size and potential of the Japanese CAD/CAM market had been a constant source of conflict between CVJ and TEL over the years. Patrick Alias wanted CVJ to achieve a market share of 30 percent by 1986, rising to 40 percent by 1990 of the total CAD/CAM market. The recent Dataquest study claimed there were 650 CAD/CAM systems installed in Japan at the end of 1982, of which 130 were CV systems. This would give CV a market share of 20 percent.

The dramatic strides IBM-Japan, Fujitsu, and Seiko made in 1981–1982, however, would indicate that CV's recent market share had slipped substantially below 20 percent. Since CV actually had 198 systems installed in Japan at the end of 1982, Alias felt strongly that the study greatly understated both the current size and growth of the Japanese CAD/CAM market. Jim Nomura also believed the Dataquest figures were inaccurate and unreliable, because they did not define what they considered to be a "system," nor did they explain how they developed their data. In his March 1983 meeting with Alias, Nomura had argued that CV/TEL actually had closer to a 50 percent market share in the Japanese turnkey systems market. Based on his own informal appraisal, Nomura felt that the turnkey market was worth about $60 million in 1982.

Patrick Alias's intuition and European experience caused him to question sharply Jim Nomura's estimate of CV's penetration of the Japanese market. He reasoned:

> Japan has a population of 116 million and the United States has a population of 230 million. The CAD/CAM market in the United States is a $500 million/year market of which CV has about a 35 percent share. If we assume that Japan's economy is at least as advanced as the U.S. economy, then the market for CAD/CAM equipment should be about $250 million, not $60 million. Since TEL's 1982 sales of CV systems—not including service revenue—were only about $30 million, TEL/CV has a 12 percent share of the Japanese market.

In addition, Alias had found in Europe that CV's market penetration was highly correlated to the amount of revenue produced per salesperson. The top European sales reps produced $3 million in revenue per year with the average sales rep producing $2 million and the weaker ones about $1 million. These figures were similar to the United States, where an average sales rep produced about $2 million in revenue. Across Europe, where there was reasonably good market information, he found that the top sales reps had about a 60 percent share. Because TEL claimed to have 30 sales reps devoted to CV, the average revenue per sales rep was about $1 million. Alias felt this was further evidence that CVJ's market share was low.

Through some European contacts, Alias had recently obtained a list of IBM's CAD/CAM customers in Japan. Of these customers, 60 percent had never appeared on TEL's call reports or loss reports. As a result, he was convinced that additional coverage was necessary in Japan. Alias also felt that low market share made each sale more difficult. In those European countries where CV had 60 percent of the market, there was a very positive market momentum. In fact, many potential customers called CV first to inquire about buying a system.

Current Situation

Alias summarized his views of the current situation as follows:

> Over the past 10 years, CV has enjoyed relatively free access to the Japanese market. Our competition has been primarily the other U.S. CAD/CAM companies. Today, however, the situation is changing; the market is becoming unstable because of the rapidly developing competition from Japanese CAD/CAM suppliers. In other words, the window of opportunity is open, and has been for some time, but it is rapidly going to slam shut unless our strategy is capable of developing significant market share rapidly. Any strategy we recommend to headquarters must therefore be capable of rapid implementation.
>
> A corollary to the goal of establishing local market share is to create a strong defensive posture in the context of our global market share. Already Japanese competition is beginning to move into the U.S. and European markets, the traditional source of CV's strength. By rapidly developing market share in the Japanese market we will limit the ability of our Japanese competitors to encroach on our areas of strength in the United States and Europe.
>
> In addition to the need for rapid implementation, another criterion for any strategy we recommend is that it must take into account our current organization and relationships in Japan. We do not begin with a blank piece of paper.

Before recommending any specific actions for the Japanese market, Alias felt it was essential (1) to develop a reasonable forecast for the CAD/CAM market in Japan, and (2) to understand all of the available strategic options.

Market Forecast

In March 1983, Alias had requested the marketing department of CVJ to forecast the growth of the CAD/CAM market in Japan. He had also requested TEL to develop a separate forecast. CVJ used a local marketing study as a base and modified it using company data and its own market intelligence. TEL had access to the same local marketing study. The results along with TEL's four-year sales forecast had been presented to him this past week in Japan. They were as follows:

TEL's Four-Year Sales Forecast

	1983		1984		1985		1986	
	Volume[a]	Market Share	Volume	Market Share	Volume	Market Share	Volume	Market Share
TEL's CV sales forecast (retail)	$ 42		$ 55		$ 75		$ 100	
TEL's market forecast (turnkey only)	187	22%	251	22%	341	22%	461	22%
CVJ's market forecast								
Total market	470	9[b]	680	8	930	8	1,200	8
Turnkey only	280	15	410	13	580	13	760	13

[a]All volume figures are millions of U.S. dollars.
[b]To be read as follows: TEL's sales forecast implies a 1983 CVJ market share of 9% of the total CAD/CAM market as forecast by CVJ.

Regardless of whether CVJ's estimates or TEL's estimates were used, the present strategy would clearly leave CV with results far below its goal of 30 percent of the total market by 1986. Even if TEL made its 1986 forecast, there would be a $260 million shortfall. Based on this analysis, Alias set the following goals for CV in the Japanese market:

CV Sales Goals, Japanese Market

	Sales Volume[a]	Market Share
1983	$ 42 million	9%
1984	109	16
1985	214	23
1986	360	30

[a]These numbers are for retail, end user revenues in Japan.

Options

On the 20-hour flight back from Tokyo, Alias reviewed his options. He wished now that Japan had gone to direct sales back in the mid-1970s when he was converting CV's European operation. In the long run, he felt that having a direct sales force would be the most effective and cost-efficient way of combating the newly emerging Japanese competition. Fujitsu and IBM-Japan both had large direct sales forces of approximately 1,500–1,800 sales representatives, some of whom were being redeployed against the CAD/CAM market. C. Itoh had 30–40 sales representatives dedicated to CAD/CAM, and Marubeni Hytech had already hired, trained, and deployed 10–15 sales reps in the last two years.

In 1983, the task of building a direct sales and service organization to replace TEL would be enormous. One applications engineer and one service engineer were required to support five installed systems, and it took 6–12 months to hire and train these support people. It took a full year to hire and train a sales representative. Based on CV's experience in the United States and Europe, an average sales representative should produce $2 million per year in revenue. However, Jim Nomura felt that $1.5 million was more realistic for Japan. A direct organization would also require supervision, administration, and managers—about one for every six or seven people. In Europe, selling and administrative expenses ran about 20 percent of sales, but costs in Japan could be expected to run higher. It was extremely difficult for U.S. companies to hire Japanese nationals. The best university graduates generally wanted to work for a company in one of the large industrial groups. Their second choice would be a smaller Japanese company that was growing rapidly. In general, the lack of job security and differences in management style made U.S.–based companies less attractive to work for.

Most U.S. companies relied on higher salaries to recruit people from their competitors. Because of employee loyalty and the consistently tight labor market, this process did not always produce the best results. This was one of many reasons why U.S. companies often entered into joint venture agreements in Japan.

In addition to sales, field service, and applications support, CV would also have to assume responsibility for the other functions and services currently performed by TEL, including:

1. Customer credit—normally 120 days. TEL's cost of credit was approximately 6 percent. CV's cost would be approximately 10 percent.
2. Shipping, tariffs, insurance (approximately 15 percent), and foreign exchange fluctuations—currently all prices to TEL were F.O.B. Bedford, Massachusetts, and payable in U.S. dollars.
3. Extended warranty—TEL provided the customary one-year warranty in Japan whereas CV only provided a 90-day warranty. CV estimated the cost of the extended warranty at 1 percent/month of the end-user price.
4. Preinstallation product/system testing, which cost approximately 1 percent of the end-user price.
5. Product modification—the hardware in all U.S. CAD/CAM systems had to be modified to conform to Japanese Industrial Standards (JIS). In addition, all software had to be converted to Japanese, including the incorporation of special Japanese Kanji figures into the system. For a completely new CAD/CAM system, this could require 30–40 person years of effort. This was currently being done 50 percent by TEL and 50 percent by CVJ at a total estimated cost of $1.4 million per new system.

Patrick Alias knew that going direct was very beneficial in Europe, but he was not sure how transferable that experience was to the Japanese market. While CV's agreement with TEL could be canceled with 30 days' notice, TEL had long-established relationships with many of its CAD/CAM customers. TEL was a fast-growing company that had earned the respect of its competitors and the confidence of its customers.

It was apparent from TEL's sales forecast that on its current course it would not reach CV's goal of 30 percent of the total CAD/CAM market in Japan by 1986. This would require a dramatic expansion of TEL's marketing efforts. For years, CVJ had been asking TEL to accelerate its sales coverage. As recently as February, Patrick Alias, on his first trip to Japan, had asked Jim Nomura to double the size of the sales force this year. Nomura's response had been that TEL was people-constrained and had been for the last five years. The company's policy, as in many other Japanese companies, was to develop its people internally by hiring the best university graduates it could and training them. TEL's management felt that this produced better results than a policy of hiring people away from other companies. The company wanted to grow as fast as possible with internally developed people. All of TEL's sales divisions were growing rapidly and Jim Nomura had to compete with other TEL divisions for available manpower. He was at a considerable disadvantage because most of the other sales divisions' products were made by TEL under joint venture agreements with U.S. companies. These companies had made long-term commitments to TEL not only as a distributor but as a manufacturing partner. Jim Nomura responded to Alias's request for more coverage as follows:

> First, I think that the CCS division has been very successful at obtaining its fair share of our company's available manpower for CV over the past few years. I would like very much to expand our sales coverage more rapidly—even double it. To do that, I need the support of CV. Our first step should be to establish the joint venture which TEL has been proposing for the last five years. TEL and CV are still "dating" after all these years, while TEL and its other U.S. suppliers are married. We have joint ventures with them and both parties have long-term commitments to each other. With a joint venture arrangement I would be in a stronger position to compete for manpower and could more rapidly expand the sales coverage. The joint venture would also help our quest for market share by strengthening our local engineering support. It would also handle final system assembly and checkout, as well as local program development and product adaptation. As needed, it could also develop any custom hardware that was requested for the Japanese market. TEL would provide the joint venture with trained people, local hiring capability, bank credit, and Japanese management know-how. CV would provide the technology and general engineering support in exchange for a 5 percent licensing fee and half of the joint venture's profits. Sales would continue to be handled entirely by the CCS division of TEL.
>
> If a joint venture is not possible, then CV can help me expand faster (1) by taking over the full responsibility for servicing and supporting our installed base of systems, and (2) by assuming full responsibility for all product adaptation, and all pre- and postinstallation support of new customers. This would allow me to redeploy my available manpower for better sales coverage. I am very anxious to increase the size of our sales force, but TEL needs more support and/or more commitment from CV in order to achieve increased market share in Japan. In the past few years TEL's performance in the Japanese CAD/CAM market has been outstanding—with some support and commitment we could do even better.

See Exhibit 5 for TEL's manpower chart for CCS and Exhibit 7 for TEL's five-year sales performance on CV systems.

Alias had explored the purchase of TEL's service and support operation by CVJ. However, TEL felt a strong commitment to support its existing customers and because of its policy of lifetime employment, TEL would not transfer its people to CVJ.

Regarding a joint venture with TEL, Jim Berrett and CV's other senior managers were strongly opposed for the following reasons:

1. Japanese management in a joint venture tended to have stronger allegiance to the Japanese half-owner.
2. There were numerous examples of Japanese companies not needing their American partner a few years after a joint venture or licensing agreement had been signed.
3. CV might lose control of its product in Japan if local sourcing was aggressively pursued.

Another option for Alias was to supplement TEL's marketing efforts with additional distributors, sales agents, or CVJ's own direct sales force. It was not clear whether TEL would tolerate this type of arrangement. TEL's other businesses were growing rapidly—recruiting capable people was its major constraint.

CV had not actively pursued additional distributors, but several capable distributors had approached it over the past few years. All were anxious to enter the CAD/CAM market. Most suggested an exclusive agreement either replacing TEL or giving them exclusive rights to locations other than the Tokyo area, where TEL had 70 percent of its sales and service coverage. Other suggestions included dividing the market by industry, application, named accounts, or some combination of these. Most of these distributors preferred that CVJ handle all new product adaptation, field service, and application support.

Another alternative for expanding distribution channels in Japan was for CVJ to enter into multiple distribution arrangements with trading companies associated with the 16 major industrial groups. As a stand-alone trading company, TEL was limited in how it could approach many of the companies associated with industrial groups. In the past three months, Alias had had several discussions with two large trading companies—Toyota and Sony. Toyota Trading Company had about 150 general salespeople and was willing to dedicate at least six salespeople to CV the first year. The trading company did not have the expertise to properly handle the CAD/CAM systems, however, and CV would be responsible for all technical training, service, and support. Sony Trading Company was interested in a similar arrangement of dedicating six sales and sales support people. Both companies were willing to adhere to CVJ's suggested pricing schedule and would expect a 7 percent commission on all sales.

Alias was confident that CVJ could work out an agreement with Toyota Trading, Sony Trading, and/or other large trading companies not currently selling CAD/CAM equipment. Members of large industry groups bought the best products available. They were not obligated to buy from other companies within their group even if a member of the group produced a similar but inferior product. They were also not obligated to buy products from their own trading company, although the trading company usually had good access to the key decision makers. Trading companies sold to everyone and were motivated primarily by volume and profit considerations. They were expert at identifying prospects, but they were not particularly interested in doing a lot of hand-holding, complex demonstrations, or presales support and analysis. As with most Japanese companies, the trading companies were only interested in entering into long-term agreements, but they did not require exclusive distribution rights.

Alias was also intrigued by the possibilities of using the current CVJ organization to expand market coverage. The CVJ organization had grown rapidly in the past two years with quarterly expenses climbing to a current rate of $1.4 million. After three months on the job, Alias was still uncomfortable about the amount and quality of support being provided by the CVJ organization. It seemed to be a growing bureaucracy with little or no responsibility for achieving sales goals. This concern was shared by Jim Nomura, who thought TEL's efforts were not well supported by CVJ in spite of its growing organization.

Over the past two years CVJ had hired six salespeople away from other CAD/CAM suppliers. These people were currently supporting TEL's sales effort and could be converted to sales if CV discontinued the exclusive distribution agreement with TEL.

Patrick Alias knew that achieving a 30 percent share of market in Japan by 1986 was essential to CV's global strategy. He also realized that any plan he developed for building market share in Japan must fully consider TEL's long-standing relationship with CV and its potential reaction.

CHAPTER 27
Signode Industries, Inc. (A)

Signode Industries' packaging division manufactures steel and plastic strapping. In 1981, the company underwent a leveraged buyout. The chapter focuses on the packaging division's need to maintain high profitability in a declining market for steel strapping. Since 1974, Signode has been losing 1 percent per year of the steel strapping market. Since then, there has also been significant erosion of prices. The division president is faced with (1) decreasing price to increase market share, or (2) maintaining/increasing prices to increase cash flow. The specific decision revolves around the potential adoption of a price-flex system that is designed to authorize selective discounting by the division's sales personnel.

Introduction

In early January 1984, Gary Reed, president of Signode Industries' Packaging Division, was preparing his presentation for the national sales meeting later that month. One important element of his presentation would be Signode's response to changing steel prices. Just two months before, the major U.S. steel companies had announced a 6.8 percent increase in the price of cold rolled steel—the raw material used in the manufacture of Signode's primary product, steel strapping.

Historically, the steel strapping industry had passed these price increases directly to the customer. Signode's sales force, however, had responded to the announcement with emphatic complaints about continued price cuts by competitors and about the company's significant price differentials. Signode's major competitor, Alpha Corporation, had already announced an increase in its book prices by 6.8 per-

David May and Gordon Swartz prepared this case under the supervision of Rowland T. Moriarty. Copyright © 1985 by the President and Fellows of Harvard College.
Harvard Business School case 586-059 (revised April 1990).

cent for a "select group of customers." The sales force, however, feared that actual prices would remain constant, as Alpha was selectively cutting prices in an attempt to gain share.

Worried by the continued price cutting, Reed had visited each of the three regional sales offices during December. In the great majority of his meetings, Reed found Signode's powerful and respected sales force clamoring for no price increase and the authority to cut prices selectively. At one meeting, Jack Davis, one of the regional managers, had presented an idea he called price-flex, which was designed to allow sales representatives to selectively discount the book price for steel strapping consumables by as much as 7 percent in order to meet competition. Davis maintained that price-flex would allow Signode to continue charging premium prices to service-oriented customers, while lowering prices for those customers who purchased on a commodity basis. Davis also argued that ignoring price-flex or another competitive pricing plan would destine Signode to further market share losses.

Reed knew that Davis had a point. Though the company had been the market leader in the steel strapping business for 25 years, the past decade had seen Signode's market share decline from 50 percent in 1977 to its current 40 percent. From this perspective, the proposal was very appealing: with price-flex to meet competitive conditions, Davis and the sales force promised a 5 percent to 10 percent increase in Signode's market share.

However, Reed's response to the price-flex proposal was also constrained by corporate financial needs. Signode had recently undergone a leveraged buyout that had increased its long-term debt by $300 million. In addition, the company had aggressive plans for acquiring and growing new businesses into the 1990s. With high debt and no access to public equity markets, Signode needed the domestic Packaging Division to generate as much capital as possible.

Reed planned to use the annual sales meeting to address the sales force's concerns about competitive discounting and market share erosion. He also wanted to announce Signode's reaction to steel price increases and his decision on pricing policy.

Corporate Background

In 1983, Signode Corporation had sales of $658,737,000 and was, as noted, the market leader in the steel strapping industry. (See Exhibit 1 for corporate and packaging division financial information.) The corporation had started in 1914 as the Seal and Fastener Company, producing and marketing patented steel strap joints and application tools. In an attempt to establish strong brand recognition, the company changed its name to Signode, from the Latin *signus,* meaning seal, and *nodum,* meaning joint. Signode purchased finished steel strapping from steel mills and then sold it direct under the Signode name. Though the steel strapping industry had a very difficult time during the Great Depression, Signode responded to the difficult business environment by increasing technical assistance to its customers.

With the end of World War II and through the 1950s, Signode registered strong growth. It reduced costs by backward integrating. Whereas it once had purchased

Exhibit 1 Consolidated Financial Data (dollars in thousands)

	1979	1980	1981	1982	1983
Signode Corporation					
Revenue	$695,183	$695,504	$700,252	$650,387	$658,737
Gross margin	207,161	201,708	200,730	186,392	204,431
Direct expense	108,127	115,146	121,249	116,507	115,508
Selling expense	56,996	58,884	64,824	64,070	59,488
Other expense (income), net	17,705	11,798	20,626	31,967	20,207
EBIT	81,329	74,764	58,855	37,918	68,716
Interest expense (income)	2,432	3,792	(541)	118	45,054
Tax	36,588	33,137	22,714	16,639	2,778
Net earnings	$ 42,309	$ 37,835	$ 36,682	$ 21,161	$ 20,884
RONA	23.1%	19.2%	14.5%	8.5%	15.7%
Packaging Division					
Revenue	$298,264	$285,777	$311,469	$285,114	$285,950
Cost of sales	207,500	195,408	218,579	195,766	181,473
R&D expense	2,810	3,335	3,473	3,762	2,879
Freight expense	0	0	0	0	0
Gross margin	87,954	87,034	89,417	85,586	101,598
Selling expense	24,677	23,705	26,736	25,708	24,178
Materials management expense	11,001	12,037	11,737	10,792	12,560
General and administrative expense	8,597	7,031	7,446	6,489	8,547
Direct expense	44,275	42,773	45,919	42,989	45,285
Other income	0	41	96	73	550
Operating income	43,679	44,302	43,594	42,670	56,863
Other (income) and expense	8,485	9,898	10,235	10,596	9,975
EBIT	$ 35,194	$ 34,404	$ 33,359	$ 32,074	$ 46,888
RONA (fully allocated)		17%	16.1%	13.8%	29.9%

the finished strapping, Signode began purchasing the rolled steel, then slit and finished the strapping itself. Signode increased its research and development efforts, developing automated and air-powered strapping tools. It opened new regional steel strapping plants and sales offices to improve customer service. In conjunction with these developments, Signode also doubled the size of its sales force and became the market leader.

During the 1960s the company's prosperity was based, in part, on the growth of the cotton and brick industries. In 1962, Signode added plastic strapping to its product line. Through that decade and into the 1970s, Signode grew through acquisition and the consolidation of its overseas markets. During the 1982 recession, with its stock price undervalued, Signode attracted the attention of famed takeover specialist Victor Posner. Determined to retain control of the company, Signode management took the corporation private. It was the largest leveraged buyout in U.S. corporate history.

Signode's Organization

Although previously organized along functional lines, Signode switched to a divisionalized structure in 1979. The Packaging, International, and Fastener and Industrial Products divisions became profit centers; finance and research and development were maintained as cost centers. In 1983, the International Division, which had posted a poor earnings record for several years, had revenues of $234 million. The Fastener and Industrial Products Division, which was viewed as an umbrella for Signode's diversification into new product lines, had sales of $138 million. The corporation's main source of cash flow to cover interest and expansion expenses was the Packaging Division, which had sales of $286 million. The Packaging Division was responsible for all domestic sales of steel and plastic strapping systems.

Fifty-nine percent of the Packaging Division's revenues came from sales of steel strapping systems. The balance came from sales of plastic strapping systems. Of steel strapping systems revenues, 79 percent was from the sale of steel strapping consumables, 5 percent from the sale of machines, 7 percent from the sale of hand tools, and 9 percent from the sale of other goods, including seals used to fasten the steel strapping.

Packaging Division Products

Steel Strapping

Signode steel strapping was used by businesses to bind products for shipping. The strapping could bind together a shipment of two-by-fours, seal the box in which a washing machine was being shipped, or secure a stack of bricks. Small or infrequent users of strapping usually applied the strapping with a hand tool that may or may not have been specially designed for the customer's specific packaging needs. If the strapping process was the last step in an integrated assembly line—as might be the case with a washing machine—it would probably be applied by a custom-designed power strapping machine. Signode's engineering department would provide custom-designed strapping machines, but the steel strapping consumables applied by the machines could be supplied by any competitor.

Steel strapping was specified by two criteria—size and grade. Size referred to the width of the strapping, and Signode produced over 170 standard sizes of steel strapping. The grade referred to the thickness and strength of the strapping. There were three standard grades of strapping in the steel strapping industry: Apex, Box Band Magnus (BBM), and Heavy Duty Magnus (HDM). Twelve strapping sizes/grades represented 73 percent of all strapping sales.

Signode also produced custom sizes and grades of strapping, primarily for larger customers. It was the only supplier of custom strapping. These custom orders represented only 6.5 percent of total sales of steel strapping. Table A outlines applications and Signode's sales for each grade.

TABLE A Steel Strapping Grades, Uses, and Sales for Signode, 1983

Grade	Use	Percent Sales
Apex	Packages and corrugated boxes	33.3%
Box Band Magnus (BBM)	Bricks and medium weight steel packages (tin plate)	26.8%
Heavy Duty Magnus (HDM)	Rolls of steel and freight car bracing	33.4%

Plastic Strapping

When Signode started producing plastic strapping in 1962, the market for plastic strapping consumables was only $10 million. By 1983 that market had grown to $170 million, of which Signode's share was $90 million (53 percent). Growing at approximately 4 percent per year, the plastic systems market was stealing share from the low end of the steel systems market. The top grades of plastic strapping could, in some cases, be used as a substitute for Apex and BBM steel strapping. This substitution loss amounted to about 2 percent of the steel strapping market per year.

Tools and Equipment

The application of steel and plastic strapping required specialized tools or machines. Signode produced more than 550 standard types and sizes of steel strapping machines and tools in 1983, ranging from simple hand tools to fully automatic customized power strapping machines. (See Exhibit 2 for pictures of steel strapping tools and equipment.)

Along with its standard product line, Signode also designed custom tools and machines to fit the buyer's production lines. Few custom tools were made, and they accounted for less than 1 percent of steel strapping systems revenues. Steel strapping machines were nearly all custom made, and as a result demand was quite uncertain. For example, although 200 units had been purchased in 1983, fewer than 100 units were expected to be sold in 1984. Each machine had a head that tensioned and sealed the strapping. The heads were built to standard Signode design specifications, while the superstructures of the machines were custom built to the needs of specific plants. About 25 percent of steel strapping consumables were applied by this specialized power strapping equipment.

Signode's plastic strapping machines and tools could be used only with Signode plastic strapping because of strapping specifications and tolerances. Once customers purchased a Signode plastic application device, they were committed to purchasing only Signode strapping. Although demand for steel machines had stagnated over the past several years, the installed base of plastic strapping machines was still growing.

Chapter 27   Signode Industries, Inc. (A)   **481**

EXHIBIT 2   Steel Strapping Tools and Equipment

Hand Tools

Manual tensioners

Signode hand tensioners allow operators to bring strap to desired tension with minimal interruption and strap waste. There are four basic types of tensioners for steel strapping. Each tensioner type fulfills specific packaging needs. The manual tensioner types available include the feedwheel type, the push type, the windlass type, and the rack and pinion type.

Feedwheel type—for general use

The feedwheel tensioner has a serrated feedwheel which engages the strapping firmly. There is no limit to the amount of slack it can pull out of the strap. Fast and easy to use, it requires the use of painted and waxed strapping and is designed for use on flat surfaces.

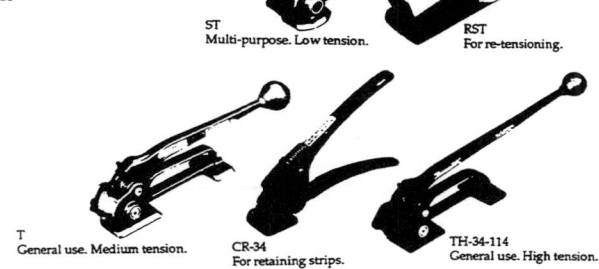

C-38-34
Multi-purpose. Low tension.

ST
Multi-purpose. Low tension.

RST
For re-tensioning.

T
General use. Medium tension.

CR-34
For retaining strips.

TH-34-114
General use. High tension.

Power Strapping Machine (M200 Series)

Packaging Division Organization

Gary Reed was president and COO of the Packaging Division. (See Exhibit 3 for an organization chart.) An engineer by training, Reed joined Signode after graduating from Bradley University in 1956. He worked his way through the sales organization into positions of general management, where he proved his abilities by turning around several smaller divisions. He noted that Signode's culture sometimes led salespeople to offer services to customers without knowing costs or effect on market share. As Signode came out of the 1982 recession, Reed realized the environment had changed:

> We were not going to recover as we had in the past. Steel strapping was a mature product. With the market moving toward commoditization, could Signode continue to differentiate its steel strapping business indefinitely?

EXHIBIT 3 **Organization Chart**

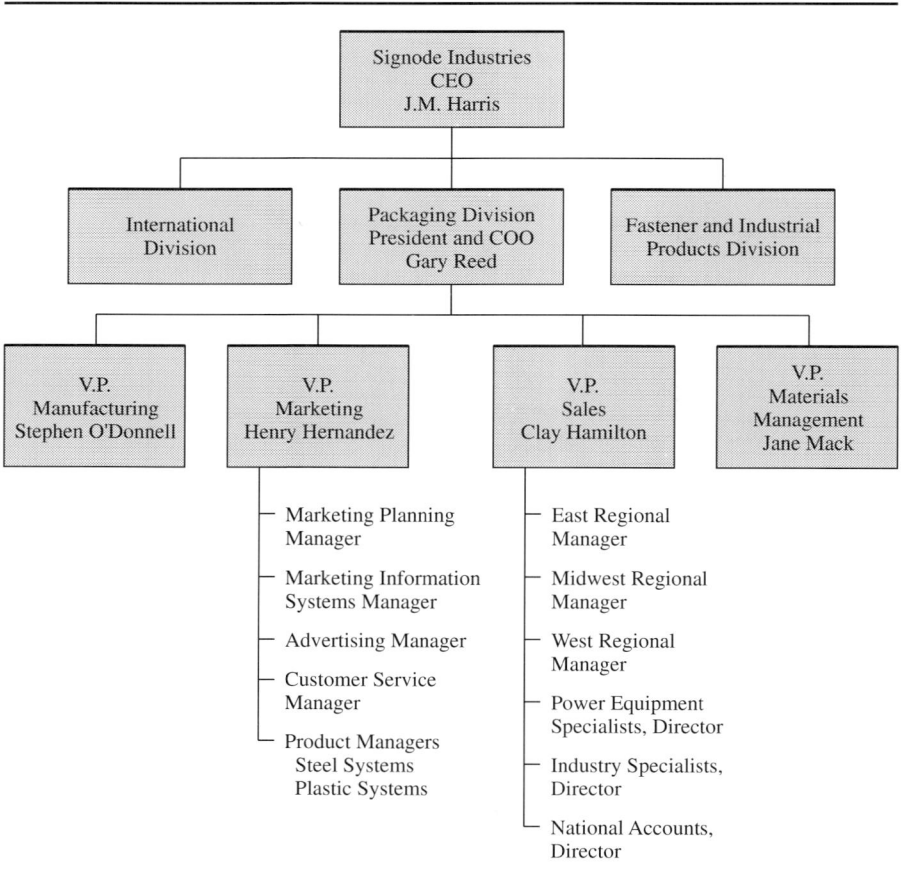

Sales and Marketing

When Reed took over the Packaging Division in 1982, he was determined to improve its marketing efforts. To this end, he appointed Henry Hernandez vice president of marketing. Reed had worked with Hernandez before and had confidence in his abilities.

In his new position, one of Hernandez's major responsibilities was the development of more sophisticated methods of measuring and segmenting the market. At Reed's behest, Hernandez quickly established product managers to oversee the marketing process for both steel and plastic strapping systems. It was believed that the product managers would help eliminate the traditional "black magic" the sales force had used in its market analysis.

Clay Hamilton, the division vice president of sales, had joined Signode in 1959 and, like Reed, had worked his way up through the sales organization. In 1983, 180 salespeople were reporting to Hamilton through 24 district managers and 3 regional managers. During the 1982 recession, Reed and Hamilton had cut the sales force from 235 to 180.

Although the sales force was organized geographically, Signode had traditionally developed markets by specializing some of its sales representatives by industry. Signode experts would study an industry's unique strapping needs, design specialized equipment to meet those needs, and then follow up with service and sales of strapping consumables. Because of this systems sales approach, the Signode sales force maintained multiple contacts within customer organizations, ranging from vice presidents of manufacturing and operations to plant managers and purchasing agents. During the 1970s, Signode also had experimented with the use of distributors to serve the lower end of the market, but the company had not been satisfied with the results.

Salespeople were compensated with a base salary and a volume bonus system. The marketing and sales organizations together set dollar sales quotas at the beginning of each year. Salespeople earned a 2 percent bonus on sales over their quota. The average salesperson in 1983 earned $35,000 per year, of which 70 percent was salary and 30 percent bonus.

In addition to its sales representatives, Signode employed two groups of specialists to assist in systems selling and account service. Power equipment specialists helped the field sales force with equipment sales, and industry specialists assisted on sales to customers in important industry segments. These specialists developed sales training programs to explain equipment applications, increase selling skills, and promote better technical knowledge of Signode's equipment line. The specialists also helped with the preparation of equipment and industry surveys and ROI justifications.

The director of national accounts also reported to Clay Hamilton. Signode's five national account managers (NAMs) targeted the 250 largest accounts and managed them in cooperation with the field sales force. The NAMs called on senior executives, made presentations on how Signode reduced customers' costs, and negotiated national, multilocation purchase contracts. Local relationships were handled by the district sales representatives.

Manufacturing and Materials Management

Signode's manufacturing and materials management efforts were also organized functionally. As the Packaging Division's vice president of manufacturing, Stephen O'Donnell managed the production of all custom and standard strapping and strapping equipment. O'Donnell, with Signode since 1958, had worked his way into general management through the manufacturing function. O'Donnell believed that steel strapping would continue to be a profitable, cash-generating business through the 1980s. It was, he said, a matter of knowing that "a cash cow can be fed and curried and nurtured for as long as the world will let you."

To continue the business profitably, O'Donnell sought to make Signode the low-cost producer in steel strapping systems. Signode was already the low-cost processor of cold rolled steel into steel strapping, but its higher raw materials costs and overhead prevented it from being the low-cost provider. There was also the problem of the shrinking market for steel strapping machines. The production of custom equipment absorbed a large amount of management time and scarce engineering and design resources. Because Signode had never been able to earn a profit on the construction of custom machines, O'Donnell strongly argued that Signode should cease production of custom machines and supply only a line of standard power strapping equipment.

Jane Mack, the head of materials management since she joined the corporation in 1980, sought to reduce Signode's materials costs by taking a more aggressive stance with materials suppliers, especially those in the steel industry. Mack had not yet altered Signode's tradition of purchasing only domestic steel, because the steel companies were important customers as well as suppliers: in 1983, the Big 8 steel companies had purchased 13 percent of Signode's steel strapping production. Analysis showed, however, that if Signode could buy imported steel at a 6 percent decrease in raw materials cost, it would break even on the profits forgone from the loss of the Big 8 steel companies as customers.

In addition, Mack consolidated inventory and reduced costs by closing seven warehouses. Sales managers, however, saw the inventory reductions as cutbacks in service. They argued that the warehouse closings were especially damaging because they were coincident with unprecedented differentials between the price of Signode steel strapping and that of its competitors.

Steel Strapping Market

The steel strapping industry was closely tied to the cycles and overall health of the industrial economy. Industry shipments of steel strapping consumables had declined from a high of 479,000 tons in 1973 to 360,000 tons by 1983. The total dollar sales of steel strapping was approximately $330 million. During this period, imports increased and began to play a role in the low-price segment of the market. Through the 1970s, domestic competitors had continued to add production capacity. In 1983 industry capacity utilization was estimated to be between 60 and 70 percent.

TABLE B Signode's Market Segmentation

Segment	Annual Dollar Volume	Shipping Quantity
National	Over $23,000	Carload (20 tons)
Large	$8,000–$23,000	Carload or truckload (13 tons)
Midrange	$3,500–$8,000	Less than truckload
Small	Under $3,500	Skid (0.6 ton)

Market Segmentation

Signode segmented its accounts based on annual dollar volume and shipping quantity, as shown in Table B.

Signode's five national account managers were responsible for the 250 largest accounts that did business across two or more sales regions, though they closely tracked only the top 180. Signode's market share had remained stable in the national and large accounts, but profitability in these accounts had varied widely, with contribution rates ranging from 21 percent to 45 percent. (See Exhibits 4 and 5 for more data by account size.)

There was a great deal of movement between segments of Signode's customer base: 44 percent of small-segment customers in 1983 had not bought any Signode products in 1982; 22 percent of 1983's midrange accounts had been small accounts in 1982, while 23 percent of large accounts had been midrange or small accounts the previous year. This movement, however, was not as pronounced among the national

EXHIBIT 4 Sales Volume, Contribution, and Product Use by Account Size

	Small	Midrange	Large	National Accounts	Total
Sales Volume and Contribution					
Percent of total strapping market	19%	22%	23%	36%	100%
Signode share 1977	35	44	45	55	50
Signode share 1983	25	34	39	54	40
Contribution	54	42	34	28	36
Percent of sales time	12	35	20	33	100%
Product Use					
Apex	62	46	23	20	
Box Band Magnus	16	21	40	30	
Heavy Duty Magnus	22	32	35	45	
Custom strapping	0	1	2	5	
	100%	100%	100%	100%	

NOTE: These estimates were provided by the industry specialists and reflect the lack of agreement within Signode regarding true market share by segment and product line. Thus, the numbers do not necessarily agree with all data in the case text.

Exhibit 5 Signode Strapping Sales by Account Size

	Purchase Size		
	Small (Skid: 0.6 ton)	Midrange (Truckload: 13 tons)	Large[a] (Carload: 20 tons)
1983 sales ($000)	$14,000	$29,200	$89,800
Percent of strapping sold	11%	23%	66%
Tons shipped	13,412	31,875	103,307
Average price per ton	$1,043	$916	$869
Number of customers	21,550	3,609	1,428
Account Migration, 1982–1983			
Percent of increase from lower size		22%	23%
Number of new customers	9,435	648	132
Number of lost customers	9,177	669	136

[a]Includes the 250 national accounts.

accounts. Experience taught that once a national account was lost, it was extremely difficult to get back.

Signode also segmented the market by industry, which was a natural outgrowth of its historic market development strategy. The corporation's 98 percent market share in the cotton industry and its 82 percent share in the brick industry were the two most dramatic examples of the success of this segmentation scheme. Signode quite literally grew up with these and similar industries, providing specialized service and equipment to meet unique strapping needs. By 1982 Signode's eight largest target industries accounted for 32 percent of Apex strapping sales, 70 percent of Box Band Magnus sales, and 75 percent of Heavy Duty Magnus sales. (See Exhibit 6 for strapping sales by product and industry.)

Exhibit 6 Segmentation by Industry (Percent)

Industry	Percent of Total Market	Signode's 1977 Share	Signode's 1983 Share	Product Usage		
				Apex	BBM	HDM
Primary metals	18.0%	50%	42%	9%	12%	79%
Forest products	12.0	50	47	26	46	28
Paper	5.6	48	48	62	14	24
Metal service	3.9	39	37	14	28	58
Synthetic fibers	3.9	26	31	7	85	8
Cotton	3.3	98	98	0	0	100
Brick	3.1	86	82	0	100	0
Transportation	2.2%	40%	39%	56%	18%	26%
	52.0%					

NOTE: These estimates were provided by the industry specialists and reflect the lack of agreement within Signode regarding true market share by segment and product line. Thus, the numbers do not necessarily agree with all data in the text.

Long-standing relationships with these industries meant Signode was sensitive to their perceptions of the strapping industry. Though the feedback was not always what Signode wanted to hear, it could be powerful. For example, an executive from a large steel company commented:

> We're paying for product innovations that were developed 10 to 15 years ago. Our market is shrinking. We don't need new tools or machines. We need steel strapping at cheaper prices to run through our existing tools and machines.

The marketing department was very concerned about customer price sensitivity and its relationship to the service component of Signode's value-added system. To improve Signode's understanding of its account base, Hamilton asked the regional and district sales managers to evaluate their accounts based on (1) relative price paid and (2) service consumed. Looking at the top 164 accounts and then further into the top 1,200 accounts, sales managers ranked them on a scale of 1 to 10. Those accounts paying the highest price for Signode steel strapping were indicated by a 10. Those paying the lowest price were given a 1. The accounts were then evaluated on a separate but similar scale for service consumed. Service included applications review and engineering, free parts, unbilled time of service personnel, demonstration tools, tool repair, custom strapping machine design, and sales calls. The results of this survey for the top 164 accounts are shown in Exhibit 7, where the two separate evaluations (price paid and service consumed) are combined into one matrix.

Competition

There were six major competitors in the steel strapping industry. In 1983, these six and Signode accounted for 92 percent of steel strapping shipments—down from 95 percent in 1977. (See Exhibit 8 for more data by competitor.) Aside from Signode, none of the industry competitors produced custom steel strapping or machines. Many competitors imported their machines and tools or sold another manufacturer's equipment. Indeed, some did not even carry a line of equipment, but sold only strapping. No competitor provided the level of service that Signode could provide.

Because of its market leadership, Signode's book price was the standard market price. A competitor would set its book prices at some discount off Signode's price, and the discount would usually reflect the level of service provided (e.g., lesser service would carry a higher discount). Traditionally, Signode had raised its steel strapping prices in tandem with the cost of raw materials. Its competitors usually followed suit, raising their book prices a similar amount. (See Exhibit 9 for a comparison of steel raw materials cost and HDM prices.)

Alpha. Signode's major competition in the steel strapping business was Alpha Corporation. A subsidiary of Lake Steel, which had sales of $835 million in 1983, Alpha sourced its steel from its parent corporation and sold strapping at a book price roughly 95 percent of Signode's. Its 21 percent market share was evenly split, with 50 percent of its sales in Apex strapping and 50 percent in Magnus. Until 1978,

Exhibit 7 Top 164 National Accounts

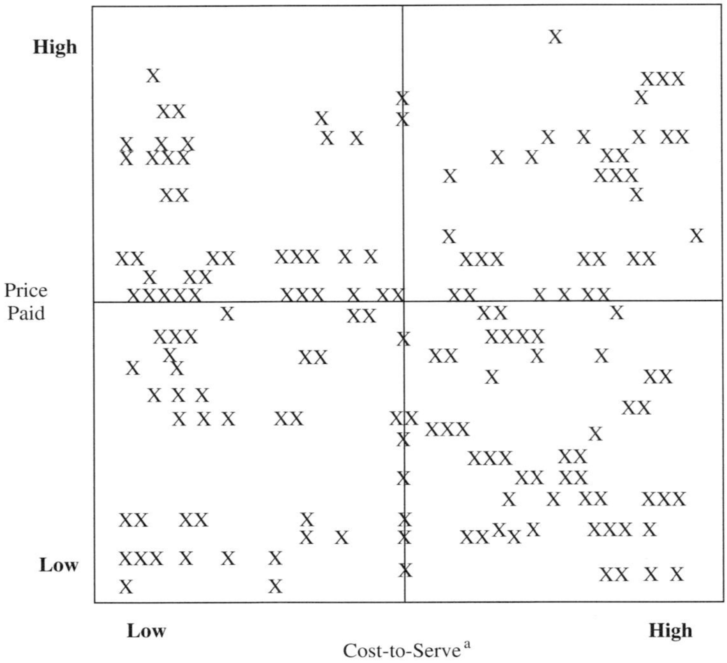

[Scatterplot with axes: vertical axis "Price Paid" from Low to High; horizontal axis "Cost-to-Serve"[a] from Low to High. Accounts plotted as X marks distributed across all four quadrants.]

NOTE: A similar scattergram (distribution of accounts) was found for Signode's top 1,200 accounts.

[a] Cost-to-serve includes sales expense, unbilled repair, parts, tools, and application and engineering services.

Alpha had been a full-line provider of both standard and custom steel strapping, tools, and machines. In that year, Alpha announced its withdrawal from the custom machine and strapping market and cut back on the level of service it provided. After the 1978 announcement, Alpha began importing its tools and machines. Unlike

Exhibit 8 Data on Industry Competition (dollars in millions)

	Signode	Alpha	Sanford	Bentley	American Metal	Jersey Steel	Plymouth
Corporate sales, 1983	$659	$835	$984	$100	$1,700	$30	$80
Steel strapping sales, 1983	$133	$70	$30	$33	$17	$13	$10
1983 Capacity utilization	71%	82%	63%	90%	53%	90%	70%
1977 market share[a]	50%	22%	10%	6%	3%	2%	2%
1983 market share	40%	21%	9%	10%	5%	4%	3%
Sales force	180	50	23	25	48	15	8
Sales volume through distributors	Less than 1%	32%	55%	50%	0%	15%	25%

[a] Imported and other steel strapping sold through distributors had a market share of 5% in 1977 and 8% in 1983.

EXHIBIT 9 Comparison of Steel Cost and Strap Prices for Magnus, 1973–1983

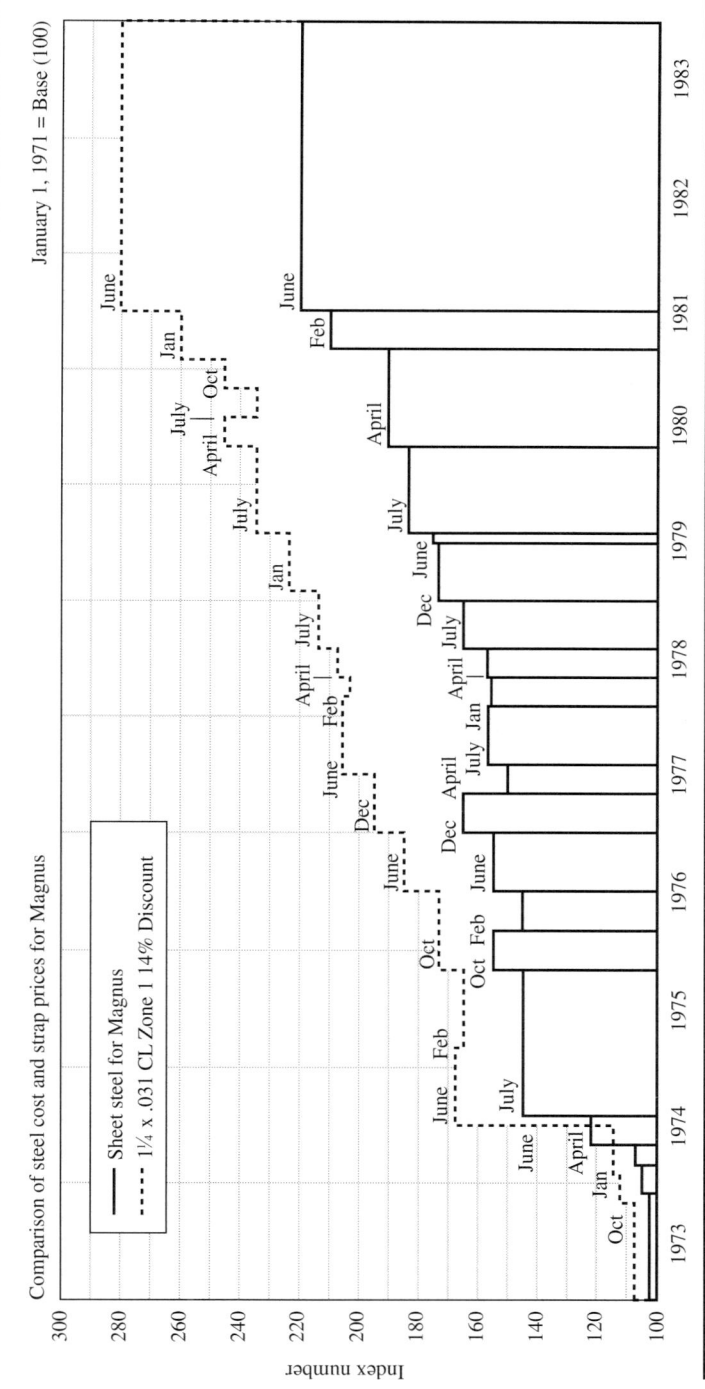

NOTE: Sheet steel prices do not include the 6.8% increase announced in November 1983.

Signode, Alpha used distributors, selling approximately 32 percent of its volume through this channel, with the balance of its sales handled by a 50-person sales force.

Sanford. A subsidiary of the Sanford Works, the Sanford strapping division held a 9 percent market share while pricing at about 93 percent of Signode's price. Selling 45 percent of its product through a 23-person direct sales force, Sanford's product mix was 32 percent Apex and 68 percent Magnus. Though it purchased steel on the open market, Sanford's overhead costs were thought to be less than Signode's. Sanford imported its strapping tools and machines and did not provide any service.

Bentley. With a 1983 market share of 10 percent, Bentley also set its strapping price at approximately 95 percent of Signode's book. Its product mix was 25 percent Apex and 75 percent Magnus, with 50 percent of the volume going through a 25-person direct sales force and the remainder through distributors. Bentley was known to have a strong marketing orientation, and it contracted for service from outside suppliers. Steel was obtained from its parent, the Marion Steel Corporation. Though Bentley produced some of its own tools, it purchased its line of power strapping machines from another supplier.

American Metal. Selling only Magnus strapping, and only through its 48-person direct sales force, American Metal held a 5 percent market share. A commodity seller with no known marketing department and no service, its strapping generally was priced 10 percent below Signode's. American Metal imported its tools and produced only one type of machine.

Jersey Steel. This company sourced its raw materials on the open market and held a 4 percent market share. Its product line was 39 percent Apex and 61 percent Magnus and was sold predominantly (85 percent) through a 15-person direct sales force. Jersey Steel averaged a 7 percent price differential from Signode. Its steel strapping production costs were thought to be higher than Signode's. Jersey Steel produced some of its own tools but did not sell machines and did not provide service.

Plymouth. Plymouth kept a 10 percent price differential on sales to its 2.9 percent of the market. It sourced its steel on the open market and sold only Magnus, with its 8-person sales force handling 75 percent of all sales. Plymouth did not sell power strapping machines and offered no service but did produce its own line of strapping tools. It had a highly concentrated customer base that was thought to be well covered by its limited sales force.

Distributors. Three hundred independent distributors played an important role in servicing small- and medium-sized customers. Although they previously had dealt exclusively in the products of one manufacturer, distributors now carried a broad line of competing products, which they sold on the basis of profit margin. Signode studies showed that while distributors did increase sales volume to small accounts, they did so at reduced profit margins for the producer. Distributors generally carried some standard strapping tools and equipment manufactured by independent U.S. and foreign companies. Based on reports from his regional managers, Hamilton believed that distributor discounting posed a major problem in the midrange segment of the market. Signode's book prices were competitive with those of the distributors, but discounting by distributors made Signode's prices 10 to 20 percent higher.

Pricing in the Steel Strapping Market

Because Signode's raw materials accounted for approximately 70 percent of the cost of steel strapping, sophisticated customers could easily determine "fair prices" for the products and services received. (See Exhibit 10 for strapping cost data.) Although customers in many industries had been willing to pay a price premium when purchasing a strapping system, it was exceedingly difficult to justify higher prices for consumables after the initial introductory period. Nonetheless, Signode attempted to use the relationships it established to recover the loss it sustained on the design and installation of machines through sales of strapping, parts, and service at higher profit margins. Until the mid-1970s, Signode succeeded with a strategy summarized by one sales executive as "we won't take a nickel out of the price for anyone."

Starting in the early 1970s, however, customer buying behavior had begun to change. Pressures to reduce costs led to an increased sophistication of buyer purchasing departments. Traditionally, Signode and many of its competitors had designed specialized machinery for customers, sold them below cost, and then reaped profits on the sale of consumables. During the 1970s, however, increased competition within the strapping market along with cost-cutting pressures from buyers led to an unbundling of the traditional product package. Some customers would now buy their specialized machinery below cost and then meet their requirements for strapping through a closed bid process. Customers also began to increase the frequency but decrease the size of their purchases; shipments of greater than 36,000 pounds declined from 52.9 percent of total strapping sales in 1980 to 47.9 percent in 1982. In 1974, this trend toward the unbundling of product and services led Signode to start charging most customers for machine service.

EXHIBIT 10 **Signode's Steel Strapping Cost Structure**

	Apex	BBM	HDM
Raw materials as a percentage of total costs	72.9%	66.4%	77.3%
Other variable costs as a percentage of total costs	14.8	18.0	8.9
Variable costs as a percentage of total costs	87.7	84.4	86.2
Fixed costs as a percentage of total costs	12.3	15.6	13.8
	100.0%	100.0%	100.0%

After the 1975 recession, Alpha reassessed the steel strapping industry as a slow-growth market. As a result, it cut its sales force by 50 percent, serving only its largest customers direct. In addition to trimming costs, Alpha began selectively offering its large accounts 5 percent discounts off its standard prices, which were set 5 percent below Signode's standard steel strapping prices. While smaller competitors were already discounting at that level, Alpha's position as the second-largest producer meant that this price discount represented a special challenge. To counter the general discounting and respond to Alpha's move, in 1976 Signode instituted a 5 percent reduction on the price of HDM strapping in all markets.

The price cut, however, did not discourage continued discounting by Alpha, Bentley, Sanford, and other competitors. For example, in 1977 Alpha responded to Signode's HDM price cut by keeping the 10 percent price differential for large accounts and extending the discounting on all grades of strapping to other market segments. Midrange accounts received an 8 percent discount, and small accounts received a 6 percent discount off Signode's prices. To protect its market share position, that same year Signode responded with an 8 percent discount on all products for 34 of its selected largest accounts that purchased more than 25 carloads of steel strapping per year.

Signode sales managers reported that the company continued to lose share. In 1978, Signode boosted the discount on all products to 14 percent for all of its national and large accounts. It also extended discounts of 8 percent to midrange accounts and 4 percent to small accounts. The corporation also started to charge selectively for tool repair and replacement parts. The competition maintained its price differential of 5 to 10 percent off Signode's discounted (not book) price.

Alpha's 1978 decision to cease production of custom tools and machines had left Signode as the only full-service supplier. From 1979 to 1981, the market seemed to stabilize and Signode regained approximately 3 percent of the market.

The 1982 recession brought reports from the field that competitors were increasing their discounting. Market information was uncertain, but it seemed that Alpha and Sanford were offering selective discounts (in addition to their book differential) of between 5 and 10 percent off their book prices. Jersey Steel and Plymouth were selectively discounting roughly 10 percent to 15 percent off their book prices. Bentley and American Metal seemed to be leading the discounting by selectively offering as much as 15 to 20 percent off their book prices. Throughout this period, Signode attempted to uphold the price umbrella by refusing to increase either selectively or generally its discounts. It continued to lose share.

At this point, Signode actually had three pricing levels. First was the book price—the pre-1978 standard pricing levels. In 1982, very few customers paid the book price. Second was the standard "4-8-14" percentage discounts to the small, midrange, and large segments of the market. Almost all customers received these price discounts, and in all but name, they had become Signode's standard prices. Finally, a process of additional selective discounting had evolved. Many of the very large and national accounts bought their strapping through a competitive bidding process. When Signode salespeople found they were being severely underbid on a very large contract with an important customer, they would request permission to

TABLE C Distribution of Price Discounts, 1983

	Percent of Signode's Accounts	Percent of Signode's Dollar Volume
No discounts (book price)	9%	1%
Standard discounts only (4-8-14)	90	89
Additional discounts[a] (4-8-14 discounts and special discounts)	1	10
	100%	100%

[a]To be read as "1% of Signode's customers, representing 10% of its sales volume, received discounts in addition to the standard discounts."

lower prices further than the standard discount to meet this competitive situation. The request would be passed up through the ranks of sales management until it reached Hamilton. With Reed and Hernandez, Hamilton would then decide what price Signode should bid on the contract. This process was in no way standardized; each case was evaluated on its own merits. Table C shows that most of Signode's customers received no additional discounts.

In November 1983 the Big 8 steel companies announced a 6.8 percent increase in the price of strapping steel. Signode's major competitor, Alpha Corporation, had already announced book price increases of 6.8 percent for a select, but unnamed, group of customers. It was unclear, however, how much Alpha's or other competitors' actual prices would change. Reed believed he had three possible courses of action.

Reed's Options

First, Reed could increase Signode's strapping prices to offset the increased price of cold rolled steel. This pricing strategy would remain consistent with the company's traditional policy of passing on raw materials cost increases directly to the customer. Reed knew, however, that the sales force had responded to the announced steel price increase with intensified complaints about Signode's price differentials and had pleaded for no price increase. They feared that Signode's competitors had increased their book prices, but had decided to maintain current actual price levels in an effort to gain share.

Second, Reed could maintain Signode's current book prices. Because reports indicated that customers in the midrange and small segments were particularly responsive to low prices and a range of product choices, Hamilton became a strong advocate of the "no increase" option. He argued that the Packaging Division would need increased market share to satisfy the corporation's cash flow requirements. Hamilton also asserted that increasing prices could cause serious damage to the sales force's morale.

Third, Reed could institute the price-flex proposal as outlined by Davis. After evaluating the market and the price-flex proposal, Hernandez agreed that this was a good choice—one that could combine price increases and discounts. Hernandez believed that the price-flex policy essentially would give the sales force an efficient means of performing the same kind of selective discounting that Reed, Hamilton, and Hernandez had already been doing.

Reed had pondered the options but had not yet decided what he wanted to say at the January sales meeting. To begin his analysis, Reed wrote down his goals:

- Maintain profitability.
- Halt market share erosion.
- Provide cash to the corporation.
- Bolster sales force morale.

Reed had to anticipate the market impact of his pricing policy. Also, he had to develop a detailed implementation plan. Finally, he would need to present a complete explanation of his reasoning to the most powerful and respected sales force in the strapping industry.

CHAPTER 28

Becton Dickinson & Company: VACUTAINER® Systems Division

Becton Dickinson's management team is negotiating a contract with personnel at Affiliated Purchasing Group (APG), a large hospital buying group. The immediate issue is how to respond to APG's demands concerning pricing, branding, and distribution terms. These decisions have to be made in the context of a changing health care industry environment which is moving in the direction of cost control. Hence, the longer-term issue is, How should BDVS conduct its business in an increasingly difficult marketplace?

On Thursday, August 1, 1985, William Kozy, national sales director for Becton Dickinson VACUTAINER® Systems (BDVS), and Hank Smith, BDVS's vice president of marketing and sales, slumped into their seats on the evening flight from Chicago to Newark. They had just completed their fifth round of negotiations in as many months with the materials manager of Affiliated Purchasing Group (APG), a large hospital buying group. Historically, BDVS had supplied most blood collection products bought by individual APG-member hospitals. But in April, APG had announced its intention of initiating group purchasing of one brand of blood collection products for all member hospitals. Since then, Kozy and Smith had represented BDVS in repeated negotiations with APG, while APG had also been negotiating with BDVS's competitors.

The subject of the negotiations was the pricing and delivery terms of a proposed purchasing agreement between APG and BDVS. Traditionally, all of BDVS's products had been sold through its distributors, who also negotiated prices for those (and other) products directly with hospital customers. In recent years, however, BDVS had begun a new form of sales agreement, known as a "Z contract," in which BDVS

Frank Cespedes and V. Kasturi Rangan prepared this case.
Copyright © 1991 by the President and Fellows of Harvard College.
Harvard Business School case 592-037 (revised May 27, 1993).

negotiated prices and quantities directly with large accounts but supplied its products through one or more of its authorized distributors.

The August 1 meeting with APG had been an all-day session, at the end of which both sides agreed that BDVS would submit its final proposal by August 15. At issue were the specific prices and terms for BDVS's two major products. In addition, there were questions raised regarding which distributors would be used to service the contract, and APG negotiators had urged BDVS to consider manufacturing a private label for APG.

"They're bringing out the big guns this time," noted Kozy as the plane began to taxi down the runway. "They certainly are," agreed Smith, "and we'll have to decide what we do about that. Al Battaglia wants to meet with us tomorrow at 1 PM about the APG contract. Let's review the situation one more time and make our recommendations."

Company Background

Becton Dickinson (BD) manufactured medical, diagnostic, and industrial safety products for health care professionals, medical research institutions, industry, and the general public. Sales in 1984 were $1.127 billion, with 75 percent coming from U.S. operations (see Exhibit 1). The company had three business segments—Laboratory, Industrial Safety, and Medical Products—each a profit center with separate marketing responsibilities. Medical Products had three divisions: (1) needles, syringes, and diabetic products, (2) pharmaceutical systems, and (3) VACUTAINER blood collection systems.

Becton Dickinson VACUTAINER® Systems Division (BDVS)[1]

See Exhibit 2 for a BDVS organization chart. Reporting to Hank Smith, vice president for marketing and sales, were three product managers, each responsible for one of the division's product groups, and a sales director, William Kozy, responsible for achieving sales targets through six regional managers. Alfred Battaglia had held several financial functions before assuming the role of division president.

Products

BD introduced blood collection products in the late 1940s. BDVS was formed as a business unit in 1980 with three major product groups having total 1984 sales of $90 million: venous blood collection (about 70 percent of BDVS sales) consisting of VACUTAINER tubes and needles, capillary blood collection consisting of MICROTAINER tubes and lancets, and microbiology systems consisting of culture tubes

---

[1] Both VACUTAINER® and MICROTAINER® are registered trademarks of Becton Dickinson and Company.

Chapter 28   Becton Dickinson & Company

Exhibit 1   Summary of Selected Financial Data (years ending September 30, thousands of dollars, except per share data)

	1984	1983	1982
Operations:			
Net sales	$1,126,845	$1,119,520	$1,113,921
Gross profit	498,128	469,077	478,291
Gross profit margin	44.2%	41.9%	42.9%
Interest income	23,824	18,211	15,147
Interest expense	22,757	32,511	32,336
Income before income taxes[a]	92,908	33,652	106,198
Income tax provision (credit)	29,505	(2,278)	29,506
Net income	63,403	35,930	76,692
Financial position:			
Current assets	$565,526	$553,281	$557,242
Current liabilities	245,794	190,222	229,523
Current ratio	2.3	2.9	2.4
Pretax income as percent of sales	8.2%	3.0%	9.5%
Net income as a percent of sales	5.6%	3.2%	6.9%
Return on net operating assets	8.2%	5.8%	10.6%
Return on equity	10.5%	6.1%	13.3%
Additional data:			
Capital expenditures	$82,324	$91,031	$130,008
Research and development expense	57,735	55,149	49,308
Number of employees	17,700	19,000	21,200
Summary by Business Segment			
Health care:			
Medical product sales	$668,757	$685,275	$685,553
Laboratory product sales	260,828	264,234	266,425
Total health care sales	929,585	949,509	951,978
Segment operating income	108,178	100,069	130,342
Percentage of income to sales	11.6%	10.5%	13.7%
Industrial safety:			
Sales	$197,260	$170,011	$161,943
Segment operating income	22,635	4,616	15,839
Percentage of income to sales	11.5%	10.5%	13.7%

[a] 1983 income was significantly affected by a one-time nonrecurring charge.
Source: Company annual reports.

and specimen collectors. Each product group accounted for about 33 percent of BDVS's 1984 operating income.

Venous blood collection systems consisted of a needle and vacuum tube used for collecting blood from a patient's veins. VACUTAINER was the BD brand name for a broad line of tubes and needles designed to meet hundreds of differing needs in hospitals, medical laboratories, and physicians' offices. (See Exhibit 3 for sample products.)

EXHIBIT 2 Blood Collection Systems Division

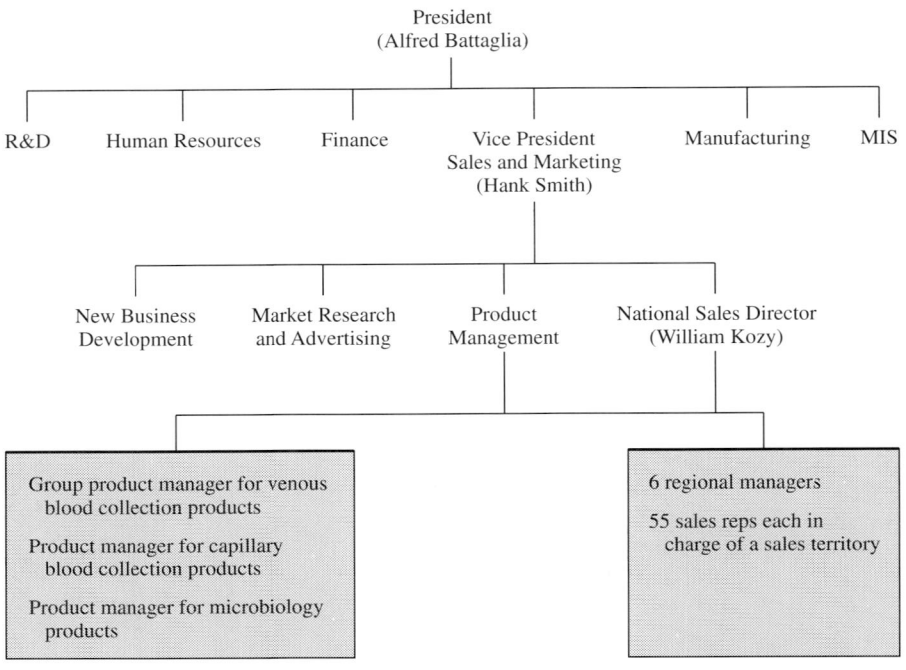

In venous blood collection, the tubes were coated with reagents to preserve the integrity of the specimen (the stoppers on the tubes were color coded to indicate the specific reagent inside). The laboratory technician, known as a phlebotomist, collected blood in different tubes depending on the type of test required by the patient's doctor.

Evacuated-tube blood collection was considered superior to the older needle-and-syringe method in providing specimen integrity, convenience, and lower costs. BD was the pioneer in converting the market to evacuated tubes. According to industry sources, BD had an estimated 80 percent market share in the United States, where nearly 100 percent of venous blood collection had been converted to evacuated-tube methods (worldwide, evacuated tube methods accounted for less than 40 percent of blood collection).

Capillary blood collection systems consisted of a lancet for pricking the patient's finger and a tube (MICROTAINER® was the BD brand name) used for blood collection and testing. MICROTAINER tubes used capillary action and gravity for collecting blood samples of smaller volumes than those generally collected by the venous method. MICROTAINER systems could be used for the same blood tests administered through VACUTAINER systems, but the common applications for MICROTAINER were in single-tube collections for infants, children, and geriatric patients.

The division marketed VACUTAINER and MICROTAINER systems as complete blood collection systems, but other suppliers' needles and lancets could be used on BD tubes and vice versa. On average, about 2.5 tubes were used per needle, with an estimated 1985 U.S. market, in units, of 800 million tubes and 320 million needles.

Microbiology systems provided a sterile environment for transferring blood specimens from the collection to the testing site. The division's microbiology tubes and collectors were all marketed under the VACUTAINER brand name.

BDVS had the broadest line of blood collection products in the industry. Peter Trow, sales representative for BDVS, noted:

> In this business, quality is not merely a function of needle sharpness or the integrity of the reagents. We also offer the widest range of tubes, and that's crucial. Big hospitals and labs run a multitude of tests, and they require product assortment and color-coding schemes to make their jobs easier. That is part of their definition of quality.

EXHIBIT 3 Sample Products

Sterile VACUTAINER Brand Evacuated Tubes
After 40 years, the goals and achievements of the VACUTAINER Brand Tube line are still unique. VACUTAINER Brand products offer unique benefits for the laboratory valuing the most extensive research and development program . . . an unequaled depth of product line . . . and an unrivaled commitment to specialized service. It's all here, exclusively with VACUTAINER Tubes.

   Here is the most comprehensive line of evacuated blood collection tubes available today   All sterile for safety. And featuring the widest array of tube sizes, draw and approved formulations . . . for chemistry, hematology, coagulation studies, special procedures, and blood banking.

   Here are the most extensively researched and documented tubes you'll find   They have to be. That's the extra commitment we bring as the people who not only manufacture them, but pioneer their development as well. Every VACUTAINER Tube is backed by in-depth clinical and/or research studies. Data is available on request.

   Here are the most significant tube introductions and improvements seen anywhere in recent years   We improved blood collection tubes for trace element studies, therapeutic drug monitoring, and coagulation studies. We've developed new tubes for special procedures like activated clotting time (ACT), LE cell preps, and STAT tests. We've expanded our choice of tubes for serum preparation. Starting with our top-of-the-line SST™ (Serum Separator Tube with gel barrier material), we added our new CAT™ (Clot Activator Tube), and then improved our standard red-top tube with a new hemorepellent stopper. For laboratories that prefer their own labeling system, we now offer a new line of VACUTAINER Tubes with SeeThru labeling that provides all the essential information without impeding visibility of the specimen.

   Here is the caliber of service support available only through VACUTAINER Systems   . . . the company that stands behind every tube you use. Becton Dickinson VACUTAINER Systems is capable of meeting your special needs because we're not just a manufacturer, but researchers and originators ready to anticipate and respond to changes in your diagnostic procedures. Our sales representatives are accessible specialists in the laboratory field. Our nationwide distribution network is always ready to get you the supplies you need, when you need them. Our technical service team is available for immediate consultation (call toll free 800-631-0174). And, to help you train your staff for the best venous blood collection techniques, our educational materials—publications, films, and sound/slide programs—are at your disposal.

   The following pages contain the latest information on our complete line of Sterile VACUTAINER Tubes and VACUTAINER Needles.

Exhibit 3 (*concluded*)

VACUTAINER Brand Needles and Accessories

The VACUTAINER System offers a wide selection of blood collection needles and accessories that meet both demanding technical requirements and patient needs during venipuncture. Sterile needles are available for single sample or multiple sample collection, with standard or thin-wall cannulae, in peel-apart packages or plastic cases, and in lengths and gauges you require.

Improved VACUTAINER Multiple Sample Needles feature the most up-to-date improvements for sharpness and ease of use. A new point configuration, special polishing, and a new lubrication process allow extra smooth vein entry and reduce "drag." Laser inspection of *every needle* detects even microscopic flaws for virtually flawless quality control. All needle hubs and shields are color-coded for quick identification of gauge. New tamper-evident labels protect against inadvertent use of an already opened needle.

There is a VACUTAINER Holder/Needle Combination designed to fit any VACUTAINER Blood Collection Tube or VACUTAINER Culture Tube. Available with choice of single sample or multiple sample needles, with standard or small diameter holder. VACUTAINER Holder/Needle Combinations are sterile, single-use units that assure protection of the sterile pathway from patient to blood collection tube. Preassembled, they offer the additional advantage of eliminating assembly and clean-up time requirements. Also available are VACUTAINER Reusable Holders in three sizes to meet any need. And sterile, single-use Luer Adapters—unique to the VACUTAINER System—that allow the use of a variety of attachments (needle holders, catheters) under a single venipuncture, sparing the patient unnecessary trauma.

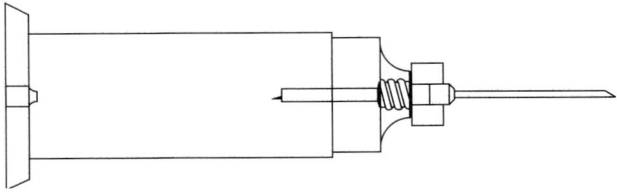

Cost-containment pressures resulted in a 1.0 percent compounded annual decline in hospital blood testing between 1983 and 1985. Forecasts indicated hospital blood testing would decline through 1987, but an aging U.S. population should increase testing somewhat in subsequent years. Testing in commercial labs and physicians' offices was expected to be 40 percent of total blood testing by 1990.

Total microcollections were forecast to increase 5 percent annually through 1990 as less-expensive, easier-to-use equipment motivated physicians to do more testing in their offices than via a hospital or commercial lab. Battaglia also noted that blood collection technology was changing rapidly:

> The clear technological trend is to enable end users to do more of the diagnostic testing. This means more testing can be done in nonlaboratory settings such as doctors' offices. In turn, that has implications for our distribution network, which tends to be built around lab distributors rather than the medical/surgical distributors who sell to nonlab locations. The technological developments also place more technical selling demands on our sales force.

Industry Background

Blood collection products were used in hospitals, commercial laboratories, and many nonhospital health care centers.

Hospitals. In 1985, approximately 7,000 U.S. hospitals performed 70 percent of all blood tests. Blood collection was generally performed at the patient's bedside and the sample then sent to a hospital laboratory for testing. The 1,800 largest hospitals (200 or more beds each) accounted for 50 percent of the market for medical equipment and supplies.

Within hospitals, the buying process for medical supplies, including blood collection products, was complex and changing. The primary contact of a BDVS salesperson varied depending upon usage requirements and the purchasing process in an individual hospital. Robert Giardino, senior sales representative for BDVS, noted:

> Blood collection tubes are a key product for a hospital lab; if the specimen is not collected properly, the lab has many problems. Hospitals order tubes frequently; most have a standing weekly order with one or more distributors for tubes.
>
> The hospital's chief lab technician is usually the person responsible for testing, ordering supplies, and handling administrative matters. In a large teaching hospital, this person might have an MD or a PhD; in other hospitals, it would be someone who came up through the lab ranks. On average, there are six subsidiary lab departments, each headed by a supervisor who reports to the chief lab technician.
>
> Purchasing influences vary, depending on the specific product. In general, the "bench people" [i.e., medical technicians in the lab] have product preferences, and these people tend to be concerned with the best quality and not price. Among the bench people, VACUTAINER is the best-known brand of blood collection tubes. But the department heads and chief lab technicians have budgets to meet. Increasingly, upper levels of hospital administration, and especially the materials managers [who perform a role analogous to that of purchasing agents in industrial concerns] are more influential. These people tend to come from different backgrounds than the lab people do, and they are always price sensitive.

In most hospitals, medical supplies accounted for 10 to 15 percent of a hospital's total costs, while the logistical expenses associated with supplies made up another 10 to 15 percent. Labor costs usually accounted for at least 70 percent. Blood collection products typically accounted for less than 5 percent of the total supplies purchased. A smaller, 100-bed hospital might purchase 40 cases of tubes (each case contained 1,000 tubes) and 20 cases of needles (each case contained 1,000 needles) annually, while a large 1,100-bed hospital, such as Massachusetts General Hospital, purchased about 1,700 cases of tubes and 800 cases of needles annually.

Commercial Laboratories. In 1985, 700 commercial labs in the United States performed about 25 percent of all blood tests. Larger national labs had 15 to 20 lab locations for which the company purchased blood collection products centrally. In these labs, the purchase process for blood collection products was similar to that in large hospitals. Most commercial labs, however, were smaller, single-location companies where the owner-manager often supervised all purchases personally. In both large and small labs, according to Giardino, "the purchasers are cost conscious, because commercial labs compete with each other primarily on price."

Commercial labs analyzed blood samples sent to them by physicians or small health care centers that had collected the blood but lacked either equipment or expertise to perform tests. Many commercial labs also performed blood tests for hospitals for a fee. A significant percentage of a commercial lab's total revenues came from blood collection and testing.

Nonhospital Health Care Centers. In 1985, these accounted for about 5 percent of blood collection and testing in the United States. But easier-to-use and less-expensive technology, as well as changing patterns in health care, indicated that nonhospital centers would account for increased proportions of blood testing in coming years.

In 1985, there were approximately 250,000 physicians in 180,000 offices throughout the United States. A number of physicians—often 50 to 60 per group—were affiliated with forms of group medical care. These physicians were increasingly performing in their offices many medical activities previously subcontracted to commercial labs or hospitals.

Other nonhospital sites—such as surgicenters, emergency centers, and freestanding diagnostic centers—were also increasing in number. They were expected to perform a higher proportion of medical activities during the coming decade, including blood collection and testing.

Market Trends

A *Newsweek* article stated:

> Few industries have gone through such intense trauma in the past two years as the market for health care. New cost containment pressures have forced a wave of cutbacks: hospital use has dropped precipitously, hospitals have shaved their own costs dramatically, and an estimated 100,000 jobs have been lost in a range of health care fields. Out of such chaos a new order seems destined to emerge.[2]

In 1983 a change in how the U.S. government reimbursed hospitals for Medicare patients (40 percent of all hospital patient days) affected the entire health care industry. Previously, hospitals had been reimbursed for all costs incurred in serving those patients. Most observers agreed this cost-plus system did not reward hospitals for efficiency. Federal legislation in April 1983 provided for a change (over a four-year period) to a payment approach based on diagnosis-related groups (DRGs).

Under the new system, the payment to a hospital was based on national and regional costs for each DRG, not on the hospital's costs. Moreover, the national and regional averages were to be updated, so that if hospitals improved their cost performance, they would be subject to stricter DRG-related payment limits.

---

[2] April 15, 1986, p. 79.

By 1985 the impact had been dramatic. In 1984, hospital admissions fell 4 percent—the largest drop on record, according to the American Hospital Association; the average length of a patient's hospital stay fell 5 percent to 6.7 days, also the largest drop ever. For the first time, admissions of people over the age of 65 fell. Nonhospital treatment—especially in-home treatment—was expected to account for larger proportions of health care. Conversely, estimates indicated that the number of hospital beds would fall to 650,000 in 1990 from one million in 1983.[3] In their place, it was expected that a variety of smaller, short-term health care facilities would proliferate.

Thus, in 1985, many hospital administrators felt that, for the first time, they faced effective, increasing competition and a need to reduce costs. One response was the acceleration of a trend toward the formation of multihospital chains and multihospital buying groups. Both types of organization were intended to increase the purchasing power of hospitals for equipment and supplies. In 1985, about 45 percent of all U.S. hospitals were affiliated with multihospital chains, and it was predicted that 65 percent would be so affiliated by 1990. Similarly, in 1985 most hospitals were members of buying groups.

Multihospital chains were usually for-profit hospitals that purchased most supplies and equipment through centralized buying organizations. In these chains, individual hospitals submitted purchase requirements and preferences for specific products, but price and delivery terms were negotiated centrally. Buying groups were looser affiliations of not-for-profit hospitals. Like chains, purchases for buying groups were handled centrally, but individual hospitals were often free to accept or reject the terms negotiated on a specific item by the central buying group. Thus, if a given hospital's administration or lab personnel had a strong preference for a given brand, and the buying group had negotiated a volume discount for a different brand, that hospital might purchase its tubes separately while purchasing other items through the centralized buying group. In addition, many hospitals belonged to several buying groups, purchasing different items through different buying groups depending upon the product, specific prices, and other factors. One BD manager noted:

> The chains and buying groups structure negotiations on the premise that they can deliver so many thousands of beds to the manufacturer with the best price. But the actual strength of these groups varies. In some, all of their hospitals purchase through the centralized procedure. In others, a large percentage of the member hospitals do not adhere to the centralized procedure. The result is that the purchasing leverage differs from one group to the next.
>
> In addition, individual hospitals belong to a number of different buying groups, and often switch from one group to the next. The result is that the various buying-group headquarters organizations in effect compete actively with each other to attract and retain hospital clients. Nonetheless, there is no doubt that chains and buying groups have increased the pricing pressures on both manufacturers and distributors of health care products in recent years.

---

[3] Cited in "Hospital Suppliers Strike Back," *The New York Times,* March 31, 1985.

Competition

Competition in the blood collection market was primarily among BD and two other firms. Terumo, a Japanese company, was a global competitor with a 1984 U.S. market share of about 18 percent in evacuated blood collection tubes and nearly 50 percent in blood collection needles. Sherwood Medical Corporation's Monoject Division was predominantly a U.S. competitor with a U.S. market share of about 2 percent in tubes and 15 percent in needles.

Over the past seven years, BDVS had maintained about an 80 percent share of the U.S. evacuated blood collection tube market while increasing its average unit price from about 6 cents to 8 cents. During that time, Terumo had increased its share from 10 percent to 20 percent while maintaining its price at about 6.5 cents per unit. In blood collection needles, however, BDVS's share had dropped from 40 percent to 30 percent during this period, while Terumo had doubled its share from 25 percent to 50 percent. In needles, BDVS and Terumo charged approximately 7.5 cents per unit, while Sherwood charged about 10 cents per unit.

A primary objective for BD in both tubes and needles was to maintain a leading market share. Management believed that Terumo was also committed to increasing its share in all segments and would continue to price aggressively. BD planned to combat such competition through accelerated new product developments and annual improvements in product quality, while using its strong market share to become the lowest-cost producer in all product segments.

An important element in BD's marketing strategy was what one executive termed "quality aggression." Since BD had vertically integrated into the production of components such as glass tubes and rubber stoppers, it could keep a tight hold on quality. In addition, BD could process reagents and chemicals in its own plants to especially demanding specifications and pioneer in new tube sterilization techniques that demanded large capital investments in radiation equipment. As one manager noted, "This raises our costs but also forces our competitors to raise their costs even more, since our higher volume allows us to amortize the capital investments over a larger base."

In the past, major companies, including Corning Glass, Abbott Labs, and Johnson & Johnson, had participated in the blood collection market but had then withdrawn. However, BDVS management believed new technologies could provoke renewed competition from these firms as well as from companies that might enter the market from a base in computer equipment, other forms of medical diagnostic equipment, or biotechnology.

BDVS Marketing and Sales Program

BD's blood collection products were initially sold through the Medical Products group pooled sales force. In 1980, however, separate sales forces were established for VACUTAINER products and a number of other Medical Products divisions. Battaglia explained:

The basic reason for the reorganization was that the different products were sold to different buyers within hospitals and had different selling requirements. Our division's products require our salespeople to speak with phlebotomists, nurses, physicians, and other technical people as well as the administrators and materials managers at an account. The salespeople must also know a great deal about the people and procedures in the various hospital labs.

In addition, developments in blood collection technology also made our product line wider and required salespeople to learn more about more complex products. Our new product development plans also supported a move toward a separate VACUTAINER sales force.

In 1985, BDVS had 55 sales representatives organized into territories based on the number of hospital beds in a given area. Territories ranged from 10,000 to 20,000 beds. All hospital, commercial lab, and distributor accounts within a territory were the responsibility of that territory rep. Territory reps reported to one of six regional managers, who in turn reported to William Kozy, the national sales director.

Each BDVS sales rep had about 100 accounts and typically made five sales calls daily: four on hospital labs and one on either a distributor or nonhospital lab. A large metropolitan hospital might receive two or three calls monthly, while a small rural hospital might receive one or two calls annually. One rep noted:

> Our sales strategy has traditionally been to sell from the bottom up: We try to work with as many of the bench people as possible—that is, the lab technicians who actually use blood collection products, who care about the quality of what they use, and who will complain to the administrators if they do not get the product they want. BD has a reputation for being more responsive than other firms to end users.
>
> I think we've maintained our market share because of this philosophy. In recent years, I've seen a number of instances where materials managers wanted to standardize their purchases around a less-expensive blood collection product, but the lab people complained and insisted on our product.

During the past year the division had introduced a new needle and had placed major emphasis on converting accounts from competing needle brands. Several sales promotions in 1985 for VACUTAINER needles gave sales reps cash awards for conversions. Results had been very positive, including the conversion of nearly 66,000 beds from competitive needles and a substantial increase in market share for VACUTAINER needles during a four-month promotion campaign (January 1, 1984, through February 28, 1985).

Distribution

BDVS sold its products through 474 independent distributors who fell into two categories: laboratory products distributors and medical-surgical products distributors. A laboratory products distributor called on hospital and commercial labs and carried a range of items such as glassware, chemicals, spectrometers, lab coats, and thousands of other supply items as well as tubes and needles. According to one BDVS executive, "Lab products distributors feel they must carry blood collection products, which hospitals order regularly, because hospitals often order the more expensive, higher-margin items along with those staple products." According to industry trade journals, price competition for large volumes had reduced distributor gross margins on blood collection products from an average of 25 percent down to about 12 percent. Medical-surgical products distributors, on the other hand, called on physicians' offices and other nonhospital sites and carried items such as gowns, wheelchairs, examination tables, and other products in addition to tubes and needles. Their margins on blood collection items rarely dropped below acceptable levels.

Battaglia noted that the distribution policies of BDVS and other BD divisions were developed and executed separately:

> We use many of the same distributors other BD divisions do, but the importance of various distributors to different divisions can vary significantly. For example, most of our sales are through lab products distributors, while other divisions sell more of their products through medical-surgical distributors. Those two types of distributors attend different conventions and speak different languages. In addition, we sell nearly all of our products through distributors, but some other BD divisions have a greater percentage of direct sales.

Nationally, there were over 1,000 distributors of hospital/medical supplies, but the 10 largest accounted for nearly 80 percent of hospital supply sales made through distributors. At BDVS, its 6 largest distributors accounted for more than 65 percent of division sales, the 50 largest for 85 percent, and 67 of the division's 474 dealers for nearly 95 percent of division sales.

BDVS's largest distributor was American Scientific Products (ASP), a division of American Hospital Supply Corporation (AHS), which in 1984 had total sales of $3.45 billion.[4] ASP was the largest lab products distributor in the United States, with an estimated 40 percent market share among distributors of products to hospital and commercial laboratories. In 1984, ASP accounted for a similar share of BDVS's sales.

ASP had 21 warehouse locations in the United States. It had installed computer terminals in major hospitals and become an important part of their logistical systems for purchasing supplies. According to ASP, for every dollar a hospital spent on a product, the hospital also spent nearly an additional dollar on acquiring and storing that item. Thus, less-costly order entry and delivery could have a significant impact for supply items.

ASP paid higher commissions to its salespeople for selling AHS products. One AHS vice president was quoted as saying: "We manufacture 45 percent of what we distribute, but our manufactured products represented 70 percent of our profits last year. Before long, we hope to manufacture 65 percent of what we distribute."[5]

Terumo and Sherwood products were also distributed by ASP. Between 1979 and 1981, according to estimates by industry sources, over 70 percent of Terumo's U.S. sales went through ASP. Beginning in 1981, BDVS managers sought to build

---

[4]In 1985, American Hospital Supply merged with Baxter-Travenol, Inc., a manufacturer of medical equipment. The merged company was known as Baxter-Travenol and had 1985 sales of approximately $5 billion.

[5]"Hospital Suppliers Strike Back," *The New York Times,* March 31, 1985.

its relationship with ASP. BDVS managers held frequent meetings with ASP management, and BDVS salespeople were encouraged to devote more time to sales meetings and product training sessions with ASP branches. In addition, as one BDVS manager noted, "We made clear to ASP our commitment to maintaining our market share and product leadership in blood collection systems and hoped they would support that objective." In 1985, BDVS was ASP's number-one supplier of blood collection products. It was estimated that all BD products accounted for about 10 percent of ASP's sales (making BD one of ASP's top suppliers) and that BDVS products accounted for about 25 percent of the BD products sold by ASP.

Other major distributors for BDVS were Curtin-Matheson Scientific (CMS), which had 20 warehouse locations and sold primarily to hospital labs, and Fisher Scientific, which had 20 warehouse locations and sold primarily to medical schools, research centers, and industrial labs.

In total, BDVS sold through six national distributors, with the remainder of its distribution network composed of regional chains and small local distributors. In most market areas, four or five different distributors sold BDVS products. One manager commented:

> Our relatively intensive distribution is a result of several factors. One is a legacy from when we were part of the BD division. Because BD sells syringes to a very fragmented physicians' market, intensive distribution is important there, and we retain many distributors that began selling VACUTAINER products when we were not a separate division. Another factor is that established relationships between a small local distributor and a lab have traditionally been important in the blood collection products area. As a result, you sometimes must sell through a certain local distributor to break into an account.
>
> Also, since the DRG regulations, hospitals are more conscious of inventory carrying costs. As they cut stocking levels and order more frequently, some hospitals look more favorably on a supplier whose products are available from a number of different distributors in the area. If there is ever a problem with getting product from one distributor, the hospital knows there is backup stock available at another in the area.

By contrast, Terumo sold its products primarily through ASP and CMS, the two largest national distributors. Terumo initially entered the U.S. market with needles in 1970 and tubes in 1972, selling through smaller West Coast distributors. In the mid-1970s, however, Terumo established a joint marketing agreement with Kimball Glass, one of ASP's major suppliers of lab products. Smith explained:

> Kimball opened the door for Terumo at ASP, which had been reluctant to take on an unknown line of blood collection products. ASP soon found, however, that Terumo's line provided them with an alternative to VACUTAINER. Terumo developed the relationship by focusing on individual ASP reps in individual branches: They worked closely with those reps to create a champion for their products in the branch.

Changing Buyer Behavior

During the 1980s, the distributor and end user marketplace was changing significantly. According to a senior executive of one large national distributor of hospital supply products:

In the past, our customer was the pathologist, chief technologist, or lab manager. This person's responsibility was to produce quality diagnostic tests on specimens brought into the lab and to do it as fast as possible. A key was to ensure that an adequate supply of products was on hand at all times. It was also the element that these people were least prepared to deal with. Most lab managers and chief technologists had risen to their positions on the basis of their clinical skills, not their purchasing skills. In addition, they didn't particularly enjoy the purchasing part of their jobs.

Major national distributors flourished in this environment, with the distributor-served portion of the market growing at 10 to 17 percent annually throughout the 1970s. Also, distributors generally paid little attention to costs, because customers primarily wanted service and were willing to pay for it. After all, the lab was a true profit center then: Hospital reimbursement procedures allowed any increased operating expenses to be passed on to customers.

Those days are gone. First, the customer is different. Buying influence has moved out of the lab in most hospitals. Most decisions on products purchased from distributors are now made by professional purchasing people, who require that traditional levels of service be provided along with lower costs. In addition, the buying influence is in many instances moving beyond the hospital purchasing department to the corporate purchasing department of national multihospital systems. Some distributors probably have over half of their total sales in these national accounts.

Finally, while most distributors currently serve the hospital and commercial lab markets, little attention has been paid by distributors to the fastest growing customer segment, the physicians' market, which includes surgicenters, emergency centers, and diagnostic centers as well as the offices of individual doctors. All trends point toward more volume in these locations and less in the hospital.

In this environment, distributors must lower costs. I believe many distributors will carry only two—or even one—vendors' brands in many product categories in exchange for lower prices from those vendors. Moreover, distributors can reduce inventory, transportation, and some administrative costs through consolidation of their product lines.

BDVS Response

BDVS instituted a Z contract, in which prices and order quantities were negotiated directly with hospitals but still delivered through distributors. Often Z-contract prices with large buying groups were 30 to 40 percent lower than list prices. Under a Z contract, as with other BDVS contracts, BDVS's distributors received a set commission from BDVS for stocking, shipping, and billing the hospital.

One BDVS manager explained that "some hospitals negotiate with us and then shop among our distributors for the best price at that level of the chain. They force our distributors to compete away a portion of their commission on Z-contract orders." With Z-contract customers, a BDVS sales rep called on the buyer 30 to 60 days before the contract expiration date to gather information about the customer's product requirements and any competitive inroads at the account. This information was entered on a Critical Information Questionnaire, which suggested a selling price and which the rep submitted to the regional manager. One sales rep estimated he spent 25 percent of his time on contract negotiations:

Until recent years, only four or five of my accounts were on Z contracts, but now almost all are. That means more paperwork and legwork. It also means less time spent with the bench people and more time with purchasing people. I've also been spending more time in negotiating seminars, since these contract sessions can be difficult and tense. I've been in the business for nearly 15 years; selling in the health care industry is more complicated, and less fun, than it used to be.

By 1985, most BDVS venous blood collection products and approximately 20 percent of the division's capillary and microbiology products were sold through Z contracts. Many of BDVS's hospital customers were affiliated with several different buying groups, each of which had separate Z contracts with BDVS. While there were approximately one million hospital beds in the United States, Z contracts encompassed nearly 2.8 million hospital beds by 1985.

Affiliated Purchasing Group

Affiliated Purchasing Group (APG) was founded in 1975. A group of independent, not-for-profit hospitals were affiliated as shareholders with a central organization that provided various services for member hospitals, including purchasing programs. APG's motto was "In unity there is strength," and the group sought to use the power of centralized purchasing while maintaining local autonomy among member hospitals.

APG headquarters personnel negotiated national purchasing agreements with suppliers, but member hospitals were free to make individual purchases separately with manufacturers or distributors of the products. APG purchasing staff monitored national and regional costs, and these data became the basis for their contract negotiations with manufacturers and distributors. The aim, according to one APG manager, was to "pay the lowest price available."

From a group of 20 hospitals in 1975, APG included more than 500 hospitals by 1985, accounting for more than 10 percent of all U.S. hospital beds and nearly 2 million annual admissions. Many large, prestigious hospitals affiliated with medical schools were APG members. In 1985, APG had national purchasing agreements with about 100 medical equipment suppliers, and the number of such agreements has grown consistently in recent years.

In addition to group purchasing, APG offered other services to member hospitals, especially for hospital administrative personnel. APG maintained a database on department administrators at APG-member hospitals, and this database was made available to APG hospitals seeking new managers. The intent was to offer administrators an opportunity to move among APG hospitals while retaining quality administrators within APG-affiliated hospitals. APG maintained a similar database on doctors. The group also coordinated a program that brought together doctors, nurses, and administrators from different APG-affiliated hospitals to discuss cost-reduction opportunities and develop specific action plans. The program allowed member hospitals to compare their costs by product line, therapy type, and department.

APG had been aggressive and innovative in other areas. It had recently established a private-label program in which it sought to have its suppliers use the APG trademark on products sold through APG purchasing agreements. By mid-1985, this private-label program encompassed a dozen product categories, and APG expected to add 30 to 40 additional products by 1986. According to James Wilson, APG's vice president for materials management and the person who had initiated many of APG's recent programs, APG eventually hoped to private-label "virtually all" products sold through APG purchasing agreements.

In early 1985, Wilson also announced APG's intention of establishing its own distribution network. Throughout 1985, APG negotiated with a number of smaller, regional medical products distributors to provide warehousing, trucking, and related functions for hospitals that purchased under APG agreements. APG then sought to have its suppliers distribute their products to APG-affiliated distributors who, in return for a larger share of the high-volume APG contracts, distributed products for lower margins than hospital supply distributors had traditionally received.

Wilson announced that the program would eventually involve a national order-entry system linking these distributors with APG-affiliated hospitals. He expected that, if the system could achieve sufficient utilization by suppliers and APG member hospitals, it could lower the hospital's costs by 3 to 12 percent on most supply items.

By mid-1985, both the private-label and distribution programs were being aggressively promoted by APG materials management. Some manufacturers had agreed to participate in these programs, while others had rejected participation. BDVS's management knew of at least two manufacturers that had not been awarded APG contracts after rejecting participation in these programs. At the same time, distributors not part of the APG distribution network, including the large national distributors of hospital supply products, were reportedly ready to stop supporting (and perhaps sever agreements with) manufacturers that agreed to the program.

Negotiations with APG

In 1982, APG had first sought to standardize its purchase of needles and tubes and had demanded substantial price reductions from BDVS. BDVS had resisted negotiating prices and terms directly with APG headquarters and had continued dealing separately with individual hospitals. Then APG established a national purchasing agreement with Terumo. BDVS's field salespeople were able to retain most sales of BDVS tubes at individual APG-affiliated hospitals, in part by lowering prices when necessary on a hospital-by-hospital basis.

APG subsequently established a group of field personnel charged with promoting the importance of compliance with APG-negotiated contracts at member hospitals. In turn, BDVS field salespeople soon reported that their Z relationships with many accounts in the APG system seemed to be suffering. One salesperson noted:

> There was a period in which I couldn't get phone calls returned from people I had done business with for years. This was especially true of certain administrators who had introduced APG programs in their hospitals. The word on the street was that APG personnel were bad-mouthing us with their numbers. I don't think this appreciably affected my

actual volume with individual departments in hospitals, but it certainly made life uncomfortable. In addition, the experience made the whole issue of compliance by member hospitals with national purchasing agreements more visible and important for APG.

In response, BDVS managers sought to mend fences with certain administrators and with APG headquarters personnel. One manager recalled:

> We held meetings with these people in different regions and explained over dinner that our actions had been based on a reasonable business decision intended to retain our presence in those accounts and nothing personal had been intended. There is definitely an emotional dimension to business situations like this, and it's important to establish lines of communications with important individuals.

Following this series of meetings, BDVS field salespeople reported a "better atmosphere" at certain hospitals.

In April 1985, Wilson announced his intention of establishing a new national purchasing agreement for blood collection products. He asserted that the supplier awarded the contract would receive 90 percent of the business in these product lines from APG-affiliated hospitals. Informally, one APG manager also informed BDVS that APG considered the blood collection agreement to be a "showcase program in which a high degree of compliance by member hospitals is important to us: we'll work for that." BDVS management estimated that VACUTAINER products currently represented more than 80 percent of the venous blood collection tubes and 40 percent of the needles purchased by APG hospitals, totaling about $6 million in 1984 purchases from BDVS.

In contrast to 1982, BDVS management in 1985 decided to negotiate directly with APG headquarters. Management felt that the APG system had grown considerably during the past three years, the central purchasing organization had increased its strength with member hospitals, and there was more risk in refusing to negotiate. Kozy recalled:

> These meetings with APG in Chicago were tense. At the first meeting, they dramatically announced that 90 percent of their business was available to the vendor with the right price. We then surveyed our sales force and, based on their contacts with users at APG affiliates, concluded that a substantial portion, but not 90 percent, of our business with these hospitals was at risk.
>
> At the next meeting, the APG manager pulled out a thick binder with the price of *every* item purchased by *every* member from *every* supplier. At the third meeting, out came another binder with their estimates of prices in our product category to all other hospital-buying groups in the United States. This is a difference from previous negotiations: They are very well prepared this time around.
>
> At a fourth meeting, they announced they had received bids from our competitors and wanted to know if we would meet their prices, which were considerably lower than our list prices and, because of the volume involved, lower than our prices on other Z-contract accounts.

Traditionally, BDVS products were sold through its authorized distributors, such as ASP, to APG-affiliated hospitals. At the start of the new negotiations with APG, Kozy noted:

We told our distributors we were negotiating a potential contract with APG and that the negotiations had the potential to be bloody: If we lost the contract, we would be very aggressive in seeking to retain business at end user accounts and wanted their support, even if the contract went to another supplier whose products they also distributed. Since then, our distributors, who do lots of business with APG-member hospitals, have sought ongoing information about developments.

The Guns of August

At the fifth meeting on August 1, Kozy and Smith proposed a Z contract with prices approximately 20 percent higher than competitors' proposals. The proposal required APG to deliver within 90 days of the initial contract date 95 percent of their member hospitals' purchases of venous blood collection tubes and 90 percent of their purchases of blood collection needles. If these targets were not achieved within 90 days, prices on BDVS products covered by the contract would automatically increase by 5% during the remaining 21 months of the proposed two-year contract agreement.

APG negotiators rejected this proposal and gave BDVS until August 15 to submit a new proposal. They also announced that they wanted all blood collection products covered by a national purchasing agreement to be part of the private-label program and thus carry the APG logo. They also wanted all products covered by the agreement to be supplied through distributors affiliated with APG, and they provided a list of these distributors. The list did not include most of BDVS's major distributors. According to the APG negotiators, moreover, BDVS's competitors had maintained their original pricing proposals and had agreed to both the private-label and distribution demands.

CHAPTER 29
Manage Customers for Profits (Not Just Sales)

Many companies have found that high sales volume does not automatically mean high profits. Among the factors that do affect customer profitability are geography, order size, and extra attention to keep the account. Some customers simply cost more to serve. Other will pay any price to get a certain product. If companies want profits and not just sales, they should start by understanding the differences among their customers. Careful analysis of customers and products will steer sellers into more profitable markets. Sellers should know the exact amount and origin of costs: Understand their profitability dispersion and set prices according to the value customers place on each product, focus strategy according to their knowledge of customers and their own strengths, install information and other systems to support a chosen strategy, and analyze profit dispersion and rethink strategy continually.

High sales volume does not necessarily mean high income, as many companies have found to their sorrow. In fact, profits (as a percentage of sales) are often much higher on some orders than on others, for reasons managers sometimes do not well understand. If prices are appropriate, why is there such striking variation? Let's look at two examples of selling and pricing anomalies:

• A plumbing fixtures manufacturer raised prices to discourage the "worthless" small custom orders that were disrupting the factory. But a series of price hikes failed to reduce unit sales volume. A study of operations two years later revealed that the most profitable orders were these custom orders. The new high prices more than compensated for costs, customers weren't changing suppliers because of high switching expenses, and competitors had shied from short runs because of the conventional wisdom in the industry.

This reading was prepared by Benson P. Shapiro, V. Kasturi Rangan, Rowland T. Moriarty, and Elliot B. Ross.
Copyright © 1987 by the President and Fellows of Harvard College.
Reprinted from *Harvard Business Review* 65, no. 5, September–October 1987, pp. 101–8.

- A prominent producer of capital equipment, realizing it was losing big sales potential in its largest accounts, started a national account program. It included heavy sales support with experienced account managers; participation by high-level executives; special support like applications engineering, custom design services, unusual maintenance work, and expedited delivery; and a national purchase agreement with a hefty graduated volume discount.

Customers, however, viewed the program as merely a dog-and-pony show, having no substance. To convince the skeptics, top executives personally offered greater sales and service support and even more generous discounts.

Sales finally turned upward, and this "success" justified even higher levels of support. But profit margins soon began to erode; the big national accounts, the company discovered, were generating losses that were large enough to offset the rise in volume and the profitability of smaller, allegedly less attractive accounts.

Clearly these two companies discovered that it costs more to fill some orders than others. The plumbing fixtures executives raised prices precisely because they knew it was costing them more to fill small custom orders. The capital equipment company willingly took on extra costs in the hope of winning more sales. Management in both companies recognized that their price tags would vary, the first from boosted prices on custom orders, the other because of volume discounts. But executives in both companies failed to see that the cost and price variations would cause profound differences in the profitability of individual accounts and orders.

Many companies make this mistake. Managers pay little attention to account profitability, selection, and management. They seldom consider the magnitude, origins, and managerial implications of profit dispersion. In this article, we examine three central aspects of this important factor:

Costs to suppliers.
Customer behavior.
Management of customers.

Costs to Suppliers

Profit, of course, is the difference between the net price and the actual cost-to-serve. In terms of individual accounts and orders, there can be dramatic differences in both price and cost.

Despite legal constraints that encourage uniformity in pricing, notably the Robinson-Patman Act, customers usually pay quite different prices in practice. Some buyers can negotiate or take advantage of differential discounts because of their size or the functions they can perform themselves, like in-house maintenance or technical support. And some customers exploit deals and promotions more than others. Moreover, the costs of serving customers and filling orders can vary significantly.

Presale costs vary greatly from order to order and account to account. Geography matters: Some customers and prospects are located far from the salesperson's home base or normal route. Some customers require seemingly endless sales calls, while others place their orders over the telephone. Some must be courted with top-level executives backed up by sophisticated account management techniques, while others need little special effort. Such variations in cost reflect differences in customers' buying processes or the nature of their buying teams. (Some teams are large and geographically and functionally dispersed; others are small and concentrated by location and/or function.) Finally, some customers demand intensive presale service, like applications engineering and custom design support, while others accept standard designs.

Production costs also vary by customer and by order. Order size influences cost, as do setup time, scrap rate, custom designs, special features and functions, unusual packaging, and even order timing. Off-peak orders cost less than those made when demand is heavy. Fast delivery costs more. Some orders call on more resources than others. A company that inventories products in anticipation of orders, however, will have difficulty tracing production costs to particular orders and customers. Accounting policies and conventions, furthermore, often cloud the distinctions in product costs.

Distribution costs naturally vary with the customer's location. It also costs more to ship via a preferred transportation mode, to drop ship to a separate receiving location, to find no back-haul opportunity, or to extend special logistics support like a field inventory.

Postsale service costs also differ. Sometimes customer training, installation, technical support, and repair and maintenance are profit-making operations, but businesses often bundle such services into the product price and the buyer pays "nothing extra" for them. For some items, including capital equipment, postsale costs are heavy.

Thus there are variations among customers in each of the four components of cost: before-the-sale expenses, production, distribution, and after-the-sale service. Moreover, if prices and costs do not correlate, the distribution of gross income will have a dispersion that is the sum of the individual price and cost dispersions, and thus much greater than either. Of course, prices and costs are often viewed as correlated, but our research suggests that they usually aren't—which produces a broad dispersion of account profitability.

With real cost-plus pricing, profitability could be uniform across customers despite wide variations in both costs and prices. But there is evidence that prices seldom reflect the actual costs in serving customers (though they may be somewhat related to production costs). In many businesses, the difference between the highest and lowest prices realized in similar transactions for the same product is as much as 30 percent, not including quantity discounts.[1] Look, for example, at the relationship between prices and total costs in one month's orders for a manufacturer of pipe resin (see Exhibit 1). The diagonal line indicates a price level equal to costs. If gross margin were the same on all orders, the orders would all lie along a line parallel to the

---

[1] See Elliot B. Ross, "Making Money with Proactive Pricing," *Harvard Business Review*, November–December 1984, p. 145.

EXHIBIT 1 Wide Gross Margin Dispersion for a Pipe Resin Manufacturer for One Month

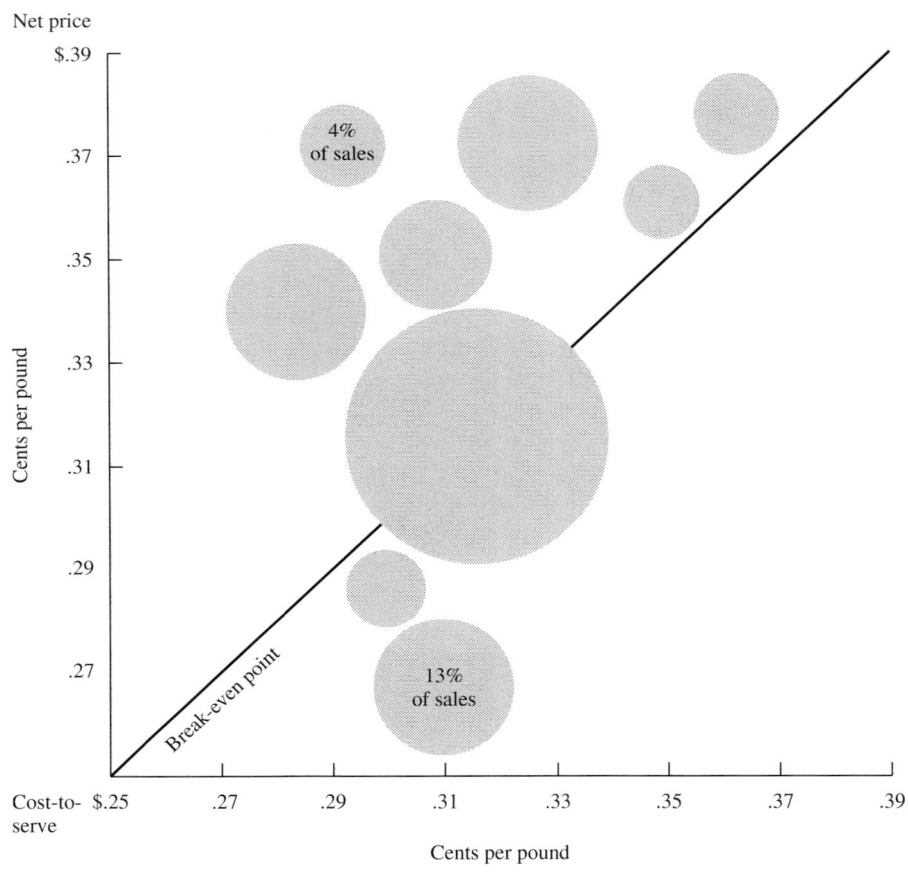

diagonal line. Instead, they are widely dispersed. Nearly 13 percent of sales volume resulted in losses of about a nickel a pound, while about 4 percent of volume generated an 8-cent profit. The rest fell somewhere between.

This pattern is not unusual. In a wide variety of situations, we have consistently observed a lack of correlation between price and the cost-to-serve. Some orders and customers generate losses, and in general the dispersion of profitability is wide.

Customer Behavior

It is useful to think of customers in terms of two dimensions: net price realized and cost-to-serve. To show graphically the dynamics of the interplay between seller and buyer, we have devised a simple matrix (see Exhibit 2). The vertical axis is net

EXHIBIT 2   Customer Classification Matrix

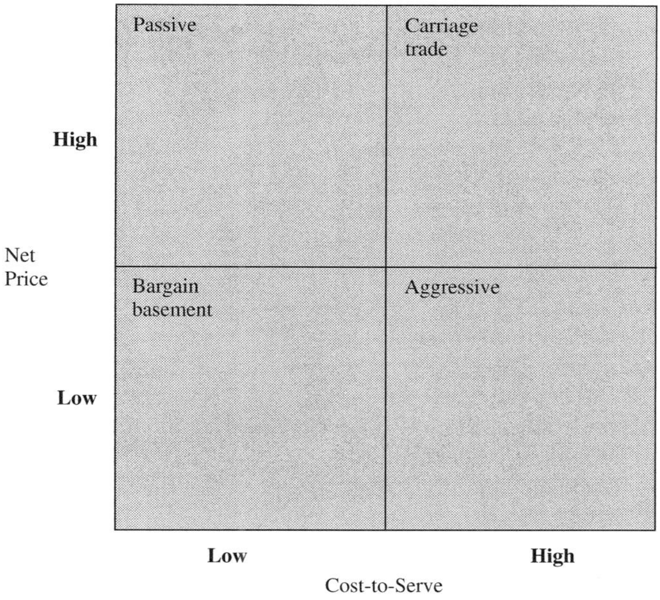

	Low Cost-to-Serve	High Cost-to-Serve
High Net Price	Passive	Carriage trade
Low Net Price	Bargain basement	Aggressive

price, low to high, and the horizontal axis is cost-to-serve, low to high. This categorization is useful for any marketer. The *carriage trade* costs a great deal to serve but is willing to pay top dollar. (This category would include the customers of our introductory example, who placed small orders for high-cost custom plumbing fixtures.) At the opposite extreme are *bargain basement* customers—sensitive to price and relatively insensitive to service and quality. They can be served more cheaply than the carriage trade.

Serving *passive* customers costs less too, but they are willing to accept high prices. These accounts generate highly profitable orders. There are various reasons for their attitude. In some cases the product is too insignificant to warrant a tough negotiating stance over price. Other customers are insensitive to price because the product is crucial to their operation. Still others stay with their current supplier, more or less regardless of price, because of the prohibitive cost of switching. As an example from another industry, many major aircraft components cannot be changed without recertifying the entire aircraft. And in some cases vendor capability is so well matched to buyer needs that cost-to-serve is low though the customer is receiving (and paying for) fine service and quality.

Aggressive customers, on the other hand, demand (and often receive) the highest product quality, the best service, and low prices. Procter & Gamble, boasting an efficient procurement function, has a reputation among its suppliers for paying the least and getting the most. Aggressive buyers are usually powerful;

their practice of buying in large quantities gives them leverage with suppliers in seeking price deals and more service. The national accounts described in the second example at the beginning of this chapter drove hard bargains with the capital equipment supplier.

Marketing managers often assume a strong correlation between net price and cost to serve; they reason that price-sensitive customers will accept lower quality and service and demanding customers will pay more for better quality and service. Thinking in terms of service and quality demands unfortunately deflects attention from the critical issue of cost-to-serve. In addition, weak cost accounting practices that average costs over products, orders, and customers often support the high-cost, high-price myth. But as we have seen, costs and prices are not closely correlated.

A supplier of industrial packaging materials recently analyzed the profitability of its large national accounts. For each one it calculated approximate indicators of net price and cost-to-serve, based on averages of the aggregate values of a year's transactions. Top officers expected to find most of its customers in the carriage trade quadrant and the rest in the bargain basement. They were shocked when the results put about half of the 164 large customers in the passive and aggressive quadrants (see Exhibit 3).

We believe this pattern is more common than is generally recognized. Among the various factors influencing buying behavior, the most important are the customer's situation and migration patterns.

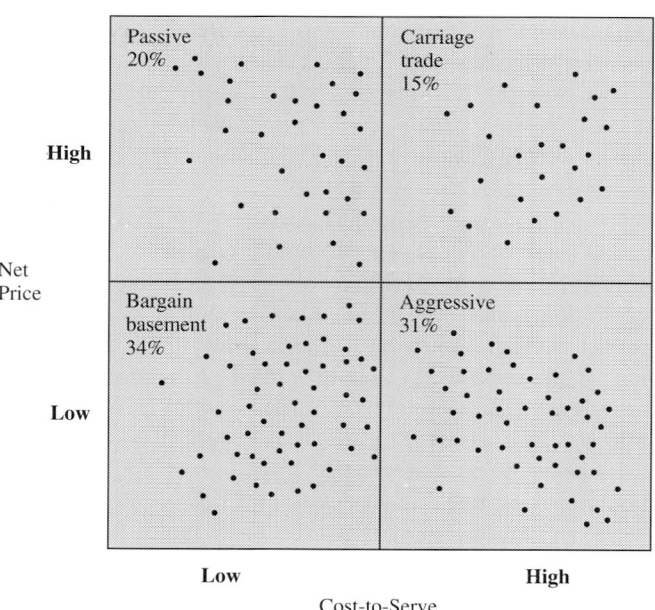

EXHIBIT 3   Customer Matrix of an Industrial Packaging Materials Supplier

Customer's Situation

Four aspects of the customer's nature and position affect profitability: customer economics, power, the nature of the decision-making unit, and the institutional relationship between the buyer and seller.

As we all know, fundamental economics helps determine a buyer's price and service sensitivity. Customers are more sensitive to price when the product is a big part of their purchases, more sensitive to service when it has a big impact on their operations. Independent of economics, buying power, of course, is a major determinant of the buyer's ability to extract price concessions and service support from vendors. The power of big customers shows in their ability to handle many aspects of service support in-house—like breaking bulk—for which they demand price adjustments. Sometimes small customers also wield considerable power. A technological innovator that influences industry standards commands the eyes and ears of suppliers. Thus, the relationship of cost-to-serve and customer size in this industry is not clear without careful measurement.

In respect to the decision-making unit, the purchase staff is generally sensitive to price, while engineering and production personnel are sensitive to service. These roles will affect decisions, depending on who most influences vendor choice and management.

Naturally, this element is bound up with any relationships that have built up between the buyer and seller. Long-standing friendships, long histories of satisfactory performance, and appreciation for any special help or favors all tend to make customers reluctant to pressure suppliers for price and service concessions. Procter & Gamble rotates the responsibilities of its purchasing department members to discourage the development of strong personal relationships with vendors.

Migration Patterns

Changes in organizational buying behavior and competitive activity can produce predictable patterns of change in customer profitability. Often a relationship begins in the carriage trade category. Customers need extensive sales and service support, insist on high product quality, and do not worry much about price if the product is new to them. They need the functionality and will pay for it.

Over time, however, as the customers gain experience with the product, they grow confident in dealing with the vendor and operating with less sales and service support or even without any. The cost of serving them is likely to decline, and they are likely to become more price sensitive. In addition, the buying influence of the customer's procurement department often grows, while the role of engineering and operating personnel diminishes. This shift of course reinforces the tendency toward price sensitivity and away from service concerns. Finally, through rival product offerings (often at lower prices), customers gain knowledge that improves their competence with the product and thus their ability to demand price concessions and lessen their dependence on the vendor's support efforts.

If the customer perceives the product as trivial (as in the case of office supplies) and therefore does not seek it avidly, price sensitivity will not necessarily increase as service needs abate. In terms of the matrix of which Exhibit 2 is an example, migration will be toward the passive and bargain basement areas. If the buyer values the product and it is complex or service sensitive (like CAD/CAM equipment), the buyer may pressure the supplier for price reductions even while service requirements remain high. The migration tends to be downward from the carriage trade toward the aggressive quadrant, as in the case of electrical generation equipment for utilities. In commodities like pipe resin, a combination of customer experience, expanding influence of the purchasing staff, and increasing competitive imitation often leads customers into the bargain basement category.

Management of Customers

The shifts toward the bargain basement and aggressive quadrants are part of the general tendency of products to evolve from high-margin specialties to low-margin commodities. The dispersion of customer profitability we have observed can be managed. We suggest a five-step action program: Pinpoint your costs, know your profitability dispersion, focus your strategy, provide support systems, and analyze repeatedly.

Pinpoint Your Costs. Manufacturers can usually measure their factory costs better than costs incurred by the sales, applications engineering, logistics, and service functions. For instance, few companies have a sense of the cost of unscheduled executive effort to handle the demands of aggressive customers. So it seems likely that customer profitability varies more widely in businesses where a large percentage of the total expenditure is incurred outside the factory. This would be the case in many high-tech companies that have low manufacturing costs but spend a great deal on sales, design engineering, applications engineering, and systems integration.

Because many specialty products are custom designed and manufactured and carry heavy nonfactory costs, the cost dispersion for these products is greater than for commodities. But as we pointed out in our pipe resin example, profit dispersion can be high even in a commodity product.

Costs incurred at different times in the order cycle have different effects on the true cost to serve the customer or order. In major sales with long order cycles and long lead times, the presale effort may begin several years ahead, and service under warranty may extend several years after installation and billing. If the cost of capital is 15 percent, a dollar spent two years before the billing of the customer is worth $1.32, and a dollar spent three years after billing is worth only 61 cents at the time of delivery. Companies with long lead times and order cycles, such as sellers of power generation equipment and commercial airliners, with long-term, substantial service liabilities, evidently have cost dispersions much larger than average, except where progress payments balance out cost flows. These companies need particularly good control systems and management judgment to measure costs and act accordingly.

Companies with poor cost accounting systems have no way to determine order, customer, product, or market segment profitability. Consequently, their cost control and management systems will be weak, and the result is likely to be above-average dispersion of costs. The sales manager of a large office equipment supplier who lacked adequate cost information described his situation thus:

> It's management by anecdote. Salespeople regularly make passionate pleas for price relief on specific orders. When I press them for reasons, they say "threat of competitive entry." When I ask them if a cutback in service would be acceptable to make up for the price decrease, they give me a resounding no! What choice do you have in the absence of cost data, except to go by your judgment of the salesperson's credibility? I've wrongly accepted as many bad price relief requests as I've rejected.

An effective cost accounting system records data by product, order, and account, and records costs beyond the factory, including selling, transportation, applications or design engineering, and even unusual, unprogrammed activities like investments of blocks of corporate management time. Presale, production, distribution, and postsale service costs should all be recorded, analyzed, and related to orders and accounts.

Of course, there are enormous difficulties in creating and maintaining such a system. But even a system that estimates such costs only approximately can help a great deal. Twice a year, for example, one industrial company calculates the cost of serving three sizes of customers (large, medium, and small) and two sizes of orders (truckload and less-than-truckload) for a representative sample of accounts and orders. During the following six months, sales managers use these numbers to guide their decisions on price-relief requests.

Know Your Profitability Dispersion. Once costs are known, the company can plot them against realized prices to show the dispersion of account profitability, as in Exhibit 2. Clearly the framework must be adapted to the characteristics of the business. Similarly, the price axis should be defined in a meaningful way. Since list prices are often misleading, use some sort of net price. However, discounts should not be double-counted under costs as well. The ultimate objective is a measure of net profit by customer and order. Tracking cost and price data by order is an essential first step in building an account profitability matrix.

Companies that know their costs and use cost-plus pricing schemes will find most of their accounts in the bargain basement or carriage trade quadrants of the matrix. Though this pattern is perfectly reasonable, sales management should try to develop accounts in the passive quadrant. Many such customers will accept higher prices because they like the product so much. The cost to them of negotiating a lower price (or better service) outweighs the extra benefits they would get. The passive quadrant represents a region of maximum value for both the seller and the buyer.

A dispersion of profits is no bad thing; only not knowing it exists is. The best managed companies know their costs well and set prices on the basis of product value to customers rather than cost-to-serve. So they have some accounts in the passive categories. In fact, their profit dispersion will be greater than that of companies pricing on a cost-plus basis. The worst managed companies, ignorant of their costs and setting prices mainly in response to customer demands, are likely to have a large number of accounts in the aggressive category, with, obviously, pessimistic implications for profitability.

Focus Your Strategy. The next step is to use your knowledge of cost, price, and profit dispersion to define a strategy for managing your accounts. Here the company defines its personality. The low-cost, low-service, low-price provider would be in the lower left of a profitability matrix, while the company that offers differentiated and augmented products, intensive service, and customization—and, therefore, more value added—is in the upper right quadrant. Because any company's capability is necessarily limited, it cannot span the entire dimension. If it tries to, the poor focus will leave the company vulnerable to competition. This will allow rivals to jump into the aggressive quadrant with high service and low prices, drawing customers away from both the bargain basement and carriage trade quadrants. The result for the stretched-out company is reduced profitability.

The company has two strategy decisions to make. One is to locate the center of gravity or core of the company's business along the axis. The other is to define the range along the axis it will cover.

The fundamental choice to be made is the selection of customers, for companies that reside in a given quadrant will *generally* produce orders in that quadrant. Customers in each quadrant of the profitability matrix behave in a distinctive manner. The supplier has to decide which behavior is most consistent with its strengths. For instance, in an industry with high transport costs, like cement or sand, a customer located at the maximum practical distance from your plant is likely to be in one of the right-hand quadrants—for you. For a competitor whose plant is located near the customer, that account will probably be in a left-hand quadrant. Unless you can form a carriage-trade relationship with that customer—realizing high prices because of the value of your services—you would do better to concede the account to your competitor.

Provide Support Systems. Unless it wants to follow a policy of cost-plus pricing, the company needs to develop processes and systems that will help it manage the profitability dispersion. The company's information system should produce reports based on order, customer, and segment profitability, not just on sales. Management must be oriented toward lateral cooperation among functions. A procedure that simply rewards salespeople for high unit sales and manufacturing personnel for low-cost production is unlikely to lead to the most profitable order mix.

Price-setting rates special attention. Companies that operate in the bargain basement and aggressive quadrants of the profitability matrix must often set up centralized offices to price large orders and screen customers' demands for services. A "special bids" group is often the only way to give the quick replies and careful analyses such orders require. Such a group can best balance financial implications, production and operating capacity, and customer needs, without giving away the store. Since carriage trade customers value the supplier's extra services, a cost-plus pricing policy may be appropriate for them. Finally, pricing for the trade in the passive quadrant has to be based on the value the customer places on the product.

The analysis, strategy, and customer negotiation functions must be kept separate. A men's and boys' coat manufacturer we know of is a good example of what happens when this rule is ignored. The owner's three sons headed divisions serving the department store, discount store, and export markets, while the owner himself managed the private-label business. He called on the three big general merchandise chains (Sears, Ward, and Penney), one of which gave him almost all of his business. The sons' divisions were very profitable, but the private-label unit was a big money loser.

Why was this so? Before a son went out to negotiate an order, the owner stressed the need to get high prices, keep costs reasonable, and secure orders that fit the company's abilities. The father analyzed large orders for profitability. But when the father went to talk to his biggest customer, no one pressured him to keep profits up. He consistently caved in to demands for lower prices, higher service, and better quality. His sons felt powerless to analyze his orders for profitability. The lesson: The same person should not set profit goals and negotiate with customers.

The more services a company provides, the more coordination is necessary among the engineers, field-service staff, and other functionaries in delivering the product and service. Likewise, the more a company increases its cost-to-serve, the more important interfunctional coordination becomes. Low-cost, low-price, low-service bargain basement operators don't need and can't afford elaborate logistics, field service, and other coordinating mechanisms. Carriage trade customers can't operate without them.

Deciding what strategic choices to make requires maintaining market research, pricing analysis, and cost-accounting functions. While these are high-leverage operations in which small investments can yield high returns, in hard times companies often view them as nonessential overhead expenses. This shortsighted attitude can be very damaging.

Repeat Analysis Regularly. A one-shot profit dispersion and strategy analysis is of little use. Buying behavior and migration patterns, like markets and competitors, are dynamic. Migration patterns gradually dilute a company's account selection and management policies.

Cumberland Metals (a disguised name) made pollution control components for the Big Three auto companies in the mid-1970s. Margins were very good, reflecting the high value the auto companies placed on the product, their lack of experience with pollution control, and the absence of competition. The entry of competitors in the early 1980s and, on the customers' part, a shift in influence from engineering to procurement staff signaled a fundamental migration in their buying behavior, but Cumberland management ignored the warning signs. This inattention caused long-standing customer relations problems and a prolonged earnings slump.

Cumberland Metals is unusual because it had only three large accounts. The loss of accounts and orders from the carriage trade quadrant is normally a matter of erosion.

How often a company should analyze profit dispersion and strategy depends on the rate of change in the market and in technology. In many cases, a once-a-year analysis integrated with the annual marketing plan makes sense. In high technology or other rapidly changing industries, a more frequent review may be better. In any case, the main difficulty lies in setting up good systems to track costs, prices, and profits; once the supporting information is available, the analysis is not difficult to perform.

Manage the Dispersion

A custom fabricator of industrial equipment, though operating at capacity, was losing money. The obvious problem was low price levels for the industry. Investigation, however, pointed to a mixture of poor pricing, poor cost estimating, and a lack of knowledge of profitability dispersion. Some bids were too aggressively priced: After winning contracts, the company then lost money on them. Executives had structured other bids to "make good money," basing them on inflated cost estimates. Astute competitors costed these bids better, handled the price negotiations more skillfully, and won the contracts. So the fabricator was winning only unprofitable bids.

The electrical products division of a large corporation, on the other hand, understood the importance of profitability analysis. It carefully analyzed its costs, developed a proactive pricing approach, and meticulously selected orders, products, and customers that fit its production competence and capacity. After a thorough before-and-after review, the financial analysis department at headquarters declared that the division had gone from a 5 percent loss to a 10 percent profit on sales in a glutted, static commodity market.

When meticulous analysis, a sensible strategy, and effective implementation are combined, a company can manage its profitability dispersion to generate profits, not just sales.

CHAPTER 30

Close Encounters of the Four Kinds: Managing Customers in a Rapidly Changing Environment

This chapter describes four kinds of selling: (1) transaction, (2) systems, (3) major account management, and (4) strategic account relationships. It discusses the advantages, disadvantages, and risks of each kind of selling, with a special emphasis on how to construct strategic account relationships which embody importance, intimacy, and longevity for both the vendoring and the buying companies.

"Get close to your customers and do what they want—be customer oriented!"
"Don't give away the store!"
"Selling is dead, there was respect, and courtship, and gratitude in it. Today it's all cut and dried, and there's no chance for bringing friendship to bear or personality."[1]
"Customer relationships are more important than they have ever before been!"

There are many different ways to think about the role of selling and customer relations in a very complex world. Perhaps the truest statement about relationships between buyers and sellers was in *Death of a Salesman,* by Arthur Miller. But, it wasn't made by Willy Loman, the salesman. It was made by his devoted wife, Linda: "It's changing, Willy, I can feel it changing."[2]

The management of account relationships, particularly those between organizations such as businesses or between businesses and major institutions such as governments, has grown more varied and more difficult. We need new ways to look at selling and serving customers.

There are four distinct ways to sell. We begin by examining these with an emphasis on the differences among them, and their relative strengths and weaknesses. The last half of this chapter focuses on the most complex form of selling—strategic account relationships.

Benson P. Shapiro prepared this note.
Copyright © 1988 by the President and Fellows of Harvard College.
Harvard Business School note 589-015.
[1]Statement by Willy Loman in Arthur Miller, *Death of a Salesman* (New York: Viking, 1949), p. 81.
[2]Ibid., p. 74.

Strategic account relationships receive this attention because they are new and very complex, replete with traps and expenses. They do not receive this attention because they are a panacea or even because they are appropriate for every vendor. They are not! The best way to understand their usefulness is to compare them with simpler, yet very serviceable approaches.

Four Approaches to Selling

For many years—indeed, back to the days of open markets and caravan traders—personal selling was a fairly simple activity, consisting of a single exchange or a series of exchanges. This type of selling can be called transaction selling. During the last couple of decades we have seen the introduction and development of three more sophisticated forms of selling: systems, major accounts, and strategic account relationships. This section describes the three new approaches, and differentiates them from each other and the earlier transaction approach.

Transaction selling has evolved into an organized approach to making exchanges. The exchange is generally quite discrete, with a product moving from seller to buyer and money moving in the other direction after some period of negotiation and information exchange. This approach is still used for a wide variety of somewhat simple products ranging from office furniture to some standard electronic products to raw materials. The sale is either a one-time exchange or one transaction in a continuing series of exchanges; the product is often purchased on the basis of physical attributes, availability, convenience, or price. The seller views each sales transaction as the culmination of the immediately preceding activities. Any degree of relationship is viewed by the seller as a series of transactions separated by downtime for servicing the account.

Systems Sales

The advent of complex systems required that the transaction approach be supplemented by more concern for customer benefits and the integration of system components. The system consisted of separate pieces, including individual capital equipment, parts, supplies, and services. Office and factory automation systems are typical examples, but petrochemical complexes and textile mills also fit the systems description. The systems sale necessitated the introduction and development of new sales techniques such as team selling, in which several different departments or functional areas (applications engineering, design, field service, etc.) of the vendor become involved in the sales process.[3]

Systems sales also appeared where the system was not in a physical form but was a program. In consumer package goods, for example, the system may be a pro-

---

[3]Benson P. Shapiro and Ronald S. Posner, "Making the Major Sale," *Harvard Business Review*, March–April 1979, pp. 68–79.

motional program involving several different product lines, national advertising, cooperative advertising, and in-store promotions. The system can also be a related set of services, such as a cash management or mobilization service sold to a company having many locations and bank accounts. The system involves more than "one piece" and is a major sale.

The systems sale differs in size and complexity from the transaction sale, and the ratio of service time between sales to actual selling time increases. But, the heart of the activity remains the sales transaction. There is still a tendency to view the time between sales as downtime. The sophistication of the approach has changed but the fundamental philosophy has not.

Major Account Management

The increasing size and complexity of sales and the development of purchasing approaches like national contracts and master purchasing agreements led to more intimacy and permanence in buyer–seller relationships. Instead of buying a product or service, or even a set of products and services as in the systems purchase, the customer literally wanted to purchase a relationship with a vendor. The sales response was major account management, frequently called national account management because customers transcended regional sales boundaries. Major or national account management is becoming the crème de la crème of personal selling.[4] It is still evolving and its popularity is growing rapidly. At its core is an account manager who quarterbacks the vendor's approach to the customer and husbands the selling company's resources for the customer's benefit. Primary issues in national account programs include the organizational structure[5] and the quality of support provided by functional groups beyond the sales operation such as manufacturing and field service.[6] Its essence is a continuing relationship with a major vendor based on intense, well-coordinated service support.

Account management represents a change in sales philosophy. The actual sales transactions "are seen as the punctuation marks of a larger relationship. Sales are a 'natural fallout.'"[7] At this point in the development of sales approaches, the whole concept of selling changed. In essence, as shown in Exhibit 1, the shift was from a transaction orientation to a relationship orientation. The systems sale was simply a more important and more complex transaction. Major account management, however, was a change in fundamental philosophy. Exhibit 2, based on a chart by Thomas V. Bonoma, highlights the differences between transaction selling and relationship creation.

---

[4]See Benson P. Shapiro and John Wyman, "New Ways to Reach Your Customer," *Harvard Business Review,* July–August 1981, pp. 103–10; Benson P. Shapiro and Rowland T. Moriarty, Jr., "National Account Management," Marketing Science Institute, Cambridge, Mass., 1980, and "National Account Management: Emerging Insights," Marketing Science Institute, Cambridge, Mass., 1982.

[5]Benson P. Shapiro and Rowland T. Moriarty, Jr., "Organizing the National Account Force," Marketing Science Institute, Cambridge, Mass., 1983.

[6]Benson P. Shapiro and Rowland T. Moriarty, Jr., "Support Systems for National Account Management Programs," Marketing Science Institute, Cambridge, Mass., 1983.

[7]Quote from a speech by Thomas V. Bonoma, formerly of the Harvard Business School.

Exhibit 1 Four Selling Approaches

Transaction
System Sale } Transaction Orientation

Major Account Management
Strategic Account Relationship } Relationship Orientation

Account management is expensive and difficult. It can only be used for major customers. And to be effective, it absolutely must be seen as a *philosophy of customer commitment,* not just a collection of advanced persuasion techniques. Its essence is superior customer responsiveness based on outstanding support systems. It goes beyond selling and has laid the foundation for strategic account relationships.

However, major or national account management, with all of its opportunities and rewards, as well as significant investments and costs, cannot satisfy the evolving needs for some closer, more permanent vendor–customer relationships. Joint product, service, and infrastructure developments have led to even more intimate buyer–seller relationships, which can be described as strategic account relationships. Such relationships are a subset of coalitions formed among companies that may be related as competitors, buyers and sellers, or sharers of jointly useful technology or resources.[8]

Strategic Account Relationships

Strategic account relationships are a new and specialized approach so there are few publicly documented examples; furthermore, several with which I am familiar are proprietary and thus beyond discussion. It is instructive, however, to look at several examples.

Exhibit 2 Transactions and Relationships

Transaction Selling	*Relationship Creation*
1. Selling dominates learning	1. Learning about the customer is intense and dominates selling
2. Talking dominates listening	2. Listening dominates talking
3. Persuading the customer is product driven and benefits focused	3. Teaching the customer is need driven and problem focused
4. The goal is to build buyers and sales through persuasion, price, presence, and terms	4. The goal is to build relationships through credibility, responsiveness, and trust

[8] See for example Michael E. Porter, *Competitive Advantage* (Free Press, New York, 1985), pp. 191–93 for a discussion of licensing and Joseph L. Bower and Eric A. Rhenman, "Benevolent Cartels," *Harvard Business Review,* July–August 1985.

The first is the Hartford Component Company, a disguised manufacturer of a somewhat specialized component for measuring instruments. Hartford competed directly with several other companies who used the same technology and with others whose components were based on competing technology. One of Hartford's primary customers, New Haven Instrument (NHI), made measuring instruments for chemical analysis and medical diagnosis. Some of its products were based upon the Hartford component. After several months of negotiation, based upon years of successful vendor–supplier relations, the companies agreed to a joint development effort. Hartford management understood that to develop its technology further it needed more product use knowledge, additional technical expertise in several related engineering disciplines, and an assured outlet for its new product, which would take substantial time and funds to develop. NHI faced intense worldwide competition and needed a "technological leg up" to improve its position. It lacked the ability to develop its component technology and wanted to leverage its strong customer relationships, applications knowledge, and skill in related technologies. Neither of the companies, each with sales of $50 million to $200 million, wished to merge, but each needed something more important, intimate, and permanent than their previous preferred vendor–major customer relationship.

Their strategic partnership involved a joint development effort, information exchange, and a carefully developed sales agreement which gave NHI a temporary exclusive purchase agreement for the components and Hartford an assured source of sales. Despite the high cost, substantial required level of cooperation and integration between vendor and customer organizations, and the requisite loss of autonomy for each, both organizations believed the arrangement was successful and worthwhile. Each, because they managed the relationship well and had carefully defined expectations, gained a great deal.

This example demonstrates the three attributes upon which strategic account relationships must always be based:

1. Importance.
2. Intimacy.
3. Longevity.

Importance usually involves three forms of interdependence: financial, technological and/or design, and strategic. Either the vendor or the customer must be exceedingly important to the other financially. Sometimes the companies, as in the Hartford–New Haven case, are mutually important to one another financially. Technological and/or design cooperation is at the heart of most strategic partnerships. Shared technological and/or design development is the element that *most* separates situations appropriate for strategic account relationships from those more appropriate for selling. Strategic importance is usually based on the technological/design relationship supplemented by the financial importance of one to the other.

Intimacy and longevity flow from the nature of the necessary relationship. Companies cannot do *joint* development without sharing intimate technological, design, and operating information. Trust is a critical ingredient in the relationship because it enables the intimacy.

Longevity is necessary to protect the intimacy, and to enable the partners to reap the financial rewards. The investments have long and hopefully high payouts. Longevity ensures a relationship during the payout period after the investment period.

Another strategic account relationship is that between the EDS (Electronic Data Systems) part of General Motors and what was the Information Systems (IS) portion of AT&T. EDS had substantial skills in integrating computers, telecommunications gear, and software to customer systems. AT&T IS sold telecommunications equipment, computers, and related equipment; it did not have sufficient systems integration skills to satisfy all its customers. EDS and AT&T IS signed a systems integrator agreement under which EDS was considerably more than a distributor because of the size and significance of the systems integrator role.

In another strategic account relationship, Fujitsu Fanuc Ltd., a Japanese robot vendor, established a joint venture with General Motors. The joint venture gave Fanuc a window on factory technology and robot application beyond what it could gain as a more traditional vendor. The joint venture, which sold robots and related factory automation equipment to GMC and other customers, enabled GMC to better understand and capitalize on rapidly evolving robot technology. It also gave GMC greater financial return from its factory automation development work because it gained returns on sales to other customers.

Comparisons and Applications

Exhibit 3 describes the four types of sales approaches. On the left is the transaction approach, with systems selling, major account management, and strategic account relationships each representing evolutions in sophistication and horsepower. Most important are the differences in goal and essence. The transaction and systems approaches emphasize sales, while the major account and strategic relationship approaches emphasize the mutuality of a long marriage. As we move from left to right we see the impact of the sale and the approach increase for both buyer and seller. Thus, the organization level and size of the buying and selling teams increase, as does the length of the relationship.

However, the relative amount of vendor effort also increases. Integration and information flow within the vendor organization expand in response to the increased effort and because of the degree of customer responsiveness and service required. As we move from left to right on the chart, the relative amount of account work done by the sales force decreases and the amount done by supporting functional units such as manufacturing, field service, logistics, and so on, increases. *This means that more and more of the salesperson's time must be spent on internal coordination and service support and less in customer persuasion.* The best relationship managers have as much internal as external focus, a paradox to most old-time salespeople. The salespeople must have broad account-related goals instead of narrow sales-related goals.

Because of the effort involved, a vendor can support only a few strategic account relationships. Most customers will be systems or transaction customers. Some will be major accounts.

EXHIBIT 3 The Four Types of Sales Approaches

	Transaction	Systems	Major Account Management	Strategic Account Relationship
1. Goal	Sales and satisfied customers	Systems sales and satisfied customers	The position as preferred supplier	An enduring, intimate relationship
2. Essence	Product sales because of performance, price, and effective selling	Integration benefits from good support and team selling	Intense service through account management	Company-to-company bonding with an institutional relationship leading to a shared destiny
3. Impact on buyer	Lowest			Highest
4. Impact on seller	Lowest			Highest
5. Organizational level and size of buying team	Lowest			Highest
6. Organizational level and size of selling team	Lowest			Highest
7. Length of relationship	Shortest			Longest
8. Relative amount of vendor effort	Lowest			Highest
9. Information needs at all levels of vendor	Lowest			Highest
10. Vendor management integration needs	Limited			Highest
11. Sales force goals	Narrow—sell products			Broad—manage the partnership
12. Number of customers appropriate for each approach	Most or some	Most or some	Not many	Very small

NOTE: In some industries such as electronics the transaction sales are called box or piece part sales to contrast them from systems sales.

Exhibit 3 describes the most appropriate sales approach. Since transaction selling is the easiest and cheapest, it should be used wherever possible. When products become complex and sophisticated, shift to the systems approach. For many companies that is all that will be needed!

When the importance of individual customers grows, and the customers need intense service because of the nature of their buying process and dependencies, the seller must switch to major account management and relationship selling. The shift must be a philosophical one—a commitment to customer service and responsiveness. It is not just the use of improved techniques. Major account management is indeed a powerful tool, but it is expensive in terms of support and integration cost and effort. It is an efficient competitive weapon only when it is justified.

Finally, for the few situations where customer importance (financial, technological and/or design, and strategic), intimacy, and longevity are high, use the most potent weapon: strategic account relationships. It is the most expensive because of support and integration demands, and loss of autonomy, but it is justified where the relationship must be long and intimate, and where the rewards are strategic.

Simply put, the message is, use the cheapest tool (see the transaction column in Exhibit 3) wherever possible. Escalate [to the right] only when necessary and justified.

Why Get Closer?

If transaction selling is so much cheaper and easier than the three other types, do we need systems selling, major account management, and strategic account relationships? When are they justified?

Systems selling evolved because of product changes and the resulting changes in the customer's buying process. Some products became more complex, with more separate parts and services, and the pieces had to fit together. The added complexity meant that other people and departments had to become involved in the purchase. When machine tools, for example, were relatively simple, the engineer at the customer company could give a clear specification to the purchasing agent, who could negotiate for a good price. While there might be a few conversations between the engineer and purchasing agent, the communication was generally simple and the coordination needs limited.

As machine tools were replaced by complex multipurpose machining centers, the whole buying process changed. What had been a simple stand-alone machine purchase became a complex systems purchase. Process engineers, product design engineers, manufacturing management, logistical personnel, procurement executives, and financial specialists had to get involved. The machining center changed the way various departments operated, the role of inventory and product variety (oops, the product and marketing managers need to be involved!), the whole concept of coordinated engineering, manufacturing, and logistics, and the risk of downtime. Service and support became complicated. New types of suppliers were needed.

Successful vendors developed better sales techniques to match the more complicated buying process and product configuration. Systems selling was the integration of these techniques into a new sales approach.

Additional, broader changes in the environment, however, forced the quantum change to major account management. Mergers, acquisitions, bankruptcies, and differential growth led to a smaller, more concentrated account base in many industries. In some, such as the market for commercial jet engines and aircraft, as few as a dozen customers control the market. These became do-or-die customers. They had to be approached well. Economic concentration brought added changes to the buying and selling organizations. There were more buying, receiving, using, producing, inventorying, shipping, and selling locations. Sales calls had to be made on more customer locations from more different sales locations. As well, the sales effort had to be coordinated with more support (manufacturing, inventorying, etc.) locations.

The communication and coordination needs entered another sphere. It was not about one or a few systems, or one or a few large, complex transactions—it was about a total vendor–customer *relationship*. And to make matters worse, the dispersion was not simply geographical. It involved many buying and selling organizational jurisdictions. The problems of internal coordination at the vendor became as important as vendor–customer coordination.

At the same time, the impact of *vendor,* not just product choice, increased substantially. Experience, good and bad, of computer buyers especially influenced views of vendor importance. Because computers of different manufacturers could not talk to one another in the 1960s, 1970s, and early 1980s, commitment to a product was a long-term commitment to a vendor and a technological approach. Thus, it was natural that a computer vendor, IBM, led the development of major and national account marketing.

Individual transactions and annual vendor-to-customer sales increased dramatically in size. Bonds between vendor and customer became more intimate. Coordination became difficult. The risk of a poor choice soared. Also, major and national account management became a fad. Those who thought it was a collection of advanced sales techniques failed. Those who saw it as a new philosophy of vendor–customer cooperation and internal vendor coordination, and who were able to make it work despite organizational inertia, complexity, and jurisdictional warfare succeeded. The difference between success and failure was clear and involved many functions. Better customer relationships enabled vendor engineers, for example, to do a better job of developing new products. The new products improved the relationship, and the better major account marketer grew further ahead of the disorganized, disoriented competitor. The better sales approach led to greater business success.

In some businesses, the vendor–customer relationship grew even closer. Joint technological work was the cause in many but not all situations. An interesting marketing-oriented situation developed at NutraSweet, where a patented sweetener made the company a primary supplier to Coca-Cola and Pepsi-Cola. NutraSweet's "branded ingredient strategy" linked its marketing strategy inextricably to its customers. The transactions were large and the dollars very great. More important, however, NutraSweet and Coke *and* NutraSweet and Pepsi had a long-term interest in promoting NutraSweet-branded diet soft drinks. Such joint marketing, operating, and/or technological dependencies led to strategic account relationships.

The evolution of the four sales approaches is really the history of more complex responses to more demanding customer purchase initiatives. Systems selling arose because of buyer demands beyond those which could be filled with the traditional transaction approach. Major account management represented a still more powerful approach to greater customer opportunity. The antecedents for the strategic account relationship approach lie in original equipment manufacturer (OEM) industrial marketing and in franchised distributor arrangements. Suppliers of complex, important components to OEMs have found it necessary to do joint development and engineering work together. The proprietary nature of the products and interfaces developed led to long-term relationships. A manufacturer of numerically controlled machine tools, for example, is typically locked in to a computer control vendor for a five-year or so generation of controls. Thus, the *minimum* commitment of the OEM machine tool maker to the control vendor is five years.

Franchised distributors in the industrial, commercial, and consumer sphere (e.g., McDonald's and Dunkin' Donuts) have intimate, long-term relationships with the franchiser who supplies a mixture of branded marketing and advertising, technical support, capital equipment, and merchandise. The long-term intimate relationship of the franchiser and franchisee is a strategic account relationship with a very specific legal definition.

Because the four different sales approaches offer such different rewards and involve such different costs, they must be applied to the right situations. Transaction selling will be ineffective where major account management is needed, and strategic account relationships will be wasted where major account management will do. Thus, accounts and prospects must be segmented for different approaches.

Segmenting Accounts and Prospects

Given the differences among the four different sales approaches in cost and impact, it is appropriate to consider which accounts and prospects might be appropriate for each approach. Much has been written about market segmentation, but the approach here focuses primarily on segmenting an existing customer base.[9]

The easiest way to segment customers is by size: typically, there are more small customers than large ones. If they are ranked by size from largest at the top to smallest at the bottom and are visualized as a pyramid (see Exhibit 4), the increasing width of the base indicates the increasing number of smaller amounts. This simple approach is a useful beginning.

The account volume can often be visualized in a pyramid or triangle (see Exhibit 5) that is upside-down with a large base at the top. That is because the few large accounts typically comprise a disproportionate amount of volume. The point at the bottom comes from the many accounts that represent a small percentage of total volume.

The largest accounts also often demand and perhaps justify more service and customization per dollar or unit of volume. This is reflected in the right-hand triangle on Exhibit 5, which has a wider top than the middle triangle, which reflects sales volume.

A simple approach is to apply the transaction sales approach to the smallest accounts (labeled micro in Exhibit 4), the systems approach to the next, and so on up to the strategic account relationship approach at the very top for the few largest

---

[9]For more on commercial/industrial market segmentation see Thomas V. Bonoma and Benson P. Shapiro, *Segmenting the Industrial Market* (Lexington, Mass.: D. C. Heath and Company, 1983); Benson P. Shapiro and Thomas V. Bonoma, "How to Segment Industrial Markets," *Harvard Business Review,* July–August 1984; and Thomas V. Bonoma and Benson P. Shapiro, "Evaluating Market Segmentation Approaches," *Industrial Marketing Management,* October 1984.

EXHIBIT 4 The Customer Pyramid

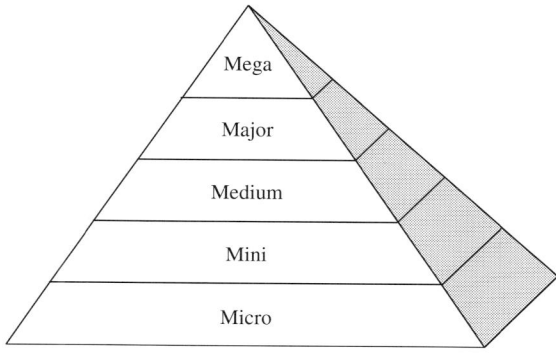

mega accounts. This method is mechanistic and heavy-handed but better than a random approach. However, it neglects sales potential, account profitability, customer needs, and vendor rewards beyond sales volume and profits.

Expanding beyond Size

Potential is easy to add to the process. The simplest way is to use the pyramids and triangles to represent realizable potential instead of only current sales volume. The same general shape is likely to appear, but the approach is more future-oriented. Specifying potential requires some careful analysis of each account, a good place to begin effective account planning.

Account profitability can be added by using the account profitability matrix (Exhibit 6), which separates accounts (and orders) by realized price and cost-to-

EXHIBIT 5 Customer Potential and Customer Demands

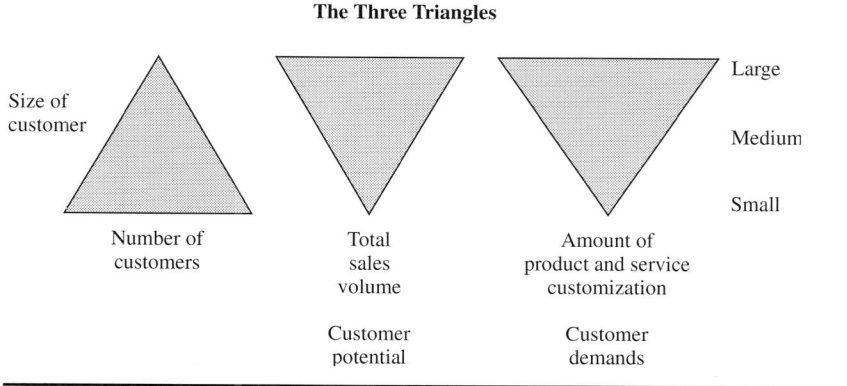

EXHIBIT 6   The Customer/Order Profitability Matrix

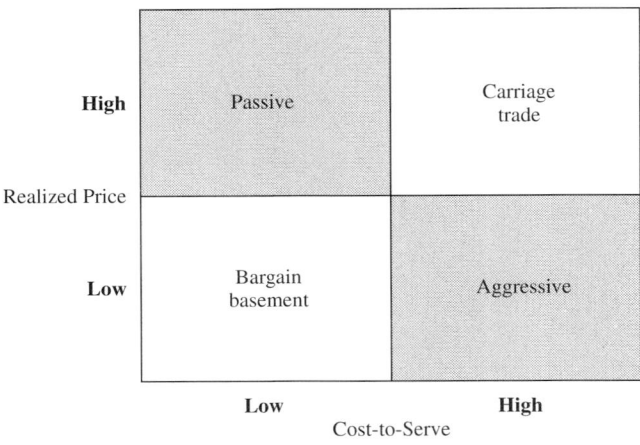

serve. "Passive" accounts, which pay high realized price and are inexpensive to serve, are more attractive than "aggressive" accounts, which pay low realized prices and are expensive to serve.[10] This approach requires an account profitability analysis system and fairly well-developed account plans to determine which accounts will provide incremental profitable business. Such pro forma analysis is important because the cost of serving an account with the strategic account relationship approach is much higher than with the transaction and systems sales approaches or even major account management.

There is no reason to use a more expensive approach when customer needs and prospective vendor rewards do not justify it. Wherever possible the least expensive, easiest approach (to the left on Exhibit 3) should be used. Only a few customers will justify the strategic account relationship approach, and a fairly small number relative to the account base will justify major account management in most vendors.

The accounts and prospects most likely to demand these advanced approaches are also usually the accounts most sensitive to *vendor* quality and performance as opposed to price, *product* quality and performance, rapid availability, and convenience. Commodity markets are characterized by buyers who emphasize price. Specialty markets are made up of buyers who want either rapid availability, convenience, *product* quality and performance, or *vendor* quality and performance.[11] The specialty buyers who are sensitive to vendor quality and performance are most appropriate for the advanced sales approaches.

---

[10]"Manage Customers for Profits (Not Just Sales)," Benson P. Shapiro, V. Kasturi Rangan, Rowland T. Moriarty, and Elliot B. Ross, *Harvard Business Review,* September–October 1987.

[11]For more on these distinctions, see Benson P. Shapiro, "Specialties versus Commodities: The Battle for Profit Margins," Harvard Business School case no. 587-120, Boston, 1987.

Finally, some accounts have special attributes that make them appropriate for special account relationships. An account providing an entry into a new marketplace, technology, or manufacturing process may be attractive far beyond its current sales volume and profitability or future potential for volume or profitability. A good example of such an account occurred in a high-technology material supplier. A mid-sized account was identified for strategic account relationship treatment because it was a consistent technological leader in the company's most important market. The materials supplier felt that being close to the technological cutting edge was in many ways more important than current volume. The account was viewed, because of its technical prowess, as the account of the future.

Some strategic accounts will help the vendor to manage product mix in a strategic sense. Such an account might, for example, take rejected product that is not up to specification for other customers but is much better than scrap. This can have a major impact on operations and profitability.

Finally, other attributes which make an account appropriate for strategic account relationship development include industry visibility and image and "ability to work with." When we confront implementation, we will give more consideration to ability to work with.

If we define *strategic accounts* as those appropriate for the development of strategic account relationships, we would include the following characteristics as criteria:

1. Current sales volume.
2. Future sales potential.
3. Current profitability.
4. Future profitability.
5. Strong customer service needs.
6. Strong customer interest in *vendor* quality and performance.
7. Entry into a new market, technology, or manufacturing process.
8. Impact on product mix.
9. Industry visibility and image.
10. Ability to work with.

Ideally, a strategic account will be high on all criteria. But often one or even several criteria will have to be sacrificed in some situations. The list indicates the need to go beyond current volume and even current profitability. Myopia is dangerous when planning for the long term. Perhaps the only more dangerous trap is to select too many strategic accounts so that none gets the amount of attention it needs.

Special Services for the Few

The amount of special sales and service attention provided and the number of strategic accounts can be combined, as shown in Exhibit 7. The vertical dimension is the number or percentage of accounts receiving special effort and the horizontal

Exhibit 7 Allocation of Customer Support

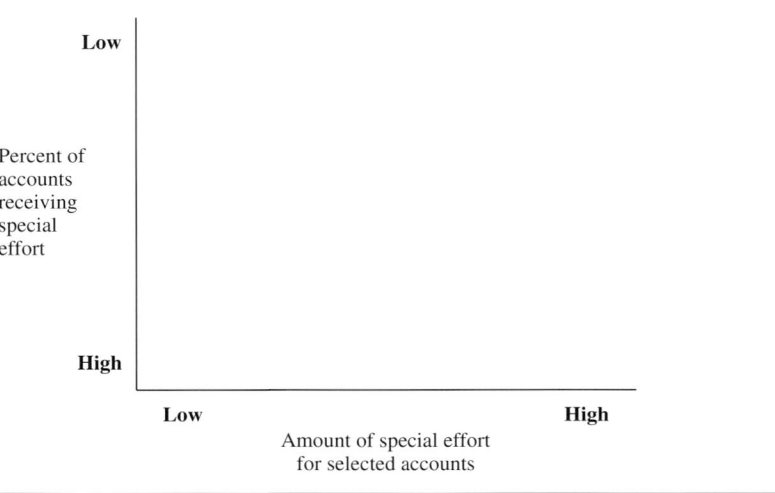

dimension is the amount of the special effort. On the upper right, a few customers get major special attention. In the lower left, many customers get little differentiation. The line between the two (lower left to upper right as shown in Exhibit 8) can be a constant cost line. The choice of giving a great deal of special effort to each of a few customers versus less-special effort each to a larger group is indeed strategic.

Exhibit 8 Allocation of Customer Support

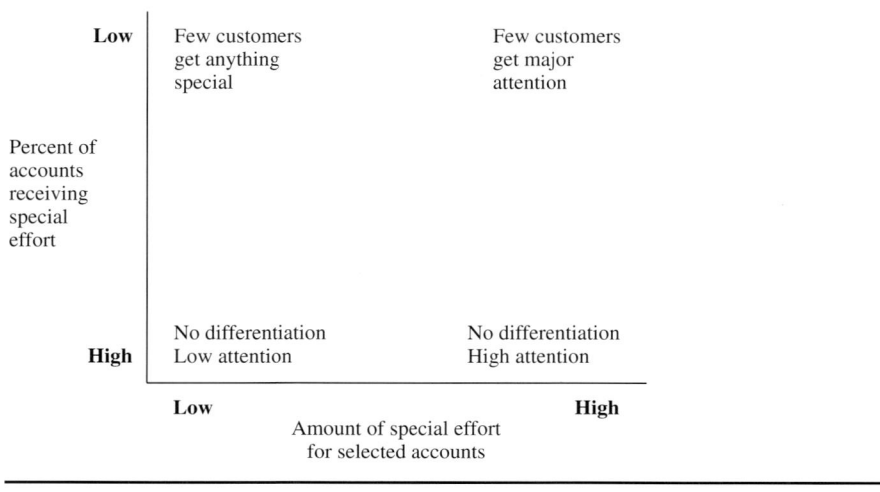

If the account base is concentrated (few customers and prospects comprise a large percentage of potential) and the accounts are interested in special services, then the upper right-hand corner of intensively nurturing a few accounts with the strategic account relationship approach will pay off. A more dispersed account and prospect potential and/or less responsiveness to special services suggests less differentiation for a larger group of accounts.

One problem with Exhibit 7 is that it is somewhat unidimensional. Perhaps a more complete way to look at the total account and prospect base is to ask what number should get each type of sales approach. Nonetheless, the issue is raised boldly by Exhibit 7.

Now that we have examined the four different sales approaches and seen that most vendors will have a mixture of the four, we turn to a deeper analysis of strategic account relationships. Before we do so, however, it is necessary to emphasize that these complex relationships are not appropriate to every vendor or to every customer of any vendor. They get special attention here because they are new and complex. Little is understood about strategic account relationships and even less has been written. We begin with the customer's view, the best place to begin.

What Do Strategic Account Relationships Provide to Customers?

The essence of strategic account relationships is the provision of a special set of efforts by the vendor. These efforts must provide a long-term competitive advantage to the customer. The customer hopes to get some mixture of technological, operational, and strategic benefits from the approach.

Most strategic account relationships are fostered by intense and rapid technological development. The need for technological specialization and integration has forced customers to look beyond their boundaries for the skills and resources they need. Often the two partners must integrate their technologies and design their products with one another. Because the technology is so pervasive and the integration so complex, the level of sharing must be high. Design and development must often be performed jointly with a great deal of frequent cutting and fitting.

Many customers and prospects seek operational rewards from the strategic account relationship vendor. Sometimes these fall out from the technological integration, at other times they are the primary benefit.

Evolving approaches to manufacturing such as just-in-time force intimate operational coordination. And because components, equipment, and systems exchanged in a strategic partnership are often customized with no second source and no other prospective customers, the operational integration system has fewer safety valves and alternatives than more traditional approaches. Thus, sales forecasting and capacity planning must be joint. Higher levels of technological and design integration create the need for greater operational integration.

The relationship between NutraSweet and its primary customers is an example of operational benefits focused on joint marketing interests. Consumer franchiser-franchisee relationships such as McDonald's and Dunkin' Donuts are another example of marketing benefits to the relationship.

By their nature, strategic account relationships work only in situations where the relationship is at the heart of the strategy of both companies. This is because the cost and effort involved in making a strategic partnership can only be justified if there is a strategic need. The cost and effort are not justified and will not be provided unless the need is clear to the relevant and powerful managers on both sides of the relationship as well as to the lower level people who must actually do the work. General Motors needed Fanuc's factory automation skills to survive and prosper in a hostile competitive environment. Fanuc needed a large, worldwide base of leading edge, high-volume customers, advanced applications knowledge, and factory involvement to develop its leading position in robots. Both companies needed each other to prosper.

How Are Strategic Account Relationships Nurtured?

Strategic account relationships require importance, intimacy, and longevity. The intimacy sets the tone for the very nature of the relationship. The technological, operational, and strategic integration lead naturally to the high level of organizational integration that must be present in strategic relationships. This is not the typical salesperson–purchasing agent relationship. It also goes far beyond the still evolving team and multilevel selling approaches that developed in the 1970s and early 1980s, to some extent, as parts of major account management. The organizational integration must extend to many parts of the vendor and customer organizations. Engineers must talk to engineers, production people must talk to one another, and top management must get together as well.

Sometimes employees of the seller must be located in the facilities of the customer to work together, or even to operate equipment. In the chemical industry, some vendors have found it advantageous or even necessary to operate leased equipment at a customer site. This raises a raft of issues about integration, including everything from union contracts to cafeteria and parking privileges.

Old-fashioned arm's-length organizational relationships are not enough; the relationships must be person to person. In many cases, the success of a person in the vendor or customer organization is more dependent on a personal relationship with someone in the partner organization than with anyone in his or her own. The designers must work at a high level of cooperation and intimacy, often melding different technologies and philosophies.

The organizational and personal integration can only take place between a vendor and a customer who have some common values and culture. That is unfortunate because sometimes the greatest strategic and technological rewards might come from working with a company quite disparate from your own. The likelihood of success, however, tends to go down in such a situation. Management support on both sides and unusual organizational arrangements might help, but there are disparities that cannot be bridged regardless of the amount of goodwill, effort, and potential reward.

Finally, there is financial integration. The strategic bond here is so great that a typical financial relationship is often too weak to reflect it. Some strategic account relationships work on a typical "I make it, I sell it, you buy it, and you pay for it" basis. But much more likely are arrangements that better reflect the relationship. Certainly outright acquisition is one approach. Formal joint ventures such as GM-Fanuc are much more likely. Other approaches include development contracts, supply contracts, licensing, and very strong informal relationships. Seldom does the buyer ask for bids for a specified product. Instead, the development is joint and the financial relationship attempts to reflect the sharing of risk, contribution, and reward. Roy Shapiro has captured a great deal about these new types of relationships in "Toward Effective Supplier Management: International Comparisons."[12]

Integration beyond the Vendor and Customer Relationship

The integration in a strategic partnership must extend sometimes beyond the two partners to the vendor's suppliers and the customer's customers. The system is sometimes so complex that other levels in the supply chain or distribution channel must be involved to provide all the needed strategic, technological, operational, and financial horsepower.

Finally, integration within each of the partners must be stronger than in a normal company. Roy Shapiro argues that the purchasing, engineering, and production functions in the customer company must become more integrated to deal with suppliers in strategic account relationships. The vendor organization must also be well integrated. Everyone must sell and service the strategic partner. If the engineering and sales functions cannot operate well together, it is hard to believe that they will be able to work with customers in an intimate relationship.

All this integration must be justified by substantial rewards.

The Rewards

Strategic account relationships offer the selling company the opportunity to leverage its skills and resources, develop long-term customers, and build strong competitive positions. Companies in a wide variety of industries have understood the rewards and opportunities. Some have reached them successfully, others have failed.

Strategic account relationships do not necessarily represent a way station between acquisition, which in a sense is the ultimate form of strategic partnership, and the more arm's-length forms of buyer–seller relationships. Instead, they can represent a continuing vendor–customer relationship which is very special because of the rewards it offers to both parties. The exchange of knowledge, including "soft" management skills and competence as well as "hard" technological capability, is at the

---

[12]Harvard Business School Working Paper 9-785-062.

core of many strategic account relationships. The seller can learn how its product is used and develop unique applications approaches. The customer is willing to share such knowledge with an outsider because it expects to gain knowledge and unique support for its new activities.

If the partnership is with a distributor, the supplier gets the commitment of resources to its product line, and the investment of the distributor's organization in unique capabilities useful only for the supplier's product line. For example, distributor salespeople may spend substantial amounts of time learning the benefits of the products, their competitive positioning, and the ways in which they can best be sold. Distributor engineers will learn the minutiae of interfacing the vendor's product with their customers' products and systems, and distributor service people will learn how to maintain and repair the equipment. The distributor is willing to make the commitments because of the permanence and intimacy of the relationship. In the distribution realm, the strategic account relationship is different more in degree than in nature from a solid, close, but typical major or national distributor–vendor relationship.

The permanence of the relationship leads naturally to a long-term customer commitment. The sales and the knowledge exchange lead to a stronger competitive position. Sometimes, for example, a vendor cannot afford to invest in a major new product without the long-term commitment of a customer to ensure the profitability, or at least to limit the financial risk, of the venture.

In some industries, the astute choice and effective management of strategic account relationships is a critical determinant of success. The choice and management of the partnerships presents some major traps, however.

Traps

The traps can be divided into four groups:

1. Attempting to develop too many strategic account relationships.
2. Picking poor strategic account partners.
3. Allocating too few resources to the relationship.
4. Losing sight of the importance of cultural compatibility in the relationships.

Because the relationships are so intensive and extensive, it is possible for a company to maintain only a few strategic account relationships. Some companies have a very concentrated customer and prospect list with few existing and potential accounts and a high proportion of sales potential in an even smaller number of them. These companies often have little choice but to develop several, or at most a few, strategic account relationships. But even companies with very extensive prospect and customer lists cannot have more than a few strategic account relationships given their attendant high demands on resources and time.

One of the most subtle forms of strategic account demands is product and service customization. If the customization is major and, as is often the case, affects the whole vendor organization and product line, the vendor will be torn apart by too many strategic account relationships. Each account will pressure the vendor to emphasize its needs and approach. If the vendor has too many conflicting pulls, it will be able to satisfy none well and, perhaps more sadly, will lose its own internal organizational coherence and end up with a poorly integrated, incoherent product line.

If the vendor can only have a few relationships, and if the relationships are strategic, it is clear that the choice of the accounts is critical. A poor choice leads to wasted resources, but that is not the major cost of the poor choice. The highest cost of a poor choice is usually the opportunity lost to develop an effective strategic account relationship with another customer or prospect. Instead, a competitor may move in and reap long-term rewards. The choice of accounts is particularly hard when it is impossible to have strategic relationships with two accounts who compete intensively with one another.

The criteria for choice, and their priority, must be set very carefully indeed. They should include:

1. A leading-edge technical and/or operational capability.
2. A willingness to share in joint technical and/or operational development.
3. A willingness to make the vendor an important part of the customer's business activities, including frequent meetings with a wide variety of functional units within the customer organization.
4. Substantial sales potential.
5. Long-term profit potential.
6. An existing relationship as a basis for the partnership.
7. Good cultural fit.

The technical and/or operational capability and development in criteria one and two above must relate to activities of clear strategic importance to the vendor. The capability might be "hard" as relates to a scientific or engineering capability or "soft" as relates to a particular form of operational capability such as marketing, service, or manufacturing.

Some companies have attempted to develop strategic accounts without devoting enough resources to each relationship. Sometimes this is because they have tried to develop too many account relationships, or have chosen to use strategic account relationships where they are not justified and supportable. At other times, they underestimated the cost and commitment needed.

Four forms of resource starvation have been particularly typical:

1. Not assigning enough top management skill and power or enough technical and functional expertise to the relationships. The strategic accounts justify and require the best staffing and attention.
2. Using a sales-oriented approach when more skills in engineering, production, service, financial, and so on, are needed. This is not a standard sale; it is a long-term, intimate partnership.

3. An unwillingness to develop custom products and services for each strategic account. The custom nature of each partnership is one of the major limitations in the number that can be developed. If each relationship needs a separate product line, and the base business needs its own product line, the total diversity must still be supportable by the engineering, production, service, and logistics functions.
4. If personal relationships are to develop, people must spend time together. Travel and telephone budgets must be extensive enough to support relationship and trust development. And the managers and experts working on the accounts must have adequate time available to do the job. Some might have to move to the partner's location on an extended, but temporary, basis. The drain of international partnerships with the attendant travel (jet lag is a real cost!) is very high indeed.

Patience is an important part of nurturing strategic account relationships. One top-level executive complained to me, "We have been at this strategic account relationship thing for three whole months and sales at the account aren't up!" Major account management takes a long time and strategic account relationship development takes even longer. Many months are needed to build a good personal relationship and even longer to build the deep institutional bonds of the strategic account relationship approach. Patience is particularly important when the joint projects involve major technological development or when the customer is a mature, cyclical company. The down cycle is often the best time to build strategic relationships but the more visible benefits such as sales increases will often not accrue until the up cycle.

Another particularly good time to build strategic account relationships is when the supplier industry is oversold and the customer is in desperate need of support. Short-term optimization of profits by such maneuvers as price gouging or allocation of scarce products to new customers instead of established ones can cost dearly over the business cycle and make it absolutely impossible for a vendor to establish the deep trust needed for this type of relationship.

The life cycle of the relationship dictates that, as in most situations, the investment must be made before the rewards can be reaped.

Finally, some companies have neglected to understand the delicate mating of cultures which leads to successful relationships. Some pairs of cultures are hard to integrate and some impossible. Partnerships require compromise and constant joint nurturing to succeed.

Implementation—Building Institutional Relationships

Although strategic account relationships are fairly new, it is possible to suggest some guidelines for success. Some are similar to those for acquisitions, an even more intimate and permanent relationship. The critical issue is the human management of the relationship, which must engender something closer than the typical buyer–seller relationship but cannot be internal management such as in an acquisition.

To avoid the traps:

1. Develop only a few strategic partnerships. Recognize that some customers will be transactional customers, some systems customers, a limited number major or national accounts, and a very small number strategic account relationships. If the number of such partnerships goes beyond being countable on one's fingers, the relationships won't be truly strategic!
2. Choose accounts who meet the explicit chosen criteria and who share a long-term vision of the future. If the relationships are to be strategic, they must be long term. If they are to be profitable, they must last long enough to generate revenue after the expensive, initial investment period. Look at them as long-term company-to-company relationships, not as related to one product, technology, or worst of all, one deal.
3. Allocate enough resources to the relationship. If the resource allocation is parsimonious, the relationship is doomed.
4. Understand that the relationships involve a substantial loss of autonomy. Decisions will no longer be made only on the basis of the needs and desires of one organization, but on the joint needs and desires of both partners. This loss of autonomy is one of the primary costs of strategic account relationship. The loss will be most severe in those activities which are closest to the heart of the relationship—often product design and technology choice.
5. Develop a financial relationship that reflects the long-term needs and interests of both parties, and which is flexible enough to adjust to changing conditions (if it is a long-term relationship, conditions will change), and explicit enough to avoid arguments about interpretation. It helps to identify, discuss, and clarify issues which are likely to create problems in the future. The relationship should be so intimate and pervasive that parts of it cannot be "swept under the carpet" in hopes they won't be noticed. Instead, the disagreements will fester until the infection destroys the relationships. There are a great many financial forms that the venture can take. All the relevant ones from supply contracts to joint ventures should be explored to find the optimum mix of flexibility and explicitness.

Finally, we turn to the management of the relationship. If the partnership is to succeed, the relationship must be institutional. That is, it must supersede the relationship between any two individuals and become a relationship between organizations.

Major account relationships depend upon an able account manager who can mobilize internal resources to support the account and who can call on many people at the account with confidence and competence. The account manager becomes the primary node in the communications network:

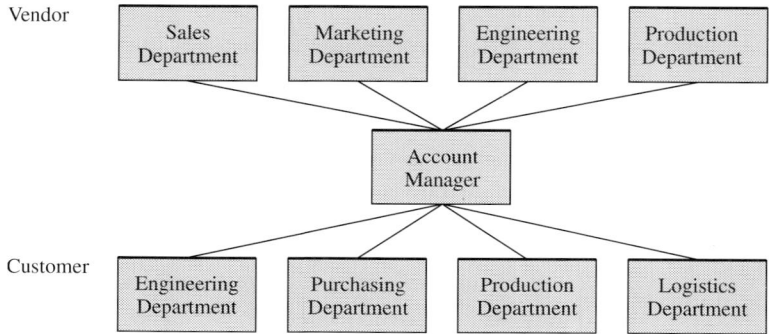

A true strategic account relationship cannot operate with one primary node. There must be intense communication among many vendor and customer functions:

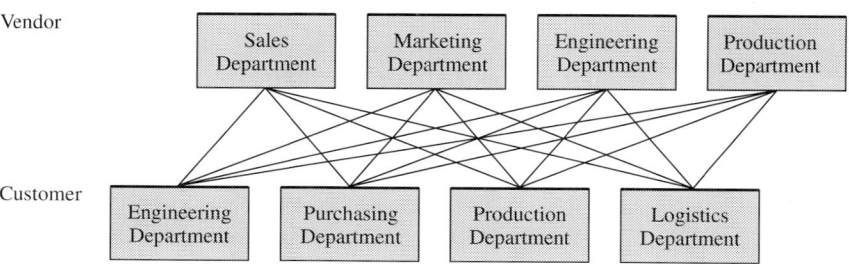

The problem with this scheme is that the communication can easily become unmanageable and uncoordinated as well as inefficient. One approach that appears to work well in many situations is to have a senior partnership team consisting of two top-level executives, one from the vendor and one from the customer, and a group of senior functional executives who manage and coordinate the partnership. In a way, this idea imitates the joint venture board of directors, but in a much more informal and day-to-day oriented way.

The senior partnership team should not replace or limit other direct communications. Instead, it should manage and coordinate the relationship, and nurture cross-company integration and communication at all levels in all functions. If the engineers do not talk to one another, for example, the benefits of the partnership will not accrue, but the costs will.

National account management has been described as a case of making and keeping promises to customers.[13] This view is appropriate in all four sales approaches, even transaction selling. But it is especially true in the relationship-building activities of major account management and strategic account relationships. Because of the long-term nature of the activities and results, yesterday's promises

---

[13]Benson P. Shapiro and Rowland T. Moriarty, Jr., "Support Systems for National Account Management Programs: Promises Made, Promises Kept," Marketing Science Institute, Cambridge, Mass., 1983.

must be kept tomorrow. When the promises are not kept, it hurts the present relationship which can have long-term impact because of the strategic nature of the relationship. The great upside opportunity of strategic account relationships puts emphasis on unmade promises as well. The unmade promise is, in essence, a lost opportunity. It sacrifices the long-term return from the relationship in the same way that unkept promises hurt the present situation.

Concluding Note

Before we considered strategic account relationships we looked at all four kinds of selling. Transaction selling is inexpensive and very utilitarian where it is appropriate. Systems sales are useful for the larger, more complex transactions. When the philosophy moves from one of transactions to one of relationships we encounter major account management. Relationship selling is not just a better set of techniques for making sales: It is a different philosophy based upon continuity and trust. When the importance, intimacy, and longevity of the relationship warrant it, the vendor should move from major account management to a strategic account relationship.

Strategic account relationships are a response to the need to develop and manage more complex, and more permanent, partnerships between suppliers and customers. They are expensive and difficult but they can offer great benefits when used selectively and implemented well. Undoubtedly some companies will view them as a panacea. They are not. In fact, in most industries they will supplement and enhance only a small part of the company's sales and marketing effort. They differ in intensity and degree, but not truly in nature, from major and national account management; they differ in fundamental nature from transaction and systems selling, however. There are four kinds of close encounters in selling, but one is closer than the others.

CHAPTER 31

Segmenting Customers in Mature Industrial Markets: An Application

In mature industrial markets, segmenting customers on size, industry, or product benefits alone is rarely sufficient. Customer behavior regarding trade-offs between price and service also becomes an important criterion. In this chapter, we offer a framework to enable such buying-behavior-oriented microsegmentation of industrial customers. We apply our framework to segment the national accounts of a large industrial company and show how the results of our segmentation study may be used to redirect the firm's resources and customer segments.

Segmenting is the art of identifying distinctive customer groups that exhibit homogeneous needs. The point of segmentation is to be able to tailor the marketing mix to address the unique needs of the various segments. A number of bases for segmentation have been offered in the literature, including:

- Demographic descriptors such as geography, standard industrial classification code, and account size.
- Product end use or application.
- Buying situation.
- Customer decision-making style.
- Customer buying behavior.
- Customer benefits.

Market segmentation designs based on product benefits are widely recognized as the state of the art and superior to traditional segmentation schemes based on industry type or customer size. Coles and Culley,[1] for example, illustrate how DuPont segmented its market for Kevlar by three unique customer benefits:

V. Kasturi Rangan prepared this note.
Copyright © 1994 by the President and Fellows of Harvard College.
Harvard Business School note 594-089.

This note is adapted from V. Kasturi Rangan, Rowland T. Moriarty, and Gordon Swartz, "Segmenting Customers in Mature Industrial Markets," *Journal of Marketing* 56 (October 1992), pp. 72–82. Reprinted with permission of the American Marketing Association.

[1]Gary J. Coles and James D. Culley, "Not All Prospects Are Created Equal," *Business Marketing* 71 (May 1986), pp. 52–58.

- For potential fishing boat owners: Kevlar's lightness promised fuel savings, increased speed, and the ability to carry fish weight.
- For aircraft designers: Kevlar had a high strength-to-weight ratio.
- For industrial plant managers: Kevlar could replace the asbestos used for packing pumps.

Such segmentation schemes, though very useful for new products, are too broad to leverage marketing-mix resources as the product-market matures. By then, competitors are able to offer equivalent products, and many buyers may therefore be unwilling to pay a price premium. This is especially true of industrial raw materials and supplies that are hard to differentiate by functions and features alone. Steadily and deliberately, as the market becomes a commodity, price and service become important buying criteria for some customers. Only by further segmenting each macro segment (be it demographic, end-use applications, or benefit) can a marketer really begin to understand the heterogeneity in buying behavior.

Product life cycle (PLC) theory contends that prices tend to drop as the product market matures.[2] Two underlying forces cause that trend. The first is customer learning during the PLC. As the product matures, many customers who by now are totally familiar with the product's characteristics, functions, and features no longer require the same intensity of product information that was once provided by its supplier. As a result, they are unwilling to pay the cost of such services. The second force is the result of competitive action that in a mature market makes equivalent products at similar or lower prices available to customers.

Given this market dynamic, customers in mature markets may be aligned along the two dimensions of price and cost-to-serve[3] (see Figure 1). Customers who demand a low price will be offered a no-frills product accompanied by minimal service, and customers who value an augmented product will pay a higher price and receive the full complement of services. Price differentials due to product quality differences are small because competitors, by then, are able to offer more or less equivalent products. Thus, any major price variations stem from differences among services provided. Customers who receive the core product pay less because it costs less to serve them than those who demand and value the full service.

In keeping with this rationale, firms operating in mature environments expect to align their customers along the value axis in Figure 1. The southwest quadrant (C) represents a core, no-frills product without much service, and the northeast quadrant (B) represents an augmented product accompanied by intensive value-added services. In both cases, the price-service offering is equitable to the seller and the buyer. The core-product customer pays a lower price and the value-added customer pays a higher price. This rationale, however, is based on the seller's expectations of how customers would behave in a mature market.

---

[2]George S. Day, "The Product Life Cycle: Analysis and Applications Issues," *Journal of Marketing* 45 (Fall 1981), pp. 60–70.

[3]B. P. Shapiro, V. K. Rangan, R. T. Moriarty, and E. Ross, "Manage Customers for Profits (Not Just Sales)," *Harvard Business Review* 65 (September–October 1987), pp. 101–8.

FIGURE 1

Potential buying behavior segments

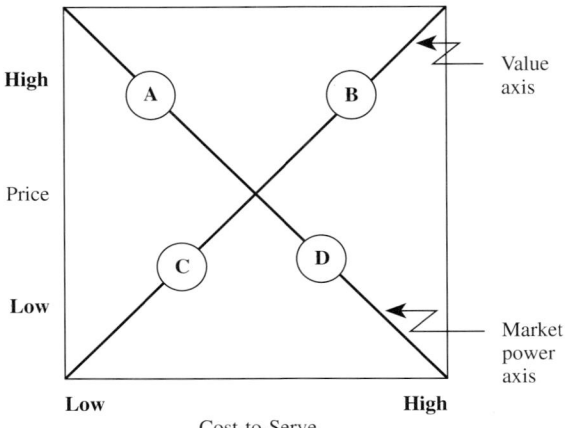

There is an alternative, which is given by the market power axis in Figure 1. Customers see only the price dimension of the matrix; they do not know the seller's cost-to-serve. Because of market maturity, however, there are usually several sellers that can offer similar products, and many customers may therefore attempt to shop around for price. Guaranteed purchase volumes and large order sizes are usually offered as the bait. As a result, customers may not necessarily align themselves along the value axis as sellers expect, but prefer to operate in quadrants C and D, depending on their knowledge of competitive offerings and their own market power.

In the northwest quadrant (A), the supplier is able to extract a relatively high price without providing the necessary services to go along with it. This is usually the result of a truly superior product offering that competitors are unable to match because of technological or other reasons (such as patent protection). Sometimes it is possible for ill-informed customers to overpay, but such a situation is unlikely to persist in the long run.

In sum, all locations above the value axis indicate that the seller is able to extract a higher value than the services it renders because customers perceive the firm's product offering as superior to competitive offerings or substitutes. Positions below the value axis usually indicate that the firm is unable to extract the full value of the services it renders with its product. Along the value axis itself, the exchange is fair. We will now describe how this framework may be used to further analyze a company's customer segments in mature industrial markets.

Database

The main purpose of this study was to validate the buying behavior framework depicted in Figure 1 and demonstrate its use for managerial action. We therefore sought a research site where the product-market environment was in the mature phase of its PLC, characterized by price pressures and the availability of equivalent competitive products. Our framework is more appropriate for mature industrial raw materials and supplies, where service rather than product characteristics is the basis for competition. We therefore sought and obtained the cooperation of the managers of the packaging division of Signode Corporation for conducting our research.[4] This division produced and marketed a line of steel strappings used for packaging a diverse range of goods such as brick, steel, cotton, and many manufactured items.

Signode, the market leader since 1948, had lost 10 share points to stiff price competition in the six years before this study. Its managers considered Signode to be the high-service supplier of steel strapping in their market. Signode was the only company to provide parts and service for repair of packaging equipment at the user firms. The packaging division also offered engineering advice on packaging needs. All other competitors provided only the steel strapping.

The company segmented its customers by size—small, medium, large, and national accounts—and within each of these segments by SIC code (e.g., primary metals, forest products, cotton, brick). Although the company did not use a buyer behavior–based segmentation scheme, its managers believed that the firm's marketing policies were structured so that low-price seekers could have a commodity product and customers who sought additional services could have a value-added product at a higher price (conforming to the behavior underlying the value axis in Figure 1). The managers suspected that such buying behavior variations existed within each size-based segment.

Because our study required an in-depth analysis of individual customer buying behavior, we focused on the company's 174 national accounts whose individual purchases of Signode's products exceeded $100,000 yearly. Collectively, these accounts represented nearly 40 percent of Signode's sales revenues. In general, one would expect to find minimal variation in such a narrow macrosegment, and if found, would only validate our conceptual framework. Signode's other segments (large, medium, and small) were much larger, ranging from 2,000 to 20,000 customers.

To operationalize our framework from Figure 1, we constructed 12 variables to capture the potential buying behavior variations in Signode's national accounts. Six of these were chosen to reflect the price-versus-service variations along the value axis, and the other six reflected the buyer power variations along the market power axis. Although this list of operational indicators may not be exhaustive, it does reflect the buying behavior dimensions that Signode's NAMs and sales reps believed to have the most influence on customer purchasing behavior. We used two sources for gathering data: in-house documents and responses from sales reps and national account managers (NAMs). Table 1 summarizes the key features of the 12 variables measured for 161 of Signode's 174 national accounts (93 percent coverage). The data collection task could not be completed in time for the rest of the 13 accounts. Although some of the data presented here have been disguised at the company's request, the segmentation approach and its implications are accurate.

---

[4] R. T. Moriarty and G. Swartz, "Signode Industries, Inc. (A)," Harvard Business School case no. 586-059.

TABLE 1 **National Account Database**

Buying Behavior Variables	Indicators Of	Source	Units	Mean
In-House documents:				
1. Relative price	Price	Sales record/NAM judgment	Discount %	5.7
2. Relative service	Cost-to-serve	Sales record/NAM judgment	1–10 scales	4.6
3. Account size (annual purchases)	Buyer power	Sales records	Dollars	556,000
4. Market share	Buyer power	Sales records	%	63
Sales force judgmental data (sales elasticity):				
5. For decrease in price	Price	NAM/Sales rep judgment	%	7.8
6. For increase in price	and	NAM/Sales rep judgment	%	22.4
7. For decrease in service	service	NAM/Sales rep judgment	%	8.4
8. For increase in service	trade-offs	NAM/Sales rep judgment	%	2.9
9. Product importance		Sales rep judgment	1–5 scales	2.9
10. Switching potential		Sales rep judgment	1–5 scales	4.1
11. Market knowledge	Buyer power	Sales rep judgment	1–5 scales	4.3
12. Decision-making process complexity		Sales rep judgment	1–5 scales	4.3

Buying Behavior Variables from In-House Documents

Given the mature stage of the market and the standardization of product features across suppliers, price versus service trade-offs were common. But since our focus was within rather than across a market segment, we measured price and cost-to-serve relative to Signode's other national accounts. Called relative price and relative service, these two measures correspond to the price and cost-to-serve dimensions, respectively. The first four variables we measured are described below:

1. *Relative price* was a measure of the higher or lower price that an account paid relative to Signode's other national accounts. Almost all national accounts received discounts from standard carload prices. Using accounting data on all transactions completed in the most recent 12 months, we computed a volume-weighted average discount for each national account. Average discounts ranged from zero to as much as 11.3 percent.

2. *Relative service* was the higher or lower level of service that an account received in relation to other national accounts. Signode's managers identified three important components of service: (1) field sales calls, (2) unbilled parts, tools, and repair work, and (3) application and engineering services. To aggregate these three components, quantitative measures for each component were first computed using their natural units. Thus, field

sales calls were measured as calls per year, unbilled work was estimated in dollars, and applications engineering in hours. These individual components were linearly converted to a 1-to-10 scale and the three rescaled measures then averaged to yield a composite score.

3. *Account size.* While various aspects of account size have been identified as influencing buying behavior, we measured account size simply as the total purchase volume of all Signode products in the most recent 12 months.

4. *Market share.* A different measure of dependency is a single supplier's proportion of business in the buyer's total purchases of a product category. We measured this as Signode's share of dollar sales volume for each account. As part of their routine sales reporting, Signode's salespeople estimated the total dollar volume of each account's steel-strapping purchases. Knowing Signode's actual sales to the account, we computed Signode's market share—an indicator of the buyer's preference for, as well as reliance on, Signode's products.

Buying Behavior Variables from National Account Reps and NAMs

We considered customer sensitivity to price and service changes to be two important aspects of buying behavior. Sales reps were asked the following question for each of their accounts: "If you were able to drop (increase) prices by 7 percent, what is your best estimate of the percentage of increase (decrease) in sales volume that would result?"[5] The 7 percent represented a level of price discounting that the management had selectively used in the past to retain certain large volume accounts in the face of competitive activity. Service elasticity was measured in the same way, except that the unit of change was broken down by its individual components for better comprehension. We thus generated four customer demand elasticities:

5. For decrease in price.
6. For increase in price.
7. For decrease in service.
8. For increase in service.

In addition to these demand elasticities, estimated the national account sales reps, four more buying behavior indicators—product importance, switching potential, market knowledge, and decision-making process complexity—were using the data collection process described above.

9. *Product importance.* Depending on the application and extent of usage, the importance of steel strapping varied over Signode's national accounts. Customers that perceived the product line to be critical were thought to devote more energy and consideration to the buying process.

---

[5]This is a widely used approach by researchers to generate quantitative judgments. The original idea was proposed by J. D. C. Little, "Models and Managers: The Concept of a Decision Calculus," *Management Science* 16, 1970, pp. B466–85.

10. *Switching potential.* Over the years, several customers had built a trusting relationship with Signode because of the product or the service or both. These customers were expected to deviate less from normal purchasing patterns, while other customers might be more likely to switch at lower levels of dissatisfaction.
11. *Market knowledge.* Regardless of the stage of market maturity, customers vary substantially in their knowledge of competitive products and prices; they search for information in varying degrees. Naturally, customers with a detailed knowledge of alternative suppliers' steel-strapping offerings were expected to use somewhat more aggressive negotiation strategies.
12. *Decision-making process (DMP).* The complexity of the buying decision-making process is a reflection not only of product and vendor characteristics but also of the buying organization's priorities and purchasing strategies. At Signode, national account reps suggested that customers with considerable leverage usually required several sales presentations and often contract-by-contract negotiation before an agreement could be reached.

Analysis and Results

To identify buying behavior microsegments, we performed a hierarchical cluster analysis based on the 12 variables of Table 1.[6] Mean values of the buying behavior variables are shown for each microsegment in Table 2.

Buying Behavior Microsegments

Segment 1: Programmed Buyers. Customers in this microsegment were small and viewed the product as a routine purchase item. They had the lowest average sales of any group and were not particularly price or service sensitive. The product was not very important or central to their operations. Compared to those in the other three microsegments, these customers had the lowest market share of Signode products.

We subsequently learned that many of these accounts used rules of thumb to allocate their purchases. They split orders among two or three vendors in fixed proportions. Signode, because of its market-leader reputation, received a major share of these purchases—on average, about 54 percent. Perhaps because of their routinized procedures, these accounts invested little effort in the buying process, either in negotiating purchases or in investigating alternative sources. In return, Signode charged them the full list price and provided below-average service. Because cus-

---

[6]In comparisons of 30 methods for estimating the number of clusters, Glen Milligan and Martha Cooper recommend the use of three statistics for determining the number of clusters: the cubic clustering criterion, the pseudo F statistic, and the pseudo t^2 statistic. We used these to arrive at the four segments shown in Table 2. See Milligan and Cooper, "An Examination of the Procedures for Determining the Number of Clusters in a Data Set," *Psychometrika* 50, no. 2 (1985), pp. 159–79.

TABLE 2 Group Means

Behavioral Surrogates	Segment 1: No. of Accounts = 54	Segment 2: No. of Accounts = 65	Segment 3: No. of Accounts = 22	Segment 4: No. of Accounts = 11
1. Relative price	0.0%	−7.9%	−10.1%	−11.3%
2. Relative service	3.6	4.9	5.6	7.1
3. Account size (sales)	$122,000	$472,000	$1,100,000	$2,100,000
4. Market share	54.2%	67.8%	71.9%	68.3%
5. Percentage increase in sales for price drop	5.6	8.9	8.7	11.8
6. Percentage decrease in sales for price raise	15.5	27.9	24.5	22.7
7. Percentage decrease in sales for service drop	5.1	9.2	12.5	12.3
8. Percentage increase in sales for service raise	1.2	3.0	5.2	7.3
9. Product importance	2.5	3.0	3.5	3.5
10. Switching potential	3.8	4.4	4.5	4.6
11. Market knowledge	4.0	4.5	4.6	4.7
12. DMP complexity	3.2	3.6	3.3	3.4

NOTES: Of the 161 complete data records, the clustering algorithm omitted nine cases as outliers. Nos. 5 and 6 are percentage increase or decrease in sales for a 7% price change; Nos. 8 and 9 are percentage increase or decrease for a unit of service change.

tomers in this segment tended to systematically allocate market share rather than evaluate the price-volume trade-offs, we characterized the purchasing behavior of this microsegment as programmed buying.

Segment 2: Relationship Buyers. Customers in this microsegment were also relatively small. The product itself was moderately important in their operations and, unlike the programmed buyers of segment 1, they were more knowledgeable about competitive offerings. While customers in this microsegment paid lower prices and received more service than programmed buyers, they also gave Signode a higher market share (67.8 percent).

Although customers in this microsegment had a propensity to switch, they were less prone to switching than their counterparts in the third and fourth segments. In addition, in comparison with their more aggressive counterparts in the third and fourth segments, these buyers did not push Signode for price and service concessions, and they paid higher prices for relatively less service. This difference in value received probably explains their extreme sensitivity to price increases. On average, a 7 percent price increase in this microsegment would decrease purchase volumes by as much as 28 percent. As these customers seemed to prefer Signode's partnership to a mere price exchange, we labeled the behavior of this segment as relationship buying.

Segment 3: Transaction Buyers. Customers in this microsegment were, on average, twice as large as the relationship buyers. They received price discounts averaging about 10 percent and an above-average service level; they had the highest sensitivity to decreases in service. The product itself was very important to their operations. Customers in this group were very knowledgeable about competitive offerings, and while valuing Signode's service offerings, they would not hesitate to switch suppliers. Because the customers here actively considered the price-versus-service tradeoffs, but often favored price over service, we labeled them transaction buyers.

Segment 4: Bargain Hunters. Customers in this microsegment were large-volume customers that received the largest price discounts (averaging 11.3 percent) as well as the highest level of service. They were sensitive to any changes in price or service; the product was very important to their operations. They were most knowledgeable about alternative suppliers and most likely to switch suppliers at the slightest dissatisfaction. Customers in this segment were the ultimate bargain hunters.

Discussion

The purpose of this study was to identify buying behavior variations in macrosegments such as national accounts. We argued that such an analysis would be useful in redirecting a company's price versus service offerings in mature industrial markets. Figure 2 shows the alignment of the behavioral microsegments with respect to the relative price and relative service variables.

At the time of the study, Signode's management was under severe pressure from its national accounts to reduce prices. The buying behavior microsegmentation and the concurrent analysis of the judgmentally generated sales elasticities, how-

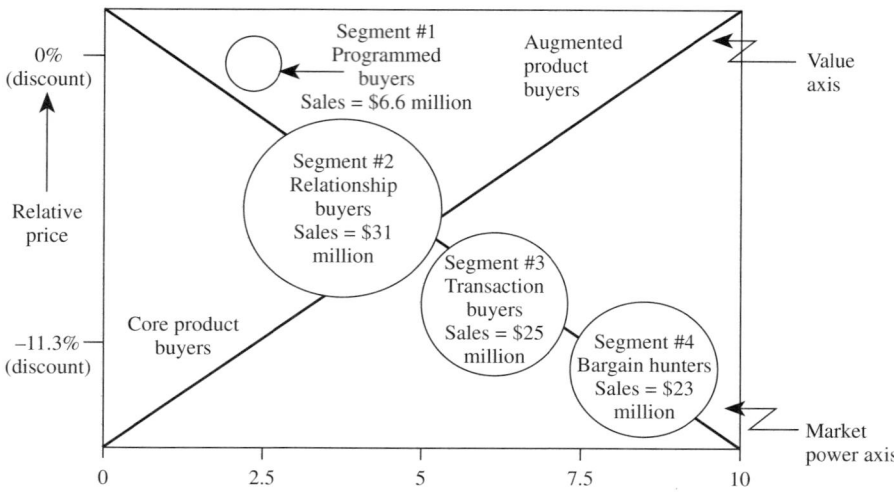

FIGURE 2
Segment profile

ever, suggested that price and service changes would not be equally effective in all four segments. When sales variations were estimated for each microsegment, Signode found that breaking even on a 7 percent price change would require total sales volume to change by about 20 percent. Similar estimates for changes in service showed that breaking even on a one "unit" service change would require total sales volume to change by 8 percent. Although these numbers should be viewed with caution because the data were gathered from salespeople in a judgmental exercise, the estimates generally suggest that:

- Decreasing price is unprofitable for Signode because the estimated increase in sales is far below the required 20 percent for every microsegment in Table 2 (see row 5 in Table 2).
- Increasing price is profitable in the programmed buyer microsegment—sales decrease of only 15.5 percent compared with a break-even of 20 percent. It exceeds the break-even number for all other microsegments (see row 6 in Table 2).
- Decreasing service is profitable in the programmed buyer microsegment because the estimated sales drop is 5.1 percent. It exceeds the break-even of 8 percent in all other segments (see row 7 in Table 2).
- Increasing service is barely profitable in the bargain-hunter microsegment sales increase of 7.3 percent compared with a break-even of 8 percent. It is far below this number for all other microsegments (see row 8 in Table 2).

It is interesting to note that programmed buyers were willing to pay a relatively higher price without demanding additional service. In a sense, these accounts were willing to pay a premium to maintain their rule-of-thumb purchase allocations to have the flexibility of buying a high proportion (46 percent) of non-Signode products. Compared with other national accounts, programmed buyers were not as sensitive to price or service changes. Instead, to increase market share in these accounts, Signode's salespeople would need to influence their customers' underlying decision-making processes. Thus, Signode management directed the sales reps handling these accounts to focus their efforts on changing the buying decision-making strategies that limited Signode's share.

The bargain hunters posed a more immediate problem. These accounts were critical to the company because of their very large size—11 accounts contributed nearly 25 percent of national account revenues. These accounts, however, also demanded the lowest prices and the highest levels of service. Worse still, bargain hunters had the highest propensity to switch to competitive suppliers. Thus, managing the bargain hunters would require considerable tact and skill to keep them from switching while countering their discount requests. To protect company margins, Signode management decided that price cutting should be used only as a defense against price cuts of competitors. Instead, Signode offered additional service in hope that this would improve sales volume beyond the estimated 8 percent break-even point. In addition, the NAMs were directed to take an active role in handling these 11 accounts.

The relationship buyers and transaction buyers of the middle microsegments had somewhat similar profiles, except that the former were less likely to press

Signode for price and service concessions. Though the relationship- and transaction-oriented customers did not pose an immediate problem, both microsegments were sensitive to price and service trade-offs. Because Signode management was concerned about the potential migration of these accounts to the bargain hunter microsegment, a separate service management group was created to explore ways of adding service value for this group of customers.

Conclusion

We believe the practice of industrial market segmentation has lagged behind the theoretical developments in the field. Although the concept of buying behavior–based segmentation was advanced two decades ago, virtually no application of the concept has been published to date. Of course, there are many important and valid reasons for this applications gap. Yet, as our research here demonstrates, considerable value can be gained by attempting to move toward buying behavior–based segmentation. A knowledge of segment behavior helped the Signode Company redirect marketing resources for profit gain.

Following the analyses at Signode, we believe that even a simple framework, such as the two-dimensional plot of price versus cost-to-serve in Figure 1, is capable of unearthing a rich subsegment of behaviors in industrial accounts. As can be seen from the figure, the diagonal equates the price to cost-to-serve for the seller. We hypothesize that the seller's profit would be roughly equal for accounts located on this axis—when customers want services (augmented product), they are willing to pay higher prices. The cross diagonal, however, represents an axis of product differentiation. Clearly, customers who demand and get high levels of services for low prices must have alternatives, just as those customers who pay high prices must find the product attractive even though they do not receive the full battery of services. Obviously, the seller's profits are likely to be higher in the northwest and lower in the southeast quadrant compared with the diagonal axis. Understandably, the segment descriptor variables and dimensions are likely to vary across applications; nevertheless, a few variables could provide rich diagnostics for management actions.

In addition, our research demonstrates a practical and implementable method for constructing buyer behavior–based segments from readily available data sources. The key, of course, is to identify variables that adequately capture the variance in buying behavior and that address a specific management problem. By selecting the segment descriptor variables to address management's concerns with price and service—two variables under Signode's control—the buying behavior microsegmentation was designed to provide useful guidance for Signode's account management policies.

We acknowledge that one application does not necessarily prove the rule, but at least it provides a benchmark for future studies. Our purpose here was to demonstrate the usefulness of our segmentation framework for managers.

CHAPTER 32
Once More: How Do You Improve Customer Service?

The authors offer a broadened concept of customer service to include core product characteristics such as performance and quality, in addition to support factors like delivery and repair. They argue that critical elements of customer service vary by phase of the order cycle (preorder, order-to-shipment, and postshipment) as well as by the type of business (flow versus project business). They conclude by providing guidelines on how to implement a customer service program in a cross-functional context.

The business community is presently flooded with articles, books, speeches, and workshops stressing the importance of keeping close to the customer as a means of achieving competitive advantage and market leadership. However, while customer service has become a dominant topic, experts repeatedly find that good service is more the exception than the rule. Is it an issue of attitudes, culture, and the lack of a "service obsession" at companies, or are other factors more relevant? What is customer service in a given situation, and how can managers diagnose internal activities that help or hinder external responsiveness?

One reason customer service workshops have not brought marked improvement is that they usually preach to the converted. Most managers realize that service is important, but often core organizational issues impede good service. Emphasizing "service culture" may momentarily galvanize the firm, but it ultimately will not help if management preaches service without addressing organizational factors.

A decade ago, *In Search of Excellence* (Peters & Waterman 1982) focused attention on the components of service, providing examples of companies and individuals that exhibited qualities of superior customer service. However, in many ways service now occupies the status of "motivation" as defined by Frederic

---

This article was prepared by Frank V. Cespedes.
Reprinted from *Business Horizons* 35, no. 2, March–April 1992, Indiana University Graduate School of Business.

Herzberg (1968) in his classic article, "One More Time: How Do You Motivate Employees?" Anxious for quick answers to a complex issue, many managers enthusiastically greet new quick fixes. Friendliness, responsiveness, and zeal become the fundamental attitudes associated with good service. Unfortunately, these attitudes are analogous to what Herzberg called hygiene factors—necessary but insufficient catalysts for obtaining the behavior and results desired.

What Is Customer Service?

Many companies define customer service as product delivery and repair. As a result, they tend to focus on delivery time, order fill rates, and billing-error minimization to determine good or bad service.

However, other factors also help determine the value of a purchase to a prospective buyer. The most obvious of these involves the product's price/performance characteristics, quality ratings as determined by the industry or respected outside rating agencies (Underwriters Laboratories in electrical equipment or *Consumer Reports* for many consumer durables), and the specifications of the product relative to the purchaser's particular requirements. But various prepurchase and postpurchase elements that add value to the item also must be seen as components of customer service. These nonproduct components include any information and ordering costs, inbound logistical costs, operation and maintenance costs, and, in many cases, disposal or trade-up costs.

Having understood that customer service should encompass broader product and nonproduct components of customer satisfaction, two ideas must be kept in mind when evaluating service efforts and goals.

First we examine value-in-use. This idea is that "the product is what the product does" (Corey 1983); the product is the total package of benefits customers receive when they buy it. This includes the functional utility of the goods; any technical assistance in applications development provided before the sale; training or repair services provided after the sale; assurances of timely delivery through the supplier's distribution network; and any brand-name or reputation benefits that help the buyer promote its product or services to customers. Benefits might also include the buyer–seller relationship itself. Particularly in industrial markets, interpersonal relationships developed among people in buying and selling organizations have intangible but real value. Conversely, the package of benefits in some situations might not include personal contact because it is more efficient to reorder or conduct other aspects of the transaction via automated, on-line systems.

The point here is that customer service should include more than product-related functions or employee friendliness. Service must encompass an entire range of possibilities by which a vendor can contribute to the customer's business operations. The ultimate economic justification for providing such services is to shift purchase criteria away from sheer price toward other value elements that help differentiate a vendor in its market.

For example, consider marketing developments in the health care industry. Since 1983, when the government changed its reimbursement procedures for Medicare patients, hospitals have encountered intense cost pressures, making them more sensitive to price. One result of this new price sensitivity was the formation of more (and more powerful) group purchasing organizations (GPOs) in which a number of hospitals made volume purchases in return for substantial price discounts. Because of the volume they represented, these GPOs were typically designated major or national accounts by most suppliers. However, as one sales director noted, "Our national account program was really a national discount program, eroding our margins and often our contacts with end users at hospitals."

Nevertheless, in recent years some suppliers have altered their marketing strategies to redefine customer service and deliver a value to GPOs extending beyond price. For example, some drug companies now bundle products—offering discounts on sole-source items when purchased along with multisource products. Such services benefit hospitals by substantially lowering transaction costs in frequently purchased product categories. These services also enable vendors to better position their off-patent products. Additionally, bundling enables vendors to negotiate multi-year contracts with GPOs across product lines, further reducing costs while increasing the vendors' "share of mind" at end-user levels. Other suppliers have developed inventory management programs which have grown in perceived value as more hospitals adopt just-in-time inventory policies. Still others give client hospitals data on the total costs of patient care in a given diagnostic category and explain how product acquisition, training, and disposal procedures affect these costs. Furthermore, some suppliers now recognize their field sales force is part of the product they sell. End-user preference for many health care products is built on the individual sales representatives' detailing and follow-up activities, as well as on the technical strength of the vendor's product.

For example, Becton Dickinson negotiates corporate contracts with GPOs, but focuses its field sales efforts on the hospital "bench people"—lab technicians and doctors who actually use the products, care intensely about the quality and reliability of what they use, and complain loudly to hospital administrators if they do not get the product they want. As one Becton Dickinson manager notes, "In recent years, I've seen a number of instances where purchasing wanted to standardize acquisition around a less-expensive product, but the labs complained and insisted on our product." The common theme in these examples is that the suppliers provided and promoted services affecting the value-in-use of their products.

In consumer packaged goods, the concentration of retail trade, availability of point-of-sale data, and direct product profit information make such services crucial in maintaining retailers' shelf space. In many industrial-product markets, strategic partnerships—and a company's position as preferred supplier—often depend on the vendor's ability to manage customer service in the broader sense. More generally, the evolving nature of production makes it increasingly difficult to distinguish between manufacturing and service businesses. As Gershuny and Miles (1983) have shown, the standard criteria used to distinguish between these two sectors are so problematic that calculating economic activity on this basis requires making many subjective or arbitrary choices. Moreover, firms' product offerings to customers now typically consist of tightly interrelated mixtures of tangible goods, real-time services, and ongoing information exchange (Norman and Ramirez, 1989), which in turn require an integrated view of production, marketing, and customer service.

One advantage of approaching service from this broader perspective is that it enables the company to develop value-based pricing policies reflecting the costs and benefits of the total product offering. In addition, this often enables the firm to differentiate a product or service traditionally viewed as a commodity. For example, L. E. Muran sells stationery, pencils, and other office supplies in a market made even more competitive in recent years by the entry of high-volume, low-priced office superstores. In response to this heightened competition, Muran and individual corporate clients jointly produce a catalog of regularly ordered items and then distribute the catalog to each of the client's secretaries. The secretaries check off what they need, and the Muran sales representative picks up the orders daily. Muran then delivers individual orders to each customer location within 48 hours and also delivers regular usage-by-department reports to customer headquarters. The director of worldwide purchasing at one such customer site notes: "We used to buy stationery, allocate space for a stockroom, and maintain four people and a supervisor to run it. Now we order all these supplies from Muran and call it our 'stockless stationery' policy."

Having understood the broader concepts of service, we recognize that customer service means different things to different customers. Many companies struggle with customer service because they treat service as a constant quality between buyer and seller—a discrete set of characteristics buyers are looking for—rather than as a variable across market settings. As a result, companies often spend much time and money developing customer satisfaction indices that serve only as exercises in pseudospecificity and mock quantification. These indices typically average different characteristics into a single set of factors that at best satisfy few individual customer purchasing and service criteria. Additionally, when efforts are made to avoid averaging, these indices become mere checklists of characteristics that are oblivious to many trade-offs between services offered and relative costs.

Critical elements of service typically vary by type of customer, as well as different phases of the order cycle and account relationship with an individual customer. For example, applications engineering or other technical services may loom particularly important for companies having few R&D or in-house service organizations. However, they are valued less by large companies with extensive R&D and in-house service personnel, where there is higher value placed on ordering ease and prompt delivery.

Several years ago, General Electric conducted an extensive audit of service factors in its industrial business units. Its findings are applicable to companies that similarly sell a variety of products in diverse markets. GE managers distinguished between what they called flow goods (standardized products usually ordered from stock and sold through distributors) and project business (semicustomized orders with substantial engineering content, typically involving various products assembled as a system by different GE business units). GE's results indicated marked

FIGURE 1

Critical elements of customer service: typically vary by phase of the order cycle and by type of business

	Preorder	Order-to-Shipment	Postshipment
Flow Business	• Accurate, timely quotations • Knowledgeable sales force	• On-time, complete, accurate shipments • Accurate, timely order tracking/status reports	• Timely, responsive complaint resolution • Quality, timely in-warranty and out-of-warranty service
Project Business	• Accessibility and responsiveness of personnel • Quality, timely application support • Product availability information	• Flexibility to react to customer changes to the order • Experienced project managers • Ownership/authority for multiproduct department orders	• Competent installation support • Accurate, timely billing • Effective spare parts support

SOURCE: "General Electric: Customer Service," Harvard Business School case no. 588-059.

differences in the service expectations of customers across the flow goods and project business order cycles (see Figure 1).

Accurate and timely quotations, and field sales representatives knowledgeable in current pricing and delivery terms and conditions, are particularly important when generating flow business orders. These products are often sold by distributors as part of a larger package of goods (most not manufactured by GE); thus, accurate and timely quotations are key to both end-users and intermediaries. In contrast, project business lead times and selling cycles are longer. Technical staffs' accessibility and responsiveness to customers' often ill-defined and evolving specifications are primary service components.

In the order-to-shipment phase, punctual and accurate shipments, as well as shipment tracking reports, are valued flow business services. Whereas the products are often relatively inexpensive and standardized, their availability is usually crucial to throughput at the customer's manufacturing plant. Consequently, reliable order shipments and tracking are especially valued. Efficient, standardized, and predictable procedures are important elements of distribution for these products. However, in project businesses, more uncertainty inherently lies in the order-to-shipment phases. Thus, project business customers value a supplier's flexibility and willingness to react to changes in the order. Standardized terms and conditions can actually become impediments to the execution of required services for these businesses. Due to this fluctuating environment, experienced project or account managers are the most important and valued promoters of customer relations.

Quick response to complaints and warranty claims are key components of after-sale service for flow goods customers. In fact, providing out-of-warranty service for these products often serves to distinguish one vendor from the next in flow product categories. As a result, a close working relationship with distributors is often an important prerequisite for good service in this type of business. However, project business postshipment service involves a different range of supplier–customer activities, including installation, training, and the maintenance of spare parts for these semicustomized system sales.

These differences must be recognized and managed, for they influence the relevant time period used in measuring service levels and costs as well as the amount and type of services inherent in achieving customer satisfaction in each type of business. For example, FileNet, a leader in the growing image processing industry, places service emphasis on applications development, system configuration, customer training, installation, and postsale maintenance and repair. It offers two distinct service contracts that provide different maintenance and repair responsiveness, based upon the customer's relative sensitivity to downtime and the availability of in-house programmers able to assist in applications development.

Many other companies are simultaneously involved in flow and project transactions with customers. Rather than use homogeneous measures of customer satisfaction, these companies must develop a portfolio of service strategies. In addition, these differences influence the degree and type of internal coordination required to provide effective service.

Customer Service and Internal Marketing

Customer service, as defined here, is inherently a multifunctional activity. This can be illustrated by considering the typical order cycle in most industrial businesses (see Figure 2). Within the selling company, as the order moves from the customer's

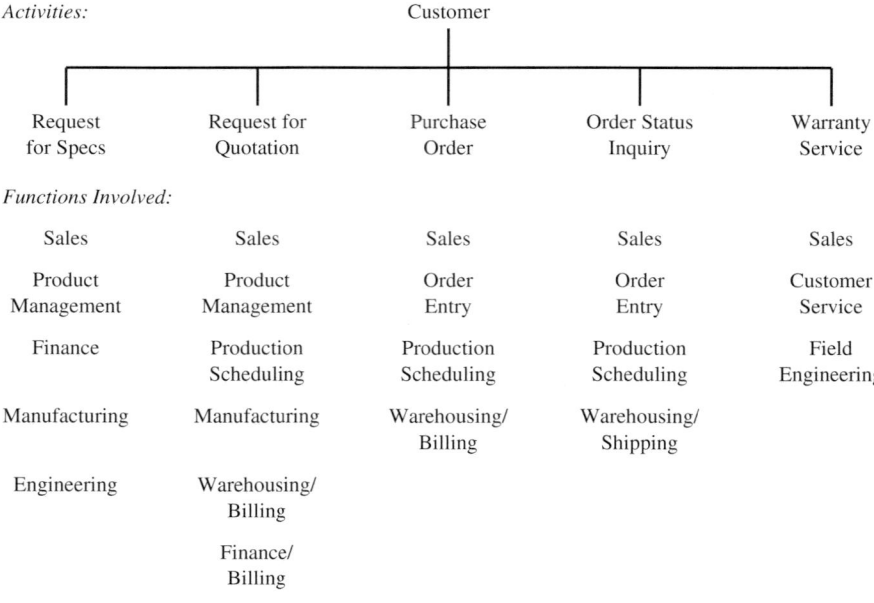

FIGURE 2

Customer service involves most functions in an organization

request for specifications and quotation to the purchase order and after-sale warranty service, the progress of an order typically involves numerous functions.

Two aspects of the order cycle are particularly noteworthy. First, field sales is typically involved in nearly all activities. Therefore, any service initiatives not recognizing field sales' role (and the implications of service changes for sales training, compensation, or performance evaluation) are likely to be short-lived or actively subverted by the company's primary customer-contact personnel. Second, though typically held responsible by the customer for any order processing problems, salespeople (or other front-line customer-contact personnel) usually have little direct authority or expertise concerning the many other areas involved in filling the order. Those most directly responsible for managing customer encounters face a series of internal marketing tasks to develop and maintain appropriate service levels. They must often persuade personnel in other functions, each of which has its own particular standard operating procedures, to help customize the order and attendant services for a particular customer.

One reason service problems persist at many companies, despite management's repeated chanting of the "keep close to the customer" mantra, is that those within the firm active in selling, marketing, manufacturing, and financing typically have different incentives and thus view the customer differently. For example, sales personnel often welcome, and argue for, product line extensions or customized solutions in an effort to cover different market segments and accounts with a variety of product configurations. However, what may seem only a minor modification to a salesperson often entails a major operating change in manufacturing, service, or product management. Product line extensions may require new processes, employee training, different production equipment or service expertise, and disrupting established (and seemingly proven) operating procedures in all areas.

Similarly, marketers usually do not need to be convinced about the importance of service; they often argue for substantial investments in same-day service, flexible terms and conditions, or no-fault/money-back service guarantees, all in an effort to "increase our share"—a typically salient goal of the marketing function in most firms. Meanwhile, finance people often evaluate a proposed investment of product design, capacity, and service in terms of quantifiable IRR, NPV, or short-term cash flow implications. And accounting affects the inputs of these calculations by allocating service overheads in ways that both sales and marketing (as well as individual product managers) often consider wrong or arbitrary (Anderson 1981; Barwise et al. 1989).

In each instance, the sources of potential conflict are clear. People in different areas of a firm typically have distinctive skills, resources, and short-term objectives. But external responsiveness requires internal coordination across these areas, placing customer service squarely in the middle of the crossfire between necessary cooperation and potential conflict. Moreover, this situation is further complicated because product-related elements receive the bulk of managerial time and attention, even though nonproduct elements of customer value are often crucial. Consider, for example, the following areas fundamental to completing tasks in any complex and time-constrained organization.

Management Responsibility. In many companies, the product elements of customer service have focused management responsibility in the form of product or brand managers, but the various nonproduct elements do not. If good service can be likened to a performance (Shostack 1985), consider that in moviemaking there is one person who is responsible for continuity—making sure the scenery in one take is congruent with the scenery for next day's filming of the same scene.

However, in most business organizations, the different activities required to develop and process an order typically have no one function or manager responsible for overseeing all the required activities. The closest thing to an order overseer in many companies is the formal customer-service staff, which usually plays a reactive role to customer complaints and has little actual authority to expedite or alter the flow of an order. The result, as one manager describes it, is the "Florence Nightingale brigade: customer-service staff trying to patch up and soothe a customer wounded in an internal war neither of them started."

In the computer industry, nearly every major vendor has recently stressed some form of systems integration provision to accommodate large clients and influential data processing buyers, who have increasing needs for smooth network communications around the world. But many of these same vendors sell and service this offering through hardware, software, and peripherals organizations that are heritages of a previous stage of competition. The result is often uncoordinated service, for separate components arrive at different times and in different quantities. Another result, as one irate computer customer recently commented, is a "pass-the-buck situation, where several product divisions are involved but nobody has control over the complete system."

Plans and Budgets. Management responsibility usually means developing formal business strategies and plans, complete with budgets and financial tracking of activities. Again, companies often have management controls in place for product-related elements, but nonproduct elements are managed on a more ad hoc basis, often without any planning process, financial controls, or method for making inevitable trade-offs among different customer groups. Indeed, the emphasis during the past decade on service culture has motivated many companies to consciously eschew plans and budgets for service activities. The tone of reasoning is: "We want our service people to be action-oriented zealots for the customer and not fettered by plans or budgets that put them in a short-term or bean-counting frame of mind."

But often the unintended result of these good intentions is that service initiatives tend to be driven by the most pressing needs at the time. The ongoing procedures of the firm do not reflect the continuing importance of service, resulting in a reactive, intermittent approach, characterized by periodic programs aimed at service excellence. In many instances, these programs actually damage the firm's service reputation: They raise customer expectations but do not deliver consistent levels of service quality, and the customer tends to focus on lapses from the promised threshold.

These programs can also damage management morale. At one large U.S. corporation, for example, the CEO had grown concerned about customer complaints, so a well-respected senior vice president was appointed to head a task force to fix service problems. However, the vice president soon found that

> customer service [is] not a new issue [here]. The Corporate Marketing files quickly coughed up numerous internal and outside reports on service dating back over 20 years. In fact, customer service has traditionally been the most studied, least engaged issue in [this] company, and even the recent top management attention [is] perceived by middle managers as just another fad.

How does the firm prevent service from becoming a fad? Because service components are typically dispersed throughout a company, planning and budgeting become important means for service realization. These seemingly bureaucratic and action-inhibiting mechanisms also make factors perceived as intangible (and therefore unimportant) more tangible to busy and resource-constrained functional areas.

Measurements and Evaluations. One reason service programs are difficult to sustain is that few managerial measures actually relate customer support expenses to profit-and-loss criteria. The cost accounting systems in most companies are set up to allocate costs by product volumes; they in turn drive the salient financial and performance measurements at the firm (Kaplan 1984). Marketing managers can track activities by brand; marketing research staff can measure product sales by region, channel, or competitor; and manufacturing managers can track variances by product category. However, even as customer service receives more rhetorical emphasis, customer data are usually absent, leaving most managers with little knowledge of account profitability. Moreover, as one observer notes, when companies do track customer support expenses, rather than product-related profitability, they usually measure it in terms of sales volume or gross margin with no allocation of SG&A costs or assets (Myer 1989).

Further, this responsibility is often vested in the sales organization staff. Their compensation is generally tied to revenue goals, giving them every incentive to endorse any service program, regardless of its profitability impact. This situation has been exacerbated in recent years as sales-automation efforts, implemented at great cost and with great attention to user-friendly technology, have tended to freeze in place obsolete accounting systems that generate little actionable data about customer-maintenance costs. The frequent result is what one manager calls "the service boomerang: based on our accounting measures, we charge toward providing certain 'value-added' services to customers; but then charge right back when the actual ROA is disappointing."

Culture-building activities may be resoundingly successful, and everyone may well realize that service is important. However, in the absence of specific measures (and the presence of continuing pressures to make quarterly earnings), service expenditures become discretionary—allocated when budgets allow and dropped when cost pressures increase. This is analogous to the typical cycle of advertising expenditures in many firms: The level of spending is actually the result rather than the cause of historical sales volumes. That is, firms tend to cut advertising spending when sales are flat or when cost pressures are most intense. But one can argue that at this juncture, advertising and service are most important.

Accountability. This is the scarcest resource in any complex organization, its dearth being particularly apparent in the area of customer service. In an effort to manage the multifunctional efforts required to provide good service, companies increasingly define service as the responsibility of all employees. But in any large organization, everybody's business tends in practice to be nobody's business. This unintentionally exacerbates the lack-of-accountability syndrome plaguing service efforts at many firms. At GE, for example, one of the first steps taken by corporate managers charged with improving service was simply to locate the people in each GE business unit primarily responsible for customer service. "We were surprised by what we didn't find," noted one executive. "There was no one person responsible for these matters in the businesses, and so no champion to raise awareness of the issues involved."

This situation can be debilitating in terms of actual service provided because, as another manager describes it, "Customer service is inherently an optics issue; it has to remain visible and a central part of someone's agenda. Otherwise, things don't happen, or they consistently happen after the fact." In most Western companies, de facto responsibility for service resides with the sales and marketing function: When dissatisfied, customers typically complain to the field salesperson, and different marketing managers are involved at nearly all points of the typical order cycle described in Figure 2. Indeed, most definitions of marketing in our business school textbooks cite customer service as central to marketing activities. When pressed for a description of their fundamental role in the organization, most marketing practitioners also cite customer service, or its fraternal twin, serving customer needs.

By contrast, responsibility for service is a less-specialized function in most Japanese firms, where engineering and manufacturing managers pursue more continuous contact with customers after the product is bought. When a Japanese company learns a customer is dissatisfied with the design of its product, it is not uncommon for the company to dispatch the design engineer, who then determines if the problem is significant enough to warrant redesign. By contrast, customer complaints in Western companies are handled much farther downstream in sales and marketing, and then brought upstream through manufacturing and product development.

Many factors account for these differences, including the now well-known differences in employment policies, manufacturing policies, and historical emphases on quality control (Aoki 1988; Mahon and Dyck 1982). But despite statements to the contrary by some Western observers, service is not everybody's business in the Japanese firm. The engineer (or manufacturing manager or product-development leader) is often held personally accountable for customer reaction. When customer service is an issue, the task facing Japanese managers is the same as for their Western counterparts: to expand and maintain their colleagues' understanding of customer needs, priorities, and preferences. It is the worst of both worlds, however, to remove product design and delivery from production and field sales—where palpable knowledge of customers and products ultimately resides—and then turn around and declare that customer satisfaction is everybody's business.

Managing Customer Retention

Given the issues outlined here, it should not be surprising that good service seems more often the exception than the rule. Improving service can start by helping management be clear about both the product and nonproduct components of customer value in the business, and then by paying attention to structures and systems that aid in the coordination of service components dispersed in the company.

In many businesses, realigning internal activities to provide better service is ultimately justified by competitive pressures. However, in the short run, this holds true only if management understands the economic value of customer retention and the factors that build and extend the buyer–seller relationship.

This has always been a salient feature of high-fixed-cost service businesses, where up-front costs of property, plant, and equipment can only be justified if the customer "stays with us" beyond the initial transaction. As a result, banks, credit card companies, airlines, and other such businesses were among the first to stress customer retention and relationship marketing programs of different sorts (Reichheld and Sasser 1990).

This imperative is also increasingly true of traditional manufacturing businesses. In these firms, new production technologies and big buyers' needs mean that suppliers must sell a system of tangible goods and intangible services, the cost of which requires customer retention over time to be economically justified for the supplier.

The marketing dynamics of customer retention at cable television companies can help illustrate issues relevant to a variety of other product-market environments. Given the cost structure of a cable franchise, the variable costs of serving an installed customer are minimal. Ideally, such customers become "annuities," as they remain part of the subscriber base and generate monthly fee revenues. In this respect, the economic value of a cable customer is the discounted value of a series of payments associated with that customer over a relevant time period. Conversely, customers become profitable to a cable franchise only after they have stayed on the system for some time. For example, one franchise found that a basic cable customer had to remain a subscriber for at least six months before the franchise recouped its costs of installing and servicing that customer. Including the amortized costs of plant construction, a basic customer had to be a subscriber for 11 months before it returned a profit for the firm. As a result, "churn" (people disconnecting the cable service for some reason) has always been a prime concern, and cable-TV firms have developed a variety of marketing programs aimed at understanding churn and minimizing its potentially devastating effects on supplier profitability.

One method of understanding customer retention is to distinguish between two types of disconnects in the customer base: those related to the product (customers dissatisfied with the franchise's particular program offerings or the quality of its transmission service) and those related to the nonproduct elements of customer value (customers dissatisfied with any of the particular transaction services or customer-support aspects of the cable franchise). In addition, there are two time periods during which the cable company can influence the behavior of customers: before and after installation of the product (see Figure 3).

FIGURE 3
Marketing dynamics of customer retention

	Preinstallation	Postinstallation
Product	I	II
• Quality	Account selection • Market segmentation • Customer education	Product policy • Product improvements • New products
• Price-performance	Sales management • Training and deployment • Sales incentives	Communications policy • Follow-up • Complaint resolution
Nonproduct	III	IV
• Transaction services	Order-entry procedures Inventory management	Account management • Team selling efforts • Sales/service coordination • Solutions orientation

• Customer support	Delivery performance
	
	Technical assistance/
	applications development
		• Responsiveness:
		   —Customer database
		   —Internal information
		     systems

In quadrant I of Figure 3, account selection and sales management policies are the primary marketing tools for managing customer retention. The goals are to attract customers whose product preferences are in line with the supplier's current product offerings and to establish sales systems that encourage a focus on such customers. In the cable business, for example, management can take some relatively simple actions at this juncture of the buyer–seller relationship: implementing marketing programs that educate potential customers about specific program offerings so that their expectations are in line with reality, or structuring sales incentives that discourage salespeople from selling pay-TV packages that customers later cancel.

In quadrant II, the supplier's evolving product policy becomes the primary marketing lever for customer retention. Many cable franchises have found that programming changes in line with the changing demographics of a franchise area are key to preserving the subscriber base. Similarly, postinstallation follow-up by the sales representative (or service personnel) can help lower the amount of churn during the first months after installation—an especially critical period for customer retention. Sending direct mail, using other vehicles aimed at explaining the purchased service in greater detail, or providing a phone number to call if there are any problems would also be helpful.

In quadrant III, the company's preinstallation transaction services and customer-support procedures should be the focus of marketing attention. Here, easy and reliable order-entry procedures, delivery performance, technical assistance (installation), and administrative procedures (contract terms and conditions) are the basis for customer satisfaction. In the cable business, joint work between the cable vendor and apartment-complex managers (or other important intermediaries between the supplier and end user) has often been the key to better performance along these dimensions of customer value. In other businesses, cooperation between the supplier and distributors, strategic alliances, and development of sophisticated information systems to expedite transactions are often critical at this juncture.

Finally, in quadrant IV, the selling company's long-term value as a supplier is the key determinant of customer retention. For marketing, this generally means paying attention to policies and programs aimed at continually improving the supplier's ability in two areas: (1) gathering and exchanging information useful in developing solutions to the customer's evolving requirements, and (2) maintaining the internal systems that are a prerequisite for external responsiveness. In the cable business, this means developing and maintaining a customer database that helps the supplier track usage patterns and continually develop appropriate programming packages and promotions. In many other businesses, however, the task is more complex, requiring changes in both the supplier's sales programs and internal costing systems. In selling, many changes in the business environment are forcing vendors to adopt account-management programs that seek to improve coordination across geographically and organizationally dispersed selling units (Cespedes et al. 1989).

But the absence of customer-level data in most companies' cost accounting systems is a major impediment. Here, activity-based cost analyses are useful because many important service costs vary, not with short-term changes in output (as assumed by most established systems), but with changes over a period of years in the design, mix, and range of a company's products, customers, and channels of distribution (Cooper 1988). This is an accounting issue that directly affects the account manager's ability to gauge the value of customer retention and so argue internally for required resources. And it indirectly affects top management's willingness and ability to be profitably oriented toward responsiveness and service.

The framework in Figure 3 is only a first look at customer retention dynamics, but it can help operationalize what "keeping close to customers" entails. By breaking down this worthy but ephemeral advice into manageable segments of the buyer–seller relationship, marketing, sales, and service managers can focus their limited time, attention, and resources on areas and actions likely to provide the best returns on customer investments.

Conclusion

How do you improve customer service? In large part, you improve it by managing the paradox inherent in a market orientation: External responsiveness (the ultimate test of marketing efforts in any firm) requires internal coordination and more attention to the organizational issues outlined in this article. These are structures and systems that customers rarely see or explicitly care about, but they ultimately elicit customer praise or customer complaints.

References

Anderson, Paul F. "Marketing Investment Analysis," in J. Sheth, ed., *Research in Marketing,* vol. 4 (Greenwich, Conn.: JAI Press, 1981), pp. 1–37.

Aoki, Masahiko. *Information, Incentives, and Bargaining in the Japanese Economy* (Cambridge: Cambridge University Press, 1988).

Barwise, Patrick, Paul R. Marsh, and Robin Wensley. "Must Finance and Strategy Clash?" *Harvard Business Review,* September–October 1989, pp. 85–90.

Cespedes, Frank V., Stephen X. Doyle, and Robert J. Freedman. "Teamwork for Today's Selling," *Harvard Business Review,* March–April 1989, pp. 44–59.

Cooper, Robin. "The Rise of Activity-Based Costing," parts 1–4, *Journal of Cost Management,* Summer 1988, pp. 45–54; Fall 1988, pp. 41–48; Winter 1989, pp. 34–46; Spring 1989, pp. 38–49.

Corey, E. Raymond. *Industrial Marketing: Cases and Concepts* (Englewood Cliffs, N.J.: Prentice Hall, 1983).

Gershuny, Jonathan, and Ian Miles. *The New Service Economy: The Transformation of Employment in Industrial Societies* (London: Frances Pinter, 1983).

Herzberg, Frederic. "One More Time: How Do You Motivate Employees?" *Harvard Business Review,* January–February 1968, pp. 35–50.

Kaplan, Robert S. "The Evolution of Management Accounting," *Accounting Review,* July 1984, pp. 404–7.

Mahon, William A., and Richard E. Dyck. "Japanese Quality Systems from a Marketing Viewpoint," *Industrial Management & Data Systems,* September–October 1982, pp. 8–14.

Myer, Randy. "Suppliers—Manage Your Customers," *Harvard Business Review,* November–December 1989, pp. 160–68.

Norman, Richard, and Rafael Ramirez. "A Theory of the Offering: Toward a Neo-Industrial Business Strategy," in Charles C. Snow, ed., *Strategy, Organization Design, and Human Resource Management* (Greenwich, Conn.: JAI Press, 1989), pp. 111–28.

Peters, Thomas J., and Robert H. Waterman. *In Search of Excellence* (New York: Harper & Row, 1982).

Reichheld, Frederick, and W. Earl Sasser, Jr. "Zero Defections: Quality Comes to Services," *Harvard Business Review,* September–October 1990, pp. 105–13.

Shostack, G. Lynn. "Planning the Service Encounter," in John A. Czepiel, Michael R. Soloman, and Carol F. Suprenant, eds., *The Service Encounter* (Lexington, Mass.: D.C. Heath, 1985), pp. 243–53.

CHAPTER 33
Automation to Boost Sales and Marketing

Forward-looking companies, by installing marketing and sales productivity (MSP) systems, are seeking increases of up to 30 percent in sales and sales force productivity. MSP systems automate routine tasks and gather and interpret data that was either scattered or uncollected before. They not only upgrade sales and marketing efficiency but also improve the timeliness and quality of executives' decision making. Viewed as a corporate strategic investment, MSP systems allow companies to exploit the synergies possible from linkages with other parts of the organization.

In the rush to automate, the marketing and sales function is the next frontier. As everybody knows, over the past decade information systems have been making great inroads in engineering and manufacturing. Automation has cut direct labor to a small fraction of production costs—an average of 8 to 12 percent in manufacturing companies. Therefore, wringing yet more cost reductions from production labor is increasingly difficult. In such technically advanced industries as computers, semiconductors, airframes, metalworking, and autos, incremental investments are now garnering diminishing returns.

On the other hand, investments in marketing and sales automation systems hold tremendous potential for productivity improvements. Marketing and sales costs average 15 to 35 percent of total corporate costs (not just production costs), so a focus on marketing and sales provides a welcome lever for boosting productivity. Moreover, the importance of marketing and sales services is growing. According to the U.S. trade representative and the National Association of Accountants, manufacturers' service activities account for 75 to 85 percent of all value added.[1] This means

---

This article was prepared by Rowland T. Moriarty and Gordon S. Swartz.
Copyright © 1988 by the President and Fellows of Harvard College.
Reprinted with permission from *Harvard Business Review* 67, no. 1, January–February 1989, pp. 100–108.

[1]James Brian Quinn, Jordan J. Baruch, and Penny Cushman Paquette, "Technology in Services," *Scientific American,* December 1987, p. 50.

that the price a product can command is less a reflection of raw materials and labor than of marketing-related services like selecting appropriate product features, determining the product mix, and ensuring product availability and delivery.

In cases we have reviewed, sales increases arising from advanced marketing and sales information technology have ranged from 10 percent to more than 30 percent, and investment returns have often exceeded 100 percent. These returns may sound like the proverbial free lunch, but they are real.

Because of the complexity of their marketing organizations, large companies are good prospects for what we call marketing and sales productivity (MSP) systems. Tangles of national account management, direct sales, telemarketing, direct mail, literature fulfillment, advertising, customer service, dealers, and distributors all offer opportunities for efficiency improvements. But even small companies that adopt MSP systems can expect impressive results.

Marketing automation investments by a $7 billion electronics manufacturer and an $8 million custom printing company each produced a first-year return of more than 100 percent. The electronics concern installed a sales support system for more than 500 salespeople. Sales rose 33 percent, sales force productivity rose 31 percent, and sales force attrition dropped 40 percent. The reduced attrition alone produced savings in recruiting and training costs that paid for the company's $2.5 million investment in less than 12 months. At the custom printer, an $80,000 investment in a minicomputer and telemarketing software returned a 25 percent increase in sales and attained payback in less than six months.

Increasing marketing productivity even a small amount can have a great impact on the bottom line. MSP systems have a double punch because they can reduce fixed costs and variable costs. Lower fixed costs mean lower break-even points. So a given percentage increase in sales produces a correspondingly larger increase in operating profits, as the chart on the next page shows. Meanwhile, lower variable costs mean that every sale contributes more to the bottom line. Indeed, because lower variable costs make the slope of the new contribution curve steeper, the absolute size of the financial advantage continues to grow as sales rise.

Despite the proven worth of this technology, few companies have automated any part of their marketing and sales functions. Even fewer appear to understand the significant strategic benefits that can accrue from marketing and sales automation; most early adopters have automated as a matter of faith rather than as part of a strategy for gaining competitive advantage. A better approach begins with an understanding of what marketing and sales automation can do, how it works, and how it can be implemented.

What the Systems Do

Distinct from general office automation systems, MSP networks are of course specific to marketing and sales. They support more intense product or service differentiation, improved customer service, reduced operating costs, and more streamlined operations. Here are some MSP systems and the tasks for which they are customarily used:

An MSP System Creates a Financial Advantage

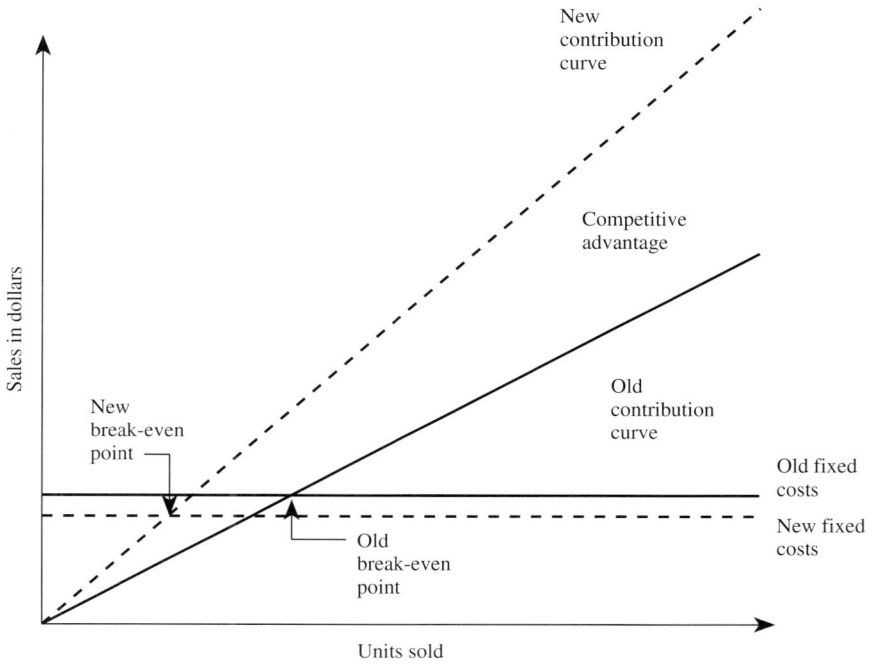

Salesperson productivity tools—Planning and reporting of sales calls, reporting of expenses, entering orders, checking inventory and order status, managing distributors, tracking leads, and managing accounts.

Direct mail and fulfillment—Merging, cleaning, and maintaining mailing lists; subsetting lists (or markets); tracking and forwarding leads; customizing letters, envelopes, and labels; generating "picking lists" for literature packages; and managing literature inventory.

Telemarketing—Merging, cleaning, and maintaining calling lists; subsetting lists (or markets); tracking and forwarding leads; ranking prospects; and prompting scripts (sales, customer service, and support).

Sales and marketing management—Providing automated sales management reports (sales forecasts, sales activity, forecasts versus actuals, and so on); designing and managing sales territories; and analyzing marketing and sales programs by such criteria as market, territory, product, customer type, price, and channel.

MSP systems can automate the work of a single salesperson, a single marketing activity like direct mail, or a company's entire marketing and sales operation. MSP systems also cut across every type of information technology from single-user PCs to networks of PCs, minicomputers, and mainframes serving thousands of users.

A simple system meets the needs of one fast-growing $25 million producer of data communications equipment that sells its products through 65 distributors. To cut down on paperwork in handling sales leads, the company adopted a PC-based MSP system. (See the flow chart showing its operation.) Compare this with the networks supporting the more than 5,000 direct salespeople of a major office automation vendor. (See the "map" showing its operation.) This vendor's system combines direct selling, distributor relationships, telemarketing, and direct mail to generate, qualify, rank-order, distribute, and track sales leads; fill prospects' requests for product and price information; update customer and prospect files; provide sales and technical product support by telephone; and automate order entry and sales reporting.

While the scales of these two networks are obviously vastly different, both of them collect, organize, and update information about every lead generated, every sales task performed, and every customer or prospect closed or terminated. What is less obvious, but no less important, is the basis both systems provide for improving marketing and sales executives' decision making.

Most MSP databases contain essential information on customers, prospects, products, marketing programs, and marketing channels. Some systems supplement the essentials with industry data (growth rates, entries, exits, and regulatory trends) and data on competitors (products, pricing, sales trends, and market shares). For most businesses, the information incorporates a subtle but important shift from other databases. Rather than focusing on products (What was the cost to produce each

A Simple MSP Flow Chart for Handling Leads

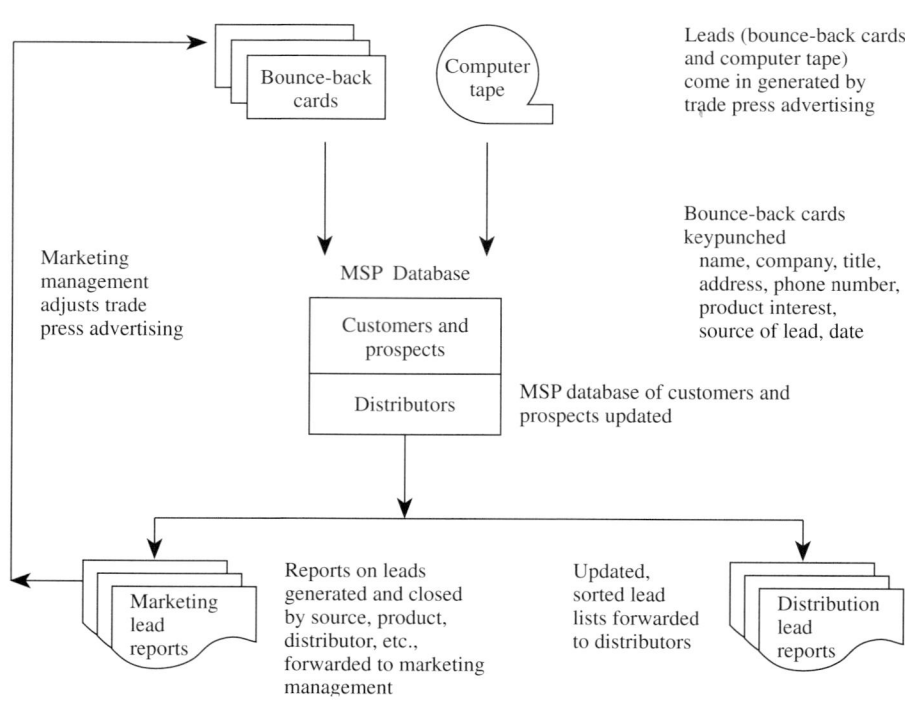

unit? How many units were made, sold, and shipped?), the MSP database is customer driven.

Whenever marketing or sales activities are performed, the database captures information that answers questions about customers and their needs. Who were the prospects? What were their interests? How were these interests generated? Which sales or marketing personnel performed which tasks? When were the tasks performed? Which follow-up tasks are required and when? Did any sales result? Gradually the database becomes a rich source of marketing and sales information, enabling management to track marketing activities and measure the results of marketing programs.

How They Aid Productivity

MSP systems improve productivity in two ways. First, automation of selling and direct marketing support tasks boosts the efficiency of the sales and marketing staff. Second, automating the collection and analysis of marketing information improves the timeliness and quality of marketing and sales executives' decision making.

These networks make direct sales and direct marketing more efficient by automating highly repetitive support tasks, like answering requests for product literature and writing letters, and by reducing the time salespeople spend on nonselling tasks, like scheduling sales calls, compiling sales reports, generating proposals and bids, and entering orders. In 1985, Xerox installed an internally developed MSP system in its southern region. Xerox credits the system with a 10 to 20 percent gain in sales force productivity and with trimming $3 million off the company's 1987 marketing support and overhead budget. By automating sales administration and support tasks, Xerox has given its salespeople more time to sell.[2]

MSP systems for direct marketing also hone the efficiency of customer contacts. For example, a system for the telemarketing function can schedule and dial calls based on the prospect's priority, prompt the telemarketer with a sales script, and automatically update customer files. At Aratex Services, a $500 million uniform supply company based in Encino, California, telemarketers using the company's old manual system each made 35 to 40 calls per day and about one sale per month. Working with an automated system, each telemarketer now makes 50 or 60 calls daily and lands three or four sales per month.[3]

Automated networks also elevate the impact of each sales communication. Access to the central database gives salespeople and direct marketers information to improve the quality of the contact, whether it is by mail, by telephone, or in person. A large financial services concern uses a telemarketing system to handle account inquiries. While responding to a customer's request or query, the telemarketer is prompted by the system to update the customer's profile information and to cross-sell other financial products.

---

[2]Thayer C. Taylor, "Xerox: Who Says You Can't Be Big and Fast?" *Sales & Marketing Management,* November 1987, p. 63.

[3]Kate Bertrand, "Converting Leads with Computerized Telemarketing," *Business Marketing,* May 1988, p. 58.

At a division of Vanity Fair that makes women's and children's apparel, salespeople use laptop PCs to access the corporate database for up-to-date inventory and order status information on 2,000 stockkeeping units. This step has trimmed the company's order cycle from more than two weeks to just three days. It also has made ordering more accurate, resulting in greater customer satisfaction, reduced order cancellations, and a 10 percent increase in sales.

In companies with many channels, MSP systems upgrade efficiency by using the central database to track and coordinate all marketing activity. Without this coordination, independent marketing groups often unwittingly pursue conflicting goals. At one multibillion-dollar office automation company, a direct salesperson had just nailed down a big order by giving a key account the maximum price discount. Before the deal was signed, however, the telemarketing group reached this customer and undercut the salesperson's price by 10 percent. Aside from the damage to its reputation, this vendor lost much of its expected margin on the sale.

This company is now installing an MSP system that will collect and organize information on all marketing programs and activities, including: (1) all customer contacts, whether by mail, phone, direct salesperson, or national account manager; (2) the status of all sales efforts; (3) the origins of all leads; (4) all leads that are being qualified internally and by whom, and all leads that have been forwarded to distributors; (5) all customers who decided to buy; (6) what and when they purchased; and (7) any incentives or promotions that helped close the deal. Coordination of information through this system is expected to prevent further embarrassments.

A Management Tool

Creation of an MSP database is an investment in astute management. The database chronicles every one of a company's marketing and sales activities, from advertising that generates leads to direct mail and telephone qualification of the leads to closing the first sale—all the way through the life of each account. It enables marketing and sales management to relate marketing actions with marketplace results.

At the $25 million data communications company whose lead-handling system we diagrammed, marketing managers use this system to evaluate media placements on the basis of sales closed. Before this procedure was in place, the company had no way to link information on leads to sales and evaluated media placements solely on the number of leads generated, not closed.

MSP systems also reduce marketing inertia because they streamline the implementation of marketing programs. For example, after designing an in-house system to organize and manage its customer/prospect files, one $2.5 million industrial manufacturer let 70 manufacturer's agents go and replaced them with in-house direct mail and telemarketing functions. The results? The company raised its accounts by 50 percent and cut marketing costs from 18 percent of sales to 13 percent.

Systems for sales force automation also drive the rapid implementation of less drastic changes in marketing programs. By using telecommunications software and laptop PCs, Du Pont's Remington Arms division has trimmed the time requirement for a national rollout of pricing and promotional programs from two weeks to less than two days.

As marketing managers become accustomed to these systems, they find new uses for them, like analyzing and modeling the buying behavior of prospects and customers. The database at Excelan, a $39 million marketer of circuit boards and software in San Jose, California, was essential in identifying a shift in customers' buying behavior from a very technical product focus to an office automation orientation. This discovery has influenced the marketing and sales managers' decisions about hiring and training employees as well as about selecting and developing new target markets.

Account histories also improve management's ability to devise and implement account management policies based on profits. By linking orders, services delivered, and prices paid with the actual costs of lead generation, preselling, closing, distribution, and postsale support, MSP systems furnish the tools for analyzing and adjusting the marketing mix. Grede Foundries, a Milwaukee producer of castings for original equipment manufacturers, has used the MSP system to develop a "perceived quality index" that yields a more complete and more accurate measure of customers' reactions than simply tracking returned goods. The system also provides pricing support. By tracking quoted prices and final selling prices, the system gives management a better idea of the price that will win a particular job.[4]

Economies of Scale?

Small businesses may gain an initial competitive edge from MSP systems because they often can adopt these systems much faster than their big counterparts. With fewer levels of management, small companies are faster on their feet in making decisions. They also tend to have simpler marketing organizations, usually relying on a single-method, single-channel selling system like a small direct sales force.

Large companies face two imposing barriers. First, they generally have both multiple layers of administration and cross-functional decision-making groups. When analyzing, evaluating, and adopting MSP systems, large companies draw in not only marketing and sales but also the accounting, finance, and MIS functions. Second—as a glance at the flow chart and map shows—their marketing organizations customarily rely on complex arrangements of communications methods and selling channels. Accordingly, their MSP systems require great sophistication and customization.

In large companies, marketing and sales automation is a high-stakes decision needing the support of many parties. In a major telecommunications company, the evaluation and selection of an MSP system called for: (1) initial screening presentations by three software vendors; (2) detailed presentations to 15 senior executives; (3) a visit by eight managers to a company with an operating MSP system; and (4) at least nine internal follow-up meetings, including presentations to the vice presidents of marketing and sales, the general managers of the ten operating companies, the directors of the MIS and MIS-procurement groups, several financial analysts, and several senior salespeople. More than 40 people had a hand in the decision. All this work occurred in a period of more than nine months after the corporate decision to automate marketing and sales.

But the story doesn't end there. Once the company had selected a $200,000 off-the-shelf system, it spent 18 months and $250,000 more installing and customizing the software. During the next two years, functional additions to the system and training of the end users added more than $1 million to the cost.

---

[4]Louis A. Wallis, *Computers and the Sales Effort* (New York: Conference Board, 1986).

Moreover, automated networks coordinate and direct sales resources—including salespeople, distributors and agents, direct mailers, telemarketers, and manufacturers' representatives—toward the highest priority prospects and customers. Hewlett-Packard's (H-P's) Qualified Lead Tracking System (QUILTS) electronically transmits inquiries to a telemarketing center, which qualifies and ranks them and electronically returns them to H-P headquarters. The company has trimmed the turnaround time for leads from as much as 14 weeks to as little as 48 hours. Hot leads are handled even faster; they are telephoned to the field sales force from the telemarketing center.[5] Similarly, field salespeople in Chevron Chemical's fertilizer division in San Francisco use laptop PCs to access rank-ordered prospect lists in the company's mainframe. At any time, the salespeople have access to leads that are only 24 hours old. Before automation, new prospect lists were printed at headquarters and mailed to the field reps, which took one to two weeks.

Finally, the MSP database is a management tool for making better use of marketing resources—that is, ensuring that they are employed to further corporate goals rather than the goals of individual marketing or sales groups. While this may sound like something management does without effort, our research shows that optimizing marketing resources is much more easily said than done. In several companies we've looked at, salespeople routinely discard hundreds or even thousands of sales leads, making little or no effort to evaluate or review them. In essence, they are dissipating the resources that generated these leads—budgets for advertising, trade shows, public relations, and other communications media.

In their defense, the salespeople complain that pursuing raw leads is a waste of time. And they are generally right. In one of these companies, salespeople who followed up the raw leads averaged only one or two sales per month, while those who followed their instincts averaged more than three. The cost of pursuing the raw leads was at least one lost sale per salesperson per month. To the salespeople, ignoring the leads was common sense. On the other hand, the advertising group, which was evaluated on the number of leads generated, was increasing its budgets to generate more and more leads. One company has solved this problem by implementing an MSP system that will use telemarketing to qualify leads before sending them to the salespeople. The system will also close the loop, allowing management to evaluate both the company's advertising placements and its sales efforts on the basis of their contributions to revenues and earnings.

Efficiencies gained through task automation and improved marketing management are interdependent and reinforcing. Task automation drives the collection of more complete customer and marketplace information, and more informed decision making targets marketing and sales activities where they are most effective. In this way, marketers get a bigger payoff from low-cost, low-impact selling methods, like direct mail and catalogs, as databases customize the timing and content of mass-marketing campaigns. At the same time, high-cost, high-impact selling methods,

---

[5]Karen Blue, "Closing the Loop: Hewlett-Packard's New Lead Management System," *Business Marketing,* October 1987, p. 74.

Map of an Integrated MSP System for a Major Office Automation Company

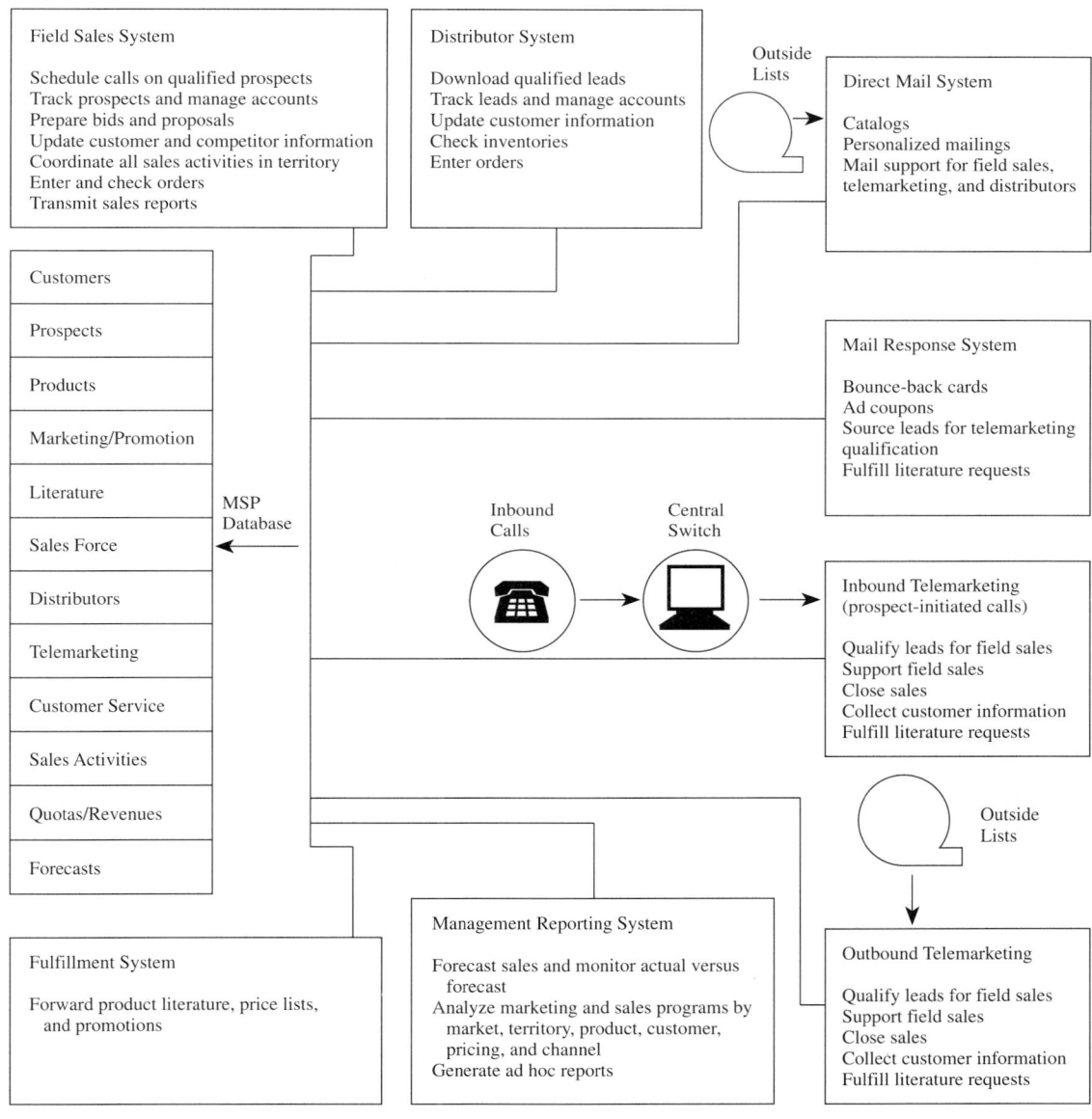

like personal selling and national account management, become more efficient as MSP systems perform routine sales support tasks, reduce nonselling time, and synchronize the use of these resources.

When you combine low-cost, low-impact methods with high-cost, high-impact approaches to gain just the right amount of stimulus at just the right time, you can obtain hefty impact at minimum cost. Hewlett-Packard, for one, has taken advantage of this synergy and has discovered the savings made possible by orchestrating direct mail, telemarketing, and personal selling.

How to Get from Here to There

The cases we have reviewed show that companies implementing MSP systems encounter many of the same barriers they would confront adopting any new technology.[6] From our observation, the process can be streamlined by following six guiding principles.

1. *Clarify the scale of the project as well as potential additions.* An audit of the marketing and sales tasks will yield these categories: those that must be automated now, those that will or may be automated later, and those that will not be automated. This simple exercise will identify marketing and sales activities that must be coordinated and focus the automation effort on getting measurable results without sacrificing flexibility.

It is important to view the project not from the perspective of the marketing groups but from a corporate perspective. With a corporate view, the company can build a "battleship"—a system that takes advantage of information-sharing and task-coordination synergies. Without this strategic perspective, independent marketing groups are more likely to invest in a number of incompatible and wasteful "rowboats." And even a rowboat can cause problems. At a big high-tech manufacturer, eight salespeople had their own PC-based sales force automation system installed. By raising issues of compatibility, data entry, and "file structure definitions," they delayed the start-up of a companywide, 300-salesperson MSP system for more than a year.

2. *Concentrate on tasks that can add value for the customer.* As in other corporate activities, marketers can get competitive advantage in two ways: by lowering costs and by enhancing the differentiation of the product or service offering. At the custom printer we referred to, streamlined job-costing and order-entry processes enable customers to price and place orders with one phone call. The real-time order-entry and order-tracking capabilities of the Vanity Fair unit's salespeople have upgraded its customer service. In both cases, customers benefit from better service, and sellers benefit from lower costs.

Other companies add value by using automation to improve the exchange of information during sales calls. The 22 salespeople in Hercules's Fragrance and Food Ingredient Group use their laptop PCs and a computer program called Flavor Briefs to consult with prospects on applications. Otherwise, Hercules salespeople would be unable to provide such detailed advice on their product line's many applications. The system saves the customer and the salesperson time and also furnishes a valuable service.

---

[6]Dorothy Leonard-Barton and William A. Kraus, "Implementing New Technology," *Harvard Business Review,* November–December 1985, p. 102.

3. *In the budget process, account for hidden costs and intangible benefits.* Budgeting for an MSP system entails overcoming three principal obstacles: high perceived financial risk, poorly understood benefits, and biased capital budgeting systems.

First, automating marketing and sales is costly. A typical hardware and software outlay per salesperson ranges from $4,000 to $7,000—so automating the tasks of 100 field salespeople can cost between $400,000 and $700,000. In addition, if the MSP system must communicate with other corporate information systems, it is likely to require the development of specialized minicomputer, mainframe, or communications networking software.

Department-level telemarketing or direct mail systems range in price from $30,000 to more than $100,000. Sales or marketing management software may up the price another $30,000 to $100,000. Of course, the cost of tying all these pieces together depends on how many pieces there are, where they are located, and how they communicate. It would not be unusual for a company with 500 salespeople as well as telemarketing, fulfillment, and direct mail operations to spend between $3 million and $5 million on integrated MSP hardware and software.

But the budget process must anticipate and account for hidden costs too. In a number of cases we studied, in-house information was so scattered and communications equipment so incompatible that simply preparing a customer list required a major effort. Other hidden costs include system customization, expert consulting, and end user training. Depending on the circumstances, these services can double or even triple the overall cost.

Because malfunctioning of an automated marketing system can threaten a business's revenue stream, it's advisable to budget for the cost of two systems—automated and manual—until the network has proved out. Naturally, all these expenses ratchet up the perceived financial risk of MSP automation.

On the other side of the equation, estimating the full financial benefit of an MSP system is extremely difficult. Tangible productivity gains, like increases in selling time and cost reductions on telephone campaigns, can be gauged fairly accurately. But intangible productivity gains, like better marketing decision making, more responsive customer service, and deeper understanding of customers, are much more difficult to track.

Still, it would be a mistake to ignore them, especially since capital budgeting processes are often biased against intangible productivity investments. Furthermore, few marketing managers and even fewer sales managers know much about their companies' capital budgeting processes—especially when huge investments in information technology are at stake. Senior executives have to take care that the process remains flexible enough to give MSP automation a reasonable evaluation.

An MSP system is a strategic investment for the whole corporation. But unlike other assets that are consumed over time, the more it is used, the more valuable it becomes. So it should be viewed as a long-term asset, not as the expense of a functional group. And, needless to say, senior management must match the scale of the company's investment to the scale of the project. Otherwise, fragmented marketing budgets will foster fragmented automation. The result, as noted above, may be many MSP rowboats with little or no coordination or compatibility.

4. *Make any tests realistic.* Because launching a full-scale network can be tremendously risky, most companies hedge their bets first by piloting automation on small portions of their marketing operations. A single function, like telemarketing or personal selling, is usually the test site. If this pilot is successful, the company adds more functions.

This ramp-up strategy, however, has serious drawbacks. It permits no insight into the complexity of coordinating multiple marketing and sales activities. Though single-function solutions may yield gratifying returns, evidence of their true worth may also stay hidden until they are combined into a system that demonstrates synergy. Consequently, estimates of financial returns based on single-function pilots may be negatively biased.

Finally, critical performance limitations may remain hidden unless the complexity and scale of the test parallel the system's actual use. One big manufacturer's telemarketing pilot ran flawlessly, providing the telemarketers with a steady stream of calls and instant access to customer profiles and scripts. But eventual integration of telemarketing with other MSP networks seriously degraded the performance of the overall system. Every time the telemarketers asked for new information during a call, they were confronted by blank computer screens for more than 40 seconds. As the business manager put it, "That's a long time to talk about baseball."

A company with a multichannel, multimethod marketing system is better off with a pilot plan that automates a multifunctional subset of the marketing organization. In this type of pilot, an integrated system, encompassing all marketing and sales functions, is installed for a single division, region, product line, or customer group. This experience is likely to be more realistic than the single-function approach.

5. *Pinpoint the roles and responsibilities of those selecting, designing, and operating the system.* Even standard MSP systems, though they may be touted as off-the-shelf products, require extensive customization. This necessity complicates the selection or design process in a number of ways.

- The process requires expertise in technology (computers, data communications, and software) as well as in marketing and sales.
- Naturally, a company's existing MIS systems are likely to constrain the choice (or development) of an MSP system.
- Marketing professionals and MIS professionals rarely speak a common language, and they often approach marketing automation projects with different perspectives. While marketing thinks about functionality (e.g., Will the system help perform marketing and sales tasks?), MIS people often focus on technical considerations (e.g., Will the system interact with other corporate information systems? Who is responsible for ensuring the integrity of corporate databases?).

It's senior management's job to make sure that the MIS and marketing professionals talk to each other and work together. It's not easy. An MIS group may automate its conception of marketing and sales only to discover later that the automated system does not actually work. Everybody knows of cases in which the MIS department loads the sales force down with reams of report forms to complete and return to headquarters. Of course, much of the requested information is irrelevant from the salesperson's standpoint, and the report forms end up in the same round file as the old lead cards.

During the long, complex process of designing and implementing a major MSP system, responsibilities sometimes become diffuse and project accountability gets blurred. In one case we know of, poorly defined responsibilities for MIS and marketing have caused big headaches. Bickering over cost allocations and database controls has made the company's $1 million MSP system useless. The MIS group will not allow marketing to access the corporation's databases. But the marketing group's computer budget is too low to keep the marketing database up-to-date. (Not surprisingly, headquarters viewed the entire MSP development process as a marketing expense instead of a corporate investment.)

6. *Modify the technology and the organization to support the system.* As in every instance in which management implements new technology, it must pay close attention to the attitudes of people in the organization. In successful MSP implementations that we have seen, both the organization and the MSP system have gone through an interactive process of change—altering the technology to fit the marketing and sales environment, then altering the environment to fit the technology.

To be useful, for example, the MSP database obviously must contain accurate, up-to-date information. Because obtaining this information requires salespeople to use the system and to support the information collection process, they have to become adept at using the new technology. Problems can result, however, if the end-users lack computer skills or if they are uninterested in using the system.

Training can overcome skill problems (if enough money is budgeted and enough time set aside), but lack of interest is harder to deal with. Experience suggests that the best way to sell the sales staff on the network is to demonstrate that it can give every user something back. That is, by helping salespeople or telemarketers work more productively, MSP systems can boost not only the company's sales but also *their* sales and *their* compensation.

For many companies, postponement of automation of the marketing function may seem to be a good way of skirting a difficult decision, but this do-nothing posture condemns the organization to being a marketing laggard. It may also be a costly mistake. Early adopters of MSP systems have gained superior competitive advantage. Compared with their "manual" competitors, they perform selling tasks with greater economy and impact. They know their customers better and can tailor their sales communications to supply just the right amount of sales stimulus at just the right time. Overall, they craft and control their marketing programs more intelligently. In the long run, the competitive barriers they establish may change the nature of marketing in their industries.

In view of this impressive record, some marketers about to embark on automation may embrace unrealistically high expectations. But MSP systems cannot work miracles. They will not offset a poorly conceived or poorly executed marketing strategy. They will not compensate for an inferior sales force, and they will not sell inferior products. Complex MSP systems are difficult to implement, and the associated returns, like any other lasting accomplishment, have to be earned.

Chapter 34

Reorienting Channels of Distribution

Traditionally, distribution channels have been viewed as vertical marketing systems where responsibility was transferred from one layer to the next, like passing a baton in a relay race. Distribution channels in the future are likely to look more like horizontal alliances of suppliers and intermediaries, all with the aim of efficiently and effectively addressing customers' real needs. These transitions, driven by an underlying change in the economics of production and distribution, are leading to distinct trends in the distribution industry. In this chapter, we focus on three primary trends: hybrid channels, multiple channels, and shorter channels. After exploring the challenges managers face as they reorient their distribution, we highlight the effects of such changes on supplier–intermediary relationships.

Distribution channels of the future are likely to look distinctly different from their counterparts of the 1970s and even the 1980s. These transitions are being driven by changes currently sweeping the customer and competitive environment—proliferation of information technology, polarization of customers (consolidation on the one hand, and fragmentation on the other), manufacturing systems that can mass-customize, and quick shipment distribution logistics. As a result, many distribution questions that were once considered central are no longer so regarded. For example, the dilemma of direct versus indirect channels does not seem to be much of a puzzle to managers anymore. Instead, new priorities of a strategic nature are being raised as practitioners and researchers attempt to cope with the dynamics of a changing business environment.[1] Can channels serve to create competitive entry barriers? Can they enhance product differentiation? Can they enable customer intimacy? Can

---

V. Kasturi Rangan prepared this note.
Copyright © 1994 by the President and Fellows of Harvard College.
Harvard Business School note 594-118.

[1] V. Kasturi Rangan, Raymond E. Corey, and Frank Cespedes, "Transaction Cost Theory: Inferences from Field Research on Downstream Vertical Integration," *Organization Science* 4, no. 3 (August 1993), pp. 454–77.

FIGURE 1

Channel options: traditional view

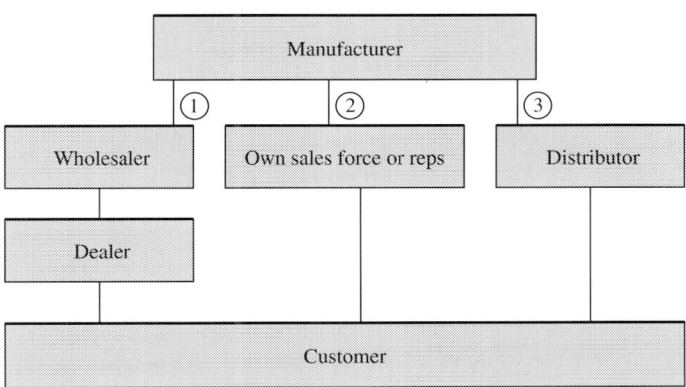

they cushion suppliers' exposure to uncertainty? Such questions seem to be of far more interest to managers building distribution channels today. It is useful to ask why this definitive shift in channel management emphasis is appearing. Fundamentally, it boils down to the nature of the distribution work. Environmental forces have changed its underlying economics and characteristics.

Traditionally, distribution channels have been viewed as vertical marketing systems where responsibility was transferred from one layer to the next, like passing the baton in a relay race. Thus in Figure 1, under option 1, the manufacturer would send a truckload shipment to the wholesaler, who then broke bulk and sold to the dealer, who in turn stocked the product and persuaded the end user to buy. If the product needed after-sales service, the end user took it back to the dealer, who also maintained and repaired the product in the field. Even though the product may have passed through several layers in the distribution system, the end user relied solely on the dealer for the fulfillment of a complete bundle of channel functions, such as information, inventory, and repair.[2] Others in the vertical system played a supporting, backstage role. The wholesaler, in this case, broke bulk and provided a wide assortment of products for the dealer's selection, but the customer fulfilled all its requirements—assortment, lot sizes, information, and repair—from the dealer and dealer alone. Manufacturers could access customers through alternative channel systems as well—directly (or through reps) or through one-step intermediaries such as distributors. These are shown as options 2 and 3 in Figure 1. But no matter which system was used, the end user fulfilled its channel function requirements mainly from one source. It was uneconomical to unbundle and allocate functional responsibility over several channel members.

A small customer that bought through the dealer channel, in Figure 1, might have actually preferred to get technical information directly from the supplier, but because of the small lot size of its purchases, it would have to seek product information as part of distribution support from the local dealer. It would be simply too

---

[2]See Louis W. Stern and Adel I. El-Ansary, *Marketing Channels,* 4th ed. (Englewood Cliffs, N.J.: Prentice Hall, 1992), pp. 1–41.

costly for the supplier to contact and provide this information directly, and costlier still for the end user to await product shipment from the factory. Even though the customer was not fully served in regard to the information function, overall it was still better to get the channel bundle from the dealer than not at all. By the same token, a large customer that bought directly from the sales force might have preferred not to pay cash and not to carry inventory, but that was the price of doing business directly with the supplier.

A small customer that bought through the dealer channel, in Figure 1, might have actually preferred to get technical information directly from the supplier, but because of the small lot size of its purchase, it would have to seek product information as part of distribution support from the local dealer. It would be simply too costly for the supplier to contact and provide this information directly, and costlier still for the end user to await product shipment from the factory. Even though the customer was not fully served with regard to the information function, overall it was still better to get the channel bundle from the dealer than not at all. By the same token, a large customer that bought directly from the sales force might have preferred not to pay cash and not to carry inventory, but that was the price of doing business directly with the supplier.

All this has changed with the information and technology revolution of the 1990s. Direct marketing and database marketing and its variations have enabled sellers to contact far-flung and often small customers for only a fraction of the cost of a direct sales call. Local distributors may no longer be the only cost-efficient alternative. Computer-aided quick shipment systems enable transporters to schedule and dispatch less-than-truckload orders with more or less the same speed and efficiency as full loads. The customer, therefore, does not suffer any inconvenience or product unavailability. Flexible manufacturing systems allow suppliers to produce small lots at only a marginally higher cost than scale-efficient large orders.[3] In short, the economics of manufacturing and distribution have changed. Traditional thinking suggests that transactions involving complex exchange of information and intensive investments would be best served direct, and those characterized by simple exchange and less-intensive investments would be best served indirect.[4] In the current environment, this conventional wisdom is under attack. The roles of the intermediary, the distributor, and the dealer are all evolving. New forms of direct channels are emerging, and indirect channels are getting shorter (fewer intermediary layers). The role of the distributor buffer between the manufacturer and the retail dealer is under threat in several business environments.[5] Firms will face unique opportunities and challenges as they adapt their channels to this changing environment.

However, what is sauce for the goose is sauce for the gander: Distributors have experienced the benefits of information technology too. In many cases, because of

---

[3] See "How to Bolster the Bottom Line," *Fortune*, Autumn 1993.

[4] Oliver E. Williamson, *The Economic Institutions of Capitalism* (New York: Free Press, 1985), pp. 85–102.

[5] As examples are too numerous to cite, we provide two illustrations: "GE Component Motors Operation," Harvard Business School case no. 587-157; and "Distributors' Links to Producers Grow More Fragile," *The Wall Street Journal*, October 28, 1992, sect. B, p. 2.

the assortment and variety of products they handle, they have been better able to exploit the economies of scope from information systems. Moreover, distributors in general have steadily updated their technical investments in channel systems. Chemical distributors, for instance, have innovated product safety systems, pharmaceutical distributors have innovated information systems, computer distributors have innovated customer support systems, and so on.[6] In all, distinctions between manufacturer and distribution channel capabilities in taking the product to market have blurred. This has put the customers and end users in the driver's seat. They have a wider channel choice and, in many cases, the option of unbundling channel functions and sourcing them from the most efficient member. It is not unusual for a customer, therefore, to seek information directly from the supplier as a prelude to negotiations on product specifications, quality, quantity, and prices, while retaining local distributors for effecting delivery and providing after-sales service.

To put it simply, the concept of channel strategy has been turned on its head. Instead of viewing the problem as one of choosing which intermediaries can reach the customer, the new approach is how customers' channel requirements can be efficiently addressed. It starts with the customer, not with the supplier, and the focus of the analysis is on channel functions, not intermediaries.[7] Channel selection is not an afterthought, but rather an integral part of the strategy of being customer oriented. In the following section we discuss three broad channel trends and their implications for channel managers.

Hybrid Channels

This is a channel structure in which the supplier and its channel partners share in the execution of the channel functions. That is, the supplier may perform some of the channel functions (e.g., sales negotiation and order generation), while its channel partners may perform the rest (e.g., physical distribution and order fulfillment). Other channel members might specialize in yet more channel functions (e.g., after-sales service). In essence, in the channel system the parts work together, with certain members specializing in certain channel functions. See Figure 2. The key distinction between this hybrid channel and the conventional channel is the horizontal nature of the task allocation. The customer's total needs are satisfied by a team of channel partners (including the supplier), each specializing in a few tasks. In the conventional model, the hand-offs were vertical, with each member performing a full bundle of channel functions required of the next level.

As suggested earlier, the trend toward functional specialization (and therefore horizontal channels) is being driven by customers' desires to receive products and services in the most cost- and time-efficient manner. This means that channel

---

[6]See "Who's Winning the Information Revolution," *Fortune,* November 30, 1992.

[7]Louis W. Stern and Frederick D. Sturdivant, "Customer Driven Distribution Systems," *Harvard Business Review,* July–August 1987. Also see V. Kasturi Rangan, M. Menezes, and Ernie P. Maier, "Channel Selection for New Industrial Products: A Framework, Method and Application," *Journal of Marketing* 56 (July 1992), pp. 69–82.

FIGURE 2

Hybrid channel

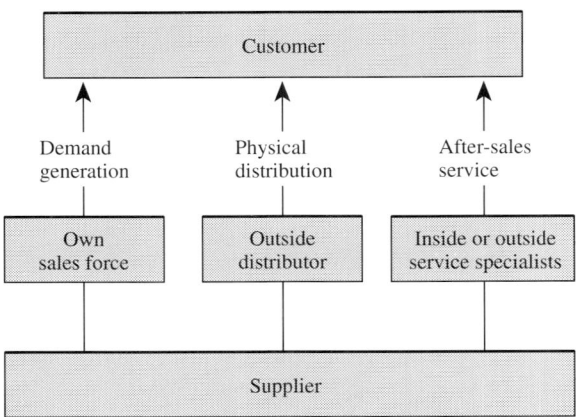

functions may have to be unbundled and offered separately, especially for the larger customers.

The health care industry abounds with hybrid examples. Becton Dickinson's Vacutainer Systems division negotiates directly with all large hospital buying groups for its blood collection needles, syringes, and accessories.[8] When the deal is finalized, Becton Dickinson signs a Z-contract with the concerned hospital buying group and provides a list of its authorized distributors. Becton Dickinson's distributors effect the physical distribution—ordering, storing, and supplying products to the appropriate hospital at the desired time in desired lots. They are able to do this at an efficient cost given the plethora of other products they already supply the hospitals. Thus, order entry and fulfillment costs are only incremental. At the same time, the cost-containment environment in the health care industry makes it attractive for buyers to negotiate directly on high-volume/high-value orders, and the competitive environment makes that necessary for suppliers as well. It gives them better control on sales, profits, and market shares.

The computer industry is also rich in hybrid channels. Witness the rise of value-added resellers (VARs) that tailor solutions for customers in niche markets—banking, retailing, CAD-CAM, and so on. While VARs provide the specific knowledge regarding the software, they have to work closely with computer vendors for hardware equipment and system configuration. Customers need hardware and software integrated in order to address their problems, but the channel expertise is such that it takes two members to put together the perfect solution.

But with new channel forms come new management challenges; the biggest one has do with channel compensation. Because the channel member interfacing with the customer is no longer responsible for performing the full bundle of channel functions, it cannot be expected to receive a margin or commission structure similar to the traditional system. Ideally, channel members under the new system should be compensated only for the functions they perform. But herein lies a catch. All members in the hybrid system must adequately perform their functional responsibilities

---

[8]"Becton Dickinson & Co.: Vacutainer Systems Division," Harvard Business School case no. 592-037.

FIGURE 3

The free-riding problem

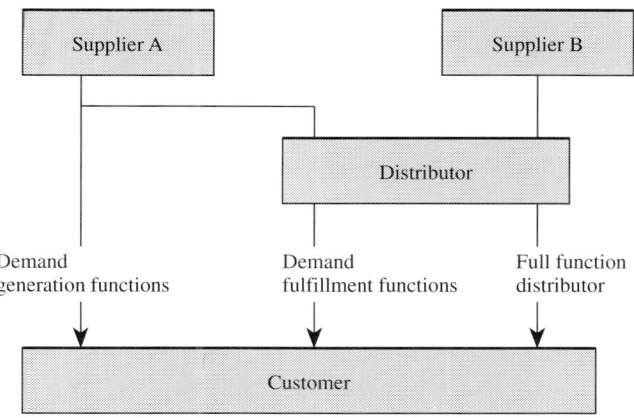

for the final sale to occur. If one member fails to do so, the whole team suffers unless some other team member covers up for the errant colleague. Such a system is open to abuses of free-riding, and the most valuable player often ends up bearing the cost most. The reward, however, is shared by all. At least, in the traditional vertical system, poor performance correlated directly with lower sales and therefore lower margins. In the new system, poor performers could earn rewards for someone else's efforts.

Managing a hybrid system requires strong leadership. The team captain has to ensure an equitable allocation of work as well as reward. This is easier said than done because in reality an outside channel member will often be part of other competing channel systems as well. For instance, in Figure 3, a distributor who is a functional specialist in Supplier A's hybrid channel system and a full-function player in Supplier B's vertical channel system could end up overallocating its resources to Supplier B. That is because its commissions are likely to be higher from B because of the full-function support it provides. Moreover, without this distributor's efforts sales of Product B and the associated commissions would be at risk. Whereas for Product A, other channel members may be pulling in the demand anyway. A heavy-handed carrot-and-stick approach is hardly likely to motivate loyalty or dedicated effort, and higher distribution margins would only violate the economic premise of hybrid channels.

Hybrid channels are very costly to monitor and administer, and seem to work only in environments that can afford high channel margins. That way distributors can be motivated by the carrot of commissions. In low-margin industries, hybrid channels seem to work only for market leaders. Such suppliers usually bring their market clout to lead their hybrid channel partners. Free-riding, for instance, is punishable by loss of orders, and in this case by a big amount. A leading industrial supply company, for example, calls on many of its accounts directly, but routes all its orders through its distribution network—a classic hybrid system. A free-riding distributor, however, will not get the company's nod. The company has multiple distributors in the same market area. Those who don't play by the rules do not get mentioned warmly by the sales force when writing the order. Theoretically, the customer could still buy from the free-rider but they rarely do so because of the influence of the direct sales channel. Thus, a combination of carrot and stick does the trick. Unfortunately, for weaker suppliers, the hybrid channel coordination costs often exceed the benefits of functional effectiveness. Such firms then have to trade off effectiveness for the simplicity and functional aggregation of the vertical arrangement. They may have to rely on full-function distributors to compete with the specialized hybrid channels of the market leaders. Alternatively, if market segment coverage is not an issue, such firms might be able to offer hybrid support for certain selected market niches.

Multiple Channels

Not to be confused with hybrid channels, multiple channels reflect the range of channels available to a customer. A buyer of personal computers, for example, could buy the same model (often the same brand) from a direct mail catalogue or a computer superstore or a computer specialty store, each at a different level of price and service. Ideally, these different service levels are meant to reflect the needs of the differing buying segments. So the expectation is that a consumer who is price sensitive but very knowledgeable about product features and specifications would order from a direct-mail catalogue. But the customer who seeks a lot of product information and education from the channel might prefer a computer specialty store. Additionally, this customer would need the reassurance, hand-holding, and local service of the specialty store. While sound in theory, unfortunately consumers do not come neatly segmented into such air-tight compartments. There is a lot of inter-segment movement across purchase occasions. Moreover, with accelerating product life cycles, proliferation of products, and fragmentation of customer segments, multiple-channel approaches are often the only way to provide market coverage. Different customers with different buying behaviors will seek out channels that best serve their needs.

So what is the problem? As shown in Figure 4, the real issue rests with the leaky gray area in the middle, which permits infiltration of customers from the adjoining segments. These are customers that patronize both the full-service channel as well as the low-price channel. As long as the higher price is a fair reflection of the higher service, they will be channel loyal, but if the service is unnecessary or can be obtained at a lower cost than what the price premium would justify, customers will cross over to the low-price channel. In a number of business environments, presales service is a public good which customers can experience without a purchase commitment. For example, nothing precludes a customer from getting a full-function demonstration from a computer specialty store, and then sourcing product from a low-cost mail order retailer. The customer takes the full-service channel for a free ride.

Another type of conflict occurs in multiple channels when a full-product-line distributor uses a loss-leader strategy to steal customers from competitors. Consider

FIGURE 4

Multiple channels

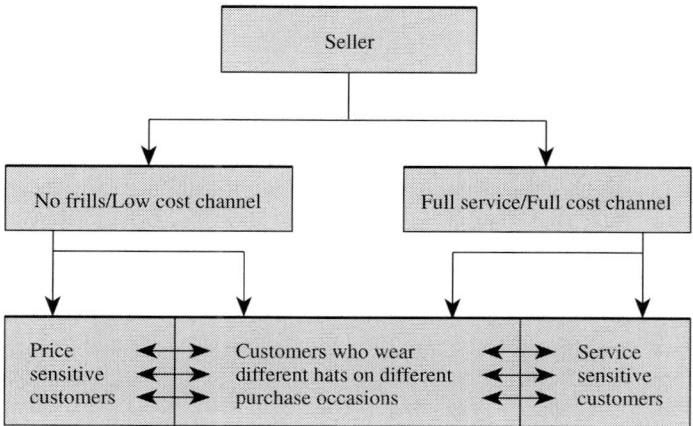

the channel illustrated in Figure 5. The company wishes to segment its market by large and small customers. The large customers buy high volume Z machines, and occasionally for their smaller plants a small number of X machines. Distributor A is set up to address this market exclusively. Distributor B, on the other hand, is set up to address the smaller customers who need X products.

Because of its technical complexity, if we assume that the distributor margin for product Z is substantially higher than that for X, it is easy to see how channel conflicts can occur. Distributor A could undersell product X because its overheads are already covered by the high-margin Z operation. This will certainly upset B's operations and lead to customer cross-overs. Of course, the opposite could happen if distributor margins for X are greater than for Z, and B undersells A. In this case, even though the large customer cannot cross over to Channel B (because the Z product is unavailable in that channel), the customer could nevertheless feel gouged and dissatisfied with its distributor (i.e., A), causing acrimonious debates and conflicts. In a

FIGURE 5

Multiple channel conflicts

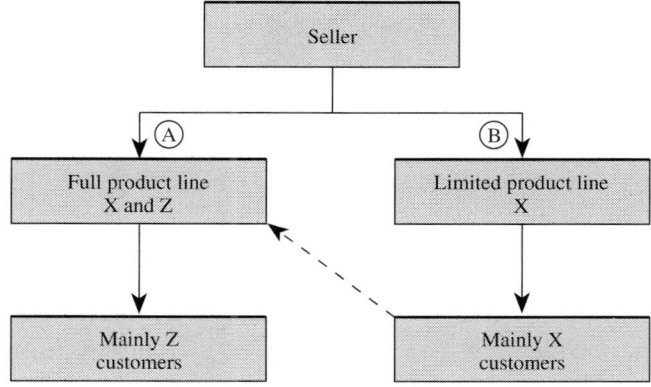

nutshell, the problem is caused by a lethal mixture of leaky market segmentation and price differentiation in the multiple channel network. What is the solution?

The common approach to managing multiple channels is to demarcate products and models by channels. Thus, direct comparisons are minimized. The demarcations, of course, work well when there are true feature differences between products. At times, in spite of product differences, competing channels will be able to offer similar problem-solving capabilities by patching/bundling products appropriately; for example, personal computers for workstations, and workstations for minicomputers. A potential solution, in such cases, is to render the patched product price uncompetitive. Such a measure restores legitimacy to the principal channel. Other channel coordination mechanisms to promote cooperation, such as joint incentives or customer partitioning, work only when one of the channel members happens to be a supplier-owned channel (e.g., own sales force or captive distribution). It rarely works when the multiple members are all independent. In our experience, the product demarcation approach is as effective as any other conflict-reduction mechanism we have seen. And when used in conjunction with other methods, it results in quite effective channel management. It has one other advantage: providing a seller the option of organizing sales and distribution channels by product line. There still has to be considerable coordination across products and channels in terms of customer segmentation, product demarcation, and pricing, but all of it is internal to the company. Once a product is priced and enters a sales channel for a particular customer segment, there is no confusion externally in front of the customer.

Multiple channels are more widely prevalent in fast-changing, as opposed to stable, market environments. When the product-market matures slowly, the channel profile usually evolves and stabilizes to reflect the needs of the new consumer buying pattern: The channel adapts to the customer buying pattern. Even if multiple channels are necessary to reflect market plurality, each channel is clearly specialized to serve a specific buying pattern. Crossovers are less common. Witness the rise of discount stores in the late 1970s and early 1980s. They were clearly targeted to the value conscious shopper, even while the service conscious shopper continued to patronize the specialty stores. The two channels often stock, display, and sell different brands, and attract a very different clientele. Another example comes from the power tool industry. Black & Decker sells its Quantum line through Wal-Mart, while its De-Walt line is routed through hardware specialty stores. While one goes for the DIY (do-it-yourself) customers, the other goes for the professional craftsman. But such is not the case in the more dynamic industries. Computer models that start their life in specialty stores gravitate to the catalog retailers in less than six months. The early buyers may not face channel dissonance, but the latecomers always do. While they may seek the service of the specialty outlet, the price of the discount outlet is too tempting to pass. Moreover, in dynamic environments customers' shopping and buying behaviors themselves are ever changing. Customers' buying criteria and customer segments are transient and dynamic as well. Multiple channels will be as common as are these environments in the 1990s.

Shorter Channels

As the economics of distribution changes, the functions of certain distribution levels are being rendered superfluous. There is a trend toward shorter channels. Of all the various intermediary types, the role of the master distributor or the wholesaler is possibly the one most at risk. See Figure 6. With the advent of quick shipment distribution logistics, retailers do not lose much time anymore in ordering directly from the supplier. And again from the supplier's side, with the availability of modern information technology, tracking and responding to retail-level orders are vastly more manageable. Information technology and quick shipment logistics have vastly diminished the need for dual inventories in the pipeline. In an intensely competitive environment, the extra margin saved at the master-distributor level then becomes a price advantage at the customer level. Witness the rise of retail-distributors like W. W. Grainger in the electrical goods industry. With over 300 stores, selling about 40,000 SKUs (stock-keeping units), Grainger has forced a reorientation in the industry. Both the seller and the dealer view the master distributor as the unwanted fat in the system. The rise of Home Depot in the construction industry, and Terminix and Orkin in the pest-control industry, are further examples of the general trend.

Ironically, in many industries master distributors were set up by manufacturers that did not have the inventory carrying capacity, the geographic reach, or the capability to fulfill small orders. The master distributor served as the essential conduit to retail distribution. But retail dealers have become larger and more sophisticated in handling both suppliers and customers. For small retail dealers, which still need extra support in product assortment or credit, master distributors may be the only way to go. But only those master distributors will survive that proactively use the advances in information and logistics technology to their advantage and combine that with excellent service of small orders. Such opportunities for success are likely to be limited in the future.

From a supplier's point of view, then, a key task is to manage the transition. Those suppliers that have successfully used a master-distributor channel in the past

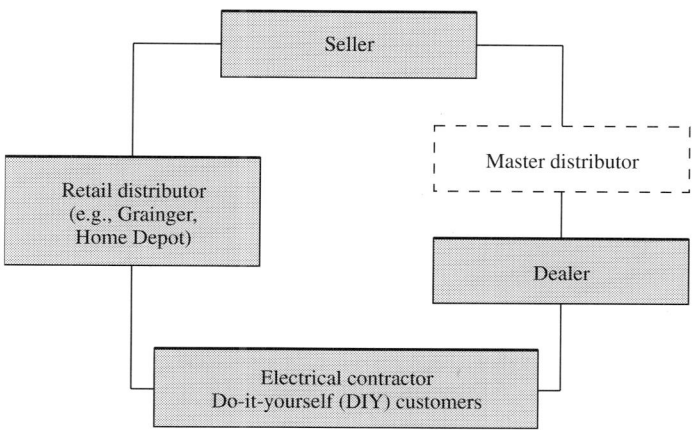

FIGURE 6

The role of master distributors

will find it hard to bypass this level. The upfront investment is daunting, and the risk of failure serious. After all, the master distributors performed the inventory-carrying and credit-advancing functions. They own all the relationships with the dealer accounts. Moreover, the potential order sizes may appear too small for effective fulfillment. Newer and more nimble competitors, however, will almost always choose the cost-efficient alternative of skipping the master-distributor level. As the supplier (with the master-distributor channel) loses revenue, share, and profits, the pressure to change may be tremendous, but the will to change is usually lukewarm, especially for the traditional leaders and large incumbents. Their entrenched relationships with these master distributors are high, and it is not as though these channel partners are unwilling to slice their margins or increase their channel efforts. In fact, they are not the cause, but rather the victim of changed economic circumstances.

Suppliers attempting to change in a half-baked, staged manner have inevitably failed. One cannot redress the situation by selectively shorting the channel for big dealer accounts, leaving master distributors to serve the smaller accounts. There is no way they can survive the subsequent intrabrand price competition that their customers—the small dealers—will face from large dealers who now have direct supplier access. One cannot have one's cake and eat it too. There are only two solutions. Either bite the bullet and shorten the channels once and for all, or do everything possible to bolster the master distributor's operations. The channel-shorting option is best implemented when the market is growing rather than shrinking. Another opportunity might be to implement the change simultaneously with the launch of a new range of very attractive products. Essentially, the timing should be such that the pull-through demand is strong enough to offset the lack of distributor push-through. This initial wave is necessary to realign and consolidate relationships with new channel partners. American Cyanamid, in 1985, overhauled its channels for Agricultural Chemicals simultaneously with the launch of a series of breakthrough new products. The new product success legitimized new channels, garnered dealer enthusiasm, and enabled a rapid implementation of the new margin structure.

Alternatively, suppliers could choose to work very closely with their master distributors and help them transform their distribution business. They should be trained to integrate the new economies offered by information and logistics technology to shape their business. If need be, suppliers should invest in such a transformation, treating the master distributors as their own master warehouse. Master distributors who are willing to throw their weight behind one or a few noncompeting suppliers will obviously enhance their chances of being selected for such special partnerships. Independent master distributors with multiple supplier affiliations have no choice but to constantly innovate their distribution operations merely to survive.

Conclusion

Regardless of the structural form, distribution channels of the future will certainly be more interactive with the customer. In many cases, customers will be able to modify products to suit their unique needs. Even now, some environments provide that latitude. Computer customers, for example, can almost transform their entire hardware system by the choice of the software and accessories. But in the future, given the increasing speed of the feedback loop, suppliers will find it necessary to offer a menu of features and functions rather than prepackage them into set product configurations. The Frito-Lay story is well known. Its route salespeople enter in call data (by store) into a hand-held computer—shelf stock, shelf space, competitor stock, promotion activity, and other such field level data. This information is uploaded to the main computer every evening, and by dawn the next day such information from all markets is processed by the mother computer, and an optimal field-level call plan is worked out for every sales representative across the country—products, assortments, prices, promotions, and the like.

The auto industry is moving toward offering customers a wider array of customizing options (control panels, leg room, interior and exterior trim, etc.), all for delivery within two or three weeks. Future distribution channels will truly have to receive in addition to transmitting channel functions. Current channels are hopelessly inadequate in this regard. Customer complaints and returned goods are usually accepted through an auxiliary channel, which is often not a part of the core distribution system of a company. Channels will have to accept their new role as a two-way communications network gracefully if they are to be really customer responsive, not just customer oriented. This can be accomplished within the structure of hybrid channels, multiple channels, or even conventional vertical marketing systems, but clearly a lot more data and information have to be shared and exchanged among the channel partners to make the two-way network a reality. Traditionally, the supplier controlled product information and the channel controlled market information, and they each used their power bases to, at times gently and at times rudely, lean on each other. While the supplier usually expected channels to deliver sales output, the channel expected a return-on-investment. It was a sales versus margin battle that manifested itself in many interesting standoffs as illustrated in Table A.

TABLE A Contentions

Manufacturer	Distributor
• You must carry a full line of all the products we make. No cherry picking.	• We can try, but we can't sell "dogs." We should concentrate on our strong points.
• We need you to concentrate on our products.	• We need exclusive territories.
• We need your active involvement in selling new products and developing new markets.	• It is very costly to do so. How will you compensate us for the effort?
• We need to know about y(our) customers in greater detail.	• We don't keep such records. (". . . Not a chance—They'll start selling directly.")
• You need to improve your sales effort.	• You need to improve your sales promotion.
• Your channel margins are too high.	• Your prices are too high.
We need to work together.	*We agree.*

But ultimately, as Table A concludes, sellers and distributors needed each other in order to reach the end customer. While the supplier and distributor battle each other, the real war is for customers, and often in the past this got translated into a desire for channel control. There was a confusion of the means for the end. In the future, channel alliances will have to energize and help each other win the competitive battle. They need to get the cake first, before they can quarrel about its allocation.

One should not, however, naively interpret this to mean that the future will see minimal channel conflicts. Quite to the contrary, as pointed out in our discussion of shorter channels, hybrid channels, and multiple channels, administering the new channels demands tremendous leadership. Issues of free-ridership, allocation of financial discounts, product and customer demarcation norms, and so on are all likely to occupy a full plate. There is one difference. These are conflicts all aimed at directly improving the system's effectiveness in addressing the customer's needs. The customer was forgotten in the old model (Table A) but will in fact be at the center in the new.

CHAPTER 35

Managing Hybrid Marketing Systems

Companies are creating new hybrid marketing systems that promise to become the dominant marketing design. These systems offer greater coverage and reduced costs, but they are also harder to manage. Managers can make the task easier with a "hybrid grid," a map that illustrates the combination of channels and tasks that will optimize cost and coverage. Another tool, a marketing and sales productivity (MSP) system, can help managers create customized channels and service for specific customer segments.

There was a time when most companies went to market only one way—through a direct sales force, for instance, or through distributors. But to defend their turf, expand market coverage, and control costs, companies today are increasingly adopting arsenals of new marketing weapons to use with different customer segments and under different circumstances. In recent years, as managers have sought to cut costs and increase market coverage, companies have added new channels to existing ones; they use direct sales as well as distributors, retail sales as well as direct mail, direct mail as well as direct sales. As they add channels and communications methods, companies create hybrid marketing systems.

Look at IBM. For years, IBM computers were available from only one supplier, the company's sales force. But when the market for small, low-cost computers exploded, IBM management realized that its single distribution channel was no longer sufficient. In the late 1970s, it started expanding into new channels, among them dealers, value-added resellers, catalog operations, direct mail, and telemarketing. IBM had built and maintained its vaunted 5,000-person sales force for 70 years. In less than 10 years, it nearly doubled that number and added 18 new channels to communicate with customers.

This article was prepared by Rowland T. Moriarty and Ursula Moran.
Copyright © 1990 by the President and Fellows of Harvard College.
Harvard Business Review, November–December 1990, pp. 146–55.

Apple Computer also started out with a clear and simple channel strategy. It distributed its inexpensive personal computers through an independent dealer network. But when the company began to sell more sophisticated systems to large companies, it had to change. Apple hired 70 national account managers as part of a new direct sales operation.

In adding these new channels and communications methods, IBM and Apple created hybrid marketing systems. Powerful forces lie behind the appearance of such hybrid systems; all signs indicate that they will be the dominant design of marketing systems in the 1990s. At the same time, smart managers recognize the high risks of operating hybrid systems. Whether the migration is from direct to indirect channels (such as IBM) or from indirect to direct (like Apple), the result is the same—a hybrid that can be hard to manage.

The appearance of new channels and methods inevitably raises problems of conflict and control-conflict because more marketing units compete for customers and revenues; control because indirect channels are less subject to management authority than direct are. As difficult as they are to manage, however, hybrid marketing systems can offer substantial rewards. A company that can capture the benefits of a hybrid system—increased coverage, lower costs, and customized approaches—will enjoy a significant competitive advantage over rivals that cling to traditional ways.

Examples of hybrid marketing systems extend beyond high-tech businesses such as computers to older industries such as textiles, metal fabrication, and office supplies and to service industries such as insurance. Many of the examples in this article are high-tech companies because the accelerated pace of high-tech industries foreshadows trends that tend to occur more slowly in other industries. The trend to hybrid systems, however, appears to be accelerating in many industries. According to one recent senior manager survey, 53 percent of the respondents indicated that their companies intend to use hybrid systems by 1992, a dramatic increase over the 33 percent that used those systems in 1987.

Two fundamental reasons explain this boost in the move to hybrids: the drive to increase market coverage and the need to contain costs. To sustain growth, a company generally must reach new customers or segments. Along the way, it usually supplements existing channels and methods with new ones designed to attract and develop new customers. This addition of new channels and methods creates a hybrid marketing system.

The need to contain costs is another powerful force behind the spread of hybrid systems, as companies look for ways to reach customers that are more efficient than direct selling. In 1990, the loaded cost of face-to-face selling time for national account managers can reach $500 per hour; for direct sales representatives, the average is about $300 per hour. Selling and administrative costs often represent 20 to 40 percent of a company's cost structure and thus have a direct effect on competitive advantage and profitability. For instance, Digital Equipment's selling and administrative costs in 1989 were 31 percent of revenues; for Sun Microsystems, the figure was only about 24 percent.

Given such economics, many companies are pursuing techniques such as telemarketing, which costs about $17 per hour, or direct mail, which runs about $1 per customer contact. A marketing strategy built on such low-cost communications methods can yield impressive results. Tessco, a distributor of supplies and equipment for cellular communications, emerged as one of the industry's fastest-growing competitors by relying on low-cost communications methods. Tessco generates leads through direct mail and catalog operations; it uses telemarketing to qualify sales leads, make its sales pitch, answer questions, and close the sale. It then follows up each sale with service telemarketing and maintains accounts through an automatic reordering process. The result: Tessco enjoys significantly lower costs than most of its competitors, which continue to rely on traditional methods such as direct sales.

Wright Line's Problems

Despite the proliferation of marketing methods, few companies pay sufficient attention to the design of marketing systems or seek to manage them in ways that optimize coverage and costs. Indeed, most companies decide to add new channels and methods without a clear and realistic vision of an ultimate go-to-market architecture. These decisions are usually made separately and independently—and often swiftly as well. As a consequence, companies can find themselves stumbling over their hastily constructed, overlapping hybrid system.

Consider how an ill-conceived and mismanaged hybrid system contributed to the 1989 hostile takeover of Barry Wright Corporation. Many factors made the Massachusetts–based company vulnerable, but a principal cause of its troubles was the performance of a major subsidiary, Wright Line, Inc. A leading supplier of accessories used to store, protect, and provide access to computer tapes, diskettes, and other media, Wright Line was struggling vainly to halt the erosion of its market position.

Wright Line's troubles stemmed from a decision made in the early 1980s to reorganize its marketing and sales functions. Previously, the company had sold its products exclusively through a direct sales force. Although the company had been growing rapidly and adding new sales reps every year, Wright Line's management was alarmed by several trends: inability to increase market penetration, declining sales productivity, high turnover of sales reps, and what appeared to be a fundamental shift in the market away from the company's traditional stronghold in large, central computer installations.

After analyzing these trends, Wright Line supplemented its direct sales force with additional marketing channels and communications methods.[1] The company formed two new units: a direct marketing operation to handle midsize accounts through direct catalog and telephone sales, and a unit to serve small accounts and to

---

[1] Channels are either direct or indirect. Methods are the communications options companies can use to reach potential customers; they may also be direct or indirect. For example, through a direct channel, a company may use account managers, a sales force, or telemarketing. The same methods may also be used singly or in combination through indirect channels.

A simple graphic captures the elements of a hybrid marketing system. Along the top are the basic marketing tasks required to obtain and maintain customers: generation of leads; qualification of these leads; presales activities, such as sales calls to woo specific customers; closing the sale; provision of postsales service; and ongoing management of the account.

Along the side of the grid are the various marketing channels and methods used to reach customers, ranging from elaborate direct to elaborate indirect options. The shaded areas represent one possible approach through a direct channel: direct mail to generate leads, telemarketing to qualify leads and manage presales and postsales activities, and a direct sales force to close deals and manage the account on an ongoing basis.

The hybrid grid can be a useful diagnostic tool to identify points of overlap and conflict in a marketing system. It can also aid in the design of a new marketing system tailored to the needs of specific customers. As a marketing map, the grid depicts the situation at a particular moment and needs to be updated as changes occur.

The Hybrid Grid: The Elements of a Hybrid Marketing System

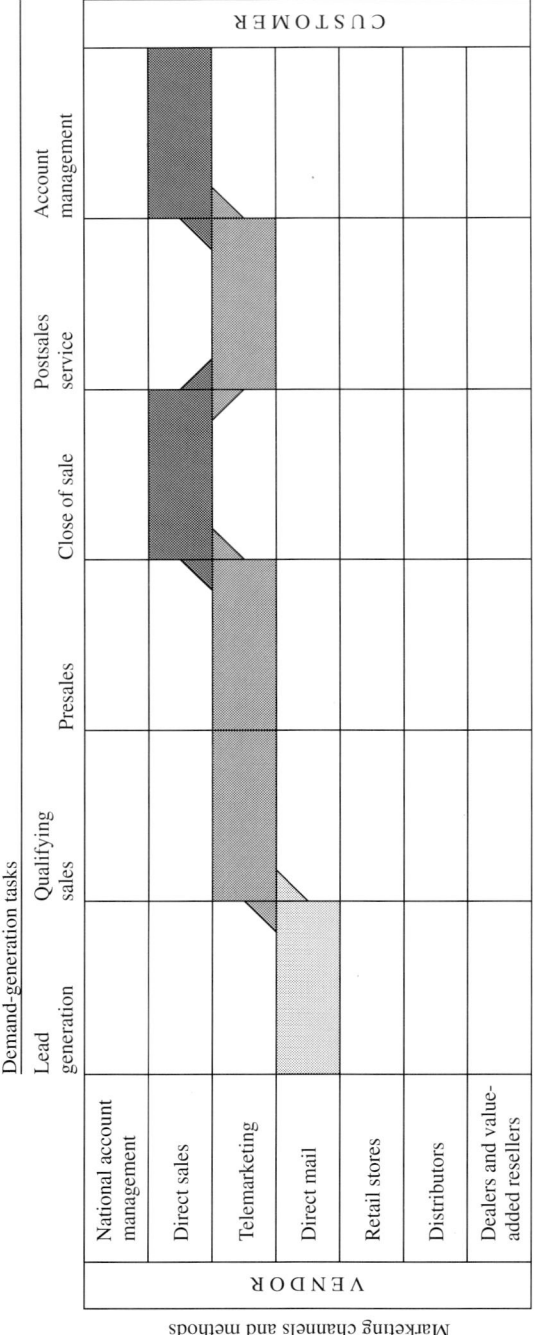

attract nonusers through indirect channels. Management's goals were to combine the advantages of high-quality personal selling to major accounts with lower-cost, increased coverage of smaller accounts.

Signs of trouble appeared almost immediately. By 1985, the reorganization had yielded declining growth rates, diminishing market share, and plummeting profits. Inside the company, strife over account ownership was rampant, and turnover among the direct sales reps reached an all-time high. Worst of all, Wright Line's customers grew confused and angry after encountering different sales offerings of the same products under widely disparate terms and conditions. Wright Line's best customers became alienated, and its margins shrank as major accounts ordered the company's products from discount suppliers.

By the time new leadership tried to untangle the mess, it was already too late. Its stock weakened by Wright Line's rapidly eroding market position and declining profitability, Barry Wright Corporation was taken over in 1989.

The Barry Wright story is an extreme example of an increasingly evident problem. Fewer and fewer major industrial or service companies go to market through a single channel or a "purebred" channel strategy that matches a specific product or service to an exclusive segment. Rather than designing an ideal distribution strategy, companies tend to add channels and methods incrementally in the quest to extend market coverage or cut selling costs. Unfortunately, such actions typically result in conflict and morale problems inside the marketing organization and confusion and anger among distributors, dealers, and customers on the outside.

Mapping the Hybrid

At the heart of the problem of designing and managing hybrid systems is the fundamental question of what mix of channels or communication methods can best accomplish the assortment of tasks required to identify, sell, and manage customers. The trick of designing and managing hybrid systems is to disaggregate demand-generation tasks both within and across a marketing system—recognizing that channels are *not* the basic building blocks of a marketing system; marketing tasks are. This analysis of tasks and channels will identify the hybrid's basic components and permit managers to design and manage the system effectively.

A map of tasks and channels—what we call a hybrid grid—can help managers make sense of their hybrid system. (See "The Hybrid Grid" on page 602.) A hybrid grid, for example, can be used to illustrate graphically what happened at Wright Line and what might have happened differently.

Before its reorganization, Wright Line used direct sales for all demand-generation tasks and all customers (see the chart "Wright Line's Marketing System: What It Had"). When it reorganized in 1982, Wright Line wanted the direct sales force (unit 1) to perform all demand-generation tasks for big customers, the new direct response unit (unit 2) to concentrate exclusively on midsize customers (using catalogs and telemarketing), and the new third-party and resale unit (unit 3) to market to

Wright Line's Marketing System: What It Had

Marketing channels and methods (VENDOR)	Demand-generation tasks					
	Lead generation	Qualifying sales	Presales	Close of sale	Postsales service	Account management
National account management						
Direct sales	ALL CUSTOMERS					
Telemarketing						
Direct mail						
Retail stores						
Distributors						
Dealers and value-added resellers						

(CUSTOMER)

small customers and nonusers through indirect channels (see the chart "What It Wanted").

Instead, Wright Line wound up with a marketing system that was neither what it wanted nor what it needed (see the chart "What It Got"). The three marketing units were performing all of the demand-generation tasks for many different types of customers. Units 1 and 2 bickered constantly over account ownership. To avoid losing accounts, for example, some sales reps improperly classified accounts to hide them from the direct response marketing division. Those who complied were frustrated by guidelines that prohibited them from calling on smaller and midsize accounts in their territories and growing with them. The activities of unit 3 added fuel to the fire. Among major customers, purchasing managers who read catalogs and received visits from the sales reps of office supply vendors found that Wright Line products were available at a substantial discount off the direct sales price.

In many respects, Wright Line's experience was typical, both in terms of the problems the company faced and its approach to solving them. Management's effort focused on identifying new channels that could be added to or substituted for all of the marketing tasks performed by the existing direct sales force channel. But this approach incorrectly assumes that each channel must perform and control all demand-generation tasks. The hybrid grid forces managers to consider various combinations of channels and tasks that will optimize both cost and coverage.

In addition, the company assumed that certain channels could best serve all the needs of certain customer segments. Hence, units 1, 2, and 3 were aligned with big, midsize, and small customers. The process of aligning high-cost channels—that is, the direct sales force—with big customers and low-cost channels with small customers is very logical, if that is the way customers buy. In Wright Line's case, however, customers bought from multiple sales channels. The attempt to use a single channel to reach a single customer group resulted in severe channel conflicts, along with customer confusion.

The design of an effective hybrid system depends not only on a thorough understanding of channel costs but also on a thorough understanding of buying behavior. When a new channel is added to service a particular customer segment, the segmentation scheme must clearly reflect the customer's buying behavior—not just the channel costs of the company. The design of an effective hybrid system requires balancing the natural tension between minimizing costs and maximizing customer satisfaction. In Wright Line's situation, the hybrid design was driven by costs, without regard for buying behavior.

Wright Line's fatal flaw was basing its marketing strategy on what was best for the company, not what was best for its customers. In focusing its costliest marketing resources on the targets with the highest potential payoff and devoting less-expensive resources to less-promising accounts, it ignored the buying behavior of its customers. Too late, Wright Line discovered that its customers could not be segmented so neatly, nor would they conform docilely to the company's perception of its most efficient channel structure. Its hybrid system was intended to lower costs and increase coverage. Instead, Wright Line lost control of both its channels and its customers.

Wright Line's Marketing System: What It Wanted

Marketing channels and methods	Lead generation	Qualifying sales	Presales	Close of sale	Postsales service	Account management
VENDOR						
National account management						
Direct sales	BIG CUSTOMERS					
Telemarketing	MIDSIZE CUSTOMERS					
Direct mail						
Retail stores						
Distributors	SMALL CUSTOMERS AND NONCUSTOMERS					
Dealers and value-added resellers						
CUSTOMER						

Wright Line's Marketing System: What It Got

Marketing channels and methods (VENDOR)	Demand-generation tasks					CUSTOMER
	Lead generation	Qualifying sales	Presales	Close of sale	Postsales service	Account management
National account management						
Direct sales	BIG, MIDSIZE, AND SMALL CUSTOMERS					
Telemarketing		BIG, MIDSIZE, AND SMALL CUSTOMERS				
Direct mail						
Retail stores						
Distributors	BIG, MIDSIZE, AND SMALL CUSTOMERS					
Dealers and value-added resellers						

The hybrid grid illustrates how Wright Line might have successfully designed and managed its hybrid system (see the chart "What It Needed" on page 609). The company could have used direct mail and response cards to generate leads among potential customers of all sizes and to perform most other tasks for small accounts. It could have used telemarketing to qualify leads among big and midsize prospects and determine approximate order size. It could have routed qualified prospects interested in buying a certain amount of equipment to direct sales reps. (Qualified prospects that turn out to be current national accounts would be turned over to the appropriate national account managers.) To midsize customers, it could have made phone calls to close sales and handle accounts; a direct sales rep or a national account manager could have performed these tasks for larger customers. For all customers, telemarketing could have been used for postsales tasks like reordering.

This version assigns demand-generation tasks to various channels, balancing both cost and customer buying behavior. Distributors were a principal part of Wright Line's setup. But this approach avoids using indirect channels, thereby allowing the company to maintain broad coverage without sacrificing control of pricing and product policy. (Of course, indirect channels are appropriate and necessary in many situations.) By establishing boundaries around genuine segments and building bridges across tasks, Wright Line might have gained the advantages of expanded market coverage and cost-effective marketing management without losing control of its marketing system and its customers.

Managing Conflict in Hybrid Systems

Conflict is an inevitable part of every hybrid system. When a company adds a channel or substitutes a new communication method within a channel, existing stakeholders—sales reps, distributors, telemarketers—invariably resist. And why not: Each faces a potential loss of revenue as well as competition for ownership of customers. In seeking to build and manage a hybrid system, therefore, companies must recognize and communicate the existence of conflict as the first and most important step.

The next step is to assess the magnitude of the conflict, asking some simple but penetrating questions: How much revenue does the company have in conflict? (Revenue is in conflict whenever two or more channels simultaneously attempt to sell the same product to the same customer.) Where is this conflict? How do channels and customers react to it? How much management time is devoted to dealing with the conflict?

The answers to these questions will vary by industry and by company, but some generalizations are possible. Clearly, a company with no revenue in conflict may be sacrificing coverage, failing to attract new customers by focusing too narrowly on a particular segment. Indeed, a certain amount of conflict in a hybrid marketing system is not only inevitable but also healthy. On the other hand, as the Wright Line story illustrates, conflict that is pervasive across channels is debilitating and potentially destructive.

Wright Line's Marketing System: What It Needed

Marketing channels and methods (VENDOR)	Demand-generation tasks					CUSTOMER
	Lead generation	Qualifying sales	Presales	Close of sale	Postsales service	Account management
National account management			BIG	BIG		BIG
Direct sales						
Telemarketing		BIG AND MIDSIZE	MIDSIZE	MIDSIZE		MIDSIZE
Direct mail	ALL	S M A L L			ALL	SMALL
Retail stores						
Distributors						
Dealers and value-added resellers						

Of course, the concept of having revenue in conflict is alien to many CEOs and senior managers, particularly those who are accustomed to using only a single channel. They should seek a point of balance where conflict is neither too little nor too much. Although the location of this point depends on many variables—as a rule of thumb, destructive behavior occurs when 10 to 30 percent of revenues are in conflict—managers can estimate it by monitoring feedback from customers and marketing personnel. When phone calls and letters become angry, or when a significant portion of management time is absorbed in mediating internal disputes or dealing with customer complaints, warning bells should go off.

Bounding the Conflict

After they determine the amount and location of conflict, managers can establish clear and communicable boundaries and specific and enforceable guidelines that spell out which customers to serve through which methods.

Most companies observe some natural boundaries in the marketplace—areas defined by the interaction between buyer behavior and channel costs. Typically, companies target the largest and most profitable customers for some form of direct personal selling and serve smaller, less-profitable accounts through less-expensive methods. The problems arise with those customers residing somewhere in the middle: midsize accounts or markets with fuzzy boundaries, such as large national accounts that use a combination of centralized and decentralized purchasing practices that vary by product, location, or order size.

In this no-man's-land, neither the customer's buying behavior nor the company's transaction economics indicates definitively which method is the most effective way to serve the customer. Because no single method is clearly superior or appropriate, several may compete with each other—an example of a situation where clear boundaries will not work. These no-man's-land customer segments should be identified and clearly communicated to all marketing units so they know they will have intracompany competition.

Once the "jump ball" selling situations are identified, it is easier to construct barriers where natural segments exist. Boundaries between classes of customers are frequently couched in terms of sales, but effective boundary design involves much more than spelling out who makes which sale. It should instead indicate who owns and who doesn't own certain customers. Boundary mechanisms that help achieve this goal are generally based on customer characteristics, geography, and products.

Customer Characteristics. Customer size is a familiar boundary criterion. One large computer manufacturer specifies that for its banking customers, its value-added resellers (VARs) should sell to small community financial institutions with less than $250 million in assets. For larger institutions, the manufacturer should sell through its direct sales force or some combination of that group and a third-party software supplier.

Order size provides another standard for drawing boundaries. A leading maker of PCs, for example, specifies that orders for more than 25 units must go through its direct sales force and orders of less than 5 units through independent dealers. Either direct or indirect channels may handle orders in the no-man's-land between 5 and 25 units.

Customers can also be classified by decision-making process or decision-making unit. A manufacturer of specialty and commodity chemicals uses a direct sales force to sell specialty chemicals because the purchasing process for these products is complex and requires several engineers to develop specifications and participate in supplier selection. The company's commodity products, however, are most often bought by a purchasing agent, and price is the key consideration. Hence, commodity chemicals are handled by distributors.

Finally, customers can be categorized by industry, particularly when there are genuine differences both in the product, price, and service package and in the expertise demanded of salespeople. The paper industry is a good example of differences in end use or applications. A different channel serves each of the four major end-use groups—newsprint, magazines, office products, and business forms.

Geographic Boundaries. Bounding by geography is clear and easy to enforce. A major manufacturer of computer-aided design/computer-aided manufacture (CAD/CAM) systems sells its offerings in the United States and Europe through a direct sales force; in Japan, it uses an exclusive distributor. The company has little difficulty preventing major conflict (except in global accounts) because the channels are physically separated. Many companies serve large, urban markets through some form of direct sales and use distributors or reps to cover less densely populated areas.

Product Boundaries. Xerox used product boundaries when it entered the personal copier market. It sells midrange and high-end machines through a combination of direct sales and dealer distribution; it sells low-end machines exclusively through retail channels. Electronics and appliance stores, mass merchants, department stores, and an American Express direct mail program are all sources of Xerox personal copiers. The company has tried to avoid excessive conflict among these different retail channels by producing distinct models for each. The basic model 5008 personal copier was designed in three different versions so retailers would not compete with one another over an identical product.

Boundary mechanisms will help contain and control conflict when it arises, but they do not—and should not—eliminate it. It is impossible to hermetically seal each segment or customer group. Astute marketers identify and communicate to their channels not only those areas where clear boundaries exist but also those where they are either impossible or impractical.

Managing Channel Additions

Maintaining order in a hybrid marketing system is a complex administrative challenge. The addition of new channels and methods inevitably requires modifications to existing reporting relationships, organization structure, and management policies with respect to motivation, evaluation, and compensation. The stakes are high since organizational moves issue a strong signal about the direction of change and top management's commitment to it. In the past decade, for example, Wang Laboratories struggled through three separate attempts to create an indirect sales organization to supplement direct sales of its products. Each new attempt foundered after meeting entrenched resistance inside the company. Indeed, Wang's inability to solve this problem is a hidden cause of its much-publicized troubles in recent years.

Although each hybrid system presents unique challenges to managers, two general administrative guidelines may be helpful. First, decisions about structure and support policies should conform to the overall goals of the marketing system. Each potential configuration should be measured against the obvious tests: Will it satisfy customers in the most cost-effective manner? Will it maximize the prospect of achieving greater coverage and control throughout the system? Will it limit destructive conflict inside the organization?

Second, the timing of changes in structure and policies should reflect a realistic assessment of revenue flows through various channels and methods over time. In a large company, for example, it is extremely unlikely that a new channel or method will account for a significant fraction of total revenues in its first year. A new indirect channel added to a system dominated by a direct channel may account for 3 to 5 percent of revenues in the first year and perhaps 20 percent by the fifth. During such a transition, management should weight its policies heavily in favor of the new channel to ensure its success.

Management sends the most powerful and immediate signals through the compensation system. Companies with hybrid systems rely heavily on compensation policies to reinforce new boundaries and routinely subsidize new activities during transition periods. The most common approach involves paying personnel in the older units to allow personnel in the newer units to make the sale. An example reveals the reasoning behind such a tactic. A large computer company was struggling with the familiar problem of adding low-cost direct methods and indirect channels to supplement its direct sales force. In seeking to motivate the direct sales reps to relinquish revenue responsibilities, the company considered three options: a penalty, a modest incentive, and a strong incentive.

In weighing the penalty option, the company reasoned that requiring direct sales reps to forfeit commissions on each sale that should be made elsewhere would discourage them from stealing sales from new units. The risks of such an approach, however, seemed overwhelming: The company saw that conflict and petty rivalries were bound to erupt throughout the marketing organization as soon as it instituted the policy.

The modest incentive option would entail paying direct sales reps a portion of their normal commission when the new units made a sale. On reflection, this solution appeared too cumbersome. It would be difficult to determine appropriate compensation levels and to define and enforce a policy that would avoid sending mixed signals.

In the end, the company chose the strong incentive option—and eventually implemented it successfully. After a thorough analysis of long-term costs and benefits, the company paid the direct sales reps their normal commission for every sale regardless of whether they were responsible. Once the new units became established, the company phased out this system of double pay.

Orchestrating a Hybrid System

Once a hybrid system is up and running, its smooth functioning depends not only on management of conflict but also on coordination across the channels and across each selling task within the channels. Each unit involved in bridging the gap between the company and the customer must "hand off" all relevant information concerning the customer and the progress of the sale to the next appropriate unit.

A recent technical tool called a marketing and sales productivity (MSP) system can be an invaluable aid in coordinating customer handoffs.[2] Beyond this, an MSP system can help a company combine and manage distinct marketing approaches to produce customized hybrid channels. An MSP system helps serve customers by identifying and coordinating the marketing methods best suited to each customer's needs. In other words, it allows the development of customized channels and service for specific customer segments.

An MSP system consists of a central marketing database containing essential information on customers, prospects, products, marketing programs, and methods. All marketing units regularly update the database. At any point, it is possible to determine previous customer contacts, prices quoted, special customer characteristics or needs, and other information. These systems can significantly lower marketing costs and increase marketing effectiveness by acting as a central nervous system that coordinates the channels and marketing tasks within a hybrid system. With a fully integrated MSP system, it is now possible to know how much it costs to acquire and maintain a customer—essential data in understanding a company's marketing productivity.

Data Translation, a small manufacturer of computer peripherals, installed an in-house MSP system to manage its hybrid marketing organization. At the outset, the company could not afford to hire sales reps but instead generated leads through trade advertising that featured an 800 number. Interested prospects received the company's catalog; they were also encouraged to call and speak to an inside sales representative about products. All contacts with prospects were tracked by the MSP system. Inside sales reps were supported by a group of technical engineers who handled customer inquiries. When Data Translation later added a direct sales force, it continued to rely on its MSP system to coordinate various marketing tasks, including generating leads and dealing with customers who call.

Coordinating the handoffs within its hybrid system and knowing the cost of acquiring and maintaining its customers gives Data Translation significantly lower marketing costs than its competitors. These lower costs translate directly into competitive advantage and bigger margins.

---

[2] For an analysis of these systems, see Rowland T. Moriarty and Gordon S. Swartz, "Automation to Boost Sales and Marketing," *Harvard Business Review,* January–February 1989, p. 100.

Capturing the Benefits

Staples, a Massachusetts–based office supplies company, is achieving outstanding growth through clever allocation of marketing tasks based on what it has learned about customer behavior. At its birth in the mid-1980s, Staples's founders decided to offer discounted office supplies in a retail superstore format, targeting white-collar companies with up to 100 employees. Staples encouraged customers to accept a free savings card that granted additional discounts and, more important, allowed the company to track purchases and to build up a customer database.

Armed with this information, management discovered that its penetration of businesses with 2 to 10 employees was good, those with 10 to 20 not so good, and those with more than 20 quite weak. Customers in the latter two segments wanted more service. In response, Staples started accepting phone orders and added a delivery service. It has also used direct mail, telemarketing, and catalogs and has considered adding a direct sales force to handle large accounts. An MSP system orchestrates and monitors the entire hybrid system and provides management with performance and productivity information on each marketing element. Staples credits much of its success to the design and implementation of its hybrid system.

Many signs indicate that hybrid systems will be the dominant design for going to market in the 1990s. How a company manages its system will help determine its fate in the marketplace. A company that designs and manages its system strategically will achieve a powerful advantage over rivals that add channels and methods in an opportunistic and incremental manner. A company that makes its hybrid system work will have achieved a balance between its customers' buying behavior and its own selling economics. A well-managed hybrid system enables a marketer to enjoy the benefits of increased coverage and lower costs without losing control of the marketing system. Further, it enables a company to customize its marketing system to meet the needs of specific customers and segments.

In sum, a company with a successful hybrid marketing system will accomplish the following:

- It will recognize that the design and management of its marketing system is a powerful weapon in an increasingly competitive and continually shifting battle for customers.
- It will construct its marketing system using marketing tasks, not entire marketing channels, as the fundamental building blocks.
- It will anticipate, recognize, communicate, and contain conflicts inherent in the marketing system.
- In designing boundaries between customer segments, it will strike a balance between too loose and too strict limits.
- It will form policies and an organizational structure that allow new channels to grow, minimize internal conflict, and reinforce segment boundaries.

- It will exploit information technology and other managerial tools to coordinate handoffs of customers and accounts from one channel or method to another and eventually develop customized marketing systems for each important customer or segment.

"Do you ever get the feeling we're not the only global marketplace in the universe?"

Cartoon by Nick Downes

SECTION IV Managing Product Market Diversity

CHAPTER 36
Managing Market Complexity: A Three-Ring Circus

In this chapter, we propose models of organization that address the various product-market environments posed by the product life cycle. We frame these changes along the two dimensions of uncertainty and diversity. We offer three sets of organizational characteristics to reflect the three stages of market development: entrepreneurship and innovation (Stage I), efficiency and dedication (Stage II), and expansion and coordination (Stage III). Contrary to current wisdom, we argue that form (or structure) is as important as process. We conclude with illustrative case examples.

In Chapter 20, "Beating the Commodity Magnet," we presented a framework for viewing the market life cycle that emphasized two important decision variables, price and cost-to-serve. We traced the price/cost dynamics as the market matured. The four strategies we discussed had implications, not only for price and service levels, but also for other aspects of the marketing mix, such as new products and distribution channels. The focus of that chapter was on marketing strategy. Here we pick up that theme and attempt to understand the underlying causes that drive the commodity cycle. Our attempt in this chapter is to take an overarching marketing organization viewpoint, rather than focusing primarily on marketing strategy.

A simple but effective way to characterize the market maturity process is along the two dimensions of uncertainty and diversity. Uncertainty stands for technological uncertainty, end-use uncertainty, manufacturing uncertainty, and all the other unpredictable events that accompany the birth and development of a brand new product-market, and diversity stands for variety and proliferation in products, applications, and customer segments.[1]

This note was prepared by V. Kasturi Rangan.
Copyright © 1994 by the President and Fellows of Harvard College.
Harvard Business School note 594-119.

[1] See Jeffrey Pfeffer and Gerald R. Salancik, *The External Control of Organizations* (New York: Harper and Row, 1978), for a detailed discussion of *uncertainty*. See Howard E. Aldrich, *Organizations and Environments* (Englewood Cliffs, N.J.: Prentice Hall, 1974), for *heterogeneity*. Our *diversity* construct is similar. Also see Gregory G. Dees and Donald W. Beard, "Dimensions of Organizational Task Environments," *Administrative Sciences Quarterly*, March 1984, for an update on measurement and operational indicators of the uncertainty and diversity constructs.

FIGURE 1

Market life cycle: Key drivers

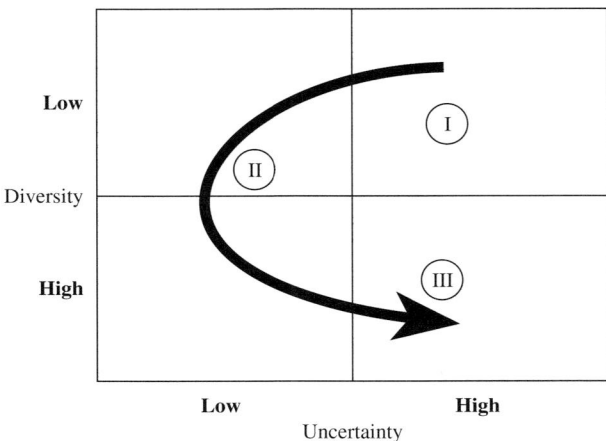

There is an inevitable, incessant rhythm to the market life cycle depicted in Figure 1. Usually, a focused group of customers will find applications for a new technology and adopt it; this is in Stage I. If the technology and its application are successful, a period of predictable growth follows, in Stage II; both suppliers and customers are knowledgeable, comfortable, and satisfied with the product-market exchange. As more customers seek the product, applications proliferate and competitors with the appropriate capabilities join the fray. This leads to a more diverse environment with a higher degree of uncertainty—Stage III. Such a market evolution has implications for how a business is organized and how the industrial marketing function is executed. If businesses are to be successful, different stages imply different organization systems.[2]

Stage I: Entrepreneurship and Integration

An initial product introduction, when the technology is new to the world, usually involves a high level of risk for both the seller and the buyer. The seller may not have mastered the technology or the manufacture of it in commercial quantities. Doubts about its problem-solving capabilities linger, and the product or its application has to be proven in the field. The initial adopters face similar uncertainties. The new product must deliver the promised functionalities, which may involve changes in the buyer's manufacturing and marketing systems as well. Anything could go wrong. Under these circumstances, buyers need considerable technical support and hand-

---

[2]The arguments we present in this paper have been inspired by the seminal works of Paul R. Lawrence and Jay Lorsch, *Organizations and Environments* (Boston: Harvard Business School Press, 1967), and James D. Thompson, *Organizations in Action* (New York: McGraw Hill, 1967). Follow-on work by many authors, such as R. Miles and C. Snow, *Organizational Strategy, Structure, and Process* (New York: McGraw Hill, 1978), are all relevant but are too numerous to cite here.

holding—a close buyer–seller relationship. One way for buyers to absorb uncertainty in this early period is to target customers or customer segments that would potentially value the new technology highly enough to take the added risk accompanying it. A sensible product/market strategy is one of focus on a few key products in a few key markets. Only after the technical uncertainties and risks have been mastered does it make sense to broaden one's product line and application base.

In this "high uncertainty/low diversity" environment, sellers obviously need a good working relationship with their customers, and this can only come with close coordination among their engineering/R&D, manufacturing, marketing, and sales functions. In small organizations this is usually addressed by providing managers with broad cross-functional responsibilities. It is not unusual in some companies for manufacturing managers to do the selling and customer servicing, just as sales managers schedule the shop floor in others. And, of course, the CEO or the president often becomes involved in the day-to-day details of all the functions, from purchasing to customer service.

In large companies, given their sheer volume of activities, such a general management orientation may not be feasible. But the various functions will still have to work very closely to overcome the hurdles of bringing the new product to market in a timely, effective manner. Figure 2 illustrates the interfunctional dependencies in a typical new product development process. Regardless of how it is done—either having functions with cross-functional responsibility, or having them all specialized but tightly integrated and coordinated—an essential requirement of the early market life cycle is that organizations have a high degree of participation, involvement, and

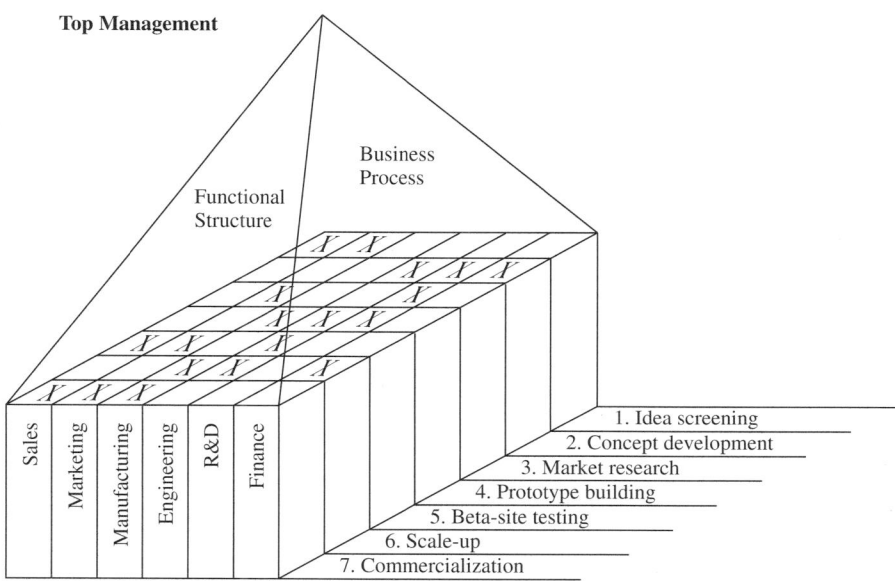

FIGURE 2

The new product development process

flexibility among the functions in developing, manufacturing, and marketing the product.[3]

Stage II: Efficiency and Dedication

In Stage II, both the sellers and the buyers feel a lot more comfortable with the technology; uncertainty levels are much lower than they were at the product launch stage. The sellers by now have mastered production, giving customers with similar application needs—who were watching from the sidelines—the confidence to adopt the new product. In fact, competitive considerations in their end-use markets will force these buyers to accelerate the new product adoption. While the market segment may still be focused, the number of user customers in the few segments will rapidly increase.

The challenges of managing technological uncertainties are now replaced by the challenges of managing scale. Suppliers will need to design, make, and sell products in large numbers. This will require dedicated attention to the functions. For example, distributors will specialize in holding stock and providing customers ready availability, the marketing department will focus on setting prices and generating demand, and the production department will specialize in making and shipping product. Essentially, as the firm settles down into a more certain environment, efficiencies of marketing and manufacturing operations become an important determinant of profit. The demand patterns by now are well known and by effectively serving that demand at low cost, firms are likely to improve sales, share, and profits. As the market life cycle advances, therefore, a firm will usually attempt to specialize and aggregate responsibilities by function. At this point, flexibility and participation are replaced by specialization and centralization. Members or departments that specialize in particular functions will own authority as well as carry responsibility for effecting those tasks.

In order to succeed, organizations must adapt to this changing environment. An interfunctional organization, suitable for entrepreneurship, will now need to transform to a functional structure. But the complexity and challenge of a modern organization are such that even as one product line matures, another may be about to be launched. As such, the integration and flexibility required of new product-markets as well as the scale and efficiency required of predictable and growing product-markets must coexist within the same organization.

The point is simple: As the market life cycle in Figure 1 advances, both functional specialization plus business process integration and coordination are needed. In small companies this is much easier to achieve. In larger operations, the sheer size of the marketing, manufacturing, or R&D operations requires dedicated functional management. Even if managers started out as generalists, the intensity of the job is certainly bound to turn them into specialists. Hence the need for a structure

---

[3]For a more detailed explanation see Steven C. Wheelwright and Kim B. Clark, *Revolutionizing Product Development* (New York: Free Press, 1992), chap. 7.

FIGURE 3

The order fulfillment process

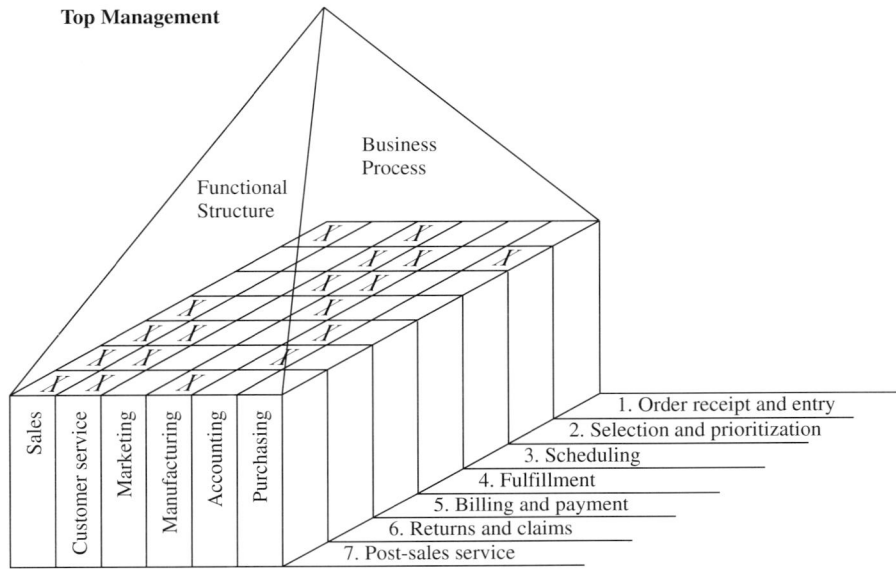

that formally encourages integration and coordination among the functions. Many brilliant entrepreneurs have been burned at this transition. They have been either unwilling or unable to accommodate the winds of change.

It is not the new product development process alone that needs a cross-functional orientation; the customer acquisition and retention process can be just as cross-functionally demanding. The latter consists of all those activities that differentiate the product/service offering in the eyes of the customer leading up to the initial sale and then repeated sales of the product. Figure 3 illustrates the interfunctional dependencies in a typical order-fulfillment activity.[4] It should be obvious from a comparison of Figures 2 and 3 that the set of functions and also the nature of their coordinating tasks are different across the different processes. Unless an effective mechanism exists to coordinate these crucial processes, one could well end up with two powerful engines pulling in opposite directions.

Consider the "customer retention process." It requires a constant monitoring of customer sentiments with regard to various aspects of the business, for example, product reliability, order fulfillment, and service response. But one cannot unilaterally raise these services higher and higher to reach a perpetual state of customer delight. First, such an option may not be financially optimal. But more important, each external customer satisfaction measure also reflects an internal process such as quality enhancement, low-cost manufacturing, or just-in-time logistics. Until and unless the external customer satisfaction process is synchronized with the internal quality management process, uncoordinated enhancement efforts will not be

---

[4]Benson P. Shapiro, Kasturi V. Rangan, and John J. Sviokla, "Staple Yourself to an Order," *Harvard Business Review,* July–August 1992.

all that effective. Furthermore, while customer satisfaction might be a key process to ensure customer retention, the new product development process or the order generation process might be the key lever to acquiring new customers. What is needed is value enhancement, not only for the customer, but also for the company and its shareholders. One should not forget that while each of these processes is cross-functional, its center of gravity usually rests with one or a few functions. For example, few would deny the centrality of R&D in new product development, and that of marketing in its commercialization. Similarly, few would deny the importance of manufacturing and customer service in order fulfillment. Functional strength is required for effective leadership in process management and also to serve as the focal point for synchronizing activities across processes. Only in this way can value for the customer be translated to value for all.

While the bigger crime, in many companies, has been top management's myopic rush to reorganize structure without consideration to the underlying core processes, some senior managers have shown undue haste for business process reengineering. In their anxiety to be market-driven, they are quick to abandon functional structures in favor of process management by teams. While the latter is bound to deliver short-term results, its long-term sustainability is doubtful in the absence of functional nourishment and nurturing.[5] While the core processes provide the essential circulation system and the nervous system for a business, without the skeleton of the structure, it would be impossible for the processes to fulfill their goals effectively.

Stage III: Expansion and Coordination

The evolution of the market life cycle to Stage III is usually accompanied by other related changes in the product/market environment. What previously was a relatively focused market with specific applications and known competition from a few key players has grown considerably more diverse. Market maturity is usually accompanied (even precipitated) by the appearance of competitors with similar product offerings. Customers, by now completely familiar with and knowledgeable about the product, demand special services to fulfill their unique requirements. Market growth slows in Stage III as most of the readily available potential has been exhausted. In addition, uncertainty has by now returned, this time in the form of demand volatility as firms battle for share in a mature market. As manufacturers scramble to differentiate their products in the different segments, product variety, customer segments, buying behavior, and channel arrangements begin to proliferate. Confronted by such diversity, firms have little choice but to coordinate across customers, customer segments, products, channels, and geographies. Product decisions have to be viewed in the context of the business unit's other products, sales

---

[5]The popular press is full of process reengineering examples. See, for example, "The Search for the Organization of Tomorrow," *Fortune,* May 18, 1992, and "The Horizontal Corporation," *Business Week,* December 10, 1993. For a detailed explanation of process reengineering concepts see Michael Hammer and James Champy, "Reengineering the Corporation," *Harper Business Press,* New York: (1993).

FIGURE 4

Managing a complex business environment

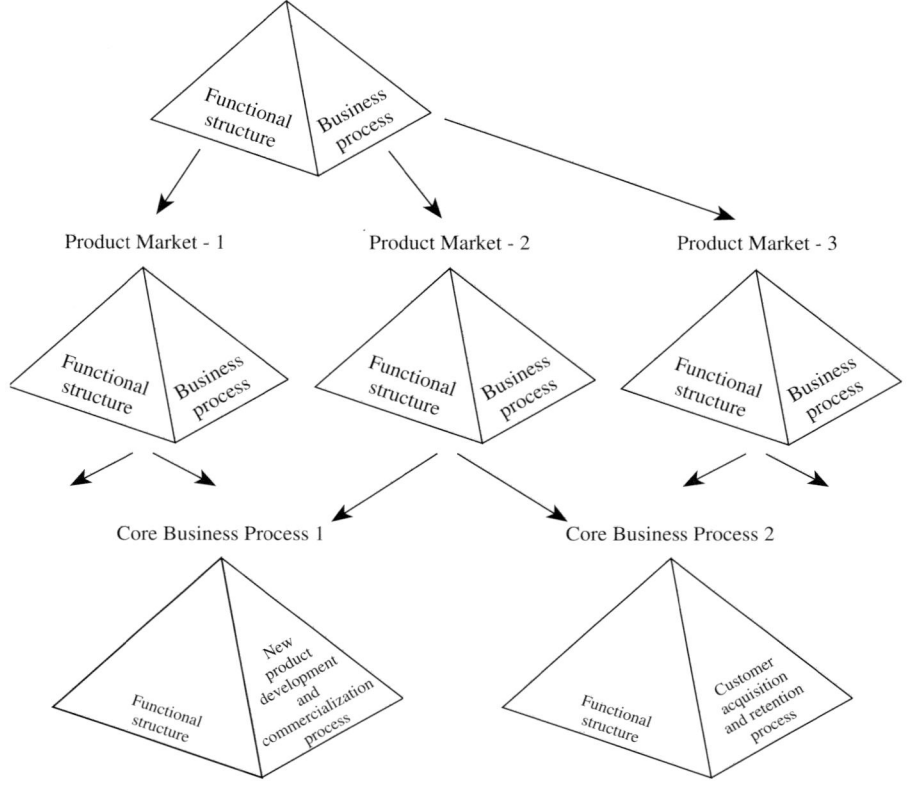

force decisions must be harmonized in the context of a firm's overall distribution channels, and marketing decisions have to be made in the context of a firm's corporate strategy.

The task of managing such a business environment is truly challenging. The complexity goes up exponentially. The different optimal functional structures and core business processes for the different product/market businesses all must be integrated into an overarching organizational system. See Figure 4. The company in that example operating in three product-markets will have to coordinate across a minimum of six core business processes and three functional structures. It is highly unlikely that these structures and processes will be consistent with one another given the company's conscious decision to participate in three different product-market segments. Yet, coordination will be necessary given an underlying common technology, shared operational resources, or overlapping customers across the three business segments. Thus, the organization will need interdepartmental, interfunctional, and interdivisional coordination. It will need flexibility, speed, efficiency, integration, and coordination all at once. "It is a three-ring circus," as the CEO of one such corporation proclaimed. "One has to manage new products, mature products, and product-market diversity, all simultaneously. When the bear has done its trick,

FIGURE 5

Organizational tasks over the market life cycle

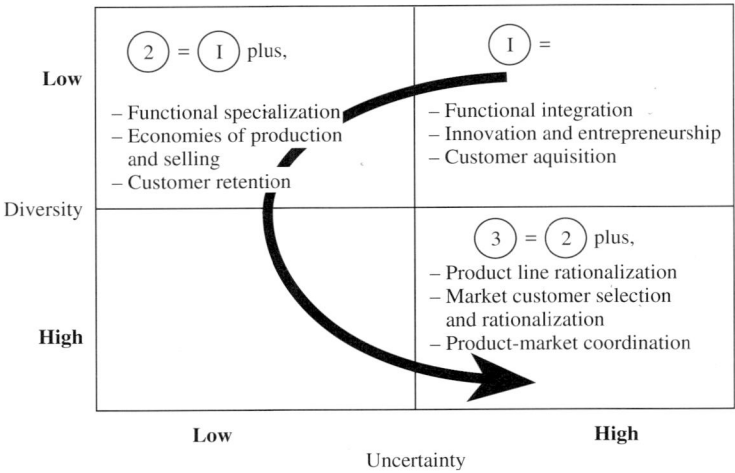

the ringmaster has to turn to the elephant. And when those two have been coaxed to deliver their act, the ringmaster has to sweat out the inclusion of the lion for the grand finale. The management style suited for one is most ill-suited for the other." Firms that are able to cope and manage the complexity are likely to receive high rewards because of product-market coverage; the risks are equally high for firms that cannot.

The dynamic of the market life cycle forces organizations into increasingly complex forms. It is not merely a question of changing from one form to the other. As shown in Figure 5, the Stage III organization is more complex than a Stage II organization, which in turn is more complex than a Stage I organization. At each stage the organization has to manage an additional level of complexity. Not every company in the market is doomed to escalating complexity, however. Firms, after all, can choose to play in whichever environment they wish. This, in fact, has been offered as a definition of strategy. A Stage II organization, for instance, can be considerably less complex if its managers decide to take a strategic focus on mature markets, a quite successful and sustainable approach under the right circumstances. It would then alleviate the necessity to organize for entrepreneurship and integration (new products), in addition to efficiency and dedication (mature products). Similarly, Stage III firms might choose to focus only on a few nonoverlapping product markets. Some of these might be new product ventures and other mature products, but as long as these businesses do not compete for the same customers, it should be possible to split the company into a Stage I and Stage II organization, focusing on different businesses.

In spite of a company's best efforts to reorganize, there is bound to be some amount of competition among its various divisions. Even so, it might be less costly for the corporation to allow some interdivisional rivalry, rather than attempting to coordinate heterogeneous divisions, because a shoddy transformation into a Stage III organization could stifle entrepreneurship and speed; teamwork degenerates into an activity wherein minutes of the meeting are kept and hours wasted. The result is a never-ending business decline to focused niche competitors in every niche. The only way to compete may be to cut the ties (real or imaginary) with the company's other business. IBM's move in 1992 to set up a PC company (separate from its mainframe and minicomputer businesses) may have been motivated by such arguments.

Case Studies and Conclusions

Consider the case of General Electric's Engineering Plastics division (GE Plastics or GEP).[6] With sales of about $5 billion in 1990, it was the largest engineering plastics company in the world. In 1957 it began with a successful polycarbonate product trademarked Lexan, which could be used to replace glass. In 1964, GEP introduced yet another resin, trademarked Noryl, which could be molded and blended with other resins to produce items such as personal computers, TV cabinets, and automotive dashboards. In 1988, with the acquisition of Borg-Warner's chemical operations, it added a low-end plastic, ABS, with applications in a wide array of consumer products such as kitchen appliances.

In the 1970s, the engineering plastics market was in its early growth stage (exceeding 25 percent per year). Automobile, appliance, and computer companies were the early adapters. New applications had to be carefully developed. Price was not an issue because plastics were replacing metals, which were heavier, costlier, and more expensive to process or machine. GEP approached this market with a strong emphasis on market development. After 1985, however, this scene changed. GEP found itself competing against other plastics, and in particular the cheaper blends, as customers who had first entered the market with a highly engineered product began to selectively downgrade their requirements. While overengineering was the accepted rule when metal parts were replaced with plastic, as companies became more familiar with plastics and their abilities, they became more willing and able to achieve an acceptable end-product performance with a lower-end, lower-priced plastic. The buying decision, purely engineering-driven in the 1970s, began to migrate toward price, manufacturability, and product availability.

When GE Plastics first entered the market with its polycarbonate product, the only significant competitor was Bayer. As its product line grew, so did its competition. When GE Plastics introduced Noryl, it went head-to-head against Du Pont's Nylon. Likewise with the addition of ABS, it gained another formidable opponent in Dow. Thus, from a single, focused product market, the company moved slowly but steadily to a multiproduct market with many competitors and slow (single digit) growth in the 1980s.

Obviously, this situation required a change in organization structure. In the 1970s the company was organized along product divisions. That is, the polycarbonate product had its own dedicated manufacturing, technology, and marketing

---

[6]"GE Plastics," Harvard Business School case no. 591-029.

resources; other products were similarly organized. The product-based structure had served GEP very well for many years; indeed, it was credited with much of the company's explosive growth during the early 1980s. At that time, penetrating new markets—converting customers from steel or concrete—was critical. A bottom line of profit and loss was clear for each product, and product loyalty was strong. The optimal organization created a sense of ownership, team responsibility, and accountability. Employees were encouraged to view themselves as general managers and entrepreneurs. But in the 1980s such a structure caused problems. First, competition among product divisions confused customers. Plastics cannibalized its own product lines in front of customers. A senior GE Plastics manager put it this way: "The Lexan marketing rep told the customer that Lexan was best, then the Noryl rep said that Noryl was best. Customers asked us, 'Will the real GE Plastics please stand up?'"

Second, the product division duplicated many tasks. Each business unit tried to be independent, so each operated distinct groups for MIS, finance, customer service, and purchasing. Finally, every product champion was also a product defender. The product-based structure established and entrenched vested interests.

In 1985, the company changed to a functional structure. See Figure 6. Worldwide it had three geographies (Americas, Europe, and Pacific). Within each geogra-

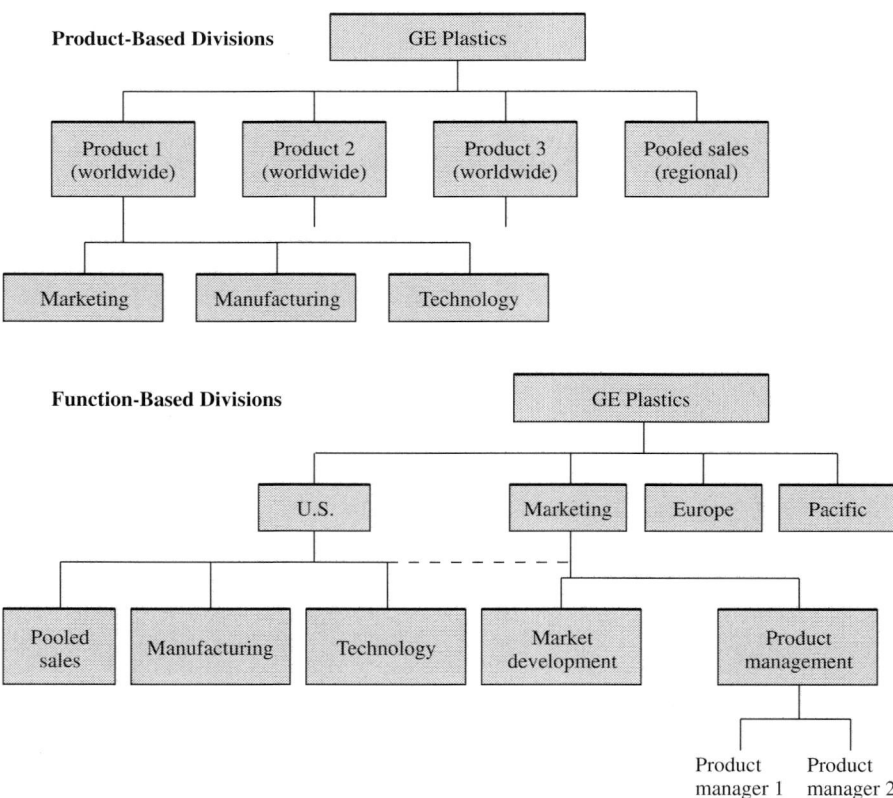

FIGURE 6

GE plastics: Organizational transition

phy, marketing, sales, manufacturing, and technology were common functions for all products. The profit-and-loss responsibility now resided with the geography head. Product managers, who reported to the marketing director, served as the focal point for product-related decisions. In the new structure, the product manager was the critical link for coordination within GE Plastics. Marketing and product management became worldwide functions, with only a dotted line into the geographies.

Then in 1989, the U.S. auto industry entered a period of deep recession followed by the computer and appliance industries shortly thereafter. GE Plastics entered the classic Stage III—high-diversity, high-uncertainty environment. It was in multiple, overlapping product markets with intensive competition for a stagnant, if not mildly declining demand. But because GE Plastics' three products all competed with each other to a significant extent, and because all three products were often bought by the same customer, it had no choice but to play the "Three Ring Circus," an entrepreneurial, flexible organization for developing new products and applications, a cost-efficient and interfunctionally integrated organization for building customer loyalty and profits, and a well-coordinated organization across product divisions and geographies to ensure external consistency and uniformity.

Other conglomerates, such as Europe's ASEA Brown Boveri, with $25 billion sales in 1990, present a different kind of challenge.[7] The company participates in approximately 50 business areas (BA) worldwide, including power transmission, robotics, steam turbines, and metal casting. The company operates about 1,100 factories and employs 250,000. The BA leader for power transformers, for example, is responsible for 25 factories in 16 countries. Fortunately, however, in spite of its staggering business diversity, the company's complex task of organizing itself is aided by the lack of product-market overlaps among its various businesses. Unlike GE Plastics, the product divisions do not cannibalize each other's revenues but are stand-alone, independent businesses. It is possible, therefore, for ABB to organize itself with daring simplicity. See Figure 7. ABB's global matrix consists of two dimensions. Along one dimension is the classic global network consisting of the worldwide head of the business area, who is responsible for product-market strategy and performance without regard for national borders. On the other dimension is the traditionally organized national company. Thus, the head of ABB's robotics company in Norway is charged with manufacturing and marketing industrial robots in Norway and providing capacity for exports according to the business unit's worldwide production plan. But the various heads of their respective business companies in a country also report to the country head. In Germany, for example, ABB's national company, with over a dozen businesses, reports a revenue of $4 billion and acts like a national company employing nearly 36,000 people. The head reports to a board of directors and prepares financial statements comparable to other German companies.

The beauty of ABB's organization is that each cell in the matrix represents an independent stand-alone company. Cell X could be the industrial robotics business

---

[7]William Taylor, "The Logic of Global Business: An Interview with ABB's Percy Barnevik," *Harvard Business Review,* March–April 1991.

FIGURE 7

ASEA Brown Boveri's matrix organization

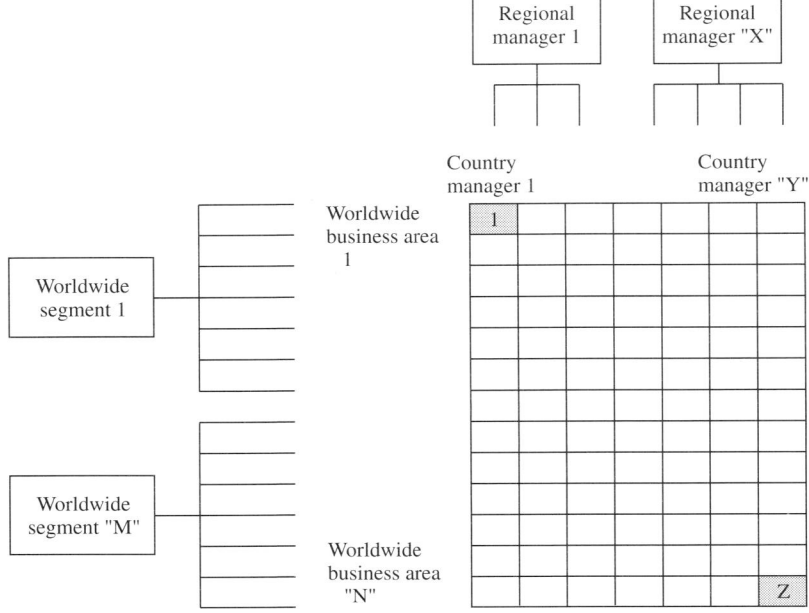

in Norway and Cell Z could be the power transformer business in Germany. The businesses within each country (i.e., column 1 or column Y) do not compete for customers and have dedicated manufacturing and engineering facilities. The only thing they compete for is resources. Across the countries, however, businesses could well compete with each other for the same customers. This is especially true of global businesses like locomotives. There is therefore a need for worldwide coordination, which is provided by the business area leader. Even predominantly local businesses need coordination, because it may be cheaper for ABB to produce all in one or a few countries for shipment to demand areas, rather than local production all over the world. Here is where the "geographies" could butt up against the "businesses," and such issues are coordinated at the top by the executive committee.

Not all companies, however, are at one extreme (GE Plastics) or the other (ABB). Often, it is a challenge to even figure out what the synergies and overlaps are. Millipore Corporation,[8] for instance, a $750 million company with an Analytical Instrumentation business and a Membrane Separation business, struggled with exactly that question. Both divisions often sold to the same customer. While the analytical instruments salespeople sold to the process control laboratory, the membrane sales force sold to the operations people. There were overlaps, but no cannibalization. They sold different products. But most important, one product was in a highly competitive mature market and the other was still a growing market with limited competition. The company's management had either to design a comprehen-

---

[8]"Millipore Corporate Strategy," Harvard Business School case no. 594-009.

sive Stage III organization or alternatively develop two: a Stage I (for new products) and a Stage II (for mature products) organization. Not an easy decision to make under any circumstances.

With increasing globalization in the 1990s, the coordination problem is demanding more attention. A large proportion of industrial customers are global, with worldwide manufacturing and sales. This introduces a different kind of market overlap—product and pricing decisions across geographies have to be coordinated, because the customer is the same! But at the same time it is important to recognize that the manufacturing and marketing environment in the geographic areas (e.g., Europe, the United States, and Japan) are considerably diverse, justifying an independent administration.

There are no easy solutions, and it is not our intention to pretend that there are. We strongly argue, however, that organizations should carefully evaluate their product-market environments before undertaking a reengineering effort. Clearly, different environments will necessitate a different process for focus. We also emphasize the need for structural anchors. It is fine to break the functional walls, but the interfunctional processes need to be coordinated in order to make a holistic and effective contribution. Without strong leadership at key links of the process chain, and a creative system to coordinate these links, managing a complex environment could be the equivalent of managing chaos.

Finally, an organization can effectively alter the environment in which it chooses to play by altering the portfolio of its product-markets. The bottom line: Strategy is all about product-market selection, and organization is all about the systems, processes, and structures necessary to effectively address customers' needs in the selected product-market.

CHAPTER 37

Barco Projection Systems (A): Worldwide Niche Marketing

Barco, based in Belgium, is the worldwide market share leader in the high-performance end of the industrial projection system business, with a 55 percent share in graphics applications. Sony holds overall market leadership through its dominance in the lower-price/performance video and data segments. Barco's planned product development program is based on assumptions of Sony's gradual migration up the performance spectrum. This assumption turns out to be incorrect as Sony surprises Barco and the rest of the industry with introduction of a "superdata" projector at performance levels beyond Barco's. Rumor has it that the innovation will be priced 20 to 40 percent below the market level as well. Barco must decide whether to maintain its previous development program or pull resources to start up a new project to beat Sony.

On Saturday morning, September 23, 1989, Erik Dejonghe, Frans Claerbout, and Bernard Dursin met to draft a crucial presentation that Dejonghe was scheduled to make to the Barco N.V. board of directors on the following Monday. As the senior vice president and chief operating officer (COO) of Barco N.V., with responsibility for Barco's Projection Systems division (BPS), Dejonghe had to respond to the recent move of a BPS competitor that threatened the heart of the division's sales. Claerbout, the general manager of BPS, and Dursin, in charge of managing Barco's distribution subsidiaries and coordinating the worldwide marketing of projectors, had both worked closely with Dejonghe to formulate the company's options.

One month earlier, the Sony Corporation surprised BPS and the rest of the industry with the unveiling of its 1270 "superdata" projector at the Siggraph trade show in Boston. Sony's product had seized first place at Siggraph as the industry's highest-performing projector from BPS and its BG400 projector. More damaging

---

This case was prepared by Krista McQuade under the supervision of Rowland T. Moriarty.
Copyright © 1991 by the President and Fellows of Harvard College.
Harvard Business School case 591-133.

still, the 1270 was rumored to be priced 20 to 40 percent below the established market price in its performance class. The industry saw the 1270's positioning as an attempt to widen the market through lower prices. For BPS—a small, batch manufacturer—the 1270's combination of low-price and high-performance threatened to collapse its traditional market segmentation, and to bring prices down to untenable levels. Dejonghe estimated that BPS stood to lose as much as 75 percent of its forecasted 1990 profits.

Sony's introduction of the 1270 had been timed to prevent competitive response; the industry's most important trade show, Infocomm, was scheduled to take place in the United States in January. Major customers, industry analysts, and dealers would be there, and BPS's performance would determine its sales for the rest of the year. Dejonghe, Claerbout, and Dursin had sketched out their pricing and product development options, and they weighed each one carefully as they plotted BPS's strategy for the following months.

Barco's Projection Systems Division

Barco Projection Systems (BPS) was the second largest division of the Barco N.V. group, with 350 employees, and turnover of 1.39 billion Bfr (Belgian francs), or $35 million, in 1988 (Exhibit 1).[1] Headquartered at Kuurne, Belgium, 15 km from Barco's main facilities at Kortrijk, the division had been formed in the early 1980s as a result of Barco's interest in the emerging technology of video projection. Throughout the 1980s, the division had grown rapidly. In 1988 it represented 23 percent of Barco N.V.'s turnover of 5.98 billion Bfr ($150 million).

Background: Barco N.V.

Barco N.V. began operations in 1934 as a producer of radio broadcast receivers. In 1948, it built its first television (TV) receiver, and from then on, consumer TV formed the bulk of its sales. As a small company, Barco was able to compete successfully by carving out a market on the basis of its R&D strength and product quality. From 1955 to 1975, the company grew rapidly and expanded into broadcast monitors and professional video equipment. At the end of the 1970s, however, during the global recession that followed the 1977 oil supply shock, demand for Barco's consumer products sagged. In response, the company redefined its focus from consumer to industrial markets. In 1989, Hugo Vandamme, Barco's president and CEO, looked back on that period:

> We knew that as a small, batch manufacturer we could not have continued to survive in markets for consumer products. Instead, we redrew our strategy to try and focus on top-of-the-line products in niche markets. In one instance, in 1983, we went as far as to say

---

[1]For this case, one U.S. dollar is equal to 40 Belgian francs. The actual value of the dollar was extremely volatile during the historical period covered.

Exhibit 1 Key BPS Financial Data, 1988–1989 (in millions of Bfr)

	1988		1989	
	Bfr	*$US*	*Bfr*	*$US*
Turnover	1,387	$34.7	1,983	$49.6
Direct production costs	772	19.3	815	20.4
Total production overhead	40	1.0	45	1.1
Marketing and R&D	130	3.3	170	4.3
Depreciation and charges	138	3.5	329	8.2
Income before taxes	307	7.7	624	15.6

Note: In addition to sales of video, data, and graphics projectors, BPS turnover recorded sales of projector accessories. In 1988, this category amounted to 168.5 million Bfr ($4.2 million); in 1989 it was 239.3 million Bfr ($6 million).
Source: BPS.

no to a customer asking for 15,000 computer monitors. We were able to turn that order down because we had spread our operations out and become involved in other markets. We had set out with a clear vision of who we wanted to be, how we wanted to operate, and where we wanted to compete. Vision is what counts.

The company's strategy throughout the 1980s consisted of three key elements. First, Barco committed itself to becoming a leader in a variety of distinct, but complementary, niche markets. The company entered a new activity only if it had an in-depth knowledge of the market and the technology involved, and if it could be among the top three manufacturers. The second element of Barco's strategy was a strong commitment to research and development; throughout the 1980s, between 8 and 10 percent of its annual turnover and 15 percent of the company's employees were dedicated to R&D. And third, in addition to growth in its businesses, the company sought a growing presence in international markets in sales, product development, and production. In 1988, Barco launched a global expansion campaign for acquisitions and joint ventures abroad. Three major acquisitions in the first half of 1989 totaled 4.4 billion Bfr ($110 million). In that same year, Barco reorganized its operations into seven autonomous divisions, each with its own research, product development, production, marketing, and sales.

In 1989, with 2,400 employees, Barco N.V. was positioned as one of the top three worldwide manufacturers in each of its product lines: automated production control systems, graphic arts, computer-aided design, and industrial projection. As a result of the company's early 1989 acquisitions and expanding sales in several key markets, turnover was expected to grow 50 percent in 1989. A number of international awards testified to Barco's technological lead in several fields. In 1988, for example, the company received the international Emmy Award for its studio monitors. The year after, BPS won the Hi-Vi Silver Award in Japan, given for the product contributing the most to electronic visualization technology.

BPS Organization within Barco N.V.

As part of the divisionalization of Barco N.V.'s operations in 1989, President Hugo Vandamme and Senior Vice President Erik Dejonghe divided responsibility for products between them; BPS reported to the latter. Dejonghe, who assumed his current position at the time of reorganization, was part of the team that propelled Barco's industrial projection activities throughout the 1980s. Joining Barco in the early 1980s as the product and project manager for special activities, he was promoted in 1983 to president of the division that fabricated TVs and large-screen projectors. Frans Claerbout was head of the R&D department for that division, while Bernard Dursin was in charge of its marketing and sales. Dejonghe, Claerbout, and Dursin worked closely together on projectors throughout the 1980s.

In 1989, Claerbout was promoted to vice president of Barco N.V. and was named general manager of BPS. Dursin, also named a Barco N.V. vice president, became the general manager of Barco International, a group that managed the marketing of certain Barco product lines worldwide, including projectors. Claerbout's and Dursin's offices remained within shouting distance of one another, however, and they continued to collaborate on projectors. Dursin continued to manage relations with the division's distributors, and, in addition, he played a leading role in setting the prices for projectors worldwide. Three regional marketing managers, who reported directly to Claerbout, were responsible for sales support to all of the division's distributors. Camiel Derijcke replaced Claerbout in 1989 as the chief engineer in charge of product development at BPS. However, Claerbout continued to make the final decisions. (See Exhibit 2 for BPS's organization chart.)

BPS Products

BPS designed, manufactured, and marketed sophisticated video projectors for industrial applications. Unlike movie projectors, which operated by shining white light through an image recorded on celluloid film, video projectors recreated an image electronically. Barco's projectors could be connected to TVs, VCRs, and most recently to computers. They were used to project images and information stored in these media onto large screens, for large-audience viewing (see Exhibit 3 for a diagram of the unit). BPS did not invent video projection, but throughout the 1980s, it played a key role in the development of niche market applications for the technology. By 1989, BPS had developed three lines of projectors: video, data, and graphics.

All of BPS's projectors were based on the same design concept and comprised three major components—tubes (3), lenses (3), and electronics. The division's product line was built primarily around a 7" tube. BPS's strength had traditionally been in electronics; given the same lens and tube combination, BPS was able to achieve measurably better performance in each of the main areas of evaluation than its competition. In 1989, the most important considerations in evaluating the performance of an industrial projector were brightness (measured in lumens), image quality, and resolution. A projector's three components worked together to provide particular

EXHIBIT 2 The Management of Barco Projection Systems, 1989

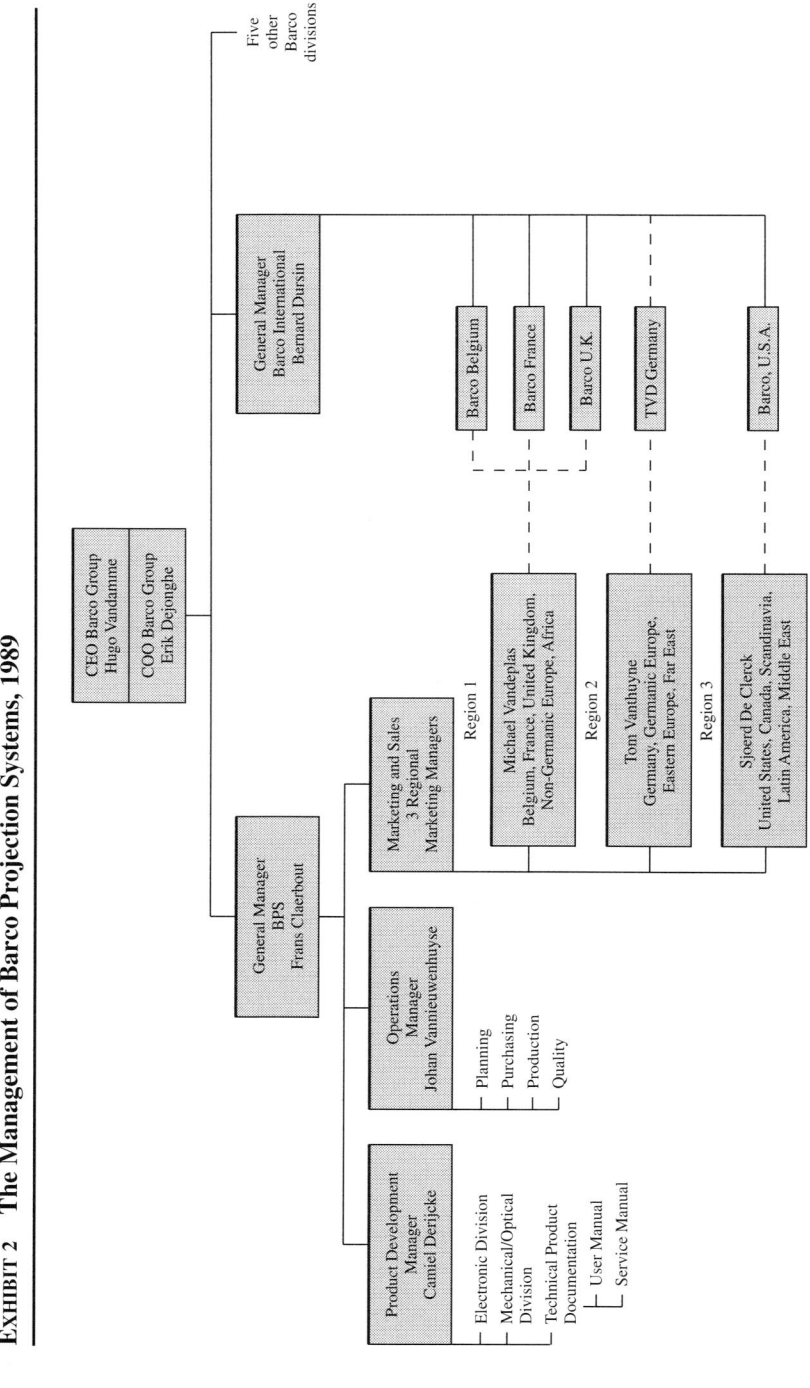

Note: Non–wholly owned distributors not shown here reported jointly to Barco International and the appropriate regional marketing manager.

Exhibit 3   Projector Diagram

Projector Side View

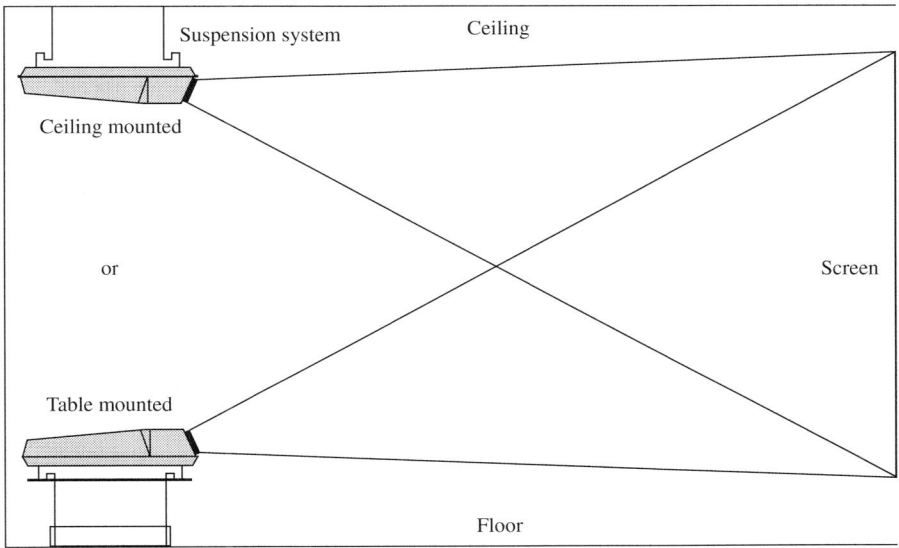

Projector Top View

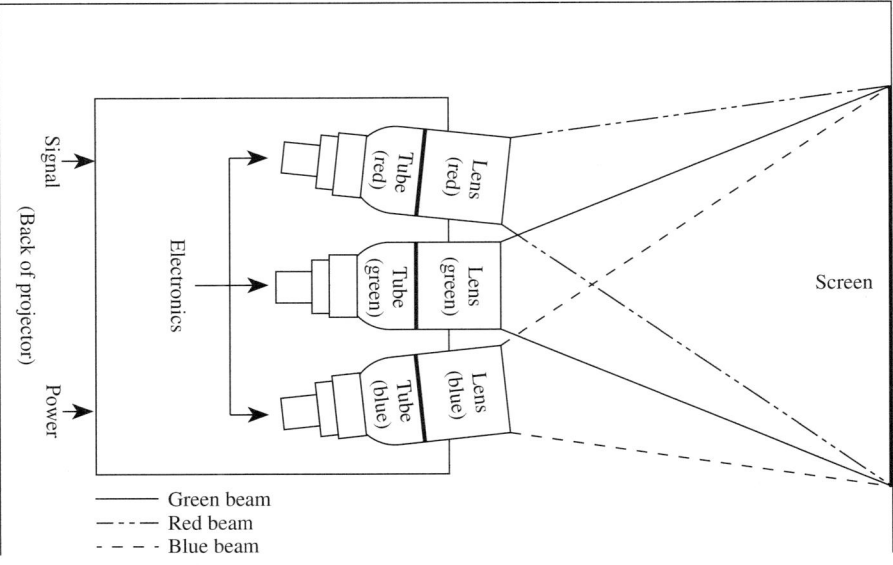

NOTE: A projector functioned in three stages. First, the information contained in an electronic signal was split into its color (red, green, blue) content. Next, each color's information was redrawn by the electrons of the projector's tubes, one for each color. Finally, the three resulting images were passed through magnifying lenses and projected in sync onto the screen for a full-color image.

results. In general, the tubes, lenses, and electronics represented 15 percent, 20 percent, and 50 percent of the projector's cost structure, respectively. The housing and mechanics represented an additional 15 percent.

What differentiated BPS's product lines was *scan rate,* or scanning frequency, which measured the speed at which a projector was able to read and process incoming electronic signals. BPS used scan rate to segment its markets; as the sophistication of the application for BPS projectors increased, scan rate increased. BPS's *video* projectors were designed for compatibility with standard video sources, such as broadcast TV and VCR, and scanned at 16 kilohertz (kHz), or 16,000 lines per second.[2] Its *data* projectors scanned at 16 kHz to 45 kHz, and were capable of displaying input from personal computers as well as video sources. Its *graphics* projectors, BPS's most sophisticated products, scanned from 16 kHz to well above 64 kHz, and accepted input from the powerful computer-aided design and manufacturing (CAD/CAM) systems, as well as from video and data sources. A projector needed to match the scan rate of its source for a clear picture to result; Barco's graphics projectors would not be compatible with any computer scanning higher than 64 kHz. BPS was continually upgrading the scan rates of its most sophisticated projector line to match advances in computer technology.

In 1989, BPS had well-established sales for its video and data lines in a variety of entertainment, training, and presentation markets. Board rooms, training centers, discotheques, classrooms, airplanes, and betting shops around the world had all installed Barco projectors. The monthly sales log of one of BPS's European distributors, for example, listed the sale of four data projectors to the Commission of the European Economic Community (EEC) for video conferencing, five video projectors to a chain of holiday resorts for entertainment rooms, and five data projectors to Groupe Bull, a large French computer company, for training centers. IBM had been one of BPS's best customers throughout the 1980s, having decided in 1984 to equip all of its U.S. training centers with Barco projectors.

In addition, BPS was pursuing a number of more specialized markets for its projection technology, such as process control and simulation. Data and graphics projectors were used for these specialized applications. In 1989, BPS installed a series of projectors in the process control room of the U.S. Union Pacific Railroad, which displayed more than 23,000 km of track on a 200 foot-wide screen. Barco projectors could also be found at the process control centers for the English Channel Tunnel project, in factories, and in flight simulation rooms for military and aerospace applications.

Evolution of BPS's Product Lines and Markets

Barco N.V.'s involvement in projection systems began in 1981, when it developed a video projector for showing motion pictures in airplanes. The projector, called the Barco Vision 1 (BV1), was priced at 450,000 Bfr ($11,250), and sold strongly in the U.S. and European markets. As the company began to investigate other applications

---

[2]Note: 16 kHz = 30 frames of information per second $\times$ 533.3 lines per frame.

for its technology, Dejonghe, Claerbout, and Dursin presented their views on the future of projection to Barco's board of directors. They believed the company could pursue one of three directions: (1) It could downgrade its technology to suit consumer video applications, (2) it could upgrade its technology for long-distance, high-performance video projection, (3) or, it could enter the untested market for computer applications.

In their presentation to the board, Dejonghe, Claerbout, and Dursin related discussions of a possible computer-compatible projector that they had had with one BV1 customer, IBM. Developing the computer application, they learned, was feasible, but scan rates would have to be increased to match a computer's faster electronics. Moreover, the projector would have to be designed with enough flexibility to be used by computer companies with different standard scanning frequencies. But Dejonghe and the others felt that the complexity of the application would work to Barco's advantage, keeping larger firms out of the market. They also thought it had the potential to expand projection markets significantly. The board voted to follow their suggestion, and made Dejonghe the new president of the TV and projector division.

In 1983, the sales of that division at Barco were split 80 percent to 20 percent between TV and projectors. Dejonghe set out to reverse that ratio. By the end of 1983, BPS had introduced the BarcoData 1 (BD1)—the first computer-compatible projector on the marketplace. Priced at 540,000 Bfr ($13,500), the BD1 was able to scan to 18 kHz, and was immediately successful in corporate presentation markets, as well as others. In 1984, BPS introduced two more projectors—the BV2 (395,000 Bfr, $9,875) and the BD2 (590,000 Bfr, $14,750), which incorporated engineering advances that permitted higher scan rates, and thus broader compatibility. From 1984 on, BPS's video and data lines continued to evolve, keeping pace with breakthroughs in design, improved components, and, in the case of data projectors, with ever-changing computer technology. In 1986, BPS began work on a graphics application for its technology.

BPS developed its graphics projectors to handle input from CAD/CAM sources, which required the upgrading of a data projector's scanning frequency to 64 kHz and above. (BPS's most powerful data projector at that time, the BD3, scanned up to 32 kHz). Dejonghe recalled how the division's market segmentation scheme was formalized:

> I remember the meeting when we decided to create a graphics segment of the marketplace for a machine scanning at 64 kHz and above. Limiting the scan rate on our data projectors would frustrate some end users. Our plan was to respond to that frustration by offering a graphics projector. We could have made it one machine, but we could not have sold it for the highest price.

Dejonghe, Claerbout, and Dursin decided to limit video-only projectors to a scan rate of 16 kHz; data projectors to a scanning range of 16 kHz to 45 kHz; and graphics projectors, their newest line, to a scanning range of 16 kHz to 64 kHz and above. In June 1987, BPS introduced its first graphics projector, the BarcoGraphics 400 (BG400), for 1 million Bfr ($25,000). The BG400 was the industry's most

EXHIBIT 4 BPS Product Evolution, 1982–1989

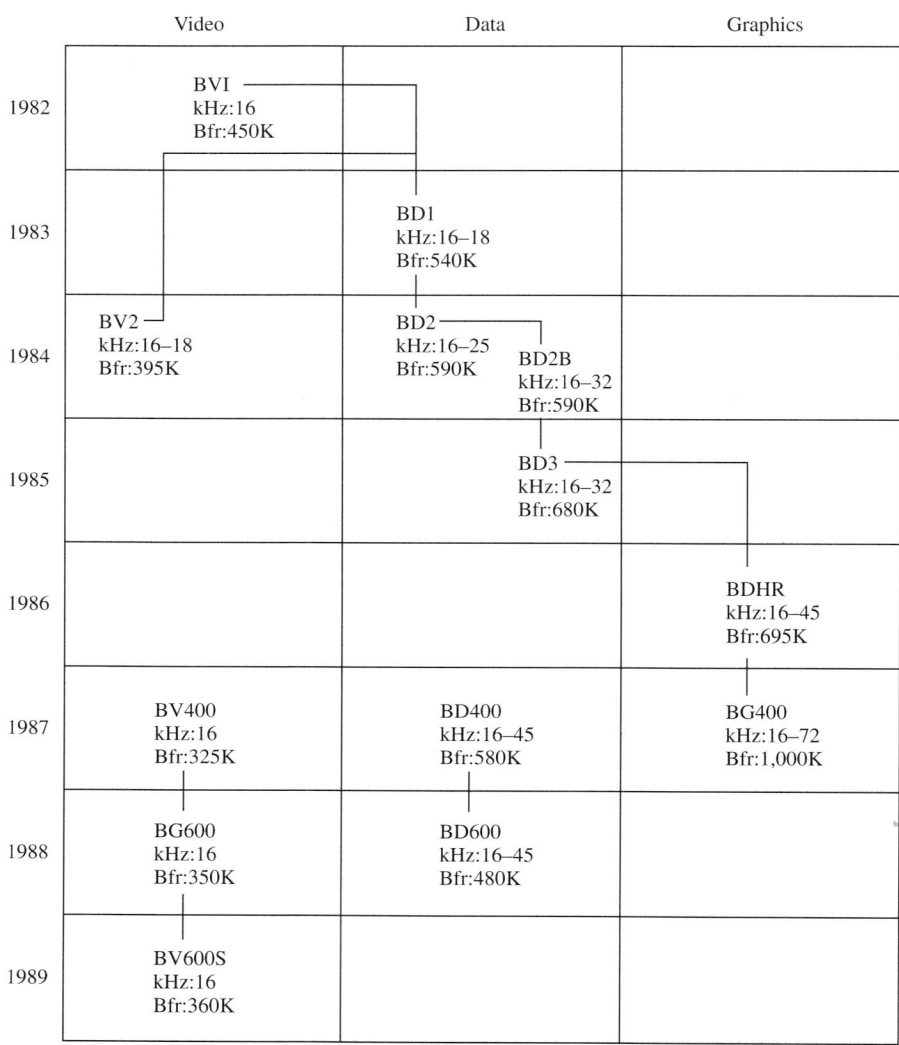

NOTE: This diagram contains principal 7″ projector introductions only; modifications and special-application projectors are not included.
SOURCE: BPS.

sophisticated high-end projector, scanning at up to 72 kHz. By 1989, the price of the BG400 had come down to 960,000 Bfr ($24,000). (Exhibit 4 displays a time chart of BPS's product evolution.)

By September 1989, BPS was looking toward its next generation of product introductions—digitally controlled projectors. Currently, all adjustments to the settings of a BPS projector were carried out manually. The new projectors would incorporate digital technology to allow a projector's mechanisms to be controlled by a hand-held remote-control unit. BPS planned to introduce the technology into the data segment of its marketplace first, and then into its graphics and video segments. BPS engineers had reached the beta test point for its first digital data projector, to be called the BD700, and were completing all modifications. The BD700, to be priced at 640,000 Bfr ($16,000), was scheduled for full production and delivery in October 1989.

Frans Claerbout summed up the forces driving the evolution of Barco's projection product line throughout the 1980s as (1) the constant search for the best possible image, (2) flexibility toward inputs, and (3) increasing user-friendliness. Product evolution, he explained, was "more a result of engineering solutions to problems that arose, than of a specific development plan." Barco's competition in industrial projection had adopted its practice of segmenting its markets by scanning frequency. Video, data, and graphics had become the standard terms for each market by 1989.

Projector Markets

Through 1994, the worldwide market for projectors was expected to grow 8.5 percent per year. Growth rates for the video, data, and graphics segments of the market, however, varied widely (see Table A).

The largest market for industrial projectors in 1989, across all segments, was North America, with 50 percent of total unit sales. Western Europe and the Far Eastern market followed, with 36 percent and 12 percent, respectively, of total unit sales. The five-year annual market growth predicted for these regions was 9 percent, 11.5 percent, and 18 percent.

TABLE A The Worldwide Market for Industrial Projectors, 1988

	Units (%)	Predicted Growth 1989–1994[a]	Price Range
Video	63%	.8%	200,000–280,000 Bfr ($5,000–$7,000)
Data	33%	12.3%	320,000–600,000 Bfr ($8,000–$15,000)
Graphics	4%	40.2%	800,000–960,000 Bfr ($20,000–$24,000)
Total	100%	8.5%	200,000–960,000 Bfr ($5,000–$24,000)

[a]Estimated average annual growth.

BPS in 1989

In September 1989, the data segment of the marketplace represented the heart of BPS's sales for both units and revenues (see Table B). The video segment was moving toward commodity, and BPS was concentrating less and less of its effort in this area. In the high end of the marketplace, BPS was the acknowledged technological leader. BPS estimated its worldwide market share, based on the total number of units sold, at 8 percent in video, 23 percent in data, and 55 percent in graphics.

Through 1994, BPS predicted that its video, data, and graphics unit sales would grow 1.4 percent, 12.3 percent, and 25 percent respectively per year. It anticipated that the worldwide market for industrial projection would continue to expand for at least five more years before being superseded by new technologies. In 1989, the division's principal products were the BD600, which scanned to 45 kHz, and the BG400, which scanned to 72 kHz. The two projectors sold in 1989 for 480,000 Bfr ($12,000) and 960,000 Bfr ($24,000), respectively (Exhibit 5). BPS's main line of video projectors sold for 280,000 Bfr ($7,000). BPS sold 4,400 units in all three categories in 1988.

Distribution

In 1989, BPS had a two-step distribution system with 45 distributors and approximately 400 dealers worldwide.[3] The division owned four of its distributors—in Belgium, France, the United Kingdom, and the United States—while the other 41 operated independently, but were Barco-exclusive for projectors. Fully owned distributors represented 61 percent of BPS's total unit sales, 61 percent of its revenues, and 59 percent of its margins. By individual product, they represented 57 percent of unit sales, 53 percent of revenues, and 50 percent of margins for video projection; 61 percent of units, 60 percent of revenues, and 57 percent of margins for data pro-

TABLE B BPS Sales by Segment, 1988

	(%) Units	(%) Revenues	(%) Margins
Video	35%	23%	20%
Data:	53	54	51
Percent BD600 of total data	79	67	NA
Graphics:	12	23	29
Percent BG400 of total graphics	85	80	NA
Total	100%	100%	100%

NOTE: Includes sales to captive BPS distributors.

---

[3]BPS could only estimate the number of dealers that carried its products worldwide, since most independent distributors were reluctant to disclose exact figures.

EXHIBIT 5   Barco's Product Positioning, August 1989 (pre-Siggraph)

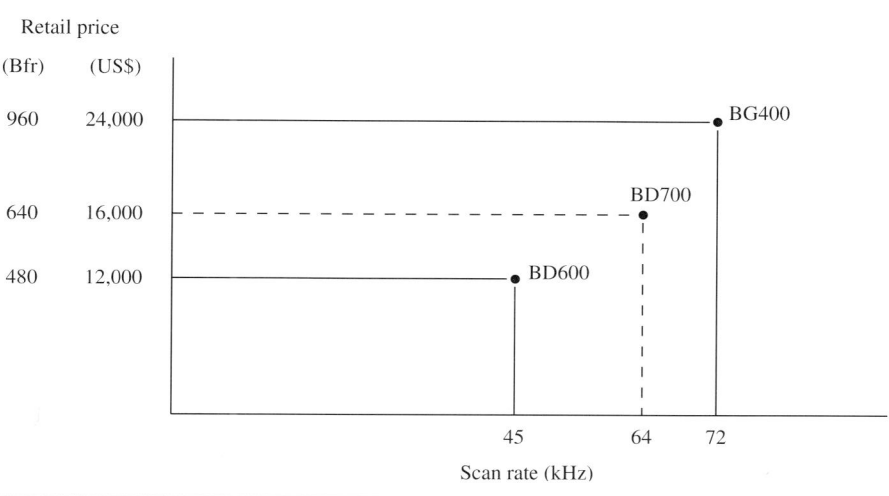

jection; and 75 percent of units, 71 percent of revenues, and 70 percent of margins for graphics projection.

BPS started selling its video projectors in Europe and the United States in 1982, through Barco's video distribution network. When the division entered the data projection market in the mid-1980s, these distributors had been required to invest in training and to add technical personnel. In Belgium, BPS had always handled its own distribution. In the United States, Barco had established a wholly owned distribution subsidiary in 1986 after the insolvency of its distributor. In France, a key market where the distributor had not kept up with the necessary investment, BPS had acquired its operations in 1988.

In Germany, a market which represented 5 percent, 9 percent, and 12 percent of video, data, and graphics unit sales, respectively, in 1988, the owner had consistently refused a BPS offer of purchase. In 1989, he had three years remaining in his contract with BPS. Regional Marketing Manager Tom Vanthuyne explained why he would have preferred to own the German distributor:

> Independent distributors tend to think short term. They are not willing to invest in advertising, or to broaden the number of dealers they work through because they want the margins themselves—for example, they prefer going direct on large accounts. When does it make sense to buy? Until now, we've done it when there were problems in our key markets. In the case of my German distributor, although it is doing OK, it is not making as much money for Barco as it is for itself. That market could be bigger; recently we lost a deal of 600 video units simply because our distributor there was not prepared to cut its margins.

For each product, BPS established a distributor price in Belgian francs. The distributors, in turn, set their own price to dealers. On average, prices in the United States

Table C   BPS's Pricing Index

	List Price	Actual Price	Comments
BPS	100	100	41% direct cost, 59% gross margin
Distributor	142	142	30% margin, 12% import duties and freight
Dealer	204	173–184	List price calculated with 30% margin Street price incorporates discounts of 10%–15%

were a consistent 15 percent lower than in Europe. The typical pricing relation approach appears in Table C.

Dealers carrying Barco projectors ranged from "box" dealers to systems dealers. The box dealer, normally found in large cities, sold projectors on the basis of cost alone, providing no service or expertise. Twenty percent of BPS's dealers were "box," while 90 percent of box sales were video projectors. Systems dealers, at the other extreme, had the know-how to integrate and install packages of equipment according to the end user's individual needs. Often these systems involved more than one brand of equipment. Given the complexity of Barco projectors—particularly its data and graphics models—80 percent of the company's dealers were the systems type.

Projector dealers typically carried three manufacturers' projectors, selecting a line for the low, middle, and high ends of the market, although these could overlap. In addition, projector dealers rounded out their sales with other audio-visual equipment such as overhead projectors, lighting, screens, and consumer electronics. A typical dealer in the United States had turnover ranging from 120 million Bfr ($3 million) to 800 million Bfr ($20 million). About 8 to 10 percent came from after-sales service.

Although a dealer's ideal margin on projectors was 30 percent, fierce competition resulted more often in margins of 15 to 20 percent, and occasionally a dealer would go as low as 5 percent to preserve a customer. Dealer overhead, however, averaged greater than 5 percent. Margins on service were higher, typically 25 to 35 percent, and sometimes as high as 70 percent. Dealers processed information from manufacturers, held vendor fairs and training sessions, and sent mailings. Barco's dealers were required to attend sales and technical courses given by the distributor, and to hire a certain number of Barco-approved technicians. In return, BPS promised price protection for unsold units at a time of a price drop, and stable pricing between the time of the first customer contact and the final order, generally a period of three to six months.

Barco projectors had a reputation among dealers for the highest quality final image and excellent reliability once fully installed. Dealers complained, however, that the machines were unnecessarily complex—designed to win awards, and not be friendly to the end user. They frequently encountered complications in installing the equipment. End users, too, often found BPS's control panels and instructions too complex. BPS's engineers contended that many of the problems arose when the instruction manual was disregarded.

The typical end user purchased a new projector every five years. With an eye to ever-increasing computer scan rates, customers tended to purchase more performance in a projector than they needed.

Competition

In 1989, three companies competed with Barco in the data and graphics segments of the market for industrial projection: Sony, Electrohome, and NEC. Several other firms, including Panasonic, Mitsubishi, and General Electric, competed primarily in the video and low-scanning data segments of the marketplace, and were not considered major competitors to BPS. In data projection, Sony held the largest percentage of the marketplace, followed by Barco, Electrohome, and NEC. In graphics, BPS was in first place with 55 percent of the market. BPS's only major competition in the graphics segment was Electrohome, with 44 percent (see Table D). Exhibit 6 lists the products of each major competitor.

Sony

The Sony Corporation, headquartered in Tokyo, Japan, was a diverse manufacturer of consumer electronics, with 1988 turnover of 460 billion Bfr ($11.5 billion). Industrial projectors were manufactured at its Sony Projectors division, and were estimated to represent 1 percent of the total company's turnover. Sony was the main player in the video segment of the projection marketplace, with 50 percent of all units sold. In data, too, Sony held 49 percent of total units sold; however, its most powerful projector in 1989, the 1031, scanned at 35 kHz. In 1988, the company's product mix was 66 percent video and 34 percent data, on a total of 15,000 units.

TABLE D   Market Share of the Major Competitors, 1988, as Percent of Total Units Sold

		Barco	Sony	E.H.	NEC	Other
Europe	Data	35	35	8	6	16
	Graphics	55	—	43	—	2
N. America	Data	16	62	14	8	—
	Graphics	60	—	40	—	—
Far East	Data	15	30	7	23	25
	Graphics	15	—	80	—	5
General Total	Data	23	49	11	9	8
	Graphics	55	—	44	—	1
	Total*	25	45	14	8	8

NOTE: To be read horizontally; Barco held 35% of the market for data projectors in Europe, versus Sony's 35%, Electrohome's 8%, and so on.
*Omits video.

EXHIBIT 6 Products of the Major Manufacturers, August 1989

Manufacturer	Model	Scan Rate (kHz)	Light Output (lumens)	Resolution (# lines)	Retail Price (Bfr)	Retail Price (US$)
Barco	BD600	16–45	600	1,600	480,000	$12,000
	BG400	16–72	400	2,000	960,000	24,000
Sony	VPH1031	16–35	300	1,100	420,000	10,500
Electrohome	ECP2000	16–36	400	1,280	344,000	8,600
	ECP3000	16–50	650	1,280	580,000	14,500
	ECP4000	16–70	650	1,280	960,000	24,000
NEC	DP1200	16–35	475	800	420,000	10,500
	GP3000	16–54	600	1,100	640,000	16,000

NOTE: Light output and resolution were used in addition to scan rate to measure a projector's performance on the world marketplace. Brightness increased with the number of lumens; however, the human eye could discern only large increases; for example, the eye perceived a 1,000 lumen projector as 50% brighter than a 100 lumen projector. With resolution, the larger the number of lines, the better the quality of the final image. Barco believed that its projectors had the highest light output of all the competitors; however, due to differences in the standards used to calculate lumens, light output was difficult to compare between companies.
SOURCE: BPS.

Typically, Sony projectors were positioned below Barco's in terms of performance (scan rate, brightness, image quality, and resolution), and were, on average, 15 percent lower in price. BPS guessed, in addition, that Sony had fewer engineers dedicated to projection than BPS. BPS expected Sony's next product introduction to be a higher-performance data projector, introduced in the fall of 1989, with an upper scanning limit between 46 kHz and 50 kHz. The division also expected Sony to enter the market with a graphics projector in late 1990.

Sony sold projectors through its network of captive commercial video distributors worldwide. In turn, these distributors worked with over 1,500 dealers across the globe. It was estimated that 50 percent of Sony's dealers were box dealers. Extensive dealer coverage—Sony had 500 dealers in the U.S. market versus BPS's 100—resulted in a low street price for Sony projectors. While dealers used 30 percent margins to figure list prices on both Sony and Barco projectors, Sony units were typically discounted 15 percent for the final sale, while Barco units were discounted 10 percent. Dealers tended to prefer to sell Barco, because they received not only a higher price, but a higher percentage of that price. In general, however, dealers did a higher volume in Sony. In 1989, few dealers could survive without the Sony volume; an estimated 80 to 90 percent of professional audiovisual dealers worldwide carried Sony video equipment. Among dealers, Sony had a reputation for reliability and low price.

Sony Components and BPS. Sony had entered industrial projection in 1985, with the 1020 video projector. Although it was slower than Barco's video projectors at that time, it had a sharper focus, indicating a better quality tube. Upon closer examination, BPS engineers found the tube, manufactured in-house at Sony Components, (a division of Sony Corporation), to be far superior in quality to Clinton's, BPS's United States–based supplier.

In late 1985, Frans Claerbout traveled to Japan to investigate the possibility of buying from Sony Components. The division, which remained independent from Sony Projectors up to the chairman's level, agreed to supply Barco, and six months later the first Sony tube was introduced in the Barco Data 3 (BD3). Measured by lumens, Barco was able to achieve better brightness with Sony's tube than Sony itself. Barco terminated its supply relationship with Clinton, and Sony became its sole supplier. Claerbout commented on the relationship:

> Our relationship with Sony is a strange one. We are competitors with Sony projectors, yet we source from their in-house supplier. To obtain tubes that suit our needs, we share a certain amount of technical and developmental information with Sony Components, while they keep us abreast of their latest developments. The fact that we rely on them for an important component makes us vulnerable, but at the same time we think that they value our business because we bring their manufacturing costs down. I would say that over the course of our relationship with Sony Components, I think that they have treated us fairly.

In one instance in 1987, however, Sony introduced a video projector with a tube that Barco had not seen; BPS subsequently purchased the tube, which appeared in its BD600.

In 1989, BPS was actively seeking other tube suppliers. All other tubes available on the market were either inferior to Sony's, more expensive, or both. Many firms manufactured tubes suited to consumer video applications, including Hitachi, Toshiba, Thomson, and Philips, but only the Sony tube had the quality necessary for high-end video projection. Sony, Barco, and Electrohome all sourced tubes from Sony Components. To protect itself against a sudden supply freeze, BPS kept a three-month supply of tubes in-house, and two months of orders in transit from Sony.

BPS spent 90 million to 100 million Bfr ($2.25 million to $2.5 million) annually for approximately 20,000 Sony tubes, which represented around one-fifth of Sony Component's projector tube business. One tube cost between 5,000 Bfr ($125) and 18,000 Bfr ($450), depending on size and quality, and BPS negotiated continuously with Sony to get the prices down. Altogether, perhaps 35 percent of Sony Component's business was noncaptive. Operations Manager Johan Vannieuwenhuyse observed: "Any time Sony wanted to squeeze us out, they could raise the price of their tubes. We would be dead in the water six months before finding another source. But I don't think they will. When we discuss other suppliers, we are taken seriously." Erik Dejonghe agreed:

> Sony has told me that their ultimate goal is to be 50 percent an industrial supplier, and 50 percent a consumer supplier—not to beat Barco in projection. I am making a bet that they continue to supply us reliably. They need competition to survive, and we are the only competition on whom they make substantial amounts of money.

In February 1989, Sony Components contacted BPS about a new 8" tube that it was developing. BPS received its first sample of the product in June, and its engineers were running tests on its performance capabilities. The face of the tube was square, rather than the conventional rectangular shape, and the product was significantly more costly than the 7" tubes that BPS was currently sourcing from Sony. BPS engineers had considered incorporating the new tube in the BD700 data projector, but had decided against the idea because it involved redesigning the shape of the projector's chassis, and sourcing a new lens to match.

Other Competitors

Electrohome. Electrohome was a privately held Canadian electronics manufacturer, with 1988 turnover of 5.6 billion Bfr ($139.8 million). Industrial projectors were the most successful group in its Electronics division, which had turnover of 2.5 billion Bfr ($62.5 million) in 1988. Electrohome operated in the data and graphics segments of the marketplace only, and was BPS's largest competitor in graphics. In terms of unit sales, Electrohome was the third largest player, behind Sony and Barco, with 1,585 units sold in 1988. Its product mix was 73 percent data and 27 percent graphics. Worldwide, the company had an estimated 11 percent of total data units sold, and 44 percent of graphics units.

Electrohome was estimated to have comparable distribution strength to BPS, with close to 100 dealers in the U.S. market; 80 percent of Electrohome's dealers were systems specialists. Given the intense competition between BPS and Electrohome in graphics, it was rare to find the two manufacturers' products sold by the same dealer. In general, Electrohome's products were priced just below BPS's. Together with BPS, it was viewed as having higher quality projectors than Sony.

NEC. NEC was a major Japanese manufacturer of electronics, with 1988 turnover of 876 billion Bfr ($21.9 billion). The company sold video and data projectors, with a product mix divided 48 percent and 52 percent between the two. NEC had pioneered digital convergence technology in the marketplace, introducing a digital data projector in 1987 that became the market standard. The company had not captured as much market share as expected, however, in part due to its inefficient distribution network. Originally, NEC projectors had been sold through the company's well-established network of computer dealers. When sales proved disappointing, NEC granted an OEM agreement to the United States–based General Electric Corporation (GE). In 1988, the company sold 1,799 units through its own network, and another 1,200 through GE. The company was estimated to hold 4 percent of the video market worldwide, in terms of units, and 9 percent of the data market.

The Sony 1270 Introduction

In August 1989, at the Siggraph trade show in Boston, Sony previewed a projector whose performance shocked Barco and the rest of the industry. Introduced as a "superdata" projector, Sony's new model—the 1270—had the power to scan to 75kHz, placing it in a market for high-performance graphics applications that BPS could not enter. In addition, the 1270 featured the new 8" Sony tube, which gave it higher marks than the BG400 in brightness, image quality, and resolution. Price rumors at

Siggraph, however, placed the unit in BPS's data range, at 600,000 Bfr to 800,000 Bfr ($15,000 to $20,000). If these rumors proved true, such performance had never been available on the market for such a low price. Erik Dejonghe, Bernard Dursin, and Sjoerd de Clerck, the regional marketing manager for the United States, were the Barco representatives at Siggraph that afternoon. Sjoerd de Clerck described the scene:

> Sony had chosen the U.S. market for its kickoff preview. They had one preproduction unit set up in a very small booth, and their presentation was quite low-key. But the 1270 was a show-stealer. It was a magnificent product. I spent two days at the booth, in a crowd of people, trying to find out as much as I could.

Dejonghe and the others were not so much surprised by a Sony introduction, as by the type of projector the 1270 turned out to be. There had been rumors, spread mostly by dealers, about an impending Sony introduction earlier in 1989. Erik Dejonghe explained:

> Barco had a pretty good idea that Sony was bringing out a new product, but we had expected it to be a direct competitor for the BD600. We thought it would be a 46–50 kHz machine, priced 10 to 15 percent lower than ours. In response, we planned to introduce a 64 kHz digital upgrade of the BD600 (the BD700) by October. We planned to maintain the 960,000 Bfr ($24,000) price tag on our BG400 until we introduced a digital version (the BG800) in late 1990. Then we expected Sony to introduce a 75 kHz graphics projector in 1990, priced somewhere near 800,000 Bfr ($20,000). All of our projections, however, were based on the assumption that Sony would respect our "vision" of the marketplace. The 1270 did just the opposite. Its positioning threatened to take a lot of money out of the industry.

Sony had announced that it would begin a roll-out of the 1270 in its major markets in November. The company planned the largest-ever publicity campaign in the history of its involvement in industrial projection; for example 15,000 customers, dealers, and distributors had been invited to the 1270's preview in France, and 5,000 to the preview in Belgium. Regional Marketing Manager Michel Vandeplas commented:

> It is obvious that Sony is not interested in competing with Barco and Electrohome for a few hundred projectors per year in the graphics segment. Instead, their aim is to reconquer our data and graphics markets, and, to do it, they need to break their market image as a mass producer of low-end products.

Although the price reports on the projector could not be confirmed, confusion reigned in the marketplace. Dealers were panicked about the possibility of a low-priced graphics projector from Sony, while Barco distributors were anxious to know how Barco planned to react. In early September, in an effort to calm the market, Barco had spread the word that it did not believe the rumors about the low price of the 1270. Privately, however, BPS management was worried about the potential for significant erosion of its market share. On the plane ride home from Boston, Dejonghe calculated that BPS stood to lose as much as 75 percent of its forecasted 1990 profits.

Saturday, September 23, 1989

As Saturday morning turned into afternoon, Dejonghe, Claerbout, and Dursin continued to weigh the options that confronted them. Mindful that BPS risked losing up to 75 percent of its forecasted 1990 profits, they had yet to reach agreement on the course to recommend to the board on Monday.

Pricing Options

Sony had targeted the U.S. and European markets with its 1270, markets which represented 83 percent of BPS graphics revenues and 91 percent of its data revenues. In the month since Siggraph, Dejonghe, Claerbout, and Dursin had given considerable thought to the potential impact of the 1270 for the rest of 1989 (October, November, and December) and 1990. By their estimations, if the BG400's price remained unchanged and the 1270 was priced at 800,000 Bfr ($20,000), the BG400 could lose 30 percent of its market share, or 153.8 million Bfr ($3.85 million).[4] At 600,000 Bfr ($15,000), the Sony 1270 threatened to capture 60 percent of the BG400's market share, or 307.5 million Bfr ($7.69 million). In addition, at this lower price point, Dejonghe and the others were concerned that the 1270 would cause significant share erosion of the BD600, priced at 480,000 ($12,000).

How should the BG400 and the BD600 be priced in response to the Sony 1270? For each machine, there were the questions of how much, if any, of a price change to implement, which markets to lower prices in, and over what time frame. Dursin reported that BPS's German distributor was feeling the pressure of the 1270 most severely, and had been calling for a significant price decrease since Siggraph. In early September, the president of the distributorship had declared:

> The German market is the second largest consumer of BG400s in the world. Our dealers inform us that Sony is taking advance orders on its 1270 in Germany. We need to protect this market, and to do it, we need to drop the price on the projectors drastically and immediately.

The French distributor, too, was experiencing market pressure to announce a price decrease on the BG400. In the U.S. market, however, the distributor was adamantly opposed to lowering the price. Regional Marketing Manager Sjoerd de Clerck had described the reasoning behind this opposition:

> It goes without saying that Barco cannot win a price war against Sony. Lowering our price might drive Sony to lower theirs further, and we could not follow. We might never be able to recover our price positioning on graphics machines. In addition, a drastic price

---

[4]BPS estimated that graphics sales for the last three months of 1989 would reach 106.7 million Bfr ($2.67 million), making the total for the year 426.8 million Bfr ($10.67 million). Assuming 25 percent growth for the following year, the 1990 graphics revenue estimate was 533.5 million Bfr ($13.34 million). The 15 month revenue estimate was thus 640.7 Bfr ($16.02 million), of which 80 percent, or 512.56 million Bfr ($12.8 million), could be assumed to be sales of the BG400. A 30 percent loss in sales of the BG400 would total 153.8 million Bfr ($3.85 million), while a 60 percent loss would total 307.5 million Bfr ($7.69 million).

drop would damage our reputation among recent, and hopefully repeat, BPS customers. Our only option is to develop a competitive projector."

Frans Claerbout was concerned about moving too quickly to lower the BG400 price—in markets where Sony was not coming out strongly, it would be the equivalent of giving away profit. He wanted to wait on confirmation of the Sony price before making any pricing decisions. In direct contrast, Dursin felt strongly that BPS should preempt the pricing of the 1270.

Product Development Options

The team also had a series of product development options to consider in light of the Sony 1270 introduction. Early in 1989, BPS's development plan had been sketched out according to the division's expectations of increased competition in the data segment of the marketplace. The plan called for the introduction of the digital BD700 by October, followed by the development of the digital BG800 for a late 1990 introduction. Twenty-seven man-months were required to complete the BD700 project, while 180 man-months had already gone into the project. In addition, BPS engineers were working concurrently on four other projector-related projects.

BPS could continue along its development schedule as planned, introducing the BD700 on time in October for immediate production and delivery. The projector was BPS's first digital model, and also incorporated an improved generator and a scanning frequency of 64 kHz. Sales of the BD700 in 1990 were expected to show an increase of 25 percent in incremental sales over the forecasted revenue of the BD600, representing some 171.7 million Bfr ($4.3 million).[5] By September, BPS's German distributor and several others already had orders for the BD700, priced at 640,000 Bfr ($16,000), on their books. Claerbout understood the importance of the on-time completion of the BD700 project, for both his engineers' morale and his customers. At the same time, however, the BD700 would not beat the performance of the 1270 at Infocomm in January 1990.

Alternatively, BPS could use the advances made in the BD700 development as a springboard to a digital graphics projector. Dejonghe estimated that BPS engineers could develop a graphics version in two to three months, working from the BD700's chassis, tubes, and lenses, with the sole addition of higher scanning frequency to match that of the 1270. If this option were pursued, the introduction of the BD700 would have to be postponed until December, causing delay in the delivery of the projector to advance-order customers. Also, with BPS's standard 7" tube, the digital graphics projector would still be inferior to the 1270 in terms of light output, picture quality, and resolution.

BPS's third option was to turn immediately to the development of the BG800. As originally planned, it was to be a digital upgrade of the BG400. Faced with the

---

[5]Data revenues were predicted to reach 912.7 million Bfr ($22.8 million) in 1989, and, assuming 12.3 percent growth for the next year, 1,025 million Bfr ($25.6 million) in 1990. Sixty-seven percent, or 686.8 million Bfr ($17.2 million), in 1990 could be assumed to be sales of the BD600. The BD700 was expected to increase data sales 25 percent over the BD600, representing 171.7 million Bfr ($4.3 million).

threat from Sony, however, the BG800 now had to be designed to surpass the 1270's performance. This would require a scanning frequency well above that of the 1270's—at least 90 kHz—as well as the incorporation of the Sony 8" tube for the best possible performance. Dejonghe had received confirmation from Sony Components that it would be willing to start supplying the tube immediately. The 8" tube required a special lens, however, and BPS's traditional lens supplier, U.S. Precision Lens of Cincinnati (USPL), had no compatible product. Although in the past Barco and Sony sourced lenses from the same supplier, Sony had worked with a Japanese firm, Fujinon, to develop the lens that appeared in the 1270. Dejonghe was not sure that Fujinon would supply Barco as well.

Claerbout estimated that the development of the BG800 with at least 90 kHz of scanning frequency and new tubes would require at least 80 man-months. In addition, he felt strongly that the projector would have to be ready in time for Infocomm if it was to be effective against the 1270. Meeting that deadline would require the cessation of all other BPS development projects from October 1 on, including the BD700. He voiced a number of concerns about committing BPS's resources to such a drastic move:

> My engineers have been working overtime on the development of the BD700 since midsummer. Now, we're considering a move that would require the indefinite postponement of the BD700 project, and an even greater commitment on their part. Overtime would be a given, but they'd also have to be willing to give up vacation days until Infocomm at least. We have the capability to produce a great machine, and a machine that is superior to the 1270. But the compression of its development could have repercussions on the quality of the final product. In addition, we don't know yet when the 1270 will actually hit the marketplace, how it will be priced, or how the customers will respond to it.

In addition to these considerations, Claerbout gave the BG800 only a 40 percent chance of making the Infocomm deadline.

CHAPTER 38

Fabtek (A)

In June 1991, Fabtek management is presented with four attractive orders. Each order represents a different mix of customer opportunity and manufacturing demands for Fabtek, which is a $30 million producer of custom equipment manufactured from an exotic material, titanium. The chapter provides a fair amount of detail on Fabtek's pricing approach and raises several issues about bid pricing, such as the potential for using different markups on labor and materials. Fabtek's manufacturing constraints and the demands of the four orders are quite explicit. The company has to decide which orders to accept at what prices for what delivery.

Introduction

In mid-June 1991, the senior management of Fabtek's Fabrication Division was grappling with a problem unprecedented in the company's 15-year history. Because of an acute shortage of capacity and increasing customer dissatisfaction with late deliveries, the company's marketing vice president, Amy Vitali, and the Fabrication Division's vice president of operations, Rob Lightfoot, had to agree on which of four potential orders the company should accept and how it should bid on them. Each of the orders represented a different customer situation, mix of labor and materials, and mix of manufacturing talents, so a direct comparison among them was difficult. Stanley Ho, Fabtek's president, had advised them to work it out themselves, but reminded them that a quick decision was necessary "if we're going to be able to fit *any* of them into our shop schedule."

This case was prepared by Benson P. Shapiro, Rowland T. Moriarty, and Craig E. Cline.
Copyright © 1992 by the President and Fellows of Harvard College.
Harvard Business School case 592-095.

Fabrication Division

Early History. The Fabrication Division was the second-largest industrial fabricator of titanium in the United States. Corporate and sales offices for the company, as well as its primary fabricating facility, were located in Philadelphia.

Fabtek was one of the first companies to provide titanium products for industrial use. Before the mid-1970s, titanium had been used almost exclusively in the aerospace industry because of its light weight and high strength. It wasn't until the price dropped (from $20 per pound for some alloys used in aerospace to $5 per pound for industrial titanium sheet and plate) and its corrosion resistance was demonstrated, however, that titanium became competitive for some applications with stainless steel, copper and nickel alloys, brick-lined steel, fiberglass, and other products used to counter corrosion. Even in 1991, titanium won the industrial applications battle only if (1) it could outlast competitive metals to such an extent that it was less expensive overall or (2) it was the only industrial metal that could do the job. Nevertheless, Ho was enthusiastic about titanium's potential and estimated that its industrial use would grow by 15 to 20 percent per year during the foreseeable future.

Growth. From its inception, Fabtek's principal business was fabrication of titanium equipment for industrial corrosion-resistant applications. The company had little involvement in the aerospace industry. Over time it added technical staff, participated in industry symposia, sponsored technical papers, and studied developing titanium markets. Active consulting and field services, such as field repairs and corrosion analysis, developed from these efforts.

In addition to the fabricating business, Fabtek sold titanium metal and specialty hardware (pipe fittings, bolts, nuts, pipe flanges) to the industrial market. The two organizations shared a common raw materials inventory. The corporation also purchased titanium in ingot and semifinished form and converted it (using steel mills that rented time on their machinery on a price-per-pound basis) to finished product forms, such as bars or plates. As business expanded, these activities were separated into a materials profit center that included metal trading, warehousing, and conversion.

In 1986 and again in 1988 capacity expansions were made in Philadelphia and efforts toward geographic expansion followed. During the 1980s a subsidiary was formed in Montreal, a branch was opened in Texas to serve the petrochemical markets, and a small, bankrupt titanium wire mill was acquired. In addition, a small subsidiary was formed in Brazil to take advantage of the rapid expansion of basic industries, such as pulp, occurring there. (Exhibit 1 provides corporate financial data.)

Organization. Operations was headed by Rob Lightfoot (who previously had been involved in Fabtek's marketing area). It consisted of two engineers who evaluated customer product designs to determine the best manufacturing processes, two drafting people, two estimators who calculated the cost of manufacture for pricing, and several administrative and clerical people. In addition, operations' shop, which was nonunion, had 78 employees in three sections: fabrication, welding, and the

EXHIBIT 1   Corporate Financial Summary, 1988–1990

	1990	1989	1988
Net sales	$31,155,402	$26,317,527	$23,137,485
Expenses:			
Cost of sales and engineering	26,351,184	22,077,768	18,604,803
SG&A	4,587,780	3,089,676	2,141,031
Interest, net	529,023	301,479	228,462
	$31,467,987	$25,468,923	$20,974,296
Income (loss) before provision (credit) for taxes on income and minority interest in subsidiary	(312,585)	848,604	2,163,189
Taxes on income	(179,400)	417,600	1,017,300
Net income before minority interest in subsidiary	$(133,185)	$431,004	$1,145,889
Minority interest in subsidiary	(11,145)	22,791	0
Net income	$(144,330)	$453,795	$1,145,889
Financial position:			
Current assets	22,170,168	13,502,616	13,072,680
Working capital	641,322	976,062	1,997,385
Property and equipment, net	2,129,571	1,510,308	848,172
Inventories:[a]			
Raw materials	6,496,350	5,215,398	4,832,166
Work-in-progress	8,898,744	4,282,422	4,909,455
Long-term debt	535,278	831,000	822,000
Stockholders' equity	2,654,223	2,798,553	2,326,758

[a] Inventory is stated at the lower of cost (substantially on a first-in, first-out basis) or market.

machine shop. Additional fabrication capacity was available in the Texas and Montreal facilities, but these were primarily intended to serve their respective regional markets and were operating at full capacity through 1991.

Fabtek's marketing organization was headed by Amy Vitali; it included two regional managers located in Philadelphia and Texas, the titanium metal sales group, and a customer service function. In addition, the company was represented by several manufacturers' representatives who operated both in the United States and abroad.[1] (Exhibit 2 shows the organization chart).

Markets and Customers

Fabtek had over 90 significant customers in 11 markets:

1. General chemicals—pressure vessels, tanks, heat exchangers, shafts and mixers, pumps, valves, piping, blowers, and anodes for chlorine.

---

[1] A manufacturers' representative was an independent company or salesperson who sold products of related but noncompeting companies for commissions on the sales.

EXHIBIT 2 Fabtek's Organization Chart

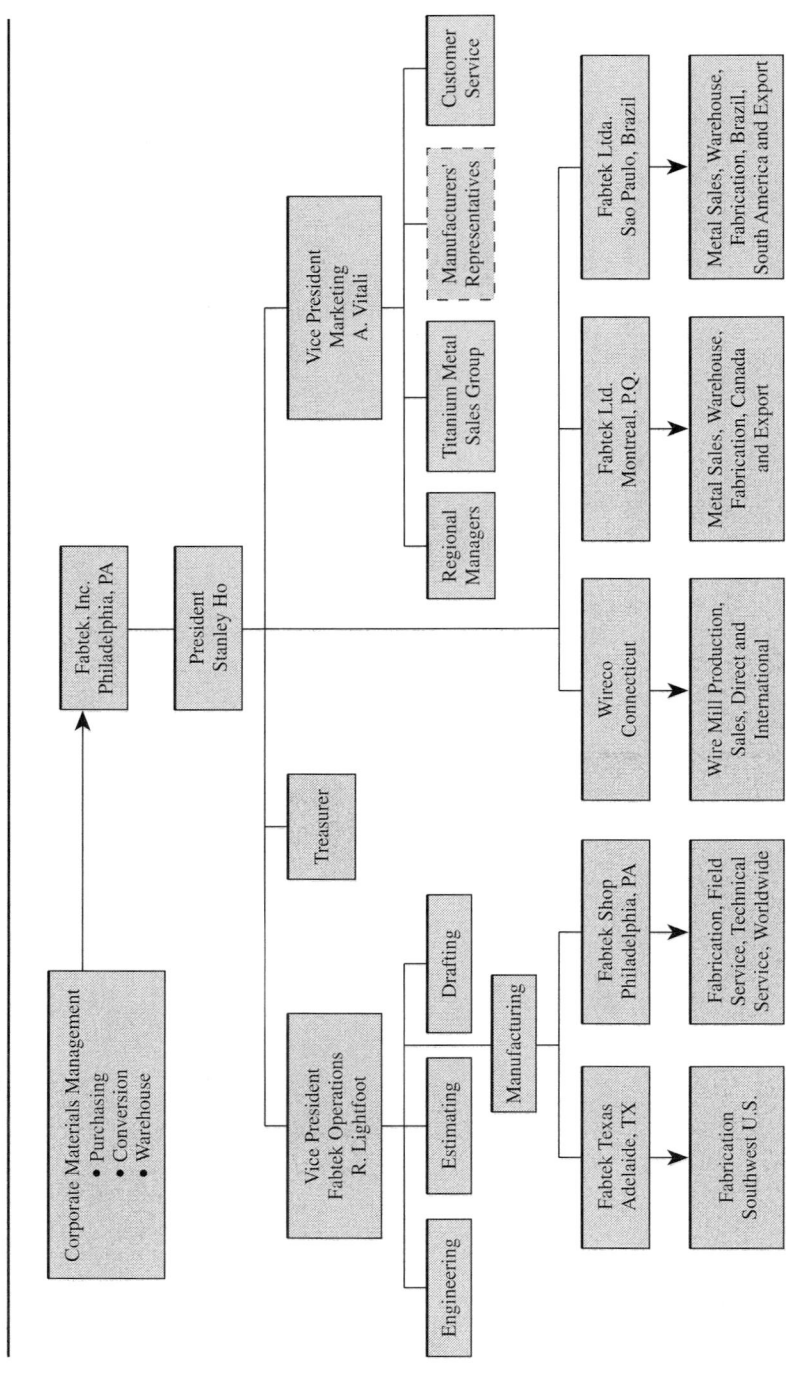

NOTE: The intimate ties between the Fabricating Division's operations and the rest of the company make it impossible to separate the Fabtek organization from that of the Fabrication Division.

2. Pulp and paper—bleaching equipment, chemical preparation vessels, and piping.
3. Basic metals—cathodes for copper and vessels for hydrometallurgy.
4. Petroleum—heat exchangers for refineries, down-hole equipment, and hot-oil coolers for production.
5. Pollution—heat exchangers, vessels, pipe for municipal waste oxidation, air scrubbers, and blowers.
6. Fibers—chemical equipment for various polymer intermediate products.
7. Water desalinization—heat exchangers, tubing, and piping.
8. Marine activities—high-voltage undersea electrical connectors, diver rescue chambers, and research submarine components.
9. Electric power generation—tubes for surface condensers.
10. Food—corrosion-resistant equipment for pickle solutions.
11. High-performance toys—12-meter sailboat parts, race cars, and golf clubs.

The majority of Fabtek's customers were located within a 500-mile radius of Philadelphia, but the firm also shipped worldwide. Customer orders ranged from $75 to $6 million, with $150,000 being typical. Approximately 20 percent of Fabtek's customers provided 80 percent of its business.

Close business and personal relationships existed between the Fabtek staff and certain customers who gave Fabtek a considerable percentage of their titanium business. One customer, Refco, typically represented 15 to 20 percent of sales each year. Two other companies accounted for 10 to 15 percent of sales on a fairly regular basis. In early 1990, Fabtek's management established a corporate policy of allowing a maximum of 20 percent of its business to reside with one customer and 30 percent to be in one market area.

Competition

Fabtek had five major competitors, none of which was located in the immediate area. The largest was in Ohio and had annual sales of $49.5 million. The others were scattered across the country and had annual sales of between $6 million and $30 million in competitive titanium work, with $18 million being average. Fabtek had an estimated 16 percent share of a total industrial titanium fabrication market of just under $150 million. It had a reputation for higher quality, but also a higher price, than most of its competitors.

Forecasts

Fabtek's sales and equity had grown steadily from 1985 to 1988, but 1989 sales were disappointing. In 1990, despite record sales of $31.2 million, the company experienced its first net loss. Management felt that the 1989 and 1990 results were more a consequence of erratic pricing and unstable market conditions than internal problems. The titanium industry had been operating at a significantly lower level than in 1987 and 1988. Capital spending on process equipment, refinery expansion, pulp and paper projects, and chemical construction had been well below anticipated levels in 1990 and was not expected to increase significantly in 1991.

Manufacturing Process

Although titanium had several fabricating peculiarities that required special skills, some operations—such as shearing, machine work, and forming—closely paralleled those used in precision fabrication of certain stainless steels.[2] In fact, the company often was able to subcontract excess machine work to local precision machine shops. Heat treatment, thermal cutting, and especially welding were generally considered the most difficult operations. Because titanium was a reactive metal, it was easily embrittled by increases in its gas content (primarily oxygen and nitrogen, but also most other elements). Melting titanium, such as in welding, or heating it above 1,200°F caused it to react instantly with air, absorbing oxygen and nitrogen and becoming brittle and useless. Consequently, cleanliness and special inert-gas welding techniques were required to produce good welds.

Fabtek used its strong competence in welding as a major selling point. One executive noted: "We feel that our expertise lies in high-quality welding. Over 80 percent of our jobs involve welding." This reputation for outstanding welding was supported routinely by radiographic, ultrasonic, and liquid penetration inspection of each weld.

The company had 33 welders who were graded from A to D, according to their ability to handle difficult work. In addition, Fabtek had several automatic welding machines. Finally, various helpers and trainees assisted the welders. (Shop capacity is shown in Exhibit 3.)

Costs. Generally a product's cost had five components, with manufacturing overhead averaging about 200 percent of direct labor cost:

Component	*Range*	*Average*
Raw material	30%–65%	45%
Direct labor	5–20	9
Manufacturing overhead	10–40	18
Subcontracting	10–15	12
General and administrative costs and profit	10–25	16

The company's objective was to have cost of goods average 80 percent, with 85 percent the upper limit.

---

[2]Shearing was cutting titanium sheets to a specified size. Machining used lathes, mills, drills, and other chip-forming high-precision tools to obtain close tolerances. Forming, done on plate or bar rolls or on a press brake, bent the item to its ultimate shape.

EXHIBIT 3 Fabtek's Operations' Shop Capacity

	Number of People		
	Day Shift	Night Shift	Total
Welding			
Welder A	7	3	10
Welder B	3	1	4
Welder C	5	6	11
Welder D	6	2	8
Trainee	2	—	2
Helper	7	7	14
Auto A	1	1	2
Auto B	—	—	—
Auto C	2	2	4
Auto trainee	1	—	1
			56
Fabrication			
Layout mechanic	2		2
Mechanic	2		2
Fab A	1		1
Fab B	1		1
Trainee	4		4
Helper	3		3
			13
Machine Shop[a]			
Machinist 1st Class	3	—	3
Machinist 2nd Class	1	—	1
Operator A	1	—	1
Operator B	2	1	3
Trainee	1	—	1
			9

[a] Additional machine capacity could be obtained through subcontracting.

Existing Situation. Shop backlog had reached a critical level in June 1991 (see Exhibit 4). This was the first time the company's booking exceeded its capacity by a significant margin. Delivery history for the past several months had been, in the word of one operations executive, "horrendous." Although routine orders were going out on time, most major or complex jobs were late. Delivery times had increased from an average of 8 to 10 weeks in 1987 to 16 to 60 weeks, depending on complexity and size, in 1990. Another operations executive added: "The main reason many customers are still coming back to us is our quality. There also aren't many other people who fabricate titanium."

According to a third operations official, one factor underlying Fabtek's capacity problem was the difficulty the company had hiring and training qualified welders.

Exhibit 4 Fabtek's Shop Schedule as of June 1991

	June 1991			July 1991			August 1991			September 1991		
	W	M	F	W	M	F	W	M	F	W	M	F
Backlog	7,200	1,670	2,350	6,800	1,040	2,050	4,200	900	1,050	4,200	1,100	1,050
Capacity	6,920	1,560	2,250	6,920	1,560	2,250	6,920	1,560	2,250	6,920	1,560	2,250
Difference	(280)	(110)	(100)	(120)	520	200	2,720	660	1,200	2,720	460	1,200
Cumulative	(280)	(110)	(100)	(160)	410	100	2,560	1,070	1,300	5,280	1,530	2,500

	October 1991			November 1991			December 1991			January 1992		
	W	M	F	W	M	F	W	M	F	W	M	F
Backlog	5,000	1,350	1,500	4,120	1,300	1,070	4,700	700	800	5,000	400	1,350
Capacity	6,920	1,560	2,250	6,920	1,560	2,250	6,920	1,560	2,250	6,920	1,560	2,250
Difference	1,920	210	750	2,800	260	1,180	2,220	860	1,450	1,920	1,160	900
Cumulative	7,200	1,740	3,250	10,000	2,000	4,430	12,220	2,860	5,880	14,140	4,020	6,780

	February 1992			March 1992			April 1992			May 1992			Total		
	W	M	F	W	M	F	W	M	F	W	M	F	W	M	F
Backlog	4,050	560	1,150	4,220	660	1,500	4,300	750	1,350	4,300	640	1,020	58,090	11,070	16,240
Capacity	6,920	1,560	2,250	6,920	1,560	2,250	6,920	1,560	2,250	6,920	1,560	2,250	83,040	18,720	27,000
Difference	2,870	1,000	1,100	2,700	900	750	2,620	810	900	2,620	920	1,230	24,950	7,650	10,760
Cumulative	17,010	5,020	7,880	19,710	5,920	8,630	22,330	6,730	9,530	24,950	7,650	10,760	24,950	7,650	10,760

NOTES: Welding and fabrication helpers and trainees were each counted as 50% of a regular welder or fabricator for planning purposes. Data assume each welder, machinist, and fabricator works 2,080 hours per year. W = Welders; M = Machinists; F = Fabricators.

The labor market around Philadelphia and our need for highly skilled workers make it difficult to find new people, especially because we can't offer much higher than average pay. The competition's shops are generally located in less-expensive areas, and we must be careful to keep our labor costs competitive. Even hiring a new welder as part of our regular work force is difficult. If we're lucky, we can find one or two a month. Then it takes between two months and two years to train them to be A level, depending on whether they were welders before. For many jobs the welders must also qualify under the ASME Boiler Code, which is expensive but necessary for A and B level welders. This situation is even more critical because the majority of our jobs require A and B level welding.

This official felt, however, that the major underlying factor was Fabtek's lack of reliable information on the shop's actual capacity at any given moment.

In the past, marketing would ask us if we had capacity available for a job before they quoted on it. But in recent months late material deliveries and problems on two major jobs have swelled our backlog, which has extended delivery dates on existing jobs. These fill the capacity marketing thought would be open for the jobs we had just bid, thereby pushing ahead *their* delivery dates. Consequently, marketing no longer believes our capacity forecasts; they simply go ahead and book the order for the longest delivery they can get away with, which, of course, adds to our capacity problem. It's a vicious cycle.

Lightfoot concurred with his subordinates; he felt marketing only recently had become realistic about the capacity limit and thus willing to work with operations to improve the company's delivery schedule. He observed:

We started Fabtek because we were excited by what we could do in the industrial market. In fact, Stanley Ho has made it our basic operating philosophy "to make money by moving titanium." It's been fun, and that's largely what kept us going—until now. At present we are faced with declining profits and a delivery crisis. Something has to be done, and perhaps being more selective in taking orders will do it.

From an operations standpoint, he felt several criteria could make an order attractive:

1. The job is technically challenging.
2. The job fits with Fabtek's high-quality image and capabilities.
3. The company's engineering expertise is utilized.
4. The job is long-run and repetitive.
5. The company has experience with similar products.
6. Specifications and job scope are clear.
7. For larger orders, progress payments can be negotiated (payments made on labor and material as applied, over the course of the contract, rather than all at the end).
8. Overall contribution before SG&A (sales, general, and administrative expenses) is near 20 percent of the product's price.

Marketing

Fabtek's fabrication and titanium metal sales were under the direction of Amy Vitali in marketing. She spent an estimated 60 percent of her time on fabrication sales and the remainder on metal sales. Similarly, the two regional sales managers each devoted 10 percent of their time to fabrication sales, and a manufacturers' representative in California handled both fabricated products and titanium metal sales. Generally, however, Fabtek relied on advertising in trade publications, industry symposia participation, and trade shows for fabrication sales. Also, Ho, Lightfoot, Vitali, and other staff people who had close relationships with customers usually handled their accounts personally. Lightfoot, for example, had close ties with certain Refco officials and thus handled all but the smallest details of this account. As one executive observed, "Most of the management people here have two or three job functions, and almost anyone can make a sale."

Bidding Process. One of the principal tasks of the people in marketing and sales was to make sure that Fabtek was on the bid lists of potential customers. Once a request for a quote was received, marketing sent it to operations for estimating (to obtain a quote as well as an estimated delivery date). Marketing then modified the quote to reflect market conditions and corporate goals.

The company had a bid success rate of 15 percent. Vitali felt this percentage was somewhat low compared with the industry average, but pointed out that only one of seven requests for quotes was "solid." She thought a more serious problem was the price competitiveness that had recently gripped the market, forcing Fabtek to play pricing games.

> Our aggressive posture has been a reaction to forces in the market more than a philosophy. As the titanium market stabilizes, which I'm sure it will eventually do, we will be better able to formulate an effective strategy about taking orders, rather than being freewheeling and reactive. This is a serious concern of mine because we haven't been able to maintain market share in the last year. We've got to pick our shots better—but we can only become more selective if we get the opportunity to call the shots.

Possible Changes. Vitali felt that the company had to become more selective about the high-risk custom jobs it took; she was also in favor of diversifying Fabtek's business among customers and markets. "We have an excellent relationship with Refco, but what do we do if they represent 30 to 40 percent of our business and then suddenly stop sending us orders?" She believed Fabtek would eventually move away from custom fabrication and become more involved in developing proprietary products. She also felt that the company had to determine its costs more accurately. "We've got to target our markets better to be sure we are using our resources to their maximum potential." To do this, she felt that marketing had to get better information out of Fabtek's operations concerning costs and capacity availability.

Vitali's preferred criteria for taking an order were as follows:

1. The job is similar to what Fabtek had built before.
2. The design is simple and the cost estimate reliable.

3. The job has good payment terms (progress payments on labor and material as applied).
4. The market area has potential for further development.
5. The job allows adequate delivery time.
6. Price is not the primary factor in the customer's decision.

The Four Prospective Fabrication Orders

In mid-June 1991 Vitali and Lightfoot met to decide whether to accept each of the prospective orders: Refco, Pierce-Pike, Worldwide Paper, and Kathco. Prices were fixed for the larger two orders but still had to be determined for the smaller two. In addition, both Vitali and Lightfoot had been uneasy about the entire bidding process and wondered if it should be changed. Lightfoot, for example, thought perhaps the company should expect a greater markup on labor than on materials. He explained that the material cost estimates tended to be much more reliable than the labor estimates. He thought:

> that we should be paid more for the greater uncertainty of the labor estimates. Overruns on costs—almost solely labor costs—were a prime reason for our poor 1990 profit performance. Right now our bidding procedure makes no differentiation between labor and materials. Maybe the customer should pay for some of the uncertainty in labor costs through a higher markup.

Exhibit 5 shows cost estimates and Exhibit 6 the projected shop load for each order.

EXHIBIT 5   Cost Estimates for the Four Prospective Orders

	Refco (petroleum refining)		Pierce-Pike (wastewater treatment)		Worldwide Paper (paper)	Kathco (electrodes)
Selling price	$6,000,000		$3,900,000		≈$2,400,000??	≈$1,500,000??
Material	2,100,000	(35%)	2,250,000	(58%)	1,080,000	960,000
Labor:						
Welding	600,000		105,000		132,000	
Machining	156,000		18,000		15,000	30,000
Fabrication	99,000		42,000		45,000	60,000
Total labor	$ 855,000	(14%)	$ 165,000	(4%)	$ 192,000	$ 90,000
Factory overhead	1,710,000	(29)	330,000	(8)	384,000	180,000
Subcontracting	300,000	(5)	390,000	(10)	450,000	—
Total factory cost	$4,965,000	(83%)	$3,135,000	(80%)	$2,106,000	$1,230,000
Contribution (before SG&A)[a]	$1,035,000	(17%)	$ 765,000	(20%)	≈$ 294,000??	≈$ 270,000??

NOTE: "≈" means approximately.
[a]SG&A = Sales, general, and administrative expenses.

EXHIBIT 6 Projected Shop Load for the Four Prospective Orders

	Refco			Pierce-Pike			Worldwide Paper			Kathco		
	W	M	F	W	M	F	W	M	F	W	M	F
1991												
June	100	100	—	50	50	—	—	—	—	—	—	—
July	1,500	600	—	1,400	100	—	1,000	200	—	—	400	—
August	2,000	700	—	1,150	100	50	1,000	300	400	—	600	1,800
September	1,800	200	—	1,000	50	150	1,000	200	500	—	200	800
October	1,900	100	500	1,200	50	250	1,000	130	1,000	—	200	900
November	2,000	200	500	1,000	100	300	2,000	—	600	—	200	700
December	2,000	700	1,000	600	300	350	1,000	—	—	—	100	700
1992												
January	2,000	800	1,000	500	250	500	650	—	450	—	—	—
February	2,000	600	1,000	—	—	500	—	—	—	—	—	—
March	2,500	600	1,000	—	—	500	—	—	—	—	—	—
April	2,500	800	500	—	—	150	—	—	—	—	—	—
May	2,500	500	500	—	—	—	—	—	—	—	—	—
Post-May	12,000	2,800	500	—	—	—	—	—	—	—	—	—
Total	34,800	8,700	6,500	6,900	1,000	2,750	7,650	830	2,950	—	1,700	4,900

NOTE: W = Welders; M = Machinists; F = Fabricators.

Refco

Refco, Fabtek's largest single customer, was one of the world's leading engineering contractors. Refco and its competitors (e.g., Bechtel, Brown and Root, and others) designed and constructed large projects around the world. Like most contractors, Refco specialized—concentrating on petroleum refineries and petrochemical plants.

Several years earlier Refco had developed a specialized piece of machinery to perform certain refinery operations under demanding pressure, temperature, and corrosion conditions. Refco had supplied many of the units in stainless steel, but corrosion failures and increasing corrosive process requirements caused a gradual shift to titanium. The units, nicknamed *Whoppers* because of their large size and hamburger shape, had to be made to exact tolerances and with great care in welding. Fabtek had worked closely with Refco in developing the design. From time to time, Refco also had come to Fabtek for other titanium pieces—usually large process vessels, such as reactors, requiring a good deal of welding and fabrication. As far as Fabtek's management could ascertain, Fabtek was the only outside titanium fabricator in the world that Refco used. On the other hand, Refco did some in-house fabrication of superalloys and titanium at its large Rotterdam manufacturing facility.

As an engineering contractor, Refco had a trained staff of field welders and welding supervisors; however, they did little titanium work because of the unique properties of the metal. Industry rumors that Refco would set up a fabricating facility for superalloys and titanium had been circulating for the past four years. According to Lightfoot (who, among Fabtek's managers, knew Refco best), Refco's executives were totally unwilling to discuss this possibility except with "Cheshire cat–like smiles." Lightfoot believed Refco was unhappy about Fabtek's long delivery schedule and occasional late deliveries and doubted its ability to handle very large requirements expected in the future.

In May 1991, Refco had come to Fabtek with a request for production of an above-size Whopper, which soon became known as a *Super Whopper*. The purchasing/subcontracting specialists at Refco stated that they were willing to pay $6 million. Refco had offered to pay for 80 percent of direct "material and labor as applied" in four installments. Thus, each time 25 percent of the work was done, Fabtek would receive 20 percent of the cost of materials and direct labor. Thirty days after delivery Fabtek would be paid for the completed piece. (Refco always paid its bills on time.)

To be completed on time, the Super Whopper would have to enter production at Fabtek in June. It was certain that the first progress payment, and perhaps the second, would come in Fabtek's 1991 fiscal year, which ended in October.

In 1990, Refco had purchased $4.5 million worth of products from Fabtek. Not counting the Super Whopper order, its 1991 purchases from Fabtek were expected to be $6 million (out of Fabtek's projected $36 million in sales).

Pierce-Pike

For almost four years Vitali had been pursuing business with Pierce-Pike, a company that specialized in constructing proprietary wastewater treatment plants. Pierce-Pike was the subsidiary of a large chemical company and had developed a strong position in a rapidly growing market. Until early April 1991, it had shown no interest in giving business to Fabtek. All its work was shared by Fabtek's largest competitor and its number-four competitor in the market.

In April, Vitali had received a request for proposal on a pressurized reactor from Pierce-Pike. She was ecstatic; it represented a partial victory, or at least some interest, following a long battle. After some difficult pricing decisions, Vitali quoted $3.9 million on the job, although she had some concern whether Fabtek could do the job in the hours estimated. The reactor involved some unusual fabrication with which Fabtek was inexperienced. On the other hand, both Vitali and Lightfoot had decided it was important to develop this capability.

On June 13, Fabtek received the order, which it could refuse. Its original quote had contained a note indicating that Fabtek might not have enough capacity to fill the order. Vitali believed Pierce-Pike's two existing sources had capacity available, but she had heard that Pierce-Pike was unhappy with the quality of both, especially the larger one. Also, Pierce-Pike was willing to make progress payments only on raw material.

Worldwide Paper

Worldwide Paper was a large integrated producer of pulp, paper, and fabricated paper products. In the late 1980s, its process development laboratory had tested a new piece of equipment made entirely of titanium. The scale-up to pilot plant and small production units had gone smoothly. Now, Worldwide was putting its first full-sized production unit out for bid. Although earlier units had been made of less-corrosion-resistant materials, this one was to be made of titanium. From Vitali's point of view, this order had a particularly interesting facet:

> For some time we have been anxious to develop a line of proprietary items. It would ease our management task and enable us to train employees on standard work, which is less demanding than custom work. It would smooth our work flow and enable us to begin to develop a sales force. Right now we don't have a standard product line, so we can't have a regular sales force.
>
> Worldwide is willing to license this item to its manufacturer. If we get the bid, we can then develop it into a standard product line. There is little opportunity for customization in the primary part of the unit, so it could be a standard product.

Lightfoot was equally excited about acquiring or developing a standard product line. In addition, he saw the opportunity to add a new capability to Fabtek's operation:

> The $450,000 subcontracting involved is for special heat treatment. It is going to cost us that much because we have to move very large parts between our plant and the subcontractor. Furthermore, this subcontractor is really taking advantage of us, because they are one of the very few facilities that can do this type of heat treating. If we made the piece as a standard product line—even at a relatively low volume—we could develop the heat-treating competence in-house with a payback of a matter of months, including the transportation savings.

Vitali suspected that the cost estimators had been very conservative in their calculations. She could not be sure of the prices that competitors would offer, but she believed the $2.4 million range to be about right. She stated, "Someone will come in lower—probably in the $2.1 million range. A couple may be at $2.25 million. But we have the quality to command some sort of premium over our competitors."

This order offered no progress payments but required a penalty of 0.1 percent of the contract price for each working day that the complete order was late. There was no incentive for early delivery.

Kathco

The fourth order was fairly straightforward. Kathco was a metal refinery that manufactured its own titanium electrodes for purifying manganese. In the spring and summer of 1991 its sales were high. During 1991 the company had a new electrode production facility under construction. Construction was delayed, so Kathco had an important shortfall in its electrode availability.

Kathco had solicited bids from only Fabtek and one competitor because it knew the companies well. Fabtek had a good relationship with Kathco. But this order was clearly a "one-shot deal": Once Kathco's plant was operating, it could supply all of Kathco's needs.

Other Considerations

Fabtek also made money by buying, warehousing, and selling titanium. The added volume from any one of these orders would affect all metal purchases. The total effect was difficult to predict because of changes in the metal suppliers' strategy and pricing, but it was generally considered good for the company. As a rule, net profit varied from nothing to about 4 percent of material cost estimates. Gross profit was a little higher but varied substantially.

The shop capacity estimates considered only the availability of labor on a straight-time, two-shift basis (that is, during normal working hours). It was possible to have people work overtime, although some resented it—especially in the summer. Overtime was expensive (150 percent of regular labor rates) and usually resulted in lower productivity and quality. Over the short run, however, it was the only feasible way to increase capacity. Skilled third-shift personnel were unlikely to be available, at least in the near future. More important, Fabtek's limited facility size might make overtime or a third shift impractical, because there would be no room to store work in process.

CHAPTER 39
Xerox Corporation: The Customer Satisfaction Program

In August 1990, the president and executive vice president of Xerox were reviewing the progress made on its customer satisfaction program. The emphasis placed on the program, the success of the program to date, and the drive to achieve the corporate goals of customer satisfaction motivated this review. At Xerox customer satisfaction is the Number 1 priority, ahead of return on assets (ROA) and market share. This chapter focuses on analyzing the strategic role of the customer satisfaction program, its goals, and the action steps for implementation. Also described are the customer satisfaction measurement system, the data analyses, and follow-up. To increase customer satisfaction and to drive the organization to higher levels of performance top management believed that Xerox should offer a satisfaction guarantee. Market research had been conducted on customer responses to four different types of guarantees. A decision had to be made regarding the type of guarantee to introduce.

We achieve customer satisfaction through dedication to quality in everything we do.

Xerox Corporation 1987 Annual Report cover
In both our businesses, customer satisfaction is the key to our success.

Xerox Corporation 1988 Annual Report cover
The Malcolm Baldrige National Quality Award.

Xerox Corporation 1989 Annual Report cover
Xerox people are on a crusade to be the industry leader in all aspects of customer satisfaction. And we're making good progress. We have improved customer satisfaction by 35 percent. Dataquest now rates our products as number one in five out of six market segments. Datapro has named our 1090 copier the "best overall copier in the world."

Paul Allaire, President, Xerox 1989 Annual Report

This case was prepared by Melvyn A. J. Menezes and Jon Serbin.
Copyright © 1991 by the President and Fellows of Harvard College.
Harvard Business School case 591-055 (revised January 12, 1993).

Xerox embarked on an ambitious program in the early 1980s to regain its eroded leadership in the copier industry—an industry it virtually created with the introduction of its model 914 in 1959. During the 1970s, Xerox customers had become disappointed with Xerox quality and service, and the company lost significant market share to domestic and Japanese competitors.

An obsession with quality and customer satisfaction, cost reductions, restructurings, and new products helped Xerox stem its eroding market share and regain market leadership in multiple markets and multiple market segments. Xerox gained 1 to 1.5 points in market share every year since 1983.

The Leadership Through Quality strategy had been in place since 1983, and customer satisfaction had become the first corporate priority since 1987. All this appeared to have paid off: Xerox Business Products and Systems won the prestigious Malcolm Baldrige National Quality Award in 1989, the nation's highest award for quality. Established by an act of Congress in 1987, this highly competitive award was given annually to outstanding American companies that had implemented total quality strategies and had significantly improved customer satisfaction.

In July 1990, Paul Allaire, president, and Wayland Hicks, executive vice president and head of Xerox Marketing and Customer Operations, decided to take some time off from otherwise hectic schedules to review the progress on customer satisfaction. They wondered whether it needed any changes or the introduction of some new programs.

The Copier Industry

The worldwide copier market was mature and intensely competitive. In the United States, copier placements (sales and rentals) had grown at a slow rate of 2.9 percent CAGR (compound annual growth rate) between 1984 and 1989; service and supplies were the rapidly growing sources of revenue in the industry (see Table A).

Xerox categorized the copier industry into three product markets, discussed below.

Low-Volume Market. Copiers in this market were designed to make fewer than 5,000 copies per month and cost less than $4,000. Over time these machines were

TABLE A **Estimated Revenues in the U.S. Copier Industry (in billions of dollars)**

	1984	1989	1994 (expected)
Sales	$ 3.9	$ 4.7	$ 4.6
Rentals	3.3	3.6	4.6
Service	3.1	5.4	5.8
Supplies	3.0	4.3	4.9
Total	$13.3	$18.0	$19.9

becoming more reliable and users were performing more of their own maintenance. This market witnessed explosive growth in the late 1970s and was the fastest-growing market until the late 1980s. By 1990, that growth flattened. Due to intense competition, copier prices and margins in most markets declined steadily through the 1980s, but especially in this low-volume market. Canon, Sharp, Xerox, Mita, and Ricoh were the major players.

Mid-Volume Market. These copiers were designed to make up to 100,000 copies per month and cost between $4,000 and $60,000. This market, which had the highest overall growth in 1989, was where Xerox had always earned the most revenue and profit. At the lower end, there was intense price pressure, while at the top end, there was relatively less price cutting. Xerox, Canon, Mita, Ricoh, and Konica were the major players.

High-Volume Market. These copiers cost over $60,000. This market, primarily because of the high product-development costs, was a high-margin business. As you moved from the low-volume to the high-volume market, more machines were leased and fewer bought outright. In the high-volume market, the lease-to-sale ratio, although declining, was 80:20 in 1990. Competition was based primarily on service and product features. Xerox and Kodak (which purchased IBM's copier business in 1988 when IBM retreated from the business) were the major competitors; Canon, Konica, and Lanier competed in the lower end of this market.

The major producers were developing new products that utilized digital copying technology as opposed to light/lens technology. Some analysts expected that market growth in the nineties would be driven by "smart" multifunction devices that combined copying, faxing, scanning, and electronic printing functions. Competitors with direct sales forces would have an advantage because the complexity and pricing of these machines was too high for effective dealer distribution. Color copying represented another potential growth area. The color copier market was expected to grow from about 6,000 units ($354 million in revenues) in 1989 to almost 60,000 units ($2 billion in revenues) by 1994.

Competition

The copier market was extremely competitive, with 23 companies battling for market share. However, Xerox was the only full-line supplier with products ranging from the low end of the low-volume to the high end of the high-volume. Based on total number of unit placements, Canon was the market leader, followed by Xerox and Sharp (see Exhibit 1). Canon's placements were primarily low-volume, low-priced personal copiers, though Canon did have a presence in the mid- and high-volume markets. In terms of copier industry revenues, Xerox was the market leader with a high market share in the higher-priced mid- and high-volume markets, which also provided significant service and supplies revenues. Xerox had by far the largest service organization in the industry and was the largest paper and supplies distributor as well.

EXHIBIT 1 Placement of Copiers (in units), 1989

	Product Market			
	Low-Volume	*Mid-Volume*	*High-Volume*	*Total*
Canon	28.6%	9.7%	12.5%	23.0%
Xerox	11.3	26.5	45.1	15.2
Sharp	18.6	7.4	—	14.6
Mita	8.4	9.0	—	8.4
Ricoh	5.0	8.5	—	5.7
Konica	4.8	8.0	7.7	5.3
Minolta	3.3	2.7	—	5.1
Lanier	4.8	3.7	3.7	4.4
Savin	1.6	7.3	—	3.2
Kodak	—	2.2	31.0	1.1
Others	13.6	15.0	—	14.0
Total	100.0%	100.0%	100.0%	100.0%
Proportion of total units	80.5%	17.0%	2.5%	100.0%
Proportion of revenues	38.7%	31.3%	30.0%	100.0%
Proportion of total copies	28.9%	31.1%	40.0%	100.0%

Company Background

In 1989, Xerox Corporation, headquartered in Stamford, Connecticut, had revenues of $17.6 billion and net income of $704 million. It had two divisions: (1) Business Products and Systems, which handled all document-processing businesses (1989 revenues: $12.4 billion; net income: $488 million), and (2) Xerox Financial Services, which handled insurance and other financial services (1989 revenues: $5.2 billion; net income: $216 million).

History

In 1959, the Haloid Company launched its model 914 office copier, the first viable xerographic office copier and considered by many to be one of the most successful single products ever made. Haloid renamed itself Xerox in 1961.

Protected by a ring of patents, Xerox achieved phenomenal growth and completely dominated the world copier market through the 1960s and into the early 1970s. After settling antitrust actions with the FTC, Xerox agreed to license its technology to competitors and to end pending patent suits. IBM and Kodak entered the business in 1970 and 1975, respectively, focusing on the high-margin, high- and mid-volume markets. Japanese companies concentrated on mass producing low-volume machines. By the early 1980s, IBM and Kodak gained significant market share in the high-volume market, and Japanese companies created and began to dominate the emerging low-volume market. Also, Japanese producers began to compete in the mid-volume market, and, by 1990, some of them were offering or announcing products to compete in the high-volume market.

During the 1960s and 1970s Xerox diversified into a number of new businesses. It purchased mainframe-maker Scientific Data Systems in 1969. A decade later, the business, a large-scale failure, was sold. Other diversification efforts included entry into a range of office computing businesses, including word processors and document processing workstations, networks, facsimile equipment, electronic typewriters, scanners, impact and laser printers, software, and medical imaging systems. In the early 80s, Xerox diversified in a new direction through its financial services acquisitions.

Xerox with its monopoly culture, its large bureaucracy, and its forays into new businesses, had difficulty responding to the new competitive pressures in its flagship copier business. Costs and product prices were higher than the competition's, quality and perceived quality had declined, and market share and return on assets had fallen to alarming levels.

Around 1980, Xerox realized that the Japanese had a 40 to 50 percent cost advantage in the copier business and that they were selling machines for almost what it cost Xerox to produce a machine. Despite the emerging competition, Xerox continued to grow, but net income declined as a percentage of revenues. By 1980, Xerox's market share was severely eroded in all product segments of the copier business. Its share dropped from almost 100 percent in the 1960s to under 40 percent in 1980.

Turnaround

Beginning in 1980, Xerox undertook a number of initiatives to respond to the increased competition and the company's declining market share. The company was restructured and developed a philosophy emphasizing quality, led by chairman and CEO David Kearns. He instigated a strong quality movement, in the belief that quality would drive costs down and that getting it right the first time would eliminate costly repairs and replacements and would prevent the unnecessary breakdowns that drove customers away. Kearns and top management strove to drive the quest for quality throughout the organization.

Quality at Xerox was defined as "meeting the customer's existing and latent requirements." Xerox believed that becoming more customer and competitor oriented was critical. It began to use competitive *benchmarking* (the continuous process of measuring products, services, and practices against the toughest competitors and those companies renowned as leaders with respect to reliability, cost, and service), to improve quality, and achieve cost reductions. By 1983, it developed a corporatewide quality program called Leadership Through Quality (LTQ), which emphasized preventing defects and meeting customers' expectations. Training all employees in quality tools and processes was a major part of the plan, and quality-related goals were set for each year through 1987.

The effort led to some successes. The ratio of support staff to manufacturing worker was reduced from 4.5 in 1980 to 1.5 in 1987, smaller product development teams helped shorten the product development cycle by 30 percent and reduce the amount of labor required to bring out a new machine by 40 percent, and the number of parts vendors was reduced from 5,000 in 1980 to 400 by 1987, resulting in higher quality standards, better pricing, and 99.2 percent of parts arriving defect-free. By some estimates these efforts helped Xerox save as much as $2 billion in the document processing business.

Xerox underwent another major restructuring in 1988, refocusing its document processing line on its core copying business. It also focused on new technologies, including color copiers and "smart" multifunction copiers. Xerox Medical Imaging was closed, the electronic-typewriter production capacity was cut back, and the workstation business was closed. Xerox expected to achieve a payback on the 1988 restructuring within three years and to position itself to achieve its goal of 15 percent pretax ROA by 1990. Xerox's ROA, which peaked at 19 percent in 1980, was 11.1 percent in 1988 and 12.6 percent in 1989.

Business Products and Systems (BP&S)

BP&S developed, manufactured, marketed, and serviced a broad range of document processing equipment. BP&S products and systems were produced in 15 countries on five continents and marketed in 140 countries by a direct sales force of about 15,000 and a growing network of dealers and distributors. It maintained a worldwide service force of about 30,000 technical representatives.

BP&S's three largest product lines—Copier/Duplicators, Printing Systems, and Document Systems—were sold and serviced by the three general sales and service operating companies: United States Marketing Group (USMG), Americas Operations (handling Canada, Latin America, the Middle East, and North Africa), and Rank Xerox (handling 80 countries, including the European Community).

United States Marketing Group (USMG)

USMG, which handled the marketing of BP&S's main products in the United States, consisted of nine functional areas, including sales, service, business operations, marketing support, services support, finance, information management, personnel, and administration. The first three functions managed the field organization, which consisted of five regions and 65 districts.

Starting January 1, 1990, the regions and districts were managed as partnerships of the three functional areas (sales, service, and business operations) with the district partnership reporting to the regional partnership, which in turn reported to headquarter's functional managers. The heads of sales, service, and operations at the district (and regional) level operated as equal partners on management decisions and planning processes.

Decision-making authority was decentralized down to the regional and district partnerships. District partnerships were given increased responsibility to resolve customer problems and to take advantage of business opportunities, but were accountable to corporate policies and inspection. Districts had authority to allocate manpower resources among the functional areas within the overall district head count limit. Regions and districts also had flexibility in advertising investments, though they had to choose from a menu of headquarter options that they could customize to local markets. Profit and expense planning (including revenue growth, profit growth, and expense targets) were generated from the district level upward.

In 1990, USMG had four goals:

1. To become an organization with which customers were eager to do business.
2. To create an environment where every employee could take pride in the organization and feel responsible for its success.
3. To grow profits and increase Xerox presence at a rate faster than the markets in which it competed.
4. To use Leadership Through Quality principles in everything it did.

Customers

Xerox categorized its customers into four segments:

1. Commercial Major Accounts (CMA): These were Fortune 500 firms and, although accounting for only 5 percent of Xerox's customers, they accounted for about 32 percent of its copier revenues.
2. Named Accounts: These were large commercial accounts that were non-Fortune 500 firms. They accounted for about 18 percent of Xerox's customers and 28 percent of its copier revenues.
3. General Markets: These were all other commercial accounts, and accounted for 62 percent of Xerox's customers and about 15 percent of its copier revenues.
4. Government/Education: These customers accounted for 15 percent of Xerox's customers and 25 percent of its copier revenues.

The first two groups were segmented further into large and small accounts. The average large Named Account provided the same revenues as the average small Commercial Major Account, and there were a larger number of large Named Accounts than small CMAs.

For most customers, product reliability was the top priority. As one Xerox executive put it: "Copiers are not exciting. Most customers don't notice copiers until they break down. Like toasters, they are just a convenience; they should be reliable and look reliable as well."

Apart from product reliability, purchase criteria varied by segment. In the low-volume segment, the emphasis was more on price than on service. These customers wanted the best possible quality at the lowest possible price. In the mid- and high-volume segments, service was a critical purchase consideration. (The relative importance of various purchase criteria for equipment and service purchase decisions for the mid- and high-volume segments is given in Exhibit 2.) Xerox and Kodak maintained their own national service organizations. Equipment service for other vendors was handled by dealer service organizations or by third-party service

Exhibit 2 Relative Importance of Major Criteria in Equipment and Service Purchase Decisions

	Commercial Major Accounts			Named Accounts		
	Small	*Large*	*Overall*	*Small*	*Large*	*Overall*
Equipment Purchase Decision						
Reliability	0.30	0.34	0.32	0.41	0.38	0.40
Ease of operation	0.17	0.24	0.21	0.20	0.07	0.13
Completeness of product line	0.21	0.11	0.16	0.10	0.20	0.15
Service quality	0.29	0.30	0.29	0.18	0.27	0.23
Price	0.03	0.01	0.02	0.11	0.08	0.09
Service Purchase Decision						
Technical Expertise	0.35	0.45	0.40	0.33	0.45	0.39
Professionalism	0.26	0.10	0.18	0.18	0.10	0.14
Guaranteed response time	0.23	0.34	0.28	0.35	0.29	0.32
Variety of contract offerings	0.09	0.10	0.10	0.05	0.11	0.08
Price	0.07	0.01	0.04	0.09	0.05	0.07

organizations, a significant emerging trend. Large service organizations such as TRW offered service either directly to customers or via exclusive relationships with producers or dealer organizations. Hicks saw an opportunity for Xerox to gain, through its service capabilities, a competitive advantage over its rivals in the U.S. and global markets.

Distribution

Historically, all Xerox products were sold directly by the Xerox sales force. However, the company recently began to distribute low-volume and low-priced mid-volume machines through dealer networks, and the lowest-priced machines through consumer retail channels.

For the copier industry as a whole, dealers were the primary distribution channel. In 1989, according to industry specialist Dataquest, 54 percent of placements went through the dealer channel, 26 percent via the direct sales force, 10 percent via the retail channel, 9 percent via national or regional distributors, and 1 percent via alternate channels (mail order, agents, telemarketing, etc.). Dataquest estimated that in 1994 dealers would account for 42 percent, the direct sales force for 27 percent, retail channels for 16 percent, distributors for 10 percent, and alternate channels for 5 percent of copier sales.

Product Line and Pricing

Although a copier appeared to be a dull, boring, and simple product, it contained some very sophisticated technology: chemical, electronic, optical, and mechanical science all wrapped in one box. For engineers, it was a tremendous technical and intellectual challenge to combine these different technologies and at the same time ensure that the product was easy to use.

In 1990, Xerox had two lines of copiers—the 10 series and the 50 series. The 10 series of Xerox copiers, introduced in 1982, helped Xerox regain significant market share. It also helped revitalize the company's financial outlook and rejuvenate its morale and fighting spirit. In 1988, Xerox introduced the 50 series of copiers. In 1990, Xerox had 18 copiers, 4 in the low-end (1020, 1025, 5012, 5014), 9 in the mid-range (1040, 1045, 1048, 1055, 5018, 5028, 5042, 5046, 5052), and 5 in the high-end (1065, 1075, 1090, 9900, 5090). It regained market share in the low- and mid-volume segments and preserved its high share of the high-end market. Xerox copiers ranged in list price (base unit) from $2,440 for the 5012 to $154,000 for the 5090.

Most Xerox copiers carried a 30-day warranty, in line with industry practice. Some of the high-volume machines carried a 90-day warranty. The new 50 series low- and mid-volume copiers (5012, 5014, 5018, and 5028) were launched with a three-year warranty. The longer warranty was an aggressive marketing tool to accelerate new product acceptance and to communicate the products' higher reliability to customers, dealers, and the Xerox sales force. These copiers utilized user-replaceable cartridges, which replaced many of the parts that were likely to need frequent servicing.

Customer Service

USMG provided maintenance and installation of Xerox as well as third-party products, including PCs and printers. Revenues from customer service were approximately $2 billion in 1989, making Xerox the country's third-largest service business (behind IBM and DEC). Customer service employed 18,000 people, with 15,000 in the field and additional staff of about 3,000, including a telephone support staff of 1,000.

Customer service at Xerox had several dimensions: fixing/repairing units; providing operating systems support, interface, and integration; communicating with customers; resolving customer issues after installation; providing technical product support; selling services; and giving feedback to manufacturing, sales, marketing, and administration.

Customer service was run as a cost center, with cost as a percentage of revenue being a very important consideration. Some managers believed that customer service should operate as a stand-alone operation and be a profit center.

The quality of customer service was measured on the following criteria: (1) customer satisfaction, based on customer surveys; (2) the expense-to-revenue ratio; (3) reliability; and (4) service billing errors. The focus on customer satisfaction, originally initiated in customer service, continued to be championed by customer service. Centralized parts support enabled customer service engineers to order parts online and improved the availability of parts in local inventory. In 1985, service marketing was established as a separate organization to focus on the growth of service revenues.

As a result of these kinds of efforts, customer service improved Xerox's service delivery capabilities and reduced service costs. Actual average response time improved from about 5.75 hours in 1987 to 4.75 hours in 1989. Customer satisfaction with service equipment repair had improved to 96 percent. Customers' wait time on the phone when calling the Service Support Centers improved more than 40 percent (and was 20 percent better than the industry average), with most customers waiting fewer than 20 seconds.

Customer Satisfaction at Xerox

During the period 1980 to 1986, Xerox had three corporate priorities: return on assets (ROA), market share, and customer satisfaction. There was no particular order to the three priorities, yet most people focused on ROA, which had a goal of 15 percent. No specific quantitative corporate goals were set for market share and customer satisfaction.

Studies conducted in 1987 concluded that customer satisfaction had not been a top priority in the day-to-day management of Xerox's businesses. However, the senior management team at Xerox was convinced that success in customer satisfaction would lead to success in the other two priorities. Customer satisfaction, the team believed, would drive an external focus and give the voice of the customer a critical role. It decided that customer satisfaction should become the Number 1 corporate priority, which, in September 1987, it announced in a series of management communications meetings and published materials. As President Allaire put it:

> We can be the industry leader in all aspects of customer satisfaction. That is our goal. It is our strong conviction that if we meet our customer's expectations, we will improve market share, and if we improve market share, we will improve our financial performance and shareholder value.

In November 1987, the senior management team issued to the operating units a set of requirements and guidelines to ensure that customer satisfaction (CS) became their first priority. These requirements and guidelines focused on reorienting the company at every level to CS as the first priority, and were used by the units to prepare their own operating strategies and plans to meet CS goals and business objectives. Operating units were given the authority and options to respond to their customers' requirements with a range of approved products, services, or solutions that would maximize CS for their markets. They were to delegate those authorities and options to the appropriate organizational level, allowing it to respond easily to customers' requirements.

In March 1988, President Allaire asked that a common, core system of measures for managing and improving customer satisfaction be established for use by all operating units worldwide. Each operating unit had been using its own method for surveying customers, asking different questions, and using different scales. In Brazil, for example, customer satisfaction was measured on a two-point scale, while

Canada used a five-point scale. Hence it was difficult to do any cross-comparisons or determine whether a particular dissatisfaction problem was endemic to one office, a region, an operating company, or the entire organization.

Based on the best methods in use, a common set of guidelines was formulated for tracking and measuring customer satisfaction. In August 1988, the senior management team approved the proposed framework of measures and issued a complete set of requirements and guidelines to all operating units for measuring, managing, and improving customer satisfaction. The units could customize their systems so long as they complied with the mandatory requirements and stayed within the guidelines. The common, core system was implemented by all operating units by January 1, 1989.

Vision and Goals

In 1990, Xerox's vision for customer satisfaction was that "100 percent of Xerox's customers are very satisfied or satisfied with our products and services through the elimination of defects and errors in our work processes and the achievement of world-class benchmark quality and value in our products and other deliveries to the customer."

The corporate goal was that by 1993 Xerox should be recognized as the industry benchmark in customer satisfaction in all business areas. This goal had two components: For the external world, the goal was to exceed competitive benchmarks for customer satisfaction in all major business areas and to exceed competitive benchmark quality and reliability in all services to the customer by 1993. For the internal world, the goal was that by 1993 Xerox products should meet customer requirements and exceed competitive benchmarks in quality; there should be fourfold improvements in reliability, a tenfold reduction in defects and errors in the work processes and deliverables that impact the customer, a 50 percent improvement in cost, and time to market should be reduced by 12 months.

Top management believed that to achieve this vision and these goals, it needed market-driven business strategies, product strategies, and investments that were determined by customer requirements and expectations. Top management also believed that it was critical that the vision and goals be communicated systematically through each level in the organization to ensure understanding, capability, and commitment. Fundamental to success was the assurance of quality by problem diagnosis, identification of root causes, and corrective actions.

Action Steps

Several actions were taken to enhance customer satisfaction. Management leadership was particularly important. Senior managers in the operating units became role models for appropriate behaviors relative to the customer, by personally taking the lead in acting to totally satisfy customer requirements and resolving customer complaints. They promoted and participated in programs that placed them in direct contact with customers.

Another action was ensuring that all employees developed a proactive attitude, role, and work emphasis focused on customer satisfaction. Every customer contact by a Xerox employee was viewed as an opportunity to manage the customer's experience with, and perception of, Xerox. Employees who had no direct customer contact focused on supporting those who did.

A customer satisfaction code of conduct was developed for all employees. CS was introduced into all training curricula, where employees learned about the Leadership Through Quality tools and processes. CS training was provided to all frontline employees.

At the end of 1988, customer relations groups (CRGs) were initiated at headquarters and at the regions and districts. At each district, the CRG consisted of two to six people. Its objective was to have direct customer contact so it could follow up on dissatisfied customers and customer complaints and to resolve issues better and faster. Problems reached the CRG in one of the following ways: customer surveys, internal sales or service problem referrals, customer losses or contract cancellations, and nonconformance costs such as machine replacement, accommodation, and sales refusals or reversals.

The perceived benefits of the customer relations group were in staying close to the customer, having a cross-functional focus on customer issues, and having a customer closed-loop process that identified problems, resolved them, conducted root-cause analyses, and provided recommendations for avoidance or elimination. The group hoped to be predictive rather than purely reactive. It hoped to resolve issues before receiving negative feedback and to identify potentially dissatisfied customers based on frequency of service, changes in billing history, changes in service contracts, deteriorating supply purchases, and so on.

The regions and districts were reorganized in 1990 as partnerships of sales, service, and business operations. Previously, the sales, service, and business operations used to report to the regional and headquarters levels, and there was not much teamwork at the local district level.

Local empowerment was another tool for increasing customer satisfaction. Processes and systems were developed and authorities were modified to enable first-line sales, service, and administration teams in the branches and districts to rapidly and effectively respond to customers and resolve complaints. All employees were made to feel accountable for CS and to act accordingly. Rewards and recognition programs were modified to ensure that they supported the CS objectives. The bonus plan for general managers, for example, included CS criteria.

Other major steps included the establishment of customer support teams for postsale follow-up, establishment of a Customer Complaints Management System, improvements in technical service, information systems, and telephone systems. Zero-defects programs were implemented for continuing quality improvement of those internal processes that directly impacted external customers.

Measurement of Customer Satisfaction

Xerox believed that a critical aspect for achieving CS was the development of tools to continuously measure, manage, and improve customer satisfaction. Two major

EXHIBIT 3 Customer Satisfaction Improvement Model

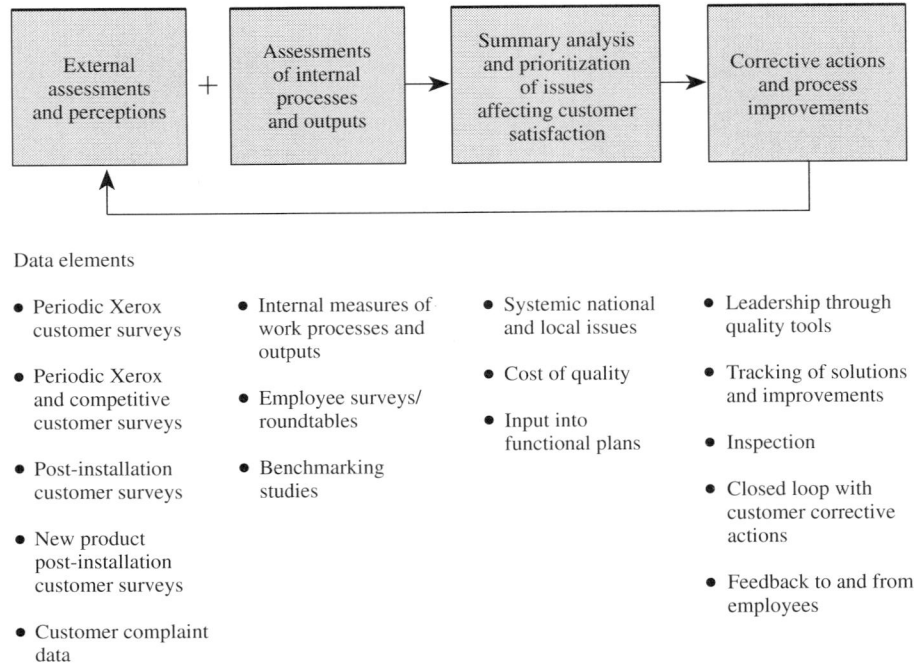

sets of data were developed and utilized: (1) external customer feedback data, which included a series of customer satisfaction surveys as well as a Customer Complaint Management System, and (2) internal quality and quantity measures of Xerox work processes and outputs that delivered products and services (see Exhibit 3).

The External Measurement System

Customer perceptions and market outcomes that resulted from implementing the strategies and action plans were monitored through the external measures of customer satisfaction. The external customer feedback data system consisted of surveys (to solicit from customers their satisfaction with all areas of their interaction with Xerox) and the Customer Complaint Management System, which captured any unsolicited feedback from customers. Four sets of surveys were used: (1) a periodic survey of a random sample of Xerox customers, (2) a postinstallation survey of all Xerox customers within 90 days of a new installation, (3) a new product postinstallation survey of a random sample of customers with new products during the launch phase, and (4) a blind survey of Xerox's and competitors' customers to establish benchmark levels of customer satisfaction and to determine Xerox's competitive position.

Periodic Survey. Each month, USMG mailed surveys to 40,000 randomly selected customers; 50 percent were sent to key operators, 25 percent to decision makers, and 25 percent to administrators. About 10,000 surveys were returned to Xerox. The surveys queried customers about satisfaction on a number of levels: overall satisfaction with Xerox, likelihood of acquiring another product from Xerox, likelihood of recommending Xerox to a business associate, and satisfaction with several different aspects of the products, services, and support (see Exhibit 4).

The key measure tracked was the overall satisfaction. Customer satisfaction was measured on a five-point semantic differential scale (very satisfied—very dissatisfied). Each month, the percentage satisfied (those who marked either very satisfied or somewhat satisfied) was analyzed in terms of a three-month rolling average, the prior month, the current month, actual year-to-date, and percent of planned target. Results were tracked by district, region, product, product type, and customer segment.

The results of the periodic surveys were used to flag problem areas and measure the effect of corrective actions for individual products, districts, and customer segments. The results were used quite extensively by product managers (to set product, district, and function targets), product development teams, customer relations groups, and various functional areas.

Postinstallation Survey. This survey was administered 7 to 90 days after installation of a machine and enabled the respondent to register any problem, enabled the local field unit to respond rapidly with corrective actions, and allowed Xerox to collect data for work process improvement. Often more than one survey was required: one as soon as possible after the installation, and another within 90 days to cover different interactions and aspects of the transaction.

The operator received the survey, which focused on the product (product performance against expectations, copy quality, ease of use), the sales process (responsiveness of the sales representative, fulfillment of commitments), the order process (availability of product, ease of understanding the options), the delivery process (timing, correctness, attitude of crew), the installation process (time to install, time lag between delivery and installation), and the support activities (user training, manuals and documentation, ease of contacting Xerox). Any dissatisfaction detected was followed up for quick resolution.

New Products Postinstallation Survey. This survey was sent to a random sample of customers just after the launch of a new product to help identify any problems that customers might face with the new product. It served as an early warning system for new product performance.

Competitive Benchmarking Customer Satisfaction Survey. This was a critical tool for comparing Xerox to its key competitors in terms of customer satisfaction and perceptions of the products and services. Other purposes of this survey were to identify which suppliers were the benchmarks in satisfying the customer, and what were customers' requirements and preferences in the quality of products and

Section IV Managing Product Market Diversity

EXHIBIT 4 Xerox Customer Satisfaction Survey: Decision Makers

This questionnaire should be completed by the individual who makes decisions about the acquisition of _____.
Please focus on your experiences in the product areas mentioned as you complete the questionnaire.

	Very Satisfied	Somewhat Satisfied	Neither Satisfied nor Dissatisfied	Somewhat Dissatisfied	Very Dissatisfied
Section I: General Satisfaction					
1. Based on your recent experience, how satisfied are you with Xerox?	☐	☐	☐	☐	☐

	Definitely	Probably	Might or Might Not	Probably Not	Definitely Not
2. Based on your recent experience, would you acquire another product from Xerox?	☐	☐	☐	☐	☐
3. Based on your recent experience, would you recommend Xerox to a business associate?	☐	☐	☐	☐	☐

	Very Satisfied	Somewhat Satisfied	Neither Satisfied nor Dissatisfied	Somewhat Dissatisfied	Very Dissatisfied
4. How satisfied are you overall with the quality of:					
a. Your Xerox product(s)	☐	☐	☐	☐	☐
b. Sales support you receive	☐	☐	☐	☐	☐
c. Technical service you receive	☐	☐	☐	☐	☐
d. Administrative support you receive	☐	☐	☐	☐	☐
e. Handling of inquiries	☐	☐	☐	☐	☐
f. Supplies support you receive	☐	☐	☐	☐	☐
g. Xerox user training	☐	☐	☐	☐	☐
h. Xerox supplied documentation	☐	☐	☐	☐	☐

Please complete 4*i* and 4*j* only if you are the decision maker for systems products (printers, workstations, personal computers and wordprocessors)

i. Your Xerox supplied software	☐	☐	☐	☐	☐
j. Xerox systems analyst support	☐	☐	☐	☐	☐
k. Telephone hotline support	☐	☐	☐	☐	☐

	Very Satisfied	Somewhat Satisfied	Neither Satisfied nor Dissatisfied	Somewhat Dissatisfied	Very Dissatisfied	Not Applicable
Section II: Sales Support						
5. How satisfied are you with Xerox sales representatives with regard to:						
a. Timeliness of response to your inquiries	☐	☐	☐	☐	☐	☐
b. Frequency of contact to review your needs	☐	☐	☐	☐	☐	☐
c. Frequency of contact to provide information about new Xerox products and services	☐	☐	☐	☐	☐	☐
d. Product knowledge	☐	☐	☐	☐	☐	☐
e. Application knowledge	☐	☐	☐	☐	☐	☐
f. Understanding of your business needs	☐	☐	☐	☐	☐	☐
g. Accuracy in explaining terms/conditions	☐	☐	☐	☐	☐	☐
h. Ability to resolve problems	☐	☐	☐	☐	☐	☐
i. Professionalism	☐	☐	☐	☐	☐	☐

EXHIBIT 4 (concluded)

Section III: Customer Support

6. What was the purpose of your most recent call to Xerox?
   ☐ *Inquiry* ☐ *Problem* ☐ *Haven't called, can't answer (skip to Question 10)*

7. How long ago did you make this call?
   ☐ *less than 3 months* ☐ *3–6 months* ☐ *6–12 months* ☐ *Greater than 12 months*

8. What Xerox function did you contact?
   ☐ *Sales* ☐ *Service* ☐ *Billing* ☐ *Collection* ☐ *Supplies*
   ☐ *Telephone Hotline Support* ☐ *Systems Analyst* ☐ *Group Customer Relations*

	Very Satisfied	Somewhat Satisfied	Neither Satisfied nor Dissatisfied	Somewhat Dissatisfied	Very Dissatisfied
9. How satisfied are you with the support you received?	☐	☐	☐	☐	☐
a. Ability to get to the right person(s) quickly	☐	☐	☐	☐	☐
b. Attitude of Xerox personnel who assisted you	☐	☐	☐	☐	☐
c. Ability to provide a solution	☐	☐	☐	☐	☐
d. Time required to provide a solution	☐	☐	☐	☐	☐
e. Effectiveness of the solution	☐	☐	☐	☐	☐
f. Overall satisfaction with support received	☐	☐	☐	☐	☐

10. What specific things can we do to increase your satisfaction with Xerox, our products, and our services? Thank you for your feedback!

Your Name _____
Position   _____
Tel #   _____   *Account #*
Date   _____   *123456789*

services. This annual survey focused on the various vendors and brands and used the same core questions as the periodic survey. However, in this survey, the identity of the sponsor was not disclosed.

Internal Measurement Process

The common, core system of measures also required matching external customer assessments of Xerox products and services to the appropriate internal quality measures and standards for the work processes and outputs that produced those deliverables. Xerox management could routinely monitor and inspect internal performance as a leading indicator of CS and as leverage in acting to improve output quality and CS. The process included setting and monitoring quality measures of the internal work processes and deliverables that impact the customer and parallel the customer satisfaction measures. The objective was to provide leading indicators of Xerox performance and improvement opportunities.

Xerox determined which processes impacted each area of customer interaction and installed systems to measure and monitor these internal processes. For every diagnostic question asked in the periodic and postinstallation surveys, there was one or more internal standards and measures that indicated Xerox performance in the applicable work processes or deliverables. Examples of internal measures included service response time, number of billing errors, and number of training hours per sales rep. Benchmark standards were set for all processes (i.e., response time should be less than four hours, or billing errors should be less than 2 percent, or all sales reps should have four hours of training with a new product).

Data Analyses, Review, and Follow-Up

Information on customer satisfaction was received from various sources such as the surveys, the customer complaint management system, the district partners, and the field reports. The data were analyzed to identify segment-specific satisfiers (factors that increased customer satisfaction) and dissatisfiers (factors that when not available in the right amount led to customer dissatisfaction).

Customer satisfaction was reviewed frequently and at various levels in the organization. A customer satisfaction improvement meeting, attended by the president of USMG, the president of development and manufacturing, the senior vice president of worldwide marketing, and their direct reports, was held once a quarter for one day. This meeting covered CS results, strategic enablers, CS corrective actions, new product status and future-product customer requirements. Cross-functional teams were assigned to follow up and to initiate quality improvement teams (QITs).

A Customer Satisfaction Improvement Network meeting of representatives from all major operating units worldwide met once a quarter for one to two days. On the agenda were customer satisfaction issues that included survey processes, targeting methodology, benchmark studies, CS results and targets, business results and targets, and best practices. On a regular basis, data were distributed to regions and districts for use by all functional areas so that corrective measures could be taken and results tracked.

At USMG, the senior management team met once every two months for two hours to review customer satisfaction. This group focused on the Top 10 dissatisfiers, the progress made on achieving the CS targets, and the actions to be taken to improve customer satisfaction.

In addition, the USMG customer satisfaction team met for two hours twice a month to follow up on the actions initiated at the customer satisfaction improvement meeting and the USMG senior staff meeting. This was a cross-functional team and consisted of members from service, marketing, administration, the headquarters customer relations group, development and manufacturing, and worldwide marketing.

The next step in the customer satisfaction process was to manage a corrective action process that responded to customer dissatisfaction indicators, off-standard internal measures, and performance improvement opportunities. All concerns, including those from customers who indicated through the survey that they were somewhat or very dissatisfied, were acted upon very quickly. About 10,000 complaints per month (150 per district) were followed up. About 35 percent came from the surveys, while the balance were from letters or telephone calls. Personal contact was made with the customer and the problem resolved within 48 hours with a closed-loop follow-up system. The districts' customer relations teams did the callbacks. Planned head-count reductions were likely to reduce the size of the customer relations team by one rep per district, unless a district decided to reallocate personnel from another function.

Root causes of problems were categorized and tracked. The most significant problems involved equipment performance and service, where surveys had revealed that customer expectations were higher than Xerox performance. Corrective measures included setting higher reliability requirements (less than one call per month) on new products, providing dissatisfied customers with better machines, and improving response time for service.

Actions were taken to improve customer satisfaction in weak market segments such as General Markets, which constantly had the worst CS performance and was furthest from the 1990 target at 84.2 percent in the first quarter. This segment was targeted at 87.3 percent, which was needed to reach the overall target of 1990 by year-end and represented 11,000 machines that needed to move from "dissatisfied" to "satisfied." Likely causes of the problems encountered by General Markets were (*a*) lack of account ownership, (*b*) frequent account rep changes (*c*) time and material prices perceived as excessive, and (*d*) low priority in the service-call queue.

Specific actions were also taken for products with below-target CS ratings. For example, retrofit programs were in place to improve the performance of some problem 50 series copiers. Midvolume copiers as a group were below customer satisfaction performance targets, mainly because these machines were generally treated with less care by customers. Midvolume machines were the orphans of the copier world, generally placed in common areas for use by a large group of people, as opposed to a low-volume or high-volume machine that had one or a few operators who took good care of the machine.

Results

Xerox set year-by-year, overall customer satisfaction targets: 90 percent in 1990, 94 percent in 1991, 97 percent in 1992, and 100 percent in 1993. These targets were broken down by customer segment and product line. The percentage of satisfied customers increased significantly in all customer segments (see Exhibit 5).

Overall customer satisfaction targets were also set for each partnership. These were, typically, based on the overall improvement required and the previous performance of the partnership relative to internal and competitive benchmarks. Partnerships with the largest variance were expected to improve the most.

EXHIBIT 5 **Percentage Satisfied by Customer Segment (three-month rolling average reported quarterly)**

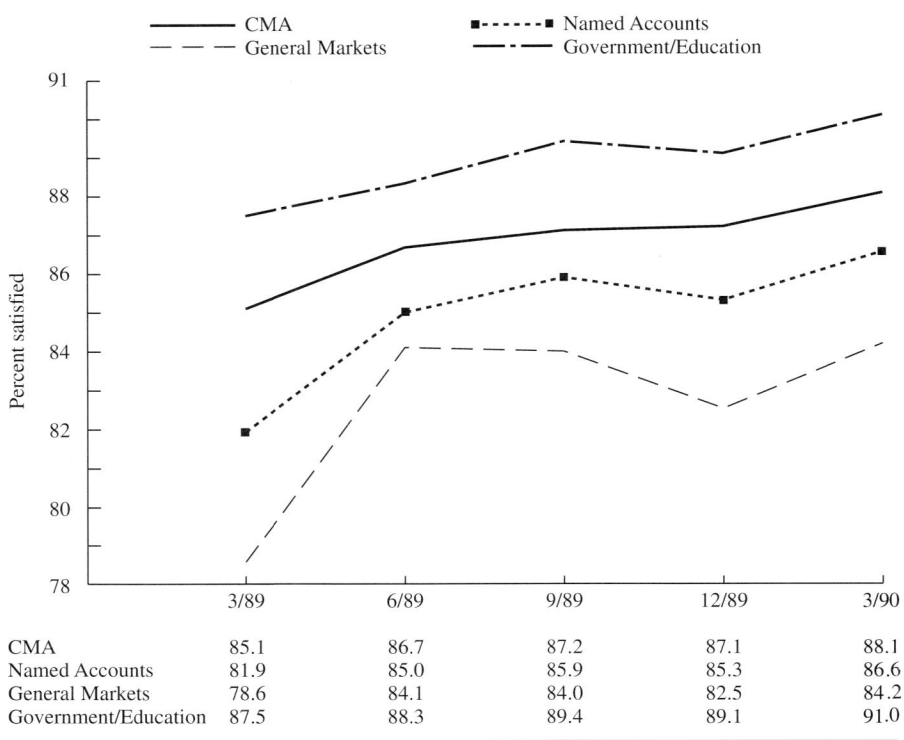

	3/89	6/89	9/89	12/89	3/90
CMA	85.1	86.7	87.2	87.1	88.1
Named Accounts	81.9	85.0	85.9	85.3	86.6
General Markets	78.6	84.1	84.0	82.5	84.2
Government/Education	87.5	88.3	89.4	89.1	91.0

The management leadership actions and the focus on changing employee attitudes began to pay off. Prior to these actions, customer satisfaction was the responsibility of the service organization, while sales and business operations did not have much of a customer focus. Customers had complained about lack of follow-up and postsale support by sales reps who seemed to disappear as soon as the order was signed. Sales reps had focused on new business and had an attitude of "sales at any cost." Many customers were frustrated with inaccurate billing and the difficulty of doing business with Xerox. When a customer problem had involved cross-functional areas, as many did, it seemed as though the sales, service, and administration people did not talk to one another, making it difficult and frustrating to find a solution.

With the district offices as partnerships, their empowerment to resolve customer issues without getting approvals at multiple levels, and the use of customer satisfaction measurements for performance appraisal changed the day-to-day customer interactions. All partners and employees felt responsible for customer satisfaction. Here are the comments of the three partners of one East Coast district:

District service manager: Three years ago I never went on a sales call; now I go on about three per month. We were not always focused on listening to the customer. We focused on fixing a machine rather than fixing a broken customer who happened to have a Xerox equipment.

District business manager: Every customer contact—"the 1,000 moments of truth"—is now considered an opportunity to improve customer satisfaction with and perception of Xerox.

District sales manager: We are more customer focused than ever before. Five years ago, there was not that much excitement about customer satisfaction. Today customer satisfaction is everything.

Customer Guarantee

In November 1987, top management of Xerox had considered offering a satisfaction guarantee because it expected that a guarantee would lead to greater customer satisfaction and would also drive the organization to higher levels of performance. It wanted to come up with a guarantee that would be difficult for Xerox's competitors to emulate, especially those in the mid- and low-volume segments who distributed through dealers. However, it thought that such a guarantee should be offered only after ensuring that the Leadership Through Quality tools and processes as well as the focus on *The Customer* were implemented, and that Xerox was able to consistently perform and deliver on the guarantee. By February 1990, it believed that Xerox had achieved those targets and that the organization was ready to guarantee satisfaction.

Most senior managers believed that a money-back guarantee was the way to go. Based on brainstorming and exploratory research, however, they decided to examine four types of guarantees: (1) a service guarantee (e.g., "If your machine is not operating 98 percent of the time, you will receive 10 percent off your next invoice"); (2) a money-back guarantee (e.g., "If you are not satisfied with the product or vendor, you can return your machine, no questions asked"); (3) a product performance guarantee (e.g., "If your machine does not perform at its original specifications or better for at least three years, we will replace your unit at no charge"); and (4) a product-fit guarantee (e.g., "If the product does not meet your needs, you can trade it in for full credit toward any other product").

During May–June 1990, Xerox conducted market research to gather inputs from various customer segments to develop a unique guarantee. The research consisted of focus groups and a telephone survey. In the first phase, focus groups were conducted in three cities to test reactions to the four broad categories of guarantees. Several key messages came from the groups:

- The credibility of a guarantee was tied to the reputation of the vendor.
- The length of the guarantee was critical; less than a year was viewed as a normal warranty at best, and at worst, a desperate sales ploy. If a guarantee was for unlimited time, respondents believed that the customer paid a premium.
- Any guarantee could be significantly strengthened by making the customer the sole arbiter.

- For the service guarantee, response time (how quickly a firm responded to a call) was viewed as more appropriate than machine up-time.
- The money-back guarantee was viewed by some as low vendor commitment (i.e., being too easy for the vendor to walk away from).
- The product performance guarantee should be at the customer's request, with no questions asked, for the life of the contract.
- The product-fit guarantee was considered by many to be inappropriate. Many focus group members indicated that customers did not want to switch equipment, but only wanted the equipment to work well and be right for their needs.

Based on the focus groups' research, Xerox decided (1) to drop the product-fit guarantee from further consideration, (2) to substitute response time for up-time in the service guarantee, and (3) to change the product performance guarantee to this wording: "If your machine does not perform up to your satisfaction for at least three years, we will replace it at no charge at your request." Thus, the three guarantees tested in the second phase of the study were:

1. A response-time guarantee, which involved a commitment to send a service person to the customer site within a specified time after the service call was received.
2. A performance guarantee, under which Xerox would commit to a certain customer-oriented level of service or product satisfaction. Xerox would replace the machine with another of equal or greater capability at the sole discretion of the customer.
3. A money-back guarantee under which the customer would receive a refund if dissatisfied.

In the second phase of the research, 560 customers (Xerox and non-Xerox), selected from all five customer segments, were surveyed by telephone. The focus group results were used to develop a questionnaire for the telephone survey. The major findings from the survey are presented in Exhibit 6.

Some competitors already offered a guarantee. Kodak had just begun a new campaign touting their "Bend Over Backwards" customer guarantee. Advertised in *Time, Business Week,* and other highly visible publications, Kodak's guarantee of product replacement was at Kodak's discretion and covered a three-year period. Canon also offered a performance guarantee, while Pitney Bowes guaranteed response time, performance, and a parts and supplies price protection. Lanier offered a 98 percent up-time guarantee.

Whichever guarantee alternative was chosen, Xerox planned an extensive marketing and advertising campaign, its biggest in 10 years, around the new guarantee. The guarantee would apply to all Xerox products for a period of three years or for the term of Xerox financing, whichever was longer, and the machines had to be serviced by Xerox (and not by third parties) throughout the guarantee period. Though Xerox executives believed that it would be difficult to link sales specifically to the guarantee, they expected that the guarantee would increase sales by 5 to 10 percent.

EXHIBIT 6   Feedback from the Telephone Survey of Customers, 1990

	Agree	Disagree
General		
Guarantees are a meaningful way to protect the customer	90%	10%
All guarantees are pretty much the same	30%	70%
A company that offers a better guarantee makes a superior product	35%	65%
A better guarantee on a quality product does not increase cost	45%	55%

Consideration

About 63% of those who heard about a guarantee took some action, such as calling for more information, asking for a demo or trial, considering a new vendor, or switching vendors; 37% did nothing on hearing about a guarantee.

Almost half of those who took some action on hearing about a guarantee switched vendors (63% took action, 29% switched vendors).

Named Accounts were most likely to respond to guarantees in the consideration process, exceeding the average by 5%–10%. General Markets were the least responsive.

Decision Factors

In terms of the decision process, the percentage of respondents who thought that guarantees were equal to or more important than the following major criteria were as follows: price (46%), features (42%), vendor reputation (50%), and experience with the vendor (46%).

General Markets and Government/Education were most sensitive to price and features. Among them, 35% view guarantees as equally or more important than price.

Guarantees were equal to or more important than prior experience or vendor reputation for all segments except General Markets where prior experience was more important.

Preferences

Customers allocated 10 points over the three guarantee offerings as follows:

	Service Response	Product Performance	Money Back
Customer segments:			
CMA	3.7	3.6	2.7
Named Accounts	3.4	3.6	3.0
General Markets	3.6	3.2	3.2
Government/Education	3.3	3.5	3.2
Total	3.4	3.6	3.0
Product markets:			
High-Volume	3.7	3.3	3.0
Low- and Mid-Volume	3.3	3.7	3.0

Current Situation

Supporters of the money-back guarantee thought it was the only option strong enough to achieve the desired effects—to mobilize the organization and differentiate Xerox's offering from competitors. As one Xerox manager said, "Kodak already offers a performance guarantee, and any competitor could match the rather amorphous 'performance guarantee.' Significant results require a dramatic offering."

EXHIBIT 6 (continued)

Believability

The percentage of respondents who said that such a guarantee was believable:

	Service Response	Product Performance	Money Back
Customer segments:			
CMA	73%	78%	58%
Named Accounts	62%	73%	61%
General Markets	63%	70%	61%
Government/Education	59%	75%	68%
Total	**63%**	**74%**	**62%**

The top "Do Not Believe" reasons were as indicated by the following percentage of respondents:

Too open-ended	28%	12%	
Never seen it happen	14%		13%
Unrealistic/Ineffective	15%		24%
Company will try to disregard the guarantee		11%	14%
Will try to repair, not replace		17%	
Company sets rules or specs		13%	

Expectations

Who would you expect to offer a guarantee? (Numbers represent the percentage of respondents who said that they would expect that company to offer a guarantee.)

	Canon	Kodak	Xerox	Other Manufacturers
High-Volume:				
Xerox Users	9	35	76	10
Xerox Nonusers	9	30	47	15
Total	9	33	63	12
Low- and Mid-Volume:				
Xerox Users	16	5	59	23
Xerox Nonusers	19	6	32	17
Total	18	6	38	18
All Respondents	**15**	**12**	**42**	**16**

Other managers thought that a money-back guarantee carried negative connotations and was a "low-commitment" alternative. They thought that a performance guarantee was a better option because it required a higher commitment from Xerox, which customers really wanted. They thought the offering could be differentiated on the basis of who determined whether performance met the customer's requirements. Under existing industry practice, the vendor determined whether the product met the performance criteria. Letting the customer make this decision would be a significantly different, value-added offering to the customer.

EXHIBIT 6 (concluded)

Current Practices

Guarantees typically covered the following items, as indicated by the following percentage of respondents:

	Parts and Labor	Response Time	Uptime	Copy Quality
CMA	83%	42%	36%	22%
Named Accounts	78	38	34	21
General Markets	82	36	31	16
Government/Education	83	47	46	19
Total	**80**	**40**	**38**	**20**

Response time guarantees typically guaranteed response times of four hours (46%), two hours (21%), same day (20%), or next day (13%).

Response Time Needs

What response time will really satisfy you? (Numbers represent the percentage of respondents who indicated that particular amount of time.)

	One Hour	Two Hours	Three Hours	Four Hours	Same Day	Next Day	Total
Customer segments:							
CMA	7%	22%	9%	32%	22%	8%	100%
Named Accounts	10	17	11	25	28	9	100
General Markets	2	11	6	12	52	17	100
Government/Education	9	12	7	20	34	18	100
Total	**8**	**16**	**9**	**24**	**31**	**12**	**100**
Product categories:							
High-Volume	9	27	13	29	17	5	100
Low- and Mid-Volume	8	11	7	22	37	15	100
Total	**8**	**16**	**9**	**24**	**31**	**12**	**100**

Supporters of the response-time guarantee pointed out that competitors had already made response time a critical attribute and that Xerox had to compete on that. Other managers believed that a response time guarantee would not provide enough incentive for all functional areas of the company. Some thought that Xerox did not have the process capacity to guarantee response time and that the option would be too complicated because it would require different response times and pricing based on geographic location (i.e., rural versus large city), among other factors.

Hicks and the other top executives had to decide what type of guarantee Xerox ought to offer.

CHAPTER 40

Millipore Corporate Strategy

Millipore, a $750 million high-technology company made and marketed two sets of products: (1) liquid chromatography equipment and supplies and (2) high-precision filtering equipment (essentially membranes). These products were marketed worldwide by three separate divisions in three separate geographies to a variety of end-use customers. The company's management had to resolve the inherent diversity of its niche-marketing strategy with the economies possible with potential aggregation. This automatically then led to the question of organizing and implementing the marketing effort.

Millipore's meteoric rise in the 1960s and 1970s heightened expectations within the company and on Wall Street of consistent annual growth in excess of 20 percent. The company's sales had grown from $1 million in 1960 to $235 million in 1980 to $750 million in 1991. With its slowing growth rate in the 1980s, the situation came to a head in the fourth quarter of 1990, when the company reported a steep downturn in earnings (see Exhibits 1 and 2). Wall Street reflected its assessment by devaluing Millipore's stock from $37 to $27. Recognizing the growing gap between its target growth rate of 15 percent and actuals, John Gilmartin, Millipore's CEO, initiated a series of changes that temporarily reversed the decline in earnings. Changes included a complete restructuring of its Waters Chromatography division, the dissolution of its Milligen division, some hard-nosed cost cutting, and a far more disciplined approach with regard to new product opportunities.

"What we did in the early 1990s is hardly a long term solution to the strategic path I have set for the corporation," stated Gilmartin:

This case was prepared by Robert W. Lightfoot under the supervision of Nitin Nohria and V. Kasturi Rangan.

Copyright © 1993 by the President and Fellows of Harvard College.

Harvard Business School case 594-009.

EXHIBIT 1 Millipore, Sales and Income, 1960–1991 (in millions)

Year	Sales	Operating Income	Net Income
1960	1	n/a	n/a
1965	6	2	1
1970	18	4	2
1971	21	5	2
1972	25	6	3
1973	31	7	4
1974	57	13	7
1975	71	17	9
1976	89	20	11
1977	118	27	15
1978	158	33	19
1979	195	36	22
1980	234	31	19
1981	256	18	11
1982	272	22	33
1983	292	28	21
1984	332	35	30
1985	367	42	32
1986	443	53	39
1987	529	65	48
1988	622	76	55
1989	658	69	53
1990	703	39	28
1991	748	85	60

SOURCE: Annual reports, Moody's.

To put it simply, we have a $310 million chromatography business that is growing at about 5 percent, a $230 million analytical membranes business that is growing at about 8 percent, and a $210 million process membranes business that is growing at a little over 10 percent. When you add up the three we are at a 8 percent growth trajectory when our corporate objectives are to grow at 15 percent. My goal for the organization is threefold: (1) 15 percent sales growth, (2) 10 percent profit on sales, and (3) 10 percent return on assets.

In order to achieve these goals, "We need to identify and exploit new product and new market opportunities. Our goal is to have 40 percent of our sales come from new products launched in the recent three years," declared Gilmartin. The corporation had increased its R&D spending in recent years to promote this goal. "I am somewhat disappointed," expressed Gilmartin "that in spite of all our R&D activity, we are unable to bring new products to markets quickly and efficiently."

Another strategic area of concern to Gilmartin was the whole notion of customer satisfaction. "Our fundamental premise is a simple one. That we can achieve our mission and vision, execute our strategy, and accomplish our goals, by focusing religiously on satisfying customers. It is really that simple, and everything is sec-

EXHIBIT 2 Millipore Summary of Operations, 1976–1991 (in thousands, except per share and employee data)

	1991	1990	1989	1988	1987	1986	1981	1976
Net sales	$747,979	$703,162	$657,515	$621,893	$528,743	$443,092	$255,803	$88,636
Cost of sales	336,165	312,422	292,827	272,222	237,096	196,362	125,914	34,806
Gross profit	$411,814	$390,740	$364,688	$349,671	$291,647	$246,730	$129,889	$53,830
Selling, general, and administrative expenses	268,672	256,483	241,130	226,784	187,640	161,112	97,817	28,615
Research and development expenses	58,001	60,907	55,032	47,066	39,305	32,837	13,886	5,309
Restructuring charge	—	34,750	—	—	—	—	—	—
Operating income	$ 85,141	$ 38,600	$ 68,526	$ 75,821	$ 64,702	$ 52,781	$ 18,186	$19,906
Other income, net	—	—	3,149	—	—	—	—	—
Interest income	6,182	6,723	3,914	3,450	2,234	3,066	1,874	—
Interest expense	(13,408)	(9,907)	(8,226)	(6,543)	(3,319)	(3,762)	(6,320)	—
Income before income taxes	$ 77,915	$ 35,416	$ 67,363	$ 72,728	$ 63,617	$ 52,085	$ 13,740	$19,852
Provision for income taxes excluding nonrecurring tax benefit	17,531	7,615	14,483	18,180	15,904	13,021	3,514	—
Income from continuing operations	$ 60,384	$ 27,801	$ 52,880	$ 54,548	$ 47,713	$ 39,064	$ 10,226	—
Income from discontinued operations	—	—	—					
Net income	$ 60,384	$ 27,801	$ 52,880	$ 54,548	$ 47,713	$ 39,064	$ 10,928	$11,310
Net income per common share:								
Income from continuing operations	$2.17	$1.00	$1.90	$1.96	$1.70	$1.40	$.38	$.405
Net income per common share	2.17	1.00	1.90	1.96	1.70	1.40	.40	.405
Cash dividends declared per share	$.47	$.43	$.39	$.35	$.31	$.27	$.155	$.055
Financial Data								
Working capital	$250,711	$224,691	$246,107	$249,277	$165,995	$165,421	$ 96,037	$49,231
Capital expenditures, net	48,119	68,331	56,734	46,650	42,746	30,014	21,831	
Depreciation and amortization	29,181	28,741	24,757	23,504	22,117	18,692	8,973	
Property, plant and equipment, net	255,468	235,662	189,241	162,588	142,480	116,964	82,668	
Total assets	783,706	734,339	650,621	576,149	479,757	398,065	252,319	85,284
Long-term obligations	102,452	103,347	104,048	104,978	5,497	12,094	34,364	
Shareholders' equity	$478,160	$434,853	$406,948	$365,547	$330,918	$289,657	$152,155	$65,284
Number of employees at year-end	5,755	6,132	5,868	5,832	5,202	4,868	3,860	1,673

SOURCE: Annual reports.

ondary to that fundamental premise," declared John Gilmartin. In his view, two components of customer satisfaction deserved close attention:

- Customer-sensitive presales systems.
- Customer-friendly selling cycle.

The former pertained to issues concerning order generation and the latter to order-fulfillment activities, including field service and technical support.

In order to rally the company to address the subject of customer satisfaction, Gilmartin had promoted a companywide initiative called Managing for Excellence (MFE). Developed by Gilmartin with his executive committee in 1991, MFE was seen as embodying a set of beliefs and practices by which Millipore would achieve customer satisfaction through an operational focus on continuous improvement in all spheres of activity. MFE, it was hoped, would lead to improved profitability and greater market share in the high-value-added separations business.

Several key process inefficiencies were uncovered as a result of the MFE initiatives. Most importantly, Millipore's internal focus within vertical organization units made cross-functional interfaces inefficient, and sometimes combative. Moreover, even within vertical chimneys, managers and supervisors were found to devote an inordinate amount of time on non-value-added activity. Strategic decisions were constantly made by (or pushed up to) the top of hierarchy. "We have to address these process inefficiencies in any strategy discussion we may seek," emphasized Gilmartin. "After all, we desire to be world leaders in our industry through unparalleled customer satisfaction, and the only way we can deliver this to our customers is via effective cross-regional and cross-functional processes," he concluded.

Company History

During the Second World War, European drinking-water supplies and testing laboratories were destroyed, resulting in massive water-pollution problems and the threat of water-borne diseases. To address these concerns, a German scientist developed a crude microporous membrane filter to detect bacteria in drinking water. When information about this technology was made available after the war, the California Institute of Technology perfected a membrane and the U.S. government awarded a contract to the Lovell Chemical Company of Watertown, Massachusetts, to begin pilot production of the membrane. Seeing potential beyond the single application of drinking-water analysis, a Lovell engineer named Jack Bush purchased the rights to the membrane production process, and in 1954 founded the Millipore Filter Corporation.

By varying the size and density of pores on a plastic sheet, Jack Bush could filter almost any microscopic particle out of almost any fluid. The entrepreneurial chemist hoped he could find marketable applications for the membrane technology, and in the early 1960s he recruited Dee d'Arbeloff to help him commercialize the technology. D'Arbeloff did so by searching the world for high-value-added applications and speaking with potential users in an array of industries.

Millipore grew rapidly during the 1960s and 1970s by applying its membrane separations technology to diverse market niches. The company's membranes were used to separate particles or organisms in analytical lab instruments and to filter impurities in the manufacture of pharmaceuticals, semiconductors, chemicals, food, wine, and other beverages. They were also used to filter intravenous solutions for medical patients, to monitor bacteria levels in water, and to purify water for industrial, scientific, and medical uses.

Following d'Arbeloff's vision of creating a broad-line separations company, Millipore also grew through mergers, acquiring Worthington Biochemicals in the mid-1970s to expand into diagnostics, and Waters Associates in 1980 to catapult Millipore into a new area of analytical technology, liquid chromatography, a technique for making precision separations of complex chemical mixtures into their individual components. To separate a chemical mixture using liquid chromatography, the mixture was injected into a solution and the liquid pumped at high pressure through a column of dense packing material. Because some components moved through the packing column more slowly than others, mixtures could be characterized by the time it took each component to pass through the column. These were then analyzed to determine the composition of the original solution. With 1979 sales of $60 million, Waters was about one-half Millipore's size at the time of the acquisition.

The merger with Waters arose out of the friendship between d'Arbeloff and Jim Waters, president of Waters Associates. Tired of running the business, Jim Waters approached d'Arbeloff on Christmas Eve 1979 with a proposal to merge the two companies. Because Millipore and Waters shared many of the same corporate customers, d'Arbeloff and Waters anticipated many synergies from the merger. Both companies sold to analytical laboratories of pharmaceutical companies and other research institutions such as universities. D'Arbeloff made no major changes to the organization following the merger, preferring instead to run Waters and Millipore as two separate companies. Only in Europe did the two companies consolidate to save administrative expenses.

Beginning in 1985, a series of tragedies befell Millipore's management. After a short struggle with cancer, Dee d'Arbeloff died in July 1985. Just nine months later a helicopter carrying d'Arbeloff's successor Jack Mulvany (who was only 47 years old) crashed, killing him, the vice president of Science and Technology, and a company researcher. After the accident, the board appointed Bill Shippey, the president of Waters, as the COO and John Gilmartin, the president of the Membranes business, as the CEO. Gilmartin came from a background in finance and had been brought into the company to rationalize the financial side of the business in 1979.

Unexpectedly thrust into the leadership of Millipore, Gilmartin reorganized the firm several times during his first few years as CEO. First, he experimented with pushing decision making lower in the organization, allowing the niche-focused strategic business units to have more autonomy. Coordination still took place at the group- or division-head level, but divisions were seen as collections of strategic business units, each going after its own marketplace. According to Gilmartin: "That strategy didn't pan out. Too much was approved after too cursory an analysis. As a result, we failed at most of the businesses that were out of the traditional area in which we operated." Strategic business units chased opportunities pell-mell, failing in part, in Gilmartin's view, to take advantage of core business opportunities closer to their existing markets and technologies. Gilmartin concluded there was a need for higher-level accountability, largely because management talent was not developed enough at the lower, strategic-business-unit level. In response to this situation, Gilmartin pulled decision making back to the division-head and corporate levels and cut back significantly on investments in start-up "new business" activities. "The centralization phase was important to get a handle on costs and a more disciplined approach to our activities," reflected Gilmartin, "but we cannot survive in the complex environment of the 1990s if decision making is not delegated down the organization."

Division Strategy and Structure

In 1992, Millipore's organization structure (see Exhibit 3) consisted of four divisions that each had profit and loss responsibility: Analytical Group, Process Group, Waters Chromatography Division, and an international sales division, called Intertech, for markets in Asia, Africa, and Eastern Europe. These divisions were supported by several shared corporate resources, including the traditional finance and administrative functions, core R&D, as well as common distribution and membrane manufacturing (shared by the Process and Analytical groups). Though each division was responsible for its own sales and marketing, their field marketing organizations were co-located in both the United States and in subsidiaries abroad. Exhibit 4 provides sales data by product line, technology, and geography.

Analytical Group

The Analytical Group "sells little devices to labs," according to its president, Geoff Woodard. Analytical served about 20 market segments, including such diverse businesses as air monitoring, lab water purification, drinking water microbiology, and life sciences. For the most part, customers were commercial, university, and government R&D labs (such as Upjohn, Genentech, Harvard University, and government water supply departments). They used Millipore's analytical products, primarily membranes, to test for impurities in water and other fluids, and to test the levels to which such contaminants could be filtered. Millipore had about 20,000 customers in the United States, and half of its sales came from core products, membrane-based devices invented in the 1960s and 1970s. Priced between $15 and $1,000 per package, these core products were consumables purchased frequently by lab purchasing agents. In the United States and Europe they were sold by a direct sales organization, primarily a direct mail and telemarketing operation.

With 30 percent market share in this business, Millipore was the clear leader. Competition was fragmented and often local. Millipore had a strong brand loyalty, which was enhanced by the company's reputation for high quality and the fact that many items were replacement modules for other Millipore systems. Woodard wondered, however, whether his division could enhance its profitability by cutting prices and buying market share.

EXHIBIT 3 Millipore Organization Chart, March 1992

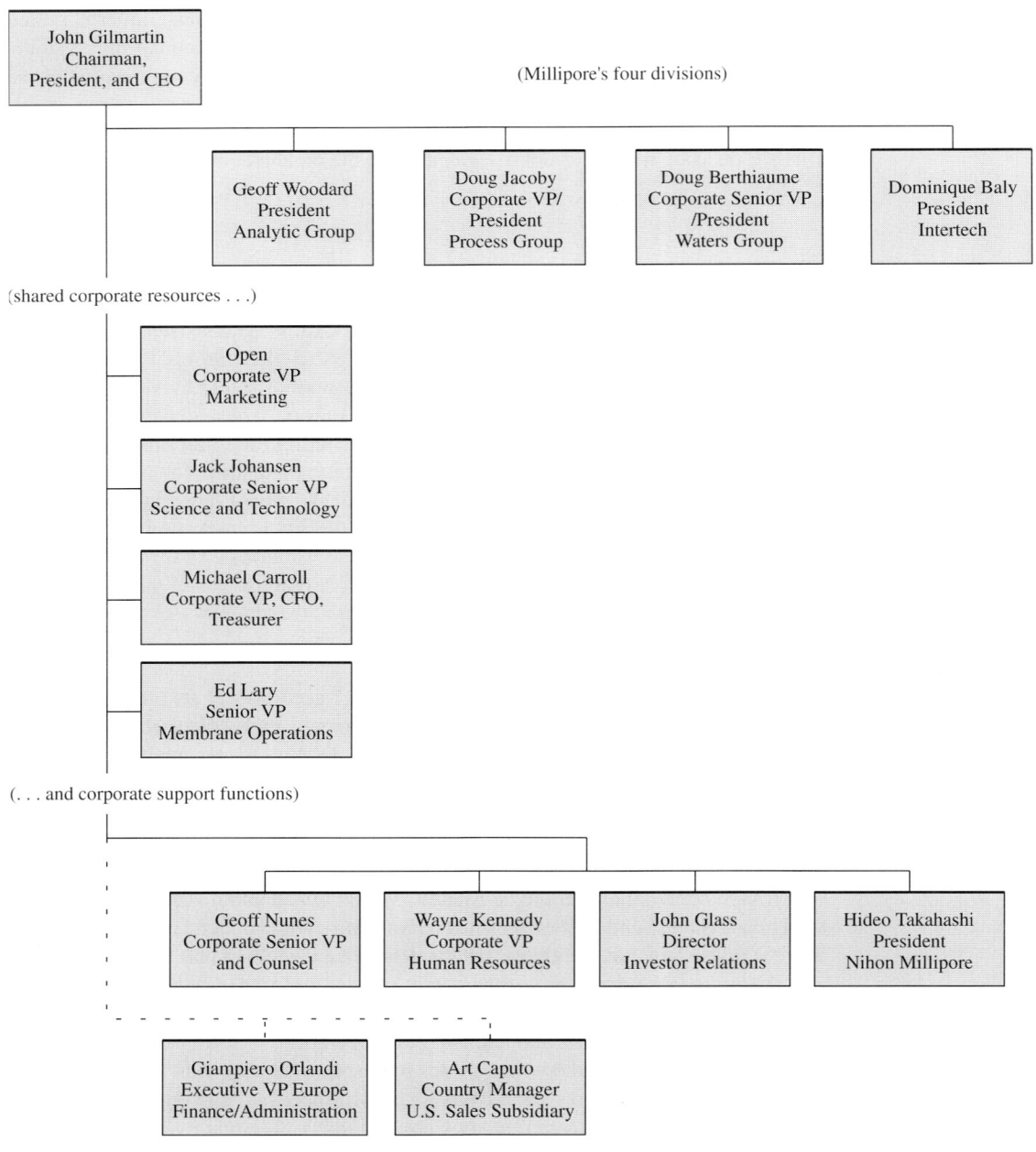

SOURCE: Casewriter depiction of organization from company data.

EXHIBIT 4 Five Years' Revenue Review by Technology/Market/Geography ($ in thousands)

	1991	1990	1989	1988	1987	Five-Year Growth Rate
Sales by Product Line and Technology						
Analytical:						
Membranes	$145,909	$139,358	$124,612	$123,241	$110,773	9%
Chromatography	265,412	259,693	242,574	230,741	207,944	8%
Other	42,429	38,638	29,698	18,824	6,392	96%
Subtotal	453,750	437,689	396,884	372,806	325,109	11%
Purification:						
Membranes	257,476	226,156	186,981	170,307	130,084	19%
Chromatography	26,454	26,669	24,739	29,059	20,884	10%
Other	10,299	12,648	7,726	6,751	12,405	—
Subtotal	294,229	265,473	219,446	206,117	163,373	17%
Total	**$747,979**	**$703,162**	**$616,330**	**$578,923**	**$488,482**	**13%**
Sales by Market						
Industrial[a]	$512,219	$476,104	$427,617	$399,406	$329,015	14%
University/government	178,016	172,504	139,568	133,195	110,810	15%
Patient care/medical research	57,744	54,554	49,145	46,322	48,657	3%
Total	**$747,979**	**$703,162**	**$616,330**	**$578,923**	**$488,482**	**13%**
Sales by Geographic Area						
United States	$274,718	$267,627	$250,218	$230,010	$203,827	9%
Western Europe	234,201	230,391	183,824	176,077	152,085	14%
Japan	171,279	136,205	120,123	112,838	86,206	18%
Other[b]	67,781	68,939	62,165	59,998	46,364	11%
Total	**$747,979**	**703,162**	**$616,330**	**$578,923**	**$488,482**	**13%**

[a]Under "Industrial" was included industries such as pharmaceutical, biotechnology, chemical, and microelectronics.
[b]This included sales to Latin America, Africa, Eastern Europe, and other countries in Asia except Japan.

The rest of the business came equally from the lab water purification line (called Milli-Q and ranging in price from $2,300 to $8,300) and from life sciences instrumentation. Millipore had 30 percent market share in the lab water purification business. About 10 salespeople sold the countertop lab water purification systems in the United States. Life sciences instrumentation was a new business for Millipore. Unlike Millipore's earlier products, these represented high-ticket instruments such as DNA sequencers, ranging from $15,000 to $100,000. The Analytical Group had 10 additional dedicated salespeople devoted to life sciences in the United States, each with a particular area of expertise and each dedicated to selling particular lines of life sciences products. Competition for life sciences products was dispersed among many equipment manufacturers serving many different markets.

Woodard thought of half his $230 million business as core and 70 percent of core business as undifferentiated. He felt that even where Millipore had a quality edge, some products were effectively undifferentiated: Customers simply did not know or care whether they were higher quality. Brand loyalty ran strong, however, especially where customers had historical protocols calling for the use of Millipore products.

To retain market share, Woodard hoped to enhance customer service wherever he could. His personal customer service goals included answering customer calls within one ring, same-day order entry and shipment, 48-hour delivery, and good technical support for those who wanted it. (Core users generally did not need technical support in this business.) Woodard also hoped to build other capabilities, such as a "Wal-Mart type capability in the inventory side of the business" so that the Analytical Group could have higher line fill with lower inventory levels.

In order to retain its market leadership, Woodard planned to grow the membrane business at about the rate of its markets. Key competitors like Gelman, Pharmacia, and Pall were all estimated to have less than 10 percent market share in this business. In the life sciences instrumentation business, however, Millipore lagged behind ABI, Pharmacia, and BioRad. The Analytical Group's organization chart is shown in Exhibit 5.

EXHIBIT 5 Millipore—Analytical Group Organization Chart, 1992

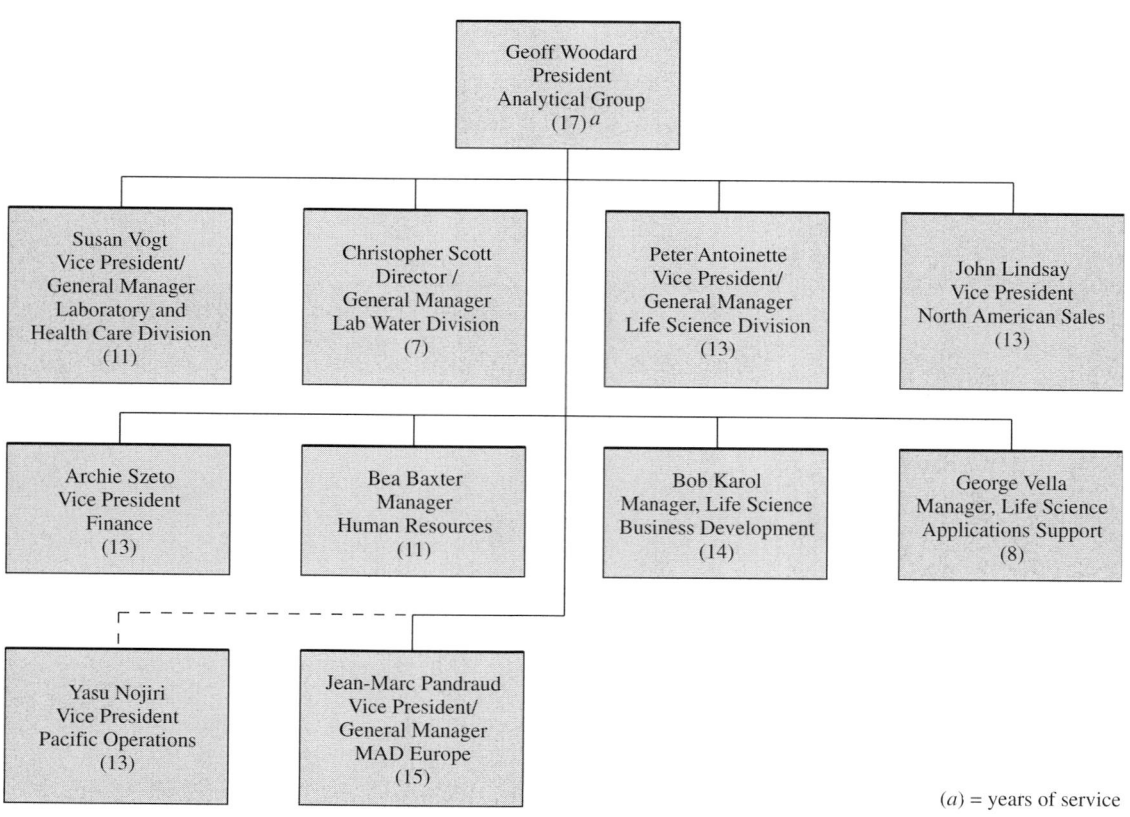

(a) = years of service

Process Group

Process Group products were based on technology that was similar to the Analytical Group's—membranes for removing contaminants. But unlike the Analytical Group, the Process Group sold membranes in large sizes for purification in manufacturing processes. Process Group customers, therefore, usually did not include government or university labs, which generally did not manufacture products. Rather, commercial manufacturers of pharmaceuticals, microelectronics, and food and beverages were the principal relevant target customer groups. The individuals who made buying decisions for process group products were usually manufacturing or process managers. Process group products were sold by about 40 application specialists (in the United States) to customers in pharmaceutical, microelectronics, and other industries.

In 1991, with nearly 40 percent of the Process Group's revenues, the pharmaceutical business had been experiencing double-digit growth per year. Since 1985, it had increased market share by a few points. Doug Jacoby, president of the Process Group, believed Millipore's reputation for quality was its key asset in this business. Pharmaceuticals customers relied on Millipore for validation of purity as well as separations in the production process. Because every drug production process required approval from the Food and Drug Administration, manufacturing processes, once they received approval, tended to remain unchanged for many years. Thus, a supplier's customer base was often very stable.

Though equally big, the Microelectronics Group was a very different type of business. In contrast to pharmaceuticals, this technology-driven business changed rapidly, and consumers usually demanded quick response time. Remaining on the cutting edge of technology was crucial for success, so Jacoby was willing to buy technology from outside to leverage Millipore's distribution capabilities. Every three to four years, the technology advanced as manufacturers tried to remove different types of contaminants from the production process. Jacoby's most recent challenge was to remove dissolved substances from gases and chemicals. In spite of the dynamic nature of the microelectronics industry, suppliers such as Millipore usually were kept informed of the industry's requirements. In the words of a Millipore manager, "The customer's needs are usually known well in advance, and we succeed provided we get an appropriate product out on time."

Jacoby thought of Process Systems, which designed, assembled, and sold membrane-based systems to industrial customers, as his third major business. Most of these process systems ranged in price between $35,000 and $50,000, although some cost as much as $1.2 million. Millipore bought approximately 85 percent of the material for these systems from OEMs. The remaining 15 percent represented membrane separation equipment manufactured by Millipore. Doug Jacoby, the group's president, felt that the systems business represented an excellent growth opportunity for Millipore.

While Jacoby recognized that he would get growth out of his three main segments, he also looked to the food and beverages industry for some growth. He did not generally place high hopes on the food and beverage industry because it was a low-margin business. Thus, his strategy was to exploit niches "opportunistically" in this segment, which he expected to grow at less than 10 percent annually.

Jacoby was optimistic about meeting his division's 14 percent growth targets in markets growing at 10 percent per year, although he had different visions for each of his three main businesses (pharmaceuticals, microelectronics, and process systems). The Process Group was the market leader in its business segment with approximately 25 percent of the $800 million market in 1991. Its largest competitor, Pall, had an equal share of the market, and other competitors were small, each with less than 5 percent of the total market. Unlike its main competitor, Millipore focused primarily on providing the separation downstream in the manufacturing process at the point-of-use. Upstream (or front-end) purification was used extensively in the industry, but Millipore's managers had historically felt it was relatively less critical and therefore the less-value-added part of the business. The Process Group's organization chart is shown in Exhibit 6.

Waters Chromatography Division

With sales of $310 million, Waters was the largest division of Millipore. With about 100 field sales people and another 100 technical support people (in the United States), Waters had the largest salesforce of any of the three divisions. A large majority of Waters' sales were core businesses (primarily high-pressure liquid chromatography, or HPLC, systems). Chemical columns (which were disposables for HPLC systems) were about a fifth of the division's sales.

Waters Chromatography produced analytical instruments (big-ticket systems consisting of different modular parts, including pumps, injectors, detectors, recorders, and other accessories) and column packing materials (relatively inexpensive "disposable" items that were replaced after every 100 to 1,000 uses). The purpose of most Waters products was not to filter out impurities, but to assess and control the quality of various samples.

Waters' core customers were primarily industrial labs in the chemical, pharmaceutical, and food and beverage industries engaged in quality control, investigative research, and production method development. The lab scientist who did chromatography work was usually different from the one who used membrane separation devices (although these scientists often worked for the same companies). Applications were varied, such as soft drink analysis kits that quality control labs used to measure the concentration of substances such as caffeine or aspartame sweetener in soda drinks. Customers were experienced, repeat buyers interested in efficiency, value, and, increasingly, automated data storage and retrieval. The high price of Waters' instruments—up to $50,000—made chromatographic instruments important capital expenditure items. Millipore believed the core segment was moving away from a separations focus toward quality assurance and traced its market share erosion to this trend. Competition had moved from technology-dependent instruments used for detection to reliable user-friendly systems capable of detecting and storing a multitude of test results.

The industry leader in HPLC for more than 20 years, Waters had nearly 25 percent market share in 1990. Competitors like Hewlett-Packard, Shimadzu, Beckman, Dionex, and Pharmacia all had less than 10 percent of the market. The industry was

EXHIBIT 6 Millipore—Process Group Organization Chart, 1992

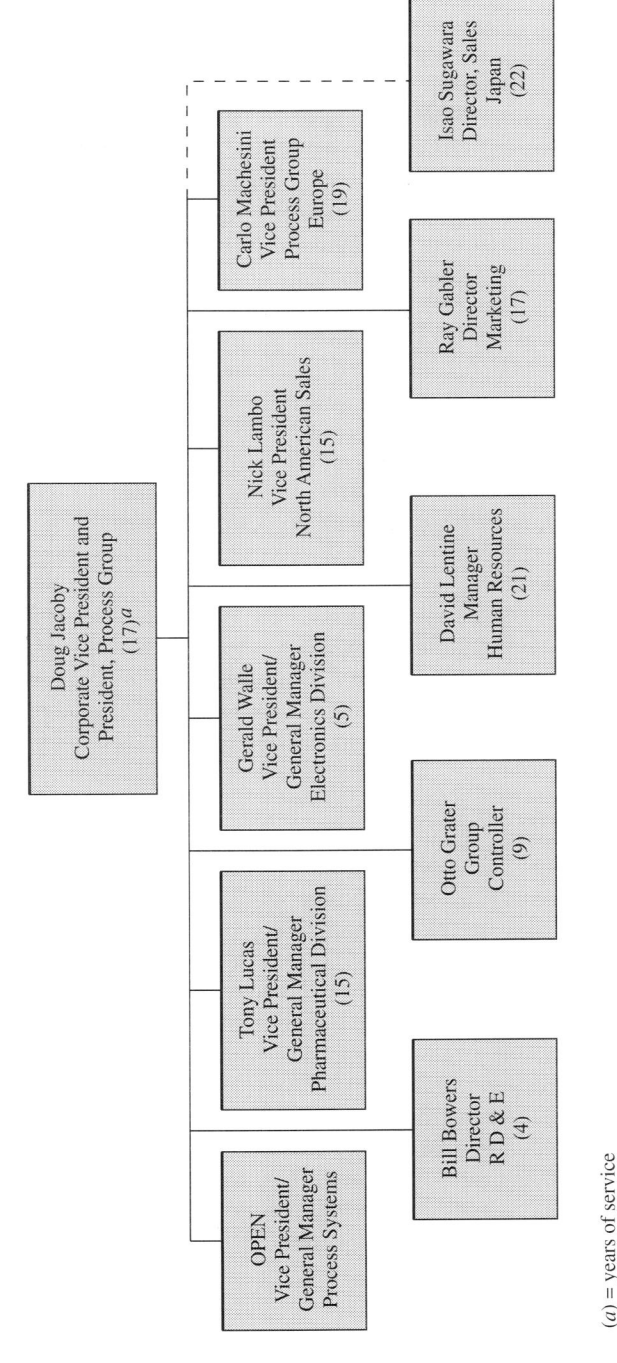

(a) = years of service

considered to be in the mature part of its product life cycle with low entry barriers and increasing competition.

Since becoming president in 1990, Doug Berthiume had engineered a turnaround of Waters by focusing on core products. He argued that Waters' prior management had tried to develop new products as a source of growth in the late 1980s at the expense of their core business; without a developed marketing organization, he contended, those product development efforts failed to achieve their potential. Therefore, Berthiume focused on manufacturing and development to improve quality in Waters' core business; he hired a marketing expert from outside and he established a five-year plan to shore up the core HPLC capability.

Overall, Berthiume expected that continued efforts to improve "blocking and tackling" would allow Waters to grow its core businesses faster than in the past five years, but still somewhat less than the market's anticipated growth rate. To reach higher division-growth targets, he felt Waters would need new products incorporating new technology, such as mass spectrometry, which could grow into a $50 million to $60 million business. Capillary separations using liquid chromatography and electrophoresis also offered growth prospects, as did the electronics business. Berthiume estimated that getting into that market could support a $50 million business. These new growth prospects raised his overall growth target for the division to double digits.

A key management issue for Berthiume was when to change his division's organizational structure, which he thought would have to be modified to grow Waters as he planned from $300 million in sales to $500 million. The current functional structure, he argued, would eventually have to be replaced by a market-oriented organization. Waters' organization chart is shown in Exhibit 7.

Intertech

Intertech developed markets in geographical areas with unique requirements that were inappropriate for direct divisional management because of either size or remoteness. Intertech sourced its product needs from Millipore factories around the world.[1] Where practical, Intertech's intent was to grow these markets to be large enough that they could be turned over to the divisions. Intertech accounted for approximately 10 percent of Millipore's sales. About 80 percent of Intertech's business came from 10 countries. Millipore expected Intertech to grow at about 12 percent per year. Dominque Baly, Intertech's president, had different strategic plans for each of the four regions in which Intertech sold Millipore's products. Asia was growing the most quickly, and Baly saw Millipore's constraints in this market as internal, not related to the market. Accordingly, Baly was managing the business for growth, not necessarily profitability. Reflecting his vote of confidence in Asia, Intertech moved its headquarters to Hong Kong in 1992. Baly's goal for the former

---

[1] Intertech did have some manufacturing capabilities in Brazil and India, but these were really only ways to circumvent local restrictions in countries with strict local content laws.

EXHIBIT 7 Waters Chromatography Division Organization Chart, 1992

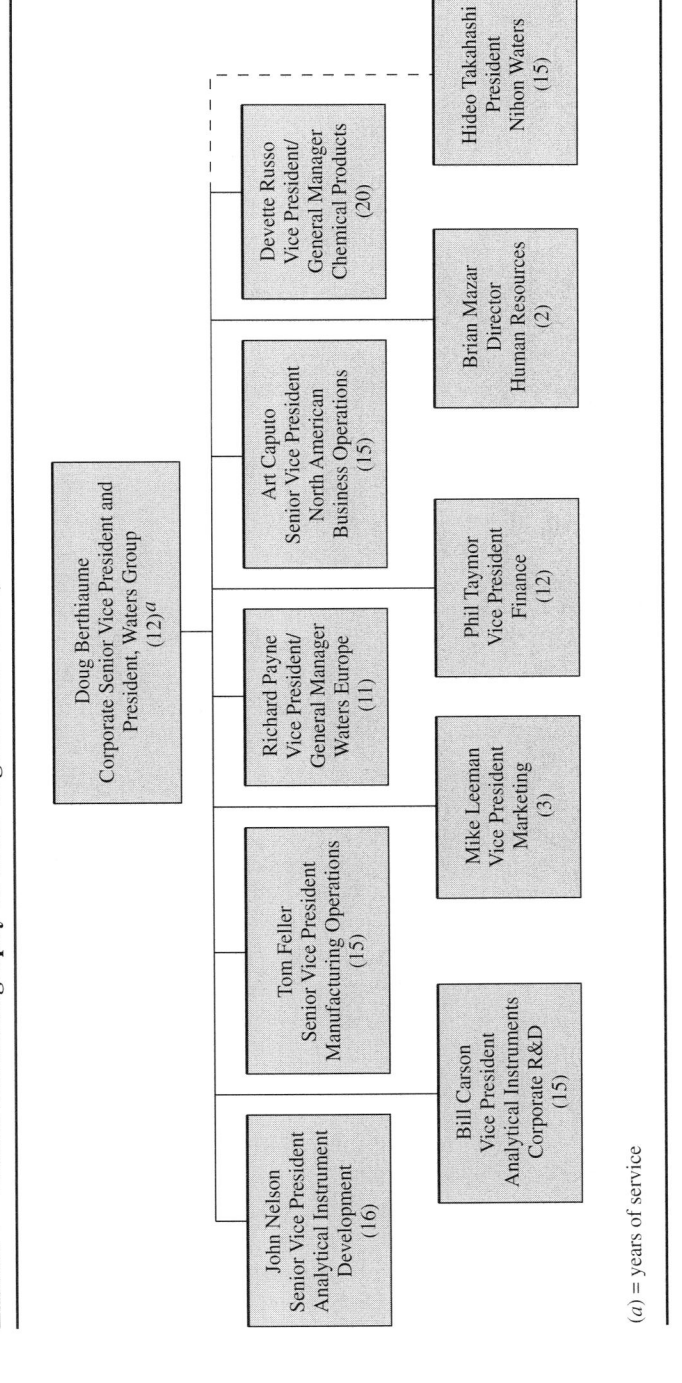

(a) = years of service

Eastern bloc and and the former Soviet Union, in contrast, was to maintain a presence, service customers, and "wait and see" what opportunities developed. Baly argued there was no strategic reason to do anything but marketing there. Intertech was quite active in the Middle East, but Baly did not expect it to grow quickly due to the small population and the industry infrastructure. Baly's highest hope for African markets was to be a good distributor. Finally, in Latin America, Intertech was forced to be flexible in order to weather the downturns in the economic cycles. Mexico, at the present time, was an exception to this rule because of its large population, proximity to the United States, and abundance of foreign investment. Because that market was still growing, Baly pursued a growth strategy there as well.

Worldwide Sales and Marketing

Overseas markets were increasingly important to Millipore (63 percent of its sales came from outside the United States in 1991). Millipore operated subsidiaries in most major European countries, headed by a country manager. In most circumstances, country managers had line responsibility for a division, acting as its sales head. In addition, they were responsible for local administration. But country managers did not have responsibility for sales of products not under their direct divisional charge. That was left to the appropriate divisional sales managers who reported up through the divisional structure to the headquarters at Bedford, Massachusetts, for Analytical and Process groups; and Milford, Massachusetts, for the Waters Chromatography Division. The country manager, who was one of the three divisional sales VPs in each subsidiary, had direct line responsibility only for administrative issues such as order-entry, shipment, and invoicing. All three product divisions shared common distribution warehouses and logistics facilities worldwide.

Though it appeared somewhat complex, this subsidiary structure reportedly worked quite well. While we were unable to study Millipore's international operations in much depth due to time and resource constraints, the few international managers we talked to indicated that in most cases the relationship between country managers and the divisional sales managers was amicable and productive. Indeed, the subsidiary structure often promoted and facilitated cross-selling products from different divisions to the same client. It also enabled Millipore to present a unified front to large multinational clients that had product and service needs that cut across the various divisions and geographies.

The U.S. sales operations had recently been remodeled along the same lines as Millipore's international subsidiaries. Art Caputo, VP of Waters' sales, served as U.S. country manager while John Lindsay (analytical products) and Nick Lambo (process membranes) headed up their respective sales divisions and reported to the country manager for administrative issues only. In addition, Peter Hay was responsible for shared services provided for all three divisions, and he too reported to the country manager. The U.S. sales operations were headquartered at Marlborough, Massachusetts, away from Bedford (worldwide headquarters for analytical and process membranes) and Milford (worldwide Waters chromatography products).

Research and Development

Core R&D supplied divisions with long-term research for product development in addition to conducting some research of its own on core technologies with potential long-term payoffs. Approximately 80 percent of the corporation's $66 million R&D budget was spent on divisional product development projects and the rest on core R&D. The divisional R&D budgets were allocated more or less in proportion to their sales revenues. According to Millipore's technology vice president, roughly 50 percent of the R&D budget was spent on incremental new products and the other half on "change the name of the game" kinds of innovations.

The initiative for division product development came up from the division. Each of the three divisions had its own unique new product development system. The Analytical and Process groups were decentralized into market-focus business units. Project ideas were submitted by marketing, sales, and R&D people, and allocation of resources was made by the general managers of the business units and divisional presidents. Resources for new membrane development to support divisional projects were allocated by the core membrane vice president for R&D, who was also responsible for allocating resources to core research projects. The process was iterative, often involving ranking of projects based on their market potential and strategic importance with the final cut being made by budgetary constraints. At Waters, the procedure was somewhat different. Top managers from each functional area constituted a New Product Committee. Marketing, sales, R&D, manufacturing, and overseas country heads were all part of this committee. They each brought in ideas supplied to them by their constituencies, and the committee as a whole then decided on how to allocate its resources.

Major Strategic and Organizational Issues

All That Glitters Is Not Gold

"New products and markets are everything," stated John Gilmartin, "and unfortunately, that is a challenge for us now. We need to become much more market driven."

A divisional R&D manager agreed:

Ten years ago, it was really not that difficult to be an innovation leader. There was a clear consensus in the market as to what would be the next new product, and there was very little competition. So we simply plugged away and came away with many winners. Now we have to juggle many balls. The technology is complex and diverse. One has to take bets and hope that competition does not leap-frog. Marketing has to absorb the uncertainties and guide us. They are the eyes and ears of the company.

Jack Johansen, the senior vice president of corporate R&D, however, was very frustrated with the lack of vision and foresight characterizing most divisional new product development work. He regretted that the central research labs could not be more long-term focused. This is the inevitable result of Millipore niche-market orientation; everyone is caught in their own sandbox. "Our new product development and launch processes seem to be a matter of R&D convenience," said one sales manager.

In spite of these frustrations, the company reported a rash of new products.

New products are key to generating increased sales and we made significant progress in this area in 1991. For the pharmaceutical market, we introduced a number of new products, including Optiseal™ filter cartridges for sterilizing fluids and Aerex™ filter devices for sterilizing gases. A priority in biomanufacturing is ensuring viral-free product and we introduced Viresolve™ systems in 1991 to meet this need. These are the first membrane-based systems that provide validatable, physical removal of viruses from protein product streams. We also, in 1991, introduced large-scale ceramic systems for antibiotic and drug purification.

In microelectronics, we further expanded our line of gas purification products that are critical to manufacturing complex microelectronics devices. These new Waferpure™ products, which remove molecular contamination from gases used during manufacturing, are the direct result of a joint venture we formed in 1991 with Advanced Technology Materials of Danbury, Connecticut. The joint venture, called Novapure, is focused on developing gas purification products for the microelectronics industry.

In the life science research area, we started shipping our new BaseStation™ Automated DNA Sequencer in the fourth quarter of 1991. Customer interest is strong, and we look forward to success with this product in 1992. We also introduced a number of new HPLC columns for protein purification, new chemistries for DNA synthesis, and new peptide purification devices in 1991.

Our chromatography development and marketing groups focused their efforts in 1991 on preparing for the most significant launch of new Waters™ HPLC products in several years. In January 1992, we introduced a new automated sample handling device, the Waters 717 Autosampler. The LC Module™ System, a compact automated chromatography system developed and sold successfully in Japan, was adapted and recently introduced in Europe and the United States. At the March 1992 Pittsburgh Conferences on Analytical Instrumentation and Applied Spectroscopy, we launched the first of our Millennium™ family of information management systems, the Millennium 2010 Chromatography Manager. Millennium systems represent a new approach to laboratory instrument data management and control. Eventually, Millennium systems will provide customers with the power to network all of their separations systems in a user-friendly Windows™ software environment.

These new product introductions, as well as other products to be launched later in 1992, signal a new era of competitive strength for our chromatograph business.

To further that objective, we entered into an agreement in December of 1991 to acquire Extrel Corporation of Pittsburgh, Pennsylvania. Extrel, with sales of about $13 million in 1991, has leading-edge mass spectrometry technology. This technology will accelerate our development of LC-MS instrumentation and it has important applications in several of our key growth markets.

"The annual report is right," added one sales manager, "but it never told you how much we have sold. If only we took all that new product money and put it into developing what the field wants, we would be better off. I would bet that more than 75 percent of successful new products we have launched in the last five years have been field initiated. They are incremental, all right, but they make big bucks."

Mike Carroll, the finance vice president, provided the following perspective:

> Product/market planning at Millipore is more a list of opportunities than a well-measured, prioritized list of projects. We are spread too thin. We don't get into the wrong opportunities, but we often underestimate the cost of pursuing them.

Where Does the Buck Stop?

The pursuit of new products and market opportunities was, in Carroll's view, symptomatic of a general lack of accountability at Millipore. Commenting on the culture of accountability at Millipore, Gilmartin observed:

> The hi-tech ideology that prevails at Millipore is that vision counts and that product performance and product differentiation count. We do not pay enough attention to how our vision impacts our financial performance or to how customers really view the value and differentiation of our products.

Descriptions of Millipore's strategic planning process shed further light on the culture of accountability in the firm. The starting point of Millipore's strategic planning process were annual five-year plans presented by strategic planning units. Each business division contained strategic planning units which handled marketing and product development for specific products within the division. The mission of the strategic planning units was to identify market niche opportunities and define the competitive posture of Millipore in that niche. Ed Ward, director of corporate planning, described the purpose of the strategic planning units: "The strategic planning units are focused on the customer. By a close awareness of what the customer is doing, we can develop products well suited to their needs." Furthermore, as Mike Carroll, Millipore's chief financial officer, noted, strategic planning units were intended to be "entrepreneurial and to allow the company to respond flexibly to changing markets—forming and disbanding such units as market opportunities presented themselves or disappeared."

In 1992 there were 20 strategic planning units. Each of these units was required annually to submit a worldwide plan that conveyed what the group hoped to accomplish in the next year and over a five-year horizon. The plans were presented to the corporate planning committee (which consisted of the top corporate executives of the firm). After the plans were presented, there was a separate meeting (the original plan proposers were not present at this meeting) during which the corporate planning committee reviewed the plans as a whole and arrived at a corporate point of view on priorities and resource allocation. This point of view was communicated in writing to both planning unit heads and the presidents of their groups. This provided the basis for discussing and deciding future direction.

Ward prepared a quarterly report of sales performance against the targets set for the strategic planning units for the top management to review. More detailed performance tracking was left to the divisions. Nevertheless, Ward felt that the performance criteria for the strategic units were not well defined. There also appeared, in his view, to be insufficient connection between rewards and performance against plans.

Reflecting on the lack of accountability, Wayne Kennedy, the firm's vice president of human resources, pointed out that Gilmartin was "not a big fan of either managing-by-objectives or pay-for-performance. He does not want compensation to be the tail that wags the dog." The lack of clear performance feedback, Kennedy felt, resulted in a great deal of ambiguity about what the performance standards of the firm *really* were: "What are the criteria by which we measure our success or failure? If you went around this company and asked different people, I bet you would not get the same answers from everyone."

Mike Carroll disagreed with Kennedy. He felt confident that everyone in the company was clear about the financial targets for the corporation: "Everyone knows that we want to grow at 15 percent and achieve a return on sales of 10 percent as well as a return on assets of 10 percent." "The key problem," he continued, "is not that people don't know what the criteria for success are. The problem is that the divisions do not feel like they own and control the firm's assets and hence don't feel any responsibility to make the best use of these assets." It was critical in his view that the divisions increasingly look beyond sales and sales growth and manage receivables, inventory, assets, and the like: "People lower down in the organization need to make tough trade-offs. We need to give the divisions all the information and accountability to make the key decisions regarding resource allocation." In general, he argued: "We should not be so top-line focused—we need a more balanced outlook."

Reach Out and Touch Someone!

According to John Gilmartin:

> We are no longer a small niche player in a handful of focused markets. We are the technology and market share leader in what is fast becoming a tough global business. The real challenge is for us to learn to operate within a matrix organization deriving synergies from our diversity and economies from our size, without losing our spirit for innovation and growth. The trick is to identify real customer needs to which Millipore's capabilities can be directed in $25 million to $50 million, or larger, market niches with few competitors.

Not only would Millipore have to manage an ever-increasing number of segments to maintain its growth while following a niche strategy, but Gilmartin believed Millipore would have to become more flexible to meet customers' rapidly changing needs. "Our customer base is diverse and constantly changing," said Gilmartin, "so we constantly have to restructure ourselves to best serve the needs of the marketplace." In Gilmartin's view, the new decentralized structure required horizontal communication three or four levels below the top, both across functions within each division and across divisions.

> In a $25 million to $150 million company, it is possible [for the CEO] to be Moses and hand down the tablets [with commandments for the masses to follow]. With as much diversity as we have, however, we need to empower people at different levels of the organization. As you empower them, these people find that what they *need* to do their jobs lies across traditional boundaries via dotted lines.

Millipore formalized cross-functional and cross-divisional communication in some areas, creating a multitude of committees, including the European Executive Committee, the Human Resources Council, the Science and Technology Council, and the Capital and Appropriations Committee. Other efforts sought to build companywide capabilities, such as, for example, the Managing for Excellence initiative to focus the business on the customer. Still, Gilmartin hoped for cross-functional and cross-divisional communication and coordination at other levels.

Despite the value that top executives placed on horizontal processes, various managers questioned the value of horizontal processes. Said Wayne Kennedy of the many councils and committees, "Some of these committees are useful, and others are sterile. The standing committees are not very useful. They should probably be disbanded and focused on key processes." In some cases, the horizontal processes confused people "about who makes the decisions, in terms of which person and which organization," and contributed to "a lack of clarity in the organization."

A senior divisional manager expressed his frustration: "It is annoying to go to these various committee meetings where nothing gets done. We all diligently make our contributions to the minutes of the meeting and go back to doing what we were doing before anyway."

The idealized type of communication of which Gilmartin spoke, however, ran across the grain of Millipore's traditional corporate culture, which emphasized the free-wheeling pursuit of growth through new product development. Managers described those who were successful at the company as "entrepreneurial" and "growth-oriented"; Gilmartin referred to traditional Millipore employees as "gun-slinging cowboys." Wayne Kennedy, the corporate vice president for human resources, summed up his assessment of the Millipore culture:

> We're an organization where people rely too much on authority and not on influence and building networks. Our people development philosophy is that you're left to sink or swim. A common profile of our employees is that they are harsh, smart, opinionated, and aggressive.

A survey conducted in mid-1991 of the worldwide management group revealed that 73 percent of the vice presidents and directors and 66 percent of all respondents did not feel that decision making at Millipore was delegated to the lowest possible level. Moreover, 48 percent of the VPs and directors and 47 percent of all respondents felt that risk taking was not encouraged at Millipore. Individuals were seen as proactive about generating lists of exciting new projects and proposals, but those same individuals did not generally wish to take responsibility for choosing between the proposals. Instead, they constantly sought approval from superiors, absolving themselves of responsibility for any failed proposals. As a result, said one manager:

> We maintain we're decentralized, but, boy, are we centralized! Everybody really *wants* decentralization and believes in it, but the result of our forecasting systems, our budget, and our capital requests is that things go too high up. Easily, things are decided one or two levels higher than they should be.

One sales manager expressed his opinion:

> Nobody asks us about strategy. Many times the company forgets that we are the ones who bring in the business; we see and seek customers every day. Unfortunately, top management in this company is overly enamored with centralized decision making. That is fine if that leads to success, but I don't sense that. The company would be better off adopting a "ground-up" decision-making structure.

Offering his interpretation of this somewhat contradictory data, John Gilmartin stated:

> Frankly, I am puzzled myself. Look at our organization structure, it is extremely divisionalized. Many of our critical management processes, like for example, new product development, are once again delegated down to individuals or teams in the divisions. Yet when I talk to my managers, there is this overwhelming cry for decentralization. I am not sure we have been able to put our finger on the real problem.

One Plus One Plus One Equals . . .

"Four or five or even more," argued John Gilmartin enthusiastically. "We have to creatively exploit the interdependencies across our three businesses and geographies. After all, the technologies and customers are often common. The question is not whether there are interdependencies, but how to promote them and in which areas."

Several corporate managers at Millipore echoed Gilmartin's view. They cited the successful integration of Waters and Millipore sales subsidiaries in Europe and Japan as examples of how operating interdependencies had been realized. Between 1984 and 1986 what had previously been separate sales subsidiaries were integrated with resultant cost savings, delivery and service improvements, and increased skill levels of employees.

Another example offered was a recently launched product called Concep. Developed in record time, this bio-separations system had been conceived by the Life Sciences Division of the Analytical Group and was reduced to practice by core R&D. It combined the fluid-handling capabilities of Waters with the membrane separation capabilities of the Analytical Group. The electronics development, documentation, and final assembly of the product were supplied by the Sterimatics Division, the fluidics sub-assemblies were supplied by Waters, and marketing and sales by Analytical.

A new product in the prelaunch phase, called Helicon-D/Prep Scale, was cited as evidence of the potential to capitalize on common customers. In this case the Analytical and Process groups were collaborating on plans for selling the product most effectively to their common customers.

Several other senior executives had somewhat pragmatic, though fully supportive, views of cross-divisional integration. "Look at companies like Johnson & Johnson," pointed out one. "They make a diverse range of products for health care. They are heavily divisionalized, but the Johnson & Johnson umbrella and the power of their unity and integrity comes clearly through. Frankly, he said, "it is our lack of imagination and perseverance that keeps us from coming together as a corporation. Unfortunately, people put narrow divisional interests above that of the corporation."

One senior manager, however, confessed: "If you want to know my honest opinion: No, I don't think much will be achieved by attempting to homogenize three fairly different businesses. Millipore could best exploit its markets and technologies by staying focused within each division. But at the same time," the manager said, "this is one instance where I would be absolutely delighted to be proved wrong."

This manager cited several examples of unsuccessful efforts to capitalize on the interdependencies between the old Millipore and Waters. In the mid-1980s, Millipore created a process chromatography product line within a division called Millipore Systems Division (MSD). The rationale was that many customers needed separation technology. Whether this was achieved by HPLC or membrane technology was irrelevant. The division was supposed to focus on customer needs, selling users the best technology—membrane or chromatography—for their specific applications. The result, he recalled, "was that the division acted as two separate units that never came together as an organization. The two divisions often presented two differing solutions to the customer."

Again, in 1986 Millipore set up a division to make analytical instruments, data systems, chemicals, reagents, and other consumables for analyzing, synthesizing, and sequencing nucleic acids and proteins. The new division, MilliGen, was to serve the rapidly growing life sciences market using membrane, chromatography, and electrophoresis technologies. Products included DNA sequencers, DNA synthesizers, peptide synthesizers, and corresponding disposables. Millipore even supported the effort by acquiring two companies to develop life sciences—Biosearch in 1988 and the Bio Image division of Kodak in 1989. Despite the eventual promise of life sciences, however, Millipore management decided MilliGen was unjustifiable as a separate division and folded its businesses into existing divisions in 1991.

Conclusion

Millipore's mission, vision, and goals were stated as follows:

Mission

To be the worldwide leader in the eyes of our customers, employees, shareholders, and suppliers in the high-value-added separations industry. To achieve leadership through a global focus on customer satisfaction, employee participation, and technological excellence. To improve the quality of life through products which advance achievement in science and technology.

Vision

By 1995, we will achieve the highest possible level of responsiveness to customers and be fully dedicated to all aspects of customer service. We will listen to our customers and tailor our efforts to satisfy their needs and expectations. We will be recognized by our customers as technology and quality leaders.

Our global organization will be designed for consistency of purpose: to satisfy the customer. There will be minimal layers of management and short cycle times. We will provide a workplace which promotes openness, trust, and participation, and is strengthened by the diversity of our people.

Our people will be competent and committed to the organization's mission, vision, and values. We will focus on continuous improvement and total quality in everything we do.

We will act responsibly to protect the environment. We will be recognized by the communities in which we live and work as an excellent employer and corporate neighbor.

Goals

Our financial goals are:
- 15 percent sales growth.
- 10 percent profit on sales.
- 10 percent return on assets.

"There is no way we will achieve these goals if we linearly extrapolate our strategies into the future," said Gilmartin. In an effort to generate fresh thinking, John Gilmartin convened a conference of 75 senior Millipore managers from around the globe. According to Gilmartin, the purpose of the conference was to seek ideas on how the growth gap might be bridged.

> While I am not looking for tactical suggestions, I do not want the conference to degenerate into an academic reinvention of our mission and vision statement, either. It would be best for us all to roll up our sleeves, open up our minds, and hammer out the key strategic issues we must address to meet our mission, vision, and goals. Be it a business issue or an organizational issue, we need to identify them and come up with actionable approaches to address the weaknesses.

CHAPTER 41

GenRad, 1990 (A): At a Crossroads in Electronic Test

GenRad is a pioneer in the electronic test instrument industry and a market share leader in printed circuit board automatic test equipment (PCB ATE). By 1990, it had experienced a deteriorating market position and poor financial performance for the last several years. The market for PCB ATE had changed rapidly, with testing requirements becoming much more complex, demand stagnating in the United States, customers seeking lower-cost testing strategies, and new entrants creating brutal competition in GenRad's main markets.

As he prepared for the annual strategic planning session with his staff in July 1990, Bob Anderson, GenRad president and CEO, pondered the changing environment his company faced. GenRad had pioneered and still was market share leader in the printed circuit board automatic test equipment (PCB ATE) industry. But as its key customers—U.S. electronics manufacturers—faced tough times in their own markets, their demand for this equipment had stagnated. Moreover, printed circuit board testing requirements had become more complex and customers were seeking lower-cost testing strategies. Competition among industry players, as a result, was brutal.

GenRad's market position was deteriorating; in fact, its continued poor financial performance over the past several years had caused some industry experts to wonder if the company would ever return to its healthy profits and double-digit growth of the late 1970s.

This case was prepared by Raphael R. Carty and Benson P. Shapiro.
Copyright © 1991 by the President and Fellows of Harvard College.
Harvard Business School case 592-045.

Company Background[1]

The General Radio Corporation (renamed GenRad in late 1976) was founded in 1915 and pioneered the electronic test instrument industry. Renowned for technical excellence—and the supplier of choice for engineers who first designed and tested electronic equipment in the 1920s and 1930s—GenRad boasted a number of firsts in the electronic test and measurement industry.

An interesting GenRad business policy was the decision to allow only very controlled, self-financed growth of its business. The policy was designed to maintain a commitment to the highest-quality premium products and to a close-knit family atmosphere within the company. The downside of this policy was that it allowed new entrants, such as Hewlett-Packard (founded in 1939) and Tektronix (founded in 1946) to ride the post–World War II electronics boom and eclipse GenRad by the 1950s. By 1954, Hewlett-Packard was the new industry sales leader. With stronger competition and market growth at the low end of the market, price competition increased and GenRad found profitability (in terms of GenRad's return on net worth) eroding from 11 percent in 1946–1955, to 9 percent in 1956–1965, and finally to 6 percent in 1966–1969.

In 1967, top management embraced a policy of more rapid sales growth and focused on a narrower product line. Also, R&D investment as a percentage of sales leapt from 9 to 10 percent (in earlier periods) to 14 percent. In addition, GenRad expanded the sales and service force dramatically and made two corporate acquisitions to gain presence in high-growth markets.

By 1972, with financial systems that had not kept pace with GenRad's growth, GenRad posted an unanticipated loss of $2.3 million (on sales of $33 million). In the wake of these setbacks, management rationalized the product line further and the R&D plan was cut. The printed circuit board automatic test equipment (PCB ATE) market, which GenRad had established in 1969, was seen as a major growth opportunity and received a good share of the reduced R&D funding, however. Profitability returned in 1975.

Over the 1980s, GenRad became focused increasingly on the PCB ATE business and expanded into product areas to complement their PCB ATE successes, with such products as a logic simulator (used to verify the design of an electronic circuit), a sophisticated test program development environment for GenRad ATE systems with links to the logic simulator, and quality management software used for tracking problems and predicting failures.

After large losses from 1985 to 1987, Bob Anderson was named the new president and CEO in January 1988 and formed a new top-management team pledged to return GenRad to profitability. By closing its Phoenix facility, at a write-off of $10 million, and reducing headcount, GenRad began to reduce its losses. In 1990, approximately 50 percent of the company's business was done overseas; about 35 percent of total revenues were in Europe, with the remainder in the Far East. Exhibit 1 shows financial data. In 1989, GenRad had $188.9 million in total revenue.

---

[1]This section includes some material from earlier GenRad cases: "GenRad" (No. 279-002) and "GenRad, Inc. (A)" (No. 482-029).

Exhibit 1 Selected Financial Data (dollars in thousands)

Statement of Operations	1989	1988	1987	1986	1985
Revenues:					
Sales of products	$151,297	$167,504	$160,011	$146,069	$162,060
Sales of services	37,609	38,355	37,556	30,990	24,402
Total revenues	**188,906**	**205,859**	**197,567**	**177,059**	**186,462**
Cost of goods sold:					
Cost of products sold	70,663	72,492	72,849	69,566	79,538
Cost of services sold	21,850	23,036	22,054	18,160	13,829
Total cost of goods sold	**92,513**	**95,528**	**94,903**	**87,726**	**93,367**
Gross margin	96,393	110,331	102,664	89,333	93,095
Selling, general, and administration expense	68,956	71,888	68,784	72,692	78,822
Research and development expense	27,682	30,656	30,570	29,940	37,739
Reorganization charges	3,000	10,000	34,500	4,435	13,405
Subtotal	**99,638**	**112,544**	**133,854**	**107,067**	**129,966**
Total operating expenses	192,151	208,072	228,757	194,793	223,333
Operating income/loss	(3,245)	(2,213)	(31,190)	(17,734)	(36,871)
Other income (expense):					
Interest income	2,402	2,318	1,554	970	202
Interest expense	(5,376)	(5,929)	(6,739)	(6,364)	(4,018)
Other net	528	(309)	(318)	4,521	221
Subtotal	**(2,446)**	**(3,920)**	**(5,503)**	**(873)**	**(3,595)**
Income (loss) from continuing operations before income taxes	(5,691)	(6,133)	(36,693)	(18,607)	(40,466)
Income taxes (benefit)	399	105	352	750	(3,557)
Income (loss) from continuing operations	(6,090)	(6,238)	(37,045)	(19,357)	(36,909)
Discontinued operations:					
Loss from discontinued operations	—	—	—	(10,465)	(15,345)
Income tax benefit (provision)	—	—	—	(73)	—
Subtotal	**—**	**—**	**—**	**(10,538)**	**(15,345)**
Net income (loss)	**$(6,090)**	**$(6,238)**	**$(37,045)**	**$(29,895)**	**$(52,254)**
Stock price	$4 to 8 3/4	$6 1/8 to 12 3/4	$6 1/8 to 18 5/8	$5 1/8 to 14 1/4	$8 to 19 3/4
Number of employees	1,869	1,998	2,113	2,063	2,534
Stockholders' equity	$60,946	$66,889	$72,939	$105,654	$132,414

SOURCE: GenRad annual reports 1986 to 1989.

Testing Electronic Equipment

Electronic equipment (e.g., computers, televisions, telecommunication switches, sophisticated appliances, radar systems) consisted of components like resistors, capacitors, inductors, transistors, and integrated circuits.[2] These components were embedded into printed circuit boards (PCBs), which in turn were assembled into completed systems (see Figure A). The printed circuit boards provided the "smarts" to govern the equipment's operation. Testing for defects could and did occur at all stages of the process, as depicted in Figure B (see also Exhibit 2).

---

[2] An integrated circuit was an array of interconnected circuits built into a single chip.

FIGURE A

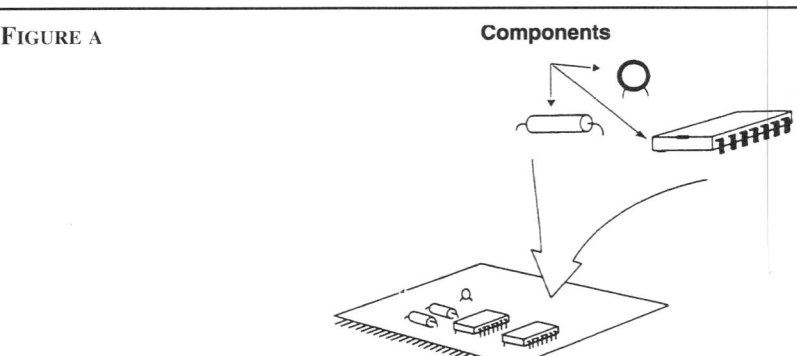

Printed circuit board

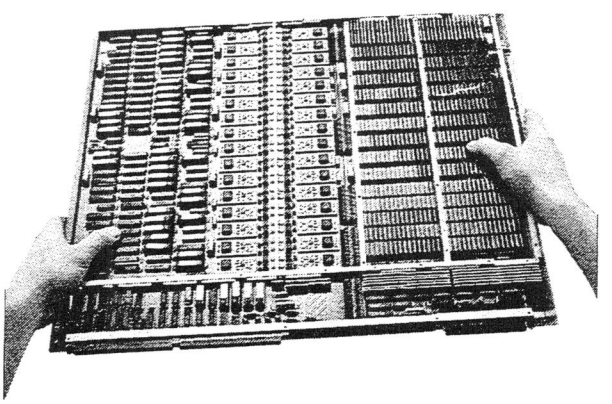

FIGURE B

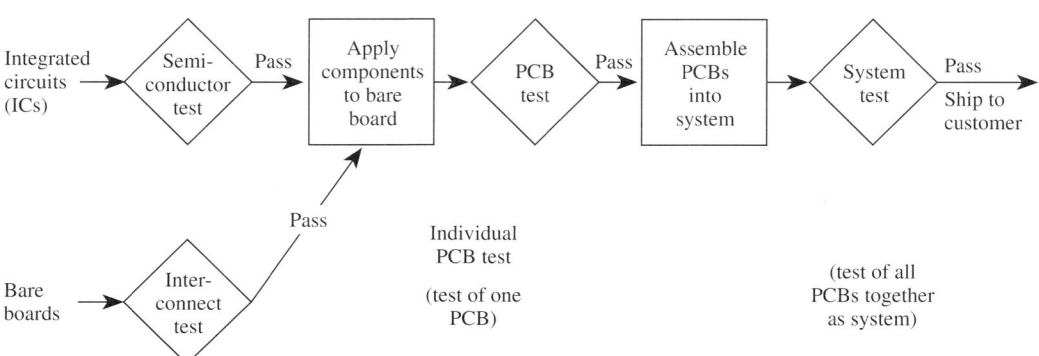

EXHIBIT 2   Typical Printed Circuit Board Defects

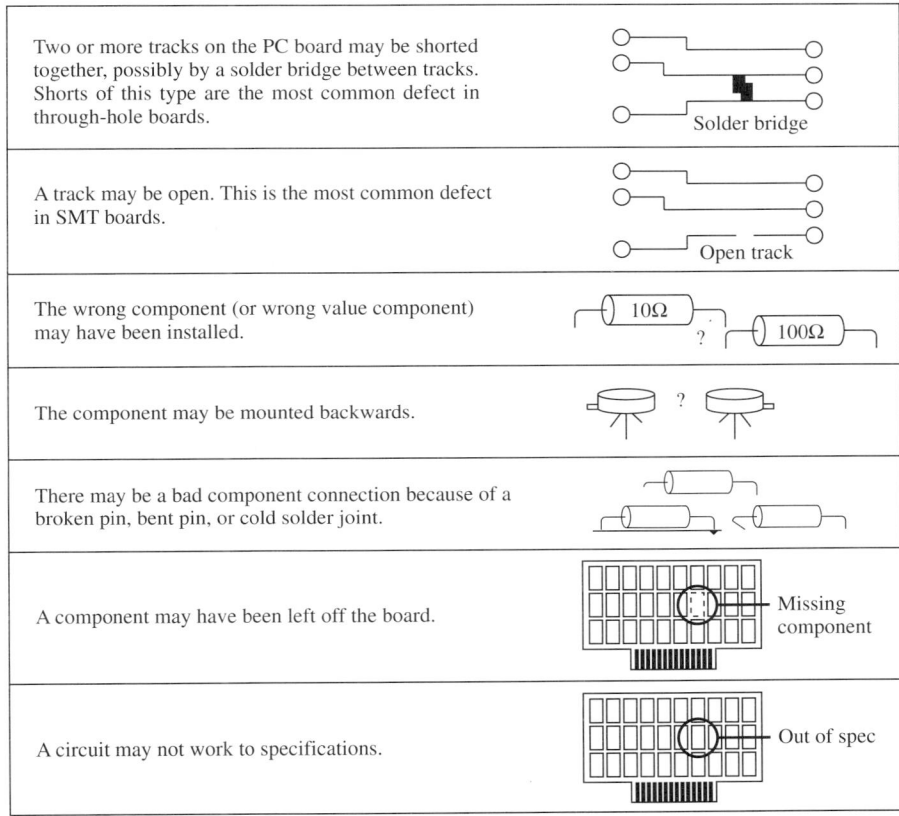

SOURCE: Deborah Graham, *Introduction to Multistrategy Testing,* GenRad, 1989, pp. 2–3.

PCB board assemblers/manufacturers tested their bare boards (i.e., without components), incoming components, and finished boards. Systems manufacturers tested incoming assembled boards, subassemblies of several boards, and completed systems. In the event of system failure, systems manufacturers also had repair and service technicians who tested completed systems, subassemblies, or individual PCBs at a customer site. Vertically integrated manufacturers like IBM might perform several steps in the process: manufacturing components, assembling PCBs, and building and servicing computer systems.

Equipment used for testing PCBs ranged from simple stand-alone machines/instruments to "rack and stack" (R&S) units, which were assembled relatively cheaply from standard stand-alone machines/instruments priced from $10,000 to $40,000, to PCB automated test equipment (ATE) priced from $25,000 to $1,000,000. A typical PCB ATE system, priced about $200,000, consisted of instrumentation used to make tests and measurements under the control of a computer programmed by the test engineer. A key feature distinguishing PCB ATE systems from the less-costly R&S systems was the sophisticated software environment used for developing test programs for each board tested, operating the test system, and providing detailed diagnostic information for each board defect found. This software allowed a less-skilled technician to operate a PCB ATE system in place of a test engineer who was needed to operate an R&S test system. (See Appendix for further details.) Automated test equipment was also available for testing semiconductors (i.e., integrated circuits) and bare boards. In 1990, GenRad competed in printed circuit board testing only.

The economics of finding and repairing faults in printed circuit boards encouraged detecting problems at the earliest possible stage. Finding and repairing a faulty integrated circuit at the incoming inspection cost about 50 cents. Finding a failure with PCB ATE at each successive stage resulted in a 10-fold increase: $5 at the board-level test; $50 at the system-level test; and $500 if the failure was discovered after installation at a customer site.

Technicians at the manufacturing or service site operated the test equipment but it was primarily specified and purchased by test engineers and their managers. Test engineers also developed test programs (to operate the PCB ATE system) and fixtures (to physically attach a printed circuit board to the PCB ATE system) for every new PCB designed by the product development organization. In addition, test engineers had to go back and modify test programs and fixtures for any change to the product design.

According to a GenRad account manager a typical PCB ATE system sale began with the key technical buyer, the test engineer. He added:

> PCB ATE systems users such as manufacturing operators and field service workers may have some input on their preference, but their influence is severely limited in comparison to the test engineer.
>
> The economic buyer is the manufacturing management, with the director of manufacturing (or director of operations) at a $100 million to $500 million facility making the purchase decision, largely based on input from the test engineering area. Unless it's a very low-end ATE system, the vice president to whom the director of manufacturing reports has the final sign-off on the capital appropriation to purchase the PCB ATE system.
>
> In situations where the purchase of the PCB ATE system is part of a broader effort (such as a total quality management project in which the objective is not just testing but also to improve the overall process), there may be a purchase committee formed. In these cases, I would have to sell each player individually and find an internal champion for GenRad on the committee.

The Market for Printed Circuit Board Testers

Printed circuit board ATE systems, GenRad's principal business representing more than 60 percent of corporate revenues in 1988, were categorized by three different applications, as Figure C demonstrates.

FIGURE C

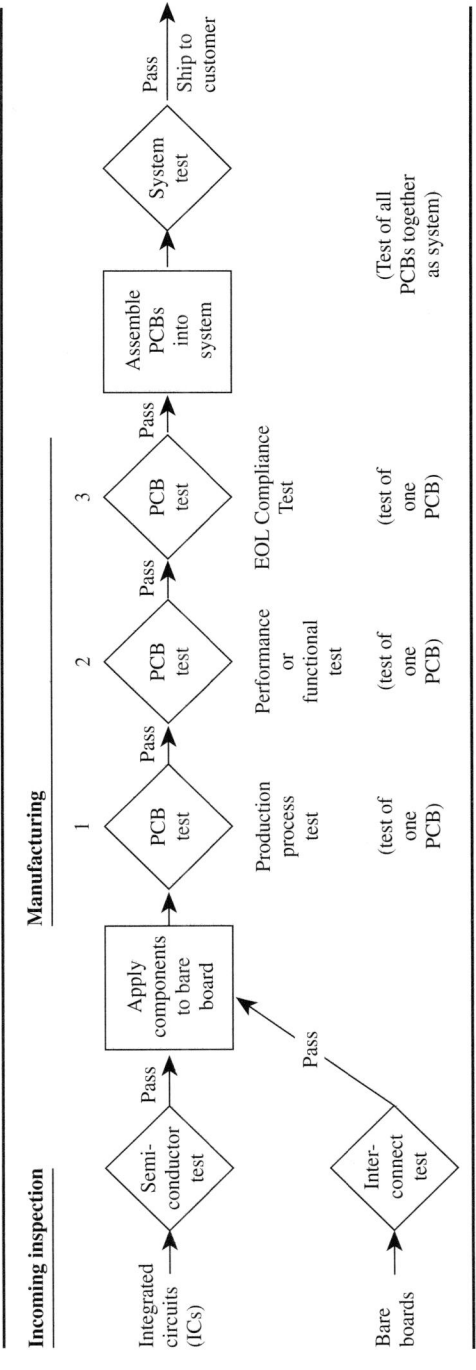

1. Production process testing, which tested for problems in the production process such as short circuits, open soldering, missing components, and the like, and answered the questions: "Did you build it right? Are all the right parts there?" This application was the second to be automated by the design of PCB ATE systems and was a market area in which GenRad was the leader, followed by Hewlett-Packard as the No. 2 vendor.
2. Performance testing, which tested for subtle aspects of PCB operation, such as timing differences, and answered the question, "Does the PCB perform as specified in the product design?" This was the first application to be automated by PCB ATE systems replacing manual rack and stack systems, and it was a market area in which GenRad (No. 3 position) competed with Teradyne (No. 1 position) and Schlumberger (No. 2 position).
3. End-of-line (EOL) compliance testing determined whether the PCB's operation complied with certain quality standards. For example, in the telecommunications industry, regulatory bodies tested for strict compliance with standards for quality of transmission service provided. For this step in the PCB production process, customers most often used the cheaper alternatives of rack and stack instruments or a "hot-bed" (i.e., a mock-up of the final system circuitry into which the PCB would be placed). But GenRad management saw this area as a potential application for a new kind of PCB test system which could provide detailed measurements as well as pass/fail test results.

Although it demonstrated compound annual growth of 28 percent from 1969 to 1988, the PCB ATE market's performance increasingly tracked the overall U.S. economy's business cycles in recent years. Accordingly, the PCB ATE market suffered downturns in 1971, 1975, 1985–86, and 1989, and a slowdown in 1981–82. In fact, it had never recovered completely from the 1985–86 downturn, resulting in a compound annual growth rate from 1983 to 1988 of only 2.9 percent.

Despite a flat market in the United States from 1983 to 1988, there was some growth in overseas markets for PCB ATE systems, especially Japan and Korea and, to a lesser degree, Europe. (See Exhibits 3 and 4.) GenRad management noted that overseas markets exhibited stronger demand for <$100,000 PCB ATE systems than the U.S. market, as shown in Exhibit 5. They saw two reasons for this disparity. First, differences in the electronics equipment created demand for different types of PCB ATE systems. In the United States, defense contractors (primarily aerospace) and computer manufacturers produced larger printed circuit boards which required the more expensive test systems, whereas in Japan consumer electronics manufacturers with much simpler and smaller PCB designs could use less-expensive test systems. Second, during the rapid buildup of electronics industries in Japan during the 1980s, Japanese manufacturers made major investments in training and in process improvements to increase the quality of their operations. With fewer defects, Japanese electronics manufacturers began to use lower-cost PCB ATE systems at earlier stages in their production process. In fact, two aggressive low-end

EXHIBIT 3 Five-Year Worldwide PCB ATE Market Sales and Growth by Price Point Segment

Price of PCB ATE System	Sales (in millions)						CAGR 1983–1988	Estimated CAGR 1988–1993
	1983	1984	1985	1986	1987	1988		
>$1,000,000	$51.0	$50.0	$45.0	$20.0	$40.5	$47.0	(1.6%)	5.0%
$500,000 to $1,000,000	18.7	43.5	45.5	79.0	90.0	94.0	38.1	5.0%
$250,000 to $500,000	148.1	209.6	178.1	172.5	203.5	188.5	4.9	7.5%
$100,000 to $250,000	235.4	246.8	193.4	171.0	137.0	198.1	(3.4%)	5.5%
$25,000 to $100,000	66.9	68.4	74.2	65.1	87.8	83.1	4.4	8.5%
<$25,000	23.9	26.2	29.3	34.9	20.7	17.8	(5.7)	7.9%
Total	544.0	644.5	565.5	542.5	579.5	628.5	2.9	6.5%

NOTE: CAGR = compound annual growth rate.
SOURCE: Adapted from Prime Data, *Automated Test Equipment Industry Service,* I (October 2, 1989), Tables 1.1-2a and 1.2-1a.

PCB ATE vendors in Japan, Okano and Tescon, built their business by addressing this need.

There was also greater usage of less-expensive test systems in Europe in 1989. Again, with fewer computer and military manufacturers, there was less need for high-end test systems. Some of the largest European countries had major national producers (Rohde and Schwarz in Germany, Marconi in England, and Spea and Tecnost in Italy) which competed for low-end to some mid-range PCB ATE system sales primarily within their home markets. These vendors did not attempt to compete with much larger players, such as GenRad and Teradyne, in the more expensive market segments.

Market Segmentation

The PCB ATE market was segmented principally by type of test technology, price point, and industry served (see Tables A and B). The initial distinction by type of test technology was into *functional testers,* which tested the actual operation of the PCB, and *in-circuit testers,* which tested individual components on the PCB. (See Appendix for more explanation of PCB ATE test technologies.) Market data available on the PCB ATE industry was organized by test technology (functional or in-circuit) versus price point. At the high-end price points, for both functional and in-circuit testers, some of the other technology was included. Hence a high-end, in-circuit tester had some functional test capability and vice versa. These mixed technology systems were referred to as combinational or multistrategy.

In terms of segmentation by industry served, John Lyons, a GenRad product manager, described the key industries which used PCB ATE systems, summarized in Table B.

Recently, vendors had begun to offer PCB ATE systems with features tailored to the needs of specific industries.

Exhibit 4 PCB ATE Market Size (demand) by Geographic Region

1989 In-Circuit Test Market = $457M

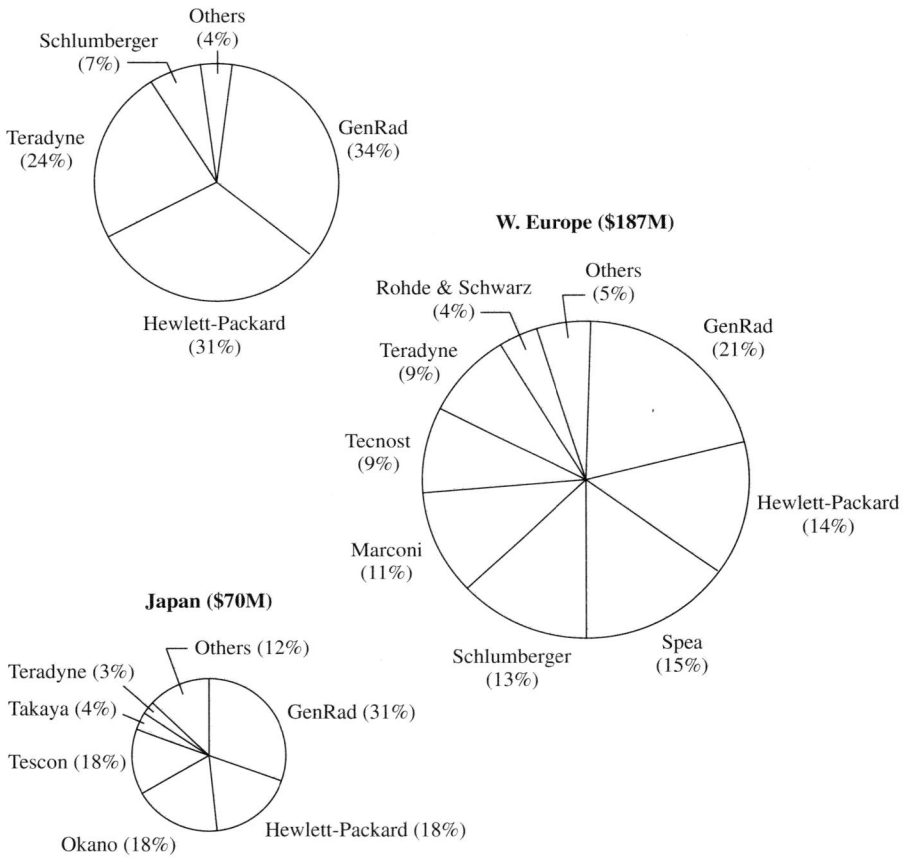

USA ($150M)
- GenRad (34%)
- Hewlett-Packard (31%)
- Teradyne (24%)
- Schlumberger (7%)
- Others (4%)

W. Europe ($187M)
- GenRad (21%)
- Spea (15%)
- Hewlett-Packard (14%)
- Schlumberger (13%)
- Marconi (11%)
- Tecnost (9%)
- Teradyne (9%)
- Others (5%)
- Rohde & Schwarz (4%)

Japan ($70M)
- GenRad (31%)
- Hewlett-Packard (18%)
- Okano (18%)
- Tescon (18%)
- Others (12%)
- Takaya (4%)
- Teradyne (3%)

Source: GenRad.

Total PCB ATE Market Size (demand) by Georgraphic Region

	1983	1988
United States	58%	40%
Europe	20	22
Japan	17	27
Rest of world	5	11

Source: Adapted from Prime Data, *Automated Test Equipment Industry Service*, I (September 8, 1989), Table 2.2-2.

EXHIBIT 5 **Prices of In-Circuit PCB ATE Systems Bought by Geographic Region in 1989**

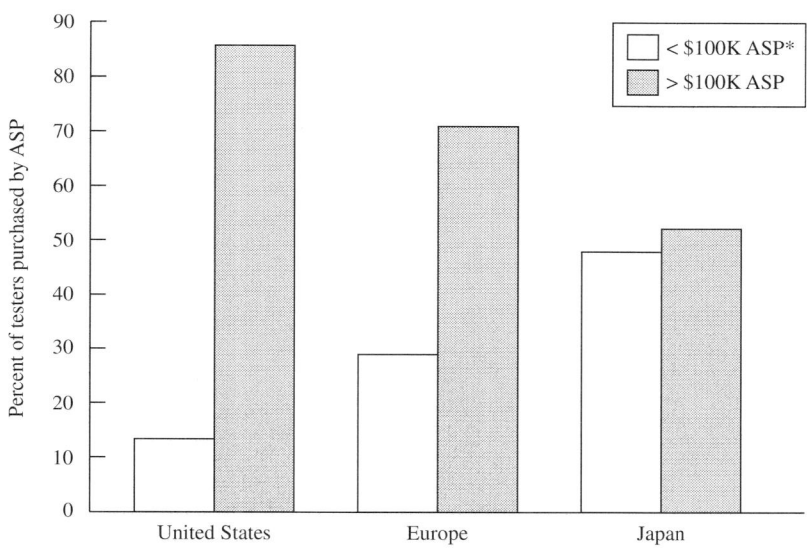

*ASP stands for average selling price.

SOURCE: GenRad.

TABLE A **1988 Worldwide PCB ATE Sales**

	Total Market		In-Circuit Segment		Functional Segment	
Price Point	Percent of Sales	1983–1988 CAGR	Percent of Sales	1983–1988 CAGR	Percent of Sales	1983–1988 CAGR
High End						
>$1 million	8%	(1.6%)	6%	45.7%	19%	(1.6%)
$500K–$1 million	15	38.1			29	37.5
Midrange						
$250K–$500K	30	4.9	37	10.4	19	(14.9)
$100K–$250K	31	(3.4)	47	(2.1)	8	(11.9)
Low End						
$25K–$100K	13	4.4			18	1.4
<$25K	3	(5.7)	10	8.4	7	(5.7)
Total	100%	2.9%	100%	4.2%	100%	1.2%
	$628.5 million		$380.5 million		$248.0 million	

SOURCE: Prime Data, *Automated Test Equipment Industry Service,* I (October 2, 1989), pp. 1.1-7, 1.1-8, 2.1-4, 3.1-5, and 3.1-6.

TABLE B

	Size of Worldwide Market Opportunity	Significant Vendor Presence		
		GenRad	HP	Teradyne
Telecommunications	Large	½✓	✓	✓
Computers	Large	✓	0	½✓
Automotive	Large	✓	0	0
Consumer electronics	Medium	✓	✓	0
Military (including U.S. Department of Defense, prime contractors, and aerospace companies)	Medium	½✓	0	✓
Industrial equipment and controls	Medium/Small	✓	✓	0

KEY: 0 = No significant presence; ½✓ = Some presence; and ✓ = Significant presence.

Competition

PCB ATE rivalry increased substantially over the later 1980s as existing vendors began to compete on price to gain market share in the face of flagging customer demand and as new entrants entered the market with low-end systems. These new low-end systems cannibalized purchases of mostly midrange PCB ATE systems in a way analogous to how personal computers and engineering workstations decreased demand for minicomputers and mainframes in the computer industry. Another factor that fueled competition was the fragmented industry structure, which encompassed more than 24 competitors—some in just a few price points of either functional or in-circuit testing. Although GenRad was the overall market share leader, it was absent from, or had a very small share of, several market segments by price point. Moreover, from 1983 to 1988, GenRad maintained its position as the PCB ATE market leader but lost share, as Figure D indicates.

As Table C shows, separating the market into functional versus in-circuit testing further demonstrates market fragmentation as some vendors, such as Hewlett-Packard and Spea, had a significant presence in in-circuit but not in functional testing. (See Exhibit 6 for a more detailed breakout of the functional and in-circuit segments by price-point and competitor.)

GenRad management viewed Teradyne and Hewlett-Packard (HP) as their most formidable competition. Schlumberger was roughly at parity with HP in terms of overall market share but was seen as losing ground and not as significant a long-term threat.

Teradyne

Teradyne, an early player in the semiconductor device test ATE market in the 1960s, entered the PCB ATE market in the early 1970s. In 1980, Teradyne intro-

FIGURE D

Worldwide PCB ATE sales

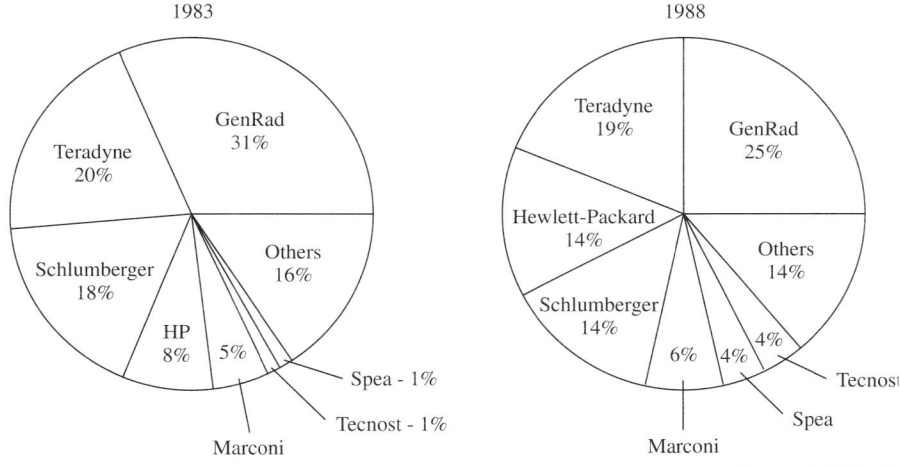

SOURCE: Prime Data, *Automated Test Equipment Industry Service* I (October 2, 1989), p. 1.7-4. Reprinted by permission.

duced the L200, the first high-end, functional tester to be priced at $1 million, thus avoiding head-to-head competition with GenRad, which was strongest in the in-circuit test market and in the functional test market at lower price points. Teradyne dominated the very highest tier of the functional segment by 1988 (see Exhibit 6). In 1989, it unveiled the L35X and L39X product lines, which replaced the L200 at the high end of the market.

To complement its success at the high end of the market, in 1987 Teradyne purchased Zehntel (a vendor of lower priced and lower performance in-circuit test systems) to gain entry into the fast growing low-end market segment. Teradyne maintained Zehntel as a separate brand and touted Zehntel systems as the "art of

TABLE C Total Worldwide PCB ATE—1988

Rank	Market Share	In-Circuit Rank	In-Circuit Market Share	Functional Rank	Functional Market Share
1. GenRad	25%	#1	32%	#3	16%
2. Teradyne	19	#3	14	#1	25
3. Hewlett-Packard	14	#2	22	#12	<3
4. Schlumberger	14	#4	10	#2	19
5. Marconi Instrument	6	#6	7	#6	5
6. Spea	4	#5	7	—	—
7. Tecnost (Olivetti)	4	#7	5	#8	<2
Leaders' combined market share	**86%**		**97%**		**68%**

SOURCE: Prime Data, *Automated Test Equipment Industry Service* I (October 2, 1989), pp. 1.3-2 and 1.3-3.

EXHIBIT 6 Detailed 1988 Worldwide Market Shares by Price Point

Price Range	1988 Sales Millions	%	CAGR 1983–1988	CAGR 1988–1993	Teradyne Sales	%	Schlumberger Sales	%	GenRad Sales	%	John Fluke Sales	%	Computer Automation Sales	%	Marconi Sales	%	Summation/Support Sales	%	GAI Sales	%	Wayne Kerr Sales	%	Tecnost Sales	%	Others Sales	%
Functional Test Market Segment																										
>$1 million	$ 47.0	19%	(1.6%)		$41	87%	$ 0	—	$ 6	13	$ 0	—	$0	—	$0	—	$0	—	$0	—	$0	—	$0	—	$0	—
$500,000 to $1 million	72.0	29	37.5		17.0	24	27.0	38	19.0	26	0	—	3.0	4	0	—	0	—	2	3	0	—	1	1	3	4
$250,000 to $500,000	48.0	19	(14.9)		5.0	10	20	42	Withdrew		0	—	10.5	22	1.5	3	0	—	4.5	9	0	—	4.5	9	2	4
$100,000 to $250,000	19.8	8	(11.9)		Withdrew		Withdrew		Withdrew		2	10	2	10	4.5	23	0	—	0	—	0	—	0	—	11.3	57
$25,000 to $100,000	43.4	18	1.4		Withdrew		Withdrew		14.0	33	.5	1	0	—	5.5	13	6.5	15	0	—	5.5	.3	Withdrew		11.4	26
<$25,000	17.8	7	(5.7)		0	—	0	—	Withdrew		15.5	87	0	—	0	—	0	—	0	—	0	—	0	—	2.3	13
Total	248.0	100	1.2	10.8[a]	63.0	25	47.0	19	39.0	16	18.0	7	15.5	6	11.5	5	6.5	3	6.5	3	5.5	2	5.5	2	30	12

[a] Estimate.

SOURCE: Adapted from Prime Data, *Automated Test Equipment Industry Service I* (October 18, 1989), Tables 2.1-2a, 2.2-1, and 2.3-1.

EXHIBIT 6 *(concluded)*

Price Range	1988 Sales Millions	%	CAGR 1983–1988	CAGR 1988–1993	GenRad Sales	%	Hewlett-Packard Sales	%	Teradyne Sales	%	Schlumberger Sales	%	Spea Sales	%	Marconi Sales	%	Tecnost Sales	%	Wayne Kerr Sales	%	Others Sales	%
In-Circuit Test Market Segment																						
>$500,000	22.0	6	N/A		2	9	0	—	18	82	0	—	0	—	0	—	2	9	0	—	0	—
$250,000 to 500,000	140.5	37	10.4		35.5	25	56	40	16	11	21	15	2	1	1	.7	6	4	0	—	3	2
$100,000 to $250,000	178.3	47	(2.1)		79.5	45	29.0	16	18.0	10	10.0	6	14.3	8	19.5	11	5.5	3	0	—	2.5	1
<$100,000	39.7	10	8.4		3.5	9	0	—	3	8	7	18	10.2	26	5.5	14	6	15	2.5	6	2	5
Total	380.5	100	4.2	3.2[a]	120.5	32	85.0	22	55.0	15	38.0	10	26.5	7	26.0	7	19.5	5	2.5	.7	7.5	2

[a]Estimate

SOURCE: Adapted from Prime Data, *Automated Test Equipment Industry Service I* (October 24, 1989), Tables 3.1-2, 3.2-1, and 3.3-1.

simplicity" for the low end. Zehntel also offered midrange PCB ATE systems, which had achieved little market success.

In comparison to GenRad, Teradyne had done more to lessen its financial dependence on the cyclical PCB (and semiconductor) ATE market by acquiring cash-generating growth businesses such as a computer backplane[3] manufacturer (representing 15 percent of 1988 sales) and a telecommunications test equipment manufacturer (representing 14 percent of 1988 sales). In 1987, Teradyne had acquired two computer-aided engineering (CAE) companies (Aida Corp and Case Technology) to form a CAE division (representing 6 percent of 1988 sales). Inasmuch as CAE was a growth market in 1988, the new CAE division was expected to become an additional future source of cash.

Teradyne's ability to penetrate foreign markets with semiconductor ATE systems, especially the Far East, was another strength. In terms of financial strength, after losses of $21.1 million on sales of $377.7 million in 1987 and $3.29 million on sales of $462.3 million in 1988, Teradyne earned a profit of $10.2 million on sales of $483.6 million in 1989.

Commenting on Teradyne's strategy in June 1990,[4] Teradyne president Alex d'Arbeloff said: "We've got to gain market share. We've got to do it at the expense of other players. We've got to play globally."

Hewlett-Packard

Hewlett-Packard (HP) entered the PCB ATE area in the early 1980s with the HP3060, a midrange in-circuit test system aimed squarely at GenRad's core business represented by the GR227X product family discussed below. By 1988, HP had PCB ATE sales of $88 million and had become the Number 2 vendor of in-circuit test systems (see Exhibit 7).

GenRad management believed that HP was attempting to bracket GenRad's GR228X product line by offering the HP3065 (introduced in 1984 as a replacement for the HP3060) priced lower than the GR228X product line and the HP3070 product line priced higher than the GR228X product line. (See Exhibit 7 for relative positioning of GenRad and HP product lines.) The HP3070, HPs highest-performance PCB ATE product line, was introduced in 1989. GenRad believed that HP's approach was to position the HP3070 as offering higher performance than the GR228X for only a little more cost and a little less performance than the GR275X for a significantly lower cost. GenRad management believed that HP's sales force was being more aggressive than GenRad's in setting customers' expectations on product performance.

Perhaps HP's greatest advantage in the PCB ATE market was its superior credibility with customers as a long-term business partner due to its financial strength and its position as both the Number 1 overall instrument vendor and Num-

---

[3]A backplane was the internal communications channel which interconnected different components of a computer system.

[4]Thomas Kiely, "Teradyne's Paradox," *New England Business,* June 1990, p. 58.

EXHIBIT 7 **PCB Test Market Segmentation**

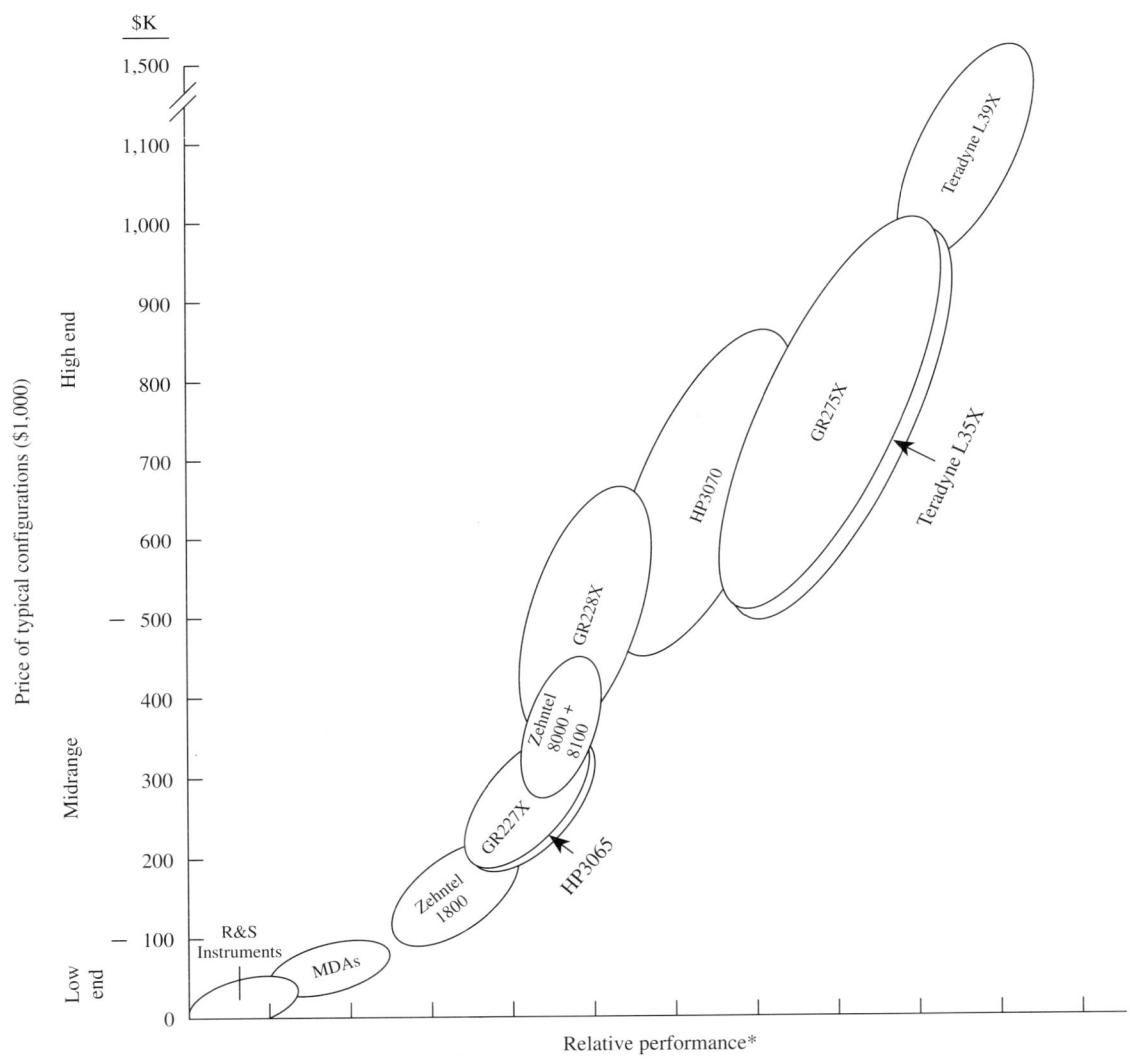

*Relative performance is a combination of the following PCB ATE system performance measures (estimated by GenRad management): system speed, accuracy, and throughput (i.e., PCBs tested per hour).
SOURCE: GenRad.

ber 3 computer vendor. HP sold itself as a "manufacturing expert" and invited PCB ATE customers in for factory tours where they saw HP PCB test systems in action and integrated into HP PCB production process. In addition, as the Number 1 instrument vendor, HP had more "feet on the street" overall and used that greater sales force presence to learn of potential PCB testing business before GenRad or Teradyne.

GenRad's field personnel believed that for inexperienced PCB ATE customers, HP had a very strong product line—if the customer did not need very-high-performance PCB ATE. But they believed that experienced PCB ATE customers appreciated GenRad's superior test development software offerings and the more experienced GenRad sales force.

GenRad

Product Line and Market Definition

GenRad's entire product line of PCB ATE systems (GR227X, GR228X, and GR275X) could perform both in-circuit and functional testing. The GR227X product line had been designed originally as an in-circuit tester and was later modified to include functional test capability over time. With the increasing trend of adding functional test technology to in-circuit test systems (and vice versa), GenRad management had become dissatisfied with functional versus in-circuit test technology as the primary way of segmenting the PCB ATE market. Accordingly, GenRad was among the first to shift to segmenting systems by which aspect of the PCB was being tested: the production process, called process testing, or the product design, called performance testing (see Figure C). The rationale was based on the fact that low-end to midrange test systems detected faults in the manufacturing process. Low-end test systems detected up to 80 percent of defects in a PCB, whereas midrange test systems detected up to 95 percent. The time to develop a test program to test a PCB ranged from days for the new low-end test systems to weeks for the midrange test systems.

In contrast, high-end systems tested subtle aspects of a PCB's performance to detect any deviation from the PCB design. Use of a performance test system, after process testing had already been done, increased the percentage of PCB defects found from 95 to 99 percent. It typically required months of effort to develop test programs for the high-end performance test systems.

The GR227X and GR228X product lines spanned the midrange of the PCB ATE market and represented GenRad's core business. (See Exhibit 7.) The GR227X product line was introduced in 1978 and rapidly became the best-selling GenRad PCB ATE product line. The GR227X product line included several models. Although initially priced in the $100,000 to $250,000 range, in 1989 GenRad made minor cost improvements and repriced downward a model of the GR227X to the $65,000 to $175,000 price range to combat encroachment from manufacturing defect analyzers (MDA)[5] and low-end systems such as Teradyne's Zehntel product line. Some GenRad managers viewed this as a defensive measure, since the

---

[5]Manufacturing defect analyzers detected only the most basic manufacturing defects (e.g., a missing device); they would not detect if the wrong device/component was installed or whether it was installed backwards.

GR227X was an older product family and the response came after several years of new competition at the low end. GenRad's success in the midrange market segment, according to these managers, had diverted management attention from the low-end threat, thereby delaying GenRad's response. The GR227X product line was used in a variety of customer environments and in 1989 had achieved good penetration of the computer and telecommunications[6] marketplaces.

The GR228X product line, which debuted in 1988, was priced in the $250,000 to $500,000 range and was positioned as a higher performance test system that was fully compatible with the GR227X. The first model of the GR228X was designed to replace the highest-performance model of the GR227X product line for high throughput testing (i.e., high volume tested per hour) of large, complicated printed circuit boards which were especially important for the computer and telecommunications markets. The GR228X delivered this higher level of performance through new technology that allowed more rapid test program generation and faster test program execution. Later models of the GR228X extended the product line downward, bringing the new higher-performance testing to smaller, less-complicated printed circuit boards, and upward, enabling GR228X systems to test even larger more complicated boards with special-purpose circuitry called ASICs (application specific integrated circuits) described in the Appendix. By 1989, the GR228X product line had been sold successfully into the computer, consumer electronics, and contract manufacturing marketplaces.

The GR275X product line was introduced in 1987 and marked GenRad's entry into the >$750,000 priced, high-performance test systems market segment. GenRad had made a public statement of intent to deliver such a system in early 1986 to help the sales force defuse the competitive threat from Teradyne in major accounts. In addition, the GR275X offered Genesis a leading edge software environment to ease the task of test program development. This offering enabled GenRad to retain leadership in the software component of PCB ATE systems. For many years GenRad's slogan had been: "The difference in software is the difference in test." Later GR275X models pushed the entry level price down to $600,000. By 1989, the GR275X had been sold successfully into the computer and military marketplaces.

GenRad management believed that GenRad had achieved several competitive advantages in the PCB ATE market, including the largest installed base (there were significant switching costs for a customer to convert a PCB testing operation from GenRad's proprietary technology to competitors' systems); technology leadership—especially in test program software development; and a sales force which provided a superior level of presales technical consulting and postsales problem resolution.

In recent years, GenRad sought to diversify its businesses beyond PCB ATE by acquiring some test and measurement businesses as well as developing focused test and measurement solutions aimed at higher-growth markets. Automotive Test

---

[6]The GR227X product line was sold to telecommunications equipment manufacturers for process testing, not end-of-line (EOL) compliance testing.

Products produced test equipment used to test the electronic subsystems of cars. They were used in dealership service centers to diagnose problems during the consumers' warranty period and beyond. Structural Test Products focused on mechanical test and measurement solutions. They produced systems to create vibration in a wide range of products (cars, satellites, computers, etc.) via shaker machines and then analyze the resulting vibration modes to predict structural problems. Design Automation Products produced a suite of software CAE (computer-aided engineering) tools that simulated how an electrical circuit still in design would perform when finally executed in silicon. It allowed designers to revamp their designs to maximize the performance of the circuit before the costly step of actual fabrication took place. These three businesses were expected to represent about 20 percent of GenRad's total revenue in 1990.

Company Culture

Like many electronics companies that followed, GenRad's original contribution to the market was technical excellence. Consequently, the R&D organization was seen as the primary line function having the strongest voice in resource allocation decisions which shaped GenRad's product strategy and served as the training ground for future general managers (program directors were most typically drawn from engineering management).

According to GenRad management, GenRad's product strategy focused on high-end, premium products in order to compete in market segments with attractive returns and to "solve the [industry's] toughest testing problems." Some GenRad managers believed that this sense of mission led to overinvestment in the midrange to high end of the market (sometimes without sufficient market data to substantiate this position) and underinvestment in the low end of the market. GenRad's failure to adequately address the <$100,000 PCB ATE market segment was noted as the most recent example. In addition, they maintained, this orientation toward the "toughest testing problems" made GenRad's New Product Development organization reluctant to use technology developed outside of the company, wanting only to develop products which could be differentiated by GenRad's engineering expertise.

This desire to provide a unique GenRad technical contribution was seen by some as another sign of the engineering function driving GenRad decision making and as slowing GenRad's ability to respond to new customer needs and competitive threats. But others countered that failure to be first to market was not necessarily a problem: "We may not be first [to market] but we will have the best product." In addition they argued that GenRad was not inwardly focused but rather had an "intuitive marketing ethic" which was best demonstrated by GenRad's devotion to providing the highest level of customer service and product quality in the industry—even through years of losses and recent layoffs. Furthermore, they contended, GenRad's strength was not in building point product solutions to current customer needs but rather in its ability to create a long-term strategic vision and leapfrog competitors' offerings in the marketplace. GenRad's creation of the PCB ATE industry in 1969, in-circuit test technology in the mid-1970s, and sophisticated test program development environments in the 1980s were cited as examples of GenRad innovating its ways to leadership.

GenRad Organization

The New Product Development organization (see Exhibit 8) was responsible for product design, development, and marketing activities. The organization was divided into several product lines, each headed by a program director who acted as a "mini–general manager" managing both R&D (product design and development) and product marketing. Program directors were measured on meeting targets (cost, product features content, and delivery schedule) for products under development. The R&D and product marketing organizations were responsible for new products, enhancements to existing products, and maintenance of existing products. The engineering manager and team were measured on performance versus plan on development cost, schedule, and product feature set. Product marketing was measured on how closely the product feature set matched customer needs. It was responsible for proposing product structure, computing an initial sales forecast, and making a preliminary pricing recommendation.

The Operations Department included Manufacturing Engineering and Manufacturing. Toward completion of a design, especially of new hardware products, a design engineer would begin to work closely with a manufacturing engineer. After testing, a formal hand-off was made to Manufacturing. For a software product the process was far simpler: Design Engineering released a debugged software master tape to Operations which then performed a final verification test and mass-produced the software. Operations was measured on a number of expense and schedule targets.

The Tactical Marketing Department was responsible for bringing a product to market, including final pricing, positioning, internal introduction (training the sales force), and external launch. Like the Manufacturing Engineering Department, Tactical Marketing depended on a hand-off from Product Marketing to perform its function. Tactical Marketing was measured on its effectiveness in supporting the field and ability to stay within their budget.

The Marketing, Sales, and Support organization included Tactical Marketing, Account Management, Field Support, and Customer Service, and was responsible for meeting sales order targets and maintaining customer satisfaction. In the United States, the sales representatives managing customer accounts and application engineers performing pre- and postsales support were organized geographically into seven districts, each managed by a district sales manager who reported to the North American sales manager. Wholly owned national subsidiaries sold and serviced GenRad products in Europe (and the Middle East) and these subsidiaries reported to the European sales director. For the Far East and South America, GenRad products were sold through a variety of distributors (joint ventures and manufacturers' representatives).[7] Sales were measured on orders booked versus target. In addition, there was a small telemarketing organization which sold products priced below $30,000 in the United States.

---

[7]Manufacturers' representatives were distribution companies which sold products on commission but did not take title to the goods.

EXHIBIT 8 GenRad Organization Chart

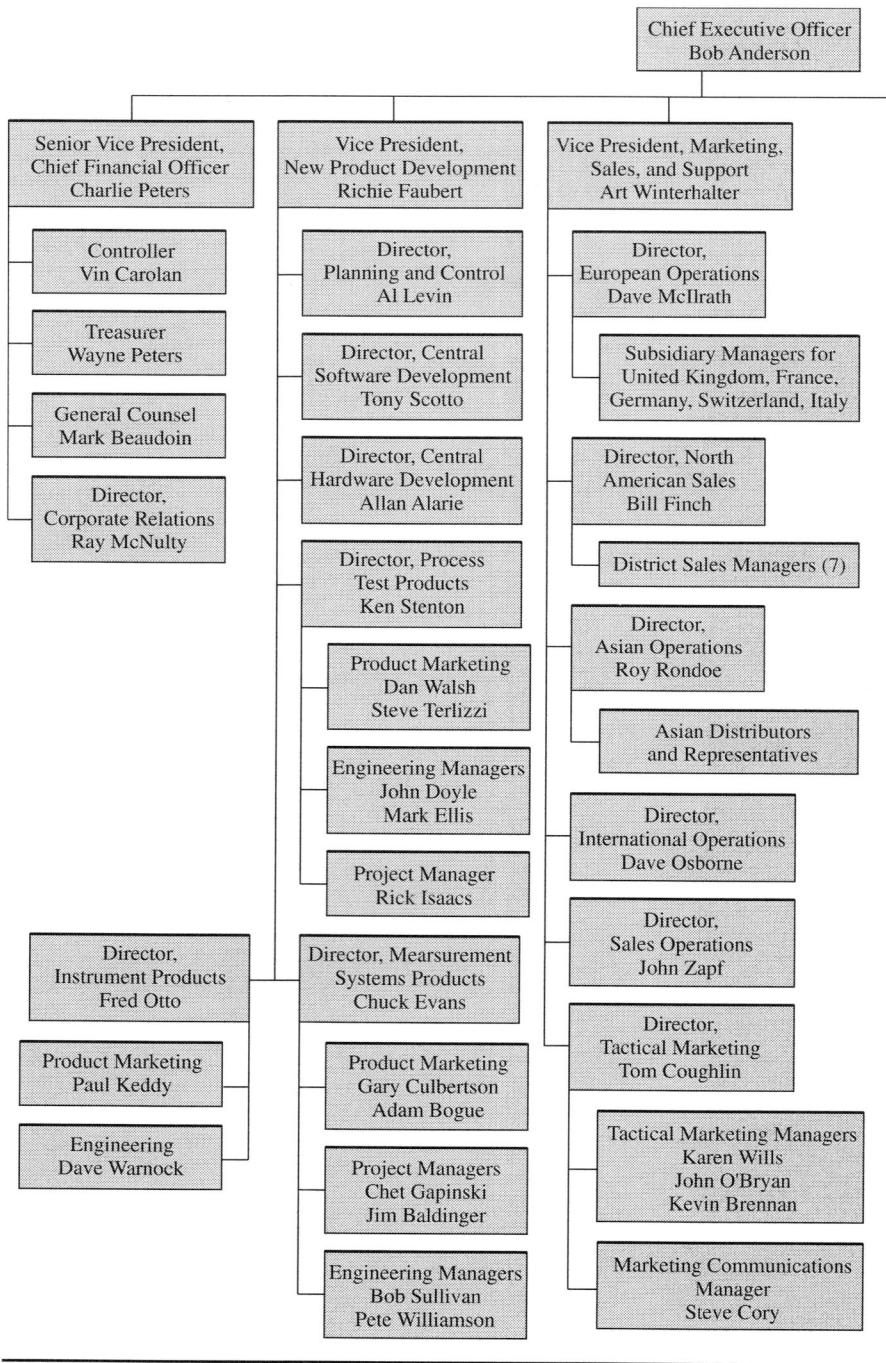

EXHIBIT 8 **GenRad Organization Chart** (*concluded*)

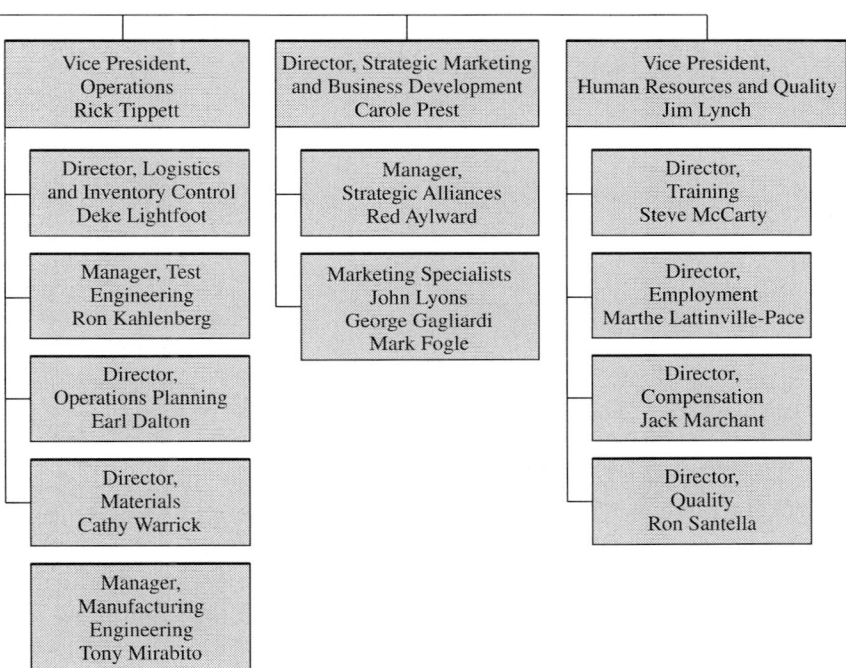

The Customer Service Department provided customer training, hotline phone assistance, technical experts to back up the field support engineers, input to product planning and product serviceability requirements, and technical training on field support of new products. Customer Service was measured on customer satisfaction.

GenRad believed it had a unique competitive advantage in the willingness of application engineers in the field and customer service engineers at headquarters to help customers get the most out of their equipment and, in some cases, to go above and beyond the call of duty. In fact the sense of duty which motivated such action typically came from individual engineers and was reinforced by management. It was such a part of the culture that assistance was given quite often without considering the cost to GenRad of doing so.

New Product Planning and Development Process

In 1987, GenRad introduced a New Product Planning process to ensure high quality product releases. The process was driven by the program director and had three formal checkpoints for top management (CEO and staff) review before a full set of resources was committed to develop the product and bring it to market:

1. *Three-year plan.* The program director reviewed his or her three-year product strategy annually with the CEO and top management. The highest priority items were assigned to an engineering manager and product manager for further investigation.
2. *Core product definition.* The program director, working in conjunction with the engineering manager and product manager, identified a target market, specific customer needs to be met, and product features. Although a very preliminary return on investment (ROI) was completed, the key test was how well the proposed product would meet customer needs. At the end of this phase a project manager (reporting directly to the program director) was appointed to shepherd the project through the next phase and product development process.
3. *Project proposal.* In this phase, a project manager worked with each functional area to put together an overall plan, including specific manpower requirements from each functional area, an overall development schedule showing dependencies, called a PERT plan, and a return on investment (computed based on the specific manpower requirements and an updated pricing recommendation). In addition, the product development organization would complete their investigation and reach consensus (between R&D and Product Marketing) on the proposed product feature set.

When the project proposal was approved by top management, the project entered the product development phase.

Over the course of new product development, a project manager—often from Manufacturing—served as the leader of the interfunctional project management team composed of the engineering manager representing R&D; the product manager representing Marketing until Tactical Marketing picked up responsibility; the support leader representing the Customer Service and Field Support organization; and the Operations leader representing Manufacturing Engineering, Quality Engineering, Purchase, Materials Control, New Product Manufacturing, Mechanical Computer Aided Design (MCAD), Computer Aided Engineering (CAE)/board design, and Standard Manufacturing.

Rick Isaacs, a project manager, pointed out some of the issues facing project teams:

> One big problem has been the hand-off from Design Engineering to Manufacturing Engineering. Back in the 1970s there was a very close, cooperative relationship between these groups with lots of two-way communication. Unfortunately, during the 1980s, this relationship broke down—Design Engineering threw the prototype "over the wall" to Manufacturing Engineering. We've begun to address this organizationally with a new initiative called concurrent engineering, which is basically having the design engineer teamed together with the manufacturing engineer from the very beginning of design, not just at the end. The idea is for R&D to become sensitive to how their design impacts test engineering and beyond.
>
> Another issue is that the Operations and Support leaders are typically less experienced than their peers on the project management team, and the Operations leader is overloaded with the number of Operations departments that he is representing.
>
> One more problem is the handoff from Product Marketing to Tactical Marketing. It's not always clear where one drops off and the other picks up. It ends up consuming a lot of project management time.

Carole Prest, the director of Strategic Marketing and Business Development, added:

> Given the serial handoff nature of our product development process, creativity had been traditionally owned by the New Product Development Department with other departments, such as Manufacturing and Tactical Marketing, viewing their roles as pretty rigidly fixed. I want my department to serve as a strategic gadfly to get downstream functional areas to look at things differently and explore ways in which they can be creative and add value to the end product: to become proactive as opposed to just reactive.

Prest's Strategic Marketing and Business Development Department had been formed in spring 1990 for three main purposes. First, it was responsible for long-term strategic market planning including market definition, selection, and requirements analysis. In particular, this department worked with New Product Development and others to find ways to creatively deploy GenRad strengths to take advantage of new market opportunities. A closely related second function was to improve the strategic decisions made by program directors by working with them on product planning and development teams. And third, this group was working to improve the quality of GenRad marketing, chiefly through performing analysis so that important strategic decisions were, in GenRad's lingo, "fact-based" (i.e., supported by much broader market data and analysis).

The Evolving Situation

Customers' New Needs

As he contemplated the future, Bob Anderson knew his customers' problems were rapidly changing, as were the approaches they used to solve them.

The mid-to-late 1980s were a difficult period for PCB ATE vendors, because with little growth in sales revenue to fund R&D costs, customer needs for PCB ATE became much more difficult to satisfy. Life cycles of electronics products shortened as manufacturers increased the pace of new product introductions. GenRad's customers were cutting the time from product design to production, which put pressure on PCB ATE vendors to help them shorten product testing cycles and better integrate design with the testing.

The miniaturization of electronic circuits continued to crowd more and more circuits onto a printed circuit board making the job of gaining access to individual components for testing more difficult. With more functionality crowded onto a printed circuit board, the cost of failure increased because it was harder to find the defect and a PCB was more costly to swap out. Increasingly, customers needed a way to test high volumes of very complex PCBs.

Paradoxically, even as their testing requirements became more difficult to meet and led to more sophisticated PCB ATE systems, customers found it much harder to justify the large capital appropriations for these systems, leading to experimentation with a number of strategies to lower the cost of PCB testing:

1. Design-to-test linkages providing the ability to transfer output from the PCB design directly into the test program generator to decrease test engineer time spent on development of test programs.

2. Distributed test strategies in which smaller, inexpensive test systems targeted for specific purposes were placed strategically throughout the PCB manufacturing process, thereby off-loading expensive midrange and high-end systems. This reduced the customer's need to buy another midrange to high-end test system in cases where the customer needed many different kinds of testing to be done. One GenRad customer commented, for example, "I would rather buy 10 $100,000 machines focused on specific tasks than another $1,000,000 multistrategy test system." The low-end test systems used in this way ranged from manufacturing defect analyzers (MDAs), costing approximately $30,000, to low-end functional and in-circuit test systems. While some testing needs could be off-loaded to smaller, less-expensive test systems the distributed test strategy would not replace demand for sophisticated test systems (ranging from $250,000 to $1,000,000 plus) that were needed for the precision of testing results delivered by higher-priced systems.

3. Built-in self-tests in which PCB designers incorporated circuitry into the PCB during the design which would allow the PCB to test itself, thereby reducing the need for PCB ATE systems.

Test Technology Trends

In addition to the new PCB testing approaches were some significant changes in PCB test technology in the late 1980s (see Appendix).

First, as electronic manufacturers improved the quality of their PCB manufacturing processes, it decreased the need for in-circuit testers which were used primarily for testing the production process. In the late 1970s, in-circuit testing had grown much more rapidly than functional testing. But by the mid-1980s this trend reversed with demand for functional testing increasing to test newer, higher performance PCBs and to test areas of a board where access was not possible for in-circuit testing.

Second, a new approach, called boundary scan, emerged as a way of testing complex boards where access to individual components was not possible. Based on technology developed by IBM, boundary scan enabled intermediary components on a board to allow a test signal to be passed on to the target component (under test) and to return the result. An industry committee of vendors and customers was formed to create an industry standard for boundary scan.

Third, there was a movement from closed test systems with proprietary technology to open test systems using industry standard technology. An example was the VXIbus standard which was designed to provide an improved interface for communications between instruments and computer control systems. Standards such as VXIbus lowered entry barriers and mobility barriers within the PCB ATE market, allowing existing competitors and new entrants to enter market segments more quickly.

With these challenges in mind, Anderson drew up questions that the strategic planning session would have to address:

- How should GenRad's PCB ATE product strategy evolve? Where should growth come from?
- What accommodations would the firm have to make?

Appendix: History of PCB ATE Technology[8]

The automatic test equipment market had grown rapidly as the miniaturization of electronic circuits transformed many industrial and consumer products. This period can be broken into three generations. In the early 1960s, printed circuit boards were fairly simple with the logic composed of transistors (and other discrete semiconductors) connected together on the bare board. Testing such boards required a test engineer to assemble a collection of rack and stack (R&S) instruments into a test system and then to test every possible logic state of the board. It typically took three to four

---

[8]Includes excerpts from GenRad's *Introduction to Multistrategy Testing* by Deborah Graham, 1989.

minutes to test the dozen or more possible states. This was called functional testing because the engineer was testing how the board would function in every possible case.

Rack and Stack Installation

With the development of integrated circuits (ICs, which shrank an entire printed circuit board into a tiny component) as mounted components, boards became so complex that testing time stretched to as long as 3 to 4 hours. Manual PCB testing was becoming impractical and in some cases, the highest cost element of the finished product. This led GenRad to introduce the first printed circuit board automatic test equipment (PCB ATE) system in 1969. By combining a minicomputer with several instruments and equipment to connect the board being tested, GenRad provided a system which could be programmed to automatically execute a variety of tests. This approach cut test times from hours to seconds and shifted the focus of test engineers from assembling hardware to developing test software.

The next wave of electronics miniaturization, which culminated in large-scale integration (LSI) logic in the late 1970s, again taxed test engineers as the density of ICs on a board increased dramatically and problems occurred in attempting to isolate which IC was at fault. The next generation in ATE was in-circuit testing, which provided a way to test each circuit on the board individually. The underlying

PCB ATE System

assumption was that if each circuit worked individually, then the board as a whole would work. Thus, in-circuit testing emerged as the preferred testing strategy for the most complex PCBs.

During the 1980s new technologies of PCB design created problems with in-circuit testing leading to a third generation of ATE systems called combinational (or multistrategy) testers, which employed both in-circuit and functional testing to test a PCB thoroughly. One technology was the application-specific integrated circuit (ASIC), which gave semiconductor manufacturers the ability to customize ICs with the unique logic needed for a particular product design rather than to build the product out of off-the-shelf ICs. The problem was that a fundamental premise upon which in-circuit testing was based was the existence of a "test library" containing all of the standard parts which could be used in the design of the PCB. But since each ASIC was a custom part, such standard models could not exist. This issue necessitated the creation of design-to-test linkages so that the output of the software used to design the ASIC (called logic simulators) could provide input directly into the ATE system's test generation software

The second major new technology issue was the creation of surface mounted devices (SMDs) through a manufacturing technique which allowed ICs to be mounted directly on the board's surface instead of the traditional method of mounting ICs through holes on the board. This technique provided the means for even greater density of ICs on a PCB, but at a cost of not providing the access needed to perform in-circuit testing. A new technology, called boundary scan, might provide a way to access ICs for which direct physical access is impossible by sending a signal through intermediary ICs. This technology was only beginning to be implemented in the late 1980s; instead, functional testing was used on those areas of the board (called clusters) where access for in-circuit testing was not possible.

CHAPTER 42

General Electric Plastics: Organizing the Marketing Function

In an attempt to keep GE Plastics at the forefront of the world engineering plastics market in an increasingly commoditizing environment, its management had to resolve:

1. *The role and responsibilities of the product management function: What should the structure look like for the 1990s?*
2. *The role and responsibilities of the marketing and sales functions: How could they best leverage their efforts to gain customer loyalty?*
3. *The system for coordinating the service needs of the company's global customers: How to take advantage of GE's international presence?*
4. *How to maintain the spirit of entrepreneurship in a $3.5 billion company?*

General Electric Company (GE), headquartered in Fairfield, Connecticut, is one of the largest and most diversified firms in the world. GE has 14 major lines of business, organized into three major categories: core manufacturing, services, and technology. General Electric Plastics (GEP) is part of the technology group. In 1987, GE had $40.5 billion in sales and $2.9 billion in net income. The plastics business, headquartered at Pittsfield, Massachusetts, represented 6.8 percent of sales for the corporation and 17.5 percent of profits.

General Electric's plastics business operation, first established in 1930, achieved worldwide engineering plastics sales of $50 million in 1969. By 1978, sales exceeded $500 million. In 1989, including a full year of revenues from a recent acquisition, sales exceeded $3.5 billion. Roughly 55 percent of those revenues were from U.S. operations, 35 percent from Europe, and a little less than 10 percent from Japan and other countries in the Pacific rim.

GE Plastics (GEP), with estimated market shares of roughly 45 percent in the United States, 30 percent in Europe, and 20 percent in Japan, had emerged as the

---

This case was prepared by V. Kasturi Rangan and Steven Michael.
Copyright © 1990 by the President and Fellows of Harvard College.
Harvard Business School case 591-029 (revised March 22, 1993).

worldwide leader in the engineering plastics market. The company's profitability was nearly 20 percent above the chemical industry average. Top management expected the plastics business at least to keep pace with industry growth in the coming decade.

Glen Hiner, who became the CEO of the division in 1978, was widely hailed as the chief architect of this success story. *Business Week* in 1988 rated him as one of the six best managers in corporate America. In early 1990, Hiner looked ahead to the coming decade:

> The theory goes that a firm should adapt its organizational structures and systems to reflect the changes in product, market, and competitive environments. We want to be one step ahead. We prefer to anticipate and design the organization to be ready for the environment.

Harbig Garabedian, GE Plastics's organization and staffing manager, echoed that viewpoint:

> We are doing so well that the first reaction is, Why fix anything that isn't broken? But we don't subscribe to that view. When there is no pain, there is often no pressure for change. In our rapid rise to a $3.5 billion dollar business, we are bound to experience some calcification, some bureaucracy. We want to remain entrepreneurial. We want to be ready for the complex environment of the 1990s.

Of the several organizational issues that were currently challenging GEP managers, the following were foremost on Mr. Hiner's mind:

1. The role and responsibilities of the product management function: What should the structure look like for the 1990s?
2. The role and responsibilities of the marketing and sales functions. How could they best leverage their efforts to gain customer loyalty?
3. The system for coordinating the service needs of the company's global customers: How could they best take advantage of GE's truly international presence?
4. How could they maintain the spirit of entrepreneurship in a $3.5 billion company?

These questions had to be answered in the context of two recent successful organizational transitions. Prior to 1985 the company organized itself by product lines, each with an independent manufacturing and marketing organization as well as profit and loss responsibility. The 1985 reorganization eliminated product line distinctions, and divisions were now organized around functions such as manufacturing or marketing. In 1988 GEP acquired Borg Warner Chemicals, which enabled the company to add a significant product to the lower end of its engineering plastics product line. The move expanded revenues by over 30 percent.

The Product

Plastics, also called synthetic resins, were a group of materials formed from long strings of organic molecules. Called plastic because when heated, they could be shaped, and when cooled that shape remained, plastics were generally classified as

EXHIBIT 1 Classification of Thermoplastic Polymers

Commodity	Transitional	Engineering	Performance
PET (unfilled)	ABS/SAN	Modified PPO*	Fluoropolymers
Polyethylene	Acrylics	Nylon*	Polyamide-imide
Polypropylene	SMA copolymer*	PBT*	Polyarylate*
Polystyrene		PET*	Polyetheretherketone*
Polyvinylchloride		Polyacetal*	Polyetherimide*
		Polycarbonate*	Polyethersulfone*
		Alloys/blends*	Polyimide
		SMA terpolymer*	Polyphenylenesulfide*
			Polysulfone*
High volume	High volume	Medium volume	Low volume
(1 MM tones/region)	(0.5–1 MM tons/region)	(40–100 KT/region)	(0.1–10 KT/region)
High processability	Good processability	Good processability	Least processable
Low thermal stability	Medium thermal stability	Good thermal stability	Excellent thermal stability
Simple chemistry/process	Intermediate chemistry/process	Intermediate chemistry/process	Complex chemistry/process
Low price	Medium price	Higher price	Highest price
2%–5% growth per year	4%–6% growth per year	5%–8% growth per year	10%–15% growth per year

*Included in Chem Systems' Engineering Plastics Study.

either engineering or commodity. An engineering plastic was more difficult to shape and to manufacture than a commodity plastic, but far easier than metal. They were harder, stronger, more heat resistant, and more chemically resistant than commodity plastics. A list classifying all plastics is included as Exhibit 1.

The physical properties of engineering plastics enabled them to replace steel, iron, aluminum, or other metals and alloys in many products. Virtually all industries used plastics in some way, but engineering plastics were particularly successful in electrical and electronic products, automobiles, construction, and appliances.

The engineering plastics market was big and getting bigger. Sales had averaged a 7.3 percent increase each year for the past 10 years, and the industry expected continued growth rates of about 10 percent per year through the 1990s.

For purposes of this case, four specific plastics will be discussed: polycarbonate (PC), nylon, modified polyphenylene oxide (PPO resin), and acrylonitrile-butadiene-styrene (ABS).

1. *Polycarbonate* was introduced in the United States in 1957 by GE Plastics. Extremely rigid and tough, PC could withstand both high impact and high temperatures, although it did not resist chemicals well. As originally formulated, PC was transparent; its first application was to replace glass in many uses to reduce breakage. Windows, signs, head lamps, and lighting fixtures remained one of the largest uses for PC. Other typical applications for (opaque) PC included microwave cookware, filter housings, bottles, lamp housings, nameplates, food processor bowls, and audio compact disks. In

1988, the top three markets for polycarbonate were: glazing (windows), 24 percent; automotive products, 14 percent; and electrical/electronic products, 13 percent. Polycarbonate represented about 34 percent of demand for engineering plastics by weight, and U.S. demand was expected to rise at 8 percent per year until 1995. GE's trademark for its polycarbonate was LEXAN.

2. *Nylon* was introduced in 1941 by Du Pont. In certain formulations, nylon could be applied in engineering applications. It was not as resistant to impact as polycarbonate, but it could withstand higher temperatures and had higher chemical resistance. Nylon's primary market was in automotive products (34 percent of sales), followed by film and coating (14 percent), and electrical and electronic products (13 percent). Nylon was commonly used for electrical connectors, fender extensions, power tool housings, food packaging, and lawn and garden equipment. About 34 percent of the engineering plastics sold in the United States was nylon (measured by weight), and demand was expected to rise 7.2 percent per year through 1995. GE Plastics did not make nylon.

3. *PPO resin* was introduced by GE Plastics in 1964 as a product that could withstand extremes of chemistry. PPO resin could be manufactured into a variety of shapes and alloyed with other resins; it was typically used in personal computers, auto instrument panels, wheel covers, pump housings, fuse boxes, and TV cabinets. Major markets included business equipment, 25 percent; appliances, 20 percent; and automotive products, 15 percent. PPO resin sales represented about 15 percent of total engineering plastics sales by weight, and U.S. demand was expected to rise 7 percent through 1995. GE sold its modified PPO resin under the NORYL trademark.

4. *ABS* was produced in greater volumes and sold at lower prices than the plastics discussed above. It represented the low end of engineering plastics in performance, with strength and resistance above commodity plastics but less than PC, PPO resin, or nylon. ABS was used for telephones, refrigerator liners, and sporting goods. Major markets included automotive products, 21 percent; appliances, 20 percent; and construction products, 15 percent. GE's trademark for its ABS product was CYCOLAC resin.

Exhibit 2 compares the physical properties of the four leading engineering plastics and Exhibit 3 shows the 1989 U.S. consumption of the various plastics categories by weight.

Plastic products were sold in an almost infinite variety of formulations. For example, plastics were commonly mixed under high heat and pressure to generate an alloy or blend to satisfy specific applications. The alloy combined the best features of its component plastics. Alternatively, the plastics were compounded with fillers or enhanced with additives to deliver a certain property, for example, flame retardance. Thus, a plastics producer could formulate a portfolio of grades, alloys, and mixtures formulated from the basic products.

Many automobile bumpers were made of XENOY resin, an especially tough GE Plastic blend of polycarbonate and polyester. Another GE alloy, GEMAX resin,

Exhibit 2   Physical Properties of Four Leading Engineering Plastics

	PC	Nylon	PPO	ABS
Impact	Very high	Good	High	Good
Strength	High	Very high	High	Good
Electrical	Good	Very good	Good	Good
Chemical	Fair	Good	Excellent	Fair
Thermal	Good	Good	Good	Fair

SOURCE: Adapted from the *Rauch Guide to the Plastics Industry,* p. 114.

Exhibit 3   1989 U.S. Consumption of Plastics (in million pounds)

Engineering Thermoplastics:	
Polycarbonate	600
Nylon	600
PPO resin	260
Other engineering thermoplastics[a]	290
Total	1,750
ABS	1,250
All other plastics[b]	55,000

[a]Polyester-based thermoplastics such as PBT, PET, and other high-performance plastics. GE manufactured several such resins: VALOX, GELOY, ULTEM, and SUPEC resins.
[b]Commodity plastics such as polyethylene, polypropylene, polyvinyl chloride, polystrene, and the like.
SOURCE: Adapted from *Modern Plastics,* January 1990.

a combination of PC and PPO resin, was used in side panels and doors of cars. GEMAX resin was strong, yet it shaped well, allowing the automotive designers great freedom in auto body styles. CYCOLOY resin, another GE offering, was an alloy of ABS and PC. In 1989 approximately 40 percent of GEP's worldwide sales came from LEXAN resin-based products, about 35 percent from CYOLAC resin-based products, and 20 percent from NORYL resin-based products.

The Molders

The final product of a plastics manufacturer like GE Plastics was a bag of pellets, sold by the pound. The plastic pellets were placed into a molding machine, which heated and shaped the plastic into the desired application—a bumper, a computer casing, a hair dryer. A plastic was molded; a metal was stamped, pressed, or cast.

Many different molding technologies existed, but the two most common were injection and extrusion. In an injection process, the plastic was heated, then injected as a liquid into a mold that shaped the plastic. As it cooled, the plastic solidified into the desired dimensions. A bumper, for instance, was injected. In an extrusion process, the plastic was subjected to great pressure and some heat, then forced through an opening that shaped the plastic in two dimensions. The product was then cut into the desired length. A pipe, for instance, was extruded.

The plastic raw material was shipped from the factory to the molder's site where it was melted and formed. Sixty percent of production was shipped to molding shops owned by the manufacturer of the final product. For example, General Motors had 12 molding shops located near auto assembly plants. These shops were called captive molders.

The remaining 40 percent of plastics sales were received by independent molding shops, which bid against one another to supply the final product manufacturer. Molding was described by one industry participant as a "down-and-dirty business," characterized by tough competition. Large OEMs (original equipment manufacturers) usually used both captive shops and independent molders to meet their needs.

Independent molders ranged from sophisticated companies with the latest manufacturing technology to mom-and-pop operations. Approximately 8,300 independent and 10,000 captive molding shops of all sizes composed the molding industry in the United States.

Original Equipment Manufacturers (OEMs)

OEMs used plastics as a raw material from which to build their own products—commonly, cars, airplanes, packaging material, appliances, electronic equipment, and building supplies. The choice of material depended upon its moldability (i.e., how well the plastic flowed to fill a particular mold and maintain proper dimensions after cooling) as well as its ability to endure the environment of the final product. For some applications, the product had to withstand a sudden physical shock (like a car bumper); for others, strong and sustained mechanical stress (like a window). Some had to endure high heat (a hair dryer); others had to withstand electrical or magnetic fields (computers); some needed to survive chemical assaults.

Customers faced a trade-off among performance, delivery, customer support, and cost. Though performance was uppermost in the customer's mind, price competition was stiff for most plastics. Prices varied widely across applications and across products.

Market boundaries for plastics were extremely fluid. For any given application, the designer might consider several brands of a specific plastic (LEXAN resin versus another manufacturer's polycarbonate), another chemically different but functionally similar plastic (offered by one or more plastics firms), as well as various metals, all of which met required standards of performance and price.

Plastics cost more per pound of material than metals, but the assembled cost of the final molded product (e.g., a bumper) was usually lower, for several reasons. First, the molding process cost less than stamping. Second, tooling costs were much lower, reducing changeover time and increasing manufacturing flexibility. Third, plastics required fewer and simpler assembly steps. Usually, plastics did not need to be welded or painted. Plastics could be molded into more complex shapes than metals. Finally, plastics were lighter than metal, so fewer pounds made more parts.

To sell the product effectively, the vendor had to satisfy two levels of customers in the distribution channel. First, the vendor had to convince the OEM to choose its plastic for a given application. Here, the product competed primarily on engineering tests, specifications, and final component cost. Second, the vendor had to serve the molder with timely product delivery, competitive pricing, and technical service. Here, vendors competed to raise molders' productivity, so manufacturing performance became an important buying criterion.

The Competition

The list of firms that manufactured engineering plastics read like a *Who's Who* of the global chemical industry. Firms such as Allied Chemical, Hoechst Celanese, ICI, Amoco, Monsanto, and Eastman Chemical (part of Kodak) all offered products in these markets. Four companies, generally considered to be leaders in the field, are profiled in detail in Exhibit 4: Bayer/Mobay, BASF, Dow Chemical, and Du Pont.

EXHIBIT 4   Profiles of Competitors

Bayer, a West German chemical company of worldwide scope, had 1988 sales of 40.5 billion DM, with income after taxes of 1.9 billion DM ($22.7 billion and $1.1 billion, respectively). It manufactured plastics, agricultural chemicals, organic and inorganic chemicals, pigments and dyes, as well as a wide variety of health care, chemical, biotech, and photographic products.

The Polymer Sector, containing plastics, in 1988 accounted for 7.1 billion DM in sales ($4 billion) and 385 million DM ($216 million) in operating income. The firm manufactured polycarbonate, as well as high-end plastics for advanced engineering applications. Bayer announced plans to nearly double its capacity to manufacture PC. Its U.S. subsidiary, Mobay, had $2.0 billion in sales and $113 million in net income in 1988.

BASF, another West German chemical company, in addition to making plastics, drilled for oil, made basic chemicals, agricultural chemicals, and dyestuffs; it also manufactured paints and printing systems. In 1986 BASF had 18.7 billion DM in sales ($9.6 billion) and 710 million DM ($364 million) in net income. The company operated worldwide; its U.S. subsidiary, BASF Corporation, had $3.6 billion in sales and $188.5 million in pretax earnings.

In the plastics business, BASF made several products that competed indirectly with PC, PPO resin, and PI, including polyether ketones, polysulfones, and composites. BASF was the leading producer of high-end engineering plastics in Europe, and had a significant presence in Japan. Plastics sales accounted for 6.3 billion DM ($3.2 billion) in 1986.

Dow Chemical, headquartered in Midland, Michigan, in 1987 had $13.3 billion in sales and $1.2 billion in net income. About 40% of Dow's sales came from basic chemicals, while the rest came from plastics, drugs, and consumer products. The firm manufactured commodity plastics such as polystyrene and transitional products like ABS. The market for engineering plastics was a new and growing business for Dow.

Du Pont, in Wilmington, Delaware, considered by many to be the most formidable chemical company in the world, had operations in agricultural and industrial chemicals, biomedical products, fibers, paints, and finishes. The firm had significant coal and oil operations as well. In 1988, Du Pont had sales of $32.9 billion and net income of $2.2 billion.

The Polymer Products group contributed $4.3 billion in sales and $404 million in after-tax operating income to the corporation. As the inventor of nylon, Du Pont could lay claim to being the inventor of engineering plastics. It currently competed primarily at the high end of the performance spectrum with liquid crystal polymers, and at the low end with nylon and nylon derivatives.

The leading competitor both in the United States and Europe to GEP's most important product, LEXAN resin, was Bayer, a West German firm. Considered a formidable technology giant and a tough competitor, Bayer had a major share of the polycarbonate market in Europe, but was only a distant second in the United States. Bayer held the European patents to the polycarbonate formula until 1971. Only after Bayer's patent expired could GE set up its own manufacturing in Europe. GE's share of polycarbonate was about 60 to 70 percent in the United States, and about 30 to 40 percent in Europe.

There was no major direct competitor for NORYL resin on a worldwide basis, though several small Japanese firms produced close substitutes. In terms of its engineering properties, however, nylon, manufactured by Du Pont, Bayer, BASF, and Monsanto provided tough indirect competition.

In ABS, GE currently had a 45 to 55 percent share in the United States. Its European share was about 40 percent. Major worldwide competition came from Dow, Monsanto, and Bayer.

The sheer scale of chemical operations was such that new firms found it quite expensive to enter this industry; investment for a minimum efficient plant required $500 million to $700 million in 1989. Consequently, future global competition was likely to be primarily among the seven major manufacturers: Du Pont, Bayer, BASF, Dow, Monsanto, Hoechst, and GE. Japanese firms were expected to give tough regional challenges, but not considered likely to supplant the seven major players in the next five years. While competition in general was increasing worldwide, recent investments by competitors like BASF and Dow in polycarbonates were a major source of concern at GEP.

Organization of GE Plastics

In 1990 the firm was organized geographically, with autonomous divisions in the Americas, the Pacific, and Europe. Each region was organized functionally, with manufacturing, marketing, sales, and technology forming the key functions; the regions each reported on a profit-and-loss basis to Hiner. Exhibit 5 presents the GE organization chart. The vice presidents for sales, manufacturing, and technology reported directly to the regional general managers, whereas the marketing directors had only a dotted line relationship; they reported directly to the worldwide marketing and product general manager at the Pittsfield, Massachusetts, headquarters. For day-to-day operations, however, marketing directors sought the guidance and leadership of the regional general manager.

Manufacturing was effected in several plants worldwide. Each plant also included a technology group responsible for short-term product and process engineering. At the world headquarters for the technology division at Pittsfield, several teams of chemists, engineers, and material scientists performed basic research on long-term product development. In addition, GEP's marketing group had several application development centers worldwide, which provided customer application support and research. Exhibit 6 shows the location of all GE Plastics manufacturing and applications development facilities worldwide.

EXHIBIT 5 GE Plastics' Organization Chart

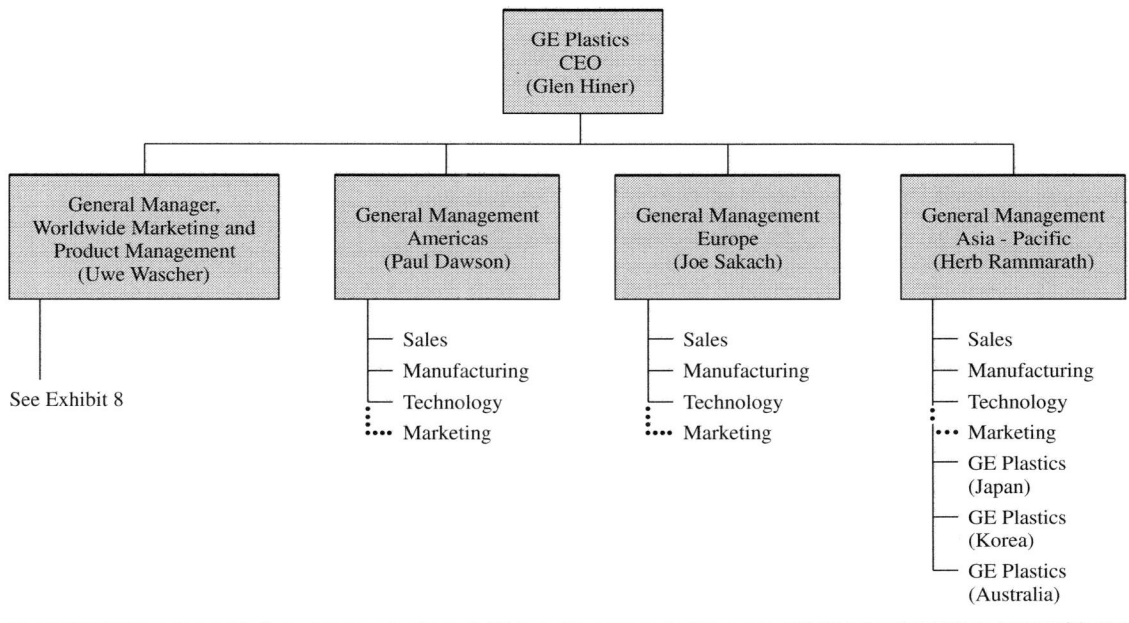

GEP Americas: The Introduction of the Functional Organization

The functional structure was implemented only in November 1985. Before that, GEP was organized by product. Three major product groups—the LEXAN Products Division, the NORYL Products Division, and the Crystalline Polymers Division—formed the heart of the business. (The ABS product came in 1988 with the acquisition of Borg Warner Chemicals.) See Exhibit 7 for a pre-1985 organization chart. Each division had dedicated resources for manufacturing, technology, and marketing. Even in the old structure, however, the sales force was shared, and they sold the full line of products.

A major impetus for the new functional structure was its success in Europe when implemented there in 1981. According to Paul Dawson, who headed the European operations at that time, "We were able to become market-oriented as a result, when previously we were sales-oriented."

The product-based structure had served GE Plastics well for many years; indeed, it was credited with much of the company's explosive growth during the early 1980s. At that time, penetrating new markets, converting customers from steel or concrete, was critical. A bottom line of profit and loss was clear for each product, and loyalty to product was strong. Vigorous competition (internal and external) created a sense of ownership, responsibility, and accountability. Employees were encouraged to view themselves as general managers and entrepreneurs.

EXHIBIT 6 GE Plastics Facilities

GE Plastics headquarters—Pittsfield, Massachusetts
European headquarters—Bergen op Zoom, Netherlands
GE Plastics's manufacturing plants:
    Mt. Vernon, Indiana, making primarily LEXAN resin and blends
    Selkirk, New York, making primarily NORYL resin
    Burkville, Alabama, making primarily LEXAN resin

    Tlaxcala, Mexico, making primarily LEXAN resin and NORYL resin
    Campinas, Brazil, making primarily NORYL resin

    Bergen op Zoom, Netherlands, making all products

    Melbourne, Australia, making all products
    Moka, Japan, making all products
    Takaishi City, Japan, making intermediate products used to produce NORYL resin

    In addition, GEP operated compounding plants in Brazil, Hong Kong, and Korea. It had also announced a joint venture in Korea to produce LEXAN resin by 1992.

GE Plastics's manufacturing plants acquired from Borg Warner:
    Washington, West Virginia, making ABS
    Ottawa, Illinois, making ABS
    Bay St. Louis, Missouri, making ABS
    Oxnard, California, making ABS
    Morgantown, West Virginia, making specialty chemicals
    Carville, Louisiana, making intermediate products for ABS
    Geismar, Louisiana, making intermediate products for ABS

    Other ABS facilities are in the Netherlands, Scotland, France, Mexico, and Japan. In addition, the GEP company had announced its intentions to put up an ABS plant in Cartagena, Spain, by 1993.

Applications development centers:
    At applications development centers, GE Plastics houses molding equipment and technical specialists to assist customers with their plastics applications.

    Pittsfield, Massachusetts, serving the East
    Southfield, Michigan, serving Detroit
    Lisle, Illinois, serving Chicago
    Mississauga, Ontario, serving Toronto and the rest of Canada
    Norcross, Georgia, serving Atlanta
    City of Industry, California, serving California
    Bergen op Zoom, Netherlands
    Milan, Italy
    Evry, France
    Manchester, United Kingdom
    Russelsheim, Germany
    Gotemba, Japan
    Dandenong, Australia

Nonetheless, problems were evident. First, competition among product divisions was confusing customers. Plastics cannibalized its own product lines in front of customers; NORYL resin in particular suffered from this internal competition. As Paul Dawson said: "The LEXAN marketing rep told the customer that LEXAN was

Exhibit 7 Plastics Business Group, Pre-1985 Americas Organization

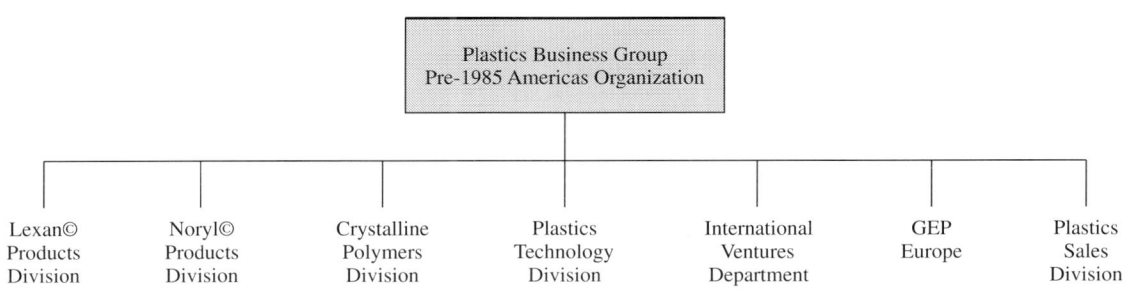

best, then the NORYL rep said that NORYL was best. Customers asked us, 'Will the real GE Plastics please stand up?'"

Second, the product divisions duplicated many tasks. Each business unit tried to be independent, so each operated distinct groups for MIS, finance, customer service, and purchasing. Clearly, savings could be achieved by consolidating some of these functions.

Finally, every product champion was also a product defender. The product-based structure established and entrenched vested interests.

Under the new functional organization, the Americas operation was headed by Paul Dawson, vice president and general manager, and included the territories of Canada, North America, Central America, and South America. Reporting to Dawson were the functional chiefs in manufacturing, technology (R&D), and sales.

Uwe Wascher, vice president and general manager, marketing, had two roles. In one, he was the worldwide head of marketing and product management, reporting to Hiner; in the other, he was chief of the Americas marketing operation. Wascher, a German national, ran the European marketing function before coming to the United States to head up a product group in the pre-1985 organization.

The sales division was organized to serve the molder. Sales reps called on individual molding shops, arranged delivery, fulfilled orders, and handled complaints. The sales force had 130 reps, each in an exclusive territory. Each rep sold the full range of GE Plastics' products. Some territories (like Detroit) were worth $80 million, but the average was $13 million. Any given territory had 70–100 customers, but 80 percent of value came from 20 percent of the orders. Reps were measured on growth against a budget based on the previous year's sales. About 30 percent of compensation was incentive based. The best reps made $85,000, the best managers $110,000. The sales force reported through 17 district managers and to three regional managers, to the sales vice president at GE Plastics' Pittsfield headquarters.

The marketing functions were divided into market development, marketing technology, and product management. Exhibit 8 shows the organization of the marketing department.

EXHIBIT 8 GE Plastics: Functional Organization

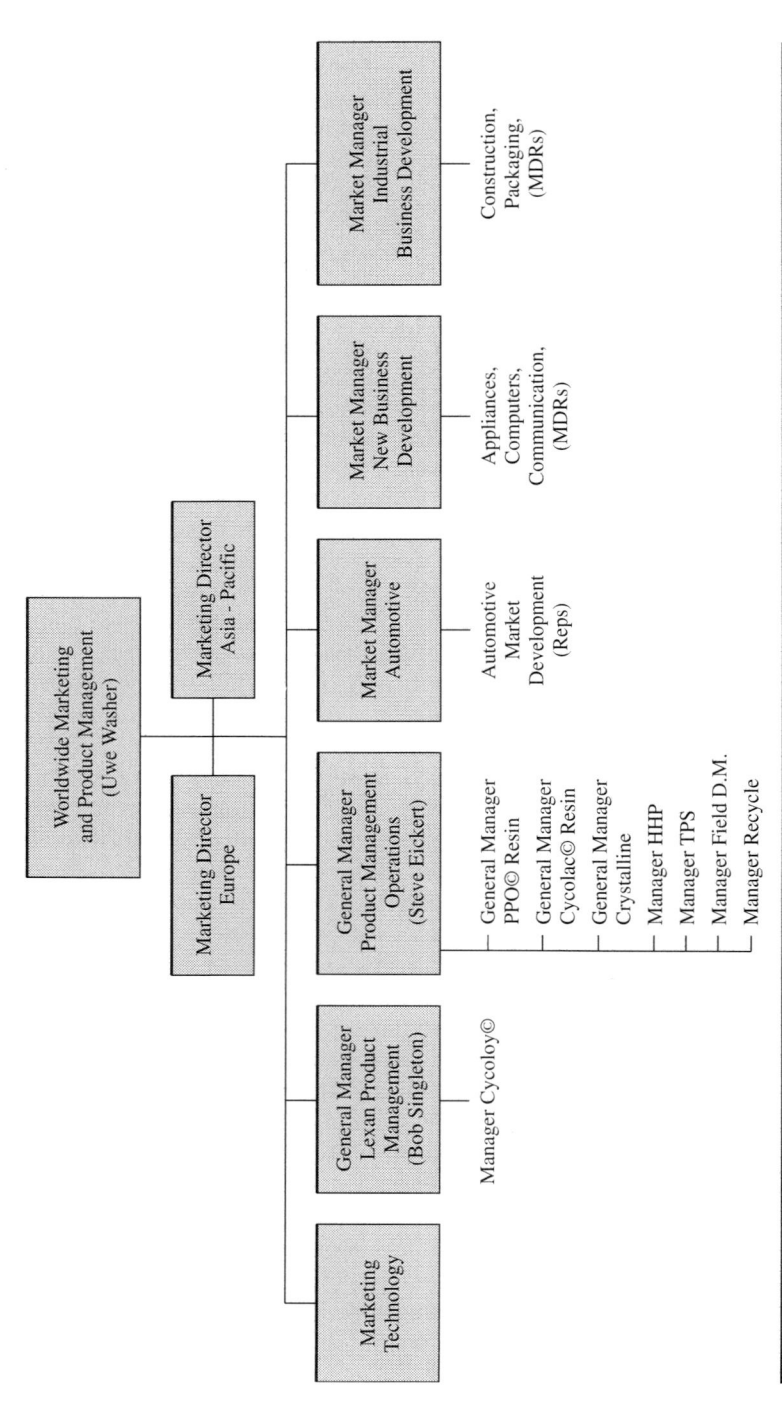

Market development reps (MDRs) served the OEM, the final customer. These specialists worked with individual customers such as Ford Motor Company to find new applications for plastics and to assist designers in the use and testing of plastics. They were supported by an Applications Development Center, with six locations in the United States, staffed by design engineers. In addition, GE Plastics had developed a computer-aided design system to be used by the customer's designers through a computer hookup.

There were about 80 MDRs plus the headquarters staff to reach the OEM. This far outstripped the marketing organization of any of GE Plastics' competitors. Market development reps were assigned to field offices based on the area's industrial base; for example, northern California had many electronics reps. MDRs reported into a field marketing manager (roughly equal to a sales district manager), who in turn reported into HQ Marketing, which was organized by programs or departments such as automotive, appliances, electronics, and so on. By and large, an effort was made to align each MDR with one department or program.

Under the new functional structure, the marketing function was the most dramatically affected. MDRs were assigned to a market, but authorized to select from all possible resins and blends the best one to meet the customer's needs. Product division–based competition was ended. Once the product was approved and specified, the sales rep would arrange to deliver the pellets to the molder and service the customer's routine requirements. As business continued with that account, if the customer needed only to reorder, it was through the sales rep; the MDR was not involved. But if the customer wanted to reconsider product features or attributes, the MDR would return.

The MDRs coordinated routinely with their sales counterparts. In a broad sense, the sales reps "serviced" what the development reps "sold." The OEMs specified the plastic but the molders bought and processed the plastic. Thus, the two reps had to communicate regularly on status of program development, orders, and customers. But coordination challenges arose when an OEM had molding facilities outside the local sales rep's territory.

An MDR in Minneapolis, for instance, serving the 3M Company purchasing headquarters would have to coordinate with the sales rep in California, where 3M's molding plant was located. If the sales rep and MDR did not already know each other, few formal systems or processes promoted such coordination. In addition, the MDRs were compensated on the basis of new business developed, whereas sales reps were compensated on total volume booked. The sales reps at times complained that MDRs spent too much time chasing new business, while the competition was eroding current business. The MDRs, in turn, complained that sales reps did not show the patience and perseverance to develop new businesses and customers.

The pricing quotations were given by the sales division, and sales reps were authorized to quote only book prices. Sales management had some latitude for price discounting within the range set by product management. Beyond those limits, pricing decisions had to be cleared with headquarters' product management.

The marketing technology function helped the customer manufacture and mold the plastic component effectively. For example, in a new application that an MDR had developed, the technology staff would become involved with the OEM customer, helping to determine how the application could be molded, and throughput improved, and how much the final cost of the manufactured part would be. Later, as the plastic component was being manufactured, the molders of that OEM would call marketing technology personnel with questions and problems, trying to improve yield. In addition, this department operated the Polymer Processing Development Center at Pittsfield, which had the newest and the best molding machines to test new applications and techniques. About 100 people worked in this department.

When the product divisions were abolished in 1985, so was the position of division general manager, who had unified and directed product strategy and tactics. Responsibility for the product under the new organization was assigned to a product manager. The central tasks of the product manager included product business strategy, competitive intelligence, pricing strategy, investment planning, resource allocation across functions, long-range planning, and forecasting. One high-ranking executive put it more succinctly: "The product manager is the quarterback."

Unlike the other marketing and sales functions, product management was a global function. Two product general managers, Bob Singleton and Steve Eickert, headquartered at Pittsfield, had about 10 product managers reporting to them. An equal number of product managers were located outside Pittsfield at Bergen op Zoom (European headquarters) and Tokyo (Asian headquarters), and reported to their respective regional marketing directors, as well as to the worldwide product managers at Pittsfield, Massachusetts. The two products general managers reported to Uwe Wascher, the general manager for worldwide marketing and product management.

GEP Europe and Asia Pacific

GEP organized its European operations along a classic matrix structure. There were country managers (United Kingdom, France, Germany, Benelux, Italy, Spain, and Eastern Europe) who were administrative (liaison) heads for all manufacturing, marketing, technology, and sales operations for a group of countries. The reporting lines and real authority, however, resided with the functional heads at Bergen op Zoom. Each country had a sales manager with several field sales reps. The marketing reps worked closely with the sales reps, but reported through market managers to the marketing director at Bergen op Zoom. It was GEP's philosophy to staff all country personnel with local nationals who were familiar and comfortable with the local language and culture. Several of these individuals, as they ascended the management ranks, occupied positions in GEP's worldwide operations.

The Asian operations, on the other hand, were somewhat more fragmented. GEP (Japan) was owned 51 percent by GE, 40 percent by Mitsui Petrochemical Company, and 9 percent by Nagase Ltd. (a trading company). All sales in Japan were effected exclusively by Nagase, whom GE managers considered an effective sales agent. Nagase also operated as GE's nonexclusive agent for other countries in that region with offices in Hong Kong, Kuala Lumpur (Malaysia), Singapore, and Taipei (Taiwan).

In addition to GE (Japan), the Pacific operations consisted of 100 percent GE-owned subsidiaries in Australia and South Korea. Countries like Australia, Korea, and New Zealand had independent sales managers, whereas the company operated through sales agents in Hong Kong, China, Singapore, Thailand, and several other Asian countries. On paper, GEP attempted to operate its Asian division along the lines of the matrix structure in Europe. The functional heads in Tokyo were ultimately responsible for all manufacturing, marketing, sales, and technology operations in the region. In practice, however, because of varying manufacturing and sales partners, the GEP Asia-Pacific headquarters served as an inspired coordinator rather than a leader.

The Acquisition of Borg Warner Chemicals

In September 1988, GE Plastics bought the chemical operations of Borg Warner Chemicals for $2.3 billion. Borg Warner, with worldwide sales of about $1.25 billion, was the leading supplier of ABS and its blends in the U.S. market. It was headquartered in Parkersburg, West Virginia, with four major plants in the United States and others in Europe. With this move, GE added a product it did not manufacture and doubled its number of plants and its poundage of sales.

Several reasons were given for the acquisition. First, ABS filled a hole in the product line. Frequently, ABS was the low-cost polymer substituted for one of GE Plastics' engineering grades. Executives at GE Plastics felt that it would be easier to manage this "erosion" if they offered the next level of product. One manager explained:

> At first, the customer orders a plastic with characteristics that exceed initial requirements. There is a tendency to "overdesign" because no one wants to make a mistake. After the properties of the plastic have been tried and tested, the customer may try to cut costs with a lower grade or a lesser product.

Erosion was estimated to affect 20 percent of all applications; thus, ABS would serve as a defense line. Moreover, ABS offered a different and a cheaper material for use in GE Plastics' alloys and blends.

Second, the Plastic Service Centers (Polymerland), with 11 distribution centers in the United States, a captive distribution arm of Borg Warner, was included as part of the acquisition. In 1989 Polymerland had sales in excess of $250 million, mainly ABS, of which over 50 percent came from GE brands and blends. The rest was procured from other plastics manufacturers. Unlike many in the industry, GE Plastics never used independent distributors, thus missing some small and midsize customers. Polymerland made it possible for GE to reach these customers that were too costly to contact directly. The centers also offered potential to add valuable new functions for customer service, such as custom formulation. One possibility seriously considered was to use the centers as recycling centers—gathering scrap plastic and reprocessing it for new use.

Product Management at the U.S. Headquarters

Role

The product manager was the key to the success of the two major reorganization efforts—first, the move to the functional structure and, second, the acquisition of the ABS product line. According to Dawson, the U.S. general manager, "While the MDR is GEP's Outside Guru, the product manager is GEP's Inside Guru." In the new structure, the product manager was the critical link for coordination within GEP. Contacts with every part of the business were required for success. The functional vice presidents described their dealings with the product manager as follows:

> The product manager gives manufacturing all the six month tactical directions—the production mix, the allocation, the staffing levels. (*Manufacturing VP*)
>
> For sales, the product manager works to set prices and to develop volume discount schedules. Also, the product manager allocates scarce product during shortage, and seeks outlets when inventories are too high. These judgments are based on the individual customer and the competitive situation. (*Sales VP*)
>
> Another task is to set priorities for R&D. The product manager is in charge of developing products for special applications. She or he manages the deadlines. Say we need a new product for cars for 1990. The product manager has to work the schedule with manufacturing and technology. I tell my people to view themselves as though they are on the PM's staff. Make sure the PM understands your trade-offs, and you understand the PM's priorities. (*Technology VP*)
>
> Few people realize that the product manager serves as chief strategic planner for the product. A PM must determine if new capacity is needed, how much to build, and in which geographic region of the world. Clearly this analysis must be built on demand forecasts and competitive conditions worldwide. (*Marketing Director*)

Positioning the product was also a key task of the product manager. The product portfolio—the original resin plus its alloys and blends—because of new inventions and the addition of ABS, was more densely packed than ever. But each item in the portfolio required positioning, and priorities had to be set within the portfolio—which item to emphasize, which to phase out.

One product manager described the portfolio problem:

> Certainly this is our most important function. If you look at our LEXAN resin product line, depending on the grades, we price between $2.75 and $1.65 per pound. Our NORYL resin price range is between $2.30 and $1.30 per pound, and CYCOLAC resin from $1.65 to $1.00. The overlaps are significant, and depending upon plant utilization and raw material cost fluctuations, the total cost of manufacturing may not vary that much among these products. We have to mix a lot of numbers, judgments, and just plain gut feel before we all agree on which product to push in a given application.

Resources

To accomplish these tasks, the product managers had little direct authority. They did not have direct control over the budget, nor did they participate in the performance reviews of other functions. Although product managers usually had access to Hiner, they could not count on resolving every dispute through the time-consuming process of going up the chain of command. Instead, they had to rely on influence—communication, coordination, and personal relationships.

The product manager's success was judged on many factors, including margin, average selling price, and volume increase over the previous year. But less-quantitative measures were equally important, such as penetrating an important new market or managing a technological breakthrough. Product managers were also judged on intangible but critical abilities to be team players and to secure the most for the team.

But the product manager was not judged on the bottom line, the overall profitability of the product. Thus, the product manager was not a general manager. In the new structure, only Glen Hiner and three general managers (Americas, Europe, and Pacific) had profit and loss responsibilities.

Criticism

The system of product managers clearly had its critics. First, some managers felt that replacing a powerful business unit chief with a product manager with no formal authority cost the company speed in its decisions: "Speed to market is critical here. The life cycle is very short, but the reorganization has destroyed vertical coordination. No one can make a decision. We might make better decisions, but we definitely make slower ones."

Second, the broad nature of the product manager's job led to some resentment. According to one manager:

> Now they've become a monster. We can't get rid of them. They're developing their own subculture. PM shouldn't be a place to punch a ticket—it should be a window into technology as well as a chance to improve one's skills at coordination. Now they've turned into a brand manager, looking for things to do. They are appropriating responsibilities.

The new functional structure offered no flag to rally around. In the old divisional structure, team identities and working relationships were forged around the product, even down to slogans (e.g., "ULTEM marches on!"). Claimed a product manager:

> This change from a dedicated product organization to a functional matrix has left us with no clear identity. It forces people to identify more with the company than with the product. In the old days there were people who would take a bullet for LEXAN resin. You can't duplicate that kind of loyalty for anything.

Many executives felt that the old entrepreneurial spirit was lost. Decisions formerly made by a single product division head were now made by a committee. "Bureaucracy has now become a part of corporate life," complained a senior executive.

Other executives felt that the consultative style slowed the company. One described the difficulty: "It's harder to invent new products. Too much coordination and teamwork is required. We have gained synergy but lost creativity. And all this coordination begets politicking."

Many managers at GE Plastics had variously argued that in fact nothing was wrong with the new functional structure. What was needed was some clarity and redefinition of the product managers' roles and responsibilities. It was the process and not the system that needed attention, they suggested. A product manager offered this view:

> Business is not the same as it was five years ago. The market is very tough, and when things go wrong, the product management function takes the rap. That draws attention away from the real issues in the field. Do we really present ourselves as a unified and united supplier of premium engineering plastics to the customer? In many cases we don't. Product management, marketing, and sales have all got to work together in unison; we cannot pull in different directions.

Problems of Global Marketing

Pressure for Uniformity

There was considerable concern at the top as to how best to organize for the global environment of the 1990s. As manufacturing moved beyond national boundaries, suppliers did the same. Auto companies, for example, expected to be able to secure polymer for bumpers at their factories on four continents. One executive summarized the key issue:

> The problem is compounded when we consider "transplants" [the Japanese companies with manufacturing facilities in the United States]. Our Tokyo marketing staff calls on designers at a company's headquarters in Japan while sales guys here are banging on the plant's door in Tennessee. That's not just cross-functional coordination, that's global coordination—not just across marketing and sales, but across Americas and Pacific. How do we deal with multinational firms?

A senior product manager, echoing this interpretation, added:

> Businesses are all getting global. Whether companies are global or not, they have to act globally because key competitors are often global. So everybody in the industry, whether a leader or not, has to keep up with the technology. The computer companies like IBM, Apple, Nixdorf, Siemens, and Honeywell started the global revolution. But now appliance companies are getting global. Look at Electrolux, for instance. I would guess that 50 to 60 percent of our U.S. customers (OEMs), 40 percent of European customers, and 80 to 90 percent of Japanese customers are all global. But that does not mean that we have to offer them uniform prices all over the world. Customers will continue to demand that and we'll continue to say no. Our production capacities, constraints, and costs are different from country to country. We cannot do business by offering the lowest common denominator. Being global goes beyond pricing, and our customers understand that. They seek consistent and uniform product policy, technology development, and applications engineering.

The drive for uniform product policy, technology, and applications engineering favored the players who could organize themselves globally. GE had several advantages because of its presence in three important regions of the world. But with that advantage came unexpected problems. A top manager explained his most recent dilemma with respect to a global camera manufacturer:

Chapter 42   General Electric Plastics

We were in keen competition with Bayer's BAYBLEND [a blend of polycarbonate and ABS] in the United States. So we sold them our CYCOLOY resin [GE's brand name for a similar blend] here, but the [camera] company's headquarters in Japan now wants the same there. That really gets our Japan managers very upset. They have always sold NORYL resin there, and have maintained a profitable position because of our strong position for NORYL resin in Japan. Specifying CYCOLOY resin would open up the competition from a whole host of equivalent Japanese blends, and they are now really worried about their long-term market share.

Diversity

Describing the differences among the United States, Europe, and Japan, GEP's worldwide marketing manager Uwe Wascher explained:

The United States is rather commerce oriented, whereas Japan and Europe are more scientific/engineering oriented. In the last decade Japan has led the way in terms of production technology and process improvements; the United States lags behind. In the United States, the buying mentality focuses on cost per pound, whereas in Japan and Europe, the engineering and innovation considerations often supersede price.

Take a concept like JIT, for instance. In the United States just-in-time means that the manufacturer wants the parts or components in time, often overnight. On the other hand, in Japan, JIT means that the manufacturer will instigate the supply chain process just-in-time for the supplier to efficiently complete the order fulfillment. The actual supply itself might take a couple of days or weeks depending upon the nature of the order. Such a process fosters partnership rather than an adversarial attitude. Relationships with customers, consequently, are stable, loyal, and very partnership-oriented in Japan and Europe. Once an early commitment is established, the business is ensured.

The United States, on the other hand, is a haven for the free market: very competitive, with multiple vendors. It is very difficult to know where the business will go. Though engineers are involved, purchase managers and administrators have a bigger say here. On the positive side, there is less need to invest in engineering resources up front, but unfortunately the chances of getting the business are less clear until late in the game.

Regarding the need for improved effectiveness in Japan, Wascher added:

The notion of Japan Incorporated is true. They have more cooperation among companies and fewer lawyers. A Japanese plastics company would always prefer to buy from a Japanese rather than a foreign company. The Japanese plastics players are all small in relation to GE, Bayer, Dow, and the like. I don't see how they can have cost or technology advantages, yet they dominate the Japanese market. They are not so good at basic research. They are outstanding in applications. We certainly need a stronger customer base in Japan. Their auto companies will teach us new and innovative ways to use and mold plastic. We need that because applications drive our business. But we shouldn't forget the other Asian countries—actually they are the fastest growing markets for our plastics anywhere in the world.

GEP's European operations, on the other hand, were considered to be in excellent shape. A top GEP executive observed:

We have a much better spirit of camaraderie and teamwork in our European operations. The country managers and sales and marketing personnel are all local nationals. Within each country they work together as a tight-knit unit, and do the best they can to come out looking good to headquarters [i.e., Bergen op Zoom]. The British, French, German, and other teams compete to show how good they are. That doesn't happen in our U.S. operations; our three regions are too vast and too diffused to generate that kind of spirited rivalry.

"We are much stronger than Bayer," claimed Mr. Wascher.

Bayer is a West German company; we are a European company. As an American company starting off in Holland, we were forced to go with a national sales/marketing team in each country. Unlike Bayer, which had the luxury of a home market and could extend its arms from Germany, we could not. By force of choice we had to be pan-European. Without doubt, English will become the de facto pan-European language after 1992, consequently giving us further advantages.

Growth with Stability

While Hiner and his team were proud of GEP's achievements and contributions in the context of the GE corporation's other 14 major businesses, leadership also had its responsibilities. Jack Welch, the chief executive of the GE corporation, had clearly and unequivocally communicated to Hiner that GE Corporate needed GEP's financial leadership, at least, for the next five years. To put it simply, while GEP reorganized itself to meet the challenges of the 1990s, there would be no room for a slowdown of its excellent performance.

CHAPTER 43
Variety versus Value: Two Generic Approaches to Product Policy

This chapter follows the dynamics of product line evolution in an industry as a whole. It traces six phases starting with a custom design on to the coalescing of demand and supply around a dominant design. The cycle of proliferation then repeats itself as suppliers and customers attempt to find new ways to differentiate their offering and make profits. This chapter discusses the underlying interactions between the suppliers and customers, as well as suppliers among themselves, that drive the tension between "diverse specification" and "universal benefits."

The marketing executive exploded:

We are in the cosmetics business. We can't offer a lipstick line with fewer than 36 colors. Our customers buy color. We even call the industry "*color* cosmetics." If you can't make 36 colors in your factory, we should get someone who can!

The manufacturing manager stood up, looked away from the conference table and retorted:

You have never understood finance and profits! You only think about sales. You have no conception of inventory management, setup costs, and return problems. In fact, you don't know a damn thing about business. All of our product lines are too long! In each one a few items make up most of our volume. But, no, you need a "full line." We aren't going to introduce still another line with 36 colors because my people and I just won't do it.

He then stalked from the room.

This confrontation is one of many which occurs on a regular basis. The issue is product line length. The sides are generally drawn between marketing and sales managers on one side demanding "a full line" and manufacturing and logistics people on the other fighting for "a more rational approach to product line management."

This note was prepared by Benson P. Shapiro.
Copyright © 1987 by the President and Fellows of Harvard College.
Harvard Business School note 587-119.

The problem is important in many industries. The heat it generates is often overwhelming. The anger and frustration permeate management meetings and lead to deeper, broader interfunctional schisms.[1] And there is little light to be shed on the problem. It seems often to be a matter of bias and "professional dogma."

The purpose of this chapter is to shed light on the topic and to provide a general framework for analysis. It will not address the question of whether or not to add a particular item to a product line.[2] Instead, it provides a conceptual framework for understanding the different points of view and a process for making decisions about product line length. Perhaps most important it demonstrates the dynamic nature of product line length decisions. The appropriate length at one time is probably not going to be the appropriate length at another. Most of the focus here will be on industrial and commercial products instead of consumer products. The thinking can be applied to all product areas, however, perhaps even including services.

The best place to begin to understand product line management is with the customer and the way in which customers choose among competing products.

Industrial Customer Trade-Offs

Customers want two substantially different sets of product attributes or characteristics: *universal benefits* and *diverse specifications.*[3] Universal benefits are those product attributes which every customer wants; for example, durability and reliability. Customers' willingness and ability to pay for these attributes differ, but all would prefer a more durable or more reliable product over a less-durable or less-reliable product at the same price.

Diverse specifications, however, are not attractive to all customers. Some actively want them and some actively do not. In the consumer goods market, most of the differences in desires for diverse specifications come primarily from differing tastes. One man prefers a paisley tie, while another actively dislikes such a tie. Other diverse specifications relate to size. The small-footed woman wants the size 5 shoe which would be of no use to the large-footed woman.

In the industrial marketplace, diverse specifications occur because of the fit between the product and other parts of the customer's usage system. The fit can be physical or can relate to the operating traditions of the user. A chemical plant that is piped in 10-inch stainless steel piping will not find 9- or 12-inch piping easy to fit into its system. The 32-bit computer manufacturer (the number of bits measures the size of the units processed) will not be able to use 16-bit memory units. Machine operators accustomed to working with a brand of equipment will generally prefer to

---

[1]For more on marketing/manufacturing frictions, see "Can Marketing and Manufacturing Coexist?" by Benson P. Shapiro, *Harvard Business Review,* September–October 1977, pp. 104–14.

[2]For more on a process to add or delete items see Barbara B. Jackson and Benson P. Shapiro, "New Way to Manage Product Line Decisions," *Harvard Business Review,* May–June 1979, pp. 139–49.

[3]These terms were coined by Peter Patch, a doctoral candidate at Harvard Business School, based upon the work of Kelvin Lancaster, a British economist.

stay with that brand unless there is some clear reason to change. Deere bulldozer operators will not, in all likelihood, welcome a change to International Harvester or Caterpillar.

Separation of attributes into universal benefits and diverse specifications makes it easier to discuss the customer's product choice decision: The decision comes down to trade-offs among various universal benefits and between universal benefits and diverse specifications. For example, one customer might prefer more durability at a higher price than a second customer who is more price sensitive. Both want durability and low price, but the second is relatively more interested in price and less in durability. Still another customer might accept the low level of durability and pay the higher price but only for a product that included a diverse specification of great interest. Our three customers thus have the following interests:

	Low Price	Long Durability	Diverse Specification
Customer 1	Low	High	No
Customer 2	High	Low	No
Customer 3	Low	Low	Yes

The marketer who looks at this situation has a series of decisions to make regarding product policy. The important assumptions underlying the decisions are:

1. At any given price, all customers prefer more durability.
2. At any given level of durability, all customers prefer a lower price.
3. Customers trade off price for durability.
4. Some customers want diverse specifications and are willing to pay more, accept lower durability, or both.

The decisions which the marketer has to make are:

1. What durability level to offer.
2. What to charge at each level.
3. What diverse specifications to offer.

The first and third of these decisions focus primarily on product policy. The second, also related to product policy, is primarily concerned with pricing. The second is also a much-less-permanent decision because price can be changed much more easily than product policy.

Underlying the two product policy decisions is another decision that is even more fundamental: the number of items in the product line. There seem to be two essentially different approaches, given this discussion of diverse specifications and universal benefits.

Two Approaches to Product Policy

One product policy alternative is to develop a *variety*-oriented product line that stresses the fit of each item to divergent customer needs. The variety will include two kinds of diversity. One kind is in the trade-off of universal benefits against each other. In the example above, the items in the product line would vary in the durability and price of each item. The line might begin with a low-price/low-durability unit; each successive unit would have increasing durability at a higher price.

The second kind of diversity involves diverse specifications. Each item in the line would have a different mixture of diverse specifications in addition, perhaps, to the different mix of universal benefits deriving from the first form of diversity.

Returning to our simple example of one diverse specification and two universal benefits (price [or low price] and durability), we might picture the product line as follows:

	Price	Durability	Diverse Specification
Item 1	High	High	No
Item 2	Low	Low	No
Item 3	High	Low	Yes

This line has three items and covers the feasible set of possibilities. A low-price, high-durability product would not be possible because it would not be profitable: Durability adds cost.

If one expands the example to multiple levels of durability and price, and several universal specifications, the product line increases in potential size and diversity:

Durability	Diverse Specification A	Diverse Specification B	Diverse Specification C
High	Yes	Yes	Yes
•			
•			
•			
High	Yes	No	No
•			
•			
•			
Low	No	No	No

If the number of universal benefits increases, the size and diversity of the potential product line increases further.

Because the variety approach to the product line views this diversity as an opportunity, the variety marketer attempts to offer many items. A variant of this approach is to offer a smaller number of items in a segment of the possible offerings. The theory is the same: Offer a product that best meets the customer's desire for both a unique set of diverse specifications and a unique mix of universal benefits. Each customer or perhaps each usage or purchase situation is approached as an opportunity to be met.

Developing an item for each unique mix of universal benefits trade-offs and diverse specifications is, however, expensive. The product line must consist of many items or an intense coverage of a limited area of the market, which implies an engineering function which can either custom design each item or design many different items efficiently. The manufacturing operation must cope with the production of many different lots with low unit sales. The logistics function must be able to process and monitor many small orders and to ship a diverse set of small individual orders. The applications engineers and repair people must be able to handle custom designs or a great diversity of designs. Finally, the salespeople and/or distributors must be able to help customers choose among the many options. All of this support is expensive and cannot be spread over many units per item.

The variety product line can be profitable only if the customer values the unique mix of product attributes (trade-offs among universal benefits and specific choices of diverse specifications) enough to pay for the intense service and a profit. (I will return to the issue of how to operate in a variety approach after I discuss the second product line approach.)

Some customers are willing to compromise their interest in a specific mix of universal benefits and diverse specifications in order to save money. They will trade off a particular mix of universal benefits and give up diverse specifications in return for more of another universal benefit—low price. The price can be lowered substantially because of the different operating logic behind this product line. The central concept to the customer is *value:* utility per dollar.

The value-oriented product line does not meet the needs of individual customers or usage or purchase situations. Instead, the opportunity to obtain more universal benefits per dollar, even if diverse specifications are sacrificed and even if the mix of universal benefits is not ideal for the customer or situation, causes the customer to purchase the product. While the variety product line attempts to *meet customer needs,* the value product line attempts to *pull customer demand to an alternative* item that provides better value or more utility per dollar.

The value approach works because the limited product line leads to economies in the engineering and design, manufacturing, logistics, applications engineering, field service, and sales functions. There are few designs, so engineering costs are amortized over many units. The short product line leads to long production runs with attendant opportunities for learning curve savings and the application of automated manufacturing technology. Setup time is amortized over the long runs. Logistics has a simpler job with fewer different items to order, inventory, and ship. Applications engineers and field service people can more efficiently support the short line. And salespeople have a faster, easier story to tell and less to learn.

EXHIBIT 1   Value versus Variety

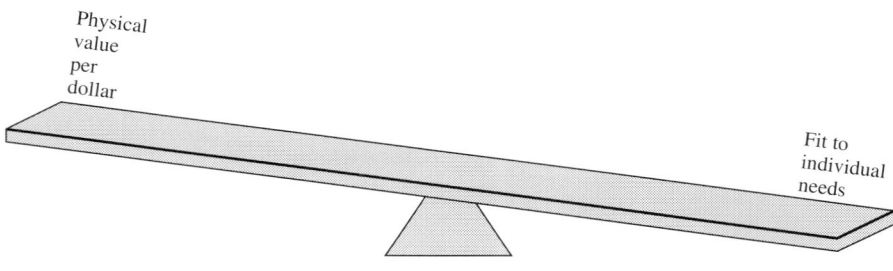

To the customer, the trade-off is between the *fit to his or her individual needs* of the variety approach or the *higher physical utility per dollar* of the value approach. Exhibit 1 shows the trade-off.

From the customer's point of view, the nature of the trade-off will be driven by three things:

1. The utility of diverse specifications and a unique mix of universal benefits.
2. The utility of price.
3. The price difference between the unique item that fits the customer's needs and the compromise item which offers more physical utility per dollar.

The price difference, item 3 above, in turn, is determined by the cost differences between providing the unique item and the compromise item, and the marketer's pricing approach.

Variations on the Variety Theme

Before looking more deeply into the marketing implications and the dynamics of change between value and variety product lines, I would like to create a more detailed taxonomy of product policies by dividing the variety-oriented approach into two further approaches. (See Exhibit 2.)

At the exhibit's right-hand extreme is the custom-designed item. These items can be, within the limits of feasibility, designed and built to meet the precise trade-offs in universal benefits and the precise set of diverse specifications desired by a customer. If, for example, the customer wants a retail display case which is 19 feet, 3⁵⁄₃₂ inches long, the custom-design manufacturer can supply it if the tolerances can be met and if the size is not too great to be accommodated in its factory. If the manufacturer can operate to a tolerance of 1/32 of an inch and can accommodate cases up to 20 feet long, it can make any case between the minimum feasible, let us say 2 feet, in 1/32 inch increments up to 20 feet. Thus, it has a product line of 18 feet (20 – 2) times 12 inches per foot times 32 32nds per inch, or 6,912 variations. It is easy to see that if the manufacturer offers a range

EXHIBIT 2   Variety—Special Purpose and Custom Design

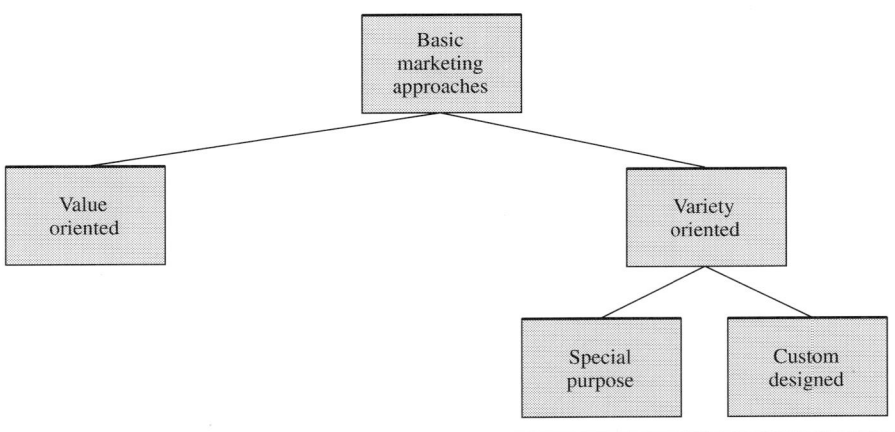

of custom heights and widths, materials, lighting options, cooling and heating options, and so on, the line for a product as simple as a retail display case can become long indeed. It will not be infinite because there are tolerance and size limits, but it can grow very fast because of the multiplicative nature of the combinations.

The custom-designed product line includes a great deal of service content in engineering and design, specification, applications engineering, field service, and sales. Custom-designed products can be mechanical, electronic or electrical, or chemical. One can, for example, purchase custom-compounded chemicals. Some custom products such as power plants are even built at the customer's site. It is difficult to differentiate between the marketing of a service and a truly custom on-site constructed product.

Special-Purpose Products

Because the cost of true custom-designed products is so high, some marketers offer a more limited form of variety: special-purpose items. Often, these products are custom built from a standard set of basic units with accessories and options. A lathe, for example, may be offered in several basic sizes, but with a variety of options concerning motor size, feeds, speeds, control electronics, and the like.

We see the same distinction in the consumer goods area where homes and clothing (e.g., suits and dresses) can be purchased as custom designs and autos from some manufacturers can be specified with a wide range of options and accessories (special purpose).

In some situations, the special-purpose units are not custom built. Instead, the manufacturer has a broad product line designed to meet the precise needs of many customers, or purchase or usage situations. The difference between custom-designed and more standard special-purpose items is just like the distinction between the variety and the value orientations. Custom-designed products offer more fit to a specific need in terms of trade-offs among universal benefits and choice of diverse specifications than special purpose units, unless the special-purpose unit has the precise attributes the customer desires. As the number of relevant universal benefits and diverse specifications increases, the likelihood of a special-purpose unit offering the precise mix any given customer wants goes down. Thus, in the move from custom designed to special purpose, the process of compromise has begun. As one moves further to the left in Exhibit 2 from special-purpose variety to value, the amount of trade-off increases. The lure of a lower price for greater physical utility convinces the customers to trade off precise fit for more physical utility per dollar.

In the value-oriented product line a manufacturer can offer only a few items. The customer makes the compromise to obtain the greater physical value per dollar.

Who Wants Variety?

To the industrial customer, the utility of the added variety will be a function of:

1. The utility of the diverse specification.
2. The utility of the unique trade-offs among universal benefits desired.
3. The customer's sensitivity to price.
4. The vendors' price policies as reflected in the price difference between the good-fit custom-designed products or special-purpose products and the more compromised value-oriented items.

While it is impossible to predict all situations, it is possible to generalize about the four factors above.

By and large, the utility of diverse specifications varies greatly by situation. In general, diverse specifications are more important than trade-offs among universal benefits. Interest in diverse specifications is probably the most powerful market segmentation variable, and does the most to define the limits of a product's applicability. A company, for example, with Apple Macintosh computers cannot use accessories, supplies, or software designed only for IBM and IBM-compatible personal computers. Many diverse specifications are binary; that is, they either exist or do not. Most of the remainder are discrete, such as the size of piping which, in large-process pipes, is in inches. Thus, diverse specifications are normally not an issue of "a bit more here" or "a bit less there." They either are or are not. Paper is either legal size (14 inches long) or it is not. Such variables are thus powerful determinants of buying behavior.

In addition, diverse specifications are analytically difficult to handle because they are discontinuous and their relationship to purchase intentions or purchase behavior is discontinuous and very bumpy. Hence, while an increase in durability may increase buying intentions—and thus sales—gradually, introducing a diverse specification will cause an abrupt change. The difference can be seen in the graphs on the next page:

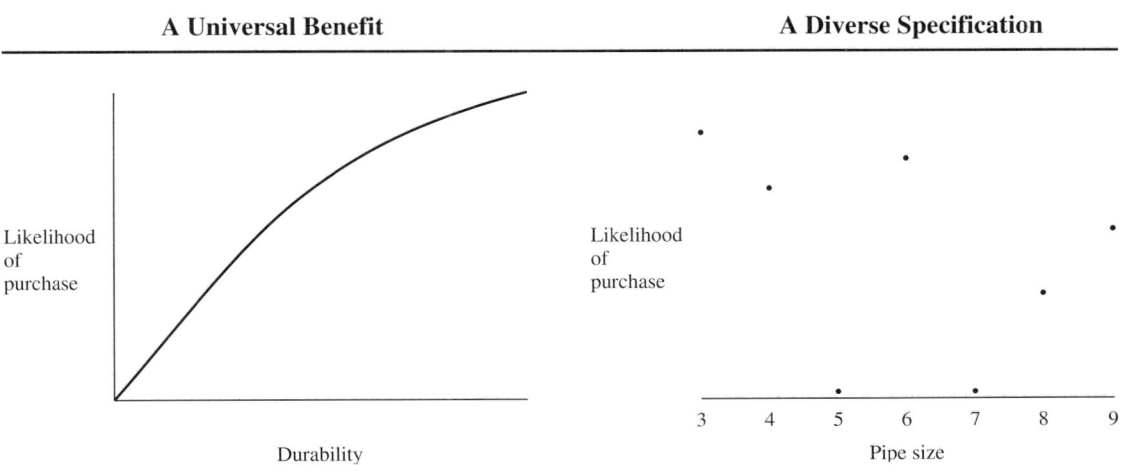

In the graph on the right, purchase is possible only at pipe sizes of 3, 4, 6, 8, and 9 inches. Sizes between the inches do not sell at all, and even 5- and 7-inch pipe does not sell.

Most buyers who want fit and are thus interested in the variety-oriented (special-purpose and custom-designed) product lines are interested more in diverse specifications than in universal benefits. It is easier to compromise among universal benefits because of their more continuous nature. Therefore, unique positions in the trade-off among universal benefits are less important and less powerful to the buyer, and thus to the seller, than unique collections of diverse specifications.

The trade-off between price, on the one hand, and the unique collection of universal benefit trade-offs and diverse specifications, on the other, tends to depend upon the impact of the product on the customer's performance system and on the customer's cost position. Products with high cost-impact and low performance-impact tend to be more amenable to the value approach because the customer is price sensitive and relatively attribute insensitive. This leads to the chart shown in Exhibit 3.

The diagonal going from lower right to upper left in Exhibit 3 also is a price sensitivity diagonal. Customers in the upper left will be more price sensitive. This means that the most appropriate pricing policy for a vendor is to obtain higher margins in the lower right and to decrease margins as the product moves toward the upper left.

The underlying driving force then becomes the customer's interest in product attributes compared to the customer's interest in price. The interest in product attributes breaks down into the interest in diverse specifications and the interest in a unique trade-off among universal benefits. The interest in diverse specifications, as argued earlier, is likely to be higher.

EXHIBIT 3 **Product Line Appropriateness as a Function of Customer Impact**

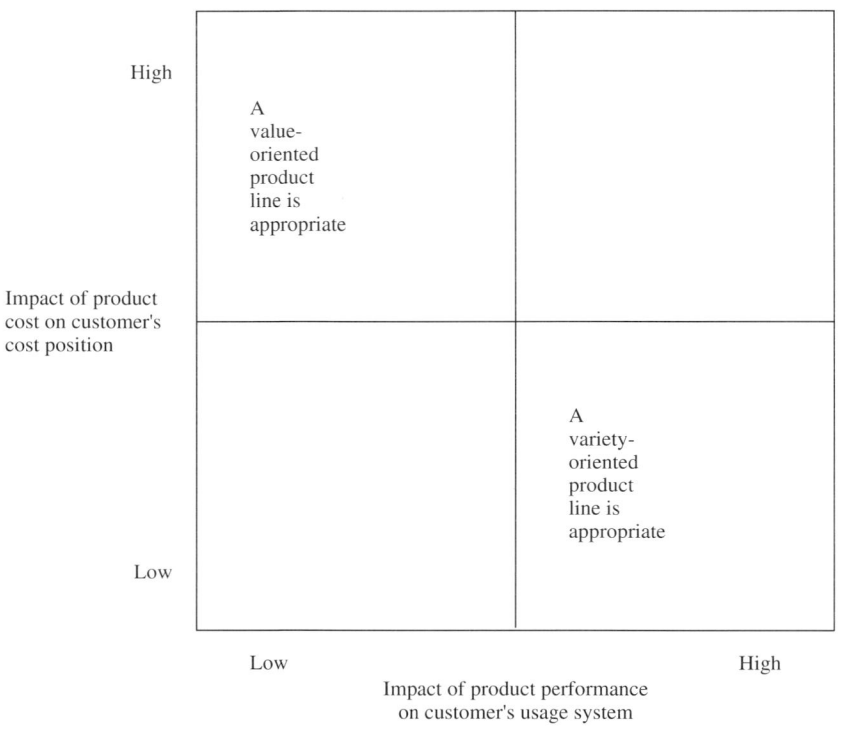

The Dynamics: The Product Evolution Trajectory

Innovation and change in product lines can be related to the variety and value approaches by the product evolution trajectory. Almost every industrial market begins with a few customized units which are experimental attempts to mate a technology and a need. At this stage, neither the customer nor the supplier knows what is possible or what is needed except in the broadest terms. The potential benefits for the customer and potential profits for the vendor are great, so both devote substantial support to the project. Early computers and robots and most industrial markets have gone through this type of embryonic period. We now see it in integrated factory automation systems, robot vision systems, and local area networks to connect telecommunications and computer equipment.

As the industry develops, it evolves into a phase of special-purpose units to do things that would otherwise not be possible. Computer-controlled machine tools maintain tolerances and provide efficiency not previously possible, for example. Engineered plastics, offering new combinations of characteristics, is another example.

A Dominant Design Arises

At some point in the development of the industry a dominant design arises that provides great universal benefits per dollar. This creates a value-oriented product line. Because the universal benefits per dollar are very high and in all likelihood fairly well positioned with regard to the trade-offs most customers want to make among universal benefits (otherwise it would not develop into a dominant design but would stay as a special-purpose product), growth comes fast. The rapid growth encourages increased production and greater marketing expenditures to spread the word. The production and marketing investments resonate with each other and grow with the market, encouraging competition and coalescing product lines around the new dominant design.

Often the market will develop with two subsets of the value-oriented dominant design. One will be oriented toward higher performance at a greater price and the other will be a stripped-down model offering lower universal benefits at a lower price. The market develops in this fashion because neither vendors nor customers can make fine or difficult distinctions in trade-offs among universal benefits. One group of customers, however, seems more interested in greater universal benefits and another in lower prices. The distinctions are coarse but further market segmentation is difficult. This is particularly true for products that are considerably more complex than the alternatives they replaced. Small business telecommunications equipment would be a good example.

The dominant design and its imitators lead to narrow product lines with few items. Competition tends to be on the basis of universal benefits. The market, both supply by vendors and demand by customers and prospects, coalesces around the dominant design and its close substitutes. Unit volume grows. Prices decrease because of greater manufacturing and marketing economies.

The Demise of the Dominant Design

Over time, however, customers grow more sophisticated in the use of the product, and vendors attempt to gain relief from the intense competition around a limited number of fairly comparable items. Some try to differentiate themselves by service and relationship; others, however, begin to offer important product variations for distinct market segments. Both customers and vendors can now define market segments and particularly diverse specifications, as well as new combinations of universal benefits, because of the growing experience base they have. Customers want special products with unique combinations of attributes, and vendors are anxious to find protected market niches, especially as growth in the core of the market abates. Product proliferation continues until a new technological breakthrough creates the opportunity for a new dominant design.

It is worthwhile to explore the rate at which these changes occur and the driving forces behind them. The relative importance of a close fit to the customer's product specifications on the one hand, and low price on the other, is a primary driving force. The more important the fit, as evidenced by the impact of product attributes on the customer's operating system, the faster the move to proliferate will be, and the slower will be the coalescing around a dominant design. On the other hand, a customer orientation toward price sensitivity will speed the move toward the dominant design and slow proliferation.

Another driving force is the possible differences among products: differentiability. The following circumstances tend to lead to more differentiability, and more and faster proliferation:

1. Number of relevant product attributes.
2. Range of variation across these attributes.
3. Importance of the attributes.
4. Difficulty in measuring the attributes and comparing products.
5. Inability of competitors to duplicate one another's attribute combinations.

A third driving force is the ratio of diverse specifications to universal benefits. By and large, diverse specifications with their discontinuous nature drive the process toward proliferation.

Technological opportunities in terms of the ability of product design engineers to develop a good compromise among universal benefits are a fourth driving force. Closely related is a fifth driving force: the technological opportunities for process engineers to develop scale economies and experience curve benefits. The greater the ability to develop a compromise product and the greater the economies of producing a limited line, the greater the speed to the dominant design and the slower the move to proliferation.

Finally, if the product can be customized in the field by manufacturer service centers, distributors, or the customer, the move toward proliferation will be slowed because the benefits of variety can be gained without proliferation in the factory. In many industries, combinations of short product lines and economical field customization have led to a good mixture of customer benefits.

It is useful to review the driving forces and to categorize them by customer or vendor so that the diversity of influences can be seen:

Force	Source
1. Relative importance of customer fit and price	1. Customer
2. Differentiability	2. Customer and product
3. Ratio of diverse specifications to universal benefits	3. Customer and product
4. Product design opportunities	4. Vendor
5. Economies of scale and experience curve benefits	5. Vendor
6. Field customization	6. Customer/vendor

It is also interesting to note the impact of the product itself on the driving forces. Differentiability is somewhat a function of the product. Computers have many attributes and ways to vary the attributes, while sand offers limited capabilities for differentiation.

A final note on the driving forces is the extent to which the vendors can affect the forces by communication and persuasion. A supplier who wants to encourage proliferation might do so by convincing customers of the importance of diverse specifications. Clearly, such an approach has limitations and is not easy, but it should be explored.

Structural Impact on the Industry

The product evolution trajectory (PET) seems to be a continuing process in many industries and to have substantial impact on the way a company and, indeed, a whole industry develops and evolves. It is instructive to look at the impact of the PET on industry structure and on the way companies must operate to succeed.

The initial phase of the PET begins with the introduction of a few custom-designed and -built units that enable the customer to do tasks previously not feasible. This custom-product phase can last for between a few years and quite some years as the customers and suppliers seek ways to work together with a reasonable set of designs. A critical management skill at this point is the selection of profitable market opportunities. Custom designing, building, and installation is expensive. Vendors who are not careful in identifying the profitable opportunities in terms of market segments, customers, applications, and profits will fail. Pricing is also a critical skill. Many of the hungry pioneering vendors will price their wares too low because they are anxious to "buy into opportunities." Many of the early pioneering firms will invariably fail.

The custom-design phase eventually leads to the development of a smaller set of special-purpose items. They tend to focus around applications identified during the earlier stage. In general, the product is still sold very much on the basis of the fit between the product and its application. At this stage, the vendors must offer considerable sales and technical support. Successful vendors invariably succeed as much through field execution as product design. In fact, a close working relationship with customers is the *only* way to garner the applications and technological information necessary to improve designs. Careful choice of markets and customers remains critical during this phase as well as the first phase.

As the industry continues to grow, a standard dominant design appears. This design tends to make radical changes in the manufacturing, engineering, technical service, marketing, and sales functions of the vendor. The switch from the special-purpose units to the dominant design tends to be accompanied by a major shakeout in the industry. Customers find it much easier to compare different vendors because the dominant design provides an implicit industry standard. In addition, customers have grown more experienced in making good judgments and more confident in their judgments. Competitors have become more imitative of one another's successful design and service features.

During the dominant design phase, industry demand tends to coalesce around a few suppliers and their more or less comparable designs. The lower prices made possible by the lower costs of the shorter product line and resultant long runs, accompanied by substantial industry growth, tend to lead toward an emphasis on a more commoditylike approach to marketing. The ratio of performance to price becomes exceedingly important in the customer's decision-making process. This standard dominant design phase can be easily seen in the microprocessor, personal computer, and robot industries. (Some industries do not grow enough to justify the development of a dominant design, and forever stay oriented toward special-purpose designs.)

The critical skills change abruptly from phase II, special-purpose products, to phase III, the dominant design. Customer and application selection and custom-design skills cease to be important while cost-sensitive product and process engineering and manufacturing move to the fore. The successful vendors of the dominant design must be able to manage rapid unit growth because of both market size and market share growth. Organizations become large, more professional, and more specialized. The loose confederation around special customer needs gives way to a more disciplined approach to volume manufacture, distribution, and sales. The cost structure shifts as product lines narrow. "Commoditization is under way!"

Over time, the customers' interest in having their unique needs met and the vendors' constant search for ways to generate additional sales and profits lead to the development of special-purpose units for market segments of limited size. The fourth phase is driven as much by the vendor's search for market niches which offer growth and profitability as by customer needs. As phase III continues and the dominant design ages, unit volume growth abates and sometimes ends, perhaps even with declines. The drive for growth continues and various suppliers cut prices in attempts to spur growth and gain share. Eventually, market size does not respond to price cuts and costs go down more slowly than prices. Profit pressure grows to intense levels and vendors search for relief.

In this new phase, the market tends to fragment, with the emphasis being the provision of units that meet the unique needs of various market segments, as opposed to the coalescing which took place in the dominant-design phase. The fragmentation continues until a new design emerges which is so attractive to all customers, or to many customers, that it encourages demand to converge on another, dominant design, one that is more advanced. This convergence is again often accompanied by increasing concentration in the industry and a shakeout of marginal producers who cannot respond to the new dominant design.

As the industry continues to evolve, it will go through a series of cycles involving fragmentation followed by coalescing. The fragmentation tends to be driven by the amount of diversity in customer needs and by the ability of the industry to provide that diversity at a reasonable cost. Exhibit 4 shows the cycles in the PET.

Two industries demonstrate the continuing process of coalescing and fragmentation which can occur over a long period despite relative maturity in the industry.

The Day the Dalmatian Cried

The fire engine industry has traditionally been terribly fragmented but now seems to be coalescing. In fact, the strength of the change was so great that American La France, once the strongest competitor in the industry, was forced to close. Appar-

EXHIBIT 4   **Product Evolution Trajectory: Product Line Breadth**

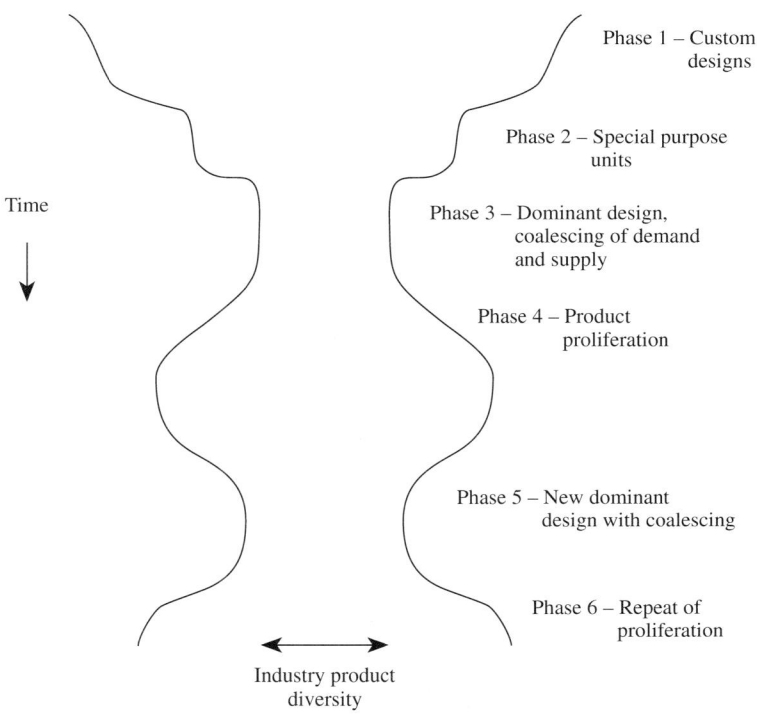

ently, the coalescing was forced by a "shift from custom vehicles to cheaper commercial ones" (*American Metal Market,* January 28, 1985, p. 14). Commercial fire engines are of a much more standard design than the custom ones. Custom units cost between $250,000 and $450,000, while commercial trucks cost between $150,000 and $200,000. Current economic factors and pressures on municipal budgets have forced fire departments to be more cost conscious and less sensitive to their apparent unique needs in their purchase decisions.

The change in the customer buying process was accompanied by a major change in the competitive situation. A new competitor, Emergency One, arose. Emergency One builds its fire engines primarily from aluminum instead of the steel used by other older competitors. The aluminum assembly, combined with a more standard product, enables Emergency One to assemble a unit in 45 days versus six months for American La France. There are also other major differences in the way the two companies operate.

The change in competition often accompanies or causes the industry to move toward a dominant design. It is not unusual for the newest competitor to offer the dominant design and thus to energize the latent customer interest in high universal benefits per dollar. In the Emergency One example, the owner of the company did not even have industry experience.

Neither American La France, nor its parent, Figgie International, seemed to recognize the changes, or were able to move fast enough to incorporate them. It is interesting that when they did recognize change was necessary, they had to hire an outside design organization to develop new models. That relationship ended in a lawsuit.

From Consolidation to Fragmentation

In clear counterpoint to the fire engine example is the current move in the integrated circuit business from general-purpose to custom and semicustom products. For example, Intel, previously a leader in the general-purpose, dominant-design part of the market, is making a "mad dash" to move into more customized products (*Business Week,* August 12, 1985, pp. 25 and 28). Here, the industry is changing in the opposite direction from the fire engine example. Customers are becoming increasingly sensitive to performance, and decreasingly sensitive to costs because of the general and strong degradation of integrated circuit prices. At the same time, various changes in manufacturing and engineering technology are enabling circuit vendors to offer more customization more easily at a lower price.

International Marketing Implications

The variety-versus-value conceptualization can be applied to international marketing. Each country can be viewed as a single market segment. Then the variety-versus-value issue becomes the question of developing a unique product or product line for each separate country. The variety orientation would lead to a separate product or product line for each country, while the value orientation would lead to a more universal or world standard product. Professor Theodore Levitt has made an impassioned plea for greater standardization[4] because, he states, all people want pretty much the same thing. On the other hand, there are many examples of products failing in new foreign markets because the foreign customers rejected a product not customized to their situation and needs.

Probably the greatest experiential evidence in favor of Levitt's approach is Japan's success with limited product lines. Japanese manufacturers stress a universal product line with little customization. Even in automobiles, their products tend to be similar from one country to the next, offering a standard set of accessories as opposed to the custom-built orientation of American manufacturers. This approach builds well upon the renowned ability of Japanese manufacturers to upgrade competitive designs in small ways and to manufacture standard products with great efficiency.

---

[4]Theodore Levitt, "The Globalization of Markets," *Harvard Business Review,* May–June 1983, p. 92.

The original export mentality of the Japanese companies and the long distance (cultural as well as geographic) between them and their customers probably almost forced the approach on them. It also fit well with their background as a more subsistence economy and their willingness as a people to be more standardized than societies like the United States which grew richer earlier. I suspect that countries just emerging from or still in the economic development process have a greater interest in higher universal benefits per dollar than in more diverse specifications. Certainly Henry Ford's success with his Model T in the United States's days of intense economic development emphasized a value orientation at the sacrifice of variety ("You can have any color you want as long as it is black!").

The variety-versus-value issue will probably have to be carefully approached in each industry and perhaps in each country group. It certainly seems to me that a doctrinaire approach like Levitt's is unlikely to succeed in situation after situation despite the author's impressive credentials and colorful rhetoric. The variety-versus-value choice is more likely to be driven by the forces described above.

Management Implications

There are two distinct sets of management implications of the variety-versus-value and product-evolution-trajectory thinking.

The concept of the product evolution trajectory emphasizes the importance of being able to identify the transition points in the industry. It is unpleasant to be a custom-oriented manufacturer (like American La France) when the industry goes to a dominant design. Often the shift to a dominant design is spurred by price sensitivity on the part of the customer industry which leads to a diminution of orders, as well as the emergence of the value-oriented dominant design.

The ability to enter with a dominant design at the right point can add considerably to corporate profits. Kearney & Trecker, for example, introduced its MM-180 numerically controlled machining center as a simple, limited variety unit to appeal to smaller machine shops as well as its traditional larger industrial manufacturing customers. The product met overwhelming success in 1979 and helped to move the industry substantially away from its earlier variety orientation based on special-purpose custom-built units. Demand for the MM-180 tripled company goals in the first two years after introduction.

It is just as painful to be a value-oriented supplier (like Intel) when the industry moves toward fragmentation. Common wisdom suggests that industries only consolidate. The striking example of the integrated circuit business shows that sometimes at least some industries go the other way.

Substantially different skills and a totally different orientation are needed to operate in the value and variety markets. The narrow-product-line orientation of the value approach requires the discipline not to proliferate the product line beyond a few economically produced items. The items must be well positioned to meet the needs of the largest market segments and to draw customers from other market segments. The strength of the line must revolve around maximum universal benefits per dollar. Effective process design and efficient manufacturing, logistics, service, and sales functions are necessities. Product designers must constantly fight to keep the product line narrow and economical (in terms of universal benefits per dollar) for the customer.

At the other extreme, the custom producer must be responsive to unique needs, particularly diverse specifications. It must identify and service many small segments with unique products. The sales force must be able to paint the picture of the benefits of custom products and must focus on the unique needs of customers. Applications engineers must be responsive yet efficient in meeting custom needs. The manufacturing function must be flexible so that it can accommodate the range of products needed. Since most custom-designed products are sold through a bidding process, the company must be able to set bid prices well; otherwise, it will lose bids that would have been profitable and win only those which lead to losses. Finally, because each order is a different item, functional integration among sales, marketing, manufacturing, engineering, and applications engineering is an absolute necessity. In custom producers, the profits are made at the interfaces of the functions, not in any single function.

The special-purpose product line is broad but not unlimited. Management must be sensitive to the need for variety without becoming a custom-oriented producer by accident. Product positioning and a total limitation on the number of items in the line is important. Of particular importance for this type of vendor is being close to the customer so that it can make the critical trade-offs between more items, perhaps at a lower unit volume per item, and not being responsive to a market segment. This approach requires management to walk a tightrope between the value-oriented limited product line and the custom-design supplier.

CHAPTER 44

What the Hell Is "Market Oriented"?

This chapter explains the concept of market orientation in a new, unconventional way. It helps the reader to understand that market orientation is an interfunctional process with distinct characteristics and much more than "being or getting close to the customer." It stresses data gathering, the nature of the decision-making process, and implementation.

The air hung heavy in French Lick, Indiana. A tornado watch was in effect that morning, and the sky was black. In a meeting room in one of the local resort hotels, where top management of the Wolverine Controller Company had gathered, the atmosphere matched the weather. Recent results had been poor for the Indianapolis-based producer of flow controllers for process industries like chemicals, paper, and food. Sales were off, but earnings were off even more. Market share was down in all product lines.

As the president called the meeting to order he had fire in his eyes. "The situation can't get much more serious," he proclaimed.

> As you all know, over the past couple of years everything has gone to hell in a handbasket. We're in deep trouble, with both domestic and foreign competition preempting us at every turn. The only way to get out of this mess is for us to become customer driven or market oriented. I'm not even sure what that means, but I'm damn sure that we want to be there. I don't even know whether there's a difference between being market driven and customer oriented or customer driven and market oriented or whatever. We've just got to do a hell of a lot better.

"I couldn't agree with you more, Frank," the marketing vice president put in. "I've been saying all along that we've got to be more marketing oriented. The marketing department has to be more involved in everything that goes on because we represent the customer and we've got an integrated view of the company."

This reading was prepared by Benson P. Shapiro.
Copyright © 1988 by the President and Fellows of Harvard College.
Reprinted from *Harvard Business Review* 66, no. 6 (November–December 1988), pp. 119–25.

The CEO scowled at him. "I said *market* oriented, not marketing oriented! It's unclear to me what we get for all the overhead we have in marketing. Those sexy brochures of yours sure haven't been doing the job."

There followed a lively, often acrimonious discussion of what was wrong and what was needed. Each vice president defended his or her function or unit and set out solutions from that particular standpoint. I will draw a curtain over their heedless and profane bickering, but here are paraphrases of their positions:

Sales VP: "We need more salespeople. *We're* the ones who are close to the customers. We have to have more call capacity in the sales force so we can provide better service and get new product ideas into the company faster."

Manufacturing VP: "We all know that our customers want quality. We need more automated machinery so we can work to closer tolerances and give them better quality. Also, we ought to send our whole manufacturing team to Crosby's Quality College."

Research and development VP: "Clearly we could do much better at both making and selling our products. But the fundamental problem is a lack of *new* products. They're the heart of our business. Our technology is getting old because we aren't investing enough in R&D."

Finance VP: "The problem isn't not enough resources; it's too many resources misspent. We've got too much overhead. Our variable costs are out of control. Our marketing and sales expenses are unreasonable. And we spend too much on R&D. We don't need more, we need less."

The general manager of the Electronic Flow Controls Division: "We aren't organized in the right way—that's the fundamental problem. If each division had its own sales force, we would have better coordination between sales and the other functions."

Her counterpart in the Pneumatic Controls Division: "We don't need our own sales forces anywhere near as much as we need our own engineering group so we can develop designs tailored to our customers. As long as we have a central R&D group that owns all the engineers, the divisions can't do their jobs."

As the group adjourned for lunch, the president interjected a last word.

> You all put in a lot of time talking past each other and defending your own turf. Some of that's all right. You're supposed to represent your own departments and sell your own perspectives. If you didn't work hard for your own organizations, you wouldn't have lasted long at Wolverine, and you couldn't have made the contributions that you have.
>
> But enough is enough! You aren't just representatives of your own shops. You're the corporate executives at Wolverine and you have to take a more integrated, global view. It's my job to get all of you coordinated, but it's also the job of each of you. I don't have the knowledge, and nothing can replace direct, lateral communication across departments. Let's figure out how to do that after we get some lunch.

All Right, What Is It?

Leaving the Wolverine bunch to its meal, I want to make a start in dispelling the president's uncertainty. After years of research, I'm convinced that the term *market oriented* represents a set of processes touching on all aspects of the company. It's a great deal more than the cliché "getting close to the customer." Since most companies sell to a variety of customers with varying and even conflicting desires and needs, the goal of getting close to the customer is meaningless. I've also found no meaningful difference between "market driven" and "customer oriented," so I use the phrases interchangeably. In my view, three characteristics make a company market driven.

Information on all important buying influences permeates every corporate function. A company can be market oriented only if it completely understands its markets and the people who decide whether to buy its products or services.

In some industries, wholesalers, retailers, and other parts of the distribution channels have a profound influence on the choices customers make. So it's important to understand the trade. In other markets, nonbuying influences specify the product, although they neither purchase it nor use it. These include architects, consulting engineers, and doctors. In still other markets, one person may buy the product and another may use it; family situations are an obvious illustration. In commercial and industrial marketplaces, a professional procurement organization may actually purchase the product, while a manufacturing or operational function uses it.

To be of greatest use, customer information must move beyond the market research, sales, and marketing functions and "permeate every corporate function"—the R&D scientists and engineers, the manufacturing people, and the field-service specialists. When the technologists, for example, get unvarnished feedback on the way customers use the product, they can better develop improvements on the product and the production processes. If, on the other hand, market research or marketing people predigest the information, technologists may miss opportunities.

Of course, regular cross-functional meetings to discuss customer needs and to analyze feedback from buying influences are very important. At least once a year, the top functional officers should spend a full day or more to consider what is happening with key buying influences.

Corporate officers and functions should have access to all useful market research reports. If company staff appends summaries to regular customer surveys, like the Greenwich commercial and investment banking reports or the numerous consumer package-goods industry sales analyses, top officers are more likely to study them. That approach lets top management get the sales and marketing departments' opinions as well as those of less-biased observers.

Some companies that have customer response phones—toll-free 800 numbers that consumers or distributors call to ask questions or make comments—distribute selected cassette recordings of calls to a wide range of executives, line and staff. The cassettes stimulate new ideas for products, product improvements, packaging, and service.

Reports to read and cassettes to hear are useful—but insufficient. High-level executives need to make visits to important customers to see them using their industrial and commercial products, consuming their services, or retailing their consumer goods. When, say, top manufacturing executives understand how a customer factory uses their products, they will have a more solid appreciation of customer needs for quality and close tolerances. Trade show visits provide valuable opportunities for operations and technical people to talk with customers and visit competitors' booths (if allowed by industry custom and show rules).

In my statement on the first characteristic, I referred to "important" buying influences. Because different customers have different needs, a marketer cannot effectively satisfy a wide range of them equally. The most important strategic decision is to choose the important customers. All customers are important, but invariably some are more important to the company than others. Collaboration among the various functions is important when pinpointing the key target accounts and market segments. Then the salespeople know whom to call on first and most often, the people who schedule production runs know who gets favored treatment, and those who make service calls know who rates special attention. If the priorities are not clear in the calm of planning meetings, they certainly won't be when the sales, production scheduling, and service dispatching processes get hectic.

The choice of customers influences the way decisions are made. During a marketing meeting at Wolverine Controller, one senior marketing person said, "Sales and marketing will pick out the customers they want to do business with, and then we'll sit down with the manufacturing and technical people and manage the product mix." Too late! Once you have a certain group of customers, the product mix is pretty much set; you must make the types of products they want. If sales and marketing choose the customers, they have undue power over decisions. Customer selection must involve all operating functions.

Strategic and tactical decisions are made interfunctionally and interdivisionally. Functions and divisions will inevitably have conflicting objectives that mirror distinctions in cultures and in modes of operation. The glimpse into the meeting at French Lick demonstrates that. The customer-oriented company possesses mechanisms to get these differences out on the table for candid discussion and to make trade-offs that reconcile the various points of view. Each function and division must have the ear of the others and must be encouraged to lay out its ideas and requirements honestly and vigorously.

To make wise decisions, functions and units must recognize their differences. A big part of being market driven is the way different jurisdictions deal with one another. The marketing department may ask the R&D department to develop a product with a certain specification by a certain date. If R&D thinks the request is unreasonable but doesn't say so, it may develop a phony plan that the company will never achieve. Or R&D may make changes in the specifications and the delivery date without talking to marketing. The result: a missed deadline and an overrun budget. If, on the other hand, the two functions get together, they are in a position to make intelligent technological and marketing trade-offs. They can change a specification or extend a delivery date with the benefit of both points of view.

An alternative to integrated decision making, of course, is to kick the decision upstairs to the CEO or at least the division general manager. But though the higher executives have unbiased views, they lack the close knowledge of the specialists.

An open decision-making process gets the best of both worlds, exploiting the even-handedness of the general manager and the functional skills of the specialists.

Divisions and functions make well-coordinated decisions and execute them with a sense of commitment. An open dialogue on strategic and tactical trade-offs is the best way to engender commitment to meet goals. When the implementers also do the planning, the commitment will be strong and clear.

The depth of the biases revealed at the French Lick gathering demonstrates the difficulty of implementing cross-functional programs. But there's nothing wrong with that. In fact, the strength of those biases had a lot to do with Wolverine's past success. If the R&D vice president thought like the financial vice president, she wouldn't be effective in her job. On the other hand, if each function is marching to its own drum, implementation will be weak regardless of the competence and devotion of each function.

Serial communication, when one function passes an idea or request to another routinely without interaction—like tossing a brick with a message tied to it over the wall—can't build the commitment needed in the customer-driven company. Successful new products don't, for example, emerge out of a process in which marketing sends a set of specifications to R&D, which sends finished blueprints and designs to manufacturing. But joint opportunity analysis, in which functional and divisional people share ideas and discuss alternative solutions and approaches, leverages the different strengths of each party. Powerful internal connections make communication clear, coordination strong, and commitment high.

Poor coordination leads to misapplication of resources and failure to make the most of market opportunities. At one point in the meeting at French Lick, the vice president for human resources spoke up in this fashion:

> Remember how impressed everyone was in 86 with the new pulp-bleaching control we developed? Not just us, but the whole industry—especially with our fast response rate. Even though the technology was the best, the product flopped. Why? Because the industry changed its process so that the response rate was less important than the ability to handle tough operating conditions and higher temperatures and pressures. Plus we couldn't manufacture to the tight tolerances the industry needed. We wasted a lot of talent on the wrong problem.

Probably the salespeople, and perhaps the technical service people, knew about the evolving customer needs. By working together, manufacturing and R&D could have designed a manufacturable product. But the company lacked the coordination that a focused market orientation stimulates.

Action at Wolverine

Just about every company thinks of itself as market oriented. It's confident it has the strength to compete with the wolf pack, but in reality it's often weak and tends to follow the shepherd. In marketing efforts, businesses are particularly vulnerable to this delusion. Let's return to French Lick to hear of such a sheep in wolf's clothing.

"Look at Mutton Machinery," the vice president of manufacturing was saying.

They've done worse than we have. And their ads and brochures brag about them being customer oriented! At the trade show last year, they had a huge booth with the theme "The Customer Is King." They had a sales contest that sent a salesperson and customer to tour the major castles of Europe.

The sales vice president piped up.

They should send their salespeople for technical training, not to look at castles. We interviewed two of their better people, and they didn't measure up technically. The glitzy trade show stuff and the sexy contest don't make them customer oriented.

No, slogans and glossy programs don't give a company a market orientation. It takes a philosophy and a culture that go deep in the organization. Let's take a look at Wolverine's approach.

It's unlikely that any company ever became market oriented with a bottom-up approach; to make it happen, you need the commitment and power of those at the top. In gathering everybody who mattered at French Lick, Wolverine was taking the right step at the start. And from what we have heard, clearly they were not sugarcoating their concerns.

By the end of the first day, the executives had decided that they knew too little about their own industry, particularly customers and competitors. After a mostly social dinner meeting and a good night's sleep, they began at breakfast on Day 2 to develop a plan to learn more. They listed 20 major customers they wanted to understand better. They designated each of the 10 executives at the meeting (CEO, 6 functional heads, and 3 division general managers) to visit the customers in pairs in the next two months; the sales force would coordinate the visits. All 10 agreed to attend the next big trade show.

They assigned the marketing vice president to prepare dossiers on the 20 customers plus another 10, as well as prospects selected by the group. Besides data on the customer or prospect, each dossier was to include an examination of Wolverine's relationship with it.

Finally, the group singled out seven competitors for close scrutiny. The marketing vice president agreed to gather market data on them. The R&D vice president committed herself to drawing up technical reviews of them, and the financial vice president was to prepare analyses of financial performance. The seven remaining executives each agreed to analyze the relative strengths and weaknesses of one competitor.

Spurred by the president, the group concluded on Day 2 that barriers had arisen among Wolverine's functional departments. Each was on its own little island. The human resources vice president took on the responsibility of scrutinizing cross-functional communication and identifying ways to improve it.

Back at headquarters in Indianapolis, the top brass did another smart thing: It involved all functional leadership so that line as well as staff chieftains would contribute to the effort. Top management quickly pinpointed the management information system as a major point of leverage for shaping a more integrated company view. Therefore, the president invited the MIS director to join the team.

Top management also decided that the bonus plan encouraged each function to pursue its own objectives instead of corporatewide goals. So the controller teamed up with the human resources vice president to devise a better plan, which won the approval of top management.

As a new interest in communication and cooperation developed, the president perceived the need to make changes in structure and process. Chief among these were the establishment of a process engineering department to help production and R&D move new products from design into manufacturing and the redesign of managerial reports to emphasize the total company perspective.

The management group, more sensitive now to the ways people deal with each other, awoke to the power of informal social systems. To make the salespeople more accessible to headquarters staff, the sales office at a nearby location moved to headquarters (over the objections of the vice president of sales). The effort to promote interfunctional teamwork even extended to the restructuring of the bowling league. Wolverine had divided its teams by function or division. Now, however, each team had members from various functions. Some old-timers snorted that that was taking the new market orientation too far. But in a conversation during a bowling league party, the head of technical field service and a customer-service manager came up with an idea for a program to improve customer responsiveness. Then even the skeptics began to understand.

The analyses of customers and competitors identified an important market opportunity for Wolverine. The management group diverted resources to it, and under the direction of the Pneumatic Controls Division general manager, a multifunctional task force launched an effort to exploit it. Top management viewed this undertaking as a laboratory for the development of new approaches and as a showcase to demonstrate the company's new philosophy and culture. Headquarters maintained an intense interest in the project.

As the project gained momentum, support for the underlying philosophy grew. Gradually, the tone of interfunctional relationships changed. People evinced more trust in each other and were much more willing to admit responsibility for mistakes and to expose shortcomings.

Unfortunately, some people found it difficult to change. The sales vice president resisted the idea that a big part of his job was bringing customers and data about them into the company as well as encouraging all functions to deal with customers. He became irate when the vice president of manufacturing worked directly with several major customers, and he told the president that he wouldn't stand for other people dealing with *his* customers. His colleagues couldn't alter his attitude, so the president replaced him.

Wolverine's sales and earnings slowly began to improve. The market price of its stock edged upward. Internally, decision making became more integrative. Some early victories helped build momentum. Implementation improved through cooperation very low in the ranks, where most of the real work was done.

Imitate Larry Bird

A year after Wolverine's first meeting in the French Lick hotel, the management group gathered there again. A new sales vice president was present, and the newly promoted MIS vice president/controller was also there.

This time the executives focused on two concerns. The first was how to handle the inordinate demands on the company resulting from the new push to satisfy important customers. The second was how to maintain Wolverine's momentum toward achieving a market orientation.

Attacking the first item, the group agreed to set major customer priorities. At hand was the information gathered during the year via industry analysis and executives' visits to top accounts. Available to the executives also were several frameworks for analysis.[1] Some accounts fit together in unexpected ways. In some situations, a series of accounts used similar products similarly. In others, the accounts competed for Wolverine's resources.

It took several meetings to set priorities on customers. The hardest part was resolving a dispute over whether to raise prices drastically on the custom products made for the third largest account. Wolverine was losing money on these. "Maybe not all business is good business," the R&D vice president suggested. That notion was pretty hard for the team to accept. But the CEO pushed hard for a decision. Ultimately, the group agreed to drop the account if it did not accede to price increases within the next six to eight months.

On the second matter, the management group decided it needed a way to measure the company's progress. The approach, everybody understood, had to be grounded in unrelieved emphasis on information gathering, on interfunctional decision making, and on a vigorous sense of commitment throughout the organization. They recognized how easy it is to get complacent and lose detachment when examining one's own performance. Nevertheless, the executives drew up a checklist of customer-focused questions for the organization to ask itself (see table below).

Self-Examination Checklist

1. **Are we easy to do business with?**
   - Easy to contact?
   - Fast to provide information?
   - Easy to order from?
   - Make reasonable promises?

2. **Do we keep our promises?**
   - On product performance?
   - Delivery?
   - Installation?
   - Training?
   - Service?

---

[1] They used the account profitability matrix described by Benson P. Shapiro, V. Kasturi Rangan, Rowland T. Moriarty, and Elliot B. Ross in "Manage Customers for Profits (Not Just Sales)," *Harvard Business Review*, September–October 1987, p. 101.

3. **Do we meet the standards we set?**
    Specifics?
    General tone?
    Do we even know the standards?
4. **Are we responsive?**
    Do we listen?
    Do we follow up?
    Do we ask "why not?" instead of "why?"
    Do we treat customers as individual
       companies and individual people?

5. **Do we work together?**
    Share blame?
    Share information?
    Make joint decisions?
    Provide satisfaction?

Two years after the company changed its direction, a major customer asked the president about his impressions of Wolverine's efforts to become market oriented. Here is his response:

> It's proved to be harder than I had imagined. I had to really drive people to think about customers and the corporation as a whole, not just what's good for their own departments. It's also proved to be more worthwhile. We have a different tone in our outlook and a different way of dealing with each other.
>
> We use all kinds of customer data and bring it into all functions. We do much more interfunctional decision making. The hardest part of all was account selection, and that really paid off for us. It also had the most impact. Our implementation has improved through what we call the three Cs, communication, coordination, and commitment. We're getting smooth, but we sure aren't flawless yet.
>
> Last night I watched the Pacers play the Boston Celtics on TV. The Celtics won. Sure they've got more talent, but the real edge the Celtics have is their teamwork. At one point in the game, the Indiana team got impatient with each other. They seemed to forget that the Celtics were the competition.
>
> That's the way we used to be too—each department competing with each other. A few years ago we had a meeting down at French Lick where everything came to a head, and I was feeling pretty desperate. There's a real irony here because French Lick is the hometown of Larry Bird.
>
> When I think about the Celtics and Bird, what working together means becomes clear. If each Wolverine manager only helps his or her department do its job well, we're going to lose. Back when the company was small, products were simple, competition was unsophisticated, and customers were less demanding, we could afford to work separately. But now, our individual best isn't good enough; we've got to work as a unit. Bird is the epitome. He subverts his own interest and ego for the sake of the team. That's what I want to see at Wolverine.

CHAPTER 45

Staple Yourself to an Order

It's fashionable today to talk of becoming "customer oriented." But no matter how many companies flatten their organizations or empower frontline workers, the simple truth is that every customer's experience is determined by the order management cycle (OMC): the 10 steps, from planning to postsales service, that define a company's business system. The authors "stapled" themselves to an order in the 18 companies they studied, literally following it through each step of the OMC. Based on this practical, hands-on approach, they point out potential gaps throughout the order management cycle. The authors offer a process for streamlining order-cycle management.

It's fashionable today to talk of becoming "customer oriented." Or to focus on that moment of truth when customers experience the actual transaction that determines whether or not they are completely satisfied. Or to empower frontline workers so they can delight the customer with their initiative and spunk.

None of this advice, however, focuses on the real way to harness the customer's interests in the operation of a company. The simple truth is that every customer's experience is determined by a company's *order management cycle* (OMC): the 10 steps, from planning to postsales service, that define a company's business system. The order management cycle offers managers the opportunity to look at their company through a customer's eyes, to see and experience transactions the way customers do. Managers who track each step of the OMC work their way through the company from the customer's angle rather than their own.

In the course of the order management cycle, every time the order is handled, the customer is handled. Every time the order sits unattended, the customer sits unattended. Paradoxically, the best way to be customer oriented is to go beyond cus-

---

This reading was prepared by Benson P. Shapiro, V. Kasturi Rangan, and John J. Sviokla.
Copyright © 1992 by the President and Fellows of Harvard College.
Reprinted from *Harvard Business Review,* July–August 1992, pp. 113–22.

tomers and products to the order; the moment of truth occurs at every step of the OMC, and every employee in the company who affects the OMC is the equivalent of a frontline worker. Ultimately, it is the order that connects the customer to the company in a systematic and companywide fashion.

Moreover, focusing on the OMC offers managers the greatest opportunity to improve overall operations and create new competitive advantages. Managers can establish and achieve aggressive goals—such as "improve customer fill rate from 80 to 98 percent," "reach 99 percent billing accuracy," or "cut order cycle time by 25 percent"—and force otherwise parochial teams to look at the entire order management cycle to discover how various changes affect customers. When the OMC substitutes for narrow functional interests, customer responsiveness becomes the overriding goal of the entire organization, and conflicts give way to systemic solutions. The best way for managers to learn this lesson and pass it on to their whole work force is, in effect, to staple themselves to an order. They can then track an order as it moves through the OMC, always aware that the order is simply a surrogate for the customer.

A Realistic Walk Through the OMC

The typical OMC includes 10 activities that sometimes overlap or interact (see "The Order Management Cycle: Inside the Black Box"). While OMCs vary from industry to industry and are different for products and services, almost every business, from the corner ice cream stand to the global computer company, has these same steps. In the following discussion, a number of important lessons will emerge that explain both the customer's experience with a company and that company's ability to achieve ambitious cost and quality goals. For example, as we walk an order through the OMC, note the number of times that the order or information about it physically moves horizontally from one functional department to another. Since most companies are organized along vertical functional lines, every time an order moves horizontally from one department to another it runs the risk of falling between the cracks.

In addition to these horizontal gaps, a second lesson to be learned from tracking the OMC is the likelihood of vertical gaps in knowledge. In field visits to 18 different companies in vastly different industries, we invariably found a top marketing or administrative executive who would offer a simple, truncated—and inaccurate—description of the order flow. The people at the top couldn't see the details of their OMC; the people deep within the organization saw only their own individual details. And when an order moved across departmental boundaries, from one function to another, it faded from sight; no one was responsible for it or the customer.

A third lesson concerns the importance of order selection and prioritization. In fact, not all orders are created equal; some are simply better for the business than others. The best orders come from customers who are long-term, fit the company's capabilities, and offer healthy profits. These customers fall into the company's "sweet spot," a convergence of great customer need, high customer value, and good

fit with what the company can offer. But in most companies, no one does order selection or prioritization. The sales force chooses the customers, and customer service representatives or production schedulers establish the priorities. In these cases, the OMC effectively goes unmanaged.

Finally, the fourth lesson we offer involves cost estimation and pricing. Pricing is the mediator between customer needs and company capabilities and a critical part of the OMC. But most companies don't understand the opportunity for or impact of order-based pricing. Pricing at the individual order level depends on: understanding the customer value generated by each order, evaluating the cost of filling each order, and instituting a system that enables the company to price each order based on its value and cost. While order-based pricing is difficult work that requires meticulous thinking and deliberate execution, the potential for greater profits is worth the effort. And by gaining control of their OMCs, managers can practice order-based pricing.

When we started our investigation of the order management cycle, we recognized first that the OMC, in fact, begins long before there is an order or a customer. What happens in the first step, *order planning,* already shows how and why bad customer service and fragmented operations can cripple a company: the people farthest from the customer make crucial decisions and open up deep disagreements between interdependent functions right from the start. The contention and internal gaming that we saw in order planning is an effective early warning sign of the systemwide disagreements that plague most order management cycles.

For example, people close to the customer, either in the sales force or a marketing group at company headquarters, develop a sales forecast. At the same time, a group in the operations or manufacturing function drafts a capacity plan that specifies how much money will be spent, how many people hired, and how much inventory created. And already these functional departments are at war. Lamented one production planner, "The salespeople and their forecasting 'experts' are so optimistic and so worried about late deliveries that they pad their forecasts. We have to recalculate their plans so we don't get sucked into their euphoria." From their side, marketing people counter distrust with equal distrust: "Production won't change anything, anyhow, anywhere." Ultimately, the people deepest in the organization and farthest from the customer—production planners—often develop the final forecast used to hire workers and build inventory.

The next step in the OMC is *order generation,* a stage that usually produces a gap between order generation, order planning, and later steps in the cycle. In our research, we saw orders generated in a number of ways. The sales force knocks on doors or makes cold calls. The company places advertisements that draw customers into distribution centers or retailers where they actually place an order. Or, increasingly, companies turn to direct marketing. But regardless of the specific marketing approach, the result is almost always the same: the sales and marketing functions worry about order generation, and the other functions get out of the way. Little coordination takes place across functional boundaries.

At the third step, *cost estimation and pricing,* battles erupt between engineers who do the estimating, accountants who calculate costs, a headquarters group that oversees pricing, and the field sales force that actually develops a price. Each group questions the judgment, competence, and goals of the others. Working through the organizational barriers takes time. Meanwhile, of course, the customer waits for the bid or quote, unattended.

Order receipt and entry comes next. It typically takes place in a neglected department called customer service, order entry, the inside sales desk, or customer liaison. Customer service representatives are usually either very experienced, long-term employees or totally inexperienced trainees. But regardless of their experience, customer service reps are, in fact, in daily contact with customers. At the same time, these employees have little clout in the organization and no executive-level visibility in either direction. That means customer service representatives don't know what is going on at the top of the company, including its basic strategy. And top management doesn't know much about what its customer service department—the function closest to customers—is doing.

This unlinked group of customer service reps are also often responsible for the fifth step in the OMC: *order selection and prioritization,* the process of choosing which orders to accept and which to decline. Of course, the more carefully companies think through order selection and link it to their general business strategy, the more money they stand to make, regardless of physical production capacity. In addition, companies can make important gains by the way they handle order prioritization—that is, how they decide which orders receive faster, more complete attention. However, these decisions are usually made not by top executives who articulate corporate strategy but by customer service representatives who have no idea what the strategy is. While customer service reps decide which order gets filled when, they often determine which order gets lost in limbo.

At the sixth step, *scheduling,* when the order gets slotted into an actual production or operational sequence, some of the fiercest fights erupt. Here sales, marketing, or customer service usually face off with operations or production staff. The different functional departments have conflicting goals, compensation systems, and organizational imperatives: production people seek to minimize equipment changeovers, while marketing and customer service reps argue for special service for special customers. And if the operations staff schedule orders unilaterally, both customers and their reps are completely excluded from the process. Communication between the functions is often strained at best, with customer service reporting to sales and physically separated from production scheduling, which reports to manufacturing or operations. Once again, the result is interdepartmental warfare.

Next comes *fulfillment*—the actual provision of the product or service. While the details vary from industry to industry, in almost every company this step has become increasingly complex. Sometimes, for example, order fulfillment involves multiple functions and locations: different parts of an order may be created in different manufacturing facilities and merged at yet another site, or orders may be manufactured in one location, inventoried in a second, and installed in a third. In some businesses, fulfillment includes third-party vendors. In service operations, it can mean sending individuals with different talents to the customer's site. The more complicated the assembly activity, the more coordination must take place across the organization. And the more coordination required across the organization, the greater the chance for a physical gap. The order is dropped and so is the customer. The order ends up on the floor, while different departments argue over whose fault it is and whose job it is to pick it up.

After the order has been delivered, *billing* is typically handled by people from finance who view their job as getting the bill out efficiently and making the collection quickly. In other words, the billing function is designed to serve the needs and interests of the company, not the customer. In our research, we often saw customers who could not understand a bill they had received or thought it was inaccurate. Usually the bill wasn't inaccurate, but it had been put together in a way more convenient for the billing department than for the customer. In one case, a customer acknowledged that the company provided superior service but found the billing operation a source of constant aggravation. The problem: billing insisted on sending an invoice with prices on it. But because these shipments went to subcontractors, the customer didn't want the actual prices to show. The finance function's response: How we do our invoices is none of the customer's business. Yet such a response is clearly self-serving and creates one more gap—and possibly a loss to the company—in the cycle.

In some businesses, *returns and claims* are an important part of the OMC because of their impact on administrative costs, scrap and transportation expenses, and customer relations. In the ongoing relationship with the customer, this ninth step can produce some of the most heated disagreements; every interaction becomes a zero-sum game that either the company or the customer wins. To compound the problem, most companies design their OMCs for one-way merchandise flow: outbound to the customer. That means returns and claims must flow upstream, against the current, creating logistical messes and transactional snarls—and extremely dissatisfied customers.

The last step, *postsales service,* now plays an increasingly important role in all elements of a company's profit equation: customer value, price, and cost. Depending on the specifics of the business, it can include such elements as physical installation of a product, repair and maintenance, customer training, equipment upgrading, and disposal. At this final step in the OMC, service representatives can truly get inside the customer's organization; because of the information conveyed and intimacy involved, postsales service can affect customer satisfaction and company profitability for years. But in most companies, the postsales service people are not linked to any marketing operation, internal product-development effort, or quality assurance team.

At company after company, we traced the progress of individual orders as they traveled the OMC, beginning at one end of the process where orders entered, concluding at the other end where postsales service followed up. What we witnessed was frustration, missed opportunities, dissatisfied customers, and underperforming companies. Ultimately, four problems emerged, which are tied to the four lessons discussed earlier.

- Most companies never view the OMC as a whole system. People in sales think that someone in production scheduling understands the entire system; people in production scheduling think customer service reps do. No one really does, and everyone can only give a partial description.
- Each step in the OMC requires a bewildering mix of overlapping functional responsibilities. As "Why Orders Fall Through the Cracks" on the next page illustrates, each step is considered the primary responsibility of a specific department, and no step is the sole responsibility of any department. But given the fact that responsibilities do overlap, many disasters occur.

Why Orders Fall Through the Cracks

Customer	Steps in the OMC	Sales	Marketing	Customer service	Engineering	Purchasing	Finance	Operations	Logistics	Top Management
Plans to buy	1. Order planning		■					■		Coordinates
Gets sales pitch	2. Order generation	■								Sometimes participates
Negotiates	3. Cost estimation and pricing		■					■		Sometimes participates
Orders	4. Order receipt and entry			■						Ignores this step
Waits	5. Order selection and prioritization		■							Sometimes participates
Waits	6. Scheduling							■		Ignores this step
Waits	7. Fulfillment							■		Ignores this step
Pays	8. Billing						■			Ignores this step
Negotiates	9. Returns and claims	■								Sometimes participates
Complains	10. Postsales service			■				■		Ignores this step

The OMC is everybody's job, but overlapping responsibilities — and lack of management involvement — often lead to confusion, delays, and customer complaints.

Leading role ■   Supporting role ▨

- To top management, the details of the OMC are invisible. Senior executives at all but the smallest operating units simply don't understand the intricacy of the OMC. And people with the most crucial information, such as customer service reps, are at the bottom of the organization and can't communicate with the top.
- The customer remains as remote from the OMC as top management. During the process, the customer's primary activities are to negotiate price, place the order, wait, accept delivery, complain, and pay. In the middle of the OMC, they are out of the picture completely.

Of course, today top managers know that customer service and customer satisfaction are critical to a company's success. In one company after another, managers pursue the same solutions to problems that crop up with customers. They try to flatten the organization to bring themselves and nonmarketing people into direct contact with customers. But while flattening the organization is a fine idea, it's not going to solve the real problem. No matter how flat an organization gets, no matter how many different functions interact with customers face to face—or phone to phone—what the customer wants is something else. Customers want their orders handled quickly, accurately, and cost-effectively, not more people to talk to.

Here's what top managers *don't* do: they don't travel horizontally through their own vertical organization. They don't consider the order management cycle as the system that ties together the entire customer experience and that can provide true customer perspective. Yet all 10 steps are closely tied to customer satisfaction. Because the OMC is an intricate network that almost guarantees problems, top management's job is to understand the system so thoroughly it can anticipate those problems before they occur. That means managers must walk up and down and from side to side, every step of the way.

What's Wrong with Their OMCs?

Consider two brief case studies. One is taken from a specialty materials producer, the other from a custom capital equipment company, but both exemplify the three most common and debilitating problems that plague OMCs.

At the specialty materials company, when customers complained about order cycle time, top managers responded by increasing the work-in-process inventory. As a result, the company could meet customer specifications from semifinished goods rather than starting from scratch. At the custom capital equipment company, when customers complained about slow deliveries, this company increased its manufacturing capacity. As a result, the company always had enough capacity to expedite any order.

Both solutions pleased customers. In addition, the first solution pleased that company's marketers and the second solution pleased that company's operations department. But neither solution pleased top management because, even after several quarters, neither produced economic returns to justify the investments. In fact, both solutions only made matters worse. At the specialty materials company, marketing staff took advantage of the increased work-in-process inventory to take orders and make sales that used up that inventory but didn't generate profits. And at the capital equipment company, manufacturing staff relied on the increased capacity to meet marketing demands but allowed productivity to slide.

The next step both companies took was predictable. Top management, frustrated by the failure of its solution and concerned over continuing squabbles between departments, called on managers across the organization to rally around "making superior profits by providing top quality products and excellent service." Top management translated *top quality* and *excellent service* into catchy slogans and posters that decorated office cubicles and factory walls. It etched the "superior profit" objective into the operating budgets of higher level managers. And it formed interfunctional teams so managers could practice participative decision making in pursuit of the new, companywide goal.

At the specialty materials company, a star sales manager who had been promoted to general manager set up an interfunctional executive committee to assess quarterly revenue and profit goals. We attended one meeting of this new committee. As the general manager sat down at the head of the table to begin the meeting, he expressed concern that the division was about to miss its revenue and profit goals for the second consecutive quarter. Committee members responded by pointing at other departments or making excuses. The vice president of sales produced elaborate graphs to demonstrate that the problem was not caused by insufficient order generation. The vice president of operations produced detailed worksheets showing that many orders had come in too late in the quarter to be completed on time.

However, given their new joint responsibility for profits, both sides agreed to put aside such arguments and focus on "how to make the quarter." All agreed to ship some customer orders in advance of their due dates because those items could readily be finished from available work-in-process inventory. While this solution would delay some long cycle-time orders, the committee decided to sacrifice these orders for the moment and take them up early in the next quarter. And immediately after the meeting, committee members started executing the plan: salespeople called their customers and cajoled them to accept early delivery; manufacturing staff rescheduled the shop floor.

Because of its small size, the custom capital equipment producer didn't need such a formal mechanism for coordinating activities. The CEO simply inserted himself into the daily workings of all functional areas and insisted on hearing all customer complaints immediately. While visiting this company, we heard a customer service representative talking on the telephone to a customer who had just been told her order would be late. The customer objected and asked for an explanation. After much hemming and hawing, the rep explained that her order had been "reallocated" to another customer who needed the product more. The customer on the phone, who purchased products from the company in a relatively large volume, demanded to speak to the CEO and, under the new policy, was connected right away. When the CEO heard this important customer's complaint, he instantly plugged the order back in at the top of the priority list.

In spite of such heroic efforts at both companies, however, customer service continued to slump, and financial results did not improve. At the materials company, customers who expected later delivery of their orders received them unexpectedly early, while those who needed them early got them late. At the capital equipment company, small customers who didn't know the CEO personally or didn't understand the route to him found their orders continuously bumped. At both companies, there was no real progress toward genuine customer satisfaction, improved service, or enhanced profits. Neither company had come to terms with the three critical problems embedded in their order management cycles: horizontal and vertical gaps, poor prioritization of orders, and inaccurate cost estimation and pricing.

The specialty materials company suffered from a fundamental horizontal gap: the marketing and manufacturing departments didn't share the same priorities for customer value, order selection, and order urgency. The real solution to this problem was to encourage and reinforce an understanding between these two critical OMC elements; both the marketing and manufacturing departments needed to address how their order management cycle generated customer value and where they were dropping customer orders in the horizontal handoff. Instead, the company introduced an expensive buffer to cover over the gap between the functions—a semifinished inventory—and, when that failed, it decided to sacrifice real customer service to serve its own short-term financial needs. The immediate solution, simply shipping orders based on the amount of time it would take to complete them, merely pushed the problem from one quarter to the next without addressing the system failure. When the next quarter rolls around, top management will still have to contend with horizontal gaps, a lack of order selection and prioritization, and the inability of their order flow to generate value for the customer.

The same underlying systemic problems existed at the custom capital equipment producer. However, because of the small size of the organization, this company took a simple, politically expedient solution—let the CEO decide—and superimposed it on an expensive financial solution—add manufacturing capacity. If the company suffered from vertical gaps before, where people down in the trenches failed to understand the strategy developed up in the executive suite, the CEO's intervention in customer orders only made the gaps worse. The CEO's involvement didn't address the systemic problems; he merely substituted his judgment and knowledge for that of lower-level employees. The detrimental effects on employee morale more than offset any immediate gains in customer appreciation. Had the CEO invested his energy in helping employees understand how each order creates customer value, has specific costs attached, and involves a certain amount of processing time—and communicated the importance of the whole OMC—he would have generated more customer satisfaction, greater employee morale, and higher profitability without adding expensive manufacturing capacity.

How Can I Fix My OMC?

It takes hard work to improve a company's order management cycle. Most successful efforts involve three basic elements: analysis, system focus, and political strategy. Each plays a different role in overall upgrading of the OMC and requires different implementation techniques, so let's look at each in turn.

1. Analysis: Draw Your OMC—and Chart the Gaps. In the course of our research, we visited a number of companies that were actively engaged in reviewing their OMCs with an eye to improvement. But only two companies had made progress; significantly, both had begun by trying to understand the whole OMC from start to finish. And they hadn't created a diagram on a single sheet of paper or a standard report format. Rather, one of these companies had built war rooms: two adjacent, bunkerlike offices. The walls of both rooms were made of poster board coated with color-coded sheets of paper and knitting yarn that graphically charted the order flow from the first step to the last, highlighting problems, opportunities, and potential action steps. With its multiple and overlapping sheets of paper, the entire chart easily exceeded 200 feet in length.

This visual tool made it possible for different people from different functions and levels in the organization to accept the OMC as a tangible entity. Everyone could discuss the order flow with a clear and shared picture in front of them. And by representing the OMC as a visible, tangible system, the chart guaranteed that disagreements over problems would focus on facts rather than on opinions about how the OMC worked.

A second type of successful analysis requires companies to look at the OMC from the customer's point of view. For example, at one company, the in-house measurement system found that 98 percent of all orders went out on time. But another detailed survey noted that only 50 percent of customers said they were satisfied with deliveries. The company was unable to reconcile the two reports until managers looked at the issue from the customer's angle and compared it with their own point of view. For instance, the customer survey measured the date when the customer actually received the order, but the company's internal system was based on the date when it shipped the order. If an order consisted of 100 items, and the company correctly shipped 99 of the items, the internal report recorded a 99 percent perfect shipment. But the customer, who needed all 100 items before work could begin, recorded the order as a complete failure. And if the order contained an incorrectly shipped item, the company did not register the mistake at all. Of course, the customer did because an incorrect item could easily interfere with his or her ability to get on with the job. Once this company recognized the difference between its perspective and the customer's, it switched to the customer's view as the basis for its tracking system.

Finally, successful companies have explicitly stated that their goals are satisfied customers, higher profits, and sustainable competitive advantage without compromising any of them. One company realized that, while it currently relied on extensive competitive bidding, it would have to start tracking its own win-loss percentages by type of customer, geography, type of order, and other relevant data to meet its larger goals. Managers could then use such data to analyze the relationship between the company's prices and its competitors as well as between volume and price. That, in turn, could translate into better price and market share and less effort wasted on unattractive or unattainable business.

2. System Focus: Put the Pieces Together, Move across Boundaries. Analyzing the order management cycle should underline this fundamental point: the OMC is a system, and executives must manage it as a system. The goal, of course, is to fit together the horizontal pieces into a unified, harmonious whole. To encourage such alignment, managers have a number of tools at their disposal. For example, through the company compensation system, managers can introduce joint reward plans that encourage employees to take a systemwide view of company performance. Or in designing performance measurements, managers can include numbers that reflect performance across boundaries or throughout the system.

Perhaps the most powerful tool managers can use is interfunctional or interdepartmental investments in projects. These expenditures not only bring different units closer together but can also result in substantial financial returns to the company. Of course, in most companies, project champions drive the decisions in the capital budgeting process. Most project champions embrace projects in their own departments or functions. Projects that cross boundaries tend to be orphans because they lack champions; even with champions, such projects require difficult, time-consuming negotiations and are often deferred or fail outright. But precisely for this reason, projects that cross department boundaries can create an integrated atmosphere. When the CEO or chief operating officer personally back investments, the whole organization gets the message that these investments reflect a new perspective. Significantly, interdepartmental projects, usually underfunded for years, often deliver the greatest returns to the company in terms of real improvements and financial results.

A company's information technology system can also play an important role. Computer technology is a crucial tool for integrating many steps of the order management cycle. Direct computer links with customers and integrated internal computer systems, for example, typically result in lower costs and better analysis. And while order processing was one of the earliest activities to be computerized in many companies, it's now time to update and reengineer such systems. When managers walk through the entire OMC, they have the opportunity to ask whether each step can be improved with a computer or, perhaps, eliminated altogether given new technology and processes. With more reliable computer systems, for instance, is manual backup still required? Or can data be captured at the source to avoid repeat entry and inevitable clerical errors?

All of these human resource, management, and information technology tools reinforce the idea, represented by the OMC, that the basic work of the company takes place across boundaries. And because obsolete or unnecessary tasks hinder coordination, all pieces of the system must fit together to meet customer needs in a seamless fashion.

3. Political Strategy: Staple Yourself to an Order. Given that the order management cycle is critical to so many daily operating decisions, it is often at the center of all political maneuverings in a company. Realistically, OMC politics will never go away; working horizontally in a vertical organization is always difficult at best. In our research, we saw hardnosed CEOs and high-ranking divisional general managers forced to admit defeat when confronted with stonewalling functional staffs. We watched young, analytically focused managers with innovative ideas face lack of interest, distrust, and selfishness—and fail miserably. The only people who can succeed at interdepartmental management are usually hardened veterans who understand company politics and can cash in favors. But even they won't succeed without visible support from the top.

One way to improve the situation in any company is to close the loop between the service providers and the strategy setters or, in other words, to tie the company closer together through the order management cycle. Managers should try what we did in our research: we "stapled" ourselves to an order and literally followed it through each step of the OMC. When managers do this, descending from the executive heights into the organization's lower depths, they come into contact with critical people like customer service reps and production schedulers. Reps, schedulers, order processors, shipping clerks, and many others are the ones who know fine-grained information about customer needs. For example, customers might want the product delivered in a drum rather than a bag, or prefer plastic wrapping to Styrofoam.

For most executives in most companies, there is simply no organizational setup for listening and responding to people at all levels. The McDonald's policy of having executives regularly work behind the counter is a worthwhile example of creating such an opportunity. Requiring top managers to work as cashiers and cooks sends a message about the company's values to all staff and enables executives to experience the OMC firsthand.

However, this idea can degenerate into an empty gesture or just another management fad. Take, for example, CEO visits to customers that become official state visits in which corporate heads discuss company relationships at a level of abstraction that has little to do with reality. In most businesses, managers can learn more from salespeople, customer service representatives, production schedulers, and shippers than from a customer's CEO.

All too often, managers who try to focus on internal conflicts directly without charting the OMC find themselves thwarted by politics and recalcitrant employees. But the wall charts and interdepartmental measurements engendered by focusing on the OMC can create an overall vision that transcends vertical politics. The customer is not involved in organizational infighting, and when a company takes on the customer's perspective, politics must take a different and more productive turn.

What Happens After I Fix My OMC?

When companies improve their order management cycles, there are three important benefits. First and foremost, they will experience improved customer satisfaction. Companies will fill orders faster, become more accurate, and generally keep their promises to customers. A well-run OMC has a huge impact on customers: Most OMCs perform worst when demand is greatest, which means that the largest number of customers experience service at its poorest quality. Fixing the OMC reverses that downward trend.

Second, interdepartmental problems will recede. When the OMC is not working well, it both reflects and causes monumental internal strife in a company. People in each department feel they are working hard to achieve their goals; they feel let down by other functions when customer service or financial performance fails to measure up. In the absence of unifying efforts and signs of improvement, the infighting can take on a life of its own and become even more divisive than the operating problems that started the battle. A systemic view helps everyone understand that all departments are interdependent.

Finally, companies will improve their financial performance. We saw companies lose sales, waste labor, and fumble investments because of poor order management cycles. Typically, companies throw money at their problems, building excess capacity, adding inventory, or increasing the body count, all of which are expensive and none of which solve the real problem. The simple fact is that when an OMC is poorly managed, greater sales, lower costs, higher prices, and smaller investments all seem impossible. But when the order management cycle works efficiently, a company can achieve these goals—and more.

CHAPTER 46

High-Tech Marketing: Concepts, Continuity, and Change

The world of high technology is characterized by unusually high levels of market and technological uncertainty; this chapter offers a thorough overview of how that uncertainty affects marketing strategies and tactics. The authors' pragmatic discussion focuses on the distinguishing characteristics of high-tech marketing, the issues that arise from those differences, and how managers can adapt fundamental marketing techniques to address those issues.

Since the late 1970s, interest in "high-tech" marketing has skyrocketed. An industry of market research companies like International Data Corporation, Dataquest, and the Gartner Group has expanded rapidly to provide competitive intelligence and market forecasts for companies that buy and sell technology-intensive products. Regis McKenna, an eminent high-technology marketing consultant, and William Davidow, an Intel executive turned venture capitalist, have written best-selling books that address high-tech marketing issues. The academic community has also been caught up in the enthusiasm; professors have written textbooks and developed courses about high-tech marketing. Several universities now offer a high-tech MBA degree.

Articles about the marketing victories and defeats of companies in the computer, telecommunications, and biotechnology industries have flooded the business press. A generation of high-tech entrepreneurs with a flair for marketing has captured the imagination of the U.S. business community. People like Steve Jobs, founder of Apple Computer and NeXt, Bill Gates of Microsoft, and H. Ross Perot, founder of Electronic Data Systems (EDS), have achieved the celebrity status of rock stars and folk heroes. *High tech* has become synonymous with high excitement.

There has been plenty of hoopla about the fact that high-tech marketing is not the same animal as other product or service marketing. It would be easy to fill a

---

This reading was prepared by Rowland T. Moriarty and Thomas J. Kosnik.
Reprinted from *Sloan Management Review* 30, no. 4 (Summer 1989), pp. 7–17.

library shelf with books and articles that drive that point home. But sales and marketing professionals are not surprised that they might have to sell software, soap, and services three different ways. They are looking for pragmatic advice about how they should adapt their plans and practices, and how to avoid blind alleys and potholes as they drive their marketing machines into high-tech terrain.

The first objective of this article is to provide a framework that explains *why high-tech marketing is different.* The second is to *identify the key issues that arise from these differences.* The third is to assess implications for managers with specific suggestions about *how they should adapt their marketing policies* to increase their chances of success in the fast lane.

Why Is High-Tech Marketing Different?

There is a great deal of confusion about the factors that differentiate high-tech marketing from other kinds of marketing. To clarify the issue, let's begin with the word *technology*—the easy part of high technology.

Technology = Knowledge, Skills, and Artifacts. Technology has been defined as "the practical knowledge, know-how, skills, and artifacts that can be used to develop a new product or service and/or a new production/delivery system. Technology can be embodied in people, materials, cognitive and physical processes, plant, equipment, and tools."[1] This definition includes both product technology (which is embedded in the product itself) and process technology (which is part of the production/delivery system). It also encompasses "management technology," the knowledge of how to market the product and run the business.[2]

High Tech = High Uncertainty about Technology and the Market. Now the hard part—the *high* in high technology. If we define technology as knowledge, skills, and artifacts, it becomes clear that every organization uses a variety of technologies to create and deliver value. What makes high-tech marketing unique? At first glance, there seems to be no consensus among the experts. Consider these three definitions from the marketing literature:

- The U.S. Bureau of Labor Statistics labels any industry having twice the number of technical employees and double the R&D outlays of the U.S. average as high tech.[3]

---

[1] R. A. Burgelman, T. J. Kosnik, and M. Van den Poel, "The Innovative Capabilities Audit Framework" in *Strategic Management of Technology and Innovation,* R. A. Burgelman and M. Maidique, eds. (Homewood, Ill.: Richard D. Irwin, 1987).

[2] N. Capon and R. Glazer, "Marketing and Technology: A Strategic Coalignment," *Journal of Marketing* 51 (July 1987), pp. 1–14.

[3] W. L. Shanklin and J. K. Ryans, Jr., *Marketing High Technology* (Lexington, Mass.: D. C. Heath, 1984).

- Regis McKenna asserts that high-tech industries are characterized by complex products, large numbers of entrepreneurial competitors, customer confusion, and rapid change.[4]
- William Shanklin and John Ryans apply the high-tech label to "any company that participates in a business with high-tech characteristics: the business requires a strong scientific/technical basis; new technology can obsolete old technology rapidly; and as new technologies come on stream their applications create or revolutionize demand."[5]

On the surface, these three definitions illustrate a divergence of opinion about what constitutes high technology. However, two underlying dimensions link the definitions and distinguish high-tech from low-tech marketing situations.

The first dimension is *market uncertainty*—ambiguity about the type and extent of customer needs that can be satisfied by the technology. Ted Levitt has argued powerfully that the difference between selling and marketing is that "selling concerns itself with the tricks and techniques of getting people to exchange cash for your product. . . . Marketing . . . view[s] the entire business process as consisting of a tightly integrated effort to discover, create, arouse, and satisfy customer needs."[6]

Unfortunately, using customer needs as the foundation for marketing in high-tech settings is problematic, because potential customers often cannot articulate what they need. McKenna's and Shanklin and Ryans's definitions of high-tech marketing both include elements of market uncertainty.

Why are the needs in the marketplace likely to be more uncertain in a high-tech situation? Figure 1 shows five questions that frequently raise market uncertainty. First, confronted with a radically new technology, customers may not understand what needs the technology could satisfy. A common example of this problem is the first-time purchase of a microcomputer. Many managers have been forced to choose between desktops and laptops, PCs and Macintoshes, without fully understanding how each would help perform various management tasks.

Second, customer needs, once known, may be subject to rapid and unpredictable changes as the environment evolves. Computer software to support income tax preparation in the face of changing federal tax codes is an example of a product facing a moving target.

Third, there may be questions about whether the market will eventually establish technical standards with which the products must be compatible if the buyer hopes to use them with other products, people, or organizations. The debate over VHS and Betamax formats in the early years of VCRs is an example of this type of market uncertainty.

---

[4]R. McKenna, *The Regis Touch: Million-Dollar Advice from America's Top Marketing Consultant* (Reading, Mass.: Addison-Wesley, 1985).

[5]W. L. Shanklin and J. K. Ryans, Jr., "Organizing for High-Tech Marketing," *Harvard Business Review,* November–December 1984, p. 164.

[6]T. Levitt, "Marketing Myopia," *Harvard Business Review,* September–October 1975, p. 26.

FIGURE 1

Sources of market uncertainty

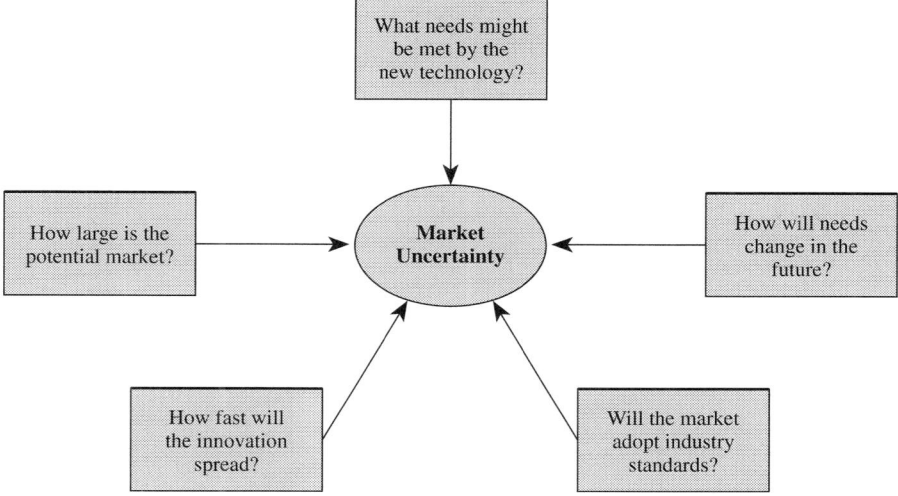

Fourth, predicting how fast a high-tech innovation will spread is difficult. An example is the difficulty market researchers have had predicting the future unit sales of innovations ranging from videocassette recorders to office automation systems.

Finally, all the preceding questions make it difficult to determine the size of the potential market. For example, in 1959, IBM turned down an offer from a startup called Haloid Corporation to invest in a new total xerographic technology because a consulting study predicted that the total market for the Xerox 914 was a mere 5,000 units. A decade later, Haloid (which became Xerox Corporation) had sold 200,000 of the 914s and was a billion-dollar company.

A second dimension that distinguishes high-tech marketing is *technological uncertainty*. Market uncertainty is not knowing what the customers want from the new technology. Technological uncertainty is now knowing whether the technology—or the company providing it—can deliver on its promise to meet needs, once they have been articulated. Technological uncertainty is higher where technology is new or rapidly changing. All three definitions cited above allude to this form of uncertainty.

Figure 2 shows five potential sources of technological uncertainty. The first is a lack of information about a product's functional performance—whether it will do what the seller promises. When computer time-sharing systems were being adopted in the 1970s, both buyers and sellers of computers often encountered this uncertainty when trying to establish the response time (how fast the computer responded to a user at a terminal) of different machines under different usage conditions. Vendors made glowing promises about response time that were difficult to compare across suppliers without the expensive benchmark testing that few customers had the time to conduct.

Second, the company supplying the technology may not have an established track record for delivery. Several situations may elicit uncertainty over delivery. The tendency of computer hardware and software manufacturers to miss promised

FIGURE 2

Sources of technological uncertainty

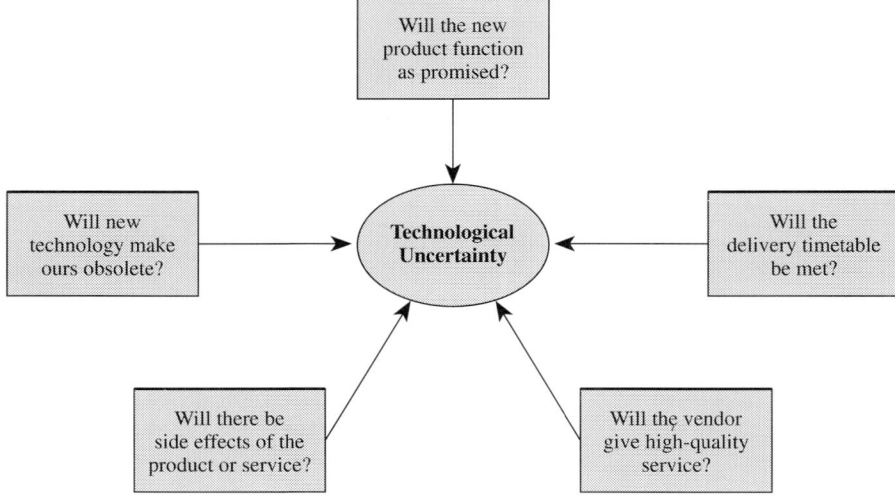

delivery dates for new products is the rule, rather than the exception. Such practices have led to a new term, *vaporware*, which refers to products promised to the marketplace that may never be completed or delivered. Long after the first shipment of new products, shortfalls in the quantity available may occur as the result of manufacturing capacity constraints, often because of a bad guess about the potential market demand for a high-tech product. For example, in 1988, a shortage of dynamic random access memory chips led to shortages of products from many hardware vendors that relied on the chips for their desktop computers. Uncertainty about delivery may also arise from doubts about whether the supplier is financially healthy enough to stay in business. Buyers are reluctant to purchase from a firm that is showing red ink, because of the uncertainty that it raises about the future supply of additional products, parts, and service. While negative cashflow is by no means limited to high-tech firms, the long-term financial viability of a startup is usually more uncertain than that of an older company with an established record of financial performance.

Third, there is uncertainty about whether the supplier of a high-tech product will be able to provide prompt, effective service. Elsewhere we have noted that high-quality service is critical across a variety of high-tech and low-tech settings.[7] However, uncertainty about service in high-tech marketing is raised by the limited data about how the new technology will behave in the field. More mature technologies, like those found in washing machines, televisions, and automobiles, have decades of experience with problems and solutions that reduce uncertainty about what might go wrong and which steps will best resolve each problem. Newer technologies have no track record, so even if the service technician arrives quickly, whether or when the breakdown can be repaired is uncertain.

---

[7] R. T. Moriarty and T. J. Kosnik, "High-Tech versus Low-Tech Marketing: Where's the Beef?" Harvard Business School case no. 588-012.

Fourth, the technology may have unanticipated side effects. In the 1980s, the increased use of microcomputers and computer networks was accompanied by an increase in unauthorized access to business and government computer systems. The press reported numerous threats to businesses, including embezzlement and computer fraud, violations of privacy, confidentiality, and even of the national defense.

Finally, technological uncertainty may arise because of questions about technological obsolescence—whether and when the market will turn to another technology to replace the current generation of products. The risk of obsolescence may occur long after a technology has found a stable market. Uncertainty can also occur when a new technology is first introduced if customers cling to their old approach just long enough to leapfrog the new technology and select an even more advanced approach introduced later. The marketer's risk in moving too quickly is that leapfrogging by competitors' products may send the new technology to an early grave. Such uncertainty surrounded the introduction of compact disc audio systems in the 1980s. The sales of these players were just beginning to take off when digital tape players that promised the same quality of sound at a much lower cost were announced. Uncertainty about whether digital tape would render the technology obsolete, even before it had achieved widespread acceptance, led many potential buyers to "wait and see."

Figure 3 shows that high-technology marketing involves high levels of both market and technological uncertainty, and contrasts high-tech marketing with three other types of marketing. The first is *low-tech marketing,* the application of known

FIGURE 3

A taxonomy of marketing situations based on technological and market uncertainty

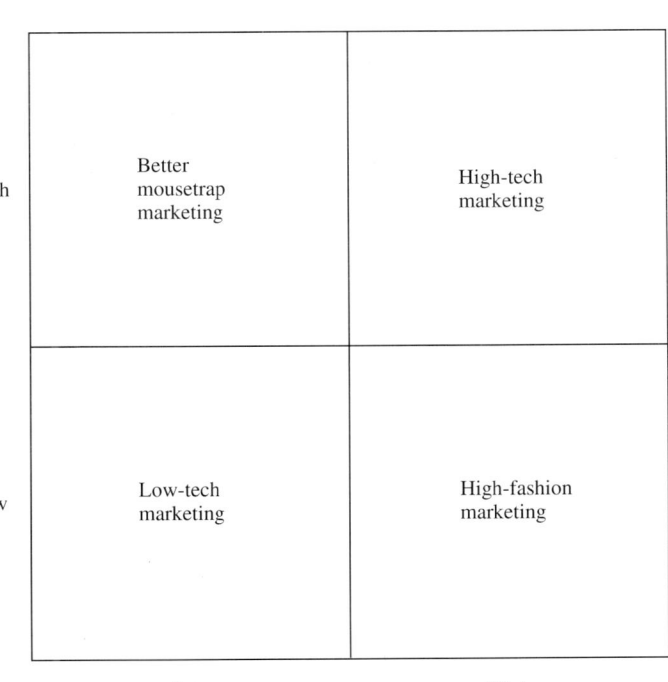

technology to meet well-established needs. Examples include a variety of mature products ranging from milk and coffee to grinding wheels and steel strapping. The second is *better mousetrap marketing,* in which new technology is introduced to solve an age-old problem. An example of this situation is a new drug, administered in familiar tablet form, which cures cancer or helps the buyer lose weight. The needs to be satisfied are clear. Whether the new mousetrap will do a better job is uncertain in the early stages. The third situation is *high-fashion marketing,* in which the technology changes relatively slowly, but consumer tastes are difficult to predict. Products in this category include designer jeans, running shoes, and motion pictures.

The next section discusses the key issues that arise from the combination of technological and market uncertainty in high-tech marketing. Some of the conclusions, as well as the practical implications, are also applicable to high-fashion or better mousetrap marketing.

Critical Issues Facing High-Tech Marketers

If increased technological and market uncertainty are the major differences between high-tech and low-tech marketing settings, what issues does uncertainty create that must be addressed to succeed in the high-tech arena? Five major issues seem to arise frequently for high-tech marketers.

• *How do we master an ever-expanding set of skills?* High-tech marketing and sales professionals must build enough expertise in the key technologies to understand their market potential and build credibility with their counterparts in engineering and R&D. They must also learn enough about their customers' business functions and industries to spot potential applications that the market has not yet discovered. Thus, the minimum acceptable breadth and depth of knowledge is greater in high-tech settings than it is in low-tech settings.

• *How do we abandon skills and knowledge that become obsolete?* Technological uncertainty and rapidly evolving customer preferences lead to shorter life cycles for products and technologies. One paradoxical implication for high-tech marketers is that, although they have to know more about technologies, markets, and applications, the useful life of their knowledge is shorter.

• *How do we coordinate skills, resources, and information across different functions in our company?* Marketing and sales professionals in technology-intensive businesses must often span functional boundaries to get the expertise, attention, or manpower they need to solve customers' problems. When the technology is new and unproven, the skills of R&D, manufacturing, and field service people are more critical than they are with a mature product or technology. When the market's needs are unclear, improved communication among marketing, sales, manufacturing, and R&D stimulates ideas for new products. Such communication also ensures that existing products are enhanced as the market's needs evolve. Cross-functional interaction allows marketing, which has the best information about customers, and R&D, which best understands the limits of technologies, to pool information and thereby better manage both forms of uncertainty.

- *How can interfirm alliances best cope with technological and marketplace changes?* The 1980s have been marked by an increasing number of marketing alliances between suppliers and customers, between manufacturers and distribution channels, among suppliers of complementary products (e.g., computer literature and software), and among competitors. Developing these is an important way to build trust, facilitate the flow of information, and encourage customers or consultants to serve as "beta test sites" to run a new product through its paces.

  Eric von Hippel has pointed out another benefit of strong supplier-customer relationships: lead customers are a major source of new product ideas. In a study of more than 160 product innovations, he discovered that lead customers—not marketers—originated ideas that led to commercially successful new products.[8]

- *How can we provide continuity in the face of constant change?* High levels of technological and market uncertainty create excitement and innovation, but they also introduce tremendous stresses on high-tech companies, the people who work in them, and the relationships between people and organizations. Unless sales and marketing managers are able to develop mechanisms to provide continuity in change, employees, customers, and suppliers could become disposable, or begin to feel that way. For many a weary veteran of high-tech marketing campaigns, the paradoxical search for continuity in change is as difficult as putting a stake in the ground during an earthquake. However, if this problem were insoluble, high-tech marketing would be a game that could be played only by very young people in very young organizations. The continuing success of "old dogs," like H. Ross Perot and Ken Olsen, and of relatively old companies, like Hewlett-Packard and IBM, suggests that a few high-tech marketers may have found a clue.

Marketing Tactics When Uncertainty Is High

At a recent research colloquium one of us gave in southern California, we asked a computer company manager what he thought of the discussion. He replied, "It was worth coming. I spent about $300 on a roundtrip plane ticket from San Francisco and my room for the night. If I pick up a couple of practical ideas I can use on the job next week, I'll break even. I got two helpful hints during the three-hour session, and another great insight from one of the other participants at the coffee break." His concern, shared by most marketers we know in high-tech environments, is how to get past the "What?" and "So what?" questions that fascinate most professors to the "Now what?" implementation question that concerns marketers in the trenches.

This section has both bad news and good news about the "Now what?" question. The bad news is that practitioners and academics alike are learning how to do high-tech marketing as they go along. That is not surprising, if you accept the fact that it is impossible to eliminate market and technological uncertainty in high-tech settings.

---

[8] E. A. von Hippel, "Users as Innovators," *Technology Review,* January 1978, pp. 31–39.

The good news is that certain high-tech organizations have discovered clever ways to adapt traditional marketing practices to their special situations. Paradoxically, they have discovered that focusing on marketing fundamentals is one of the best ways to provide the continuity in change so crucial to the long-term success of people and organizations.

The remainder of this section provides action recommendations for each of the five issues, with examples from leading high-tech companies.

Broadening and Deepening the Skill Set

Successful high-tech marketers need to have a basic understanding of the technology, the customer's industry, and the customer's business functions. How do we increase the breadth and the depth of our marketing and sales teams' skills?

Part of the solution is *creative recruiting*. Many computer companies heavily emphasize a technical undergraduate degree for candidates seeking sales and marketing positions. While this deepens the sales force's technological skill, it leaves gaps in detailed knowledge of customers' industries and business functions. In contrast, a leading software and systems integration firm, American Management Systems (AMS), learned not to rely exclusively on people with education and experience in information technology. AMS has created a "functional specialist" career path and now hires fast learners with hands-on experience in their customers' business functions. Teaching functional specialists what they need to know about computers is easier than teaching computer scientists the intricacies of consumer loans or public-sector accounting.

Another part of the solution is *creative training that gets sales and marketing professionals closer to customers*. A training simulation widely adopted by computer hardware manufacturers has salespeople and sales managers live in a customer organization for a week and deal with a major technology purchase from the buyer's perspective. Various salespeople play the roles of a customer's division general manager and vice presidents of finance, marketing, sales, manufacturing, and management information systems. By walking in the customer's shoes, sales professionals gain insights not easily acquired by simply talking about, or even listening to, their clients.

Some high-tech marketers invite loyal customers and recent "rejectors" (buyers who recently selected a competitor's products over their own) to lead discussions about the buying process during marketing and management training. This approach is not recommended for those whose egos bruise easily. Candid criticism about product line flaws or mistakes made in the selling process can be painful in the short run. However, the lessons learned may reduce the pain of lost sales in the long run.

The third, and perhaps most enduring, way to broaden and deepen the skill set is through *creative job assignments*. While on-the-job training occurs in every company and industry, a few high-tech firms have used it in particularly clever ways to enhance the skills of those who create and market their products. One leading systems consulting firm routinely teams relatively new programmers and systems analysts with its most seasoned business developers in competing for new business. The new employee accompanies the veteran "rain maker" on calls to the prospective customer, is encouraged to ask questions in meetings to determine the client's needs, writes parts of the proposal, is involved in estimating the work's scope, and plays a key role in presenting the proposal to the prospective customer. If the business is won, the programmer or analyst becomes a member of the implementation team. He or she can communicate the subtleties of the business problem and the client organization more powerfully than if the partner handed the word down from on high. In the long run, letting employees taste the thrill of winning business and the agony of losing a sale early in their careers provides a sense of the big picture.

Another company, Manac Systems International, develops and markets software products to support law office functions such as time keeping, billing, and storage and retrieval of documents. Most of Manac's customer support is done via a telephone hot line. Clients call with a problem and are forwarded to one of the customer support staff, with whom they walk through the facts to solve the problem. Hot line support is not unique; virtually every computer company has such an organization. What *is* unique is the way Manac staffs this function. Unlike most companies, which hire full-time customer support workers, Manac has all its programmers and application consultants (who test the programs and write the documentation and training manuals) take turns on the telephone watch. Each programmer and application consultant has telephone consulting duty for two full workdays each week.

One advantage of having the software and manual writers on the phone is the customer's exposure to people with the best knowledge of the technology and its application. A second advantage is that the technical people develop a much deeper understanding of how law offices function. Ironically, although Manac does not have a separate marketing department, it is one of the most marketing-oriented high-tech companies we know.

Abandoning Knowledge That Has Lost Its Relevance

How can we learn to recognize when the world has changed and to abandon once-successful marketing approaches that have outlived their usefulness?

One of the most powerful ways is to teach marketers to think in *future perfect* terms. Stanley Davis uses the term as the title of his book about linking strategy, science, technology, and organization. He suggests that implementing a strategy in a radically new context requires an organization's leaders to "lead from a place in time that assumes you are already there, and that is determined even though it has not happened yet." He cites an earlier definition of this new sense of time from Karl Weick:

> The actor projects this [future strategy] as if it were already over and done with and lying in the past. . . . The fact that it is thus pictured as if it were simultaneously past and future can be taken care of by saying that it is thought of in the *future perfect* tense.[9]

---

[9] S. M. Davis, *Future Perfect* (Reading, Mass.: Addison-Wesley, 1987).

For those who may think the suggestion that high-tech marketers be future perfect sounds far-fetched, consider these examples of future perfect behavior from successful high-tech marketing companies.

Between 1970 and the present, American Management Systems has successfully implemented numerous complex information systems. As they tackle each new custom-built system, they work closely with clients to develop the strategic concept of how the completed system will add value to the organization. Together, consultant and client create a "system concept" that describes in the present tense, *as though it already existed,* the tangible details of people and technology interacting in new ways to create information, respond to requests for changes, and perform new functions in the parts of the organization the system will support. AMS's future perfect visualization of the strategy for a high-tech product is unique. The founders have used future perfect projective techniques to articulate their own marketing strategy over five-year time horizons—a lifetime in the software and systems consulting business.

Apple Computer's corporate university, Apple University, recently introduced a series of learning programs for its managers, called Living Programs™, that also adopts a future perfect approach. At one of these programs, the Apple Management Seminar, groups of more than 100 managers spend four days living life at Apple five years in the future. They are formed into self-managing teams of 20 to 25 people and given the task of creating a product, using cutting-edge computer technologies, to help solve a problem that Apple will face in the future, or to communicate what Apple will be like in the future to new Apple employees. Apple senior managers, including CEO John Sculley, visit the seminar and conduct sessions. The learning and the concrete products Apple managers have developed during these programs are nothing less than astonishing compared with what other competent and dedicated marketers accomplish expending much more time and effort in management seminars and on the job.

In short, rapid change renders strategies based on the lessons of the past obsolete even before they can be implemented. High-tech managers can avoid becoming victims of their experience by thinking and acting in future perfect terms. This winning philosophy is captured by a recent quote from hockey star Wayne Gretsky: "I don't go where the puck is—I go where it is going to be!"

Building Cross-Functional Collaboration and Communication

Product design, manufacturing, sales, and marketing professionals need to improve their cross-functional communication and understanding of customer needs if they are to design, make, and market products that provide value. Several methodologies show great promise of enhancing cross-functional activities and communication. For example, Quality Function Deployment (QFD) originated at Mitsubishi in 1972, and was piloted at Digital Equipment Corporation, AT&T, and ITT in the late 1980s.[10] Through a series of graphical forms, customer desires for intangible product

---

[10] J. R. Hauser and D. Clausing, "The House of Quality," *Harvard Business Review,* May–June 1988, pp. 63–73.

qualities are linked to a specific, physical product attribute. For example, customers' desires for sportiness in a car may be linked to the presence of bucket seats or the shape of the automobile. Then the physical product attributes are linked to design choices, technologies, components, or engineering specifications for the product.

Takeuchi and Nonaka and Hayes, Wheelwright, and Clark describe how well-managed companies have organized the development of new products to enhance cross-functional communication and reduce the time between conceiving and launching a new product.[11] Both approaches recommend a great deal of interaction among marketing, sales, field service, R&D, and manufacturing throughout the process. This degree of interaction contrasts with traditional approaches to new product development, in which one function dominates the process for one phase, and then passes the baton to another function at a later phase.

In addition to new methodologies for product design and project management, many high-tech firms are using management development and training to foster cooperation and communication across the borders traditionally erected between functions, business units, and countries. AMS and IBM use organizational and team-level simulations to give participants hands-on experience in developing group solutions to problems often encountered on high-tech project teams. Data General invites sales, field service, and R&D professionals to join its marketers as full participants during a series of marketing leadership development programs. As part of the Data General programs, cross-functional teams apply new tools and techniques to marketing problems currently faced by the organization.

Using Interfirm Alliances Effectively

There are numerous examples of alliances in high-tech settings. In 1985, Digital Equipment Corporation established a Manufacturing Corporate Accounts Management (MCAM) program, in which manufacturing executives familiar with cutting-edge technology in Digital's operations met with their counterparts in the firm's leading customer organizations to exchange ideas on how to use new technology. The MCAMs also worked with Digital's manufacturing, marketing, sales, and product development organizations to cross-fertilize ideas in different functions.

Between 1985 and 1988, alliances between computer hardware and software vendors who constituted one "channel" to the customer markedly increased. For example, Tandem Corporation, the manufacturer of NonStop computers, built a group of 100 specialists responsible for developing relationships with third-party software manufacturers. In the following year, it tripled the number of alliances with software suppliers. *Systems Integration Age* has reported a significant rise in the number of relationships between computer software companies and consulting firms that specialize in customizing software, installing it, and training users.[12]

---

[11]H. Takeuchi and I. Nonaka, "The New New Product Development Game," *Harvard Business Review,* January–February 1986, pp. 137–46; R. H. Hayes et al., *Dynamic Manufacturing: Creating the Learning Organization* (New York: Free Press, 1988).

[12]"SIA Alliance Report," *Systems Integration Age,* February 1988, pp. 6–19.

Numerous biotechnology, semiconductor, and computer companies are also forming global strategic alliances to help match the financial strength of larger partners with the creativity of high-tech startups, or to marry the products and technologies of one partner with the market presence, access to customers, and knowledge of distribution channels of another.

As alliances proliferate, it is important to think carefully about how to select and then implement a portfolio of partnerships. Kosnik has pointed out five potential stumbling blocks of global alliances.

- Different partners are organized differently for making marketing and design decisions, leading to *problems in coordination.*
- A company with special competence may align itself with multiple firms that are bitter competitors, leading to *problems of cooperation and trust.*
- "Allies" with the best combination of complementary skills in one country may be ill equipped to help one another in other countries, leading to *problems in implementing alliances on a global basis.*
- The rapid pace of technological change virtually guarantees that the best partner tomorrow may be different from the best partner today, leading to *problems in maintaining alliances over a long time period.*
- The tendency of each partner to want as many allies and as few enemies as possible will make it difficult to say no to any alliance, leading to *problems in establishing unique competitive advantage.*[13]

A framework to compare what each partner "brings to the party" is summarized in Figure 4. Any venture requires a mix of:

- Resources (money, information technology, people, and time).
- Relationships (with customers, channels, and influential people).
- Reputation (breadth of a firm's visibility and depth of its credibility).
- Capabilities (technological expertise, industry experience, functional competencies, creative talent, managerial know-how, marketing skill, and knowledge of the countries in the target segment).
- Chemistry and culture (the compatibility of styles and values of the firms and people who work in them).

Each potential partner may offer a different mix of the above ingredients in each of the countries where the marketing will occur. This framework provides an approach to compare alternative partners and to assess the strengths and weaknesses of a proposed partnership in different country markets.

Focusing on Fundamentals to Provide Continuity in Change

The rate of change in both technologies and markets has accelerated relentlessly in the last decade. High-tech products careen from the uncertainty of development and

---

[13]T. J. Kosnik, "Stumbling Blocks to Global Strategic Alliances," *Systems Integration Age,* October 1988.

FIGURE 4

What does each partner bring to the party? A framework for evaluating strategic alliances

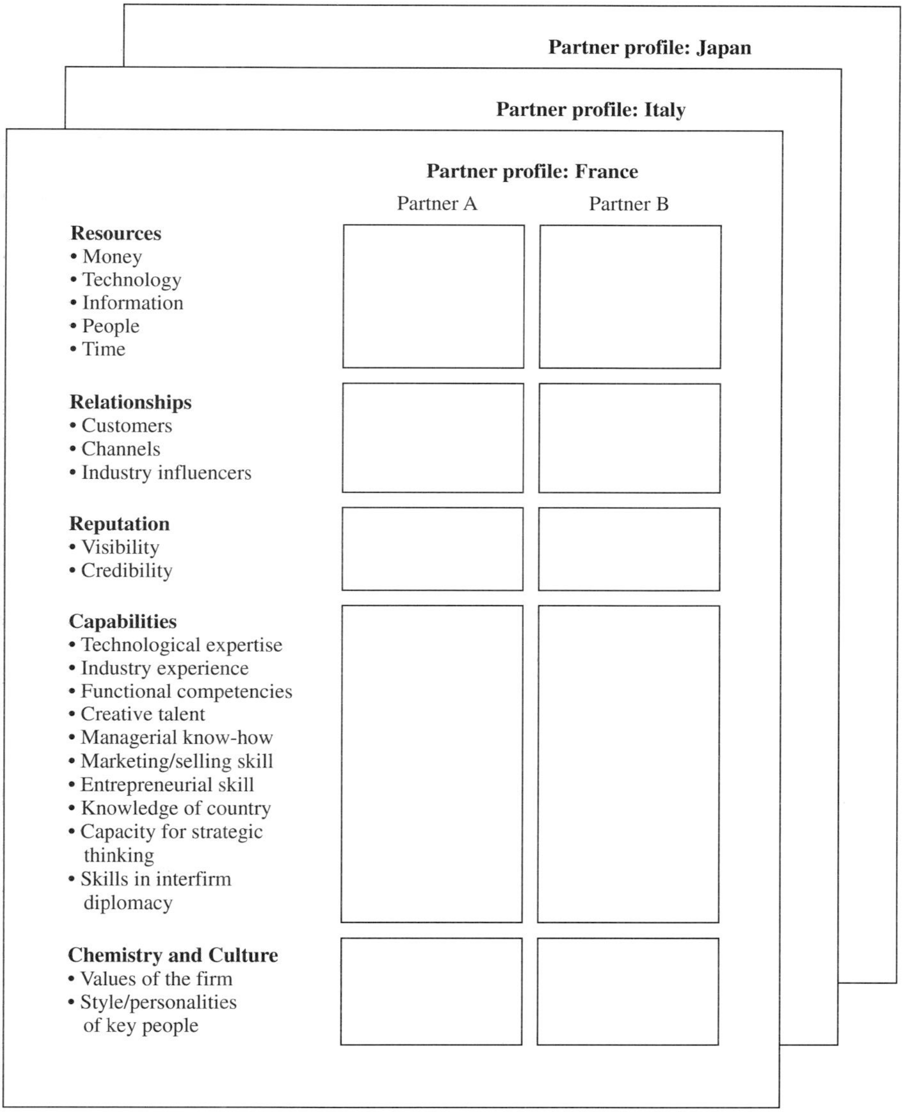

Partner profile: Japan

Partner profile: Italy

Partner profile: France

	Partner A	Partner B
Resources • Money • Technology • Information • People • Time		
Relationships • Customers • Channels • Industry influencers		
Reputation • Visibility • Credibility		
Capabilities • Technological expertise • Industry experience • Functional competencies • Creative talent • Managerial know-how • Marketing/selling skill • Entrepreneurial skill • Knowledge of country • Capacity for strategic thinking • Skills in interfirm diplomacy		
Chemistry and Culture • Values of the firm • Style/personalities of key people		

launch through the phases of growth and product maturity in a span of months rather than years.[14] In the process, high-tech marketers experience both the excitement of a roller coaster ride and the stress of combat. In the midst of this chaos, some form of stability is needed if both people and companies are to achieve sustained success over the decades that mark the life cycles of organizations and marketing careers.

---

[14]G. Stalk, Jr., "Time—The Next Source of Competitive Advantage," *Harvard Business Review,* July–August 1988, pp. 41–51.

To provide continuity in change, focus on the fundamentals. The first element of this focus is a set of company values. IBM's values—respect for the individual, customer service, and commitment to excellence—are widely known by employees, customers, and others in the marketplace. So too are Hewlett-Packard's seven corporate objectives in the areas of profit, customers, fields of interest, growth, people, management, and citizenship. Unfortunately, corporate values have been trivialized in the 1980s; almost every company has drafted a statement of shared beliefs. In their rush to cover all the bases, many companies espouse such a large number of conflicting values that they lose their meaning. There are too many values to remember, and even if the mission statement is consulted, it is often impossible to determine how to make trade-offs between conflicting values. If corporate values are to provide continuity, they must be both memorable and meaningful for decisions in the trenches.

The second element of focus is targeting market segments and customers. Partly as a result of an engineering-driven heritage, many technology companies believe the key to success is in creating great products, then selling them to anyone who has the money. But the faster technology and markets change, the more impossible it is to be all things to all customers. Consider the market selection decision of Steve Jobs at NeXt, who developed a new generation of personal computers and focused its introduction on the college and university marketplace. Some industry observers scoffed that the focus was too narrow, but we think not. Undoubtedly financial institutions, manufacturing companies, and other target segments had potential uses for the NeXt machine. Few industry observers thought that NeXt would *always* confine itself to colleges and universities. But as a starting point, Jobs understood that trying to stretch a start-up company's marketing and sales resources across a broad range of customers was a recipe for failure. Focus rarely requires marketers to say "never" to opportunities; it often requires them to say "not now."

NeXt is an exception to the practice of most high-tech companies. In contrast, consider the segmentation strategy of a minicomputer manufacturer competing for market share with companies 10 to 50 times its size. The company recently announced it was confining itself to three target segments: government, manufacturing, and service industries around the world. The only specifically excluded segment is the scientific/engineering marketplace! Unless the company sharpens its focus considerably, it will be stretched too thin to achieve a dominant position in any segment. As competition intensifies, the company will risk being gradually overrun by larger competitors that can throw greater resources at any market opportunity. Carl von Clausewitz, a nineteenth century Prussian military strategist whose theories have become popularized by twentieth century business authors, stresses the importance of massing one's forces at the enemy's weakest point to achieve victory on the battlefield.[15] Focusing on target segments is the only way a small high-tech competitor can hope to win against much larger adversaries. In a global marketplace, even the largest companies are not large enough to be all things to all customers for all time.

---

[15]C. von Clausewitz, *On War* (Princeton, N.J.: Princeton University Press, 1976).

High-tech salespeople who have to make quarterly sales quotas, and high-tech entrepreneurs who are wondering if they can make the next payroll, often resist our advice to focus narrowly, since it means sacrificing some opportunities in the short run. We understand their dilemma. In fact, a certain amount of opportunism is not only acceptable but essential if marketers are to capitalize on the volatility of their environment. At the same time, however, maintaining discipline and composure in the heat of battle is essential for continued success.

The third element of focus is product policy. If focused market selection suggests that we can't be all things to all customers, focused product policy implies that most high-tech companies can't even be all things to *some* customers. Specific decisions that should be used to focus a company's product policy include the following.

- The amount of standardization versus customization—that is, the extent to which the marketer will adapt the physical product to meet special customer needs. Manac refuses to customize its software products to meet the needs of a single law firm. Many of its competitors customize, for a fee. However, Manac releases a new version of its software every six to twelve months. If customization were done, implementation of new releases would be a nightmare. Thousands of law firms would call to find out how to add the customized patches from their old versions to each new release.
- The amount of service to offer with the product. Computer hardware manufacturers offer widely varying amounts of education, service, and technical support. They also either charge customers separately for the service or bundle it with the product. Unfortunately, competitors who have not managed the service component carefully wind up bundling lots of free service with their products. This lack of focus squeezes their profits between competitors that give better-quality service and charge for it and those that give less service but offer lower prices.
- The breadth of product line—that is, the number of different types of product categories. Intel's decision to manufacture workstations, rather than limit itself to semiconductors, expanded the breadth of its product line.
- The depth of product line—that is, the number of models available within a product category. Apple recently announced new models of Macintosh computers but retained the existing models; this increased the depth of the Macintosh line.
- Industry standards versus proprietary technology. High-tech companies must decide between adhering to a voluntary set of technical standards for the industry and using a specialized, proprietary technology to solve customer problems. Debates on industry standards sometimes drag on for years, leaving companies that are trying to develop new products bewildered and behind schedule. Customer pressure for industry standards appears to be increasing. At the same time, the number of factions warring over which approach will become the standard is rising. The dilemma these conflicting trends pose for product policy is critical. Many companies are attempting to hedge their bets by simultaneously developing new products that adhere to differing technological standards. Unfortunately, playing it both ways is extremely expensive and tends to lengthen the time necessary for product development, as people, management attention, and finances are stretched to the limit. Only the largest competitors have the resources to pursue multiple industry standards at the same time.

We have limited our discussion of fundamentals to shared values, target market selection, and product policy. Other basic marketing tactics, such as pricing, advertising, sales force management, and distribution channel management, also merit the attention of high-tech marketers. However, if market selection and product policy are not focused, quality execution on the other marketing variables will rarely save the day. Conversely, if high-tech marketers clearly articulate their values, steadfastly commit to their customers, and are disciplined in their product policy decisions, they can make more than their fair share of mistakes elsewhere without suffering a fatal setback.

Conclusion

This chapter began with a claim that high uncertainty about technology and the marketplace was the underlying difference between high-tech and other environments. This uncertainty gives rise to marketing problems that successful high-tech companies address with creative adaptation and a focus on fundamentals. Holding this delicate balance of flexibility and focus promises to be the foremost challenge facing high-tech company leadership in the 1990s.

Chapter 47

Logic of Global Business: An Interview with ABB's Percy Barnevik

Percy Barnevik, president and CEO of ABB Asea Brown Boveri, has boldly, yet simply, reorganized ABB as a model of competitive enterprise: an organization that combines global scale and world-class technology with deep roots in local markets. He offers a detailed guide to the theory and practice of building a "multidomestic" enterprise. He describes ABB's matrix system and a new breed of global managers.

William Taylor: Companies everywhere are trying to become global, and everyone agrees that ABB is more global than most companies. What does that mean?

Percy Barnevik: ABB is a company with no geographic center, no national ax to grind. We are a federation of national companies with a global coordination center. Are we a Swiss company? Our headquarters is in Zurich, but only 100 professionals work at headquarters and we will not increase that number. Are we a Swedish company? I'm the CEO, and I was born and educated in Sweden. But our headquarters is not in Sweden, and only two of the eight members of our board of directors are Swedes. Perhaps we are an American company. We report our financial results in U.S. dollars, and English is ABB's official language. We conduct all high-level meetings in English.

My point is that ABB is none of those things—and all of those things. We are not homeless. We are a company with many homes.

Are all businesses becoming global?

No, and this is a big source of misunderstanding. We are in the process of building this federation of national companies, a multidomestic organization, as I prefer to call it. That does not mean all of our businesses are global. We do a very good

---

This reading was prepared by William Taylor.
Copyright © 1991 by the President and Fellows of Harvard College. All rights reserved.
Reprinted from *Harvard Business Review,* March–April 1991, pp. 91–105.

business in electrical installation and service in many countries. That business is superlocal. The geographic scope of our installation business in, say, Stuttgart does not extend beyond a 10-mile radius of downtown Stuttgart.

We also have businesses that are superglobal. There are not more than 15 combined-cycle power plants or more than three or four high-voltage DC stations sold in any one year around the world. Our competitors fight for nearly every contract—they battle us on technology, price, financing—and national borders are virtually meaningless. Every project requires our best people and best technology from around the world.

The vast majority of our businesses—and of most businesses—fall somewhere between the superlocal and the superglobal. These are the businesses in which building a multidomestic organization offers powerful advantages. You want to be able to optimize a business globally—to specialize in the production of components, to drive economies of scale as far as you can, to rotate managers and technologists around the world to share expertise and solve problems. But you also want to have deep local roots everywhere you operate—building products in the countries where you sell them, recruiting the best local talent from the universities, working with the local government to increase exports. If you build such an organization, you create a business advantage that's damn difficult to copy.

What is a business that demonstrates that advantage?

Transportation is a good one. This is a vibrant business for us, and we consider ourselves Number 1 in the world. We generate $2 billion a year in revenues when you include all of our activities: locomotives, subway cars, suburban trains, trolleys, and the electrical and signaling systems that support them. We are strong because we are the only multidomestic player in the world.

First, we know what core technologies we have to master, and we draw on research from labs across Europe and the world. Being a technology leader in locomotives means being a leader in power electronics, mechanical design, even communications software. Ten years ago, Asea beat General Electric on a big Amtrak order for locomotives on the Metroliner between New York and Washington. That win caused quite a stir; it was the first time in 100 years that an American railroad bought locomotives from outside the United States. We won because we could run that track from Washington to New York, crooked and bad as it was, at 125 miles an hour. Asea had been pushing high-speed design concepts for more than a decade, and Brown Boveri pioneered the AC technology. That's why our X2 tilting trains are running in Sweden and why ABB will play a big role in the high-speed rail network scheduled to run throughout Europe.

Second, we structure our operations to push cross-border economies of scale. This is an especially big advantage in Europe, where the locomotive industry is hopelessly fragmented. There are two companies headquartered in the United States building locomotives for the U.S. market. There are three companies in Japan. There are 24 companies in Western Europe, and the industry runs at less than 75 percent of capacity. There are European companies still making only 10 or 20 locomotives a

The Organizing Logic of ABB

ABB Asea Brown Boveri is a global organization of staggering business diversity. Yet its organizing principles are stark in their simplicity. Along one dimension, the company is a distributed global network. Executives around the world make decisions on product strategy and performance without regard for national borders. Along a second dimension, it is a collection of traditionally organized national companies, each serving its home market as effectively as possible. ABB's global matrix holds the two dimensions together.

At the top of the company sit CEO Percy Barnevik and 12 colleagues on the executive committee. The group, which meets every three weeks, is responsible for ABB's global strategy and performance. The executive committee consists of Swedes, Swiss, Germans, and Americans. Several members of the executive committee are based outside Zurich, and their meetings are held around the world.

Reporting to the executive committee are leaders of the 50 or so business areas (BAs), located worldwide, into which the company's products and services are divided. The BAs are grouped into eight business segments, for which different members of the executive committee are responsible. For example, the "industry" segment, which sells components, systems, and software to automate industrial processes, has five BAs, including metallurgy, drives, and process engineering. The BA leaders report to Gerhard Schulmeyer, a German member of the executive committee who works out of Stamford, Connecticut.

Each BA has a leader responsible for optimizing the business on a global basis. The BA leader devises and champions a global strategy, holds factories around the world to cost and quality standards, allocates export markets to each factory, and shares expertise by rotating people across borders, creating mixed-nationality teams to solve problems, and building a culture of trust and communication. The BA leader for power transformers, who is responsible for 25 factories in 16 countries, is a Swede who works out of Mannheim, Germany. The BA leader for instrumentation is British. The BA leader for electric metering is an American based in North Carolina.

Alongside the BA structure sits a country structure. ABB's operations in the developed world are organized as national enterprises with presidents, balance sheets, income statements, and career ladders. In Germany, for example, Asea Brown Boveri Aktiengesellschaft, ABB's national company, employs 36,000 people and generates annual revenues of more than $4 billion. The managing director of ABB Germany, Eberhard von Koerber, plays a role comparable with that of a traditional German CEO. He reports to a supervisory board whose members include German bank representatives and trade union officials. His company produces financial statements comparable with those from any other German company and participates fully in the German apprenticeship program.

The BA structure meets the national structure at the level of ABB's member companies. Percy Barnevik advocates strict decentralization. Wherever possible, ABB creates separate companies to do the work of the 50 business areas in different countries. For example, ABB does not merely sell industrial robots in Norway. Norway has an ABB robotics company charged with manufacturing robots, selling to and servicing domestic customers, and exporting to markets allocated by the BA leader.

There are 1,100 such local companies around the world. Their presidents report to two bosses—the BA leader, who is usually located outside the country, and the president of the national company of which the local company is a subsidiary. At this intersection, ABB's "multidomestic" structure becomes a reality.

year! How can they compete with us, when we have factories doing 10 times their volume and specializing in components for locomotives across the Continent? For example, one of our new plants makes power electronics for many of the locomotives we sell in Europe. That specialization creates huge cost and quality advantages. We work to rationalize and specialize as much as we can across borders.

Third, we recognize the limits to specialization. We can't ignore borders altogether. We recently won a $420-million order from the Swiss Federal Railways—we call it the "order of the century"—to build locomotives that will move freight through the Alps. If we expect to win those orders, we had *better* be a Swiss company. We had better understand the depth of the Swiss concern for the environment, which explains the willingness to invest so heavily to get freight moving on trains through the mountains to Italy or Germany and off polluting trucks. We had better understand the Alpine terrain and what it takes to build engines powerful enough to haul heavy loads. We had better understand the effects of drastic temperature changes on sensitive electronics and build locomotives robust enough to keep working when they go from the frigid, dry outdoors to extreme heat and humidity inside the tunnels.

There are other advantages to a multidomestic presence. India needs locomotives—thousands of locomotives—and the government expects its suppliers to manufacture most of them inside India. But the Indians also need soft credit to pay for what is imported. Who has more soft credit than the Germans and the Italians? So we have to be a German and an Italian company, we have to be able to build locomotive components there as well as in Switzerland, Sweden, and Austria, since our presence may persuade Bonn and Rome to assist with financing.

We test the borderlines all the time: How far can we push cross-border specialization and scale economies? How effectively can we translate our multidomestic presence into competitive advantages in third markets?

Is there such a thing as a global manager?

Yes, but we don't have many. One of ABB's biggest priorities is to create more of them; it is a crucial bottleneck for us. On the other hand, a global company does not need thousands of global managers. We need maybe 500 or so out of 15,000 managers to make ABB work well—not more. I have no interest in making managers more "global" than they have to be. We can't have people abdicating their nationalities, saying "I am no longer German, I am international." The world doesn't work like that. If you are selling products and services in Germany, you better be German!

That said, we do need a core group of global managers at the top: on our executive committee, on the teams running our business areas (BAs), in other key positions. How are they different? Global managers have exceptionally open minds. They respect how different countries do things, and they have the imagination to appreciate why they do them that way. But they are also incisive, they push the limits of the culture. Global managers don't passively accept it when someone says, "You can't do that in Italy or Spain because of the unions," or "You can't do that in Japan because of the Ministry of Finance." They sort through the debris of cultural excuses and find opportunities to innovate.

Global managers are also generous and patient. They can handle the frustrations of language barriers. As I mentioned earlier, English is the official language of ABB. Every manager with a global role *must* be fluent in English, and anyone with regional general management responsibilities must be competent in English. When I write letters to ABB colleagues in Sweden, I write them in English. It may seem silly for one Swede to write to another in English, but who knows who will need to see that letter a year from now?

We are adamant about the language requirement—and it creates problems. Only 30 percent of our managers speak English as their first language, so there is great potential for misunderstanding, for misjudging people, for mistaking facility with English for intelligence or knowledge. I'm as guilty as anyone. I was rushing through an airport last year and had to return a phone call from one of our managers in Germany. His English wasn't good, and he was speaking slowly and tentatively. I was in a hurry, and finally I insisted, "Can't you speak any faster?" There was complete silence. It was a dumb thing for me to say. Things like that happen every day in this company. Global managers minimize those problems and work to eliminate them.

Where do these new managers come from?

Global managers are made, not born. This is not a natural process. We are herd animals. We like people who are like us. But there are many things you can do. Obviously, you rotate people around the world. There is no substitute for line experience in three or four countries to create a global perspective. You also encourage people to work in mixed-nationality teams. You *force* them to create personal alliances across borders, which means that sometimes you interfere in hiring decisions.

This is why we put so much emphasis on teams in the business areas. If you have 50 business areas and five managers on each BA team, that's 250 people from different parts of the world—people who meet regularly in different places, bring their national perspectives to bear on tough problems, and begin to understand how things are done elsewhere. I experience this every three weeks in our executive committee. When we sit together as Germans, Swiss, Americans, and Swedes, with many of us living, working, and traveling in different places, the insights can be remarkable. But you have to force people into these situations. Mixing nationalities doesn't just happen.

You also have to acknowledge cultural differences without becoming paralyzed by them. We've done some surveys, as have lots of other companies, and we find interesting differences in perception. For example, a Swede may think a Swiss is not completely frank and open, that he doesn't know exactly where he stands. That is a cultural phenomenon. Swiss culture shuns disagreement. A Swiss might say, "Let's come back to that point later, let me review it with my colleagues." A Swede would prefer to confront the issue directly. How do we undo hundreds of years of upbringing and education? We don't, and we shouldn't try to. But we do need to broaden understanding.

Is your goal to develop an "ABB way" of managing that cuts across cultural differences?

Yes and no. Naturally, as CEO, I set the tone for the company's management style. With my Anglo-Saxon education and Swedish upbringing, I have a certain way of doing things. Someone recently asked if my ultimate goal is to create 5,000 little Percy Barneviks, one for each of our profit centers. I laughed for a moment when I thought of the horror of sitting on top of such an organization, then I realized it wasn't a silly question. And the answer is no. We can't have managers who are "un-French" managing in France because 95 percent of them are dealing every day with French customers, French colleagues, French suppliers. That's why global managers also need humility. A global manager respects a formal German manager—Herr Doktor and all that—because that manager may be an outstanding performer in the German context.

Let's talk about the structures of global business. How do you organize a multidomestic enterprise?

ABB is an organization with three internal contradictions. We want to be global and local, big and small, radically decentralized with centralized reporting and control. If we resolve those contradictions, we create real organizational advantage.

That's where the matrix comes in. The matrix is the framework through which we organize our activities. It allows us to optimize our businesses globally *and* maximize performance in every country in which we operate. Some people resist it. They say the matrix is too rigid, too simplistic. But what choice do you have? To say you don't like a matrix is like saying you don't like factories or you don't like breathing. It's a fact of life. If you deny the formal matrix, you wind up with an informal one—and that's much harder to reckon with. As we learn to master the matrix, we get a truly multidomestic organization.

Can you walk us through how the matrix works?

Look at it first from the point of view of one business area, say, power transformers. The BA manager for power transformers happens to sit in Mannheim, Germany. His charter, however, is worldwide. He runs a business with 25 factories in 16 countries and global revenues of more than $1 billion. He has a small team around him of mixed nationalities—we don't expect superheroes to run our 50 BAs. Together with his colleagues, the BA manager establishes and monitors the trajectory of the business.

The BA leader is a business strategist and global optimizer. He decides which factories are going to make what products, what export markets each factory will serve, how the factories should pool their expertise and research funds for the benefit of the business worldwide. He also tracks talent—the 60 or 70 real standouts around the world. Say we need a plant manager for a new company in Thailand. The BA head should know of three or four people—maybe there's one at our plant in Muncie, Indiana, maybe there's one in Finland—who could help in Thailand. (See the insert "Power Transformers—The Dynamics of Global Coordination.")

Power Transformers—The Dynamics of Global Coordination

ABB is the world's leading manufacturer of power transformers, expensive products used in the transmission of electricity over long distances. The business generates annual revenues of $1 billion, nearly four times the revenues of its nearest competitor. More to the point, ABB's business is consistently and increasingly profitable—a real achievement in an industry that has experienced 15 years of moderate growth and intense price competition.

Power transformers are a case study in Percy Barnevik's approach to global management. Sune Karlsson, a vice president of ABB with a long record in the power transformer field, runs the business area (BA) from Mannheim, Germany. Production takes place in 25 factories in 16 countries. Each of these operations is organized as an independent company with its own president, budget, and balance sheet. Karlsson's job is to optimize the group's strategy and performance independently of national borders—to set the global rules of the game for ABB—while allowing local companies freedom to drive execution.

"We are not a global business," Karlsson says. "We are a collection of local businesses with intense global coordination. This makes us unique. We want our local companies to think small, to worry about their home market and a handful of export markets, and to learn to make money on smaller volumes."

Indeed, ABB has used its global production web to bring a new model of competition to the power transformer industry. Most of ABB's 25 factories are remarkably small by industry standards, with annual sales ranging from as little as $10 million to not more than $150 million, and 70 percent of their output serves their local markets. ABB transformer factories concentrate on slashing throughput times, maximizing design and production flexibility, and focusing tightly on the needs of domestic customers. In short, the company deploys the classic tools of flexible, time-based management in an industry that has traditionally competed on cost and volume.

As with many of its business areas, ABB built its worldwide presence in power transformers through a series of acquisitions. Thus, one of Karlsson's jobs is to spread the new model of competition to the local companies ABB acquires.

"Most of the companies we acquired had volume problems, cost problems, quality problems," he says. "We have to convince local managers that they can run smaller operations more efficiently, meet customer needs more flexibly—and make money. Once you've done this 10 or 15 times, in several countries, you become confident of the merits of the model."

Karlsson's approach to change is in keeping with the ABB philosophy: Show local managers what's been achieved elsewhere, let them drive the change process, make available ABB expertise from around the world, and demand quick results. A turnaround for power transformers takes about 18 months.

In Germany, for example, one of the company's transformer plants had generated red ink for years. It is now a growing, profitable operation, albeit smaller and more focused than before. The workforce has been slashed from 520 to 180, throughput time has been cut by one-third, work-in-process inventories have decreased by 80 percent. Annual revenues have fallen $70 million per year to a mere $50 million—but profits are up substantially. Today the German manager who championed this company's changes is in Muncie, Indiana, helping managers of a former Westinghouse plant acquired by ABB to reform their operation.

ABB's global scale also gives it clout with suppliers. The company buys up to $500 million of materials each year—an enormous presence that gives it leverage on price, quality, and delivery schedules. Karlsson has made strategic purchasing a priority. ABB expects zero-defect *continued*

Power Transformers—The Dynamics of Global Coordination

suppliers, just-in-time deliveries, and price increases lower than 75 percent of inflation—major advantages that it is in a position to win with intelligent coordination.

Sune Karlsson believes these and other "hard" advantages may be less significant, however, than the "soft" advantages of global coordination. "Our most important strength is that we have 25 factories around the world, each with its own president, design manager, marketing manager, and production manager," he says. "These people are working on the same problems and opportunities day after day, year after year, and learning a tremendous amount. We want to create a process of continuous expertise transfer. If we do, that's a source of advantage none of our rivals can match."

Creating these soft advantages requires internal competition and coordination. Every month, the Mannheim headquarters distributes detailed information on how each of the 25 factories is performing on critical parameters, such as failure rates, throughput times, inventories as a percentage of revenues, and receivables as a percentage of revenues. These reports generate competition for outstanding performance within the ABB network—more intense pressure, Karlsson believes, than external competition in the marketplace.

The key, of course, is that this internal competition be constructive, not destructive. Since the creation of ABB, one of Sune Karlsson's most important jobs has been to build a culture of trust and exchange among ABB's power transformer operations around the world and to create forums that facilitate the process of exchange. At least three such forums exist today:

- The BA's management board resembles the executive committee of an independent company. Karlsson chairs the group, and its members include the presidents of the largest power transformer companies—people from the United States, Canada, Sweden, Norway, Germany, and Brazil. The board meets four to six times a year and shapes the BA's global strategy, monitors performance, and resolves big problems.
- Karlsson's BA staff in Mannheim is not "staff" in the traditional sense—young professionals rotating through headquarters on their way to a line job. Rather, it is made up of five veteran managers each with worldwide responsibility for activities in critical areas such as purchasing and R&D. They travel constantly, meet with the presidents and top managers of the local companies, and drive the coordination agenda forward.
- Functional coordination teams meet once or twice a year to exchange information on the details of implementation in production, quality, marketing, and other areas. The teams include managers with functional responsibilities in all the local companies, so they come from around the world. These formal gatherings are important, Karlsson argues, but the real value comes in creating informal exchange throughout the year. The system works when the quality manager in Sweden feels compelled to telephone or fax the quality manager in Brazil with a problem or an idea.

"Sharing expertise does not happen automatically," Karlsson emphasizes. "It takes trust, it takes familiarity. People need to spend time together, to get to know and understand each other. People must also see a payoff for themselves. I never expect our operations to coordinate unless all sides get real benefits. We have to demonstrate that sharing pays—that contributing one idea gets you 24 in return."

—William Taylor

It is possible to leave the organization right there, to optimize every business area without regard for ABB's broad collection of activities in specific countries. But think about what we lose. We have a power transformer company in Norway that employs 400 people. It builds transformers for the Norwegian market and exports to markets allocated by the BA. But ABB Norway has more than 10,000 other employees in the country. There are tremendous benefits if power transformers coordinates its Norwegian operation with our operations in power generation, switchgear, and process automation: recruiting top people from the universities, building an efficient distribution and service network across product lines, circulating good people among the local companies, maintaining productive relations with top government officials.

So we have a Norwegian company, ABB Norway, with a Norwegian CEO and a headquarters in Oslo, to make these connections. The CEO has the same responsibilities as the CEO of a local Norwegian company for labor negotiations, bank relationships, and high-level contacts with customers. This is no label or gimmick. We *must* be a Norwegian company to work effectively in many businesses. Norway's oil operations in the North Sea are a matter of great national importance and intense national pride. The government wouldn't—and shouldn't—trust some faraway foreign company as a key supplier to those operations.

The opportunities for synergy are clear. So is the potential for tension between the business area structure and the country structure. Can't the matrix pull itself apart?

BA managers, country managers, and presidents of the local companies have very different jobs. They must understand their roles and appreciate that they are *complementing* each other, not competing.

The BA managers are crucial people. They need a strong hand in crafting strategy, evaluating performance around the world, and working with teams made up of different nationalities. We've had to replace some of them—people who lacked vision or cultural sensitivity or the ability to lead without being dictators. You see, BA managers don't own the people working in any business area around the world. They can't order the president of a local company to fire someone or to use a particular strategy in union negotiations. On the other hand, BA managers can't let their role degrade into a statistical coordinator or scorekeeper. There's a natural tendency for this to happen. BA managers don't have a constituency of thousands of direct reports in the same way that country managers do. So it's a difficult balancing act.

Country managers play a different role. They are regional line managers, the equivalent of the CEO of a local company. But country managers must also respect ABB's global objectives. The president of, say, ABB Portugal can't tell the BA manager for low-voltage switchgear or drives to stay out of his hair. He has to cooperate with the BA managers to evaluate and improve what's happening in Portugal in those businesses. He should be able to tell a BA manager, "You may think the plant in Portugal is up to standards, but you're being too loose. Turnover and absenteeism are twice the Portugese average. There are problems with the union, and it's the managers' fault."

Now, the presidents of our local companies—ABB Transformers in Denmark, say, or ABB Drives in Greece—need a different set of skills. They must be excellent profit center managers. But they must also be able to answer to two bosses effectively. After all, they have two sets of responsibilities. They have a global boss, the BA manager, who creates the rules of the game by which they run their businesses. They also have their country boss, to whom they report in the local setting. I don't want to make too much of this. In all of Germany, where we have 36,000 people, only 50 or so managers have two bosses. But these managers have to handle that ambiguity. They must have the self-confidence not to become paralyzed if they receive conflicting signals and the integrity not to play one boss off against the other.

Isn't all this much easier said than done?

It does require a huge mental change, especially for country managers. Remember, we've built ABB through acquisitions and restructurings. Thirty of the companies we've bought had been around for more than 100 years. Many of them were industry leaders in their countries, national monuments. Now they've got BA managers playing a big role in the direction of their operations. We have to convince country managers that they benefit by being part of this federation, that they gain more than they lose when they give up some autonomy.

What's an example?

Finland has been one of our most spectacular success stories, precisely because the Finns understood how much they could gain. In 1986, Asea acquired Strömberg, the Finnish power and electrical products company. At the time, Strömberg made an unbelievable assortment of products, probably half of what ABB makes today. It built generators, transformers, drives, circuit breakers—all of them for the Finnish market, many of them for export. It was a classic example of a big company in a small country that survived because of a protected market. Not surprisingly, much of what it made was not up to world-class standards, and the company was not very profitable. How can you expect a country with half the population of New Jersey to be profitable in everything from hydropower to circuit breakers?

Strömberg is no longer a stand-alone company. It is part of ABB's global matrix. The company still exists—there is a president of ABB Strömberg—but its charter is different. It is no longer the center of the world for every product it sells. It still manufactures and services many products for the Finnish market. It also sells certain products to allocated markets outside Finland. And it is ABB's worldwide center of excellence for one important group of products, electric drives, in which it had a long history of technology leadership and effective manufacturing.

Strömberg is a hell of a lot stronger because of this. Its total exports from Finland have increased more than 50 percent in three years. ABB Strömberg has become one of the most profitable companies in the whole ABB group, with a return on capital employed of around 30 percent. It is a recognized world leader in drives. Strömberg produces more than 35 percent of all the drives ABB sells, and drives are a billion-dollar business. In four years, Strömberg's exports to Germany and France have increased 10 times. Why? Because the company has access to a distribution network it never could have built itself.

This sounds enormously complicated, almost unmanageable. How does the organization avoid getting lost in the complexity?

The only way to structure a complex, global organization is to make it as simple and local as possible. ABB is complicated from where I sit. But on the ground, where the real work gets done, all of our operations must function as closely as possible to stand-alone operations. Our managers need well-defined sets of responsibilities, clear accountability, and maximum degrees of freedom to execute. I don't expect most of our people to have "global mindsets," to do things that hurt their business but are "good for ABB." That's not natural.

Take Strömberg and drives in France. I don't want the drive company president in Finland to think about what's good for France. I want him to think about Finland, about how to sell the hell out of the export markets he has been allocated. Likewise, I don't expect our profit center manager in France to think about Finland. I expect him to do what makes sense for his French customers. If our French salespeople find higher quality drives or more cost-effective drives outside ABB, they are free to sell them in France so long as ABB gets a right of first refusal. Finland has increased its shipments to France because it makes economic sense for both sides. That's the only way to operate.

But how can an organization with 215,000 people all over the world be simple and local?

ABB *is* a huge enterprise. But the work of most of our people is organized in small units with P&L responsibility and meaningful autonomy. Our operations are divided into nearly 1,200 companies with an average of 200 employees. These companies are divided into 4,500 profit centers with an average of 50 employees.

We are fervent believers in decentralization. When we structure local operations, we always push to create separate legal entities. Separate companies allow you to create *real* balance sheets with *real* responsibility for cash flow and dividends. With real balance sheets, managers inherit results from year to year through changes in equity. Separate companies also create more effective tools to recruit and motivate managers. People can aspire to meaningful career ladders in companies small enough to understand and be committed to.

What does that mean for the role of headquarters?

We operate as lean as humanly possible. It's no accident that there are only 100 people at ABB headquarters in Zurich. The closer we get to top management, the tougher we have to be with headcount. I believe you can go into any traditionally centralized corporation and cut its headquarters staff by 90 percent in one year. You spin off 30 percent of the staff into freestanding service centers that perform real work—treasury functions, legal services—and charge for it. You decentralize 30 percent of the staff—human resources, for example—by pushing them into the line organization. Then 30 percent disappears through headcount reductions.

These are not hypothetical calculations. We bought Combustion Engineering in late 1989. I told the Americans that they had to go from 600 people to 100 in their Stamford, Connecticut, headquarters. They didn't believe it was possible. So I told them to go to Finland and take a look. When we bought Strömberg, there were 880 people in headquarters. Today there are 25. I told them to go to Mannheim and take a look at the German operation. In 1988, right after the creation of ABB, there were 1,600 people in headquarters. Today there are 100.

Doesn't such radical decentralization threaten the very advantages that ABB's size creates?

Those are the contradictions again—being simultaneously big and small, decentralized and centralized. To do that, you need a structure at the top that facilitates quick decision making and carefully monitors developments around the world. That's the role of our executive committee. The 13 members of the executive committee are collectively responsible for ABB. But each of us also has responsibility for a business segment, a region, some administrative functions, or more than one of these. Eberhard von Koerber, who is a member of the executive committee located in Mannheim, is responsible for Germany, Austria, Italy, and Eastern Europe. He is also responsible for a worldwide business area, installation materials, and some corporate staff functions. Gerhard Schulmeyer sits in the United States and is responsible for North America. He is also responsible for our global "industry" segment.

Naturally, these 13 executives are busy, stretched people. But think about what happens when we meet every three weeks, which we do for a full day. Sitting in one room are the senior managers collectively responsible for ABB's global strategy and performance. These same managers individually monitor business segments, countries, and staff functions. So when we make a decision—snap, it's covered. The members of the executive committee communicate to their direct reports, the BA managers and the country managers, and the implementation process is under way.

We also have the glue of transparent, centralized reporting through a management information system called Abacus. Every month, Abacus collects performance data on our 4,500 profit centers and compares performance with budgets and forecasts. The data are collected in local currencies but translated into U.S. dollars to allow for analysis across borders. The system also allows you to work with the data. You can aggregate and disaggregate results by business segments, countries, and companies within countries.

What kind of information does the executive committee use to support the fast decision making you need?

We look for early signs that businesses are becoming more or less healthy. On the 10th of every month, for example, I get a binder with information on about 500 different operations—the 50 business areas, all the major countries, and the key companies in key countries. I look at several parameters—new orders, invoicing, margins, cash flows—around the world and in various business segments. Then I stop to study trends that catch my eye.

Let's say the industry segment is behind budget. I look to see which of the five BAs in the segment are behind. I see that process automation is way off. So I look by country and learn that the problem is in the United States and that it's poor margins, not weak revenues. So the answer is obvious—a price war has broken out. That doesn't mean I start giving orders. But I want to have informed dialogues with the appropriate executives.

Let's go back to basics. How do you begin building this kind of global organization?

ABB has grown largely through mergers and strategic investments. For most companies in Europe, this is the right way to cross borders. There is such massive overcapacity in so many European industries and so few companies with the critical mass to hold their own against Japanese and U.S. competitors. My former company, Asea, did fine in the 1980s. Revenues in 1987 were 4 times greater than in 1980, profits were 10 times greater, and our market value was 20 times greater. But the handwriting was on the wall. The European electrical industry was crowded with 20 national competitors. There was up to 50 percent overcapacity, high costs, and little cross-border trade. Half the companies were losing money. The creation of ABB started a painful—but long overdue—process of restructuring.

That same restructuring process will come to other industries: automobiles, telecommunications, steel. But it will come slowly. There have been plenty of articles in the last few years about all the cross-border mergers in Europe. In fact, the more interesting issue is why there have been so *few*. There should be *hundreds* of them, involving *tens of billions* of dollars, in industry after industry. But we're not seeing it. What we're seeing instead are strategic alliances and minority investments. Companies buy 15 percent of each other's shares. Or two rivals agree to cooperate in third markets but not merge their home-market organizations. I worry that many European alliances are poor substitutes for doing what we try to do—complete mergers and cross-border rationalization.

What are the obstacles to such cross-border restructuring?

One obstacle is political. When we decided on the merger between Asea and Brown Boveri, we had no choice but to do it secretly and to do it quickly, with our eyes open about discovering skeletons in the closet. There were no lawyers, no auditors, no environmental investigations, and no due diligence. Sure, we tried to value assets as best we could. But then we had to make the move, with an extremely thin legal document, because we were absolutely convinced of the strategic merits. In fact, the documents from the premerger negotiations are locked away in a Swiss bank and won't be released for 20 years.

Why the secrecy? Think of Sweden. Its industrial jewel, Asea—a 100 year-old company that had built much of the country's infrastructure—was moving its headquarters out of Sweden. The unions were angry: "Decisions will be made in Zurich, we have no influence in Zurich, there is no codetermination in Switzerland."

I remember when we called the press conference in Stockholm on August 10. The news came as a complete surprise. Some journalists didn't even bother to attend; they figured it was an announcement about a new plant in Norway or something. Then came the shock, the fait accompli. That started a communications war of a few weeks where we had to win over shareholders, the public, governments, and unions. But strict confidentiality was our only choice.

Are there obstacles besides politics?

Absolutely. The more powerful the strategic logic behind a merger—the greater the cross-border synergies—the more powerful the human and organizational obstacles. It's hard to tell a competent country manager in Athens or Amsterdam, "You've done a good job for 15 years, but unfortunately this other manager has done a better job and our only choice is to appoint your colleague to run the operation." If you have two plants in the same country running well but you need only one after the merger, it's tough to explain that to employees in the plant to be closed. Restructuring operations creates lots of pain and heartache, so many companies choose not to begin the process, to avoid the pain.

Germany is a case in point. Brown Boveri had operated in Germany for almost 90 years. Its German operation was so big—it had more than 35,000 employees—that there were rivalries with the Swiss parent. BBC Germany was a technology-driven, low-profit organization—a real underperformer. The formation of ABB created the opportunity to tackle problems that had festered for decades.

So what did you do?

We sent in Eberhard von Koerber to lead the effort. He made no secret of our plans. We had to reduce the work force by 10 percent, or 4,000 employees. We had to break up the headquarters, which had grown so big because of all the tensions with Switzerland. We had to rationalize the production overlaps, especially between Switzerland and Germany. We needed lots of new managers, eager people who wanted to be leaders and grow in the business.

The reaction was intense. Von Koerber faced strikes, demonstrations, barricades—real confrontation with the unions. He would turn on the television set and see protesters chanting, "Von Koerber out! Von Koerber out!" After a while, once the unions understood the game plan, the loud protests disappeared and our relationship became very constructive. The silent resistance from managers was more formidable. In fact, much of the union resistance was fed by management. Once the unions got on board, they became allies in our effort to reform management and rationalize operations.

Three years later, the results are in. ABB Germany is a well-structured, dynamic, market-oriented company. Profits are increasing steeply, in line with ABB targets. In 1987, BBC Germany generated revenues of $4 billion. ABB Germany will generate twice that by the end of next year. Three years ago, the management structure in Mannheim was centralized and functional, with few clear responsibilities or accountability. Today there are 30 German companies, each with its own president, manufacturing director, and so on. We can see who the outstanding performers are and apply their talents elsewhere. If we need someone to sort out a problem with circuit breakers in Spain, we know who from Germany can help.

What lessons can other companies learn from the German experience?

To make real change in cross-border mergers, you have to be factual, quick, and neutral. And you have to move boldly. You must avoid the "investigation trap"—you can't postpone tough decisions by studying them to death. You can't permit a "honeymoon" of small changes over a year or two. A long series of small changes just prolongs the pain. Finally, you have to accept a fair share of mistakes. I tell my people that if we make 100 decisions and 70 turn out to be right, that's good enough. I'd rather be roughly right and fast than exactly right and slow. We apply these principles everywhere we go, including in Eastern Europe, where we now have several change programs under way. (See "Change Comes to Poland—The Case of ABB Zamech.")

Why emphasize speed at the expense of precision? Because the costs of delay are vastly greater than the costs of an occasional mistake. I won't deny that it was absolutely crazy around here for the first few months after the merger. We *had* to get the matrix in place—we couldn't debate it—and we *had* to figure out which plants would close and which would stay open. We took 10 of our best people, the superstars, and gave them six weeks to design the restructuring. We called it the Manhattan Project. I personally interviewed 400 people, virtually day and night, to help select and motivate the people to run our local companies.

Once you've put the global pieces together and have the matrix concept working, what other problems do you have to wrestle with?

Communications. I have no illusions about how hard it is to communicate clearly and quickly to tens of thousands of people around the world. ABB has about 15,000 middle managers prowling around markets all over the world. If we in the executive committee could connect with all of them or even half of them and get them moving in roughly the same direction, we would be unstoppable.

But it's enormously difficult. Last year, for example, we made a big push to squeeze our accounts receivable and free up working capital. We called it the Cash Race. There are 2,000 people around the world with some role in accounts receivable, so we had to mobilize them to make the program work. Three or four months after the program started—and we made it very visible when it started—I visited an accounts receivable office where 20 people were working. These people hadn't even *heard* of the program, and it should have been their top priority. When you come face-to-face with this lack of communication, this massive inertia, you can get horrified, depressed, almost desperate. Or you can concede that this is the way things are, this is how the world works, and commit to doing something about it.

So what do you do?

You don't inform, you *overinform.* That means breaking taboos. There is a strong tendency among European managers to be selective about sharing information.

We faced a huge communications challenge right after the merger. In January 1988, just days after the birth of ABB, we had a management meeting in Cannes with the top 300 people in the company. At that meeting, we presented our policy

Change Comes to Poland—The Case of ABB Zamech

Last May, Zamech, Poland's leading manufacturer of steam turbines, transmission gears, marine equipment, and metal castings began a new life as ABB Zamech—a joint venture of ABB (76 percent ownership), the Polish government (19 percent ownership), and the company's employees (5 percent ownership). ABB Zamech employs 4,300 people in the town of Elblag, outside Gdansk. In September, two more Polish joint ventures became official—ABB Dolmel and Dolmel Drives. These companies manufacture a wide range of generating equipment and electric drives and employ some 2,400 workers.

The joint ventures are noteworthy for their size alone. ABB has become the largest Western investor in Poland. But they are perhaps more significant for their managerial implications, in particular, how ABB is revitalizing these deeply troubled operations. The company intends to demonstrate that the philosophy of business and managerial reform it has applied in places like Mannheim, Germany, and Muncie, Indiana, can also work in the troubled economies of Eastern Europe. That philosophy has at least four core principles:

1. Immediately reorganize operations into profit centers with well-defined budgets, strict performance targets, and clear lines of authority and accountability.

2. Identify a core group of change agents from local management, give small teams responsibility for championing high-priority programs, and closely monitor results.

3. Transfer ABB expertise from around the world to support the change process, without interfering with it or running it directly.

4. Keep standards high and demand quick results.

Barbara Kux, president of ABB Power Ventures, negotiated the Polish joint ventures and plays a lead role in the turnaround process. "Our goal is to make these companies as productive and profitable as ABB's operations worldwide," she says. "We don't make a 'discount' for Eastern Europe, and we don't expect the change process to take forever. We provide more technical and managerial support than we might to a company in the United States, but we are just as demanding in terms of results."

ABB Zamech has come the furthest to date. The change program began immediately after the creation of the joint venture. For decades, the company had been organized along functional lines, a structure that blurred managerial authority, confused product-line profitability, and slowed decision making. Within four weeks, ABB Zamech was reorganized into discrete profit centers. There are now three business areas (BAs)—the casting foundry, turbines and gears, and marine equipment—as well as a finance and administration department and an in-house service department. Each area has a leadership team that generates the business plans, budgets, and performance targets by which their operations are judged. These teams made final decisions on which employees would stay, which would go, what equipment they would need—tough-minded business choices made for the first time so as to maximize productivity (employee and capital) and business area profitability.

The reorganization was a crucial first step. The second big step was installing ABB's standard finance and control system. For decades, Zamech had been run as a giant overhead machine. Roughly 80 percent of the company's total costs were allocated by central staff accountants rather than traced directly to specific products and services. Managers had no clear idea what their products cost to make and thus no idea which ones made money. Tight financial controls and maximum capital productivity are critical in an economy with interest rates of 40 percent.

Formal reorganization and new control systems, no matter how radical, won't have much of an effect without big changes in who is in charge, however. ABB made two important decisions. First, there would be no "rescue team" from Western Europe. All managerial positions, from the CEO down, would be held by Polish managers from the former Zamech. Second, managers would be selected without regard to rank or seniority; indeed, there would be a premium on young, creative talent. ABB was looking for "hungry wolves"—smart, ambitious change agents who would receive intense training and be the core engine of Zamech's revival.

Most of the new leaders came from the ranks of middle management. The company's top executive, general manager Pawel Olechnowicz, ran the steel castings department prior to the joint venture's creation—a position that put him several layers below the top of the 15-layer management hierarchy. Employees had already elected him general manager shortly before the creation of ABB Zamech, so he looked like a good choice. The marine BA leader *continued*

Change Comes to Poland

had been a production manager in the old Zamech, another low-level position, and the turbines and gears BA manager had been a technical director.

"We put in place a management team that lacked the standard business tools," Kux explains. "They didn't know what cash flow was, they didn't understand much about marketing. But their ambition was incredible. You could feel their hunger to excel. When we began the talent search, we told our Zamech contacts that we wanted to see the 30 people they would take along tomorrow if they were going to open their own business."

Next came the process of developing a detailed agenda for reform. The leadership team settled on 11 priority issues, from reorganizing and retraining the sales force to slashing total cycle times and redesigning the factory layout. Each project was led by a champion—some from top management ranks, some from the other "hungry wolves." A steering committee made up of the general manager, the deputy general manager, the business area managers, and Kux meets monthly to review these critical projects.

To support the change initiatives, ABB created a team of high-level experts from around the world—authorities in functional areas like finance and control and quality, as well as technology specialists and managers with heavy restructuring experience. Team members do not live in Poland. Kux says it is unrealistic to expect top people to spend a year or two in the conditions they would find in Elblag. But they visit frequently and stay updated on progress and problems.

The logistics of expertise transfer are more complicated than they sound. For example, most of the Polish managers spoke little or no English—a serious barrier to effective dialogue. So ABB began intensive language training. "If Polish managers want to draw from the worldwide ABB resource pool, they must speak English," Kux emphasizes. "Most communication doesn't happen face-to-face where you can have an interpreter. Last May, I couldn't simply pick up the phone and talk to the general manager. Today we speak in English on the phone almost every day."

Of course, speaking on the telephone in English assumes a working telephone system—a dangerous assumption in the case of Poland. Thus, another prerequisite for effective expertise transfer was creating the infrastructure to make it possible. ABB has linked Zamech and Dolmel by satellite to its Zurich headquarters for reliable telephone and fax communications. (It is now easier to communicate between Zamech and Zurich and Dolmel and Zurich than it is between Zamech and Dolmel.) In January, ABB Zamech began electronically transferring three monthly performance reports to Zurich—another big step to make communications more intensive and effective.

Once it created the communications infrastructure, however, ABB had to reckon with a second language barrier—the language of business. To introduce ABB Zamech's "hungry wolves" to basic business concepts and to enable them to transfer these concepts into the ranks, ABB created a "mini MBA program" in Warsaw. The program began in September, covers five key modules (business strategy, marketing, finance, manufacturing, human resources) and is taught by faculty members of INSEAD, the French business school. Sessions run from Thursday evening through Saturday noon, use translated copies of Western business school cases, and closely resemble what goes on in MBA classes everywhere else.

The change program at ABB Zamech has been under way for less than a year, and much remains to be done. But it is already generating results. The company is issuing monthly financial reports that conform to ABB standards—a major achievement in light of the simple systems in place before the joint venture. Cycle times for the production of steam turbines have been cut in half and now meet the ABB worldwide average. A task force is implementing a plan to reduce factory space by 20 percent—an important step in streamlining the operation. ABB will draw on the Zamech experience as it begins the reform process at Dolmel and Dolmel Drives.

"You can change these companies," Kux says. "You can make them more competitive and profitable. I can't believe the quality of the reports and presentations these people do today, how at ease they are discussing their strategy and targets. I have worked with many corporate restructurings, but never have I seen so much change so quickly. The energy is incredible. These people really want to learn; they are very ambitious. Basically, ABB Zamech is their business now."

—William Taylor

bible, a 21-page book that communicates the essential principles by which we run the company. It's no glossy brochure. It's got tough, direct language on the role of BA managers, the role of country managers, the approach to change we just discussed, our commitment to decentralization and strict accountability. I told this group of 300 that they had to reach 30,000 ABB people around the world within 60 days—and that didn't mean just sending out the document. It meant translating it into the local languages, sitting with people for a full day and hashing it out.

Cannes and its aftermath was a small step. Real communication takes time, and top managers must be willing to make the investment. We are the "overhead company." I personally have 2,000 overhead slides and interact with 5,000 people a year in big and small groups. This afternoon, I'll fly up to Lake Constance in Germany, where we have collected 35 managers from around the world. They've been there for three days, and I'll spend three hours with them to end their session. Half the executive committee has already been up there. These are active, working sessions. We talk about how we work in the matrix, how we develop people, about our programs around the world to cut cycle times and raise quality.

I'll give a talk at Lake Constance, but then we'll focus on problems. The manager running high-voltage switchgear in some country may be unhappy about the BA's research priorities. Someone may think we're paying too much attention to Poland. There are lots of tough questions, and my job is to answer on the spot. We'll have 14 such sessions during the course of the year—one every three weeks. That means 400 top managers from all over the world living in close quarters, really communicating about the business and their problems, and meeting with the CEO in an open, honest dialogue.

Let's discuss the politics of global business. For senior executives, the world becomes smaller every day. For most production workers, though, the world is not much different from the way it was 20 years ago, except now their families and communities may depend for jobs on companies with headquarters thousands of miles away. Why shouldn't these workers worry about the loss of local and national control?

It's inevitable that a global business will have global decision centers and that for many workers these decision centers will not be located in their community or even their country. The question is, does the company making decisions have a national ax to grind? In our case the answer is no. We have global coordination, but we have no national bias. The 100 professionals who happen to sit in Zurich could just as easily sit in Chicago or Frankfurt. We're not here very much anyway. So what does it mean to have a headquarters in Zurich? It's where my mail arrives before the important letters are faxed to wherever I happen to be. It's where Abacus collects our performance data. Beyond that, I'm not sure if it means much at all.

Of course, saying we have no national ax to grind does not mean there are any guarantees. Workers will often ask if I can can guarantee their jobs in Norway or Finland or Portugal. I don't sit like a godfather, allocating jobs. ABB has a global game plan, and the game plan creates opportunities for employment, research, exports. What I guarantee is that every member of the federation has a fair shot at the opportunities.

Let's say you're a production worker at ABB Combustion Engineering in Windsor, Connecticut. Two years ago, you worked for a company that you knew was an "American" company. Today you are part of a "federation" of ABB companies around the world. Should you be happy about that?

You should be happy as hell about it. A production worker in Windsor is probably in the boiler field. He or she doesn't much care what ABB is doing with process automation in Columbus, Ohio, let alone what we're doing with turbines outside Gdansk, Poland. And that's fair. Here's what I would tell that worker: We acquired Combustion Engineering because we believe ABB is a world leader in power plant technology, and we want to extend our lead. We believe that the United States has a great future in power plants both domestically and on an export basis. Combustion represents 80 years of excellence in this technology. Unfortunately, the company sank quite a bit during the 1980s, like many of its U.S. rivals, because of the steep downturn in the industry. It had become a severely weakened organization.

Today, however, the business is coming back, and we have a game plan for the United States. We plan to beef up the Windsor research center to three or four times its current size. We want to tie Windsor's work in new materials, emissions reduction, and pollution control technology with new technologies from our European labs. That will let us respond more effectively to the environmental concerns here. Then we want to combine Combustion's strengths in boilers with ABB's strengths in turbines and generators and Westinghouse's strengths in transmission and distribution to become a broad and unique supplier to the U.S. utility industry. We also have an ambition for Combustion to be much more active in world markets, not with sales agents but through the ABB multidomestic network.

What counts to this production worker is that we deliver, that we are increasing our market share in the United States, raising exports, doing more R&D. That's what makes an American worker's life more secure, not whether the company has its headquarters in the United States.

Don't companies like ABB represent the beginning of a power shift, a transfer of power away from national government to supranational companies?

Are we above governments? No. We answer to governments. We obey the laws in every country in which we operate, and we don't make the laws. However, we do change relations *between* countries. We function as a lubricant for worldwide economic integration.

Think back 15 years ago, when Asea was a Swedish electrical company with 95 percent of its engineers in Sweden. We could complain about high taxes, about how the high cost of living made it difficult to recruit Germans or Americans to come to Sweden. But what could Asea do about it? Not much. Today I can tell the Swedish authorities that they must create a more competitive environment for R&D or our research there will decline.

That adjustment process would happen regardless of the creation of ABB. Global companies speed up the adjustment. We don't create the process, but we push it. We make visible the invisible hand of global competition.

Index

ABB Asea Brown Boveri
  organizing logic, 825
  reorganization, 823–841
ABB Zamech, 838–839
Account histories, using MSP, 579
Account profitability matrix, 535–536
Account relationships, beta testing and, 326
Account size, 553
Account volume, 534
Addition to product family, 68
Add-on/enhancement of product, 68
Administrative costs, 600
Advertising, 79–80
Affiliated Purchasing Group, contract negotiation, 495–512
After-sales-service, generic channel function, 332
Aggregate project plan; see Project plans
Aggressive customers, 517–518
Alias, Patrick, 452, 453, 456, 458, 469, 470
Alignment with current market
  risk and, 299
  technology commercialization and, 293–294, 298
Allaire, Paul, 667, 668
Alliances and partnerships, 270
Analysis of competitive products, 310–311
Analysis of customer perceptions, 309–315
Analytical Group (Millipore), 696–699
Analytical instruments, 99–123
Anderson, Bob, 714, 715
Announcement, implementation issue in ROLM Corporation case, 209–210
Anticipated need, new solution based on, 296–297
Apple Computer, hybrid marketing system, 600
Application engineering, channel function priority, 333
Applied research, 284–285
Approaches to selling; see Sales approaches
Asset recovery operations, Rank Xerox, 224–225
Assortment, generic channel function, 332
Atlas Copco
  background, 424–426
  distribution network, building of, 422–436
  distribution strategy, 428–436
  franchising, 422–423, 435–436
  Industrial Compressors Division, 426–427
  stationary air compressors, 423–424
Attraction power, 51
Automation
  effect on labor, 573
  for sales and marketing, 573–585
Availability, generic channel function, 332
Aziz, Fouad, 172–173, 174

Bach, John, 360, 361, 363, 366–370, 372–374, 375–376

Backlog, implementation issue in ROLM Corporation case, 210–213
Bailey, Kristin, 261
Balcom, Jim, 76, 77–78, 80, 81
Baly, Dominique, 705–706
Barabba, Vincent, 74
Barco Projection Systems
  background, 633–634
  competition, 645–648
  competition by Sony, 632–633
  distribution, 642–645
  evolution of product lines and markets, 638–641
  introduction of Sony 1270 projector, 648–649
  in 1989, 642–645
  organization of BPS, 635
  pricing options, 650–651
  product development options, 651–652
  products of BPS, 635–638
  Projection Systems division, 633–641
  projector markets, 641–642
  September 23, 1989, 650–652
Bargain basement customers, 517
Bargain hunters, 556, 557
Barnevik, Percy, interview, 823–841
Barry Wright Corporation, hybrid marketing system, 601–603
Baumgart, Paul, 413
Beckman, Sara, 288
Becon, Glenn, 288
Becton Dickinson & Company
  background of, 496–500
  changes in buyer behavior, 507–509
  competition, 504
  distribution, 505–507
  financial data, 497
  industry background, 501–504
  marketing and sales program, 503–509
  market trends, 502–503
  negotiations with APG, 510–512
  products, 496–500
  sample products, 499–500
  VACUTAINER Systems Division, 496
Bender, Howie, 174
Benefits
  categories of, 55, 56
  classes of, 55, 56
Benefit variables, 309–312
Beninga, Cheryl, 259
Bennett, Bob, 257, 259
Berrett, Jim, 452–453, 456, 458
Berthiume, Doug, 705
Beta testing, 64, 320–329
  defined, 322
  test site interests, 327–328
  validity of, 325–327
Better mouse trap marketing, 812
Bidal, Bill, 261

Bidding process, Fabtek, 662
Bid pricing, Fabtek, 653–667
Billing, 797
Blood collection products, as commodity business, 346
Booz Allen & Hamilton, technology commercialization statistics, 281
Borg Warner Chemicals, acquisition by General Electric Plastics, 759
Box dealer, 644
Branding, contract negotiation and, 495–512
Brand-use status, industrial segmentation and, 38–39
Breakthrough products, 67–71
  relative importance of, 71
Breakthrough projects, 268
Bundling of products, 561
Bush, Jack, 695
Business model, Northern Telecom, Norstar, 175–179
Business process integration, 622–623
Business-to-business marketing
  complex buying/selling process, 5–6
  concentrated customer base, 6
  customization, high level of, 7
  defined, 3
  derived demand, 4–5
  external linkages, 4–6
  internal linkages, 6–7
  management challenges, 7–10
  order fulfillment mechanism, 7
  technology, emphasis on, 6–7
Buyers
  changes in behavior of, 507–509
  motivation of, 54–56
  perception of selling company, 56–57
  powerful, 51–54
  value of purchase to, 560
Buyer-seller relationships, 41
  at initial product introduction, 620–621
Buyers' personal characteristics, 35, 43
Buying behavior variables, 552–554
Buying center, 49–51
  defined, 49
Buying group, negotiation with, Becton Dickinson & Company, 495–512
Buying psychology, 46–60
  gathering information, 57–59
Buying roles, 49–51
Buying/selling process, complexity of, 5–6

Caputo, Art, 102, 112, 706
Carriage trade, 517
Carroll, Mike, 709–710
Carroll, Robert, 419
Carter, Dennis L., 248, 255
Centers, Mike, 97
Centralization, with MSP, 578

842

Index

Channel additions, hybrid systems, 611–613
Channel benchmarking, 333–335
Channel compensation, hybrid channels, 590–591
Channel conflicts, 593–594
Channel design framework, 331–338
    description of process, 338–341
Channel function requirements, 332–333
Channel options
    evaluation of, 336
    feasibility of, 335–336
Channel overlaps, 336–338
Channels of distribution, 9–10; *see*
    Distribution channels
Channel strategy for new market,
    Computervision Corporation, 452–475
Channel structure
    hybrid channels, 589–592
    multiple channels, 592–594
Chaparral Steel, research at, 284–285
Chemicals, Rohm and Haas, 148–162
Chief executive officer (CEO), roles and needs
    of, 48
Chief pilot, roles and needs of, 48
Christensen, Clayton, 292
Clabough, James, 437–438, 441, 450, 451
Claerbout, Frans, 632, 633, 635, 639, 641,
    647, 650, 651, 652
de Clerck, Sjoerd, 649, 650
Coercive power, 51
Collaboration, cross-functional, 816–817
Commercialization, new products, 63–75
Commissions, hybrid channel systems and, 591
Commoditization
    differentiation strategies, 351–356
    early warning signs of, 348–349
    General Electric Plastics, 745–764
    industry dynamics, 357–358
    key concepts, 349–351
    timing, 356–357
Commodity businesses, 345–346
Commodity cycle, 345–359
Commodity magnet, 347–349
Communication(s)
    cross-functional, 816–817
    low-cost methods, 600–601
    MSP and, 577
    of product concept, 299–300
    Rank Xerox, 220
    Techsonic Industries, Inc., 84
Communications strategy, Rank Xerox, 232–235
Company culture, GenRad, 734–735
Company services, pricing of products and, 312
Company technology, industrial segmentation
    and, 38
Compatibility of new product with existing
    product line, 198, 205
Compensation policies, in hybrid marketing
    systems, 612
Competition
    American companies in Japan, 463–466
    Barco Projection Systems, 645–648
    Becton Dickinson & Company, 504
    in copier industry, 670–671
    Cumberland Metal Industries, 368–369
    distribution channels and, 586
    driving technological improvements,
        294–295
    Fabtek, 657

Competition—*Cont.*
    General Electric Plastics, 751–752
    Signode Industries, Inc., 487–491
    time-based, 283–284
Complementary product availability, channel
    function priority, 333
Components, 4
Computer industry, hybrid channels in, 590
Computervision Corporation
    Applicon and, 464
    Calma and, 463
    channel strategy for new market, 452–475
    competition in Japan, 463–466
    current situation, 470–475
    C-V Japan, 459–463
    financial data, five year summary, 454
    Fujitsu and, 464–465
    history of, 453
    IBM-Japan and, 464
    international operations, 450–463
    Japanese CAD/CAM market, 466–470
    market forecast, 470–471
    products, 453–456
    Seiko and, 465
    Tokyo Electron Limited (TEL), 456–459
Concentrated customer base, 6
Conflict, in hybrid marketing systems,
    608–611
Consumable supplies, 4
Consumer goods, demand for, 4
Consumer markets
    differentiated from industrial markets, 3
    purchasing decisions, 5
    segmentation of, 35
Contract negotiation, Becton Dickinson &
    Company, 495–512
Cooper, Robert, 289
Coordination
    across channels in hybrid marketing
        systems, 613
    cross-functional and interdepartmental, 10
    of sales resources, automated networks
        and, 580
    in Stage III, 624–627
Copiers, Rank Xerox, 215–243
Core rigidities, 290–291
Corporate jet purchase, buying psychology
    and, 47–49
Cost accounting systems, 520–521
Cost/benefit analysis
    of channel options, 336
    by customers, 307–309
Cost/benefit tradeoffs, 313–315
Cost containment, 600
Cost estimation and pricing, 795
Cost minimization, 606
Cost-plus pricing, 515
Costs
    pinpointing, 520–521
    to suppliers, 514–516
Cost structure, relationship to price, 318–319
Cost-to-serve, 516–518
    customer alignment in mature industrial
        markets, 549
    market life cycle and, 619
Cost variables, 312–313
Cousins, Doris, 139
Creative job assignments, 814–815

Creative recruiting, 814
Creative training, 814
Credit terms, channel function priority, 333
Critical capabilities, 278–280
Cross-functional collaboration and
    communication, 816–817
Cross-functional coordination, 10
Cross-functional team, for product
    development, 63–64
Crowley, Frank, 227, 234, 235, 237, 240, 242,
    243
Cultural diversity, and strategic account
    relationships, 540–541
Cumberland Metal Industries
    background, 361
    competition, 368–369
    contract period, 369–371
    curled metal, 361
    EGR development, 362–363
    entry into automotive market, 362–369
    market opening for, 363–365
    negotiations with Beta Motors, 372–376
    organization, 361
    precontract negotiations, 365–368
    pricing, 366–368
    relations with Beta Motors, 371–372
    reorganization, 371
Cumberland Metals Industries, beta testing, 324
Current markets
    barrier to technology commercialization,
        291–292
    technological potential, alignment with,
        293–294, 298
Custom-designed item, 770–771
Customer alignment, in mature industrial
    markets, 549–550
Customer base, 6
    relationship with, 198
Customer behavior, profitability and, 516–520
Customer capabilities, industrial segmentation
    and, 39–40
Customer characteristics, 609–611
Customer demands, driving technological
    improvements, 294–295
Customer input
    on breakthrough product development,
        67–69
    on incremental product development, 69–70
    on new product development, 66–67
    Techsonic Industries, Inc., 76–98
Customer location, industrial segmentation
    and, 38
Customer management, for profits, 513–524
Customer needs
    high-tech marketing, 808
    industrial pricing and, 306–319
    Millipore, 118–119
Customer perceptions
    analysis of, in pricing, 309–315
    Millipore, 108–109
Customer price sensitivity, 487
Customer profitability, 513–524
Customer purchasing approaches, 35, 40–41
Customer relationship
    large customer, Peak Electronics, 377–396
    over product life cycle, Cumberland Metal
        Industries, 360–376
Customer retention, 569–571

Customer retention process, 623–624
Customers; *see also* Buyers
  aggressive, 517–518
  benefits of strategic account relationships, 539–540
  classification of, 609–611
  cost-to-serve, 516–517
  evaluation of products by, 307–309
  hybrid channels and, 589–592
  industrial customer trade-offs, 766–767
  large, relationship with, 377–396
  management of, 513–524
  multiple channels and, 592–594
  negotiation with, 360–376
  net price realized, 516–517
  partnering with, in product development, 303
  preparation to buy, 120
  product choice decisions, 767
  Rank Xerox, 228–232
  Rohm and Haas, 155–157
  segmenting by size, 534, 551
  segmenting in mature industrial markets, 548–558
  sensitivity to price, 519
  sensitivity to service, 519
  for shadowed new products, 72–73
  sophistication of, 775
  United States Marketing Group (Xerox Corp.), 674–675
  value, and, 769–770
  working relationship with, 621
  Xerox customer guarantee, 687–689
Customers, analysis of
  for profitability, 513
  using MSP, 579
Customer satisfaction
  customer retention process and, 624
  external measurement system, 680–683
  internal measurement system, 683–684
  maximization of, 606
  measurement of, 679–684
  Xerox Corporation, 668–691
Customer segmentation
  in mature industrial markets, 548–558
  by SIC code, 551
  by size, 534, 551
Customer segments, homogeneous, 331
Customer service, 559–560
  accountability, 568
  description of, 560–564
  internal marketing and, 564–568
  management responsibility, 566
  managing customer retention, 569–571
  meaning to customers, 562–564
  measurement and evaluation, 567
  order fulfillment and, 624
  plans and budgets, 566–567
  United States Marketing Group (Xerox Corp.), 676–677
Customer service workshops, 559
Customization, 7
  in integrated circuit business, 780

D'Arbeloff, Dee, 695, 696
Database marketing, distribution channels and, 588
Davidow, William, 806

Davis, Stanley, 815
Dawson, Paul, 754, 755, 760
Dealer sales, Ohmeda (BOC Group), 397–421
Dean, Yank, IV, 77–78
Death of a Salesman, 46, 525
Decentralization, global business, 833–834
Deciders, 50–51
Decisionmaking, by executive committee, 834–835
Decision-making process, 554
  MSP and, 577
Dedication, 622–624
Dejonghe, Erik, 632, 633, 635, 639, 647, 649, 650, 651
Delivery, uncertainty about time of, 809–810
Delivery terms, negotiation of, 495–512
Delusionary new products, 74–75
Demand
  derived demand, 4–5
  estimation of, 5
Demand-side strategies, 357
Demographics, 35, 37–38
Demos, beta sites used as, 324–325
Derijcke, Camiel, 635
Derivative projects, 267
Derived demand, 4–5
Design in advance of market, 293–298
  challenges in, 298–304
Detailed market study, 64
Development map, 267–273
Development resources, 265–266
Development risks, 65
DiDeo, Tony, 113, 114
Differentiation of physical product, 350–351
Differentiation strategies, 351–356
  market focus strategy, 355
  process innovation strategy, 354–355
  service innovation strategy, 356
  value-added strategy, 352–353
Digital Equipment, time-based competition, 283
Direct accounts, Atlas Copco, 433
Direct mail, for cost containment, 600
Direct mail and fulfillment, 575
  price for systems, 583
Direct marketing
  distribution channels and, 589
  MSP and, 577
Direct sales force
  Ingersoll-Rand, 443
  Ohmeda (BOC Group), 397–421
Discounting, selective, Signode Industries, Inc., 476–494
Display, Atlas Copco, 433
Distinctive competencies of corporation, 284
Distribution
  Atlas Copco, 422–436
  Barco Projection Systems, 642–645
  Becton Dickinson & Company, 505–507
  contract negotiation and, 495–512
  management of multiple channels, 437–451
  Rank Xerox, 220
  Sony projectors, 646
  Techsonic Industries, Inc., 82–84
  train of, traditional, 587–588
  two-step system, 642
  United States Marketing Group (Xerox Corp.), 675

Distribution channels, 4, 9–10
  coordination, for new products, 244–263
  database marketing, effect of, 588
  design of, 330–342
  direct marketing, effect of, 588
  hybrid channels, 589–592
  Intel Corporation, 244–263
  management of multiple channels, 437–451
  multiple channels, 592–594
  policies and guidelines, 449
  reorientation of, 586–598
  Ring Medical, 143–146
  Rohm and Haas, 159–160
  shorter channels, 595–596
  strategic priorities, 586
  as vertical marketing systems, 587–588
  vertical or horizontal, 586
Distribution costs, 515
Distribution industry, trends in, 586–598
Distribution network, 422–436
Distribution strategy
  Atlas Copco, 428–436
  Computervision Corporation, 452–475
  for new market, 452–475
Distribution system, Ingersoll-Rand, 443–448
Distributors
  benefits of information technology to, 588–589
  Ohmeda (BOC Group), 397–421
Diverse specifications, 766–767
  utility of, 772–773
Diversity
  different mixture of diverse specifications, 768–770
  General Electric Plastics, 763–764
  in market maturity process, 619
  in Stage III, 624
  value-oriented product line, 769–770
  variety-oriented product line, 768–771
Dominant design, 775
  demise of, 775–777
Dreyfuss, Henry, 302
Droege, Arthur, 422–423, 426
Drone aircraft, 25–29
DuPont, market segmentation by, 548–549
Dursin, Bernard, 632, 633, 635, 639, 649, 650
Dyer, Tom, 76, 78

Efficiency, 622–624
  MSP systems and, 577
Ehlers, Norman, 381, 382
E.I. duPont de Nemours Company, utility pricing by, 308–309
Electrohome, competition with Barco Projection Systems, 648
Empathic design, 300–302
Ennis, Mike, 163, 167, 168, 170, 171, 172, 174, 183, 185
Entrepreneurship, 620–621
Environmental leadership program, Rank Xerox, 225–228
Environmental marketing team, Rank Xerox, 227–228
Estimation, of demand for industrial products, 5
Evaluation, 567

Evolution of product to meet uncertain need, 297–298
Expansion, in Stage III, 624–627
Expert power, 51, 52
External linkages
    complex buying/selling process, 5–6
    concentrated customer base, 6
    derived demand, 4–5
    distribution channels, 4
    industrial marketing, 4–6

Fabtek
    bidding process, 662
    capacity shortage, 653
    competition, 657
    customers, 655–657
    Fabrication Division, 654–655
    forecasts, 657–658
    growth, 655
    manufacturing process, 658–661
    marketing, 662–663
    markets, 655–657
    organization, 654–655
    prospective fabrication orders, 663–666
    shop backlog, 659–661
Field testing, Northern Telecom, Norstar, 181–182
Final business plan, 64
Financial performance, new product development and, 264
Fister, Mike, 248, 263
Focus groups, 78, 79, 80, 301
    advertising based on, 80
Follow-on services, 347
Ford Motor Company
    minority supplier development program, 380–382
    relationship with Peak Electronics, 377–396
Foreign company, building of U.S. distribution network, 422–436
Forster, Dave, 125, 133, 139, 141, 143, 144, 145, 147
Franchised distributors, 534
Franchising, Atlas Copco, 422–423, 435, 436
Fry, Arthur, 72
Fulfillment, 796
Functional organization, GEP Americas, 753–758
Functional performance of product, uncertainty about, 809
Functional specialization, 622–623
Future need, determination of, 296–297

Gabler, Ray, 113, 114
Garabedian, Harbig, 746
Gatekeepers, 49, 50
General Electric Plastics
    acquisition of Borg Warner Chemicals, 759
    competition, 751–752
    diversity, 763–764
    generation of consumer interest by, 299–300
    GEP Americas, 753–758
    GEP Asia Pacific, 758–759
    GEP Europe, 758
    growth with stability, 764
    management of complexity, 627–631
    molders, 749–750

General Electric Plastics—*Cont.*
    organization, 752–753
    original equipment manufacturers, 750–751
    pressure for uniformity, 762–763
    problems of global marketing, 762–764
    product description, 748–749
    product management at U.S. headquarters, 760–762
General management orientation, 621
GenRad
    company background, 716
    company culture, 734–735
    competition, 725–732
    customers' new needs, 740
    electronics testing equipment, 719–720
    financial data, 717
    Hewlett-Packard, 730–732
    history of PCB ATE technology, 741–744
    market for printed circuit board testers, 720–724
    market segmentation, 723–724
    new product planning and development process, 738–739
    organization, 735–738
    product line and market definition, 732–734
    product-marketing strategy, 715–744
    Teradyne, 726–730
    test technology trends, 741
Geographic boundaries, 611
Geography
    effect on customer profitability, 513
    presale costs and, 514–515
Gill, Frank K., 248
Gilmartin, John, 106, 692, 693, 695, 696, 707, 710, 711, 712, 714
Global business
    ABB Asea Brown Boveri reorganization, 823–841
    obstacles to global restructuring, 835–840
    politics of, 840–841
Global coordination, 829–830
Global manager, 826–827
Global organization strategy, General Electric Plastics, 745–764
Gnodde, David, 15, 24
GNP; *see* Gross national product
Govaerts, Val, 215, 227, 231, 235, 238, 240, 242, 243
Green consumerism, Rank Xerox, 221–224
Greene, Harold, 204
Green products, Rank Xerox, 215–243
Gross national product (GNP), business-to-business activity as percentage of, 3–4

Haas, Otto, 149
Halpert, Mark, 415
Hamilton, Clay, 483, 493
Hay, Peter, 706
Headquarters, role in global business, 833–834
Health care industry, hybrid channels in, 590
Heavy equipment, 4
Hernandez, Henry, 483, 493
Herzberg, Frederic, 559–560
Hewlett-Packard
    GenRad and, 730–732
    immersion in environment of user, 302
    product definition project, 285–288

Hewlett-Packard—*Cont.*
    Qualified Lead Tracking System (QUILTS), 580
    shortening product life cycles, 282
    tracking trends to determine future needs, 297
    user needs considered at, 294–296
High-cost channels, alignment with big customers, 606
High fashion marketing, 812
High-tech, defined, 807–808
High-tech marketing, 806–807, 806–822
    better mouse trap marketing compared with, 812
    broadening and deepening of skill set, 813–814
    continuity in change, 818–822
    creative job assignments, 814–815
    creative recruiting, 814
    creative training, 814
    critical issues, 812–813
    cross-functional collaboration and communication, 816–817
    customer needs, 808
    differentiating factors, 807–812
    high fashion marketing compared with, 812
    high-tech, defined, 807–808
    interfirm alliances, use of, 817–818
    literature about, 806
    low-tech marketing compared with, 811–812
    market uncertainty, 808–809
    recognizing obsolete marketing approaches, 815–816
    tactics, 813–822
    technical standards, 808
    technological uncertainty, 809–812
    technology, defined, 807
Hillback, Elliott, Jr., 415
Hiner, Glen, 746, 752, 764
Hirama, Will, 404
Ho, Stanley, 653
Holloway, Bob, 389
Homogeneous customer segments, 331
Hoodes, Donald, 426, 440
Human factors; *see* Buying psychology
Hybrid channels, 336–337, 589–592
Hybrid grid, 599, 603–608
Hybrid marketing systems, 599–615

IBM Corporation, hybrid marketing system, 599
Immersion in environment of user, 302
Implementation of product launch, ROLM Corporation, 207–213
Incentives, in hybrid marketing systems, 613
Incremental products
    relative importance of, 71
    Techsonic Industries, Inc., 81
Independent distributor network, Ingersoll-Rand, 443–444
Industrial customer trade-offs, 766–767
Industrial marketing; *see* Business-to-business marketing
Industrial markets
    differentiated from consumer markets, 3
    products sold in, classification of, 4
    segmentation of, 35–45
Industrial membranes, 99–123
Industrial pricing, 306–319

Industrial products and services, size of market for, 3–4
Industrial segmentation, 35–45
   Millipore, 110–111, 117–118
Industry knowledge, industrial segmentation and, 37
Industry life cycle, 273–274
Industry structure, PET and, 777–778
Influencers, 49–50
Information flow management from beta site, 326–327
Information systems, Ring Medical, 124–147
Information technology
   distribution channels, effect on, 588–589
   MSP and, 575
Ingersoll-Rand
   buying behavior, 447–448
   distribution system, 442–448
   multiple channels, management of, 437–451
   rationale for multiple channel system, 447
   spare parts sales, 446–447
   Stationary Air Compressor Division, 441–443
   stationary air compressor market, 438–441
Initial screening, 64
Initiators, 49, 50
Innovation
   incremental versus radical, 66, 67–71
   of product delivery system, 351
   relation to variety and value approaches, 772
In Search of Excellence, 559
Installed base, implementation issue in ROLM Corporation case, 213
Insurance industry, hybrid marketing systems, 600
Integration, market complexity and, 620–622
Intel Corporation
   coordination of distribution channels for new products, 244–263
   math coprocessors, 252–253
   microprocessors, 249–252
   overdrive processor, 253–263
   overview of, 246–248
Interdepartmental coordination, 10
Interdependencies among divisions, 712–713
Interfirm alliances, use in high-tech marketing, 817–818
Internal linkages, 6–7
   customization, high level of, 7
   order fulfillment mechanism, 7
   research and development, 4
   technology, emphasis on, 6–7
Internal marketing, customer service and, 564–568
International marketing, variety *versus* value in, 780–781
Intertech (Millipore), 705–706

Jacoby, Doug, 701, 703
Japan
   CAD/CAM market in, 466–470
   competition of American companies in, 463–466
   market potential, 469–470
   unique market characteristics, 467–469
Jensen, Ray, 380, 381, 382, 385

Job assignments, creative, 814–815
Jobs, Steve, 66
Johansen, Jack, 102, 707
Johnson, Jack, 15, 25, 33

Kearns, David, 672
Kennedy, Wayne, 711
Kitplanes, 32–33
Kleinschmidt, Elko, 289
Known need
   improved solution for, 294–295
   new solution for, 295–296
Kodak, time-based competition, 283–284
Kozy, William, 495, 511, 512
Kummer, Karl, 227, 228, 232, 234, 235, 237

Labor, effect of automation on, 573
Lambo, Nick, 120, 121–122, 706
Laptop PCs, MSP and, 578
Laswell, Harry, 252, 253, 255
Lauer, Clinton, 381, 386
Launching of product; *see* Product launch
Launch planning, Millipore, 99–123
Launch strategy, 121–122
Leadership Through Quality strategy (Xerox), 669, 671, 679
Leahy, Tim, 100
Le Roux, Philippe, 15, 16, 20, 22, 33–34
Levitt, Theodore, 310
Life cycle cost, 205
Light aviation, 29–32
Light equipment, 4
Lightfoot, Rob, 653, 654, 661, 663, 666
Lindsay, John, 706
Logistics, generic channel function, 332
Lot size, generic channel function, 332
Low-cost channels, alignment with small customers, 606
Low-tech marketing, 811–812
Lundy, Bob, 198, 199, 204–214

Macey, Joan, 148, 149, 160, 161, 162
Macher, P.E., 394, 395
Mack, Jane, 484
McKenna, Regis, 806, 808
McLean, Peter, 127
Major account management, 527–528
   justification of, 532–533
Malcolm Baldrige National Quality Award, 669
Mall studies, 301
Management challenges in business-to-business marketing, 7–10
Management of marketing
   industrial segmentation and, 36
   MSP and, 578–582
Managers, cross-functional responsibilities, 621
Managing for Excellence (Millipore), 695
Manufacturing, order fulfillment and, 624
Manufacturing constraints, Fabtek, 653–667
Manufacturing operations, Rank Xerox, 219
Manufacturing resource planning system, 293
Map of tasks and channels in hybrid marketing system, 603–608
Mapping projects, 267–273
Market analysis
   industrial segmentation and, 35
   research on product success/failure, 288–290

Market complexity
   case studies, 627–631
   efficiency and dedication, 622–624
   entrepreneurship and integration, 620–622
   expansion and coordination, 624–627
   GE Plastics, 627–631
Market coverage, increase of, 600
Market creation
   risk and, 299
   technology commercialization and, 293–294, 298
Market definition, Millipore, 109–110
Market development reps (MDRs), 757
Marketer, decisions regarding diverse specifications, 767
Market focus strategy, 355
Market growth, in Stage III, 624
Market identification, wrong market, 297
Marketing and sales productivity systems (MSP)
   customization of, 584–585
   direct mail and fulfillment, 575
   economies of scale and, 579
   estimation of financial benefit of, 583
   implementation guidelines, 582–585
   large companies as prospects for, 574
   as management tool, 578–582
   MSP databases, 576–577
   PC-based, 576
   productivity improvement and, 577–578
   ramp-up strategy, 584
   sales and marketing management, 575
   sales force automation, 578–579
   salesperson productivity tools, 575
   telemarketing, 575
   uses of, 574–577
Marketing automation, 573–585
Marketing challenges, Ring Medical, 141–146
Marketing inertia, MSP and, 578
Marketing mistakes, in new product development and commercialization, 66–75
Marketing operations, Rank Xerox, 219–220
Marketing plan, review of, 161–162
Marketing program, Northern Telecom, Norstar, 179–180
Marketing resources, MSP for, 580
Marketing strategy
   review of, 161–162
   Rohm and Haas, 160–161
Marketing systems
   hybrid marketing systems, 599–615
   Ohmeda (BOC Group), 397–421
Marketing tasks, analysis of, 603
Market knowledge, 554
Market launch, 64
Market life cycle, 619–620
Market oriented, 783–791
Market position, new product development and, 264
Market potential, Japanese, 469–470
Market research
   beta testing, 320–329
   high-tech marketing, 806
Market research firm (MRF), 78
Market segmentation, 8
   diverse specifications, 772
   GenRad, 723–724
   in mature industrial markets, 548–558
   Signode Industries, Inc., 485–486

Index

Market selection, industrial segmentation and, 36
Market share, 553
    Signode Industries, Inc., 476–494
Market studies, Techsonic Industries, Inc., 84–85, 90, 94
Market uncertainty, high-tech marketing, 808–809
Market windows, 282
Mass marketing, 75
Master distributor, 595–596
Matthews, Ross, 174, 175, 182
Matthews, Stephanie, 141
Mature industrial markets
    product life cycle theory, 549
    segmenting customers in, 548–558
May, Chuck, 382, 383, 386, 389, 390, 394, 395
Mazda, rotary engines and, 19
Measurement and evaluation, 567
Metal fabrication, hybrid marketing systems, 600
Micromanagement of project development, 266
Midttun, Helge, 127, 132
Migration patterns, 519–520
Miller, Arthur, 46, 525
Millipore
    accountability, 709–710
    Analytical Group, 697–700
    communications, 710–712
    company history, 695–697
    competition, 114–117
    corporate background, 100–107
    division strategy and structure, 697–707
    interdependencies, 712–713
    Intertech, 705–706
    LC/MS project, 107–112
    Managing for Excellence, 695
    new product commercialization, 99–123
    Process Group, 701–703
    product launch, 120–122
    product/market planning, 707–709
    research and development, 709
    strategic and organizational issues, 709–713
    summary of operations, 694
    virus removal commercialization, 113–114
    Waters Chromatography Division, 703–705
    worldwide sales and marketing, 706
Minority-owned business, Peak Electronics, 377–396
Minority supplier development program, Ford Motor Company, 380–382
Moore, T.E., 325
Motivation
    of buyers, 54–56
    for service, 559–560
Motorcycle manufacturing, 15–34
Mowery, David, 288
MSP databases, 576–577
    as management tool, 578–582
Multidivisional organization, Millipore, 692–714
Multidomestic enterprise, 824
    organization of, 828–833

Multiple channels, 592–594
    management of, 437–451
    rationale for, 447

Naming of product, 118
National regulations, Rank Xerox and, 238
Navigation products, 93–97
Neale, Bill, 377
NEC, competition with Barco Projection Systems, 648
Negotiation with customers, Cumberland Metal Industries, 360–376
Nested hierarchy, 36, 37, 43–45
Net price realized, 516–517
New core product, 68
New markets, technological potential requiring creation of, 293–294, 298
New product commercialization, 63–75
    Millipore, 99–123
New product marketing, Ring Medical, 124–147
New product planning and development, GenRad, 738–739
New products
    coordination of distribution channels for, 244–263
    design of channels of distribution, 330–342
    development and commercialization, 7–8
    failure rates for, 63, 330
    Intel Corporation, 244–263
    Techsonic Industries, Inc., 76–98
New product taxonomies, 66–68
Next generation product, 68
NG (company), 15–34
Nomura, Jim, 457, 458, 469
Northern Telecom
    business model, 175–179
    business products division, 166–168
    field test, 181–182
    Greenwich investment proposal, 163–170
    marketing program, 179–180
    Norstar development program, 174–175
    product definition, 180–181
    product development, 171–187
    product launch, 171–187, 182–185
    product line extension, 163–170
    project planning, 163–170
    reseller analysis, 168–170
    Vantage product line, 172–174
Norton, James Lansdowne, 16
Norton Group PLC
    choice of product, 15–34
    drone aircraft, 25–29
    history of company, 16–21
    light aviation, 29–32
    motorcycle market, 22–25
    scope of operations, 21
    ultralight aviation (kitplanes), 32–33
Nunley, Al, 97
NutraSweet, joint marketing interests, 539–540

O'Donnell, Stephen, 484
OEM, 748–749
Office supplies, hybrid marketing systems, 600
Ohmeda (BOC Group)
    anesthesia equipment, 410–413
    architectural products, 416
    company background, 398–400

Ohmeda (BOC Group)—Cont.
    dealers, 404–406
    direct sales, 406–408
    infant care, 415
    marketing changes, 400–403
    marketing channels, 404–408
    markets, 408–416
    North American Field Operations, 416
    options, 421
    organization, 400
    patient monitors, 413
    respiratory therapy, 413–414
    suction therapy, 414–415
    U.S. sales, 417–421
Olsen, Den, 395
Operating variables, 35, 38–40
Opportunity costs, 65
Order fulfillment, 624, 796
    urgency of, 41–42
Order fulfillment mechanism, 7
Order generation, 795
Order management cycle (OMC), 792–793
    analysis, 802–803
    benefits of, 804–805
    billing, 797
    case studies of, 798–801
    cost estimation and pricing, 795
    fulfillment, 796
    lessons regarding, 793–795
    order generation, 795
    order planning, 795
    order receipt and entry, 796
    order selection and prioritization, 796
    political strategy, 804
    postsales service, 797
    returns and claims, 797
    scheduling, 796
    system focus, 803
Order planning, 795
Order receipt and entry, 796
Orders, size of; see Order size
Order selection and prioritization, 796
    Fabtek, 653–667
Order size
    effect on customer profitability, 513
    industrial segmentation and, 42
Organizational structure, Millipore, 692–714
Original equipment manufacturers (OEM), 750–751
Owens, Ed, 125, 132, 133, 139, 140, 141, 143, 144, 145, 147

Paboojian, Dennis, 207
Partnering with customers, in product development, 303
Passive customers, 517
PBX equipment, ROLM Corporation, 198–214
Peak Electronics
    agreement with Ford, 385
    attempt to discontinue relationship, 394–396
    background, 379–380
    beginning of operations, 389–392
    contract with Ford, 386–389
    financial difficulties, 392–394
    initiation of relationship with Ford, 382–385

Peak Electronics—*Cont.*
  relationship with Ford Motor Company, 377–396
  Yancy, Earl, 378–379
Penalties, in hybrid marketing systems, 612
Perceived quality index, 579
Personal buyer characteristics, 35, 43
Person to person relationships, in strategic account relationships, 540
Petty, Judy, 140
Phone systems
  Northern Telecom, Greenwich investment proposal, 163–170
  Northern Telecom, Norstar launch, 171–187
  PBX equipment, ROLM Corporation, 198–214
Physical attributes of product, in analysis of customer perceptions, 310–312, 313–314
Pickering, Wendy, 365, 366
Platform projects, 268–269
Platforms, 273–275
Polinsky, Joe, 363, 365
Pope, Dean, 423, 426
Post-It Notes, as example of shadowed new product, 72
Postsale service costs, 515
Postsales service, 795
Potential product lines, Rank Xerox, 235–237
Power, types of, 51–53
Powerful buyers
  identification of, 54
  types of, 51–53
Power structures, industrial segmentation and, 40
Power transformers, 827–828
Preliminary business analysis, 64
Preliminary market assessment, 64
Preliminary technical assessment, 64
Presale costs, 514–515
Price, Carl, 179–180
Price concessions, in mature markets, 347
Price erosion, Signode Industries, Inc., 476–494
Price-flex system, Signode Industries, Inc., 476–494
Price-performance ratio, 313–315
Price-sensitive customers, 518
Price strategy, 306, 307
Pricing
  based on marketing-related services, 574
  CAD/CAM systems, 467
  contract negotiation and, 495–512
  customer price sensitivity, 487
  diverse specifications and, 767
  Fabtek, 653–667
  market life cycle and, 617
  profitability and, 513
  in steel strapping market, 491–494
Pricing of products, 8–9
  analysis of customer perceptions in, 309–315
  buying psychology and, 46–47
  cost structure and, 318–319
  customer needs considerations in, 306–319
  Millipore, 119–120
  product planning and, 317–318

Pricing policy, Rank Xerox, 240
Pricing terms, negotiation of, 496–512
Processed materials, 4
Process Group (Millipore), 701–703
Process innovation strategy, 354–355
Process technology, 807
Product, type of, matching with development process, 64–65
Product acceptance, Rank Xerox, 237–238
Product application, industrial segmentation and, 42
Product attributes, 766
  price, trade-off with, 773
Product boundaries, 611
Product bundling, 561
Product choice decisions by customers, 767
Product commercialization, new products; *see* New product commercialization
Product concept, communication of, 299–300
Product customization, generic channel function, 332
Product definition, Northern Telecom, Norstar, 180–181
Product definition project, Hewlett-Packard, 285–288
Product development, 64
  acceleration of, 65
  beta testing, 320–329
  cross-functional team, 63–64
  failure rate of new products, 63
  Hewlett-Packard product definition project, 285–288
  Millipore, 104–107
  new product commercialization, 63–75
  NeXT computers, 66
  Northern Telecom, 171–187
  Norton Group PLC, 15–34
  research on product success/failure, 288–290
  stages in, 64
  timing of beta testing, 326
Product development process
  flaws in, 63
  matching with product type, 64–65
Product development program, Barco Projection Systems, 632–652
Product differentiation strategy, 350
Product evaluation, by customers, 307–309
Product evolution to meet uncertain need, 297–298
Product evolution trajectory (PET), 774–780
  fire engine industry, 778–780
  integrated circuit business, 780
Product guarantees, Rank Xerox, 240–243
Product importance, 553
Product information
  channel function priority, 333
  generic channel function, 332
Production costs, 515
Production ramp up, 64
Productive sales calls, in buying psychology, 58
Productivity, MSP systems and, 573–574, 577–578
Product launch
  failure of, 63, 148–162
  implementation of, 198–214
  launch strategy, 121–122
  Millipore, 111–112, 120–122

Product launch—*Cont.*
  Northern Telecom, 171–187
  Northern Telecom, Norstar, 182–185
  Rank Xerox, 215–243
  recycled parts, built from, 215–243
  Ring Medical, 124–147
  Rohm and Haas, 148–162, 160–161
  ROLM Corporation, 198–214
  Sony Walkman, 74–75
Product life cycles, 282, 347–348
Product life cycle theory, 549
Product line evolution, 765–782
Product line extension
  Northern Telecom, 163–170
  project planning for, 163–170
Product line management, Intel Corporation, 244–263
Product lines, potential, 235–237
Product management, General Electric Plastics, 745–764
Product-marketing strategy, GenRad, 715–744
Product-market strategy, Millipore, 692–714
Product planning, pricing and, 317–318
Product policy
  custom-designed item, 770–771
  different mixture of diverse specifications, 768–770
  diverse specifications and, 767
  price relationship with, 313–315
  product versus value, 765–782
  Ring Medical, 141–143
  special-purpose products, 771–772
  variety-oriented product line, 768–771
Product positioning, delusional new products, 74–75
Product quality assurance, generic channel function, 332
Product replacement, Northern Telecom, 163–170
Product status, industrial segmentation and, 38–39
Product technology, 807
Product warranty, channel function priority, 333
Profitability
  cost and price variation, effect on, 513–514
  costs to suppliers, 513–514
  customer behavior, 516–520
  customer situation, effect of, 519
  in declining market, Signode Industries, Inc., 476–494
  migration patterns, effect of, 519–520
  segmenting accounts and prospects, 533–536
  strategy, focus of, 522
  support systems, 522–523
  variety product line, 769
Profitability dispersion, 513, 521–522
Profit dispersion analysis, 523–524
Profit margin, 644
Profits, customer management for, 513–524
Programmed buyers, 554–557
Project development, micromanagement of, 266
Project mapping, 267–273
Project planning
  Northern Telecom, 163–170
  for product line extension, 163–170

Index

Project plans, 264–280
Project SAPPHO, 286–288
Pun, Cesar, 257, 259
Purchase decision
    people involved in, 48
    powerful buyers, 51–54
Purchasers, 50, 51
    impact of sales approaches on, 531
Purchasing approaches, 35, 40–41

Rabino, S., 325
Rank Xerox
    asset recovery operations, 224–225
    communications, 220
    communications strategy, 232–235
    company background, 216–221
    competition, 220–221
    customers, 228–232
    distribution, 220
    environmental leadership program, 225–228
    environmental marketing team, 227–228
    green consumerism, 221–224
    manufacturing operations, 219
    marketing operations, 219–220
    national regulations and, 238
    organization of, 216, 219
    potential product lines, 235–237
    pricing policy, 240
    product acceptance, 237–238
    product guarantees, 240–243
Rash, Bill, 253
Raw materials, 4
Recruiting, creative, 814
Reed, Gary, 476, 477, 483, 493–494
Reference accounts, beta sites used as, 324–325
Relationship buyers, 555, 557–558
Relative channel profile, 334
Relative price, 552
Relative service, 552–553
Repetitive tasks, MSP and, 577
Replacement motors, as commodity business, 346
Resale, goods purchased for, 3
Research
    from basic to applied, 284–285
    on product success/failure, 288–290
Research and development, 4, 269
    from basic to applied research, 284–285
    centrality in new product development, 624
    Millipore, 707
    shadowed new products and, 71–72
Research of customer base, 78–79
Reseller analysis, Northern Telecom, 168–170
Resource allocation, Norton Group PLC, 15–34
Returns and claims, 797
Reward power, 51
Ring Group of North America, Inc., 127–132
Ring Medical, 132–133
    HCS-100, 133–141
    marketing challenges, 141–146
    new product marketing, 124–147
    Ring Group of North America, Inc., 127–132
Risk, in product development, 299

Rohm, Otto, 149
Rohm and Haas
    company background, 149–152
    competition, 157–159
    customers, 155–157
    distribution channels, 159–160
    Kathon, 154–155
    marketing strategy, 160–161
    metalworking fluid biocides, 152–155
    product launch failure, 148–162
    sales and profits, 150–151
ROLM Corporation
    company background, 199–201
    competition, 204
    growth years, 201–203
    implementation, 207–213
    new product launch, 198–214
    product lines, 200
    SIGMA, 204–206
    technologic concerns, 203–204
Rotary engines, Norton Group PLC, 15–34
Roundtree, W. Dekle, 397, 400, 401, 404, 405, 413, 414, 415, 416, 421
Ruggieri, Paul, 124, 125, 130, 131, 132, 143, 145, 146, 147
Ruttenberg, Valerie, 408
Ryans, John, 808

Sales
    automation and, 573–584
    human side of; see Buying psychology
    types of selling, 525–547
Sales and marketing management, 575
Sales approaches
    application of different types, 530–532
    comparisons of different types, 530–532
    justification for different types, 532–534
    major account management, 527–528
    strategic account relationships, 528–530
    systems sales, 526–527
    transaction selling, 526
Sales audit, in buying psychology, 58–59
Sales force
    preparation to sell, 120–121
    productivity of, 577
    raw leads, followup of, 580
Sales forecasting, Millipore, 122
Sales managers, 46
Salesperson productivity tools, 575
Sales promotion, beta testing used for, 324
Sales resources, coordination of, 580
Sales strategies, 46
Sales volume, income and, 513
Scale, management of, 622
Scheduling, 796
Secondary wave planning, 276–278
Security, implementation issue in ROLM Corporation case, 209
Segmentation criteria, 35, 36–43
Segmentation of industrial markets; see Industrial segmentation
Segmenting customers, 607
    in mature industrial markets, 548–559
Sekhri, Paul, 100, 113, 115, 119, 120, 122
Selective discounting, Signode Industries, Inc., 476–494
Seller, impact of sales approaches on, 531
Selling; see Buying/selling process

Selling approaches, based on buyer motivation, 55–56
Selling costs, 600
Semiconductors, Intel Corporation, 244–263
Service
    after-sales-service, 332
    Atlas Copco, 432–433
    high-technology, uncertainty about, 810
Service industries, hybrid marketing systems, 600
Service innovation strategy, 356
Services, 4
    pricing of products and, 312
    special services for selected accounts, 537–539
Shadowed new products, 71–73
    shadowed, defined, 71
Shanklin, William, 808
Shephard, Carole, 227, 234, 235, 238, 242
Ship yield, 392
Shorter channels, 595–596
SIC code, customer segmentation by, 551
Signaling properties of beta testing, 325
Signode Industries, Inc.
    competition, 487–491
    corporate background, 477–479
    financial data, 478
    general background, 476–479
    manufacturing and materials management, 484
    organization of, 479
    organization of packaging division, 482–484
    plastic strapping, 480
    pricing in steel strapping market, 491–494
    sales and marketing organization, 483
    steel strapping, 479–480
    steel strapping market, 484–487
    tools and equipment, 480–481
Site selection for beta testing, 325–326
Situational factors, 35, 41–42
Size of company, industrial segmentation and, 38
Smith, Hank, 495, 507, 512
Social responsibility, management of, 10
Sonar depth sounders, 76–98
Sony Corporation
    competition with Barco Projection Systems, 645–648
    introduction of 1270 projector, 632–633, 648–649
Sony Walkman, launch process of, 74–75
Special account relationships, 537
Specialization, 622–623
Special-purpose products, 771–772
Stage-gate system, 65
Staples, Inc., hybrid marketing system, 614
Status power, 51, 52
Steady stream sequencing, 275–276
Steel strapping, as commodity business, 346
Stewart, Alan, 173–174
Strand, Dave, 99, 108, 110–111
Strategic account, defined, 536
Strategic account relationships, 528–530
    benefits to customers, 539–540
    choice of accounts, 541
    customers applied to, 536–537
    implementation, 544–547

Strategic account relationships—*Cont.*
   integration in, 541
   justification of, 533–534
   management of, 545–547
   nurturing of, 540–541
   problems of, 542–544
   rewards of, 541–542
Strategy, for managing accounts, 522
Strategy analysis, 523–524
Superglobal business, 824
Superlocal business, 824
Supplier-customer misperceptions, 66–67
Suppliers
   costs to, 514–516
   hybrid channels and, 589–592
   reorientation of distribution channels, 586–598
   shorter channels and, 595–596
Supply-side strategies, 357
Support systems, profitability and, 522–523
Support tasks, MSP and, 577
Surveys, 301
Switching potential, 554
Systems, 4
Systems dealer, 644
Systems sales, 526–527
   customers applied to, 534–537
   justification of, 532
Szuluk, Charlie, 386

Targeted selling, buying psychology and, 47
Target market, Ring Medical, 134–137
Task automation, 580–581
Taxonomies, new product, 66–68
Taylor, William, interview, 823–841
Technical standards, high-tech marketing uncertainty, 808
Technological obsolescence, 811
Technological potential
   alignment with current markets, 293–294, 298
   development of products based on, 295–296
Technological uncertainty
   defined, 809
   delivery date, 809–810
   obsolescence, 811
   product's functional performance, 809
   service and repair, 810
   unanticipated side effects, 811
Technology
   of company; *see* Company technology
   defined, 807
   emphasis on, 6–7
   high-tech marketing, 806–822
   role in product development, 67–69
   ROLM Corporation, 203–204
   strategic account relationships and, 539
Technology commercialization
   design in advance of market, 293–305
   distinctive competencies of corporation, 284
   Hewlett-Packard product definition project, 285–288
   market windows, 282
   research, 284–285
   statistics on, 281

time-based competition, 283–284
   user needs, 288–293
Technology push, 297
Techsonic Industries, Inc.
   company background, 77–78
   customer, importance of, 80
   depth sounder market, 81–82
   marketing, 82–84
   navigation products, 93–97
   new product development by, 76–98
   new product options, 84–89
   VHF marine radio, 89–93
Telemarketing, 575
   for cost containment, 600
   price for systems, 583
Telephone; *see* Phone systems
Teradyne, 726–730
Test market, 64
Textiles, hybrid marketing systems, 600
Time-based competition, 283–284
Timing
   of beta testing, 326
   implementation issue in ROLM Corporation case, 210
Training
   Atlas Copco, 433–434
   creative, 814
Transaction buyers, 556–558
Transaction costs, 561
Transaction selling, 526
   customers applied to, 534–537
Trial production, 64
True yield percentage, 392

Ultralight aviation (kitplanes), 32–33
Uncertain need, solutions for, 297–298
Uncertainty
   high-tech marketing, 808–809
   initial product introduction, 620–621
   in market maturity process, 619
   in product development, 299
   in Stage III, 624
   technological, 809–812
United States Marketing Group (Xerox Corp.), 673–674
   customers, 674–675
   customer service, 676–677
   distribution, 675
   product line and pricing, 675–676
Universal benefits, 766
   diverse specifications *versus* trade-offs, 772–773
   dominant design and, 775
Urgency of order fulfillment, industrial segmentation and, 41–42
User evaluation of future products, 299–300
User needs, 288–293
   product development based on, 294–298
   tools and mechanisms for understanding of, 300–304
User reaction, elicitation of, 299–300
Users, 50, 51
   as developers, 302–303
   myopia about needs, 292–293
Utility of product, 772–773
Utility pricing, 308

Value-added strategy, 352–353
Value-in-use, 560–561
Value-in-use strategy, 353
Value of purchase, 560
Value-oriented dominant design, 775
Value-oriented product line, 769–770
   dominant design and, 775
Value pricing, 308
Vandamme, Hugo, 633
Vandeplas, Michel, 649
Vannieuwenhuyse, Johan, 647
Vanthuyne, Tom, 643
Variety marketer, 769
Variety-oriented product line, 768–771
   custom-designed item, 770–771
   diverse specifications versus trade-offs, 773
   profitability of, 769
   special-purpose products, 771–772
Variety versus value, 775–783
   international implications, 780–781
   management implications, 781–782
Vendor relationships, in business-to-business marketing, 6
Vertical marketing systems, distribution channels as, 587–588
VHF marine radio, 89–93
VideoDisc, as example of delusionary new product, 74
Vitale, Richard J., 388
Vitali, Amy, 653, 655, 662, 663, 665, 666
Von Hippel, Eric, 302

Warranty, channel function priority, 333
Wascher, Uwe, 763–764
Waters, Jim, 696
Waters Chromatography Division (Millipore), 703–705
Webster, Thomas, 405, 408
Weick, Karl, 815
Wholesaler, at risk, 595
Wilson, Edith, 277–288
Win ratio, 206, 207
Witteck, Charlie, 125, 132, 133, 143–144, 147
Woodard, Geoff, 697–700
Worldwide marketing, Barco Projection Systems, 632–652
Write Line, Inc., hybrid marketing system, 601–608

Xerox Corporation
   company background, 670–673
   copier industry, 669–670
   current situation, 689–691
   customer guarantee, 687–689
   customer satisfaction at, 677–687
   customer satisfaction program, 668–691
   history, 671–672
   United States Marketing Group, 673–677

Yancy, Earl, 377–396

Zaltman, Gerald, 74
Z contract, 495–496, 508–509, 512